UNITED EMPIRE LOYALISTS

ENQUIRY INTO THE LOSSES AND SERVICES
IN CONSEQUENCE OF THEIR LOYALTY

Evidence in the Canadian Claims

SECOND REPORT
OF THE
BUREAU OF ARCHIVES
FOR THE
PROVINCE OF ONTARIO

By Alexander Fraser

Part II

(Pages 705-1376) with index for Parts I and II

CLEARFIELD

Originally published as
Second Report of the Bureau of Archives for the
Province of Ontario, Part II, 1904 (published in Canada 1905)

Reprinted by Genealogical Publishing Co., Inc.
Baltimore, Maryland, 1994

Library of Congress Catalogue Card Number 93-80414

Reprinted for Clearfield Company by
Genealogical Publishing Company
Baltimore, Maryland, 2010

ISBN, Part II: 978-0-8063-1406-8
ISBN, the two-part set: 978-0-8063-1404-4

Made in the United States of America

SECOND REPORT

OF THE

BUREAU OF ARCHIVES

FOR THE

PROVINCE OF ONTARIO

BY

ALEXANDER FRASER,
PROVINCIAL ARCHIVIST

1904

PART II.—(pp. 705-1376) with index for Parts I. and II.

PRINTED BY ORDER OF

THE LEGISLATIVE ASSEMBLY OF ONTARIO

TORONTO
Printed and Published by L. K. Cameron, Printer to the King's Most Excellent Majesty
1905

Produces order from L.-Col. Brown to the late Saml. Williams to send in his Negroes to fort Cornwallis, dated April, '81. With certificate that 3 Negroes were accordingly sent & that they were captured.

NEW CLAIM.

591. Case of JOHN BONNELL, formerly of Georgia.

1786.
July 27.

(48).

Claimant appears & says he was in Georgia about 80 miles from Savanah, when it was evacuated & could not join the Brit. when they evacuated. Should have gone with them, could he have got down in time. This was in 1781. He staid in Georgia till summer 1784, then went to St. Augustine. Did not hear of the act till he came to Augustine. Now resides at Coppendoch in tnis Province.

Says he joined the Militia under Col. Brown at St. Mary's. Served with him about 9 months. Went into Georgia, served till 3 weeks before evacuation of Charles town, when he had leave to go up the Country. Says he staid 2 years. Had no opportunity of going before. His Father lived upon O'Geetchie in Georgia & Claimant had 60 Head of Cattle on his Farm of his own. Claimant was then 20 yrs. of age. His Father is now in that Province.

When Genl. Prevost went from Charles town, Claimt. went up to fetch his Cattle down to Savanah. Thinks this was in 1781. Had got his Cattle & was carrying them away when he was taken by Rebels and made a Prisoner. The Rebels made a Prize of his Cattle. 4 Horses; lost when he was taken Prisoner. Left them on a farm near his Father. They were afterwards taken by the Rebels.

PETER OGELVIE, Wits:

(49).

Knew Claimant. He lived on O'Geetchie some time after troubles began. He went to E. Florida to join the Rangers under Col. Brown in E. Florida. Believes he came to Georgia with Col. Brown's men. Cannot say how he came to be absent from Savanah. Says that he believes that Claimant afterwards was lurking about & if he had been discovered would have been apprehended & put to death.

Thinks he had a large stock on his Father's Farm. Heard he was taken Prisoner, with some of his Cattle. Cannot say how many he had on his own farm. Had 3 or 4 horses of his own purchased during the war.

Claimant says that while he was in Georgia the Rebels were after him & threatened to murder him. Says he had not an horse or Company, which was his reason for not going sooner to E. Florida.

Says his Father gave him 10 Cows on his marriage. The rest he had raised. His Father gave him them on his marriage.

JOHN OGELVIE:

Says Claimant's Cattle were marked different from his Fathers.

They were marked in the ears.

45a AR.

other Sons. Was exchanged. He continued to serve during the war.

Went from Augusta at the same time with Govr. Tryon for England. Witness has heard he arrived at Portsmouth in the Beginning of last winter & died there. Witness believes he did not arrive in London.

Witness is his eldest Son. Has 2 Sisters, Jane & Susan, alive and 2 Brothers who are now in E. Florida under Spanish Government.

His 2 Brothers in E. Flor. are named Abner & Wilson. Has a Brother William now in the Bahamas.

By Laws of North Carolina all real estate goes to the eldest son. Jane Williams married Nathaniel Ashley. Susan married Drury Fort. Both the Husbands were Loyalists & went from S. Carolina. Abner & Wilson Williams were also Loyalists & served in the war. Has another Brother, Jacob, now in England.

Samuel Williams was possessed of a Saw Mill & Grist Mill on Peder River with a large Tract of Land adjoining. Wits. thinks 7 or 800 acres. Took up some himself & bought other parts. Not a great Deal cleared. He built both the Mills. Finished about a twelve month before the Troubles began. Vals. them at £7 or 800 Ster. There were about 20 acres clear. (46).

Wits. vals. the Land with the Mills at £7 or 800 Ster. His Father had Deeds. Heard that they were advertized for sale. Witness had an Interest in these Mills & had paid 100 guis. to his Father & was to have paid more & was to pay £150 more, for which he was to have a moiety of the Mills without the Land. Produces affidavit from Willm. Williams taken in the Bahama Islands, stating that his Father had a Company in E. Florida Rangers & gives an acct. of his serving under Col. Brown with Certificate from Genl. MacArthur that he believed the afft. true.

Saml. Wills. had 4 Negroes at Fort Augusta. He had recd. an order to send them to the works. Wits. saw the order to his father from Col. Brown. The same as the order to Witness. They were all taken there; 3 valuable ones & a likely Boy about 14. He had 5 horses taken at Augusta.

Wits. is told to send an acct. about his Father, whether he is dead or not, & whether he made a Will. (47).

MARTIN WEATHERFORD, Wits:

Knew Samuel Williams. He was one of the first who left his home. One of the most Loyal. He & his sons served all the war. He was a Captn. in Florida Rangers.

Heard of his having a very good Saw Mill. Knew that he had Negroes. He was at Fort Augusta & taken Prisoner there.

Letter produced from Geo. Lecker in London to Messrs. Limburner & Co. at Quebec stating the Death of the late Samuel Williams. Certificate produced from Lt.-Col. Thos. Brown of the Loyalty & services of the late Samuel Williams & his Family in Strong Terms, stating services.

1787. Dec. 24.

Produces valuation of Property by Captn. John Legat & 3 others.

45 AR.

JOHN FOWLER, Wits.

Solomon Fowler was a Relation of Claimant's, from the first declared in favour of Brit. Served as Captn under Col. De Lancey & Lost his Life in the Service. Knew his farm in East Chester, remembers him long in Possession. It had been in one family. Thinks about 200 acres, most of it clear. He thinks more than 150 acres. Has known such Lands sell for £6, 7 or 8 per acre. Some £10. Vals. it at £2,000 New York Cury.

Has heard that Solomon Fowler made a Will in Favour of his Wife. Thinks owing to his being taken off suddenly he made no other Will.

Rachel his first Child died an Infant without children. All the family of Fowlers are Loyal. Claimt. is a Steady Loyalist.

N.B.—It seems as if Mrs. Fowler was likely to return to the States. Her Children being there & she having no settlement in this Prov.

MR. ISAAC WILLIAMS, Wits.

(23). Knew Solomon Fowler, loyal from the first, knew his farm in East Chester, it had been in the Family. Remembers Solomon Fowler a great while in Possession. 3 parts of it tillable, wd. sell for £8 or 9 per acre. James Hunt is now in Possession. He bought it of the States. Her maiden name was Hunt. Her family are great Rebels.

Further Evidence in Case of JOSEPH PAXTON, V. Vol. 4, 120.

Produces Copy Will of Wm. Paxon dated 1731, whereby Testator gives 200 acres to be surveyed at the East End of his Tract to James Paxon & his Heirs.

By the Will the Claimant's Mother was to have half the Profits of real Estate, during her Life. She died in 1777. James Paxon died without a Will.

Claimt. is his eldest son & Heir.

Produces Letter from James Hicks dated at Abury April 19, 1786, in which he says that the Council have made a Resolution not to give any Certificates or memr. of forfeite. Estates, and as Claimant's Estate was made over to the Pensylvania University, it was not in his Power to procure him any evidence to avail anything.

Produces Return from the Sheriff in Bucks County whereby he Certifies that 200 acres are allotted as the right of Joseph Paxton, on a Division of the Estate of James Paxton, under Writ. to (24). the Sheriff, Certified as a Copy of Sheriff's Return by Saml. Benezer, Bucks Co., April, 1786.

August 19. Further Evidence in Case of PATRICK WALL.

Produces Copy of Will of Crean Brush dated Octr., 1777, by which he gives his Estate real & personal to his wife Margaret for

Col. Jas. De Lancey, was killed in the year 1780, attacking a party of Rebels at Horse Neck.

Produces Certificate of Col. James De Lancey to Loyalty of Capt. Solomon Fowler to his activity at first & that he lost his Life afterwards in the Service, Anapolis, Aug., 3, 1786.

Solomon Fowler was possessed of a Farm in E. Chester, con sisting of 200 acres. Came to him from his Father & Mother. It had been in the Family a great while. His Father left it to be sold, his Mother bought it & gave it by Will to Claimt's Husband. He had been long in Possession of it. A large Dwelling house 6 rooms on a floor, a large Mill house, a large Barn, 3 Orchards. Almost all Cleared, just enough Wood for the purpose of Repairs & Fewel. Most of it Tillage & Meadow. Ten fields well fenced. Vals. it at £2,000 New York Cur.

Produces Office Copy of Will of Solomon Fowler bearing value it at £2,000.

Produces Office Copy of Will of Solomon Fowler bearing Date 1763, whereby he gives all his Estate to his Wife & Daughter Rachel, his then only child, and in case of the Death of Rachel, gives the whole real & personal to his Wife & her Heirs & Exrs, Rachel Fowler is dead without Issue. This estate has been confiscated & sold.

Produces Copy of Conviction agst. Solomon Fowler.

Produces Certificate from Isaac Stoutenburg one of the Comrs. of forfeited Estates. That he & Philip Van Cortlands sold 29 June, 1785, a Tract of Land in West Chester Co. of Solomon Fowler, forfeited by his Conviction to one James Hunt in considn £1,000.

Produces Certificate from the Treasurer, Gerard Banker, that he recd. 254.4.6. from Thomas Barton due to Solomon Fowler, for the use of the State, recd. on 11 Novr., 1784, Signed Gerard Banker. (21).

Claimt. says that she made enquiries about her Dower, but was told by a Lawyer whom she consulted, that it would be in vain to make any application.

Her Husband had several children, after the Date of his Will. Seven children were living, the eldest son Edmund is in Demerery, rest in New York.

Lost five Horses, 4 taken from the farm at E. Chester, when her Husband went to Long Island, taken on acct. of her Husband having joined the Brit. The fifth was lost at Williams Bridge where Solomon Fowler lost his Life.

Lost a Cart, a Yoke of Oxen, 3 Cows, taken when her Husband went to Long Island, 19 Load Wheat in the Ground destroyd, some taken from the Barn, about 12 Bushel, Oats, fowls, furniture, Implements of husbandry. (22).

They took away a Negroe, they used him very ill & beat him. He got away & got home & died in 3 weeks. She thinks in consequence of his ill usage.

Claimant now lives at Granville.

(18).

Co. subject to his Wife's Right of Dower. Signed John Brown, Clerk Genl. Court.

Produces Copy of Inquisition taken 29 March, 1780, before Escheator, which finds that Claimt. Campbel Calvert & Co., possessed 2 acres called the Thistle Distillery.

Produces Certificate from John Pendleton, Auditor of Accts. for the Commonwealth of Virginia, stating that it appears by Report of Commrs. appointed by Act of Assembly to ascertain the Losses in Norfolk, that the Distillery was valued at 6,000, that 17 houses of Neil Jamieson were valued £2,173, equal to Specie. Destroyd before 1 Jany., 1775, and it appears by the Returns of the Escheator that a Lot belonging to Neil Jamieson, in Norfolk was sold for £34,100, Aug., 1780, when Scale of Depreciation was 70 to 1.

Produces affidt. as to Tobacco burnt at Rocky Bridge by Brit. Troops, under Gen. Philips, April, 1781, 53 Hds. Property of Mess. Glasford & Co.

Certificate that 2 houses belonging to James Lisle & burnt by Genl. Arnold, were worth £330, & the Tobacco houses at Richmond burnt by Ld. Cornwallis were worth £1,220.10.

Then I give and Bequeathe unto my son, Stephen, and to his heirs & Assigns for ever all my Right & Title to the Land and the Store standing thereon, adjoining the great Bridge at the Head of Norwalk Harbour, also the remaining third of my Lands in the Common Field situate at Georgias Hill so called.

(19).

The above and foregoing ―――― Coppy of that Part of the last Will & Testament of James Hoyt, Desd. of the Real Estate that he Bequeathed to his son Stephen. Witness, Goold Hoyt, one of the Exects., Abijah Odel, Wm. Peters.

NEW CLAIM.

1786.
August 12.

603. Case of SARAH FOWLER, Widow of Solomon Fowler, late of New York, for Herself & Children.

MRS. SARAH FOWLER Says.

She staid at New York after Evacuation. Her husband's estate had been Confiscated, it laid at East Chester, it lay between the Lines so that the Rebels could not get it. Just before Evacuation Mrs. Fowler took Possession, but was afterwards turned out by a person who had got a Lease from the Comrs. of forfeited Estates. She disputed & there was an Ejectment brought by this Lessee who at last got Judgment & she was turned out. Says she kept Possession 1 year or more.

Her Husb. Solomon Fowler was a native of America, settled at East Chester when Troubles broke out. At first opposed all the Measures of rebels in Training, &c. on acct. of which he was disarmed. Concealed some time & joined the Brit. at Long Island.

(20).

Soon after their landing, was appointed a Captn of Militia under

Produces Copy Conveyance from Luckin Thorndike, Israel Hutchinson, Dummer Jewett, the Commrs. of forfeited Estates, of a Parcel of Land in Salem on part of which the Mansion House formerly of Claimant stands, to Elias Heskel Derby in considn £6,050, in Massts. Govert. Securities. They sell the same in fee & warrant the same in the name of the Commonwealth, to the Purchaser in fee.

Produces Copy of Deed from Wm. Hynd to Col. Brown of 12 acres in Marblehead in a Place called the Plain farms in Consid. £50 Curt. Passable Money New England, 1728.

Produces Copy of Deed from John Marston to Col. Saml. Brown of a Parcel of Land in Stage Point in Salem, Contains about 3 acres in considn £54 Cury, dated 1718.   (16).

Produces Deed from Wm. Saunders to Col. Saml. Brown of 100 acres within Township of Salem in consr £400 Cury., dated 1711.

Produces Copy of Deed from James Derby to Col. Saml. Brown of a house & Land in Salem in considn £60 Cury., dated 1716.

Produces Copy of Deed from Jos. Flint, to Col. Sam. Brown, of 3 or 4 acres in Salem in Considn of £50 Cury., dated 1722.

Produces Certificates to Claimts being possessed of a Pew in Meeting house at Salem & vals. at £20 Str. Signed Jas. Jeffrey Clerk of the Proprietors of Meeting house, April, 1786.

Produces Certificate that Claimt. was entitled to 2-3 of 18 & ½ Common Rights in Great Pasture of Salem which have been sold by Commrs. of Confiscated Estates, signed Jos. Clough, Clerk of Proprietors, April, 1786.

Produces Certificate that Col. Saml. Brown was one of original 20 Associate Grantees of Land in Penobscot. 5,000 acres to each share. Silvanus Burn, Proprs. Clerk, May, 1786. Certificate that Claimt. was owner of one half the aforesaid share in 1774.   (17).

Produces Certificate signed John Downing, Peter Boyer, Committee for settling with Comrs. of Sale, that Comrs. of Sale sold in Co. of Worcester Lands the Property of Claimt. to amount of £2,450 Lawful, equal to £1,860 Str.

N.B.—Claimt's Agent Joseph Blaney says in a Letter, he is informed the Commrs. sold 1,700 acres for the sum mentd. in the above Certificate.

As to Property in Connecticut, Produces affidavit of Ebenezer Backus that he knew Claimant's Estate in Colchester, Lime & New London, tho' not exact No. of acres, very valuable from its situation, good farms & builds., well timbered, as valuable as any Land in Province. Divided into farms, vals. it at 15 Dollars per acre.

(539). Further Evidence in Case of NEIL JAMIESON, V. Vol. 6, p. 53.   August 11.

Produces Copy of Inquisition taken 28 March, 1780, before Mathew Godfrey, Escheator of Co. of Norfolk, which Inquisition finds that Claimt. possessed a Lot in Norfolk, and 93 acres in the

Further Evidence in Case of THOMAS YOUNG, V. Vol. 2.

LT. COL. JOHN FANNEN, Wits.

Has heard all Claimant's family were turned off Steven's Creek & that one Williams was settled on it. Heard that Claimt. had Land on Pimlico Sound. Knew of some of his Negroes & heard that they were in Possession of a Rebel. He was very Loyal, suffered great Hardships.

NEW CLAIM.

1786.
August 10.

602. Case of MICHL. WALLACE, Partner with John Wallace & Co., late of Virginia.

(14).

No part of the New Claim is admitted by Comrs. except the articles relating to Sloop Industry & Cargo taken by the Roebuck Man of War.

Claimant Sworn Saith.

The Company were settled at —— in Nansemond Co., Virginia. Michl. & John Wallace & Co. on breaking out of the Troubles all took part with the Brit. & was obliged to leave the Country on that Acct. His Partners were never in America, but continued to reside in Scotland. Claimt. is Native of Scot. Settled in America in 1771.

Were in Possession of a Sloop called the Industry, thinks it was taken Novr., 1775. It was in James River, had been fitted out from his own stores. Was going up James River in order to get out of the way of the Rebels. Was taken in James River by a

Tender from the Roebuck. Thinks the knowledge of the Prohibitory Act arrived about a week before his vessel was taken. Cargo was rum, Wine, &c. Claimt. has been informed the Cargo was used by Sr. Andrew Hammond's fleet. The vessel was afterwards burnt at Norfolk by Ld. Dunmore's order in May, 1776.

Has heard there was a Condemnation of this ship & Cargo at a Court of Admiralty appointed by Lord Dunmore at Norfolk. Vals. the Sloop & Cargo at 997.15.10. Virginia Cury.

Claimant's Partners are five in No. This was a joint concern.

(15).

August 11.

(543). Further Evidence in Case of GOVR. BROWN. Vol. 6, p. 107.

As to property in Massachusetts.

Produces Copy of Deed from Jos. Bowditch to Claimt. of a piece of Land in Southfield in cons. £75 Lawful, 1764.

Produces Copy of Deed from Saml. Sarasy to Col. Saml. Brown of parcel of Salt Marsh in Salem County, 1 acre & ½ in considn £20 passable Money, 1728.

Produces Deed from Ebenezer Bowditch to Claimt. of a Lot in Salem containing 4 acres & ½ in considn £200 Lawful, 1760.

100 acres Clear. His Father had been in Possession of it 24 or 25 years ago. It has been Confiscated & sold as Claimt. has been told. His name was in the Bill of Attainder. Could have sold it for 20sh. Str. per acre. There were fine Improvements on it, a very good house, Barn & another Smaller house, orchards.

No. 2. 200 acres on Broad River, purchased of William Crank & Elias Brock 14 or 15 yrs. ago in Considn of £100 Prov. Money. Cleared 100 acres, built 3 houses, had need to let the houses & cleared Land at £10 Provn. per ann.

Has heard these Lands are Confiscated & Sold, one Hamilton & Woods were in Possession when Claimant heard last. Claimt. lost his Deeds, they were in his Trunk & plundered, when his house was rifled by Rebels.

No. 3. 250 Acres in Sandy River, purchased of Curtis Culon since the War. in Considn £500, S. Car. Cur.,Paid him in horses at the old Rates. Claimant lived there, cleared 60 acres, built a good house. There were other houses, vals. at 20sh. Str. per acre.

Had 2 Negroes, Rebels took them from his house, after Claimt. joined the Brit. Army, never got to any of his family. Prime Negroes, 27 Horses left at different places, on his joining Brit., which he thinks fell all into the Hands of Rebels, some very valuable, worth £8 Ster. each on an average, 30 Cattle, 70 Hogs, Household furniture & Tools, has a child now in the State of South Carolina. (12).

Claimt. says he was in the Course of the War, after joining the Brit. taken Prisoner twice, Was once put in Gaol, but made his escape & joined Lord Cornwallis.

MR. THOS. YOUNG. Wits.

Knew that Claimant was appointed Lieutenant Col. of Militia,

---

by Lord Cornwallis. He was much employed, did a great deal of Duty. chiefly under Col. Balfour after he went to Charlestown. He was much distinguished & a great Deal of Trust reposed in him.

Knew No. 1, Left by his Father. Wits, saw the Will & knows that Land was given by his Father to all his Sons. Remembers Claimant in Possession of this Land. A great Deal clear. A very great Improvement. All his Brothers were Loyal & were obliged to quit that part of the Country. Thinks none of them can have only a part of the Family Estate.

Knew No. 2. Heard that he purchased of Crank, had purchased long before his Father's Death. Land was very valuable on Broad River, the best Land in that Country. Heard that Claimt. had Negroes. A great many horses & Cattle. (13).

AUGUSTINE HOBB, Wits.

Knew Claimant, he served as Lieutenant Col. Militia. Witness served under him. Knew No. 3, 50 or 60 acres clear, purchased just as troubles began.

recollection that it was in the Fall of the year 1783 that he delivered his Memorial.

(9).   THOS. YOUNG, Wits.

Says he was at Augusta when Col. Fannen made out his claim He made out his Claim before John Mills. Wits. had valued his Estate & was sworn bef. Just. Mills. Heard it was to go by Tinsley. It was in the same Fall when Witness sent his by Col. Hutchins, which was in the fall, 1783. Samuel Branning, Witness & a 3rd person were the Apraisers, all sworn before Just. Mills. Capt. Tinsley was a Captn in the Light Dragoons under Col. Balfour. Wits. heard he was going to England.

Claimt. says Col. Hutchins was gone a little while before he went to Augusta, is quite sure he gave it to Capt. Tinsley in the same fall as Col. Hutchinson went away from Augusta.

He sent it by Captn Tinsley, because Captn Tinsley's Claim had the Province Seal affixed to it along with Claimants.

He is a native of America, resided in Camden District on his own Property when Troubles broke out, joined the Brit. at Hudson's Ferry in March, 1779, had been frequently called upon to join the American Militia & refused, & had been imprisoned on that acct.

(10).   Joined Genl. Prevost, was first Captn Militia under Col. Turnbul, was appointed Lieutenant Col. of Militia by Lord Cornwallis. He thinks in Jan. 1781 was constantly in service, was in the Engagement at Parker's Ferry. Had there a Troop of horse under Major Fraser.

After Tarletons Defeat at the Cow Pens had the care of the wounded men to conduct them to Camden, his Party were attacked & defeated. Wits. escaped being taken, was frequently employed by Lord Cornwallis, both to get him Information & in Service.

Produces Certificate from Govr. Tryon, June 1784, that Claimt. was appointed Lieut. Col. of Militia by Lord Cornwallis and to his Loyalty.

Produces Certificate from Jas. Robinson, Lt. Col. S. C. Royalists to Claimt's Services as Lieut. Col. Militia & to his Loyalty, April, 1784.

Produces Certificate from Genl. MacArthur to his Loyalty & serving as Lieut. Col. Militia, July, 1784.

Produces Certificate from Several Officers of Militia to Claimts Loyalty & sufferings. Rob. Cunningham, Thos. Fletchall & sevl. others Jany., 1782.

Claimt. came from Augustine to this Province, is now settled in Argyle, is to have Land in the Tusket.

(11).   Claimant was possessed of 250 acres on broad River. Had it from his eldest Brother by Deed of Gift, after his Father's death. About a year before the War. It was left by his Father's Will to Claimant, but Claimant took a Deed of it from his eldest Bror. says it was a Lease & Release from his Bror.

No. 3. 3 acres & 1-2 called Sheep Pasture, had it under his Father's Will, vals. at £35.

No. 4. 4 acres of Woodland in Danbury, purchased of Mathew Stawe. Produces Deed from Mathew Stawe by which the Premises are Conveyed to Claimant in Considn £3.10, dated 16 Nov., 1775. Claimt. says he gave other Lands which he had under his Father's Will in exchange for these Lands, vals. £5.

(7).

Produces Copy of Conviction. Produces apraisement on the Oath of Danl. Dibbel & Ezra Dibble to Valuation of Estate as above.

Produces Certificate from Joseph Cook, Judge of Probate that Major Taylor & Ezra Dibble were appointed by Orders of the Court of Probate to sell so much of Estate of Claimt. as might be sufficient to pay his Debts. 30.10.6.

Produces Copy of particulars estate as delivered in at the Court of Probate, agreeing with the before mentioned acct. Stating the Land to have been distributed to Claimant under his Fathers Will. Produces Copy of Sale from Major Taylor and Ezra Dibble of No. 3, for 30.10.6.

Produces Copy of Sale from John Lawrence, Treasr. of No. 1 in Considn. of £42. Claimt. says part of the Dwelling house was burnt, after he left it, which made it of less value, fire happened in 1778 by Lightning. Rebels in Possession. Claimt. thinks it worth £100 in that state. Produces Copy of Sale from John Lawrence, Treasr. of No. 2, in considn of £70.3. Produces Certificate of Sale of No. 4.

THEOPHELUS CHAMBERLAIN, Wits.

(8).

Knew Claimant, recollects his joining the Brit. He went to them on acct. of his Loyalty. Knew that he was on Lloyd's Neck, under Col. Upham, looks upon him as very Loyal.

Knew No. 1. He had it from his Father, remembers him in Possession. His Mother had ½ of it, vals. it at £150 Con. Cur. Knew No. 2, remembers the family in Possession.

ISACC HOYT, Wits.

Claimt. certainly from the first Loyal. Knew his Father's Property, understood he came to part of it, the whole of No. 1, worth £250. Knew No. 2, val. £14 per acre. Knew No. 3, val. £10 per acre.

NEW CLAIM.

601. Case of Lieut. Col. JOHN FANNEN, late of S. Carolina.

1786. August 10.

Claimt. Sworn Saith.

He was at St. John's, E. Florida. He made out his Claim in the Fall, 1783. Made out at Augusta before Justice Mills. gave it to Capt. Tinsley who said he was going to England. Gave it Capt. Tinsley a few days after Col. Young left Augusta, says on

(5).

Knew No. 2. Remembers him in Possession. He lived there. His house was burnt by the Rebels soon after Claimt. joined the Brit. Knew No. 3, on Beaver Dam.

Lands on O'Gretchie very good. Has seen £5 pr. acre given for clear Land. Rebels have the Lands in Possession. He had a very pretty stock. He had Horses of different kinds, saddle & working horses, about 100 Cattle, all left on the place to the mercy of the Rebels & the Rebels had them. Sheep, Hogs, Goats.

NEW CLAIM.

1786.
August 7.

600. Case of COMFORT BENEDICT, late of Connecticut.

Reason assigned that he delivd. his Claim in Oct. 1783, to John Andrews who was going to England, to be delivered by him to Commrs.

JOHN ANDREWS, Wits., Sworn, Saith:

He was at New York in the Fall of '83. About Novr. '83, 2 persons call'd on Wits. One was Claimant. He lodged papers

with Witness to carry to England to lodge with Commrs. & made out a Letter of Attorney to Wits. Wits. took charge of this. Sail'd for Eng. Nov. 28. Still has the papers. He left his chest & trunk at Plymouth & they did not arrive till April or last March in London.

Wits. says he lodged other Claims. Mr. Simpson was his Agt. & he paid Mr. Simpson 5 gns. for each memorial. Claimant's Claim was so small & with not having the money to pay Mr. Simpson, was the reason for not delivering the Claim.

(6).

Claimant Sworn Saith: He was at New York in the Fall, 1783; delivered his Claim to John Andrews in Oct. or Nov. '83. Heard he was going to England, which was his Reason for sending it by him.

He is a native of America. Settled at Danbury in Connecticut when troubles began; at first sided with Brit.

In March, 1778, was draughted into Continental Troops. Was carried under a guard to Newhaven to serve in American Army. Made his escape in 4 or five Days. Concealed himself at Newtown; got within Brit. Lines in Long Island in June following. Served und' - Col. Upham on Lloyds Neck. Col Upham had th ; Command of the Refugees after Claimant went away. All his property was seized.

Continued at New York till Evacuation, then came to this Province. Is now settled at Dartmouth.

Was possessed of No. 1, 1-2 one house & builds &c., in Danbury. Had this by Will of his Father, he died in 1772. Claimt. entered on his Death. Claimt. had half & his Mother the other half. Vals. it at £140 Con. Cur.

No. 2. A Lot in Colepit Hill, consisting of 6 acres had it under his Father's Will, consisted of an orchard & good plough Land. Vals. at £70.

James Wright. Produces papers by which it appears the acct. was made out before Jas. Hume, C.I., Novr., 1783. One part went to England under Seal of Province. Produces duplicate now. Never heard of Col. Hutchinson since.

He is a native of North Britain. Came to America with his Father & Mother in 1752 or thereabouts. Was settled in S. Carolina at first. Went in 1775 to Georgia & settled there. Joined the Brit. at Augusta as soon as they came, under Genl. Campbell; had a Commission as Lieutenant of Militia under Col. Medley; had a Captn.'s Commission. Produces Captn.'s Commission from Sr. James Wright. Commission of Capt. of a Troop of Horse Militia, dated Oct., 1781. (3).

Produces Certificate from Col. John Douglas of Georgia Militia that Claimt. had served in his Regiment with a Troop of Horse, & to his activity in service & Loyalty, St. Augustine, 1st March. 1784.

Do. from Col. Thos. Brown, K's Rangers in strong terms.

Produces Certificate from Sr. James Wright to Claimant having been appointed Captn. of Militia to his active serv:ces & Loyalty & recommending him to Govr. Tryon, 4 July, 1782.

Produces Certificate to his Services & Loyalty, Thos. Brown Arch. MacArthur, Saml. Raworth, April 19, 1784.

Claimt. continued in Service till Evacuation of Savannah, then went to Augustine. Came to this Province in 1784. Now settled in Chisencook.

Was possessed of 300 acres on O'Gretchie River, Georgia Drew this in the year 1775, or beginning of yr. 1776. Cost him £8. Cleared 15 acres. Began building a Grist Mill. Had built some other small builds. Did it himself. Vals. it at £200 Geor. Cury.

200 acres in Rocky Comfort, 8 miles from the other; purchased after the other in 1777 or 1778, in Considn. £15. 12 acres Clear. Built a house. Lived there with his family. Vals. it at £45. (4).

150 acres on Beaver Dam, 1 mile & ½ from the other, purchased after the last in Considn. £10. 50 acres Clear. Vals. it at £50.

Had a Negro Boy 12 years old. His wife left him with a friend. He was found out & sold by Rebels, worth £50. 6 Riding Horses, 6 Working Horses, mare & colt, taken from the place by Rebels. Some by chance might be taken by the Indians.

136 Head of Cattle, taken by Col. Parkers men, Rebels. 100 Hogs, 25 Sheep, Goats, Furniture & Tools. Produces affidt. from 3 persons to the valuation of Claimant's Property as in his Schedule.

WILLM. MORRIS, Wits., Sworn, Saith:

Knew Claimt.; that he joined the British at Augusta, & servd. faithfully & Loyally during remaining part of War. Knew his land on O'Gretchie, about 300 miles. Knew him in Possion, 6 or 7 yrs. ago.

THE EVIDENCE.

New Claim.

1786.
August 3.

598. Case of ROBERT SLOANE, late of S. Carolina.

(1).

Claimant says he went from Charlestown to East Florida. Was near St. Augustine; about 30 miles from it, at a place called St. Johns Went to St. Johns in Aug.; was there all the Fall of 1783. He was sick & likely to die & could not go to Augustine till Jany., 1784. There heard of the Act. Made out his claim in Feby. Says no ship went from Augustine till Capt. Montgomery went, which was in the spring. Sent his Claim by Capt. Montgomery. Produces Capt. Montgomery's Recept for his Claim, April 1784.

Says he is a native of Scotland. Settled in America in 1767, in 96 District; brought about £70 with him. Had 200 acres in 96 Dist., drew them himself in March, 1768. Cleared 50 acres; built a house & Barn, & made orchards. There had been former improvements which Claimant bought for £20. Lived there when Troubles began; served once in American Militia against the Indians; was fined for not serving; joined the Brit. after Reduction of Charlestown, then joined Militia under Col. King. Then went to Georgia; was in the seige of 96 by Genl. Green. Afterwards went to Orangeburg & to Charlestown. On Evacuation went to East Florida.

(2).

Was possessed of 200 acres in 96 Dist. Vals. them at £150. Produces Valuation of 3 persons on Oath, who value them at £100.

Had 35 Horses. He had bought a stock of breeding mares, English breed. Vals. them at £9 Ster. pr. head. 200 Head of Cattle; bought a stock at first, reckoning young & old together. The horses & cattle were taken by the Rebels after Seige of 96. 80 Hogs, 260 bushels Corn. Cash in his house £22. He was robb'd of it by a party from Essex. Merchant goods of which he was robb'd, Furniture, Tools.

Is told he must produce Witnesses to show his ill Health at St. John's, and to proof of his Property.

Produces Certificate from Wm Shaw, Master Master at Halifax, that Claimant arrived in Cargo Packet from Augustine, and was mentioned as a Loyalist. Now resides near Submacady.

New Claim.

1786.
August 5.

599. Case of EDWARD CRAWFORD, late of Georgia.

Claimant Sworn Saith:

He was at St. Augustine in the Fall of '83. Gave his Claim to Col. Hutchins in Novr., 1783. Claimant was acquainted with Col. Hutchins when he lived in Peder, which was his reason for giving the Claim to Col. Hutchins. Sent at the same time a Letter to Sir James Wright. Claimant had served under Sr.

PROCEEDINGS

OF

LOYALIST COMMISSIONERS

HALIFAX, 1786.

VOL. IX.

BEFORE COMMISSIONER PEMBERTON.

Claimants.

	MSS. Folio.		MSS. Folio.
Benedict, Comfort	5	Maxwell, William	35
Bownell, Isaac	25	Neeley, Major	29
Brown, Gov.	15	Paxton, Joseph	23
Crawford, Edward	2	Robie, Thomas	25
Donaldson, William	39	Sloan, Robert	1 and 44
Fanning, Lieut.-Col. John	9 and 48	Taylor, Nathaniel	45
Fowler, Mrs. Sarah	19	Wall, Patrick	24
Jamieson, Neil	18	Wallace, John	35
Wallace, Michael	14 and 35		

Produces Certificate of Conviction of Claimt. for joining the Enemies of the State. Produces a Certificate from Aaron Dunham, which mentions rect. of Cash from Moses Tucker. Claimt. says Moses Tucker purchased his Land.

Produces affidavit of Jonathan Woodruff to Claimt.'s Estate at Elizth. Township being worth £750 Pen. Cury., & to its being confiscated & to his personal property, worth £282 Pen. Cury.

Admits he owed about £70 Pen. Cury.

Left all the Stock in the Schedule mentioned on his farm, & values them as in Schedule.

30 Had of Cattle, 16 Sheep, 3 Hogs, 3 Horses, Wagon, Slay, Furniture, all taken by Americans.

Claimant says he was frequently employed by Genl. Skinner, Genl. Vaughan, & Col. Manhood, while the Troops were at Amboy & from Staten Island as a guide & to collect intelligence, for about 3 years for which he never recd. anything, except a few dollars from Gen. Skinner.

(61). Capt. Cameron of the 37th Regt., certifies to Mr. Pemberton, that he always understood Claimt. to have been an active, zealous Loyalist, that he was frequently employed by the Commander officers from Staten Island, and that the greatest Reliance was laid on his Information.

into American Militia which was his reason for going off when he did & joining Brit. (58).
Was taken Prisoner. Got afterwards to Charlestown & Continued with Brit. till Evacuation of Charlestown. Now lives at Maagash.
Had 166 acres in Mecklinburg Co., bought it in 1771 or 1772. Gave £104 N. C. Cur. for it. 40 acres clear. Claimt. built a small house & repaired another.
16 head Cattle taken by Rebels. 4 horses, 16 Hogs, 200 Bushels of Corn, Some wheat & oats, furniture & Tools, Flax.

New Claim.

597. Case of SAMUEL SMITH, late of New Jersey.   1786. July 31.

Claimant affirms:

That he delivered his Claim to Stephen Skinner. Genl. Skinner's Brother, at New York in Oct., 1783, to be delivered in England. He was then going to England. Stephen Skinner wrote him one Letter after his arrival, in which he said he had not then delivered his Claim, but if anything was wanted from Claimant he would write to him again. Claimt. has not heard from him since.

He is a native of America. Resided at Elizth. Town, New Jersey, when Troubles broke out. When Troops landed from New York into New Jersey under Lord Cornwallis, met them at Elizth. Town, & by request of Genl. Skinner, to get information of the movements of Continental Army; furnished the Brit. army with information. (59).

Was taken up on suspicion of Supplying Brit. Army with Provisons. Was carried Prisoner to Chatham; was confined a short time; made his escape to Amboy. Never could return home, but continued within Brit. Lines till Evacuation of New York. Now settled at Anapolis.

Produces Certificate from Major James Campbell that Claimant was reckoned a Loyalist & confidentially employed by Genl. Skinner, July, 1786.

Produces Certificate from John Hicks, Depty. Inspector King's Provn. Tran, to Claimant's joining the Brit. on Lord Cornwallis entering Jersey; his services & Loyalty.

Produces Rect. of Stephen Skinner for the Claimt., delivered Oct., 1783.

Was possessed of 110 acres with House & builds in Elizth. Township, Co. of Essex. The Deed was delivered to Stephen Skinner; purchased in 1770 of Jonathan Marsh, in Considn. £500 Pens. Cury. Produces Deed from Jonathan Marsh, his father, to Jonathan Marsh of 100 acres in Elizth. Township, more or less in Considn. £79 Pen. Cur., dated 1758. The Deed from Jonathan Marsh, the son, to Claimt. is in England. (60).

Claimant built upon the Place in addition to the former house & improved the Place. Vals. at £7 per acre. It has been sold by Commrs.

(56).

Servd. a short time as a Militia in the Works at Brooklyn, Long Island. Kept guard often. Continued within the Brit. Lines during the War. Came to this Province on Evacuation of New York. Now settled at Anapolis.

Was possessed of 100 acres in the Co. of Bucks. Had been possessed many years. Came to him by his Father's Will, tho' he had been possessed before.

Produces office Copy of his Father's Will, whereby he devises this Estate to Claimant for Life, after his Decease to the Heirs of his Body. His Father died in 1774. Claimant continued in possession. There has been no Recovery Suffrd. His children are now in the State of Pensilvania. Was very good Land; 80 acres meadow & Tillage, & about 20 acres Wood.

Would have let for more than £30 Pens. Cur. pr. ann. Vals. at £8 or 9 pr. acre.

This has been confiscated & sold. Produces Certificate from Geo. Wall, Agent for fo.feited Estates in Bucks Co., that Claimant had been attainted of High Treason, in consequence of which his Estate, consisting of a Tract of 100 acres in New Britain became forfeited, and was advertized & sold at public Auction.

Produces affidt. from James Hutchinson of Anapolis; Knowledge of Claimant's Estate & to Valuation & to Loyalty.

(57).

Lost Horse, Wagon & wearing apparel, taken & plundered by the mob on acct. of Claimt.'s Loyalty. Horse worth £25, wagon 14, wear. apparel 19.

ISAAC STEV. HUTCHINSON, Wits.:

Knew Claimt. He always opposed the exercise & training of Rebel Militia. He was ill used on that acct. Always declareu in Favour of King & Brit. Govrnt. Thinks he was obliged to leave his home on acct. of his Loyalty. He went within the Brit. Lines. Heard frequently that he assisted at the Works of Brooklyn. Knew his Estate in New Britian Township, 100 acres; had been his father's; good land, with a large interval; on the side of a small River. Land adjoining sold for £7 pr. acre. Wits. thinks this would have sold at that price. Heard he was plundered by mob on acct. of his opposing the measures of Reb-

NEW CLAIM.

1786.
July 28.

596. Case of JACOB BLEWER, late of Mecklinburg Co., North Carolina. V. Vol. 2, p. 19.

EVIDENCE IN THIS CLAIM TAKEN DE BENE ESSE.

Claimt. appears & being Sworn, Saith:

He is a native of America. Resided in Mecklinburg Co. when Troubles broke out. Always sided with the Brit. Joined the Brit. at Canada in 1780. Lord Cornwallis commanded. Continued with him above a 12 month. Claimt. had been draughted

NEW CLAIM.

594. Case of HENRY GREEN, late of S. Carolina.

1786.
July 28.

Claimt. Sworn Saith:

(54).

He resided at Rawdon; gives the same reason for not sending his Claim as John Sanderson.

He is an Irishman by Birth. Came to America about 17 or 18 yrs. ago. Settled in 96 Dist.; joined Loyal Militia at the fight at 96, under Cunningham. Joined the Brit. again before the seige & continued to serve till reduction of Charlestown. Came away on Evacuation of Charlestown.

Produces Certificate from Col. Peavis that Claimant was in the engagement against the enemy at 96 in 1775. Was in Prison in the year 1776, by the enemy, & to his activity & Loyalty.

Produces Certificate from Quarter Master Genl. Department in S. Carolina, that Claimt. had been employed as a Blacksmith in his Majesty's Serv., Novr., 1781.

Was Possessed of 600 acres in 96 Dist.

1. 150 drawn by himself, by his mother & step father.
2. 150 acres.
3. 100 by his Uncle.
4. 100 by an Aunt.
5. 100 by Purchase.

Has lost his Grant & Deeds. Not much Improvt. on No. 1; 10 or 15 acres clear on No. 2; a good house & shop. No improvmts. on No. 3; Do. on No. 4. 9 acres clear on No. 5. Gave £150 S. Car. Cur. for it. 16 Head Cattle, sold at Vendue when Claimant joined the Brit. Afterwards lost a mare & colt, taken by the Rebels. 3 more Horses, 60 Hogs.

(55).

SAML. PROCTOR, Wits.:

Knew Claimt. He joined the Brit. early. Know that he had several Lots of Land in 96 Dist.

Know No. 2. Considerable Improvmts. upon it. 12 or 13 acres Clear. Know No. 5. Knows Claimt. had paid for Clearing 6 acres. There was none Clear. He had a Considerable Stock of Cattle.

595. Case of JOHN MEREDITH, formerly of Pensilvania.

1786.
July 28.

Claimt. Sworn Saith:

He is a native of America. Was settled in Township of New Britain, Co. of Bucks, Pensilv. Took part from the first with the Brit. Discouraged all Rebel associations. Was obliged to quit home because he declared against the measures carried on by the Rebels. Left home in June, 1777. Did not get to New York till July following. Was obliged to quit his home. Gave information to Genl. Pigot at New York of the Situation of Rebels.

(52).

Was possessed of 250 acres in 96 Dist. Drew it himself. Had cleared 25 acres; a good house, Barn & 2 Stables. Has been in Possession 16 years. It is now in hands of Rebels.
Left 3 horses, 12 head Cattle—left on his Plantation. Rebels had them. 60 Hogs, furniture, Cash.

MAJOR NEELEY, Wits:

Remembers Claimant. Came in & joined Militia after reduction of Charles Town. He continued to serve after that. Knew a Plantation of which he was said to be the owner. A good Plantation. There might be 30 acres clear. Cattle & horses & Hogs. The family were driven off from the Property.

1786.
July 28.

593. Case of DANL. BOWEN, late of New Jersey.

Claimant appears, being sworn saith:

He is a native of America. Was settled in Cumberland Co., New Jersey, when Troubles began. At first took an active Part against the Rebels. Joined none of their Associations. Was carried before one of their Committees & gave security to appear at next Q. Sess. Had been fined for not joining the Militia. Joined the Brit. at Philadelphia, Aug. 1777. Acted as a guide to the Army in several Instances. Raised a Company of West Jersey Volunteers & was appointed Captn.

Produces Commission from Sr. Wm. How, appointing Claimt. Captn. in Regt. Loyal New Jersey Volunteers, 21 March. 1778. Has now half pay. Regiment was draughted in about 6 months. Claimant was seconded. Continued at Long Island during the war.

Came to this Province in Octr., 1783, & is now settled at Wilmot. Produces Certificate from Major Vandyke, Commandr. of late West Jersey Volunteers, that Claimant joined Brit. at Philadelphia, acted as a Guide, raised greater part of a Company & was appointed Captn. and to his Loyalty, 20th March, 1786.

(53).

Claimant was possessed of a Lot consisting of ½ acre in Rhodes Town, Co. of Cumberland. Purchased the Ground in 1770, in two Lots, in Considn. of £10 Jer. Cury. Built 2 houses, Wood house, brick house, finished in 1775. Cost £400 Jers. Cur. They are Confiscated & sold.

Produces Certificate of Sale of House & Lot from Aaron Dunham. Lost personal property left at his house. His stock was seized by the Rebel Militia & he believes some part was saved by his friends. Lost 1 Cow, 3 Hogs; all taken by the Militia. 2 acres of Wheat on the ground.

Certificate from Aaron Dunham; mentions sale of several trifling articles of personal Property.

Produces Deposition from Willm. Kelsay, one of the Commissioners of forfeiture, that he recd. from Claimt.'s Bror. a Bond for £177 Jers. Cur. from Moses Crosley, and a note for £6 from Elias Shepherd. It appears from Aaron Dunham's Certificate that these sums were paid to the State. Produces Kelsay's Rect. to his Bror. for the said Bond & Note.

Knew him from time he was a child. Thinks he had 50 or 60. Believes he was sick, which made him stay so long in Georgia. Some were drove off from O'Geetchie & some from Briar Creek—at different times. Thinks it was in the course of more than a year. His father had Land at Briar Creek. Heard he was taken Prisoner & lost some of his Cattle then. (50).

N.B.—Claimant appears a suspicious character & his acct. scarce credible.

(589). Further Evidence in Case of Col. PIERSON. July 27

WILLM. MEEK, Wits:

Says he knows Claimant's Plantation in 96. 30 or 40 acres clear. Saw Horses, Cattle, Hogs. Has seen the Place where his Mother lives. It is a Clever Place.

Further Evidence in Case of THOS. YOUNG. July 27

MAJOR NEELEY:

Knew Claimant. Knew him first in 1779. He was then brought in Prisoner & confined in the same Gaol with Wits. in 96 Dist. Knew that he afterwards joined the Brit. & served as Captn. under Witness & continued to serve during the war. Has been at his Plantation on Steven's Creek. Was there before the war. Remembers him in Possession. Seemed a good Plantation. Several houses built. Thinks it must have been Confiscated & sold. There were Negroes about his house.

MARTIN WEATHERFORD, Wits:

Knows Claimant. He was an active Loyalist & suffered frequently. Knew his Plantation at Steven's Creek. Remembers him in Possession some years. They were good Lands. There were several Builds. He had Negroes, a considerable stock of Cattle & Horses. Heard he had some fine Horses. (51).

NEW CLAIM.

592. Case of JAMES JONES, late of S. Carolina. 1786. July 27.

Claimt. appears & being sworn says:

He resided 72 miles from St. Augustine. As soon as he heard of the act, sent down his Claim to Mr. Mills who was a Justice of Peace. He was so ill he could not go. It was about the time Captn. Thos. Young sent his Claim. Mills sent word he could not accept it, because Claimt. was not present. It was brought back to Claimant because Mills could not send it. Claimant was then too ill to move from home.

He is a native American. Settled in 96 Dist. Was obliged to serve in American Militia at first & to take oaths. Joined the Brit.

after Charles Town was taken. In Militia under Major Neeley & continued to serve during the War. Came from St. Augustine last April, 12 months. Now settled at Dartmouth.

Life or her Widowhood, whichever last longest. Directs the Estate to be sold to raise £3,000 if his Wife is Married. She is to have only her 3rd for her Life, 2-3 between 3 Daughters, V. vol. 5, 103.
Produces Inventory of Crean Brushs real Estate with Valuation at 6,287 Lawful by 2 Appraisers.
Produces Inventory of personal Estate amounting to £380. Afterwards Produces Copy of Order for the Comrs. of forfeiture

to sell the sd. Crean Brush's Estate.

Further Evidence in Case of ISAAC BOWNELL, V. Vol. 2, 128. August 19.

Produces Certificate of Judgement for assisting the Army of Great Brit. Produces Certificate of sale from Aaron Dunham of 2 Lots.
Produces Certificate of David Olden, Agent for selling forfeited Estates that he sold a Lot in Amboy forfeited Estate of Claimant, March, 1786. (25).

604. Case of THOS. ROBIE, late of Massachusetts Bay. 1786. August 23.

Claimt. Sworn Saith.

He is a native of America, lived at Marblehead when Troubles broke out, did not take an active part, but shew'd himself inimical to the measures of the Rebels. Left Marblehead about the 6th May, 1775 & came to this Province, thought himself hardly safe in person as he had been threatened. He was reckoned a Tory & they were told the Tories would be put in the front of the Battle. Hostilities commenced on the 19th April. Claimant left New England in May following, broughts away some of his effects, there was then no Impediment to bringing away his effects if he had

Convenience of Trunks .. Vessels. Says his name was in the list Act ofPrecription. Left his house chiefly in the care of his Wife's Grandmother.
In 1776 his house was entered upon by a Committee. Part of the effects were sold by his Wife's Grandmother, part of the effects were stole. The house was his own, built it himself. Purchased the Land about 1772 in considn £140 Str. Built the house at about £750 Str. There were two Mortgages upon it, one for £400 & the other for £800. No Interest having been paid, as Claimt. had no advantage of the house, the sum is now large, admits the Mortgages are to the full value of the Estate now. The Mortgagee took Possession in 1783, but have since brought an action here for the Debt and got Judgement. Claims Debts £1,410. (26).
Produces an Acct. of Goods in his store in Decr., 1777, then seized by a Committee & sold. Produces Affidt. of Richard Harris that in Dec., 1777, several articles were then in Possession of the Committee as the Property of Claimant & sold, & the money, amounting to £427.19.11 Lawful Mon. of sd. State paid by the Committee of whom Harris was one to Henry Gardner, Treasurer.

Produces Rect. by Henry Gardner, Treasury Office, 18 Jany. 1780, recd. of Committee of Marblehead 427.19.11 of the Estate of Thos. Robie. Claimt. cannot fix the sterling amount of this sum.

Produces further Acct. from Fras. Felton that Claimt's Estate real & personal was taken Possession of & that several articles of personal Estate was sold.

The Act produced mentions only Sundry articles in the Hardware Business. Fras. Felton was one of the Marblehead Committee.

Produces affidt. from Richd. Harris that Committee took Possession of Claimant's house & Land at Marblehead & leased & improved the same for the Benefit of the State. Vals. them at £40 per ann. Rent.

In Octr., 1783, one of the Mortgagees got Possession. Produces Certificate from Genl. Thos. Gage dated London, 5 Ap., 1776, that Claimt. did before 19th Apr., 1776, deliver in writing a Declaration purporting his hearty Disapprobation of the Measures adopted by the Americans against Supremacy of Brit. Parlt.

It appears that the sum paid into the Treasury is in Sterling very little £20 or 30. According to several Letters from Claimant's friends in Marblehead, but Claimant says many of his effects were stollen out of his store, after they took Possession of it.

Produces an acct. of several articles sold by his Wife's Grandmother to amount of £209, laid out in Government Notes.

FOSTER HUTCHINSON, ESQ., Wits.

Knew Claimt. understood him a friend to Brit. Govermt. and an enemy of the Measures pursued by the Americans. Is satisfied he is amongst the persons proscribed.

He was amongst the persons who address Govr. Hutchinson. He never recanted, some of them did.

REVD. MR. WEEKS.

Knew Claimt. Considered him as a friend to Brit. Govr. always. Knew he had a brick house at Marblehead. Kept a store, chiefly in the Hardware Business. Left the Country early, came away before Trials & Proscriptions in general, but all the persons who addressed Govr. Hutchinson & did not recant were he thinks proscribed.

THOS. BROWN Wits.

Claimt. signed the address to Govr. Hutchinson. Remembers seeing his name in the Newspapers, proscribed as an Enemy to his Country & people, forbid to have any Dealings with him. This was owing to his signing the address to Govr. Hutchinson. He had declared against New Importation agreement.

Some of the persons who address Govr. Hutchinson recanted. Claimant never recanted.

Had a large Store & good Business. He suffered greatly in Trade in Consequence of his Declaration of his Principles, and of signing the address. His Business was almost ruined by it.

605. Case of Major NEILEY, late of South Carolina. 1786. August 25.

Claimant Sworn Saith.

He was at St. Augustine in the Fall of 1783. Thinks in Novr. Made out his Claim in the Autumn, 1783, sent it home by a ship of Mr. Moss's which was wrecked on the Bar of St. Augustine in the Winter, 1783.

Made out another Claim in Nov., 1783, to be carried by Col. Thos. Browne. Produces affidt. from Col. Thos. Brown that the Claim thereto annexed is a Duplicate of the Original Claim sent Home by Col. Browne to Mr. Geo. Randal, London, in Novr, 1783 (29). Sworn before John ——— Just. P., New Providence Bahama Isls. May, 1786.

Claimant saith he has not heard of Mr. Randal. Claimant had served with Col. Brown & was well acquainted with him, which was the reason for sending by him, making him his attorney, Claimt. says he thought this had been delivered which was his reason for not sending home a New Claim.

There was no New Claim delivered, except the address to the Comrs. at Providence which was brought by Captn Hood to this Place & which Claimant says he thought would be tantamount to a Claim.

This address was signed by Claimant Decr., 1785.

Claimant says they had not seen the Comrs. notices requiring Affidt. of the Reason which prevented Delivery of former Claims.

He is a Native of America, settled in 96 Dist. when Troubles broke out. From the first took part with Brit. Took arms in the year 1775, joined Col. Brown & Genl. Cunningham, was in the engagement at 69 in 75. Escaped into the Cherokee Country, came back in the year 1776 with some mon. and was waylayed by a Party of Rebels near 96 & shot thro the Body with 2 Balls, left for dead in the spot. Continued there very dangerously ill, afterwards got home, laid about 9 months before he recovered. (30). Remained at home till Col. Campbell penetrated as far as Augusta in 1779. He sent several Gentn. into ye Country to raise the Loyalists. Claimant raised a body of men accordingly & joined the Militia; a party of about 600 were raised & were going to join Col. Campbell and cut off at a Place called Kettle Creek.

Claimant was then gone to bring up a party of 150 men. His party were afterwards cut off. Claimant made his escape, but was obliged to deliver himself up on Terms. His party were all imprisoned 29 in No. and tried for their Lives. Claimant was tried & Convicted & sentenced to die in 12 Days, but was discharged on arrival of Govr. Rullege. Produces his discharge, on giving

Security in £10,000 Bail for good Behaviour & not to return to the District where his family were during the War.

Remained in the Bounds to which he was confined, but in Beginning of 1780 went into 69 Dist., remained concealed there until Sr. Henry Clinton laid seige to Charlestown; joined Col. Peavis at that time. Who came from Sr. Hen. Clinton to raise ye Militia.

(31). After Charlestown fell the Militia rose openly and reduced the Country to Allegeance, about 100 miles square. Claimant raised a large Body & was with them in the service. Col. Innes came up & took ye command. Afterwards Col. Balfour arrived, was appointed Major in Col. Thos. Pearson's Regiment Militia in 1780.

Produces another Commission from Col. Balfour in 1781, to same Rank. Continued to serve during the War, served under Col. Ferguson, served all the War.

Went to St. Augustine on Evacuation of Charlestown. At the end of the War went to Bahama Islands, means to settle at Abaco. His family are at Providence.

Produces Certificate from Govr. Tryon to Claimant's Loyalty & recommending him on his leaving East Florida, June, 1784.

Produces 4 Affidts. to giving same acct. of Claimants loyal Conduct & Services as above stated by Claimant himself & to his Losses being very Considerable. All sworn at New Providence, June, 1786.

Produces Certificate from Col. Brown to Claimants Loyalty, great & Early Services & the Expenses he was at and to his subsequent services as Major Militia. Confirmed by Genl. MacArthur. Produces several Letters from Col. Stewart to show he was in his Confidence & Employd by him in Service.

Was in Possession of:

(32). No. 1—400 acres on Saladu River, purchased 200 acres 18 years ago, gave £15 or 20 for it, bought a man's right & improved it, drew the other 200 acres himself, 50 acres Clear, a dwelling house & various builds., one orchard, vals. it at 20 Sh. per acre, lived here.

No. 2—150 acres near the former, purchased before the war in Considn. £20, nothing done upon it.

No. 3—100 acres on Eucra River, left to Claimt. by his Bror. 15 years ago. Claimant was in possession, about 10 acres Clear, house & Barn. Vals. it at 10 Sh. per acre.

No. 4—400 acres on Eucra, purchased about 12 yrs. ago for £30, unimproved.

Thinks th se Lands are sold, has had Letters from a friend of his that his Lands are sold. His name was on the List of persons banished.

Produces Schedule of personal Estate:

5 Negroes, 2 taken off from Claimant's Estate by a party of Rebels who came from Camtuch against the Estates of the Loyalists, 2 were lost at the seige of 96 in the year 1781, 2 first were

worth £50 each, the 2 others £40 each, lost another at Charles town, stole from him.

Wagon & Team. Entered into his Majesty's Service by Genl. Cunningham, appraised at £107 Ster., 4 horses taken in service, Fees for Doctor, Gaol Expenses, Debts.

30 Head Cattle taken from his farm, 10 Sheep, 5 horses & mares, Corn, furniture & Tools, 42.

(33).

THOS. YOUNG, Wits.:

Knew Claimant. Very early distinguished himself by his Loyalty & was very active, was with him about the time of Reduction of Charles town, he was very——— in bringing the Country to Allegeance.

Knew No. 1—That he had Land there, but does not know the Quantity. Knew other Lands reported to be his near the former. Knew him to have Negroes, Cattle & horses and a good Stock.

JAMES JONES, Wits.:

Knew No. 1—About 50 acres Clear, good Builds.

No. 2—A valuable Tract, 15 acres clear, has some five Negroes, Horses & Cattle, he had a great Character for his Bravery & activity & performed great Services in bringing the Country into subjection after Reduct. of Charles town.

COL. PEAVIS, Wits.:

Remembers Major Neeley, he was very early in declarg. his sentiments, very active, remembers his activity in bringing the Country under Allegeance on reduction of Charles town. He was the first who joined Wits., he was very badly wounded, heard of his being tried for his life. Knew his activity on many occasions. Speaks highly of his Exertions. Knew No. 1, very good Land, 50 or 60 acres Clear. Vals. it at 10 Sh. per acre.

(35).

No. 2—Very fine Land, no Improvements.

606. Case of Executors of WILLM. MACLELLAN.

1786.
August 28.

Claim is entered Jas. Wallace & Co., but should be in the names of Michael & John Wallace & Willm. Maxwell.

MICHL. WALLACE, Wits.:

Appears, says he is one of the Executors named in Wm. Maclellan's Will. The Claim was lodged by James Wallace, Bror. of Wits. & Brother in Law of the Testator, Wm. Maclellan.

Wm. Maclellan resided at Tarborough, N. Carolina, had been settled there many years, came from Scotland. He was one of the persons proscribed & banished in the year 1776 on acct. of his loyalty, in which he went to England. Came to New York afterwards & went from thence to Charles Town, where he died in 1782. Made a Will. Produces Copy of Will bearing date 1781, Whereby Wm. Maclelland after payment of Debts & Legatees, he directs residue to be delivered amongst his Sisters Children, appoints Mich. Wallace, John Wallace & Wm. Maxwell Execrs.

(36). JAS. WALLACE, Wits.:

Says the Claimt. lodged in the name of Jas. Wallace & Co. Was lodged by his friend in England, to whom he sent home his acct. & was intended to be a Claim for the Property of the late Willm. Maclellan. Witness sent home the Estimate but gave no directions as to whose name it was to be lodged in, sent home at same time Copy of the Will.

Wm. Maclellan, Testator, lived in Tarborough, refused the Oath of Allegiance to the States & was proscribed & banished, his name is in the Act of Assembly on which he went to England. Returned afterwards & died at Charles Town.

Sent him Copies of his Title Deeds, the original Deeds are in Georgia with John Wallace, one of the Executors.

He was possessed of several Tracts of Land, 1 Tract near Tarboro of 100 acres, Wm. Maclellan lived there, remembers him in Possession till he went away. A second Tract of 50 acres, five Lots in Tarborough, remembers him in Possession.

Produces Copy of Proceedings of a County Court at Edgcomb, Whereby it appears that Mrs. Hill was summoned to show what right she had to the property formerly Wm. Maclelland's, then in (37). her Possession. It appears that Maclellan transferred all his property to James Hill, since deqd., but the transfer is set aside as fraud & the property is Confiscated.

Witness knew his Negroes, 9 in number, val. £70 per head, some very valuable, 3 horses, 1 mare, 13 Cattle, 40 Hogs, Corn, Chair, Furniture, all these articles are declared to be Confiscated in the Proceedings of the Sd. County Court.

Witness gives an acct. of the Sale of the above mentioned difft. Lots of real Estate from an acct. given him by a person who was at the Vendue.

Will Contains Legacies, to his Mother £100. She lives at Edinburgh. James Wallace, £400, he resided last in Charles town, but is now settled there. Michl. Wallace in Halifax, John Wallace in Georgia, Wm. Maxwell, New York, £50 each. The Children of his Sister now reside at Glasgow. Debts 2120.

Copy of the Will is produced in hand writing of James Wallace, Witness, which he says he copied himself from Original Will.

Produces acct. under the hand writing of James Hill of the several articles purchased by him of Wm. Maclellan, being all the above property.

Witness says Mr. Maclellan took a Bond from James Hill for the Amount, but Hill conveyed the whole back again afterwards.

Produces the Bond from James Hill dated in June, 1777, for £2000. Bond is by James Hill, Jonas Johnson, Isaac Lessumes & Henry Hart. The three last, the Witness says, were merely as Securities in £4000 in Consid. to pay £2000 North Car. Cur. on 1st Day Jany., 1784. The Lands were Conveyd back by James Hill to Wm. Maclellan in July, 1777.

(38).

Produces Advertizement in *Virginia Gazette*, July 16, 1785, for Sale of the Several Articles above mentioned, sold by Wm. Maclellan and in Possession of Mrs. Hill.

Witness is told he must get the Original Title Deeds from Georgia.

NEW CLAIM.

607. Case of WM. DONALDSON, late of Virginia.

1786.
September 2.

Claimant sworn:

Says he came from New York to Shelburn in Novr., 1783, heard of the Act but not with any certainty. Never expected so much would come of it, but hearing Parson Walter was going to England, thought he would try what success his application would have. He was engaged in building a Log house 2 miles & ½ from Shelburn, & therefore was too late to send his Claim by him, left it with Mr. Knox, a Notary at Shelburn, to be sent to Mr. Walter, it was sent to Halifax but Dr. Walter was gone, it was sent after him to England, but arrived too late.

(39).

Dr. Walters Certifies that he recd. the Claim in England, but it came too late. Claimant says Dr. Walter told him it was 8 Days too late.

Produces Letter of Attorney to Dr. Walter which apprs. to have been drawn up 20 Feby., 1784.

Says he is a native of Scotland, came to America in 1763, settled at Portsmouth in Virginia, resided there when Troubles began, sided with the Brit. Govmt. at first. Was applied to to take the Oath to the States, which he refused. Joined Lord Dunmore on his first coming to Portsmouth.

When Lord Dunmore went away he gave Claimant Leave to stay to settle his affairs. Claimant accordingly staid six weeks after Lord Dunmore went away. He was put in Confinement, was brought before 2 Rebel Cols. & ordered to depart & not come within 2 miles of the Town. Claimant accordingly went, having Concealed his property in a friend's house retired into the Country & about 4 or 5 months afterwards was taken up & sent to Williamsburg Gaol, kept there 4 weeks. While he was in Williams

(40).

Gaol the house where his effects were was broken open by a mob & plundered.

Claimant was carried before Govr. Hendrie & discharged on giving Security for good Behavr. After this he kept Concealed. Joined Genl. Mathews at Portsmouth as soon as he came there in 1777 or 1778, continued with him & acted as a Guide to the Army to Col. Doyle & Major Despard, continued with the Army & went with them to New York. Went with the Army on their way to Charles Town, but was taken Prisoner on his voyage & carried Prisoner to Charles town & kept in Prison 4 months, so remained till Charles town was taken, then released. Remained at Charles town 18 months as a Volunteer. Went to Virginia, was taken Prisoner again, was Exchanged, joined Lord Corn-

wallis at Portsmouth, continued with him till he was taken Prisoner. Had a Store with the Army. Staid after Lord Cornwallis was taken Prisoner. Was on Parole. Produces his Parole dated 30th Nov., 1781.

Had leave to go to Cabin Point for recovery of his health Decr., 1781, staid 13 months at Cabin Point, was ill, thence went to New York & staid till Evacuation, & on Evacuation came to Shelbourn. Now resides at Barrington.

(41).

Produces affidt. of John Malcolm Herbert, taken before James MacEwen, at Shelburn, to Loyalty of Claimant & to his having had a shop & store at Norfolk, that he heard of his sufferings & Losses. Saw him afterwards at Charles town in Business again. Heard of his being taken Prisr. & of his Losses.

Produces affidt. of James Dunn to Claimants Loyalty, that he had a store at Portsmouth, was ill treated, imprisoned, his store plundered. Heard of his being taken Prisoner again going from Charles town to Virginia & losing his effects.

Had an house in York Town, took a Lease of the Ground as soon as the Army went under Lord Cornwallis, built a house upon it & left it there. Says he had Leave to stay behind when Lord Dunmore left Portsmouth. A party came down against Lord Dunmore & plundered his store, 1 Hd. Molasses, 3 Vinegar, 3 Barls. do., Tobacco, various articles, these articles were carried away.

12 months afterwards went away & packed up his effects & left with Mr. Thos. Stewart & they were plundered, chiefly Dry Goods.

As Claimant was going from Charles town to Portsmouth he was taken Prisoner by a Body of men who plundered his property, lost 5 Punchuns of Rum, this was on the Eastern Shore, done by a parcel of Plunderers, 2 Hds. of Sugar, 3 Bbls. of fine Powder Sugar, 2 Pipes of Maderia. This was on the Eastern Shore Hog Island.

(42).

Claimant meant to convey these things to Portsmouth, 3 Quarter Casks Wine, 1 Barrel Beef, vars. other articles.

Lost 4 Negroes, 3 were plundered from him on the Eastern Shore, a Wench & 2 Children, the other was taken by a mob from him near Portsmouth as he was going from Charles town, Cattle & horses at different times, all plundered.

Furniture, Tools, James River Bank Bills, Debts about £300 due to him.

JAMES AMOT, Wits:

Says he was apprentice to Claimt. before Troubles began, he resided in Portsmouth. From the first took part with the Brit. He joined Lord Dunmore on his first coming to Portsmouth, he continued with Lord Dunmore while he staid. Staid behind with leave as Wits. thinks.

He was treated very ill after Lord Dunmore went away, rebels came down upon them when Lord Dunmore went away & plundered the Refugees who were the most active. They then took some things from Claimant, Wits. cannot say exactly how much. He kept a grocery store, Vinegar, Molasses.

Afterwards he packed up his effects in Barrels, Wits. helped pack up. All dry goods, 3 or 4 Barrels, they were removed into the shop of a Blacksmith, Mr. Stewart. He was sent to Williamsburg Gaol. While in Gaol he sent word to have these Things removed. Wits. had got Carts to remove them, Stewart persuaded Claimants Wife to let them continue. The next Day they were all taken away. Witness saw mobs about. Stewart had been tarred & feathered. Mobs were raised against the friends of Government. (43)

He had then a Negro Wench & one Child who went afterwards to Charles town, and Witness understood they were lost when Claimant was on the Eastern Shore Hog Island, going from Charlestown to Virginia, and many other things were then lost, plundered by Rebels as Witness heard.

He afterwards bought another Negro in Virginia after his return from Charles town who was taken from him by the Rebels, as Claimant told Wit.

Witness cannot ascertain the value of his store at Portsmouth. Says it was a pretty little store. 3 Horses, 2 Cows & Calves, these he had at first left behind when Claimt. went with the Brit.

He had other Cattle afterwards when he returned from Charles Town. Heard they were taken by Rebels.

Cla'mt. left Furniture when he left Ports mouth with one Cheny. Witness heard it was plundered. Claimant cannot value his store with any exactness, had a Negro Wench with 1 Child at Ports mouth, she had afterwards another Child at Charles town.

Claimant was removing from Charles town, he had landed his goods from a Brig that was driven on Shore & had secured the effects in the Custody of one Arthur Upshaw. The Mob came down & plundered all the things & took ye Negroe Wench & 2 Children. (44).

The Negroe boy he bought ofterwards & lost him in Virginia. The Mob came & plundered him. Claimt. had bought Cattle at a Vendue which had been plundered by the Refugees, he left 18 of these Cattle behind, which were taken by Rebels.

1786.
September 5.

[600]. Evidence in the Case of ROBT. SLOAN, V. first Page.

Produces affidt. of Saml. Smith taken before Neil Robertson, Just. Peace, Island Cape Breton, that Claimt. was dangerously ill in the Fall, 1783, that Witness assisted to move him to Town

Augustin to house of James Lyle, where he lay long ill.

Produces Affidt. from Jas. Lyle that Saml. Smith brought Claimt. to Witness' House in the Fall, 1783, that he was then very ill & continued long ill.

WILLIAM WALLACE, Wits.:

Knew him in South Carolina, heard he joined the Brit. after reduction of Charles town, heard him reported to be a Loyalist & to have been concerned in Skirmishes agst. Rebels, has been on his Lands, reported to be 200 acres in 96 Dist., betwixt 15 or 16 acres clear, had seen one horse that he rode, breeding mare & Colt. He was reported to have a large stock of horses and of cattle, but more of Horses.

(45).

SAML. PROCTOR:

Knew Claimt., he was in the English Camp after fall of Charles town. Understood him to be supporting the English Army. Has been on his Lands once, 200 acres, not much clear, stock small when Witness was on the Place, a good while ago.

September 25.

608. Examination taken de bene esse in the Case of NATHANIEL TAYLOR, now residing in Canada, formerly of Massts.

SAMPSON SALTER BLOWERS, Esq., sworn, saith:

Knew Claimant, he lived at Boston, he was uniformly Loyal, actively so, was much persecuted on acct. of his Principles. He was Deputy Naval Officer thro' the Province of Massts., a Son of the late Sr. Frances Bernard was Principal, he had held it for several years. He had held it under Mr. Bernard's Predecessors in office, Communabus Annos. Thinks it was worth £500 Mass. Cury. He had an appointment from Mr. Bernard, thinks it very improbable any other Person should have been appointed to supersede him, but supposes he would have continued to act.

He continued to act after it had become a matter of Danger for the King's officers to act, & after many of the King's officers had been threatened & had resigned. He left Boston with the Troops, he could not have staid afterwards.

(46).

WILLM. TAYLOR, Esq., Wits., Brother to the Claimt., sworn, saith:

The Claimant was native of America, resided at Boston. When Troubles began he had then the office of Deputy Naval Officer in the Port of Boston for 20 yrs. before. Deputy Naval Officer thro the whole Province for about 4 years, he was Deputy to Mr. Bernard. Witness does not exactly know the Terms between his Brother & Mr. Bernard.

From the first of the Troubles he was uniformly attached to the Brit. Government, he was particularly active at the time Govr. Hutchinson commended. He left Boston when the Troops did. He was proscribed, his name is in the first Act.

His Property was chiefly personal, he had some real Property, 2 pieces of Ground in Boston, building Lots, but there was not any building upon them.

The cffice was formed of Mr. Barnard, a very lucrative office, imagines it worth £600 Ster. per An.

GEORGE BRINDLEY, Esq.:

Knew Claimant at Boston, from the first looked upon him as perfectly Loyal, & he continued uniformly so. He was Deputy Naval Officer at first of the Port of Boston for several years. At commencement of Troubles he was Deputy to Mr. Bernard, thinks that Deputation extended to several other Ports, thinks it extremely unlikely he should have been turned out, he had been long in the office, even from his Infancy. Witness did not know the Terms he was upon with Mr. Bernard.

Claimt. was much respected in his office & had a great Knowledge of it & he therefore thinks he would not have been turned out, does not know the value, but says he supported a large Family handsomely out of it. Has generally understood that these Deputies continued while they conducted themselves well.

(47).

GREGORY TOWNSEND, Esq.:

Knew Claimant at Boston, always heard him reckoned a faithful Loyal subject. Knew him intimately & is convinced of his Loyalty. He declared his Loyalty from the first.

He was proscribed early. Was obliged to leave Boston when the Troops went away. He was in Possession of the office of Deputy Naval Officer from a Boy, he had been in the office at Commencement of the Troubles, thinks Mr. Bernard was the Principal. Does not know what Terms he was upon with Mr. Bernard. Looks upon it as a permanent office, unless for misbehaviour. He was a man of excellent Character & thorough Knowledge of the office. & therefore very unlikely to be turned out.

The appointment was lucrative. Witness does not exactly know the value, thinks it supported him & his Family, who lived handsomely upon it.

(48).

September 29.   Further Evidence in the Case of COL. FANNING.

Captn. DANL. MACNEAL, Wits., sworn, saith:

He lived formerly in N. Carolina. Knew the Tract of Land which from General Report he understood to be Col. Fanning's, & had so understood for several years, it was near Cape Fear River, thinks about 640 acres, some clear, not much. Improvmts. not Considerable.

There was a road thro the Land which Wits. often w nt. Land near the road excellent, he understood the other parts were equally good. Thinks what he saw would sell at 2 Gns. per acre, tho there were little clearings upon it. Clearances were in bad order, but the Land excellent, Improvmts. ordinary. Knew he had a House at Hillborough, heard of his having Lands at the Hawfields.

N.B.—Much too high.

(49).

PROCEEDINGS

OF

LOYALIST COMMISSIONERS

St. JOHNS, 1786.

Vol. X.

BEFORE COMMISSIONER PEMBERTON.

Claimants.

	MSS. Folio.		MSS. Folio.
Acherly, Isaac	60	Kipp, Samuel	55
Brisband, John	65	Lutkins, Hendric	21
Brown, John	66	Mabee, Peter	59
Bunnel, Solomon	37	Obrien, John	69
Callahan, Mrs. Rebecca	17	Perine, John	47
Covert, Abraham	61	Ruggles, Brigadier Gen. Timothy	1
Fowler, Jonathan	39	Smith, Arthur	24
Fowler, Mrs. Sarah	50	Smith, Samuel	12
Golding, Nathaniel	64	Sneden, Stephen	12
Hatfield, Isaac, Jr.	37	Tobias, Joseph	40
Horton, Solomon	67	Tolten, James	60
Jones, Josiah, Simeon, Stephen and Jonas	30, 36 and 51	Vincent, Charles	62
		Willett, Walter	7
Jones, Mrs. Mahitabel	34	Williams, Frederic	44

47 AR.

THE EVIDENCE.

1786.
October 13.

609. Case of Brigdr. Genl. TIMOTHY RUGGLES, late of Hardwick, Co. of Worcester, Massachusetts.

Claimant sworn, saith:

(1).

He is a native of America, born in Massts., resided at Hardwick, took an active part in favour of Government in the French War, the War before the last, served under General Amherst, was the oldest officer & had the Command of the Provincial Troops. Had the Honor of particular Commendations for his Conduct in a Battle near Lake George, took the French General Prisoner. At the end of the Campaign after the taking of Montreal, he retired to his Country Employment at Hardwick. He was second to Genl. Haviland, who Commanded one of the Divisions against Montreal.

Was residing at Hardwick on his own Estate when the Troubles broke out. Always a friend of Brit. Govnt. In the Disturbance about the Stamp Act, a Congress was chose to sit at New York, Claimant was chose one of that Congress by the Province of Massts. with 2 others, of whom Otis was one, attended that Congress. When he saw how violent they were, he dissented from their measures & would not sign an address because it denied the Power of Parlt. to bind the Colonies. On his return was reprimanded by the House of Representatives at Massts. for his unfaithful Discharge of his Duty.

In consequence of this Reprimand, he moved for Leave to Publish the Reasons of his Conduct, which was at first granted, but afterwards retracted, but he afterwards published them at his own Expense & Risk.

(2).

His publication quieted People in general, tho' many violent people were his enemies, yet he was so popular that he was returned representative to the House of Assembly. He continued there in great measure unmolested till there came out a mandamus for a new Council. Claimant acted under that mandamus as one of the Council. He had formerly refused a seat at the Council Board, but on this conjuncture of affairs, he was induced to accept the appointment, finding many people were alarmed & afraid to come forward & declare their Sentiments & many had refused.

This particularly marked him as an object of Persecution to the Rebel Party. On his way to join Genl. Gage he was assaulted by a Mob & got thro' them at great Hazard about 10th Aug., 1774. Never returned home. Went to Salem. On Evacuation of Boston came with the Troops to Halifax. Went to New York, came from thence on Evacuation. Now settled at Aylesford. Was amongst the first persons proscribed. His Property has been all Confiscated.

Produces a Gazette printed at New York in 1775, mentioning Thomas Gage & Timothy Ruggles as proto Rebels & Wicked Parricides.

Produces a Letter wrote to him while at Boston to caution him against secret attempts upon his Life, then thought to be concerted.

Produces appointment from Sr. W. How to Claimt. to be Commandant of all the Comps. of Loyal Associated Volunteers, dated Octr., 1775.

Was possessed of an Estate consisting of Seven Farms in Harwick, one Farm in Prince town & some Land in New Hampshire.

No. 1—His Homestead Farm, purchased part by his Father in 1739 in Considn. of £500, made other purchases afterwards. Consisted altogether of about 400 acres, had been long in Possession, built upon it & improved it, a good mansion House well finished, 2 Barns & outhouses, about 300 acres clear. Had let it. The rent was to be paid by improvement of farm. (3).

No. 2—A Pine Plain Farm on Ware River, purchased in 1753 in Considn. of £200 lawful. Consists of 103 acres.

No. 3—The Cooper Farm with several pieces, containing about 150 acres.

No. 4—The Cox Farm, containg abt. 150 acres, these two last Farms were in Claimts. Possession, but his Son was upon them. These Farms were well improved with good orchards, Stone Walls, Houses & Barns on each.

No. 5—His Billings Farm, consisting of upwards of 100 acres.

No. 6—His Gate Farm, consisting of upwards of 100 acres.

No. 7—Farr Place with a Tract adjoining called Winslows, about 100 acres.

Three Pews in the Meeting House.

No. 8—Part of the Pot Ash Farm in Prince Town, consisting of about 500 acres.

Thinks his Hardwick Estate consisted of about 1,100 acres, Vals. it at 12,000 Stn., including his part of the Pot Ash Farm in Prince town. It was a fine Situation. Hardwick laid about midway from Connecticut River & the Places from which Cattle are usually driven for the Stall feeders. There was a fair twice a year at Hardwick. Had it in Contemplation to have turned his farm to a grazing farm & values it on that Idea. (4).

Produces an Inventory of the Claimts. Estate taken by 5 Appraisers appointed by the State of Massts. in 1777, who agree with the above acct. as to Quantity of Land. Produces Copy of Grant of Pot Ash Farm which appears to have been granted in Jany., 1764, by the House of Representatives to Claimant in Considn. of his important services during the late War, more particularly while Commander in Chief of the Troops of the Province furnished

---

for Reduction of Canada.

Claimant had at different times parted with about 2-3 of this. 1-3 was left, consisting of about 500 acres.

Produces Letter from his Agent, Timothy Paine, from Worcester Co., informing him that his Estate had been declared Confiscated & disposed of, sends him Copy of the Valuation by 5 Appraisers, Nov. 7, 1785.

(5).

Produces an acct. from the Registers office in Co. Worcester, where all Conveyances of Land are registered, Containing Conveyances of Land to Claimt. to the above amount in 21 Lots. There was a Mortgage on two farms for £300 lawf.

Claimant says the Schedule of his personal Estate delivered at the office is a true acct. of the valuation just. He set down all the particulars according to the best of his Recollection in order to be as exact as possible not with a view to enhance the value of his Estates.

Has a Pension of £200 per Ann. v. Mandamus Council.

Claimant had the office of Inspector of Unclaimed Lands in New Hampshire. Produces grant of this office during his Majesty's Pleasure, with a Yearly Salary of £300 per Ann., Dated 1770. This Salary was paid about the time Claimant came int) this Province. At the time Claimant was doing the Duties of this appointmt., it was attended with Considerable Expense, so that he did not Clear much by it, as he thought himself obliged to pay those expenses. Most of those expenses would not have returned again so that he thinks he should have cleared £250 per Ann. by it.

Produces Certificate from Committee appointed to settle with Committees of Sale, stating the neat Proceeds of real & personal Estate of Claimt. amounted to 1231.14 lawful, dated Boston, 15 Novr., 1785.

Produces Letr. from Agent dated Novr. 17, 1785, which says that part of the Estate set off to the Claimts. Wife for 3rd is not included in Certificate above mentioned.

(6).

JOHN RUGGLES, Witness:

Knew the Estate at Hardwick, it Consisted of seven farms. No. 1—He thinks it about 400 acres. His father lived there. Farm well fenced & improved. Land in excellent cultivation, on an average best lands would sell at 20 Dollars per acre, unimproved Lands at 1-3.

No. 2—Knew that farm.
No. 3—Knew that farm.
No. 4—Knew that also very well. The two last farms as good as the Homestead.
Knew also No. 5, equally good with the Homestead farm.
Knew also No. 6, adjoining former, equally good.
No. 7—Equally good.
No. 8—Potash farm in Prince Town, not so good as Homestead. but very valuable.

His father had 34 horses. 50 Head of Cattle, of which 10 were oxen.

RICHARD RUGGLES, Wits., Son of Claimant:

Knew the Estate at Hardwick very well. Consisted of about 7 farms. No. 1 Homestead farm, vals. it at £10 per acre altogether, including builds.

No. 2. Knew that farm. Had a large Quantity of Intervail Land. No. 3 & No. 4 equally good with the Homestead. No. 5 & No. 6 adjoining equally good. No. 7 equally good. No. 8 in Princetown. His father had sold some of these Lands. Some of it very good. (7).
His mother has now part of the Homstead, & part of another farm for her 3ds. The eldest son lives with her. Thinks there were 40 horses, near 100 head Cattle, 50 Sheep or more.

Certificate produced that Claimt.'s real Estate in Massts. was sold as forfeited, excepting Part assigned to his Wife while she continues in the States. Signed John Fessenden, Willm. Paige, who were two of the Committee. 1787. February 22.

NEW CLAIM.

610. Case of WALTER WILLET, formerly of Pensilvania.   1786. October 16.

Claimant sworn saith:

In Jany., 1784, he resided at Granville. Heard of the act in Jany. Thos. Oldfield sent Marines on Board the Renown. Was then with Claimt. He made out his Claim. Got some Papers from the States, gave them to Mr. Oldfield, who was then going to England & made Mr. Oldfield his attorney, who expected to sail in a few days, but his ship was delaid, & did not sail so soon.

Produces a Letter from Clementson & Denton, his new agents in London, dated Octr., 1785, who say that Lieut. Oldfield has lodged Claimant's memorial with them, but they could do nothing with it as it was too late. Claimant thinks the Renown sailed a little time after Lieut. Oldfield left him.   (8).

Says he is native of America. Resided in Bucks Co., Pensilvn., when Troubles broke out, in Septr., 1777. Joined the Brit. Army under Sr. Wm. How, just before the Battle of Germantown. Was with the army & frequently employed by Sr. Wm. Erskine to get Intelligence.

In April, 1778, held a Commissn. as Lieut. of Bucks Co. Light Dragoons in Captn. Sandford's Troops. Was attached to the Queen's Rangers under Col. Simcoe in 1779. Was with him when he was taken near Brunswick. Commanded the advanced Guard that Day. Had seven men killed & wounded that Day.

Went to Savanah. Was attached to Tarleton's Legion, 1780.

and about June, 1780, was incorporated with the Legion, and now receives half Pay as Lieut. of the Legion.

Came to this Province from New York before evacuation. Was chose agent for the officers of the Legion. Now settled at Granville.

Was possessed of a Farm in Bucks Co., consisting of 173 acres. Had it by marriage. It had been the Estate of Thos. Harding. Thos. Harding has 2 durs., one named Martha, the other Rachel. He died many years ago, & the Estate came to his 2 Daughters. Claimant married the eldest Daughter, Martha. In 1767 a Division was made of the Estate between the 2 Sisters.   (9).

Produces Copy of the Proceedings in the Court of Common Pleas, Bucks Co., on a Partition of the Estate in 1767, whereby it appears that 172 acres of the Estate late of Thos. Harding are assigned to Claimt. & Martha, his Wife, as her Right. The other moiety is assigned to the other sister.

Produces office Copy of Covenant to lead use of Recovery, by which it is covenanted that a Recovery shall be suffered of the Lands, & they settled to the use of Claimant & his Heirs, dated 14 March, 1775. Enrolled in Ct. of Com. Pleas. Produces Copy of Writ of Execution whereby it appears the said Recovery was suffered agreeably to the aforesaid Covenant in March, 1775.

(10). Says he was proscribed and his Estate Confiscated both real & personal. Produces Copy of Certificate from George Wall, dated April 18, 1786, whereby he certifies that he had recd. from Martha Willet £7,000, the purchase money for the Confiscated Estate of Walter Willet 23 Aug., 1779. With affidavit from Isaac Hicks that the above is a true Copy from the original Certificate in Mrs. Willet's Hands, and that he was well acquainted with the hand writing of said George Wall, reputed agent of Confiscated Estates & believes the Hand writing of the original Certificate to be the sd. George Waters. Sworn before Timothy Taylor, one of Judges of Common Pleas, April, 1786. This £7,000 paid by Martha Willet was Congress money. Claimant's Father & Mother in Law let her have the money to purchase it.

He cannot say what the Congress money was worth at time of purchase. Says his Father & Brother in Law borrowed this money & have been sued for it, but the Estate was sold again to pay the money. What it was sold for he cannot tell.

Claimant's Father, Brother in Law, Wife & seven children are all living there. Whether they live on the Estate he does not know. He does not know whether the Estate is absolutely sold. Says this Estate is worth £12 Pensila. Cur. per acre. It has been appraized by two appraizers at 20 Dollars per acre, amounting to

£7.10. Claimt. therefore values it at £7.10 per acre. Says his wife has behaved very ill & he is now at variance with her.

His personal Estate was Confiscated & sold at Vendue. All his personal Estate was seized soon after he joined the Brit. Army & sold.

3 Mares, 2 Cows, 32 Sheep, 8 Tons Hay, 100 Bushels Wheat, Wagon, Cart, Beds & furniture. All these were sold & nothing restored afterwards to his wife.

(11). Says that by the Laws of Pensilvania his Wife is now her own mistress, & can purchase the same as if divorced. It is considered as a **Divorce**.

SAML. WILLET, Wits., saith:

Claimant came in the Fall 1783. Saw Claimt. in April, '84. He then told him he had sent his Claim home by Mr. Oldfield. He saw Mr. Oldfield a few weeks before who told him the same. The Renown went in the course of that summer. Knew his farm in Bucks Co. It had been the Wife's Estate. He was offered £12 per acre for it 2 yrs. before. Thinks it was worth less when Claimt. left it.

Knew his personal Estate. Says it was taken for use of Continental Army. Whether sold he cannot, but thinks they were sold. A Brooding mare, 2 young Mares, 32 Sheep, 2 Cows, other things taken afterwards. Thinks Congress money in 1779 was as 5 to 1.

Produces office Copy of Conveyance by Commonwealth of Pensil. in March, 1778, to Martha Willet of a Plantation consisting of 172 acres in Consideration of £7,000 Cury., renting it to be the Estate forfeited by Claimt.

November 27.

Further Evidence in the Case of SAML. SMITH, of New Jersey.

Claimt. lost 110 acres in Elizth. Township. Purchased of Jonathan Mash in Considn. 500, 17 yrs. ago. Vals. £750.
34 Cattle, 3 Horses, 3 Hogs, 16 Sheep, Household furniture, vars. or. articles.

(12).

SAML. MOOR:

Knew his Farm. Has been upon it. Heard of his purchasing it of one Mash. Thought to have got it cheap. He much improved it. Heard he had a good stock & had many Cattle taken from him before he left home.

NEW CLAIM.

611. Case of STEPHEN SWEDEN, late of New York.

1786.
October 17.

Claimt. sworn saith:

He was at New York in Octr., 1783. Had heard of the act & delivered his Claim to Mr. Joshua H. Smith at New York. He was a Lawyer & drew it up for the Purpose of being presented to ye Commrs. Pd. him 2 gns. & ½ for it. Never heard from Mr. Smith about it. Mr. Smith gave Claimt. his address where to write to him in England, which he produces & says it is Mr. Smith's Hand writing.

Says he is a native of America. Resided at East Chester when Troubles broke out, on his own Estate. On Troubles breaking out, declared himself a friend of Brit. Govert., but signed first Association on the recommendation of Govr. Tryon as represented to Claimt. by Jos. Gedney & Col. Hunt. Joined the Brit. the day they landed on York Island in 1776. Carried several persons who were coming to join the Brit. Returned home but joined the Brit. at Ward's House & chiefly continued with them, but went occasionally from within the Lines to visit his Family who continued at East Chester. In about a year & half his Family came to him at New York, there continued till evacuation. Acted on two occasions as a Guide to the army. 1st, when a Detachment went from Ward's house to Melesquan, 2nd, the next summer went

(13)

as a guide to a party under Genl. Tryon against Genl. Heath. Produces a protection from Sr. Wm. How, given at Ward's House 27 Oct., 1776. Signed, Robt. Mackenzie.

Produces Certificate to his Loyalty & that he had been persecuted by the Rebels & obliged to quit his Property from Col. Stephen Delancey. To same effect from Jas. Delancey.

Was possessed of—

No. 1. A Farm at East Chester, consisting of about 66 acres. Had it by Deed of gift from his Father.

Produces Deed from his Father Saml. Sweden, whereby in Considn. of fatherly Love he gives 50 acres more or less in East Chester, dated 1 March, 1767.

(14). Produces Deed from John Odell, whereby he bargains & sells to Claimt. a piece of Salt Marsh containing 1 acre &·½ in Considn. of £18 Cury., dated 11 Jany., 1773. Had about 14 acres & ½ left by his Father's Will. He died in April, 1778. Has not the Copy of the Will.

The Farm was in very good order. A good Dwelling house & builds. Claimt. had built the Buildings himself. A good orchard & good Deal of fresh meadow. 20 acres of fresh mead. About 20 acres Tillage, rest Wood & Pasture. Vals. it at £13 Cury. per acre.

This Estate has been sold by Trustees appointed by Supreme Court to pay the sum of £1,200 Cury., which Claimant owed for another Estate which he had purchased.

Both the Estates were sold to pay the Debt. Has been informed that both together they did not amount to sufficient to pay the Debt. His Estate he thinks sold so low in consequence of its being damaged by the Troops, both the British & American Troops.

(15). Was possessed of another Farm in Harrison's Precinct, consisting of 200 acres. Produces Deed from James & Peter Innis, whereby they bargain & sell to Claimt. a mess. & Tract containing 200 acres in Harrison's Precinct in Considn. 1,600 Cur., dated 3 Apl., 1776.

Claimt. says he paid £400 part of purchase money, chiefly in paper money. £1,200 was left unpaid for which Claimt. gave 3 Bonds in the sum of £400 each, to be paid yearly. Have put these Bonds in suit & the Estates of Claimant have been sold to pay this Debt. Vals. this at 1,600, the price he gave for it. Says at the time he purchased, paper money was as good as hard money.

Lost a Negroe worth £60. Taken by a party of Rebels from his farm. Heard he was afterwards sold. Lost a yoke of oxen, taken by Rebels. Do. 2 Cows, 3 Horses. Lost 2 oxen, 2 Cows, taken by Brit. & Hess Troops.

Produces a New York *Packet*, May, 1785, wherein is an advertisement for sale of the above mentioned two Estates, from the Trustees for all the Creditors of Claimant. Said to be the Property of the Trustees of all the Credrs. of Claimt. Trustees are Thomas Thomas, Jesse Hunt & Benjn. Stromson. Claimt. supposes they were Trustees appointed by the Supreme Court. He had made no such Trustees himself.

ROBERT DICKSON, Wits:

Knew Claimt. at East Chester. Has known him since 1774. He was very Loyal. When Brit. first landed on Long Island, he assisted in conveying several Loyalists to the Brit. in Company with Joshua Pell & others. Considers him as uniformly Loyal. Knew his Homestead at East Chester, which he had, as Wits. understood, from his Father. Has heard it vald. at £800 Curcy.

JONATHAN ANDERSON, Wits:

Knew his Farm in Harrison's Precinct. Worth £1,600 Cur. It had been sold 2 years before for £1,800. He was always considered a friend of Government.

COL. BERRY HUNT, Wits: (16).

Knew Claimant. At first he was not so well attached as Wits. wished, but afterwards he was a true friend to Brit. Govert. He was once appointed a Committee man for the Rebels & acted as one, but on Brit. landing on Long Island he joined them & had a Correspondence with them. He once with anor. Committee man called on Witness & wanted him to sign an Association. Continued steady after he joined the Brit. N.B.—Claimt a shabby Loyalist.

Knew his Estate at East Chester. He had it from his Father. Vals. it at £7 or 800.

Heard of his purchase of another Estate in 1776 for £1,600. Knew of his having a Negroe. Heard he was taken by one Stephen Ward, a violent Rebel & sold. Heard of the sale of both his Estates, for a Debt of 1,200.

The Estate having been damaged & there being arrears of Interest made his Estate sell for less than enough to pay the Debt. Thinks when he purchased the second Estate, it was an improper time.

612. Case of REBECCA CALLAHAN, Widow of Charles Callahan, formerly of Province of Mayne, Massts. 1786. October 17.

Claimt. sworn saith: She is Widow of Charles Callahan, late of Pownalburg. He was Native of Ireland. Was settled at Pownalburg, before the Troubles began. From Beginning he declared himself a friend of Brit. Govert. (17).

In the year 1777, he was so persecuted that he left his Home & went to Halifax. He had been in the sea farring way. He had the Command given him of an armed Sloop called the Genl. Gage. He continued as Commander of this Sloop for 2 years, when he was cast away & lost his Life on the Nova Scotia Coast. He was then going to pilot a Sloop of war called the North to Spanish River.

Claimant continued at Pownalburg till 1778, then was obliged to quit it. 3 months after her Husband had left her, the Rebels came & seized all his Estate, real & personal, dispossessed Claimt. of her Husbs. property. Sold his personalities by auction. She was obliged to fly & came to this Place. From thence she went to Halifax.

His real Estate was advertised for sale, but was not sold. Claimant has since been & taken Possession of it; found it much damaged. The house was greatly damaged, but she was suffered to take Possession of House & Lands.

(18). The real Estate consisted of an House in Pownalburg & 240 acres of land. Claimant's Husband died without a Will. He left a Brother as she thinks, who was in the West Indies, but she has not lately heard of him. She had in Possession, when the personal property was seized, Furniture worth £200. It was a large house, 2 story high. 3 yoke oxen, 9 Cows, 3 Horses, 14 Sheep, farming utensils worth £40. These articles were seized by one Nathanl. Thering, who was appointed agent by the Judge of Probate, & produces office Copy of Appointment of Nathanl. Thering, which states that Charles Callagan had fled to the enemy & absented himself more than 3 months, leaving Estate of more than £20 value. Therefore the Judge of Probate appoints the sd. Nathanl. Thering agent with power to take Possession of all the Estate of sd. Ch. Callagan & to dispose of the same according to Law, & to pay Debts & to return an Inventory to the said Court. Dated 17 Nov., 1777.

In pursuance of this Power Mr. Thering took Possession & sold the personal Estate.

She says her Husband owed no Debts. There were no claims on his Estate. She has had no claims for his Debts since his Death.

Claimant says she left her Brother in Possession of the real Estate, who is since dead. His son she thinks is in Possession.

Produces several Letters from some of the Committee of Correspondence, stating Charles Callagan to be a disaffected person. Summons from Committee of Safety and Complaint to Judge of Probate, desiring him to appoint an agent for his Estate.

(19). Says she should prefer living here if she could. Means to try & sell her Estate at Pownalburg & live here. If she cannot sell it, supposes she must live upon it. Taxes must be paid & so much laid out to put the Estate in Repair, that she cannot live upon it unless she has something on first going to it.

N.B.—I infer from this, that she hopes to get something from G. Brit. to enable her to go & take Possession of her Estate. She assures ye Commrs. by memorial yet she has no Intention to live in New England.

Produces Commission to Charles Callagan to be Commander of Sloop Genl. Gage from I. Wilson, Judge of Ct. of Probate, Dominica, 22 Aprl., 1778.

REVD. MR. BAILEY:

Knew the late Mr. Charles Callagan. He lived at Pownalburg. On breaking out of Troubles he immediately sided with

---

Government. He was obliged to quit his house in consequence of persecution from the Rebels. Went to Halifax, was employed as Commander of the Sloop Gen. Gage, in which he lost his Life when he was piloting a sloop of war.

There was then a Brig preparing for him at Penobscot. Knew his House & farm. His House very elegant, just finished, well furnished. Vals. furniture £200. Thinks it could not be less. 3 yoke of oxen, 9 Cows, 3 Horses, 14 Sheep, farming utensils, £40. Remembers this Property was seized & sold. Heard of no debts on the Estate. Supposes the money was returned into ye Court of Probate for use of the State. (20).

Mrs. Callagan has got Possession of the real Estate, but Witness thinks it can be of no value to her. The Estate is so damaged & she is so proscribed she cannot live there. Speaks of Claimant's ill Treatment after her Husband fled.

Mr. JOHN MACNAMARA, Wits:

Knew the late Charles Callagan. He was very loyal. Obliged to quit Pownalburg in consequence of being called upon to serve in American Army, which he refused & being persecuted on that acct. was obliged to fly. His Estate was soon after seized & his personal Estate sold; furniture worth £200. Had oxen, horses, & farming utensils. Thinks he did not owe a Copper.

Charles Callagan had a Bror. who left America 14 years ago. Heard of his being in West Inds. 4 yrs. ago. 1787. June 14.

Produces Certificate, dated 10th April, 1787, from the Revd. Mr. Bailey & sevl. respectable Inhabitants of Annapolis that Claimt. has resided there sevl. years & that they cannot learn she has any Intention of removing.

NEW CLAIM.

613. Case of HENDRIC LUTKINS, formerly of New Jersey. 1786. October 18.

Claimt. sworn saith:

He came to this Province in fall of 1783. Heard of the act (21). a few Days after he had arrived here. With all expedition drew up his Claim & left it with Major Brown; that he shd. send it away to Halifax to go to England. Major Brown said he sent it right away to England. Major Brown told him he had sent them. They were safe enough.

He is native of America. Lived at Hackinsac in New Jersey when Troubles broke out, on his own Estate. From the first beginning took part with Brit. Govert. Signed no Association with Rebels. Joined the Brit. Army under Genl. How as soon as he came to Hackinsac. Continued with the Army; went to Staten Island & then to New York, staid till Evacuation & then came to

---

this Prov. & is now settled in Clements Precinct. Lives with one Van horn. Acted once as a Guide to the Army. Was possessed of 20 acres of land at Hackinsac. Purchased 2 acres many years before ye Troubles. Produces Deed from Isaac Kess to Claimt. of a piece of Land in Precinct of Barbadoes in Considn. of £12.5 Cury. of New York, dated Nov., 1772.

(22).

This was 2 acres. Vals. them at £6 per acre. An orchard upon it. Had 20 acres from his Father by Will. His Father died about 15 yrs. ago. Had it before his Father's Death. Continued in Possession. Produces a Release from his 2 Brothers reciting that Claimt. was entitled to these Lands, containing 20 acres under his Father's Will & releasing all their Rights, dated 1783. Claimt. says he was the eldest son, & released his Rights to some other Lands to his Brothers, which he did in order to Confirm what he knew was his Father's Intention, to avoid Disputes, as there was some Doubt about the Will.

There was a small house, 5 acres Meadow, 4 acres Wood, the rest Tillage, 3 miles from Hackinsac. Vals. it at £6 per acre. All this Land has been sold. Produces Certificate of Judgement & Confiscation.

Produces Certificate from James Board, one. of the Commrs. for the County Bergen, of Sale of Claimant's real & personal Es-

| Real Estate, 16 acres & 3 Qrs............... | £473.3. 9 |
| Personal Estate .... | 284.1.10 |

This is in Congress Money.

N.B.—Claimt. seems a fair man.

Says his personal Estate was seized & sold, consisting 1 horse, val. £20; furniture & farming utensils, £40, undervalued.

JOHN FRANCIS RIERSON, Wits:

(23).

Claimt. came to this Province in fall 1783. Understood he had his Claim made out at Major Browns to be sent to England. Witness advised him to it, & it was done. From the first Day Claimt. was a good Loyalist. His only 2 Sons & a Son in Law were in the Brit. Army.

He joined the Brit. in the Fall 1776 when Troops came first to Hackinsac. He served as a Volunteer & did Duty with Witness frequently. Continued with the Brit. Troops, attending on Skinner's Corps, frequently serving as Volunteer the whole war.

Knew his Estate purchased of Isaac Kepp, about 2 acres. It was all an orchard, joining to his Land, lignt land, but situation good. Vals. it at near £10 per acre. Knew the Lands he had from his Father. Claimt. was the eldest Son. The Father divided his Estate between all his Sons. Thinks Claimt.'s share might be about 20 acres. It was light land, 5 acres meadow very good. Vals. it at £10 Cury. per acre altogether.

This being a small Parcel of Land would fetch more than a large Parcel. Knew his horse, very good. Worth £15 York Money. Furniture & Farm utensils worth £50.

NEW CLAIM.

1786.
October 20.

614. Case of ARTHUR SMITH, late of New York.

Claimant sworn saith:

He was in the Province in the Fall of 1783. Resides in Granville Co., 18 miles from Anapolis. His Wife came to him in Novr.

She brought the Act of Parlt. amongst other Papers. Claimt. did (24).
not meet with Act of Parlt. till Jany., 1784, then went to Col. N.B.—Ought to
Beverley Robinson to have his Claim drawn up & sent home, who have sent us as soon as his wife
sent it home to his Father, Col. Robinson, then in England, but arrived.
it arrived in England too late.
 Produces Certificate from Col. Bevy. Robinson that Claimt. N.B.—Claimt.
applied to him in Beginning of the year 1784 to have his Claim seems to have applied time
forwarded to the Commrs. which he forwarded to his Father, then enough.
in England, to lay before Commrs., but it arrived too late.
 He is a native of America. Lived in Orange Co. when Troubles broke out. From the first sided with the Brit. Govert. Was a Prisoner when the Brit. Army first came to New York. Had been taken up & committed to Prison by the Provincial Congress on

acct. of his Principles. Was in Confinement at Fisk Hill when Brit. came to Long Island, then was suffered to go home on Parole. In beginning of 1777 was taken up again & released on Parole. In May, 1777, taken up & close confined in Orange Co. Gaol. In June committed prisoner on board a prison ship. In Aug. following made his escape & joined the Brit. Army at Hackinsac in Septr. Continued with the Army in Government service, employed by Col. Willard who was in the Commissary Department, in purchasing Horses, Cattle &c., for the Army. (25).
 In Novr., 1778, was taken Prisoner, while he was upon Government service, going to make purchases. Was taken prisoner on Long Island. Kept Prisr. till March, '80, then escaped, & got to New York, there continued till he came to this Province, which was in the Fall 1782. Now settled at Willmot. His Wife & family came to him from New York in the Fall 1783.
 Was possessed of 257 acres in Orange Co. Produces Deed from John & James MacGreer to Claimant of Lot No. 7 in Chesacook Patent in Orange Co., containing 157 acres in Considn. £141 N. York Cur., dated 1757.
 Produces Deed from Philip Livingston to Clarmt. of Lot No. X in Chesa Cook Patent in Considn. £175 New York Cury., dated 1764.

 This Lot No. X consisted of 100 acres. They were unimproved Lands when Claimt. purchased them. Claimt. built an house, good Barn, 4 barracks. The 2 Lots joined. Cleared almost the whole estate. It was chiefly Intervaile. Lived upon it. 3 orchards upon it. Was within 14 miles of Town of Gochen. Was offered for this estate £2,000 York Cury. 3 years before the Troubles, including the Crops on the ground. Vals. it at £2,000 York Cury. This estate has been Confiscated & sold.
 Produces New York *Packet*, dated Octr. 12, 1780, containing a summons from the Sheriff of New York for Claimant to appear (26).
& traverse the Indictment found against, otherwise there would be Judgement against him.
 Has been informed by many People that this Estate was Confiscated & sold. Some of his own Family have been on the Estate since it was purchased by Saml. Brewster.

Says he had other Lands but having no Deeds he made no Claim. Lands on Long Island, but has not heard wher. they are Confiscated, given by his Father. Had 22 Rights in Brookhaven & South haven, Long Island, given by his Father by Deed of Gift, worth £1,000, but has not heard whether they are Confiscated. Had 225 acres in Orange Co. 12 miles from his before mentioned Estate, laid in Banker's Patent. Had it by Deed of Gift from

his Father in Law. Says it is Confiscated, but he has no evidence of it.

Claimt. is told he must get Certificates of Sale of the 2 Lots comprising his Estate of 257 acres. Imagines his lands on Long Island may have been seized by his eldest Brother & be in Possession of it in his Children.

Claimt. had it by Deed of Gift from his Father. The eldest Bror. sided strongly with Americans. Is since dead as Claimant has heard. The 225 acres may possibly be secured by his former Tenant, who is Grandson to his Father in Law, from whom Claimt. had it.

(27).
Had 8 yoke of oxen, 50 Cows, 24 3-yr. old Steers & Heifers, 18 2-yr. old, 20 yearlings. His whole stock was about 150 Head. 14 Horses, 160 Sheep, 30 Hogs, Farming Utensils, Tools, Corn & Boards, Household furniture, chiefly destroyed by the Rebels. Vals. furniture at £100.

This property was seized & sold at public Vendue.

JOSHUA OKES, Wits:

Knew the Claimant, not much till lately. Heard he had been persecuted by the Rebels on acct. of his Loyalty. Heard he was always reckoned a Loyalist. Heard that he had been imprisoned. After ye Peace was in Orange Co. & saw the estate which was reported to have been his when he lived. Saml. Brewster was in Possession. Had bought it of the Commissioners. A great Deal of Meadow, 60 or 70 acres. A great Deal of cleared Land besides

heard his moveable Estate was all sold by the Comrs. Thinks the Land would have sold altogether at 10 Dollars per acre. Wits. saw Saml. Brewster a little time afterwards, who said he had sold the Farm.

JAMES SMITH, Wits:

Son of Claimant. Says his Father was several times imprisoned on acct. of his Loyalty. Was imprisoned on board a prison ship, made his escape & went within the Brit. Lines. He served in the Commissary Department purchasing Provisions till he was taken Prisoner on Long Island.

(28).
Knew the Land in Orange Co. About 260 acres. He lived upon it. Thinks there were near 100 acres meadow. The Land was chiefly cleared. Had better than 100 head of Cattle, 14 horses, good farming stock. His house well furnished. Has heard of these Lands being Confiscated.

JOHN SMITH, Wits:

Son of Claimt. Remembers his Father was several times imprisoned on acct. of his Loyalty. He was always on the part of the British. Remembers his being on board the Prison Ship & making his escape & going within Brit. Lines. Wits. was at home when they came & seized his Father's Estate. All the moveables were sold at Vendue. They afterwards seized & sold the Land.

Witness has been since the Peace on the Land. Sely & Little were in possession when Wits. was there. Heard they bought it of Brewster for £1,400.

Remembers when his Father's moveables were sold. A great many Cattle & Horses were sold. Left only one Cow for his Mother. They sold everything. His Mother bought 2 Cows & 1 horse.

BENJAMIN BADCOCK, Wits:

Knew Claimant. He was always a Loyalist. Frequently imprisoned. He was on board the Prison Ship. Remembers his moveables being seized by the Commrs. Col. Marvill came & took ye Inventory. Saw the sale. 150 horn Cattle, 14 horses, 170 Sheep, 30 Hogs, farming utensils, household furniture. Saw these articles sold. Mrs. Smith had 1 Bed, 1 Cow.

Knew he had a large Estate. About 250 acres. A great Deal cleared. The Improvements had all been done by himself. Near 100 acres Mead. clear. Near 100 acres new Plough Land. Has heard this Land has been Confiscated; that Brewster bought it.

Nov. 27. Produces certificate of sale of personal estate, and of real estate to amount of 100 acres, with Letter from Major Bashley stating the difficulty of getting ye Certificate for real estate, but saying he is confident the whole was sold.

(29).

615. Case of JOSIAH SIMEON STEPHEN & JONAS JONES, late of Massts.

1780.
October 21.

JOSIAH JONES appears & being sworn says:

He & his Bros. Claim as Heirs to his Father who died in 1776. He died without a Will, leaving eleven Children. Nathan, the eldest son, now living in the States. Elisha, who died in this Province leaving a Widow & children. Israel now living in the States. Daniel who lived in the States now dead., having left a Widow & children. Elias in the States. Claimant Josiah in Nova Scotia. Ephraim now in Canada, who has served in the Brit. Army the whole War. Josiah who now appears & lives at Sisseboo, Simeon who lives in New Brunswick. Stephen who lives at Sisseboo. Jonas who lives in England. He left also one Daughter married to Issa Dunbar who lives in the States.

Claimant says his Mother also is living & now lives in the States. His Father had a considerable landed Estate in Midsex Co., Massts. By his dying without a Will his Estate goes amongst all his children, 2 shares to the eldest son. His Mother has no Jointure, but is entitled to her Dower.

(30).

Says his Father Elisha Jones was a native of America. Lived in Midx. Co. He had always been a friend to Brit. Government. Opposed all their Town meetings. Declared his sentiments openly.

,In 1775 he was then Col. of Militia of the Co. of Midx. and raised the Militia in order to oppose the violent measures of the Insurgents. He was obliged to keep a guard of Militia round his own House for fear of being attacked. His Life was in Danger which was the Reason that he kept this Guard. Before Hostilities began, the Mobs had come so often against him that he was obliged to leave home & went to Boston in the Fall 1774. Continued there to declare the same sentiments. Three of his sons were with him in Boston, and after the Battle of Lexington, embodied in Militia (31). under Gen. Ruggles. Josiah & Stephen, two of the Claimts. & Elisha who is dead.

His Father continued in the same Loyal Principles till his Death. Gen. Gage always consulted him & placed the greatest confidence in him. He died in 1776.

Claimant, Josiah, lived in New Hampshire when Troubles began. Always took the part of ␣overt. Left home on 19 April, 1775. Was obliged to go, as he was then so persecuted by Mobs, the whole Family having made themselves obnoxious by their ⸺Loyalty, that he could not stay. Went to his Father at Boston. Continued under Protection of Brit. Arms. Was sent to this Province by Gen. Gage to procure Forage for the Army. In coming to this Province was taken Prisoner but made his escape & in 1776

served in the Militia under Gen. Ruggles. They consisted of Loyalists who were embodied at Boston. Served till Boston was evacuated. Went with the army to Halifax, then went with the army to New York, having an employment in the Secretary's office under Captn. Mackenzie. Continued in this employment till the year following then was employed in the office of the Inspector of Provisions, Francis Rush Clarke. Went with ye Army to Philadelphia, afterwards employed in the Commissarys Line at New York. Was then in Govr. Wentworth's Genl. Volunteers & served till the Fall 1782, then came to this Province.

His Father was possessed of—

(32). No. 1. 2,900 acres in Adams, Massts. His Father had a grant of it many years ago, above 20 years ago. This is still unimproved. The Grant was from the Province by purchase. Claimt. does not know what consideration was given. Vals. this at 11 Shills. per acre, Ster. This is Confiscated.

No. 2. 5,200 acres in Partridge Field. His Title was the same by Purchase from the Province, 20 years ago. The Land continues as it was. Vals. this at 11 shils. per acre. Produces a Quit Claim from Governor Bernard relative to this Estate.

No. 3. 674 acres in Pitsfield & Washington, purchased by his Father of Charles Prescot. Produces Deed from Charles Prescot to Elisha Jones of 600 acres in Considn. £133, 1,750. Vals. this at 15 shil. per acre. His Father had been offered this. The Land was unimproved, but from its situation very valuable.

No. 4. 75 acres at Weston in Co. of Midx. This he had from his Father. There was an elegant mansion house, & various builds. All the Land clear & improved, except what was kept for wood. Vals. £1,000 Ster. Produces Release from Elisha Jones' Brothers & sister to this Property.

No. 5. 70 acres in West Town called Allens Farm, purchased of David Allen. Produces Deed from David Allen to Elisha Jones of 70 acres in Weston in Considn. £250, 1,758. Vals. this at £350. His Father had much improved it.

No. 6. 44 acres in Jerico purchased 15 yrs. ago of Randal Davies. Has seen the Deed. Vals. this £150 Ster. It was chiefly mowing Land, 15 miles from Boston. (33).

No. 7. 85 acres in Nonsuch. Produces 4 old Deeds to his Father of land in Nonsuch. Various considerations, exceeding 85 acres in Quantity but his Father sold part. This is chiefly in Weston, Notick & Sudbury, about 15 miles from Boston. Improved by his Father. Vals. at £382 Ster.

No. 8. 60 acres in Prince Town purchased 25 years ago, then unimproved. Since improved by his Father, now consisting of Pasture. Vals. at £150 Ster. Produces old Deed from Isaac Jones of Release to Claimant of this Land.

Produces Copy of Libel by the Attorney Genl. against his Father & Certificates of Sale agreeing with the above acct.

Says his Mother has made application for her 3ds. but has got nothing. His Brothers who have continued in the States have got nothing except what was given by their Father in his life time. They are in Hopes of recovering some Lands not included in ye Confiscation.

616. Case of Mrs. MAHITABEL JONES, Widow of Elisha Jones. October 21, 1786.

Claimant sworn saith

She is the Widow of Elisha Jones. Elisha Jones lived in Boston Govert. when Troubles broke out. He joined the Brit. at Boston. Went to his Father then. He was with the Army till he came to this Province, in the Fall 1782. He had been employed in the forage & wagon Department. He died in Jany., 1783, without a Will, leaving 7 children. His eldest son Elisha now of age is at St. Johns. His 2nd Son Alpheus & a daughter, Mahitabel, are in the States. Sereno, Upham, Asina, Unice, Robert are with their Mother. She claims a share for herself & children to the Estate of her Husband's Father for which see the preceding Case. (34).

Her Husband was possessed of—

No. 1. 105 acres in Adams. He had it by Gift from his Father 16 or 17 years ago.

No great improvements. Produces Copy of deed from Register of grant to Elisha Jones of Pitsfield in Considn. of his building a Saw Mill by Elisha Jones. John Murray & Nathan Jones, 1768. Says he built a Saw Mill according to the above Considn.

48 AR.

No. 2. 230 acres in Pitsfield. Produces Copy from Register's office of Deed, whereby Elisha Jones in considn. of fatherly love grants, Elisha Jones, his son, 230 acres in Pitsfield, 1761.

Her husb. lived at Pitsfield; built an house & barns & had a good store. 100 acres under Improvement.

(35).
No. 3. 20 acres in South End Square, taken in execution for a Debt of £40 lawf. Mon.

No. 4. 18 acres, part of Lot No. 27, in Pitsfield, taken for a Debt.

Produces Certificate that the above mentioned Lands, being the estate of Elisha Jones, late of Pitsfield, were forfeited to the State, from Court of Com. Pleas held for Berkshire, Feby., 1783. Produces Copy of Libel by Attorney General, which describes the Lands as above. N.B.—No Certificate of Actual Sale.

Her Husband was in Possession of all the moveables contained in the Schedule, which she says are properly valued. They were all taken from her after her Husband went away by the Committee & sold at Vendue. They returned a few articles to Claimant. Now lives in Township of Digby at Sisseboo.

Says she was in the Country when her Lands were sold. She claimed her 3rd but they would not allow her anything. Says she was in the House when the moveables were sold. They were sold by the Committee, Valentine was Chairman.

JOSIAH JONES, Wits.:

Says his Brother in Law Elisha was a Loyalist from the first. He servd. as Lieut of a Co. of Loyalists under Genl. Ruggles, & was with the Army the whole War.

(36).
No. 1. He had an Estate in Adams of 105 acres; given by the Proprietors in Considn. of his building a Mill. He built the Mill. Improved. the Lands; built an house.

No. 2. Had a farm of 230 acres in Pitsfield, given by his Father, which he had greatly improved. He lived there. There was an elegant mansion & fine orchards.

Knew No. 3. He understood it was his Bros.'; heard of No. 4 being his Brother's. These Lands have been sold under Confiscation, as Witness has heard from his Bror., who he thinks was at the sale, & from others. Col. Vanskerk was the purchaser & now lives on it.

Looks at the Schedule of Moveables. Thinks he had the articles therein comprized.

(615). Further Evidence in the Case of JOSIAH JONES.

Says he practised in the Profession of the Law. Was settled in New Hampshire. His Clear profits £50 Ster. pr. ann. Claims for sufferings & expenses while in Concord Gaol.

ELISHA WILLIAMS, Wits.:

Says his Professional Income he thinks exceeded £50 pr. ann.

New Claim.

617. Case of SOLOMON BUNNEL, late of Massts. 1786. October 22.

Claimt. Sworn Saith: He came to this Province in the Fall, 1782; staid at Anapolis till the Spring, '83. Went to Sisseboo 17 Septr., 1783. Heard of the Act; that there was to be Compensation made, but did not hear of the limited time. (37).

Claimt. admitting that he heard of intended Compensation in the Fall 1783, & having taken no steps in Consequence of that Information, is told his Claim cannot be admitted.

New Claim.

618. Claim of ISAAC HATFIELD, Junr., late of West Chester, Prov. New York. 1786. October 22.

Claimt. Sworn Saith:

He lived in this Province in the Fall, 1783, at Digby. Heard of the Act in the Fall, about the time of Evacuating New York. Many people neglected to send. He was doubtful whether he should send any Claim. In Jany. or Feby., 1784 he delivered his Claim to Mr. Harday; he said he was then going to England. Claimt. delivered it at Halifax. It must have been early in Feby. or late in Jany., 1784.

He is a native of America; resided in West Chester Co. when Troubles broke out. On breaking out of Troubles, from the first took part with Brit. Was required by rebels to serve in their Militia, & to sign their Association, which he refused. In consequence of this he made himself obnoxious. They fin'd him which he refused to pay, & he was obliged to quit home.

Joined the Brit on their first Landing on Long Island. Joined as Volunteer in Queen's Rangers. Continued all that winter in that service. Had the Command of a Company. Afterwards joined Col. Delancey. Afterwards had a Commission as Captn. in West Chester Militia and then Lieutenant Col. in same Militia. Continued in the service during the War, at his own expense; has no half pay. Came to this Province from New York in Sumr. 1783. Now settled at Digby. (38).

When he left Home in 1776 he lost 18 Head Cattle, 4 Horses, farm horses, 50 Sheep; left them on his farm in West Chester when he went away. Heard of some being taken by one person, some by another, some for fines.

While Claimt. was stationed at King's Bridge with Commission from Govr. Tryon as Lieut. Col., he was attacked about Jany. 1780 at his Quarters, the house set on fire, & he lost cash £32.13.3. House, furniture, £13.1.4. Cloaths 58. Lost Horse, Vals. 42. It was kill'd in action at the time his Quarters were attacked. He was taken Prisoner & carried to New England; remained Prisoner about 3 months. Claims for expenses, £30.

THOMAS KEPP, Wits.:

Knew Claimant. He was always reckoned a Loyalist. Witness came within the Lines in 1779. He then servd. as an officer in West Chester Militia. In the Fall he raised the Regiment of Militia and had the Commission of Lieut. Col. Witness served with him. He acted as Lieutenant. Remembers the attack on his Quarters at Morris House near No. 8, King's Bridge, Jany., 1780. The House was burnt. Claimant was taken Prisoner.

(39).

Claimt. lost Clothes, furniture, — of his horses, money; he lost one horse shot by his enemy, worth 40 gns., a very fine horse. He remained Prisoner 3 months. He was then exchanged.

October 23.

Claimt. produces Comn. from Govr. Tryon dated 16 Nov., 1779, appointing him Lt. Col. Commandr. West Chester Refugees.

NEW CLAIM.

619. Case of JONATHAN FOWLER, late of New York.

1786.
Oct. 22.

Claimt. appears, Sworn Saith:

He came from New York just before the last Embarkation. Had heard of the Act. Some persons sd. that Claimant's Estate was confiscated; some said not.

Produces a Letter dated 30 March, 1784, which mentions that it was said his Estate was not confiscated, owing to a mistake of the Sheriff. Claimant has no doubt but that in fact his Estate was confiscated, tho' he did not know it for a certainty till lately. Did not hear of the mistake of the Sheriff till he recd. the above mentd. Letter.

(40).
Seems a very fine man.

Claimant is told that as he took no steps till after Expirn. of Act of Parlt., and as the reason he assigns that he was led to suppose there might be no Confiscation from a mistake of the Sheriff, was not known to him till the Expiration of Act, His Claim cannot be admitted.

620. Case of JOSEPH TOBIAS, late of Dutchess Co., New York.

1780.
Oct. 22.

Claimt. Sworn Saith:

He is a native of America; resided in Dutchess Co. when the Troubles first broke out, on his own Estate. From the first declared his sentiments in favour of Brit. Govnt.; never signed any American Association or served in their Militia. Joined the Brit. Oct. 1776 at King's Bridge. Servd. that Fall with the Loyal Volunteers under Major Rogers. After Fort Washington was taken went to Long Island with a Pass from Genl. How. Continued on Long Island till he was taken prisoner. Was kept a prisoner at Norwalk in Connecticut State for 6 months. Then made his escape & joined the Militia Troop under Col. Hamilton. Continued there till taken Prisr. a secd. time. Was put in Gaol at Hartford & let out on a Bond, near 2 years. Was paroled to come to New York & negotiate an exchange which he effectuated. Continued there till taken into confinement in consequence of Writ by a person who had bought his Estate. His Bror. gave Bail immediately. Continued in Dutchess Co. till the Spring 1786, then came to this Province, and now lives with his Bror. Christian at Digby. Has been here ever since his arrival from ye States. Lived with his Brother in Dutchess Co. who had been Bail for him on an Estate of his Bror.'s. His Bror. now keeps a Store. Claimant acted as Clerk to him. (41).

Was possessed of 160 acres in Dutchess Co., given by his Father's Will. Has not a Copy. Could not obtain it from the office. His Father died in 1774. Christian Tobias is his eldest son and heir. His Father left him this Estate. Says he was in Possession 3 or 4 years before his Father's Death & was in Possession when he joined the Brit. Then left his effects upon it. Built a Saw Mill upon it; the whole was under fence; 20 acres meadow, almost all the rest plough land. One House & Barn. Vals. it at £1,000 York Cury.

Says his real Estate was seized by the Rebels in 1778 or 1779 & sold.

His moveables were seized soon after he joined the Brit. & sold. Produces Certificate from Henry Livingston, Jur., of sale of his personal Estate to amount of £188 & upwards, Aug. 1777. Henry Livingston, Jur., signs himself one of the Commrs.

Produces office Copy of Judgment agst. him & that he forfeit his real & personal Estate. Judgment signed Feby. 1782. Says his real Estate was sold in 1777. Nathanl. Platt bought it. He is now in Possession of it. Says he tried to get Certificate of the sale of his real Estate, but could not obtain it.

Says his reason for staying was his being taken by a Writ at (42). the Suit of Nathanl Plat. Does not know what the Writ was, or what sum his Bror. gave Bail for, but it was not a large sum. Nothing has been done on that Writ ever since. Does not know what sum Nathl. Plat swore to in taking out the Writ. Thinks his Bror. gave Bail for £60.

His personal Estate Consisted of:

20 Head of Cattle, 5 Horses, 60 Sheep, 5 Hogs, farming utensils £10, Tools. Says his intention is to stay with his Brother, Dr. Tobias at Digby.

Gives additional Reasons for staying; that his wife was ill; she died in 1784; has 2 sons now living in the States; one with Claimant's Mother in Law, the other with Claimant's Sister. Says he acted as Clerk with his Bror., Thos. Tobias, who lived in

---

Dutchess Co., but had no share in Profits of Business. His name was not made use of as a Partner.

Dr. CHRISTIAN TOBIAS, Wits.:

Bro. to Claimant. Says he lived in Dutchess Co. on Lands adjoining Claimant's. Thinks his Bro. never signed any Rebel Association or served in their Militia. Witness & Claimant left the Country together; both joined the Brit. at King's Bridge in Octr. or Novr, 1776. Does not recollect that he served that Fall.

(43).

Claimt. got a Pass & went over to Long Island. He was there doing business when he was taken Prisoner & carried into Connecticut. This was on acct. of his Loyalty. He was at that time employed in Trade. Returned to Long Island after his Confinement in Connect. Served in Militia under Col. Hamilton.

Witness came to this Province in the Fall 1783. Says his Bror. was in the Country & servd. with a Writ of Suit of one Plat. His Brother Joseph was Bail for him. His Bror. Thos. is in Trade. Joseph, Tobias, Claimant lived with Thomas. Wits. thought it likely Claimant recd. some Benefit from the Business. Did not Consider him as merely Clerk.

Expects that he now means to settle with Witness. Intends to apply for Land. Wits. has supported him since he has been here, but means he should get Lands.

Says his Bror. was possessed of 160 acres in Dutchess Co.

He had it from his Father in his life time. Confirmed by his Father's Will. Witness is eldest son & Exer. & is satisfied this Estate was left to his Brother.

It was good Land. There was a Saw Mill upon it. Vals. it at £1,000. A good orchard & good mowing ground. One Plat has bought the Estate, on the Sale by the Commrs.; his stock was good. Thinks he must have had 20 Head of Cattle, 5 Horses, a good many Sheep.

NEW CLAIM.

1786.
Oct. 23.

621. Case of FREDERICK WILLIAMS, late of New York.

Claimant Sworn Saith:

(44).

He came from New York about June or July, 1783. Returned to fetch his wife & family from New York. Staid there about 4 or 5 days, then set off for this Province on his return; had a very bad passage & did not get to Anapolis till about the beginning of the New Year, 1784. As soon as he arrived he drew up his Claim & sent it to Halifax to be forwarded to Col. James Delancey, then in London. It was forwarded accordingly, but arrived a few days too late.

Says he is a native of America. Lived at West Chester on Frogs Neck when Troubles broke out. At first appeared neuter & was quiet, but signed no Association nor servd. in the Militia. Joined the Brit. as soon as they landed on Frogs Neck. Had done them service before by dispersing Protections, by giving them information of the Rebel Works. He sent an acct. of their strength to Sir Wm. Erskine & Gen. How. On the Brit. landing Claimant joined them, at a great risk, having been pursued & in Danger of being intercepted. Embarked in the Boat with Gr. Wm. Erskine & Gen. How. Continued with them till sent forward with a Co. of Light Infantry. Gave information of the ground to Col. Musgrave, who was wounded in an engagement while Claimant was with him. Returned with the Troops to New York.

After this returned home in 1777. Had a Commission as Captn. in Col. James Delancey's Regmt. of Militia.

Produces Commission dated 31 March, 1777. Has no half pay. Servd. during the War; raised upwards of 100 men. Came away in the Sumr. 1783. Now settled at the Head of St. Mary's Bay.

Has made over his landed Estate to a Relative who has hitherto preserved it.

Lost.—13 Oxen, 7 Cows, 8 Young Cattle, 2 Hogs, 45 Sheep. They were taken by the Americans at different Times from his farm. Does not know what use they were put to. His House was burne & effects in it by a party of Rebels. Val. £50.

Lost 8 Horses taken away by Rebels. They were kept for the service, & some lost in service. Lost a Negro Man. He was taken by the British & served in Rogers' Co., & died. Lost a negro man & a Negro woman, & 4 Boys, taken when house was burnt by the Rebels.

Lost a ferry Boat taken by Rebels. New, worth £50.

Lost some articles by Brit. Troops, Negro before mentioned, forage to amt. of £15. Claimt. was with the party who took Col. Wells from His Encampmt., & Col. Green at another time.

JACOB VEAL, Wits.:

Knew Claimt. in Frogs Neck. He was a Loyalist. Joined the Brit. early at Frogs Neck. He had afterwards a Commission as Captn.; was always out with the Army, & continued to serve during the War. Remembers that he lost many cattle, 40 or 50, taken by the Rebels; 40 Sheep. Remembers his house burnt. Remembers negroes taken by the Rebels, who came to plunder him as being a Loyalist, engaged in arms agst. them. He lost a Negro man & a Wench & 3 or 4 Children. Lost many effects from his house. He lost a Considerable No. of horses, some in service and some taken by the Rebels when his house was burnt.

THOMAS BAYEUX, Wits.:

Knew that Claimant had a place at Frogs Neck. Knew that he served as Captn. under Col. Delancey; believes during the whole War.

MAJOR HUGGERFORD:

Knew Claimant; from the first considered him as a Loyalist. He joined the Brit.; served as Captn. in Wits' Regiment of West Chester Refugees. He distinguished himself by his activity & Bravery. Witness employed him oftener than any officer in the Regiment & was always satisfied with his conduct. Remembers that at one time a large quantity of Cattle were taken from him by the Rebels. Remembers that he had Negroes. The Parties that came down for this purpose, came particularly with a view against the property of distinguished Loyalists. He continued to have the Command of a Post at Frogs Neck during the War.

GIDEON PALMER, Wits.:

Claimant had a great many horses & cattle. Lost all at different times. Remembers his house being burnt, & he lost at that time a Negro Wench & several Children.

(47).

1786.
October 23.

622. Case of JOHN PERINE, late of New Jersey.

Claimant Sworn Saith:

He came from New Jersey on purpose to have his Claim heard; means to settle here if he is spared by his family, but has lived in the States ever since the Peace. He is a native of America; lived in Monmouth Co. when Troubles broke out, on his Father's Estate, with his Father. From the first took part with the Brit. Signed an Association but sorely against his will. Says the paper of Association was burnt in 1777. Joined the Brit. at Amboy. Did not serve but kept within the Lines during the War. Lived chiefly on Staten Island or New York.

On Evacuation of New York remained on Long Island. His family is now in New Jersey. He now & then visits his family, but does it clandestinely.

Says he assisted Captn. Moody when he went to Philadelphia & brought him in safe to the Lines, also assisted a person sent out by Captn. Moody.

Was possessed of a Lot of Land in Midx. Co. in Township of Amboy; he bought it at Sheriff Sale. Produces Deed from Sheriff dated 1772, whereby it is conveyd. to Claimt. in Considn. 14 Cur. N. Jersey. It is about 15 acres. Vals. at £5 pr. acre

(48).

No. 2. Was possessed of 172 acres in Amboy Township; Had it by Deed of Gift from his Father. Produces Deed bearing date 1763. This Land was in fine improvement. 20 acres Meadow. Above 100 in the Whole Clear. A good house. Vals. it at £1,000.

No. 3. Had 47 acres in the same Township. Purchased of one Longfield, 4 or 5 years before ye Troubles, at £6 pr. acre, New Jersey Cury. Has lost the Deed. Vals. it at £6 pr. acre.

All this Estate has been sold by the Commissioners. Says the Certificates of Sale of his real & personal Estates were left at Halifax at one office by Gibertson.

Says he had 30 Head of Cattle, 11 Horses, 30 Sheep, 11 Hogs, farming utensils, house furniture. Says his effects are enumerated in the Schedule sent to our office and there rightly valued.

All this was seized on his going away & was sold.

His wife & family bought in some of the moveables at the Vendue; not a large part. One Vorehese is now in Possession of his landed Estate.

He had Debts; a Mortgage due to him, which he says were his reasons for staying. Altogether above £200.

THOS. HOOPER, Wits.:

Knew Claimt. & has been well acquainted with his conduct during the War. He was certainly very Loyal. Thinks his staying in the States ever since the Peace has been in order to get money due him, and that he had not the means to convey himself & large family away. His Family are all there. But Witness is satisfied that during t e War he conducted himself as a Loyalist. Remembers that he assisted & protected Captn. Moody. Witness was in Company with him. (49).

Knew No. 2. It was a very good farm. Vals. it at £5 Cury. per acre.

Thinks he & his Family would come under the Brit. Government if he had the means. Says he is a very deserving & honest man & always had that Character.

N. B.—The Claimant seems a very good man but an Inhabitant of the States.

ISAAC BONNEL, ESQ.:

Knew Claimant. Considered him during the whole War as a Loyal subject, & that he had suffered on acct. of his Loyalty. He was on Staten Island while Witness was there several years.

Witness Considered him as a suffering Loyalist. Thinks he was unable to leave the States from the lowness of his circumstances, his family being large, and that he staid to collect Debts. Witness speaks of him as a very fine man.

Further Evidence in Case of SARAH FOWLER. 1786. October 24.

Claimant appears. Produces Office Copy of the Will of Rachel Fowler whereby she gives 2-3 of her real Estate at Hutchinson's to her son, Solomon Fowler, & his Heirs, in Considn. that he pays £100 to Each of her 3 daurs., Rachel Palmer, Hannah Butler, & Abigal Fowler. Will dated 1761. Rachel Fowler died soon after making his Will. Produces Rects. for the Legacies to Tests., 3 Daurs., dated in 1762. (50).

Produces Copy of a Mortgage on Solomon Fowler's Estate of a Tract of Land in East Chester to the Loan office for £100 Cury., dated 1771. The Estate Consisted of 200 acres, a double house, a mill; there was an house which was destroyed during the War.

All her children are in the States except the eldest, who is in Demerary.

THOMAS HUGGERFORD, Major of the West Chester Refugees, Wits.

Remembers Solomon Fowler. He was a Captn. in the West Chester Refugees. Joined the Brit. on Long Island. He was killed in an Engagement at Horse Neck in Connecticut.

Saw his farm at East Chester. Was with him then during the War. A Considerable Farm, Well Cleared & Cultivated. Land was very valuable in that situation.

He left a large family; by the Law of the Province the Estate of person who died without a Will goes amongst all children. The eldest son has a double share.

FREDERIC WILLIAMS, ESQ., Wits.:

(51).

Knew Solomon Fowler. He joined the Brit. Troops very early. He was appointed a Captn. in the West Chester Refugees. He was killed at Horse Neck in a Skirmish. Witness was with him; they were attacking an house where there was a picket.

Knew his Farm. It was a very compact, good farm; thinks about 200 acres. Vals. it at £8 York Mon. pr. acre. By Laws of New York, Wits. thinks the eldest son is entitled to the Lands of person dying intestate.

Solomon Fowler's eldest son is now about 14 or 15. Witness supposed he is in the States.

October 24

615. Case of STEPHEN JONES, one of the Sons of the late Elisha Jones, of Massts.

Claimt. appears & being sworn saith:

He is the youngest son but one of the late Col. Elisha Jones. See before the Case of Josiah Jones.

Produces Copy of Memorial presented to the Lords Commrs. of his Majesty's Treasury, presented in 1781, accompanied with copies of Certificates from Genl. Gage, Lord Percy, Gen. Burgoyne, Sir W. How, Govr. Wentworth, Genl. Ruggles, Col. Small, to the Loyalty & services of Col. Jones & of his Family & their sufferings. Lord Percy mentions particularly the Loyalty of Josiah, Elisha & Stephen & that they servd. in the corps under Genl. Ruggles.

(52).

Genl. Burgoyne particularly certifies as to Jonas Jones, who served in his army & is now in England.

Sir Wm. How also certifies strongly in favour of Stephen Jones. Col. Small speaks highly of Col. Jones & thinks his Death was occasioned by his sufferings & maltreatment.

Produces Copy of a Letter from Ld. G. Germain to Sir Guy Cooper, speaking in high terms of Commendation of Stephen Jones & recommending him to the Treasury.

In consequence of this application, Josiah, Elisha, Simeon, & Stephen recd. £100 each, & Stephen £100 more for his expenses. Stephen was the person presented the memorial. Josiah, Elisha & Simeon were abroad.

Produces a News Paper called Massts. *Spy*, dated Novr. 6, 1783, containing advertisement for the sale of part of his Father's Estate.

Claimant joined the Brit on the Day of Lexington engagement. Joined Lord Percy as he was coming to the assistance of Col. Smith & carried the first certain news of the number of the enemy who were collecting to Genl. Gage who ordered another Brigade to support Lord Percy.

Claimt. was employed by his Father in the Command of a foraging party from Boston. Went with the Troops & returned with them to New York. Was then in the Commissary Department.

Servd. under Genl. Ruggles during the Blockade of Boston. In Feby., 1781, Claimant went to England & returned on Octr., 1781, to Carolina with Col. Thompson & there served as adjutar* to the Cavalry. Since that had a Commission as Cornet in King's American Dragoons, given by Sir Guy Carleton. (53).

Says that he had Genl. Leslie's particular thanks for his Conduct in one engagement which Col. Thompson had with Genl. Maryon on the Santee River. He was slightly wounded on that occasion & knock'd off from his Horse. Has now half pay as Cornet. His Father died without a Will, on which Claimt. says the real Estate goes to all the children, the eldest taking a double share.

His Brothers, who are now in the States, were settled on Estates which they had from their Father before the War, and are now in possession. There are other parts of his Father's Estate unconfiscated, which there is a probability of being recovered by his Brothers in the States. Should that be the Case, they will obtain portions of their Father's Estate equal to the shares of the other Brothers, who have staid under Brit. Govrnt.

He agrees in general with the acct. given by Josiah Jones, of the State of the Family. Nathan Jones, the eldest son, lived at Penodscot while possessed by Brit. Troops; was there as Volunteer during the Blockade. The Place where he lived is now given up to the States.

Claimant says that the children provided for by the Father in his life time, before they share in the rest of the Estate which the Father dying intestate leaves, they must bring into the acct. what they have recd. from their Father. Understands the Law of the Province to be so. (54).

N.B.—He is told he must send us an acct, what Estates his Father settled on his Bros., and how much they have now in Possession of their father's Estate, whether thus settled or recovered as not having been confiscated.

Claimant has seen the valuation made by his Bror. Josiah & agrees with it. Thinks it reasonable. It is valued at the rate at which his Father used to sell his Lands. Claimant is now settled at Sisseboo.

Says the Estate now claimed is above half what he was supposed to be worth.

NEW CLAIM.

623. Case of SAML. KIPP, late of New York. 1786. October 30.

Claimant Sworn Saith:

He left New York in 1783 on 1st June, and came to Nova Scotia, & settled on his first coming at Cumberland. In conse-

quence of having heard of a Letter from Col. Delancey to Captn.
Knapp, he drew up his Claim & swore to it before James Law,
9th Nov., and gave it Gilbert Totten, Agent to Col. Delancey's
Regiment, who was to give it to Major Brace, who was going to
England as Claimt. understood & was to deliver it there to Col.
Delancey. This was about the month of Novr. Major Bruce went
(55). to Halifax. Thinks the Claim was forwarded to him there. He
went to England, but the Claim came too late to Col. Delancey's
Hands to be delivered in time.

Produces Letter from Col. Delancey in which he admits he
recd. the Claim, with many others, in No. 133, in July, 1784,
with a Copy of a note from Major Brace to Col. Delancey, dated
12 July, 1784, in which he informs him that he sends him a
Packet just recd. from Halifax, which he supposes should have
been delivered before he left the country.

Claimt. says he is a native of America; resided at North Castle in New York Prov. when the Troubles began. Never signed
any Association with the Rebels or served in their Militia. Joined

the Brit. just after the Battle at Long Island. Joined Col. Rogers and served under him as Volunteer in the Queen's Rangers
that Campaign. The next summer served under Col. Delancey
in Regt. of West Chester Loyalists. In 1779 had a Commission
as Lieut. of Capt. Knapp's Troop of Refugee & Militia Light
Horse.

Produces Commission from Govr. Tryon, dated 19 Nov.,
1779. In 1780 had a Command of a Troop under Col. Delancey.
Continued to serve under him during the War. Came in the
summer 1783 to Nova Scotia & is now settled.

Produces Certificate signed Marguard, aid de Camp to Genl.
Losberg to Loyalty & to spirited services of Claimt.
(56). Was entitled to ¼ of a farm at North Castle in West Chester
Co., left by his Father's Will. Produces Will of Benj. Kipp,
his Father, dated 3 Aug., 1780, whereby he gives the remainder
of his Estate after a few Legacies to his four sons, Willm.,
James, Saml., & Thomas. Testator died soon after making his
Will at Morrisina. His Father had been banished from his Estate on acct. of his Loyalty & persecuted by Act of the State.

He joined the British & lived within the Lines till time of his
Death. He acted occasionally as a Magistrate. He had before
had a Commission as Magis'rate. He was too old to bear arms.

The Estate consisted of 317 acres in North Castle of which
Claimant was entitled to ¼.

His Father had been in Possession 30 or 40 years. All improved. Hardly enough woodland left. 60 of Meadow in one
piece. A good house & Barn & orchard. Vals. the Estate at
2,000 New York Cury. This Estate has been confiscated.

Produces Copy of Judgement against Benjamin Kipp, Claimt.'s
Father, and Confiscation of his Estate. Claimant says the whole
has been sold, but that one of his Brothers, Willm., who continues
in the States, is allowed ¼ for his share.

Lost 2 Horses & Colt when removing within the Lines. Taken by the Enemy. 1 horse killed in service. 1 taken by enemies. 1 horse & Cow taken by French. Lost household Furniture. Had furniture in his Brother in Law's house which was burnt, and Claimant lost furniture to amount of £20. Left 2 horses on his farm which he hired. Taken by the Rebels. 1 Negro deserted to the enemy. Says he had no Half Pay, and recd. nothing for his services, except 50 Days' Pay as Captn. of a Troop of horse. Col. Delancey certifies strongly to his Loyalty & active services. (57).

THOMAS KIPP sworn saith:

He is a Bror. to Claimt. His Father Benjamin was banished for his Loyalty & proscribed & joined the Brit. in Nov., 1778. Died within the Lines. His Estate was confiscated.

The Claimant joined the Brit. soon after the Battle of Long Island. Continued to serve during the war. Benjamin Kipp died in 1780, having made his Will, & left the Remr. of his Estate to his 4 Sons. Willm., eldest son, now in the States. James who came to this Country since dead. His Wife & Son are gone to the States, his eldest Son is an Infant. Saml. Kipp, 3rd. Bro., the Claimant. Thomas the present Witness who lived at Digby.

The Will has not been proved. It is attested by Mary Free, Thomas Kipp, Wits., Saml. Kipp, a Cousin of Claimants, Benjamin Kipp had an elder Son, who died in his Life time, named Jesse who has left a Son named Benjamin who lives in the States and is Heir at Law. Witness says that if his Father had died without a Will, or the Will is set aside, the whole goes to the Heir at Law by Laws of New York. The Land was sold. Willm. Kipp is allowed to hold his part ¼ of the Estate. (58).

The farm consisted of 317 acres & ½. Vals. it at £2,000. Knew that Claimant lost horses on moving within the Lines. Thinks he left horses behind him when he joined the Brit. Knew that he lost horses in service.

JAMES DICKENS, Wits:

Knew the Estate of Benj. Kipp, but not particularly, but vals. Lands situated as those were in West Chester at £6.10 or 7 New York Curr. per acre. Thinks it was an average Price for Lands in that situation. Comrs. admit oss proved on ccision.

Claimant is told he must get Certificates of the Sale.

NEW CLAIM.

624. Case of PETER MABEE, late of New York. October 30.

Claimt. sworn saith:

He came from New York in June, 1783, settled in Cumberland. Sent his Claim by Col. Delancey. V. Case of Samuel Kipp.

(59).

Is native of America. Lived on Cortland Manor when Troubles broke out. Joined the Brit. in 1781. Was quite a Boy, which was his reason for not joining before. Served in Captn. Kipp's Troop in Col. Delancey's Regt. Served 2 years. Came away at the end. Had no real Estate. Lost 4 horses, 2 Saddles, Arms & Cloathing in Service. He served as a Seargent all the time. It does not appear that this Claim was sent to Col. Delancey.

He is told that his Claim cannot be admitted, his name not being in Col. Delancey's List, but that he is no sufferer as he would not have been entitled to Compensation from us.

NEW CLAIM.

1786.
October 30.

625. Case of ISAAC ACHERLY, late of New York.

Claimt. sworn saith:

He came from New York in June 1783. Sent his Claim home by Col. Delancey. V. Case of Saml. Kipp.

Served 3 yrs. in Col. Delancey's Regt., 1st as private then as Seargt. Lost 6 Horses in service. Provided horses at his own expense. The horses were taken. Produces his Discharge from Col. Emerchies Regt. in 1779. Afterwards with Col. Delancey.

(60).

NEW CLAIM.

October 30.

628. Case of JAMES TOLTEN, late of New York.

Claimt. says: He came from New York in Septr. 1783. Settled in Cumberland. Sent his Claim by Col. Delancey. V. Case of Saml. Kipp.

Served in Col. Delancey's Regt., & before Col. Delancey had it, as a private. Lost 2 horses in service. Paid £12 York Cury. for one, the other was taken out of the Country.

NEW CLAIM.

1786.
October 31.

627. Case of ABRAHAM COVERT, late of New York.

Claimant appears & being sworn saith:

He came from New York in the Fall 1783. Sent his Claim home to Col. Delancey.

He is a native of America. Resided in Dutchess Co. on an hired farm. Signed no Association, nor served in Rebel Militia. Fined for not serving. Joined Col. Delancey in April, 1781. Says he did not join sooner, being confined to his Farm on security given by his friends. Had a Commission as Lieutenant, and acted in that capacity during the war. He resided on a Farm hired of Roger Morris. He had a Lease. The Lease was to continue while he paid Rent, at £3 per 100 acres. Had the Power of selling but the Land lord took 1-3 of the Purchase money. The Improvements were his own. (61).

Had 117 acres in Fredericksburg. There was an house & Barn and other builds. Purchased it 16 years ago of his Father for £100. Built an house & Barn. Planted an orchard. Did it all himself, therefore cannot say what he laid out. Cleared 15 acres meadow. Cleared 40 acres upland. Fenced it himself. Says all this estate has been sold. His family were turned off about six Days after he left home. Vals. it at £300.

The Land was seized as belonging to Roger Morris & sold. John Berry & John Maclean bought Claimt.'s Improvements.

Lost 6 Cows, left on his Place when he left home & they were seized. A mare taken by the Rebel army. A horse left at home & seized, and farming utensils, £20. Charges for fines taken from him £195.

Says he was advised to stay by General Clinton. His fines amounted so high from his continuing among them so long. Is now settled at Fannings Burg, called Ramsbay.

CAPT. KNAPP, Wits.

Knew Claimant. Considered him as a Loyalist from the first. Thinks he joined Col. Delancey's Regt. about 1781, then served as Lieutenant during the war. Knew his Plantation. It was on Phiiips Patent. Vals. the Improvements between £2 & 300. On sale the Landlord took a fine, 1-3 was the highest. All this Land has been sold. He had a considerable stock. Understood they were immediately seized when he joined the Army. (62) Loyal, bore arms; lost improvements, 6 cows, 1 horse, farm; returns.

NEW CLAIM.

628. Case of CHARLES VINCENT, late of New York. 1786. October 31.

Claimt. appears, sworn saith:

He left New York in the sumr. 1783. Sent his Claim by Col. Delancey.

Is a native of America. Lived at Fish Kill, Dutchess Co. Joined the Brit. as soon as they landed in 1776, at New Rochell. Served as Volunteer in Queen's Rangers. Continued with them till they went to Philadelphia. Was detained by sickness. Served in Col. Delancey's Regt. afterwards, as a private & continued during the war. Settled in Cumberland.

Vals. it too high.

Had 46 acres at Fish Kill. Had it by Gift from his Uncle, four years before the war began. His Uncle had no children. It was under good cultivation; 2 or 3 acres meadow clear. 4 or 6 acres upland on which he had raised one crop of wheat. The rest unimproved. A common house. Vals. it at £10 per acre. The whole together he vals. at £10 per acre.

(63)

Was seized on his going away & Confiscated. Left Corn in his neighbours barn. 40 Bush. Wheat, 70 Bush. Buckwheat left it there. His neighbours took it, on acct. of his having joined the Brit., & sent his wife & family after him to New York. 5 Hogs, furniture, £15, taken by a Capt. Hill, a rebel Capt. who came & turned his wife away from his farm. Has been informed one Macgill lives upon it. Has no Witness present.

There appears the name of Charles Vincent of Bateman's Precinct in Anstey's List, but this appears not to be the Claimant.

Is told he must prove Confiscation.

NEW CLAIM.

629. Case of NATHANL. GOLDING, late of New York.

Claimt. sworn saith:

1786.
October 31.

He came from New York in the sumr. Sent his Claim to Col. Delancey.

He is a native of America. Lived at North Castle. Joined the Brit. in Long Island in 1777. Served with Col. Fanning as a private 2 yrs., then served at Morrisina with Bearman, Hatfield & then Delancey acted as Seargent. Served till end of war. Now settled at Ramsbay. Had an house at North Castle, built by himself, on the road & partly on Quinby's Land. He had Leave from Quinby. Lost 2 horses, taken by Capt. Simcoe. 2 Cows, 7 young Cattle. They were at North Castle, on Moses Quinby's Land. They were plundered by what he calls Skinners.

(64)

Lost cloathes, furniture; taken by the same Persons called Skinners. Charges for cash being laid out by him on recruiting service.

Says his house had cost him £30. He lived upon it a little while. Built it near Quinby's Land. One Davis, an acquaintance of Claimants, is now on it. Says beside his own labour it cost him £6 or 7.

Says he had raised Cattle on Quinby's Land, which was rented by his Mother. 2 Cows & some young cattle. Admits he himself had a small share in plunder taken by the Troops who sided with the Brit.

Produces Col. Fanning's allowance to Claimt. later on recruiting service.

TIMOTHY DANIELS, Wits:

Knew the house at North Castle. Claimant built it. He did the Carpenter work himself. Appears to know nothing of the matter & drunk.   N.B.—Hardly anything to be allowed.

NEW CLAIM.

630. Case of JOHN BRISBAND, late of New York.

Claimt. sworn saith: 1786. October 31.

He left New York in the sumr. Sent his Claim to Col. Delancey.

He is a native of Ireland. Settled in America about 5 years before Troubles began. Resided at Saratoga. Joined the Brit. in 1777. Served as Volunteer in Col. Jessup's Regiment. Was soon taken Prisoner, brought to Æsopus Gaol. Escaped to New York. Continued at New York 2 yrs., then joined Col. Delancey. Served during the war, as seargent. Came to this Province. Now settled at Fannings Borough.   (65).

Was possessed of 109 acres at Saratoga. Purchased of Cornelius Kyler in Considn. £120 New York Cur., 5 yrs. before ye Troubles. Paid part, was to pay the rest by Instalments. None clear when he bought it. Cleared 40 acres. Built an house & Barn. Vals. it at £300.

Does not know what is become of it. Says he does not claim for it as it is not Confiscated. Lost 2 yoke of oxen at Saratoga, taken by Americans, because he was a Tory. 2 horses; lost in Morrisina when he was in service. Had one killed. Lost 3 Cows & 4 Calves, taken from his farm at Saratoga; taken because Claimt. had joined ye British. Lost apparel & furniture & utensils, taken from his house at Saratoga. Vals. them at £108. 2 Horses left on the Farm.   N.B.—No such name in Ansley's list.

Too high.

JAMES BRISBAND, Wits., Son to Claimt.:

Says his Father joined the Brit. in 1777. Was taken Prisr. afterwards. He served in Col. Delancey's Regt. till end of the war. He had on his farm at Saratoga 2 yoke of oxen, 2 Cows & 4 Calves, 2 mares & 2 Colts, part of his furniture & part of his farming utensils, not many. All these things were on the farm at Saratoga, taken by parties of Rebels sent on purpose to take ye things belonging to Tories. They seemed to shew orders for seizing these things.   (66).

N.B.—To be allowed for those articles.

NEW CLAIM.

631. Case of JOHN BROWN, late of New York.   1786. October 31.

Claimant sworn saith:

He left New York in the sumr. 1783. Sent his Claim home to Col. Delancey.

N.B.—A very fair man.

(67).

Native of England. Settled in America 7 or 8 years before the Rebellion. Lived at Horse Neck. When Troubles began, joined the Brit. in 1777, at King's Bridge. Served with Col. Delancey then under Col. Hamilton, afterwards with Col. Emerick as private, then with Col. Hatfield & continued in service the whole war. Now settled at Fannings Borough.

Was possessed of house & 5 acres in Horse Neck. Purchased the Land at 50 shills. per acre & built a new stone house. Made a stone fence & planted fruit trees of various kinds. Vals. it at £50. Lost Wheat, Household stuff, one Cow.

THOMAS MERIT, Wits:

Knew his Land at Horse Neck, about 5 acres. He purchased it some years before ye Troubles. He built an house & greatly Improved it. Vals. it at £50 York Cury. He had one Cow. Heard particularly that Rebels took his Land & Cow & goods, because he joined the Brit.

N.B.—Claimant to be allowed almost the whole of his Demand.

NEW CLAIM.

1786.
October 31.

632. Case of SOLOMON HORTON, late of New York.

Claimt. appears & being sworn saith:

He left New York in the summer 1783. Sent his Claim to Col. Delancey.

Is a native of America. Lived on Philips Manor. Went within the Lines in 1777. Took an Oath of Allegiance at New York in 1777. Produces Certificate by the Mayor of New York. Produces Pass from Col. Fanning. Joined Col. Delancey about 2 years before end of the war. Kept Guard at Col. Delancey's Mill, 6 or 7 months. Afterwards did work with his Wagon & horses. Looked upon himself as under Col. Delancey. Now settled at Ramsbac.

(68)

Was possessed of a Farm at Philips Manor, as Tenant. About 130 acres. Had it from his Father, about a year or two before he left home. The House & Buildings & fence he calls Improvements, these belonged to the Tenant. This house & buildings built by his Father, cannot value the builds. All this was cleared Land except 12 or 14 acres.

He says his Father may be upon it now. He had a Writing from his Father. Says he went to the Landlord with his Father. His Father said Col. give my Land to my Son Solomon. He said very well. Does not know that anything was done by ye Col. or the Claimant, father's name was Samuel. Claimant has an elder Bror. now living near Cumberland. His Father sided with Americans, and Claimant says he now lives upon it for his life by

Agreement, when he gave it to Claimant. Vals. the Improvmts. &c. at £500.

Lost a yoke of oxen, 2 young Cattle, 5 Cows, 7 young Cattle, 3 Horses.

Claimant was taken Prisoner just before the Battle of the White Plains. Left all the above articles on his Farm at Philips Manor. Heard they were taken by Rebel Army. They drove all in the Place belonging to friends or foes. Took his furniture & farming utensils. Taken by the rebel army. Vals. them at £80.

Had a small house at Morrisina, built on Morris Land. Had no leave from Morris. Had a Protection from Genl. Tryon. Vals. this house at £15. Lost Pork & grain to amount of £35; in an House at Morrisina. Claimt. lived there. It was burnt and the above articles destroyed. Burnt by a party who came to take them. Col. Hatfield & several others were taken Prisoners. Has no Witnesses present. (69).

N.B.—His farm on Philips Manor is too highly valued, but it does not appear to be lost. May be allowed for yoke of oxen, 1 yoke young Cattle, 3 Horses, 5 Cows.

NEW CLAIM.

633. Case of JOHN OBRIEN, late of New York.

1786.
October 31.

Claimant appears, being sworn, saith:

He left New York in sumr. 1783. Sent his Claim to Col. Delancey.

Is a native of America. Lived in Dutchess Co. Joined the Brit. in 1780. Served in Capt. Kipp's Troop. Served during the war, as a private. Was possessed of a farm in Dutchess Co. Came to him on his Father's death. He died 3 years before Claimant joined the Brit. without a Will. Estate came to Claimt. as eldest son & Heir at Law. It consisted of 214 acres in Fredericks Burg. 20 acres mead. clear. 150 acres Plough land clear, the rest wood. Was in Possession 3 yrs. till he joined the Brit. Bels. it was Confiscated & sold. His Uncle bought it. Vals. it at £400.

Does not appear in Anstey's List. Claimt. is told he must get Certificate of Confiscation.

Lost 1 yoke of oxen, 4 Cows, 20 Sheep, taken from his farm by Col. John Hyat, a Rebel, on acct. of Claimants joining Brit. Had been his Fathers. Lost 1 horse in action, 1 horse saddle & bridle, 1 2-yr. old Colt, suit of Cloathes, taken by the enemy at Morrisina. (70).

ABRAHAM COVERT, Wit:

His Father had a Farm in Dutchess Co., lease Land under Col. Morris, about 200 acres. His Father died without a Will, about 6 years ago. Thinks the estate would have been divisible among all the children. There were 6 children. The Claimt. was no more in Possession than his mother & the rest of his Bros. & Sisters.

There was a considerable stock on the Farm.

(71). N.B.—Claimt. entitled only to 1-7 of his Father's Property.

PROCEEDINGS

OF

LOYALIST COMMISSIONERS

ST. JOHNS, 1786.

VOL. XI.

BEFORE COMMISSIONER PEMBERTON.

Claimants.

	MSS. Folio.		MSS. Folio.
Ackerly, Obadiah	45	Jones, Mrs. Mahittable	43
Angivine, John	34	Kerch, Robert	2
Angevine, Peter	21	King, Mrs. Kesia	1
Botsford, Amos	22	Knapp, Titus	7
Brown, Jonas	49	Lloyd, Mich.	34
Cornwell, Samuel	46 and 48	Merrit, James	16
Crawford, John	35	Paine, William, M.D.	62
Eccles, James	6	Palmer, Lieut. Gideon	31
Embree, Joseph	17	Pugsley, John	8
Embree, Samuel	4	Purdy, Gabriel	13
Fowler, Amos	38	Rundle, Jabez	22
Gleeson, John	10	Seaman, Stephen	9
Gordon, James	38	Smith, Abraham	3
Hayt, James	52	Teed, John	19
Hunter, John	15	Trenchard, Henry	12
Hyat, Nathaniel	18	Wilson, John	18
Jones, Elisha	46		

THE EVIDENCE.

NEW CLAIM.

1786.
October 31.

634. Case of KESIA KING, Widow of James King, late of New York.

Claimant sworn saith:

Her Husband, James King, lived in Ulster Co., New York, on his own Estate. He joined the Brit. in Oct., 1777. He afterwards served in Capt. Purdy's Co. as a private till his Death in the year 1780. He died near New York. Made a Will & left Claimant his Estate.

Claimant came in the year 1779 to New York. Lived at Morrisina. Came to this Province in sumr. 1783. Sent her Claim to Col. Delancey. Now lives in Cumberland.

(1). Her Husband was possessed of 192 acres in Ulster Co. He bought it of Jacob Garrow. Left it by his Will to Claimant. About 20 acres clear, a Log House & small orchard. Vals. it at £250. Thinks it rather too high valued.

Says she was turned away from this Estate, & they said her Husband had forfeited it. Does not know what has been done towards Confiscation, nor knows that it is sold. She was turned away & traveled on foot to New York. Lost a mare, val. £8. Lost several other articles, taken from her, when she left the Place, but did not put in her claim, because her Husband might have Debts to that amount.

ROBERT CATCH, Wits:

Knew James King. He joined the Brit. in 1777, & served in Capt. Purdy's Co. Went to a Place called Bergen Point. Died there in 1780. Made a Will in 1778, whereby he gives his wife all his Estate, real & personal. Attested by 3 Witnesses. The Claimant Kesia came within the Lines in 1779.

Claimant seems an honest poor creature.

Knew James King's Estate in Ulster Co.; 192 acres. Remembers James King in Possession. He bought it of one Jacob Garrow. About 20 acres clear. Heard that some persons who had been in the Rebel Army, particularly John Stevens, was in Possession of it.

(2). N.B.—Name of James King does not appear in Anstey's List.

NEW CLAIM.

1786.
October 31.

635. Case of ROB. KERCH, late of New York.

Claimant appears & being sworn saith:

He left New York in sumr. 1783. Sent his Claim to Col. Delancey.

He is a native of America. Lived in Ulster Co. Joined tne Refugees under Col. Hatfield in 1779. Served all the war, till he came to this Province. Now settled in Cumberland. His

Father, William Kerch of Ulster Co., had acted as Lieut. of Militia.

In 1777 came within the British Lines. Continued ill & died in 1778. Left a Will, and gave Claimant an Estate. Produces his Father's Will, dated in 1778, whereby he gives a farm of 118 acres, which he bought of Jacob De Gorma to his Sons, Robert, Job, David, William. Attested by 3 Wits. Note.—Seems an estate in tail, which is given them.

Claimant's share is 1-4 of 118 acres. Vals. the whole at £240. Heard that one Ebenezer Gilbert was in Possession. Cannot say it was sold. Name does not appear.

KESIA KING, Wits:

Knew the Farm which belonged to Claimant's Father. Remembers him in Possession of it. He was Lieut. of Militia. He was a Loyalist. Went in the Brit. Lines & lost all by being a Loyalist. The son, Robert Kerch, has served a great while in Delancey's Corps. Claimant seem a fair man.
(3).

His Brothers are in the States. He says they are not in Possession of the Estate.

NEW CLAIM.

636. Case of ABRAHAM SMITH, late of New York. 1786.
November 1.

Claimt. sworn saith:

He left New York in Sumr. 1783. Sent his Claim to Col. Delancey.

He is a native of America. Lived in West Chester Co. Always declared himself a friend to Brit. Govert. Went within the Brit. Lines about 3 yrs. before the Evacuation.

He went within the [Brit. Lines] because he was plundered for harboring refugees. He lived 8 or 9 miles beyond ye White Plain, between the Lines. Was plundered of Ten Tons of Hay & 70 Bush. Oats by Rebels. Horse & 3 Cattle, taken by the Brit. Troops. Was robbed of £18 Cash, & horse by 2 Scouts. Claimant was attacked on the Road. Household furniture, plundered at difft. Times by the Rebels. Not to be allowed anything strictly.

Never signed any Rebel Association & was always ready to assist the Loyalists. (4).

ELIJA SMITH, Wits:

Claimant was always called a friend to Govert. Protected & harboured Loyalists. He lived between ye Lines. Was plundered at different Times. Plundered by the Rebels of furniture & horse taken on ye road & money.

NEW CLAIM.

637. Case of SAML. EMBREE, late of New York. 1786.
November 1.

Claimt. sworn saith:

He left New York in Sumr. 1783. Sent his Claim to Col. Delancey.

He is a native of America. Lived at Morrisina, when the Troubles began. Never signed any Rebel Association. Joined the Brit. on their first coming to Morrisina. Col. Delancey formed a Company of Militia of which Claimant was one. Continued to serve. Had a Commission as Lieut., first in Col. Delancey's Regt.

in 1777, th n under Major Bearman, then served again under Col. Delancey. Served the whole war. Now settled at Cobblegate Mountain.

Was possessed of 120 acres at Morrisina. This Land was purchased about 2 yrs. before the war of Col. Lewis Morris. Col. Delancey made the Purchase for him for £900 New Y. Cury. Claimt. paid the money. Had a Deed. Says the Deed is left at New York April 9. Produces Deed as above.

(5). Col. Lewis Morris got a Judgement against him for Trespass in cutting Timber to make oars for the use of the Brit. He says he had not done the Tresp., but the Judgement was got under the Trespass Act & Col. Lewis Morris got Possession. It was sold by the Sheriff on the Execution, & Morris bought it.

Produces Letter from Solomon Avery, Tenant of the Farm, to let Claimant know his Farm was sold by Sheriff, 22 Aug., 1785, & that Morris bought it. Produces Proceedings. Vals. the Farm at £900.

Lost 8 horses, taken at different times by Rebel parties from his farm; 2 Cows do, furniture &c. Plundered at difft. times to amt. of £100. Thinks the plundering was general. Lost a great Deal when the houses were burnt at Morrisina.

TOBIAS KNAPP, Wits:

Knew the Estate which Claimt. had at Morrisina. Understood that Col. Delancey had purchased it for him. Saw Claimt. have the money to go & pay for it. Saw £3 or 400. He had been possessed of it some time before Witness knew him. Witness went to live with him in 1779. Lived with him 2 years. Col. Delancey had been one of his securitys in purchasing. Thinks there must have been 120 acres, chief part cleared. Very valuable, thinks £8 or 900. Lost several horses in Service.

NEW CLAIM.

1786.
November 1st.

638. Case of JAMES ECCLES, late of New York.

Claimt. sworn saith:

Sent his Claim to Col. Delancey. He lived in Dutchess Co. Joined Col. Delancey in the year 1780. Served with him as a private to end of war. Now settled in Cumberland.

(6). Lost 1 horse at Morrisina, plundered, when the houses were burnt. Lost one horse a year before he left home. He was taken Prisoner at the time, because he was suspected of intending to go to Brit. Col. Henry Ludington took the horse & at the same time took Claimt. Prisoner. Was taken Prisoner at Morrisina & kept close Prisoner 2 yrs. & 4 months at Lancaster, Philadelphia & other Places.

Wearing apparel lost at Morrisina, when ye houses were burnt.

HENRY PEERS, Wits:

Remembers that Claimt. served under Col. Delancey. He lost an horse at Morrisina; plundered. A very good one.

NEW CLAIM.

639. Case of TITUS KNAPP, late of New York.   1786.
November 2nd

Claimant sworn saith:
Left New York in Septr., 1783. Sent his Claim to Col. Delancey.

Lived at North Castle. Joined the Brit. at Morrisina in 1779. Joined the West Chester Refugees. Served till the end of the war as Seargt.

Left one horse in the Country at North Castle on the farm of Thos. Clapp, taken by the Rebels from the farm, after he was a prisoner on suspicion. Lost 2 horses in Morrisina while he was in service. Lost 2 Cows & 2 Calves. He was sending them into the Brit. Lines. Had bought them to send them into the Brit. Lines. This was before he joined the Brit. in 1779. Lost a Watch & money & Wearing apparel, taken from him at Morrisina.

(7)

SAML. EMBREE, Wits:

Remembers Claimt. in service. Heard he left an horse in the Country, in the care of a friend. Saw one horse of his taken from a stable at Morrisina. Claimt. was taken Prisonr. at same time. Heard he had bought 2 Cows & 1 or 2 Calves to send into ye Brit. Lines & they were taken. Resides in Cumberland.

NEW CLAIM.

640. Case of JOHN PUGSLEY, late of New York   1786.
November 2nd.

Claimt. says he left New York in June & sent his Claim by Col. D.

Is a native of America, resided at Philipsburg. Joined the Brit. at White Plains in 1776. Served as a Guide. Served as Lieut. & Adjutant to West Chester Refugees. Produces Certificate from Melyanum Aid de Camp to Genl. Losbing to his having served as Adjutant—to his zeal and Loyalty.

Produces Certificate from Col. Emerick to his Loyalty & particular services. Served till Evacuation of New York, then came to this Province. Now settled at Cumberland.

(8).

Lost a Negro. He would not come to Nova Scotia. He had worked 2 years during the later part of the War—so Claimt.

was forced to leave him behind. Claimt. sd. he came away sooner than he thought of & had no opportunity of getting him. He had worked with Capt. Williams. The Negro is now at West Chester. Lost 6 horses while in service. Cow lost at Morrisina— taken by the British. Wheat taken away from Philips manor by the Rebels.

Had about 100 acres of Land adjoining Courtland manor. Came to him on his Father's death. His Father was killed by the Rebels. He died without a Will in 1779. Claimant is eldest son.

Seems a very good man, has strong certificates, may have a compensation for his lands.

His Father had bought this Land of ———— in Considn. £300, New Y. Cury., 4 or 5 years before the War. His Mother was on it when he heard last. Whether she is warned off he does not know.

Says he was promised 100 guins. by Col. Emerick for going into ye Country. Was absent 3 weeks & performed the service at great Risk.

JOHN GLEASON, Wits.

(9).

Knew Claimant's Father. Remembers him in Possession of an Estate in Courtland manor. A free Estate. Remembers his father in Possession, a good House, Orchard & Barn. Thought it a good farm. Heard that the Grandfather bought it for the Father of Claimant. Wits. says he has bought Land of this goodness for £4 or 5 per acre. He heard his Father was killed by the Rebels. Claimant was the eldest son. Goes to the eldest son by Law of New York.

NEW CLAIM.

1786.
November 2nd.

641. Case of STEPHEN SEAMAN, late of New York.

Sworn saith:

He left New York in Sumr., 1783. Sent his Claim to Col. Delancey.

Lived in Dutchess Co. Joined the Brit. immediately after their coming to New York—in 1778.

Served with Major Bearman, then Hatfield, then Delancey. Continued till end of the War as a private. Now settled in Cumberland. Lived on an hired farm in Dutchess Co.

(10).

Lost 2 Oxen, 2 Cows, 2 young cattle, 2 horses, 20 Sheep, part of household furniture, utensils, Tools, Wheat 60 Bushels, 40 Bushels Corn. All this he left at home when he joined the Brit.

Rebels came to get it as soon as he went away & seized it on acct. of his Loyalty. They let his wife have a Cow, but they sent her within the Lines & took away the Cow. Lost a Cow afterwards within the Lines. It was plundered & was robbed of some Cash.

MOSES SIMMONS, Wits.

Knew Claimant. He went early within the Brit. Lines. Served a great while—till end of the War. He lived on an hired farm. Left, when he went away, Horses, Cows, 2 young Cattle, Sheep, furniture. Saw all these things sold after Claimt. went away. Heard of his having oxen. <small>To be allowed.</small>

NEW CLAIM.

642. Case of JOHN GLEESON, late of New York. <small>1786. November 2nd.</small>

Claimant says he left in Sumr., 1783. Sent his Claim to Col. D.

Lived in North Castle. Joined the Brit. in 1779. Joined Major Bearman. Continued to serve during the War. Now settled on Cobblegate Mountain.

Was possessed of a farm of 120 acres in West Chester Co. Produces Deed from James Burns to Claimt. of 120 acres in West Chester Co., in Considn. £400, 13 Feby., 1776. The Troubles had begun. Says he paid the Purchase Mon. in old Money except £66. The Land is now in Possession of James Leggat who has 2 Tenants upon it. <small>(11).</small>

After Claimt. bought it built a Log house & builds. Made 9 fields. Set out an Orchard. He laid out £200. Lost 1 horse at Morrisina taken by Rebels, 1 do. Left 25 sheep on the Farm when he went away. 100 Bushls. Wheat, farming utensils & English goods taken from his house at North Castle to amount of £40 or 50. Says he was in Debt £332. Offered his farm & his Books to his Creditors, which they would not take. Has 200 or £300 due to him. <small>To be allowed.</small>

Produces Certificate from six Justices to his Loss Goods by Water on his Coming into the Country. Brought several Things with him. Came to Cumberland & going from Cumberland to Mickam the Boat was lost & Claimt. lost Cash £100, Household furniture, Cloathes for himself & family, £100. <small>To be allowed.</small>

JEREMIAH MERRIT:

Knew Claimant. Remembers that he servd. in Col. Delancey's Regt. a good while. Knew his Farm at North Castle, bought of James Burnes.

He had a good stock on his farm. Remembers he left soon when he joined the Brit. Remembers his bringing furniture from New York & heard of its being lost.

STEPHEN SEAMAN, Wits.

Remembers that Claimant served a long time with Col. Delancey. Heard he brought a Considerable Property with him from New York & that he lost it. To be allowed for Cattle on his farm & his Loss on removal.

NEW CLAIM.

November 2nd.   643. Case of HENRY TRENCHARD, late of New York.

Sent his Claim to Col. D. Lived in Harrison's Purchase, West Chester Co. Joined Brit. 1777. Joined Guides & Pioneers, then served under Major Bearman, then Delancey. Seargt. Continued to serve during the War. Now settled at Cobblegate Mountain.

(12).   Lost 7 horses while in service under Col. Delancey. Bought them & pd. ye Cash for them. When he left home left furniture Val. 40, Shop & Smith's Tools 28. Lost 2 Cows in Morrisina. Wearing apparel lost at Morrisina. The goods left at his house when he went away were seized by the Rebels on acct. of his going away.

JOSEPH SEERS, Wits.

Remembers that Claimant joined the Brit. Knew his Shop. He had very good tools. He left them behind him. He left a good deal of Furniture and very good Cloathes. Heard they were taken on acct. of his joining the Brit.

To be allowed a Trifle for Things left at his House when he went away.

NEW CLAIM.

November 2.   644. Case of GABRIEL PURDY, late of New York.

Sent his Claim to Col. D. Lived on Philips' manor. Joined the Brit. at the time of the Battle of White Plains. Served with

(13).   Col. ———, then with Major Holland, in the Guides & Pioneers, afterwards in Col. Delancey's Regt. as Seargent. Served till end of the War. Now settled in Cobblegate Mount.

Was possessed of the Improvmts. on a Leasehold farm in Philips manor. His Father was possessed of the Farm & gave it Claimt. His Father sd. he would have his name taken off the Book. Claimant's name put on. His Father told him the Col. Sd. he would do it. Claimant was in possession of it. The lot contained 140 acres. Vals. Improvmts. at £300 Exclusive of the Cols. fine.

Left various articles on his farm when he joined the Brit. Thinks the H·'riar· took them alm·st all.

Says his Grandfather left by ye Mother's side 160 acres of Land on the White Plains to be divided in different shares. Val. his interest at £75. His Grandfather was a Loyalist, but remained on his Place during the War.

HENRY PURDY, Wits.

Claimt. served great part of the war. He joined the Brit. early. Knew the farm in Philips' Manor which belonged to Claimant's Father. His father told Wit. he had given it to 'Claimt'. Witness & Claimt. are Brothers. Wits. knows his Father intended he should have it, but is dubious whethe rye

Conveyance was made by the Col. His Bror. was in possession of it & raised grain. His Father is living.

Witness has heard that his eldest Bror. has purchased it, & is now in Possession. Thinks he had purchased the whole fm. The name of Claimt. shd. have been substituted for his Father in Philip's Books. Thinks if it was not done it was owing to the Distresses of the Times, which were then beginning in 1775. (14).

Vals. the Improvmts. at £300 besides what was to be paid to Col. Philips.

Produces Lease & Release from Samuel & Winifred Purdy, Father & Mother of Claimt. to Jacob Purdy, Henry, Gilbert, Gabriel, Saml. & Gilb., Jun., of all the right which Saml. & Winifred had in the estate of the Grandfather under his Will. They state this right to be ¼ of the Grandfrs. Estate, 1782. Loyal, bore arms to be allowed for improvements legacy.

NEW CLAIM.

645. Case of JOHN HUNTER, late of New York.   November 2.

Lived on Philips' manor. Joined the Brit. in 1781. Was then a young man. Continued to serve with Col. D. as private during the War. Now settled in Cumberland.

Lost horse, taken from his Mother's farm, after Claimant went within the Lines. It was taken because it was found out to be Claimants. His Bror. Claimed it, but it did not signify. Lost 3 in service. Lost Corn, etc., before he joined. Lost Cloathing. Some within ye Lines, some before. To be allowed.

ADAM IRELAND, Wits. (15).

Remembers Claimant living with his Mother & having an horse of his own. Heard he was taken after Claimt. went within the Lines because he belonged to Claimt., & heard that Claimt.'s Bror. Claimed him but they would not allow it. He was reckond. a very fine horse. He was a Stallion. He belonged to ye young man. He had bred him on his Mother's land. Had some share in the Crop on his Mother's Lands. Lost horses & Clothing in the service. It is likely enough that he retaliated.

May be allowed for one horse.

NEW CLAIM.

646. Case of JAMES MERRIT, late of New York.   November 2.

Sent his Claim to Col. D.

Joined the Brit. in 1779. Served in Delancey's Regt. till end of the War. Now settled in Cumberland. Lived in White Plains before the Troubles. Had a Negro given him by his Father just as he went within the Lines. He was taken by a Rebel party, who came plundering & sold at auction. A young negro, worth £100. Lost a yoke of oxen; taken away before Claimt. had joined the Brit.

(16). He lived with his Father. It was known that he was a Tory, and they came & took all his Creatures: a yoke of Oxen, 3 Cows, 3 head Cattle. They took these Cattle away from his Father's farm. They were sold. Lost 2 horses at Morrisina while he was in service. Left a wagon that he could not bring away from New York, Val. £20.

SAMUEL EMBREE:

Heard that his Father gave him a Negro, when he was a boy. **Came into** the Lines when Claimt. came. Witness hired him of Claimt. by the month. While he was in his Employ he was taken by a party who came plundering & sold at Vendue. Thinks the plunderers had ye money. Vals. £100 Cury.

NATHANL. PURDY, Wits.

Claimant had a pair of Steers which were kept on his Father's land. Claimt. bought them of Witt. Heard they were taken for the use of the rebel army. Did not understand that the persons who took them made any enquiries whose property they were.

Claimant seems a fair man.

SAMUEL HALIDAY, Wits.

Knew that Claimant left a Wagon behind him when they left New York because he could not bring it away. It was a very good Wagon.

NEW CLAIM.

November 2. 647. Case of JOSEPH EMBREE, late of New York.

(17). Examination *de bene esse.*

SAML. EMBREE, Wits.

His Bror., Joseph Embree, joined the Brit. at the first forming of the Militia under Col. Delancey. Served the whole War as a private. Now settled on the Cobblegate Mountain.

He lost 8 horses. Some taken privately some by parties. Taken in Morrisina by plundering parties. One taken from Witness' house, carried into the Country & sold. He was taken Prisoner & at the same time had an horse taken. Bought them all. Sometimes he had money for foraging. Sometimes got it for his share in things brought in. Bought one horse of Wits. Gave £15 for it. The apparel & Cash was taken from him when he was

taken Prisoner. Wits. is told that his Bror. need not attend on this Claim, but if he Claims a Legacy from his Father he must attend. This Legacy is left payable out of lands not confiscated but sold by Witnesses' Mother. The money is now claimed from the Estate by Col. Morris, who has got a Judgment on the Trespass Act against Joseph Embree.

NEW CLAIM.

648. Case of NATHANL. HYAT, late of New York.

Examd. *de bene esse.*

SAMUEL EMBREE: (18).

Claimt. served as Cornet sometime in Delancey Regt. Remembers that he lost 2 horses at Morrisina taken from Witness house. Another taken from his Mother's house. He had sent it up from Morrisina. It was claimed by some rebel. Lost an Ox, taken by the Legion. He was plundered of 2 Silver Watches.

Witness is told to inform Hyat that he need not attend in person.

NEW CLAIM.

649. Case of JOHN WILSON, late of New York. November 2.

Sent his Claim to Col. D.

Lived at the White Plains. Joined the Brit. in 1780. Served in Col. D.'s Regt. till end of war as a private. Now settled at Cumberland.

Lost 2 yoke of oxen. Bought them within the Lines. Partly sold one pair. The man to whom he was to sell them took them without paying the money & carried them to the Rebels. Lost the other pair. Had them at Morrisina when they were driven off, the Cattle left were taken by the Rebels. They were brought within the Lines by Country people & Claimant bought them to sell again. Lost a horse before he left his home. It was taken because he was a friend to Govnt. by a party that came against the Tories. To be allowed

Cash left with a man in Morrisina. Claimt. sent for it when he came away, but the man would not let him have it. (19).

JAMES MERRIT, Wits.

Thinks he had a horse that was taken from him before he left home. Gives the same acct. as to the 2 pr. Oxen.

NEW CLAIM.

650. Case of JOHN TWEED, late of New York. November 2.

Sent his Claim to Col. D.

Lived in West Chester Co. Joined the Brit. in 1777. Joined Major Holland. Served all the War, except when Prisoner. Served at last with Col. D. Now settled at Ramsback.

Lost a Negro. It was left to his Wife by her uncle, Isaac Covert. Claimt. never got possession of him. Isaac Covert lived in Courtland Manor. Has heard that several negroes which belonged to Covert were distributed amongst Covert's Brother's Children. Has heard this negro was sold in New England. He makes out no title.

(20). Lived in a house of his own on his Father's farm when he went away. Left 2 horses, 1 yoke Oxen, 4 Cows, 4 Cattle, 16 Sheep, Household Furniture. Left his Wife in Possession. They were taken by the Rebels who were called Guides. Took them because he had left home. Sent his Wife to Claimant afterwards.

ISAAC TEED Wit.

Claimant lived in Courtland Manor. Had 2 horses, 1 yoke Oxen, 4 Cows, 4 Cattle, 16 Sheep. He left all these things behind when he went away. They were taken by Americans because he went into the Brit. Lines. They sent his Wife after him.

NEW CLAIM.

November 2.   651. Case of PETER ANGEVINE, late of New York.

Claimt. sent his Claim to Col. D. He lived in Philips Patent. Joined in 1779. Served all the War. Now settled in Ramsback.

(21). Was possessed of 158 acres Leasehold in Philips Patent, Dutchess Co. Had them from his Father, had been in Possession 3 years. Vals. the Imprvts. at about 40sh. per acre, the Landlords generally took 1-3; in his Valuation he includes the Landlords part. Left 4 horses, 12 Cattle, 30 Sheep on his Farm. The Rebels took them & sold them. One Berry & his Party took them. Berry was a Committee man, lost a mare in service.

ABRAHAM COVERT.

Knew Claimt. He joined the Brit. early, served several years. Knew the Estate he had in Philips Patent. He had it from his Father. It was divided on his Father's death, between him & John his Bro. His Father died about 7 years ago. Witness valued the Estate. The whole was 316 acres. Claimt. was to have 1-2. Witness vald. the whole at £500. Wm. Hill was another appraiser Agreed in the Valuation. Peter was entitled to half and had half. In Possession.

They had a great Stock, there was a great Stock.

When Wits. vald. it there were 25 head Cattle, 3 or 4 horses, 20 or 25 sheep, three months after this Claimt. joined the Brit. Thinks he left the whole stock. He went off on being draughted into Militia. Heard they were all seized & sold on acct. of his going off.

NEW CLAIM.

November 2.   652 Case of JABEZ RUNDLE, late of New York.

Joined the Brit. in 1779, Served all the war as a private, settled at Cumberland.

Lost a fine horse. Lost in action, he was taken. Heard he was taken by a Scout who had it from the Americans & bought it in. Claimant bought it. The persons who took it claimed it as their property. (22).

653. Case of AMOS. BOTSFORD, late of Connecticut. November 3.

Claimant Swo.n Saith.

He is a native of America, was settled at New Haven in Connect. When Troubles began in the Profession of the Law. On breaking out of the Troubles, declared in favour of Brit. Govert., and against their measures, refused to take the Oath of Allegiance to the States, & by that means was excluded from Professional Practice. In July, 1779 went within the Lines. He had been persecuted before, but on Genl. Tryon's Expedition two of his

Brothers having acted as Guides, he had become so obnoxious that he was obliged to quit home. Went to New York. Made an offer of service and of raising men in a Corps intended to be raised, but it was not done. Continued at New York till the Fall, 1782. Came to this Country with a Letter from Sir G. Carleton to Sr. Andrew Hammond, was employd to look out for Lands for the settling of the Loyalists.

Produces Authentic Copy of a letter from Sr. G. Carleton to Sr. And. Hammond, dated Sep., 1782, recommending Claimant & 2 other persons as agent for the Loyalists, desiring him to give them assistance, and they may have access to Records of Province. (23).

Was possessed of an House & Lot in the Town of Newhaven. A Lot was an acre & ¼, purchased the Land in 1770. Produces Deed from Benj. Douglas to Claimt. for a Lot in Newhaven containing 1 acre & 1-2 in considn £150, dated 1770. Built an house after the purchase at expense of near £600. Had just finished it before the Troubles. Had built out houses & builds. Made garden fences, lived there, it was in the centre of the Town. Vals. it at £1,000 Cury. Produces Valuation by Isaac Beers & Elijah Forbes on oath before John L. C. Roem, who values it at £1,120 Lawful Mon. Cont.

This Estate has been Confiscated & sold.

Produces Copy of Conviction of Claimt & Confiscation. Produces Inventory of his Estate.

Home Lot—1-6 Grist Mill, moveables. Produces Certificate of no incumberance on this estate.

Produces certificate of sale from Jonathan Fitch, Admr. on the Estate of Claimant of No. 1.

No. 2. Was possessed of a small Tenement in North haven. Produces Deed from Saml. Clarke to Claimt. of a Lot in Northhaven in considn of £40, dated 1777, Vals. £20, Produces Certificate of no Incumbrance.

No. 3. 1-6 part of a Grist Mill in North haven. Produces Deed from James Bradley to Claimant and John Chandler of 1-3 of Grist Mill in considn. £40, 15 March, 1775, produces Certificate of no Incumbrance. Vals. his share at £20 Str. This share in Mill is included in Inventory. (24).

50 AR.

Left principal part of his furniture, val. £75 Str. at low Estimation. Books, principally Law £37 Str, 1 Cow, 60 Sheep, his personal Estate is returned in the Inventory.

Income. He practised as a Lawyer. Was at the Bar. His annual Income, he was in rect. of about £600 a year from his Profession. He states his Clear Income after expenses in supporting his family at £225 Str. Produces some of his Books by

which his Business appears to have been very extensive.

Has now the appointment of Clerk of the Peace, Ct. of Com. Pleas, register of Deeds for the Co. of Westmoreland. The annual Income scarce exceeds 30 guins. per ann. Has recd. 10sh. per day for servs. to ye Loyalists for one year, and is to have some lands. Says he has sent a power of Attorney 3 Gent. at the Bar to recover his Debts. They have recovered none & he produces an opinion from them that the State of Connecticut will not suffer a person whose Lstate has been Confiscated to maintain a suit for recovering a Debt if sd. Debt was contracted bef. Judgement of Confisn. Signed Charles Chauncey, Tom Ingersoll, Piere point Edwards, Newhaven, May, 1786.

(25).

Produces another Letter from Charles Chauncey who says he cannot inform him of any adjudicn. but their statute is that every Estate shall afterConfiscation be treateu as if the person was dead.

Says there has been an Act of Assembly authorizing his agent Charles Chauncey to collect firm debts due to Claimt sufficient for maintaining Claimant's Children at School in the States.

Produces Copy of Deposition taken by the Comrs. at home that Claimt. if he rated his annual Income at 300 per ann., rated it very low. Signed, C. Monro, July, 1785.

NEHEMIAH MARKS ESQ., Wits.

Was acquainted with Claimt. Always looked upon him as a friend of Brit. Govert. Understood that his Life would have been in Danger had he Staid, he made himself so obnoxious by assistance to the Loyalists. Knew his house at Newhaven. He built it. It was very valuable, in a good situation. His house was well furnished, he lived as gentnly. as any man in Newhaven. He seemed to be in full as much Business as any young man of the Profession & seemd. rising very fast. Wits. adds that before he left Newhaven, he gave all the Professional assistance in his Power to the Loyalists & advised them to continue firm in their allegiance.

(26).

DANL. LYMAN, ESQ.

Knew Claimt. in Newhaven. Always considered him as a Loyalist. He was obliged to leave Newhaven on acct. of his Loyal Principles. Knew No. 1. He built the house, in a good situation, a very good house, it was amongst the most elegant Houses. Does not think it would sell for what it cost building. Vals. it at £7 or 800 Ster., very low. The house was very well furnished. He was in considerable Practice, was amongst the first Lawyers,

50a AR

had a very fair character, & had the fairest Prospects. He lived very well & seemed to be laying up money.

654. Case of JOHN HORNER, late of New Jersey. November 4th.

Claimt. affirms:

He is a native of America, resided in Monmouth Co. when the Troubles broke out, took part with the Brit., went to them at Trentown, had a Protection from them. Continued within the Brit. Lines except now & then that he went out privately. After the affair at Trentown went to New York, went with the Army to Philadelphia, returned to New York, acted part of the way as a Guide, was several times called upon by Sr. Wm. Erskine to give his advice about Guides. Had a Commission as Ensign in ye King's Militia Volunteers from Sr. H. Clinton, 1779. Products Commission. On Evacuation came to St. John's, now settled at Beaver Harbour in this Province. (27),

His Estate was confiscated on acct. of his joining ye Brit. & Sold.

Was possessed of House & Lot in Monmouth Co. consisting of about 1 acre of Land, with house, shop, &c. Produces Deed from Mich. Mount to Claimant of a Lot in Township of Upper Freehold Monmouth Co. in considr. £15.12. Prov. Money, dated 1768.

Says he built house, shop & fences after he made the purchase. Vals. it £150 Prov. Mon. Could have rented it for £10 per an.

Produces Certificate from Joseph Laurence, one of the Comrs. that he sold this House and the personal Estate of Claimant.

Was possessed of a Plantation in Burlington Co. purchased of Isaac Jones. Produces Deed from Isaac Jones to Claimant of a Lot called the Tavern in Township of Hanover, Berrington Co. containing 82 acres in considr £214 Cur., dated March, 1773.

Produces Deed from the Sheriff to Isaac Jones of the Lot called the Tavern Lot in Considn £200.10, dated April, 1769.

Improved the Place considerably after he purchased it. Repaired the house, made new fences, Cleared Land, used to let it for £25 per ann. Cury. Claimant was to do the repairs. This Estate has been sold. Produces affirmation from Alexander Howard that he applied to the Comrs. of forfeited Estates for a Certificate of Sale & they absolutely refused. Vals. it at £350 Prov. Mon. 7s 6d. per dollar. (?8).

Produces affidt. from Burzilla Groon, valuing Claimt's real Estate £450, New York Cury., which Estate has been Confiscated. Valuing moveable Estate at £200. Sworn at New York before a Notary Pub.

The same valuation put on the Estate real & personal by Anthony Woodward.

Claimt. says his moveable Estate consisted of 1 horse, 2 Cows, 6 hogs, Carpenter's Tools, Timber £20, Household furniture £150.

This was seized & sold. Certificate includes personal Estate, but does not specify the Quality.

Claimt. adds that he conveyed private intelligence from Sr. Henry Clinton across the Country to the Admiral.

ANTHONY WOODWARD, Wits. Affirms:

Knew Claimt. He lived in Monmouth Co., he was a Loyalist from the first. He came in on Brit. first coming to Trentown. Went backwards & forwards after the Defeat of the Hessians at Trentown. He went to New York to the Brit. He continued with the Brit. till end of War. He had a Commission in the King's Militia Volunteers. Some of the men of that Regiment were raised, know not if all. Claimt. served in Engineers Department. His Estate real & personal was seized & sold.

Knew No. 1. It formerly belonged to Michl. Mount. Claimt purchased it & built house & shop. Vals. it Land £20. His builds. might have cost £100. No. 2. Knew No. 2. Claimt. purchased it of Isaac Joins, about 80 acres, Claimt. he believes let the Lands, there was an house upon it which was kept as a Tavern. It was a public road.

(29).

Vals. it at £300 or more.

This land was sold & bought in by his wife & sold again. She has now come into the Country. Seems to admit he valued the moveable estate too high formerly when he valued it at £200.

Knew his house & some of his persnl. Est.

N.B.—Seems to know little of his moveable Estate & to have been hasty in his first valuation.

Does not think Claimant's Wife purchased the land in Burlington till some time after the sales made by the Comrs. of forfeited Estates.

N.B.—Congress money must have been very low when his Wife purchased.

(30).

JOHN HORNER, Claimt. says:

He believes Michl. Mount bought it, and is now in Possession of it. Denies that his wife had any share in the purchase of this.

No. 2. His wife got a man to purchase it for her. His name was Joseph Taylor. He gave £1,000 & more Congress Money for it. She gave him £33 provn. Mon. in gold & Silver above the Congress Money, which he gave for it. She has now sold it, is to have £280.

His Wife bought some of the moveables by means of a friend. Knows not how much, but believes some were bought. She sold considerably of what she had bought, when she came away.

JOHN LEONARD Wits.

Knew Claimt. He resided at Monmouth Co. He was always held a Loyalist. He went early in the Brit. Lines. Continued with the Army. Knew his Est. in Monmouth Co., house & lot, decent house & shop. Vals. it at £150 Phila. Cury. 7s. 6d. pr. Dollar, has heard that Mount bought it.

Knew No. 2. Heard that it had become the property of his Wife after he left the Country. On first time of selling the Estate, they sold for a mere trifle. Produces Deed from the Comrs. John Buller & Jos. Borden, to Joseph Taylor of Lands in Burlington, the forfeited Estate of Claimt., in considn £1,005, dated 22 May, 1779. (31).

NEW CLAIM.

655. Case of Lieut. GIDEON PALMER, late of New York. November 6.

Claimt. sent his claim to Col. D.

He is a native of America, lived in Frog's Neck. Joined the Brit. soon after landing in Long Island, gave Information, joined Delancey when he raised his horse, served with him during Delancey's & Beardmore's Command, as a Lieutenant served all the War. Now settled in Westmoreland Co. this Province.

Produces Certificate from Col. D. that Claimt. had served 5 years as Lieutent. with West Chester Refugees. Produces Commission from Sir Guy. Carleton in 1783 to be Captn. of Militia destined for Cumberland.

Lost a Negroe Man. He listed in the Queen's American Rangers. A Yoke of Oxen. Claimt. bought them of 2 men in Dys. Regt. some more came from Horseneck & took them for him, 1 horse, stolen from Claimt. from the Bowry at New York. A Negro runaway, but Claimt. got him back on paying £20 to a man for fetching him back.

A Negroe, bought of Ben Townsand in Delanceys Co. during the War. He deserted to the Enemy.

Was possessed of ½ the Sloop Fame. Produces Rect. from Henry Puntein of £250 New Y. Cury. from Thos. Mulliner & Claimt. for the purchase of the Sloop Fame, 13 Decr., 1778. (82).

Claimt. had sent her at his own risk to bring a Load of Wood from Huntingdon to New York to the Army. She was taken by an American whale boat. It would have been a profitable venture, had not the Sloop been taken.

The Sloop Fame had been taken by Captn. Gardiner of the Ship Maidstone and had been condemned at the Vice Admiral's Court, New York, in 1778, before Claimt. purchased her. Produces Copy of Condemnation in 1778. Lost a small Sloop of about 30 Tons. She was at Frog's Neck taking in forage for the Army. Was taken by an American whale boat and retaken.

Claimt. pd. for her recapture £32, this was in 1780.

Left a crop in the Ground when he left New York. Left his Father & Bror. in possession of the Land, it was his Father's Land. Horse taken, left at his Father's when Claimt. went to Long Island to join the Brit, taken because Claimant had gone away to join the Brit. had a Cow, a pair of Steers & 6 Hogs, on his Father's Lands when he went to join the British.

There came a party down to his Father's & plundered nine of the above articles & many more of his own & threatened his life (33).

on acct. of Claimts having gone away to the Brit. They came immediately after Claimt. had gone away.

JOHN BAKER Wits.

Knew Claimt. Claimt. joined Brit on Long Island, remembers him well serving as Lieut. in Col. D.'s Regt. Remembers he had an horse of his own on his Father's Lands, thinks he had some stock of his own too on his farm. His Father's Estate was plundered on Claimt.'s acct. as Wits. thinks & on the Father's acct. too, as they were reckoned a Loyal family. Had a Negroe named Prince who listed in ye Queen's Rangers & died in service Had a Negro who deserted to the enemy, remembers his being part owner of the Sloop Fame.

NEW CLAIM.

November 6. 656. Case of JOHN ANGIVINE, late of New York.

Claimt. sent his Claim to Col. D.

Lived in Dutchess Co. joined the Brit. at Long Island, 1776. Served all the War, except the time he was Prisoner, as private, Now settled in Ramsback.

Was possessed of Tenant Land in Philips Patent, 158 acres, was entitled on his Father's Death, his Father Died in 1778, there was a Division made between Claimt. & his Bror. v. case of Peter Angevine, Claimt. to be allowed the same, for Estate & for Cattle.

(31).

NEW CLAIM.

November 6. 657. Case of MICH. LLOYD, late of New York.

Sent his Claim to Col. D. Native of Ireland, at Philadelphia. Joined the Brit. in 1777. First in 52 Regt. then 57th Regt. Then served with Bearman, then with Hatfield, then Col. Delancey, till end of War, now settled in Cumberland.

Lost 3 horses while in service with Col. D. at Morrisina. Left 3 behind him at New York when they came away. He is told to expect nothing.

November 7. CASE OF BRIGR. GEN. RUGGLES.

JAMES PUTMAN, ESQ.

Knew his Home Farm at Hardwick, very good Land & well fenced & in a good state of Cultivation, good house & builds. & good Conveniences Thinks this fairly worth £5 Ster. including the Buildings, does not know the other parts of his Estate.

He had a remarkably fine Breed of horses, that used to sell at an higher Price than any other Person's Horses in the Province The old Genl. used to set an higher value upon them than other people did.

NEW CLAIM. (35).

658. Case of JOHN CRAWFORD, late of New York.

November 6.

Sent his Claim to Col. D.
Lived at Pondridge in West Chester Co. Joined the Brit. in the year 1780. He was persecuted, beat & abused. Was tried for his Life on suspicion of being Pilot, was taken by a mob who were going to hang him, he had a large family could not leave them. Thinks he did not sign any Rebel Association. Was fined for not serving in Militia he came to Delancey but was not able to serve but continued with him and worked at the Trade of Cordwainer & Shoemaker till Evacuation of New York. Now settled at Cumberland.

Was possessed of 60 acres of Land with house & Barn in West Chester. Had 40 acres by his Father's Will. Produces Copy of Will of his Father John Crawford, whereby he gives his son John the Claimant, 40 acres of Land, dated 1770.

Robert, the eldest son, is dead, leaving Children. Claimant had been in Possession of these Lands 3 or 4 years before his Father's Death continued in possession till 1780 built an House & Barn upon it, bought 20 acres adjoining to the above about 1771, of his Brother James Crawford at 40sh. per acre, improved & fenced it. The whole lot was valuable Land, near 20 acres Meadow, about 20 acres Plough Land, Vals. it at £400.

This Estate has been Confiscated, Produces Judgement against Claimt. & Confiscation of his Estate, does not know who has bought it, nor who is in Possession. Heard that Capt. Jos. Lockwood & Amos Scofield were in Possession.

(36).

Lost 4 Oxen, they were all taken for fines, 2 Cows & 6 young Cattle, taken for fines. Claimt. himself sold some & paid fines with the money. 2 Cows were taken as he was coming into the Lines. Withdraws claim for 20 Sheep as they have been sold & he has got the money, lost 2 horses, 1 taken for a fine, another taken after he was within the Lines, plundered Indian Corn growing on a small piece of Land that he had hired.

JAMES CRAWFORD, Wits.:

Claimt. was always Considered as a Loyalist & ill treated on that aqct. He was much abused by the Mob. Heard he was tr'ed for his Life. He was Considered as having piloted the Brit. Army from King's Bridge to Bedford, he was tried for it & acquitted. He had 60 acres of Land, 40 under his Father's Will, he purchased 20 acres of Witness, at about 40 Sh. per acre.

He was in Possession of 40 acres before his Father's Death. It was understood in the family that he was to have what was left by his Father's Will forever. He was Clear of Debt. Vals. the 40 acres at £10 per acre. Knew that he had a good stock. The eldest son of the elder Brother Robert is now living at Boston. The Son is now of age.

(37).

TITUS BROWN, Wits. :
Claimant was always a Loyalist, suffered as much as a man could & live. Knew his Land, he had it from his Father & Brother, Vals. the land at £8 per acre, he means Cultivated Lands would fetch £8 New York Curcy.
His Stock was mostly taken for fines.

NEW CLAIM.

November 7.   659. Case of AMOS. FOWLER, late of New York.

Claimt. came to Cumberland in Oct., 1783, sent no Claim home that year.
Is told his Claim cannot be admitted.

660. Case of JAMES GORDON, late of Georgia.

November 8.   Claimt. sworn, saith:

(38).   He went to America in 1772, in Consequence of a Proclamation from Sr. James Wright to make a Settlement in Georgia & engaged in that undertaking with Mr. Jonas Brown & Mr. Thos. Brown, afterwards Lieut. Col. King's Rangers. They were at a considerable expense in preparing for this undertaking. Carried a great many indebted servants.

There being some Difficulty about making a settlement in the Frontier as intended, Claimant purchased a place in S. Carolina for a Temporary settlement & settled the persons whom he had brought with them. Afterwards, in obtaining Lands from Govr. Wright. He parted with the Settlement in S. Carolina & removed into Georgia & settled on Broad River, was settled there when the Troubles broke out. One of his Partners, Mr. Thomas Brown, being young & active & violent against the rebel measures, used to attend their meetings & oppose their measures. Claimt had the same sentiments but did not declare them with so much warmth.

On acct. of Col. Brown's open Declaration, a party came down to their settlement and took him Prisoner, carried him to Augusta, tarred & feathered him. Col. Brown went after this to Saludu River. Claimt. & he had concerted measures with Cunningham who was raising a party thereabouts to come & join them in order to get Possession of Augusta. Cunningham let the scheme fall to the ground. After this Brown went away to Charlestown, but Claimant staid in order to secure his Property if possible. Claimand continued but a short time on his settlement, being continually molested & having constant Depredations made upon him by persons who were forward in promoting the Rebellion in that Province, and having recd. Information of an Intention to plunder & destroy his settlement, he went away with his servants. Claimant was obliged to go on foot. Carried away what effects he could which were very few & went to back Parts of S. Carolina. Thinks this was in the summer of 1775.

(39).

Claimant looks upon the joint Concern to be from that time at an end.

He then made a purchase on his own private acct. about 8 miles below fort Charlotte on the Savanah River & settled there. Continued there quiet as well as he could, but the people of the Country inveigled away his servants. He was called upon to serve in their Militia & obliged to send a Substitute. Claimant continued there till after the Fall of Savannah in 1779, Col. Brown then coming to the Post at fort Augusta, Claimant went to him & joined him there.

The Country being at this time quiet, Claimt. returned to his Settlement. Claimt. afterwards joined Col. Conger & Col. Allen who were going to take Post at 96 & gave them what Information & assistance he could. Left them in Possession of the Post at 96 & returned to his own settlement. Continued about 2 months, having Information of Designs against him. Had got every thing in readiness to go away when a party came down, took away all his horses, seven in number. Claimant found himself obliged to quit his Settlement, packed up his things as many as he could & sent them down by a canoe & marched on foot with his Negroes thro' the woods to Augusta & joined Col. Brown, then went to Charlestown, leaving his Negroes in the charge of one Mr. Keating & left his baggage with Col. Brown.

(400).

His Baggage was lost on the Fall of Fort Augusta, and the Negroes left with Mr. Keating were taken as being known to be Claimants.

Claimant having thus lost all his property applied to Col. Balfour & by his means was appointed Deputy Commissr. of Sequestered Property. Continued at Charlestown acting in that Employment till Evacuation, then went to the West Indies; continued about 16 months in the West Inds., then came to this Country & is now settled at Musk Wash in this Province.

Claimant was Possessed of a Plantation consisting of 450 acres on the Savannah River, S. Carolina, purchased it in beginning of year 1775 of one Brown for £300 Ster., it was very valuable, 15 or 20 acres Clear, there were 80 or 100 acres of Swamp which were valuable. Had a Deed from Mr. Brown which was left in Charlestown, built an house & stable & houses for his Negroes. Vals. this Plantation £300 Ster., Houses & build. £350 Ster. This was all his own concern, with which his Partners had nothing to do. The Rebels are in Possession of it. He has endeavoured to get accts. from the Country but cannot.

(41).

Lost 15 Wo king Negroes & seven Children, he carried them with him to fort Augusta, they were taken from Possession of Mr. Keating, near fort Augusta, with whom Claimt. left them, they were taken as being known to be Claimants. They were carried away into the mountainous part of the

(42).

Country & never got back. Left furniture at his house when he went away. All the things mentioned in the Schedule which it was impossible to carry away, Val. £570 Ster.

Lost seven horses, taken from him by a party who understood Claimant was going off & came & plundered them. Lost other articles of Cloathes, Linen, Books, furniture, that were in Col. Brown's Possession when fort Augusta fell. Val. £300. Had arms in his house which were taken from him. Val. £25.10.

WILLIAM WELSY, ESQ.:

Knew Claimant in Georgia, always understood him Loyal. Remembers his going out with a large party to make a settlement in Georgia on Ceded Lands in 1773 with a number of servants. Mr. Brown, afterwards Col. Brown, was concerned in the undertaking. Witness understood they purchased and settled on the ceded Land. Col. Brown had been exceedingly active against the measures of the Insurgents, he was tarred & feathered. Understood Claimt. was soon obliged to quit the Settlement & went to S. Carolina.

On our recovering Georgia heard that Claimant came to Fort Augusta. Heard that Claimt. had a Settlement of his own, Private Concern, in S. Carolina, near Camden, having a Plantation in that part of the Country, he must have had Negroes.

Has heard that his Baggage, such as he could bring with him, was at fort Augusta when it fell & was plundered. Remembers him acting in the office of Mr. Cruden as Commssr. of Sequestered Estates, remembers him acting in that Department all the while Witness was in Charlestown, looks upon that as a trust of great Importance.

(43).

Col. Brown was much distinguished for his zeal & activity & Claimant was always considered as perfectly Loyal & firm in his attachment to Brit. Govnt.

(618). MAHITTABLE JONES, Widow of Elisha Jones of Pitsfield, Massts. V. Vol. 10, p. 77.

November 9.

ELISHA JONES, Eldest Son of the late Elisha Jones of Pitsfield appears, & being sworn, saith:

His Father, Elisha Jones, was 2nd Son of Col. Elisha Jones. He joined the Brit. at Boston & served. Was with them till his Death. He died in 1783 without a Will, leaving Claimant, his Eldest Son, & 6 other Children. For acct. of his Family & for

acct. of his Property, v. the case of Mrs. Mahittable Jones.

Claimant is 24 yrs. of age in June next.

Claimant was at School when his Father went to Boston. Joined the Brit. Army at New York when 16 yrs. of age, served as Volunteer above 3 years. He claims his share in his Grandfather's Estate.

His Father was in Possession of No. 1. One Hurd is now in Possession, he bought it of the Commrs, he paid for it by a Quantity of Boards. His Father had agreed to sell it to Hurd, but no Deed had been drawn up. His Father was to sell it for a number of Boards, he cann)t say the exact No. (44).

Knew No. 2, his Father lived upon it, Confiscated & sold. Vanskort is now in Possession, there was a Saw Mill & Grist Mill upon it, sold for £600 lawful.

No. 3 was his Father's, Vanskort is now in Possession.

No. 4 was his Fathers. No. 5—His Father was also possessed of about 80 acres, took it for a Debt, called Webb Lot, Intervail Land, cannot say who is in Possession, it has been Confiscated and sold, vals. about £100. His Father had 2 Negroes, both enlisted in the American Army.

His Father had certainly 11 horse kind, 1 yoke oxen & some young Cattle, 7 or 8 Cows, 40 Sheep, furniture & farming utensils, had Bonds & Notes which were taken from his Mother. His Father owed also a great deal of Money. No. 1 vald. at £300 Ster.

No. 2, 3, 4 at £939 Ster. by 3 Apraisers on Oath from Massts.

Says his 2nd Bror. & Sister, Mahittable, are coming from the States. The Mother & all the Brothers are to settle together at Sissiboo.

New Claim.

661. Case of OBADIAH ACKERLY, late of New York.   November 9.

Sent his Claim to Col D.

Joined D. in 1777 in the first Troop of horse which he raised, (45)· served till that Troup was discharged, then with Major Bearman, then Hatfield, then Col. D. as a Private. Now settled at Cumberland.

Lost some of his furniture before he left home, he lived in Courtland Manor. Rebels came & put him in Confinement beaouse *Claimt speaks very fairly.* he was a subject to the British & traded with them & assisted, took cloathes & furniture, val. £30 York Crcy. Lost all his horses in service, lost the rest of his furniture while in the Lines at Morrisina, lost 2 Cattle, he lived on the outlines, a party came down & took them a few Days after the Peace. Claimt. bought them of Aaron Hurd. The people who took them came in the night, were called Skinners.

New Claim.

662. Case of SAML. CORNWELL, late of New York.   November 9.

Claimt. saith: Sent his Claim to Col. D. Lived in Duchess Co. Joined the Brit. April, 1777, served under Major Holland, then Col. Emerick, then Hatfield, then Dy. as Seargent till end of the War. Now settled at Cumberland.

Abominably high.

(46).

Was possessed of an house at King's Bridge, built at his own expence during the War, within the Lines, not his own Land, 't was rebel Land, by that means lost his house. Says he gave £120 N. Y. Curcy. for the Boards, Nails & Shingles & Carpenters Work. Lost 2 horses, one killed, one taken in action. Cattle taken by Brit. Troops. Slay & horses, he was getting wood for the use of the Army under a Contract & they were taken by a Plundering Party by force of Arms. 2 horses taken in the same way, in the service, 1 horse died while he was in pursuit of Rebels. Lost Cash when taken Prisr. in 1778. Cloathes at same time, 2 horses more.

663. Case of ELISHA JONES, V. 108.

ABRAHAM FROST, Wits:

Knew the late Elisha Jones, Son of Col. Jones, lived at Pitsfield.

(47).

Remembers him in Possession of Considerable real Estate in Pitsfield, should think near 400 acres. Remembers him a good while in Possession, there was a good 2 Story house, a large Barn & other builds. Lands in very good order, a vast Deal of Clear Land. Sometimes they sowed 50 acres of Wheat. Wild Land used to sell from a Dollar to 2 Dollars. Good Meadow was very high. He cannot fix value of improved Lands as they were so seldom marketable. Wild Lands they were continually buying. Good Meadow might be worth from 15 to 20 Dollars per acre. Plough Land from 10 to 15 Dollars, 6 Sh. to Dollar.

Elisha Jones had a large stock, he kept a Tavern & large Store & had a Pot ash Work. He had an English Stallion and very fine horses.

RICHD. SQUIRE, Wits.:

Knew Claimant's Father, Elisha Jones, he was very Loyal. Knew his Farm, but not the exact particulars, it was a large farm, a good house, great Improvements had been going on for ten or eleven years. In Lanesboro Witness bought Lands with little Improvements for 20 Shils. per acre. Meadow Land would fetch £5 or 6 per acre lawful, Plough land not so much. Saw his Wife & family after Elisha Jones went away, she was in Distress & complained of being stript of every thing.

He dealt largely, had a Pot Ash—. Must have had a good Deal of Money owing him. Witness thought him in a very thriving way, he seemed to be making money.

Case of SAML. CORNWALL. V. 113.

ABRAHAM COVERT, Wits.:

(48).

Remembers Claimts serving with D. Remembers his house at Kings Bridge, he built it on rebel ground, it was a frame, rather more than an Hut, not much finished, things were very high.

New Claim.

664. Case of JONAS BROWN, THOS. BROWN & JAMES GORDON, of Georgia. V. Supra.

Claimant, James Gordon, gives the acct. of his & his Partners engaging in an adventure to make a settlement in the Ceded Lands in Georgia at Supra in his own Claim.

Claimant went out first in the year 1772 to make Preparations. Thos. Brown, afterwards Lieut. Col., arrived in the Fall, 1773, with a number of Servants. Claimant, Jas. Gordon, at first made a Purchase in S. Carolina after Col Browns arrival, they continued there some time, parted with that settlement & went to settle on the Ceded Lands about the Fall. (49).

They had obtained Warrants of Survey for 5,000 acres on Broad River, for which Deposit had been paid of 8d. per acre. This 8d. was to be accounted as part of the Purchase money, but the Price per acre was to be settled by Commrs. afterwards, the best land not to exceed 5 Shils., the worst not less than 1 Sh. per acre. These Warrants were dated in the end of 1773, or beginning. Cla'mant & Co. went on that understanding & proceeded to build houses for Servts., built houses, cleared Lands.

The Settlement was in this improving situation when the Troubles broke out. Col. Brown from the first was very active & violent in opposing the Measures of the Rebels.

In Consequence of Col. Brown's open & warm Declaration against the Measures of the Rebels, a party came down to the Settlement & took him Prisoner, carried him to Augusta.

Claimant, Jas. Gordon, continued on this Settlemt. till many of his servts. were inveigled away & he was obliged to go, this was in the later end of the Summer, 1775.

As soon as Claimant went away the Rebels came & plundered their Houses & Stores, took away their Tools, &c.

The Partnership was in Possession of the said 5,000 acres under Warrants of Survey. Vals. these at the sum given in the Deposit, £166.13.4. 38 horses at £5 each, £190, Grey Mare. (50).

No. 2—200 acres on Euchee River, purchased in 1773 in Considn. of £25 Georgia Money. Expense in getting the Conveyance, £2.10.

Claimant says that a Law was past in 1776, as he thinks, for the purpose of declaring the Estates of persons who did not reside forfeited in Consequence. Several persons who resided in the Ceded Lands got Possession of this Settlement. Claimant thinks they obtained an order or grant from the State for that purpose.

Claimant says this Property was sold before he left Charles town. He left Directions to have a Certificate of the Sale sent to him, but has not yet recd. it, but perfectly recollects his receiving unquestionable Information of its being sold & heard what it sold for.

Lost at the time this Settlement was plundered
16 Horses, £12 each... £192.0.0
Tools, Val ... 220.0.0

N.B. They had Tools of various kind, for Carpenters, Blacksmiths, Coopers, &c.

Goods in hand for the new Settlers...... £100.0.0

(51).

Wagon ... 15.0.0
Furniture ... 50.0.0
Arms, &c... 75.0.0
Cattle, about 80 in No... 70.0.0
Provisions... 50.0.0

Col. Brown is now in the Bahama Islands. Mr. Thos. Brown is now in England.

WILLM. WELSY, Esq., Wits. :

Remembers Col. Brown & Mr. Gordon coming to make a Settlement on the Ceded Lands in Consequence of Govr. Wrights Proclamation. They brought out many Servts. with them & Witness recollects that these servants went upon the Settlement. No doubt they had Tools for ye different Artifices.
Witness recollects that a great many Servts. were brought, he thinks at two Embarkations.
It was notorious that Col. Brown had been driven from his settlement & treated cruelly & horridly after he was taken Prisoner.

665. Case of JAMES HOYT, late of Connecticut.

November 14.

Claimt. sworn, saith :

He is a native of America, resided at Norwalk, Connect. Prov. When Troubles broke out was in Trade. From the first declared in favour of the Brit, but took no active part. Before the Battle of Lexington had been imprisoned on Suspicion of bringing Tea into the Country. Was taken up in 1776 on Suspicion of having Conveyed Intelligence to the Senegal Frigates, but discharged in a few days. Was much persecuted till he went within the Brit. Lines in Octr., 1777. On first joining went as a Volunteer with the Army, till his friends procured him a Vessel, it was a private trading Vessel. In the Spring, 1778, was taken by a Privateer, carried to New London & kept in Prison, was Exchanged in the Fall, after that he had the Command of the Swift Privateer. After quitting the Privateer Business went into Trade at New York. Was in Trade a twelve month till appointed Cashier to the Barrack Masters Departmt. by Col. Crosbie. He was afterwards Continued by Brooke Watson as Clerk in the Fewel Department. Came here on Evacuation of New York. Claimt. has

(52).

now half pay as Quarter Master to Prince of Wales American Regimt.

This half pay was Continued by Sr. Guy Carleton in Consequence of Certificates from several persons of Character to Claimants Loyalty & his spirited Exertions, particularly while he was acting as Volunteer.

Before he went within the Lines his property was plundered. Claimant was suspected to have secreted his Property in a Store at Stratfield, which Store belonged to his Father. The Mob came & took Possession of a Vessel called the little George belonging to Claimt. which lay at the Dock near the store. She was carried up the River & ran on shore, this was in the year 1777. The vessel was afterwards sold. Claimant does not know by what Authority, but supposes it was by Authority from Genl. Silliman. She was bought by Ward & Sherman, zealous Americans. Claimant had built this Vessel himself, her Burthen was about 30 Tons, she was new. Vals. her at £360 York Money. (53)

Claimant lost in like manner by Plunder 63 Boxes of Tallow Candles, they were thought to be secreted in his Father's Store,

as other people had sent their things up into the Country to prevent their falling into the Hands of the Brit. Troops.

A Party headed by Seargt. Halley took them as being the property of Claimant, they were afterwards carried to Fairfield & sold at public Vendue for acct. of the State. Thinks they were sold by Genl. S. Merriman, who acted as States Attorney, or Major Abels. They were sold before Claimant had gone into the Brit. Lines. The property was Condemned as having been secreted for the use of the Enemy. Vals. these at 226.16.0. (54).

There had been proceedings at the Court at Fairfield for the purpose of Condemning these Goods.

Lost 86 Boxes of Soap in the same manner, which were also Condemned, Val. 258.8.0.

The Vessel was sold after Claimt. had joined the Brit. Troops, the other goods were sold before.

The Senegals Boat had carried off his Brother's Property in order to secure it some nights before, & Claimant supposes this Circumstance made them suspicious that he had the same Intentions of Carrying off his Property likewise.

Says he & his whole Family were known to be Zealous Friends to the British Governmt. His Father suffered great Persecution on acct. of his Loyalty. He now lives at Stratfield with Sir Guy Carleton's full approbation.

---

666. Case of JOSEPH ROBINSON, Lieut. Col. of S. Carolina Royalists, Late of S. Carolina. 1786. November 16.

Claimant appears & being sworn, says:

He is a native of America, resided on Broad River, S. Carolina. Took a very early part in Favour of Brit. Government. Had a Command under Lord Wm. Campbell in 1775, as Major of

(5). Militia. About Nov. of that year was Concerned in the first Engagement at 96. Had 2,400 men under his Command. In this Engagement Claimant was successful, but his men dispersed afterwards, & on the assembly of them under Patrick Cunningham they proved unfortunate. Claimant went into the Cherokee Nation, during which time his settlement was plundered, his house burnt & his Family driven from Home.

Claimant went thro' the Creek Nation to Pensacola, thence went to Augustine, joined the Regiment of S. Carolina Royalists under Col. James at St. Johns River in East Florida, 1778. Had a Commission in May, 1778, as Lieut. Col. of that Regt., had almost the sole Command as Col. James did not often attend. Had been acting before he recd. his Commission in the capacity of Lieutent. Col. Continued to serve during the War.

On Evacuation of Charlestown went to East Florida where he staid about a twelve month after the Peace, went thence to

Jamaica & staid about a twelve month there & then came to this Province. Is now settled on the Kennibeckasis, has Half Pay.

Claimant was possessed of a Tract of Land on Broad River.

(56). No. 1, Consisted of 300 acres, purchased some years before the War, there was some little Cultivation, it was purchased partly for money & partly on Exchange of Cattle of one Boneau, a Frenchman in Charles Town. Had a Deed which was destroyed when his house was burnt. He built a dwelling house, Barn & Stables after he made the Purchase. There was about 30 acres Clear. Claimant lived upon it, it was very good land, it was valued by two Gentlemen on Oath at £3 Ster. per acre. This appraisement was sent with his Papers to England. Claimt. thinks his valuation rather too high. He had a very good Fishery upon it, which had been made by the Indians. Thinks he could have sold it for £500.

Claimant saw his name amongst the Persons whose Estates were forfeited. His Estate being early seized he believes it was shared out amongst any plunderers who could get Possession. They were not regular in keeping the acct. of Estates which were seized at that time, nor returned any regular acct. of the sales. When last he heard one John Moore was in Possession. He was a neighbour & Claimt. imagines he had purchased it.

No. 2—Another Tract in 96 District of 100 acres, purchased of Jacob Garner about 6 years before the War 'n Considn. of £30 Provl. money.

Cleared about 15 acres & built an house, Vals. it at near £100 Provl. Claimt. imagines Moore is also in Possession of this Tract.

Lost a Negroe Wench & Child. Left at 96 when Claimt. went to the Cherokee Nation. The Rebels came & plundered him, (57). took his Wife Prisoner, took ye Negroe & Child, they kept the Negroe & Child. On Claimants going away they came down & plundered his settlement. No. 1, & burnt his house, they took 5 horses. 26 Cattle, 10 Sheep, Household furniture to amt. of £60 Ster., Clothing, Arms, Wheat, Corn, Hemp, &c. in the Barn to val. of £100. He had a very valuable Library which he had purchased himself, Law Books & Books in different Languages. Had 60 Vols. of Law Books, 100.

He had the Place of Deputy Surveyor in South Carolina. The rate of Surveying was at 30 Sh. Provl. per 100 acres, he cannot estimate the annual value of it.

MOSES WHEALLEY, Wits.:

Knew Claimant before Troubles began, he was settled on Broad River. From the beginning he took a decisive part in Favour of Government. He had the Command of Militia at 96 against the Americans in 1775, he had an Engagement with them. He Commanded it was said 2,000 men & was successful. He afterwards disperst the men. (He went to the Cherokee Nation, after which they came & burnt his House. Witness saw his house & all his Goods burnt that they could get at.

Remebmers his having the Command of S. Carolina Loyalists He was Lieut. Col., was very active in forming that Regiment & served during the War.

Knew No. 1—Remembers his purchasing it & building upon it. A good Deal was Clear, 30 acres or more.

There was a Shad Fishery which was Valuable.

It was valuable Land. Wits. bought some Land on that River at 20 Sh. per acre, taking the whole together he bought about 300 acres, there were some acres Clear. (58).

Knew No. 2—It Consisted of 100 acres. Remembers Claimt. in Possession, he purchased it of Jacob Garner. When his house was burnt his stock was plundered, thinks more than 5 horses, reckons about 20 Cattle, some furniture & Books ournt, a great many things burnt. Remembers that he had a Negroe Woman & Child who were taken away & kept by the Rebels.

Witness has heard the Landed Estate was sold.

Has heard his, Claimts., name was on the Confiscation List in the Carolina News Papers.

667. Case of STEPHEN KENT, late of New Jersey.   November 16.

Claimt. sworn, saith:

He is a native of America. Resided in Woodbridge, Jersey, when Troubles broke out on his Father's farm in an house which had been built near his Father. On breaking out of the Troubles both Claimt. & his Father took part with the Brit. Signed no rebel Association. Was trained at first in their Militia once or twice but never served. Paid fines to be Clear.

In the Beginning of 1777, Claimant & his Father went to Staten Island. They were forced to quit their Home, they skulked about till they could get to Staten Island, then went to New York. (59).

51 AR.

Produces several Passes from Gen. Vaughan, Lord Cornwallis & others to Claimt. & his Father.

Claimt. produces Certificate of his Loyalty from Gen. Skinner. Produces anonymous Letter to his Father in 1775, threatening his Life for opposing the Measures of the Committee of Safety, &c.

Claimt. served as Volunteer in the Town. His Father, David Kent, died at New York in 1778, having made his Will.

His Father was possessed of 215 acres in the Town of Woodbridge. His Father had purchased some, some came from his Grandfather. His Father had been in Possession near 30 years

of almost all. Produces Deed from Stephen Kent, great Grandfather to Stephen Kent, Father of Claimt., of 140 acres, 1714.

Produces Deed from Willm. Kent to David Kent of 21 acres in Considn. £75—1751.

Produces Deed from Wm. Stone to David Kent of 75 acres in considn. 422.10 New Jersey Mon., dated 1759.

Produces Deed from John Geddes to David Kent of a Lot in Woodbridge in Considn. £84.9 dated 1762. Claimant is the only Son.

(60). Produces his Father's Will Whereby he gives that Piece of Land bought of William Stone to his 3 daughters, gives his Books & apparel and all his Lands & real Estate to his Son Stephen, the Claimt. Makes him Exect. dated 9 May, 1775. The Estate has been Confiscated & sold.

Produces Certificate from Ebenezer Ford that he & Willm. Manning, another Commr. for Co. of Midx., sold 214 acres in Woodbridge, the Property of David Kent, forfeited by his adherence to the King of Great Britain. This includes the 75 acres left to his Daughters.

The Testators 3 Daughters—Holday married & lives in Woodbridge, Rachel, since dead without Children, leaving Stephen her heir, Zernia, who lives in this Province with Claimt.

Claimt. came to this Province after Evacuation of New York, now settled on the Kennibekasis.

This Estate was between Amboy & Remingtown, on Rareton River. Says his Father was offered 7.10 per acre. It was all Clear, 2 very good houses & barns, there was fresh meadow & salt meadow. Produces Valuation by apraisers valuing Land at £7 per acre. Valuing Improvements at £550. Vals. the whole at £8 per acre, including the buidings.

JOSEPH ALWARD, Wits. :

(61). Knew David & Stephen Kent, both very Loyal. Witness was employed to get Intelligence & he found he could always depend upon them as true friends to the Loyal Party. Knew his Estate at Woodbridge, Vals. it at £7 per acre, Builds. at £550.

JOHN FORD, Wits. :

Knew David Kent, he was very Loyal from the first, had made himself more obnoxious than any one. Suffered all but Death. Was obliged to fly within the Lines, his son went with him. Stephen was also very Loyal, always opposed the Rebels. Knew his farm at Woodbridge, it consisted of two Lots, containing upwards of 200 acres, it was bought at different times. Remembers the Father in Possession a long time. One Brooks & ——— are now in Possession, they bought it of Commrs. as Witness has heard. Vals. it £7.10 per acre without the builds. Vals. Builds. at above £500, there were 2 houses & Barns & outhouses.

Claimant claims also his Father's personal Estate under his Father's Will as Execr. His Father lost 13 Cattle kind, 1 horse, very good, taken by night from his farm by a Party who came against him as being a Tory in Feby., 1777. Before they went off 3 horses, 6 Sheep, farming utensils, some articles of furniture left on the Farm when they went away. They had removed many of their things. Has Debts due to him in the States to above £20. (62).

668. Case of WM. PAINE, M.D., late of Massts. 1786. November 17.

Claimt. appears & being sworn, saith:

He is a native of America. Was situated at Worcester in Business in the Physical Line when the Troubles broke out. From the first openly declared his sentiments in favour of Brit. Govnt.

In Aug., 1774, signed a Protest against a resolution of a meeting at Worcester. Judge Putnam & others signed it, all afterwards recanted except Claimt, Judge Putnam & another person.

In Consequence of this Protest Claimt. was obliged to leave his Home very suddenly. Went to Boston & joined the Brit. Troops under Genl. Gage, went from thence to London.

In Octr., 1775, was appointed Apothecary to the Army in America. Went from London to Ireland & sailed under ye Command of Earl Cornwallis for North Carolina. Sr. Peter Parker Commanded the Fleet, arrived in N. Carolina, sailed afterwards to S. Carolina.

He was the only person able to do Business of the Hospital in that Climate, owing to the sickness of the others. Went afterwards to New York with the Fleet, attended Sr. H. Clinton to Rhode Island, there remained till Evcauation of that Garrison. Came to New York, did duty at the Hospital till ordered to travel with Lord Winchelsea to attend upon him, left Ld. Winchelsea at Lisbon, went to London. (63).

Joined the Army again in the Spring, 1782. Was appointed Physician to the Army at New York in the Fall, 1782. Was sent to Halifax by order of Sr. Guy Carleton in consequence of a malignant Fever then raging amongst the Troops at Halifax. He is now continued in the service on half Pay.

Claimant was possessed of ½ a Shop & Lot in Worcester. Claimt. was in Partnership with Shepherd & Hunt and had purchased ½ the Shop & building & Lot in Considn. of £50 Curoy. in the year 1772. Laid out money upon it afterwards. Vals. his Interest at £50 Ster. Produces Certificate of Confiscation & Sale of this Land.

Personal Estate—Produces an Inventory of all his personal effects returned by Wm. Davis, Agent on the said Estate. Valuation by 3 appraisers at £2,238.

Produces Certificate of Joseph Wheeler, Regr. of Probates, of sale of his personal Estate.

(64). Claimant had a Considerable No. of Professional Books, very valuable ones, which were sold. He has considered the Inventory of his effects & is satisfied that he values them low at £325.6.

Claimt. paid £67.10 to his former Partners in Consequence of his leaving the Place. Says he has now owing to him in the State of Massts. Debts to amount of £5,000 that money.

JUDGE PUTNAM:

Knew Mr. Paine at Worcester, he was in very good Professional Business. He distinguished himself very early as a friend to Brit. Govmt. in 1774 when Town Meetings were frequent to adopt Resolutions against the Government. In Worcester the Loyalists were not afraid to declare their sentiments at the meetings.

70 Persons at one of the meetings declared their Dissent against an unconst'tutional Resolution that had been carried by a small majority. Claimt. was one of the Protesters. Some of the Protesters were afterwards taken up. Witness was obliged to go away to avoid Persecution on this acct. Claimt. did the same rather than to recant. All that staid were obliged to recant.

Claimant afterwards served in the British Hospital, Witness believes with great credit & did great service. Witness is fully persuaded of his Loyalty.

(65). He was in Partnership with Shepherd & Hunt. Understood the Shop & Goods were between them. The Shop was new & good, not worth he thinks less than £200.

He had a house very well furnished with new furniture, it was very good furniture. Witness scarce ever saw better furniture.

PROCEEDINGS

OF

LOYALIST COMMISSIONERS

St. JOHNS, 1787.

Vol. XIV.

BEFORE COMMISSIONER PEMBERTON

Claimants.

	MSS. Folio.		MSS. Folio.
Admas, Nathaniel	2	Grey, William	29
Allward, Benjamin	9	Hoyte, Israel	37
Babbet, Daniel	6	Jones, Ed.	44
Beardslee, Zephaniah	69	Jones, Simon	31
Bedel, John	60	Laurence, William	52
Bickle, Nicholas	66	Loder, Jacob	47
Campbell, Capt. Peter	56	Macdonald, John	22
Chase, Reuben	23	Miller, Moses	5
Clark, Nehemiah	63	Millican, Benjamin	60
Cochrane, Capt. John	53	Ogden, Mrs. Rachel (nee Wetmore)	49
Cook, Zedicia	41	Partelow, Amos	7
Cowperthwaite, Hugh	39	Peters, Thomas	1
Crawford, James	15	Pickens, Andrew	68
Dickinson, Gilbert	28	Picket, David	42
Dickinson, Samuel	20	Terrill, Anthony	36
Earl, Justus	18	Underhill, Nathaniel	11
Earle, Capt. Edward	17	Vandeburg, Peter	51
Fairweather, Thomas	13	Waterbury, Silvanus	46
Flewelling, Abel	32	Wilson, John	25
Flewelling, Francis	34		

THE EVIDENCE.

NEW CLAIM.

1787.
January 22.

669. Case of THOMAS PETERS, late of New York.

Claimt. appears & being Sworn Saith:
He came from New York in April, 1783. Went up the River in May. Went up about 60 miles, near Majorfield. Continued there 2 years.
The Act of Parliament was talked of. He cannot say he could not have sent his Claim, but thought only real estates would be allowed a Compensation.

(1).

He is a native of America; resided in Dutchess Co. Declared from the first in Favour of Brit. Was frequently imprisoned. Was sent to Philadelphia Gaol & kept there 4 months. Got within the Brit. Lines at New York about Feby. 1777. Lived at Long Island during the War. Did not serve. Came away before the Evacuation. Now settled at Gage Town.
Was possessed of 10 Cows, 3 on his own farm, 7 were hired out to his neighbours, who were to return them in 3 years with Calves. This was an usual way of letting Cows; 4 2-yr. old, 3 were let out; 4 yearlings, 2 were let out; 1 pr. oxen, 1 mare, 20 sheep, 100 Bushels of Wheat in ye House, 5 Tons Hay. Produces an acct. of his personal Estate seized & sold by Comrs. of Sequestration. Signed, Peter Curtmens.

Says several Cows & Cattle were taken, which are not mentioned in the acct.

WM. PETERS, Wits.:
Says his Bror., the Claimant, was imprisoned on acct. of his Loyalty. Kept a long while in Prison. After his discharge on Parole he got within the Lines. He had considerable stock when he went within the Lines. Some let out, but had some at Home, both Horses & Cattle.

NEW CLAIM.

1787.
January 22.

670. Case of NATHANIEL ADAMS, late of New York.

(2).

Claimt. appears & being Sworn Saith:
He came from New York in the summer of the Evacuation. Went up the River to Majorfield. Continued there all the Winter. Never heard of the Act till he heard of Capt. Vand.'s going home & intending to take claims, on which he gave his Claim to Capt. V.; he had no opoprtunity before.

Is a native of America. Was settled on the White Plains as a Blacksmith. Never signed any Association. Joined the Brit. as soon as he conveniently could. Went to New York in the Spring, after the Battle of White Plains. Served one Campaign in the Guides & Pioneers; then served at Morrisina under Col. Delancey. Came away in the sumr. Now settled in King's Co.

Was possessed of one House, Barn & Shop on ye White Plains. There were five acres of Land; bought it in ye year 1770. It was sold by the Sheriff on an Execution. He gave £290 York Mon. Paid the whole in gold & silver. Says he was offered ~568 for it before he went into it. Says he repaired the House after he purchased. Vals it at £353.

This house was burnt by Col. Green by order of an American General, after the Brit. Troops left White Plains. It was burnt in order to prevent its affording shelter to Brit. Troops. 13 or 14 houses in that neighbourhood were burnt on the same Reason. Has heard one Dr. Graham, a neighbour, has taken Possession of the Land.

(3).

Had a house & land at Greenwich, Connect.; it had belonged to his Father. Came to Claimt. on his Father's Death. His mother has it for life. She is now in Possession. It was not sold when Claimant was in the Country in 1783. Lost 2 Horses at Morrisina while he served. Lost 1 Ox, 6 Cows, & some Hogs. There were taken when the house was burnt. One Stevens took them for the use of American Army, Smiths' Tools, &c., in his shop, when his house was burnt. Grain in the house.

MOSES MILLER, Wits.:

Knew Claimant. He was a Loyalist. Remembers his going within Brit. Lines. He served in Delancey's Brigade a good while. new his place at White Plains. Remembers him several years in Possession; it was bought of the Sheriff. There was about five acres of Land. Vals. the Land at near £20 per acre. There was an House, Barn & Shop. They were burnt by the Americans.

JONATHAN HANKSHURST, Wits.:

Knew Claimant. He was always a Loyalist. He went within ye Brit. Lines in 1777. He was first in the Pioneer Service, then in Delancey's.

Knew his place at White Plains. Remembers Claimt. buying it. It was sold by the Sheriff. It had belonged to one Boyd. There were about 5 acres of Land; was very valuable then. The Buildings were new. Could not have been built for less than £150. He had a good stock of Tools. He commonly—— 2 or 3 -ows, some Sheep & Hogs.

(4).

MRS. MARY BURTIS, Wits.:

Knew Claimant. He was a Loyalist. Remembers his purchasing his Place at White Plains. Dr. Graham has taken Possession of the Land & fenced it in with his own. Thinks he had 5 or 6 Cows. He had horses & hogs. His house was burnt. His shop & everything destroyed by the Rebels.

New Claim.

January 22.

(5).

671. Claim of MOSES MILLER, late of New York.

Claimt. appears & being Sworn Saith:

He came in the last Fleet from New York. Went up the River about 40 miles; staid there all the Winter. Heard of Mr. Hardy & heard of Capt. V., but was not able to send his Claim.

He is a native of America. Lived at Philips Manor; had a farm there; was taken prisoner for being a Tory. About the year 1780, went on Parsons Island near Hellgate, which was within ye British Lines, to be protected. Came away when ye Troops came away. Now settled in Queen's County.

Had a farm on Philips Manor of 150 acres; paid £0.4.6 pr. ann. Could have sold the Improvements for £500. Says he gave £440 for the improvts. 8 or 10 yrs. before ye Troubles; paid the whole. It was in York money. Had laid out money afterwards. Vals. ye Improvments £500 York Mon. Lost 200 Bush. Wheat, taken by American Army in ye year 1780. Lost 2 Horses, 32 Sheep, 16 Hogs, taken by American Army when the Brit. first came on the White Plains. The Rebels took his farming utensils & furniture.

MR. NATHANL. ADAMS, Wits.:

Knew Claimant. He was a Loyalist. Was imprisoned as a suspected Tory. He went within the Brit. Lines some time after Witness. He had a farm on Philips Manor. There was a good Barn; the House somewhat old. Heard of the American Army taking away his Corn & Things from his house. This was just before the Brit. went upon White Plains, to prevent their falling into ye hands of the Brit. Army.

New Claim.

January 22.

(6).

672. Case of DANIEL BABBET, late of New York.

Claimt. appears & being Sworn Saith:

He came from New York in the last Fleet. Had heard of the Act. When he came here, went above ye Falls; staid there 4 weeks.

On further examination, says he is sure he came here in the course of the summer. Went up the river about the first of Septr. Went to Gage Town. Had no opportunity of sending his Claim by Capt. V.

He lived at Dutchess Co.; went within the Brit. Lines; went to King's Bridge, when Stoney Point was taken. Continued within the Brit. Lines; took ye Oath of Allegiance. Went to Long Island; there worked at his trade of Blacksmith. Now settled in Gage Town.

Had a Lease of Col. Beverly Robinson's Land, 87 acres. Gave 200 for ye Improvemts. just before ye Troubles.

Had a Lot in Fredericksborough. This was on Col. Robinson's Land. Improvemts. belonged to Claimt. Gave £40 for ye Improvemts. 4 years before ye Troubles. He added greatly to the Buildings; lost 2 Horses, one was Stollen, 4 Cows, 1 Yoke Oxen, 28 Sheep, 4 2-yr. olds, 2 yearlings, Farming Utensils, Furniture, Tools. Left these things on his farm. Has been told the Comrs. seized them & sold them.

Produces Certificate to his Loyalty from Col. Beverley Robinson.

(7).

ANTHONY TIRRELL, Wits.:

Knew Claimant. He had a Lease on Col. Robinson's Land. He had a house in Fredericksburg. Agrees in acct. of his moveables.

NEW CLAIM.

673. Case of AMOS. PARTELOW, late of New York.   January 22.

Claimt. appears & being Sworn Saith:

He came to the Province in May. Went up to Majorfield, & in the fall went higher up the River at a Place 90 miles dist. from this Town. Heard of Captn. Vand.'s going to England & carrying Claims. Never heard of the Act before that time.

He is a native of America. Lived in Dutchess Co. Joined the Brit. in Jany. 1777, on Long Island. He was obliged to quit home on acct. of his Loyalty. He had refused serving in their Militia; refused signing their Associations, but admits he signed one. Served in Govr. Brown's Corps for 4 months, then put a man in his place.

Produces Leave of Absence for 10 Days from Col. Patterson. Was a Seargt. in Govr. Brown's Regt., then went to New York & there remained on Long Island till he came here. Now settled in this Town. Works at his trade as a Shoemaker.

(8).

Had a Farm of 54 acres in 9 Partners, Dutchess Co. Produces Deed from Ebenezer Reynolds to Claimt. of one moiety of 100 acres more or less in Considn. £60 New York Mon., Sep. 1772. Besides this sum of £60 he engaged to take care of two old people, relations of Ebenezer Reynolds. There was a good orchard, all under Improvemt. except 13 acres.   Vals. it at £240 York Mon. Expects Proof of Confiscation. His name appears in Anstey's List. He says one Plat first bought it.

Had 4 Cows, 36 Sheep, 5 Hogs, Wheat in stock, 20 Bushels, Hay, 7 tons; Furniture, £15; Tools. These things were left on his farm & taken on his going within ye Brit. Lines.

MATHEW PARKSON, Wits.:

Says his Bror. had from the first been Loyal. He went into ye Brit. Lines about ye Beginning 1777. He served in Govr.

Brown's Regt. His Bror. had a farm at 9 Partners, which he bought; he thinks about 50 or 60 acres, Some of it very good Land. He had some Cows & some Sheep.

NEW CLAIM.

January 23.

(9).

674. Case of BENJAMIN ALLWARD, late of New Jersey.

Claimt. appears & being Sworn Saith:

He came from New York in July 1783. Went up the River to Majorhela. Staid there a twelve month. Had no opportunity of sending his Claim.

He lived at Woodbridge; from the first he declared himself in favour of Brit. He had been often obliged to attend their Committee & imprisoned. Went to New York in the Spring after the Brit. Troops had been in the Jerseys. Continued in New York. Is now settled at Mahogany.

Was possessed of a farm of about 200 acres in Woodbridge. Bought it 20 years ago of Timothy Bloomfield. Produces Deed from Tim Bloomfield to Claimt. of 250 acres in Considn. £550, dated 1750. He sold a little of it.

He lived on this Farm. 40 acres Meadow; more than 60 acres Plough Land. Vals. it at £6 pr. acre; was offered it.

No. 2. Another Farm of about 40 or 50 acres at Woodbridge. Bought it a year after the other. Vals. it as high if not higher than first.

Produces Deed from Saml. Alward to Claimt. of 30 acres, more or less, in Considn. £200, 1759.

Produces Certificate of Sale by Ebenezer Ford, one of the Comrs., stating the No. at 315 acres.

Produces Certificate to his Loyalty from Saml. Holland, Surveyor Genl., requesting his Bror. officers to protect him & his property, dated Bridgetown, 1776. His Estate had been plundered on acct. of his being a Tory.

(10)

3 Horses, 2 Colts, 1 Colt, 7 Cows, 8 Young Cattle, furniture, Farming utensils.

JOHN FORD, Wits.:

Remembers Claimant at Woodbridge. He and his family were amongst the first to declare in Favour of Brit. Govnt. They had suffered a great deal on acct. of it. Has seen the Claimt. taken before their Committees. Heard of his Imprisonment. He went within the Brit. Lines in the Spring, after Lord Cornwallis had been in the Jerseys; Continued there during the War.

Knew No. 1. Vals. it at £6 pr. acre exclusive of Buildings; the dwelling house was very good; a large Barn. There were several other buildings. Knew No. 2. The land was equally valuable; there was no build.

He had a good stock. Knew some of his horses particularly.

STEPHEN KENT, Wits.:

Knew Claimant. He was distinguished for Loyalty. Knew No. 1. Vals. it at £6 pr. acre exclusive of builds. There was a good house, barn & various builds. Knew No. 2. Vals. the land full as high as the other. One Freeman was in possession when they heard last.

(11),

N.B.—Some of the Witnesses say that Claimt. first proposed an Association of Loyalists, and a Paper was drawn up by Genl. Skinner, and a great many signed it on Claimt.'s application. The purport of it was to support his Majesty, & the Brit. Govrnt. All Claimt.'s sons signed it.

NEW CLAIM.

675. Case of NATHANIEL UNDERHILL, of New York. January 24.

Claimt. appears & being Sworn Saith:

He came from New York in the sumr., 1783. Staid here about 4 Days. Went up the River to Majorfield. Settled there. Staid there all the Winter. Sent his Claim by Captn. Vand. Had no opportunity before.

Is a native of America. Lived in West Chester Co. Joined the Brit. in 1777. Went into New York. Joined Col. Delancey's. Served with him one year; then was in Tarleton's Legion, 3 or 4 years.

Produces his Discharge signed George Hanger, New York, 20 Oct., 1781. Continued on Long Island till he came to this Province. Now settled in Majorfield.

Produces Copy of Recommendation from George Hanger, Certifying that he had behaved with spirit, & also had been of service to Govr. Tryon as a Guide, July, 1782.

(12)

Was possessed of 2 Farms in Philipsburg. He withdraws his Claim for these Farms, having sold the Improvemts. He says he got £423 York for his Improvemts. Says in Improvmts. he reckons only Buildings; does not reckon what is laid out on ye Lands.

Lost 6 Horses; Genl. Stirling had 2; four taken by the Rebels, 2 were sold, 5 Cows, 8 Calves, 1 Yoke of Oxen, 26 Sheep, Wheat, 160 Bushels, Utensils, furniture. These things were on his Farm and were taken by the American Troops a little before the Battle of White Plains.

MOSES MILLAR, Wits.:

Says Claimt. had a large stock. Thinks his stock was lost about the Time of the Battle of the White Plains.

676. Case of THOMAS FAIRWEATHER, late of Connect.

January 24.

Claimt. appears & being Sworn Saith:

He is a native of America. Lived at Norwalk. Joined Governor Tryon about the time Norwalk was burnt. Went with Govr. Tryon within the Brit. Lines. Contin'd at Long Island. Served as Volunteer when Refugees were called upon. At first had served in Rebel Militia; took no further part. Says he was obliged to serve.

(13).

Had an Estate in Norwalk Consisting of an house & 9 acres of Land. Purchas'd it 15 years ago of Joseph Hitchcock for £215 Connect. Cury. Had improved it greatly. The Deed has been lost. There was a very good house, newly repaired. This was burnt at the Fire at Norwalk. Vals. ye house at £150. Vals. ye Land at 170 or £180 at £20 pr. acre. Does not know what is become of the Land, or who is in possession. After he came away there was one Execution for a Debt which he says was only £47, which he justly owed & they have got possession of all the land for it. They have run up the acct. so high by costs & expenses.

No. 2. Had a small piece of Land in Norwalk, which he bought of his Brother. Produces Deed from Hanford Fairweather to Claimt. of a piece of Land in Norwalk in Considn., £40 York M., dated 31st. Aug., 1775.

This Land was a Quarter of an acre with an house upon it. This house was also burnt. Vals. it at £25 lawful. Lost furniture burnt at Norwalk, to amount of £80.

(14).

Vars. articles of Provisions, Corn, Boards, lost at the same time. Tools, 1 Horse, 2 Cows 17 Sheep. These were plundered by the Rebels after ye town was burnt. Is now settled in Kingston on ye Kennebikases.

JONATHAN CATCHUM, Wits.:

Knew Claimt. He was a Loyalist. Does not know that he was so at first, but lately he has been active in helping of ye Loyalists to get to ye Brit. He went with Govr. Tryon within ye Brit. Lines.

Knew his house in Norwalk. Remembers him in Possession. It was burnt at the fire at Norwalk. It was a clean house, new repaired. Lost a good Deal of household & shop goods & tools. He had a mare. Knew 2 Cows, a flock of Sheep.

Knew No. 2. That he bought of his Bror.; there was a shop upon it. Supposes it was burnt.

SAML. CATCHUM, Wits.:

Knew Claimt. He was not Loyal at first, but was afterwards. Went within the Brit. Lines with Govr. Tryon in 1777. He had servd. in ye Rebel Militia.

Remembers some Brit. Prisoners coming to Norwalk & Claimant proposed to attack the Guard & take off the Prisoners &

he himself went to look after a Sloop, on which they were all to go on board, but the sloop not coming the scheme did not succeed.

Knew his house at Norwalk. Thinks there were about 7 acres. The house was burnt. Vals. the whole at £300. Thinks the house at 200. He lost some house furniture; lost some Tools, Provisions. He had a Mare, 14 Sheep, 2 Cows.

Knew No. 2, which he had of his Bror.

(15).

New Claim.

677. Case of JAMES CRAWFORD, late of New York. January 24.

Claimt. appears & being Sworn Saith:

He came here in May, 1783. Went up to Burton; Continued there all Winter. It is 60 miles up the River. Sent his Claim by Capt. V.

He is a native of America. Lived at North Castle, West Chester Co. Remained quiet at first. In the year 1777, joined the Brit. at New York; servd. in the Corps of Guides & Pioneers, then went to Long Island. Is now settled at Long Reach.

Had a Farm in West Chester Co. Had it from his Father, John Crawford. His Father died in 1773. His Father had a Deed which is burnt.

Produces Probate of his Father's Will, whereby he gives 57 acres to Robt. Crawford, his eldest Son, 57 acres to Archibald, John 40 acres, & gives the Residue of his Lands to James, the Claimant. Claimant had been in Possession of this Farm before his Father's Death. Continued in Possess. of it till he went within ye Lines.

There were about 80 acres, 7 acres Meadow, about 10 acres wood, the rest Plough Land, 2 story house. Vals. it at £10 pr. acre, including Builds.

Produces Judgment of Confiscation of Claimant's Estate. The last acct. he heard was that a Priest & Lawyer were living in the house.

(16).

Lost 3 horses, 1 pr. Oxen, 3 Cows, 8 Young Cattle, 24 Sheep, left on his farm; the Comrs. took part & sold it before his wife came away. Says his Father owed about £100, most of which Claimant had paid.

TITUS BROWN, Wits.:

Knew Claimant. He was always reckoned a Loyalist. In 1777 he joined the Brit. Troops; servd. with the Guides & Pioneers. Knew his Farm in West Chester Co. It was his Father's. Remembers Claimt. in Possession after his Father's Death. His Bros. had other Estates. There was a large, double house.

Vals. ye land at £10 per acre, including builds. One John Haynes, who was a leading man in the Rebel service, was in Possession after Claimt. went away.

NEW CLAIM.

January 26. 678. Case of CAPT. EDWD. EARLE, late of New Jersey.

Claimt. appears & being Sworn Saith:
He came to this Province in Octr., 1783. Went up the River to Frederickton. Sent his Claim by Hardy. The Claim was (17). delivered here by his Brother, who Continued in this Town.

He is a native of America; resided in Hackinsac when Troubles broke out; joined the Brit. in 1776 when Lord Cornwallis first came into ye Jerseys. Had a Commission as Lieut. in Col. Buckirk's Corps; afterwards had a Captain's Commission in same Regt. Has now half pay. Servd. all the War. Is now settled on the Grand Lake, Queen's Co.

Claimant & his Brother, Justus, were in Possession jointly of a farm in Hackinsac. It was left to them two jointly by their Father's Will. His Father had been dead near 20 years. The Land was not divided, Claimant being under age, so that it continued jointly in Possession of the 2 Brothers. It consisted of about 200 acres & upwards. There was a good House & Barn.

The elder Brother, Justus, was in Possession of the whole. Produces Probate of his Father's Will, whereby his Father, Silvester Earl, gives Justus Earl & Claimt. the Plantation in which he lived, equally to them & their Heirs, paying £300 when Claimt., Edward, came of age, to three Daughters of Testr. Will is dated in 1768. His Father died soon after.

Produces Copy of Judgment agst. Claimant Confiscating his Estate with Valuation by 2 appraisers at £2,000 York Cury.

NEW CLAIM.

(18).
January 26. 679. Case of JUSTUS EARL, late of New Jersey.

He is a Brother to Edward Earl. The Claim is entered in both their names. The landed Estate belonged to them equally, the moveable Estate belonged to Claimant. Says he gave his Claim to Mr. Hardy, before Mr. Hardy went to Halifax. He gave it in the joint name of himself & Bror.

Claimt. lived at Hackinsac; joined the Brit. on their first coming to ye Jerseys. Servd. first as a Volunteer. In Apl. had a Comn. as Ensign in Col. Buskirk's Regt. Had afterwards a Comn. as Lieut. Continued to serve during War. Has now half pay. Lives in Queen's Co.

Was possessed of a Farm in Hackinsac which belonged to him & his Brother, it was given by his Father's Will. The farm consisted of above 200 acres on ye survey after Confiscation, it measured he thinks 250 acres. There were between 30 & 40 acres of Meadow, 110 Plough Land, the rest Woodland. Farms in that Precinct if in good cultivation used to sell from £10 to £15 per acre.

Produces Copy of Judgement against him and Appraisement at £2,000 York Cury. The Estate was sold. Claimt. saw an advertizmt. of sale. Abraham Bardolph bought it & is now in Possession. By his Father's Will £300 was to be paid to his 3 Sisters, £100 each. One is dead; the second Hannah, married to Wm. Sorel, at Shelburne; the 3rd died in the States.

(19).

The moveable Estate belonged to Claimt. It was left on ye Farm. It consisted of 5 horses, about 20 horned Cattle, 29 Sheep, furniture, Farming Utensils, a Considerable Quantity of Corn in the Barn.

This was seized for thé use of the American Army; does not know that any part was sold by Comrs. It was chiefly pillaged & taken for use of Army.

NEW CLAIM.

680. Case of SAMUEL DICKENSON, late of New York. January 26.

Claimt. appears & being Sworn Saith.

He sent his Claim by Mr. Hardy in the Winter 1783.

He lived in Dutchess Co. On breaking out of the Troubles took part with Brit. Refused to sign a Rebel Association on which he was disarmed.

In June, 1779 went within Brit. Lines at Frogs Neck. Did not bear Arms, but kept guard & assisted the Brit. Troops all he could. Continued at New York till he came to this Province; now settled at Gage town. Had 2 Leasehold Farms in Fredericksburg. The first was in a share in a Lease made to his Father. The original Lease was by Col. Morris to his Father, James Dickenson for his own Life, Life of Gilbert Dickenson & of Claimt. On his Father's death Claimt. & Gilbert Dickenson divided the Lands. Claimant had for his share 119 acres, paying £6. Says he could have let it for £30 per ann.

(20).

He estimates his Loss by the Difference between Rent received & the Rent which he could have got.

No. 2. The other Farm was a Lease to Claimant himself for Life from Col. Morris. It was near 20 years since he had the Land. The farm consisted of 396 acres, paying 30 Bushels of Wheat. Claimt. sold 100 acres in the year 1776 & got upwards of £100 New York Mon. for it. Some part paid in Goods & some in cash. Could have let these 296 acres for £50 pr. ann. 40 acres Meadow, larger part of the residue of Estate under Improvts.

One Benjamin Crosby is now in Possession, who has bought the farm in fee under Confiscation of Col. Morris's Estate.

Lost 4 Cows, 15 sheep, 6 swine, 1 horse, farming utensils, furniture, corn, hay. Left all these things on the Farm, No. 1. They were seized or plundered after he went away.

(21). Produces an Inventory from the Auditors Office containing a few articles & amongst others a Negroe Woman who belonged to his Bror. Gilbert..

Had half a Schooner, purchased after he went within the Lines, & employd in getting wood for the Town & Garrison at New York; taken by a Privateer, vals. it at £100. Claimt. afterwards says he vals. Improvmts. at so much an acre. His own at 5 Dollars per acre.

SELICK DAN, Wit.

Knew Claimt. Always reckoned a Loyalist. Knew his Farms. He had 2 Leasehold farms under Col. Morris. Knew No. 1. Thinks it would have let for nigh £30 York Money. Knew his other farm. It had been upwards of 300 acres. He parted with some of it. Thinks ye remt. would have let for £40.

JOHN YEOMANS, Wit.

Knew Claimt. He was always reckoned a Loyalist. Knew his Farms. Knew the Farm No. 1. Thinks it would have let for near £40 per ann. Knew his other farm. Thinks it would have let for more.

NEW CLAIM.

January 26.   681. Case of JOHN MACDONALD, late of New York.

Claimt. appears & being Sworn Saith.

(22). He came from New York in Aug., 1783, went up the River to Burton Township, was there all the Winter, never heard of any opportunity till he heard of Capt. V—, sent his claim by him.

He is a native of Scotland, settled in America about 20 years ago. Lived in ye 9 Partners when troubles broke out. Was imprisoned for not signing a rebel Association & for enlisting now in the King's Army. First in Pughkepsie, then sent to Litchfield, then to Exter Gaol. Close Confinement there 9 months, broke Prison, joined the Brit. at Reduction of Æsopus, continued with the Army, was sent by Genl. Vaughan to carry Despatches to Genl. Burgoyne, found him a Prisoner. Continued with the Army. Employd. in secret services frequently, was in several skirmishes. He had been at first offered a Commission by the Rebels, but he refused it.

Lost his household goods near the 9 Partners. He lived in a school house where he taught school. The house did not belong to him, but he had furniture. Soon after he was first taken up a party came to plunder his house because he was a Loyalist. Produces an Inve..tory of Things lost. Had 2 Cows, 1 horse, furniture, Cloathes, Tin makers Tools; now lives in Burton.

JOSHUA GEDNEY, Wits.

(23). Thinks him a good Loyalist. Remembers his keeping school near the 9 Partners, lived in a school house.

NEW CLAIM.

682. Case of REUBEN CHASE, late of New York. January 27.

Claimt. appears & being Sworn saith.
Went up the River in the Summer, 1783 & staid there all next Winter; sent his Claim by Capt. V——.
He is a native of America. lived in Dutchess C., was disarmed; draughted with the Rebel Militia, on which he left ye Country and joined the Brit. in Jany., 1777. Went to Long Island. Worked at Stoney Point, and Lloyd's Neck as Carpenter. Continued in ye Brit. Lines. Now settled in Gage town.

Had a farm at Fredericksburg, one of Col. Morris's Short Lots, consisting of 130 acres; Bought it of one Wm. Lovelace, gave him £100 York Mon. for it 2 yrs. before ye Troubles. Had time allowed him for payment, paid him chiefly in Congress Money. Improved it after he bought it. Vals. it at £1 per acre. Has heard this Estate has been sold by Comrs.
Left a Stock on his farm when he went away, Grain 50 bushels, 2 pr. Oxen, 3 Cows, 3 yearlings, 1 horse, 25 sheep, 17 Hogs, Coopers & Carpenters Tools, farming utensils, these things were taken chiefly for fines, for his & his sons not serving in their Militia, some pillaged & some for Retaliation. (24).

GILBERT DICKENSON, Wits.
Knew Claimant, Considered him always as a Loyalist. Knew his farm, it was a Tenant Farm under Col. Morris. The Improvts. belonged to Claimt. Says Improvemts. of a farm well cultivated and to be reckoned worth as much as the soil itself. Used to val. the Land at 40sh. per acre. Vals. the Improvemts. on this Farm at £150. Speaks of a pr. of Oxen & some Cows.

SOLOMON MABEE, Wits.
Knew Claimant's Stock. Knew that the Rebels took a Yoke of oxen for a fine. They were sold at Vendue; heard also of a

Cow being sold. He went within ye Brit. Lines in Jany., 1777, because he would not serve with the Rebels.

SAML. DICKENSON, Wits.
Knew Claimt. Considered him always a Loyalist. Knows of a pr. of Oxen & a pr. of Steers of his.

NEW CLAIM.

683. Case of JOHN WILSON, late of Jersey. January 27.

Claimt. appears & being Sworn saith.
He came to this Province in the May Fleet. Went up to Majorville immediately; continued there all that Winter, except when he was absent at Meriamachee, says he did not hear of the (25).

52 AR.

Act till he returned from Merimachee, March, 1784.
He is a native of America. Resided in the Co. Midx. Jersey, when the Troubles broke out, joined the Brit. at Woodbridge when the Army came from the White Plains. Was in the Forage Department under Commissary. Continued within the Lines all the War; is now settled at Merimachee.

Was possessed of one Estate in Piscatua, came by his Father's Will. Produces Probate whereby it appears that his Father John Wilson gives to Claimt.—after a few Legacies, all the Remr. of his Estate real & personal, to him & his Heirs, Will dated 4 March,

---

1773. Claimant had 2 elder Brothers, who were both provided for in his Father's life time. His Father died in April, 1775.

Claimant was in Possession with his Father & continued in Possession after his Father's Death till he came away.

The Estate consisted of about 100 acres, purchased by his Father at different times. Produces Deed from Stephen Arnold to Claimt's Father of 32 acres in Considn. £30, dated 1728.

(26). Produces Deed from Charles Wilson to Claimt's Father of 9 acres in Considn. £18, 1743.

Produces Deed from Saml. Leonard to Claimt's. Father of 12 acres in Considn. £16, 1734.

Produces Deed from Robt. Martin to Claimt's Father of 12 acres in Considn £60 Cury. at 8c the dollar, 1764.

Produces Deed from Do. to Do. of 28 acres in Considn. 130 Cury. at Do., 1766.

All these lands laid in Piscatua.

Produces Deed from John Johnston to Claimt. himself of a piece of Salt Meadow in Considn. £9, 1773.

These Lands were in his Father's Possession, after he had portioned out Claimant's 2 Brothers. All these Lands laid together, near 50 acres clear. There was a large orchard, an dwelling, House & Barn. Vals. it at £1,000 York Cury. The Land has been Confiscated & sold. It has gone thro several Hands; was in Possession of Simeon Randal, and one Little, whom Claimt. heard last.

Left a stock on his Farm, 4 horses, 2 Cows, 4 young cattle, farming utensils, some furniture.

These Articles left on his Farm when he went within ye Brit. Lines, heard they were sold at public sale.

Lost 5 Cows when he served with the Army from Piscatua. He left them in the Forage Yard; heard that one Dun, a rebel, took them.

(27). SAMUEL SHARP Wits.

Knew Claimant, came off with him to the Lines in Decr., 1776, to Woodbridge, joined the Brit. Troops there. He was a very firm Loyalist. Knew his farm at Piscatua. Knew it while his Father lived. Knew the two Elder Brothers. The Father had portioned them out with other Lands. They were both settled. The Homestead was intended for the Claimt. His Father continued there till his Death, from his death he remembers

52a AR.

Claimant in Possession. Thinks ye Quantity about 100 acres. Enough of the Farm was clear.

Lands sold sometimes at 5. Sometimes at £10 per acre. This Farm was well improved, buildings good. Vals. it about £6 or 7 per acre. Has heard it was Confiscated & sold. A Rebel Commissary was the first Purchaser.

He had a good Team & was in good Circumstances.

684. Claim of GILBERT DICKINSON. January 27.

JOHN MACDONALD Wits.

Says he conversed with Mr. Dickinson about sending his Claim home. They talked of Hardy first, this was in the Winter after they came to this Province, whether before or after New Year's Day he cannot say. Wit. asked him why he did not send by Capt. Vand. There was then a rumour that Capt. Vand. was going, told Mr. D. There was a talk of Capt. Vand's going.

Witness did not himself know nor could he tell Mr. Dickenson for certain that Captn. Vand. was going. Witness came to this Town & ye Conversation was at Mr. Squeers.

N.B.—This contradicts Witnesses own acct. on his own claim, he says he was up ye Country all the Winter.

— HUNGERFORD, Wits.

Remembers Claimt. applying to Mr. Hardy to carry his Claim to England. This was in the Winter of 83, before Mr. Hardy went to Halifax. Mr. Hardy asked a Guinea. Mr. Dickenson sd. he had no money & could not get any. Does not recollect whether there were or were not other opportunities of sending to England after this. Supposes there might have been other opportunities.

(28).

NEW CLAIM.

685. Case of WM. GREY, late of New York. January 29.

Claimt. apprs. & being sworn saith.

He came to this Province in Aug., 1783 & went up the River in about 10 Days, a little below Majorville, continued there above a year.

He is a native of America, resided in West Chester Co. On breaking out f the Troubles opposed the metting of the Committees. There was Protest signed by many Loyalists against sending members to Congress. Claimt. went down to sign it & did it at the hazard of his Life. Name was advertized amongst the persons who signed the Protest, which made him very obnoxious to ye Rebels, he was carried before their Committee & fined. Left his home in March, 1777, took Refuge in the Brit. Lines at New York. Continued within ye Lines, now settled at the Head of Belle Isle Bay.

(29).

Was possessed of a Farm of about 156 acres in West Chester Co. It was not Confiscated. He has employd a man to sell it, who is likely to cheat him. He has sold it to his sons for half the value.

Was possessed of a Personal Estate when he went away, Negroe Wench, & 2 Negroe Children, 1 pr. Oxen, 4 Cows & 6 Young Cattle, 2 horses, & 1 Colt, 22 Hogs, 167 Sheep, 200 Hides, 13sh. 6d. each. Farming Utensils, Furniture. Left these things on his Farm. They were all seized & sold by the Comrs. at a Vendue.

The Negroe Wench & 2 Children were sold to Wm. Drake. Has Debts owing to him upwards of £400 York Cur.

(30). Came as a Captn of Loyalists to this Province with Commission as Captn.

MR JUSTUS SHERWOOD, Wits.

Knew Claimant. He was one of the first who opposed ye Rebels. Signed a Protest against them. Heard of his name being advertzed as one of the Protestors against the Rebels. Knew his Negroes, a Wench & 2 Children; seized & sold by the Comrs. to Witnesses Knowledge; Had the largest stock of sheep of any man in that Country, double. The Comrs. got them.

He was a Shoemaker & Tanner by Trade. Had a great many hides. He used to lay in 200 Hides in a year. His vats were full of Hides, when he went away. Comrs. got some, others were pillaged. Vals. them at about 2 Dollars each untan'd or under. When tanned they were at a double value.

Speaks to ye Damage done to his house & builds. The Troops encamped on his Lands & they did a vast Deal of Damage, out of particular spite.

PETER DOUKE, Wits.

Knew Claimant, he was forward in declaring his sentiments openly against the Rebels. He opposed Committees & Congress. Knew of his having a Negroe Wench & 2 Children.

He had a large flock of sheep, bought 55 of Witness. He was
(31). a Tanner & carried on a great Deal of Business.

January 30. 686. Case of SIMEON JONES, late of Massts. Vid. Vol. 10, p. 67.

Claimt. appears & being Sworn Saith.

He is one of the younger Sons of Col. Elisha Jones, & claims his share in his Father's Estate; his Father having died Intestate.

Claimant lived at Hevisdue, New Hampshire. Had been Clerk of the Court in the County of Cheshire. Had always declared in Favr. of Brit. Govert. Had assisted his Bror. Josiah to make his escape from Gaol. on which he was himself imprisoned & made his escape & got within the Lines in 1777. Went to New

York, served as Volunteer in Govr. Wentworth's Volunteers, then served as Lieut. in the King's American Dragoons, nas now half pay; came to this Province in April, 1783; now settled at Prince William, 20 miles above St. Anns; agrees with the acct. of the Family given by his Brothers.

Besides his share in his Father's Estate, claims for Professional Losses. He had the Place of Clerk of the Ct. in Sheshire. Had had it for five years. Was appointed by Govr. Wentworth; was worth under £100 Str. pr. ann. Vals. it at £97 pr. ann.

Claimt's name is included in the Certificate mentd. in the examinatio of Stephen Jones. Vol. 10, p. 127.

(32).

ELIJAH WILLIAMS.

Knew Claimt. Remembers his holding the Place of Clerk of the Court of Common Pleas, in Co. of Cheshire. It was hardly ever that such officers were turned out. Vals. at £100 per ann. Thinks it worth so much as that.

NEW CLAIM.

687. Case of ABEL FLEWELLING, late of New York. January 31.

Claimt. appears & being Sworn Saith.

He came to this Prov. in June, 1783. Sent his Claim by Mr. Hardy in Decr.

Is a native of America, lived in Ulster Co. Had signed a Protest against Delegates to Congress for which he was prosecuted & very ill used, in March, 1777; Went to New York for Protection; went as Pilot on Board Admiral How's Ship; carried a Brig up the North River, when the Expedition was going on agst. Danbury. Was Pilot when Fort Montgomery was taken. Was 2 years in the Engineers Department, master of a Yacht waiting on Capt. Mercer.

Continued all the War within the Brit. Lines, now settled up the River on Long Reach, ten miles from Town.

(33).

Was possessed of a Farm in Newboro, purchased 3 yrs. before ye troubles, Produces Deed from Gilbert Denton to Claimt. of 149 acres in Newburg in Considn. 390 Lawful mon. New York, Septr. 1773.

He afterwards sold 40 acres of this at £1 per acre. This was enough Land & the most inconveniently situated. Vals. it at £400 New York Cur.

Produces Valuation by Wm. Palmer at that sum who mentions in his affidt. that it had been Confiscated & Sold.

Produces Copy of Judgement & sentence of Confiscation of his Estate.

Produces Certificate from Cadwallader Colden to Loyalty of Claimt. & to his having been possessed of a good freehold Estate.

One Joseph Pierson is now in Possession. He was a Rebel Commissary.

Was possessed of 2 Yoke of Oxen, 7 Cows, 4 young Cattle, 1 Horse, 13 Sheep, furniture, Farming Utensils. Left all these things. They were seized by Comrs. & sold. His wife was on the Premises, when they came & sold the Things. The things were sold at Vendue.

MARY HUSTON, Wits.

Was a neighbour of Claimants at Newboro, Ulster Co. He had a house & farm. Remembers him in possession of it, from the first was loyal. He had stock & was considered as a man in good circumstances.

JOHN WIGANS Wits.

(34).

Knew Claimt's Farm at Newboro. Remembers him in Possession. Thinks above 100 acres, tolerably good Land, an old settled place; Considerable part of it clear. He was called a good farmer. Remembers his riding a good horse, & that he had a good Team of Oxen.

NEW CLAIM.

January 31.

688. Case of FRANCES FLEWELLING, late of New York.

Claimt. apprs. & being Sworn Saith.

He came to this Province in the Sumr. 1783. About a fortnight after his arrival went up the River about 40 miles. Never heard of the Act till they heard of Vandbs. going. Sent his Claim by him.

Lived at North Castle, West Chester Co. Lived quiet at first. Joined the Brit. at Morrisina in 1779, served 3 months under Col. De Lancey, then moved on Long Island. Continued there during the War. Now settled on Musquosh Island. Had Land but sold it before he went away. He afterwards went on another man's farm, which he had sown, but was obliged to quit, when he went & joined ye Brit. Left 9 acres of Wheat, 9 acres of Corn in ye ground, 10 Tons of Hay then cut & in Stack, taken by the Rebels. 20 Sheep left on this Place which he heard the Rebels had, 5 horses, some before he went on this farm & some after. Household furniture, Farming utensils, plundered at different times, generally paid his fines in Continental money.

(35).

JOSEPH FLEWELLING, Wits.

Claimt. joined the Brit. Morrisina, & continued within the Lines. He served a little time under Col. De Lancey. He had sold his land to his Brother, he moved in to another Place, belonging to a Rebel & carried his own stock there. A couple of horses, some sheep, some took one thing & some another.

ABEL FLEWELLING, Wits.

Always heard that Claimt. was Loyal; he parted with his

Farm to his Brother. When he joined the Brit. heard he left stock behind him.

SAML. TILLEY, Wits.

Knows Claimt. to be Loyal. He had Property, but heard he sold his Land, believes his moveables were taken, has heard so.

NEW CLAIM.

689. Case of ANTHONY TERRILL, late of New York.   January 31.

Claimt. apprs. & being Sworn Saith.

He came to this Province in May, 83, went up ye River immediately 45 miles, continued there all the Winter. Never heard of it till Mr. Hardy had gone to Halifax, then came down to this Town, & Mr. Hardy being gone, could not send it by any body else. (36).

Lived in Dutchess Co. when Troubles broke out. Always declared in Favr. of Brit. Govert., joined the— in 1779 at New York. Applied to serve in the Garrison Battalion in which his Father had a Company, but did not get it. So did not serve. Was at Morrisina, was in five expeditions as Volunteer with Col. De Lancey's Corps, now settled in Queen's Co.

Was possessed of a Tenant Farm in Fredericksburg 169 acres. His Father had a Lease from Col. Robinson of 337 acres. He gave half of this to Claimant in 1778, when he, the Father,, went within ye Brit. Lines His Father is dead, he died in Bahama Islands without a Will leaving Willm. Terrill his eldest son, his sister has half the Lease & now lives in the States.

It was a Lease for 3 Lives, his Fathers, his Brothers & his own. Vals. at £130. His Father gave £270 for the whole Lease at first. He gave it to Col. Robinson. Lost a Yoke of Oxen, 15 Sheep, 2 Heifers, Corn, &c. in ye ground, left these things on ye Farm, they were sold by Comrs. Says his Sister is in Possession of half ye Lease. Does not know who had ye other, but says it was sold by Comrs. Has old Paper Money to amount of 80 Dollars for which he claims. (37).

NEW CLAIM.

690. Case of ISRAEL HOYTE, late of Connect.   February 1.

Claimt. appears & being Sworn Saith.

He came from New York in May. Came here in May, staid here a short time. Then went up the River to Kingston. Says he lived two miles from the Road. A great many Neighbours came down in the Fall for Provisions, but Claimant says he never heard of the Act till he heard that some Claims had been sent by Mr. Harding, of which he was not informed, till Mr. Hardy had gone to Halifax.

(38).

He lived in Norwalk Connect. Joined the Brit. in 1777. had been apprehended in June preceding & carried before a committee & insulted by a Mob, imprisoned in order to be tried for his life. Broke Gaol & made his escape to New York. Sent on board a Tender for a short time. Got a Protection for cutting Wood for City of New York. Continued within the lines during the War. Now settled at Kingston.
Produces Protection in 1778 & 1779.
Had a House & 1 acre of Land in Norwalk. Purchased it in 1769. Produces Deed from Nehemiah Street to Claimt. of House & Barn in Norwalk in considn of £70 New York 1769. Laid out a great Deal in Reprs. after he purchased it. Vals. it at £100. It was sold by Commrs., one Danl. Jackson is in Possession.
Claimant was taken in 1781 when on his return, after having been taken Prisoner & then saw Jackson who has bought it. His Wife secured some of his moveables. After he had broken Gaol, they went & seized what they could get at.
Produces Appraisement made by order of the Admr. of Confiscated Estates, who value the Prems. at 350, in Connect. Money. 6 Dollars for one. Says the house had suffered by fire which made it of less value. Lost Household furniture, burnt, Tools, burnt at the Fire at Norwalk. They were in the house of his Wife's Mother.

SILAS RAYMOND, Wits.

Knew Claimant. He was from the first, Loyalist. Heard of his being taken up, & imprisoned, understood he broke Prison & came within the Lines. Knew his house & Land in Norwalk. There was about an acre of Land. Vals. it at £100. He was a shoemaker, his house was tolerably well furnished. He had tools & Implements for Trade and to keep 2 or 3 People to work.

NEW CLAIM.

February 1st.

(39).

691. Case of HUGH COWPERTHWAITE, late of Jersey.
The Wife of Claimant appears & says her Husband is so ill he cannot attend. She is told she must send a Certificate of his Illness from an Apothecary or Justice of Peace.

Mrs. Cowperthwaite being sworn saith. Her Husb. came from New York in ye Sumr., 83, went up ye River to Majorfield. Never knew of the Act, till they heard of Vand., sent his Claim by him.
Her Husband lived in Salem Co., New Jersey. He joined the Brit. at Philadelphia. He had carried Intelligence to Lord Cornwallis when he first came into the Jerseys of General Waine having crost ye Delaware. When the Brit. left the Jerseys, he kept hid, but afterwards got to Philadelphia.

Went as a guide to Col. Manhood & Major Simcoe, raised a Company under Col. Vandyke but never had a Commission. He was ill of a Fever when he should have had his Commission & did not recover, till the Regiment was draughted into other Corps. He then went to Morisina, did Duty there under Col. Delancey as a private. Witness & her Children were sent into New York, about 18 months after her Husband went away.

Her Husband was possessed of a Farm containing 260 acres in Salem Co. He had bought it of his Brother for £500, 11 years before the Troubles, had been in Possession of it till he went away. The Comrs. came & rented it for one year & then sold it. (40).

Thinks there were about 15 acres Meadow, 200 acres clear Plough land. A good Log house & new good Barn. They were offered £900 for it, a year before her Husband went away, he afterwards built a new Barn.

Produces Inquisition. Produces Certificate from Aaron Dunham of Sale of Real Estate £1815, of personal 402.

Produces Valuation by two Freeholders of Salem Co. at £44. Her Husband left 6 Cows, 9 young Cattle, 2 horses, Corn & all sorts of Grain in the Barn.

Farming Utensils, Furniture.

After her Husband went away as soon as they heard he was gone to Philadelphia, they came & seized his Things & sold them at Vendue at another Tory's house, 2 miles from the Place. They left her nothing except the clothes on her back. Says the money owing to her Husband stated in his Claim, was paid into the Comrs. (41). She was informed so by one of the Comrs.

Feby. 26. Wm. Hubbard, Justice of Peace, certifies that Claimant was in an ill state of Health & unable to attend the Comrs.

NEW CLAIM.

692. Case of ZEDICIA COOK, late of Connct.　　　　February 1.

Claimt. apprs. & being Sworn Saith.

He came here in July, went up the River directly to the upper end of Majorfield, 65 miles up the River. Was up there all the Winter, never heard of the Act till it was too late, first heard of it after Capt. Vand was gone.

Lived in Newhaven, Connect., took part from ye first with Brit. Quitted Home about 1779, he had been so tormented he could not stay. They had threatened to put him into the mines. Got to Lloyd's Neck, Continued in the Garrison there for 18 months. Was in the Barrack Masters Department for 4 or 5 Months on Long Island. Had a Lot consisting of House & Barn at Newhaven. Produces Deed from Ebenezer Townsend to Claimant of a small piece of Land in Newhaven in considn of £105 Lawful, 1769.

He finished ye house & built a barn after he purchased it. Vals. it at 150 Lawful.

Produces Certificate of there being no Mortgage.

(42)

Produces Judgement of Confiscation of real & personal Estate. Lost a Stage Wagon & 2 fine horses, taken from the Premises after he went away. They made Love to his Things. Claimant kept a State Wagon. Used to go through the different States. Vals. them at £50.

NEW CLAIM.

February 2.

693. Case of DAVID PICKET, late of Connect.

Claimt. apprs. & being Sworn Saith.

He came to this Prov. in May, 1783. Went immediately up the River, 35 miles, & then encamped till they got a surveyor & had the Lands surveyed & got to their Lots in the course of the Fall. Heard in the Winter of Mr. Hardy having carried claims home. Heard afterwards that Capt. Vand had carried Claims, but did not hear till Capt. V was gone. Afterwards explains from his circumstances that he could not know of the Act till Feby., 21st.

He lived in Stamford. Left Stamford in Septr., 1776, Joined the Brit. on Long Island. He had been advertized as an enemy to his Country. After a Trial by a Committee in Consequence of having signed a Paper to manifest his Loyalty, which was the reason of his quitting Home.

Continued with the Army in the Wagon Depart. a short time. His family were sent to him in the next Spring. Continued in the Lines.

Now settled in Kingston.

(43)

Was possessed of a House & Lot in Stamford. Land about ½ acre. Purchased about 1766, for £47, subject to a Widow's Thirds. Laid out a good Deal in Repairs. Bought the Widow's third, made an addition to ye house, vals. it at £150.

Produces Copy of Judgement of Confiscation of his real & personal Estate.

Lost Weaving Implements worth £40, furniture, Provisions, 1 Cow, 1 Steer, 1 yearling, lost 15 lbs. Tea, which he had on board a Boat & meant to sell, ½ a Schooner employed in carrying Wood. His house was plundered on Long Island & he lost some money &c. Left the things just mentioned at his house when he went away. His wife was turned off in 11 days, after he went away. She got some of the furniture away.

ISAAC BELL Wits.

(44)

Knew Claimt. at Stamford. From the first he declared his Loyalty & suffered as much as any one. Remembers his being advertized as an enemy to the state. Witness was obliged to assist his Family privately during that time. Knew his house & Lot. Remembers his purchasing it. He did a good Deal to it after he bought it. Vals. it at £160 lawful mon.

He was a Weaver & carried on a good Deal of Business. Thinks he saw 2 or 3 Looms going. He was an honest good man.

Used to see two or 3 Cattle about the Place. Was Witness to his Wife being turned off the Premises. Understood the Things had been seized.

NEW CLAIM.

694. Case of ED. JONES, late of Pensilva.   February 2.

Claimt. apprs. Says he came to this Prov. in May '83. Went up to Majorfield. Staid at Burton that winter, 60 miles off. Heard of the Act just before Capt. Vand. went, sent by him.
Lived in Bucks Co., Pensilvania. Joined the Brit. in the fall after they came to Philadelphia. Served in the Bucks Co. Militia Volunteer. Served all the War. Now settled on Spoon Island.
Had a Farm in Bucks Co. consisting of 100 acres. It belonged to his Father, Edward Jones.

He died intestate about 2 years before the Troubles, leaving several children. Claimant was eldest son. He paid his Brother & Sisters about £150 for their Interests on which he was to have the Farm before mentioned, being half his Father's Estate. 6 acres meadow, 40 acres Plough. The rest in Wood. A good stone house. Vals. it at £7.10 per acre. This has been confiscated & sold.
Lost 1 Cow, furniture, farming utensils; left on the Farm when he went away. The Rebels came & took every thing away from his Wife.
Produces Deed of Quit claim & Release from his Brother & his Sisters & their Husbs., whereby they release to him all their Rights in 109 acres in Hilltown in Considn. £176, dated 1774.   (45).
Says his Bror., Jonathan Jones, had the other half of his Father's Estate, paying the same Considn. his Sisters & Claimant as Claimt. paid.
His Bror. Jonathan is now in Pensilv. One Saml. Mackinstin is now in Possession of the Estate. He bought Claimant's share. His Bro.'s share was also Confiscated. Joseph Gruse bought it, & was in Possession when Claimt. heard last.
Is told to bring Certificate of Conficn. & Witnesses who knew his Estate. Claimt. says he saw an advertizt. for the Sale of his own Estate in a Philadelphia News Paper.

---

695. Case of SILVANUS WATERBURY, late of Connect.   February 3.

Silvanus Waterbury being so ill as not to be able to attend, which was Certified to the Comrs. by their Clerk, Mr. Betts, who went up for the Purpose of seeing him, his attendance was dispensed with & his Wife Sarah appearing for him, she was heard upon her Husband's Claim.
Silv. Waterbury lived at Stamford, Connect. He was from the first in favour of the Brit. Government. Had been active in seizing some Powder which was Conveyed up the Country for use

of the Rebels, in 1777. Went within the Brit. Lines at New York, served as a Pilot several years, occasionally.

He was obliged to stay at Evacuation of New York on acqt. of illness. He had there had a second paralytic stroke. In consequence of his continuing in New York he was taken up for back rents and imprisoned, & they were obliged to pay about £43. As soon as he was released from his Imprisonment he came away from New York; got here in June '84. Now lives in this town.

He had a House & Lot in Stamford. Purchased it about 2 years before he went to New York of James Rogers. The Deed is sent to England, together with Certificate of Confiscation.

Vals. it at £150 lawful mon. It has been valued at that sum by 2 persons of this Place, Mr. Jervas & Mr. Halley.

Household furniture. Her Husband left to the amount of £40. Witness endeavoured to secure it & put some in one place & some in an other, before she went to New York. The Committee afterwards got some to amount of £18 York mon. The rest was pillaged & on her going back she could not get any part of it. Lost 400 Dollars in the year 1776. It was Continental money. Her Husband supplied Abraham Bates, her Brother in Law, with money to purchase a Vessel & Cargo to go off from the Country. they prest everybody into their service. Joined Genl. Tryon & there sold the Cargo.

(47).

NEW CLAIM.

February 3.

696. Case of JACOB LODER, late of Connect.

Claimt. apprs. Says he came to this Prov. in July '83. Went immediately 60 or 70 miles up the River. Continued there all the winter. The first he heard was of Capt. Vands going home to England. Never heard of the Act before. Sent his Claim by him.

Lived in Stamford, Connect. Joined the Brit. in April, 1777. Had been draughted into Militia. When New York was taken they prest everybody into their service. Joined Genl. Tryon & came over to Long Island. Continued in Trade at New York.

Now settled at Majorfield.

Had a House & Lot consisting of about 11 acres in Stamford. Produces Deed from Danl. Loder to Claimt. of a Tract of 3 acres in Stamford in Considn. of £33, dated 1771.

Produces Deed from Danl. Loder to Claimt. of 6 acres in Stamford in Considn. £100 York, dated 1773. The Quantity was about 11 acres. A very good house finished after he bought the Place. The Land was orchard, Grass & Plough Land. Vals. it at 400 York mon.

(48).

This Estate is now in Possession of one Avery who purchased from the Cmrs. Produces Copy of Writ to the sheriff &c. to seize the Lands of Claimt. lying in the District of sd. Sheriff, with return by the Constable that had attached 7 acres in Stamford together with Dwelling House &c. of Claimt.

Produces Copy of Writ to Sheriff &c., requiring him to give notice to Claimt. to appear to shew cause why his Estate should not be declared forfeited.

Left his personal Estate with his Wife. His Wife came to New York about 2 years after he had gone there. They took some furniture, val. about £5.

When he went away first he left some Hides. Some his Wife sold & some were taken. About 8 Hides were taken.

ISAAC BELL, Wits:

Knew Claimt. He left the Rebel Militia as soon as he could.

He was always one of the Tory Party. Witness considered him as a good Loyalist. Knew his House & Lot; should have thought about a dozen acres. It had been his Fathers & Brothers, & Claimant purchased it. Vals. it at £300 lawful, 6sh. Dollar.

Claimt. says he owed about £27 York on the Estate, which he expects was claimed from the Estate.

A NEW CLAIM.

697. Case of RACHEL WETMORE, Widow of Benjamin Ogden, February 3. formerly of New York, Now Wife of Timothy Wetmore. Admitted for her Children Under Age.

Claimt. appears & says her first Husband was Benj. Ogden.

He lived at New York. He was apprehended as a friend of Govert. in 1775. In 1776 he was Confidentially employed by (49). Govr. Tryon. He staid on Board the Asia, then on board the Dutchess of Gordon. Went with the Troops to Long Island. Raised men for a Captns. Company in Govr. Brown's Regt., but he failed to get the Commission as Capt., but had that of Lieut. Continued as L'eut. till he lost his Life in action at Hanging Rock, S. Carolina, in 1780.

He left Claimt., his Widow and 4 Children. Rachel married to George Wetmore at Antigonish, 25 or 26 years of age. Benjamin Ogden at Antigonish. He served during the war. Has half Pay as Ensign, now 21. Albert, at Antigonish, 17 years of age, Andrew here. Her Husband left only personal Estate.

Claimant herself came to this Province in July '83. Continued here during the Winter.

Lost furniture, Tools &c., when her Husband went on Board (50). the Asia. Taken on acct. of his going to Govr. Tryon. Furniture amount of £40. Tools for turning, Tools for joiners & Carpenters' Work, 3 Sets Compleat Det. Books, 50 Boards & Stuff, Sashes & Pediments.

Produces Attestation to shew her Husband raised 45 men. Produces Wart. to enlist men in Gen. Brown's Brigade. Produces Certificate from Major Carden that Lieut. Benj. Ogden was killed in action Aug., 1780.

AZOR BETTS, Wits:

Knew the late Benj. Ogden. He was a very active Loyalist. He was the first man he thinks apprehended & confined on acct. of his Loyalty at New York. He served & lost his Life in Action. Left 4 Children, when he went on Board the Asia. He had an house well furnished. He had at sundry times things seized after he had went on board the Asia. He had a large Quantity of Joiners & Carpenters Tools; enough to supply from 12 to 20 workmen —Chiefly.

BENJ. CLOSE, Wits:

(51).

Knew Benj. Ogden. He was an active, zealous Loyalist. Knew him on Board the Dutchess of Gordon. He was confidentially employed by Govr. Tryon. His house at New York was well furnished. He had been a House Carpenter & employed a good many apprentices. Saw many Tools when Mrs. Wetmore came to Staten Island. She sd. she had been obliged to quit the house & had been stript of many things.

Andrew Ogden appeared & expressed his Desire that the money allowed him shd. be paid to his mother, & said it would be very Convenient that the money allowed for his Bror. Albert shd. also be pd. to her.

A NEW CLAIM.

February 3.

698. Case of PETER VANDERBURG, late of New York.

Claimt. appears. Says he came in the first Fleet; went up the River. Staid there all the Winter. Never heard till Capt. Vand, his Brother, went to England.

He lived at PughKepsie. Joined the Brit. when Fort Montgomery was taken. Never served. Lived within ye Lines. Now settled in Conway Township.

Lost 3 Cows, 2 horses, 9 Sheep, 7 Hogs, furniture. Left them at Pugh Kepsie, when he went within the Lines. They were seized & sold at Vendue.

NEW CLAIM.

February 3.

699. Case of WM. LAWRENCE, late of New York.

(52).

Claimt. appears. Says he came to this Prov. in Aug. '83. Went up the River to Gage town. Had no opportunity of sending but by Capt. V. Sent by him. Sure he never heard of it, till they heard of Capt. V.

Lived in Dutchess Co. Joined the Brit. at New York in 1777. Was obliged to quit home, because he would not serve with the Rebels. Did Duty as a Guard at the out Post for about a month or 6 weeks. Continued on Long Island. Now settled in Gage Town.

Had a Tenant Farm under Col. Morris, consisting of about 70 acres. Bought the Improvements of 66 acres of one Eben Hoyt, about 6 years before ye Troubles. Gave him £80 York mon. Was to pay 50 Shills. Rent. Says the Landlord used to have 1-6 part on the sale. On the first sale. The Landlord had 1-3 afterwards

1-6. Improvemts. takes in Land & Buildings. Vals. them at £160. He had much Improved the Place.

Lost 5 horses, 2 pr. Oxen, 3 Cows, 1 pr. 2-yr. old Steers, 2 Heifers, 3 yearlings, 12 Sheep, 6 Hogs, farming utensils, Corn in ye ground. Left all these Things on his Farm. They were all taken away. They were inventoried & taken away.

THOMAS CARL, Wits:

Knew Claimant; always looked upon him as a staunch friend to Government. He went within ye Brit. Lines, because he would not stay amongst the Rebels. Knew his Farm. It was a choice farm. Vals. ye Improvements at £150. Remembers 3 horses, some Cattle, Oxen & young Creatures, Sheep.

(53).

NEW CLAIM.

700. Case of CAPT. JOHN COCHRANE, late of New Hampshire. February 5.

Sarah, Wife of Claimant, appears & being sworn saith:
Her husband came to this Province in July '83. They went to Mahogany. Her Husband had a paralytic stroke before he left

New York. When he arrived here he was not capable of doing any Business. About six or seven weeks after his arrival he was taken very ill again. He Continued very ill the whole Winter; had no more strength or understanding than a Child. He is now better. If present, he could hardly be understood. His memory is gone. Thinks the journey to this might be attended with great Danger.

This acct. is Confirmed by Mr. Paddock, an Apothecary of this Town. On these circumstances the Claim is admitted & Capt. Cochrane's attendance for the present dispensed with.

Her Husb. is a native of America. Lived at Fort William & Mary in New Hampshire. Commanding officer at the Fort. Appointed by Govr. Wentworth. He was appointed in 1771. Continued in this Command till the Fort was dismantled by the Govr. order & left in Aug., 1775. He went with Govr. Wentworth on Board the Ship Canso to Boston. He was occasionally employed in the Navy. Went on a Voyage as Pilot on Board the Lively. He Continued with the Army; always ready to give them his assistance by Land or Sea.

He was employed by Genl. Prescot on Rhode Island to attack an Enemies out Post, which he performed & took ye Picket. He was on a Cruise with Mr. Leonard.

(54).

Went with Dispatches from Rhode Island to New York, and was employed on various occasions. Now settled at Mahogany. His Pay at 10s. per Day as Comr. of Fort William & Mary was Continued till Octr., '84, & has since that time been stopt. Produces Certificate from Govr. Wentworth to Claimt.'s Loyalty & active services, to his having acted as Capt. of Volunteers with Commission from Sr. W. How, and in general agrees with the acct. above given & speaks of his merits in the strongest terms & of his personal activity.

(55). Witness says her Husb. was possessed of a farm in Londonderry in New Hampshire. Produces Deed from Saml. Hogg to Claimt. of 30 acres in Londondery in Considn. of £1,000 lawful Moy., dated 1752.

No. 2. Produces Deed from Hannah Lasley to Claimt. of a piece of Land in Londondery at £1.10 lawful per acre, 1772. It measured above 80 acres. Produces Deed from Robt. Rogers to Claimt. of 12 acres in Londondy. in Considn. £15 lawf., dated 1774.

No. 4. Produces Deed from Wm. Rogers to Claimt. of 34 acres & 26 acres in Considn. £300, 1772.

Produces Valuation of the above farms by Saml. Allison & John Morrison who Value—

No. 1	£254
2	369
3	18
4	186

The name of Claimant appears 4th in the Bill of attainder, 1778.

It appears in Govr. Wentworth's Letter that Claimt. had Rights in Tamworth & Whitfield. Witness says these Rights are on the Borders. Does not know where in Vermont.

Lost Household furniture, Provs. & utensils to amt. of £150 lawful. When her Husb. went to Boston with Govr. Wentworth,
(56). about 2 months after he went, she was oraered to quit the Premises, which she did & was moving her goods, on which a Mob rose & took every thing she had, calling them ye goods of a Tory. She got part back, but lost to amount of £150 lawful. Gives an Inventory of some of the Furniture &c., which was lost. This acct. is confirmed by Deposition of Eben Louring & John Potter who were employed to convey ye goods.

February 5. 701. Case of CAPTN. PETER CAMPBELL, late of New Jersey.

Claimt. appears & being sworn saith:

He was settled at Trentown when the Troubles broke out. Joined the Brit. when they first came to the Jersey in Decer., 1776.

Had a Wart. to raise a Company in Genl. Skinner's Brigade. Had raised part of his men. After the affair at Trentown while endeavoring to join the King's Army, was taken Prisoner & sent to Philadelphia. Was kept close confined 11 months in different Gaols. Made his escape from Carlisle & joined the Brit. at Wilmington in 1777.

(57). He was not paid for his expenses or for his sufferings during confinement, not having compleated his Company he had no Pay.

Went as a Volunteer with Col. Ferguson to Egg Harbr. His Conduct was represented so favourably by Col. Ferguson on that occasion, that Claimt. was allowed to purchase a Company which he accordingly did, in Skinner's Brigade & went with Col. Allen with the first Troops under Col. Campbell to Georgia.

Was at the taking of Savannah, at the Defence of 96. Was severely wounded at Enone in South Carolina. Was shot thro. the shoulder. Went from Charles Town to New York on the Evacuation. Now settled in York Co. Has half Pay.

Was in Possession of a House & Lot in Chesnut St., Philadelphia. Had it by his Father's Will. Produces authenticated Copy of his Father's Will, whereby His Father, Thomas Campbell of Philadelphia, devises to Claimant & his Heirs his House & Lot in Chesnut Street, Philadelphia, and also 3 acres of Meadow. Will dated 1762.

Testator died soon after. Claimant was then a minor. His Guardians took Possession for him. Claimant was just of age when the Troubles broke out. He had not settled with his Guardians.

Produces Valuation of the Estate by Chas. Jervis & Thos. Conly, who state that the Estate had been sold as forfeited on attainder of Claimt. They value ye house & Lot at 5,500 Pens. Cur. The Lot of Mead. at 150.

Claimt. saw an advertizement for the sale of this Estate in a Philadelphia Paper. His Guardians used to let from £100 to 120 per ann. Pen. Cur. Claimt. was there 2 years ago. One Captn. Colwell was in Possession. He had purchased it of the Cmrs. His name appears in a Philadelphia News paper, '82, amongst those whose estates were forfeited.

(58).

He had 2 Negroes, when he joined the Brit. One of his Negroes went with his Wife to Philadelphia; was afterwards seized & sold. This was a very valuable Negroe. Claimt. gave £100 for it. The other was left in the Jerseys & he does not know what became of him.

BENJAMIN DAVIES, Wits., affirms:

Knew the house & Lot in Philadelphia. Claimt.'s Father's Estate, & left to Claimant. It was a very good House with stables & Coach house. It was a double Lot. The ground thereabouts used to let at 30s. per foot Ground Rent. Has not known a house so good as that let under £200 per ann. Speaks of 2 or 3 yrs. before the War. Thinks the Builds. would have cost £2,000 Pen. Cury. Vals. it at £4,000 at the lowest rate. Has understood it has been sold under Confiscation. Meadows in the situation where Claimt. was used to sell for £50 pr. acre.

COL. ISAAC ALLEN:

Claimt. took a decided part very early. Had a Wart. to raise a Company in Skinner's Brigade. He was taken Prisoner before he had compleated it, & kept a long while in Confinement. Claim-

(59).

ant distinguished himself in an expedition under Col. Ferguson, who spoke in high Terms of his Conduct. He went with Witness to the Southward. He was a very gallant officer & particularly distinguished himself at 96. Wits. heard Col. Moncrief speak highly of him. He was severely wounded before the affair at 96.

Knew the house & Lot at Philadelphia. It was his Fathers. Remembers hearing it was let at £120 per ann. Cannot set a value upon it.

Remembers a valuable Negroe that Claimt. gave £100 for.

Knows the person who purchased his House. Understood he purchased it of the Comrs.

Claimt. admits there is an Incumbrance of £500 Pens. Cury. on the house & Lot, which was paid off on the sale.

Nov. 27. Produces Certificates of Sale of the House in Philadelphia and of the Piece of Meadow. Produces Copy of the Mortgage upon the Estate, by which it appears it was only for £200 lawf. in 1776.

uary 5.

702. Case of JOHN BEDEL & BENJAMIN MICHEAN, late of New York.

JOHN BEDEL, one of the Claimts. appears & being sworn saith:

(60.)

He & Benjamin Michean were Partners in Trade on Staten Island. Benjamin Michean has continued on Staten Island & is there now. Claimant John Bedel continued there till May, '84, then came to this Place. Is now settled up the River.

Claimant was apprentice at New York when Troubles began. Mr. Michean was settled on Staten Island. Claimant set up a Trade for himself on Staten Island at the Fresh Kills. Two or 3 yrs. after the Troubles, entered into a Partnership with Benja-

---

min Michean & carried on Trade at a Place near Richmond. Claimt. says he removed there because Mr. Michean's store at Fresh Kills nad been plundered. Removed near Richmond as being a safe Place. Carried on a Trade with the Garrison & Inhabits. It was a valuable Trade.

Their store was plundered at this Place near Richmond by parties of the American Army, in the years '79 & '80. Claimant & his Partner had declared themselves in favour of Brit. Govert. Admits that these Parties used to plunder indiscriminately.

(61).

Claimant was taken Prisoner by a Party who plundered his store, each time. Was kept near a month, but had his Parole very soon, and was on Parole when he was taken Prisoner a second time.

The Goods which were plundered he vals. at 1,200 New Y. Cury. Lost cash to amt. of 74. Did not make out this acct. from their Books but only from their Judgement of Things lost. Says they looked upon themselves as safe, by being so near the Brit. Post at Richmond. Says that he had been active in the Militia.

Produces Copy of a Letter which Witness sent to Genl. Skinner May, 1781, in which he mentions that Claimt.'s Shop had

53a AP.

been plundered to amount of £180. This was wrote with a view of having a party to pursue the Plunderers that they might retake the Things if possible.

He does not recollect whether a party was sent, but is satisfied the Things were not returned. The party who came to the Store must have past another which belonged to a person of a doubtful Character.

Col. Bellop speaks very favourably of Claimt.'s Character & Loyalty. Says their Trade on Staten Island did not prove advantageous. Thinks they have not pd. their creditors, & been out with the Brit. Troops which had made him obnoxious to ye Rebels. & particularly pointed them out for being plundered. (62).

Produces Certificate to the Loyalty of himself & Partner. Signed by several Persons who also Certify their Belief as to the Losses of Claimt.

COL. BELLOP, Wits:

Remembers Claimt. Bedel on Staten Island. He had been an apprentice at New York. He was certainly a Loyalist. He was very active. He went frequently out with the Militia. Remembers his carrying on a Trade in partnership with Michean; the principal business was with the Garrison. Remembers he moved from Fresh Kill to a Place near Richmond. It was thought

a safe Place. Heard of his store being plundered. Witness was at Richmond & went on the alarm to ye Place. It appeared to have been plundered. They plundered the Loyalists particularly, not the stores belonging to their friends. Heard of his being plundered another time.

NEW CLAIM.

703. Case of NEHEMIAH CLARK, late of Connect.   February 5.

Claimt. apprs. & being sworn saith:

He came here in Septr., '83. He delivered his Claim to Mr. Hardy in Decr. (63).

He lived at Hertford, Connect. Had declared his sentiments in Favr. of Brit. Govert., which made him obnoxious at that Place so far, that he was obliged to remove to Reading where there were many Loyalists. This was soon after the Tea was destroyed at Boston, in 1774.

Claimant went in Feby., '75, to Hertford to settle some affairs. He was insulted & treated by a mob with great cruelty so that his Life was in Danger. He was attended by a Physician, who thought him in great Danger. He made his escape at last with Difficulty.

After his return to Reading he was taken again by a mob &

obliged to sign a Bond of £1,000 that he would not join the Brit. He was then obliged to secrete himself & got to the Brit. at Long Island in Dec., 1776, joined the Army, served as Lieut. under his Bror. in Col. Brown's Regiment, afterwards as Surgeons mate to Col. Hartehey's Regt. Afterwards appointed Surgeon to the Chasseurs under Col. Emerick. Served till that Corps was draughted, then was appointed Surgeon in Quarter Master Genls. Department. Continued in that Department till he came hither. Is now settled in York Co. Has no Half Pay.

(64). Was possessed of a house in Hertford. Produces Lease from Aaron Bull, reciting a former Lease from the South Society to Aaron Bull, for 999 years, to Claimant of half the Premises so demised for 900 years reserving 42 shils. Rent 1771. It appears by Indorsement that this Lease is entered on the Records of the Town of Hertford.

Claimant afterwards built a house, a Barn & out buildings on the Premises. He laid out £560 York Cury. Produces Valuation on Oath, by 2 appraisers at 350 lawful New Engl. Claimant let it the year he came for £12. Once to Dr. Gibson for £15. He produces a Letter from Wm. Heron, New York, who states that he had procured an appraisement of his house. Authenticated under seal of the States, which has miscarried.

Claimt. says the South Society took Possession of it & sold it to Dr. Gibson.

Lost furniture at Reading to amount of £125. Almost all this was taken by a Rebel General. They allowed his Wife scarce anything. Left a Chaise. His Business brought him in £400 lawful, one year with another. He includes bad Debts.

REVD. JOHN BRADSLEY, Wits:

(65). Knew Claimant at Hertford. He was from the first a declared friend of Brit. Govert. He suffered greatly. Was advertized as an enemy to his Country. Went with the Witness within the Lines. Served first with his Bror. in Col. Brown's Regt., afterwards as Surgeon in Col. Emerick's Regt., then in the Quarter Master General Department. Remembers his house at Hertford. the Town. All the builds. were new. Should think the whole worth £500 York Cury. Has been at his house at Reading. It seemed decently furnished. Speaks of him as a man of Honour & Integrity.

DR. HUGGERFORD:

Remembers Dr. Clarke serving in several Regts. during the war. Speaks highly to his character & Loyalty, and to the sufferings of Claimt. & his family.

JOSEPH CLARKE, Wits:

(66). Claimt. joined the Brit. early. He had suffered greatly at Hertford from Insults, from the Mob. He served in several Regts. Knew his house at Hertford. Could not have been built under £400. His business was very extensive between £3 & 400. His house at Reading was well furnished. Understood the Rebels had taken it, Nov. 26. Prods. 2 Affidts. that the South Society in Hertford granted a Lease for 999 years of a piece of Land in Hertford to Claimt. & that he built a house &c. upon it. That the Society re-entered for non payment of back rents & afterwards leased the same to Dr. Gibson with appraismt. at £260 lawful.

NEW CLAIM.

704. Case of NICHOLAS BICKLE, late of New Jersey.   February 6.

Claimt. says. He came to this Prov. in May. Went up the Kennebikasis. Staid there all ye winter. Never heard of the act during the winter. Some of his neighbours told him last winter. Lived in Humberton Co., Jersey. Was taken up & carried before the Committee. Refused to take oath to the States. Was fined £30. Was several times imprisoned, broke Gaol & got to Philadelphia where he joined the Brit. Was in Wagon Department, then worked as Blacksmith. Afterwards went to New York with the Army. Worked there as a Carpenter 2 years in the Engineer Department. Came from New York 1783. Now settled on Kennebikasis. (67).

Lost Household furniture, £130 Pens. Cur., 3 horses, Wagon, 1 yoke oxen, 1 yoke Steers, 3 Cows, several Hogs, several Sheep, Tools, Farming utencils, Grain cut, Flax cut, Potatoes, oats in ye ground.

Produces Aaron Dunham's Certificate of sale to amt. of £109. Says he lived on a hired farm. Left all these articles on the Farm. They were taken &·sold.

ANDREW DICKENS, Wits:

Was a Neighbour to Claimt. Claimt. was always Loyal. He had been imprisoned & suffered a great Deal. Broke Gaol to join the Brit. Knew he had a stock; 3 horses, 3 Cows, a yoke of oxen, some Sheep, 6 Hogs, middling furniture, Blacksmiths' Tools, Farming utensils. They were taken & sold.

NEW CLAIM.

705. Case of ANDREW PICKENS, late of New Jersey.   February 6.

Claimt. says. He came to this Prov. in June, '83. Went up the River. Staid there all the winter. Did not hear of the act till last month.

Lived in Huntindon Co. From the first declared in Favor of Brit. Govert. Was taken up before several Committees, was imprisoned, broke Gaol & joined the Brit. at Brunswick in 1777. About 40 men had raised to join the Brit. Was joined by 2 or 3 parties. On coming into Brunswick Claimt. was shot thro. the (68). thigh. His party was dispersed. He was taken Prisoner. Was afterwards sent to the Hospital. Got to the Brit. Lines at New York in Oct., 1777. Continued within the Lines. Served occasionally. Went out with parties. Worked sometimes in the Engineers' Department. Now settled on the Kennebekasis.

He was possessed of 250 acres in S. Carolina, but waives the Claim not having Proof.

Lost 4 Wagon horses, Wagon, 2 young horses, 6 head of Cattle, 28 Sheep, 19 Hogs, farm utensils, Household furniture, grain in stock, £30, Oats do, 10, Indian Corn & Buckwheat. These things were taken & sold.

Produces Inventory with Apraisment.
Produces Certificate from Aaron Dunham of Sale to Amt., £218.

NICHOLAS BICKLE, Wits.:
Was a neighbour to Claimt. He was always Loyal. He was Imprisoned; wounded. Before this he helped to raise men. 2 persons were hanged for it. Claimt. would have shard. the same fate had he not made his escape.

Knew that he had a good stock of Cattle. Large stock of sheep & hogs. Furniture very good. He had grain in the Stock. He had a larger stock than Wits.

NEW CLAIM.

(69).
February 6.

706. ZEPHANNAH BEARDSLEE, late of Connect.

Claimt. says he came in the June Fleet. Went to Majorfield; staid there all Winter. Sent his Claim by Captn. Vand. Never heard before.

Lived at Stratford, Connect. Was from the first a Loyalist. Joined Col. Ludlow at first. Suffered a great deal from cruel ill treatment which he experienced several times. Has not yet recovered. Servd. under Col. Ludlow several years from soon after the fight at Danbury till end of the War. Now settled at Westfield.

(70).

Had a small house & shop at Stratford; built it himself. Paid a trifle to the Landlord; it was his own, & he could have sold it—it having been built with leave of Col. Joseph Wooster, his Landlord. Vals. it at 30—.

Was a Weaver. He had a Loom & furniture. Everything was seized after he went off & joined the Brit. He followed also fishing; had a Boat; had a share in two Seines, 1-4 in one, 1-6 in another.

His wife was robb'd, his house & shop pulled down & every thing destroyed, when he went to ye Brit. on that acct.

COL. LUDLOW, Wits.:
Speaks very favourably of Claimt. & confirms the acct. of his having served under him most of the War.

PROCEEDINGS

OF

LOYALIST COMMISSIONERS

St. JOHNS, 1887.

Vol. XV.

BEFORE COMMISSIONER PEMBERTON.

Claimants.

	Ms. Page.		Ms. Page.
Allward, Asher	34	Harkey, David	68
Anderson, George	22	Ives, Capt. David	59
Berten, Peter	51, 62 and 75	McEwan, Patrick	4
Betts, Dr. Azor	57, 61 and 75	Montgomery, Alexander	47
Bull, Jacob	73	Montgomery, Alexander, Jr.	49 and 56
Caldwell, William	1	Redout, Maria (Mrs. Tredwell)	24
Cochran, Captain	23	Richards, Charles	6
Colden, David	35	Sealey, Benjamin	78
Cory, Mrs. Sarah	79	Smith, Daniel	63
Crannel, Bartholomew	7	Stow, Edward	27
Dickson, Joseph	18	Summers, Philip	72
Eagles, John	31	Vincent, Charles	70
Hamilton, John	5	Whepley, Oliver	20
Harding, William	75		

THE EVIDENCE.

New Claim.

February 7. 707. Case of WM. CALDWELL, late of Pensily.

Claimt. says he came to this Prov. 14th Sep. '83. Knew of the Act before he left New York, 7 or 8 days; staid over 2 nights. Went up the River to Major——— Had no opportunity till by Capt. Vand. Sent his Claim by him.
Is a native of England. Was settled in Union Township, Pensilva., before the troubles.

(1). In the year 1775 had declared his sentiments in favour of the British Govrnt. at several Town Meetings in Union Township. In consequence of which he was summoned to attend a Committee at Reading, 14 June, 1775. Was tried on 15th & sentenced to be tarred & feathered, which sentence was put in execution. 200 men in arms attended in order to see the sentence put in execution.
On the 15th two Militia officers came to his house & demanded his goods & carried them away. Claimt. was dismist & ordered to leave ye Country.
Went to Phila., purchased a house for his family & went to Virginia. Joined the Brit. at Brunswick, Feby., '77.

Served as a guide principally to Col. Mathews & to several other Detachments and continued to serve during the War.
Now settled in Queen's Co.
Produces Book containing Copy of the Order for his attendance before a Committee of Bucks Co., Pensa., 14 June, 1775.
Produces minutes of his Trial.

(2). While with the Army at Philadelphia, was employed by Jas. Galloway to go to Willm. Moor, Esq., for Intelligence. He procured the Intelligence & was taken on his return to Philadelphia & his horse & money taken from him & Maryland Bills to amount of £114.
He was tried f r his life & sentenced to be hang'd. Made his escape by bribing a Sentinel & got to Philadelphia.
Lost the following articles: Shop of Goods to the Val. of ～800 that Cury.; Waggon & 2 horses.
After his Trial in June, 1775, 2 Militia officers came & demanded his effects. Went into his shop; took Claimt.'s Waggon & horses & carried the things away. Says his Books containing the acct. of his shop Goods were lost on removal of his Family.
Lost when taken going with Intelligence from Wm. Moor, Esq., to Phila.

A horse, Cash, 56, Bills, 114. On his coming to Phia. he called at John Robt. Williams' house to bring away some money which he had lodged there, which was ye reason for his having so much.

Produces certificate from J. Galloway that Claimt. was a friend to Govt. & had been employed in its service.

Produces Certificate from Major Marlland that Claimt. had been a guide to 2nd Batal. L. Infy. & on several occasions very serviceable.

Produces Certificates from Col. Bev. Robinson that Claimt. had been employed as a guide & behaved well, also that he had a Commission to man one Whale Boat. (3).

Produces Letter of Govr. Franklin speaking of Claimt. as a brave Loyal subject.

Bought a house in ——— Street, New York, in the year 1782. It appears by his Books that he pd. £75 York Cur. for it.

One Vanrypee, now at St. Anns, is a Witness to Claimt.'s Loss.

James Callaghan, of Merimichee, is also a Witness. They were two of the Rebel Militia who took his shop goods in 1775.

708. Claim of PATRICK McEWEN, late of S. Carolina. February 7.

Claimt. says he is a native of America.

Lived in the Jerseys when Troubles began. Was called upon to serve in the Rebel Militia which he refused & went to North Carolina. There had been several Battles in the Jerseys before he went.

He purchased 100 acres of Land in North Car. Staid there about 2 yrs. After Charlestown was taken joined the Brit. Servd. with Captn. Sutherland of the 71—. Went to Camden in '96. Was under Gen. Cunningham in the S. Carolina Militia. At the time of the engagement of '96 was taken Prisr. Came from Charlestown to Nova Scotia. Now settled on Belle Isle Bay. (4).

Had 100 acres on the Waters of 2 Creek, purchased of one Knox, since ye Troubles. Gave him as good as £50 that mon. Gave a Mare & was to pay some cash.

Lost Leather & Shoemakers Tools & Clothing; left them when he went to join the Brit. Left them with one George Marshal, who was a Loyalist. There were 30 sides of Leather. Lost a horse, &c., while he was in Service.

DAVID BLACKENEY, Wits.:

Remembers Claimt.'s serving in S. Carolina Militia. Understood he came from N. Carolina; he was a shoemaker & saddler. Remembers his being taken Prisoner, when he lost a horse & saddle, &c. Understood he had some Land in North Carolina.

709. Claim of JOHN HAMILTON, late of S. Carolina. February 8.

Claimt. says. He is an Irishman. Was settled in Coty Dam Creek. Served the Brit. from the first. Served under Col. Hamilton in 96 Militia during the War. Has been in 2 or 3 Skirmishes. Joined at 96. Was at the first engagement there. (5).

Had 100 acres on ——— Town Waters. Had lived there 15 years. Had 15 acres Cleared. Had a good stock of Cattle. Speaks with certy. of 8, 2 Mares & one Horse, 12 Sheep, furniture & utensils. Left these things on his Farm. His wife & family were sent away & the things taken. Now settled on Patago Jack River, Cumberland.

Col. Hamilton delivers a Memorial for Claimt. in which he speaks of his Knowledge of Claimt.'s Loyalty & Services & his

having a Plantation & stock.

DAVID BLAKENEY, Wits.:
Remembers Claimt. serving in the Militia of 96. Has been at his house. He had a pretty Plantation on Cuffy Town Waters; a smart Clearance. He had a pretty stock, has some Cattle & Sheep.

NEW CLAIM.

February 7.

710. Case of CHARLES RICHARDS, late of Jersey.

(6).

Claimt. says he came in May, '83; went up the River soon; staid there all the Winter. Never knew of the Act till last Winter with certainty.

He lived in Elizth. Town. Joined the Brit. at New York in 1778. He could not stay—he was so harrassed. Was imprisoned. Fined; was tried for his life, so that he was forced ᴛo get away. He was tried because he was a Tory.

When he removed from Elizth. Town he endeavoured to recover his effects, but the Rebels got information & took them.

2 Yoke of Oxen, 7 Cows, 2 horses, 6 Colts, furniture, 2 Waggons.

Lost some sheep before this and a yoke of oxen & 1 Cow taken at Newark after Lord Cornwallis had been there. Whether taken by Lord Cornwallis' Army or ye Rebels does not know. Now lives in Long Beach.

February 8.

711. Claim of BARTHOLOMEW CRANNEL, late of New York.

(7).

Claimt. upon being Sworn Saith:
He is a native of America. Lived in Dutchess Co. when the Troubles began. At the first appearance of the Disputes he exerted all his influence, which was considerable, to keep people from taking any part against the then Established Govrnt.

He thought so early as 1774 that the Whig Party had Independence in Contemplation. Is not quite certain as to dates, but says that when there was a Plan for establishing Committees of Correspondence in Dutchess Co. he opposed it with all his interest & he thinks he so far prevailed as to prevent it. Continued uniformly to pursue his conduct.

In 1775 recvd. an anonymous Letter threatening his Life.

In 1776 the Congress determined to build 2 Frigates at

Poughkeepsie and a great number of ship builders came from New York who were all violent in support of the Rebellion.

About June 1776 there came an order from Congress to several Counties to summon meetings to consider about declaring Independence & taking sence of the people upon it. The Committees in Duchess Co. meeting for this purpose. Claimt. & Mr. Sneidiker were then mentioned as persons who would be likely to prevent such a measure in Dutchess Co. Claimt. being informed of the opinion entertained of by the Committees & the violent speeches against them. Thought it prudent to withdraw & went to Orange County intending to have returned home in about 3 weeks. He was taken at Goshen by a body of horse & carried before the Committee of Orange Co. He was detained 2 or 3 days. Was then taken before a joint Committee of 2 Counties. There was an order to carry him from Committee to Committee and so to have conveyed him home. The last Committee in Orange Co. thought the order irregularly & discharged him. (8).

Gives an acct. of his being persecuted in various ways. Was forced to leave his House and abscond; found it impossible to stay. In Decr., 1776 arrived in Long Island. Continued within the Lines. Came here with a Company of Refugees.

Produces threatening Letter in May, 1775, calling him Traitor & threatening vengeance.

Produces an order of a Committee for 2 Precints that he should be conveyed under a Guard from Committee to Committee till delivered to a Committee at Pughkepsie.

Had an appointment of a Dollar per Day & 5 Rations from Dr. Henry Clinton on an application to Sir Guy Carleton. He allowed him £50 pr. Quarter York Cury. This ceased on leaving New York. (9).

Has now the Appt. of Clerk of the City of St. John which is of very little profit.

Claimt. was possessed of considerable property in the town of Pughkepsie. Part of it had belonged to Peter Vanclerk, Father to Claimt.'s wife, and Claimt. had become entitled to it partly in right of his wife & partly by purchase from the Vanclerk family. It consisted of:

No. 1. 3 acres & 22-10 near the Dutch Church. Vals. this at £174.7.6

No. 2. 2 acres on the South side the Road including Dwelling House, &c., £337.10.

No. 3. 4 acres with Mills & Mill Pond; Mill Pond covered 3 acres, £1125.0.0.

No. 4. 85 acres & ½. Vals., £1442.16.

This Estate had belonged to Peter VanCleek. Claimt. married Sarah, Daughter of Peter VanCleek. He had 6 Children. Claimt.'s wife was entitled to 1-6 Part of her Father's real Estate, under his Will. Claimt. produces a Lease from himself and Sarah his wife to Lancaster Green of a 6th part of the real estate of Peter VanClerk, his wife's Father, decesd., dated 1746. This (10).

Lease was for the purpose of Conveying the Wife's Estate to the Claimt. in Fee and accordingly there was a Release the next day made to Lancaster Green and the case was examined before a Judge, which was sufficient to Convey away her interest whereupon the Estate was Conveyed to Lancaster Green in fee, but it was declared to be in Trust for Claimt. & his Heirs. The Release is Lost.

Claimt. Produces Deed of Partition between himself, Laurence, Leonard, & Peter VanCleek whereby the Estate of Peter VanCleek is divided into different Lots & distributed amongst the parties, dated in 1756.

He Produces Deeds from Peter VanCleek & Leonard Van Cleek, Conveying particular parts of their Father's Estate to Claimt. in part in 1756 in Considn. £60, the 2nd in 1762 in Considn. £700 including the Mills.

Produces an agreement on part of Sarah Van Cleek to sell her share in Considn. of £180 & £10 annually for 6 years in 1756, with receipt of the purchase money. He did not obtain the— till since the Peace, but produces it now from her & her Husband bearing Date from the time of agreement. He has parted with

(11). some of the Lands. He Produces a survey of the Estate with acct. of the quantity of the different Lots.

On examining the Deeds & Survey, the Quantity appears correspondent to the above acct., 1-4 of which the Claimt. has from his wife, the rest by Purchase from the Van Cleek Family.

The release has been lost of which he makes an affidavit.
The Mills were erected in their present state in 1759 by Claimt. & Leonard Van Cleek. Claimt. afterwards bought Leonard's share for £700.

Go on with No. 5.

No. 5. Produces Deed from John Brady to Claimt. of 17 acres in Pughkepsie in Consid. £58 York Cury. 1767.

Vals. it at £5 pr. acre.

No. 6. 35 acres in Pughkepsie. Produces Deed from John Van Denbogist to Claimt. of 33 acres in Considn. £80, 1767.

Says it measured 35 acres.

Vals. it at 5 pr. acre.

No. 7. 30 acres adjoining former. Produces Deed from Jacob Counter to Claimt. of 30 acres in Considn. of £100. 1771.

Vals. at 5 per acre.

No. 8. 45 acres Pughkepsie. Produces Deed from Barnet Lewis to Claimt. of 45 acres in Considn. of 250. 1772.

(12). Claimt. says he has had this Deed since the Peace. But the Bargain was made in 1770; in 1772 he got Possession. Was in Possession till he left the Country.

Vals. this at £5 pr. acre.

No. 9. 5 acres in Pughkepsie. Produces Deed from Thomas Boyle, Claimt. & Murray Lister of 10 acres in Considn. £48. Claimt. claims half. Vals. it at £5. 1765.

No. 10. 38 acres in 9 Partners. Produces Deed from Cor.

Osborne to Claimt. of 38 acres & ¾ in great 9 Partners in Considn. £107. 1769.
Vals. this at £7.10 pr. acre.
Used to let No. 8 at 25 pr. ann. This was in his own Possession or of his immediate Tenant.

Produces Copy of Judgment of forfeiture of real & personal Estate.

Claimt. has been informed of the Sale of his back Lands, viz. those purchased by himself that had not belonged to the Van Cleeks.

Pughkepsie was the Seat of Government during the War, and No. 2 was made use of as the Government House. The Govrnt. took Possession of his other Lands that had belonged to the Van Cleeks. Has not heard of any sale of these Lands.

When ye Govr. of New York left Pughkepsie quitted ye Premises which had been Claimt.'s. He recommended it to two Gentn., Dr. Topper & Mr. Lewiston, sons in law to Claimt., to get it if they could. They have endeavoured to do it, and presented a memorial to the Assembly for that purpose, offering to pay the mortgage, but a Claim being thrown in by Leonard Van Cleek exects. of a Debt of £1,000; the matter has been suspended since & no grant made.

(13).

He thinks if this Debt of £1,000 was out of the way they could obtain ye grant.

Says this is a mere ideal Debt; that he does not owe a farthing. Bels. Dr. Toppen is in Possession.

One Dr. Cook has located on No. 5, 6, 7 & 8 & is in Possession as Claimt. is imformed; he has paid for 5, 6, & 7, but not 8. There being some doubt about the Title on a Claim set up by Barnet, Lewis & Son on a supposition that his Father did not grant Claimt. a Deed for this.

(14).

His influence in opposition to the measures of the Rebels. Remembers particularly his opposing the— Committee of Correspondence. Thinks his influence had more weight than anything else in defeating that scheme.

Remembers his leaving Pughkepsie about the time of declaring Independence. He was imprisoned afterwards on suspicion of collecting persons to oppose that measure.

In short in everything which countenanced the commencing Rebellion, he did all in his power to oppose the measures carried on by the Rebels.

Knew his Property in Pughkepsie in general.
Knew No.1 to be their own Land in the Centre of the town as that was. Sells from 100 to £120 York Cury per acre.
Knew No. 2 Claimt. built that house himself; there was an excellent garden.
Vals. it at £1,000.
No. 3. Knows the Mills. He purchased in shares with Col. Van Cleek. The Mills were not of any great consequence when

(15).

they bought them. Claimt. afterwards bought Col. Van Cleek's share. A great Deal of money was laid out about them. The Creek was cleared at great expense. The Mill was converted into a double Mill. A great deal of money might have been laid out by Mr. Crannel upon them. These Mills must have been very valuable ——— None on which so many persons depended; having their Corn ground. Thinks it would have sold for more than £2,000 York.

Knew that he had Lands which he had purchased of the Van Cleek family to Considerable amount. Looks at the Survey and says—he remembers his being in Possession of Lands corresponding with the acct. given by Claimt. in his Schedule. This includes No. 4.

Vals. this at about £35 York pr. acre.

Remembers Claimt. in Possession of all this Est. ever since he came into the Par., which is some years before the War.

Knew No. 5 very well. Values it at between 5 & 10 pr. acre.

No. 6. Remembers Claimt. purchasing it. Vals. at the same.

No. 7. Remembers his purchasing it. Vals. at the same.

No. 8. Remembers Claimt. in possession Remembers his letting it. Witness once thought of purchasing this.

Values it at £400.

(16).

Knew No. 10. Part in 9 Partners, part in Pughkepsie. Wood Land. Bought as he recollects of Dr. Osborne.

Vals. at £10 pr. acre.

Claimt.'s house No. 1, very well furnished. He kept the Mill in his own hands. There was a considerable Quantity of flour in hand; that he understood was seized by Comrs. Some was secreted by Mrs. Crannel & some was discovered & taken.

Mr. Crannel's Business was very extensive, more than that of any other Lawyer in the Place.

HENRY VANDERBURG, Wits.:

Remembers that Claimt. was very active from the first against the measures of the Rebels. His influence was Considerable. He opposed the Plan for Committees of Correspondence.

He had a Considerable Estate that belonged to ye Van Cleek family; partly by his wife, partly by purchase from her family: Knew No. 1. Vals. the house & Lot at £800.

(17).

Knew the Mills; in valuing these mills says he must go by what he has heard of the sale of other Mills. Remembers Mills on this Stream, about a mile off sold for £3,600 York Cury.

Says he has seen the Schedule delivered in by Claimt. Remembers him in Possession of the Lands contained in the Schedule & agrees in the Valuation.

Remembers his house was well furnished. He had Wagons, Sleigh, & a ——— Stock of every kind. He had the Mill in his hands. Had a considerable stock of Flour. Heard of some being secured by his wife & afterwards discovered.

His Business was very extensive. He was high in Credit.
(There are six pages of this testimony gone.

C. H.)

NEW CLAIM.

712. Case of Jos. DICKSON, late of Connect. February 9.

Claimt. says. He came in June '83.
Says he went up the River and did not hear of it till after Capt. Vand. returned.

Is a native of America. Lived in Fairfield when troubles broke out. Joined the Brit. in 1776. Went to the Queen's Rangers where his Bro. was an officer. He sent him to recruit which he did. Was employed a good while in the service. Brought in a good many men. The next Spring enlisted in Major Stark's Regt.; (18). servd. about 2 years. Had his Discharge; afterward served with Loyal Rangers at Loyds Neck. Was in every expedition in the Sound. Servd. once as an Ensign under Col. Upham. Came here with Commission as Lieut. to ye Loyalists. Now settled in Kingston.

Had 6 acres & ½ in Norfield Par., Fairfield Co., purchased 4 years before the War of one Seth. Sherwood at 6.10 per acre. Pd. in hard money. Built an house, & cleared it. Has a Deed but left it behind him. Left it with a frienu to be put on Record.

Part taken by his Bro. for which Claimt. recd. £40, about half Quantity. The other part was taken by a person, Eben Bigsby, who pretended to have a Debt due to him from Claimt. He is now in Possession.

Says he did not owe 20sh. in ye world.
Vals. the whole Estate at £100 Cur. of that Prov.
Produces Certificates from Major Upham to his having served as Ensign, to his good Character & Loyalty.

ANDREW PATCHEN, Wits.: (19).

Remembers Claimt. joining the Brit. He was employed in the recruiting service. He served in Major Clark's Regt. under Col. Lockwood near a yr. Afterward with Loyal Refugees at Loyds.

Knew his Place. 6 acres & ½; a good house. He bought the land and built upon it. Vals. it about 100. His Bro. has part, to the Val. of ±40. One Ebenezer Bigby took ye residue on pretence of Debt. Witness was there & Bigby told him if he had not got it somebody else would, so he procured Capt. Duncans to carry on a Law Suit to get the Prems. & Capt. Duncans was to have half.

They were in possession when Witness was there.

New Claim.

February 9.

713. OLIVER WHILPLEY, late of Connect.

Claimt. says he came in May. Went up the River 100 miles. Staid at Oromokto the whole Winter. Heard nothing of the Act till they heard of Capt. Vamd. They sent their Claims to him but he was gone.

He lived at Fairfield, Cont. Joined the Brit. at Lloyd's Neck in 1777, was in the Barrack Department. Served till he had his leg broken. Staid within the Lines till he came hither. Now settled at Kingston.

(20).

Had a house & 13 acres Land in Greenwich, Fairfield Co., had it from his Father.

His Father gave him this Land in 1776, his Father went off to the Brit, Claimt. staid behind, but did not dispose of it. He joined the Brit. in 1777. Says it is Confiscated, was told so by a man who came here. His Father bought it a good while ago, had it ever since. Claimt. remembers there was 9 acres of meadow, the rest plough Land. Vals. it at £160.

Says his Father was once offered £20 per acre for the meadow.

His Father is now here came from New York to this Province. Now lives at Kingston.

Claimt. seems an honest creature.

All his Brothers & Sisters are here.

Lost 2 Cows, they were taken just after his Father went away, the Rebel Committee took them & sold them on acct. of his Father going away.

JONATHAN SCOFIELD, Wits.:

Remembers that Claimt. was a Loyalist & went within the Lines. Knew the Estate which was his Father's, heard his Father say he gave it to him. Claimt. staid after his Father left the Country. His Father gave it to him lately.

(21).

There was an house, 4 acres and meadow which used to be called 7 acres. Meadow very good, worth £10 per acre. House & Home Lot not so good. He had 2 Cows.

The Rebels Confiscated the Estate & Sold it.

DAVID SCOFIELD, Wits.:

Claimt. is a Loyalist & so is his Father. Knew his Father's Estate some years ago. His Father gave him the Estate before he left the Country. He had a house & Lot & heard of his having some Meadow.

He says his Father gave it up to him, tho' he did not give a Deed, before he went into ye Brit. Lines.

New Claim.

714. Case of GEORGE ANDERSON, late of South Carolina. February 9.

Claimt. says this Claim is for his Father's Estate, is admitted for himself & Sister, they being the Infants.

Claimt. says his Father lived in 96 Dist., S. Carolina. Served in the Brit. Army under Col. King, served about a year, died at Dorchester, was then in the Army.

Left a Widow, since Dead. 1st William, since dead with Children. 2, Claimt. George. 3rd, Elizth. in the States. 4, John, in the States. 5, James, do. 6, David, do. 7, Jane, do. 8, Susan, now with Claimt., aged 7. (22).

Claimt. has served. Served at 96 during the Seige. Was taken ill of the Small Pox, as soon as he got well went to the Army again. Was in the Militia of 96 District. Came from Charles Town to Nova Scotia, is now 23 yrs. of age. Settled on Bell Isle Bay.

His Father had 300 acres on Reedy Branch. His Father went there from Ireland near 20 yrs. ago, drew those Lands. 30 acres were Clear. Says the Eldest Son is heir to the Land.

He had 6 horses, 12 Cows, 24 Cattle, 40 Hogs, 8 Sheep, Corn, Leather, Furniture, Utensils.

Most of these things left on his farm when he went to the

Brit. Some had been taken before they were all taken off by the Rebels.

COL. JOHN HAMILTON:

Knew Claimts. Father, he was a Loyalist, died while in service in the Army. He had a Plantation of 300 acres on Reedy Branch.

His Wife & family were driven from the Place.

The Claimt. is a Loyalist, has served in the Brit. Army.

There were about 40 acres Clear. The Father had lived 15 or 16 yrs. upon it. He brought a pretty property with him into the Country.

Has seen his Estate, it was very considerable.

Claimt. is his Eldest Son now living. The Land goes to the Eldest Son. (23).

Gives the same acct. of the Family.

Susan, the youngest, now lives with Witness.

[703]. Further Evidence in the Case of CAPTN. COCHRAN.

COL. WILLARD, Wits.: February 10.

Claimt. was very forward in giving Intelligence. Joined the Brit. very early. Considers him as perfectly Loyal, no one more so & very active.

The Township of Londonderry was an Extraordinary good Township for Land, the Land was very valuable.

Has been at Claimants Places & knew he had an Estate there.

Thinks them certainly not overvalued at 10 Dollars per acre, exclusive of Buildings. His Land was in a very good part of the Town, near the meeting house. They are common farm houses. Claimt used to let them.
Has understood Claimts. Estate was amongst the first advertized for sale. Thinks the persons in the first Bill of Attainder in New Hampshire were in the same situation as the notorious C—p— in Massts.

(24). Saw the advertisement for sale.

NEW CLAIM.

February 10.   714. Case of MARIA REDOUT, late of Connect.

Claimt. says she came in May, '83. Her Hub., Ephraim Tredwell, came with her. They went up the River, immediately settled on Musquosh Island. Thinks she did not hear of the Act till about 2 years ago.

Her Husb., Ephraim Tredwell, lived in Fairfield Co. He joined the Brit. at Danbury, went with the Army to Long Island. Their Eldest Son went to Danbury with his Father, he died 'n the Brit. service. Her Husband continued at Long Island till he came to this Province. He died in '84 without a Will, leaving

8 Children, the Eldest Son, Mathew, lives with Claimt. now, 24. All the Children are in this Province.

Her Husb. had a farm of 93 acres in North Fairfield. Purchased about 15 years ago. Was in Possession till he went away. Claimt. staid 2 years after him when she went into the Lines with a Flag.

There was a chore house, very good Land, almost all meadow & Plough land. Thinks it is greatly undervalued in her schedule.

Does not know what is become of the Lands. One Bennson was in Possession when she heard.

(25). Left 20 Sheep with a neighbour which she knows nothing of since. Her Husb. was plundered when he lived at Long Island.

Things were taken out of a Vessel which belonged to her Husband. Had a Boat of his own from whence these things were taken, to value of 28.

Lost some Cord Wood, burnt at Eatens Neck, where they staid a little time before they got to Loyds Neck. The Rebels attacked their house there, burnt 10 Cords of Wood.

The Land goes among the Children. She has eight now living Nathaniel. Frederick Samuel live with their Mother, Abel Majorfield, Epheraim in St. John. Rueben with his Mother, Ruth Camb at the Falls. Rebecca with her Mother, Mary with her Mother.

———————

Now lives at Majorfield. Maintains the Children that live with her.

Is told to get Certificate of Confiscation.

NATHANIEL TREDWELL, Wits.:
Says his Father joined the Brit. at Danbury. He could not stay because he was draughted to go into Washington's Army for 9 months, on which he went into the Brit. Lines. He had a Bro. who died in the Brit. service.

His Father continued in the Lines during the War. He died here without a Will. His Father had a house & Land, 33 acres in North Fairfield. His uncle told him the Estate was Confiscated & sold for £100.   (26).

He had 20 Sheep. Knew one Biggs who bought some of them. Witness was draughted into the Militia in which he went off.

His Father was plundered of Things which he was carrying in a Boat which he meant to sell to ye garrison. Lost some things at Eatens Neck, vars. articles, money, Clothes, furniture. Near 10 Cords Wood burnt.

His Mother maintains all the Children here except Witness, who is able to maintain himself. Has tried to get Certificates of Confiscation from the States.

NEW CLAIM.

715. Case of EDWARD STOW, late of Massts.   February 12.

Claimt. says came here in June, '83. Went up the River immediately, continued there all the Winter. Did not hear of the Act till he heard of Capt. Vand going home. He then got a Copy of the Act & sent his Claim by Capt. Vamd. Could not possibly have sent it sooner.

He is a native of England. Has been at Sea from the age of nine till the last 20 or 30 years. Now between 70 & 80 years of age. Is an old Master & Commander.   (27).

Lived at Boston before the Troubles began, from the first declared himself a Friend to Brit. Govt. Had an opportunity under Comrs. of Customs to examine Cargoes going out of Boston.

He seized two Gun Cans., a pair of Swivels & a Cohorn for the use of his Majesty. He was mobbed, insulted & had Libels stuck up at his Door, his house tarred, surrounded & mobbed, his life threatened. Had 2 Centries to guard his Door. Was forced to leave Boston at the Evacuation. Came to Halifax. Went with the Fleet to New York, came from thence in '83. Now settled in this town.

Produces an Appointment from the Comrs. of Customs, Boston, to seize prohibited & uncustomed goods, 17 Jany., 1775.

Produces one of the Libels stuck at his Door abusing him in the grossest terms as an outrageous Tory.

Was Possess of
House, Land, Wharf & Buildings in Orange Street.   No 1.
Produces Deed from Abar. Scamuel to Claimt. of a Tenement or Dwelling House with Land thereto belonging, bounded on Orange Street in Considn. £124, 1758.

(28).

He laid out a great Deal in Improvements, lived upon it. It was a house 3 Story high, there was a store, Chocolate house, Garden, every thing complete. Vals. it at £650 Strg.

Was Possessed of another house in Boston adjoining to the former.

Produces Deed from Thos. Thompson to Claimt. of 2-5 of 2-3 of a Piece of Land & buildings in Orange Street, and likewise 2-5 of 1-3 after the Death of Elizth. Thompson, Mother of Thos. Thompson, who had the same for her Dower in Considn. of £80 lawf., 1768.

Says after the Purchase there was a Partition of the Estate by order of Judge of Probate. An house adjoining No. 1 was allotted to Claimt. for his share and he was to have 2-5 of the part allotted to the Widow after her Death.

No. 2.

He laid out a great Deal about it. Vals. it at 440.

Was also Possessed of a fine house & Land in Cambridge. Produces Deed from Josiah Brown to Claimt. of 2 pieces of Land in Cambridge containing 4 acres with Dwelling house, Barn & Apparts. in Considn. of £146.

Produces Plan by which it appears to measure 5 acres. He says he laid out 1,000 Dollars on these Prems. after he bought them. Vals. it at £225 Stg.

(29),

Produces Certificate of the sale of Claimants Dwelling house & Wharf in Orange Street to Benjamin Thompson for £610.

Claimt. says Benjamin Thompson was one of the Heirs of Thomas Thompson, and he thinks he has continued under this Purchase to get the other house, No. 2, which belonged to his family formerly. He thinks Elizth. Thompson, the Dowress, is living and therefore he cannot produce any Certificates of the Sale of the Lot.

Benj. Thompson having got Possession of this house & the Widow being still living this has not been sold as he imagines.

Produces Certificate of the Sale of the Estate at Cambridge.

He could not remove his Household goods & furniture on the Evacuation of Boston.

He removed his Plate & Some Artices but left a great Deal behind. There was such an Hurry & such Difficulty to remove things that he left he imagines to amount of £100 in Furniture, Tools, Loft Sails, Anchors, Cables, &c., belonging to a small Schooner.

NATHAL. DICKSON, Wits.:

(30),

Knew Claimt. at Boston. Remembers his being harissed, insulted & abused by the Mob on acct. of his Loyalty. He was as good a friend to Government as any man in the world. He met with great abuse on acct. of it.

Knew his 2 houses in Orange Street.

Knew the house where he lived, No. 1.

Grandly furnished, he had a great Deal of good furniture. Knows that he had it, not in his power to get these things away from Boston. It was a Capital house. Remembers hearing that Claimt. had detected some Rebels in carrying ut arms & ammunition & seized them for his Majestie's use. Saw him once attended by a guard to protect him. The Soldiers were obliged to keep off the mob with their Bayonets, they abused & insulted him greatly.

COL. WINSLOW, Wits. Says Claimt. was very active in opposing the rioters at Boston & was in Consequence personally insulted. He was so obnoxious that an Officer of one of the Regiments at Boston was ordered to pay attention to the safety of his Personal Property.

He was appointed to examine ——— going out of Boston, which he executed with fidelity.

NEW CLAIM.

717. Case of JOHN EAGLES, late of New York. February 13.

Claimt. says he left New York in July, 83, bound for Anapolis. Was driven by distress of Weather to Bermuda. Arrived there a little before Xmas. Would have gone to England himself from there had there been any Vessel that started for that Place. Staid there till April, no Vessel went during that time for Europe. Says no Claim was sent home from Bermuda during the time that he was there. Went from Bermuda to Anapolis in April, arrived in May, 84. (31).

Resides near this Town. He is a native American. Resided near the White Plains.

Raised a Company before March, 1776, by Direction of Genl. Tryon. Capt. Banes himself raised above 50 men. Claimt. was to have had Commission as Lieut. in the York Volunteers, but he resigned his Claim in order to get Commission as Capt. in Queen's Rangers. He raised a Company & had a Commission in the Queen's Rangers in Aug., 1776, in 1777 he was superceded with 26 other officers, from that time he remained within the Lines.

Produces Notarial Copy of his Commission as Capt. Queen's Rangers from Sir W. How, 25 Aug., 1776.

Produces Certificates from Col. Robt. Rogers, late King's Rangers, that Claimt. raised his full Company of men in 1776 & was superceded without ye Benefit of a Ct. Martial in 1777, that he acted while under his Command as a Loyal subject & continued his Loyalty tho' after distressed by the Rebls, New York, 1783. (32).

Was Possessed of 2 houses in New York. Produces Lease from Ann Leake to Jos. Gedney of a Piece of Ground in New York for 21 yrs., paying £30 yearly, 1780. No. 1.

With Indorsement by which Joseph Gedney assigns the Premises to Claimt. in Considn. £650 York Cur., May, 1781.

Claimt. says Gedney built an house on the Premises after

No. 2.	he got the Lease which he had not furnished. Claimt. furnished it after he purchased the Lease. Vals. this at £650.
	Was possessed of another house in New York. Produces Lease from the Govrs. of the College at New York to Saml. Ward, of a Lot in New York for 21 years, payment 15 Dollars annually, 20 June, 1780. With Assignment from Saml. Ward to Claimt. in Considn. 5 Gn, 10th May, 1781. He built an house on this Ground afterwards. Vals. it at £400. The first house was Confiscated as the Estate of Joseph Gedney. Produces judgment agst. Joseph Gedney. Says Lewis Morris is in Possession of the second house for Damages done on his Land.
(33).	He produces a Letter from a friend in New York mentioning that Lewis Morris is in Possession of No. 2, as is said for Damages done his Land. He resided on some Land of Ed. Philips, near the White Plains. He lost 4 Cattle at time of Battle of White Plains, thinks the Brit. Troops had them. 15 Sheep, 3 Hogs, lost furniture & farm utensils, cannot give any acct. of them. The Brit. Troops were there. The Americans had the ground first & then the Brit. Lost a mare afterwards. She was stole from the Manor of Fordham.
	One Israel Homvall, who was Comr. of forfeitures, had her. A crop of wheat destroyed at Morrisina by the French & Rebels in the year 80, when the French made a Feint of attacking New York.
	JOSHUA BARNES, Wits.: .
(34).	Claimt. raised men for the York Volunteers together with Witness. Afterwards had a Company of Queens Rangers. He purchased a house of Jos. Gedney at New York. He had another house which he had brought from Morrisina & put it up on some ground which he had hired. He had a fine mare at Morrisina taken by a Dutchman. The mare was taken up by Claimt. by a Writ, and he let him go on the man saying he would pay him. Witness understood that the man who took ye mare sold it to a Rebel officer.
Nothing to be allowed.	Worth £60.
	NEW CLAIM.
February 13.	718. Case of ASHER ALLWARD, late of Jersey.
	Claimt. says he came to this Province in July, '83, staid a week. Went up to Majorville, staid there a year. Came down

once in Novr., staid only 2 or 3 Days. The first he heard of it was when Capt. Vand. was going.

He lived in Woodbridge with his Father, went to Staten Island in the Summer, 1777, within the Brit. Lines. Worked 10 months in the Engineer Department. Continued within the Lines till he came to this Prov. Now settled in this Town.

He had some Property on his Father's farm, he had 4 horses of his own, 3 Cows. They were taken away by the Rebels from his Father's farm at Woodbridge. They were mixt with his Fathers & all taken together.

BENJAMIN ALLWARD, Wits.: (35).

Claimt. ent within the Brit. Lines soon after the Troops had been thro' Jersey. He continued in the Lines. He worked some time in the Engineer Department. He had some Creatures on his Father's farm. His Father allowed him to have them.

719. Case of DAVID COLDEN, ESQ., late of New York.   February 14.

Cadwallader Colden, an Infant of the age of 18, the only son of David Colden, deced., appears by Chief Justice Ludlow, his Guardian. Chief Justice Ludlow being sworn, saith: David Colden was second Son of Lieut. Govr. Colden, of New York. Lived on Long Island at the Commencement of the Rebellion in Queens County. Stood forward in support of Goverment. Exerted all his influence in Queens County to keep the Inhabitants there true to their allegiance. Contributed to prevent Delegates being sent to Congress, and in general Ch. Just. Ludlow speaks of the conduct of David Colden on the Commencement of the Troubles in the highest terms. Speaks of him as one of the most meritorious Loyalists of whom they considered as the head of their Party.   (36).

The trouble increasing, he joined the Brit., being obliged to take Refuge in New York.

During the War for 9 years he was Superintendent of the Police on Long Island in Conjunction with Wits. & so continued till the Evacuation.

He was attained in the first Act. He determined, however, to stay, which the Commander in Chief approved of, but the New Govr. & Lieut. Govr. of New York contrived to get him from Long Island & he went into the neighbouring of New Jersey and in about 6 months he set off for England, taking his Eldest Son, ye Claimt., with him. He arrived there in the summer of 1784. Died soon after his arriving. Witness thinks misfortunes hastened his Death.

No. 1. David Colden was Possessed of a Mansion House & Builds. on Long Island, consisting of 300 acres.

(37).

Produces Deed from John Willet & ors. to Cadwalader Colden of 140 acres on Long Island in Cons. 2,000 York Curcy., dated 1762.

Produces Deed from Thos. Gunel to Do of 23 acres Salt Meadow in Cons. 159£, 1763.

Produces Deed from John Keys to Do of 6 acres Salt Marsh, Cons. 53, 1756.

Produces Deed of Gift from Cadwallader Colden to David Colden of the above Premises, 1770.

Produces Deed from Adam Lawrence to David Colden of 88 acres Upland, 32 Marsh, Cons. 715, 1760.

Produces Deed from Saml. Cornell to Dav. Colden of 13 acres & ½ Upland, Cons. 145£, 12th Oct., 1775.

These include No. 1 in the Schedule.

Cadwr. Colden after his Purchase laid out a great deal in the Improvmts. of this Place. Meant it for his Place of Residence, built largely upon it & fenced it.

The Improvements were made at a great expense. There were two farm houses upon it.

Thinks it upon the whole undervalued in the Schedule when it is estimated at 15£ per acre York Cury.

Thinks it was worth the money to a farmer. The place next to it sold in his opinion at a higher rate.

No. 2. Was Possessed of 1,000 acres in Ulster Co.. They were originally in 2,000 Patent.

Produces Deed from Saml. White to David Colden of ¼ of 4,000 acres on West Side of the ———, Cons. 200£ 1761.

(38).

Produces Deed of Partition by which 1,000 acres is allotted to David Colden, 1765.

These Lands are unimproved. They have been valued as he thinks at 14 Shs. per acre.

Chief Just. Ludlow thinks that unimproved Lands in that neighbourhood may be valued at 14 Sch. per acre.

In Tryon Co.

No. 3. 2 Lots on South Side Mohawk River on a Tract of Butters Purchase.

Produces Deed from Hendrick Crossny, Grantee under the Crown, of 2 Lots to David Colden in Cons. 200£, 1761.

This is Vald. at 4s. per acre.

Produces Deed from Chr. Blundell, one of the general Grantees, to David Colden of 1-8 on a Tract on both sides Mohawk River in Consd. 5 Sh., 1761.

This Consists of 5,000 acres, is Vald. at 8 Sh. per acre.

Produces Deed of 2-13 of 13,000 acres on South Side Mohawk River, Culd. ——— part of McKees Purchase, Consn. 100£, 1770.

Consists 2,000 acres, Val. 4 Sh.

Produces Deed from Isaac Vrooman for Sir Wm. Johnson of 2,000 on North Side Mohawk River, Consn. 100£, 1770.

(39).

Val. at 4 Sh. per acre.

Divers Lots in Col. Croghan's Patent. Produces Deed from Cadwalr. Colden, Jr., to David Colden of several Lots in Col. Croghan's Patent in Consn. 10 Sh., Decer., 1775.
Val. 2 Sh. per acre.
Produces Deed from Col. Croghan to David Colden of Lot No. 4. Consist. of 1,000 acres in Township of Belvedere, Consn. 50£, 1772.
Vals. 3 Sh. per acre.
All these Lots in Tryon Co. are new Lands & unimproved.
No. 4. Albany Co.
Was Possessed of Seven Lots in Snyder's Patent.

Produces Deed from C—— Brush of 7 Lots in Co. of Albany on East Side of Hudson River part of 10,000 acres granted to Henry Snyder, Consn. 100£, dated 1762. Contained 1,000 acres. One of these lots has been leased in 1767 at 7.10 per Ann., Rent to commence 5 yrs. after ye Date. Vals. at 8 Sh. per acre.
Only one of these Lots has been let.
No. 5. In Charlotte, Cumberland & Gloucr. Cos.
Produces Deed from Thos. Chandler to David Colden reciting a Patent granted to Thos. Chandler & ors. in July last past of 1,000 acres in ⸺ons. 20£, Dec., 1766.

(40).

Produces Deed from And. Myers to Dav. Colden of 1-7 of 6,900 acres in Whittingham Towns. in Cons. 50, 1770.
From Cornelius Ryerson of 1-29, being 1,000 acres in Readsborough Patent in Cons. 50, 1772.
From Peter Stoutenbouyt of 1,000 acres in Hilsboro in Cons. 50£, 1770.
From John Willet of 1,000 acres in Dunmore, Cons. 50, 1770.
From Robt. Doughty & Geo. Hicks, of 4,000 acres in Besboro, Cons. 100, 1770.

From John Kelly, of 2,000 acres in Kingsborough in Cons. 162, 1771.
From Dr. Bunekerhoff, of 1,000 acres in Halton, Cons. 50£, 1770.
These Lands in Vermont are Valued at 3 sh. & 3d. per acre.
All these Grants are Grants from New York Govt.
Chief Justice Ludlow says in a Contest in the year 1773, when there were several Ejectments brought for Lands in Bennington which involved the Question between the Rights of New York & New Hampshire, he endeavoured at a Compromize & he took all the Pains he could to form a Valuation of the unimproved Lands, which he fixt at last after the best Information he could obtain at 1 Dollar per acre.
Mr. Colden had no other Title but under the above mentioned Deeds. Had no immediate Tenants.
All the above Articles David Colden possessed by Purchase. He was entitled to other Property under the Will of Cadwallader Colden, Sr., his Father.
Produces Probate of the Will of Cad. Colden, Whereby he gives 1-5 of his real & personal Estate to his Son, David Colden.

(41).

No. 1.

Does not mention the consideration.

(42).

(43).

In Tryon Co.
Cadwallader Colden, Snr., was possessed of 5 Lots of Glens Patent.
Produces Patent to Patrick Maclaghey & Andrew MacDowen of 5 Tracts in Glens Patent, 1783.
Produces Certificate from Caderwallader Colden, Jur., that he had the Deed from Pat. Maclaghey & And. MacDowen to Caderwallr., Senr., formerly in his Possession, but could not procure it. Certifies that the sd. Conveyance was a Conveyance of all the Lands granted to Pat. Maclaghey & And. MacDowen.
David Colden's share in these Lots amts. to 965 acres. Val. at 8 Sh. per acre.
Produces a Deed from Col. Croghan to Cadwallader Colden of 40,000 in Tryon Co. in Cons. 1,840 in 1771.
Produces Original Patent to Skinner & from thence to Geo. Croghan in 1770. David Colden's share is 7,788. Vals. at 2 Sh. Cader. Colden had 6,000 acres by Deed from John Kelly, 23rd Sep., 1775.
Produces Certificates taken before a Notary Public from Geo. Falliett & Phil. Kearney of their having inspected a Deed from John Kelly, Cadwllr. Colden, of 6,000 acres near the Susquehana, Tyron Co., Sep., 1775.

David Colden's share amounts to 1,200 acres. Val. at 2s. 6d.
Caderwallader Colden was in Possession of 2 Tracts in Dunmore of 9,000 & in Hillsbora of 9,000.
No. 2. Produces Certificates from Geo. Falliot & Phil. Kearney, attested before a Notary Public, of their having inspected the Conveyances of Cadwallader Colden of the above mentioned Tracts in Dunmor & Hillsbora in 1770 & Conveyance of 5,331 acres in Readsborough in 1783, in Trust for the Legatees under the Will of Cadwallador Colden. Dav. Colden's share in the 2 first Tracts is 3,600 acres. 1,066 acres in the Readsborough Lands. Vald. at 3s. 3d. per acre.
Cadawallader Colden Ser. died in the Fall 1776 he appointed Cadawallader Colden, Jun., David Colden & Eliz. Delancey Execrs.
Cadawallader Colden was the only acting Execr. He possessed himself of the Personal Estate of the Testr.
David Colden died in London in 1784, leaving Cadawallader D. Colden, the present Claimt., his Eldest Son, now settled in St. Johns, Alice Colden in New York Prov., Mary Colden do, Eliz. Ann. do, Catharine do.

His Wife survived him but is since dead.
Produces Will of David Colden, Whereby he gives all his Lands in the Cos. of Ulster, Albany & Tryon to Claimt. in fee, except the Lands comprized in his Father's Will.
He gives the Flushing Estate & the Estate left by his Fathers Will and his personal Estate, except a few Legacies to his Wife, Claimt. & 4 Sisters in equal shares.
The Flushing Estate is that in Long Island.
The Lands in Charlotte, Cumberland & Gloucester, except those in Readsboro, to his Wife & 4 daughters in equal shares.

The Readsboro Lands to Claimt. He appoints Cadwallader (44).
Colden, Jr., Chief Justice Ludlow & his Wife & Mr. Watts his
Executors.

The 4 Daughters are now Infants, living with their uncle,
Cadwallader Colden, in New York. The outstanding Debts due
to Cader. Colden, Ser., amount to 7,468. David Colden is entitled
to 1-5.

David Coldens personal Estate.

Outstanding debts £579, the rest of the personal Estate has
been in a great measure disposed of in maintaining the family.

David Colden had the office of Surveyor General of New
York, to which he was appointed in 1774, during good Behavior.

Produces Grant of the office dated 20 Decer., 1774.

Govr. Tryon was then at home. The Lieut. Govr., Cadwallader Colden, made this Grant to his Son.

Col. Fanning was at home & procured the appointment by means of Govr. Tryon.

His grant was antedated so as to bear date before the appointment of David Colden. This was done by the Treasury at home and it was a grant during pleasure. (45).

The annual profits from this office would have been at least £500. If arrears are to be allowed it would be for 10 years.

The Chief Justice says that he applied for a Pension for the Widow & Children of David Colden, which he thought he should have procured, as the merits of David Colden had been so very eminent.

But as the Widow & daughters were in the States of New York he could not procure it. He procured £30 pension for the Son, whom he left in England with Col. Farmington.

The Son applied to the Board that he might have his Pension continued when at New York, which was not allowed, & by going without that Leave he lost his Pension.

The Chief Justice says he left him without much money to support him & he believes Col. Farington was rather tired of keeping him, or of contributing to his suport, & gave him leave or rather wished him to go.

The Chief Justice sent for him from New York; has been appointed his Guardian by the Govr. here, and has placed him with Wiley to study law, and now supports him. As far as his right as Guardian goes, he means to keep him here and he is satisfied that the young man himself has no thoughts of returning.

Claimant himself speaks of his determined Resolution to abide (46).
under the British Government.

Chief Justice says. He should have sent for the children if he could have got a pension for them. They are now supported on the Charity of their Uncle. The eldest daughter is to come here this summer. The rest of the family would come hither if they could have nothing to support them. As far as his Power goes he means they should.

The Uncle who has supported them in ye States has a Family of his own.

Chief Justice Ludlow certifies by Letter to the Commrs. that

4 Miss Coldens are arrived in New Brunswick, Nov. 27.

COL. LUDLOW, Wits.:

Agrees with Chief Justice in his acct. of David Colden's Loyalty & Services.

He was one of about 12 or 14 who made a Protest against a Provincial Congress. Was very well acquainted with the Property on Long Island. Was called upon once to Value it with Mr. Maceons; they vald. it at 4,500. Thinks it is worth that since Nov. 27. Produces Certificate of Sale of David Colden's Estate in Queen's County.

(47).

NEW CLAIM.

February 15.

720. Case of ALEX. MONTGOMERY, late of New York.

Claimt. says he came to this Province May '83. Went up the River to Burton very soon. Staid there all the Winter. Never came to this City once during ye Winter. Had no opportuntiy of sending by Capt. Vand—. Sent it by him. He is a native of Ireland. Came to America in 1754; lived in Spencer Town when Troubles. Declared his sentiments at first in favour of Govrt. Was summoned often & often before their Committees for being a Tory. Was too old to serve himself but sent his two sons into the British service. They were taken Prisoners & kept in Prison 18 months. Claimt. supplied them with necessaries while they were at Pughkeepsie.

His sons sent him a Letter, which fell into the hands of the Rebels, and on that acct. they persecuted him more & more. Left his house and went to his mother in law's. Staid there two months. On his return home they sd. he had been with the enemy. 30 people came armed to take him. He jumped out of a window, made his escape into ye woods & got to the Sound, & was going in a Boat to Long Island; was taken prisoner, carried back; then lost his papers, but made his escape. Got into ye Brit. Lines. Continued there till he came to this Province.

(48).

Had a Lot of Land with house & Buildings in Spencer Town. Containing 78 acres. Gave a Deed of it to one John Taylor before he left home. He did this in order to secure it. Sold it for £400, not half the value, and has not received any part of the money. He had taken Lands in exchange for others since ye Commencement of ye War. Gave Lands that cost him £800 for them.

Had a Lot in Col. Jessup's Patent above Albany, Purchased 3 years before the War of Col. Jessup; this lies in Kaiodyrascras.

Purchased at 5sh. York money pr. acre. He paid Col. Jessup by furnishing provisions for him & his servts., by finding him Board & Lodging. Says two men have been put upon it & have made some improvements. Claimt. was never there himself.

Says it would have brought 20s. pr. acre before ye War began.

Lost Wheat in the Barn taken from him as being a Tory; taken for the use of the Continental Army. Vals. about £20.

Lost a Mare, taken from him while making his escape. (49).

Produces Copy of Deposition of one Thomas Gardiner to his Knowledge of Claimt. being possessed of the Lands mentioned in his Schedule.

NEW CLAIM.

721. Case of ALEXANDER MONTGOMERY, Jun., late of New York. February 15th.

Evidence De Bene Esse.

Alex. Montgomery, Snr., says his son came here in Sumr., '83. Went up the River. Is now settled at Gage Town. He served with Col. Uphraim & Col. Hewlet on Lloyds Neck, and on Expeditions in different Places almost all the War.

Gresham Lockwood, Father of Witness' wife, left by will a Lot of Land of 10 acres in Greenwich to Witnesses' wife. She dying in his Life Time he added a codicell that is was to go amongst his children.

Testr. died about the beginning of the War. One David Brown was in Possession of the Lot in Trust for Witness. Children by Witness' order says that he gave security in £700 to act as Guardian for his children to the Cr. of Probat, but never got possession himself, but directed David Brown to take possession. (50).

David Brown has left it as Witness believes; perhaps his Brother in Law may be in Possession, one Willm. Hurry, who has married Witness' sister.

There was 16 acres notmen tioned in the Will, which will go amongst all the Children; there were 9 children. Witness' wife was one of the children. John, his eldest son, now amongst the Genoese, Alexander, the Claimt., Archibald, aged 22, at sea; Hugh, infant, at Sea; David, infant, here; Mary, married, in the States; Sarah & Susannah now here.

Knew the Lot of Land in Greenwich very well; thinks it is vald. at 6£ pr. acre.

Vals. it at that.

The 16 acres were more valuable; they were valued at £15 pr. acre.

His son, Alexr., was taken Prisoner when endeavouring to make his escape within the Brit. Lines.

Lost Cash, &c., to amt. of £20. He was taken Prisoner a 2nd time while on Government service. Suffered a long Imprisonment.

Witness says he had furnished him with money to carry him off within the Brit. Lines.

His son is very ill with a swelling in his arm & could not come to St. Johns.

NEW CLAIM.

February 15.   722. Case of PETER BERTON, late of New York.

Claimt. says he came here June '83. Went up St. Johns River about 24 miles, at Oak Point. Came down in the first part of the Winter, thinks after Xmas.

Says he staid but one night. Knew of no opporty. but of Cap†. Vand.'s, but Capt. Vand was gone.

He is a native of America. Has been in the sea faring Line. Has been master of a ship since the year 1756 to 1770. Was settled at New York as mercht. at the commencement of the War. Declared in favr. of Brit. Govrt.

He was called upon to take a Commission in the Rebel Militia, which he refused. This made him suspected. He was persecuted, & he thought he could not stay safely any longer. Went to Long Island in Feby., 1776. May following was obliged to secret himself till Brit. Troops came. Then took Possession of his Place again & continued in Long Island. Came here Capt. of Loyalists.

(52). Produces his Commission. Produces Protections for himself & family after Brit. Troops arrived in Long Island.

Was possessed of a Farm in Long Island; purchased part in 1776 & part in 1780; about 22 acres near New Town; cost him £1,500 New York Mon. Only 300 pd. in Congress Mon. Vals. it at 1,500.

It has been seized by one Frances Lewis, who was one of the joint owners with Claimt. of Sloop Dolphin, which was taken by his Majesty's ship Argo. He says the sloop was sent to sea against his consent & therefore he has a claim on Claimt. for the Loss & has seized his Land on that acct. Supposes he got judgment against him for a Debt.

Was possessed of 5-8 of Sloop Commerce, 60 tons. She was taken Oct., 1775, by his Majesty's ship King Fisher at Sandy Hook on her return from Charles Town, with the Corps of Col. Edw. Fenwick.

Mr. Thos. Ming then & now of New York had the other 3-8 Capt. Mountague brought her into New York in the year 1776. Claimt. asked what right he had to her. He said she was condemned at Halifax.

(53). Produces the orders of the Capt. of the Sloop by which he is dir'cted to carry the Body of Col. Fenwick to Charles Town & to return as soon as he can to take Passengers back, but no goods.— 10 July, 1775.

She was ready to return when she was taken possession of by orders of a Rebel Committee & employed by them 27 or 28 days; thinks this was the Pretence for Capt. Mountague's seizing it.

Produces Bill of Sales of the whole Sloop Commerce for £133 from the ship builders, Robert Baker & Thos. Dodge, 1774.

This was only for the Hull. The Rest of the Expense in fitting her for Sea amoun s to above £770. Vals. her at £800 as fit for Sea.

Claimt. has sold 3-8 and is entitled to 5-8.

Had ½ the Sloop Ranger. Burthen, bet. 40 & 50 tons. Had left her to Wm. Vandeusent, who was removing to Amboy. He was to pay 30 Shils. pr. Day & to run the risk of her being ship wrecked.

She was taken in March, 1776, by his Majesty's ships at Sandy Hook. She was scuttled & sunk.

Produces Bill of Sale of 1-4 for £60 in 1774; of his original 1-4 from the ship builder for £25.

Vals. his half at £120 when sunk. (54).

Was possesed of 1-8 of the Dolphin, burthen, 120 tons. She was on her passage to England from a Whaling Voyage to the Coast of Brazil & taken by his Majesty's ship Argo in March, 1776, at Dominica & there condemned.

Produces office copy of Condemnation of Sloop Dolphin & her cargo as belonging to persons inhabiting within the Province of New York, by the Admiralty Court at Dominica, 18 March, 1776.

He had 1-8 of the Dolphin, the other 7-8 belonged to persons who were friends to the Rebel Cause. Claimt. was ship's Husband, and as such had the Direction of her.

Vessel & cargo was consigned to Neave & Co., London. Her Cargo was 256 Barls. Spermacets Head matter.

Vals. the vessel at £1,500
The Cargo 1,536
                                                                1,260

She sailed from New York, Aug., 1775. The Custom House was then open and it was properly cleared then.

Thinks the Custom House was shut soon after. Thinks there was no Rebel Custom House at New York during ye War.

Had £100 Int. in the Whaling Copany at New York, bought in 1773 & 1774. The Co. consisted of 60 or 70 subscribers. Their (55). stock was about £10,000. The Co. had 4 Brigs., 2 Sloops; they had made one voyage; were on the 2d., when most of the vessels were taken by ye King's ships. One Sloop got back with her cargo; this was divided amongst the Proprietors, but the Tories were excluded.

Lost 5,350 Square feet white oak, 9 masts, &c., intended for the use of the Navy at home. This was on Carter's Hook in Feby., 1776, when Claimt. left New York. Part was taken by the Rebels, part carried on board his Majesty's transports, part was carried into ye King's Yard.

Had 8 4-pounders; they were seized by a Rebel Committee in the Winter, 1776; taken from Ross's Wharf.

He had 2 Boxes of Small Arms which he destroyed to prevent their getting into the Hands of the Rebels.

Had goods in his store when he quitted New York, according to his Inventory. They were all taken after he went away. He heard that two Captns. of Privateers with their crew broke open

(56) the store & divided the stores between them; even fought for them; they were almost all in the shipping way.

Had a little store in Long Island which was plundered in Aug., 1776; thinks they were general plunderers. Was plundered of a Penace & Pettiangre in New Town Creek about ye same time.

(721.) Continuation of Evidence in Case of ALEXR. MONTGOMERY, Jnr.

February 15.   CAPT. IVES, Wits.:

Speaks of Alexander & Archibald; they served within his Knowledge. Came very young to the Army. They were very Loyal & good young lads.

JAMES HAIT, Wits.:

Remembers their both serving; they were very active & serviceable; the 2 Montgomeries were mentioned as excellent soldiers.

Knew a man at Greenwich of the name of Gersham Lockwood. He was a man of some property. Speaks of their bravery in boarding a French vessel in the Sound; the number on board were double that of the asasilants; the vessel was taken.

NEW CLAIM.

February 16.   723. Case of AZOR. BETTS, late of New York.

Claimt. Says. He came to this Province in May, '83. He was in the Physical Line. Went up the River in 3 weeks. Continued there that summer & the ensuing Winter. Sent by Capt. Vand; had no opportunity before—did not hear of it before.

(57).

He is a native of America. Settled in New York in the Practice of Physcn. From the first declared in Favour of Brit. Govrnt. Was confined by a Committee for carrying Intelligence on Board the Duchess of Gordon & Asia., and for attempting to spike same at King's Bridge. Was banished to Œsopus by the Provincial Congress. He returned to New York. Was confined again. Made his escape just before New York was taken. Got to the Brit. & came in with them.

Was made Surgeon of Queen's Rangers by Genl. How; was afterwards suspended with many other officers.

Had a Warrant as a Capt.'s Lieut. in the King's American Rangers. He recruited men in consequence of this Warrant.

Was 18 months at the Post at Morrisina as Surgeon by Request of Col. Delancey & Major Haggerford.

There being a great want of a Surgeon at Morrisina, he got Leave of Absence to go there, where he acted as Surgeon. Came away in the first Fleet to this Place.

(58).   After his return from Œsopus the Claimt. was tried by the Provincial Congress for carrying Intelligence to ye Enemies &

was sentenced to die, and was lying in Gaol under that sentence just as the Brit. troops came.

About the time of his first confinement by order of the Committee, the Rebel Barrack Master went and broke open his house.

His Books, his Medicines & furniture were lost at that time. The damage done to him was at least £50. They went in search of him & were attacked by a mob.

Was in Possession of a house in New York jointly with Capt. Purdie. Began it in 1779. It was on Corporation ground with a reserved Rent of ½ a Joe, payable after ye War. This was finished in that & the ensuing year.

This hou e he Vals. at £600; Claimt.'s share at £300. His Practice was worth £500 per ann.

NEW CLAIM.

724. Of CAPT. DAVID IVES, of New York. February 16.

Claimt. says came in May, '83. Went up the River to Oro, 2 months. Staid there; did not come down in the Winter. Sent by Capt. Vand.; this was the first he heard of the Act.

He is a native of America. When troubles broke out was in Charlotte Co., now Vermont. Informed the Comr. at Ticonderago that General Arnold was coming against that place. Went to Canada. Joined the Brit. under Genl. Carelton the Sumr. after. Was employed by Genl. Carleton to carry Despatches into the Country. Did not get back that Winter. The next Spring was taken Prisoner; was tried for his life under Genl. Wayne at Ticonderago & condemned & was under sentence of Death, when Genl. Burgoyne came before that place. Was then forwarded to Albany & so to Œsopus & thence to Litchfield. Was released there on giving Bail of £1,000. A year after he got to New York. Was at first in Quarter Master's Department, during (59).

which time he was taken Prisr. & carried to Hertford Gaol. Kept 3 months.

Afterward had a Commission as Captn. in the Associated Loyalists. Servd. at Lloyds Neck, first under Major Hubble, then Major Upham. Servd. till end of the War. Now settled in Burton.

Had 1,000 acres in Township of Shoreham, Charlotte Co., Vermont.

Had cleared & improved 20 acres. Purchased 2 Rights & ½ in Shoreham Township for 15£ a Right. Purchased of one Rose, 3 yrs. before the war. 2 Rights & ½ contained 1,000 acres.

Had 100 acres in Puttney purchased for 25£ 3 yrs. before the war. (60).

100 acres in Wells bought of Titus Ives. He bought 300 acres for £4.10, & sold 200 for 30£. Claims for ye other 100 acres.

375 acres in Mouleton, purchased for 15£ 3 years before the war.

The patentees of whom he purchased held under New Hampshire Grants.

He had a considerable Stock in Shoreham Township when he was beginning his Improvmts.

4 Oxen & 1 horse, were taken by the Committee when he was taken Prisoner & carried to Ticonderago.

Farming utensils taken at same time sold at Vendue.

2 Cows were taken in Connect. on pretence of a Debt. All his Lands in Vermont have been sold as he hears for payment of Taxes.

When taken Prisoner while serving in Quarter Master Generals Department lost Cloaths & some horses. These horses were hired by Claimant & James Hoyte of two persons who have brought an action against Hoyte & he has brought an action against Claimt. & obtained Judgement in the inferior Court at Sunbury.

JOSHUA BLISS, ESQ.:

(61). Certifies to his activity & Loyalty & good character. Served a year or more under Witness at Lloyds Neck. He was very spirited & ready to do his duty.

723. Continuation of AZOR. BETTS.

MRS. WITMAN, Witness:

Remembers Claimt. at New York. Distinguishes himself early by his Loyalty. He was continually harrasd. Amongst the first persecuted.

Remembers his being carried before a Committee before he was banished to Œsopus.

His house was very well furnished. She heard he had his Things taken away & destroyed.

He was in good Business. Had a great Deal in the Insartation way.

Geo. Leonard certifies to his bravery & conduct as an officer & Loyalist.

722. Continuation of Case of PETER BERTON.

WILLIAM PAGAN, ESQ., Wits:

Knew Claimt. He was an active Steady Loyalist. He was formerly Master & Commander of a ship belonging to Leave & Co.

(62). Afterwards set up as a merchant. Did Business with Leave & Co., Merchts. in Land.

Remembers that he had a share in the Sloop Commerce. As far as he recollects of the Sloop should suppose it cost between 7 & 800£ fit for Sea.

Remembers that he was concerned in a Sloop employed in the whaling Business. Thinks it probable that this vessel was Consigned to Neave & Co.

Is of 120 Tons Burthen & completely fitted out for the Whaling Business. Thinks this Sloop might be worth 1,500 or near it. The Cargo as described in the Schedule was very valuable.

Speaks highly of his Character as a man & his public conduct. He had a share in the Whaling Co. of 100£.

A NEW CLAIM.

725. Case of DANL. SMITH, late of Connect. February 16.

Claimt. says. Came in May, '83. Went to Majorfield. Never heard of the act till Dr. Betts told him that Capt. Vand was going home. Sent his Claim by him. He was down here, but it was on business. He made no stay, but returned directly. (63).

Lived in New Milford, Lichfield Co., Connect., when Troubles broke out. Declared at first in Favr. of Brit. Govert. Was one of the opposers of Committees. Was before their Committees & confined.

In 1776 went to Long Island. It was the Day Fort Washington was taken. Was employed in bringing off Loyalists, the ensuing winter. Had a Warrant for raising men in Connect—he ———— a good many. In March, 1777, was apprehended—Broke Gaol after a Confinement of some months, got within the Lines in Octr. Lived in Long Island & New York.

Went out occasionally on various expeditions. Served as a guide in the exped. against New Haven, Fairfield & Norwalk. Continued within the Lines till end of the war, except the time that he was kept as a Prisoner.

Now settled in Burton.

Was Possessed of a House & Lot in New Milford, consisting of 113 acres.

Produces Deed from Eliz. Taylor to Claimt. of a Tract in New Milford, part of Lot No. 21, containing 14 acres & ½; Considn. 20£.   No. 1.

Produces Deed from Elnathan Curtis to Claimt. of 108 acres in Cons. 210£, 1762.   (64).

Produces Deed from Elnathan Curtis to Claimt. of 2 acres & 1 Quarter, with a Dwelling house; Cons. 90£, 1762.

One acre & ¼ of this was taken for a Debt. 8 acres purchased by his wife from ye Commrs. Therefore he deducts these 2 parcels. Claims now for 113 acres. He had laid out a great Deal cf Money in Improvemts. He had kept a public house.

Vals. it at 1,000£ lawful.

Produces Copy of Writ to Sheriff &c. of Lichfield to seize Claimt.'s real estate, he having joined the Ministerial Army 1777, with Indorsement by the Constable that he had seized several Pieces of Land & Dwelling House of Claimts.

Produces a Lease of Claimt.'s Estate for a year from the Admr. in the year 1780 at £10.16 per an. Part of the Estate had been disposed of before this.

Produces a Lease from 2 of the Committee in 1777 of part of Claimt.'s estate for one year at 10£.

His Wife was allowed part for her dower, but on his coming away, the whole is to be sold, & his son had a Letter that says it was advertized for sale since Claimt.'s Wife came away.   No. 2.

He had a Farm in Kent Township, Lichfield Co. Produces Deed from Saml. Courwims of 55 acres in Kent in Cons. 88£, 1769.

(65).   He Conveyed away some little part himself. Pt. was taken for a Debt which reduced it to 47 acres. Produces Deed from Jethro Hatch & others to Claimt. & Jonathan Wright of 96 acres in Cons. 33£, 1773.

Says he paid the whole money, Wright paying none. Acknowledged here before a Justice that the whole belonged to Claimt.

Produces Writ to ye Sheriff to seize Claimt.'s Real Estate in Kent, March, 1777, with endorsement by Constable that he had seized 49 acres & ½, 96 acres.

Had Lands in Susquehana. Bought a Right Pierse, Son of one of the first Patentees, for 12£ 5 years before the Troubles. It lies on the outskirts towards the Indians. The settlers there have been drove off by the Indians. Had a Deed of it. It consisted of 2,000 acres. Nothing had been done but laying out Lots.

His moveables were seized at New Milford. Produces Writ from Justice of Peace to Sheriff &c. to attach Claimt.'s personal estate, Jany., 1777.

(66).   With Indorsement by the Constable of several things which he seized.

His Wife got back some of the things mentioned in the Return by the Constable but he lost all the things mentioned in his Schedule. The wheat mentioned in the Schedule taken at Kent was growing on ye ground.

Says there were no Debts, but what he has before mentioned.

Mentions several persons who are now in Possession of his Estate, who have purchased different Parts.

CALEB MALLORY, Wits:

Knows Claimt. He was from the first a Loyalist. Remembers his opposing Committees. He was taken up & confined. He went in the year 1776 within the Lines.

Afterwards was employed in raising men in Connect.

He served on several Expeditions. Served frequently with Witness.

Knew No. 1. Remembers him in Possession. Thinks somewhere about 120 acres. A very valuable farm; almost the whole was under Improvemt. Vals. it at 1,000£.

Knew his other farm in Kent, but not so well. Not so valuable as No. 1, nor so much Improved. Vals. it at 3£ per acre.

These Estates have been sold. Witness has privately been there & heard of its being sold. Was in the county when it was

(67).   Confiscated.

JOEL MURRAY, Wits:

Knew Claimt. He was always considered very Loyal. Suffered Confinement on acct. of it. Knew his Estate at New Milford, upwards of 100 acres; very valuable; almost all Improved. Vals. it at 10£ per acre.

He had another Farm in Kent not so valuable. Vals. it at 3£ per acre.

He was in very good circumstances. Had a good stock & good furniture. Was in the Country when Claimt.'s Estate was Confiscated. It was bought in different parcels by different People. It was taken from his Wife, first let, afterwards sold.

Remembers different Persons in Possession of different Parcels who purchased it. A Rebel Col., Col. Star, had part given him.

NEW CLAIM.

726. Case of DAVID HARKEY, late of North Carolina. February 17.

Claimt. says. He came in the 2nd Fleet. Went up the River before the winter. Came down once. Never heard a word till he heard of Capt. Vand. Sent by him. (68).

He lived in New Montgomery, North Car. Joined the Brit. Army under Lord Cornwallis in S. Car. in '80. Raised a Company of men as Militia in the back Country. His men were defeated. He made his escape himself & joined the Brit. in Cambleton. Staid with Ld. Cornwallis till taken Prisr. at York Town. Had 25 men under him. Was in the Commissary Department. Was 19 months Prisr. before he got to New York. Now settled on Grand Bay.

Produces a letter from Charles Stedman to shew he was concerned in the Commissary Department.

Had 300 acres in New Montgomery. Bought of Geo. Crouch in 1777, for 60£ & a horse. His Wife & children were driven off & the Land sold.

Lost 7 horses, 3 Cows & 7 Cattle, Mon. & Cloaths, Wagon, Furniture. All left behind when he went to join the Brit.. Corn in the ground.

HENRY UNDERWOOD, Wits:

Remembers Claimt. in Lord Cornwallis's Army. He had a Company of men under him in the Commissary Department. He had a Commission signed by Booth, by Lord Cornwallis order. He continued with Ld. C. till taken. Heard he had been raising Militia before he came to Lord Cornwallis. Heard he had lived very well & had a pretty Plantation. He was raising men & was to have a Company. (69).

ST. JOHN, 17TH FEBY., 1787.

This is to certify that I know David Harkey in North Carolina and that I believe him to be a Loyal Subject and have heard that he lost much in Consequence thereof.

DAVID FANNING.

(The original of which this a Copy is included in the Vol. C. H.)

NEW CLAIM.

February 17.   727. Case of CHARLES VINCENT, late of New York.

Claimt. says. Came here in July. Went up the River 40 miles. Came down in the winter. Never knew of any opportunity till he heard of Capt. Vand, but it was then too late. Now lives on the Kennebaccasis.

Lived in Dutchess Co. Joined the Brit. soon after the Battle of White Plains. He was so persecuted he could not stay. He continued within the Lines. Now & then went home privately.

(70). Served occasionally under Col. Delancey & Col. Emerick. Brought men in for them. Conducted some of Burgoyne's Prisoners to New York.

Had 200 acres in Dutchess Co. It was a tenant farm held of Mr. Rt. Gibb Livingston. Had a Lease for 3 Lives. Bought about 10 years ago, just before the war. One of the 3 Persons was dead when he bought the Lease. Gave 230£ for it. Paid it all before he came away. Some York Pap. Mon., some Jersey Pap. Money; all before ye war. Vals. it at near 500.

Had a house & 6 Lots in New York. Produces Lease from Geo. Stanton, Attorney, from Jas. DeLancey to Claimt. of 6 Lots for 21 yrs., paying 9£ annually. 24 July, 1782.

Had a Negroe Wench & Boy in Dutchess Co. His Father gave them to him. She would not come away & therefore his Wife was forced to leave her behind. Lost Wagon, Cart, yoake of oxen.

Taken for the use of the Rebel Army.

JOHN MASTIN, Wits:

(71). Knew Claimt. He was always a Loyalist. Suffered greatly He joined the Brit. very soon. He piloted Loyalists frequently within the Lines. Piloted Burgoyne's men within ye Lines.

He had a Leased Farm in Dutchess Co. Thinks he bought it of one Vincent long before the war. He was reckoned a Considerable Farmer.

He had a black girl & child.

Says the Landlord would add a new Life in the Lease for 5£. He had Cattle.

Capt. Vandenburg speaks highly of Claimt.'s Loyalty. He was serviceable in getting intelligence from the Country. The officers used to place great confidence in him. He was very useful. Col. Emerick often employed him.

NEW CLAIM.

February 17.   728. Claim of PHILIP SUMMERS, late of Jersey.

Claimt. says he came in Fall 83—went up to Majorford—sent his claim by Capt. V.

Lived in New Jersey, joined the Brit. when Genl. How came to Brunswick, was first under Genl. Meadows, acted for him. Was a soldier undr Col. Allen 7 years.

Had a house at Bound brook & 5 acres & 3-4 Land. Purchased of Henry Simpson, he gave £577 Prov. Mon. Paid at 3 times. Purchased in the year 1772.

His house was burnt. The Rebels have taken the Land. The furniture was sold at Vendue, Baker 1, Tools, &c. Had a Cow & 1 Horse. (72).

Produces affit. Geo. Bridges Rodney that Claimt. had a house Barn, &c. & 5 acres 3-4 Land in Bound brook bought of Henry Simpson.

Col. Winslow certifies that Geo. Br. Rodney is a man of Character & credit.

That Claimt. declared his sentiments openly at first—Was forward in assisting those persons who hoisted the King's Flag. Was confined, refused taking the Oath to the Rebels. Served afterwards during the War. His house was burnt on acct. of his Loyalty & a small stock & furniture taken. Col. Allen certifies to his having served under him. Understood he had property, Conjectured about £100.

NEW CLAIM LODGED AT HOME.

729. Case of JACOB BULL, late of New York.

Claimt. says—He came in 83. Went up the River; heard nothing till he heard of Capt. Vand. sent his Claim by him. February 17.

Lived in Duchess Co. Always joined the Brit. Had a Son in Col. Robinson's Regimt. Another Son with Col Delancey.

Went within the Lines, moved to Long Island. His wife & Chldren were sent to hm. Was so persecuted that he was frequently obliged to secrete in Woods. Was summoned before the Committees. Lives at the Grand Lak—.

Had 2 Tenant farms in Dutchess Co. under Robt. G. Levinston. 1 Lease of 120 acres for 3 Lives. Purchased of Christian Sacchorader, gave 300£ for it many years ago, 21 years ago, made great Improvements since. Not one of the Leases was out. Ther were fine Meadows. It was near the road which made it valuable. (73).

Vals. it at 650£.

2nd Lease for 150 acres & 50 acres Timberland. This was a lease for 3 Lives bought of the Widow Haws for 135£ 25 years ago.

Vals. it under 400£.

Says in his Memorial he Vald. his farm at £700.

There was a good house & Tan Yard on the second farm.

Had a Stock, 1 Yoke of Oxen, 1 of Steers, 10 Cows, 9 horses, 60 Sheep, 7 Hogs, Farming Utensils, Carts. These Things were seized by Comt. & sold.

Had 60£ Debts owing to him.

ABRAHAM VAN AMBURG.

Knew Claimt. He was reckoned very Loyal, and was obliged to quit his home on Acct. of his Loyalty. He had been much persecuted.

(74).
Knew one of his Farms. The first he bought many years ago. Thinks it 100 & odd acres, good Land & buildings. Such a Farm would sell for £400. Knew that he had another farm above the other. He had a very good stock. A Considerable Flock of Sheep.

He was a man in very good circumstances.

CAPT. VANDERBURG Wits.

Heard he had two excellent farms well stocked. Heard him always considered as a very honest man. Heard of his Stock & its being seized.

Has heard from his Father that he was very Loyal in his Principals. Says these Leases sold very high, almost equal to the soil right. About ½ the val. of fee simple.

725. Continuation of Case of PETER BERTON.

COL. LUDLOW says Claimant had been Master & Commander of a Ship & was settled as a merchant in New York. Speaks of him as a man of Integrity & very Loyal, decided Loyalist from the first.

726. Continuation of Case of DR. AZOR BETTS.

CAPT. RICHD. VANDERBURG.

(75).
Remembers Claimt. settled in Business at New York. He was a very zealous active Loyalist. Speaks of his services as being very great & distinguished. Understood his Practice had been extensive. Estimates his Annual Income from his Profession at £200.

He laid in Œsopus Gaol at the time Capt. Vand's Father was there & was a most distinguished Loyalist.

NEW CLAIM.

February 17.
730. Case of WM. HARDING, late of New York.

Claimt. Says: He went to Anapolis in 82. Came here in April, 83. Went to Majorville, was once down here, now settled on Bell Isle Bay. Had no opportunity of sending his Claim but by Capt. Vand.

Lived in Ulster Co. Joined the Brit. in 1776. Went on Board the Asia, and joined the Brit. at New York soon after it was taken.

Served as Pilot on the North River in ye King's Ships and served occasionally with the Loyalists under Major Ward.

Produces Certificates to his having fetched a Sloop under ye command of Capt. Dun, 1778.

Had a sloop, about 40 Tons.
Produces Bill of Sale of Sloop, crshd the Debby, within 12 loads in Consdn. £250 Curry., dated 25th Mar., 1776. (76).
When he went to New York left his sloop at Newbury Dock.
It was seized as soon as he went away to New York and was sold by Comrs. after heard that it was employd in the Continental service.
Produces Letter from one Lieut. Smith dated March 29, 1785, which mentions that the Sloop was taken & sold by the Comrs.
Had conveyed his farm to Lieut. Smith & John Flewelling for a Debt of about £40 due to Lieut. Smith & £60 due to Flewel-

ling. Lieut. Smith had cheated him in the sale of the Farm & J hn Flewelling has obliged him to give a New Bond for the Money due.
When he left Newboro they took 3 horses & one Cow.
Claimt. was despatched by Sir Hen. Clinton to the Revolters under General Wayne then near Trentown. was taken Prisoner on his return, was wounded & imprisoned, was confined to a Dungeon 3 weeks in Irons. Broke Gaol by bribing the sentries.
Geo. Leonard Certifies to his Bravery & Loyalty.
Major Upham Certifies him to be a faithful enterprising de- (77). serving Loyalist, Ditto. Amos Botsford.

MRS. HUSTIN Wits.

Remembers a Sloop which was said to be Claimt's. He left it at the Wharf at Newboro when he went to New York, he never got it again. Thinks the Comrs. took it. They took & sold ye things of the Loyalists who were off at that time.

NEW CLAIM.

731. Case of BENJ. SEALEY, late of Connect. February 17.

Claimt. says: He came in May, 83, went up to Majorfield, did not hear of the Act. He lived at Stratford, joined the Brit. at Lloyd's Neck. Sometimes kept Guard on the neck. Chopt. Wood. Continued within the Lines. He had been carried to Gaol before he went within the Lines. He was taken up by 3 officers from the committee. He was robbed of £17 in silver & gold. Lost Beef. When sent to Gaol the officer took his horse & saddle. Left some c rn on ye ground, a piece of Chintz, some furniture.
He was taken to Gaol for aiding & assisting the Loyalists. (78).

CALEB MALLORY Wits.

Knew Claimt. He was a Loyalist. He assisted Loyalists to get witin the Lines. He lost a horse. Heard of his losing a creature. He assisted Witness in carrying Despatches, he came in & brought Intelligence of an Intention to fire New York.

He was put to Gaol on acct. of having assisted Witness to get off Sound Money. He was put to Gaol & they took his horse. He had money about the same time, 3 gs. hard mon. & some Continental Money.

CHAPMAN JUDSON Wits.

Claimt. was a Loyalist, assisted Loyalists in getting away. Heard of his being plundered. He had made money by carrying Loyalists. Knew of his horse, heard he lost money.

NEW CLAIM.

February 19.
(79).

732. Case of SARAH CORY, WIDOW & THOS. CORY, ELDEST SON of GRIFFYN CORY, Deceased, late of New York.

Claimt. says: He & his Mother came in Sep. 83, came to this place, landed up the River at Gagetown, there remd. Heard of Capt. Vand, but it was too late.

Griffyn Cory lived in Courtlands Manor, West Chester Co. He had 2 Sons in the Brit. Service, he was too old to bear arms. He went to Long Island, had a Protection there, died there in Aug., 1780, made a Will a short time before his death whereby he gave his wife Sarah a Legacy 120 out of the Estate in Courtlands Manor & his moveable 20£ to 3 of his children, Claimt. & Sisters to be raised out of the said Estate.

And the rest of his Estate between his 5 Sons, to be pd. when they come of age, makes his wife Claimt. Thos. & John Cory, 2nd Son, his execrs.

He left Sarah his Widow, one of the Claimts. Thomas Claimt. John died in the Brit. service without Issue.

Gilbert at Gage Town 4 mos. Dead without Issue. Griffyn do. Lewis do. Morris do.

Claimt. Thos. has been in the Brit. service all the War, in the New York Volunteers.

(80).

His Father Griffyn had an estate in Courtlands Manor.

Produces Deed from Moses Travers to Griffyn Cory of 99 acres in Cons. 300£, 1770.

Produces Deed from Peter Secord to Griffyn cory of 82 acres in Cons. 410£, 1774.

These 3 Farms adjoined to each other, says his Father was offered 1,600£ for them.

About 30 acres Meadow, there was not more than a sufficient proportion of Timber Land.

Produces Copy of Judgement against Griffyn Cory declaring his Estate forfeit.

Joseph Osborn bought it.

There was a Mortgage of the Farm bought of Moses Travers.

PROCEEDINGS

OF

LOYALIST COMMISSIONERS

S<small>T</small>. JOHNS, 1787.

Vol. XVI.

BEFORE COMMISSIONER PEMBERTON.

Claimants.

	Ms. Page.
Barker, Thomas	15
Beaman, Thomas	7
Bears, William	52
Bellia, John	31
Bulyea, Henry	35
Burt, David	36
Cable, Mrs. Ann	74
Carpenter, Archelaus	11, 19 and 28
Compton, John	63
Colden, David	6
Cory, Mrs. Sarah	1
Dorington, John	23
Flagler, Simon	26
Flewelling, Thomas	3
Foster, Ebenezer	40, 49 and 52
Free, William	29
Gray, William	25
Green, Mrs. Elizabeth	48
Hendrick, Conrad	23
Ingraham, Benjamin	60
Jones, Edward	44
Jones, Ephriam	80
Jones, Josiah, Simeon, Stephen and Jonas	80

	Ms. Page.
Jones, Mrs. Mehitaphel	81
Morehouse, Daniel	39
Ogden, John	24
Oram, James	21
Pine, Stephen	45
Pote, Jeremiah	64
Quig, Hugh	27
Reece, Anthony	54
Secord, William	30
Shaw, John	19
Thorne, Joseph	73
Thorne, Robert	14
Underhill, William	46
Vandeburg, Richard	51
Van Tassel, Isaac	13
Vernon, Gideon	55 and 63
Wheeler, George	71
Wheler, John	33
Willard, Col. Abijah	7
Wyer, David	70
Wyer, Thomas	67
Yerxa, John	29

THE EVIDENCE.

February 19. (732). Continuation of Claim of SARAH & THOS. CORY.

(1) Claimt. Sarah says: She went up the River immediately. Never heard of the Act till she heard of Capt. Vand.
Her late Husb. lived in Courtd. Manor from the first he was a friend to the Brit. Govrt. Suffered greatly from Imprismt. & abuse. At last he was obliged to quit his home & went within the Brit. Lines at Long Island. Claimt. & family were sent to him about 7 or 8 months after he went away. He died at Long Island in the year 1780, v. acct. of his Estate Supra., besides the Mortgage to ye Loan Office on his Estate, there was some trifling debt.
Cannot say how much, has heard of one Bond. It was advertized for Sale.
Her Husb. was away in Feby., 1778. In the following April they took Possession of his Farm, let Claimt. have a Room. Took his moveables before they took Possession of the Farm. They sold the moveables at Vendue, allowed her very little.
Claimt. has been there since her Husbd. Death. One Hunt a Commissr. of forfeited then on it. One Osborn bought it afterwards. Lost 17 Cattle, 3 Cows, 1 horse, furniture, 10 Hogs, 30 Sheep, farming utensils, corn in the chamber.
All her children are now here. The eldest has served all the War.
Gilbert served in a British Privateer. Silvaneus now 22 yrs. of age, the others Infants.

(2). SOLOMON DINQUY, Wits.

Knew Griffyn Cory. He was always reckoned a Loyalist. Heard frequently of his Confinement. He came within the Lines in Feby., 1778, his family was sent to him.
Knew his Estate in Courtlands Manor, 3 Farms bought at different times. Remembers him in Possession. Above 250 acres. A very good farm, 40 acres Meadow, 160 Tilage, the rest Wood Lands. Heard him offered 1,600 York Cury. for it. He refused it. Asked 2,000 York Cury. for it. Values it at 6 or 7£ per acre.
Never heard of any Debt but the Loan Office Debt. He had a good stock of Horses, Cattle, Sheep. Thought him a man of Property. Not in Debt.
The whole to be pd. to the Mother.

JOHN YEOMANS Wits.

Knew Griffyn Cory. He was uniformly Loyal. Knew his Farm in Courtlands Manor. Remembers him in Possession. Vals. the farm near 2,000 York Cury.
Looked upon him as a man clear in his Circumstances, & not incumbered with Debt.

He had a considerable stock.
Witness understood all the family are here.

NEW CLAIM.

733. Case of THOS. FLEWELLING, late of New York. February 19.

Claimt. says he came in Aug., 83, went up the River, was not there during the Winter. Heard of Capt. Vand, came down intending to send by him but he was gone. Lived at North Castle, from the first declared in Favr. of Brit. Govt., had 4 Sons in Brit. Service. Frequently went within the Lines, but did not entirely leave Home till 1779. He had been much abused and ill treated before he went, tho old went in the service. Went with Col. Simcoe & Tarleton as a guide several times. Went frequently as a guide the first year. The 2nd year was stationed at Frogs Neck. Claimant had two of his sons with him, was afterwards 2 yrs. at Lloyd's Neck. Now settled in Queens County. (3).

Produces Certificate to his taking Oath of Allegiance to ye King.

WM. TRYON, GOVR., 1777.

Pass from Geo. Beckwick.
Was possessed of a farm in North Castle near 300 acres. 40 acres by Deed of Gift from his Father, 40 years ago.
Purchased 168 acres of Nichs. Outhouse at about 20 shils. per acre, not much improved, above 20 years ago.
37 acres purchased of Benj. Griffin 2 or 3 years after his first purchase, all new Land, at about 20sh. per acre. 25 acres purchased of one Wm. Dusenburg soon after the other purchase at near the same price, 9 acres of John Furman, 3 acres Meadow of John Miller. (4).
Has Deeds, he left them at Home, he had buried them in his Garden, took them up for fear of their being spoilt & Lodged them with a friend, but they were found out by the Rebels, the Box broken open & the Deeds taken or destroyed.
He laid out a great Deal in Improving his Farm after his Purchase. His Farm was improved almost throughout. There was no timber Land that he meant should stand.

There was a Saw Mill & other Buildings.
Vals. it at 4£ per acre York Money, two neighbours of his valued it at that Price about 1773.
After his family went away it was located by some Rebel Officers.
His Stock was seized after he got within the Lines. Thinks most of the Cattle was taken for the Army.
2 yoke of Oxen, 2 fat Heifers, 8 Cows, 3 2-year olds, 2 Yearlings, 2 Mares, 1 Stallion, 2 Colts, 62 Sheep, 4 Hogs, Wool 80 Pound, Furniture, Farming Utensils. (5).
All the above articles were taken from his Farm at Newcastle. Considerable part sold at Vendue. His name is in Anstey's List— Is told told to

end for certtfi-
cates of sale.   Was plundered at Long Island by a party who came over in Whale Boats of Arms to Amt. of 11£.

February 20.   JOSEPH FLEWELLING Wits.

Knew Claimt. at North Castle. He was always a Loyalist. Knew his Estates, some by his Daddy. The rest purchased of 2 or 3 persons, imagines it near 300 acres. Remembers him in Possession very well. Most of it improved, only a proper Quantity of Timber Land left. Vals. it at 4 or 4.10 per acre.

He had a pretty good Stock. Understood a Rebel Capt. was on it when they heard last.

THOMAS WAGSTAFFE, Wits.

Knew Claimt. He was always considered particularly Loyal. He had a farm between 2 & 300 acres. Remembers him in Possession. A Good Farm property & Stocked, 2 Yoke Oxen, Sheep, horses &c.

Remembers his coming within the Lines, he had 2 Sons in the Service.

(6).   Produces Certificate of his Character & Loyalty from Timothy Witmore.

February 21.   718. Case of DAVID COLDEN.

Chief Justice Ludlow says: He had been credibly informed that one Lewis Cornwal located on the Estate in Long Island. Mrs. Colden was turned off. Witness understands Lewis Cornwall is now in Possession.

The Daurs. of David Colden are likely to come into this Country. Thos. Colden who has now half pay & is coming hither in the Spring is a person rightly to have the Protection of them. And Capt. Willet is coming hither too. These two persons most likely to have the care of them.

February 21.   734. Case—Claim of COL. ABIJAH WILLARD, Acting Exect. to the Will of Thos. Beamson, late of Massts.

COL. WILLARD Appears.

Says Thos. Beaman died, lived at Petersham, Worcester Co. at the Commencement of the Troubles. He was very Loyal. He was Confidentially employd by Genl. Gage to go through different parts of the Country in order to find out the sense of the people. Was a guide to Genl. Smith & Lord Percy on 19th Apl., 1775. He was appointed Wagon Master to the Army by Sir Wm. How.
(7).   Continued in that employment till his Death. He was very zealous in his principals & active in his conduct. He died at Bedford, Long Island in the year, 1780.

Produces Probate of his Will, bearing date 8th Oct., 1780, whereby he gives 1-3 of his real & personal Estates to his Wife.

Gives all the Remr. of his effects to his Children, Eliz., Thos., Sarah, Ebenezer, Abigail, Joseph & Witness.

He died soon after making his Will. Col. Willard has proved the Will & acted as execr. The Widow Elizth. is now at Digby. Elizabeth his eldest Daur. is now in New England, but is coming hither. Col. Willard expects her here every day. About 22 yrs. of age.

Thos. the eldest Son, is in the Seafaring Line, Mate on Board a Sloop belonging to this harbour, but has a farm besides of 200 acres. Sarah in New England under age. Ebenezeer settled at Lancaster, just gone to New England to fetch his sisters. Abigail dead. Joseph & William, Infants at Digby with their Mother. No. 1.

Thos. Beaman was possessed of a Farm at Petersham with a Mansion house, &c. Purchased of Silvanius How in the year 1761.

The Deed has been sent to England.

Col. Willard produces a Certificate from Danl. Clap, Register of Worcester Co. that there appears on the Records a Deed from Silvanius How to Thos. Beaman of 83, May, 1761, and no Conveyance from him about 2 acres. (8).

There was a good Mansion House, Mr. Beaman lived there. He built the house himself, all inclosed & fully improved.

Vals. it at £500 Str.

Produces Certificates from Jonathan Grant, Admr. of his personal Estate, that he understood his real estate was Confiscated & sold, that he was present at the Sale.

Produces Certificate of Sale from John Fessenden one of the Comrs.

Was possessed of a Farm in Murrayfield, Hampshire Co. Col. Willard says he sold the late Thos. Branian 120 acres in Murray field in Cons. 120 Lawful in the year 1770. He built a small farm house after the Purchase, cleared 40 acres after he bought it. Set out an orchard. Vals. it at 200 Str. No. 2.

Col. Willard has seen an advertizmt. for the sale of this & has no doubt but what it is sold, expects Certificates.

He had 13 acres Timber Land in Lancaster Co. given him by his Faher by Deed of Gift many years ago. Wits. remembers him in Possession. No. 3.

Vals. it at 40sh. per acre.

Witness when he lodged the Claim did not know the particulars of his other real Estate, tho' he understood he had other Lands, but not being particularly acquainted with it did not mention it in his Claim. (9).

Produces Deed from Philip Philips to Timothy Shaw, Father 31 acres in Petersham, Cons. 30£, 1773.

Produces Deed from Silas Benter to Thos. Beaman & William Baron of 40 acres in Petersham in Con. 100£, 1772.

Remembers him in Possession of these Lands. The last let was mowing ground chiefly & Pasture.

The moveable Estate consisted of the Articles in the Schedule was sold before Mrs. Beaman left the Country, they would not allow her any part.

The family are coming as soon as possible, they have no dependence upon any persons in the States.

One of the Sons, Ebenezer, lives near Witness, is a very industrious man & means to bring his sisters from the States.

Mrs. Beaman is settled at Digby with the two youngest children, has 200 acres of Land.

COL. MURRAY, Wits.

(10). Knew Mr. Thos. Beaman, a firm Loyalist, very active. Witness recommended him strongly to Genl. Gage. He had been active & very serviceable in Collecting the sense of the Inhabitants. He was very serviceable to Lord Percy on 19th April, 1775. He was appointed Wagon Master to the Army greatly in consequence of Witness Recommend. He was a firm resolute man.

Knew No. 2. 120 acres, remembers Mr. Beaman in Possession of it. He improved it after the purchase.

Vals. it above 1£ per acre.

He had some other out Lands but Witness did not know them particularly.

Testator's Wife & some of the youngest children are now settled at Digby.

NEW CLAIM.

February 22. 735. Case of ARCHELAUS CARPENTER, late of New York.

Claimt. says he came here in 83, did not stay above 3 or 4 days, went to Majorfield, came down once. Staid here but one day. Thinks it was after Xmas. Admits that he had heard of Hardy's going before he came down.

(11). Lived in Westchester. Left home in 1777, went to New York. He had harboured a good many Loyalists & always declared in favour of Brit. He harboured 200 Loyalists at a time & victualed them. Lived in New York, then on Long Island, all the War. Now settled at Mouth of Washydoemack.

Was possessed of an Estate at North Castle, Westchester.

Produces Deed from Caleb Fowler to Claimt. of 80 acres 3-4 in North Castle in Cons 670, parted with 6 acres 3-4, 1769.

Produces Deed from Jacob Carpenter to Claimt. of 17 acres, Cons. 153, 1772.

Produces Deed from Wm. Fowler to Claimt. of 6 acres, Cons. 3£, 1769. This was Woodland.

He had on this Farm improved & fenced it. 20 acres meadow, 40 Plough, Vals. it 900£.

Produces Certificate of Sale, it sold for 490£.

30 acres Morgaged for 58£ to Loan Office.

Had another Tract in North Castle. Produces Deed from Walter Franklin to Claimt. of 125 acres in Cons. 450. Sep., 1774.

He had pd. £80 Mortgd. it for the rest, does not know what (12). is become of it. Franklin may have put somebody in Possession.

Left his moveables on his Farm. They were taken by a Committee & Sold.

3 horses, 1 yoke oxen, 4 cows, 4 young cattle, sheep, household furniture, utensils.

ROBT. THORNE, Wits.

Knew Claimt. He was reckoned Loyalist. When Witness went from the Country, there were near 200 Loyalists. Claimt. brought their Victuals. Went within ye Lines afterward.

CONS. CARPENTER, Son of Claimt.

He helped carry abundance of Victuals to Loyalists in the Woods. Abundance of times.

He staid at home when his Father went into the Lines. They came & seized his moveables. They sent Witness, his Mother & family off. They went to New York.

NEW CLAIM.

736. Case of ISAAC VAN TASSEL, late of New York. February 22.

Claimt. says: he went up the River, sent by Capt. Vand. It was his first opportunity.

He lived at Phips Manor. He sold his Land. He sold 100 acres for 100 Dollars.

Went within ye Lines in 1779, served under Delancey. Pro- (13). duces Capt. Vanderburgh Certificate to Loyalty.

Lost some wheat, taken after he left home, taken by Continentals. 30 Bushels Wheat in the Stack after he went within ye Lines. He bought a small house at Morisina.

REUBEN WATRIVERS, Wits.

Claimt. came on Philips Manor to the home of Witness's Wife's Mother to shair in the Profits, was to have 1-3.

After he went away ye Rebels took it. Knows not how much. Nothing to be allowed.

NEW CLAIM.

737. Case of ROBT. THORNE, late of New York. February 22.

Claimt. says. He sent his Claim by Mr. Hardy.

Lived in Dutchess Co. Always declared in favor Brit. Was imprisoned 2 months. Joined the Brit. 1777 at New York. Continued within ye Lines. Had a schooner, supplied the garrison with Fruit &c. Continued within the Lines all the war. Now settled at Gage Town.

56 AR.

(14).
Name appears in Anstey's list of personal estate.

Had a Lease in Dutchess on Col. Bateman's Estate. Produces Lease from Col. Bateman to Claimt. of 209 acres for the Lives of Claimt., his Wife & Son, paying 23 Bushels wheat annually, 1770. Built an house & Barn. Laid out 200£. Cleared 100 acres. Says he was offered 500£ for it. Vals. it at that sum.

Lost 6 Cows, 1 horse, 5 young Cattle, 5 Hogs, 30 Sheep, household furniture.

Produces Certificates from Capt. Vand to his Loyalty & sufferings.

THOS. BARKER, Wits:

Knew Claimt. He was always reckoned a Loyalist. Could not stay in the Country. Went off with the other Loyalists.

Has seen his farm in Bateman's Precinct. Understood he was a Tenant.

Seemed a pretty good house & Barn. A pretty Deal of clear Land. About the year 1774, as well as he can judge, such a Farm wd. sell for 500£; rather more as the Barn was so good.

Speaks of his stock particularly of between 20 & 30 sheep.

JOSHUA GIDNEY, Wits:

Knew Claimt. He was very Loyal. He had a farm in Bateman's Precinct. Considerable Deal of cleared Land; good builds.,
(15). orchard. Betwixt 70 or 100 acres appeared to have been cleared. The Price of the Improvements on these Tenant Farms varied very much. Depended a good Deal on the situation. He seemed to have considerable stock.

February 22.

738. Claim of THOS. BARKER, ESQ., late of New York.

Claimt. says. He lived in Dutchess Co. Was in the Commission of Peace. He very early, in the year 1773, exerted himself in support of Govert. Opposed the choosing a Committee for Charlotte Precinct, at a public meeting. In a great measure by Claimant's means a great majority declared against having a Committee. Claimant then drew up a Form by which the subscribers declared Allegiance to his Majesty & that they would support his Govert. This was signed by a great many. He was taken up on pretence of having enlisted men for his Majesty's service. Carried to Pughkeepsie, carried before the County Committee.

He recd. a Proclamation from his Majesty for suppressing the Rebellion which he communicated to General Tryon.

In 1776 was sent to Litchfield Gaol, Connect., thence to Pughkeepsie. Kept there 4 months; to Fish Kill, then New Hampton. Was released in Jany., 1777; went home; secreted himself in the Woods.

(16). In the beginning of year 1778, got within the Lines at New York, then to Long Island. Continued during the war. Now settled at Frederickton.

56 L AR.

Was Possessed of an Estate in Charlotte Precinct. Produces a Deed from Cornelius Van Vleit to Claimt. of a Tract in the lower 9 Partners, describing the Boundaries, consisting of 200 acres more or less, in Consd. of 500£ Cury., Decr., 1762.

His Buildings which he made after the Purchase cost him 800£. Cleared a great Deal. Stone fences, 25 acres meadow, 90 acres Ploughland.

Produces appraisment by two persons on Oath who valued it at 1,400.

Claimt. has no doubt but he could have got that sum for it. Subject to a Mortgage to Loan office of 75£.

Had a Tract in Orange Co.

Produces Deed of Gift from his Father, Thomas Barker, to Claimt. of all his right in Caskeat or New homestead in Orange Co., 1763.

There were 18 original Purchases of Cakeat Patent for 900£. His grandf. was one. The particular quantity of Land is not yet ascertained. A great Deal is still undivided. There had been some Divisions. He had a right to a Lot of 180 acres; very valuable; well improved & settled. His right has been contested by a Cousin. He had a right to another Lot of 73 acres; well improved. His Proportion of divided Lands amounted to 783 acres. Vals. it at more greatly than 600£. He had sold one Lot of 205 acres at 1£ per acre. (17).

Henry Humphries bought No. 1 and had lived upon it when Claimt. heard last. Claimant was there in June, '84. Humphreys was then in Possession. Has heard that Judge Coe located on some part of the Cakisat Patent. Has heard his son is in Possession of this Lot of 180 acres before mentd.

His moveables consisted—
3 Horses, 1 pr. Oxen, 12 Cows, 9 Cattle. Had 80 Sheep,

Furniture, 50£, farming utensils, Hay, 25 ton. They were most of them sold at Vendue.

Produces Deposition from Stephen Badgely that he was present at the sale of Claimt.'s personal estate by Commrs.

Produces strong Certificates to his Loyalty, Conduct & services from Capt. Clements & Lieut. Reed.

CAPT. JOHN HOWARD, Wits:

Knew Claimt. He distinguished himself very much by his Loyalty at first of the Troubles. Heard of his opposing Committees & proposing Declaration of Allegiance to his Majesty which was signed by many. He was active in getting people to sign it. (18).

Has been at his House in Charlotte Precinct. It was an improved farm. He used to have good horses. Witness thought him in good circumstances. He was a Magistrate of the Co. Remembers his imprisonment.

JOSHUA GIDNEY, Wits:

Knew Claimt. He distinguished himself very much by his Loyalty, Opposed Precinct meetings. Knew his Farm. A clever Place. The Land was valuable thereabouts. He seemed in very good circumstances. Witness observed a good stock.

Revd. Mr. Odell speaks to his Loyal Conduct & Character.

February 23. (735). Continuation of Claim of ARCHILAUS CARPENTER.

GILBERT PURDIE, Wits: Says Claimt. was Loyal from the first.
Knew No. 1, near 100 acres. A piece of good meadows. A good Deal of clear.
Vals. it at 8£ per acre.
He had another farm purchased just before ye troubles.

NEW CLAIM.

February 23. 739. Case of JOHN SHAW, late of New York.

(19). Claimt. says. He went up the River. He only came down once & staid a short time. Is settled in Queens Co.
He lived in Dutchess Co. Joined the Brit. in 1776 at New York. Had from the first declared in favr. of Brit. Govert. He was confined several times which obliged him to go within the Lines for Protection. His Family were sent to him in 1777.
Had a farm in Dutchess Co., inherited it on his Father's Death.
Produces Deed from Philip Philips to Timothy Shaw, Father of Claimt., of his Right & Title to Improvmts. on Gregory farm. forever. There is no date to this assignment but Claimt. says it was 15 years ago.

Says Philip Philips gave his Father the farm for services. One of the Gregorys is now living.
Says his Father was in Possession for 7 yrs. before the war. His Father died on Long Island, 1779, without a Will. It seems from Claimt.'s acct. that Gregory had had a Lease, but Mr. Philips, the Landlord, turned out Gregory and then gave the Improvements to Claimt.'s Father.
His Father made no Will. Claimt. is his only son. Has a sister living in the States.
There appears by a survey 186 acres.
(20) His Father had been a Loyalist & was confined on which he went within ye Lines, where he died. Does not know who has the Land. Says his Father improved the Place greatly after he got it.
Vals. it at 500£.
The stock was chiefly his Fathers. Some part his own. It consisted of—
4 horses, 15 Cows, 2 pr. Oxen, 8 fat Cattle, 25 head Cattle, 25 sheep, 14 Hogs, Corn in the Barn, Hay, Farming utensils. Of these 1 horse, 8 Cows, 7 young Cattle, 14 Sheep, 10 Hogs, Wheat belonged to Claimt. The rest belonged to his Father. All this was taken away after he went away.

ALEXR. BROWN, Wits:

Knew Timothy Shaw, Father of Claimt. He was Loyal. Went within the Brit. Lines for Protection. Claimt. was also Loyal & went on that acct. within the Lines. The Father died at Long Island. Claimant is his only son. He has a sister in the States.

Knew the Farm. Thinks it was given to Timothy Shaw about 1766. There was a mob by the Tenants against the Landlord, Mr. Philips. Timothy Shaw was one who assisted Philips for which & other services he gave him the farm. Witness understood that Philips gave the Gregories a Farm elsewhere, but they still made a Claim and in 1766 they turned the old man out, but he got Possession again & then staid till he went within the Brit. Lines. (21).

Is told the Gregories are not in Possession. The farm was about 200 acres, chiefly improved.

Knew the Stock. Heard of its being seized & sold. 30 or 40 head of Cattle, 4 horses, 1 yoke of oxen, 13 Sheep, 10 Hogs, Hay. Understood it was seized & sold by Commrs.

His name is in list as to personal estate to be allowed for moveables.

740. Case of JAMES ORAM, late of Pensilvania. February 24.

Claimt. says. He lived in Pensilvania Co. near Philadephia. Was a gardener, nurseryman & Seedsman. In ye year 1777 joined the Brit.in German Town. Says he refused a Capts. Commission in Rebel Army. Continued with them. Served as Conductor of horse to the field Artillery under general Cleveland. Served five years. Was with Lord Cornwallis & taken Prisoner at York Town. Was discharged at Charles town. Produces his discharge Oct., 1782. Signed Alexr. Forbes & P. Traill, who Certify his having served 5 years & behaved faithfully. Now settled on Long Reach.

He had a garden & nursery in which he lived of Mr. Gurney. He had no Lease. He left his wife there. The Rebels coming down she came into Philadelphia. All his garden was destroyed. His furniture was destroyed.

His garden was in the way of march of the Army, but had he not been a Tory they would not have meddled with him. (22).

ROSS CARVIE, Wits:

Knew Claimt. He was a Gardener near Philadelphia. Hired the garden of Mr. Gurney. He had several hundred fruit trees. It was beyond the Lines, but the Rebel Troops came with Design to injure as well Mr. Gurney as the Claimt.

He had some moveables. This was in the Fall 1777. Witness on going there found that the house was destroyed. The house was Gurneys. The nursery was laid waste.

Says that this Depredation would not have been committed had Mr. Gurney & Claimt. joined the Brit.

Speaks favourably of the character of Claimt. He was an old soldier.

Thinks 7s., 6d. per Doz. not too much for apple trees.

February 24

741. Further Evidence in Case of CONRAD HENDRICK.—v. Vol. 12, Page 140.

(23).

Mrs. Hendricks produces Will of her late Husband, Conrad Hendricks, after payment of his Debts he gives all his estate to his Wife for Life, with power to dispose of it if not disposed of then to his three children now herewith, Sarah, James & John. With Power to his wife if his son, David English, comes into this Province to give him such part of his estate as may make his share equal with the other three. Empowers his Wife to Sollicit Compensation from Government. Makes her sole Exer, Will, dated May, 1784.

NEW CLAIM.

February 24.

742. Claim of JOHN DORINGTON, late of New York.

Claimt. says. He came in May, '83. Went immediately up the River. Did not come down. Could not send till by Capt. Vand. Sent by him. Lives in Kennibickasis.

Lived in Orange Co. Joined the Brit. soon after Fort Washington was taken. He served in the 55th Regt. as private, last war. Produces Certificates to shew it after he came into the Lines. Cut wood for the Garrison & city. Continued so employed all the war. Lived some time on Long Island.

When he left Orange Co. left 3 Cows, 7 horses, 2 oxen, 2 Wagons, 7 Sheep, 100 Bushels Wheat, 50 Bushels Rye.

When he went to the Brit. these things were taken & sold. Says they were sold by one Esq. Cowper, Justice of Peace.

(24).

On further examn. says he lost 3 of the horses & one Wagon while cutting wood for the garrison & city; 4£ Cash then.

Says the Continental Army took the wheat & Rye. Produces no Witnesses.

NEW CLAIM.

February 26.

743. Case of JOHN OGDEN, late of New York.

Claimt. says. He came in July, '83. Went up to Gage town. Did not come down. Never heard of the act till last year. Now settled in Queens County.

Lived in Westchester Co. Went within the Brit. Lines on Long Island, the spring after New York was taken. He was draughted in the Militia & did not choose to serve, on which he went into the Brit. Lines.

Lost—yoke of oxen, 2 horses, 2 Cows, 2 Calves, 17 Sheep, 2 2 years old, 5 Swine, Cart, farm utensils.

Left all these things on a hired Farm. They were taken from the Place. His Wife was there. They would not let her have anything. She came to New York. Part sold by Vendue. The sheep were taken for the Rebel Militia.

Produces Certificate of his taking the Oath of Allegiance. Mathews, Mayor of New York, 27th March, 1777.

JOSEPH FERRIS, Wits: (25).

Knew Claimt. He was always reckoned a Loyalist. He went within the Lines, rather than serve in the Militia. Believes him a very honest man. Knew of his having some stock; yoke of oxen, 2 horses, Cart.

Heard of his stock being taken on acct. of his Loyalty.

(688). Continuation of Case of WM. GREY — v. B. 14, Page 74.

Says he came down in beginning Feby., '84, or end of Jany. Came on Saturday & went away on Monday morning next. Will not say positively that Hardy was gone.

Thinks he could not have advised any person to send their Claim by Hardy, as he had quareld with Hardy. Admits he heard in the winter that Hardy was going home & crd. Army Claims. Cannot answer positively whether he did or did not advise any one to send their Claim. Possibly might have done it, but does not recollect it.

NEW CLAIM.

744. Case of SIMON FLAGLER, late of New York. February 26.

Claimt. says. He came in June, '83. Went up the River. Was there all the winter, except once that he was down here. He (26). then staid only a day & a half. Did not know that he cd. send his Claim.

Lived in Dutchess Co. Joined the Brit. in New York in 1779. He had been in before and had once endeavoured to get 30 men within the Lines to join Capt. Howard. Continued at Long Island. Went out to work for the garrison.

Lost 1 pr. oxen & 1 Cow and 1 horse, taken for forces. Lost one horse when endeavouring to make his escape. Lost 4 young horses, Sled, Wagon. These last were taken & sold at Vendue, for assisting the enemy. Produces Certificate of Sales Corresponding with the last acct.

745. Further Evidence in Case of HUGH QUIG—v. Vol. 12, February 26. P. 147.

GEORGE BROWN, Wits., says he knew Claimt. in Morris Co. He came in at the first of the war. Fetched in a good many men whom he had listed.

He belonged to Brown's Brigade & brought in men to that Brigade. He had afterwards Wagons. His Lands have been sold. Witness has been there since ye Peace. One Millar bought it & rents it out for 10£ per ann. About 20 acres clear. Witness understood Claimt. had worked for Lord Sterling who paid him

(27). by giving him Lands. Witness lived near him before the war. Remembers him in Possession of this Land, which Millar now owns.

Knew his stock. Remembers 2 Stills, 8 oxen, 13 head of Cows, Wagon, 2 Carts. He was a distiller.

Heard these things were seized & sold after he went within the Lines. A guard was sent before his family got away. Witness saw the Guard.

WILLIAM CAIN, Wits:

Knew Claimt. Always Loyal; at first supported Tories. Carried them within the Lines. Victuald them at his own expense.

He went in with a good many men into the Lines. Thinks he was a soldier himself for a while afterwards in the Wagon Department.

Knew his Estate that he had from Lord Sterling. A great piece of Meadow clear. Cost him a great Deal. He had more Land.

Has been informed the Land was sold. Knew 7 Cows, 5 2-year old, 8 oxen, Wagon & carts. Two pretty large Copper Stills. Witness saw ye Cattle Vendued. Heard the other Things were vendued.

(28). Witness says he has known him supply Loyalists with food for weeks together, till he could get them within the Lines.

February 27. (735). Contiuation of Claim of ARCHILAUS CARPENTER.

FRANCIS FLEWELLING, Wits: Knew Claimt. He was very Loyal. Used to assist Loyalists. Used to help victual great numbers. Knew his Land. Thinks about 100 acres. He was in Possession 5 or 6 years before the war. Considerable mead. Lands sold from 5 to 8£, Woodland from 2£ to 3£. He had a considerable stock. Saw the Rebels take his stock. Understood it was carried to be sold at Vendue.

NEW CLAIM.

February 27. 746. WM. FREE, late of New York.

Claimt. says. He came in July. Went up the River. Never heard till he heard of Capt. Vand.

Lived on Courtlands Manor. Joined the Brit. at Frogs Neck. Served with Col. Delancey 4 years.

Lost a Heifer, taken for a fine. Left 10 Sheep on hired place. Lost a horse in service. Lost anr. in action.

JOHN YERXA, Wits:

(29). Claimt. served with Delancey. Knew he had sheep left on the Manor of Courtland. Many were lost. Cannot tell how many. Witness went to look for them. They found 4.

Supposes Continental Militia took them. The Brit. Troops had been there.

NEW CLAIM.

747. Case of JOHN YERXA, late of New York.   February 27

Claimt. says. He came in Aug. Went to Majorfield. Sent by Capt. Vand. Could not send before. Lived on Courtland Manor. Joined the Brit. in the year '80. Served with Col. Delancey as Volunteer.

One Cow taken by Continental Militia, but after he got within the Lines, he bought her & carried her in. Lost cash, taken from him & money spent in Prison.

WM. FREE, Wits:

Claimt. served under Col. Delancey. Knew the Rebels took a Cow from him, for his not serving in Militia. This was in '78, two years before he went within the Lines.

NEW CLAIM.

748. Case of WILLIAM SECORD, late of New York.   February 17.

Claimt. says he came in July. Went up to Majorville. Sent his Claim by Capt. Vand. Was down once.   (30.)

He lived in Orange Co. Joined the Brit. in 1777. Worked in the Ship yard. Produces Oath of Allegiance, Protection, Passes, Recommendation from De Veber, Justice of Peace. Came here; Lieut. of Company of Loyalists. Produces his Commission from Sir Guy Carleton.

Lost grain in the ground and farming utensils at Newboro. In the year 1766 went to Newboro. Sowed some grain there; left it. Came down to New York; left farming utensils & 1 Cow at Newboro. Moses Hunt took them of whom he had hired ye ground. Lost Household goods. Moses Hunt took some. 2 horses, one at his Fathers, taken by one Ticker after Claimt. went within the Lines. One horse left at Cownkas after, taken by one Smith after Claimt. went within the Lines.

Yoke of Steers, 2 Cows & Heifer left at his Fathers, taken by one Sicker & his Co. Sicker belonged to Militia. Has no evidence.

NEW CLAIM.

749. Case of JOHN BELLIA, late of New York.   February 27.

Claimt. says. He came in '83, in Septer. Was discharged 10 Oct. as a soldier in Capt. Halebes Company. Went up the River   (81).
in 3 or 4 days Time, 24 miles. Would not send his Claim. Produces his discharge. He lived in Philips Borough on a Tenant Farm. Joined the Brit. in Oct., '76. Went on Board the Tartar. Went on shore, was taken Prisoner; kept in Prison 6 weeks; broke gaol & joined Col. Fanning at New York. Served with him 3 years, and then 4 with Col. Beverly Robinson.

Had 200 acres in Philips Borough. Had it about 10 years before the war. His Brother in Law left it to him to take care of his Family. Col. Philips consented to its being assigned to Claimt.
He says he pd. his Bro. in Law's Debts, above 100£, besides

maintaining his Family. Pd. Col. Philips 20£.
When Claimt. went away he left his wife & family on his Farm. In 3 years time they were driven off & came to New York. The Land was almost all clear.
Left farming utensils, furniture, 5 horses, 8 Cows, 1 pr. oxen, 40 Sheep, 300 Bushels Wheat, 200 Bushels Corn, Cyder.
Left these things when he went. They were taken from his wife. His stock was taken away at once. Taken by force. Taken by one Gilbert. They were in the Rebel Militia.
One Wiley took Possession of the Land.

WILLIAM BAZBY, Wits:

(32). Knew Claimt. in Philips burg. He went to the Brit. soon in the war. Served as a Brit. Soldier. Knew his Farm. He had it 3 years before ye war. Had it of Robert Williams. One Wiley had it. He was a Rebel. He had it during the war.

Knew some of his stock. The Rebels sent a Party to take them, while he was a Prisoner, after he had been on Ship board. He had a pretty good stock.

Produces Certificates from Lieut. Ward to Claimts. having served since '78, & to his Loyalty.

JAMES BULLIA, Wits: He is half Brother to Claimt. Claimt.

went to the Brit. in 1776. He served with Col. Fanning & Col. Robinson.

Knew his Farm. A smart orchard and considerable salt & fresh meadow & almost all clear Land.

Robert Williams, his Brother in Law, owned it & made it over to Claimt. 8 or 10 years before the war. He was to take care of Robt. Williams family. Thinks he paid Robt. Williams Debts. Jacob Wiley had it, when they heard last. Philips Land was all sold. Witness supposes Wiley bought this Place. There
(33). was a Privilege of 2 Fisheries, and a fishing Dock, which Claimt. had built himself.

Knew his stock, taken by the Rebels after he went on Ship board. They were driven away by one Gilbert. Does not know what Anthony Gilbert had. Heard they were sold at Vendue.

Henry Bulyea, Father of Claimt., says his son was to take care of Robt. Williams Children till they were grown up, & put them to Trade. The small children lived with Claimt.

NEW CLAIM.

February 27. 750. Case of JOHN WHELER, late of New Jersey.

Claimt. says. He came in May, '83. Went up the River. Came down once & a while. Heard of Hardy & Vand.

Lived at Newark. Joined the Brit. in 1776 at Burash. Continued within the Lines during the war. Served now & then as Volunteer. Was twice Prisoner. Settled now on the Kennibekasis.

Had a house & Lot at Newark containing about 20 acres. Left him by his Uncle many years ago. He has been in Possession till he left home.

There was a house & Barn & 20 acres of Land, a Double house. The Land was chiefly orchard. Vals. it at 700£.

Produces Certificate of Sale. It once was let for 14£ per ann. (34).

Lost a horse & furniture &c. A good Deal has been saved. Produces Certificates of Sale of personal Estate to amt. of 28£.

STEPHEN FAREND, Wits:

Knew Claimt. He was always reckoned a Loyalist. Went within the Brit. Lines 1777. Continued within ye Lines during the war. He was a man of Estate. He had a decent kind of House. Shd. value ye house alone at about 150£. Does not know the No. of acres. Some for 20, some more. There were Home Lots, some for 7£. Outlands sold sometimes for 5£.

March 24, Mrs. Wheler. This was an Incumbrance of 100£

York Cur. A Mortgage on the Estate to Capt. Jos. French. He staid in the States.

There was a Bond of 60£ but this was not on the Estate. One Zebedee Wilson bought the Estate. He or his Son are now in Possession. Vals. it at 500£ York Cur.

Her Husb. was in Possession as soon as he came of age.

NEW CLAIM.

751. Case of HENRY BULYEA, late of New York. February 27.

Claimt. says. He came in July. Been up the River all the (35). time. Sent by Capt. Vand.

Lived on Courtlands Manor. Had ½ a farm. Went within ye Lines '81. Continued within the Lines. Had 5 Sons in the Brit. Army. His Son & he had a Farm between them of 180 acres. Bought the Improvmts. 40 years ago. Gave 25£. Afterward did a great Deal; built, fenced & planted orchard. Vals. ye whole Improvmts. at 300£.

Lost 2 horses, 2 Cows, 2 2 year olds, 2 yearlings, 2 Sheep, some Corn, taken by Rebel Militia. Taken from him because his Sons were gone into Army & he was reckoned a Tory.

ROBERT BULYEA, Son of Claimt.:

Claimt. & his Son Joseph had a farm betwixt them, 180 acres. His Father has had it a long while. There were scarce any Improvements when he first had it.

The Rebel Militia took his stock; 2 Cows, 2 horses, 2 2 yr. olds, 2 Calves, 2 Sheep, Seven Hogs.

JOHN YERXA, Wits:

Knew Claimt. He went into ye Lines towards the end of war. He was Loyal from the first. He had a farm on Courtlands Manor between him & his Son.

(36). Vals. Improvmts. at 300£.

NEW CLAIM.

February 28. 752. Case of DAVID BURT, late of Connect.

Claimt. says. He came here in Septr. Went up to Gage Town. Staid there all the winter. Did not come down once. Sent his Claim by Vand. Lived at New Haven, Conect. Joined the Brit. in April, 1777. Enlisted first in the Queen's Rangers. Was discharged at Philadelphia. Went to Long Island. Came from there to this Country. Lives now 20 miles above St. Anns.

Produces his discharge, dated 22 Decr. at Philadelphia.

Was possessed of an Estate in Ridgefield Consisting of 15 acres & ½ & ¼ of a Grist Mill.

Had 10 acres under his Father's Will. His Father died about 2 years before the war.

Purchased the rest of Joshua Tongue 14 yrs. ago for 125£ York Cur.

There was an house & Barn. Most of the Land was orchard, except about 3 acres of Woodland.

House & Barn not built for less than 150£ New York. They were on the Place when he purchased. Vals. the Land at 8£ Cur. per acre; House & Barn 100£.

(37). Produces Judgement of Confiscation of his real & personal estate. Produces certificate from Town Clerk, that he was possessed of 6 acres with Buildings &c., also 6 acres & 66 Rods, also 40 in Ridgefield in the year 1775, and that there was no Improvemts.

Produces Copy of Writ to Sheriff to seize his real estate, with return by Constable that he had seized 12 acres of Land & Buildings, also 3 acres of Woodland.

He had ¼ of a right in a grist Mill. His Father built the mill on a stream belonging to the town. The mill belonged to him as long as he kept it in Repair. Had been built many years. His Father left it to 4 Sons. Claimt. one. Had it after his Father's Death. They used to grind 90 Bushels in summer Days. Thinks his share worth 20£.

Lost moveables, 1 Cow, some furniture.

Produces Writ to Sheriff to seize his personals with return by Constable that he had seized 1 Cow & some articles of furniture which he specifies.

Produces appraisment by two Persons on oath who valued his real estate at 125.5, as Land sold in 1775. Also valued his personal est. They add that the sd. landed Estate had been sold.

(38). Says his mother has 1-3 of the Land which was his Fathers, for her Life. She is there now.

DANL. MOREHOUSE, Wits:

Knew Claimt. He went within the Lines in the year 1777. Served 8 or 9 months, in the Queens' Rangers. Knew his Estate, about 15 acres, House & Barn. Remembers him in Possession. He had good part from his Father, above 9 acres. Orchard very good. Good Woodland. Vals. it at 10£ per acre, including Buildings.

There was a grist Mill which belonged to the four Brothers. The stream belonged to the Town. The Brothers had the Mill on Condition to keep it working. Vals. the Mill at 500£.

NEW CLAIM ADMITTED IN ENGLAND.

753. Case of DANL. MOREHOUSE, late of New York. February 28.

Claimt. says, he came in Sept., was disbanded 10 Oct. Moved up the River to Barton. Sent his Claim by Vand.

He lived in Westchester Co. Joined the Brit. in 1776, before New York was taken. Served in the York Volunteers during the War.

Now settled 9 miles above St. Ann's.

Had 15 acres of Land in Courtlands Manor. Bought it of one Loudell 3 or 4 yrs. before ye War at 3£ per ann. (39).

Vals. it at £5 per acre.

Does not know that it has been Confiscated. On further examination it seems to have been only Tenant Land held under Delancey. His name is not in A1 list.

Had 3 acres of Land in Ridgefield, Connect. Part came by his grandfather Samuels Will. His grandfather died about 16 years ago. He took Possession on his Death. Bought some more of his two Brothers at the rate of 3£ per acre.

He moved from Connect. about 7 years before the War, and then he let his Land in Connect., does not recollect for what. He let it to his Brother in Law, who came to this Country.

He had 15 Sheep on Courtlands Manor left when he joined the Brit., some few farming utensils. Does not know what became of them.

DAVID BURT, Wits.:

Knew Claimt., he joined the Brit. early, served all the War in New York Volunteers. He was a very good soldier.

Knew he had a piece of Land in Courtlands Manor, 15 acres. He had it some time before the War, bought it of one Lobdel.

Claimt. lived there. Thinks it was a Tenant's farm & it must have been only Improvements.

He had some Land from his Grandfather in Connect., but Witness cannot say how much.

NEW CLAIM.

February 28. 754. Case of EBENEZER FOSTER, late of New Jersey.

(40). Claimt. says he came here in May '83, went up the River directly. Did not hear of the Act till about 15 Nov., and then nothing certain. Intended to have come down as soon as the River was froze & passable. Lives about 23 miles up the River, and did not come down that Winter any more. Said he had no opportunity of sending in the course of the Winter. He sent to Mr. William Taylor in England in the course of the Summer.

He says that the Place where he lives is about 7 miles from the Winter Road, it was a very uncommon thing to see a Winter Passenger.

Wm. Taylor Certifies that he recd. the Claim in England, but it came too late.

Was settled in Woodbridge. One of the Judges of the inferior Court.

From the first opposed the measures of the Rebels. Had influence enough to have a Committee dissolved of which he had been returned a member, and opposed the choice of other Committees tho' in vain.

(41). His conduct rendered him so obnoxious that he was frequently dragd before the Town.

When the Brit. Troops landed in Staten Island in consequence of an order from Govr. Livingstone to apprehend persons suspected, he was taken up & was confined under Bond of £1,000 for some months.

In Dec., 1776, went within the Lines, joined Lord Cornwallis at Brunswick. Lord Cornwallis gave him Protection. Had a Commission to administer Oaths of Allegiance, in consequence of which he administered the Oath to Members. This conduct marked him out as an object to the Rebels. His house was beset. General Winds with a party came with a view to take him, on which he left home & did not.

Went to Staten Island. Continued there a long time & then went to New York.

Produces Commission from Genl. Skinner to Claimt. & 3 others to to administer Oath of Allegiance, to select 10 Companies of Militia, &c., dated 3 Decr., 1776.

Claimt. was possessed of 149 acres with Buildings in Woodbridge, Midx. Co.

No. 1—72 acres came to Claimt. by Descent from his Mother, Margaret Heddon. His Mother died in 1767 or thereabouts, it came to him on her Death.

Produces the Title Deed of his Mother, Margt. Heddon, of 60 acres together with an Island of Meadows. Produces Deed (42). from Chs. Wright to Claimt. of 22 in Woodbridge in Cons. 129£, 1753.

From David Wright to Do. of 22 acres in Do. in Cons. 145£, 1754.

From Jos. Shortwell to Do. of 10 acres in Cons. 52£, 1755.
From Benj. Shortwell to Do. of 3 acres & ¼ in Cons. 14.14
E.N. In. Cur.
From Silas Walker to Do. of 19 acres in Cons. 173, 1764.
All these Lands laid together, amounting to 149 acres.
Claimt. lived there. A good house & Barn.

Vals. it from 10 to 11£ per acre, including Buildings. Besides this had 12 acres Meadow that belonged to his Mother, came on his Mothers Death. Mentioned in Title Deed.
Vals. it at £7 per acre.
Had an Estate in Bergen Co.
Produces Deed from Geo. Sly to Claimt. of 52 acres & ½ in Bergen Co. Cons. 100£ Cncy. 1771. No. 2.
Planted an Orchard & Improved.
Vals. it at 150£.
Produces Copy of Inquisition in Midsx. Co. & Judgment & Copy of Writ to the Commrs. to sell.
Produces Certificate from Aaron Dunham of sale of real & personal Estates. (43).
Produces advertisement in New York Paper for sale of 53 acres, formerly Claimts., Nov. 27, 1786.
Personal Estate—
Lost—A Negroe Woman about 15 years of age, left her at his house at Woodbridge when he went away. She was taken when his other property was seized, a yoak of Oxen, 8 Cows, 3 3 yr. old, 10 2 yr. olds, 7 Yearlings, 30 Sheep, furniture, very considerable, 25 Bushels Wheat, 200 Bushels Indian Corn, 20 Bushels Buck Wheat, 20 Oats, had 4 horses.
Left these at his farm at Woodbridge.

They were seized before his family came away.
Lost a horse on Staten Island, taken by a Party under Genl. Sullivan.
Aaron Dunham's Certificate states amount personal Estate at 145.
Judge Allen Certifies that Claimt. is a man of Integrity & good Character. He was an active intelligent Magistrate and uniformly Loyal.
He stood forward at first & took an active part.
Thinks he possessed a Clear Estate. Understood he was unincumbered & in good Circumstances. (44).
(694). Further Evidence in the Case of EDWARD JONES.

EVAN THOMAS, Wits.:

Knew Ed. Jones. He joined the Brit. at Philadelphia. Served with Buck's Co. of Volunteers.
Knew his farm, he had it from his Father, has often heard he had 100 acres, it was in Hilton Township, Bucks Co. Claimt. was possessed several years before ye War.

Vals. it about 7£ 10 per acre.
About 2 years ago Witness was there. A man was then in Possession who bought it at Vendue. It was sold by Comrs. Thinks his name was Makinstree, he was no relation to Claimt. He had a good Stock.

NEW CLAIM.

February 28.

755. Case of STEPHEN PINE, late of New York.

Claimt. says he came in May. Went up the River. Sent his Claim by Capt. Vand.
He lived in Ulster Co. Was obliged to leave home on acct. of his Loyalty. Went on Board the Dutchess of Gordon in Feb., '76, afterwards on board the Tartar. Got within the Lines & was in the Wagon Service, then entered as a guide. Was with the Army & continued in the Lines all the War. Now settled in Queens Co.

(45).

He had sold his Lands, for which he had taken Bonds, part now due.

His Lands were in Dutchess Co. He moved to Ulster Co. after he sold his Lands & carried his stock.

Left his stock when he went within the Lines on a farm he had hired. His family were sent down to him at New York. Before they came down his things were seized.

1 Yoke Oxen, 3 Cows, 2 Mares, 1 horse, furniture, farming utensils, a Loom & tackling.

Alpheus Pine, Son to Claimt.

Name not in Anstey's List but claimt seems a fair man, and the things were taken before first Confiscation Act.

He continued in the Country after his Father went within the Lines. Was at home when some Rebel officers seized his Property on acct. of his having gone within the Lines.

Sometime after his Father was gone they took farming utensils, household fu niture, the Stone house & 1 Mare. They took the Oxen before. There was a Vendue at Newboro but does not know whether their things were sold at Vendue. He says the things were taken because his Father was a Tory & had gone away.

NEW CLAIM.

(46).
March 1.

756. Case of WM. UNDERHILL, late of New York.

N.B.—This account is confirmed by Stephen Baxter

Claimt. says he delivered his Claim to Col. Robt. Rogers at New York about last Septr., '83, who promised to carry it to England.

He lived at Philipsburg, Westchester Co., joined the Brit. as soon as they landed on Long Island. Served 9 months as Capt. in Queen's Rangers, raised 162 men. Afterwards had a Wart. to raise men from Col. James Rogers. He was going after some of Burgoynes men when he was taken Prisoner. Kept Prisoner 2 yrs. & 9 months. He was on Parole when Andree came to Genl. Arnold.

Claimt. advised him to go to Capt. Kips Company in the Wood & they would get him within the Lines. He was taken soon after.

Claimt. was known to have had some Conferences with Andree, on which he was so ill used that he was left for dead on the ground. Was carried off by some of Delanceys Corps. From that staid within ye Lines all the War.

Now lives at Spoon Island.

Had a Tent. Farm of 200 acres in Philipsburg. His Father had it from the uncle or grandfr. of Col. Philips 40 yrs. ago. On his Father's Death it came to Claimt. He paid one of his Brothers something for his Interest. His Father died 30 years ago. Claimt. was in Possession till he left home. 60 acres tillable, 25 acres Meadow. Rent was 3.4.6 per ann.

Vals. it at 500£.

Isaac Waldron was in Possession, hired it of ye Comrs.

1 pr. Oxen, 1 pr. Steers, 8 Cows, 2 horses, very valuable, 62 Sheep, furniture, farming utensils. Most of these things were taken after his Conversation with Andree, in which he was said to have broken his Parole.

He lost Wheat, 150 Bushels; Buckwheat, 300 Bushels; Oats, 50; Corn.

(47).

Says Col. Simcoe offered him 56£ for one of his horses. Produces Certificates to his being brought in a number of Recruits for the Provincial Corps, &c., & to his Loyalty from Col. Winslow.

His name is in A 1 Personal List.

STEPHEN BAXTER, Witness:

Knew Claimt. Speaks very favourably of him. He entered very early in Brit. service. Raised a Company, was very active, served 8 or 9 months. He was taken Prisoner. Witness saw him in Close Confinement. He was afterwards on Parole.

Knew his farm, it was called 200 acres, supposes it was more. About 70 acres Clear. Vals. Improvmts. at £400. He had a good Stock, many Sheep.

(48).

NEW CLAIM.

757. Case of ELIZABETH GREEN, late of New York.   March 1.

Claimt. says: Her Husb. died 6 years ago last October. She came here in Aug. Went up the River. Sent her Claim by Capt. Vand.

Her Husband lived on Courtland Manor. He joined the Brit. at K'ng's Bridge. Served under Col. Emerick till they were disbanded, then served under Col. Delancey till his Death.

He had a house in Courtland Manor built by the road side, a little Log house, gave £5 for it 4 or 5 years before he went to the Brit.

Claimt. staid at this Place when her Hub. went to the Brit. Rebels came & took everything, drove her away. They took ye little furniture she had, 2 Cows & 2 Calves. Now lives at St. Ann's.

JACOB VAN WART:

Knew Claimts. Husb., he lived in Courtland Manor. Was very Loyal. Served as a Soldier.

Knew his house, stood on Witnesses Land, he hired it, could not have sold it. Witness thinks the house was his, the Witnesses. He had 2 Cows, a little furniture, thinks the People destroyed them, no young Cattle. Remembers his 2 Cows driven away by the Rebels 4 or 5 months after Thos. Green went within the Lines.

(49).

March 5. 754. Continuation of the Case of EBENEZER FOSTER.

STEPHEN FOSTER, Witness:

Son of Claimt. Says his Father from the first took a part against the Rebels. He was chose once one of tne Committee. He resigned & opposed all Committees.

He administered the Oath of Allegiance to persons in the Town of Woodbridge.

His Homestead consisted of about 150 acres, most of it Clear, only a small (part) of Woodland left.
Knew the Estate in Bergen Co.
Remembers the Negroe, she was taken away by the Rebels, all the horned Cattle, amounting to near 40. He had 6 horses.

LAURENCE FOSTER, Wits.:

Son of Claimt. He staid at Home after his Father went within the Lines. The Rebels took all his landed Estate & took his Stock. Made Witness help to drive them. They took ye Negroe. Thinks they took about 30 horned Cattle, 6 horses, 29 sheep. They took furniture at different times. Drove all the family away at last. All went to Staten Island.

(50).

JOSEPH THORN affirms:

He knew Claimts. Estate in Woodbridge, about 150 acres, very good Land. He has had it many years. It was the best part of the Country. Thinks it would go to £10 per acre Jersey Cur. Wits. had been employed in doing masons work to the house many years ago. Thinks he was Judge of the County Court.

He had Meadow besides his home Place, had a good stock.

March 6.

758. Continuation of the Case of CAPT. RICHD. VANDERBURG.

CHARLES ROBERTS, Wits.:

Says he knows the Estate late Mr. Rapalgies at Bashwick, about ?0 acres, a very good farm, there was a good house. A good stand for a public house. The Land was mostly upland, not much meadow.

Vals. it at £1,000 York Cncy.

Witness was there in July last. Mr. Wailey was in Possession.

Young Mr. Rapalgie was there. His uncle was trying to recover the Estate for him. He lost the action, which was renewed while Witness was in the Country.

It was reported that Mr. Wailey had bought it privately of Commrs. He turned out a Tailor, one Gilbert, who had taken Possession.

Capt. Vanderberg says he has had a Letter from his Brother in Law, Gilbert Bogart, then Abraham Rapalgie, the Infant, has failed in his renewed action and Capt. Vanderburg expects Proof of Confiscation & Sale.

(51).

(754). Further Evidence in Case of EBENEZER FOSTER. March 8.

WILLIAM BEARS, Wits.:

Knew his Estate at Woodbridge, No. 1, thinks about 150 acres. Remembers him offered 1,300£ for it before he made Improvemts. After the Improvemts. Vals. it at 11£ per acre.

Knew that he purchased in Bergen Co. He had a large stock. He had a Negroe Wench, thinks 5 horses.

He was a very active Loyalist from the first. Administered the Oath of Allegiance to many persons, to Witness amongst others.

NEW CLAIM.

(52).

759. Case of WM. BEARS, late of New Jersey. March 8.

Claimt. says: He came in July, '83. Went up to Majorville. Came down once in the Winter. Never heard of it till he heard of Capt. Vand. going. Sent his Claim by him.

He lived in Woodbridge. Joined the Brit. in the Fall, after they took New York. Has been in the Engineers Department ever since during the whole war. Discharged at New York.

Had a House & Lot in Woodbridge.

Produces a Deed from Job Thorp to Wm. Gadbeer of a Messuage & Land in Woodbridge. Considn. 30£, 1760.

Gadbeer was his name, but he has of late gone by the name of Beers. His name having been so entered in the Engineers Roll by mistake.

He built upon this spot, laid out some 200£. Vals. it at 200£.

It has been sold at Vendue, one Thomas Force, a Committee Man, bought it.

Left Stock on his Place when he went away. He was obliged to leave home in the night. 2 horses, 3 Cows, 12 Sheep, 2 Hogs, Household furniture, Provisions, Wheat 20 bushels, Rye, 2 Looms & tackling worth 20£, Farming Utensils.

(53).

The Rebel Troops came to his house the Day after he left it. They destroyed most of the Things.

EBENEZER FOSTER, Wits.:

Knew Claimt. He was very Loyal. Joined the Brit. at New York. Served in the Engineers Department. Knew his house & Lot in Woodbridge, about 1 acre & ¼ Land, House & Barn. His proper name is Gadbeer. Witness remembers Claimt. in Possession of this Place. He did a good Deal to it. Vals. it at 150£.

He was Clear in the World, Saving & in good Circumstances. Has frequently heard his Land was sold, bels. it to be so. The Rebels took Possession of his House, as Witness believes, soon after he went away & is satisfied he could bring nothing away. Witness speaks very favourably of his character.

NEW CLAIM.

March 8.

(54).

760. Case of ANTHONY REECE, late of Connect.

Claimt. says: He sent his Claim by Mr. Hardy.
He is a native of West Indies. Lived at Middle town, in Connect., when Troubles began. He went to Quebec & joined Genl. Burgoyne's Army in 1777, with the Promise of a Commission. Went with them on the expedition. Left him at Skeensboro with Dispatches to Sir Wm. How. He was taken on his return but made his Escape. Went to New York, recd. a Pension of ½ Dollar per Day from Sep., 1777, to April, 1783.

Served as Volunteer in the Army at Philadelphia & Charles Town.

Produces Certificate of Bevy. Robinson that he was on the List Extra guides & received ½ Dollar per Day.

He had no real Property. Is entitled to the Estate of an Uncle of his, to whom he is heir at Law. His Widow is now in Possession.

NEW CLAIM.

March 9th.

(55).

761. Case of GIDEON VERNON, late of Pensilva.

Clamt. says: He went to Campo bello, Ireland, Passmaquoddy Bay, Sep., 1783, from New York. Had not heard of the Act having passed when he left New York. The first he heard with certainty was when Mr. Hardy called there on his way from New York in Octr., '83. Claimt. sent to Mr. Hardy in Dec. following, with an acct. of his Losses desiring Mr. Hardy to take what steps were necessary, sent it by Mr. Lacy, Master of a small vessel from Shelburne. Does not know what Mr. Lacy did with the Letter, it did not come to Mr. Hardy's hands.

Had no opportunity of sending to England. No Vessel went immediately to England that he knew of. Has since heard that one vessel went in January. She went from St. Andrews, 20 miles from Campo bello, Ireland. They had scarce any boats in Campo bello Island & had not means therefore of Commnuication with the Vessels at St. Andrews. During months of Decr., Jany., February, Claimt. recollects no other Vessels but that Commanded by Lacy going from Campo bello to St. John's, and no vessel went to England during that time from Campo bello.

He lived in Providence Township, Chester Co. When Troubles began he from the first took a Loyal part. Had made himself obnoxious to the rebel Party in the year 1775 by objecting to an alteration proposed by the popular party in the Day for choosing Sheriffs, Assembly men & other officers.

(56).

Claimt. & others of the Loyal Party adhered to the Day formerly appointed for that Purpose. In Septr., 1777, left home. Went to the Brit. Army, had a Conference with Capt. Eustace & Lord Clinton. He was desired to go & make his observations in the American Army, which he did, & reported to Capt. Eustace.

A Party came in Persuit of him on which he fled & got on Board the Eagle. Was sent by Lord How with Despatches to Sir Wm. How at German town. He was frequently employd in going backward & forward from Sir Wm. to Lord How.

Remained till Philadelphia was Evacuated. After employd as guide to small Scouting Parties & sent to reconnoiters.

In Consequence of Claimts. Report a party of 60 Rifle men were surprized at Fox Chase & most of them taken. Claimt. Conducted the party who surprized them.

Went to New York with the Troops.

In Novr., 1779, was employd by Sir Henry Clinton to go with Despatches to Philadelphia & back part of Pensilvania, which he performed.

In 1781, had a Commission as Capt. of Associated Loyalists from Sir Henry Clinton, by Direction of Board of Directors.

Produces his Commission, 9 April, 1781.

(57).

Was employd in intercepting mails. He intercepted four & got two mails safe into the Lines.

He was particularly employed to intercept a mail from Philadelphia to general Green in May, 1781. He succeeded & sent it to Head Quarters.

He produces his Memorial to Sir Guy Carleton for Recompense for this Service on which appears an observation from Robt. Alexander, that Claimt. intercepted a mail from Philadelphia which was sent to Head Quarters.

Confirmed by Anthony Stewart.

Mr. Alexander was a Director & Mr. Stewart Secretary of the Board of Directors of Associated Loyalists. Both of them also say that they were informed by Govr. Franklin of Claimt. having been employd in secret Business by Sir Henry Clinton.

Claimt. has at present no half Pay.

He is now settled on the Magadary River.

(58).

No. 1. Was Possessed of 73 acres in Chester Co. under his Father's Will.

Produces Probate of the Will of his Father, Moses Vernon, Whereby he devises to Claimant 71 acres in Chester Co. Will dated 1767. Testr. died soon after.

Claimt. has been in Possession ever since till he left home.

No. 2. Purchased about 60 acres near the former. Produces Deed from Elias Vernon to Claimt. of 60 acres in Cons. 350£ Pens. Cur., June, 1774.

He lived at another house of his Brother's, but held these Lands himself.

Of No. 1, there were 5 acres meadow, 50 acres tillage.

Of No. 2, 10 acres meadow, 40 acres tillage. A farm House & Barn on each. A good orchard on one.

Vals. at 10 per acre Pens. Curcy.

---

(59).

Produces Certificates from Thos. Lewis, Agent for Sale of forfeited Estates, that he sold 2 Plantations, 160 acres, the other 42 acres in Providence Township belonging to Claimt., with appraisment by 2 persons at 75£ per acre.

Had 10 fat Bullocks taken by Rebel Militia on Claimt. leaving home, 1 yoke of Oxen Do., 11 Steers Do., 2 horses lost in Service. Hay, about 40 Ton, Potatoes, 400 Bushel.

Had a Lease of a house in New York. Produces Lease from David Clarkson of a Lot in New York to Claimt. & Jacob Ruffington for 7 years on the Rents & Covenants mentioned in the Lease, dated 1781.

Claimt. bought Mr. Buffington's Interest in the Lease.

1-3 part of the Sloop Fury purchased about 6 weeks before he left home. She was for the purpose of carrying Wheat & carried 7,000 Bushels.

She was taken by Col. Pape, a Rebel Col. 1-3 belonged to Mr. Lloyd, a Loyalist the other 1-3 belonged to a person of Doubtful Character.

Claimt. has understood Col. Pape sold it, that the owner who was not a Loyalist got his share.

Vals. his own share at 50£. He gave 65£ in Wheat for it.

Produces Instructions from Head Quarters, April, '81, for Claimt. to proceed with party under his Command on the Plan proposed. Do. from Directors of Associated Loyalists to Claimt. as Commandary on Excursion on the Delaware, April, '81.

NEW CLAIM.

March 10th.

762. Case of BENJ. INGRAHAM, late of New York.

(60).

Claimt. says: He came here in the summer, was disbanded Oct. 10. Went up to St. Ann's in 10 Days, staid there all the Winter. Knew nothing of the Act.

He lived in Co. of Albany, New York Prov. He endeavoured to get to the Northern Army under Genl. Burgoyne but could not. He returned, got to New York Decr., 1776. Served in King's American Regiment all the War, first private then Seargent.

Produces his Discharge 10 Oct., 1783. Now lives at Fredericton.

Was Possessed of a farm in Albany Co., King's District. Produces Deed from Isaac Hamlin & John Frost to Claimt. of 76 acres in Cons. 65£, 1773.

From Samuel Shaw to Claimt. of 8 acres in Cons. 8£, 1774.

From David Castle to Claimt. of 8 acres, Cons. 11£, dated 24 March, 1776. Says the Purchase was made in 1775.

From James Lockwood to Claimt. of a Dwelling house & Piece of Land in Cons. 20£, 1774.

The whole farm contained 93 acres, laid all together, 10 acres Meadow, all under fence & Improvements, except a small Quantity of Woodland. A new house. Says he improved it greatly after he bought it. Vals. it at 100£.

Produces affidt. from Alex. Montgomery, sworn at Gage Town before Wm. Tying, that he was in the Country when Committee seized the Estate of Claimt. They first had the Land & forbid his Wife to meddle with the Stock. (61)

Produces permit from these Comts. for Claimts. Wife to continue at her Habitation, which Claimt. says was his house. She continued there till the Peace. Came from New York with her Husband.

His Stock was seized by Committee & Sold. 1 yoke Oxen, Do. Steers, 7 Cows, 4 young Cattle, 35 Sheep, 6 Hogs, Farming Utensils, some little furniture, 140 Bushels Wheat in Stack, Rye 30 Bushels, 40 Oats, 150 Corn.

N.B.—His name is in both Ansteys Lists.

Produces Letter from Capt. Clements speaking very favouraby of Claimts. conduct & that he was universally esteemed by the officers of ye Regiment.

ABIJAH NEGRAHAM, Wits.:

He is Bro. to Claimt. Says Claimt. endeavoured to get .o the Northern Army. He had been imprisoned & put in Irons on acct. of his Loyalty. He could not get to Gen. Burgoyne's Army. Got to New York. Served all the War. (62)

He had a farm with a small framed house, containing 90 acres of Land & more, it was very well Improved. Agrees with Claimts. acct. of the Stock.

Was on the farm after his Brother went away. Witness took care of the family.

The Committee seized the Estate. They first rented the farm, have since sold it.

Sold the Stock at Vendue as he has been informed.

March 10.   Continuation of the Case of GIDEON VERNON.

Claimt. says he owed 80£ but had given no mortgage, it has not been claimed from the Estate, but has been demanded of Claimt. here.

JOSEPH TAYLOR, Wits. :

Knew Claimant, he was very active & considered as very serviceable to the King's Party. He was possessed of an Estate in Chester Co , thinks about 140 acres, part by his Father, part by purchase.

Vals. it at 5£ per acre.

(63).   He was in good circumstances & had a good Stock of Sheep, horses & Cattle.

Produces Certificates to his Loyalty from Dr. Paine & that Claimt. had been on several occasions confidentially employd.

Mr. Robt. Pagan Certifies in the most favourable manner of his Character & Conduct since he has been in this Country.

Ditto Mr. Clenck & Hugh MacKay.

NEW CLAIM.

March 10.   763. Case of JOHN COMPTON, late of New Jersey.

Claimt. says: He came in July. Went up to Majorville. Came down in Octr. Staid Nov. & Decr. Employd as a Bricklayer here & at Carleton.

Did not send his Claim till Capt. Vand. went, did not know it before.

Rejected.

Rejected as he was here in the Town & Carleton near 3 months of the Winter.

March 12.   764. Claim of JEREMIAH POTS, late of Massch.

Claimt. says: He is a native of America. Lived at Falmouth, Casco Bay, when Trouble broke out. He did everything in his Power against the measures of the Rebels. He happened to be one of the select men at Falmouth whose business it was to give notice of Town Meetings. Claimt. refused to notify the Meetings desired by the Rebels. In consequence of this he was persecuted. Was imprisoned several times. Had his Things taken from him by Force, so that he was forced to quit home, got away in May, 1777. Got to Nova Scotia, went in an open boat. Went from Halifax to New York in 1778. Was employd by Admiral Gambin to pilot a Vessel to New Hampshire which was going with Sir Henry Clinton Manifestoes.

(64).

Had been employd as Pilot on Board the Rainbow before that time.

When he went as Pilot of the Vessel which was carrying the Manifestoes, the Vessel was seized & the Whole Crew made Prisoners & kept in Prison during the Winter.

Went to Penobscot in 1780 & to St. Andrews in the beginning of 1784.

Produces Certificates from Capt. Osborn of the Ariadne that Claimt. acted as Pilot to the Rainbow on a three months Cruise in 1777, to the satisfaction of the Capt. & Officers.

Was possessed of a House in Falmouth, purchased it in the year 1770 of Saml. Cobb, gave a house & Land in the Country, about 12 acres, in exchange for this house & gave 100 ½ Joes in addition.

It was a Town Lot, a Dwelling house, a Store & out buildings, Wharf & Warehouse, Lime Kiln.

Buildings were all destroyed by Capt. Mowat in Octr., 1775.

The Land has been Confiscated.

Vals. the Whole at 600 Sterl.

Produces Certificates of Sale of a Lot in Falmouth and a Pew in the Meeting House.

Vals. the Pew at 12£.

At the time of the Fire at Falmouth lost a Cable worth 21.12, furniture wortht 40£.

Had also a Pew in the Church which was burnt, worth £15.

Lost the Sloop Jolly, 30 Ton Burthen. Taken from Claimt. by a Committee of Falmouth & Sold. Produces Certificates that

(65).

the Agent on the Estate of Claimt. accounted for a small Sloop, sold for 77£.

Vals. her at 150£ Sterl. Had two Scows taken at the time the Sloop was worth 40£.

Had an interest in the Schooner Favourite. Mr. Pagan was the owner of 7-16, Claimt. 9-16. She came to Falmouth the Day before the Fire. They were obliged to send her off without a Cargo. She went to the West Indies. The restraining Act had come out just before the schooner arrived there. The Master was to have got freight & carried her to England & done the best he could with her, but he could not stay at Tobago, he at last sold her at ———— for 337.10. She was worth 750£.

The Sloop Jolly which had been Claimts. was taken by the Tender of a Man of War. Claimt. got her again by paying salvage of 10£. The Rebels had her about three years, so she was not worth 80£ Crcy. when he got her.

Produces Protection from Capt. Mowat, Oct., 1775.

Mr. Thos. Myer, Wits.:

Lived at Falmouth. Mr. Pots from the first showed himself very Loyal & took an active Part. He was sent a Prisoner to the Provincial Congress at Watertown.

Knew his Lot at Falmouth, it was a very fine situation.

The buildings were all destroyed by the fire. Knew the Cable which was burnt, worth about 20£. He had removed a good deal of furniture, but lost a great Deal.

Knew his two Scows, they carried 8 or 9 Cord Wood. Remembers his having the Sloop Jolly.

(66).

ROBT. PAGAN, Wits.:

Claimt. was very Loyal, as much so as any man. Knew the Lot at Falmouth, it was in best Part of the Town.
Vals. the property at 1,000£ Sterlg.

March 12th.   765. Case of THOS. MYER, late of Massts.

(67).

Claimt. says: He lived at Falmouth when the Troubles broke out. From the first did all he could to support the Govrt. he was taken up & abused as a soldier, he refused to serve, on which he was taken up & abused by the mob, obliged to pay a fine. Was taken up to the Provincial Congress. Was obliged to quit Falmouth in 1777. Went to Nova Scotia with Mr. Pots in an open boat. Went to New York.

Commanded an Armed Vessel there & had two Smart Engagements with 2 Rebel Privateers at different times.

Went to Penobscot in the year 1780 & from thence to St. Andrew's

Produces Protection from Capt. Mowat, Oct., 1775.

Produces Attested Copy of Commission to Claimt. to Command the Brigantine British Tar, to be manned with 65 men the year 1779. He acted in this Command 9 months, during which time he had two Engagements. The vessel was so bad a sailor, that he was obliged to give her up. He then was for some time in the Transport Service.

(68).

Had a House & Lot in Falmouth, the house & buildings were destroyed at the time of the Fire by Capt. Mowat.

Produces Deed from Lewis Detters to Claimt. of a Lot in Falmouth in Cons. 170£ Conf. Mon., 1773.

He laid out a great Deal after the Purchase, it was a mere bake house when he bought it, he made it a Comfortable Mansion Laid out upwards of 100£.

Vals. it at 250.

Produces Certificates of Sale of Lot in Falmouth.

Lost furniture at same time to amount 15£.

Had ½ the Cargo of a Sloop caled the Defiance, lying at the Still house Wharf, Falmouth, & burnt.

The Cargo consisted of Lumber. Claimts. share in Lumber was £52.17.10. Produced Rect. to show he had paid so much for this Lumber, the rest of the Cargo was worth above 20, Claimts. Share, 75£.

Pew in the Church, Vals. 12£.

Schooner Mariann left at Falmouth, taken by the Com mittee, sold by them, they gave his Wife about 10£. She was worth 75£.

(69).

Built an house at Penobscot in the year 1781. There was a grant to Mr. Pagan, Mr. Wright & Claimt. of Land, each took their share & built upon it. Claimt. admits he now might sell it.

Vals. it a 500£.

Mr. Robt. Pagan, Wits.:

Claimt. has always been a Loyalist. He had the Command of an Armed Brig. of which Witness was part Owner. He distinguished himself by a very spirited Engagement & continued in that Command to the satisfaction of his Employers till the vessel was Converted into a Schooner.

Knew his Lot in Falmouth, worth 2 or 300£. Recollects that a Sloop was burnt at the time of the Fire, in which Mr. Myer was Concerned as part Owner of the Cargo.

Produces Copy of order, Nov. 28, of House of Assembly for Claimt.'s Wife to 90£ Newport or Halifax in a Casket, and that the Committee of Safety take Possession of Claimt.'s Estates, real & personal.,

766. Case of David Myer, late of Massts.   March 12th.

Thos. Myer, eldest son of David Myer, decd., appears. Says his Father lived at Falmouth. He was Tide Surveyor. He was an officer under government almost all his Life. He declared his sentiments most freely against the Rebellion, in consequence of which he suffered great abuse. He continued at Falmouth supported by Witness. When Witness was settled at Penobscot, his Father came to him there. He died at St. Andrews in March last, without a Will.   (70).

He lived in an hired house at Falmouth. Witness knew he had the furniture mentioned in the Schedule. He had nobody to assist him & Witness is satisfied it must all have been lost & it is wor h the sum stated in Schedule. Witness is his eldest son. He has 2 Sisters both in the states.

Produces the Commission to his Father in 1769 to be Tide Surveyor.

767. Case of Gen. Wheler, late of New York.   March 12th.

Nicholas Wheler, one of the younger Sons of Geo. Wheler, decd., appears. Says his Father lived in Livingstons Manor, Albany Co. He had always declared in Faivour of the Brit. Govert. He had 2 Sons in the Brit. Army. He tried 3 or 4 times to get within the Brit. Lines but could not. He was several times imprisoned. Kept several months in Prison. All his moveables were taken at different times. The Rebels drove him from his Place & sold it. He did not get within the Lines till the Peace. Came here on Evacuation of New York. Died Novr. last at Oromokte. Left a Widow Polly & 10 Children.   (71).

The eldest son & 2 Brothers & 1 Sister are now in the States. The Widow & 6 Children are here.

His Father had a Tenant Farm of above 200 acres. He had a Lease of two Lives, his own & his Wifes. Could sell the Improvets. He had 7 horses, 8 Cows, 2 pr. Oxen, 18 Heifers, 6 young Cattle, 30 Sheep, 7 Hogs, Furniture, farming utensils. Most of it was seized & sold.

Produces 2 affidavits sworn at Frederickton to the Loyalty of Geo. Wheler & his sufferings, and that his property was publicly sold. The Deponents value his Property at 7 or 800£ this Cury. Claimt. has no settlement of his own. He works at Majorville, but his home is with his mother at Oromookto. His Brother Reinhard is with his mother, older than Witness. Served in Brit. Army during the war. Elizabeth Wheler now with her mother. Edward in Majorville for work, but will return to his mother. Mary now at Majorville. Catharine with her mother. Wishes whatever is paid may be paid to his mother.

(72). Name of Geo. Wheler, Dutchess Co., is in Anstey's List.

Claimant's Father was driven from his Place & had gone to New Milford in the Fall 1782. Got in New York in April, '83. Went with him.

The Place was sold in March '83. The moveables were taken at different times. Some he sold himself to support him in Prison.

His Mother proposes that Mr. Sandys shd. be her Agent.

March.   768. Case of JOSEPH THORNE, late of New Jersey.

Claimt. says. He came to Campo bello from New York in Aug., '83. Staid there all the Winter. Removed next spring to Beaver Harbr. Now settled there. Had no opportunity of sending from Campo bello. Was settled at Pescatua, Midsex Co.,

(73). Jersey. Went to Lord Cornwallis's Army in the Winter 1776. Produces Protection from Lord Cornwallis Dec., 1776. Produces Certificates from C. Manhood of his having subscribed a Declaration agreeable to the Proclaman. by Commrs., Jany., 1777.

Carried Forage to the Army during the Winter. Was taken Prisoner with his son. Kept 3 Days there. Left Home when the Army Evacuated New Jersey. Produces Pass, dated 10 June, 1777. Had his Family removed to Staten Island. Remained there during the war. Saved two Regiments on Staten Island from being surprised by giving notice of an attack intended by Genl. Sullivan.

Had 37 acres in Piscatua.

Produces Deed from Lawrence Eikengen to Claimt. of 37 acres, 4-10 in Piscatua, Cons. 135£, dated 29 March, 1774.

He repaired it considerably. Built a New Barn.

Vals. it at 112£ Sterl. It is Mortgaged for 100£ Jersey Currency.

Produces Certificate of Sale with appraisment at 160£.

Lost a horse, taken from his house at Piscatua by the Rebels, after he had been imprisoned in the winter 1776. A party came to his house, took & destroyed his furniture, left a wagon. Col. Webster's men had taken the weels so he could not bring it off. Lost 2 horses &c. by the Brit. in Staten Island.

Produces Certificate from Col. Bellop that Claimt. came to Staten Island as a Loyal Refugee in 1776 or 1777. Speaks of him
(74). as a good subject.

NEW CLAIM.

769. Case of ANN CABLE, Widow and the Children of John March 17th.
Cable, Decd., late of Connect.

ANN CABLE, Widow:

Says she came in May, '83. Went up the River. Never came down in the winter. Never heard till Capt. Vand. was gone, of the act of Parl.

Her late Husb. lived at Glasstenberry, Connect. He went from Home in the spring & joined the Brit. in Dec., 1776.

He had a vessel of his own which served as a Tender to Capt. Askew of the Swan.

Produces Copy of Certificate from James Ayscough that John Cable served with him as Volunteer with his Vessel & 10 men from the ———.

Produces Journal kept by ——— which appears authentic, Cable. wherein he states he left home August, 1776, to go to the Kings' B. 16. Troops, but returned. Helped People over to Long Island. Went P. 164. to different Places & was at great expense to keep People faithful.

States that in Nov., 1776, he went to Horse Neck & bought (75). two vessels & left one there to be Laded. Went to Fairfield. Was carried before a Commission on Suspicion. Sent for his Brother to come round from Horseneck that they might go away together. Was carried before several Committees. Was acquitted by the Committee of Fairfield Dec., 1776. Prepared to go off. A mob collected again. His Brother came in haste to inform him that the vessel at Horseneck had been seized. The Journal goes no further.

In his acct. he states the Sloop Sally as his own. Vals. her at 246.10.

Says her Husb. lost &c., &c.

Action at Danbury to this Day 8 Feby., 1778.

As to his Loyalty, he was ready to serve on every occasion, when it was in his Power.

He died in Decer., 1779, witht. a Will. Left Ann, his Widow, John, his eldest son, aged 29; James, 24; Peter, 22; Anthony, 21; Danl., 17; Jane, 25; Marianna, 15. All in this Province & live with their Mother.

Claimt. says her Husband lost the Sloop Greenwich or Sally. She was taken at Horseneck with a cargo of Flax Seed.

He had two other vessels.

Claimt. says she staid a year & half after her Husband's De- (76). parture from Glossenbury. Went with her family. She was obliged to give up her all. They took his Books & furniture to amount near 40£. Mentions particular articles.

He had a real Estate bought in 1772 for 300£. Consisted of 25 acres with a Mill. He built a Dwelling house & stores. Has no Deeds. There was a mortgage for 409£ to one Mr. Brown. Supposes Mr. Brown may be in Possession.

WILLIAM PECK, Witness:

Remembers John Cable. He was a Loyalist. He went off to ye British in 1776. Served with a vessel along with Capt. Ayscough for a twelve month.

There was a sloop at Horseneck of 25 Tons. Witness built her for George Peck & Joseph Ferris, producing Bill of Sale to George Peck & Joseph Ferris, Consn. 103, 1771.

There appears an Indorsement by which George Peck & Joseph Ferris give up all their Right to Witness, March 31, 1777.

He cannot say what he gave. Says that John Cable bargained for her before, in the Fall 1776. The Mob took her in Decr., 1776. A guard was put over her.

(77). Witness got Possession of her in January next. She was taken again from Witness & the Cargo landed. The Rebels made a Gally of the Sloop afterwards. The Seed was put in a Store at Horseneck & burnt, when Govr. Tryon burnt the Place.

Witness considered the vessel as his own, but meant Cable should have her. Considered the Seed as Cables. Sloop Andrew was saved. He lost the Sloop Primeus & Cargo.

JAMES CALEHAN, Wits:

Knew John Cable. Remembers his serving under Capt. Ayscough with a small vessel of his own. A Brother of Claimt. came off from Glossonbury at the same time.

About Christmas, 1776, Witness had a Conference with John Cable at Fairfield & he agreed to go off with him, as they could not continue at home. John Cable had two vessels, one the Primus. The name of other Witness does not recollect. Believes it might be the Andrew. The Mob on Suspicion of their Intentions stopt the two vessels, took away the sails. When Cable & Witness were carried before a Committee they were at last cleared. Went away in January. Witness with John Cable went in the Andrew. The (78). other vessel, the Primus, sailed in Company. They were obliged to go away in a great Hurry. They thought the Mob rising & therefore Witness said they must go, or they should be taken by the Mob if they did not.

John Cable's Brother came & gave the alarm. Told them that the vessel left in his care had been seized at Horseneck.

They proceeded in Consequence of this for Huntingdon. The Andrew got safe. The Primus was lost. Vals. her at 250 Dollars. C ble lost 440 Bushels Flax Seed, 9s. 6d. per Bush.

Witness says they were obliged to retreat in this way, otherwise the vessels would have been seized. He understood both these vessels belonged to Cable. They would not have sailed at that time & in such weather, had it not been from fear of the Property falling into the hands of the Mob. Witness understood that John Cable had an Interest in the vessel at Horseneck & in the Cargo.

William Peck is a Relation of John Cable's. Conjectures that the vessel might have been Cables, tho. they thought it prudent to pass it in the name of Peck, as Cable had other vessels & there might be more Danger of getting them off.

WILLM. PECK, Witness, called again. Says the Sally was about 25 Tons. Vals. her at 206£. She was loaded with Flax Seed. Produces his Book of accts. whereby it appears that he made John Cable Debtor for 754 Bushels of Flax Seed at 3s. 9d. lawf. per Bushel, and another cash worth 4£.11. Makes him also Detter for money paid Capt. Peck, 33.9 lawf. This cash was part of Payment for the Sloop. Says he was present when John Cable bargained with Joseph Ferris & Geo. Peck for the vessel in the Fall of 1776. (79).

Says that his Reason for taking the Assignment from them to himself was because John Cable was gone off & if taken in his name the Rebels would have kept her, without any chance of getting her again.

Meant certainly that Cable should have had her. Witness paid one half for which he charged Cable. Is Cable to pay the other half now.

JABEZ CABLE:

Remembers John Cable serving under Capt. Ayscough with a Tender of his own for 6 or 7 months. Witness was Pilot to Capt. Ayscough.

The Tender was of great service to them. Cable was very active & zealous & served as a Volunteer. Has often heard Cable speak of the vessel taken at Horseneck as being his own.

JAMES CABLE, Wits:

Says that he & all his Brothers & Sisters wish that Payment should be made to the Mother. Says that his Mother had several articles of furniture taken from her when she came off & she was allowed to take very little. (80).

Claim of JOSIAH, SIMON, STEPHEN & JONAS JONES. Vol. 10, p. 30, Supra.

This is a Claim by the children of the late Col. Elisha Jones of Massts. for the real Property of their Father who died Intestate in the year 1776.

This being a Claim for the Father's Estate the Comrs. Consider all the Children, who are Loyalists themselves, as entitled to Claim for their share and therefore it is the Intention of the Comrs. to admit Ephraim Jones, one of the Sons now resided in Canada, to Claim for his share in the Estate, tho. he is not mentioned by name in the Claim.

The late Col. Jones left six children besides his, the five sons above mentioned all which six children were handsomely provided for in his Life time. Five are now in the States. One Son named Elisha, who was also provided for by the Father, died in Nova

(81). Scotia, leaving a Widow & family, who have an allowance made under the Claim entered in the name of Mehettaphel Jones and others.

The children in the States besides the Provision before mentioned, are likely to recover great part of their Father's Estate, which has not been Confiscated.

By the Law of Massts. the Estate by the Father dying intestate became divisable amongst all the children with a double share to the eldest son, and those children who had been provided for in their Father's Life time were obliged to bring in what they had formerly recd. to account which has been certified of the Attorney General of this Province.

The Sons who are now under the Brit. Government have not been provided for by their Father and if they divide all the Confiscated Estate, it will not make their share. so large as their Brothers in the States.

On this ground the Comrs. divide the Property proved to be Confiscated into five shares.

They have already named three of the Brothers and reportd them for Compensation 1-5 to each. They mean to examine Ephraim in Canada, transmit the Evidence which has been taken. They in this case as Jonas, one of the Brothers, now resides in England & will be examined there, that if the Board at home agree (82). with the Comrs. here, he may the same allowance.

This being the case of a very meritorious Family, the Comrs. have made their Report as expeditiously as it has been in their Power tho. perhaps a little out of the common course with a view to serve them as much as possible.

PROCEEDINGS

OF

LOYALIST COMMISSIONERS

QUEBEC, 1787.

Vol. XVII.   z

BEFORE COMMISSIONER PEMBERTON.

Claimants.

	MSS. Folio.		MSS. Folio.
Adams, John	85	Marsh, Abraham	89
Barnet, Mrs. Ann, (now Mrs. Hall)	40	Miller, Garret	48
Brian, Mrs. Rachel (Mrs. McIntosh)	58	Mack, John	54
Cameron, Duncan	59	Monro, Hugh	68
Campbell, Mrs. Elizabeth	30	Morris, Lieut.-Col. John	9 and 26
Cox, John	36	Orr, Thomas	25
Cruikshank, Alexander	32	Parrott, James	83
Dunham, Daniel	80	Perry, Samuel	22
Frost, James	12	Ruiter, Capt. Henry	62
Hoffnail, Michael	74	Scot, Walter	50
Holland, Samuel	2	Skimming, John	82
Hyatt, Abraham	52	Smith, Alexander	43
Jebare, Joseph	66	Stewart, William	67
Jones, Josiah, Simeon, Stephen, and Jonas	10	Swan, Thomas	56
McIlmoyle, James	45	Taylor, Nathaniel	19 and 26
Macnaughton, Alexander	1	Waite, John	46
Macneil, Archibald	11 and 14	Weber, Christian	65
Macquin, Daniel	87	Wragg, Richard	78

58 AR.

THE EVIDENCE.

NEW CLAIM.

May 5th.

770. Case of ALEXR. MACNAUGHTON, late of Georgia.

(1).

Claimt. says. He went on Evacuation of Charlestown to St. Lucia. Went from St. Lucia to Tortola & thence to St. Augustine in April, 1784. Could not send his Claim from Lucia or Tortola. Did not know of the Act till he came to Augustine. Claims many of them were sent home.

Lived in Georgia at Briar Creek. Joined the Brit. when Col. Cambell first came in—Was with the army till evacuation, then went to Charles town. Was in the Militia. Was in several engagements.

Had 200 acres in Briar Creek. Had them 15 or 16 years. Had them on first coming from Ireland. Took them up, cleared 30 acres. Heard he was on the black List at St. Augustine.

Lost 4 horses, 30 Cattle, 80 Hogs, furniture, utensils, Corn.

His home was destroyed by the Rebels and all his things plundered, after Ash's Defeat.

Capt. Wm. Read Knew Claimt.

He was very Loyal. Remembers his serving in the Militia.

Came in on Col. Campbell's Landing. Continued to serve till evacuation of Savanah.

He had a Farm on Briars Creek. He had a considerable number of Cattle.

Knew his Farm very well. A good Plantation. A good Deal Clear. Remembers him in Possession. From first he cleared it himself.

N.B.—Witness wishes to have his Militia Commission & Certificates.

Quebec.
May 21st.

771. Case of SAMUEL HOLLAND, ESQ., late of New York.

(2).

Claimt. appears & being sworn saith: He lived at Amboy, New Jersey, when the Troubles broke out. He came out to America in the year 1756, as Lieutenant in the 60th Regt. He acted as Engineer to Genl. Wolf in the seige of Louisbourg & in the conquest of this Country. He had a Company afterwards in the 60th Regiment. Was 2nd Engineer in this Province, afterwards principal Engineer. Produces his Commissions.

In the year 1764 was made Surveyor of this Province which he now holds, and about the same time Surveyor General of the Northern District of North America. Produces Commissions.

His business had carried him to Amboy where he was residing when the Troubles broke out.

The Americans wanted to make Claimant their Chief Engineer or Master of Artillery.

By General Tryon's Direction he said in the Country to get some Information. In Novr., 1775, he went on Board the Dutchess of Gordon & was sent home by Genl. Tryon with Dispatches for

Lord Geo. Germain & to give Information. In 1776 returned to America as Brevet Major & aid de camp to Genl. Hyster, Commander of the Hessian Troops. He resigned this appointment in 1777, raised the Corps of Guides & Pioneers. (3).

Went to Danbury with Genl. Tryon. Was at the taking of Fort Montgomery & on different skirmishes. He having the care of the Guides, the chief of the Intelligence went thro. his Hands. Continued in this service till 1778, when he came to this Province by order of G_nl. Haldimand. He was appointed Muster Master of the German Troops here. He continued in the Province ever since.

Has now the Place of Surveyor of this Province with Salary of 300£. Has no half pay.

His Place as Surveyor of the Northern District had no salary annext to it, but his allowance for House Rent & Provisions amounted to about 100£ per ann.

It was intended that he should have had a Benefit from the Publication of his Maps & Plans, which he had been employed in taking for ten years, but Des Barnes has cheated him out of this. He has frequently recd. the Thanks of the Board of Trade for his services.

Claimt. was possessed of 3,105 acres in the Township Rumney No. 1. & Campton called Hollandville.

Produces Grant from Govr. Wentworth of 3,105 acres in the Province of New Hampshire 1773, with a survey of the same by (4). Jas. Roudge, Surveyor General.

Before this Grant was made to Claimt. there was a Dispute between the two Townships Rumney & Campton & Claimt. could not have the grant till he had settled the dispute & paid the Demands of different Persons upon the Lands. Claimant settled with the different Townships, gave Lands to some persons & bought out others, and paid to different persons to buy out their rights. The sum of £562.8 Sterling.

He obtained a vote from the Proprietors in the Township of Campton Confirming the Grant of 3,105 acres, with exception of 500 acres to Benning Wentworth and any 100 acre Lots already laid out under ye hand of Proprietors, dated 1773. *Benning Wentworth was satisfied, and the other lots bought out.*

Produces his Books kept by George Durboge, his Clerk, by which it appears that the above sum of 562£ was expended on acct. of the Estates of Hollandville. *Produces a receipt from his agent, Ed. Everett, of a like vote from Rumney, with exception of lots already laid out. Says he bought out the lots.*

When he purchased there were about 4 Huts upon it & about 150 acres clear. Claimt. built a large house for a Tavern, 2 other Houses & Barns. Cleared 400 & some of the most valuable Lands. Had paid ½ a Joe for clearing the Interval Land. Most that he cleared was Interval Land. It cost ½ Joe first clearing & then 4 Dollrs.

He says he sold his Commission of Captn. of 60th Regiment (5). for 1,500£, all of which was laid out upon this Estate. He had granted several Leases. The Tenants were to pay out the Profits on the Lands & in the year '80 were to pay Rent. The rent in 1780 would have been worth 220£ per ann.

He was offered by a Relation 5,000£ for this Estate. Says he would have sold it for that, taking Bonds & Mortgages. Does not think he could have got such a sum in hard money.

This lies in New Hampshire in a well settled part of the Country.

Claimant's name was in the act of Proscription. It is now in Possession of several persons who had it as a Reward of their services.

One Everitt who served as Capt. in the Rebel service is now in Possession of the Tavern and Peter Mayhew is in Possession of a large Farm and all the Possessors are adverse to Claimant.

He had no Debts or Incumbrances on this estate.

(6). N.B.—It appears on his acct. Books kept by George Durboge that Claimant is in good circumstances & had a large Ballance owing to him.

No. 2. Had an Estate in Corinth, Vermont. Had 1-3 of the Township in his own right, 7,308 acres. Purchased of the New Hampshire Grantees at different times for about 136£ & got it confirmed by the New York Government. He had been in Possession from 1773, till the Rebellion broke out. Had made surveys & divided the Lands. Had let out several parcels and laid the whole out in Lots. He had pd. the expenses of getting the grants in New York.

They used to sell for a Dollar per acre. The purchasers were to pay 3d. per acre after 10 years quit rent.

Claimt. has made all this over to a friend Asher Potter to save it if Possible. Potter has not got Possession of any part. Some part has been sold to pay taxes.

He had purchased 1,050 acres in the same township in the name of his two Sons John & Henry who are trying to recover it.

A great many hundred acres were cleared by the different Tenants. He had sold a Considerable part subject to quit Rent (7). after 10 years. He had sold about 1,100 acres. The money had not been paid.

No. 3. Had 2-3 of the Township of Topsham in Vermont, adjoining to Cornith, about 16,000 acres. He purchased of the New Hampshire grantees & got the Title confirmed by New York Govrt. Had completed his Purchase in 1773.

Has been in Possession & run the boundary lines & laid out the Roads. Had not parted with this to any Tenants.

He had laid out no more than in purchasing of the New Hampshire Grantees & paid for expense of New York Grants.

Withdrawn Claim for Estate at Barnet.

No. 4. Had several undivided Rights in Rumney; a Right consisted of 350 acres. These purchases cost him about 84£ in the year 1773.

Was possessed of his several Bonds mentioned in the Schedule. There was a Mortgage from John Armory to John Watts of House & Land in New York for 1771 Dollars. Assgined by Watts to Claimt. in 1773.

Amory continued in Possession till his death, before the Rebellion. Watts being a Loyalist now in England, is not allowed to recover any thing, neither is Claimant.

Claimt. supposes the mortgage may have been paid in Paper Money to the state on Watt's acct., who has been prosecuted. Produces Letter of Abraham Lott of New York by which it appears that Aldoma Leffert bought it with the Mortgage upon it & had the Mortgage canceld., paying the money due to Watts on Mortgage into ye Treasury, Watts being a Loyalist & his Estate Confiscated. (8).

---

772. Case of LIEUT.-COL. JOHN MORRIS, late of New Jersey. May 25.

Exam. de bene esse.

ISAAC OGDEN, Witness:

Says he was acquainted with Claimt. for many years. He lived in Monmouth Co., New Jersey. He was then an officer on half pay, having served the war before last.

In 1775 he stood forward in support of the Brit. Govert. He was appointed Commissioner to take the Oaths of Allegiance in 1776. After the Trentown affair he retired to Sandy Hook & held the Post there. He raised a Regiment in Genl. Skinner's Brigade which he Commanded. Served the whole war, at least till the Regiment was reduced & was much distinguished for his Loyalty & activity. (9).

Understood he had an Estate in Monmouth Co. Does not know the value.

Knew the Family of the Leonards, one of whom has appraised Claimant's Estate. They were a respectable family. Is not particularly acquainted with the hand writing of Saml. Leonard.

Case of JOSIAH, SIMEON &c., JONES, late of Massts. (Supra). May 29.

EPHRAIM JONES, one of the sons of the late Col. Elisha Jones appears & being sworn saith:

Says he is one of the younger Sons of Col. Elisha Jones, decd., of West town & Claims the same share with his other Brothers of his Father's Estate.

He lived at East Hoosack when Troubles began. Joined the Brit. at Point au fur. Joined Genl. Ridehazte, after was with Sir Guy Carleton. Was appointed Commissary of Forage in Genl. Burgoyne's Army by Sir Guy Carleton. Was with Genl. Burgoyne & taken Prisoner at Saratoga. He continued on subsistance of 3s. 8d. per day for some time. (10).

In 1781 entered as a Volunteer in the Royal Rangers & served till that Regiment was reduced in Canada.

Is now settled above Montreal in Seventh Township. Has no appointment now or half Pay.

Was Commissary for the Loyalists but that has now ceased.

May 29.

773. Case of ARCHIBALD MACNEIL, late of Massts., Decd.

Elizabeth MacNeill, Widow of the decd. Archibald, has been appointed admr.

David Shoolbred appears in her behalf.

Says the late Archibald Macniel lived in Boston in Business of a Baker which he carried on in an extensive Line. From the first he distinguished himself by his Loyalty. He was one of the town Association. Left Boston with the Troops.

(11). In the year 1774 & 1775 the Tradesmen at Boston had refused supplying the Troops with Bread & Flour, on which occasion Mr. Macneil & a Mr. Hill engaged to do it & supplied them for a long time.

Went to Halifax on Evacuation of Boston. Came from thence to Quebec & settled here in June '85, going from this Place to New Brunswick. He was murdered by some Indians.

He had made no Will. He left a Widow, who is appointed admr. Lives at Quebec.

Eldest Son, Archibald, in Jamaica, a Clerk in the house of Balentine, Fairly & Co.

He served in the Engineer Department during almost the whole war.

Wm. Henry a Clerk with Wilson Taylor of Montreal. Eliza-

beth, Wife of Witness. Nancy, Wife of Thos. Hill, now of Boston. Sarah, unmarried, with her Mother at Quebec.

Mary, wife of John Walter, mercht. of Quebec at present as Witness thinks in England, his Wife is now at Boston, but Witness supposes Mr. Walter means to come here or to stay in England.

Produces Copy of Warrant for banishing him from the State of Massts. Signed John Hancock, 1784.

May 29.

774. Case of JAMES FROST, late of Rhode Island.

[12]. Claimt. appears & being sworn saith:

He is a native of America. Was in Quebec when the Troubles first broke out. He had come from Rode Island. Had the Command of a ship. Had been several years in the Trade to this Country. He left his Family in Rode Island.

In 1775 entered into the Brit. service. Served on Lake Champlain in different Commands, first under General Carleton & then under Govr. Haldimand's appointment. Continued to serve till the year 1782, when he was sent for to Quebec. Made Captn. of the Port there and enjoys that appointment now.

Produces Certificate from Capt. Schank to Claimt. to skill &

Services in Strong Terms.

Produces Letter from Ditto in strong terms of Commendation of Claimant's Conduct & Loyalty.

Claimt. says he was possessed of a House & Lot in New Port, Rode Island. It had been his Fathers. His Father, Millar Frost, left it him by Will. He died in 1769. Claimant was then at Sea, but took Possession as soon as he arrived at Newport. Continued in Possession. Was master of a ship & sailed to different parts of the world. His home was Rode Island. He happened to be in this Province just as the Troubles broke out. Offered his services & his ship to Sir Guy Carleton, which was accepted. The ship was fitted out as an armed ship & served him during the seige in 1775, till the winter set in. She was then hauled on shore. Claimant served in the Garrison with Commission as a first Lieutenant. After the seige was over, was ordered in service on the Lakes nl Supra. (13).

Claimt.'s Father had been in Possession a long time. He bought the land & built the house himself. Claimant was eldest son. He had a Brother living at his Father's Death, and has a sister now living. Vals. this house at 600£. It was a good house in the centre of the Town. This house has been Confiscated & sold.

Capt. Martin brought a Newspaper when this house was advertized for Sale. Capt. Martin's house was advertized in the same Paper.

Claimant has not been able to get any Certificates of Confiscation or Copies of proceedings he has wrote, but had no answers to his Letters. His Wife & family are in this Province.

His furniture was also sold at the same time. It was advertized for sale with the house.

Vals. it at 50£.

V. Vol. 11. Col Dundas's Book, 18 July, '87.

Further Evidence in Case of ARCH. MACNEIL, decd.   June 5.

DAVID SHOOLBRED, Wits:

Produces Pass for Arch. Macneil, Septr. 1774, Boston. Signed John Small. (14).

Produces Deed from Isaac Freeman to Archibald Macneil of Messuage & Land in Marlboro Street, Boston, in Cons. £660.13s., dated 1753. No. 1.

Appears a Mortgage. Witness Produces Deed from Mary Ross to Arch. Macneil of a Mess &c. in Marlboro Street for 30£ Conditionally for Payment of said sum & Interest, dated 1775. No. 2.

Produces Deed from John Hunt to Archd. Macneil of 2 Lots in Grenville containing 55 acres each in Consn. 47.13 Lawful 1768. No. 3.

Produces Deed from John Hunt to Archd. Macneil of a Lot No. 4. containing 84 acres in Granville in Consn. 36£ Lawful, 1768.

Produces Deed from John Hunt to Archd. Macneil of 2 Rights in Valentine Township, Connect., to each of which 100 acres has been already laid out in Consn. 36£, 1772. No. 5.

He had 5,000 acres in North Yarmouth, Casco Bay. These Lands had belonged to Mr. Roland Houghton. No. 6.

Roland Houghton gave by Will, dated 1744, 600 acres in North Yarmouth to his sons John & Richard & Grand children Joshua & Anna Winock, also all the Rights he had in the Islands belonging to Township of North Yarmouth equally amongst his (15).

said children. Gives the Residue of his Estate to his Widow, Ann Houghton.

Mr. Macneil married Ann Winock, one of the Legatees in the above Will mentioned. Mr. Macneil had one child by his first Wife. The child is dead & the Wife is Dead.

Produces Copy of Will of Joshua Winock, whereby he gives Arch. Macneil all his Estate, real & Personal, after payment of Debts, 1748.

Produces Deed from Anna Houghton, Widow of Rowland Houghton, whereby she conveys to Archibald Macneil one 150th part of a Gore or Tract of Land in North Yarmouth in Consn. of 10£, dated 1751.

Produces short Abstract from the Books of the Proprietor in

North Yarmouth, whereby it appears that several Rights were sold to Rowland Houghton. Signed by Proprietor's Clerk.

Produces a subsequent Letter from the said Proprietor's Clerk to Archd. Macneil relative to building an House on the Lands there, to shew Mr. Macneil was interested in these Lands.

Produces Mortgage from Amos Silvester of 40 acres in North Yarmouth, 1774.

No. 7.

(16).

Penobscot Lands. Produces a Deed from Anthony Coverley to Mary Taylor, his Daughter, of half his right which he bought of Charles Chauncey containing ten Leagues at a Place cald. Muscongus, 1765.

Taylor & his Wife, formerly Coverley, sold their Interest to Archibald Macneil.

Produces Copy of Assessment on the Proprietors of Lands in Penobscot amongst which Mr. Macneil's name appears.

SARAH MACNEIL, Witness:

Says she remembers that there was a kind of Combination amongst many of the Tradesmen not to work for the Troops, on which her Father stood forward & worked for the Army.

He always continued to shew the same Loyalty. He continued as long as the Troops staid. Went away with them. He came to Halifax & afterwards to Quebec.

He died without a Will & Mrs. Macneil is adsx.

Mrs. Macneil appears, says she has been appointed adminx.

Certificate of the sale of Mr. Archibald Macneil's Estate in Suffolk Co., Massts., for the sum of 1,000£ lawful. Signed Saml. Barnet, Chairman of Committee. Produces Valuation by 3 appraisers who value it at 2,500£ lawful & that it would have rented for 130£ lawful.

SARAH MACNEIL, Witness, says:

(17).

There was a large Dwelling House, 2 Bake Houses, Stable, garden. The bake houses & outhouses & storehouses were built after the Purchase from Freeman.

He was offered 1,000£ Sterl. before he built the house at the end of the garden.

His Son in Law, Thos. Hill, tried to buy it in, but was not allowed. He would have given 2,000£ for it.

Remembers her Father in Possession of Lands in Granville purchased of Mr. Hunt; No. 3 & No. 4. Did not hear of anything laid out by her Father after ye Purchase.

Heard also of his being in Possession of Lands in Valentine Township, No. 5.

He had Lands in North Yarmouth. She does not know how much. Mrs. Macneil, the first Wife, & her Bro. Joshua were the only Heirs to Rowland Houghton. Mrs. Macneil, the first Wife, died before her Brother Joshua.

Her Father had Lands in Penobscot purchased of a Mrs. Taylor. Thinks her Father had a Deed.

They have tried to get Certificates of Confiscation of their Lands but could not obtain them.

Her Father had a Sloop of 115 Tons. It was taken into the King's Service by Major Sheriff. Her Father therefore had neglected to get her ready to take away. It was left at Boston on the Evacuation & there sunk by the Americans. The notice was so short that her Father would not have been able to have carried it off. Her Father purchased it at auction.

(18).

He left the largest part of his furniture behind at Boston; large Glasses, Tables & one very valuable horse & chaise.

Her Husb. had Debts due 1,677£.

JOHN COFFIN, ESQ.:

Knew the late Archibald Macneil at Boston. He was distinguished from the first for his Loyalty. Witness speaks clearly & decidedly & strongly to that point. Thought him in good circumstances as he lived well. He had a great Deal of Business from the Army.

Knew No. 1. Vals. it at 1,000£ Sterl.

Heard of his having Lands in other parts of the Province.

Understood he had a large Tract about Penobscot. His house was very well furnished.

CONSTANTINE FREEMAN, ESQ.:

Knew Macneil. Heard of his having Lands in Penobscot & Grenville.

NATHANIEL TAYLOR, ESQ., Wits., says:

Knew Archibald Macneil. He always was distinguished as very Loyal. Knew his house at Boston, No. —. There was a large lot, Garden, Bake House, &c., in a public, well situated Thinks it worth between 1,000 & 1,500£. Heard of his having other Lands. Considerable property to the eastward. Understood it was a Property in what was called Plymouth Purchase, which extended from Kennebec to Penobscot. Thinks he had other Lands.

(19).

Heard he had a Sloop at Boston. Witness thinks he registered a Sloop for him & that it was left at Boston. A Sloop of that burthen, 115 tons, was worth from 200 to 400 Lawful, according to the Condition she was in.

June 6.

775. Case of NATHANIEL TAYLOR, ESQ., late of Massts.

N.B.—Evidence heard de bene esse at Halifax.

Claimant sworn saith:
He is a native of America. Lived at Boston. He was Deputy

Naval officer there. Had been in that office from the year 1755. Benjamin Pemberton was the Principal. Claimt. acted as his Deputy for many years. Afterwards acted as Deputy to the sons of Sir Francis Bernard. Produces the last appointment from John Bernard in 1772.

(20).

He was discharging the Duties of this office when the Troubles broke out. When Boston Port was shut up, he went first to Plymouth, then to Salem & executed the office there. During this time he was stationed at Salem from Aug., 1774, till after the Battle of Lexington. He was desired by Genl. Gage & the Quarter Master General to send Provisions for the King's Service to Boston which he did & sent in many vessels while he was in the Custom house at Salem in the year 1775. He understood there was a Design to seize his person & hold him as an Hostage in case Genl. Gage should seize any person at Boston, on which he made his escape & got on Board a man of war & got to Boston. Continued at Boston till Evacuation, having left a person to execute his office at Salem. Came to Halifax on the Evacuation & from thence to this Province. His name is in the first Act of Proscription.

He was possessed of 2 Lots of Vacant Land in Boston. He

had purchased the principal part 3 or 4 years before the Troubles. 1-8 part belonged to his children, the rest he had purchased for about 150£. He was offered 150£ Stel. for one, the other he sold at 100£ lawf. He had let the 2d. Lot at 6£ per ann.

This Land has not been sold. Claimant has sent a Power of Attorney to sell it, if possible. At present therefore suspends his Claim as to this Property.

When he left Boston he left considerable personal effects. He left merchandize & furniture to the value of 500£ which he could not bring away. Part has been disposed of for the Benefit of his children. He thinks about half. The rest has been lost to himself & family. It was left under ye care of Mrs. Tailor's Father who died 2 or 3 years ago. Part was seized as soon as the Rebels entered the Town.

(21).

Claimt. cannot give a very exact acct., but says he can confidently say he lost above 100£ Sterl. value. Several persons who had lost property from the King's Troops retaleated & took property of the Loyalists. He lost that way. States Debts to amount of 600£ Sterl.

His Place was worth from 450 to 500£ Sterl. after paying the Principal. It was increasing in value. It arose from Fees. He had been in the office above 20 years. It comprehended all the Ports in the Province. There was no chance of his being turned out. He recvd. fees till the Day he left Boston, March, 1776. He has now no Place or appointment. Has not recd. any Provisions.

The Claimant had advanced his Principal, Mr. John Bernard, 574£ which has not been repaid. He was also security for 200£ for Mr. Bernard which he is liable to be called to acct. for.

Claimt. was entitled in right of his Wife to half an undivided Estate in North Carolina. (22).

His Wife's name was Minott. It had been the Estate of her Mother, whose name was Morr. It came by Will to her Mother. On the Mother's Death it came to Mrs. Taylor & her Sister Elizabeth Hall as heirs, but Mr. Minot was entitled to his Life Interest in it. He died in 1784 & then Mrs. Taylor & her sister's right commenced, but the sister had been allowed to keep Possession in ye Father's Life time.

It was near Cape Fear. Consisted of house and 600 acres, and 500 acres near the same place. Claimt. imagines Mr. Hall is now in possession. The first parcel of land was well improved.

New Claim.

776. Case of SAML. PERRY, late of New York. June 8.

Claimt. appears & being sworn saith:

He lived at Sorel in the summer of '83. Had been there a year or two. Says he did not hear of the Act with certainty till the spring of 1784. Does not remember any Claims sent home from thence at that time.

Came in the spring 1784 to Quebec & sent his Claim by Captn. Gomersal that Fall. Does not think any Claims went from Sorel in the Fall '83, except some that might have been carried by Col. Jessup.

He lived at Saratoga. Was always a friend to Govert. Was going off in 1776 to Col. Jessup to have come with him to Canada. He was taken Prisoner & Confined.

In 1777 joined Genl. Burgoyne's Army at Ticonderago. Served with Col. Jessup, brought in 47 men. Served till Genl. Burgoyne's Retreat, then made his escape & got to Canada. (23).

He neglected to get a Commission tho. he brought in a sufficient No. of men to have obtained one had he asked it at first. Now lives on Bay Chaleur.

He had 111 acres at Saratoga in the Township of Parmintown. This was a new township. Laid out in Lots 3 or 4 years before the War.

He bought about ye sumr. 1773, at a Dollar & ½ per acre. Pd. 2-3 of it. Then unimproved. Bought it of Lefferts, one of the Proprietors. Had a Deed. Vals. it at 40sh. per acre, York Cury. Has heard that it was to be sold. There remained 45£ due on the Purchase money.

Lost 2 horses. The Rebels got them. 2 Bullocks, 6 Cows, 2 yearlings, 3 Calves, 30 Hogs, taken by an American Committee after he joined Genl. Burgoyne.

Lost Wheat, oats & Corn, near 500 Bushels, but ye Indian Coru was in the ground.

Lost furniture & farming utensils, taken in same manner. One of his Brothers tried to save some but could not.

(24). Produces list of No. of men whom he carried in amounting to above 40. Produces affidavit of Isaac Man, Junior, & of Mrs. Loes Naughton to Loyalty & good character of Claimant & his appearing in good circumstances. Man's affidt. mentions Claimt.'s joining the Brit. at Ticonderago.

JAMES WITTSER, Wits:

Knew Claimt. Remembers his joining Genl. Burgoyne's Army. He brougu̇ in between 40 & 50 men of which he was looked upon as Commander. He continued to serve that Campaign.

Knew his Land in Parmintown, 10 miles to West of Saratoga. Thinks he had 50 acres clear. He had it between 3 or 4 years. A snug house. He seemed to have a good stock. He had horses, oxen, Cows & was in a thriving way. Speaks strongly to his Loyalty. Often went with messages to him on secret service from Col. Jessup. He was informed by several Loyalists that Claimt. supplied them in the Woods.

NEW CLAIM.

June 8.   777.   Case of THOMAS ORR, late of New York.

Claimt. says he was at Montreal in Sumr. '83, 9 miles from Montreal at Busherville. Did not hear of the Act, or of any Claims going home during that year. Was at Montreal several times. He was then a Soldier in Col. Jessup's Regiment. Heard a flying report.

He lived at White Creek near Fort Edward in 1777. Joined
(25).   the Brit. at Skeensboro. Was first in the Bateaux service, then in Major Jessup's Regt. Was taken at Saratoga. Came back to Canada, was discharged in 1784. Produces his Discharge. Now settled in Quebec.

Had 78 acres by Lease from Dr. Clarke. Had the Lease in 1774. 7 years free & then to pay 1 sh. per acre.

Had cleared 6 acres & built a Log House. Left a small crop standing. Left cloaths & furniture & money. Left at home.
Is told.   They were taken by Rebels because he joined the Brit.

Produces 2 affidts. to his Loyalty & Character.

Produces Lease from Dr. Clarke, dated in 1776.

(775). Further Evidence in the Case of NATHANIEL TAYLOR.

Claimt. produces Copy of Wills of Maurice Moor, dated 1742, whereby he gives to his daughter Elizth. Brown & her Heirs 600 acres on Prince George's Creek where she then lived.

Elizabeth Brown afterwards married George Minot. She died in 1747, leaving Mrs. Taylor & Mrs. Hall her only Daughters.

There was a mansion House & other buildings on this spot. Land well Improved.

Mrs. Taylor was interested in a Tract of Land near the former. Claimt. produces a Letter from his agent, stating that a Tract of 1,000 acres granted to Maurice Moor had descended on Death of a Mrs. Corbyn amongst 4 persons as Heirs to Maurice Moor of whom Mrs. Taylor is one. (26).

Claimt. thinks the first Lot would have sold for 10 sh. per acre. Vals. the 2nd at ye same.

(772). Further Evidence in Case of JOHN MORRIS. June 10.

Claimt. sworn saith:

He lived in New Jersey. Had been an officer in the war before last in '47. Produces Commission.

In 1775 took an active part in favor of Brit. Govrt.

Was appointed to administer ye Oath of Allegiance in 1776.

He joined Sir Wm. How in July, 1776, on Staten Island. In Dec., 1776, went to Monmouth Co. to administer ye Oath of Allegiance, which he did to numbers. Raised a great many men with whom he joined the Brit. Forces & served.

In Decr., 1776, was appointed Lieut-Col. Commander 2 Batal New Jersey Volunteers. Continued to serve till the Regt. was draughted into other Batallions on which he was seconded 1782. He came to this country on Evacuation of New York. (27)

Was possessed of—

250 acres of Land with House & outhouses in Shrewsbury Township, purchased in 1773. Produces Deed from William Pearce Ashfield to Claimt. of a Tract at Trenton Falls, Shrewsbury Township, Mon., in Cons. 1,200 New York Cury.

Produces Survey of Land in 2 Pieces 1 55 acres, the other 224 & a 3rd piece above 50, which and the Boundaries of the Deed, but Claimt. admits he sold some which reduces it to 250 acres.

He made Improvements by Buildings after he purchased.

The Part he sold he sold at 10£ per acre.

Vals. the Estate at 8£ per acre.

Produces Certificates from Saml. Leonard valuing Claimt.'s Estate, real & personal, 2,900£ & Certificate from John Smith to Mr. Leonard's Character.

This Estate was seized when Claimt. joined the Royal Army & has been sold.

Produces Letters from his Agent in New Jersey, Saml. Brien, stating that Proceedings had been against him. Says he could get Certificates of sale of his Estate & Copies of Proceedings but had no money to pay for them.

Produces affdt. from Edward Antell sworn before a Magistrate, at 3 Rivers, that Claimant's Estate at Trenton & Rivers had been Confiscated & Sold. (28).

He was indebted to Mr. Walton 600£ & Interest. He lived at New York. He did not Claim on the sale of Claimant's Estate. Walton had a Bond but no mortgage from Claimt.

He had lands at forked River. Produces Deed from David Ogden to Claimt. of 1,200 on forked River in Consn. 1,145, 1768. He sold 700 acres to one Woodmansey.

In 1775 he sold 500 acres to John Holmes. John Holmes gave a Bond & Mortgage on these Lands for 628£ in 1775. Gave also 2 Bonds as Collateral Security.

He has continued in Possession & sold the Lands.

Lost 2 Negroes, seized when he joined the Brit. Army. Horses & stock as in Schedule. Says he lost ye whole. Heard they were sold.

(29). Claimt. says he has no half pay. He has been struck off the half pay List on acct. of having recd. half Pay as Lieut. in 47th Regiment while he received full Pay as Lieut.-Col. in Provincial Regiment. This appears in a Letter from Wm. Cullen, dated July, 1785. Says in fact he recd. Lieutents half Pay the whole time he served.

He recd. a Letter, dated Aug., 1784, informing him he was then on the Provincial half Pay List.

Claimt. not knowing that Provincial half Pay would be granted had then drawn for his Pay as Lieut. in 47 Regt.

After receiving Information of Letter sent in Aug he drew for his Provincial Half Pay.

Thinks his drawing for both, which was a mistake, has occasioned his loosing both.

He has recd. 100£ temporary Provision. Produces Certificates of Confiscation & Aaron Dunham's acct. of Produce on Sale of real & personal Estate.

1787, June 16. 778. Case of ELIZTH. CAMPBELL, Widow of Moses Campbell, now Elizabeth Finlason, late of New York.

Claimt. being sworn saith:

Her Husband was a native of Scotland. Had been a Seargent in war before last. Was settled on Lake Champlain when the Troubles broke out. On Major Allen Campbell's Lot between Crown Point & Ticonderago. In the last Rebellion he joined Genl. Fraser immediately. Was afterwards employed in Indian Department. Continued so employed till he died in 1781.

(30). Produces Certificate to his character from Col. John Campbell who adds that Genl. Fraser sd. he had been very useful to him in 1776 & 1777.

Produces Certificates from Genl. Fraser in strong Terms to entitle him to 8 Rations, with several Certificates to his Loyalty & activity & the service he rendered Genl. Fraser.

He has left a Widow, the Claimt. & 8 Children. Alexander, eldest son, now lives near Johnstown — of age. Elizabeth Bland Allen. Nancy, now Mrs. Sutherland. Catherine, Isabell, James & John. All in this Province.

4 Young Infants live with their Mother. Elizabeth Bland lives in this Town. Mr. Sutherland lives in Point Murellea Township. Allen in same Township, the other four live with their Mother.

He had 200 acres in Major Campbell's Lot, granted at the end of war before last. He had cleared about 20 acres, built an house, Barn & Outhouses. One of the Rebels now lives upon it. Does not know of any Confiscation or Sale. It was a good Tract but does not know how to value it, thinks £250.

Lost 2 horses, Wheat in the Barn, 100 Bushels, Carpenter's Tools, Household Furniture, farming utensils.

Most of these things taken by the Rebels when her Husband first joined Genl. Fraser. (31).

Lost Hay, Boats, Buildings, &c. Destroyed after General Burgoyne's Defeat. Does not know by whom they were destroyed.

Alexander Campbell appears, Eldest Son of James Campbell. Says he is 21 years of age. Entitled as he supposes to the Lands. Lives at Mr. Noel's, Shoemaker, in this Town.

CAPT. FRASER, Wits.: Says he knew the late Moses Campbell. Remembers he joined the Army in 1776 & Served the Campaign in 1777, he was a remarkably good man for his line of Life & active & Loyal.

Knew his Lot, it was about 5 miles above Crown Point. A tolerably good house, an appearance of Considerable Improvemts. He seemed in Circumstances to support his family tolerably well. Major Allen Campbell had a large Lot of Land there & Moses Campbell h d been a Seargent in the same Regiment.

779. Case of ALEXANDER CRUIKSHANK, decd., late of New York. June 16.

CATHERINA, Widow of Alex. Cruikshank, dec'd., appears:

Says her Husband died about last August, 2 year, without a Will, left 3 Children, 3 Girls, Elizabet., Ann, Sarah, all Infants, now living with Claimant. (32).

Her Husband was a native of Scotland. Lived in Albany, had been settled there some time when the Trouble began. He always declared in Favour of Brit. Government, on which he was imprisoned & kept in Prison 9 months. He had been at New York in beginning of 1777, it was thought he had been to carry Information. On his return he was taken up on Suspicion of having carried Information to the King's Troops. Was first in Œsopus Gaol, then on Board a Prison Ship till he made his Es-

cape & joined Genl. Burgoyne, continued with him till they were taken at Saratoga on the Capitulation. Came to Canada. Resided in Canada till his Death. Claimt. lives in this Town.

Her Husband was possessed of No. 1 House & Lot in Albany. It belonged to John Klyne & was purchased by her Husb.

Produces Deed from John Klyne to Alexander Cruikshank of

(33).

House & Lot in Albany, as also of another Lot adjoining the above in Consd. 1,500, 10 Dec., 1776.
Produces the Old Title Deeds of John Cleine.
There was a good 2 Story House where they lived, an Orchard & Outhouses & a small house which was let out to a Silversmith at 8£ per Ann. On the 2d lot was a Tan Yard & 3 Several Buildings, let out at 40£ per Ann.
Bought in Decr., 1776, paid paper money. Claimant took Possession in the Spring following, her Husband being then ;n Gaol. After her Husband joined Genl. Burgoyne, they came to the House & turned Claimant out, seized the household furniture, seized 2 horses. The horses were sold & part of the furniture, but Claimt. saved some trifling Articles. The rest in the Schedule were sold.

She looks at the Schedule & says most of the Things were seized when she was turned out of Possession of the house.
Before her Husb. purchased the House of Clein, he lived in a house near the Dutch Church, where he kept a shop. Claimt. had got the Things out of this shop, lodged them with a person who made away with most of them. These are the first Articles in the Schedule.

(34).

Her Husband had a Negroe Wench. Produces Bill of Sale of a Negroe Wench for 70£ in the year 1777. She was taken by the Rebels & sold. They found her out at Albany. Claimant was in hopes to have saved her but could not.
Produces Copy of Notice from the Sherif of Co. of Albany, amongst others, for Alexr. Cruikshank to appear to an Indictment found against them for adhering to the Enemies of the State. Unless he appeared, Judgment would be entered & his Estate, real & personal, forfeited.
The House & Lot was sold, one Hornebec, a Dutchman, is in Possession.
Does not know that her Husband owed any Debts.
Says her Husband was offered 500£ for the Bargain he had made after the Purchase.

MAJOR EDWARD JESSOP, Witness:

Says he knew the late Alexr. Cruikshank. He was settled of Albany. Speaks to his Loyalty. He joined Genl. Burgoyne in 1777, previous to which he had been Confined. Continued with the Army till they were taken at Saratoga.
Thinks he was included in the Convention. Knew his house in Albany, it was a very good house, it had been one Clyne's, thinks it worth abt. 800£ Cncy. Heard the house was seized & the Widow turned out.

(35).

Before the Troubles he had been in Trade as a Retail Shop Keeper, in Considerable business.
Understood the Widow was in Possession of the house purchased of Cline & had been in Possess. for some time, & supposes she carried furniture, &c. there.

LIEUT. PHIL. LANSING, Wits.:

Knew the late Alexr. Cruikshank. He was a Merchant in Albany. Was truly Loyal. Was very ready to give assistance to the Loyalists. Kept a shop in an house of Witness Father's. He afterwards purchased Cline's house. Mrs. Cruikshank kept Possession of the house, their furniture was removed there. Witness had often been there, house seemed well furnished. The

Comrs. took Possession of the house. Speaks of one Mase. Vals. the Lot bought of Cline at 1,200£.

780. Case of JOHN COX, late of New Jersey.   Juue 18.

Claimt. appears:

He is a native of America. Lived in Woolwich Township, Gloucester Co., when Troubles broke out. Was a seafaring man.

From the first declared against the measures of the Rebels. (36). Refused to take up their arms, or serve in their Militia, on which his property was seized for fines.

When Lord How's Fleet came up the Delaware in 1778, Claimt. had been taken Prisoner for giving Information to ye Fleet. Made his escape, went on Board the Eagle. Served occasionally by Land at Billings port, being acquainted with the Country.

Was also Employd in carrying Provisions to Garrison at Philadephia when Philadelphia had charge of some sick & wounded & went round to New York.

Got a Privateer at New York which he Commanded for 2 years. Afterwards settled at Vendue Master at New York.

On Evacuation of New York went to Antequa. Has been ever since in the West Indies, Trading in the Islands, is now settled at St. John's, in Island of Antiqua.

Produces Affidt. from Capt. Cozens to Claimants Loyalty & Services & to his Information that Claimts. Estate, real & personal, had been Confisated & Sold.

Produces Affidt. from Capt. Wallis Urim to Claimts. Loyalty. That he had been taken Prisoner for giving Intelligence to the Army & Navy in 1778. His property plundered, that he made his Escape & joined the Fleet, and speaks to Claimants services.

Produces Letter from Capt. Cayton stating that Govr. Frank- (37). lin & Mr. Shoemaker had recommended Claimant as a Loyal, good subject. Produces Letter from Thos. Ashton Cox that Claimt. was recommended to him as an honest man & good Loyal subject.

Claimt. was P ssessed of 150 acres with 2 Dwelling Houses No. 1. at Woolwich, Gloucester Co., near the Delaware, given him by his Father.

Produces Deed from his Father of 100 & [a blank] acres in Woolwich Township in Cons. 200£, dated 1767.

59 AR

(38).

There was then a Mortgage on the Estate to Mathew Gill, which he paid off.

Claimant Produces Certificates from James Bowerman Prothonatary that the Mortgage was paid off to Mathew Gill.

Claimt. when he paid off the Mortgage got a Sheriff's Deed to Confirm the Title, and purchased it of the sheriff. Produces the Sheriffs Deed dated 1769, Whereby it appears the Land was 150 acres.

Claimant lived in one of the houses, let the other at 20£ per Ann. The farm consisted 30 acres Meadow, the rest Arable & Woodland, not more Woodland than necessary. Vals. it at 1,500£ Pensil. Curcy. Meadow was valued at 30 or 40£ per acre, Pensilv. Curcy. Other Lands worth 4 or 5£ per acre.

It has been sold. Saw an advertisement for sale. There was a Debt to the Loan Office of 100£. Phoenix Fezelow is now in Possession, he purchased of the Commrs. at Public Sales.

Was possessed of 23¼ near the other. Produces Deed from the Sheriff of Co. Gloucester to Claimt. of 23¼ acres in Woolwich Township in Consdn. 40£, April, 1776.

Says the Consn. £40 was inscribed by the Sheriff in the Deed, but that in fact it cost above 100£, paid in ready money.

Vals. it at 210£.

11 acres meadow, the rest Swamp.

His personal Estate was seized when he gon on board the Fleet. They plundered his house, took 3 Horses, 11 Cattle, 40 Sheep, Hogs, furniture & utensils, very good, cost him a good Deal of money. Rebels sold them at Public Sale.

They took a Negroe, but he made his Escape from them. Claimt. has lost him.

Produces Valuation of his Personal Estate by Isaac Justuson, Jesse Richards, as in Schedule delivered.

EVAN GRIFFITH, Wits.:

(39).

Says he lived in Pensilvania. Remembers Claimant, just after the Army came to Philadelphia, being with them & assisting both the Army & Fleet. Went with them to New York. Understood he had good Property in Gloucester Co., has been near the Place, but never on the Spot. Lands along the River are very valuable. Meadow Land well diked. Witness has known sell at 40£ per acre Pens. Woodland about 6. Understood from the neighbourhood that all Claimts. Estate, real & personal, had been Confiscated & Sold.

Produces Certificates of Confiscation & Sale of Plantation in Woolwich and appraisement at 600£ New Jersey Curcy., and Aaron Dunham's Certificates of Sale of real & personal Estate.

NEW CLAIM.

781. Case of ANN, formerly Widow of CONRAD BARNET, now June 18.
HALL.

Claimt. appears:

Says she lived in Montreal in the Fall 1783. Sent her Claim to Mr. Powell in England.

This is Confirmed by Certificates from Wm. Dunmore Powell, that he received the Papers in England & did not lodge them because Mr. Foster told him a personal Examn. of Claimant was necessary.

Says her late Husb., Conrad Barnet, was a German. Lived at Still Water. He was a soldier the War before last, shows his discharge from 47 Regt. He was too old to serve this War, was taken up and put in Gaol for supporting his King in 1777, by it appears Certificate of Philip Skene that he was imprisoned 6 months. Produces a Pass from Philip Skene, Aug., 1777. (40.)

Produces a Pass for Conrad Barnard, his Wife & 3 Children, Aug., 1777.

Her Husband had been to give Generel Burgoyne Information. The Rebels came & seized his Things & took away all the Cattle & Every Article of Property.

Claimant & her Children went into the Woods. She & her husband & Children afterwards came into Canada. Her Husband died 3 months after he came into Canada, at La Prairie. He made his Will but the Will was lost.

By the acct. given of the Will it appears he left his Esfate to his Wife & Children, therefore the Estate must go as the Law directs.

He left John, the Eldest Son, William, Mary, all Children.

Her Husband was in Possession of a Leased farm at Still Water, held, under General Skylr, 150 acres, paying 7£ per Ann., it was forever.

Her Husband had made all the Improvemts. himself, a block house & Stables & Barn & Orchard, 100 acres Clear & good fences. On an Exchange once proposed the Estate was valued at 600£ York. (41).

Has heard her Husband say it was worth 600£.

Produces Certificates from Major Gray & many other officers that Conrad Barnet of Stil Water was obliged to leave the Place for his Loyalty with his Wife & Children.

When her Husband had been to give Genl. Burgoyne Information, the Rebels came & seized his Property.

14 Cows, horses, 6 Steers, & all the articles mentioned in the Schedule. They were seized by the Continental Army.

PHILIP P. LANSING, LIEUT.:

Knew the late Conrad Barnet. Remembers him settled at Still Water. He was a worthy, good man & a true Loyalist & was driven into Canada with his Wife & family.

He had a Lease from Genl. Skyler, thinks about 150 acres. Lease forever, paying of Produce 1-10th. Remembers him in Possession some years.

He had made great Improvements, he had built house & outhouses. The Landlord would have had 1-3 of Purchase money in the Sale. It would have sold at £20 sh. an acre, this includes the Landlord's fine.

(42).
Allowed £205.

Knew him to have a good Stock. He was a very industrious man.

Claimt. Produces the Lease which appears a Lease from Philip Skyler to Conrad Barnard & his heirs forever, paying 10th part of the produce annually. Says the Landlord had settled the Rent at £7 per Ann. with her Husb.

Claimant now livs in St. Lawrence Suburbs. Is at the Expense of Educating her Children which seems confirmed by some Certificates.

ELLIAS WILLARD, Wits.:

Says he has lately resided at Still Water, near the Place where her Husband lived. Knew the farm, thinks about 150 acres. Genl. Skyler has let this farm & another joining farm lately & there are now new Tenants upon them. Understood they were Leases for years. Has heard of the family being in good Circumstances. It seemed a good farm.

NEW CLAIM.

June 18.

782. Case of ALEXR. SMITH, late of Philadelphia.

Claimant appears:

(43).

Says he sent his Claim to Mr. Powell in England, sent it from hence in the Fall, 1783. Mr. Powell Certifies he recd. the Claim but did not deliver it because he understood the personal appearance was necessary at Examn.

He is a native of North Britain. In 1769 settled in Philadelphia. Was a White Smith by trade. Had a good Deal of Trade there.

On the Troubles breaking out declared against the Rebels. Signed no Association. When Troops came joined them immediately. Left Philadelphia on the Evacuation on Board the Fanny to New York. Came from there on Evacuation. Now settled here.

Produces Certificates to his Loyalty from S. Shoemaker. Ditto from Danl. Cox & that Claimt. was proscribed & lost an Estate in Philadelphia & in Cumberland Co.

He had a house & Shop at Philadelphia.

No. 1.

Produces Deed from Jacob Ducke to Isaac Craig for a Lot in Pine Street, paying 23 Dollars per Ann. for ever, with Assignment from Isaac Craig to Claimt. in Consn. 5£, 1773.

Says he built an house & Shop after he bought it. Vals. it at 250£ Pensil. Crcy., exclusive of the stock.

Says he could not carry any of his Shop goods, left to Value of 25£ behind him.

Produces Certificates signed J. Sproat, Secry., that a Lot of Ground & Shop, late Alexander Smith, was Confiscated & vested in the University & rents at 30£ per Ann. (44).

He had an Estate in Cumberland Co., consisted of 270 acres. No. 2.

Produces Deed from James Scott to Hugh Gilmore of 100 acres in Bedford Co., the same as Cumberland, in Consn. £9.18s, dated 1771, Assigned to Claimt. in 1771, Considn. was 60£. He produces several Rects. to show payment.

Says this was called a 100 acre Lot, it was on Dunlap Creek, it measured in fact 270 acres. He built house, Barn, &c., after the purchase. 20 acres Clear. Vals. it at 200£.

Produces Letter from his Agent in Philadelphia inclosing a

Certificate of the Confiscation of his Property in that City. Says he can do nothing as to the Lands to the Westward, the Return not having been made to the office from thence, but says there is no Doubt of the Confiscation.

Govr. Penn has paid the Debt stated in Claimts. Memorial.

New Claim.

783. Case of JAMES MCILMOYLE, late of New York. June 18.

Claimt. says:

He was at Montreal in the Fall 83. Gave his Claim to Mr. Kyln at that time, he was then going to England. (45).

He is a native of Ireland & Lived in Balstown, New York State. Joind. Gnl. Burgoyne at Skeensboro in the year 1777. Served in the Engineer Department. Made his Escape a few Days before the Army was taken at Saratoga. Got to Canada & has there continued.

Lives at Aswegatchy.

Had been in Gaol before he joined Genl. Burgoyne on acct. of his Loyalty.

In ye year 1777 after he joined Burgoyne a Rebel Capt. named Collins went to his Father's house, took his Father's

Cattle, Claimant's Cloaths & Watch & Carpenter's Tools. Capt. Collins was a neighbour of Claimant's. Does not know what he did with things taken. Claimt. had a watch which he brought from Ireland.

Says Collins had an order from the Commander of the Rebel Army against all disaffected persons in that settlement.

Produces Certificates to his Loyalty & spirit & that he had Conducted a good many Loyalists from this Province into Canada. Signed John Nairn, Major 53rd.

(46).
June 20.

784. Case of JOHN WAITE, late of New York, decd.

Jane, the Widow of John Waite, appears:

Says her Husband died 2 years ago. Has left Seven Children. Her Eldest Son, George, appears.

Her Husband was a native of England. Settled in America about 13 years ago.

Settled on Sir John Johnson's Lands, in Tryon Co. Had 3 Sons & 2 Sons in Law in the King's Service, on which the Rebels came & burnt their house on that acct., took Witness & her Husband Prisoner & Confined from May to Christmas, took the Cattle when they burnt the House.

She & her Husband made their Escape & came to this Country. All her Children are in this Province.

Her Husband had a Lease of 150 acres on Sir John Johnson's Land 13 years ago, they were to have it 5 years for nothing & then to have a Lease & pay as others pd.

Her Husband had built an House & Cow house. Cleared 14 or 15 acres.

(47).

2 Cows, 2 Hogs, Household goods & Tools brought from England burnt in the house. Now lives with her Children.

GEORGE WAITE says:

If this true U.E. Loyalist.

His Father lived on Sir John Johnson's Estate. When the Family first came to America they heard of the Battle of Bunkers Hill. His Father landed at New York, then went up to Johnstown, in Tryon Co., & settled there

If claimt can be found, must explain it. John Prescott says it was August, 1775, when he landed with Waite at N. York from England.

Witness & 2 Brothers & 2 Brothers in Law were in the King's Service, on which his Father & Mother were persecuted & imprisoned. Heard the house & all their property was burnt. They had 1 Cow, 1 heifer, 2 hogs, there were Tools & farming utensils & some furniture. Heard they were destroyed.

NEW CLAIM.

June 20.

785. Case of GARRET MILLER, late of Cambden, Charlotte Co.

Claimt appears:

Says he was at Sorel in the Fall of '83, sent his Claim home by Major Leake in Nov., '83, but he did not deliver it.

He is a native of Ireland. Came to America in 1772. Went first to Virginia, afterwards settled in Campden, New York Prov. in the year 1775. Joined the King's Army at Crown Point in 1776. Was taken Prisoner in 1777. Served under Col. Peters. Was continued a Prisr. for 2 years. Made his Escape & came into this Province. Now lives at Sorel.

(48).

Says he bought a Lot of one Peter Sparling in Campden in 1774, it consisted of 188 acres was to pay 110£ York Money.

Had pd. between 30 & 40£.

He produces a Bond from Peter Sparling dated 31 Decr., 1774, in the sum of 200 on Condition to Convey to Claimt. his right & Interest in the Township of Campden on or before 1st Novr., 1776, on payment of £110.

Robert Sparling never made the Deed because the money was not pd.

Says he gave his Bond to Sparling for the money. Sparling

is a Loyalist & Claimt. heard he was at Halifax.

Says he Cleared 12 or 13 acres.

The Commrs. took it away, took it from his Wife while Claimt. was a Prisoner, sent her away.

Vals. Land unimproved at 12sh. & 6 per acre. Could have sold it.

28 acres were Clear when he bought it.

Vals. improved Land at £3.15 per acre.

He lost 1 Cow, 1 Steer, 1 Heifer, 1 Calf, Hogs, Tools, &c., Utensils, Wheat in the ground, when he left home.

(49).

These things were plundered or destroyed before his Wife was driven away by the Americans.

PETER MILLER, Wits.:

Says he remembers Garret Miller purchasing a Lot in Campden of one Sparling. Thinks there were 180 acres. Remembers his joining the King's Army at Crown Point, he served as a Quarter Master Seargent, he was wounded & taken Prisoner. Remembers having a yoke of Oxen, 2 Steers, 2 Cows, Tools, Mare & Colt.

Witness sold a yoke of oxen & 2 Steers for him in Genl. Burgoyne's Army. Heard the rest were taken by the Rebels.

Says the Claimt. had made Considerable Improvements. Cleared 9 acres himself. Unimproved Land sold at 20 sh. or 12 sh. York Money.

NEW CLAIM.

786. Case of WALTER SCOT, late of New York. June 21.

Claimt. says: He resided at Montreal in 1783 & has been here ever since. Sent a Claim in the Fall by Lawyer Powel, delivered it to him when he was going to England, but he afterwards returned it.

(50).

He is a native of Ireland. Came to America 2 years after the French War. Settled at Still Water, lived there when the Rebellion broke out. At first took the Part of his King. Was Imprisoned for a Tory. His Sons joined the Brit. Troops. He was kept in different Gaols in the year 1776 from June to Christmas, then released to his own farm & there was on Parole till Genl. Burgoyne came.

Claimant & 2 Sons joined Genl. Burgoyne & continued with him till he was taken, then came to Canada. Now lives at Isle Aux Noix.

Produces Certificates to his Loyalty & Pass from Philip Skene. In Certificates Philip Skene remembers Claimts. Imprisonment.

He had 200 acres under a Lease from Genl. Skyler.

Produces Lease from Phil. Skyler to Claimt. forever of 198 acres, paying £4.19.3 annually after the year 1772 & paying Taxes, &c., dated 1768.

Says he had a house & 2 Barns, 2 Stables & other outbuildings & cleared 130 acres, had 2 orchards.

Genl. Skyler has got the Land again & has let it.

(51). After he had joined Genl. Burgoyne's Army his stock was all taken.

7 Horses, 15 Cows, 4 Steers, 150 Bushels of old Wheat in the house, Hogs, 20 Sheep, furniture, Cloaths.

Taken by the Rebels, heard they were sold.

CAPTN. LA MOTT, Wits.:

Knew his farm. Knew Claimt. at Still Water, good Land, well situated. Speaks of his Loyalty & that of his family. He had many Cattle. Lived in Comfortable circumstances. Has other attested Witness with Provisions, &c., for ye Indians, &c.

LIEUT. PHILIP LANSING, Wits.:

Knew Claimt., he lived at Still Water. He was very Loyal, he & all his Family. Heard of his Improvement.

Claimant & his Sons joined Genl. Burgoyne. Came into this Province before the Convention.

He had a Lease under Genl. Skyler.

Claimt. was a hard working, industrious man & did a great Deal to his farm. Had 100 acres or near it clear. Buildings were in good state. He had planted Apple Trees. It was Land well situated. Claimt. cd. have got a large sum for it, 30 Sh. per acre taking it all together. He had a Considerable Stock which he bels. was taken by the Rebels. Parties from the Rebel
(52). Army & Militia used to come particularly to seize the property of persons who had shown themselves well affected towards ye Brit. Govt.

A NEW CLAIM.

June 22. 787. Case of ABRAHAM HYATT late of New York.

Claimt. being sworn, saith:

He came into Canada in the year '80. Lived at St. John's all the Fall of '83. Gave a Claim to Capt. Mices to forward to Quebec in the Fall of that year, but it was too late.

Now lives on Masisco Bay on Lake Champlain within the Province of Canada, 15 miles from the Isle au Noix Settlement.

He is a native of America, lived at Skenackady, Albany Co.

When Troubles began joined Genl. Burgoyne in the year 1777. Servd in Capt. MacAlpine's Corps. Had not servd in Rebel Militia. Was at Saratoga. Was ill at the time of the Convention. Continued at his own Place till the year 1780. Was several times fined. At last was put in Gaol, kept 3 or 4 weeks, then discharged on Bail.

Went off on account of the Persecution he met with.

He had a farm of his own in Ball Town, 100 acres, purchased of Beriah Palmer about 3 years before the War, gave 2 Dollars per acre, it was Wild Land. Sd. he had cut down the Wood of 3 or 4 acres. Vals. it at 30 Sh. per acre. (No. 1.)

Does not suppose the Rebels have taken possession of it. (53).

Had a Tenant farm 125 acres at Skeneckady. Had a Lease, bought a year before ye War. Abraham Fundy was the Landlord. (No. 2.)

Claimt. had an Assignment of the Lease, which was for 16 years. Was to have the Land till end of the Lease, then give it up, he had nine years to come.

He made Improvemts., some buildings, about 30 acres were clear.

Lost 5 horses. His Wife sold some of them, 4 out of the 5, 16 Sheep lost by the Indians & Continentals while he was in Burgoyne's Army.

Lost Cattle & Cows. His Wife disposed of some before she came away, 8 Hogs, furniture was partly plundered, his Wife sold some.

Had some Boards which were taken by a neighbour, a Rebel.

JAMES MACYLMOIL, Wits.:

Knew Claimt. before ye War. He joind Genl. Burgoyne & servd the Cmpaign. He had a farm at Skmackyda where he lived. He followed ye Trade of a Shoemaker & had stock about the house.

A NEW CLAIM.

788. Case of JOHN MOCK, late of New York.

(54). June 22.

Claimt. appears & being sworn, saith: He lived at St. John's in the Fall of 1783. Sent his Claim by Capt. Leake, he did not arrive in time.

He is a native of Germany. Came to America 20 years ago, settled near Albany. When Troubles began joined Genl. Burgoyne at Fort Edward & Servd that Campaign as a soldier. Was at Saratoga, got away before Burgoyne & came there, is now settled in Massisco Bay.

Had a farm near Albany, about 130 acres. He took it up & Cleared it, at least 60 acres Clear, a new framed house & builds.

It belond to Rancellor who lived at Albany & had a large Estate. His time for payment of rent was just coming, he had no Lease, would have had one if the Troubles had not come on. Vals. it at 300£.

Rancellor now resides at Albany & has sold the Lands that had belonged to the Tories.

Seems a very honest man. (55.)

Had 6 horses, 4 oxen, 4 Steers, 8 Cows, 2 young Steers, 2 Heifers, 54 Sheep, 16 Hogs, furniture, utensils, 300 Bushels Wheat in the Chamber, 200 in Straw, Wagon.

Taken by the Rebel Army when Burgoyne was taken.

PHILIP DAYRICH, Wits.:

He knew Claimt. He joined Burgoyne's Army & Servd the Campaign. He was always considered very Loyal. Knew that he had a farm about 9 or 10 miles from Albany. Remembers him in Possession before the War. It was held of one Rancellor, there were fine Improvemts. upon it, he could have sold the Improvemts. There was a new frame house & good Builds.. He had Cleard a fine Piece of Land.

Vals. it at about 300£ York Curcy.

He had a very large stock, all taken by the Rebels on acct.

of Claimt. being a Tory.

June 22

788. Case of THOMAS SWAN, late of Massts.

Claimt. appears, says:

He is a native of America, lived at Groughton, Co. of Midx. on a farm of his own & was also in Trade.

On breaking out of the Troubles he took part of the Brit. Govt. He had shown the same Principles before, when he lived with a person who opposed the non Importation against which Claimt. also did. This had made him obnoxious, he was obliged to leave his Home. He left home in April, 1777, took Refuge with the Army, first Escaped to Rhode Island & after to New York.

(56).

In 1779 His family were driven away by order of the State of Massts. & came to Claimt.

Claimt. servd as a Volunteer in Govr. Wentworth's Volunteers & went on several Parties with them.

Before Claimt. left home, he had made over his Landed Property to his Brother for fear of its being lost under the Act of the Assembly past against Absentees.

His Brother has sold it for Paper Money & the Estate has

not been Confiscated, but by his Brothers taking Paper Money the whole is lost.

When he went away some of his Property was plundered by his neighbours.

His Wife & family disposed of some. He left the articles mentd. in the Schedule.

Is now settled at Montreal.

He had purchased the farm above mentd. about the commencement of the War, it consisted of 100 acres, finely improved & in good Condn, gave 45£ lawf., paid some in hard money, some in Paper. (57).

He thought as the War was putting an end to Trade, particularly as he had opposed the Non Importation Agreement that it was the best way to his money, &c., in the Purchase of Lands.

His Claim was given in by a friend at home without any particular Directions from Claimt. & his friend has given in several Charges which Claimt. would not have made.

Says he served with George Leonard in his Naval Excursions. Claimt. speaks of his present Distresses.

ROLLAND SPARKS, Wits.:

Knew Claimt. at New York. He served in Wentworth's Volunteers. Was on frequent Excursions with them. Was active in the service. Witness was in the same Company in which Claimt. servd. W.s on Board one of Mr. Leonard's vessels in his Expeditions.

A NEW CLAIM.

790. Case of RACHEL BRIAN, late Widow of James Macintosh, New York.   June 22.

Claimt. appears:

She & her late Husb., James MacIntosh, were at St. John's in the Fall of '83. Her Husband died last March, 2 years ago. Made a Will & left everything to Claimt. Left no Children. (58).

Her Husb. was a native of North Brit., was a soldier in War before last, settled at Ticonderago before ye Troubles on a Tenant farm. He would not take arms with the Rebels. He joined Genl. Burgoyne as soon as he came, piloted the Army cross the Lakes. Continued with the Army. Was in the Convention. Came to Canada.

Produces several Passes. Produces order from Genl. Fraser mentioning that James Macintosh had been entirely ruined by the Rebels & allowing 3 Rations.

Her Husband had 215 acres near Ticonderago, purchased 9 years before ye Rebellion. He cleared 40 acres. A good dwelling house & Barn.

The Rebels burnt the house on acct. of her Husb. joining ye Brit. Army. Thinks her Husb. pd. 60£ for it.

Had the stock mentioned in the Schedule all taken by the Rebels when her Husb. joined Genl. Burgoyne.

Says they kept a public House & had a great many articles of various kinds. They used to carry on a little Trade, & she says they had all the things mentioned in the Schedule. (59).

Her present Husband belongs to the 31st Regt. Is to send the Will & Leases.

NEW CLAIM.

June 23.

791. Case of DUNCAN CAMERON, late of New York.

Claimt. says:

He was at Port Chamblee in the Fall '83; all the Fall. Had the care of the People who worked at the King's Saw Mill. Was under Capt. Twiss in the Engineer Department. Sent a Claim to Major Leake to be carried to England in the Fall '83.

He is a native of Scotland. Came long ago to America. Lived at a Place called Mapletown, 36 miles from Albany.

Had. declared his sentiments from the first in Favor of Brit. Govert.

In Aug., 1777, joined Genl. Burgoyne. Served with the Loyalists under Col. Foster. Brought 30 People in with him. On Col. Fosters Death the Loyalists were Commanded by Capt. McKoy. They were afterwards joined to Sr. J. Johnson's Regt.

Had the Commission of Ensign. Served during the Campaign.

(60). Came to Canada after Convention of Saratoga. Was in the Engineer's Department till the year 1784. Has now half Pay as Ensign. Settled on Lake Champlain.

Had a Tenant farm of 160 acres in Mapletown, near Bennington, but not in Vermont.

Had a Lease from Alex. Colden, dated 1769. It was a Lease forever, paying 1 sh. per acre rent.

Took it as Wild Land. Built a house & Barn & had improved 60 acres. They were well cultivated & fenced.

It was hired of Alexander Colden. He used to be called Governor from his or his Father's being Lieutent. Govr. of New York. Was Post Master General.

Claimt. had leased out 80 acres, half the Estate, receiving £6. 3s. yearly.

Claimt. was to be answerable for ye Rent to Govr. Colden. About 12 acres of these Lands were cultivated when he let it off.

Vals. the 80 acres which he reserved for himself at 170 or 180£ York Money.

The part which Claimt. held has been Confiscated & sold. It was sold at Albany.

The tnt. of the other 80 acres enjoys them still, but does not
(61). pay the rent. This is a loss of £2.5 annually to Claimt.

He made a Claim of 1,500 acres in Vermont in the Claim sent Home by Major Leake, but withdraws it.

When he joined Genl. Burgoyne his stock was seized; 8 Cattle, 5 horses, 30 Sheep Stacks of Wheat, Peas, oats & Corn, Barley, Hay, Utensils. Saved his furniture.

There were Parties sent from the Rebel Army to seize the property of Tories. A Party was sent from Bennington under the Command of Isaac Clark who took Claimt.'s Property.

JOHN RUYTER, Wits:
Remembers Claimt. serving the Campaign in Burgoyne's Army. He lived at Mapletown. Heard he had a great farm. Has been thro' the Place where Claimt. lived, but did not particularly know the Lands.

1787, July 1st.

Claimt. produces Lease forever, dated 2nd Octr., 1769, from Alexr. Colden to Clt. of a Lot of Land in the E. Side of Hudsons River, Albany Co., containing 160 acres in Consn. of Clt.'s discharging the Quit Rents due & to become due & also to paying 1s. pr. a. pr. an. after 5 years from the Date of the Lease.

Also Deposition of James Williamson, dated 28th April, 1780, taken before the grand Jury at Albany, charg. Clt. with having joined the British Army.

Produces appraisement at 3£ per acre by Thos. Sickel who mentions that 79 acres & ½ have been sold as Claimt.'s property by ye Court of Forfeiture.

(62).

NEW CLAIM.

792. Case of CAPTN. HENRY RUITER, late of New York.   June 23.

Claimt. says: In the Fall of '83 he was at St. Johns. He sent a Claim by Major Leake; gave it him in the Fall of '83.

Is a native of America. Lived in Pitts town when the troubles broke out. From the first declared against the measures pursued by the Rebels. Was obliged to leave Home & had been sculking in the woods till he could join Gen. Burgoyne. Joined him in Aug., 1777. Carried in several men. Was first under Col. Foster, then McKoy & afterwards under Major Rogers. Had a Capt.'s Commission under Major Rogers, in the Kings' Rangers. Has now half Pay. Resides on Caldwells Manor, Lake Champlain.

Had 260 acres in Pits Town. Produces Deed from Wm. Smith to Claimt. of 303 acres in Pits Town in Consn. 272£ York. dated 30 June, 1774.

Had pd. some & given a Bond for the rest. He had sold about 40 acres. After ye purchase he built a Saw Mill. Cleared about 50 acres. Built a house & another small house.

(63).

Vals. it at near 700£.

The Estate has not been sold. It has been taken Possession of by several persons. Has heard it was advertized for Sale. His name was amongst the Persons indicted.

No. 2. Had a Lot in the New City. Produces a Note by which Jacob Lansing promises to give a Deed to Claimt. of a Lot in the Township of Stonecody in Cons. 25£, dated 1768. Claimt. never had the Deed.

No. 3. Had a Lease in Hsick. Lived there before he went to Pits Town. It belonged to Danl. Bratt. Was to have had a

Lease for 40 years. Was to have been paid for the Improvemts. He had sold the Improvemts.

When he joined Burgoyne he left 20 head of Cattle, 13 horses, 10 Sheep, Farming utensils & furniture. He got some, but most were taken by the Rebel Army, chiefly by one Capt. Bentley & Captn. Wright, 2 days after ye Battle of Benningyon.

Produces an order by which his family were banished from the State of New York in 1780.

HERMANUS BEST, Wits:

(64).
Knew Claimt. at Pits Town. Always considered him as a Loyalist.

He joined Genl. Burgoyne. He had a farm at Pits Town. Claimt. had bought it several years. Bought it of Ch. Just. Smith. He had built a Saw Mill. 30 or 40 acres clear. He had built a Dwelling house & lived there. Witness did not particularly know the Land.

Witness vals. such Lands, Wild, at a Dollar or more. Clear Land at 4 or 5 Dollars.

He had a good stock & seemed in good circumstances.

Produces Albany Gazette with advertizmt. for the sale of the Equity of Redemption of Claimt.'s Estate in Pits Town.

NEW CLAIM.

June 23.
793. Case of CHRISTIAN WEBER, late of New York.

Claimt. says: Was at St. Johns in the Fall '83. Gave a Claim to Major Leake in Feby., '84. He was then going to England by the way of New York.

Is a native of Germany. Lived at Claveroak, Co. of Albany. Joined Genl. Burgoyne in the year 1777, at Patent Kiln. Served in Jessup's Regt. as Captn. Served the Campaign. Came to Canada after the Convention of Saratoga. Was afterwards on the new arrangement made Lieut. in Sir John Johnson's Regt. Has now half pay.

(65).

Claimt. was in Possession of 30 acres in Cloveroak, 30 miles from Albany, which he had from his Father in Law. This was vacant Land when taken Possession of by his Father in Law, Christian Haver. He possessed it many years; gave it Claimt. in 1773. He had no Deed, but Claimed it by possession.

One Rancellor also Claimed it, pretending to have an Indian Deed.

Claimt. had also taken Possession of 100 acres of Vacant Land adjoining in 1773.

Claimt. did not send in his Claim for the Land, because he did not think it would be lost, but he finds a Committee man has got Possession of it.

There was a good framed house, which Claimt. had built himself. The Land was good, all clear.

Vals. this Lot of 30 acres at 150£ York Money.

Lost 2 Cows, 2 Heifers, 18 Sheep, 14 Hogs, furniture & utensils. The Rebels took them in the winter 1778. There was an order from a Committee for seizing Claimt.'s effects. They took 5 Slay Loads of effects from the House. Some shop goods & different things were taken. Above the value in Schedule in the year 1781. The Rebels took 2 Trunks of Cloaths & other Things which he had secreted & was endeavouring to bring away with her to Canada. (66).

Produces affidt. of Christian Haver sworn before Herr Ruiter to Claimt.'s personal Estate being taken by Rebels, and that Claimt. had a farm. Cannot say how much Land & that a Rebel Capt. moved into it.

794. Claim of JOSEPH JEBARE, late of New York. June 25.

Claimt. says: He is a native of America. Lived at Saratoga when Troubles broke out. Joined the Brit. Army at Fort Edward in the year 1777. Worked in a Blacksmith's shop with the Army. Continued till Burgoyne was taken, then came to Canada. Now lives in this Town.

Had a Lease from Genl. Skyler of 60 acres. Had it about 4 years, but had no Deed. He had made Improvemts; cleared a Dozen acres & built a house.

Lost 2 horses & 3 Cows. The Rebels took farming utensils, furniture.

JOHN PLATT: Claimt. joined the Army in 1777. He worked for the engineers. He had a little Farm hired of Genl. Skyler & a little stock. He was a poor man. He came into the army & came to the Province with ye Loyalists. Witness always considered him Loyal. (67).

NEW CLAIM.

795. Case of WILLIAM STEWART, late of New York. June 25.

Claimt. says: He is a native of Scotland. Was settled in New York State at Cambridge near Albany. Served in American Militia 2 Days when General Burgoyne came into the Country. Deserted from Militia. Continued with him till he was taken. Served under Major Hughes. Came to Canada. Now lives at Montreal.

Lost a horse & some Cloaths, taken and sold directly after he joined Genl. Burgoyne. Taken by one of the Rebel Committee men. Does not know what became of it. He had Debts owing him, great part of which he has recovered since.

JOHN SKIMMING, Wits:

Speaks to Claimt.'s Loyalty. He had a horse & some good Cloaths.

They were plundered when Claimt. & Witness joined the Brit. Army, owing to his having joined the Brit. Army.

(68).
June 26.

796. Case of HUGH MONRO, late of Albany Co., New York.

Claimt. says:

He is a native of Scotland. Had been a Seargent the war before last. After the Peace settled in America. Lived near Albany on the Kydoseros Patent. When the Troubles broke out joined one of the Rebel Meetings or Associations. In July, 1777, joined Genl. Burgoyne; was appointed to Captns. Rank. First served in Jessup's Regt., afterwards had the Command of a Company of Batteaux men. Continued till Burgoyne was taken, then came to Canada; then went into the Engineer's Department under

Capt. Twiss at Quebec. Was so employed about 2 years. Now settled in Oswegatchy. Has not half pay.

Produces Certificates from Capt. Shank that Claimt. joined him at Saratoga with his Company of Batteaux men in Sep. 1777. Speaks very favourably of his Conduct, and that he was wounded while doing his duty.

Produces a Certificate from Capt. Wilcox that Claimt. had the care of transporting Provisions from Fort Edward & to his good Conduct.

(69). Produces Certificate from Capt. Twiss that he had been employed under him in Engineers Department after Aug., 1779, to January, 1781, without additional Pay & to his good Conduct.

Was possessed of—

No. 1. 279 acres in Kayodoscros Patent, purchased of Mr. Isaac Low in 1771. Purchased at 20 sh. per acre.

Purchased a large Tract in 2 parcels & sold all except one parcel of 279 acres. He purchased the whole at 20 sh. pr. acre. There was a Mortgage to Isaac Low of 300£ York Cury. on this Estate of 279 acres. Vals. it at 25 sh. per acre Halfx. Cury.

There was a place for a Mill on this Lot.

The whole of this is valued by Major Jessup, Capt. Jones & Mich. Hofnayl at 207£ Hal. Cury. Has been informed that the Place was sold.

Is told to get certificate.

No. 2. Had a Lease of 300 acres in the said Patent, 1 mile from ye other Tract, called Fort Miller. Took it in 1776, Fanning Fisher. It was a Lease forever at 15£ York Cury. per ann.

Had a Lease but it is lost. The Landlord took the Land on Claimt.'s going away.

Claimt. took the Improvemts. for a Debt of 70£. Laid out money afterwards; lived there.

(70). Vals. the Improvemts. at 125£.

Claimt. sold a Tract before mentd. for 1,400£ to one Robt. Hoaksley in 1776. He was also to saw a thousand Logs for Claimt. The Logs were sent to the Mill in the Winter 1776. Hoaksley sold the Land to Platt who was to saw the Logs. Part was sawn after Burgoyne's Depart., then Logs & Planks were all taken by the Rebels for rebuilding the Barracks. Says they were known to be his Boards & Planks & taken as such.

Vals. them at 287.10.

Had also some other Boards & Planks which Claimt. had left at the same Mill.

Vals. them at 28.15.

Hoaksley & Platt were both Loyalists.

Hoaksley was with Burgoyne. Platt went into Canada.

When he joined Genl. Burgoyne he left Negroes & his other property with his Wife at No. 2.

Lost 2 Negroes, man & woman, 5 Cows & 2 Horses. His Wife was driven away & went down to Albany.

The Negroes were driving the Cattle & horses. The horses were taken away from the Negroes at Stillwater. The Negroes & Cattle were taken by the Rebels. He does not exactly know when. Says his Wife did not dispose of them. Lost also farming utensils & furniture, at his house. Plundered by the Rebels after he joined Genl. Burgoyne. (71).

MICHL. HOFNAIL, Wits:

Knew Claimt. He was always considered a Loyalist. Joined Genl Burgoyne. Had the Command of a Company of Batteaux men. Served the campaign. Was afterwards in the Engineer's Department in this Province.

Remembers his purchasing a large Tract of Mr. Low. Sold a good deal. Kept about 2 or 300 acres. Remembers the Lot that he kept. The Land was some of it, that in the Front very good.

Vals. it at 20 sh. per acre.

Knew his Lease at Fort Miller, No. 2. He lived there. The

Improvemts. were good.

Heard of his having Logs at a Mill which were taken by the Rebels. He had a Negroe man & woman.

JOHN JONES, Wits:

Knew Claimt. He was always Loyal. Joined Genl. Burgoyne. Was Capt. of a Company of Batteaux men.

Knew that he had part of a Tract, purchased of Mr. Low in Kayodos reas Patent. Witness with Major Jessup made a Valuation of these Lands and estimated them at 207£ Hal. Cury.

He lived at Fort Miller. Witness had valued them Improvemts. with Major Jessup after Deductions for Rent &c. at 125£. Has seen a Negroe man & woman at his house, horses & cows His house was Comfortably furnished. (72)

Witness knows nothing of Claimt.'s right to the Logs, but if the numbers was as represented by Claimant says they are rightly valued.

MAJOR JESSUP, Wits:

Knew Claimt. He served as Capt. of a Co. of Batteaux men. Knew of the small Tract purchased of Isaac Low. Does not speak of knowing him in Possession, but understood the Purchase of a large Tract was made some years before the war.

60 AR.

Vals. what was left at 3 Dollars per acre.

Knew the ground at Fort Miller. Heard of his taking a Lease of it.
Vals. the Improvements at 125£.
Did not know of the Claimt.'s Right to the Boards, &c., but if he had such Right they are properly valued in the Schedule.

JOHN PLATT, Wits:

Bought a Tract of Land of Mr. Hoaksley who bought it of Claimt. The Land was sold for a sum of money, he thinks 1,400£, & the Purchase was to said 1,000 Logs for Claimant, Witness taking the Bargain was obliged to saw the Logs.

When Witness took Possession in 1777, there were a great many Logs drawn to the mill for sawing which belonged to Mr. Munro. Witness himself sawed 431. There were more Logs ready. He cannot speak to the exact No., but there were a great many, besides what Witness sawed.

(73).

JOHN WRAGG, Witness:

Remembers a great many Logs at the Mill which had been purchased by Mr. Platt. Did not hear whose the Logs were, but there were many at the Mill in the year 1777. A great many were sawed. A great many Piles of Boards & Planks were taken away by the Rebels. Saw them taken. The rebels said they took them for the use of Congress.

NEW CLAIM.

June 27.

797. Case of MICHL. HOFFNAIL, late of Kingsbury, in New York.

Claimt. says. He lived in the Sumr. 1783 near Chamblee. In Octr. went on Business to Lachine. There was told by Major Jessup that he was outlawed and that his estate in the States would be lost, which he thought was safe. He came back thro' Montreal & was going to Albany to recover his Estate, it having been Confiscated after the Peace, but heard at St. Johns it was too late & did not go.

(74).

His home was near Chamblee during this Time.
His Estate had been Confiscated since the Peace.
All the Proceedings have been since ye Peace.
He lived in Kingsbury when Troubles broke out. Never was in their Militia. Refused serving as an Assembly man. Joined Genl. Burgoyne at Fort Ann. Assisted in conveying forage & Provisions. Was employed on Secret Service by Major Jessup & Capt. Fraser. Being suspected he was obliged to fly & came into Canada. Went back to Albany in '84, having some houses there that had been secured to him. He exchanged the Houses for 600 acres on Killingland Creek, when he settled within the American Lines. Now settled there.

Produces Certificate from Major Carleton to enable Claimt. to Provisions. St. Johns, 1780.

No. 1. Had a Lot in Kingsbury, No. 10, containing 242 acres, purchased in 1771 for 20s. per acre of Joseph Smith. Built 2 Mills under one Roof & a Blacksmith's Forge. Built an house & Barn. There were 50 acres clear. Says he laid out 2,000 Y. Curry. on ye Place.

Vals. it at 1,500 York Cury.

Produces proceedings whereby it appears he was indicted, 25 July, 1783. Final judgement entered 29 Dec., 1783.

Col. Williams located upon the spot, who sold it to Henry Hart. Claimt. has brought an eject. against Hart, but has not been able to get a hearing. (75).

Produces Valuation by 3 Appraisers who value it at 1,500£.

Says all his Deeds & Papers were taken by the Rebels from Mr. Adams, in whose care Claimt. had left them.

No. 2. Had another Lot in Kingsbury, No. 18. 242 acres purchased in 1775 of James Mackennice & ors., for 500£. He had a Mortgage before on the Lands. Altogether cost him 500£. There was a great Deal of clear Land; 70 acres clear. He moved a great Deal of Hay. Vals. it at 500£.

The Heir of the person of whom Claimt. bought it has got Possession & holds it, having found out that Claimt. had lost the Deed. So that it is not Confiscated at present.

No. 3. Had 750 acres, Charlotte Co., in the Artillery Patent, bought in 1772 of James Panton. 40 or 50 acres were clear when he bought it. Claimt. Leased 250 acres of it.

He had not paid the whole money & has been obliged to pay 150£ that he owd upon it for which he gave a Bond.

Vals. it at 20 sh. per acre. It is valued by 3 appraisers at 562£.

This is Confiscated. Does not know who is in Possession. Dr. Williams has got a Deed of it. Hart bought it. Claimt. had brought Ejectmt. against Hart but cannot get a hearing. (76).

His furniture, Cattle,, &c., were taken at his House at Kingsbury. Plundered and taken by the Indians of Burgoyne's Army.

MAJOR JESSUP, Wits:

Knew Claimt. Always looked upon him as a Loyalist. Witness had such Confidence in him, that he employed him in Secret Services in Associating the Loyalists, which he performed to Witness's satisfaction.

Is satisfied of his Loyalty. He frequently assisted & gave Intelligence to ye Loyal Party.

Remembers the house where he lived at Kingsbury. It was a comfortable house. Remembers the Mills. There was a good Deal of Clear Land.

CAPT. JOHN JONES, Wits:

Knew Claimt. Is satisfied perfectly of his Loyalty. He was considered as a person in whom the Loyal party might place full confidence. Knew No. 1, his Lot in Kingsbury, 242 acres. Remembers him in Possession. He had Mills.

Vals. it at 1,500 York mon. He laid out a great Deal after the Purchase.

(77). Knew No. 2. Understood from all the Parties that he purchased it in 1775. Vals. it 500£.

Understood he had Lands in the Artillery Patent. Some of the Lands are good. Knows the Appraisers. Thinks them competent & good Judges of Land.

His House was well furnished.

Mentions several Instances of Assistance given to the Loyal party, and to his having performed several pieces of service.

Speaks very favourably of him. Thinks he intends to return within the Brit. Govrt.

NEW CLAIM.

June 27. 788. Case of RICHD. WRAGG, late of Saratoga, New York.

Claimt. says. He was at St. Johns in the Sumr. & Fall of '83. Sent a Claim by Capt. Abbot in '83. It did not arrive in time.

Is a native of England. Settled in America 20 years ago. Lived at Saratoga, when the Troubles broke out. Always declared in Favour of his Majesty. Assisted several Loyalists employed in Secret Services. Was the first man who found a Pilot to conduct the friends of Government into Canada in 1775.

(78). His conduct had made him obnoxious to ye Rebels. He was put in Gaol. Was persecuted & obliged to quit his Home.

In 1779 came into Canada, settled at St. Johns. Was foreman at the King's Works in the Smith's Business. Now resides there. Produces his Discharge from Gaol in Dec., 1776, on giving security for good Behavr. &c.

Produces Certificates to his Loyalty by Sir John Johnson & Danl. MacAlpin. Annexed to a Petition to Govr. Haldimand.

He had 386 acres of Land in Saratoga. Produced Deed from John H. Beechman to Claimt. of 386 acres in Kayodoscens Patent in Consn. 220£ Cury., dated 1773.

He gave 33£ more for Improvements. He built a shop & Stables. 60 or 70 acres were clear. Vals. at 300£.

It has been Confiscated & advertized for sale.

His horses & cattle were taken by Burgoyne's Army. His furniture was destroyed in like manner. His Wheat & Corn were destroyed. Utensils, &c., Provisions were taken by the Army.

JOHN PLATT, Wits:

Knew Claimt. at Saratoga. Always considered as a staunch Loyalist. He gave assistance repeatedly to Loyalists in Distress.

(79). He assisted Witness when he was going into Canada to carry Intelligence respecting the Motions of Genl. Montgomery's Army. Knew of the Business on which Witness was going. Supported his

Family in his absence. Witness went once to his assistance when he was in Albany Gaol. He was much persecuted. He made his escape from there. His family were sent away from Saratoga.

He had a Farm at Saratoga. Remembers him several years in Possession before the war. It was a valuable Place. 60 acres or more cleared.

He had a good stock; 4 or 5 Cows, 5 or 6 Horses, Tools. The Horses were taken by Burgoyne's Indians. A great many things were taken by the Rebels, after Burgoyne's defeat.

WILL. STEWART, Wits:

Read in the York Papers advertisement for the sale of the Lands of Richd. Wrag in Saratoga.

NEW CLAIM.

799. DANIEL DUNHAM, late of Kingsbury, New York. June 27.

Claimt. says. He was at the River De Chine 1783. Made up his acct. and gave it to Major Jessup in Oct. in order to be sent to England. Their Quarters were during that Winter at De Chaine.

7 Leagues from this Place.

Is a native American. Lived in Kingsbury. In the year 1777 joined Genl. Burgoyne, but did not stay with the army. Did not return to Kingsbury, went to different places. Joined the Brit. in the year 1780, at Crown Point. Served till the war was over, part of the Time as Seargt. in Jessup's Corps. Produces his Discharge. Lives at Oswegachy. (80)

Had 30 acres at Kingsbury, purchased of Capt. Jones. Is not certain whether in '74 or '75. Had no Witness. Gave 60 Dollars in old Currency. He cleared 4 acres & built an house.

Vals. at 30£. Is informed it is sold by the State.

Hired some Lands of a person who had taken Possession of

Vacant Lands belonging to Mr. Bayard. Took them in 1776 at a Rent of 8£ per ann.

Had a share in a saw mill in Kingsbury Common. 1-16 share. He helpt to build it. It did not cost him much, besides Labour. Cost 10£.

A Robet. Magee takes 2 horses from Kingsbury in 1777 & a Gun. 2 Cows lost since the year 1780. His Wife was sent away & his utensils & furniture were taken. They were on a Place belonging to another person, when his Wife took shelter in Argyle Township.

CAPT. JOHN JONES, Wits:

(81). Remembers Claimt. at Kingsbury. He went to the Army in 1777, but did not stay. He afterwards joined at Crown Point. Considered him as a Loyalist. Speaks favourably of his character & services.

Claimt. bought 30 acres of Land in Kingsbury of Wits. He thinks in 1775. He was to pay 10 sh. per acre York Money. It was paid or settled in acct. in the year 1775. He had not a Deed, but Witness would have given him one at any time. Claimt. had a share in a saw mill, 1-16. Witness speaks of Claimt. having frequently assisted persons of the Loyal Party. Heard of his having lost horses & cattle, between 1777 & 1780. He lived in Argyle Township.

June 27. 800. Case of JOHN SKIMMING, late of New York.

Claimt. says: He lived in New Cambridge, Albany Co. when Troubles began. He joined the Brit. at Skimesboro in the Fall of 77. Continued with Genl. Burgoyne, was employed as a Clerk by Genl. Burgoyne; was taken at Saratoga. Came into Canada with the Loyalists, have continued there since in the Quarter Masters Department. Now employed in Capt. Genevay's Office.

(82). Lost a Trunk with his Cloathes & Money. Left at New Cambridge when he joined Genl. Burgoyne. It was concealed in a friend's house. Mr. Charles Gorden at New Cambridge. His friend was a Loyalist & had joined Genl. Burgoyne. A parcel of Rebels came & plundered the House & took Claimts. things amongst others. Cash 10 gs. Cloathes 35 York Cury.

Produces affit. from Charles Gorden in whose custody the things were left to Claimt's Loss to the above amount.

The party that plundered Gorden's house came for that Purpose because he was a Loyalist.

June 30. 801. Case of JAMES PARROTT, late of Cambridge, Dist. Province of New York.

Claimt. says: He is a native of America, resided at Little White Creek, Cambridge Dist., when Troubles broke out. He took part of Govermt. he signed the first Association, joined the Brit Army at Crown Point in 1776. Served in Major Jessup's Regt. as Lieutent. Has served all the War. Now lives at Cataraqui; has ½ pay as Lieutent. His Estate was confiscated & sold after he joined the Brit. Army.

(83). He was possessed of 100 Acres in Little White Creek, purchased 7 or 8 years before the War, purchased of one Leake in Consd. of 80£. It was New Land. He laid out a great Deal about it. Improved 80 acres, built a Log House & Barn.

Vals. it at 600£ York Mon.

It was mortgaged to the Loan Office for 50£ of which part was pd. The Loan Office have seized the Land & sold for the Debt.

Produces Certificates of Conviction. Produces Certificates of the late Loan Office from which it appears that there was only due 39£.15 to the Loan Office in 1777, & not for 8£ afterwards.

Had 7 Horses, 20 Cattle, furniture, utensils, 300 Bushels Wheat, Corn, Wheat in the Stock, Oats standing, Hogs, Sheep. These things were taken by town Comrs., 2 Days after the Battle of Bennington. Some sold by public Sale.

CAPTN. CORELL, Witness.

Knew Claimt. Considered him always as a Loyalist. He joined the Brit. at Crown Point in 1776 & continued to serve. Was Lieutent. in Witness's Company.

Knew his Farm. Remembers him in Possession some years before the War. It was a well Improved; 2-3 of it well Improved. He built a Log House. Vals. it at 5£ per acre N. York Cury.

Has heard it has been sold by the Loan Office under Pretence of a Mortgage.

He had a considerable stock. Thinks he had 20 Cattle. He was a very industrious farmer & in good circumstances. (84).

HUGH MUNRO, Wits.

Knew Claimt. Considered him always as Loyal. He joined in 1776 & served. Knew his farm, a very excellent farm, good house & Barn. Vals. at £5 per acre.

JOHN LEAKE, Wits., Father in Law to Claimt., Says when his Son in Law joined the Brit. his stock seized by persons sd. to be Commrs. part was sold. He had a large stock of horses, Cattle & Wheat. His Land was taken by the State. Witness offered to pay what was due to the Loan Office, which they would not take, it was sold afterwards by the Loan Office. *Claimant a good man.*

NEW CLAIM.

802. Case of JOHN ADAMS, late of Pits Town, N. York Province. *June 30.*

Claimt. says: He was at Sorell in the Fall 83. Said he did not know of the Act till 85. *Shuffled and prevaricated.*

He is a native of London, came to America in 1764, was settled at Pits Town, joined the Brit. Army at Bennington in 1777. He, his Father in Law & Brother took 2 Rebel prisoners. Joined a Detachment of Genl. Burgoyne's Army. Continued with his Army till ye Convention. Came to Canada at the Convention. Now settled at Sorell.

(85).   Had 40 acres improved near Pits Town, took it in 1771. It was King's Land. He settled without a Grant. Made improvements. There was a Claim to this by Mr. Munro.

Built 2 houses. His Improvements he values at 120£, in this he reckons only the Clearing of the Ground, House & Barn, vals. at 40£.

Does not know whether the Lands are sold.

In 1777 after the Defeat at Bennington all his moveables were taken. All the Corn was in the ground. They took his utensils & furniture.

After Burgoyne's Defeat when coming into Canada, he was seized & had his money taken by an officer & 3 militia men.

His Father in Law was seized at the same time. He was executed afterwards for having taken one of the Rebels in their way to Bennington.

He was also entitled to a Lot in Albany in right of his Wife. Produces Deed from several persons to Wm. Rogers of a Lot with ¼ part Tanning Utensils in Consr. 15£, 1760.

His Father in Law died in 1778, left it by Will to Claimt's Wife. This was a Town Lot without any buildings. Does not know that it has been Confiscated. John Rogers, Brother in Law
(86).   to Claimt., says Claimt. joined Genl. Burgoyne's Army in 1777. Staid with Burgoyne till the defeat at Saratoga.

He had some Lands near Pitts Town. He took Possession of some vacant Lands & made good Improvmts. A twelvemonth after he was on it. Heard of Munro & others claiming it.

After the Battle of Bennington Claimt's furniture, Utensils, & Corn were taken because he was with the British.

He had money with him & was coming to Canada after Burgoyne's Defeat.

Understood they took his money from him.

Jun 30.   803.   DANL. MACQUIN, late of Ulster Co., New York.

Claimt. says: He is a native of Ireland, settled in America in 1765. Settled in Ulster Co. Was there when the War broke out. Took an active part with Govrt. tho he signed the first Rebel Association in 1775. He raised men for his Majesty, for which he was afterward taken up & confined twice & sentenced to die, but made his escape, got to New York, joined Col. Fanning's Regt. Served as Lieut. 3 years. Had afterwards a warrant for
(87).   a Co. in Col. Ludlow's Battalion, but did not get his Commission, not having raised a sufficient No. of Men. He had raised 14 men. Has no half pay at present, lives at Cataraqui.

Produces Certificates by persons in the States that Claimt. had been imprisoned & sentenced to Death on acct. of his Loyalty,

& that he was possessed of considerable Property, and that a Capt. of Militia sold his effects.

Says he was possessed of 150 acres in Ulster Co. bought of Capt. Leak 5 years before the War. The first time of paymt. was not till after Commencement of the War. He was to pay 50£ after expiration of 5 years. He built a house, barracks & cleared ½ the Land. The Troubles coming on he did not pay the money, but charges for Improvmts £300 York Cury. Says his Improvts. cost him £500. Capt. Leak has since sold the Lands.

He lost his stock, 14 Cattle, recking. 4 Oxen, 1 horse, 1 mare, utensils, furniture. Shop goods to amount of 1,100 New York Cury.

All these things were taken while Claimt. was in the Brit. Army. Everything was sold at a public vendue, except the Shop goods which were plundered.

He laid in his shop goods in 1775 to amount of 1,500. Thinks he had not sold £200.

Has sent a particular acct. home & to the Commrs. at Halifax. His stock was chiefly dry goods. He owes the money to the Merchants with whom he dealt. (88).

He had a Pottash Work on his Lands. Lost his Kettle worth £33, Two Tuns of Potash worth £30 Sterling per ton.

Says the great part of his shop goods were plundered. He went after the Peace with Permission into the Country to look after his effects but was seized by the Mob, robbed & driven away.

He had 43,000 Staves of which he has given a particular acct. Hogshead staves sold at £10 a 1000 before the War, other staves £5 per 1,000.

V. Vol. 21, p. 59.

NEW CLAIM.

804. ABRAHAM MARSH, late of Albany County.   June 30.

Claimt. says: He was at Carleton Island in the Fall of 83. He was discharged there from the 84 Regt.

He is a native of America. Resided at Shaftesbury, Albany Co., at present Vermont, but used to be called Albany Co. Joined the Brit. in 1777, served with Genl. Burgoyne, was with him at (89). Saratoga. Afterward joined 1st Batal. 84. Served with them as private during the War. Now settled in Johnstown.

He had a house Lot at Shaftsbury, bought it 14 years ago for £16. He built a house & Shop, had a Bark Mill & Tan House.

Produces Certificates by 2 persons that Claimt. lost by Confiscation to amnt. of £280 Lawful.

Seems a fair man.

Produces Certificate from Thos. Chittendon that Claimt's Estate at Shaftsbury was Confiscated. He left a good many hides, thinks about 60.

CAPT. COVELL, Wits.

Speaks particularly of his Loyalty, & good character. He had a Lot with exceding good Preparations for a Tannery at Shaftesbury.

Witness says: That in Vermont State they have paid no attention to New York Grants, considering them as no Title.

They have Confiscated when the Claim has been under the New Hampshire Grants, considering them as a good Title.

(90). Gives Claimt. a very good character in every Respect.

PROCEEDINGS

OF

LOYALIST COMMISSIONERS.

MONTREAL, 1787.

Vol. XX.

BEFORE COMMISSIONER PEMBERTON.

Claimants.

	MSS. Folio.		MSS. Folio
Auger, Frederick..	41	Jones, James	62
Ball, Jacob	11 & 28	McKee, Alexander	74
Bender, Philip	67	MacDonel, Randel	21
Buck, Philip	44	Mabee, Lewis	66
Carman, Michael	2	Millard, Thomas	30
Chisholm, John	51	Obenholt, Widow	38
Claus, John	37	Park, (Parker), James	55
Clindinning, James	46	Petrie, Hanjoist	31
Coon, John	17	Philips, Richard	20
Clement, Joseph	23 & 49	Philip, William	1
Crysler, Adam	13 & 53	Pickard, William	18
Depu, John	68	Rose, Donald	54
Dobson, Isaac	80	Secord, Solomon	78
Elliott, Matthew	69	Servos, Daniel	4
Field, Mrs. Rebecca	56	Sherwood, Capt. Justus	4
Frelick, Benjamin	26	Skinner, Timothy	61
Friel, John	8	Smith, Frederick	40
Gerty, George	77	Thomas, Michael	42
Gerty, Simon	76	Thompson, Archibald	55
Griffyn, Joseph	2	Turner, Edward	59
Hare, Mrs. Margaret	33	Walker, Jacob	45
Heanor, Henry	36	Warner, Christian	27
Heaslip, James	22	Wheaton, John	9
House, George	65	Windron, Hendrick	82
Hoverland, Andrew	64	Wintemute, John	43

THE EVIDENCE.

Aug. 9th.

805. WM. PHILIPS.

Claimt. says he resided at Varren in the Fall 80, & all that Winter. No Loyalist there but himself. Knew nothing of the Act till too late.

He is a native of America, resided near Albany. From the first declared his principals in favour of Brit. Govert. So early as 1777 was imprisoned & confined some days on acct. of his Loyalty. In 80 he came into Canada, joined Sir John Johnson. He was not a soldier, but staid with the Army some time, then worked at his trade of a hunt.r.

(1).

He had frequently given assistance to Loyalists, harboured & protected them at his own expense. Produces an acct. of several persons whom he had assisted & protected.

Lost 2 Horses, 2 Cows, Cattle, furniture Utensils. All left behind him when he went away. Sheep, Hogs, taken by friendly Indians.

Montreal, 12th March, 1788.

Produces Certificate from Capt. Thos. Fraser, Loyal Rangers to Claimt's Loyalty & Service to different Couting Party, during the War, 2nd March, 1788.

Aug, 11th.

806. MICHAEL CARMAN, New York.

Claimt. Apprs.

He is a native of Germany, went to America 1750, was settled in Tryon Co. when Rebellion broke out. He was too old to serve, but always declared in favour of Brit. Govert. His son Richd. & Son in Law joined the Brit. Army in 1776.

The Claimt. was driven away in 1781, came into Canada.

(2).

He had a Lease from Sir Wm. Johnston of not quite 100 acres. Claimt. is now near 80 years of age, is to send his Lease by his Son in Law who will also give a faithful acct. of his property.

The Son Michael Carman, has also sent a Claim but it is for property included in his father's Claim. Vi Bound Vol. 12, p. 165.

N. C.

807. Case of JOSEPH GRIFFYN, late of New York.

Claimt. appears.

Aug. 13th.

Says he resided in the fall of 83 with his Regt., Major Jessups, till they were discharged, he sent his Claim by Major Jessup.

The late Isaiah Griffyn was a native of America, lived in Albany Co., joined Genr. Burgoyne in 1777 He lost his life in 1778 from Illness & fatigue while in the Service.

He left a Wife, now in the States. Claimt. his eldest Son in this Province. Rosel with Claimt. both ye two Brothers are Infants. They appear.

The landed Estate has been saved & therefore he withdraws his Claim.

Claims for a share in his father's personal Est. for himself & 2 Bros. Claimt. joined Genr. Burgoyne in 1777 & served all the War, was discharged from Major Jessup Regt. (3).

His father lost, 5 Horses, 10 Sheep, farming utensils, Cloathing, 4 Hogs.

These thi..gs taken when his Father joined Gen. Burg. They were taken by the rebels.

Produces Nov. 27th Major Jessups Certificate to Loyalty & Services.

Produces affidt. from Hannah Allen sworn to before Justice White to Isaiah Griffyn personal estate as above & to its being taken by the Rebels.

808. Further Evidence in Case of Capt. Justus Sherwood. Aug. 18th

Claimt. priduces letter from Govr. Haldimand from which it appears he was confidentially employd in secret service of Importance.

Produces a parcel of old Deeds much injured. They appear to be purchases made by Claimt. between 72 & Jany. 75 of different Parcels of Land & Rights in different Townships in Vermont, appearing to Correspond with the Acct. given by Claimt. on his first exanination. The Considern. cannot be exactly made out. Seems to have been small. (4).

Claimt. says he purchased Land held under the New Hampshire Grants.

809. Claim of Danl. Servos, late of New York. N. C.
Aug. 22.

Claimt. says he resided at Niagara in the Fall of 83, & the ensuing Winter. In Nov. 83, he gave in a Claim to his commanding officer Col. De Pyster to be sent to England, which Claim never arrived in England in time.

Sent a 2nd Claim in Consequence of notice from J. Gust Hope as soon as he possibly could.

Is a native of America. Resided in Tryon Co. New York Prov.

Claimt. his Father & Brother had declared in Favr. of the Brit. His Father, Brother & Claimt. were all imprisoned at different times. Claimt. was imprisoned in Johnstown Gaol in Aug. 1778. They went off. They could not stay any longer. They (5). went on service. Went to Niagara, joined in 1779, had a company of men as Lieut. in the Indian Department, produces his Commission from Genl. Haldimand in 1779, Continued in that service during the War. His Brother served also in the same Department.

Produces Instructions from Col. Johnson, Col. of the six nations to Claimt. in 1780. His Father was killed by a Party of the Rebels at the Time. He was endeavouring to collect a party to

come off in the summer, 1778. He was attacked by a Rebel Party. Claimt. was in Company. His father was shot. Claimt. left the Country at that time.
Has not at present any half pay.
The Claim is for the Estates of his Father. His father Christopher was killed in 1778. He died without a Will. He left a Widow, Clara, now in the Colonies.
Claimt. Eldest Son, 2 Jacob now here, 3rd Bro. Infants now

in the States, 5 Sisters in the States.
His Father had 1,500 acres on Charlotte River. His father purchased it of Sir Wm. Johnson about the year 1770. The Deed is lost. He gave other Lands in exchange for it. It was uncultivated when he took it.

(6). About 90 acres clear, 2 Dwelling Houses, 2 Barns, 2 Mills, a Grist Mill & Saw Mill. A Large House for making Potash. Values the Farm at £3,000 York Cury including Buildings, the Mills & the Potash House.
Vals. the 2 Mills at £700 which are included in the above Estimate. Vals. the Potash House at £120.
This Estate has been sold. Part of it has not yet been sold.
His Mother has not been allowed anything for her Dower.
Claimt. says he saw an advertisement for the sale in a rebel News Paper.
None of his family are in Possession of any part of the Estate. His Father lost a personal Estate consisting of 12 horses, 21 Head Cattle, 25 Sheep, 40 Hogs, furniture, Utensils for farming, Blacksmith & Weaver's tools, 3 large Kettles, utensils for Potash Work, Valued at £350 at the lowest.

These Utensils were left on the Premises when they went away & sold by the Rebels.
The Potash House & Works & all the Buildings were burnt by the Rebels.
Produces 2 affts. that Claimt's Father Possessed the real & Personal Est. as contained in Schedules & that they are fairly valued by Claimt.
Says there were no Debts on the Estate.
N.B.—His name appears in Anstey's List.
He is told to produce Certificates of Sale.

(7). ADAM CHESTER Wit.
Knew Claimt's father Christr. He was killed by the Rebels. He died without a Will, leaving Claimt. his Eldest Son. Knew his estate in Charlotte River. He bought it of Sir Wm. Johnson. Gave other Lands for it. Remembers him settled there sometime before. Above a 1,000 acres. A good Deal was clear. Speaks of 40 or 50 acres but cannot ascertain the No. There was a good D..lling house, 2 Mills, a grist Mill & Saw Mill. He had a Potash Work on ye Premises. Vals. Clear Land at £5 per acre. Vals. unimproved at 20s. per acre. The Mills cost old Sevors a good Deal of Mon y. Thinks pretty near 500£. Knew the Pot-

ash Works, 2 Kettles, the principal expense is in the Kettles. Has

heard the Estate has been sold. Claimt's Father had a large stock Blacksmiths tools, furniture, &c. He had good Horses. Everything was taken away by the Rebels.

Produces Certificates to Loyalty & Services from Col. Butler.

810. Claim of JOHN FRIEL, late of New York.   Aug. 22.

DEBORAH FRIEL, Widow of Claimt. appears.   (8).

Says her late Husb. was a native of Ireland. Settled in America 20 years ago, lived at John's Town, Tryon Co.

He joined the Brit. at the Beginnnig of the Rebellion. He at first joined Col. Claus & Sir John Johnson in 1775. He staid some time with them. He then returned home, staid a year, during which time he was imprisoned for 18 days. In 1777 he joined the Brit. Troops again, served under Sir John, served till brought up to Niagara by Col. Johnson. He died 3 years ago without a Will, leaving Claimt., his Widow & 3 Children, 1 girl grown up & married to Saml. Cox & 2 boys, children all there now live with the Mother.

Her Husb. had a Lease from Sir Wm. Johnson for ever at 6£ per an. d ted 1771.

Her Husb. had improved it, cleared 10 or 20 acres. Claimt. herself was driven from it. The Rebels took it & rented it at 9£.

Her Husb. lost 2 Cows, & 1 Calf, furniture. All these things were taken by the Rebels, on acct. of her Husb. having joined Sir John's Corps. They were taken from Claimt.

Produces Certificates to the Loyalty & Services of the late John Friel & that he joined the King's Troops at Commencement of Rebellion from Sir John Johnson.   (9).

811. Case of JOHN WHEATON, late of New York.   Aug. 23rd.

Claimt. says:

He resided at Detroit in the Fall of 83 & all the ensuing Winter. Heard nothing of the Act.

Heard of the 2nd Act. in Consequence of Orders sent from Genl. Hope last year. Sent as soon as he possibly cd. after these orders came to Detroit.

Is a native of America, lived at Schenectady, Albany Co. In Sepr., 1777, joined Genr. Burgoyne, served as an Artificer attachd to Capt. McAlpines Corps. Continued with the Army till his Depart. got afterwards to Lake George & from thence to Ticonderago & afterwards to Canada.

Was in the King's Works under Capt. Twiss at St. John's. Came up here in the Spring of 83, was here all the summer, went in the fall to Detroit, is now settled at Detroit.

(10).

Has a House & lot in Schenectady, a town Lot, purchased in 1774 of Albert Vider in Considn 200 York Mon.
The Deed is in the States, made no Improvts, vals. it at the same sum. It has been confiscated & sold.
Produces advertisement for the sale of House & Lot of John Wheaton, late of Schenectady, Name is in Anstey's List.
Produces Letter from his Bro. informing him that it was sold.
It consisted of 2 small houses. He let one for £5 per an.
Lost his tools, Carpenters tools, furniture, Cloaths, Lost a Cow, 2 Hogs.
Richd. Stephens, Wits. Knew Claimt. He was always consid. a Loyalist. He joined Gen. Burgoyne, belonged to Capt. McAlpine's Corps & went to Canada. He bought a House 2 or 3 yrs. before ye Troubles of one Albert Veder in which he lived, Vals. it at near 200£. He was a Carpenter, had a lot of Tools.
Produces Certificate to Loyalty & services from Sir John Johnston.

N. C.
Aug. 23.

812. Case of JACOB BALL, late of Albany Co.

Claimt. says he resided at Niagara in the Fall of 83 & all that Winter. Did not know of any act in 83. Sent his Claim as soon as he could after Genrl. Hope's orders last year.
Is a native of America, resided near Albany when the Rebellion broke out, took part with the King from the first, kept quiet as well as he could but was fined & imprisoned.

(11).

In 1778 left his Home & joined Butler's Rangers, had a commission as Lieut. in Butler's Rangers. Served during the War. Has now half pay.
Produces his Commns. in 1779 & 1780. Says he did not join Gen. B. in 1777 as he could not with safety attempt it. The Posts being held by the Rebels. He sent to enquire of Genl. Burg in Summer 77 & they brought him word that he was to stay for a better opportunity. He was troubled so much that he could not stay at home.

Can only be allowed for improvements.

Had 100 acres of Land on Rancellors Manor. He had settled without any Deed above 20 years ago. He had cleared 100 acres, had built a framed house & barn & Potash Works.
They wanted the settlers to take Leases, but they refused, but they agreed to pay the 10th part of the Profits, but never got a Lease, as by the death of Stephen Rancellor the Father, it came to his Son who was an Infant.

The Potash Works was made 2 years before ye War. The Place is about 20 miles from Albany, Vals. it at 5£ per acre.

Too high.

Says he estimates the Land at 10£ per acre but considers the Seigniors Right at worth half.

(12).

Vals. his House, Barn & Potash Works at 700£. The Potash Works includes buildings, 2 Kettles, the 2 Kettles cost 50£. He includes a Ton & ½ of Potash, A Ton of Potash worth 50£.
Produces notice from one Nichs. Marschs to Claimant's Wife to quit the Premises in 83.

Produces a Cancelled Bond by which his Wife & Son bound themselves in the sum of 200£ to Nichs. Marschs to quit the Premises in a months time, dated May, 1784.

As to Lands at Schorhara it was some Land he had from his elder Bros., who is now in Possession.

Lost 15 Horses, 30 Cattle, 30 Sheep, 30 Hogs, farming Utensils. Left all these things on his farm when he went away in 1778. The Rebels took them away in the year 1780.

Produces affts. from 3 persons to Claimt's Loss as above specified & to the valuation.

Claimt. says Marschs is a Relative to Rancellor & may possibly have some Claims to the Lands on that acct. N. C.

Is told to get a certificate of the vals. Certificates to Loyalty.

813. Claim of ADAM CRYSLER, late of Albany Co.   Aug. 23.

Claimt. says:

He resided at this Place in the Fall '83 & the ensuing winter. Sent a Claim home by Col. Butler. Sent another Claim afterwards in consequence of orders from the Commanding officer. (13).

Is a native of America. Lived at Schohary, Co. of Albany, when Rebellion broke out.

He declared from the first in Favr. of his Majesty. He was carried frequently before the Committees.

He went from home in 1777 towards fort Stanwix with 35 men. Was taken sick by the way. Sent his men forward. When he recovered he returned towards home to collect his men together who had been dispatched. He himself made his way to Niagara & served first as Lieut. in Col. But Rangers, afterwards in the Indian Department. Has not at present half pay.

Now resides near Niagara.

Produces a sort of Journal of his Services from March, 1777, under ye Comands of Col. Butler & Johnston, from which he appears to have been much employed & to have been very active & to have gone through a great Deal.

Had a Farm in Vrooman's Patent. Cannot tell ye exact No. of acres. His Father bought it many years ago. He has been dead 35 years. Claimt. is his eldest son. It came to him on his Death, & he has had ever since. It lies on Schohary river. He used to sow 40 skepples of wheat. There were meadows & grass grounds besides. 40 acres arable, clear 4 or 5 acres meadow. He describes the lots as containing 35 or 36 morisons. A morison is 2 acres. Thinks this farm about 70 or 80 acres. A good House & Barn. Vals. it at 1,000£. (14).

Cannot tell what has been done in respect to the Confiscation or Sale.   Greatly too high.

Produces Deed from Cornelius Van Alestyn to H——Cresler of half a Tract at Huntersfield in Vrooman's Patent & half of a fifth part of undivided Land called Œsopos in Considn. of 260£ York Cury., dated 1749. The moiety of undivided Lands has been sold. No 1.

No. 2.	A Lot of Land in Schohary in Wm. Bough's Patent. Wm. Bough was Claimt.'s Uncle. He got the Patent many years ago.

He gave Claimt. a Lot 30 years ago.

Claimt. kept it for firewood. It was totally unimproved. Produces Deed from Wm. Bough to Claimt. of 89 acres at Schohary in Cons. 6£ Cury., dated 1762, besides the Consn. Money. Claimt. says he was at great expense in obtaining the Patent, 2 acres with a Grist Mill on Bough's Patent bought sometime before the Rebellion by his Brother. Built ye mill afterwards.

The Mill cost 200£. Vals. it at 800£. This mill has been burnt down by the Indians. It was done by mistake. The Indians understanding it to belong to a Rebel.

Enormous.

Produces Deed from Baltiza Cresler to Claimt. of 2 acres on Wm. Bough's Patent in Consi. 10£, dated 1776. Claimt. built the mill after he made the purchase.

(15).

No. 4. Had a share in a Saw Mill on Bough's Patent. Claimt. & 3 others, all named Bough & Related to Claimt., built the Mill 20 yrs. ago. Says it was in work but did not bring any Profit. He used it chiefly for his own Board & fences.

No. 5. A Lot in Baests Patent on Cobers Kiss; 30 acres Claimt. had it from his Step Father. It was a great way off from Claimt. None of it improved.

Produces Deed of Gift from Michl. Helzenger to Claimt. of 34 acres in Baest's Patent on the Schohary, 1765.

No. 6. A Lot on Charlotte River in Swart's Patent, abt. 80 acres. His Father was one of the Patentees. He has this share from his Father. None of this improved.

Produces a Patent to Vrooman Swarts, H. ―――― Cresler of Lands 24 miles west from Schohary, dated 1743. Condition in the Patent is to cultivate 3 acres for every fifty, within 3 years.

Lost 14 Cattle, 8 Horses, 5 Sheep, 20 Hogs, Wheat 300 Skepples, Farming utensils, 1 Waggon.

(16). They were taken away by the Rebels in 1777, after he left Home, & have been all sold.

His name appears in Anstey's List.

Produces 2 affdts. that Claimt. was in Possession of the estates above specified & that the acct. was just.

One of the Deponents is D. Servos vs̄. his evidence in fra.

I believe he is a good man.

Produces Certificates to Loyalty from Col. Butler.

Is told to get Certificates of Sale.

N. C.
Aug. 23.

814. Claim of JOHN COON, late of Albany.

Claimt. says:

He was at Niagara in the Fall '83. Was too late to send his Claim to Col. Butler.

Is a native of America. Lived in Albany Co. Joined the Brit. in 1777. Joined Col. Butler's Corps & served with the Rangers 7 years as Seargt.

Had some Leased Land on Rancellor's Patent. His Father had some on which he now lives. Clearance had also some, at least 100 acres. The Estate was undivided. Claimt.'s share contained about 40 acres clear. He had a separate house of his own. (17).

His Father & eldest Bro. are now in Possession of the whole, except some which his Bro. has sold. There was a contest about this Land between Norman Shell's People & Rancellors.

He lost 2 Horses & Colt worth 50£. 1 Horse, very fine horse, 2 Cows, 6 Calves, 1 Heifer, furniture, Tools.

When Claimt. went off to join Burgoyne these things were taken by the Rebels & sold at Vendue. His Father tried to save them but could not.

Produces 2 affdts. to his having had the above Property & that his acct. was just.

JOHN SEGAR, Wit:

Knew Claimt. Remembers him in Possession of a House & Farm at Norman's Kits.

He had one fine Horse. It was taken by the Rebels & sold for £52.

He had some stock besides.

815. Claim of WM. PICKARD, late of Pensilva. Aug. 23.

Claimt. says:

He is a native of America. Lived in Susquehana in Pensilva. Always supported Brit. Govert. He & his 2 Sons left home to join Col. Butler in '77. Joined him. Served in the Rangers He & one of his sons were privates, the other was a Drummer. Served all the war. (18).

Lives now at Niagara.

Had some Land in Westmoreland, 300 acres. Had no Deed or Lease, but had made Improvmts. & lived there. He built a House & sort of Barn. There was a great dispute between Pensilva. & Connect. as to which State the Land lay within when he went to settle there. He cleared about 24 acres. His house & Barn were burnt by rebels.

He had some Land in Tryon Co., purchased of Jacob & Philip Skyler. It consisted chiefly of Islands in the Mohawk river. 3 acres of Land on the Bank. He had a Deed of it.

He gave some other Lands in exchange for it.

It was a great while ago.

He let it to Jacob Skyler of whom he purchased it when he went to Susquehana, partly for money, partly to have cattle, but has received nothing from it.

Vals. it at 150£. Has heard that it was sold by Commrs. because Claimt. was a Tory. There were about 10 acres clear of this Land. Has heard it has been bought by a nephew of Claimt.'s, who is now in Possession.

(19). Lost Cattle & Goods on Susquehana. 5 milch Cows, 2 young creatures, Grain, 24 bushels & 16, 2 horses, 8 Hogs, furniture, utensils. Left on his place when he went away. Taken by the Indians & Rebels. Lost Crop on ye ground.

Says he sometimes hears his Estates has been sold. Sometimes not.

FREDERICK SMITH, Wits: Says Claimt. had Improvemts. in Westmoreland on the Susquehana. Had cleared 20 acres. He had settled upon it. It was not conveyed to him. He built House & Barn, since burnt. Knew his other Lands in Tryon Co. His nephew now has them. He had a good stock; 5 Cows, 2 horses, 2 young creatures &c. They were taken & destroyed by the Rebels. He served in the Rangers from beginning to end of war. He had 2 Sons in the Rangers.

Maybe allowed some little for improvements, and pretty well for stock.

August 23.

816. Case of RICHD. PHILIPS, late of New York.

Claimt. says:

He is a native of America. Lived at Susquehana in 1777. left his Home & joined Col. Butler in the Rangers. Served 2 years; was then taken Prisoner & confined in several gaols. Made his escape & got to New York, from thence came to Montreal. Now settled near Niagara.

(20). Had a proprietor's right in Susquehana. It was a disputed Title, but Claimt. says he had Grants both from Pensilv. & Connect. A proprietor's Right consisted of about 4,000 acres. He had parted with 1-4. He used to sow & plow about 40 acres.

N.B.—Says this land was better than that in the Schohary for which Chrislor charges so high.

Says he had paid a set of Blacksmith Tools & 40 Dollars for it. He had a Log House & Barn. He did it all himself. Vals. clear Land at ½ Joe pr. acre.

He says the Pensilva. Title used to be reckoned the best. The Connect. Govt. have got it.

Lost all his Stock & utensils.

He had 6 Horses, 5 Cows, yoke oxen, 5 young Cattle, 6 Sheep, 40 Hogs, taken by Connect. Govt. & sold by them when he went away. His Papers & Deeds were all taken away & his House plundered.

PHILIP BUCK, Wits.:

Knew him on the Susquehana. He had considerable Improvemts, 30 or 40 acres clear. He settled there in 1772. He was taken Prisoner & confined some time. He got away once, was taken again. From thence he escaped to New York.

He had a good stock. Thinks the Rebels had them, not the Indians or Rangers. His stock was gone before they came.

A fair man, to be allowed improvements and stock.

N. C.
August 24.

817. Claim of RANDEL MACDONEL, late of Tryon Co.

(21). Claimt. says:

He resided at Niagara in the Summer '83 & the ensuing winter.

Is a native of Ireland. Went to America many years ago. Was settled on Mohawk river, Tryon Co. Joined the Brit. at Fort Stanwix in 1777. 4 Sons went with him to the Brit. Army. Served in Col. Butler's Rangers as a Seargt. Served all the war. Now lives at Niagara.

Produces Certificates to Claimt.'s Loyalty, good conduct & services from Col. Butler.

Lived in a Leased House of Sir Wm. Johnstons. Had no Land of his own. Had 15 Cattle, 9 Horses, Sheep, great many Hogs, do. furniture, Cloaths, utensils, taken by the Rebels after he joined the Brit.

Produces affdt. by 2 persons of his being possessed of the effects above specified & that they are moderately valued.

BARNABAS SKRAN: Knew Claimt. on the Mohawk. He had considerable stock, 8 or 9 horses. He had a plentiful stock. Witness left home before Claimt. did. He had the stock at that time. Heard the Rebels took his things. He had a good Waggon & good farming utensils. Satisfied claimant had a pretty good stock.

818. Claim of JAMES HEASLIP, late of Albany Co.   August 24th.

Claimt. says: (22).

Is a native of Ireland. Went to America '74. Was settled at Beaver Dam, 20 miles from Albany. Settled on Pataroon Land. Was to pay a 10th part of Produce, but had got no Lease. In 1777 joined Butler's Rangers. Was a Corporal. Served all the war. Produces Certificates from Col. Butler to services & Loyalty. Do. from the Surgeon of ye Regt. & that he had been severely wounded in the service. He had built a House & cleared 12 acres. Lost the crop, 1 Cow, 1 mare, utensils, furniture, Cloaths, taken by the Rebels. Seems a fair man. To be allowed as much as we can, on acct. too of his having been severely wounded.

819. Claim of JOSEPH CLEMENT, late of New York.   N. C.
   August 24th.

Claimt. says:

He resided at Montreal during the Sumr. '83, & in the Fall at Quebec.

He delivered his Claim to Sir John Johnston late in the Fall at Montreal. Says he waited to deliver his Claim to Sir John, as Sir John had told him he was going to England & would take care of it. Sir John actually set out to go to England that Fall by way of Halifax.   (23).

Is a native of America. Lived on the Mohawk river, Tryon Co. Joined the Brit. at 1777. Joined Gen. Burg. Carried 40 or 50 Indians in with him. Served during the war in the Indian Department, as Lieut., sometimes as Volunteer. Now lives near Niagara. Has no ½ pay.

Had a Farm at Trepas Hill on the Mohawk, part of Hansen's Patent. The farm consisted of 300 acres. Was his Fathers.

Produces Deed from Nichs. Hansen to Joseph Clement, Claimt.'s grandfr., of 850 acres in Considn. 635£, dated 1749.

Claimt.'s grandfather left this to Claimt.'s Father & 2 Brothers.

This Estate was divided. Claimt.'s Father purchased some of his elder Bro, which made his share above 300 acres.

Claimt.'s Father joined the Brit. at beginning of Troubles. Served as Lieut. in Indian Department. Died in '81. Made a Will. Produces the Will.

Testr. gives his Estates to his Wife during widowhood, afterwards gives Claimt. all his Low lands & part of his uplands.

Adjoining the rest of the uplands he gives to his other two sons, John & James. Will is dated 1770.

(24). Claimt.'s share. The Low lands & Claimt.'s share in the uplands make 145 acres. Produces Plan of the Estate, which corresponds with the above acct.

There were 3 houses on the Low Lands, an orchard; 60 acres clear. Vals. the clear Lands at 15£ pr. acre, York Cury. Vals. ye unimproved Lands at 40 sh. pr. acre.

His Mother & Brothers are now living & live at Niagara.

Claimt. did not know of his Father's Will when he gave in his Claim & he gave in a Claim for the whole Estate as Heir at Law.

His mother, Catharine, came to this Province in '80. His secd. Bro., John, came in '80. He has served as Lieut. in the Indian Department. The 3rd. Bro., James, came into this Prov. Has been in the Storekeeper's Department.

The Family were all active in support of Brit. Govt. His 2 Bros. were young lads when Claimt. left the Country. They came into this Country on acct. of attachment to Brit. Govrt.

N.B.—The Conviction appears against the Father in Anstey's List.

Claimt. is told to get certificates.

The Farm has been sold. Heard that one Henry had bought it.

(25). His 2 Bros. were entitled to remaining part of the Farm, 155 acres in the uplands of which 15 acres were clear. Vals. them at 40s. pr. acre. They had a share in a saw mill. It belonged to 6 Proprietors in Hansen's Patent. His Father had 2 shares. Chiefly used for sawing boards for their own Houses & fences. Thinks a share worth about 20£.

They had a Negroe taken from his Mother. A Rebel officer is now in Possession of him. Horses, Cows, live stock, furniture, farming utensils.

Produces Certificates to Loyalty & Service from Col. Butler.

Produces affidt. from 2 persons to the amount of Claimt.'s Losses as above.

Says there were no debts on the estate.

ARENT BRADK, Wits:

Says he knows the Family of Clement. They were all Loyal.

Joseph, the Claimt., joined the Brit. early. The Father & Brothers & Mother all came away.

Knew the Farm at Trepes Hill. Remembers the Father in Possession. Thinks it better than 300 acres. There were 60 acres cleared; good Buildings. Some part of the upland clear. Vals. ye Low land at £20 pr. acre. Vals. upland at 40sh. per acre. Col. Butler had Lands adjoining which he used to sell at that rate. They had a very good stock. They had 2 Negroes & a wench. I Negroe & the wench came with them. The other Negroe is in Possession of a person in the Colonies. (26).

N.B.—Look in Col. Butler's determination as he had lands adjoining

Understood all the moveables were sold by the Commissrs.
The family were in good circumstances.

820. Claim of BENJ. FRELICK, late of Albany Co. August 25th.

Claimt. says:

He was at Niagara in the Sumr. '83 & the next winter. Is a native of America. Lived near Albany. In 1778 joined Butler's Rangers & served 6 years as Seargt.

Had suffered terribly before he quitted Home on acct. of his Loyalty. Obliged to quit Home. Now lives at Niagara. Produces his discharge June, '84.

Had a farm of 10 acres in the Pataroon Lands. Had no Deed or Lease. Had been settled there 6 yrs. Had cleared 10 acres, built House & Barn. Lost 2 Horses taken for fines, 2 Cows, 19 Hogs, furniture, utensils, Tools. His family were driven from the Place & the rebels took all the things above mentioned. (27).

Produces affidvts. that Claimt. sustained the Losses above mentioned.

CHRISTIAN WARNER, Wits:

Knew Claimt. He was always considered a Loyalist. He had a little farm on Pataroon Land. He had 10 acres clear, House & Barn.

He had Horses & Cows &c., being well for a beginner. Lost them all.

821. Claim of CHRISTINA WARNER, late of Albany Co. August 21th,

Claimt. says:

He was at Niagara in the Fall '83. Is a native of America. Lived near Albany. Joined Gen. Burgoyne in 1777. In 1778 came here & joined Butler's Rangers. Served dur. war as Seargt.

Had a farm on Pataroon's Land. Had been settled several yrs. before ye war. Cleared 12 acres clear & had began to clear more. Built an House & Barn.

Lost 2 Cows, 1 ox, 2 horses, 4 Sheep, 13 Hogs, furniture, utensils.

Taken by the Rebels soon after he joined Burg. (28).

BENJ. FRELICK, Wits:
Knew Claimt. He had a farm on Pataroon's Land. He was always a Loyalist. Served in Butler's Rangers.
He had more clearances than Witness.
Had rather a larger stock than Wit.
Remarks his having 3 horses. Lost 2, 3 or 4 horned Cattle.

August 25th.   Further Evidence in the Case of JACOB BALL, v. 21.

BENJ. FRELICK, Wits:
Knew Claimt. He served as Lieut. in Butler's Rangers. He was settled on Pataroon Land before ye war. He was an old settler. Had near 100 acres clear. Had a good House & Barn. Had a

Potash Work there. He had no Right to sell anything but Improvemts. Vals. these Lands at about 5£ per acre. Potash Work cost him a good Deal. Nothing very expensive about the Buildings. Thinks he had 3 Kettles.
He had a very large stock; 25 horned Cattle, 10 horses, 30 Sheep, Hogs. Most of it tak n by the Rebels & sold. Knows that
(29).   the horned Cattle & horses were sold by the Rebels.

CHRISTIAN WARNER, Wits:
Knew Claimt. He was an old settler on Pataroon Land. The same as Rancellor's Manor. He had a large Farm, about 100 acres clear, 2 houses & Barn & Potash Work. The buildings not expensive, but the Pots were. Says there was no certain rule of selling by the acre. People sold for what they cd. get.
A Lot generally consisted of 400 acres. Knew one Lot sold at 120 York Cury., but he had not near such good Lands as Claimt.
He had a very large stock; 30 Cattle, 10 or 15 Horses; all lost. Most of them taken by the Rebels.

August 25th.   822.   Claim of THOS. MILLARD, late of Pensilva.

Claimt. says:
He is a native of Am. Lived on Susquehana when the Rebeln. broke out. Was always a supporter of Brit. Govrt. Had 3 Sons in the service from 1778 to end of the war.
(30)   In 1778 came to Niagara. Could not continue at Susquehana, being known to be a Loyalist, so that he & all his family came away. Now settled near the Falls.
He had made a bargain for purchasing Lands in 1777. The purchase has not been completed, but he has been obliged to pay 100£ in consequence of his agreemt.
His moveable Estate consisted of 100 Bushels of wheat which had been harvested in 1777. Do. Ind. Corn, 2 fine horses. Stole as he was moving into Canada. . Seven Hogs, cloatus, Linen, some Flour.
More of these things were lost on a Farm which he had on Susquehana river, 16 miles below Wyboosenk.

He purchased 300 acres in 1774, for abt. 30£. Built an house. Had about 30 acres clear.

The Purchase was recorded but he has lost the Deed. He Vals. it at 100£. Had agreed to sell it for that sum. The moveables were chiefly taken by the friendly Indians. He has not heard that his land has been sold.

Claimt. seems a very fair man.

THOS. MILLARD, JR., Wits:

Says his Father purchased a Farm in Susquehana just before Rebellion. 300 acres; 30 acres clear. He lived there till they set off for Canada. The whole family came because they would not be rebels & could not stay unless they were rebels.

(31).

Wits. & 2 Bros., all that were big enough to serve, have served his Majesty during the war.

His Father had a considerable stock. Lost wheat, Corn, 2 Horses, 7 Hogs, utensils, furniture.

May be allowed.

823. Claim of HANJOIST PETRIE, of Tryon Co.

Claimt. says:

He is a native American. Lived at the German Flats when ye Rebellion broke out. Took ye part of the King. Joined King's Troops at Fort Stanwix. Served under Col. Butler. Served 4 years as private. Now lives at Niagara.

August 25th.

Was possessed of 100 acres of Land in German Flats. He purchased it 2 yrs. before the Rebellion. Gave another farm for it. 200 acres of unimproved land. Had a Deed. 60 acres clear when he purchased it. Says he built a Log House & Barn after the Purchase. He built the House himself. Vals. it at about 600£.

Does not know what is become of the Land. It was not sold lately.

N.B.—His name is in Anstey's List.

Had 5 horses, 6 Cattle, 60 Hogs, 10 Sheep, utensils, furniture, cloaths.

Left in his House & taken by the Rebels.

(32).

Produces 2 affidts. that Claimt. was in Possession of Land, stock &c., but they cannot say to what amount.

MRS. DOROTHY THOMPSON, Wits:

Knew Claimt. He was a neighbour to Wits. Lived at Barnetsfield, 12 miles from German Flats. He was very Loyal from the first & suffered a great deal from it. He went off to Fort Stanwix. He served afterwards in Butler's Rangers. Knew his Farm. He purchased it 2 years before the war. Thinks about 50 acres clear.

He was in Possession till he went away to the British. He built a house there himself. He had a pretty good stock. Some was seized by the Rebels. Some he was obliged to leave, from not being able to carry it away with him, as they fled & went thro the woods. Claimt. seemed to be in pretty good circumstances.

(33).   He had he Land of Witness's Husband & gave other Land in
exchange for it. She says it was 2 years before the war. Says
the Land her husband had of Claimt. was improved.
Is told to get Certificates of Sale.

August 25th.   824 Claim of MARGT. HARE, Widow of John Hare, late of
New York.

Claimt. says:
She resided at Montreal in '83. Gave her Claim to Major
Leake. He was going to England that year. He set off but he did
not get to England in time.
Her husband, John Hare, was a native of America. Lived
in Johnstown when ye Rebellion broke out. He joined the Brit.
in 1776. Was a Captn. in Indian Department.

Lost his Life in an Engagement at Fort Stanwix. He made
a Will. Left his Estate to Claimt. during her Widowhood & then
to his Children.
Wits. eldest Son. He has served in Butler's Rangers. 3
Daughters, 2 in this Prov. under age; 1 married in the States.
(34).   Claimt. came herself in June with her Daughters in '83.
Says she was kept by one of the Rebel's Commissr. of —— or she
would have come in sooner. Says he stopped her as an hostage.
Her Husband was Possessed of an Estate at Johnstown which
has been sold, but they have not received all the money.
Her Husb. lost various articles in 1776 when Gen. Skuyler
came against them in that settlement. His House was plundered.
Delivers an acct. in her husband's hand writing. The amt. is
It is over-   40£, but seems to be for Provisions taken from the house & some
charged in the household goods plundered. This was in Jany., '76.
acct.
In June following his house was plundered by a party of
Rebels under Col. Draten & other Rebel officers. Buildings were
damaged and fences were destroyed.

The late John Hare had a Lease from Sir Wm. Johnston. He
was to have had a Lease for 10 years, but the Deed was not made.
The house & place were near the Gaol. John Hare was under
Sheriff. The Gaol was made a Fort of by the Rebels & in making
the Fort they made use of Timber from Mr. Hare's house to amount
(35)   of 25£. They took his Fences for burning. They took boards,
iron, staples, &c.
Greatly over-   Produces an acct. of Damage done to amount of 100£ & up-
valued.   wards.
Claims also for Loses of office of Under Sheriff. Produces
Seems to be a Deport in 1775.
loss from bad
neighbors.
WM. HARE, the eldest Son:
Says his Father made a Will. Witness entered in Butler's
Rangers in the yr. '80. Served till they were discharged. Served
as a Volunteer. Witness was at Home when his Father's house was
plundered by Skuyler's party. Remembers when the Rebels took

Possession of the Gaol & fortified it. They took Timber & Boards of his Fathers to make a Block house at the Gaol. Damaged his House. Took ye fences to burn. Damaged his Corn & other property.

---

825. Claim of HENRY HEANOR, late of Ulster Co.   August 25th.

Claimt. says. He is a native of Germany. 22 yrs. ago came to America. Lived in Ulster Co. Was in Butler's Rangers. Served 3 years.

Had Land from Mr. Livingston, about 80 acres, for 2 Lives. himself & Son, paying ½ a Skipple for 2 acres. Had not a Lease.   (36). Had cleared 34 acres. Built house & barn.

Vals. his Improvmts. at 100£.

Lost 4 Cows, 7 Hogs, 3 Sheep, 100 Bushels Wheat, all his furniture, utensils.

Taken by the Rebels when Claimt. went to the Brit. Army.

JOHN WRAIGHT, Wits: Knew Claimt. He was a Loyalist. He went to Canada & joined the Rangers. He had a Son in the Rangers. He had a Leased farm about 80 acres. He had made Improvemts. Had cleared 30 or 40 acres.

He had 7 or 8 horned Cattle, Sheep & Hogs, furniture. Witness saw some of his things. Sold at Vendue by the Rebels.

---

826. Claim of JOHN CLAUS, late of Tryon Co.   August 27th.

Claimt. says:

He was at Niagara in the Fall of '83 & the ensuing winter.

Is a native of Germany. Had been settled many years in America. Lived at Cobus Kill, Albany Co. Joined the Brit. in '77, at Fort Stanwix. Served under Col. Butler 7 years as Corporal.

Produces his discharge.

Had 200 acres in Cobus Kill, Albany Co., since called Tryon   (37). Co.

Produces Deed from Wm. Banyard to Claimt. of lot No. 10, containing 203 acres near Cobus Kill in Cons. 125£ Cury., 1771.

Recited to be part of Tract of 7,000 acres granted to several persons in 1761.

He worked upon it after the Purchase. He had cleared 10 acres, built a House & Barn.

Says he had paid some of the purchase money, not all. Vals. it at 200£.

It has been sold by ye Comrs. Claimt. has seen the person who bought it, who told him what he had paid for it.

Had 4 horses & 3 Cows, & 1 Heifer, furniture & utensils. The Rebels took them & sold them at Vendue, after Claimt. went away.

Claimt. was wounded in Service.

JOHN STEVENS, Wits:

Claimant a fair man.
(38).

Knew Claimt. Knew his Farm. Was shown his Farm after Claimt. went away. There were buildings & some clearances. It had been sold by the Comrs. Had not known the Place formerly, but knew that Claus had a Farm there. Knew of 2 horned Cattle which the Rebels took. Saw some of his cloaths which ye Rebels took. He had also some Horses.

August 27th.

827. Claim of WIDOW OBENHOLT, late of Pensilva.

The oldest son of John Obenholt appears. Claimt. affirms.

That this is a Claim of his Father's Estate. It is entered in his Mother's name, but was sent home by Claimt. & was intended to be a Claim for the whole family.

His Father, John Obenholt, was a native of America. Lived in Bucks Co., Pensilva. He aided the Brit. all he could. Joined them at New York in the year '80. He had been active in assisting Brit. officers to get cross the Delaware, this being known he was obliged to fly. He had been committed for high Treason, broke Gaol & got to New York. Died there in '80. Made no Will.

Left Elizth., his Widow, now living in Bucks Co. Claimt., his eldest Son. John, now about 16 years of age, now in the Colonies.

(39).
No Loyalist. nor any of the family now living.

Claimt. lived with his Father when the Rebellion broke out. He staid till his Father went to New York. Claimt. had been active in carrying some of the soldiers who were taken Prisoners under Burg. He went to New York once or twice on this business to carry in Prisoners, on no other occasion. Continued in the States till last Fall.

His Father had a farm, 6 miles, in Bucks Co., purchased 24 or 25 yrs. ago. There were 200 acres, a grist mill, 2 houses & 2 Barns. The Deeds are in the Colonies but a Copy has been sent to England. Thinks his Father gave 700 or 800£ for it. This Estate has been valued at 1,100 Pensilv. Curry. It has been confiscated & sold. A Certificate of Sale is sent to England.

His Father had considerable moveable Estate, which were seized & sold.

3 horses, 5 Cows, 12 Sheep, 6 Hogs, considerable furniture, Hay, taken & sold.

August 27th.

828. Claim of FREDERICK SMITH, late of Pensilva.

Claimt. says:

He is a native of Germany. Settled in America after the last French War. Resided on Susquehana when the Rebellion broke out. Joined the Brit. early, thinks it was in '77, served all the war as private under Col. Butler. Had 2 Sons with him in same Regiment.

(40).
Nothing but improvements.

Produces his discharge.

He had 300 acres on Susquehana in Westmoreland, these were the Disputed Lands. To that he had no Deed. Took them up

some years before the War. Had Cleared 30 acres, had built house & Barn.
Lost 2 horses, 3 Cows & Heifer, 5 Hogs, furniture, Crop on the ground.

WM. PICHARD, Wits.:
Knew Claimt., he served all the War. Knew his Place on the Susquehana, about 300 acres, he had some acres Clear, he had built a house & Barn. He had not quite so much clear as Wits.
Knew his Stock, 2 or 3 Cows, 2 Horses & several other things. Resides at Niagara.

829. Claim of FREDERICK AUGER, late of Pensilva. August 27th.

Claimt. says:
He is a native of Germany. Came to America 30 years ago. Lived on the Susquehana when the Rebellion broke out, joined Col. Butler, served 7 years with him as private.
He had 2 Sons in the same Regiment.
He had half a proprietors Right on the disputed Land on the Susquehana, gave 72 Dollars for it, his ½ right was 2,000 acres   (41).
Says he went to Susquehana in 1772, Cleared 20 acres, built a good house & Stable.
Lost 4 Cows, 3 3 year old Heifers, 2 2 yrs. old, 3 Calves, 7 Sheep, 14 Hogs, large am. furniture, utensils, 60 Bushel grain, 80 Bushel of Ears heads Corn. All lost by the Indians & Rangers.

MICHL. SHOWERS, Wit.: Knew Claimt. He served in Butler's Rangers from the time that the Susquehana was cut off by Col. Butler. He had Lands on the Susquehana. He had ½ in Proprs. Right, it was the Disputed Land. He had a Clearance, house & Barn, about 20 acres Clear. He settled there about 1772. He had a pretty large Stock, taken by the Indians & Rangers.

830. Claim of MICHL. THOMAS, late of Susquehana river, August 27th. Pensilva.

Claimt. says:
He is a native of America. Lived on Susquehana. When Rebellion broke out joined Col. Butler in Oct., '78. Served all the War except the last year. He was discharged, being old & having a large family.
Produces his Discharge in '83.   (42).
Had disputed Lands on Susquehana, 300 acres. Took it up in 1772, had cleared about 30 acres, built upon it. He had this Estate of 300 acres allowed him in order to settle a right to preserve it. He had under Connect. but had got a Promise to have it Confirmed by Pensilva.
Lost Stock, 4 Cows, 1 yoke oxen, 10 Sheep, 8 Hogs.
The Rangers had these things, his furniture utensils he was obliged to leave when he quitted his Place.

A very fair man; admits that he thinks Col, Butler or ye Commander in Chief ought to pay for his cattle.

FREDERICK AUGER, Wit.: Knew Claimt. He & Wits. went together to join Col. Butler. He had a farm on the Susquehana, 20 acres Clear & good buildings. He had oxen, heifers, Cows, &c., lost them by the Rangers & Indians. He left all his furniture & utensils behind.

August 27th. 831. Claim of JOHN WINTERMUTE, late of Pensilva.

Claimt. says:

He is a native of America. Was settled on the Susquehana when Rebellion broke out. Joined Col. Butler in 1778, served all the war as a Corporal.

Had ½ a proprietors Right on Susquehana disputed Land, had it from Connect. Govt., about 1772. Says he paid 160 Dollars.

(43). He had Cleared 60 acres. The Lot which he had consisted of 300 acres, built upon it, half a Right consisted of 200 acres.

Lost 10 Horses, 6 horned Cattle, besides 10 Cows, 42 Sheep, 30 Hogs. The Indians & Rangers had all these Things in '78.

N. B. to be allowed for mprovements. He had a large stock, most of it taken by the Rangers.

When he came away he left furniture, utensils, &c., behind him.

MICHL. SHOWER, Wits.:

Knew Claimt. He joined Col. Butler's Rangers & served. He had ½ proprietors Right on the Susquehana. He settled about a year before Wits. Thinks he had 60 acres Clear.

The most reasonable Clearing 20 sh. per acre. 3£ the highest, has known it done for 10 sh.

He had a large stock, 9 Cows & many other Creatures.

His Cattle, &c., were taken by the Indians & Rangers. He left his furniture, Tools & utensils behind.
Col. Butler Certifies strongly to the Loyalty of Claimt. & all his family.

August 27th. 832. Claim of PHILIP BUCK, late of Susquehana.

(44). Claimt. says:

He was at Niagara in '83. Is a native of Germany. His Parents brought him while an Infant. Lived on Susquehana, joined in 1777 at Fort Stanwix, continued in Butler's Rangers till he was taken Prisoner. He was exchanged to New York in 1778, came from thence to Niagara, joined the Rangers again. continued to serve all the War.

He had a Proprietors Right on Susquehana, settled in 1771, paid ten Dollars. 15 acres Clear, built a house, Barn & Barrick.

Lost 2 Cows, 2 young Creatures, 4 Sheep, 20 Hogs, furniture, utensils, Grain, 100 Bushel.

Lost grain, 20 Hogs by the Rebels when he went away in '77. The Indians had his other Cattle in '78. His furniture & utensils were left behind.

MICH. SHOWERS, Wits.:

Knew Claimt. He had settled on the Susquehana. He had 20 or 25 acres Clear & very good Buildings. He joined the Brit. a year before Wits. did. Knew his Stock.

He was in a pretty good way. Heard he lost part of his stock by the Rebels. He lost other things afterwards by the Indians & Rangers. He has suffered very much this War by Imprisonment. Claim't a very good man.

833. Claim of JACOB WALKER, late of Pensilva.   August 27th. (45).

Claimt. says he came to America 50 years ago. Lived on Delaware River when Rebellion broke out. In '78 joined Col. Butler. Served in the Rangers all the War as private.

He had 200 acres Northampton Co. on the Delaware, took it up from the office at Philadelphia at 15£ per 100 acres, Quit Rent, had it about 5 yrs. before the War, had done nothing, had a Deed. Had been at Expense of Surveying, the whole came to 30£ Pens. Crcy. Should have Cleared it if the War had not come on. Hs had an Improvemt. about 5 miles from this Place where he lived.

He lost all his stock there. A Scouting Party of the Rebels came up against 4 or 5 people, amongst whom Claimt. was one, who were Loyalists, 2 were killed, 2 taken Prisoners. Claimt. made his Escape. This was in the Winter of '78. N. C.

They took 2 Horses, 20 Hogs, 7 Deer Skins, furniture, utensils.

JOAL WESTBROOK, Wits.:

Knew Claimt. he joined Butlers Rangers in '78. Knew of his having an Estate on the Delaware. He had taken it up at the office at £15 per 100 acres.

He had the Lands surveyed. Witness saw his Deeds. Witness lived with him. (46).

He had 2 Horses & other Things.

There came up a Scouting Party against the Loyalists who lived in that neighbourhood & took them. They killed one or two people at the same time.

834. Claim of JAMES CLENDENNING, late of New Jersey.   August 28th.

Claimt. says he was at Niagara in '83. Is a native of America. Lived in Sussex Co., West Jersey, when the Rebellion broke out.

Was always a friend to Brit. Govnt.

Never served in American Militia. Signed one Association. Claimt. and 2 of his Sons left their home in May, '78, he was so persecuted he could Stay no longer, he & both his Sons went into Butler's Rangers in the Fall, '78. Served till the Regiment was disbanded. He & his 2 Sons served as privates. They are all now in this Settlement.

No. 1.

(47).

He had 180 acres, part in Noleton, part in Hardwick Township, Sussex Co.
Produces Deed from Ebenezer Cowell reciting that a certain Tract of unlocated Land has been taken up & surveyed & properly recorded in the Surveyor's office in Burlington & Conveyd to the sd. Ebenezer Cowell in Consn. of 20£ lawful Curcy., the same Tract amounting to 180 acres, to Claimt., dated 1768.
This was Proprietors Land in the Western Division. He lived on this Spot. He Cleared 40 or 50 acres, there was a Log house & Barn, an orchard. Has known Land grubbd. for 20 or 25 sh. per acre.
Vals. Wood land at 20 sh. per acre. Vals. Cleared Land at 3£ per acre.
Says the Land has been Confiscated & Sold.

No. 2.

Had also taken up 200 acres more in the Western Division. Produces Deed from Ebenezer Cowell to Claimt. of 200 acres in Consn. 30£ Lawful, 1774.

With Certificates by the Surveyor Genl. that the Land had been Surveyed & was Conveyd accordingly in pursuance of a Warrant from the Proprietors in 1774, with Certificate of the Conveyance being recorded.

Allowed what he gave for it.

The whole Expense was about 30£. He had begun to make a Clearance & built an house. Vals. it at 20 sh. per acre.
Says this Land has been Sold.
Lost 1 Cow, 9 Sheep, 3 Horses, Carpenter's Tools, farming utensils.
These things were seized & sold.

(48).

WILLIAM MAN, Witness:

Has known Claimt. since he was here. Has understood he & his 2 Sons have served in Butler's Rangers. The Agent Loyl-Comrs. for the Western Division, whose name is Joseph Gascoign, told Witness that Claimts. 2 Places had been Sold. One was sold for £125 Certificate Money, does not remember what the other sold for, but remembres the Agt. said it was sold. The Conversation was this last Spring. Witness was in the Jerseys and was thinking of purchasing the Place, which made him Enquire about it.
Has seen No. 1. there was a Clearance. but cannot say how many acres. Vals. Cleared Land there at 20 sh. pr. acre.

Wild Land at 2 Dollars, he has known it sell at that Price with some little Improvmts. Not quite so valuable if the Improvemts. had not been begun.

Sale proved but Claimt is told to get Certificate if he can.

Knew No. 2 better, that was the one he meant to purchase. There was some little Improvements. Judge Simms was to have sold it to Witness. Wits. was to pay 5£ above the Certificate Money, 125£. Witness cannot say what the Val. of the Certificate Mon. was.

Resides at Niagara.

Further Evidence in Claim of JOSEPH CLEMENT. V. 47.

JOHN CLEMENT apprs.: (49). August 28th.

Says he lived with his Father when the Rebellion began, he was then a boy. In '80 he came into the Province & servd as Leut. in the Indian Departmt. Claims his share in the real Estate of his Father left by his Will. Has heard the Uplands Vald. at 40 sh. pr. acre. Says 15 acres at least were Clear of the Uplands, 60 acres of the Lowlands were Clear. Remembers his Father had a fair Stock.

Is willing that his Elder Bro. shd. receive his Share.

Says his Father had 2 Shares in a Saw Mill, he purchased one for 25£ he thinks.

Says he withdraws his Claim unless Government gives him to the full amount of what he asks, which is 40sh. an acre for the Uplands, taking in the 15 acres Cleared Land.

JAMES CLEMENT, 3rd Son of Jno. Clement, appears:

He lived with his Father in '81, he went within the Brit. Lines, was put in the Store Keeper's Departmt., afterwards went as Volunteer with the Rank of Ensign. Claims his Share in the Uplands. Says one of the Houses is on the Uplands. (50).

Says he withdraws his Claim unless Government gives all that he asks. Says his oldest Bro. does the same.

ELIZA CLEMENT, Widow of Lewis Clement, appears:

Says she is the Widow of Lewis Clement, he died in '81. He served from beginning in the Indian Departmt. as Lieut. & Interpreter. Says he made his Will, gave her the Estate during her Widow hood, but says she supposes the personal Estate on her Death goes amongst the Children. Claimt. herself left Home 7 yrs. ago & came into this Province.

There were about 60 acres Lowland Clear.

Some of the Uplands Clear.

Joseph Clement, the Eldest Son appears & desires to leave the whole Claim to the Determination of Commrs. for himself, his Mother & 2 Brothers. Says they did very wrong. August 29.

Her Husband had a Negroe, a very good labourer, he is now in Possession of Major Fenders, supposes he bought him.

10 Horses, 10 horned Cattle, 25 Hogs, 15 Sheep, furniture, farming utensils, the furniture and the farming utensils were taken by the Rebels & sold in the house at a Vendue. (51).

Says she agrees with her 2 Sons that she withdraws her Claim unless Governmt. allows the whole of their Charge of 2,000£ York Curcy.. and says her Eldest Son does the same.

835. Claim of JOHN CHISHOLM, late of Albany Co. August 29.

Claimt. says: He lived at Niagara in '83. Is a native of N. Brit. Arrived in America in 1774, settled in Tryon Co., joined the Brit. in 1777, joined the Indians & came into Niagara & served in the Indian Department al the War.

62 AR.

A fair man.

Took up 150 acres in Courtright's Patent in 1774, it was lease Land forever, paying 6d. per acre. It cost him nothing to take up. He had Cleared 6 or 7 acres, had built an House. Vals. it at 20£, exclusive of buildings.
Lost 4 head of Cattle, taken by the friendly Indians. Left his furniture & Blacksmith's tools at his house, he could not bring them away, the Rebels have got them.

DONALD ROSS, Wits.:

(52). Knew Claimt.
He served in the Indian Department 6 or 7 years.
He had a farm on Courtright's Patent. He settled there before the War. He had Cleared 9 or 10 acres, had built an House. He had a stock of Cows, he had some Blacksmith's tools, some Furniture.
Capt. Jos. Brant certifies to his services without pay.
Resides at Niagara.

August 29.

Further Evidence in the Case of ADAM CRESLER. V. 20.

DANIEL SERVOS, Wits.:

Knew Claimt., he came in in '77, served in Butler's Rangers & in the Indian Department.
Knew No. 1. Thinks there were near 50 acres Clear, remembers him for many years in possession.
(53). The Land was very valuable. Vals. it at 10£ the highest, 5 or 4£ the lowest for Clear Land, his was pretty good.
Knew he had Land in Boughs Patent.
Knew No. 3. The mill was built about a year before he went away. Thinks it cost 400£ building. Knew that he had a share in a Saw Mill.
Knew he had Land in Cobus Kill and on Charlotte River. He had a very good stock of Horses, Sheep & Cattle.
Heard it was all taken & sold by the Rebels.

N. C.
August 29th.

836. Claim of DONALD ROSS, late of Sussex Co., N. York.

Claimt. says he was at Niagara in '83. Is a native of Scotland, came to America in '74, settled on the Head of the Delaware, joined the Brit. in 1777, went with the Indians was in the Indian Department, served all the War.
Had settled on 100 acres, the Land belonged to a man of New York named Banyard. Had no Lease, settled in 1775, he had Cleared 8 or 9 acres, built an House, had been at no Expense.
(54). Was going to have a Pot Ash Work, had 2 Kettles cost 20£. Had 3 more partners but he had paid 11£ for the Kettles, had several things in his house besides.
4 Partners had settled on this Place. Says he Cleared the Land after the War began.

62a AR.

John Chisholm. He knew Claimt., he served in the Indian Departmt. He settled on Lands at Head of Delaware in '75. With Lease or Deed 4 settled on the same Place. They had 2 Kettles, Stock & furniture. Knew that Claimt., Wits. Bro., had 7 Cows, 2 oxen, 2 young Cattle. There was an House. 3 of the Partners had been with Capt. John Macdonell. Wits. saw the Cattle sold by one Col. Harper. Capt. Brant Certifies to his services. *Claimt to be allowed ⅓ this stock and 5 £ for kettles.*

837-838. Claim of ARCHIBALD THOMPSON & JAMES PARK, late of Tryon Co. *N. C. August 29.*

Claimt. ARCH. THOMPSON being sworn saith:

He was at Niagara in '83.

Is a native of Scotland, came to America in '73, joined the Indians in '75, served during the War.

He & James Park settled together on John Harper's Land in Tryon Co. Never had a Lease or Deed, were to have had if the disturbance had not come on. They had Cleared a little before the disturbances, thinks about 12 acres in the whole before they left, had built a Log House, had 2 horses, 5 horned Cattle, Cloathes, furniture. Says they joined Capt. Macdonell first in Aug., 1877, joined the Indians under Brant in '78. *(55).*

James Parker, Claimt., says he came from Scotland with Archibald Thompson. Settled as Partner in Tryon Co. Went from Home with him & served in the Indian Departmt. They took up 100 acres, had not pd. anything, had not any Deed or Lease. They were to have paid 20£. They Cleared 12 acres before they went away, most of it before ye Rebellion broke out.

They had 2 horses & a Colt, 4 Cows & some young Cattle, the Rebels got them all.

JOHN CHISHOLM, Wits.:

Knew both Claimts., they went off with Witness & several other Loyalists. They served in the Indian Departmt. They had Land from Col. Harper in Tryon Co.

Thinks they Cleared 13 acres.

He saw 2 Horses, 3 or 4 Cows, and altogether a nice Stock. *Good men to be allowed a little.*

Capt. Brant Certifies to their Services & that they acted as Volunteers.

---

839. Claim of REBECCA FIELD, Widow of George Field, late of Pensa. *August 29.*

Claimt. says:

Her Husb. died 2 yrs. ago. He resided at this Place in the year. 8. *(56).*

Her Husb. was a native of America, lived on the Susquehana. In '78 he came to Niagara & joined Col. Butler. Claimt. came with her Husb. he also brought 3 Sons. Her Husb. and Sons all served in the Rangers during the War. They could not live at home, they were so persecuted. Came away in a great hurry or they would have been sent to Gaol.

Produces Certificate from 2 Witnesses that Geo. Field on his Death bed declared he gave every thing to his Wife on Condition that she paid 3£ to each of his Sons.

He left Daniel, Eldest Son, now at Detroit, who served in the Rangers.

Gilbert & Nathan both here, they served in ye Rangers.

Her Husb. had 300 acres on the Susquehana, this was not disputed Land. They had not got a Deed. Her Husb. bought it of one Daniel Rees in the year 1774, he was to give 300£ Pens. Money. He was to pay by finding other Vacant Lands & taking them up for Daniel Rees. Says her Husband had done this & taken up a good Deal of Land for Rees. Enough to pay all except 40 or 50£.

(67). The Land was Wild & unimproved, they Cleared about 40 acres, planted an orchard, built an house. Lived 3 years upon it.

Says the Land has been since sold by Danl. Rees. Says it cost 40 sh. to Clear Land then pr. acre, sometimes more, now & then less.

Says her Husband had other Lands in Partnership with Dr. Plunket, taken up at the office, of which she can give no acct., but says Dr. Plunket is probably now in Possession.

They brought most of their stock, left 2 or 3 Calves, 15 Hogs, all their furniture, Cloathes, 2 Sets Blacksmith Tools. 2 Horses were taken away before they went by the Rebels & sold, 3 Rifles.

EDWARD TURNER, Wits.:

Knew Geo. Field. Witness came with Geo. Field & his 3 Sons in '78. They left the Country on acct. of their Loyalty. They served in the Rangers.

Geo. Field had bought 300 acres of one Rees, was to pay £300 in other Land. He settled upon them about 1773. He had Cleared 40 acres & built an house. He left all his furniture, Blacksmith Tools, 2 Sets, a great many Hogs. He had lost 2 horses before taken by the Rebels.

(58). Witness does not know how much Geo. Field had paid on the purchase money.

Has heard it was sold under Confiscation as being forfeited. He was told so by one John Allen who was in the Country at that time.

NATHAN FIELDS, the youngest Son appears:

He & his Father & 2 Bros. left their Home in '78. Came
Very good here & served in the Rangers. Is willing that his Mother should
people receive his Share, answers the same for his Brother Gilbert. Says the Estate was sold by Daniel Rees again.

Isaac Dobson says he was authorized by Daniel Field to say that he consented all the payments should be paid to his Mother.

840. Claim of EDW. TURNER, late of Pensilva.   N. C. August 29.

Claimt. says he was at Niagara in '83. He is a native of America. Was settled on Susquehana. Came from home in 1778. There were families of Loyalists came away to join the Brit.

His Father came with him, joined the Rangers, died in the service. First joined the Rangers, server 9 months, then was in the Navy Service on the lakes during the War.   (59).

His Father died without a Will, leaving Claimt. his Eldest Son. Sarah now married to Gordon Avery, his Widow, 2 daughters, Children, who live with Claimt.

His Father, Moran Turner, had an Estate in Northumberland on the Susquehana, this was not the disputed Lands.

Produces Locations from the office at Philadelphia.

| 300 acres | 1769 | 50 acres | 65 |
| 300 acres | Oct., 1775 | 150 acres | 1776 |

The Locations are in different names, but all belonged to his Father. The Expense of Location was 5£ per 100 acres to the Proprietor besides other Expenses.

He had also 2 Islands in Susquehana one hundred acres each, Island his Father bought, the other Island he took up.

There were Improvements on all the Locations, on the 2 Island there were 10 acres Clear & an orchard. He built there.

Says he Vals. the Land altogether at 10 sh. per acre.

His Father was driven off before he quitted the Country. Claimt. heard it was advertized for Sale.

Left furniture, utensils, Hogs & a few Creatures behind, they carried away their Cattle.   (60).

REBECCA FIELD, Wits.:

Knew Claimts. Father, he & his Son both left the Country on acct. of their Loyalty. They served in the Rangers. Has been on the Father's Lands. Knew both the Islands, they belonged to the Father. There were not any of them on the disputed Lands.   Claimt seems a very good man.

There were Considerable Improvemts. on the Islands & on other Lands of the Fathers.

NATHAN FIELD, Wits.:

Knew Morris Turner's Land. He cannot say how much, but speaks particularly to ye 2 Islands. Remembers him in Possession before the War. There were Considerable Improvemts. on both the Islands.

SARAH ANN, Mother to Claimt., appears: August 31. N. C.

Says she is willing all the Payments should be made to her Son, the Claimt. Says she has the Deeds from those persons in whose name the Locations were made.

August 29.

(61).

841. Claim of TIMOTHY SKINNER, late of New Jersey.

Claimt. says he left Jerseys Septr., '83, arrived at St. John's 24th Octr. Wintered at Sorel. Came to Niagara the next Summer.
Is a native of America, lived in Sussex Co. Never came into the Brit. Lines during the War. Says he was always a friend to the Brit. Govt., declared his Sentiments, was taken up in April, '77 & Committed to Gaol. He was kept 6 months in Close Confinement. This was part of his Sentence.
Produces Certificate under Hand of Wit. Livingston Gov. dated July, 1777, reciting that Claimt. had been fined 150£ & sentenced to 6 monts Imprisonment & that part of his Imprisonment was pardoned. Says he laid in Gaol some time not being able to pay his fine. The whole time of his Imprisonment was about 14 months.

No Loyalist.

Says he could not make his Escape. Afterwards he continued at Home till Sep., '83. Saved good part of his Estate.
Claim is for his fine & Imprisonment.
Produces Rects. to prove Payment of his Fine.
NATHNAIEL PETIT, Esq.: Knew Claimt., looked upon him as a friend of the Brit. Govnt. during the Rebellion. Remembers his being Imprisoned on acct. of his Loyalty. He was kept Close Prisoner 6 months & fined. He had been tried by a Court of Oyer & Terminer.

(62).
August 30.

842. Claim of JAMES JONES, late of Kingstown, New York.
Claimt says: He is a native of America. Lived in Ulster Co. when the Rebellion broke out. He had been taken Prisoner because he would not join the Rebels. He had been Clerk to a Company of Militia before, which made the Rebels more angry that Claimt. refused to join them. He was kept Prisoner 3 years, Close Confined & in irons 9 months. Could not get away till '80. Came to Col. Butler's Rangers & served in these Rangers till the end of the War.
Now lives near Niagara at 10 Mile Creek.

He had 52 acres in Kingstown, Ulster Co. It was Corporation Land, on a Lease forever, paying 12 Skipple of Wheat Annually. Had the Lease about 3 years before the Rebellion. His Wife staid behind him. The Corporation made her give up the Lease & gave her 20£.
Claimt. had Cleared about 20 acres. There was a good Log house & an apple orchard. Vals. it at 100£.
The Trustees of the Corporation have sold it under Pretence of Rent being due. They drove his Wife away. When he left the Place he left 10 Head of horned Cattle, 2 Horses, 14 Hogs, furniture, a great Deal, said as much as 9 Waggons carried when he first went to the Place. Most of these things were destroyed or taken by the Rebel Scouts. Col. Sneider, a Rebel Col., warned his Wife off the Premises. The furniture was destroyed or plundered at that time. Some of his Cattle were disposed of by his Wife.

(63).

Seems to have suffered a great deal and appears a fair man.

He saved one Waggon load of furniture.
Claimt. Expenses while in Gaol 60£. Grain in the ground. Produces Certificate to his Loyalty & Services from Peter Ball, Lieut. of the Rangers.

PETER WINNEY, Wits.:
Knew Claimt. had some Land of the Corporation of Kings- N. C. town. He had some Creatures. He was avery good Loyalist.
Wits. say him in Gaol on that acct.
Mrs. Palmer Certifies to his Loyalty.

843. Claim of ANDREW HOVERLAND, of Tryon Co.   August 30.
Claimt. says he was at Niagara in the yr. '83. Is a native of Germany. Was in the last French War. Settled in America after end of that War, resided in Tryon Co. Went to Niagara in '78 to join Col. Butler. Served all the War in the Rangers.   (64).
Had 200 acres, had it soon after the French War, gave 2 years work for it to Col. Crawford.
Had 40 acres Clear. Vals. the Clear Land at 100£, the rest at 100£ mon. Does not know what is become of it.
Had 13 horned Cattle, 3 Horses, 12 Hogs, Furniture, Uten- A poor, sils. The Rebels have taken all these things.   honest creature.

LAWRENCE BLASONS, Wits.:
Knew Claimt. He left his home to join the Brit. He would not stay with the Rebels. He served a long time with the Rangers.
He had a farm in Tryon Co., thinks about 40 acres were Clear. Remembers him in Possession long before the War.
He had a good Stock, he had 12 horned Cattle, 3 Horses.
Justice Burch Certifies that Claimt. was settled on a good Farm & had good Stock.

844. Claim of GEO. HOUSE, late of Tryon Co.   August 30.

Claimt. says he is a native of America, lived on the Mohawk River, joined the Brit. in 1777, served all the War under Col. Butler in the Rangers.
Had some Lands on the Mohawk, had no Lease but had lived (65). on them 15 years before the War. He had built an House. A good Deal was Clear before he took it, but he Cleared some more. He only Claims for the Buildings 24£, he had 4 horses & 2 Colts, Utensils, furniture, grain in the ground. Left all these things Allowed when he Came away. The Indians took some, the Rebels also took some, the most.

MRS. MARY BRANT, Wits.: Remembers Claimt. He had some Lands on the Mohawk where he lived. He had a good Claimt house & buildings which he built himself, he had some Lands a good man. Cleared. He had 4 work horses, five horned Cattle, utencils, furniture. He left them behind when he went away.

Aug. 30.

845. Claim of LEWIS MABEE, late of Tryon Co.

Is a native of America. Lived on the Mohawk. Joined the Brit. in 1777; joined Col. Butler. He could not stay without joining the Rebels. Served all the War. Now lives near Fort Erie.

Had 50 acres on the Mohawk. It was a gift from Lewis Clement, his uncle, many years ago. He cleared between 18 & 20 acres; had an excellent House & Barn & out buildings. Vals. it at 300£.

(66).

One Victor Harrison now has it. Understood he bought it from Commissnrs.

N.B.—His name in Anstey's list.

6 Horses, 9 horned Cattle, Utensils, Furniture. Left all these things on the Premises when he went away. Many of them were Vendued by the Rebels.

AUNT. BRADT, Wits.:

Knew Claimt. He left his home early in ye War & joined the Rangers. Knew his place. 50 acres upland. Remembers him being in possession. Most of it clear. A very good house. He had a good stock of cattle & horses. The things were all taken by the Rebels & his wife was sent off. Understood the things were vendued.

---

846. Claim of PHILIP BENDER, late of Pensilva.

Claimt. says he was at Niagara in '83.

N. C.
Aug. 30.

Is a native of Germany. Came very young to America. Lived at Susquehana when the Americans declared Independence. Left his home in the Spring, '77. Could not stay without taking part with the Rebels. Came off to join Col. Butler. He came with the Loyalists of his settlement and served near the end of the War as private. Produces his discharge '82.

(67).

Had 320 acres in the disputed Land on the Susquehana. Took it up in 1776; gave 70£ Pensilv. Cury. The Rebellion broke out —he had not paid all.

To be allowed.

Lost 1 Cow by Indians, 5 Sheep by Indians & rebels, Rangers. Left all his furniture behind and his utensils. Left corn & wheat, 200 Bushels in the Stack. The Rebels got some.

A very good man—to be allowed as much as we can.

His furniture was removed too fast & was found out by the Rebels. Thinks this was worth 120£ including Cloathes. Produces 2 affid. that Claimt. lost the effects & property in the Claimt.'s Schedule mentd.

JOHN DEPUY, Wits.:

Knew Claimt. He went off early to join Col. Butler.

He had a farm on the Susquehana; bought during the Rebellion. He had a good stock. He had very good furniture. There was a chest of Cloathes & Linen. It was found out by the Rebels & taken by them.

Aug. 30.

847. Claim of JOHN DEPU, late of Pensilva.

Claimt. says he is a native of America. Lived on Susquehana; joined the Brit. early; joined Col. Butler first; served under him and Col. Johnston all the War; first in ye Rangers, then in Indian Departmt. Was employed to go with Intelligence from Niagara to New York. (68).

Now lives at Fort Erie.

He produces a Commission from Gov. Trumbull in the year 1775, appointing him Lieutnt. in the 9 h Company in 24th Regiment in ye sd. Colony. Says the Chief of this Company joined the Rangers afterwards.

He had a farm on Susquehana. Produces Copy of Deed from W. Paterson to Claimt. promising to Convey 950 acres in Considn. of his Bond for 475£, dated Sept., 1773. Claimt. says he gave his Bond, of which he has paid 160£ & got his Deed.

Produces Copy of Deed from Wm. Patterson & Ph. Johnston, promising to give a Release of this right to 300 acres adjoining Claimt.'s other Lands on his paying 2 Bonds of 75£ each, Sept.,

1773. He had not paid these 2 Bonds & had not got the Deeds. To be allowed.

Was in Possession of all these Lands. Admits they were disputed Lands, but he did not know of the disputed Title when he purchased.

He had cleared about 30 acres.

Vals. the whole of his Property at 400£.

He lost 2 Cows, 2 Heifers, 30 Hogs, some little furniture & Reasonable. utensils.

All these things taken by the Rebels.

THOMAS CONDET, Wits.:

Knew Claimt. He has been much distinguished for his Loyalty & Services. One of the first men who joined the Brit. Troops.

Knew his Farm on the Susquehana. Heard he was entitled Seems a very fine man, seems to about 900 acres. Knew the place where he lived. There was a to have been very active. good clearance.

848. Claim of MATHEW ELLIOTT, late of Pensilva. (69).

Claimt. says. He resided at the Falls '83, at Detroit & either May 31. there or in the Upper Country all the ensuing winter. The time for lodging claims was expired before Intelligence of the Act reached persons in that Situation.

Says he sent his Claim under the 2nd Act to be forwarded to Halifax as soon as he possibly could, which was in May, '86.

Produces Certificates from Major Ancrane. Commanding Officer, at Detroit, dated May, '86.

That General Hope's Letter containing notice sent from the Commissrs. at Halifax, did not arrive at Detroit till 26 March,'86, & that there was no opportunity of forwarding the Claim from Detroit till 13 May, 1786.

Claimt. says the Dispatches did not leave Detroit so soon as 13 May; thinks not till July.

Is a native of Ireland. Settled in America, 1761; resided at Fort Pitt when the Rebellion broke out. From the first he did everything in his power in support of Governmt. Refused to sign all Associations proposed by the Rebels. He was at that (70). time an Indian Trader; had large quantities of Merchandise, consisting of Blankets & other articles which Congress then sitting at Philadelphia in the year 1776 applied to Claimt. for, as wanting them for the use of their Army, which he refused. The Comrs. appointed by Congress for Indian affairs at Fort Pitt, made the same application which Claimt. refused & said ue had promised the Indians to supply them with the articles then in his Possession.

In the summer just before this Transaction he had been wounded.

Company raised by Commission from Genl. Gage, of which Allen McKee was to be one of the Lieut.-Cols., John Conolly, Esq., the other, and Lord Dunmore the Col. They were never raised but fell into the hands of the Enemy.

In Oct., 1776, Claimt. left Fort Pitt with a view of going within the Brit. Lines & carrying his effects. Claimt. did not arrive at Detroit till March, 1777. He was sent by Gov. Hamilton to Quebec; from thence he went to New York, & returned by Fort Pitt again to Detroit.

(71).

He was appointed Capt. in the Indian Department in 1778 & served during the War. Was in every service in that Country during the War. At present has no half pay. Resides at Detroit.

Produces Certificates from A. McKee to Claimt.'s Loyalty, to the opposition he made at first to ye measures of the Rebels.

Appointed to command of a Company intended to be raised on that acct. for support of Government & to quel the Rebellion.

That he took the earliest opportunity of escaping to Detroit & lost his effects by the way; that in 1778 he made his escape from Detroit with Deponent; that he has ever since distinguished himself in every Campaign carried on in that Quarter during the War, & in his endeavours to retain the Indians in their attachment to his Majesty.

Produces Certificates to his zeal & activity from Lieut. Govr. Hamilton.

Produces Certificates from Col. De Pyster to Claimt.'s conduct & good behaviour in action & on every other occasion when he could show his Loyalty.

(72).

Produces Certificates from Major Mathews that Claimt. fled from the Colonies in 1776. Served during the War to the entire satisfaction of his Commanding officers & that he distinguished himself on various occasions as an active, useful & gallant Partizan. He adds that he always understood he lost a considerable Property.

He lost various articles in the Indian Trade, consisting chiefly of Cloth, Blankets, Linen, Calicoes, &c.

When he left Fort Pitt in the Fall of 1776, he had packed up these articles & had got 100 miles from Fort Pitt into the Indian Country. Claimt had gone forward.

Indians came & took all his effects. These Indians were of the Six Nations; they were of the Kuega Nation.

They said they acted under Governor Hamilton's orders. Claimt. thinks that if Governor Hamilton had not been taken Prisoner he should have been indemnified for the Loss. Claimt. says that Govr. Hamilton had given orders to stop all persons coming from that Country on a supposition that there were only Rebels who would come from that Country.

The Indians divided all his property. He made several applications to the Indian Chiefs, who said they were acting under Govr. Hamilton's orders & that he must apply to him for redress. (73).

There were 15 horse loads of Goods & two Horses. His Cloathes were also packed up in the Bales of Goods.

Vals. the Goods, Cloathes, &c., at 900£ Sterling.

The 15 horses were taken by the Indians. He left a great many horses at Fort Pitt which he could not bring away; there were 47. He was obliged to have a great many horses for the purpose of carrying on his trade. He reckons them worth 10£, one with another.

They fell into the hands of the Americans. They seized them after Claimt. went away.

Lost a Negroe, he was with the Claimt.'s Goods & horses when taken by the Indians. He was killed the year afterwards endeavouring to make his escape from the Indians to his master. N. C.

Claimt. is told to send a Deposition as to the particulars of the Goods, &c., lost, tho' at the same time I intimated to him that this matter was not, I apprehended, without one ——— to redress, and also to send Deposition as to the No. of Horses left at Fort Pitt.

849. Claim of ALEXR. MCKEE, ESQ., late of Pensilva. Aug. 31.

Claimt. lives at Detroit & sends a Letter to inform the Commrs. that particular Business in the Indian Department prevents his attendance and begging they would examine his evidence. (74).

MATHEW ELLIOTT, ESQ., Wits.:

Says he knew Claimt. He lived at Fort Pitt. His by birth an American. From the first he took a decided Part in Support of the Brit. Govnt. In 1776 he was appointed Lieut. Col. in a Regiment that was to be raised for quelling the Rebellion, of which Lord Dunmore was to be Col. Commissions were sent from Gen. Gage, but fell into the hands of the Rebels.

He was apprehended in Consequence of some letters to him falling into the Rebels Hands & imprisoned. Had a guard over him. In 1778 he made his escape to Detroit. He served afterward in the Indian Departmt. Was in every service during the War.

He is now agent for Indian affairs under Sir John Johnson. Wits. knew his Property.

Knew No. 1. Knew that he had an Estate in Lancaster Co. on the Susquehana. His family used to live there. There were 2 Farms. His Father had it & it came to him as eldest son; it were well improved & Valuable. (75).

Vals. Clear Lands at 4 or 5£ pr. acre.

Knew No. 2. He had 2 houses & several lotts at Pittsburg. He lived at one of the Houses. It was a good house; the best House there. The Lotts were small, about 40 feet in front.

Claimt. bought the House where he lived & some of the Lots from Mr. Ross before the Rebellion.

Wits. Vals. the House & the Lots adjoining at 1,000£ L. Pensilv. Knows there were 3 Lots adjoining; cannot say whether there were more.

No. 5. Knew No. 5. It was well improved. He took it up himself & improved it many years ago. Near 100 acres improved & fenced.

N. C.

There was a good house & outhouses. It was near Fort Pitt. He held it in his own Hands; lived there. It was very fine Land, worth ½ Joe pr. acre.

V. Vol. 25, 155.

Aug. 31.   850. Claim of SIMON GERTY, late of Pensilva.

MATHEW ELLIOTT, Wits.: Says that Claimt. is Interpreter in the Indian Departmts. He would have come to Niagara had he not been detained by particular Business & the Commanding officer could not spare him. He was in the Upper Country in '83.

(76).

Claimt. is a native of America. Lived at Fort Pitt. From the first declared in favour of Govrnt. He quitted Fort Pitt when Wits. & Capt. MacKee did in 1778. After he came to Detroit he served constantly in the Indian Department. He acted as Interpreter. Was out on every service.

He had Lands in Hannahs Town, No. 1; does not know how much. Says there was a Law suit about it.

Produces two Deeds of 600 acres each in Westmoreland in

N. C.

1773 & 1774 in Considn. of 6£ each from Jacob Mayor to Claimt. with affid. from Jacob Mayor, that he made Improvements on the Lands he mentions about 13 acres, but the deed & the affits. are much torn & hardly legible. Wits. thinks No. 1 included in the Purchase.

It was unimproved till lately. In 1770 this place was laid out in a Town.

(77).

Does not know that Claimt. made any Improvemts. after his purchase. Says there was an old Field which has been cleared, but was grown almost up again; might be five or six acres.

Claimant over charges greatly

Knew No. 2. It was about 4 miles from Pittsburg. He had it many years. Thinks he took it up. About 15 or 20 acres clear when Wits. saw it last. Claimt. had stock then. Knew of his having 4 horses, which Wits. understood he kept at Fort Pitt. Kentucky is about 600 miles from Fort Pitt.

Aug. 31.   851. Claim of GEORGE GERTY, late of Pensilva.

CAPT. MATHEW ELLIOTT, ESQ., Wits.:

Says that Claimt. is so high up in the Indian Country that he supposes the Comrs'. letter could not reach him.

Knew Claimt. at Pitsburg. He was distinguished from the first for Loyalty. He had been active on various occasions. He was imprisoned at different times. He broke gaol at ———— & brought off a party of the 8th Regt., who were also Prisnrs there to Detroit, he served afterwards in the Indian Departmt.

He lost a Boat ————. This was in 1778. It was on the Mississippi.

One Willing had fitted out a Boat at Fort Pitt to go on a sort privateering Party & fell in with the Boat of Claimt on the Mississippi. Thinks he fell in with it by accident & plundered it. This he supposes to have been in '78. (78).

852. Claim of SOLOMON SECORD, late of Pensilva.

Claimt. says: His Father, James Secord, resided in Niagara in the Fall of '83, & the ensuing Winter. He died the next summer. Aug. 31.

His Father was a native of America; resided on the Susquehana in Northumberland Co.; joined the Brit. in 1777. Left home in March because he would not side with the Rebels. Served first in the Rangers & afterwards in the Indian Department, as Lieut. till '82. He died in '84, leaving Claimt. his eldest son.

He made a Will & left his estate among all his children.

Claimt. was with his Father when Rebellion broke out. Claimt. & 2 Brothers joined the Brit. Army with their Father; have all served. The rest of the family followed soon. They are all in this Province. Claimt. is one of the Executors.

His Father had 300 acres on the Susquehana disputed Land, called Northumberland under Pensilva. & Westmoreland under Connect. His Father had settled about 3 years before the War. He had no grant but had agreed with the owner to pay £50 per 100 acres when Title was made out. The person who agreed to sell held under Pensilva. Govt. Thinks his Father had not paid anything. Cleared between 20 & 30 acres. (79).

Built 2 small Houses & a good Barn. Vals. improvements at 150£.

Lost 2 head Cattle, 5 horses, furniture, utensils. Left them when he went away.

JOHN SECORD, Wits.:

Knew James Secord. He left Home to come into the Brit. Lines. He brought all his family. They are all very Loyal. He & 3 of his Sons have been in the service.

Knew his Land; between 20 & 30 acres clear; a good Barn & House. He had a very good Stock. Thinks he lost 8 Cattle & some horses. N.C. A very good family; to be allowed for improvements and stock.

All to be paid to Claimt. He says he is authorized by all his Family to act for them.

853. Claim of ISAAC DOBSON, late of Pensilva.

Claimt. says he resided at Niagara in the Fall of '83 & the ensuing Winter. Aug. 31.

Is a native of America. Lived on the Susquehana when Rebelln. broke out. In 1779 came to Niagara. He left Home on acct. of his attachment to his Majesty. He had been imprisoned & could not continue in the Country unless he joined the Rebels. (80).

He had been offered by the Rebels a Captn's Commission which he refused & was put to Gaol for it. Was sutler to the Rangers for some time. Now resides at Detroit.

He had 150 acres on the Susquehana. Purchased of Geo. Field in 1774. Had a Deed, purchased it for 150£. Geo. Field had a Title under Pensilva. Govt. It was in Northumberland

It was disputed Land. But says he paid 20sh. per acre, the usual price; pd. ye money down. He built a house, 2 story high. Cleared about 60 acres & fenced them. He carried on his improvemts. to the last. Vals. it at 500£ York Cury.

Says it has been sold by Pensilva. Govnt.

Left furniture, utensils, 30 Hogs, 9 Sheep, 7 Calves, 1 2-yr. old. Left all these things behind him. Corn in the ground.

(81). Produces affidt. from Daniel Field, sworn before Major Mathews, to Loyalty of Claimt. & to his Losses as in Claimt.'s Schedule set forth.

SARAH CHEERY, Wits.:

Knew Claimt. He was always very Loyal. Left Home on that acct. Remembers his farm, he bought it of Geo. Field; he gave £150 for it. It was a year or more before the War. He improved it greatly after his purchase. Cleared 40 or 50 acres & 6 acres Meadow. Has heard it was sold. They used to Val. unimproved Land at 20sh. per acre; clear Lands went for difft. prices. He had a fair stock; brought some with him. Left a good deal behind. Gives the same acct. as Claimt. When they came away they were persued so fast they could not carry all their effects with them.

Aug. 31. 854. Claim of HENDRICK WINDRON, late of Pensilva.

Dorothy, Wife of Claimt. appears. Says her husband went to the Mohawk River about 10 weeks ago. He went to see some Relations. She expects him back every day. All his Family are here.

Her Husb. was native of America. Lived on the Susquehana River. He left Home to join the Brit. He would not join the Rebels. He was one of the first that joined the Rangers. Servd (82). all the War. Claimt. herself & family with several other families of Loyalists came in about 9 years ago. Is now settled near Fort Erie.

Her Husb. had a Farm in Susquehana. He bought under the Connecticut Title. He settled on it seventeen years ago. He had a Deed for same; 5 or 6 acres clear; there was a house; left 3 horses, 10 hogs, furniture & utensils, tools. Nothing but their horned creatures.

Produces 2 affidts. to Claimt.'s being in possession of Property mentioned in his memorial & to his losses.

Seems a poor honest chrature.

Mr. Justice Burch certifies to Claimt.'s Loyalty. Speaks

(83).

very favourably of him. Says he is only gone on a visit into the Colonies.

PROCEEDINGS OF LOYALIST COMMISSIONERS.

MONTREAL, 1787.—VOL. XXI.

BEFORE COMMISSIONER PEMBERTON.

Claimants.

	MSS. Folio.		MSS. Folio.
Arney, Jonas	109	MacDougal, Peter	97
Arney, Nicholas	110	MacGwin, Daniel	35
Austin, Joel	9	Mackenny, John	91
Baker, John	60	Mackim, James	80
Bell, Duncan	70	Maclellan, William	11
Bell, William, Jr...	73	Macnut, Mrs. Eva	106
Benson, Mathew	54	Macpherson, John	86
Brown, John	12	Macpherson, Peter	92
Brown, Mrs. Mary	29	Marsh, James	59
Brownscn, Samuel	48	Maybee, Eleanor	68
Buck (Burch), John	1 & 18	Mordoff, George	30
Buck, Mrs. Sarah	110	Orser, Jos., Heirs of	36
Carscallen, Edward	71	Park, Cyrenus	41
Cartwright, Richard	22	Parke, James	43
Chartres, George	95	Pencil, John	105 & 107
Cline, Mrs. Elizabeth	81	Perrott, James	39
Conklin, Jos...	58	Perry, Robert	51
Conkwright, Hercules	76	Peterson, Nicholas, Jr...	96
Cornelius, John	105	Peterson, Nicholas, Sr...	97
Cotter, James	65	Philips, Elisha	75
Defoe, Abraham	44	Prindle, Joel	84
Detlor, Val	78	Prindle, Joseph	83
Diamond, Jacob	87	Prindle, Timothy	83
Dingman, Garret	102	Prindle, William	82
Embury, John	79	Ramsey, James	10
Eselstine, Peter	24	Richardson, Asa	46
Fairfield, William	66	Robins, James	100
Finkle, George	75	Roblin, Owen	32
Finkle, George, Sr...	33	Rogers, William	57
Fletcher, Sax	112	Rose, Matthias	63
Fraser, Kenneth	87	Rose, Mathias, Sr...	77
Gardiner, Jacob	55	Schemerhorn, William	72
German, John	26	Shorey, David	85
Grooms, Elijah	40	Shunk, Peter	7
Hartman, David	85	Simpson, Alexander	40
Hawley, Ichobad	57	Smith, Daniel	31
Hicks, Lewis	98	Sneider, Marks	99
Hough, Barnabas	61	Snider, Simon	108
Hough, John	81	Spicer, Ezekiel	113
Hofnail, Jobert	28	Storms, Gilbert	99
Hogal, Mrs. Eliz...	39	Stover, Martin	109
Hover, Casper	25	Swartz, Simon	89
Howell, John	64	Van Alstine, Isaac	84
Jackson, David	62	Van Alstine, Mrs. Lydia	93
Johnson, James	78	Vanderlip, William	13
Keller, John	101	Vant, A...	74
Kintner, George	21	Warner, Levi	63
Lorraway, Isaac	52	Washburn, Ebenezer	50
Lorraway, Isaac, Jr...	53	Welsh, Samuel	46
Lucas, Amos	88	Williams, John	56
McGrah, Owen	104	Wiss, John	93
McTvart, James	95	Woodcock, John	103
MacArthur, Chas	112	Young, Adam	15
MacArthur, Deborah, Mrs...	111	Young, Peter	45
MacDougal, John	94		

THE EVIDENCE.

Sept. 1st.

855. Claim of JOHN BUCK, late of Ulster Co., New York Prov.
Claimt. Says:

He is a native of England. Settled in America 1772. Resided in New York. When the Rebellion broke first out. He was prest to sign an Association which he refused & retired to Albany to avoid it. Having a large Property on the Delaware he went there in 1778. Finding the disturbances increasing he found he could not return to Albany. Hearing that Col. Butler was going (1). to make an attack on the Susquehana Country & that he and the Indians wanted Provisions, Claimt. wrote to Col. Butler that he would bring him a supply of his own cattle & Such as his Interest would procure from his neighbours, on which Col. Butler sent Lieut. MacQuin and 2 Indian Chiefs & Claimt. Came off with 40 of his neighbours & 136 cattle.

From thence he returned to his Estate on the Delaware. The Rebels having Information of the part he had taken came in a large Party, surrounded his House & plundered his effects.

He was attacked in this manner three different Times, the last he was forced to make his escape & was fired at, but he escaped into the woods. From thence he got into the Indian Country & afterwards to Niagara.

He was appointed to the care of the Indian Stores. He was not able to go out on active service, but was considered by virtue of his appointmt. as being one of the Indian Department. Now settled near the Falls at Niagara.

Capt. Watson, Commanding Officer of Niagara, certified to Claimt's great Services amongst the Loyalists in the Settlemt.

Claimt. was possessed of upwards of 5,000 acres on the Dela-
(2). ware. It laid in 3 Tracts, one was call'd Pasa Conch, where he lived.

Purchased at different times between the years 1773 & Beginning of the year 1775. Chiefly of Col. Joannas Hardenburg. The first cost was upwards of £2,500.

The Conveyances not having been recorded, the Estate has not been Confiscated & Claimt. is in Hopes to secure it. Has Conveyd all his Right to Mr. James Ellis, of Skenectady, & therefore he does not claim at present, but hopes he may be allowed to apply in case hereafter it should be lost.

When the Americans attacked his House in 1778 in consequence of his having suppied Col. Butler with Provisions, they burnt all his buildings & plundered all his effects. Burnt a Dwelling House inhabited by Tenants.

His Dwelling House was a moderate one which he built himself. The other buildings were included in his Purchase. He gave £35 for the Old Barn & house & 75 for other buildings.

They destroyed all his stacks of all kinds of grain, he had 200 acres of Clear Land & must have had upwards of 50 acres in grain.

The grain thus destroyd must have been worth near £300. (3),
They destroyd his furniture, not very valuable, & took his stock.
1 Blood Stalion cost £75, 2 Blood Mares, cost £60, 1 2-year old Stallion worth 35, 8 Mares working sort, 40 Sheep, 20 Hogs, Farming Utensils, Plows, Harrows, 1 Wagon & Apparel.

Besides what he lost on his Estate at Papa Conch. He lost a Wagon, Curisell & Slay.

They were at different peoples houses & found out to be his Property & seized by the Americans & Sold at Vendue.

He had some goods Œsopus & some other goods plundered at Marble Town. Think 2 articles were chiefly Linen & Cloathes & furniture, Beds. He lost Iron Work for a Grist Mill & Saw Mill which had been finished at the forge worth £50.

Lost several articles at the Mill house, at Woodstock. Lost Tools for japanning Tin, Iron & Copper, in which Trade Clarviavi had been engaged. These Tools Cost about 100 guineas.

When Claimt. went from New York to Albany in 1775, he set up a shop there. He set up his own Trade as Japanner & Tinman & kept a store of Dry Goods besides.

After he left Albany in 1778, he sent 2 persons to fetch off his most valuable Property there. They had 3 Horse loads, consisting of Shop Goods, Cash to amount of £90, & various articles. They were seized by the Americans on the Road. They were dis- (4). covered to be Claimt's & the Persons who were conveying them away were sent to Gaol. Says this loss was near £500.

After it was known that Claimt. had made his escape to the British his shop in Albany was seized & all the remainder of his Stock in Trade were taken or made away with, many of the articles were sold at Vendue. This Loss was between 3 & £400.

Says his Shop Books were lost at the same time so that he will lose Debts due to him upwards of £200.

When Claimt. sent Home his first Claim, he thought it most likely that great part of his Property at Albany had been saved by his Friends there & he did not know what was the amnt. of the Loss when the whom he sent were conveying away his Property & it was taken from them, on which acct. it was not included in his first Claim.

JOEL AUSTIN, Wits.

Knew Claimant. Remembers Claimt. going with Cattle & Provisions to supply Col. Butler. He carried 29 Cattle of his own. Persuaded his neighbours to send theirs. They went in with 110 Cattle. The party consisted of 50 or 60 people.

Claimant had been very active in getting these people to go. He had wrote to Col. Butler to send People to meet him.

After Claimant's Return the Americans attacked his House. The first Party was commanded by Capt. Bongun. They took (5). away all they could carry. Heard of his being attacked by other Parties, & that he got out of a Window & made his escape at the Risk of his Life.

He had some fine English Horses which were taken.

63 AR.

Witness understood they afterwards took all his Moveables & burnt his Houses.

He had a large Improvement. He had a great Quantity of grain which was burnt. He had one Wagon in the Place, Ploughs, Harness, & a very large assortment of farming Utensils of all kinds. Remembers he had seen Iron Works for a Saw Mill & Grist Mill which were discovered to be his & taken. Heard he lost other things at Albany.

JOHN CHISHOLM, Wits.

Heard of three persons who were fetching off Claimt's goods from Albany being seized on the Road in 1778. Witness saw the persons who were seized & understood from them that they were removing Mr. Burch's things, which were taken & the people sent to Gaol.

THOMAS MACMIKEN, Wits.

Heard of Claimt's Losses when his things were removing from Albany, one of the persons who was removing the things had been his Housekeeper. There were effects to Considerable Amount.
(6). Hugh Alexander was one of the persons employd. They were then in number. All were taken & put in Gaol.

The Things were taken by the Americans under the Command of an American Col. Butler. Heard of Cash & Shop Goods being taken. He had a Store at Albany. Witness has been there. Witness heard that Everything at Albany which was found out to be Claimt's was seized.

After Claimant supplied Col. Butler with Provisions scouting Parties went & plundered his house at Papa Conch, they seized all he had. He escaped with difficulty, was near losing his Life. Heard that they fired at him.

He had an Excellent fine Stallion, a fine Stock of Horses. There was a considerable Stock of grain & Cattle. Witness understood that Everything that could be found was taken or destroyed.

He had considerable farming Utensils.
N.C. Witness says Hugh Alexander was prosecuted for having assisted in Carrying off Claimt's Things & his Property was confiscated on that acct. This Witness Knew himself & saw the things sold.

Witness remembers that Thos. Cornyn who was Overseer of Claimt's farm was taken up & tried & condemned for having assisted in supplying Col. Butler with Cattle, &c.
Sept. 1.

(7). 856. Claim of PETER SHUNK, late of New York.

Claimt. says he was at Detroit in 83.

Is a native of Germany. Came 25 years ago to America. Lived near Albany. Joined Capt. Brant at the Beginning of the War & afterwards was in the Rangers, served the whole War. Was badly wounded.

63a AR.

Produces his Discharge from Butler Rangers in which it is mentioned that he had been disabled by wounds from doing his Duty.

Now lives at Detroit.

Had 300 acres 9 miles from Albany. Had a Lease forever from Rancellor, paying 9 Skipples of Wheat pr. an. Had 150 acres clear. A fine orchard. A Dwelling house & Barn. Vals. it at 400. A Rebel Col. lives upon it.

Lost 8 horses, 2 mares, 2 colts, 5 cows, furniture, utensils, Grain in the Ground, 150 Bushels of Wheat in a Lot. The Commrs. of Albany took these Things after he went away.

JOHN SEAGER, Wits.

Claimt. joined the Brit. very early, long before Burgoyne was taken. He served all the War. Knew his Place at Helback, about 15 miles from Albany. It was Rancellors Land. He had better than 30 acres clear. 3 acres Meadow, he had a Partner on the Place who had more Land than Claimant, 4 horses, 3 Cows, the furniture belonged to the other man.

(8).

The other man was John Brat. He is now there. He had 150 Skipples that belonged to Claimt. himself. The Rebels got them & took away his Horses & Vendued them.

Claimt. explains that Brat & himself had 2 farms adjoining each other of 300 acres each & that he lived with Brat on his farm laterly & was to have part of it, but he does not claim for that.

Seager being called again purseveres in the first acct. So that Claimt's case remains unintelligible.

Claimt says that the Farm he Claims had belonged to old Brat. He gave it up to Claimt. He had a Deed for it. 3 years before the Rebellion he only lived one year. He went & lived with Brat afterwards.

Brat was to give him half when he died for working for him. He says that about 150 acres were clear Seager, Wits. explains that Claimt. lived with old Brat when Witness knew him. Witness thought all the Land continued to be Brats, but now believes it was Claimant's. Thinks 60 acres Clear. Speaks of Claimt. as a very honest Man.

Claimt. seems good man, tho' his acct was difficult to make out.

Never heard the Land was sold, but a Rebel is certainly in Possession of it. His name is Hank Shaver.

(9).

857. Claim of JOEL AUSTIN, late of New York.

Claimt. says he was at Niagara in 83.

Sept. 7.

Is a native of America. Lived at Papu Chink at the Head of the Delaware. Joined Col. Buller in 1778. Went up with Mr. Burch with Cattle. Served from that time all the War.

Had 2 Lots of 100 acres at Papu Chink Lease Land. 1. 100 acres for 63 years paying £4.10 per ann. Had 60 years to come. 2. The other was a Lease for ever paying £4.10 pr. an.

Had 25 acres clear in the 2. Had a house on this first. Vals. the 2 at £100.

Lost everything he had. 8 Hogs, 3 Sheep, furniture, Cloathes, Utensils, Crop on ye Ground.

A very fine man. Charges reasonably; to be allowed to the full nearly. Satisfied.	JOHN BURCH, ESQ., Knew Claimt. He went with Witness when they carried the Cattle to Col. Buller, is a very honest man & very Loyal. He served all the War. He had two Lots of Leasehold Land, 25 or 30 acres Clear. He lost all his Cloathes, of which he had a great Deal, worth 30 or 40£, & all his Property.

Sept. 1st.

858. Claim of JAMES RAMSEY, late of Tryon Co., New York.

(10).

Claimt. says he resided at Detroit in 83.

Is a native of America. Lived at Cherry Valley, Tryon Co. Continued quiet in Beginning of the War. Never joined the American Militia. When the Rangers & Indians came to that settlement Claimt. joined them. Thinks this was in 1778. Served from that time about a year with the Rangers when he was discharged on acct. of Illness & settled at Detroit. Now lives near the falls of Niagara.

He had an Estate at Cherry Valley which has not been lost. His House & buildings were destroyd by the Indians. Had part of his Stock. The Americans took 2 horses, some Cattle. He 4 horses, all his horned cattle, 30 in No., 25 Sheep, do Hogs,

Seems a good man; to be allowed, but not to amnt. of what he claims.	Cloathes. Some furniture & utensils. All left behind when he went away He had removed most of his things before ye House was burnt.

WM. MACLELLAN, Wits.

Knew Claimt. He joined the Brit. under Col. Butler. He had a farm in Cherry Valley. He had a large Stock, remembers his Buildings burnt by Indians. He left almost all his stock behind him when he went away. Carried hardly anything but the Cloathes. He was always considered Loyal.

(11).

Sept. 1.

859. Claim of WM. MACLELLAN, late of New York.

Claimt. says.

He was at Mashishi in 83.

Is a native of Ireland, went to America in 1768, resided in Cherry Valley, joined Col. Butler in 1779. Served all the War. Produces his discharge.

He had Lease Land, 50 acres forever, paying 6d per acre, had cleared near 20 acres, but he withdraws his Claim, as his Brother in Law is in Possession.

Allowed.

His House was burnt by the Indians. Lost Crop that had been harvested, burnt at the same time. Lost 2 horses by the Indians, Farming Utensils Weavers Tools, all burnt, furniture &

He is a fair man. Q. if we can allow anything.	Cloathes. Says the Indians did it, because the Americans should not find out who were Loyalists, if they had not done it the Americans would.

JAMES RAMSEY, Wits.
Knew Claimt. He was always Loyal. He joined the Rangers, served all the War.

He had a farm in Cherry Valley. His Buildings & all his effects were burnt by the Indians, thinks one reason was that the effects should not fall into ye Hands of Americans.

860. Claim of JOHN BROWN, late of Schoharie, New York Prov. ^{Sept. 1.} (12).

Claimt. Says.

He is a native of America, Lived at Schohain, Albany Co. He declared in Favour of the Brit. Govert. from first. He joined the Brit. in 81, came to Niagara. He was so persecuted he could stay no longer. He was ordered to quit the Country by the Rebels as being a Tory. Served in Buller's Rangers from 81 to their discharge. Produces his Discharge.

He had a Lot of 200 acres, bought it many years ago of George Man, paid 185£ for it. It laid in Schohary. Cleared 30 acres. built a house & Barn. Vals. it at £1,000. This has been Confiscated and sold. ^{Too high— greatly.}

He had other Land on Cobus Conk 300 acres, that belonged to his Wife. It was unimproved.

His wife had 100 acres by her Father's Will. He died 20 years ago.

The other 200 acres by her Grandfather under his Will. He died 30 years ago. Claimt. has never been in Possession. Vals. this at 20sh. per acre.

Does not know what is become of it. (13).

Lost 2 horses, some cattle, mentions 9, furniture, Utensils, the Rebels got them. ^{N.B.--His name in Anstey's list.}

ADAM CUSTER, Wits.

Knew Claimt. He was in the Rangers. He bought Lands of one Mann in Schoharie River. ^{Is told to get certificate of sale.}

Heard 200 acres & that it cost £200. Cannot tell how much was cleared. He had good Horses & good Cows. ^{Case ill supported in evidence.}

861. Claim of WM. VANDERLIP, late of Pensilv. Septemter 8.

WILLIAM VANDERLIP, 2nd Son appears.

His Father William resided at Mashishi in the Fall 83 & that Winter. He died in the Fall of 85 without a Will, having John his eldest Son now in the States. Claimt, his 2nd Son, 2 Sisters, Eliz. & Mary unmarried, who live in this Province. with Capt. Fry. They are under 2 years of age.

His Father was a native of Holland, settled in America 30 years ago, lived in the Susquehana, went into the Rangers in 1777. Served 3 years in the Rangers. Was discharged on Acct. of Illness. He then Continued in Canada.

(14).

Reasonable compared with others, but land belongs to eldest son now on the States.

Came to Niagara 3 yrs. ago. Claimt. followed his Father when he joined the Rangers. Claimant served in the Rangers a year & half. He was then quite a Boy & was discharged as being too young.

Now resides near Niagara.

His Father had 300 acres on the Susquahana, had them under Pensilv. They were disputed Lands, 50 acres clear. Charges £150 Y. Cury Lands & Buildings.

4 Horses, 4 Cows, 8 Calves, 4 Sheep, 30 Hogs, furniture, Utensils, a large quantity of grain.

There was a Barrack & 3 or 4 Stacks of grain.

After his Father went away the Rebels took the Live Stock The grain & all the Buildings were burnt by the Rebels just before Col. Buller went into that Country & cut off that part of the Country. The Americans when they returned in apprehension of Col. Butler's coming destroyed every thing.

JOHN DEPUE, Witness.

Knew Claimt's Father. He joined Butler's Rangers early & served some time. William, the 2nd Son, followed his Father & served some time in the Rangers.

———

Knew the Place on Susquehana, 300 acres, the eldest son John now resides in the Colonies, he served in the Rangers, but after the Peace returned to the States.

Is very fair. To be paid to claimt for himself and sister.

His Father had a good Stock, 4 Cows, 2 horses, 8 calves, 4 sheep, 15 hogs, furniture & utensils, a good deal of grain. The Rebels took the live Stock, burnt the other things.

September 6.

862. Claim of ADAM YOUNG, late of New York.

(15).

Claimt. Says.

He is a native of America. Lived on the Mohawk, Tryon Co. When the Rebellion broke out joined Col. Butler at Oswego in 1778. He had been imprisoned for 11 months for refusing to take an oath to the States.

He was confined in different Gaols. At last sent to Norwich Gaol in Connect. Govrt. As soon as he was released he went home. The rebels came & burnt his House & all his buildings & took away or destroyed all his Effects. The reason of this was because he had given Provisions to Loyalists who were coming to Canada. At one time he sent 74 over.

After his House was burnt he & his 2 Sons went & joined Col. Butler. He served 6 or 7 years—He had four Sons who served. Now lives on the Grand River about 60 miles from Niagara.

He had 2,600 acres on Mohawk.

No. 1. 600 acres in Youngs Patent, taken out 30 yrs. ago, there he lived, had cleared 100 acres, had 2 houses, 1 Barn, a Saw Mill, &c.

No. 2. Had 2,000 acres in another Patent, which was Called Fentie's Patent & Livingston's Patent. This was 10 miles from the other, taken up ten years before ye War. This was all unimproved.

He had a Saw Mill & a Potash Work on No. 1. Values No. 1 at £1,000 besides the buildings.
Values Saw Mill at £140.   (16).
Values Potash Work at 150.
Heard the Land was sold. His name is in Anstey's List. His horned Cattle, 6 Horses & all his Moveables were taken by the Rebels. *Is told to get certificate of sale.*
13 Horses, 12 Cows, 6 Heifers, 12 Sheep, 20 Hogs. All his furniture, Utensils, very good.
He kept a Shop of Dry Goods, he traded with Indians, Lost to amount of £150. *A very good man.*

HENRY W. NELLES, Wits.

Knew Claimt. He was always considered Loyal. Remembers him being sent to Prison for his Loyalty. Heard of his House being burnt, & all his effects taken or destroyed by the rebels. He lived at some distance from the Mohawk river in Tryon Co. Witness knew the place where he lived. It was a very fine place, well cleared. There was a Saw Mill & a Potash House upon it. He had Land also in other Patents.

Vals. the Clear Land in No. 1 at £7 per acre York Cury. Vals. the Saw Mill at £200, Pot Ash House & Work £150, Vals. the Woodland from 20 to 10 sh. per acre, according to its situation. Heard the Estate was sold.

Claimant was in Service some time in the Rangers. He had 3 sons also in the service. Thinks there was another son who died in the service.

JOHN YOUNG, Wits.   (17).

Says his Father suffered a long Imprisonment on acct. of his Loyalty. His House & Buildings were burnt & all his effects plundered & destroyd after which he went off with 2 of his sons. He served in the Rangers. He had three Sons in the Rangers, one of whom died. Witness himself served in the Indian Department. He had 600 or 700 acres in Young's Patent. Claimant was one of the original Patentees. It was an old Patent. There was a good farm clear. There was a Saw Mill & a Pot Ash Work on this Place.

Vals. Saw Mill at 200£, Clear Land at 6£ per acre. Woodland at 20sh. per acre.

He had other Lands in Patents. He had a good Stock & furniture, all was lost. He came away with scarce sufficient Cloathes to cover him.

He kept a Shop. He had always articles for the Indian Trade, thinks he saw an advertismt. for sale. There are strangers that live upon the Place.

Claims also for a 1,000 acres on the Susquehana, 30 miles from the Mohawk, bought by Claimt & Claimt's Brother of Sir John Johnson. It was purchased after the War began & Claimt's Bro. was now in Possession, but Claimt is liable to pay the whole Purchase Money to Sir John Johnson.

Further Evidence in Case of JOHN BURCH, ESQ.   September 10.

(18).

THOS. CUMMING, Wits.
Knew Claimt. Remembers his supplying Col. Butler & his Party with Provisions &c. Witness Father went with the Cattle by direction of Claimt. He went with them as far as Anguorgern when they were delivered to Capt. Colvertt. His Father was taken Prisoner when Mr. Burch made his escape from his house, was carried to Gaol, tried for his Life & Condemned but was released.
Witness lived at Mr. Burchs at Papa Chon. Remembers the Rebels coming to attack his House, it happened 3 times. The last time Claimt. made his escape, at the risk of his life. The Houses & Buildings were destroyd.

Witness made his escape at the same time. Most of his Cattle & many of his effects had been taken away on the first attack made upon his House. Thinks the grain destroyd worth £400, there were 3 or 4 Stacks of Wheat.
Knew his horses. They were taken the first time, a stallion & 2 mares, very valuable besides others. Knew that he had Property at different peoples Houses which was discovered to be his & taken.

(19).

He lost Iron Works for a Grist Mill. Thinks the prime cost of this was £40 or £50. Witness himself left it on the road. Knew of Tin Tools & Japanning Tools left at Woodstock. They were found out to be Claimt's & taken.
Knew that he had a Shop at Albany. He was sending off 3 Horse Loads of Shop Goods. They were taken at Schoharie, discovered to be his & were sold by the Rebels. A Cousin of Witness was one of the Persons employd to carry the Things away. She was sent to Gaol on that Acct.
Witness was at Albany in 77. Claimant had at that time Goods in his Shop to considerable amount.

DAVID VAN EVERY, Wits.
Says he was a Seargt. in Butler's Rangers. Claimt. sent a Letter by Witness to Col. Butler that he would supply him with Cattle & with men. Col. Butler sent one Indian Officer & Witness, who accordingly brought off a considerable No. of Cattle & men. procured by Mr. Burch. They brought a great many cattle, all procured by M. Burch, either his own or from his neighbours.

ADAM SMITH, Wits.
Knew that Claimant had various effects at the Mill House, Woodstock. Witness was the person who put the Things by. His Tools & Mahogany Bedstead, there were 2 or 3 Barrels full of Things. The Rebels found out these Things after Mr. Burch went away to be his & took them.

(20).

He was reckoned a rich man. Witness heard the Americans got all his effects. He was told so by many people.
Heard of his Loss of 3 horse loads of goods going from Albany.
April 2nd, 1785. Produces affidavit from John Lansing sworn at Albany to Claimt's Property lost at Schoharie on removal from Albany in Augst. 1778 by Janet Andrew formerly McClement, who was servt. to Claimt. & Employd in moving the Things

863. Claim of GEO. KENTNER, late of Pensilv. September 17.

Claimt. Says.

He was at Mashichi in 83, and all the ensuing winter.
Is a German, came to America 22 yrs. ago.
Resided on the Susquehana when the Rebellion broke out, joined Col. Butler in 77, was at Fort Stanwix, was taken Prisoner, was released & afterwards served in Sir John Johnson's Regt, 2nd Batall. Served till his discharge.
Produces Discharge, Resides in the 5th Township.
Had 300 acres on Susquehana, bought of Jesse Lukin, Surveyor of Land at Philadelphia in 76. He never had a deed, was to pay £18 for it. Had not paid. He cleared 20 acres, some fenced. Built a house & Stable. (21).

4 Horses, 2 Heifers, 2 Cows, 1 Yoke of Oxen, Household Furniture, farming Utensils, Grain in the House, Left at Home when he went away. Says they were taken by the Rebels.

PHILIP BURCH, Wits.

Remembers the Claimt. went to join the Brit. very early. He served during the War.
Knew his place. He had a good Clearance & good improvements. He had a good stock.

FREDERICK AUGER.

Knew the Place where Claimt. lived. He had 3 Horses, 1 Yoke Oxen, 2 Cows, farming Utensils. He left all these things on his place when he went first to Niagara.

Col. Butler says that in the Expedition in 78 under his command at Wyoming a great many Cattle were taken for the use of the Troops. Some of them from persons known at the time to be Loyalists, & from others whom he afterwards knew to be Loyalists. He never charged Government on this acct.

Mentions particularly having some Cattle of Wentermuts. Says his party killed or carried away all the Cattle they met with in the Settlement. (22).

864. Claim of RICHARD CARTWRIGHT, late of Albany Co. September 26.

Claimant says he is a native of England. Settled in America in 1742, resided in Albany when Rebellion broke out, from the first declared in favr. of Brit. Govert. Suffered both in property & person very much, in 1778 was sent from Albany to go within Brit. Lines, by the Commrs. of Conspiracies. N.B.—Aged 70; infirm.

Produces summons from the Commrs. to attend in July, 1778. With an order for his Departure, 20th July, 1778. He was conveyed away by a Guard to Crown Point. Staid at Montreal. Now settled at Cataraqui.

Says he was in Consequence of his having assisted the Loyalists & expended a great deal on that acct. He had refused taking an oath to the Americans.

(23).
To be allowed.

Produces Certificates from Sir John Johnson & 6 others to his Loyalty & to the assistance he had given Loyalists on all occasions. He had 100 acres near Cherry Valley, bought of Peter Martin in 1775, took it for Debt of £100. It was partly improved, about 10 acres cleared. No buildings but a Hut. Claimt. had entered on the Possession. Vals. it at £100 York Cury.

Lost Cloathes, Furniture & various articles from his house at Albany. They came to Claimt's house in 1778 when he had refused to take the oath & destroyed & plundered his effects to above £100 York.

Advanced Money on different occasions to Loyalists.

He suffered a 2nd time from a Mob on the King's Birthday. His house was surrounded by 3 or 4,000 People. He was beat & abused & his effects destroyd.

Laid out a great deal of Money in Support of Loyalists.

When he came away he was allowed to sell some of his effects that were left at Vendue, but great part was plundered from him, to amount of 50£.

Refers himself to Major Hughes at Montreal; seems very good man; his certificates are strong.

He was appointed to Post of Deputy Postmaster for the City and Co. of Albany. Produces his appointment from Dr. Franklin & Wm. Hunter in 1756. He held this for many years, but gave it up before the Rebellion began.

Resides at Cataraqui.

Major Hughes certified to his Loyalty in very favourable terms, & that he had been at his House where he seemed to have everything comfortable about him & to be in good circumstances.

September 26.

865. Claim of PETER ESELSTINE, late of Albany Co.

(24).

Claimt. says:

He resided betwixt Isle au Noix & Point au Fear in the Fall '83. Gave in an acct. to Mr. Robins to be sent to England in '83, but heard no more of it.

Is a native of America. Lived in Albany Co.; joined Genl. Burg at Saratoga. Continued with him till ye Convention. Served in Jessup's Corps as private till ye Regt. was disbanded. Produces his discharge.

Had Lands near Albany which he parted with before he came away, by way of mortgage, as he had not paid for it.

Lost 15 head of Cattle. Left them on his Farm. Heard they were sold at Vendue when he went away. 2 Cows, 2 Working Cattle, a Bull & some yearlings, in all 15; 7 Hogs, 6 Sheep, Carpenters' Tools, farming utensils, furniture. Resides in 2 Township.

GEORGE FINKEL, Wits.:

Knew Claimt. Remembers his serving in the Rangers. Knew his Property. Knew his stock partly; 10 or 12 horned creatures. He left everything when he went to join Genl. Burg. The Rebels took them. He had 8 sheep; he had carpenters Tools & furniture. Says the Things were taken away by the Rebels. (25).

CONRAD VAN DUSEN, Wits.:

Knew Claimt. Knew his property. He had a stock, but cannot say what quantity. Understood they were taken away on acct. of his going to Genl. Burgoyne.

866. Claim of CASPER HOVER, of Pensilva.—Died. September 26.

His second son, Jacob, appears.

Says his Father resided at Lechine in the Fall of '83 & all that winter. He died last July 12 months, leaving Henry, his eldest son, now residing in the 4th Township, & Jacob, who appears & a widow now in the 4th Township.

His Father was a native of Holland. Lived on the Susquehana. Joined the Brit. in 1777. Claimt. himself & 2 Bros. also joined. His father served some time. Claimt. & his Bro. served till their Discharge.

Reside in 4th Township.

His Father had done little improvements on the Susquehana. A house & Barn, 6 Horses, 8 horned Cattle, 9 Hogs, Tools, & furniture, 80 Bushels Wheat. All these things were on the premises when they joined the Brit. A good family.

EDWARD HICKS, Wits.:

Knew Casper Hover. He & his 3 sons all joined in 1777 to Butler's Rangers & served. The young men all the War. He had 5 or 6 Horses, 4 Cows, & young Cattle & other things. Knew that all the Creatures were taken by the Rebels. (26).

They were left on the premises when he went to join Brit. Army. Satisfied.

867. Claim of JOHN GERMAN, late of Albany Co. September 26.

Claimt. says:

He sent a Claim to Major Jessup in '83, to be forwarded to England. Resided at Sorel.

Is a native of Germany. Came young to America. Lived near Fort Edward when Rebellion broke out; joined the Brit. on Lake Champlain in 1776.

Served in Major Jessup's Regt. all the War till his discharge, when Regt. was reduced. Had also 3 sons in the service. Now resides in 4 Township.

Had Lease Lands in Saratoga District, 100 acres; the improvements were Claimt.'s. There was a good Log house & 15 acres Clear.

Left all his effects on his farm in 1776. His family staid till 1777. Left his effects on the Premises. The Rebels took all the Cattle & things they could carry away.

(27). 3 Working horses, 4 Cows, 3 2-year olds, 2 yearlings, 4 Calves, 16 Hogs, Corn, 60 bushels oats, furniture, wagon new, 8 Tons Hay.

These things were left on the Premises when his Wife went away within the Brit. Lines.

Produces Certificate from Pat Smith that Claimt. was an Inhabit. near Fort Edward & had Horses, Cattle & utensils.

JOHN LOW, Wits.:

A fair man; to be allowed. Knew Claimt. He joined the Brit. very early. Left his Stock on his Farm. His wife left the place the year following & left the Stock. Wits. saw the Rebels take them off; horses, Cows, 6 Heifers, Plough, Harrow, Wagon, & Sleighs. Saw the Wagon taken by the Rebels.

N.C. 868. Claim of JOBERT HOFNIAL, Charlotte Co., New York.
September 26. Died.

His Widow, Margaret, appears. Says her Husb. resided at Sorel in the Fall & all the winter.

He was a native of Germany. Came 23 years ago. Lived at Kinsboro, Charlotte Co., when the Rebellion broke out. He joined the Brit. in '80. Joined Jessup's Corps & served during the war.

He died 2 years ago without a Will. Left a Son, Andrew now in the 4th Township. He has served in Jessup's Regiment (28). 3 yrs. as a Drummer. Came in with his Father. He is not yet of age.

Her Husband had 60 acres in Kingsboro. His Brother gave the Land to him, but they had not cleared any part. The Brother was a man of substance. Now lives in the States.

They worked on the Brother's Land but had not cleared any part of their own. They cleared on their Brothers Land & had a House there where they lived.

Her Husband had 5 horses, 2 taken by the Rebels, 3 killed by the Rebels, 3 Cows, 2 Calves, a yoke of Steers, 10 Sheep, 3 Hogs, farming utensils, taken by the enemy.

In the year 1777 because he staid behind & would not go away into the Rebels. The Rebels suspected all persons who staid thus behind to be Tories & to stay with Intent to join Burgoyne. The Indians got some of the Sheep.

JOHN GERMAN, Wits:

A good man. Knew the late Jobert Hofnail. He was a good Loyalist. He was always Loyal. Illness prevented his coming into Canada in '77. He joined in '80. Wits. has understood he had a stock of his own on his Brother's Lands & believes they were taken or detroyed by the rebels.

N.C. 869. Claim of MARY BROWN, Widow of John Brown, Decd.,
September 26. for herself & Children.

Claimt. appears:

Her Husband, John Brown, died 10 years ago without a Will, (29). leaving Claimant & five Children now living. Four of them are now in the King's Dominion, but she does not know where. One of them, a daughter named Sally, married to one Tilney in 2nd Township.

Her Husband was a native of America. Lived in Dutchess Co. Always a friend to the King. She had 4 Sons who served in the Army under Col. Beverley Robinson. Her Husband went within the Lines in 1777. Took the Oath of Allegiance.

Produces Certificates to his taking the Oath of Allegiance.

He had a Lease farm in Dutchess Co., near the Row——, at £7 per ann.

He had 4 Cattle, 2 horses, 24 hogs, furniture, farming utensils, cloathes, fifty bushels grain, a Loom, a Fish Sein. All these things were left on the Place. When her Husb. went within the Lines Claimant went with him. Has heard these Things were Vendued by the Rebels.

Cash destroyed. Was chiefly destroyed by the Brit. Troops being Congress money.

MICHAEL CROSS, Wits:

Says Claimt. came from New York under Witness' direction (30). as the widow of a Loyalist. Does not know any thing of her Evidence Family, or their property. Speaks of her as a very industrious feeble. woman. She is now married to one Elgood.

870. Claim of GEORGE MORDOFF, late of Tryon Co. N.C.

September 26.

Claimt. says:

He was at Oswego & Cataraqui in the Fall of '83 & during the Winter.

Is a native of Scotland. Went to America in 1773. Settled in Tryon Co. Joined Sir John Johnson in '80. Staid as long as he could, tho. he gave all the assistance to the Loyalists & always declared his sentiments. Served in 2nd Batall. Continuel till discharged.

Had 100 acres; bought a Lease in the year 1773. It was a Lease from Sir Wm. Johnson to Peter Young of 100 acres, Tryon Co., Kingsboro Patent forever, paying £6 pr. an. He gave £25 York for it. There were only 2 acres clear & a framed house. He cleared 26 acres afterwards and built barn. Vals. ye whole at 100 York. Lost a mare, 1 Heifer, taken by the Rebels. Cattle, farming utensils & some furniture.

DANIEL SMITTS, Wits:

Knew Claimt. He was always Loyal. Knew his Place. He (31). bought it before the troubles of Peter Young. There was not Seems a good much clear before he bought it. He cleared a good Deal. man.

N.C.
September 26.

871. Claim of DANL. SMITH, late of Tryon Co.

Claimt. says:

He resided at Oswego & Cataraqui.
Is a native of America. Lived on the Mohawk. Joined Sr. John Johnson in the year 1778. Served all the war in the 2nd Battal.

A very good man; may be allowed the whole.

Lived on Leased Land of Sir Wm. Johnson. When he joined the Brit. he left 2 Cows, 1 Heifer, 4 Sheep, furniture, some wool.

GEO. MURDOF, Wits:

Knew Claimt. Remembers he joined Sir John Johnson, and that stock was seized on that acct. Witness was then in the Country & knew it. 3 Cows & some Cattle & household furniture.

September 26.

872. Claim of OWEN ROBLIN, late of Orange Co.

Claimt. says:

He resided at Sorell in the Fall '83.

(32).

Is a native of America. Lived in Orange Co. when Rebellion broke out. Suffered greatly. Was imprisoned & kept in Irons 13 weeks. Joined the Brit. in '79. Was employed in the Barrack Master's Department. Afterwards served in the out Posts, till evacuation of New York.

Had a Lease farm held of David Mathews in Orange Co. It was for four years or 5 years a time, but says he could have sold the Improvemts. He had lived there 10 years.

Had a Partner with him. Vals. his improvemts. at £30. Says according to the Custom, he could have sold his Labour done in making Improvemts.

Lost 8 horses, 1 Cow, 6 Sheep, 4 Hogs, Hay & Grain. Left all these things on his Farm when he went away & they were taken by the Rebels.

PHILIP ROBLIN, Wits:

Claimt. went within the Brit. Lines. He was always Loyal. He had been imprisoned before that time. He served at the out Posts.

Seems a good man.

He had part of a Lease Farm. He had made considerable Improvemts. Believes by the Custom he cd. sell the Improvemts. He had Horses & Cows &c. Left the wnole behind.

N.C.
September 26.

873. Claim of GEO. FINKLE, SER., late of Albany Co.

Claimt. says:

Claimt aged, near 70.

He resided at the River de Cheyne in '83. That Winter
Is a native of America. Resided in Clobeck Dist., Albany Co. Joined Genl. Burgoyne in '77. Continued with him until he was taken. Came into Canada. Served with Jessup's Corps as a Volunteer. Was with them till they were discharged.

(33).

Had a Lease of 170 acres on Rancellor's Manor in Clobeck Distrist. Had a Lease from Robt. Rancellor for 3 Lives, his own, Wifes & 2 Sons. Just before the Rebellion, had given £5 for it. Had improved between 60 & 70 acres. Had built a framed House. Vals. it at £300 York. Rancellor has since sold it. He had 2 yokes of oxen, 1 yoke of Steers, 50 Hogs, 30 Sheep, Furniture, Tools. All taken after he joined Gen. Burg. by the Rebels.

PETER ASELTINE, Wits:

Knew Claimt. He joined Gen. Burg. in '77. He left his stock upon his Farm when he went away. The Rebels would have hanged him if they could have caught him for raising men & swearing them in to the King's service. He was afterwards into Jessup's Corps.

Knew his Place. It was Leased Land. A farm in general consisted of 120 acres on Rancellor Manor. Remembers his living there long before the war. A good deal was clear, 50 acres; a large framed Barn & framed House. His Lease was for 3 Lives. Vals. the Improvemts. at £300 York. He had a considerable stock of Horses & Cattle. He left them on his Place. They were taken after he joined Burg. (34).

CONRAD VAN DUSEN, Wits:

Knew Claimt. He was always a true Loyalist. He had a farm on Rancellor Manor. Thinks he had about 50 acres clear. Remembers him in Possession some years before the war began. Improvemts. on Leases for lives not so valuable as on a Lease forever. There was a good Barn & a framed House.

Vals. these improvemts. at £300 York.

Thinks his stock must have been a Dozen or 15 Cattle & 6 or 7 horses.

Further Evidence in Case of DANIEL MCGWIN, heard at Montreal. September 26.

JOHN EVERETT, Wits:

Knew Claimt. in Ulster Co. He was always considered as a Loyalist. He had a snug Farm near Newboro. Remembers him in possession about 6 yrs. before the war. Near 40 acres clear; a snug house. Vals. clear land from 2 to £3 York pr. acre. Witness was informed in 1776 by Claimt. that he had got a No. of men who would come in. Wits. took ye names to Gover. Tryon. There were about 50. Wits. returned to order Claimt. to bring in the men. Was informed he was in Prison. (35).

He had Cattle, horses. He carried on the Potash business & kept a store. Remembers Claimt. bringing in men to serve in Col. Fanning's Regt. He was Lieut. in that Corps—vi Vol. 17, April 4th. Produces affidt. taken before Neal McLean, Esq., Cataraqui, from David Flyn, that Claimt. purchased at New York in the year '80 goods to amount of £401.11.9½ of Deponent & goods of others which were sent from New York to Sag harbour in Long Island. Were taken by plundering parties. Vals. the whole between 8 & £900 York.

September 26. 874. Claims by Heirs of Jos. ORSER, Decd., late of Philips Manor, Prov. of New York.

ANN, Widow of the decd., appears:

Says her late Husb., Jos. Orser, died on his Passage from New York to Quebec in '83, without a Will, leaving Claimant, his Widow, John, the eldest Son; 5 other Sons & one Daughter. The eldest son is now in the States.

(36). Her Husb. was a native of America. Lived on Philip Manor when Rebellion broke out. From the first joined the Brit. Her Husband continued at home, being very old. In May, '82, their House was burnt by the Rebels, because three Sons were in the Brit. Army. They then went within the Lines & lived there till the evacuation of New York

No. 1. The eldest son is the only one of the family who has staid behind. The rest are here; 2nd Son, Arthur; 3, Isaac; 4, Solomon; 5, Gilbert; 6, Gabriel; 7, Rachel. He had 100 acres on Philips Manor. This was his own Land. Bought many years ago of the Patentees. He gave £200 for it. It was clear Land; all improved.

No. 2. The other Lands adjoined consisted of 95 acres. Held of

of Philips on a yearly Rent at £5, but there was no Deed.

The Land was valuable, being near the North River. Does not know what is become of it. She says the Land held of Philips always went to the Widows.

They had a fine stock which was plundered by the Rebels at different times, because they had sons in the King's Army. Speaks of 8 Cows, 3 fine young horses, Calves, yearlings, 30 Sheep, 20 Hogs. All their furniture, utensils, cloathes taken by the Rebels.

ARTHUR ORSER, Wits:

(37). He & all his Brothers have served this war, in Col. Delancey's Regt. All came to this Province except John, the eldest son.

His Father did not go within the Lines till late in the war, burnt & then he went within the Lines. Continued there till evacuation of New York.

but was known to be a Loyalist all the while. His House was
No. 1. He had 100 acres of his own Land. He bought it some years before the war. All improved.
No. 2. He had 95 acres manor Land. He lived there. That was the House burnt down.

Says that the Lands No. 1 were worth £7 pr. acre York. As to No. 2 the Land was Philips. The Improvemts. belonged to the Tenants. In general the Widows had these Lands while they continued widows & then they went to the Heir.

His Father's stock was taken away by the Rebels at different times. He used to have sometimes 30 Head of Cattle, besides Horses. Furniture went the same way. He himself is desirous that any share due to him be paid his Mother. His other Brothers desire the same.

EMMANUEL ELLIBECK, Wits: (38).

Knew the late Jos. Orser. He was always very Loyal. All his sons were in King's Army. The old man continued at Home, but he was terribly ill-used. His House was burnt. He went within the Lines at last. He had Land of his own & Manor Land. The old man often supplied Witness with Provisions for himself & other Loyalists. He had a large stock. The Rebels took the whole. Witness was often backward & forward on secret service & knew of their effects being taken by the rebels. *A very good family; to be allowed what we can.*

Isaac & Solomon, 2 other Sons, say their Father used to have 30 Head of Cattle, 8 Horses, 20 Sheep. Thinks there was as much as this taken by the Rebels. Furniture partly burnt, part taken.

The Widow used to have the Manor Lands during their Widowhood.

They all agree that whatever is allowed should be made payable to Arthur Orser, the eldest son here.

875. Further Evidence in Case of JAMES PERROT, heard at Montreal. September 26.

Produces Deed from Jacobus Lake to Claimt. of a Tract —— (39). Van Kyler Patent, consisting of 100 acres in Considn. £80. 9th year of King George 3d.

876. Further Evidence in Claim of ELIZ. HOGAL, heard at Montreal. September 26.

BUSTEYON HOGLE & JAMES, 2 Sons of Eliz. Hogle, appear: Say they came to this Province. Now live in the 2nd Township. Busteyon is 19, James 18 years of age.

They now live with James Perrot on his Lands. He married an aunt of theirs. Busteyon is the eldest son of John & Eliz. Hogle now living. Says Mr. Perrot has hitherto acted on his guardian & has maintained him. Both wish what is due to them to be paid to Mr. Perrot.

877. Claim of ELIJAH GROOMS, late of Midx. Co., E. Jersey. N.C.
September 26.

Claimt. says:

He came from New York in the summer of '83. Stopt at Sorel. Staid there all the fall & winter.

Is a native of America. Lived in Monmouth Co. Joined the Brit. in 1776. Served 6 years in Genl. Skinner's Brigade. Was discharged in '82.

Produces his discharge in '82. Was then in the privateer way. Says he was frequently employed as a spy.

Had 6 Cattle of his own. His sister bought them for him (40). during the war with her money, but his Brother in Law kept them. He had a mare taken for a Tax. Taken from his Father's Lands. He had also 6 Sheep which his sister bought for him & his Bro. in Law refused to give up.

64 AR.

N.C.
September 27.

878. Claim of ALEXR. SIMPSON, late of New York.

Claimt. resided here in '83 & the winter. Claimt. is 60 yrs. of age, much afflicted with Reumatism. Almost always in pain. Is a native of Ireland. Came to America in '62. Resided at Conogharie when Rebellion broke out. Traded with the Indians. Took the King's part at first. Was twice in Albany Gaol; 1st time ten weeks; 2nd time was imprisoned because he would not take an Oath to ye States. Came here in '80. Brought in 44 men with him. Have continued in this Province since.

He went to settle for the American Army on the German Flats in '76. He was either to do that or take a Commission or go to Gaol. He was put to Gaol, on which the Americans plundered his Liquors to amt. of £100.

(41).

Claimt a damed rascal.

Went a 2nd time to settle the American Army in the same year at the same place. On being imprisoned the Americans went & plundered his store to amount of £200.

In 1777 he took some horses to sell to Americans or any body & lost 3. They were stolen.

N.C.
September 27.

879. Claim of CYRMENS PARK, formerly of Kingsburgh, Charlotte Co.

Claimt. says:

He resided at St. Johns or the Upper Part of Canada in the Fall of '83 & winter.

Is a native of America. Lived at Kingsboro, Charlotte Co. Joined the Brit. in '77, under Burg. After his capitulation staid in the Country till '80, then came in & Joined Major Rogers.

Served in the Rangers till they were discharged as Corporal. Produces his Discharge.

May be allowed for clearing 10 acres.

Had a Lease, 150 acres in the ——— Patent, Kingsboro District. Had the Lease in '73, at £6 York pr. ann., with liberty to purchase. There was some clear when he first went & some builds. He cleared 20 acres more; built a stable.

Lost 1 ox, 1 Horse, in '77, taken after he joined Burg. at *Shecasboro*. When he came into Canada in '80, he left a stock.

(42).

Seems a very good man.

1 yoke oxen, 1 Cow, 3 horses, furniture, farming utensils, some wheat. Most of these Things were at a place where he lived after his Return from Burgoyne's Army near his old Farm, for he had been ordered off his own Farm, but says he was allowed to mow ye Hay on his Farm. Left a Hay barrack, 14 tons.

THOMAS HARRIS, Wits:

Knew Claimt. He was very Loyal. He joined Genl. Burg. at first; afterwards served in Major Roger's Corps.

Knew his Place. He had considerable improvemts. He had cleared 4 or 5 acres himself. Thinks not 20 clear in the whole. Speaks of 2 horses & a Colt, yoke of oxen. Lost some after he joined Burg. Lost others afterwards. Thinks he lost all his furniture, except what he & his wife could carry on their Backs.

---

880. Claim of JAMES PARKE, late of Charlotte Co.   N.C.
September 27

CYLL—— PARK, his Bror., apprs.:

Says his Bror. James is blind. Is now at Oswegatchie in hopes to get assistance from a Surgeon there.

He came to St. Johns in the Fall of '83. He had been imprisoned by the Americans for a year. On being released he came to St. Johns. Continued during the winter at St. Johns.

Is a native of America. Served with Burg. Continued in the Colonies till '80, then joined Major Roger's Rangers. Served till the Discharge, tho. he was a prisr. part of the time. Produces his Discharge as Seargent. (43).

He had a Lease of 150 acres in the artillery Patent at 1s. per acre Rent. He had a long lease, taken before ye War began. He cleared 25 acres, built a house & stable.

He had 1 Cow, Tools of various kinds, furniture, farming utensils. He had 150 Pine boards. All taken after he came to Canada in '80.

He was robbed of cloathes & money in '77, by a Continental Scouting Party.

JAMES JOHNSON, Wits:

Knew Claim. He joined Burg. Afterwards, in '80, was in Major Roger's Rangers.

Knew his Place, a hard farm, betwixt 30 & 40 acres improved. A Log house. Remembers him in Possession before the war. He had a pretty stock. He had a good store of Tools.

881. Claim of ABRAHAM DE FOE, late of Albany Co.   N.C.
September 27.

Claimt. says:

He resided at St. Johns in '83.

Is a native of America. Lived in Albany Co. Joined Gen. Burg. Was taken in Bennington fight. Got into Canada in '80. Served in Major Roger's Rangers till they were Discharged.

Had a farm in little Hoosick. It was a Lease of 100 acres granted by Abraham Tinbrook 14 years ago to Claimt.'s Father who gave it to his son immediately. Had cleared 15 acres. Built a house. Was to have it ten years free & then pay — pt. Produce. Vals. ye Improvemts. at 400 Dollars. (44).

A good man.

Lost 1 yoke oxen, 3 Cows, 2 Hogs, Grain of various kinds, most of it in the ground, furniture, utensils. Left these things when he went to Burg. The rebels had them.

PETER YOUNG, Wits:

Knew Claimt. He joined Burg. Was afterwards in Roger's Rangers. Knew his Place.

14 or 15 acres clear, 3 Cows, 1 yoke oxen. They were taken away when he joined Burg. All his other Things were taken.

N.C.
September 27.
882. Claim of PETER YOUNG, of Bennington, Pownal Township, Vermont.

Claimt. says:

He was in St. Johns; 2nd Balln. in St. Michels. Gave in his Claim to Major Leake in '83. Sent another to Halifax.

Is a native of America.. Lived at Bennington. Joined Burg. Was kept a prisoner. Got away as soon as he could & joined Sir Johns 2nd Battn. Served till ye Regt. was Discharged.

(45).

He had 6 acres of meadow land in Pownal given by his Father to Claimt. in 1775. He built a framed house. 2 brood mares, 1 horse, 2 Colts, 2 Cows, taken when he joined Genl. Burg.

ABRAHAM DEFOE, Wits:

Knew Claimt. He joined Burg. He served in Sir John 2nd Battalion. Knew his Place, his Father gave it to him. It was at Pownal. His Father is now here. The Rebels have got the Place. He had a Stallion, 2 Mares, 2 Colts, 2 Cows.

Knows that they were taken by the Rebels.

N.C.
September 27.
883. Claim of SAML. WELSH, late of Albany Co.

Claimt. says:

He was Isle au Noix in the Fall '83 & at St. John's during the winter.

Is a native of America. Lived at Kingsboro, joined the Brit. in Canada. Served in Major Rogers Rangers 3 yrs.

Lost 2 horses, 1 Cow, 30 Bushel Wheat, 40 Potatoes, furniture, very little, utensils. These things were at his Brother in Laws, John Ward, near Fort Ann. They were found out to be Claimts. things & taken by the Rebels.

(46).

THOS. HARRIS, Wits.:

Knew that Claimt. had 2 horses, 1 Cow, furniture, &c. Knew that he left them with one Ward & that the Americans found them to be Claimts. & took them away.

N.C.
September 27.
ASA RICHARDSON, Wits.:

Knew that Claimt. had a mare & colt & Cow & furniture. They were left with Ward. Heard they were found out & taken from Ward when Claimt. went to Canada.

884. CLAIM OF ASA RICHARDSON, FORMERLY CHARLOTTE CO.

Claimt. says:

He resided partly at Coator Cor. & Sorell in the Fall '83 & the Winter.

Is a native of America, lived in Kingsboro. Was with Gen. Burg. but was then ill, did not serve. In '80 came to Canada, was incorporated with Col. Jessup's Regimt., continued with them till they were discharged.

Produces a Pass in Aug., 1777, from Burg's. Head Quarters.

Had 21 acres of Meadow in Kingsburg, bought them 3 or 4 years before the war of one Copel in Considn. of 6£, cleared it afterwards. Vals. at 100 York. No. 1.

House & 15 acres of Lease Land in Wood Creek, bought the improvemts. Produces a Paper by which it appears he bought these improvemts. in 1772, all improved. Vals. at £40 Hal. Does not know what has become of his Land. No. 2. (47).

2 horses, 1 taken by the Indians, 1 by the Rebels, 1 Ox, 1 Cow, 2 young Cattle, Some Rebels took them by armed force from his Wife. 2 Hogs, do., utensils, furniture, taken by Rebels.

30 bushels of Wheat, various kinds of grain, some flax, 12 Tons Hay, he lost part in '77, part when he went into Canada, most of it by the Rebels.

SAML. BRUNSON, Wits.:

Knew Claimt., he was always considered Loyal, he was with Gen. Burg. at Skenesboro, afterwards went to Canada. Was in-

corporated in Jessops Regt.

Knew No. 1, 20 acres, bought of one Copel some years before ye War & was in Possession of it. Most of it improved.

Knew No. 2, there was some Improvemt., 15 or 20 acres, he lived there. He h d a pretty good Stock. The Rebels took a Considerable part.

885. Case of SAML. BROWNSON, late of Kingsbury, Charlotte Co. N.C. September 27.

Claimt. says: Old and infirm

He was at Sorel in the Fall of '83 & the Winter.

Is a native of America. Lived at Kingsbury. Came to St. John's in 1778. He could not stay, Consistant with his Principles. He had some Contract in the Engineers Departmt., afterwards joined Major Jessups, continued till he was invalided, served about 4 years. (48).

He had fifty acres in Kingsbury, his own Land, he had these fifty acres for settling on the Land 20 years ago, this was all clear. There was a good house & Barn. No. 1.

Vals. Land at £3 per acre York, exclusive of House & buildings.

He had besides, a Lease Lot of 192 acres, the Lease was for 999 years at 1 sh. per acre after 10 years, taken of Charles Ward, No. 2.

Abtthorpe, 30 acres of this improved. The Landlord has taken all this Lot, by re-entering for non payment of Rent.

He has also taken No. 1, pretending it to be part of the Lease.

Had also a Lease Lot of one Smith 15 years ago, this was 242 acres at 1 sh. per acre after 10 yrs. He had a Tenant upon it.

This has been reentred upon for Non Paymt. of Rent. This was not improved.

He had a Considerable Stock, the Cattle were taken away by the Rebels.

(49). 4 Cows, 4 Oxen, by rebels. 6 Calves, 8 hogs, by Indians, furniture, utensils.

ASA RICHARSON, Wits.:
Knew Claimt., he was a Loyalist, he joined the Brit. in '80, served with Major Jessup.
Knew his Property at Kingsbury.
No. 1. He had 50 acres of his own for settling, thinks he settled in '63, all Clear. He built a large House & large Barn.
He had also a Lease Lot from Abthorpe, a good Deal of this was Clear, the land not very valuable.
He had also a Lease Lot from one Smith, he had a Tenant of 50 acres upon it.
He had a large Stock of Cattle.

N.C.
September 27.

886. Case of EBENEZER WASHBURN, late of Rutland, Charlot Co.
Claimt. says:
He resided at Yamaska in ye fall '83 & the Winter
Is a native American, lived at Rutland, joined Burg '77, was taken prisoner, sent to different Gaols. Got into Canada in '78. Served from that time in Major Jessup's Corps as Seargt. till reduced.

(50). Had 100 acres in Rutland, bought in 1775 of Saml. Yeack, thinks he gave £120 Lawful for it, pd. in Cattle, &c., none improved. He himself improved 4 or 5 acres, there were no buildings, does not know what is become of it. Vals. it at £200 York.
Had a yoke of Steers, Horse & Cow, they were at his Brother in Laws. Taken by a Scouting party of Rebels after he joined Genl. Burg.

ROBERT PERRY, Wits.:
Knew Claimt., he joined Burg., was taken Prisnr. soon after in '78. Went to Canada again, served with Major Jessup Corps all the War.

A good man. He had 100 acres in Rutland, bought before the War, he had a Deed, Witness saw it, a little was Cleared. He had a horse, a yoke of Small Oxen, 2 Cows, they were on Witness's Lands. He left them when he went to join Burg. They were taken by the Continentals, as Witness was informed, they were known to be Claimts.

N.C.
September 27.

887. Claim of ROBT. PERRY, late of Charlotte Co.

Claimt. says:
He resided at Mashish in the Fall '83 & the Winter.

(51). Is a native of America, lived in Rutland Township, Vermont. Joined Burg. early in 1777, returned to Canada after ye Capitulation. Served in Major Jessup's Corps. Produces his Discharge.

Had 50 acres in Rutland. Produces Deed from Ephraham No. 1. Derwon to Claimt. & David Shorey of 100 acres in Rutland in Considn. of £37, dated '76.

Says this was bought in '72 & the money was paid at different times. He had not the Deed till the whole was pd., which is ye Reason that Deed bears Date in '76, half belonged to Claimt, about 30 acres Clear.

Vals. the Clear Land ½ Joe per acre to Clear it.

Produces Certificates of Sale of this Estate from John Fasset & Certificate from Thos. Chittenden of Confiscation of all Claimts. Estate.

Produces Deed from Gideon Walker of 55 acres in Rutland No. 2. in Considn. £4. 72, none Clear.

Produces Deed of 13 acres & ½ in Considn. of £4.2. '75, none of this Clear.

He had parted with 13 acres of No. 2, 1 Horse, 1 yoke oxen, Seems a good man. Cows, 6 Sheep, 6 Hogs, farming utensils, furniture.

Left them at the Place when he went away. Has been always informed the rebels took them in '77. He also had Wheat, & Corn in the ground & Grass ready to cut.

DANL. WALKER, Wits.:

Knew Claimt. Knew his Place, he bought it some years before he came away. Heard of his purchasing No. 2. (52).

EBENEZER WASHBURN, Wits.:

Knew his Place No. 1 in Rutland, he bought it he thinks in 1773. Thinks he had 30 acres Clear. Knew he had other Lands. Knew his Stock, 4 Cows, 1 Horse & other things.

N.C.

888. Case of ISAAC LORRAWAY, late of Litchfield Co., Connect. September 27th

Claimt. says:

He was at St. Michels in the Fall '83 & during the Winter.

Is a native of America, lived in Susquehana, joined the Brit. in '78. Joined Sir John's Regt. Served during the War.

Had 300 acres on Susquehana, had it 5 years, had it from the office at Philadelphia for £5 per 100 acres. A large Tract was taken up at the same time by 30 families. Had Cleared 18 acres, had built house & Barn.

Had 4 Oxen, 3 Cows, 2 Horses, Tools, utensils, furniture. A good man.

The Rebels took all their Things in 1777. Claimt. was then in Prison for his Loyalty. They took his Things & sold them at Vendue. (53).

ISAAC VAN ALSTINE, Wits.:

Knew Claimts. Lands on Susquehana, 18 acres Clear. He had 300 acres for his Share, he had a yoke Oxen, 2 young Steers, 1 Horse, 1 Mare, Tools. The Rebels took them. Witness was present. Claimt. was then in Gaol. The Things were sold at Vendue. He was in the County at the time & heard of the Sale.

N. C.
September 27th

889. Claim of ISAAC LORRAWAY, JR., late of Connect.

ISAAC LORRAWAY, Ser., appears:

Says his Son is taken ill of the Ague. He is in the Bay of Quinty. Could not possibly come.

He was at St. Michels in the Fall '83 & during the Winter. He lived at Susquehana, joined the Brit. in Canada, joined Sir John's 2 Battal. Served during the War.

He had a Lot on the Susquehana, he had it under Connect. Govnt. He took it in beginning of War, bought it of Solomon Strong, all Woodland.

ISAAC VAN ALSTINE:

(54).

Knew Claimts. Land, he bought it during the War, under Connect. Govnt., all Woodland, bought it in 1776 or 1777.

N. C.
September 27th

890. Claim of MATHEW BENSON, late of Bergen Co., E. Jersey.

Claimt. says:

He was at Sorel in '83. Is a native of America, lived in Bergen Co. Joined the Brit. at New York. He had recruited men for Col. Bayard's Regt. Served in Col. Bayard's Regt. till they went to Halifax, he was discharged there. Got in the King's Brew house, staid till Evacuation of New York.

This is very fair.

Had 30 acres. His Brother has recovered it & sold it, he withdraws his Claim.

2 Cows, 4 Horses, furniture, farming utensils, Cloathes, they were plundered by the Rebels because Claimt. was with the Brit.

N. C.
September 27.

891. Claim of JACOB GARDENER, late of Albany Co.

Claimt. says:

He was at the River Le Cheyne in '83.
Belonged to Jessups Corps.
Is a native of America. Lived in Rancellor Manor. Joined the Brit. in 1777. Went into Canada after the Capitulation. Served in Jessups Corps all the War.

No. 1. (55).

Had 120 acres on Rancellor Manor, took it 10 years before he left the Country. He had 10 years free, then forever paying the 10th part of Produce. He built a house & barn. Near 60 acres Clear. Vals. it at £100. Says it has been sold by Rebels.

No. 2.

Had 42 acres in Kenterhook District, got a grant just before Rebellion began, it had cost nothing & he had done nothing upon it.

64 acres exactly in the same way as No. 2.

No. 3.

2 yoke of Oxen, 2 Horses, 2 Colts, 6 Sheep, 7 Hogs, Utensils, furniture. These things were taken away by the Rebels when he went to Burg.

JAMES ROBINS:

Knew Claimt, he is a very good Loyalist.

He had a farm on Rancellors Manor, he had lived upon it some years, 20 or 30 acres Clear, remembers his having a yoke of

oxen, remembers a Horse.

892. Claim of JOHN WILLIAMS, late of Saratoga.

A good man.
N. C.

Claimt. says:

September 27.

He was at Mashish in '83. Is a native of Am., lived at Saratoga, joined the Brit. in '81. Came into Canada, joined Major Jessups Corps. Served during the War.

Had 200 acres of Lease Land at Saratoga He had not got a Lease but was to have had one, he had been settled 2 years before the War.

(46).

He had Cleared 40 acres, built a house & Barn. Vals. Clear Land at £3 per acre. 1 Horse, 7 horned Cattle, 10 Sheep, 18 Hogs, utensils, furniture. Lost all these things.

When the Rebels retreated on Burg arrival they took all these things because he would not go with them. They plundered all those who staid behind, considering them as Tories.

A fair man, tho' he claimed too high at first.

WM. ROGERS, Wits.:

Knew Claimts. farm, he had been settled some years before ye War. Between 30 & 40 acres Clear, he had a horse, yoke of Oxen, 4 Cows, doz. Sheep.

They were all taken on the Retreat of the Rebels.

893. Claim of WM. ROGERS, late of Saratoga.

N. C.
September 27.

Claimt. says:

He resided at Mashish. Is a native of Amer., lived at Saratoga, joined the Brit. in '76, served all the War, was 3 times prisoner.

Had 100 acres Lease Land near Saratoga. Had the Lease from one Murray. After 5 years was to pay 1 Sh. per acre, had Cleared 30 acres, built 2 houses & a Barn.

Had a horse, yoke of Oxen, yoke of Steers, 2 Cows, 18 Hogs, furniture, utensils. Lost when the Rebels retreated from Gen. Burg.

A very fair good man.

(57).

JOHN WILLIAMS, Wits.:

Knew Claimts. Place. He had a Lease farm some years before the War. About 30 acres Clear. He had a Clean Stock, 2 Oxen, Steers. All his Stock & Effects were plundered in the Retreat of Rebels.

N. C.
September 27.

894. Claim of ICHOBAD HAWLEY, late of Achington.

Claimt. says:
He resided at the River De Chene in '83. Is a native of Am. Lived at Ashington, joined Genl. Burg at Skeensboro. Made his Escape at Ticonderago. Was taken Prisoner & carried into ye Cols., obliged to run the gauntlet. In '80 got to Canada. Joined Major Jessup, served all the War.

Lost 2 horses, Joiners & Carpenters Tools, Cloathes. Lost at different times, Cloathing lost when he was taken Prisnr. near Ticenderago. Lost the other things in '80. He was then taken Prisoner, made his Escape & left the Things mentioned which were taken by the Rebels.

(58).
A good man, somewhat disordered in is mind.

ISAAC BRISCOW, Wits.:
Knew that Claimt. had Joiners & Carpenters Tools. Speaks of his Loyalty & Sufferings.

DAVID WILLIAMS, Wits.:
Knew Claimt., he was a tradesman, had Tools for Joiners & Carpenters work.

N. C.
September 27.

895. Claim of Jos. CONKLIN, late of Albany Co.

Claimt. says: Fall of '83 he was at La Chene & that Winter. Is a native of America. Lived at Albany Co., joined the Brit. as far as he could. Had 2 Sons in the Brit. Army. Was too old himself to serve. Did not come within the Lines during the War. Came in in the Spring after ye Peace.

Claims for Cattle, a Mare & Colt, 2 or 3 Cows, taken at different times on acct. of his Loyalty & for £100 fine. Was often imprisoned.

Claims nothing for Lands or Tenements.

N.C.
September 27.

896. Case of JAS. MARSH, late of Wethersfield, Vermt.

Claimt. says:
He was at St. Johns in '83. Is a native of A., lived in Vermont, joined the Brit. in '80, served with Major Rogers during the War.

Produces his Discharge.

(59).
Had 100 acres in Wethersfield, bought in '72 of Wm. Upham. Wild Land then, he Cleared 20 acres, built a house & Barn.
It is sold.
Had yoke of oxen, 2 Cows, 6 Sheep, 7 Hogs, furniture, utensils, taken by the Rebels when he left home on acct. of his joining the Brit.

LEVI WARNER, Wits.:
Knew Claimts. farm, given him by his Father in Law, 8 or 9 acres Clear when Wits. knew it. He had a yoke of Oxen, 2 Cows, when Wits. knew the Place.

897. Claim of JOHN BAKER, late of Bergin Co., E. Jersey.   N. C.

September 27.

Claimt. says:

He resided at Sorel in '83. Is a native of England. Came to America many years ago. Lived in the Jerseys, joined the Brit. at New York, continued with them all the War as a guide & Pilot.

He had some Cloathes & Household furniture burnt in the Jerseys. He was then with the Army, he had some furniture which he was endeavoring to carry to New York, the first time Lord Cornwallis was there. It was at Hackinsac after they left the Place. The Rebels set fire to the House. Estimates his Loss at £10. (60).

This was done in moving his Things.   Seems a foolish claim, it was meant as a

Lost a Cow but does not know how.

Says he never got a farthing for his services as guide and Pilot.   claim for pay as guide and pilot.

JOHN PARSAL, Wits.:

Says Claimt. was meaning to carry his things to New York. There was a fire at Ternfly where these things were. Pots, Pans & bedding he had brought them there 2 days before. It was just about the Time that Mr. Washington's Light Horse were destroyed.

---

898. Claim of BARNABAS HOUGH, late of Charlotte Co.   N. C.

September 27.

Claimt. says he resided at St. Johns in '83. Is a native of Am. Lived at Paulet, Vermont, joined the Brit. in 1777, was left sick when Burg was taken. Went into Canada in July, '78. Served in Jessups Regt. all the War.

Had 100 acres in Paulet, bought a year or year ½ before he went to Gen. Burg. Produces Deed from F. Willard of a Tract of 50 acres in Considn. of 100 York.   No. 1.

(61).

Says he gave Lands in exchange for No. 1, not Money. Does not know what the lands so given cost him. Vals. it at £100 Hal.

Produces Deed from John Stark of 50 acres in Considn. £50 York, 1775. He pd. Cattle for this Land.   No 2.

Produces Chittenden's Certificate of Confiscation of all his Estate & Fasset Certificate of Sale of No. 1 & of Confiscation of his Estate, real & personal. Vals. it at 50£ Hal. Of No. 1 15 or 16 acres were Clear. There was a Dwelling house & Blacksmiths Shop.

Had 2 yoke of Oxen, 2 Cows, 7 Hogs, utensils, Tools, taken by the Rebels in '77, when Claimt. went to Burgn.

WM. FAIRFIELD, Wits.:

Knew his Lands in Paulet, 8 or 10 acres of No. 1 were Clear. Vals. Clear Land at £3 pr. acre.

<small>Claimt. a good man.</small>
Knew No. 2, 50 acres, 3 or 4 acres Clear, no buildings. He had 2 yoke of Oxen, 2 Cows, ye other things, thinks they were plundered. He joined the King's Army in '77.

<small>N. C.
September 27.</small>

899. Claim of DAVID JACKSON, late of Charlotte Co.

Claimt. says:

<small>(62).</small>
He resided at Oswego in '83. Is a native of England. Came to America in '72, was settled at Skeensboro, joined the Brit. in '80, served in St. John's 2nd Batall.

Had 100 acres in Skeensboro, Lease Land, 20 acres Clear. 1 Horse, 4 Cattle, furniture, utensils.

<small>Claimt. a drunken dog.</small>
JAMES JACKSON, Wits.:

Claimt. had a Lease of 100 acres at Skeensboro, had it in '72. He had Cleared 14 acres.

He lost 3 Steers, 1 Horse, some furniture, a little farm utensils.

<small>N. C.</small>
900. Claim of LEVI WARNER, late of New Hampshire.

Claimt. was at St. John's in '83.

Is a native of A., lived at New Hampshire, joined Gen. Burg. Served till end of War. Produces his Discharge.

Lost Property in Claremont, New Hamps. Had a small House & Garden given by his Father, given many years ago. Says he came off in the night, left furniture, Weavers Tools, 1 Cow, 1 Heifer, 3 horses. Heard these things were taken by the Committee of the Town.

<small>(63).</small>
JOSEPH MARSH, Wits.:

Knew that Claimt. had a house in Claremont, given him by his Father. When he went to join Burg he left a stock, a Cow, heifer, Hogs, Weavers Tools, &c., thinks the Rebels had them.

<small>N. C.
September 28.</small>

901. Claim of MATTHIAS ROSE, of Albany Co.

Claimt. says he resided at Quebec in the Fall '83.

Says he delivered his Claim to Col. Peters, he was then going home to England. He told Claimt. he was going & would take care of the Claim & promised to lodge it at Home.

Is a native of A. Lived at Saratoga, joined the Brit. in '76. Went with Burg in '77, taken Prisnr. in '81, joined the Brit. again in Cana., joined Jessups Corps. Continued till the Regt. was reduced.

Had 100 acres Lease Land at Saratoga, it was a Lease for 20 years, 20 yrs. before the War. Had Cleared 20 acres, built a house, 5 horses, 6 Cattle, 10 Hogs, furniture, utensils. The Rebels took all these things on their retreat from Burg.

<small>(64).</small>
WM. ROGERS, Wits.

Knew his farm at Saratoga. Remembers him in Possession long before ye War. 15 acres Clear. Knew his Stock, 5 horses,

3 or 4 Cows, 2 young heifers, hogs, furniture, cloathes, utensils, taken when ye rebels retreated. They took all the things that belonged to persons who were with the Brit.

902. Claim of JOHN HOWELL, late of Tryon Co.   N. C.
September 28.

Claimt. says:

He was at Cataraqui in '83. Is a nat. of A. Lived at Johnstown. Joined the Brit. in '77, has served all the War in Sir Johns Regt., 3 yrs. Seargt. Major.

Had 170 acres of Land near Mayfields in Tryon Co. It was a Lease from Abraham Down about 12 years ago, came to Claimt. on his Father's Death, a Lease forever at £5 rent.   A good man.
30 acres were Clear, built a Log House & Barn. Vals. Clear Land £4 York pr. acre.
Lost 1 Heifer, 1 Cow, 7 hogs, Wagon, utensils.

ABIJAH CHRISTIE, Wits.:
Knew Claimt. from near Mayfield. There was a Considerable Clearance. He lived there. His Father lived with him. They had a Considerable Stock. His Father died at Beginning of War. It came to Claimt. on his Father's death.   (65).

903. Claim of JAMES COTTER, late of Albany Co.   N. C.
September 28.

Claimt. says:

He resided at Cot au Lac. A Detachmt. of 1st Battll. was doing duty there. Is a native of Ireland. Came to America 36 yrs. ago. Lived in Johnstown. Came with Sir John to Canada at first. Served all the War.

Had 100 acres Lease Land from Sir Wm. Johnson at £6 per Ann., Lease forever, had it a long while before Sir Wm. J's Death. Had Cleared 30 acres, built a Log house.
2 horses, 2 Cows, 3 yearlings, 5 hogs, furniture, utensils.

Rebels took them when he joined Sir John Johnson.

GEORGE MORDOFF, Wits.:   A good man.
Knew his Place, it was a Lease farm from Sir Wm. J., about 25 acres Clear. He had Cattle & horses on the Place, the Rebels had them.

904. Claim of WM. FAIRFIELD, late of Powlet Township.   September 28.

Claimt. says:

He is a native of A. Resided in Powlet Township, joined the   (66).
Brit. in '78. Served in Jessups Corps all the War.
Produces Strong Certificates to Service & Loyalty from Major Jessup.

No. 1.   had 50 acres in Powlet T. Produces Deed from Sim Sears to Claimt. of 50 acres in Powlet in Considn. £20, '75. It was not Clear when he bought it, 12 or 14 acres Clear, no builds.

No. 2.   This was 50 acres that had belonged to Abner Blanchard. He had mortgaged to one Van Slick for £20. Claimt. had bought it of Blanchard & was to pay off the mortgage of £20.

He had not got a Deed from Blanchard and it appears from several Papers produced that Claimt. was not to have a Deed till he had pd £20 to Van Slick, so that he can have no Claim excep tfor what he had paid Blanchard, which was £30 York.

Claimt. lived on this Lot.

No. 3.   50 acres in do. bought of John Abbot, produces Deed, Considn. £25 in 1776.

The War had begun, but he thought it safer to lay out his money so. 5 acres Clear, 4 withdrawn, 5 withdrawn.

No. 6.   150 acres in Powlet T. bought of Ebenezer Hulbard, produces
(67).   Deed. Considn. 169 Lawful, dated 1777.

No. 7.   Had another Lot of 50 acres bought of Hen. Markes in Powlet Towns., 15 yrs. ago. He bought a whole right for £30, he had parted with all but 50 acres, all this was Wild & Confiscated.

No. 8.   Had also 100 acres bought of Do., this has been sold for Taxes.

Produces full Certificates of Confiscation & Sale of all the above Lands Except No. 8, with Copies of the Deeds of Sale.

He produces a Valuation of his Property by 2 persons in the State of Vermont, both real & personal.

A very good man, be allowed what we can.   Lost 8 Cows, 4 yearlings, 4 horses, 35 Sheep, utensils, furniture. Taken by the American Army when Burgoyne was coming on. He says all Cattle was driven off, but those who were friends to the Americans had the Privilege to get their Cattle again.

BERNABAS HOUGH, Wits.:

Knew Claimts. Est. Knew several Pieces of Land that he had in Poulet Township.

Knew No. 1, 10 acres Clear. Knew No. 2, bought of one Blanchard, 20 acres Clear. No. 3, knew it, it was not much improved. He had other Lots. Wits. knew No. 6, 25 acres Clear.

(68).   Heard of his owning Lands in No. 7. Knew his Stock, agrees with Claimts. acct.

N. C.
September 28.   905. Claim of ELENOR MAYBEE, Widow of Peter Maybee, late of Albany Co.

Claimt. says:

She resided in Sorel in '83 Her Eldest Son, John, is 22 yrs. of age. She is married to Joseph Hoffman. Her Son lives with him.

Her late Husb., Peter, was a native of America, lived at Saratoga, joined the Brit. in '76, joined Col. Jessop. Died in

Canada the Winter of '77. He had been with Burg, served that Campaign. She went to Canada Summer after Husbs. death.

Her Husb. had 150 acres in Duchess Co., he had it by gift from his Father 20 years ago on his marriage. He lived there 4 years. 90 acres Clear, he let it when he went away. She thinks the Rent was £19 per Ann. No. 1.

He went & settled at Saratoga on Lease Land, he had a Lease for 3 Lives 8 or 9 years before the War. He had about 100 acres, rent was £4.10 York after ten years. He had improved 60 acres. Has heard a rebel officer is settled on No. 1. No. 2.

He had 2 good horses, 2 Cows, 2 Calves, 18 Sheep, 16 Hogs, furniture, utensils, Cloathes. Claimt. was in Possession of the Place. All these things were taken from her in Summer '77, taken by the Rebels because her Husband had gone to Canada. (69).

JONAS AMEY, Wits.:
Knew the late Peter Maybee, he joined the Brit. in '76, served in Burg's Campaign, died the Winter after. Knew his farm at Saratoga, it was a Lease farm, 60 acres Clear. He had been there some years before the War. He had a pretty good Stock.

MARTIN HOVER, Wits.:
Knew Peter Maybee. Remembers his coming to Saratoga.

Heard he had left a farm of his own when he came there.

906. Claim of DUNCAN BELL, late of Charlotte Co.   N. C.
                                                                       September 28.
Claimt. says:

He resided at St. John's in '83.
Is a native of Scott. Came to A., lived in Charlotte Co. Joined the Brit. in '78. Served in Rogers Rangers all the War as Seargt.

Had 3 horses lost when he was carrying Genl. Hald. Despatches. Had 2 horses at his Father's at Fort Edward, they were taken by the Rebels in '79. (70).

Had an Ox & 2 Cows at his Father's at the same time. Lost Cloathes & 2 fire locks at his Father's.

WM. BELL, Wits.:
Says he lived at Fort Edward. His Son had 2 horses, an Ox & 2 Cows, they were his property, the Rebels took them, 2 guns & Cloathes, the rebels took them when he went to Canada.

907. Claim of EDWARD CARSCALLEN, late of Charlotte Co.   N.C.
                                                                September 28.
Claimt. says:

He resided at St. Tuse in '83.
Is a native of Ireland. Came to America many years ago. Lived in Camden Dist., joined the Brit. in '76 at Crown Point.

(71).

Carried in 20 men. Served as an officer under Peters, MacKay & Jessup. Served during War.
Had 350 acres Leased Land in Charlotte Co. near Allington, had this Lease in '70, it was a Lease to 10 persons. Claimts. Share, 350 acres, a Lease forever at 6d per acre.
Cleared 50 acres, Log house & barn.
Vals. Clear Land at £3.15 per acre Hal. Crcy. Wild Land at £1 York.
Mr. Duane has got the lands again.
1 yoke Oxen, 3 horses, 1 yoke Steers, 1 Cow, 11 hogs, utensils, Cloathes, furniture Tools, taken by the rebel Army on Burg's coming.

PETER DETLOR, Wits. :

Knew Claimt. Remembers he joined the Brit. with a number of men in '76, served all the War. Knew his Place, he had it some years before the War, 2 or 300 acres, 50 acres Clear. Knew his Stock, 3 horses, & agrees with Claimts. acct.

VALENTINE DETLOR, Wits. :

Knew the farm, 350 acres, he had it 7 years before the War, 50 acres Clear. There were many partners in the Lease originally, but each had taken their share. Agrees in the acct. on the Stock.

N. C.
September 28.

908. Claim of WM. SCHERMERHORN, late of Albany Co.

ELIZ., Widow, appears:

(72).

Says she came to Canada in the fall '83. Her Husb. came to meet her at St. John's. Thinks he came Early in October. They went on her arrival to the River au Chaine & staid there all the Winter. Went thro' Montreal but made no stay.
Her Husb. was at that time almost out of his mind from his Distresses.
Her Husb. was a native of America, lived at Hilberg when Rebel. broke out.

This acct. confirmed by Rev. Mr. Stewart and Sir Jno. Johnson.

Her Husb. was very active from the first in support of the Kings cause. Joined Genl. Burg. He was taken Prisoner after Burg's. Defeat. He was to have carried Despatches from Burg. to Clinton, fell sick & was taken prisonr, kept a Prisoner a twelve month. Got to Canada afterwards. Carried a number of men. The men went into Butler's Rangers.
Her Husb. was to have had a Commission but he never got it. He continued in Canada, died in June last. Left Claimt. his Widow, John, his Eldest Son, only 12 years old & 4 other Children, all living with their Mother.
Her Husb. had 3 farms in Rancellor Manor. These were Leased Lands, Lease forever, thinks the 10th part of Produce was payable for Rent.

He bought the improvemts., there was a Considerable Clearance. All these farms laid together, he had had them for many years.

He had 6 horses, 17 Cattle, 13 Sheep, a good many hogs, a great Quantity of Grain of dif. kinds, furniture, utensils.

Says she was driven from her Place and all these things were destroyed or plundered by the Rebels.

Sir J. Johnson & Revd. Mr. Steward Certified to me strongly as to the Loyalty & Services & Sufferings of the said W. Skermerhorn.

909. WM. BELL, JUR., Charlotte Co. N. C. September 28.

Claimt. says:

He was at St. John's in '83.

Is a native of Scotland. Came young to A. Lived at Fort Edward. Joined the Brit. in '77, served ever since in Rogers Rangers.

Lost 4 horses, 2 Cows, 4 Hogs.

They were at his Father's, they were taken in '77 by the Rebels. They were known to be Claimts., he was driving the 2 cows to Gen. Burg. Army, they were taken by the Rebels.

ADAM WENT, Wits.:

Knew that Claimt. had 4 horses, they were plundered by the rebels, he had 2 Cows.

910. Claim of ADAIM VANT, late of Charlotte Co. N. C. September 28.

Claimt. says:

He resided at La Chine in '83.

Is a native of Germany. Came to A. in 1751, lived in Kingsbury. Joined the Brit. in '79, served all the War.

Had Leased Land, 15 acres in Kingsbury, 1s. per acre rent, most improved, it was a town Lot. He had built the house himself, it was a Lease forever. Vals. it at £100.

3 Cattle, 3 Hogs, utensils, furniture, taken by the rebel Comrs. after Burg's. defeat.

WM. BELL, JUR., Wits.:

Knew the Place, it was a Town Lot, 15 acres, he had built the House. Remembers 2 Cattle. He had good furniture, heard it was taken by the Rebels. Saw his House in Possession of the Rebels. A good man.

911. ELISHA PHILIPS, late of Charlotte Co. N. C. September 28.

Claimt. says he resided at St. John's in '83. Is a native of A. Lived at Kingsb. Joined in '77, served all ye War in Rogers Rangers.

Lost a horse, a yoke of Steers, Grain & Hay cut, taken by the Rebels in '77.

SAML. BROWNSON, Wits.:

Knew that Claimt. had a yoke of Steers & a horse, understood they were taken by the Rebels. He had a farm on shares, he had some Hay, thinks it was taken by Burg's. Army.

N. C.
September 28.

912. GEORGE FINKLE, late of Albany Co.

Claimt. says:

Was at Cataraqui in '83.
Is a native of A. Lived at ———, near Albany, joined in '77, served 4 or 5 years. He had some Lands but not having got his title he made no Claim. Had Stock on this Land.
6 horses, 6 Cattle, 14 Sheep, utensils, good furniture, Cloathes.

A very fair man

The rebel Rangers & rebel Comrs. took them in '77, just after Burg. Defeat. Some were sold at Vendue.

HERCULES CONKRIGHT, Wits.:

Claimt. had some Lands at Pushtain Kiln. He had horses & Cattle, 6 Cattle, 5 Horses, Sheep, a good Stock, lived well.

N. C.
September 28.

913. Claim of HERCULES CONKWRIGHT, Albany Co.

Claimt. says:

He was at Isle au Noix in '83.
Is a native of A., lived in Albany Co., joined in '77, served ever since.

(76).
A good man.

Had Stock on his Father's Land near Pushtain Kiln, 2 horses, 2 Cows, 1 yearling, 4 hogs, utensils.
All these things left with his Mother when he joined the Brit. They were all sold at Vendue.

GEO. FINKLE:

Knew Claimt. had some Stock. Knows that some were sold at Vendue.
His Mother's things & his were sold too. They were sold on acct. of his joining the Brit.

N. C.
September 28.

914. MATHIAS ROSE, Sen., late of Albany Co.

Claimt. says:

Resided at St. Johns in '83.
Is a native of A., lived at Saratoga; joined in '80. Served ever since in Jessup's. Produces discharge.
Had Leased Lands at Saratoga.

No. 1.

100 acres. A Lease for the Life of Rob. Livingston. Had cleared 50 acres. Built a clover house.

No. 2.
(77).

Had a 40 acre Lot, adjoining this was disputed Land. Claimt. took possession of it & cleared 10 acres.
Lost 16 Cattle, of all 4 were oxen, 6 horses, 20 Hogs, 6 sheep, utensils, furniture, cloathes to amt. of £60, taken by the 65a AR.

Rebels when Burg. was surrounded. Took Claimt. a Prisnr. at A good man. same time because he would not join them.
He had 2 Sons in the King's Army.

ELVE SNIDER, Wits.:
Knew Claimt.'s Property. He had considerable improvmts. on his land at Saratoga and a very large stock, 16 head of Cattle, 20 hogs, 6 horses, 6 sheep, utensils, furniture. Knows that all these things were taken by Rebels. She lived at the house at this time.

---

915. JAMES JOHNSON, late of Charlotte Co.   N. C.
Resided at Mashishe. Is a native of Ireland. Came young September 28. to Am.; lived on Artillery Pat.; joined in 77. Served ever since.
Had 125 acres in Artillery Patent. Lease was 999 years at 1s. pr. acre. Took it in '71. Cleared 30 acres. Built a house.
Had 9 Cattle, 2 horses, 5 hogs, furniture & utensils. These A good man. things were taken by the Rebels in '77.
Produces a affidavit from Cyrenens Parks & Saml. Welch, (78). that Claimt. had a farm 30 or 40 acres clear & a good stock.

Claimt. says:
916. VAL. DETLOR, late of Charlotte Co.   N. C.
                                           September 28.
He resided at Carleton Island & Le Chine.
Is a native of Ireland. Came to America in '56. Settled in Camd. Dist.; joined in '76 at Crown Point. Served during War.
Had 312 acres Lease Land in Camd. Dist. They had a Deed of a large Tract of Land amongst 10 of them. Carskallen was one —7 years before the War. They were to have fresh Deeds, each for his own share. They had not got their deeds but they had

each got their own shares laid out.
Claimt's share was 312 acres, 25 acres clear, built a House & barrack.
When Claimt. went away the Rebels turned away his wife & family & so they did to the other Families.
1 yoke oxen, 1 do Steers, 3 Cows, 13 Sheep, utensils, furniture, potatoes, corn in the ground.
Says this is not Vermont; the line runs between Canada & Ashington.

JOHN EMBURY, Wits.:   (79).
Knew Claimt.'s place. He had 16 or 17 acres Clear. He had near 300 acres. He had a yoke of oxen & cattle & sheep, taken by the Rebels on acct. of his having joined the Brit.

Claimt. says:
917. Claim of JOHN EMBURY, late of Charlotte Co.   N. C.

He was in Montreal in '83. Says he sent his Claim by September 28. Major Leake. Gave it him in the Fall.

Is a native of Ireland. Came young to Am. Lived in Canada Dist.; joined in '76. Served some time. Served in '77. Was afterwards in Engineer's Department.

Had 125 acres of Lease Land in Camden Dist., part of the Tract of which Detlor & Carskallen had some share. His share was only 125.

Had 15 acres Clear. Built Log house. Yoke of Steers, 1 Cow, 5 Sheep, 1 Mare. Taken by the Rebels.

Saved furniture & utensils.

VAL. DETLOR, Wits.:

Knew Claimt.'s place. He had 125 acres of the Leased Land for his share, 15 acres Clear. Agrees in acct. of Stock.

N. C.
September 28.
(80).

918. JAMES MACKIM, late of Albany Co.

Claimt Says:

Was at Sorel in '83. Native of Ireland. Came to A. in '74. Settled in Bennington; joined in '76. Served all the War.

Claimt, a drunken Irishman, very little to be allowed.

Had 30 acres of Land in Wilson's Patent; bought in '74; gave £10. Cleared 5 acres. 1 Cow, furniture, utensils, left behind him when he joined the Brit.

JOHN EMBURY, Wits.:

Says Claimt. had some Lands in Wilson's Patent. Does not know how much. It was bought before the War.

EDWARD CARSKALLEN, Wits.:

Says Claimt. possessed 30 acres in Wilson's Patent, before the War. He lived upon it & built a house. Does not know ye stock.

N. C.
September 28.

919. ELIZ. CLINE, late of Tryon Co.

Claimt. Says:

She was at Cataraqui in '83. Is a native of Germany. John Cline was her first Husb. Lived at German Flats. He was very Loyal. He was known to be so. Had been fined, but he could not carry arms, being infirm. He was killed by the Rebel Indians because he would no go to fight against the King. Left 6 Daughters, 5 of them are here. Soon after his death his wife & daughters came to Canada.

(81).

Good people. are told to send affidavit of Husb. loyalty and property. Their wits. was ill.

He had 100 acres of Land. Took it up 21 years ago. 75 acres cleared & fenced. A frame house & Barn, 5 Cows, 3 yearlings, 4 mares, 2 wagons, utensils, tools. She left all these things when she came away within the Brit. Lines. She would not stay with the Rebels.

She is now married to John Nicholas.

N. C.
September 28.

920. JOHN HOUGH, Albany Co.

He was at Cataraqui in '83. Is a native of Germany. Lived at Johnstown. Joined in '76; was prisoner, then joined Sir John's Corps. Served all the War.

He had some Lands but had no lease. Had some stock. 4 horses, 2 Cows, 5 Sheep, 15 hogs. The Rebels took them after he joined the Brit.

921. WILLIAM PRINDLE, late of Albany Co.   N. C.
September 28.

Claimt. Says:

He was at St. John's in '83; is a nat. of A. Lived at Skeensboro. When Burg. first came to Skeensboro joined Burg. Afterwards served in Major Roger's Rangers 4 years. Produces his Discharge.

Had a Lease of 111 acres in Skeensboro forever, paying 1s. pr. acre. 30 acres Clear. Log house. Lost 2 Oxen, 1 Bullock, 2 horses. Had let his 2 oxen to two people of whom he could never get them. 1 horse had for acct. of King's Army by Genl. Skeen., the other horse taken by the Rebels, 10 hogs taken by the Rebels.   (82).

After being driven from Skeensboro he got to Fort Edward & had some other stock. All that he had saved.

3 Horses, Wagon, Cow, 2 yearlings, furniture, utensils, Corn in Stack, Hay, 6 Hogs.

Most of these were destroyed at Fort Edward by orders of Major Carleton in the year 1780 or left when they went away.

JAMES JACKSON, Wits.:

Claimt., a lease farm at Skeensboro. 12 acres clear.
He had a Stock at Fort Edward. The rebels had some.

922. JOSEPH PRINDLE, late of Albany Co.   N. C.
September 28.

Claimt Says:

He was at St. Johns in '83. Is a Nat. of A. Lived in Skeensboro; joined in '80. Served all the War. Produces his discharge.

Had stock at Seth Sherard's house at Skeensboro. 1 horse, 2 Swine, tools, corn, hay. When he went off with Major Carleton left these things behind.   (83).

923. TIMOTHY PRINDLE, late of Albany Co.   N. C.
September 28.

Claimt. was at St. John's in '83. Joined the Brit. in '80. Served all the War.

Claimt. resided at Kingsboro. Had a stock on some lands that happened to be vacant.

2 horses, 3 cows, 4 swine, 6 small do., tools.

When Major Carleton left Skeensboro these things were left behind, part destroyed. The Rebels had 1 mare. Thinks most of the things were destroyed by Major Carleton's Party before they retreated.

WM. PRINDLE, Wits.:
Confirms this acct. of his Bros.' stock.

N. C September 28. The acct. of these 3 Bros. & Father seems true. but Q. whether we can allow for losses which happened from Major Carleton's retreat. They seem good men. N. C. September 29.	924. JOEL PRINDLE, late of Albany Co. Timothy Prindle, son, attends. His Father is very old & infirm, not able to attend. He was at St. Johns in '83. He came in ye year '80. Joined Major Carleton. Left his property at Keensboro & Kingsbury. A quantity of wood, 3 Cows, 4 Horses, Hogs, furniture, utensils, cloaths. It was impossible to move the things. They had only 1 Wagon for 5 families. 925. ISAAC VAN ALSTINE, late of Pens. Claimt. resided at Cote de Lac in '83. Is a Nat. of A——. Resided at Susquehana when Rebellion broke out. Joined in '78. Served in Sir John's Regt. all the War. Had 300 acres Land Susquehana, 5 years before the War; had no deed. Cleared 4 or 5 acres. Built a house. Lost 1 horse, driven off by the Rebels, furniture, utensils very little.
(84).	ISAAC LARRAWAY, Wits. : Claimt. had cleared 4 acres. He had been in Possession before the War. Had a mare. He had a Plough & harrow & a little furniture.
N. C. Seplember 29. (85). V. Perry's claim. A good man.	926. DAVID SHOREY, late of Charlotte Co. Claimt. says he was at Carleton Island in '83. Is a Nat. of A——; lived in Vermont on Otter Creek; joined Burg. Served in the 84th 8 years. Produces his discharge. Had 50 acres bought in partnership with Robt. Perry, vi. his claim. Produces the Deed bought in '72. Built a house, 25 acres of Claimt.'s share clear. Produces Certif. of Confiscation and of sale, 1 Cow, 4 yearlings, 14 sheep, hogs, furniture, utensils. Taken by the Rebels after he joined Burg. Produces an afft. from Robt. Perry, that Claimt. had 25 acres clear, & the stock above mentioned.
N. C. September 29.	927. DAVID HARTMAN, late of Albany Co. Claimt. Says : He is a native of Germany. Came to A—— many years ago. Lived in Albany Co.
  A good man. (86).	Joined Burg. Served all the War in Jessup's Corps. Had 150 acres at Tomparing, a Lease for 15 years for nothing. then to have it forever, paying 1 Bushel of wheat pr. ann. Had the Lease 6 or 7 years before ye War. 20 acres Clear; built House & Stables. His wife was turned off in '78. 4 horses, 4 cattle, 8 sheep, 16 hogs, furniture, utensils, sold at vendue by the Rebels.

LIEUT. HOWARD, Wits.:
Says Claimt. had a good farm, at least 20 acres Clear. Seemed to have a good stock. He is a good man. stock.

928. JOHN MACPHERSON, late of Albany Co.   N. C.

Claimt. was at Mashish in '83.   September 29.
Nat. of Scot. Came to A. in '74. Settled at Saratoga; joined the Brit. in '76. Served all the War in Jessup's.
Had 140 acres of leased Land at Saratoga from one Beakman. Seems a good man but little Had the Lease in '75 for 3 yrs. from Capt. Drummond. The can be allowed. Stock was Capt. Drummond's but he was answerable for it. A yoke of oxen, 3 cows, & 3 calves. All the furniture was Claimt.'s own property.

Affidait of Capt. Peter Drummond, dated 19th May, 1788, stating Claimt.'s property to a considerable amt. Improvements & stock.

929. JACOB DIAMOND, late of Albany Co.   N. C.
    September 29th
Claimt. Says:
He resided at St. Johns in '83.
Is a Nat. of A. Lived in Albany Co. Joined Burg. in 77. Served to end of the War in Major Rogers' Corps.
Had a Lease of 100 acres at Saratoga at 1s. pr. acre. Had it long before ye War. Had cleared 16 acres.   (87).
Had a yoke of oxen, 1 Cow, farming utensils; left them at home; ye Rebels took them.
1784.
MR. ROBINS, Wits.:
Knew his place. He had 5 or 6 acres clear. He had a yoke Very little. of oxen & cow, farm utensils.

930. KENNETH FRASER, late of Albany Co.   N. C.
    September 29th
Claimt. Says:
He was in the Hospital at Quebec; broke his arm in '83. Had sent a Claim to Major Jessup that Fall to be sent to Eng. He promised he would take it home.

Is a Nat. of Scot. Came 32 yrs. ago to America. Lived at Fort Edward. Joined in '77. Served till end of War. Produces Discharge.
Had his allowance for last War, 50 acres near Fort Edward. Cleared 25 acres & good meadow besides. Had a house there. Had 3 horses, 6 cows, 16 hogs, 4 sheep, flax 100 Wt., 50 Bushels A good man. corn, utensils, furniture. The Rebels took them from his wife. Pretty good stock.
Had a son killed by the Rebels.

931. AMOS LUCAS, late of Kingsbury.   N. C.
    September 29th
SAMUEL BROWNSON, JUN., who has married Susanna, widow   (88). of Amos Lucas, deceased, appears.

Says Amos Lucas came to Canada in the Fall '83. He was not within the Lines during the War, but was desired to stay by Dr. Smith, for the purpose of forwarding expresses. **Came to St. Johns in the Fall '83. Came from thence to Cataraqui.** He lived near Fort Edward. Had been employed in forwarding expresses & getting intelligence ever since Burg's time. He had a son in the Army. Staid by Dr. Smith's particular request.

He sold his Lands.
Lost 4 Oxen, 5 cattle, 10 sheep, 24 hogs, utensils, furniture. These things were plundered at different Times, & likely to have been by both Armies. He lost some of the things when the Americans retreated on Burg's approach.
Produces an affidt. from Elisha Philips that Amos Lucas had the stock above mentioned.
Feby. 25th produces Certificate from Thos. Sherwood that Claimt. was desired to stay to receive & procure intelligence by him from Dr. Smith.

(89 .

N. C.
September 29th

932. SIMON SWARTZ, late of Tryon Co.

Claimt. Says:
He was in Sir J. first Battn. at Montreal. Gave in Claim to Major Guy, his commanding officer, before the Regt. was disbanded.
There was an order in the Regt. for them to give in their claims.
Is a Nat. of A——; lived in Tryon Co.; joined Sir John at Oswego. Came thro' the woods with 50 or 60 men under Agitant Miller. Thinks in '76. Served till end of War. Produces his Discharge which says he had served 6 yrs. & ½.

His mother came from New York in '83.
His father, Henry, had a House and 2 Lots of Land in New York. He died in New York Govt. He never came within the Lines. On his death this place came to his mother.
He has now an elder Bro. in ye States and a Sister married to Capt. Grass. Household furniture at Bowman's Creek, at Capt. Grass' House, belonging to his mother taken by the Rebels.
Capt. Grass Says.
Henry Swarts died without a Will, so that the mother cd. have nothing but for Life in the Premises.
The eldest son is in ye Colonies. The mother came within the Lines, New York, in June '83 & from thence to Canada. She was at Sorell in '83. Says the mother would not come in before the House & builds. were burnt, 2 Tenements, stable & shop, 2 Lots worth 200.
The mother had effects at Witnesses house which were sold at vendue. Thinks to amt. of £50 York. They were taken with witnesses effects & sold at vendue, about the year '80.
The Father had provided for the eldest son in his life time.

(90).

A good man.

Told the rest of the children to be easy. What was left should belong to them. There is only a brother & sister left, besides ye eldest. The effects at Witnesses house had belonged to the old man.

933. JOHN MACKENNY, late of Charlotte Co.   N. C.
Claimt. Says: September 29th

He was at Lechine in '83.
Is a Nat. of Scot. Came last War to A——. Lived in Charlotte Co. when Rebellion broke out. He joined in '77. Served till end of the War in Jessup's Corps. Produces discharge. Had 99 acres Leased Land at White Creek; the Land belonged to Delancey. Rent was 1s. pr. acre. Lease forever. Had it 7 years before ye War. 50 acres clear. Built house & hovel; 11 Cattle, 1 mare, 4 sheep, 8 hogs, furniture, utensils. The rebels took them from his wife, because he went to the Brit.

(91).
A good man.

PETER MACDOUGAL, Wits. :
Knew Claimt.'s farm. Hhe had a Lease from Delancey. Had been 6 or 7 years on the place. Had Considerable Clearance. He had considerable stock. He was in a prosperous way.

934. PETER MACPHERSON, late of Albany Co.   N. C.
Claimt. Says: September 29th

He was at Yamoski in '83. Is a Nat. of Scot. Came to Am. in '75. Lived at Balstown. Joined the Brit. in '81. Served till end of War in Jessup's Corps. Produces Discharge.

Had agreed to purchase 112 acres in Balstown in 1775; was to pay 15sh. pr. acre. The War beginning they could not make out a title, so he had not a deed and paid nothing. He lived there & cleared 25 acres.

He had 3 Cows, 3 oxen, 1 yearling, furniture, utensils, cloathes. Left them behind in '81. Had sold 2 of these oxen & 1 Cow. The other ox had been taken by some friends who were going to the Brit. so that he left very little behind him.

(92).

N. B.—Says he came to America at Time of Bunker's Hill fight.

ABRAHAM CONKRIGHT, Wits.
Knew Claimt.'s place. He had cleared 25 acres. The Rebels took 1 Cow, 2 yearlings, grain, utensils.

935. LYDIA VAN ALSTINE, Wid. of James Van Alstine, late of Tryon Co.   N. C.
September 29th

ISAAC CROUTHER, present Husb. of Lydia Van Alstine apears.

Says his wife was at Montreal a year before the Regiment was discharged. Her first Husb. was in Sr. John's 1st Battal.

(93).

Died during War. She sent a Claim by Capt. Leake in '83. James Van Alstine left 5 children. They appear to have been all under age in '83. They are all here. The eldest son Lambert served in Sir J. Regt. as Fifer. Jas. Van Alstine had served all the War in Sir J. Johnson's Regt. Lived on Susquehana. Had Lands on Susquehana.

ISAAC VAN ALSTINE, Wits. :

Jas. Van Alstine had cleared 10 acres, built an house, had 2 Cows, 1 mare, the rebels took them.

N. C.
September 29th

936. JOHN WISS, late of Albany.

Claimt. was at La Chine in '83.
Is a Nat. of A——; lived in Albany; joined the Brit. in '80. Served till the end of War in Jessup's Corps.

And Coopers.

A good man.

Had some Lease Lands near Albany. 150 acres, lease for 10 years. Had cleared 11 acres. There were buildings. Went on in beginning of Rebellion; bought the improvmts.; pd. £25 York.
5 Cattle, 12 hogs, furniture, carpenters tools, & farming tools, taken by the Rebels, because he would not join them.
Produces a Receipt of 100 Dollars for a fine in '80.

N. C.
September 29th
(94).

937. JOHN MACDOUGAL, late of Charlotte Co.

Says he was at Quebec till Oct., then went to Mashish.
Is a natie of A——; resided in Charlotte Co.; joined Burg. Served till end of War in Jessup's Regt.
Had some lands which he sold.

A good man.

Had a stock. 6 Cattle, 3 horses, 18 hogs, furniture, cloathes, utensils. Rebels took them all, left nothing, made his mother deliver up his cloathes. Held Bayonet to her Breast.

PETER GILCHRIST, Wits. :

Knew Claimt's stock. 3 Cows, one or two yearls, 2 horses, hogs.

N. C.
September 29th

938. GEO. CHARTRES, late of Albany Co.

Claimt. Says:

Was at the River La Chine in '83.
Is a native of A——: lived at Clavinook, Albany Co.,; joined Burg. Served till end of War in Jessup's.
Had Leased Land in Rancellor's Manor. 100 acres paying 10 lbs. of produce, 20 acres clear; built a framed house. Vals. improvmts. at £300.
3 Cows, 1 Horse, 7 Hogs, utensils, furniture.

(95).

Claimt. was in Albany Gaol & in Irons. Some of the things taken there, some after he joined Burg.

A good man. Had good improvmts. Lieut Sharpe & Major Van Alstine are to be his Evd. at Montreal. Says Lieut. Sharpe had 2 or 300 acres. Thinks 100 acres clear; a good storehouse.—
Marginal note.

939. JAMES McTAGGART, late of Albany Co. N. C.
September 29th

Claimt. Says:

He was at Cataraqui in '83. Is a Nat. of Scot. Came in '74. Came to New York. Lived on the Mohawk River. Joined the Brit. in '80. Served till end of War. Produces Discharge.

Lost 1 ox, 4 horses, 75 Bushels wheat, near 100 oats, 4 tons hay.

They were on a Leased farm of Claimt.'s on Mohawk. They were taken by the Rebels after he went off becs. he went to join the Brit.

940. NICHOLAS PETERSON, JUN., late of Bergen Co., N. Jersey. N. C.
September 29th

Claimt. was at Sorel. Is a Nat. of A———. Lived in Bergen Co. Went within the Brit. Lines to New York in '76. Produces Certificates of his having taken Oath of Allegiance Sig'd (96). Tryon, 23rd Jany., 1777. Served at the out Posts with other Loyalists under Major Ward. Was at the blockhouse. Continued there till Evacuation.

Lost 1 Cow, 1 horse, 1 mare, some trifles of cloathing. These things were at his Father's, taken after he went to New York, because he had gone to join the Brit.

He had a Boat, which was cut to pieces by the Rebels because he used it for carrying Provisions to the King's Army in 1776.

CHRISTIAN PETERSON, Wits.:

Claimt. went to New York. Went with the Loyalists. Was at the Block House in Bargen Wood. Lost a Cow, Horse, Mare, Boat, Cloathing, taken by the Rebels. Some at his Father's after he went to New York, because Claimt. was friendly to A good man Govrnt.

941. NICH. PETERSON, SEN., of Bergen Co. N. C.
September 29.

Nich. Peterson, Jr., says his Father is very old & not able to walk. Says his Father was at Sorell in '83.

He lived atBergen Co. He went within the Brit. Lines about '78. He was always a Loyalist. He was so plagued that he was forced to come within ye lines. There continued till they came away.

He had some lease Lands in Bergen Co. He had been settled upon them 3 years before the War; between 15 or 20 acres (97). clear; built a clover house and barrick.

CHRISTIAN PETERSON, Wits.:

His Father had 20 acres clear. Remembers 2 horses & a Cow; Cloathes taken by Rebels. He left some furniture when he came to New York.

N. C.
September 29.

942. PETER MACDOUGAL, late of Charlotte Co.

Claimt. was at Mashishe. Is a Nat. of Scot. Came to A. after last War. Lived at White Creek. Went on Scouts with Dr. Adams. Came into Canada in '78. He was driven off his Farm because he would not join ye Rebels.

Had 100 acres in Rupert. Bought 2 Soldiers Lots after last War. Had not cleared any part. Lived on Delancey's Land at White Creek. He had 99 acres lease forever at 1s. pr. acre. Had been 6 years upon it.
Had cleared 30 acres. Had built a Clover House. Had 7 Cattle & 1 Calf; little utensils. Taken by Rebel Captn. because he would not join ye Rebels.

JOHN MACKINNEY, Wits.:

(98).
Claimt. was always a true Loyalist. He had a Lease from Delancey, 99 acres, on White Creek. Had a considerable clearance. He had 4 cows, 2 steers. Taken away by the Rebels.

N. C.
September 29.

943. LEWIS HICKS, late of Albany Co.

Claimt. says: He lived at Mashishe in '83.
Is a Nat. of A. Lived at Saratoga. Joined Burg. Served till end of War in Major Jessup's R. Had a Lease 100 acres at Saratoga. Lease for 3 Lives. They had not got the Lease, but went upon ye lands. Cleared 8 acres. Had 2 Cows, 2 Heif., 6 Hogs, furniture; all taken by the Rebels in '77.

GILBERT STORMS, Wits.:

A good man.
Very little loss.
Knew Claimt's farm. He had cleared 6 or 7 acres. He had 2 Cows, 2 Heifs., 5 or 6 Hogs, some furniture. Thinks the Rebels nad them.

N. C.
September 29.

944. GILBERT STORMS, late of Albany Co.

Claimt. was at Mashishe in '83.
Is a Nat. of A. Lived at Saratoga. Joined Burg. Served to the end of the War in Jessup's Had 100 acres Land. Had cleared 30 acres. Had built a House. Had yoke of oxen, 2 cows, 1 horse. The Rebels took them, because he went into the Enemies Lines. They took his furniture & utensils.

(99).

LEWIS HICKS, Wits.:

A gocd man.
Knew Storms' farm. He had a Lease of 100 acres, 30 clear. Had built a House, a yoke of Cattle, 2 Cows, 1 horse, 2 or 3 yearlings, furniture, utensils, taken by the Rebels because he was in the King's Army.

945. MARKS SNEIDER, late of Albany Co. N. C.
September 29.

Claimt. says he was at Yamaska. Is a Nat. of A. Lived at Saratoga. Joined Burg. Afterwards served with Jessup till end of War. Had 100 acres Leased Land at Saratoga, 6 acres clear. Had built a House, 2 steers, 3 Cows, 2 horses, 8 hogs, utensils, furniture, tools, cloathes.

Continentals took them, because he was a Tory.

SIMON SNIDER, Wits.:

Claimt. had a farm at Saratoga. Had cleared 6 acres. Had 1 mare, 2 cows, 8 hogs, tools, very valuable, farming utensils, furniture; taken because he was gone to Canada.

946. JAMES ROBINS, late of Albany Co. N. C.
September 1.

Claimt. Says:

He was at the Isle au Noix in '83. Sent a Claim by Capt. Leake & agn. by Capt. Gumersal to ——— & to Hal. (100).

Is a native of England; has been 25 years in A.; resided near Albany. Joined the Brit. in '77. Served ever since. Lieut. in Jessup's Corps. Has ½ pay.

Had a farm in Rancellor's Manor. It was a Lease for 3 Lives, his own & 2 Childn., at Rent of 14 bushels of wheat pr. ann. Had cleared 10 acres. Built a framed house & barn.

Had 3 Cows, 8 Hogs. Just before he joined Burg. a party pursued him because he had been employed in raising men. He had actually engaged about 60. He mustered 47 in the Camp.

When the party pursued him to his house they plundered everything, took or destroyed all his furniture, cloathes for himself & family, Wheat 80 Bush., 60 Bush. Flaxseed, some Plate &

Mon., all his Cattle. They took everything. His furniture was new & pretty good, Cloathes very good, part intended for sale, Worth £118 York at least. Had laid in a stock, imagining things would be dear.

A good man, had a considerable stock of movables and he lodged at his house.

JACOB DIAMOND, Wits.:

Knew Claimt.'s Farm at Saratoga. He had considerable improvements. He had some cows, his house was well furnished, he kept a store & was in good circumstances. One Capt. White lived in his house lately. He was a Rebel Capt. (101).

JOHN DUSENBURY, Wits.

Knew Claimt.'s Farm. He had 8 or 10 acres clear. He had a good house well furnished. His furniture was new & very good. He kept a store; thinks there was a considerable stock in it for cloathing. He had Cattle & Horses. Was in good circumstances.

He has the general Char. of a good man, and a man who has suffered greatly. He nearly lost his life by the Oneida Indians friends of the Americans.

N. C.
September 30.

947. JOHN KELLER, late of Albany Co.

Was at Oswego in '83. Is a Nat. of A. Lived on Hoosick River; joined Gel. Burg. Served during War in Sir John's 2nd Batal.

Had 100 acres on Hoosick River. He went & settled upon it.

Had no Deed.

Cleared 8 acres. Had a house built, cost £12. Lost a mare & colt, 1 acre corn planted. The Rebel army took the mare & Colt at time of Burg's. Acre of corn was destroyed by Rebels.

CHRISTIAN KELLER, Wits.:

Father and son seem good people. Very little loss.

Claimt. had 100 acres. Cleared 8 acres. Had a good house. Lost a mare & nice colt. The rebels took them. An acre of corn was destroyed by rebels.

N. C.
September 30.

948. GARNET DINGMAN, late of Albany Co.

Claimt. was at Cataraqui in 83.

(102).

Nat. of A. Lived at Warenbush on the Mohawk. Joined the Brit in '81. Served in Sir John's 2nd Batal., to the end of the War.

Had 160 acres on the Susquehana. No deed; took it 4 yrs. bef. ye War. Cleared 20 acres. Went from thence to Warensbush, after the Indians had been on the Susquehana. Took 50 acres there; was 2 yrs. there. Must have been in '78. When he came into Canada in '81. Left a stock at Warensbush, 2 horses, 2 cows, 5 sheep, 10 hogs, utensils, furniture. All taken from his wife after he went away.

JOHN WOODCOCK, Wits.:

Knew Claimts. Place on Susquehana, had Considerable Clearance, had settled 3 years before ye War. Went to Warrens bush. When he went away in '81 he left his stock in Witness' Custody, a Mare & Colt, 1 Cow & 1 Heifer, 5 Hogs, 7 Sheep.

His furniture was taken from his House. His Wife was Stript of every thing. The Stock was taken from Wits. house.

N. C.
September 30.

949. JOHN WOODCOCK, late of Albany Co.

Claimt. was at St. Johns in '83. Came to Canada, May, '83. Never was within the Lines during the War. Lived on the Susquehana. Moved to Warrins bush in 1779, there continued till '81.

(103).

Had assisted Loyalists to get away. He had a Son, Bros. & Son in Law in the King's Army.

Was turned off from Warrens bush in '81. Produces order for his Departure as being an Enemy to the States, Signed G. Putnam, in '81.

Had 400 acres on Susquehana, on the East Branch of Susquehana under York Govnt., bought of Banyard £40 per 100 acres, says he pd. for them. Cleared 40 acres. Lost some Cattle at Susquehana, 1 ox, 1 Heif., 2 Sheep, 2 Hogs, taken by the King's Party. Lost some furniture then.

Took a Lease in '79 for 6 yrs. at Warrns bush, paying 1-3 part of Produce, was driven from this in '81, lost Horse, 12 Sheep, Grain gathered & grain in the ground.

EVE PINSET, Wits.:

Knew his Place at Susquehana, 40 acres Clear. He helped Loyalists with Provisions. Had a good Stock at Susquehana.

JOHN CORNELIUS, Wits.:

Knew Claimt. farm held under Banyard, 20 Clear. Had a good Stock. He supported Loyalists & Spies & Scouts.

GARRET DINGMAN, Wits.: (104).

Claimt. had a large Stock then. Was reckoned a Loyalist. Was driven off on acct. of his Loyalty.

950. OWEN MCGRATH, late of Tryon Co.   N. C.
September 30.

Claimt. says he was at Oswego in '83.

Is a nat. of Am. Lived at Tryon, joined in '80, served till end of War.

Had Possession of some Land with a Lease, had 2 Cows, 1 Mare & Colt, 6 Sheep, utensils, grain in the ground. After he went away all was taken from ye family.

JOHN WOODCOCK, Wits.:   Shabby evid.

Heard Claimts. effects were taken after he left his Place.

951. JOHN CORNELIUS, late of Albany Co.   N. C.
September 30.

Claimt. was at Oswego & Cataraqui in '83. Is a nat. of A. Lived at Susquh., joined Genl. Burg. served to end of the War. Prisnr. part of the time.

Had 100 acres on Susquehana, was to give £40 pr. 100 acres in 10 yrs., had 16 acres Clear. Lost 1 horse, 2 Cows, 1 Heif., 8 Hogs. The rebels had them.

JOHN WOODCOCK, Wits.:

(105). Claimt. had 16 acres Clear on Susquehana. He joined King. Speaks of horse, 2 Cows & 8 Hogs & Heifer.

N. C.
September 30.

952. JOHN PENCEL, late of Tryon Co.

Claimt. says he was at Mashish in '83. Is a nat. of Germany. Came young to Am., resided on the Susquehana, he died 8 or 9 in Buttlrs Rangers.

His Father had 1,000 acres on Susquehana, he died 8 or 9 years ago. Claimt. had one Elder who was a Soldier with the Americans, died after his Father, killed in action. Left Sons, who are of course heirs. Says his Father had given him this land by Writing 8 years before his death & Claimt. was in Pos-

session. Says he went to ye place a year before his Father. His Father was then living on the Delaware. Came from thence to Susquehana. 6 acres clear, built a small house, 12 Sheep, 2 Cattle, 5 horses, household goods & furniture & farming utensils, all taken by the Indians. His house was burnt & his Deeds & papers destroyed.

No evidence.
(106).

His Father took up the land of Pens. Govnt. 20 years ago. No part was Cleared till Claimt. returned there himself. Refers himself to Capt. Caldwell.

N. C.
September 30.

953. EVA MACNUT, late of Tryon Co., Widow of James Macnut.

Claimt. says she now is Wife of John Pencel. She was at Mashishe in '83.

Her first Husband, Jas. Macnut, was nat. of A. Lived on Susquehana. Her Husb. had engaged to serve in Sir John's 2 Batallion in '78. He gave in his name to the Seargnt to serve. He had come into Canada & meant to join, he died in '79, Mashishe, left a Son now with Claimt. 14 yrs. of age.

He had 300 acres on Susquehana of Banyard & Wallis, was to have paid in 10 years, had not paid. Cleared 20 acres.

Lost 3 horses, 5 Sheep, 5 Hogs, furniture, Cloathes. The rebel Indians took them or killed them. Her Father, Groddus Dingman, was driven into Canada as a Loyalist — Died there in '82. He had some Stock on his farm at Susquehana which was taken or killed. She is entitled only to a share of Father's Estate. She has 5 Bros. living.

Her Mother died at Mashisho. Claimt. is entitled to the Cloathes & effects which she lost at Susquehana by the Rebels.

(107).

JOHN WOODSTOCK, Wits.:

Shal by case.

Knew James Macnut, had 20 acres clear on Susquehana, 3 horses, 5 Sheep, 5 hogs, furniture, & his Stock was taken by the

Americans. Knew Groddus Dingman, he came into Canada on acct. of his Loyalty, he had 3 horses, 1 Bull, 5 Sheep, 5 hogs, taken by the enemy.

Further Evidence in Case of JOHN PENCEL.

PETER WARTMAN, Wits:.

Knew Claimt. Remembers his living on the Susquhana, his Father & Mother lived with him, does not know what Land they had. There was a Cornfield. These were disputed Lands. Wits. thought it ye Father's Land.

954. SIMON SNIDER, late of Albany Co.   N. C.
September 30.

Claimt. was at Mashishe in '83.

Is a nat. of A. Lived at Saratoga. Joined the Brit. '77. Served till end of the War.

No. 1. Had 100 acres at Fort Edward. Produces Deed from John Lydons to Claimt. of 100 acres on East side of Hudson River, Cond. to Clear 15 acres then to pay 5 Shil. Rent within 20 years, dated 1753. Says he gave £50 York for it.

He built a house & Cleared 30 acres. It has been sold by Kyler, who claims it as it seems under Lydons, or disputes his title.

Vals. Clear Land at ½ Joe per acre.   (108).

No. 2. Had a farm also at Saratoga, had it 4 years before ye War from Lawyer Smith, had no Lease, cleared 30 acres. built a Log house & Barn, 4 horses, 2 Cows, 2 yoke oxen. 2 Calves. 8 hogs, Grain, dift. kinds in the Stack. Rebels took them after Burg. furniture, utensils.

The Corn taken by one of the Rebel Commrs.

GILBERT STORMS, Wits:.

Knew No. 2, remembers Claimt. in Possession of it, he cleared about 20 acres, he had a Considerable Stock. Heard of his having other Lands.

JONAS AMEY, Wits.:

Knew his Lands on Hudson River, he lived there before he came to Saratoga.

955. Case of JONAS AMEY, late of Albany Co.   N. C.
September 30.

Claimt. resided at Mashishe. Is a nat. of A., lived at Saratoga. Joined in '76, has served the whole War. Was a guide for Gen. Burg.

Had 190 acres Lease Land taken 10 years before the War. Lease for 3 Lives, his own, his Daughter & Mrs. Blaker at 1s. per acre. 60 acres Clear, 2 Log houses & one Barn.

3 horses, 1 Colt, 1 Cow, 1 Bull, 5 Sheep, 20 Hogs, Weavers Loom & Tackling, utensils & furniture. Left all these things when he went away, they were chiefly plundered by Scouts.

MARTIN STOVER:

(109). Knew the Place, he had 60 acres Clear. Knew his Stock, Cows, horses, Hogs, furniture, Tools, utensils, taken away by the rebels.

N. C. 956. MARTIN STOVER, late of Albany Co.
September 20.

Claimt. says he was at Mashishe in '83.

Is a nat. of A., lived at Saratoga, joined at first, served up to end of War.

Had 190 acres Leased Land for 3 Lives at 1s. per acre, Clear-
A good man. ed 63 acres.

1 Cow, 2 ox, 1 Heif., 1 Bull, 4 horses, 8 Sheep, 6 hogs. The rebels had them all in '77.

---

rebels had them all in '77 & all his furniture & utensils.

JONAS AMEY, Wits.:

Knew Stovers Place, 190 acres, 60 acres Clear, horses, Cattle. Agrees with Claimts. acct. of moveables.

N. C. 957. NICHOLAS AMEY, late of Albany Co.
September 30.

Claimt. says he resided at Mashishe in '83.

Is a nat. of A., lived at Saratoga, joined at first, has served all the War.

Had 300 acres Leased Land, had them 8 years before the War. Lease was for 3 Lives at 1s. pr. acre. Had Cleared 60
(110). acres, a Log house & builds.
A good man. 3 horses, 8 horned Cattle, 20 Hogs. Left them when he went away. Thinks they were plundered.

Tools, furniture & utensils also plundered.

GILBERT STORM, Wits.:

Knew Claimts. Place, he had about 50 acres Clear, he had a large stock, left it behind when he went away. The Rebels took it.

October 2. 958. SARAH BUCK, Widow of Bisn. Buck, late of Vermont.

Claimt. says she was at St. John's in '83. Staid there all winter.

66a AR.

Her late Husb. Bun Buck was a nat. of A., lived at Pownal. He joined in '77, he served with Sir John till his Death, died in '80. He had Lands in Pownal, cannot say how much, thinks 50 acres, got it in the first of the War. 20 acres Clear.

2 Cows, a yoke of oxen, 2 horses, little Cloathes, Grain reaped, taken by the Rebels after her Husb. had left home in order to join the Brit. Her Son also joined ye Army, he was killed by the Rebels. Left 3 Children who are now with Claimt. **Refers** to Capt. Anderson. (111).

959. DEBORAH MACARTHUR, formerly Tuttle. N. C.

She was at St. John's in '83. Is a nat. of A. First Hub. October 3. was Elisha Tuttle. Never came within ye Lines. She & her oldest Son by Tuttle Came into Canada in the Winter '77. Her Son Andrew served on board the Ships on the Lakes. **She came** into the Lines because she would not stay with the Rebels.

Her Husb. had 100 acres. Produces Deed from ———— of 100 acres in Budport in the year 1777 in Consid. £35. Husb. built house on the Place. Garden destroyed by Brit. Army.

---

taken by Indians & Sailors.

Produces Genl. ———— receipt for Do., 2 Calves & 2 hogs taken by Indians & Sailors.

Furniture & utensils taken by rebels & Brit. Army.

960. CHS. MACARTHUR, late of Albany. N. C.
October 3.

Was at St. John's in '83. Is a nat. of America, lived in Albany Co., joined the Brit. in N. York in '76, has served till end of War in Major Rogers.

Had Improvemts. on 50 acres in Kinderhook, had a Lease for 20 years, had Cleared 6 acres, had ye land 2 years before ye War. (112).

Lost 1 horse, taken when he went to N. Y. by a rebel. Left 5 Cows, 10 Sheep, 14 hogs, 2 Mares, left on his farm when he went away.

961. SEX FLETCHER, late of Albany. N. C.
October 3.

Claimt. says he was at Yamaska in '83. Discharged in Lachine.

Nat. of Germ. Been 30 years in Am., lived on Mohawk River, joined in '77, served ever since. Produces his Discharge.

Had a Lease of 100 acres between himself & Bro. 16 years ago. Lease forever, paying £6 per Ann. Cleared 30 acres.

Lost horse, 1 Cow, 1 Heifer, 4 hogs, furniture, utensils, left A good man. all these things when he went away. They took every thing away.

N. C.
October 3.

(113).

Too little
to allow.

962. EZEKEEL SPICER, late of Charlotte Co.

Claimt. says he was at De Chine in '83.
Is a nat. of A., lived at Fort Edw., joined in '81, served 3 years, 2 Sons with him.
Had 100 acres Lease for 21 near Fort Edward, bought it in '78, gave £5 York Mon. for it. Lost a litle furniture & other Articels, about £10.

PROCEEDINGS

OF

LOYALIST COMMISSIONERS.

BEFORE COMMISSIONER PEMBERTON.

Claimants.

	MSS. Folio.		MSS. Folio.
Bender, George	67	McGregor, Donel	40
Bethun, Angus	49	McGruer, John	21
Calder, Mrs. Janet	31	McIntire, Duncan	71
Caldwell, John	46	McKay, Hugh	35
Clark, Francis	45	MacKee, Alexander	85
Crislor, Philip	25	McNaughton, Donald	73
Deal, Adam	80	McLaren, Ewen	73
Everts, Oliver	90	MacDonell, Ronald	27
Fennel, John	88	MacDonell, Keneth	43
Ferguson, Israel, Richard and Farrington	68	MacLeod, Mrs. Isabel	76
		Macbain, Mrs. Isbel	59
Fitzpatrick, Peter	72	Macdonell, Allan	48
Fraser, Mrs. Isabel	60	Macdonell, Alexander	48
Fraser, William, Sr., Capt. William and Thomas	17	Macdonell, John	52
		Macdonell, John, Sr.	47
Gordon, Robert	44	Macdonell, Roderic	49 and 53
Glasford, James	78	Macgregor, John	43
Grant, Archibald	31	Mackay, Donald	77
Grant, Finlay	50	MacNaughton, Donald	73
Grant, John	81	Marsh, William	12
Grant, Peter	36	Meyers, John W.	10
Grant, William	62	Millross, Andrew	54
Hamblin, Silas	74	Murchison, Duncan	28
Hanes, Jos.	39	Murchison, John	29
Haws, George	38	Murchison, John, Jr.	29
Hindman, Samuel	41	Prentice, Daniel	81
Hofftalin, James	58	Ross, Mrs. Christiana Cameron	82
Holmes, James	1	Ross, Donald	23
Horn, Henry	66	Ross, Finley	34
Hunter, David	24	Sandford, Ephriam	7
Impey, Philip, Sr.	55	Schermerhorn, Wm.	64
Landon, Asa.	89	Snyder, John	32
Lindsey, Mrs. Abigail	37	Stuart, David	75
Lindsey, Derby	37	Weejars, Jacob	5
Livingston, Mrs. Flora	51	Whailen, David	47
McArthur, Donald	67	White, Alexander	13
McDonel, Donald	30	Wiltsee, Benoni	83
MacGevah, William	79	Yurex, Isaac	63
McGillisplate, Donald	34		

THE EVIDENCE.

N. C.
October 11.

963. Claim of JAMES HOLMES, late of N. Y.

Claimt. says he made out his Claim on the 6th Jany., 1784, & then sent by the Post to John Delancey at New York, to be forwarded to England, it arrived 10 days too late.

Produces affidt. from John Delancey that the Papers containing the sd. Claim were put on Board a Ship bound for England on 10th Jany., directed to Capt. James Delancey, but Deponent was informed by a Letter from his Bro. that they did not arrive till 6th April.

(1).

Is a native of America. Lived at Bedford, Westchester Co., when the Rebellion broke out. Had acted as Lieut. Col. of Militia & Justice of the Peace. At first he sided with the Americans. Commanded a Regiment as Col., the 4th Regimt. raised in Province of New York. On understanding there was an intention to declare Independence, he resigned his Commission at the end of the Campaign, '75. He returned to his farm at Bedford & lived retired. In April, '78, he was taken up on Suspicion of intending to join the Brit. Army. He made his Escape after 2 days Confinement. Went within the Lines at New York. Staid at New York & Long Island till the Fall 1779. He was then taken Prisnr., being out of the Lines, & was Confined 20 months in Pughkepsie, then made his Escape, got to New York in Aug., '81, joined Col. Delancey's Corps. Soon afterwards served as Lieut. Col. in his Regt. till the end of the War.

He thought at the end of the War his Estates had not been Confiscated. He went into Connecticut to go to England in '84, supposing his Claim had been sent home. But understanding his Claim had been lodged under the first Act, & not being in Circumstances to go to England, he returned to Connecticut, there lived till March, '86. Then went to St. John's, New Brunswick, but returned that Summer to fetch his Family, but his Wife could not come; he had not settled yet, his Wife and family are in Connecticut. His Wife has a small Property there, but Claimt. has lived lately on a Place belonging to a banishd Loyalist, one Capt. MacDonald. His intentions are to settle in Canada, but he has not fixt.

(2).

Produces Certificate from Fred. Philips to Claimts. Character, to his having deserted the Cause on their declaring Independence & that he has lost a Considerable Estate.

Beverly Robinson Certifies the same, not from his own Knowleuge of Claimt., but from what he has always understood.

Col. James Delancey Certifies to the same effect & that Claimt. joined the Corps of Westchester Refugees under his Command, that had the Command of almost every Party against the Enemy & distinguished himself as a brave & good officer.

Had a farm in Bedford consisting of 273 acres, part by Deed of Gift from his Father.

Produces Deed from John Holmes to Claimt. of a piece of Land in Bedford, since sold, & half a Lot that lies undivided between Grantor & Ebenezer Holmes, dated 1756. (3).

Produces Ebenezer Holmes Quit Claim to the other Moiety in 1765. He gave Land for this Quit Claim. This amounted to 163 acres.

The next, containing 110 acres, was purchased at different times. Produces 8 Different Deeds of Purchase of Small parcels at different Times between 1761 & 1774. The largest parcel was purchased in April, 1774, 73 acres & ½ for £215 York Crcy. Produces Survey Corresponding with the above acct. 10 acres purchased n 1777.

The farm was under good Improvemts, 400 fruit Trees, good Stone Walls, about 200 acres Clear, 40 acres meadow. Tolerable good farm house & Barn & out buildings. Vals it at £1,500 York Crncy.

Produces Valuation by 2 appraisers at £1,500. Produces Certificate of Confiscation & Certificate of Sale.

When he was taken Prisnr. in '78, his Negro & horse were taken, he was a valuable Negro, was taken by a Party Commanded by Major Pauling. The horse was taken at same time, both sold by order of a Committee.

Produces an affidt. that the Negroe & Horse were taken by order of a Committee in 1778, & they appraise the Negroe at £75, (4). Horse at £40, York.

He says greater part of the Debts have been paid in to the use of the State.

Produces Certificates from Gerard Banks, Treasurer, that no Claim was exhibited against Claimts. Estate, but one in a joint Bond for £172 by him & his Bror., further Certificates that public Securities had been paid in Discharging a Mortgage & 5 Bonds for £100 each due to Claimt.

BENJAMIN OGDEN, Wits.:

Knew Claimts. farm at Bedford. Remembers him in Possession, about 260 or 270 acres. It was a very good farm, fully improved, as much clear as was proper for the farm, good orchards, good Deal of meadow. Vals. it at 14 or £1,500, it used to be reckoned worth that.

Remembers his Negroe & horse being taken from him when he was taken Prisoner. He made his Escape & went into ye Lines with Wits. Thinks he was near Bedford when he was taken Prisoner a second time.

Produces Certificate from Major Murray that Claimt. & his May 24. Family arrived at St. John's from Connecticut 9th March, 1788, & that he produces a Lease dated 19th March, 1788, from (5). Madame Baberty of a House, &c., for a year.

964. Claim of JACOB WERJARS, late of Albany Co. N. C.

Claimt. says he was at Cataraqui in the fall of '83 & the October 12. Winter.

Is a native of America, lived at Cooks borough, Albany Co. When the Rebellion broke out joined Burgoyne's Army. Went into Canada after Burg. defeat, servd till end of the War. Produces his Discharge as Seargt. in Sir John Johnson's 2nd Batall., June, '84.

Winter.
Had 235 acres in Cooks Boro, Albany Co. Purchased by his Father a little before the Rebellion. Does not know what his Father gave for it, thinks it was 10s. per acre, besides Improvements. His Father gave him a Deed of it a year before the War. Claimt. is the Eldest Son. His Father now lives in the States, but not near this Place. Near 50 acres Clear, built house, &c. Says it has been sold. Vals. it at £207.
16 Hogs, Wheat, 150 Bushels, farming utensils, taken by (6). the Rebels. Cannot say anything about Horses or Cows.

EPHRAIM WERJAR, Wits.:

His Father had a farm in Cooks Boro of 235 acres, bought Michl. Cookss at the Beginning of War. His Brother lived upon it, supposes his Father gave it to him. The Rebels have got it. Michl. Cook took it again & has sold it. His Bro. lost 16 Hogs & some Wheat, a considerable quantity, and some utensils.
Called again. Claimt. says his Father bought it of Bennet & Golding, who lived at New York & they had a Mortgage of all Michl. Cooks Lands. Cannot say when he bought it, says it was before the War. Thinks he paid 10s. pr. acre for it.

His Father also bought the Improvemts. of one Thos. Sisco, ye Tenant. Says his Father bought it for Claimt., but Claimt. had his Deed from his Father. His Father had no Deed from Sisco, but he delivered Possession to Claimts. Father. Claimt. says he lived 2 years on this Place, his Father lived 70 miles off.
Cook has taken Possession & has sold the Land.
(7). Is told there is no Proof of this Estate being Confiscated or sold as forfeited.

October 22. 965. Case of EPHRAIM SANDFORD, late of Salem, West Chester, New York.

Claimt. says he is a native of America, lived at Salem, West Chester Co., New York. In '75 he went on Board the Asia to take Refuge, as he had suffered from his Sentiments being known in Favour of Brit. Govnt. In '76 joined Sir Wm. How on Staten Island, went from thence, raised 63 men, with which he joined the Army. Had a Capts. Commission in the Queen's Rangers, serv d till the Spring '77, when he was superceeded,

afterwards served as Volunteer at Fort Montgomery & other Places. Continued on Long Island & at New York till '83, then went to Nova Scotia & from thence to England. Has an allowance of £60 pr. Ann. from Home. Came from England to New Brunswick in August last.

Means to settle in this Country.

Produces Copy of his Commission from Sir W. How, Agu., 1776.

Produces Copy of Certificates to Loyalty from Govr. Tryon, Do. from Ed. Winslow, & that he mustered him as Captn. in 1776.

Do. to Services from Major Armstrong. Do from Major Grimes, & accounting for Claimts. being superceeded, which was owing to accident. A Second Batallion was to have been formed in which Claimt. was to have been a Captn. & he was removed for that Purpose from the 1st Batallion, but the 2nd was not raised & therefore he was superceeded. To same effect from Capt. McCrea & Major Armstrong & Lt. Col. French. (8).

He has recovered part of his Estate that was not sold, & therefore his Claim is now much less than it stood at first.

Was possessed of 40 acres in Reading, Fairfield Co., Connect.

His Father, Ephraim Sandford, had a Considerable real Estate at Reading. He died 24 years ago, leaving several Children, Claimt. was one of the younger Children. The Estate was distributed & this Lot of 40 acres was allotted to Claimts. Mother in part of Dower, after that to Claimt, as his proportion of his Father's Estate. She died in '77.

This is Certified by Lewis B. Sturges, Clerk of the Court of Probate & Certifies the names of the 3 persons who made such Distribution, who also Certify the same & that it contained 40 acres. (9).

Produces Copy of Conviction & forfeiture.

Produces appraisements at £6 lawful pr. acre by 2 persons.

Produces Copy of Deed of Sale by the Treasurer, John Lawrence, of part in '82, the rest has been sold since.

Produces Certificates from Thadius Benedict, appointed admt. on the sd. forfeited Estate of the Sale. Vals. at £244. 17.6.

Had a House & Land at Salem of 50 acres, he lived there. Claims for his Profits. His family were turned off & sent into ye Brit. Lines, but he has saved the Estate. His Bror. has sold it.

Lost Personal Estate. Produces Certificate of the Sale of his personal Estate to amount of £90 by 2 Commrs.

It consisted of household furniture, 3 Cows, 2 horses, 2 yearlings, Hatter's Tools.

His Loss was a great Deal more than the Estimates in the Certificates. He lost 50 Sheep, not sold by Commrs., but embezzled with several other articels.

He produces Certificates that his Estate at Salem was occupied by order of & to the use of the State of New York, & estimating the a/c. at £280. Damage done £50, Timber £20. (10).

Produces Deposition from Ebenezer Brown taken at New Brunswick to Claimts. property at Salem, that he left the same on acct. of his Loyalty & that his personal Estates was sold at Vendue. Do. from Abraham Close, taken at New Brunswick.

N. C.
October 22.

966. Claim of JOHN W. MEYERS, late of Albany Co.

Claimt. says he resided at St. John's & Isle Au Noix & Du Chene in '83. On Service resided chiefly at St. John's dur. ye Winter. Is a nat. of America. Lived in Albany Co. When Rebellion broke out joined the Brit. in '77, joined Major Jessups Corps. Staid with Burgoyne some time, but had leave to go after some Recruits. He got to New York, afterwards came to Canada with Despatches, returned to New York & in the year 1780 returned again to Canada where he raised a Company & was joined to Major Jessups Corps, servd till end of War as Capt. to half Pay. Resides at Bay of Quinty.

(11).

Had 200 acres in Cohenning's Patent, Albany Co., was to have had a Lease forever, paying 10th Part of Produce. Had the Promise, but there were infants concerned & he could not get the Lease. Went upon it in 1777, Cleared 100 acres, built house & Barn, planted orchard.

Produces an application from one Bat. Rossboone to the Commrs. requiring an appraisement of Claimts. farm as being forfeited among others, offering to deposit 1-3 part of the value. in order as it seems, to purchase under an Act of the State.

Vals. Improvemts. at £400 York.

Lost 7 horses, 4 Cows, 5 young Cattle, 30 Hogs, 17 Sheep, utensils, furniture, 140 Bushels Wheat. These things taken after he joined Burgoyne, most of them in '77 & '78.

JOSEPH SMITH, Wits.:

Lived with Claimt. as a Servt. He joined Burg., he went afterwards to New York. He from the first to the last did all he could for the Brit. Govnt. He carried Despatches to Canada. He servd at N. York under Col. Richmoor several months which was draughted into other Regimts. He afterwards raised a Company in Canada.

(12).

Seems a fair man.

Knew his Farm, 100 acres Clear. He was on it 6 years before the War. Knew his Stock, when he went from home they left 7 Horses & a good Stock behind, 4 Cows, 5 young Cattle. The Rebels got most of the things.

October 22.

Further Evidence in the Case of WM. MARSH. V. Vol. 4, P. 95.

Claimt. produces Certificates from John Collins, D. Surv., dated 6 Sep., 1787, that Claimt., his Wife & 6 Children being entitled as Loyalists to 850 acres.

Had drawn 400 in 8th Township, Bay of Quinty, & is to have a Patent in 12 months.

Claimt. says he has recovered nothing of what was his own Estate, has recovered for Children his Father's Property & got back his Bonds & Notes. Says his Father's Lands were in Dorset, his own in Manchester.

Produces Genl. Haldimand's Pass to go in ye Provinces on his private affairs, May, '83.

Produces Letters from General Haldimand who seems to have employd Claimt. in looking out for Lands for Loyalists. Mentions in one of his Letters in '84, that he had leave to go to his Family. His family were then in Vermont. (13).

His family are now in Vermont but he means to fetch them.

CAPT. COVEL, Wits.:

Says that he bels. Claimt. did not recover any of the Lands which were his own Property.

967. Claim of ALEXR. WHITE, late of Tryon Co.

N. C.

Claimt. says he left New York in the Summer '83, later end of Aug., arrived at Quebec in Septr., staid there 3 days, then went to Sorell, staid there all the Fall & the ensuing Winter. October 24.

Is a native of Ireland. Settled in America 27 years ago, lived in Tryon Co. when the Rebellion broke out, had then the office of Sheriff of Tryon Co. He opposed the meeting of rebel Committees. Took up some of the Persons who met & Confined them. As Sheriff he published a Proclamation sent by Govr. Tryon against the meeting of Committees, &c. He published this Proclamation in the County Court, in Consequence of which he was attacked by an armed mob, his house beset, till he was relieved by Sir John Johnson. Then went to Canada. (14).

Was taken Prisoner on Lake Champlain & carried to Albany Goal. This was all in '75 He was the first officer in a Civil Department that was confined. He was put in Irons, but released on Parole, to go Home. They afterwards sent him to New England, he got away from thence & in 1777 joined Genl. Burg. a few days before his ———.

He was taken again on his way to Canada & carried again to Albany. He was taken again & kept near 12 months till discharged.

Produces Certificate of his Exchange 12th Oct., 1778. After this Exchange he went to New York. He was employed some time as Barrack Master there, continued till the Summer before Evacuation, then went to Quebec. Now resides at Sorrell.

Produces his appointment as high Sheriff of Tryon County. under the Hand & Seal of Govr. Tryon in 1772.

Produces Letter which enclosed the Proclamation above mentd. dated Nov., 75.

Produces Certificate from Govr. Tryon that the Claimt. was high Sheriff, that he appointed him on acct. of his Charcater & Loyalty. Speaks of his sufferings by Imprisonmt. & in his Property & to his ardent Zeal & Loyalty.

Produces Certificates to the like effect from James Delancey, Sir John Johnson, Col. Johnson, & to the Truth of the Facts stated in his Memorial. (15).

Had 1,000 acres in the Provincial Patent near Fort Edward & Fort Ann. It was a grant in the year 1763 to 26 Proprietors. It was called the Provincial Patent, the Proprietors had been

(16).

Provincial officers the War before last. Col. Calcraft was first in the grant. The Lands had been divided in 64. The share of each proprietor was 1,000 acres. Claimant put one Tenant upon it who soon left. There was not much done upon it. Has no acct. of Sale of it. Vals. it at 10s. pr. acre.

No. 2. Had some Land in Albany Co., purchased some Soldiers Rights, about 300 acres. Had not improved it.

Claimt. was Tenant of a Farm of Sir Wm. Johnston on the Mohawk, lived there & had considerable personal Estate.

9 Horses, 6 Cows, 26 Sheep, 1 Bullock, Household furniture. Vals. near 200; Grain, Hay & Barn do. 50.

Utensils. These things were all taken in the Winter, 76. Chiefly by a Mob. His wife was driven from Home at the same time. Stript of almost everything. Left Corn growing in the Ground to amnt. of above £100.

He had a black servant at his House at this time who was taken away by the same mob.

Produces affidt. to his having all the above Property, both real & personal by Philip Cook sworn before a Master in Chancy in London Sep 85.

Sir John Johnson certifies to his Loyalty & that he had to his Belief the Property stated in his Schedule.

Vals. the Annual Income at £200 Str. pr. ann. Is certain it was worth more than that.

N. C.
October 30.

(17).

968. Claim of WM. FRASER, SNR., & CAPT. WILLIAM & THOS. FRASER, late of Tryon Co.

CAPT. WM. FRASER appears.

Says his Father, his Brother & himself resided in the Fall 83 at Yamaska, continued there all the Winter.

They are all natives of Scotland. Came to America 20 years ago. Claimt. & his Father lived at Balstown, his Bro. lived at Johnstown when the Rebellion broke out. From the first the whole family declared in favour of Brit. Govert. Wm. Fraser Sn. was then 70 years of age. Not able to serve but gave all the assistance he could to Govert.

In 1775 Claimant took part with a body of men under Col. Johnson, raised for the purpose of quelling the Rebellion.

Claimt. went from Balstown to Col. Johnson & went with him to Oswego.

Claimant Thomas was with another Party at Johnstown. They were obliged to surrender to a Party of Americans & gard Hostages.

In 1777 both Wm. & Thos. were taken prisoners with a body of about 100 men which they were bringing into Canada for the King's Army. Were carried to Albany. Made their Escape in July & joined Genl. Burgoyne at Fort Edward. Both servd. first under MacAlpine afterwards Jessup. Served all the War. Have both ½ pay as Captns.

Wm. Fraser Ser. came within the Brit. Lines in the year 80. He had left his farm 18 months before. All their furniture came in. His Father had a small Pension from Govr. Haldemand.

Claimt. Wm. & Thos. served at the Block House at Yamaska five years but went on different expeditions during that time.

Produces Certificate in 1783 from Reidezel to the good conduct of Wm. & Thos. during their Residence at the Yamaska block House in very strong terms. (18).

Do. in very favourable terms from Col. St. Leger, speaking of them both as the most confidential & Loyal among the King's subjects.

Produces Letter from Resident respecting the services at held at Claimant's desire, respecting his acts, informing him of the Commander in Chiefs full approbation of his Conduct in 1782.

Produces Letter from Resident respecting the services at the Block House in 1782, shewing the confidence placed in Claimt.

They all now live at Oswegatchie.

No. 1. They were in Possession of Leased Land in Johnstown, about 8 miles from the Mohawk, they had a Lease of 100 acres from Sir Wm. Johnstown near 18 years ago. Lease for ever paying £6 per ann. York Curv after 5 years. The Lease was in their Father's home. There were 70 acres Cleared. A good house & Barn & orchard.

Produces Lease from Sir Wm. Johnston to Wm. Fraser, Ser. of 100 acres, reserving £6 York per ann., dated 1769. Produces the appraisement of the Improvmts. at £300 York. Vals. it at the same. (19).

No. 2. They had 600 acres in Balston. Produces Deed from Dirk Lefferts & ors. to Wm. Fraser, Ser., of 200 acres Kayadosseras Patent, Albany Co. in Cons. £80, dated 1772.

Produces do. from do. to do. of 200 acres in consr. £160 York April, 75.

They had 200 acres more but have not the Deed purchased in 1773.

The whole farm laid together, about 60 acres clear. They cleared the whole themselves. It was worth 9 Dollars per acre to clear. An acre of clear land properly fenced was worth £3 Hal. per acre.

Vals. Wild Land at 6 Dollars.

Produces Certificates of their several Claimt's being convicted o Inditment.

The Stock on No.1 consisted. 4 Milch Cows, 2 horses, 5 young Cattle, 12 Sheep. 6 Hogs. Utensils. grain in the Stock of different kinds. 6 Ton Hay. All these things were left on the Premises & taken in 1777. Part were sold by Vendue. Part plundered.

Stock on No. 2 consisted 3 horses, 1 mare & colt. 6 Cows, 6 young catt   e o. oxen,, 13 Sheep,   s. 7 Hogs. 50 Bushels Wheat, 8 Ton Hay. All this was plundered in 1777. (20).

When the Claimt went to Burgoyne's Army, altho the old was at that time on the Premises. They left him nothing of any value.

THOS. FRASER appears.

& Confirms this acct., as given by his Bro. The Father William is so old & infirm that his attendance is dispensed with.

JOHN MACPERSON, Wits.

Knew all the Claimts. The whole Family were distinguished for their Loyalty from the first. The old man was always very Loyal.
Knew that they had a Farm at Johnstown.
Knew No. 2 very well. They owned 600 acres, but had improved only 200. Thinks about 30 acres Clear. There was a good Stock. Horses, Oxen & Cows. Thinks the Father sold a good Deal of the Stock when he came to Canada.

DONALD ROSS, Wits.

Very good man

Knew No. 1. Near 70 acres Clear. There was a fine stock of Cattle there. Heard of their having Lands in Balston.

N. C.
October 30.

969. Case of JOHN MCGRUER, late of Tryon Co.

Claimt. says he was at Cote du Lac in the Fall of 83. Did not come down till Xmas.

(21).

Is a nat. of Scotland. Settled in America in 1763. Lived at Johnstown when Rebellion broke out. Was imprisoned 9 months in 1776. Joined the Brit. Army in 1777. Was under Sir John Johnson at Fort Stanwix. Servd till end of War.

Had a Lease from Sir Wm. Johnston. Had no Deed. Had it only from year to year. It was near Johnstown. There were 80 acres clear when he took it. He paid Rent to Sir John. He Cleared 9 acres. He says he had agreed with Sir W. Johnston that the Landlord would pay for the Improvmts. It was to be settled by 2 Appraisers what should be pd.

Says he built a house with Sir Wm.'s Leave & Sir Wm. was to pay him when he left it. Says it cost him £60 York.

Had a large Stock, no one in that part had more.
13 horses, 10 Cows, 4 Oxen, 5 Heifers, 40 Sheep, 6 Hogs, Utensils, grain of different kinds. All these things were seized in 77, & sold at Vendue.

DANIEL ROSS, Wits.

Knew Claimt's farm. It was Sir John's Land. A good Deal of it was clear. 100 acres Clear. How much Claimt. had cleared Wits. does not know.

Knew his Stock. It was a large stock. The stock was on the Place when he left it. (22).

CAPT. WM. FRASER, Wits.

Knew Claimt's Farm. There was a large Clearance but Wits. does not know the terms on which he held. There was a considerable Stock. He had a Partner of the name of Bennet. Speaks of his Loyalty & Services.

Claimt. on being called again says his Partnership was at an end before the War began. His Partner was concerned in the Improvements, was to have half & half in the Farm, but Claimt. says he himself had the largest share in the Stock. Bennet his Partner left the farm in 1776.

CAPT. THOS. FRASER, Wits.

Says he remembers Bennet went from the Farm before Claimt., but does not know when the Partnership was at an end. There was a large Stock. Witness when he knew the stock thought it belongd. to both.

N.b. Note. It seems as if there had been no Dissolution of Partnership & that some of the Stock belonged to Bennet, tho Claimt. was to pay for it & it was left in his Possession.

970. Case of DONALD ROSS, late of Tryon Co. N. C. October 30.

Claimt. says he was at work at the Cedars in the Fall of 83. Did not come to Montreal till 2 or 3 days before Xmas. (23).

Is a native of Scot. Came to America 30 years ago. Served last War. Lived at Johnstown, joined the Brit. in 1776. Was in Sir John's Regt. Served all the War.

Had ½ a Lot of Land in Johnstown. Lease Land. Had no Deed, paid Rent from year to year, 15 acres Clear, built a house. had a Man & Colt, & Cow, Heifer, 5 Hogs, 2 Sheep, Cloathes, Utensils.

Left all these things at home when he went away. They were plundered by the Rebels because he went to ye Brit.

JOHN MAGGINIS, Wits.

Knew Claimt's farm. It was leased from Sir W. Johnstown. There was a good Piece cleared. He had some Stock. Wits. cannot say exactly how much. A good man.

971. Claim of DAVID HUNTER, late of Albany Co.—Lodged in England. N. C. October 30.

Claimt. says he sent a Claim by Major Jessup in 83.

Is a nat. of Ireland, came with his Father to America in 1774. Settled in Balstown, joined the Brit. in 1779. Served in Major Jessup's Regt. till end of the War. (24).

His Father & Mother had a Farm & Stock in Balstown, his Father died in 82 & his Mother in 83, leaving Frances the eldest son, now in Balstown, Claimt. the 2nd Son John, who served on Board the Brit. Fleet, a Daughter, now in the States. His Father & Mother died without a Will. Supposes that his Brother is now in Possession of Land & Stock.

October 30.

972. Case of PHILIP CRISLOR, late of Tryon Co.

Claimt. says: He is a native of America. Lived in Tryon Co. When Rebellion broke out joined the Brit. in 1777 at Fort Stanwix, served first in Sir John's Regt., then in Col. Butler's, to the end of the War. Resides at New Johnstown. Produces Col. Butler's Certificate to his service & Loyalty.

(25).

Had 50 acres at New ——, Tryon Co. Purchased in 1769, of one Bather Nuskall. Gave £60 York Cury. for it. Had a Deed, left behind, cleared 30 acres. Made large Buildings. Had a Blacksmith's shop there, & a building for a Potash Work.

Vals. the Farm & buildings belonging to the Farm at £450 York.

Vals. ye clear land at £5 per acre. The uncultivated Land at £1.5. There are Rebels now in Possession.

Too high.

Vals. Potash House & Works, Kettles at £650.

There were three Kettles & Iron Ladles & other Iron Works, 30 large tubs, a Tub 12s. 2 Tun boiled Potash, 5 Tun not boiled.

Had a Blacksmith shop in the same place little Tools, 500 Weight of Iron, 200 Weight of Steel.

His Potash Works & Shop, & all his effects were sold at Vendue in 1777.

He had 12 Cattle, 25 Sheep. 30 Hogs, 5 Horses, furniture, farming Utensils very good. Had Merchandise worth £30. Paper Money to amount of £80 Congress Money.

JOHN SHELL, Wits.

Knew Claimt. at New Tarlock. He was always a Loyalist. Joined the Brit. Troops in 77. Served all the War.

(26).

Knew his farm. He bought it before 70. 30 acres clear. large buildings. Vals. Clear Land £5 per acre. He built Pot Ash Work himself. It was a large Work. 2 or 3 Kettle, a good many Tubs. There was a good Deal of Potash left when he went away.

Had a Blacksmith Shop, very good Tools, a good deal Iron & Steel. Knew his Stock. 12 Cattle, 5 horses, 24 Sheep, Hogs, Good Farming Utensils. His House very well furnished. He left a little Shop & had Merchandise.

Seems a good man. Is told to get Certificates of Sale.

Some of his effects were plundered.

A good deal sold at Vendue. Some Rebels are in Possession of the Land.

973. Claim of RONALD MACDONELL, late of Tryon Co. N. C. October 31.

Claimt. says: He was about 20 miles from Montreal in the Fall of 83. Did not come down till just about the time that the Regiment was Discharged. He was on duty at ye ———
Is a nat. of Scotl. Came to America in the French War. Lived in Sir John Johnson's Land when the Rebellion broke out. Came with Sir John Johnson at first, & served all the War. Produces his Discharge last French War & this War. (27).
Lived on Lease Land of Sir John's. Charges nothing for Lease.
Lost 2 Cows, 1 Mare, 2 Heifers, 2 Yearlings, 1 Steer, 1 Bull, farming Utensils, Cloathes. Left all these things when he went away. Heard the Rebels took them.

JOHN CAMERON, Wits.

Knew Claimt's Stock. He had 6 Creatures & a mare & several farming Utensils. He left the whole behind him when he joined Sir John Johnson he came with him at first in the year 76. A good man.
He left them behind. The enemy had them.

974. Case of DUNCAN MURCHESON, late of Tryon Co. N. C. October 31.

Claimt. says he was at Le Chine in the Fall of 83. Staid there all the Winter.
Is a nat. of Scotl. Came to America in 1774. Settled with Sir Wm. Johnstown. Joined Sir John at first of Rebellion. Seved as Sergeant. Served 3 years as Conductor in the Indian Department.
Had Lease Land 50 acres, was to have had a Deed. Cleared 14 acres, built House, Barn & Stable.
Had 4 Cows, 1 Heifer, 1 Bull, 2 Calves, 1 Horse & Colt, 4 Sheep, 5 Lambs, 10 Hogs, furniture, Utensils, Cloathing, Grain in ye Barn. Left on his farm when he joined Sir John first. taken by the Rebels. (28).
His Father was bringing him 20 guins. from Scotland. His Father was in North Car. He was taken Prisoner & died there.

JOHN MURCHISON, Wits.

Knew Claimt's Farm. Thinks 14 acres clear, took his farm in '73, thinks he had some creatures, 1 horse & Colt, 4 Sheep, 6 or 7 Hogs, Utensils. A good man.
Left all these things on his Farm when he went away. They fell in the Hands of the Rebels

975. Claim of JOHN MURCHESON, late of Tryon Co. N. C. October 31.

Claimt. says he was settled at Tarbonne in the Fall 83. Came to Montreal 2 or 3 days before Regt. was discharged.

67 AR.

Is a native of Scotl. Came to America 14 years ago. Settled on Sir Wm. Johnston's Land. Joined Sir John at first. Served all the War.

Had a Lease 50 acres. Had cleared 14 acres, had 6 horned Cattle & 1 horse, 5 Sheep, 7 Hogs, furniture, Utensils, of small Value. All left behind.

(29).

DUNCAN MURCHESON, Wits.

A good man.

Claimt. came to America with Wits. Settled at Johnstown. Had a Lease of 50 acres. Cleared 14 acres. Agrees in acct. of the Stock with Claimt. All was left behind. He was not quite in such good circumstances as Wits.

N. C.
October 31.

976. Claim of JOHN MURCHESON, JUN., late of Tryon Co.

Claimt. says he was at Montreal & La Chine in the Fall 83. Gave a Claim to his Commanding Officer, Capt. Duncan. Is a nat. of Scotl. Came to America in 73.

Settled in Johnstown. Came with Sir John at first. Served all the War.

He had a Lease 50 acres. Built a Log house & cleared 12 acres.

8 Head of Horn Cattle, 1 Horse, 9 Sheep, grain, Utensils, furniture small.

Left all these things behind.

DUNCAN MURCHESON, Wits.

A good man.

Confirms the above acct. & testifies to his knowledge of the Truth. Resides in New Johnstown.

N. C.
October 31.

977. Claim of DONALD MCDONELL, late of Tryon Co.

(30).

Claimt. says he was with a Detachment of his Regt. 18 miles from Montreal. Says he gave in a Claim to his officer, Capt. Angus MacDonell. Lives at Lot No. 2. 1st Township, 2nd Concession, New Johnstown.

Is a nat. of Scotl. Came to America in 73. Settled on Sir W. J. Land. Servd all the War. Had 100 acres. Cleared 2 acres, built house & Stables, 1 Cow, 1 Heifer, Utensils & furniture, Grain.

DONALD MACGILLES, Wits.

Knew Claimt's Farm. He had cleared 2 acres. Had built

A good man.

a house, had a Cow & Yearling, with furniture & few Utensils. Left all behind. Wits. & Claimt. joined the Brit. Army together

N. C.
October 31.

978. Claim of ARCHIBALD GRANT, late of Tryon Co.

Claimt. says he was at Isle Au Noix & Montreal. Gave his Claim to Capt. Mackenzie. Produces Capt. Mackenzie's Certificate to this effect.

67a AR

Is a nat. of Scot. Came to Am. in 74. Settled with Sir Wm. J. Joined Sir John at first. Served all the War. (31).
Had 100 acres. 6 acres Clear. Built a house & barn. 4 head of Cattle, farming Utensils, furniture, grain. Left all behind. Act. confirmed by 2 Wits. A good man.

979. Claim of JANET CALDER, Widow, late of Albany Co. N. C. November 1.

Claimt. says her Husband William Calder died 5 years ago. He was a Soluier in Sir John's Regt.
He was a native of Scotl. Came to America 14 years ago. Settled on Cartwrights Patent. Joined the Brit. in 79. Served several years till his Death. She came with him into Canada.

He died in Spring, 1782. Left 3 Children. She was at St. Martin in the Fall of 83 & the Winter. The 3 Children are now with Claimt. All young. She takes care of them. She lives on River Raisin.
Her Husb. had 150 acres on Cartwrights Patent. He had a Deed. A Lease for ever, paying 6d. per acre annually. Cleared about 12 acres. Built a house & Barn & Stable. Lost a Cart, grain of different kinds.
Acct. Confirmed by John Cameron, Wits. and John Mackay Wits. Good woman

980. Case of JOHN SNYDER, late of Albany Co. N. C. November 1.

Claimt. says he was at Mashishe in the Fall 83. Went from (32). thence to St. John's. Afterwards went to New Johnstown.
Is a native of America. Lived at Saratoga. Joined Capt. MacAlpine in 77. Enlisted with him. Was soon after taken Prisoner. Got home in the Winter. Left his home & came to Canada in 80. He was promised a Lieutenancy by Capt. MacAlpine but could not get it. He therefore went & staid at Mashishe.
Had a Lease from General Skyler. No. 1.
Produces Lease from Philip Skyler to Claimt. of a Farm

Pt. of Lot No. 27, for ever, paying £4 York Cury per ann., dated 1769.
Built Log house & Barn. Cleared about 25 acres.
Had 112 acres in Palmerston. Produces Deed from Dirk No. 2. Lefferts to Claimt. of 112 acres in Considr. £44.16 York, dated 1769.
He had made no builds., but had began clearing, gave a Horse in pt. of paymt. & the rest in hard money.
Had a Stock in No. 1. Lost 3 Cows, 4 other Cattle, 4 horses, 8 Sheep, 7 Hogs,, furniture & Cloathes. These things were (33). taken in the year 1777 by the Rebels. When he returned from Imprisonment found his effects had been taken.

LIEUT. LANSING, Wits.

Speaks very strongly in favour of his Loyalty & Character. Knew No. 1. A very good place, well improved. Heard of his having No. 2.

A very good man.
He had a good Stock on No. 1. He had Horses, Cows, Sheep, Hogs.

*N. C.
November 1.*
981. Case of FINLEY ROSS, late of Tryon Co.

Claimt. says: He was in Sir John's first Regt. Gave his Claim to the Adjutant in 83., to be sent before Commrs.

Is a nat. of Scott. Came to Am. in 73. Settled in Sir Wm. J. Land. Joined Sir John at first. Has served all the War.

Had a Lease of 100 acres. Cleared 10 acres, built House, Barn & Stable.

(34).
Lost 6 Head Cattle, Utensils, furniture. Wheat in the Ground. Some wheat & grain in the Barn. The rebels took them after he joined Sir John.

A good man.

DONALD MACLEAN, Wits.

Knew Claimt's farm. He had cleared 10 acres. Had built a house, Barn &c. Knew his Stock. He had 6 Cattle, some farming Utensils. The Rebels had them.

*N. C.
November 1.*
982. Case of DONALD MCGILLES, JR., late of Tryon Co.

Claimt. says he was at Montreal in 83, gave his Claim to the Adjutant in Consequence of a regimental order.

Is a nat. of Scot. Came to Am. in 74. Settled on Sir John's Land. Joined Sir John at first. Served all the War.
Had some Lease Land 4 acres clear. built house & Barn.
1 Cow, 1 Ox, Little farm Utensils.
Left on the Place when he went away.

A good man.
Acct. Confirmed by Donald MacDonell, Wits.

*N. C.
November 1.*
983. Claim of HUGH MCKAY, late of Tryon Co., Deceased.

(35).
His eldest son Wm. McKay appears.
Says his Father died last Summer, without a Will. He was Soldier in Sir John's 1st Batal. He delivered a Claim to the Adjutant. Claimt. is the only Son. His Mother is also dead. His Father was nat. of Scot. Came to Amer. 16 yrs. ago. Settled on Cartwrights Patent, had 150 acres. He joined Sir John in 80. Claimt came with him. His Father served till end of War.

Had a Lease on Cartwrights Patent. Does not know that he had the Deed.

Cleared 9 acres & built 2 Houses & Barn. Lost Cow & Calf, furniture, some Grain. Left when they came away, the Rebels got it.

JOHN MACKAY, Wits.

Knew Hugh Mackay's Place on Cartwrights Patent. He had 9 acres clear, had a little Stock. Came into Canada in 80. Served in Sir John's Regt.

984. Case of PETER GRANT, late of Tryon Co.   N. C. November 1.

Claimt. says he was in Sir John's first Batal. Was at La Chine in fall 83.

Is a nat. of Scot. Came to Amer. in 74. Settled on Sir Wm. J. Lands. Joined Sir John at first. Served all the War.

(36).

Had a Lease of 100 acres. Cleared 10 acres, built house, barn & Stable.

Lost 4 Cows, 1 Ox, 1 Heifer, Utensils, furniture. Left the things at Home when he went away. The Rebels took them.

JOHN McDONELL, Wits.   A good man.

Knew Claimt's Farm, 9 acres clear, saw 4 or 5 head horned Cattle.

---

985. Case of ABIGAIL LINDSEY, Widow of John Lindsey, Duchess Co.   N. C. November 6.

Claimt. says she was at Sorell in '83 & all the Winter.

Her former Husband John Holmes was a native of America. Lived at 9 Partners. He came into Canada in '80, & joined Major Jessup. He was so persecuted he would not stay with the Rebels. Served till the Regt. was Discharged.

Claimt. herself came into Canada in the Spring '82. Her Husband was tried at 3 different times, fined 3 times, one £60. When he went away he left with Claimt. 1 Horse, 2 Cows, 10 sheep. The Rebels came & took them from her, because her Husband was gone to the Brit. Took all her furniture; small. Has 2 Children by her first Husband they are not at Sorell.

(37).

Produces Major Jessup's Certificate to her late Husband's Loyalty & service.

986. Further Evidence in the Case of DERBY LINDSEY, vi. Vol. 18 & 145.

Abigail Holmes gives the same acct. of Derby Lindsey's fam-

---

ily as the other Witness. But says it was time of the Peace before the old man came to Canada. He was always Loyal, & had been frequently imprisoned on that acct.

He had a large farm. He was turned off by the Rebels.

He had 3 Horses, 4 Cows, near 30 sheep. When he was turned off the premises he was obliged to leave all his stock & effects. Says the Rebels had them.

N. C.
November 6.

(38).

987. GEORGE HAWS, late of Ulster Co.

Claimt. says they left New York in July '83. Came to Canada with the other Loyalists, & continued at Sorell all that Fall & ever since.
 Is a Nat. of Germany. Came many years ago to Am. Lived in Ulster Co. when Rebellion broke out. Lived on Leased Land.
 In 1778 came to New York. Continued at New York. Lived with his Brother, who was a Butcher in New York. His family came in in '80.
 Had a Lease farm of 100 acres. When he went away he left his stock with his Farm in 3 or 4 weeks; the Commit. came & took

N.B.--Name of Urijah Haws appear in Anstey's list, means Claimt.

an Inventory of his things & sold them. Sold 5 Cows, 4 Cattle, 2 Horses, farming utensils, cloathes. All sold at Vendue.
 Lost a horse taken from him on his way to New York. Cloathes lost as his wife was sending them to New York.
 Produces affidavit from Jane Harris sworn at Sorell to Claimt.'s Loyalty & that his Property was sold at Vendue in '78.

N. C.
November 6.

988. Claim of Jos. HANES, late of Tryon Co.

(39).

Claimt. says he was at Le Chîne in Fall '83 & the ensuing Winter.
 Is a Nat. of Germ. Came to America 23 years ago. Lived at Johnstown on the Mohawk. Came into Canada in '81. Three sons joined Sir John Johnson, 1 was killed; two others served till end of the War.
 Came into Canada because the Rebels persecuted him. They would have taken his life if he had not came away.
 Lives 4 miles from Montreal, but has land in 4 Township.
 Had a Lease from Sir Wm. Johnston of 100 acres, Lease forever, paying Rent £6 pr. ann. Cleared 50 acres.

Built house, Barn, &c., planted an orchard.
 Lost his utensils, furniture, 3 Horses, 3 Cows, 24 sheep, grain, 300 Boards. The Rebels took some, but his wife disposed of some & brought some to Canada.

CALEB PECK, Wits.:

Knew Claimt. He had 3 sons in the King's Army. Claimt. was always Loyal. He came in long before the War was over.
 Knew his Farm. He had between 30 & 40 acres clear. He had 3 Horses & Cows & Sheep & a Wagon.

(40).

N. C.
November 7.

989. Claim of DONEL MCGREGOR, late of Tryon Co.

Claimt. says he was at Coteau de Lac in the Fall '83, & staid till Xmas.
 Is a Nat. of Scot. Came to America 23 years ago. Lived at Johnstown. Joined in '77. Served till end of the War in Sir John's Regt.
 Resides at the River Raisin.

Had a Lease farm of Sir Wm. Johnston. Lease forever, paying £6 pr. ann. Took ye farm originally between himself & Peter Fenny, bought his improvemts. 15 years ago. Gave £30 York for it. Had 20 acres Clear. Built House & Barn.

3 horses, 4 Cattle, 5 Hogs, utensils, furniture. Taken by the Rebels immediately after he went away.

PETER FENNY, Wits.:

Knew Claimt.'s Farm. Lease was first granted to Claimt. & witness, of 100 acres, years before the War. Claimt. bought witnesses share for £30. He pd. part, owes about £10. Cleared some afterwards. 20 acres clear in the whole. Had built house, (41). Barn & Stable. Agrees in acct. of the Stock as given by Claimt. A good man.

990. Case of SAMUEL HINDMAN, late of Charlotte. N. C. November 8.

Claimt. says he was at Chamble in '83. Staid there till he went to Bay of Chaleur.

Is a native of Ireland. Came to America in 1762. Resided at White Creek, Charlotte Co., bordering on Vermont, 10 miles from Fort Edward. Joined the Brit. in '77. Served Burgoyne's Campaign as Ensign in Queen's Rangers. Went off with the Genl. Despatches to Ticonderago the night before the Capitulation.

Came to Canada after Burgoyne's defeat. Afterwards went with Despatches for Genl. Haldimand & Lord Dorchester.

His residence was at Chamble. Three years ago went to Chaleur; is settled there.

His family are at Vermont.

Had 268 acres in Charlotte Co. bought of one J. Morien Scott at New York in 1774. Had a Deed but left it with his wife. She is now at Benington. Gave 20sh. pr. acre for it, York. Pd. part in paper mon., pt. in cash.

Cleared certainly 18 acres & began clearing a great deal (42). more, 30 acres. Says it was never reckoned Vermont. One rebel Major, Major Webster, now has it.

Vals it at £1,100 York Says he was there. The place was Q. If not fraud. sold. He does not know by whom it was sold. Is told to get certificate of

Lost 2 horses, 3 Cows, 2 Cattle, Hogs, furniture, utensils. sale and the deeds.

Capt. Mackrahin took these Things in '77, 2 Days after he left home. His wife was driven off the place. Says he is going to Vermont or his wife is coming.

Produces affidt. from one Robt. Caldwell in Chaleur Bay Seems a very that Claimt, joined the Brit. Army. That he had a Farm which character. was reckoned good Land. Deferred for further Evid.

991. KENETH MACDONELL, late of Tryon Co. N. C. November 12.

Claimt. says. He was at Isle au Noix in the Fall '83. Came to Montreal before his Discharge.

(43).

Is a native of Scotl. Came to Amer. in '73. Was settled at Johnstown. Came with Sir John at first; served till end of the War. Produces his Discharge.

Had 50 acres of Land on the Mohawk; was to have had a Lease from Sir Wm. Johnston. Cleared 7 acres. Built house, Stable & Barn. 5 Cows, 1 Mare, furniture, utensils, wheat. Left all these Things on the Place when he joined Sir John.

JOHN MACDONELL, Wits.

A good man.

Knew Claimt.'s farm, 50 acres. Had cleared 7 or 8 acres. He had 5 Cows, 1 Mare. Left all his Things on the place when he went away. In 1st Township.

N. C.
November 12.

992 JOHN MACGREGOR, late of Tryon Co.

Claimt. Says: He was at Coteau de Lac in the Fall '83.
Is a native of Scot. Came to America before last French War. Lived on a Farm of Sir Wm. Johnston's when Rebellion broke out. Came with Sir John at first. Served all the War. Produces his Discharge.

Had a Lease of 100 acres. Cleared 15 acres; built House & Stable.

Had 5 Horses, 2 Cows, 1 Heifer, utensils, furniture. Left on his farm when he went away.

DUNCAN MACARTHUR, Wits.:

(44).
A good man.

Knew Claimt's Farm. He had about 26 acres clear. He had horses & cows. Remembers 4 horses. He left all these things on his place when he joined Sir John. In 1st Township.

N. C.
November 12.

993. ROBERT GORDON, late of Tryon Co.

Claimt. says: He was at La Chine in ye fall '83. Gave in his Claim to his Commanding officer.

Is a Nat. of Ireland. Came to America 18 years ago. Was settled in Pensilv. when Rebellion broke out. Joined Sir John Johnson at Oswego in '77. Has served ever since. End of the War was a Seargt. Says he lived at Fort Pen; had saved £150. In 1776 went to New York & thence to Albany. He was imprisoned. He had hired a house near Albany. He escaped from Prison, on which the Rebels went to his house & took all his Things. Took Cash in his desk £150 York Cury. Says it was in hard cash. They took a mare, 2 cows, hogs, furniture, hay.

Refers to Lieut.
McFall as Wits.
for him.

Says he had bought 30 stand of arms. Gave a great many of them away to Loyalists. Lost 4 or 5 which the Rebels had.

Evidence deficient at present.

Produces Sir John Johnson's Certificates to service. In 1st Township.

Deferred for further Evid.

N. C.
November 12.

994. FRANCIS CLARK, late of Tryon Co.

(45).

Claimt. says: Was at Montreal in the Fall '83. Gave his Claim to his commanding officer. Produces Certificate to the fact.

Is a Nat. of Great Brit. Came to America at beginning of War before the Battle of Bunker's Hill. Went first to Pensilv., then came to New York, from thence went to Cherry Valley; joined the Brit. at Fort Stanwix in '77. Served till end of the War.

Brought some cloaths from home with him. Left them behind when he wen to New York. Whe he went to Fort Stanwix left a horse behind him at Cherry Valley.

Shoemakers Tools. The rebels got the horse & tools.

JOHN CALDWELL, Wits.:

Knew Claimt. at Cherry Valley; think in 1775 & '76. He had a horse & shoemakers tools. He joined the Brit. in '77, & left all these things behind him.

995. Claim of JOHN CALDWELL, late of Tryon Co.   N. C. November 12.

Claimt. Says: He was in Montreal in '83.

Delivered his Claim to the Adjutant.

Is a Nat. of Scot. Came to America in 1770. Was settled in Cherry Valley, 12 miles from the Mohawk. Joined Sir John at Fort Stanwix. Served till end of the War.   (46).

Had 50 acres Tenant Land. Bought the improvements of the Tenant in '75. Paid £45 York, 8 acres clear. There was a house & Pot Ash House in the Purchase. Was to have brought the soil right if War had not come on. Had 2 horses, furniture, utensils, hides.

FRANCES CLARK, Wits.:

Knew Claimt. at Cherry Valley. He had a Farm & Potash Work. Claimt.'s share was about 50 acres. There was a considerable Clearance. He had horses. 1st Township.

996. DAVID WHAILEN, late of New York.   N. C. November 12.

Claimt. says: He was at Montreal in '83. Sent in his Claim to Captain Macdonell. Produces Capt. Macdonell's Certificate to the fact.

Is a Nat. of Amer. Lived at Kingsbury, Charlotte Co. Joined Genl. Burgoyne. After his defeat came to Canada. Joined Sir John Johnson. Served to end of War. Produces his Discharge.

Had 50 acres in Kingsbury. Bought 3 yrs. before ye War. Gave £8 for it. He had 8 acres clear. When he came away he left some farming utensils. Some corn harvested. Potatoes planted. 1st Township.   (47). Seems a fair man. No evidence £15 or 20.

997. JOHN MACDONELL, SEN., late of Tryon Co.   N. C. November 12.

Claimt. says: He was at Carleton Island in '83. Is a Nat. of Scot. Came 14 yrs. ago. Lived at Johnstown when Rebellion broke out. Served all the War in the 84th Regt. Produces his Discharge.

Had a Tenant farm 50 acres from Sir Wm. Johnson. 8 acres Clear. Built House. Had 5 Cows, grain, furniture, & utensils.

Left all these things behind when he joined the Brit. Army.

A fair man.   KENETH MCDONALD, Witness:
Confirms the above acct.
Resides on Lot 14, 3rd Concess., 1st Township.

N. C.
November 12   998.   ALLAN MACDONELL, late of Tryon Co.

Claimt. says he was in St. John's first Bataln.; gave his Claim to his Commanding officer.
His Claim was heard July 23 conditionally.
(48).   He is a native of Scotland. Came to America many years ago. Lived in Johnstown. Served all the War.
Fair man.   Had a Tenant Farm, 9 acres clear. Lost 1 horse, 7 cows, furniture, Utensils.
Acct. confirmed by Alexr. MacDonell. Lot 12, 1st Con, 1st Township.

N. C.
November 12   999.   ALEX. MACDONELL, late of Tryon Co.

Claimt. says he was in Sir John's 1st Regt.; gave his Claim to his Commanding officer. Was heard in July last conditionally.
He is a native of Scotl. Came to America 15 years ago. Served all the War.
Had a Tenant Farm, 9 acres Clear. Lost a horse, 12 cows, utensils, furniture.

Fair man.   Acct. Confirmed by Allen Macdonell, Wits.:
Lives at Lot 15, 1st Conc., 1st Township.

N. C.
November 12.   1000.   RODERIC MACDONELL, late of Tryon Co.

Claim was heard in July last Conditionally.
Claimt. is a native of Scotl. Came to America 15 years ago. Served all the War.
Had Tenant Farm 100 acres, Charlotte Co., 10 acres clear.
A fair man.   Lost 1 Horse, 11 Cows, utensils, furniture.
Acct. confirmed by 2 Wits.
(49).   19 Lot, 2 Conc., 1st Towns.

N. C.
November 15.   1001.   Case of ANGUS BETHUN, late of Alb. Co.

Claimt. says he did not give his Claim. to his Commanding officer. He was at Montreal in '83. His Claim was so little that he did not give it in to his officer but says he gave his Claim to Mr. Cuyler at that time.
Is a nat. of Scotl. Came to Amer. in '73. Lived with Capt. Macdonell in Tryon Co.: joined the Brit. in '75. Served first in

Indian Department, then in Sir John's Regt. Produces his Discharge.

Lost a mare, Colt & Cow.

Says he had been working & earned a Mare, Colt & Cow. Left them with one MacDougal when Claimt. went away at Duanes Bush; lost Cloathes. He was on his journey & left them at a house, when they were taken away.

RORY MACDONELL, Wits. :

Says Claimt. had a Cow, a Mare & Colt. Says the man with whom he worked gave them to him for his Labour. He left the mare & colt with MacDougal. He carried away nothing when he went away.

MacDougal staid in the Country. He was known to be a rebel from the first. (50).

1st Township.

1002. FINLAY GRANT, late of Tryon Co. N. C. November 15.

Claimt. says. He was at Point au Lac in the Fall '83.
Is a Nat. of Scotl. Came to America 14 years ago. Was settled on Sir John's Land. Joined Brit. in '77. Served till end of War. Produces his Discharge.

Had 100 acres Tenant Farm. Had cleared 12 acres. Built house & barn. Had 2 horses, 6 Cattle, 6 Pigs, Utensils, furniture.

He left them all when he went away. His wife did not bring anything away.

RONALD MACDONELL, Wits.:

Knew Claimt.'s Farm. He had cleared 12 acres. Settled there before the War. A good man.

Agrees in acct. of the Stock.

1st Township.

1003. FLORA LIVINGSTON, Widow of Seargt. Livingston, late of Tryon Co. N. C. November 15.

NEIL LIVINGSTON, her only Son, appears :

Says his Mother is old & Sickly & not able to attend. (51)
She lived at Coteau du Lac in the Fall '83. She was there or at the Cascades all the Winter.

John Livingston, his late Father, was a Nat. of Scotl. He came to America before the War. Settled on the Delaware River. He joined Sir John Johnson at Oswego. Served all the War. Was a Seargent. He was drowned in the summer '83.

His mother & witness came to Niagara in year '80. Now resides in Johnstown, 1st Township. His Father had 150 acres on Cartwright's Patent, tenant Land. He took it in '74 or '75. He cleared about 8 acres. He then went to the Delaware. No. 1.

Had a grant of 100 acres from V. B. Livingston. This was before the War. He gave nothing for it, but at the same time he No. 2.

(52).

hired some other Land. 50 acres or more of Livingston for which he was to pay Rent. He had cleared 8 acres of the 100 acres given him. He kept both the Farms, No. 1 & No. 2, they were only 5 miles distant. His stock was on the Delaware Farm.

1 horse, 3 cows, 3 calves, 1 Bull, 9 Hogs, utensils, furniture. They were taken when his Father went away & sold by the Rebels. Wits. was there at the time.

ANGUS BETHUN, Wits.:

Knew John Livingston, deceased.
Knew No. 1. A farm on Cartwright's Patent. He had cleared some.
He went from thence to the Delaware. Had some land given him by Livingston. Had some on Rent. Cleared 7 or 8 acres. They had Stock.
Resides 1st Township.

N. C.
November 15.

1004. JOHN MACDONELL, from Cullacky, late of Tryon Co.

Claimt. says: He was at Osswegatchie in the Fall '83.
He is a native of Scot. Came to America in 73. Was settled at Johnstown. Joined at beginning of War. In the 84th Regt. Served all the War. Was discharged in '83. Produces his Discharge.
Had a 100 acres Lease Land. Cleared 15 acres. Built house & Barn & Stable. 2 horses, 1 Colt, 3 milch Cows, 3 young Heifers, utensils, furniture.
He left them when he went away.

(53).

A good man.

FINLEY GRANT, Wits.:

Knew Claimt's Farm. He had cleared 15 acres. Agrees in acct. of Stock.
Resides No. 2 Township.

N. C.
November 15.

1005. Claim of RODERICK MACDONELL, from Glen Morrison, late of Tryon Co.

Claimt. says: He was 18 miles from Montreal in the Fall '83.
Is a Nat. of Scotl. Came to Am. '74. Settled on Sir John's Land. Joined Sir John at first. Served all the War.
Had a Farm. Had cleared 10 acres. Lost 2 horses, 1 Cow, furniture, utensils, Grain chiefly in ye ground. Donald Grant, Sen., Wits.: Knew Claimt's place, 10 acres Clear. Knew 1 Cow, 2 Horses of Claimt's.

A good man.

N. C.
November 19.

1006. ANDREW MILLROSS, late of Tryon Co.

Claimt. says: He was at Montreal in '83, & delivered his Claim to Major Leake.
Is a native of England. Came to America in '73. Was settled in Johnstown when Rebellion broke out. He was imprisoned

& persecuted, but did not leave his Farm till '80. Then came to Canada. Served in Sir John's Regt .till end of the War. Produces his Discharge. Now lives in Johnstown, 2 Township.

Had 200 acres Lease Land. Had 100 acres on Lease himself. Took the Lease in '73; bought the other 100 acres in '75. They were also on Lease; paid £70 York. (54).

He had cleared about 9 acres of his own Lands. There were 27 acres Clear on the Land he bought.

1 mare, 3 Cows, 1 yoke of Oxen, 3 sheep, furniture, utensils, Considerable quantity of Carpenters' Tools.

Says he left all these things on his Farm when he went away.

Produces an affidavit from Thomas Haller sworn before Capt. Anderson, at New Johnstown, to Claimt's property as above stated, and to the sale of the Lands under Confiscation.

The Witness was not able to attend on acct. of the Illness in his Family.

ROBT. ROBINSON, Wits.:

Knew Claimt.'s Farm. He had 200 acres, 100 acres on Lease. He purchased the other; he took himself on the purchased Land near 30 acres clear. He cleared 10 on his own Land. Stock, he left all behind when he went away. *Seems a very fair man.*

1007. Claim of PHILIP IMPEY, SEN., Tryon Co.

N. C.
December 6,

Claimt. says: He was at Montreal in '83. Was in the 1st Batal. Gave his claim to Lieut. Cqnally to be sent home to England, in consequence of a Regimental order. (55).

Is a native of America. Lived on Mohawk River when the Rebellion broke out. He had always declared in favour of Brit. Govnt., tho' he signed one Rebel Association, but he was disarmed by the Rebels as they found he did not approve their principles. He was forced away from his Home in the year 1777. All his sons except 2 small children were in the King's Troops. He had six sons in the King's Service. Claimt. came to Canada with Sir John Johnston when he came up to the Mohawk River

about the year '80. He could not get away sooner. Served himself afterwards in Sir John's Regiment, first Battalion. Produces his Discharge. Now lives at Johnstown, 2nd Township.

No. 1. Had 600 acres in Glens Purchase on the Mohawk. Produces conveyance from Archibald Kennedy & J. Mallett to Claimt. of a Tract of Land part of Glens Purchase, containing 1,173 acres, in Considn. of £1,000 York Cury., dated 5th Nov., 1773.

Says he paid £575 of the Purchase Money. Produces Receipts. N.b.—There is a Receipt indorsed for the Whole. Claimt. says that Kennedy took a Mortgage of the Premises back to secure the purchase money. (56).

Claimt. had parted with all but 600 acres.

He made considerable improvements after he bought it. Cleared 40 or 50 acres. Built a frame house. Had prepared materials for a grist mill.

Claimt. understands that Capt. Kennedy & Mr. Watts, who acted as agent for Mallet & Kennedy, have got the lands again. Claimt. does not know where Capt. Kennedy now is. Thinks the whole farm with improvts. worth £1,000 York.

No. 2. Had 60 acres in Stone Araby had been Long in Possession.

Produces Conveyance from Adam Impey to Claimt. of 62 acres in Stone Araby in Considn. 5 Shils., dated 1752.

He cleared the whole of this Place & built a framed House & Barn.' Had a fine orchard.

Vals. it at £600 York. Was offered £500 for it.

The House & Buildings were destroyed by the King's Troops.

Claimt. had given a Bond & Judgment for £100 on which his creditors got Possession of the Land, but the State afterwards took it & made sale of it.

(57). Had the 3 negroes & personal Estate mentioned in the Schedule. It was seized by the Commrs. of Forfeiture in the Fall of 1777 & was sold that year.

Seems a good man. He produces an acct. of the Sale of his Things at Vendue drawn up by a Son in Law of Claimt.'s who was present at the Vendue. With the prices for which they sold.

Sir John Johnson Confirms this acct. of his Property & Certifies to his Loyalty & good character.

Claimt.'s Debts £209 York Money.

December 7. 1007. Claim of JAMES HOFFTALIN, late of Albany Co.

Claimt. says: He is a native of America. Lived at Hillsbury near Neshcat Haw, Albany Co. Joined Butler's Rangers in the year 76. Served all the War.

Had 150 acres in Sussex Co., New Jersey. His Father bought them many years ago. His Father died 40 years ago They came to him on his Father's death. He was in Possession (58). till he went to Albany Co. He then left his Brother as his Tenant.

40 acres were clear. There was a Log house. Clear Lands sold at £5 York Cy. pr. acre. The Rebels have taken the Lands. Says they turned his Brother off.

Has heard it was sold as forfeited by Claimt.

Seems a fair man. He had some Stock on his Place at Albany, the Land was not his own. He was obliged to leave his Stock, 2 horses, 3 Cows, 10 Sheep, taken by rebels. Left Utensils, furniture, when he went away.

Now settled near Niagara.

N. C.
December 7. 1008. Claim of ISBEL MACBAIN, Widow of Andrew Macbain, late of Tryon Co.

Claimt. says: She resided at St. John's in the Fall '83. Lives there now.

Her Husband was a native of Scotland. Came to America in 1774. Claimt. came with him. They took Lands on the Mohawk.

Her Husband joined the Brit. in 76. He served in Sir John Johnson's Regiment till discharged for sickness. He was taken Prisoner as he was coming to fetch his Family. He broke Gaol & made his escape.

Claimt. came the year after, during the War. Her Husband died at St. John's in 1783, leaving 2 Children both with Claimt. both Infants. (59).

He had some Lease Lands. Her Husband had not Cleared any of the Lands, but he was to have leave to Continue there.

They lost 2 Cows, 1 Bull, 2 Oxen, furniture, Flour & Wheat 14 Bushels.

Claimt. was driven from the Place by the Rebels & obliged to leave all these things.

1009. Claim of ISABEL FRASER, Widow of Simon Fraser, Deceased, late of Albany.   N. C. December 19.

Wm. Fraser, eldest Son of Simon Fraser, decd. appears.

Says this is a Claim put in for his Father's Estates by a friend of the Family & was put in in the name of his Mother. Says his Father died without a Will, leaving Isabel his Widow & eight children. Witness is the eldest, the rest of the children are with him. 5 were Infants in the Summer of 84. All agree he should act for them.

The late Simon Fraser was a native of Scotl. Came to Amer. in 73. Was settled at Mapletown, Albany Co. when Rebellion broke out. From the first he sided with Brit. Govnt. Collected many persons who came to an agreement to join the Brit. Troops as soon as they could. He joined at Skeensboro in July 77. Served till he was taken Prisoner at Bennington. He died in Albany Gaol.   (60.)   Claim admissible for Claimt & brothers & sisters.

Witness joined the Brit. Army in 77. Served in Sir John's Regt. as Lieut. has now half pay. His Mother came into the Province in 84. Witness was himself at Cataraqui in the Fall 83 & the ensuing Winter. Resides at Coteau de Lac.

Produces Letter from Judge Fraser of the active & zealous Loyalty of Simon Fraser decd. & of the sufferings of himself & family on that acct., and gives his opinion of the truth of the Acct. of Losses set forth in the Schedule.

Produces Certificate from Col. Campbell to Simon Fraser's services & of his sufferings by which his Death was as Col. Campbell thinks occasioned.

His Father had 160 acres at Mapletown, Leased. Land, taken of Alexr. Colden. Lease for ever at 1s. an acre Rent. Taken in 74. Most of it Clear when he took it. He bought the improvemts. Paid £240 York for them. He cleared about 12 acres afterwards, in the whole 124 acres clear.   (61).

The Title was under New York Govnt. His Mother has sold 100 acres of it. 60 acres of the best part she could not dispose of. This had been taken away on the Division of ye township Mapleton & Bennington in the year 1775. There was a Dispute about boundaries.

His Father had, 2 Yoke Oxen, 1 Yoke Small Oxen, 6 Cows, Calves, Heifers. Altogether about 20 head, Horse, Mare & Colt. 24 Sheep, Utensils, Some furniture, Corn & Hay in Stock.

All taken from the Premises after the Battle of Bennington. His Father was then a Prisoner in Bennington. They were taken on acct. of his having joined ye Brit. Army.

December 24.

1010. Case of WILLIAM GRANT, late of Balstown, Albany Co.

Claimt. appears & being Sworn saith:

He is a nat. of Scot. Came to America 17 years ago. Was settled at Balstown.

(62).

In 1776 he was imprisoned on acct. of his Loyalty, kept 9 months confined, joined the Brit. Army in 77. Served in Major Macalpine's Corps. Produces his Discharge in 83. Lives at Oswegatchu.

He had 279 acres in Balstown, purchased in 73, of Gasport Funday, at 2 dollars per acre. Had not paid for it & it was mortgaged back again for the whole purchase money. Cannot say how much was clear. There was a Log house. Has heard it was sold at Vendue. Says it was sold in 77. On recollection says there were 15 acres clear. There were no Clearances when he bought it.

Had 3 Cows, 3 Calves, a Yoke of Oxen, 1 Mare, 3 Colts, 2 Heifers, furniture, Utensils, Carpenter's Tools, Grain in the Stack.

Left all these Things on his Farm when he joined the Brit. They were seized & Sold at public Vendue.

Produces Deposition by James Robinson & James Macylemoile to the Truth of the above acct. Taken before Judge Fraser, Oct., 83.

N. C.
December 29.

1011. Claim of ISAAC YUREX, late of Chester Co., New York. Lodged in England.

Claimt. says: He was at Sorell in the Fall 83, and all that Winter, from thence went to Cataraqui.

(63.)

Is a native of America. Lived at North Castle when Rebellion broke out. He came to New York as soon as the Brit. Troops got Possession of it. He was so much distrest on acct. of his having been of the King's Party that he was forced to leave Home. Continued at New York till the Evacuation worked at the King's Stores. After Evacuation came to Canada. Now lives at Bay of Quinty.

He had 23 acres in North Castle, bought a little before ye Rebellion, of Nathl. Courtland, had a Deed. Gave £70 York Cury. He built an House & planted an orchard, 1-2 was Clear when he bought it. He did not want to clear any more. The Land has been taken Possession of by the Rebels.

Vals. it at £100 York. Says it was worth double. Lost 2 mares, 2 Cows, 6 Sheep, Saddles.

He left these Things on his Place when he joined the British.

Produces Deposition from Isaac & Solomon Osser, taken before Michl. Grass at Cataraqui to the truth of Claimt's acct. of Losses.

Says he is not yet settled at Bay of Quinty, was this year before last in the the State of New York. Came from there this Fall.

Michl. Grass says he looks upon Claimt. as a very honest good man. Knew he had a good Farm at North Castle. His children are now at Cataraqui. Wits. cannot form a decided opinion whether he means to Continue in this Country. Thinks if he could recover his estate at North Castle he would return, but says he has Lands here.

February 20.

(64).

Further Evidence in Case of WILLIAM SCHERMERHORN, v. Vol. 21, f. 117.

January 4.

SIMON CLARK, Wits.

Leaves several Papers that belonged to the late William Schermerhorn. The late Wm. Schermerhorn lived at his House at Montreal, left the Papers there. Witness knows nothing of his property.

There appears a List of above 100 persons as having taken the Oath of Allegiance to his Majesty, administered by Capt. Schermerhorn & agreeing to Service, dated March, 1777.

Produces a Paper signed by 60 persons at Normans Kill, May 24, 1780, seemingly to request that Schermerhorn might be one of their officers.

Produces a List of 60 persons indorsed as a List of Persons engaged by W. Schermerhorn, July, 1780.

Produces a Copy of an engagement on the part of Wm. Schermerhorn binding himself to the whole value of his estate to give Satisfaction to persons who would enlist to serve his Majesty. July, 1780.

Produces Paper of Conveyance from Frederic Wormer to John Hollomber of 60 Morrisons on Patroons Land in 1767, with Indorsement to Wm. Schermerhorn.

Produces Copy of Genl. Burgoyne's Orders Aug., 77.

Major Jessup certifies to his Loyalty very strongly, heard he had a farm on Rancellors Manor at Halleback and a good stock.

(65).

Witness remembers him serving with Genl. Burgoyne.

1012. Claim of HENRY HOVER, late of Tryon Co.

N. C.
January 10.

Claimt. says He was a Soldier in Sir John Johnsons 1st Batal. Was at La Chine in the Fall 83, gave in a Claim to Capt. Darby.

68 AR.

(66.)

A good man.

Is a native of Hanover, Came to America in 1753, Served the last French War. Lived on the Mohawk River, when Rebellion broke out. Did all he could for the King from the first. Joined Sir John's Battalion in 1780. Had five sons in Sir John's Regt. Produces his Discharge.

Produces Certificates from Major Gray of Claimt. & five Sons carried arms for his Majesty & to his good Behaviour.

Now lives in 2nd Township.

Had 100 acres Lease Land on the Mohawk, Leased of Major Fundy, Lease for ever, paying £6 York per an. Had cleared 10 acres, built house, & barn, had 3 horses, 2 Cows, 1 ox, 2 Heifers, 9 Sheep, Loom, farming Utensils.

These things were all taken after he went away & joined the Brit.

N. C.
January 10.

1013. Claim of GEORGE BENDER, late of Tryon Co.

Claimt. says: He was in Sir John Johnson's 1st Batal. Was at Cote du Lac in 83.

Is a native of Germany, came to America many years ago. Had Lands from Sir Wm. Johnston. Joined Sir John J. in 77. Served all the War. Produces his Discharge, lives in New Johnstown. Suffered very much from illness in the Woods where he came first to join the Brit.

(67).

Had 100 acres lease Land. Took it about 73. Cleared 15 acres, built house & barn. Lost 3 horses, 2 Oxen, 2 Cows, 5 Hogs, Utensils, furniture. Left all these Things when he went away.

HENRY HOVER, Wits.

Knew Claimt. He was always Loyal. Knew his farm. It was leased of Sir Wm. Johnson. He had a pretty Clearance & an orchard. 3 horses, 2 Oxen, 1 Cow, 1 Heifer, had things Comfortable about him.

N. C.
January 11.

1014. Claim of DONALD MCARTHUR, late of Tryon Co.

Claimt. Says: He was in Sir John's Regmt. Gave his Claim to the Adjutant in the Fall 83. Confirmed by Certificates

from Capt. Mackenzie.

Is a native of Scott. Came to America in 75. Produces Certificates to his Character on leaving Scotland, in May, 1775. Came to New York that year. Settl on the Mohawk, joined the Brit. in 77, at Fort Stanwix.

Served all the War. Produces his Discharge.

Purchased after rebellion.

Had 100 acres on the Mohawk, bought of Isaac Low for £20 in 1775. Cleared 14 acres, 3 Cows, 2 Calves, 1 Ox, furniture, Utensils.

JOHN MACARTHUR, Wits.

(68).

Says his Father came to America in 1775, joined Sir John Johnson in 77. He purchased Lands on the Mohawk of Isaac

68a AR.

Low in 75. Cleared a good deal. When he joined the Brit. left his Stock behind.

1015. Claim of ISRAEL, RICHARD, & FARRINGTON FERGUSON, N. C. late of Albany Co. January 11.

Israel Ferguson appears & on being Sworn saith: He and his 2 Brothers were at at St. Johns in the Fall 83. All in the King's Rangers.

Are natives of America, Lived near Fort Edward. Had a farm in Partnership, lived near each other. Israel joined the

Brit. at Skeensboro in 77. Richard joined in 78, then very young. Farrington joined in 79. Then an Infant. All served till end of the War.

Now live at the Bay of Quinty.

They had settled on Jessup's Land in Jessupsburg in 1774, which they quitted after —— some improvements. Then went to Camerons Neck. They cleared between 8 & 10 acres.

They had 300 acres on Cameron's Neck, Albany Co.

They had an agreement for a Lease from Govr. Robinson in 75, before the War broke out, settled upon ye land. When witness left it they had cleared 60 acres. Before he went away 2 horses taken. When he went away he left the Things mentioned in the Schedule on the Lands. His younger Brothers would have joined the Brit. when he did but were too young, only 13 & 12. (69).

After Israel went away his Mother & Sisters & one of his Brothers were thrown in Gaol. She came into Canada as soon as she was released. His Father came into Canada in 78.

Israel Ferguson is authorized by all the Family to receive what may be allowed for their Losses.

Produces a release from his Father to show he gives up all his Right to Compensation to his Sons, Israel receives ½ Pay as Good people.

Lieut., Richard as Ensign.

LIEUT. PHILIP LANSING Wits.:

Knew the Family. Remembers the Father employd in carrying Despatches of Consequence, giving an acct. of the Rebel Army to Canada in the year 1776. They were a very Loyal Family. Israel & his 2 Brothers served in the Rangers.

The Mother & Sisters were imprisoned at Albany. The whole Family came as soon as they could get away into Canada.

They had Cattle & Various Things taken from them by the Rebels.

LIEUT. WALTER SUTHERLAND, Wits. (70).

Knew all the three Brothers & the Father. The whole Family were Loyal. The Brothers all served. They had a Farm on Cremmes Neck. They had it before the Rebellion.

Witness was at the Place in 78. Thinks there were 40 or 50 acres Clear.

They had very good furniture & Utensils, & a good Deal of it.
Speaks of a fine Yoke of Oxen & Cows.

N. C.
January 11.   1016. Claim of DUNCAN MCINTIRE, late of Tryon Co.

Claimt says: He was at Sault de Recollect in 83. Is a native of Scotl. Left Scot in 75. Produces Certificate to his Character, 28th May, 1775, by the Minister & others.
Came to New York in the Summer 75. Settled on Sir John Johnson's Land. Came to Canada in the year 80. Served till end of War. Sent three Sons into the Army Service. 2 went at first. One was killed at Fort Stanwix. He was himself too old
(71). to go into ye Army. Staid on his Place as long as he could. He was afraid of Staying any longer, as he was a Tory. Now lives on the River Raisin.
Had a promise of a Lease of 100 acres. There was a clearance of 30 acres which he purchased, he gave 21 guins. for Improvemts. of all kinds. He had 9 head of Cattle, 3 horses, 16 Hogs, 6 Sheep, furniture, utensils.

A good man but O.   Left all these things on his Place when he went away.
HUGH CHISHOLM, Wits.
Knew Claimt's Place. He had 30 acres clear. He purchased it after Beginning of Rebellion. Knew his Stock. Agrees with acct. given by Claimt. His Wife disposed of some. All the Family are now here. They were all very Loyal. Claimt. had a Son killed at Fort Stanwix.

N. C.
January 12.   1017. Claim of PETER FITZPATRICK, Tryon Co.

Claimt. says: Was in the 2nd Batalion of Sir John's Regt. He had been confined in Albany Gaol, tried & Condemned to die by the Rebels as a Spy. Got released after ye Peace. Got here in the Fall. Heard the Claims were gone to England when he came.
Is a native of Ireland. Came to America in 1766. Lived on the Mohawk when Rebellion broke out. Served at the first of the War. Then employd in secret service. Afterwards
(72). servd till end of War. Produces Discharge from 2nd Battalion.
Had 50 acres given to his Wife by Col. Guy Johnston. She had been a servt. of his, had 14 acres clear & orchard. Built small
Seems a good man.   house, 2 Cows, 1 Mare, 4 Hogs, furniture Utensils.
Sir John Johnson confirms his acct.

N. C.
January 12.   1018. Claim of JOHN MCNAUGHTON, late of Tryon Co.

Claimt. Says: He was at Montreal in 83. Gave his Claim to ye Adjutant.
Is a nat. of Scot. Came to America in 75. Rebellion had began when he came. Went & settled on the Mohawk. Had

Lands from John Glen, 200 acres. Was to pay £20 York per 100 acres whenever they could pay. Cleared 10 acres, joined the Brit. in 77. Served all the War. Produces his Discharge.

Had 10 acres clear on the Mohawk, 3 Cows, 1 Bull, furniture, Utensils small.

1019. Claim of EWEN McLAREN, late of Tryon Co.   N. C. January 12.

Claimt. Says: He gave his Claim to his Commanding Officer in 83.

He came to America in 75. After the Rebellion began, (73). settled in Tryon Co. joined in 77. Served all the War.

Had 250 acres. Bought of John Brown. Was to pay £30 York per 100 acres. Cleared 3 acres. 1 Mare, 2 Cows, 1 Heifer, Utensils, furniture. Left all behind when he went away. A very good man.

Says New York was in the Rebels Hands when they arrived. They could not help themselves not having money to return.

1020. Claim of DONALD MACNAUGHTON, late of Tryon Co.   N. C. January 12.

Claimt. Says: He is now settled on the River Raisin. He was out of the County on a visit into ye States when the other Loyalists sent their Claims. As soon as he returned sent a Claim to Mr. Craigie. He belonged to Sir John's first Battalion. Gave his Claim to his Captn.

Is a native of Scotland, came to America in 75. Settled on the Mohawk. Joined the Brit. in 77. Servd. all the War.

Had Lands on the Mohawk, took them up after the Rebellion began, 100 acres. Cleared 5 acres, 1 Cow, 1 Mare, Utensils, furniture. Left them when he joined the Brit.

Rejected on a personal examination.

1021. Claim of SILAS HAMBLIN, late of Albany Co.   N. C. January 14. (74).

Claimt. says: He was at Sorell in ye Fall 83. Is a native of America, lived in Albany Co. when Rebellion broke out. Joined the Brit. in 1776. Served all the War. Produces his Discharge. Lives at Yamaska.

He lived at Saratoga. Had agreed for Lands there & had carried Stock upon them. Had a Yoke of Oxen, 2 Cows, 3 young Cattle, some Wheat & Hay, 4 Hogs, Utensils & furniture.

He had had Possession of these Lands some time but not A good man. having made any compleat agreement, he charges nothing for them.

Produces Certificates from Major Jessup, on the back of his Discharge to Claimt's services & having been employed in a Confidential service of Danger which he executed to Major Jessup's Satisfaction.

Knew that Claimt. had a Yoke of Oxen & some Stock.

N. C.
January 15.
(75).

1022. Claim of DAVID STUART, late of Charlotte Co.

Claimt. Says: He was at Sorell in ye Fall 83. Is a native of Scotland. Came to America in 57. Lived at Fort George when Rebellion broke out. Was from the first a friend to the King's people. Assisted in Piloting parties of Loyalists. Left his home when Burgoyne was taken. Was going to join him. Was taken Prisoner. Kept 12 months confined, got into Canada in 78. Brought his family with him, now resides at Sorell.

Had 100 acres Lease Land at Fort George, lease for ever, at £5 York Cury. had not got the Lease, but was to have had it. Had been in Possession several years before Rebellion, had 16 acres clear, built house & Stable.

Had 1 Yoke Oxen, 4 Cows, furniture, Utensils. Left them on his Place when he went away.

JOHN JONES, Barrack Master, Wits.

Knew Claimt. He was always Loyal. The Scouts of the Loyal Party used to rendezvous at his House. He was very serviceable in giving them Assistance.

He went within the Brit. Lines on acct. of his Loyalty. Heard of Improvements.

A good man.

He had 100 acres from Witness. He had been sometime upon the Land. He had cleared a good Deal. He was very diligent.

He had a pair of Oxen, 2 or 3 Cows, besides young Cattle.

N. C.
January 15.
(76).

1023. Claim of ISABEL MACLEOD, late of Tryon Co.

Claimt. says: She came to this Province years ago. She came in the Fall 83. She was unwell & could not come sooner. Brought 6 young Children, all Infants. All live with their Mother at New Johnstown.

Her late Husband Malcolm MacLeod, had been a soldier last French War. Joined Sir John Johnston at first, intending to come to Canada. He was so old that he could not go on but returned back. He was put in Gaol on acct. of having joined Sir John Johnson.

He used to harbour Scouts & give them all assistance he could. He died in 78.

He had some Tenant Land of Sir William Johnston. Had cleared 16 acres.

Furniture, Utensils, Small value, corn in the House, 30 Bushels, Sugar, Leather.

HUGH MUNRO, Wits.

Knew the late William MacLeod. He was very Loyal. Joined Sir John. Went till he could go no further. Thinks his Death occasioned by his suffering from his marching & Imprisonment. His Children were all Infants. Came into this Province soon as they could.

(77).

Wm. MacLeod had 16 acres cleared & well fenced. Thinks Claimt. very proper to have what was to be allowed, & has no doubt but that she will distribute it properly.

1024. Claim of DONALD MACKAY, late of Tryon Co.   N. C. January 15.

Claimt. says: He belonged to Sir John's 1st Batal. Gave his Claim to Capt. Mackenzie.
Is a native of Scotl. Came to America in 73. Was settled on Sir Wm. Johnston's Land when Rebellion broke out. Joined Sir John at first, served all the War. Produces his Discharge.
Had a Smart farm of 100 acres, 12 acres Clear, built house, Barn & Stable.
Had 1 Horse, 3 Cows, 2 Calves, grain in the ground, Utensils, furniture. Left all these Things on his Place when he joined the Brit.
Produces some Paper Money, old & new, about 60 dollars.   A good man.
Resides at New Johnstown.

HUGH MUNRO, Wit.
Knew Claimt's Place. He had 12 acres Clear. Agrees in the acct. given by Claimt. of his Stock. Says he joined Sir John Johnson in 76. Served all the War.   (78).

1025. Claim of JAMES GLASFORD, Tryon Co.   N. C. January 15.

Claimt. says he was at Mashishie in 83.
Is a nat. of America. Lived at the Susquehana when Rebellion broke out. Came into Canada as a Loyalist in 79. He could not stay in his own Country, having always declared himself in favour of Brit. Govnt.
He had frequently assisted Loyalists. He assisted Col. Butler & the Indian Party under him. Now resides at Mashishie.
He had taken up 100 acres Land in 74. He had not paid, but had taken Possession & made a Clearance of 8 acres. Built house & Barn. Lost 1 Mare & Colt, 1 Cow, 4 Sheep, furniture. Utensils, left behind when he came to Canada.

WILLIAM MACGEVAH, Wits.
Knew Claimt. when he lived on ye Susquehana. He was always Loyal. Left his home & came with the other Loyalists into Canada in 78. He had a considerable Clearance on the Susquehana, 2 houses & a Barn, built before ye Rebellion.
He had a considerable Stock.   A good man.

1026. Claim of WILLIAM MACGROAH, late of Tryon Co.   January 15, (79).

Claimt. says he is a nat. of Scot. Came to America in 73. Was settled on the Susquehana when Rebellion broke out. From first declared in favour of Brit. Govnt. He was obliged to leave Home. Came to Niagara with the other Loyalists in 78. Now lives at Montreal.

Had taken up 100 acres on the Susquehana, had cleared 12 acres. Built house & Barn. Left his furniture & Utensils. All his Crop was gathered.

JAMES GLASFORD, Wits.

Knew Claimt. He was very Loyal always. Came with the other Loyalists to Canada in 78.

He had a Clearance of 11 or 12 acres. Left his furniture & things behind him when he came away.

N. C.
January 16.

1027. Claim of ADAM DEAL, late of Pownal Vermont.

Claimt. says he was at Cataraqui in 83.
Is a native of America. Lived at Pownal, joined the Brit. in 77. Served till end of War. Produces his Discharge.
Now lives at Masisco Bay.

(80).

Had 45 acres in Pownal, purchased of one Osborne, purchased it for £41 York, paid most of the money for it. Says his Title was under New Hampshire Govt. There were 16 acres clear when he bought it. He cleared 10 acres more. 2 horses, 2 Cows, 3 Steers, 2 Calves, 6 Hogs, Utensils of small value.

HERMANUS BEST, Wits.

Knew Claimt. He was always Loyal. He joined the Brit. Army in 77. Went with Wits. Knew he had a farm at Pownal. He bought it before the War. One Gardiner is now in Possession. Got it during the War. Understood he left a Stock behind him when he joined the Brit.

N. C.
January 18.

1028. Claim of DANL. PRENTICE, late of Tryon Co.

Claimt. says. He was in Sir John Johnson's 2nd Batal. Sent a Claim by Capt. Leake in '83.
Is a native of America. Lived on Sir John Johnson's Land, when Rebellion broke out. Came to Canada in 1780. Says he was imprisoned & could not come sooner. Joined Sir John's 2nd Batt. in '80. Served 3 years. Produces his Discharge.

(81).

Had a farm of 130 acres hired of Sir John Johnson. Taken some years before ye Rebellion. Cleared 30 acres.
Lost 5 Cows, utensils, furniture. Left on his Farm when he went away.
Sir John Johnson certifies that Claimt. had a Lot of land from him, where he had made considerable improvemts. before the war & to his Loyalty.

N. C.
January 19.

1029. Claim of JOHN GRANT, late of Charlotte Co.

Claimt. says. He was at St. Johns in the Fall '83.

Is a nat. of Scotland. Came in '75. Came from Scotland in the summer. Went to New York. Went to Albany & so to Charlotte.

Took Possession of Lands near Fort Edward. Had 3 acres clear. Joined Burgoyne at first, served afterwards 4 years in Major Roger's Rangers.
Resides on River au Raisine.

1030. Claim of CHRISTIAN CAMERON, late Widow of Donald Ross.   N. C. January 19.

Claimt. says she came from the Colonies after ye war was over, but has 2 Infant Children who are now on the River au Raisine. The eldest, Ann Ross, lives with Finley Ross, her Brother, by Donald Ross's first Wife. The second, Mary, lives with Claimt., Alex. Ross. Donald Ross was a native of Scotland. Came to America in '63. Was settled on Sir John's Land when Rebellion broke out. Joined the Brit. at first; served about 4 years. Was at Fort Stanwix. Got an illness there & died after his Return to Canada. Left a Widow, the Claimt.. now the Wife of Wm. Cameron. She never came into Canada till the war was over.   (82).

FINLEY ROSS, his eldest Son, now under 21 years of age. He appears. Says he came into Canada in the year '80. His Father & elder Brother since dead, being in the Army. Witness staid to take care of the rest of the Family. He was then very young. They left their Home on acct. of their Persecutions. His Mother in Law & 2 sisters staid behind.

His Father had 100 acres Tenant Land on Sir John Johnson's Estate, taken in '63. He had cleared 14 acres, built house & Barn.
Lost 1 Sheep, 1 Hog, 2 Cows.
Finley Ross now lives on the River Raisine. The whole to be paid to him for himself, 2 sisters & younger Bro.   A very fair young man.

DUNCAN MACDONALD, Wits:
Knew the late Duncan Ross. He was very Loyal. Joined the Brit. in '76. Served till his Death. Left five children, Finley, Alexr. & 3 Daughters. All children when he Died. Knew his farm. He had a good clearance. Thinks 14 acres.
One of the Daughters is married to Duncan Macgregor who lives on Caldwell's Manor.   (83).

1031. Claim of BENONI WITTSER, late Albany Co.   N. C. January 22.

Claimt. says he was at St. Johns in the Fall '83. Is a native of America. Lived at Phillipstown, 14 miles from Albany. When Rebellion broke out, joined the Brit. in '77. Has served all the war. Produces Discharge from Jessup's Corps.
Lives at Oswegatchie.

Had 120 acres on Rancellor's Manor. He had not got a Lease. Bought the Improvemts. in '76. Gave Between 30 or £40, paid in Cattle. 16 acres clear when he got it. Lost 1 Horse, yoke of oxen, 3 Cows, 10 Sheep, utensils, furniture.

(84). Left on the Place when he went away to join the Brit. Produces affidavit from Jesse Lamb, taken before Ephreham Jones, Esq., to Claimt.'s Loyalty & his having the stock above mentioned.

JAMES KELSEY, Wits:

Knew Claimt.'s Place. He came in the year '76 to Rancellor Manor. He bought the improvemts. Thinks about 20 acres clear when he bought it. It was an hundred acre Lot. He had stock which he left behind when he went to Genl. Burgoyne's Camp.

January 22. Witness understood they were taken by a Rebel Committee.

Further Evidence in Case of ALEXR. MACKEE, v. Vol. 20, p. 154.

COL. JOHN CONOLLY, Wits:

Knew Claimt. before the commencement of the Rebellion. He was then settled at Fort Pitt as Deputy Superintendent of Indian Affairs. He was very active in securing the good will & assistance of the Indians to the Brit. Govert. His situation enabled him to be of great service. This was in the year 1775. Witness (85). was then acting under orders from Lord Dunmore & he found the greatest assistance from Mr. MacKee in securing the Friendship of the Indians. Witness communicated all his Plans & Designs to Claimt.

Claimt. had a Commission from Lord Dunmore in 1775 to raise a Regiment of which he was to be Lieut.-Col. The Commission was in Wits. possession, & destroyed when Wits. was taken Prisoner.

No. 1. In consequence of his conduct he made himself so obnoxious to the Rebels, that there was an order of Congress to take him up. Witness heard on which he made his escape to Detroit. Knew Lands of Claimt. on the Susquehana. No. 1.

Remembers his Father living there. Supposes the Land came to him on his Father's death. He died previous to the war some time. Claimt. was his eldest son. It was an old improved Place within 3 miles of Harris ferry in Paxton Township. Improved Lands in that neighbourhood sold very high, from 5 to £10 Pens. Cury. Does not know how much was improved, but it was settled 60 yrs. ago.

(86). There was a good Mansion House. Knows not the Quantity of Land. There was no dispute about the Lands on this part of the Susquehana.

No. 2. Did not know No. 2. These Lands in Northumberland might be disputed Lands.

No. 3. Knew that he had property in Pittsbourg.

There had been a Dispute between Pensliv. & Virginia respecting the territorial Jurisdiction. That matter was not finally settled, so that grants were not made out, but the Title of Preoccupancy was considered as being good. Claimt. must have had this Title of Preoccupancy from Mr. Ross who left Pittsburg in '76.

He lived in a Place which had been a Redoubt when the King's Troops left the Place in 1773. These Redoubts were given by Genl. Gage to different Persons.

He had surveys in Westmoreland.

Knew No. 5. It was 3 or 4 miles from Fort Pitt. It was called Chosken Island. It had been an Indian Town. There was a good Deal of cleared Land. He must have had Possession 10 years before the Rebellion. He had a good House there. It was a large survey, and a great deal cleared, both by Indians & afterwards by himself. Imagines there must have been 150 acres clear. Those lands were very valuable. They were very fertile & the Situation good.

(87).

Clear Lands in that neighbourhood have sold from 20 to 40 sh. pr. acre.

But these lands were more valuable than any others in the neighbourhood.

Claimt. had these Lands before the Dispute between Pensilvania & Virginia. It was then considered as being in Pensilv. Governt.

Claimt.'s Title was under Surveys from the Proprietor's office at Philadelphia.

Wits. has heard that this Estate has been Confiscated by Act of the State Virginia, but that Congress has since determined that it lies within the limits of Pensilvania.

Whether there has been any Confiscation by the State of Pensilvania Witness has not heard.

1032. Claim of JOHN FENNEL, late of Tryon Co.   N. C. January 24.

ELEANOR, Wife of Claimt., appears:

Says her Husband is very ill and cannot possibly attend. Her Husband was a soldier in Sir John's first Battalion. Gave his Claim in the Fall '83 to Capt. Arch. Macdonell.

He was a native of America. Lived at Johnstown when Rebellion broke out. Joined Sir John Johnson at first. Has served all the war. Now lives at Montreal. Produces Discharge.

(88).

Had 100 acres Tenant Land from Sir John Johnston.

Feb. 5. Claimt appears. He served all the war. Had 100 acres Tenant Land, 8 acres clear. Had furniture.

JOHN BOICE, Wits:

Knew Claimt. He joined Sir John at first. He had 8 acres of land Clear. Had furniture.

N. C.
January 24.

(89).

1033. Claim of ASA LANDON, late of Charlotte Co.

Claimt. says he was at St. Johns in '83.

Is a native of America. Lived in Connecticut at Salisbury when the Rebellion broke out. Joined the Brit. at Skeensboro. Was employed to carry Intelligence from Genl. Burg. to Genl. Redheazel. Had a Pass to go to his own Place from the Army after the Battle of Bennington. Found he could not stay. There were orders against him that if apprehended he would have lost his life. Got into Canada in Oct., '77. Staid at St. Johns. Continued there till he went up the Country. Now resides at Oswegatchie.

Produces Pass for himself & Family. Signed P. Skene, 1777.

Produces Certificate to Loyalty & Character from Major Jessup.

Had 200 acres in Charlotte Co. in Vermont. It was after the Battle of Lexington & after ye Battle of Bunkers Hill. He did choose to live in Connecticut Govert. Wished to get nearer the British Lines.

Produces Deed from Olive Everts to Claimt. of 100 acres in Consid. £86 Y. Cur., dated June, 1776. The other Deed was

dated about same time for 100 acres more. He paid part.

30 acres Clear when he bought it. He had Continued to improve it & fence it.

Vals. it at £200 Halifax.

Lost—yoke of oxen. They were in the King's Works. Genl. Burgoyne had them from Genl. Redhazel. Had 14 tons Hay mowed. Left a set of Tools, Flax, Wheat in the Barn; threshed 3 Bushels. Wheat in the Stack, besides utensils & Furniture.

(90).

Produces Certificates to his Character & Loyalty from Justus Sherwood, James Campbell, Alex. Campbell.

Produces Certificate of Sale by James Clayborne, Commissr. in State of Vermont.

A very good man.

Produces Appraisemt. of Claimt.'s Lands by 2 Appraisers on Oath.

January 24.

1034. Further Evidence in Case of OLIVER EVERTS—v. Vol. 18, F. 70.

ASA LANDON, Wits:

Knew Claimt. He was always Loyal. Knew his Estate at Castleton, adjoining to Wit.'s Estate. He bought it before the War.

There was excellent Intervall Land.

Vals. such Land at £3 lawful pr. acre.

As to No. 2. It was the Fathers. He does not know anything of the agreement between Father & Son. Heard ½ was the Sons.

(91).

He was in good circumstances & had a considerable stock.

PROCEEDINGS

OF

LOYALIST COMMISSIONERS

MONTREAL, 1788.

VOL. XXIII.

BEFORE COMMISSIONER PEMBERTON.

Claimants.

	MSS. Folio.		MSS. Folio
Agnew, William	77	McCaffrey, John	37
Algier, Martin	67	McDonell, Alexander	1
Annable, John	54	McDonell, Donald	6
Ault, John	77	McDonell, Jno	17
Barnhart, George	33	McDougal, John	19
Beagh, Daniel	71	McGreur, Mrs. Catharine	36
Beaker, Henry	49	McIntosh, Alexander	50
Beverley, David	35	McMullin, Donald	24
Boice, John	42	McPherson, Murdoch	6
Bowen, Luke	76	MacDonell, Hugh	1
Burrett, Stephen & Daniel	31	MacDonell, John	18
Cameron, Alexander	13	MacDonell, John	24
Cameron, Alexander Sr.	16	MacGillis, Donald	3
Cameron, Angus	16	Macdonell, Duncan	23
Cameron, Donald	25	Macdonell, John	21
Carley, Bartholomew	11	Macdonell, John	22
Caswell, Lemuel	9	Macdonell, John	23
Chisholm, William	14	Macpherson, James	20
Closson, Caleb	12	Markley, Henry	29
Cock, John Sr.	74	Mercelis, John	62
Cryderman, Mrs. Catherine	51	Morden, James	53
Dingwell, James	5	Munro, Alexander	72
Dingwell, John	5	Pickell, John	70
Dulmage, John	46	Riblin, Philip	38
Empey, Philip, Jr.	79	Ross, John	37
Ferguson, Alexander	4	Ross, Thomas	64
Ferguson, Peter	15	Ryckman, Widow	64
Fraser, Donald	27	Schick, Christian	68
Fraser, John	63	Selick, Dayle	61
Glasford, John	56	Shaver, John	29
Glasford, John Jr.	57	Sherwood, Thomas	8
Graham, Thomas	3	Staring, John	59
Grant, Alexander	7	Stoneburner, Jacob	47
Grant, Alexander; the Estate of	18	Tompkins, Israel	49
Grant, Alexander	27	Van Allin, Jacob	73
Grant, Duncan	15	Van Camp, Jacob	40
Hagart, John	25	Van Camp, Peter	41
Kennedy, Alexander	2	Waggoner, Jacob	66
Kingsbury, Joseph	78	Waldec, Martin	75
Lawrence, John	43	Wallace, William	32
Lawrence, John	79	Warner, Michael	68
Leahy, William	39	Wilson, John	47
Loucks, George	28	Wist, John	43

EVIDENCE.

N. C.
January 25.

1035. Claim of ALEX. MCDONELL, formerly of Bolesken, late Tryon Co.

Claimt. says. He was in Sr. John's 1st Battal. He was at Coteau de Lac in '83.

Is a native of Scotland. Came to America in '73. Was settled on Sr. John Johnston's Lands. Joined Sr. John at first. Served all the war.

Produces his discharge. He lost a finger at fort Stanwix. Now lives on River Raisini.

A very good man.
(1).

Had 50 acres Tent. Land. Cleared 3 acres. Built house & Barn. Had a young ox, furniture, utensils.

HUGH MCDONELL, Wit:

Knew Claimt. He came to Am. in '73. Knew his Place. Thinks 4 acres clear. Remembers the young ox.

N. C.
January 25.

1036. Claim of HUGH MACDONELL, late of Tryon Co.

Claimt. says: He was at Sorell in '83.

Is a native of Scotland. Came to Amer. in '73. Settled on Sr. J. Johnston's Lands. Continued on his Place till 1780. 2 of his Brothers went at first. Claimt. staid at Home to take care of his Father & Mother. His Father & Mother & Claimt. came all away. They Could not stay any longer. In '80 Claimt. went to Sorell. Was in the Engineer's Depart. there till the end of war.

A good man.

Now lives at River Raisini. Had 100 acres tent. Land. Had cleared 6 acres. Built house & Stable.

Lost 3 Cows, mare & Colt, farming utensils. All left behind.

ALEX. KENNEDY, Wits:

Knew Claimt. He had 100 acres. 8 acres clear. 3 Cows, mare & colt, all left behind.

N. C.
January 25.
(2).

1037. Claim of ALEX. KENNEDY, late of Tryon Co.

Claimt. says he was at Sorell in '83.

Is a nat. of Scotl. Came to America in '73. Settled in Johnson's Bush. Did not come into Canada till '80. Would not stay with the Rebels. Was in the Engineer's Department. Now lives at River Raisini.

Rented Clear Land. Had no land of his own. Had 5 Cows, 1 mare, 5 Hogs, 9 Sheep, furniture, utensils. Left all behind. Could not dispose of them.

THOMAS GRAHAM, Wits:

Knew Claimt. He was always Loyal. He had 5 Cows, 1 mare, 9 Sheep, 5 Hogs, furniture, Utensils. Left all behind.

1038. Claim of THOMAS GRAHAM, late of Tryon County. N. C. January 25.

Claimt. says he served in Sr. John Johnston's 2nd Battn. Resided at Oswego in '83.
Is a native of Scot. Came to America in '73. Was settled in Johnson's Bush. Joined Sr. John Johnson in '80. Served till end of War. Now resides at New Johnstown. Had 100 acres Tent. Land. Cleared 8 acres, built house & Barn.
Had 2 Cows, 2 Sheep, 7 Hogs, furniture, utensils, flax, 12 Bushels Ind. Corn.

ALEX. KENNEDY, Wits: (3).

Knew Claimt. He had a good Clearance. He had 2 Cows.

1039. Claim of DONALD MACGILLIS, late of Tryon County. N. C. January 25.

HUGH MACGILLIS, one of the Sons of Claimt., appears. Says his Father is very ill & keeps his Bed. & cannot attend. His Father was in Sr. John's 1st Batt. He was at Le Chine in '83. Gave his Claim to Capt. Angus MacDonnell.
He was a nat. of Scot. Came to Amer. in '73. Joined the Brit. in '77. Served till end of the war. Produces his Discharge as Seargent. Lives now at New Johnstown.
Had rented Lands. Had 3 Cows, 6 Hogs, 3 Pigs, 50 Skipples

Wheat, furniture, Cloathing.

ALEX. KENNEDY, Wits:

Says Claimt. is very ill. Knew his Stock; 3 Cows, &c. Left the Place in '77. The Stock was left on the Place.

1040. Claim of ALEXR. FERGUSON, late of Tryon County. N. C. January 25.

ALEXR. FERGUSON, his eldest son, appears. Says his Father died since his Claim was sent in. He was in Sr. John Johnston's 1st Batt. Heard he gave in a Claim to his Commanding officer.
Was a nat. of Scotl. Came to Amer. in '73. Settled on Johnson's Bush. He joined the Brit. in '77. Served till end of the war. Produces his Discharge. Left a Widow, 2 Sons, 2 Daughters unmarried, 2 other married. All in this Country. All agree that Claimt. shd. receive what may be allowed. Says he was too young to serve; not 20 yet. He came into this Country with the rest of the Family in '82, before the War was over. Came as soon as they could get away. Now lives on River Raisini.
His Father had 50 acres. Had Cleared 6 acres. Had 2 Cows, 1 ox, Flax, Some Corn, furniture, utensils. (4).

ALEX. GRANT, Wits:

Knew the late Alexr. Ferguson. He came to A. in '73. Joined the Brit. in '77. Knew his Place. He & his Bror. had 100

acres betwixt them. Alex. Ferg. had cleared more than 6 acres. He had a pretty stock. All left behind.

N. C.
January 25.   1041. Claim of JAMES DINGWELL, late of Ulster Co.

Claimt. says: He gave his Claim to Captn. J. Macdonnell in '83.

Is a nat. of Scotl. Came in 1775. Went & settled on Lands of Judge Livingston in Ulster Co. Joined at Fort Stanwix. Served all the war. Produces his Discharge. Lives on River Raisini.

(5).

He & his Bror. John had agreed to buy. They had made agreement for several Lots. Claimt. had cleared 5 acres. Left 2 horses, 2 Cows, 200 lbs. Maple Sugar, utensils, furniture.

JOHN DINGWELL, Wits:

He & his Bror. came from Scotland in May, 1775. He & his Bror. had 12 acres clear between them.

N. C.
January 25.   1042. Claim of JOHN DINGWELL, late of Tryon County.

Claimt. says. He gave his Claim to his Commanding officer in '83. Produces Certificate to that effect.

Is a nat. of Scot. Came in '75. Left Scotl. in May '75. Settled on Judge Livingston's Land. Joined the Brit. '78. Served till end of War. Had several Lots in New Stanford. Had agreed

for them. Cleared 8 acres of his own. Had 5 Cows, 1 yoke oxen, 1 horse, furniture.

N. C.
January 25.   1043. Claim of MURDOCH MCPHERSON, late of Tryon County.

Claimt. says: He gave his Claim to the adjutant in '83.

Is a nat. of Scotl. Came to A. in '73. Settled in Johnson's Bush. Joined at first. Served all the war. Produces his Discharge. Had been a soldier formerly. Produces his Discharge from 22nd Regt. New settled on River Raisini.

(6).

Had 150 acres Tent. Land. Had cleared 12 acres, built house Barn & Stable. Had 3 Cows, 3 calves, 2 Heifers, furniture, utensils. Left all behind when he went away.

DONALD MCDONELL, Wits:

Knew Claimt. Knew his Place. He had 12 acres clear. He had 3 Cows, 3 calves, 2 yearlings. Left all his Stock behind.

N. C.
January 25.   1044. Claim of DONALD MCDONELL, late of Tryon Co.

Claimt. says: He belonged to Sr. John's first Battalion. Gave his Claim to the adjutant in '83.

Is a native of Scotl. Came to America in '73. Was on the Mohawk. Had no Lands. Did not come in till year '80. He had endeavoured before & was taken Prisoner & robbed. Carried to Canada in '80. Served till end of the war. Lives on River Raisini.

Had 1 horse & 2 Cows on Murdock Macpherson's Land, some little furniture, utensils. Left behind.

ALEXR. GRANT, Wits:

Knew Claimt. Knew that he had a horse & 2 Cows. They were his own property. He left them behind.

1045. Claim of ALEXR. GRANT, late of Tryon Co.   N. C. January 25.

Claimt. says: He was in Oswego in '83. Is a nat. of Scot. Came to America in '3. Was settled in Johnson's Bush. Joined in the year '80. Served till end of War as Seargent. He was very young. Had the charge of the Family. Could not come at first. His Father John went at first.   (7).

Had 100 acres between himself & Father. His Father died in '77 soon after he joined the Brit. army. Claimt. is eldest son. Has 3 Brothers here & 2 Sisters. His Mother is also living.

There were 18 acres Clear, a good house. Had a mare & Colt, 1 Cow, furniture, utensils, Corn.

DONALD MCDONELL, Wits:

Knew Claimt's Brothers & Sisters & Mother. That they agree Claimt. shd. receive all they may be allowed. Knew the late John Grant. He joined Sr. John's Regt. very early. Died in Canada.

Claimt. is his eldest son. Knew their Farm at Johnson's Bush. This had 100 acres, 18 acres clear. Knew mare Colt, 1 Cow of theirs, &c.

1046. Claim of THOMAS SHERWOOD, late of Charlotte Co.   N. C. January 25.

Claimt. says: He was at St. Johns, chiefly in the Fall '83. Is a nat. of America. Resided at Kingsbury near Fort Edward, Charlotte Co., not Vermont. Joined the Brit. in '77. After his Retreat staid 1 year, then came into Canada & served in Major Jessup's Regt. Has now ½ Pay as Ensign. Resides at Osswigatchie.

Had 150 acres at Kingsbury. Had a Lease from Joseph Smith for 999 yrs. at 18 D. per ann. After 7 years with a right to purchase at 2 Dollars per acre. He had not made his Purchase tho. he had the money ready to do it. Claimt. says the Lease was of 242 acres granted to Seth Sherwood originally, who granted ½ the Lot by assignment to Claimt. Entered upon it 6 or 7 years before the war. Had cleared 120 acres, made ye Improvetms, after the assignment, built 1 house & 2 Barns.

Claimt. had a Brother in the Rebel service who was once in Possession of it. Lost 1 yoke of oxen, cart & chain, which were sent to Burgoyne's Camp & were lost. The Rebels got them. 1 yoke of oxen, 1 Cow, seven Swine, Hay, utnesils, furniture, some destroyed. Many articles left on his Place, when he left the Country.

CALEB CLOSSON, Wits:

Knew Claimt. He was always considered as a Loyalist. Joined Burg. in '77. Knew his Place at Kingsbury. He had

(9).

been possessed of it many years before the war. He had a Lease of a Farm of about 150 acres as Witness thinks. Thinks 100 acres were clear. An indifferent house, but 2 large Log Barns. The Lease was originally to Seth Sherwood, who assigned part to Claimt., half the Lot. Witness attested the Deed. Claimant himself made the Improvemts.

Believes Dial Sherwood, who was an officer in the Rebel Army, has the Lands now.

LEMUEL CASWELL, Wits:

Knew Claimt.'s Farm. It was in partnership between Claimt & his Bror. Claimt. was owner of half. He made the Improvements after the assignment from his Bror. Cleared 120 acres.

N. C.
January 25.

1047. Claim of LEMUEL CASWELL, late of Charlotte Co.

Claimt. says: He came from Philadelphia where he had been imprisoned in Octr., '83. Continued that Fall & Winter at St. Johns.

Is a nat. of America. Lived near Fort Edward. Joined Genl. Burg. Attended the Camp with his Team, where he was taken. Claimt. staid about 12 months, then came into Canada. Joined the King's Rangers. Served till end of war. Was taken prisoner on an expedition into ye Colonies & kept imprisoned from 6 Octr., '81 to 7 May, '83. Produces his Discharge as Seargt. Lives at Oswegatchie.

Had 240 in Kingsbury. Had a long Lease for 999 yrs. at 1s. per acre. Took the Land in '73. Cleared 30 acres, built house & Barn.

(10).

Had a Deed of 240 acres in Vermont. It was a right in Weybridge near Otter Creek. Purchased in 1760 for £10 York. Had done nothing. Lost 1 yoke oxen, 2 horses, 2 Cows, 2 young Cattle, 6 Sheep, furniture, utensils. Most of these things taken after he left the Country to join the Brit.

Produces Certificate to his Loyalty & to his having been employed in Secret Service with great Hazard & to his having been taken while so employed & tried for his life, from Justus Sherwood.

THOMAS SHERWOOD, Wits:

Knew Claimt. He was considered always as Loyal. He joined Genl. Burgoyne's Army with his Team. Came into Canada in '80. He was frequently employed on Secret Service. He was taken & tried for his Life. One Lovelace, who was taken with him, was hanged. Knew his Place. Thinks 242 acres; 30 acres cleared, house & Barn. He was in good circumstances. Had oxen & Cows.

January 25.

1048. Claim of BARTHOLAMEW CARLEY, late of Charlotte Co.

Claimt. says: He is a native of America. Lived at Fort Edward. Was always a friend to the Brit. Govert. He was very young when Burgn. came into the Country. Did not join till '81, but gave assistance to Loyalists. Was employed in carrying Despatches. Came into Canada & joined Jessup's Regt. in '81 & served till end of war. Produces his Discharge. Now lives at Osswegatchie.

(11).

Had a Tenant Farm of 140 acres at Fort Edward. It was a Lease from Henry Cuyler to Joseph Jellet in 1772, which was assigned to Claimt. Joseph Jellet was Claimt.'s grandfather. Produces Lease of 140 acres for 21 yrs., dated in 1772. There appears an Indorsement that Joseph Jellet gave this up to Claimt. There were 30 acres improved. Improved by Claimt.'s Grandfather. Says the Assignment was made in '78. He gave a note to pay £43. Cuyler has entered upon it & granted a new Lease.

Lost 2 horses, 8 Tons of Forage, farming utensils. Left on his Place.

THOMAS SHERWOOD, Wits:

Knew Claimt. Considered him as Loyal. When Witness went on service, he was informed Claimant was to be trusted, which he found. Claimt. brought recruits & gave assistance. He came to Canada afterwards & served.

Knew his Place. It was his Grandfathers. A considerable clearance. Thinks 20 acres clear. They had a good Deal of Hay. Speaks of horse & Cow.

(12).

1049. Claim of CALEB CLOSSON, late of Charlotte Co.

N. C.
January 25.

Claimt. says: He was at St. Johns in ye Fall '83.

Is a native of America. Lived at Fort Edward. Joined Genl. Burgoyne at Skeensboro. Was in Major Jessup's Regt. till end of the war, but has been chiefly employed in Secret Service. Now lives at Osswegatchie. Produces Certificate from Justus Sherwood to his having been employed in Secret Service 2 yrs., which he executed very faithfully. Produces Instructions while he was going on Secret Service from Major A. Dundas. Produces his Discharge from Jessup's Corps as Seargt.

Had 250 acres at Fort Edward. It was a Lease from Genl. Skene to Oliver Barker. The lease was granted 15 years ago. It was a Lease for 999 years. Oliver Barker was Claimt.'s Step Father. He died before the war. Claimt. entered on the Place on his Death. Made the Improvements himself. Cleared 5 acres entirely, 15 nearly cleared, built Log house. Had 4 Tons of Hay at another Place, which he left behind him when he went away.

MR. THOMAS SHERWOOD, Wits:

(13).

Knew that Claimant was much employed on Secret Service. Thinks he gave as much satisfaction as any one of his Rank in such employment. Knew his Place. He built a small house & improved 10 acres. It had been his Step Fathers. He died before the war & Claimt. made the Improvements.

Seems a good man.

N. C.
January 26.

1050. Claim of ALEXANDER CAMERON, from Invermorrison, late of Tryon Co.

Claimt. says: He gave his Claim to the adjutant in the Fall '83.

Is a native of Scotland. He came to America in '73. Settled in Johnson's Bush. Joined the Brit. at first; served all the war. Produces his Discharge. Lives at New Johnstown..

Had 100 acres Tenant Land. Had cleared 10 acres, built house, Barn & stables.

Had 4 Cows, 1 calf, 1 ox, 2 Heifers, utensils, furniture. Left all behind. His Wife disposed of nothing.

A good man

ALEXR. GRANT, Wits:

Knew Claimt. He came from Scotland in '73. Had 10 acres clear. He left it very early. He had a pretty good stock.

N. C.
January 26.
(14).

1051. Claim of WILLIAM CHISHOLM, late of Tryon Co.

Claimt. says: He gave his Claim to the adjutant in the Fall '83.

Is a native of Scotl. Came to Amer. in '73. Settled in Johnson's Bush. Joined the Brit. in '77. Served all the war. Produces his Discharge. Lives on River Raisini.

A good man.

Had 100 acres Tenant Lands. Had cleared 9 acres, built house & stable. Had 4 Cows, 1 Hog, furniture, utensils. Left all behind when he went away.

ALEX. CAMERON, Wit:

Knew Claimt. Knew his Place. He had cleared 9 acres. 3 or 4 Cows.

N. C.
January 26.

1052. Claim of PETER FERGUSON, late of Tryon Co.

Claimt. says: He gave his Claim to Capt. MacKenzie in ye Fall '83.

Is a nat. of Scotl. Came to Am. in '78, settled in Johnson's Bush. Came with Sir John at first. Served till end of War. Produces his Discharge. Now lives on River Raisini.

A good man.

Had 50 acres of Tenant Land, had Cleared 6 acres, built house & Stable. Had 3 Cows, 1 ox, 1 Heifer, utensils, furniture. Left all behind.

ALEX. GRANT, Wits.:

(15).

Knew Claimt. Knew his Place. He & his Brother Alex. had 100 acres between them, had separate Houses, they had Cleared between 14 or 15 acres. Claimt. had $\frac{1}{2}$ that Quantity for his share. He had some Cows.

1053. Claim of DUNCAN GRANT, late of Tryon Co. N. C. January 26.

Claimt. says: He was in Coteau de Lac in '83, belongd. to Sr. John's 2 Batt.
Is a nat. of Scotl. Came to Amer. in '73, settled in Johnson's Bush, joined Sr. John at first, served all the War. Now resides at New Johnstown.
Had a Tenant Farm, had Cleared 7 or 8 acres, had 8 horned Cattle, 5 Sheep, 1 Hog, Corn, furniture, utensils, all left behind.

DUNCAN MACDONEL, Wits.:
Knew Claimt., he joined Sr. John at first. Knew his Place, 8 acres Clear, he had 8 Cattle, 5 Sheep, furniture, utensils.

1054. Claim of ANGUS CAMERON, late of Tryon Co. N. C. January 26.

Claimt. says: He was at St. Michells in '83.
Is a nat. of Scot. Came to America in '73, settled in Johnson's Bush. He joined in '77, served till end of War. Produces his Discharge. Lives at River Raisini.
Had 100 acres Tenant Land, had cleared 8 acres, had 2 Cows, Corn, utensils, furniture. (16).
A good man.

ALEX. GRANT, Wits.:
Knew Claimant., he settled in Johnson's Bush in '73. He had near 12 acres Clear. He had some Cows, &c., left behind.

1055. Claim of ALEXANDER CAMERON, SENIOR, from Glenmorrison, late of Tryon Co. N. C. January 26.

Claimt. says: He was at Le Chine in '83.
Is a nat. of Scot. Came to America in '73, settled in Johnson's Bush, joined the Brit. in '79, served till end of War. He now lives in New Johnstown.

Had 100 acres, had cleared 20 acres, built house & barn, 1 horse, 11 Hogs, 1 Sheep, Goods, furniture.

JOHN MACDONELL, Wits.:
Knew Claimt He joined Sr. John on his second Journey from that part of the Country to Canada, he had cleared 20 acres, he had 1 Horse, 11 Hogs, &c.

1056. Claim of JNO. MCDONELL, from Inveroucht, late of Tryon Co. N. C. January 26. (17).

Claimt. says: He gave his Claim to Capt. MacDonald in the Fall '83.
He is a nat. of Scot., came to America in '73, settled in Johnson's Bush, joind Sr. John on his second Expedition, served till end of the War. Lives on River Raisini.

Had 50 acres, had cleared 10 acres, had 3 Cows, 2 horses, 1 Heifer, Corn, furniture, utensils.

ALEX. CAMERON, Wits.:

Knew Claimt. Knew his Place, he had 10 acres clear. He had 3 Cows, 2 Horses & Heifer.

N. C.
January 26.

1057. Claim of JOHN MACDONELL, from Tomachraiskie, late of Tryon Co.

Claimt. says: He gave his Claim to Capt. Anderson in '83.

He is a nat. of Scot., came to America in '73, settled in Johnson's Bush, joined in '77, served till end of War. Produces his Discharge.

Had 100 acres, had cleared 15 acres, built house, barn, & Stable, cellar.

A good man.
(18).

Had 5 Cows, 1 Bull, Corn, Sugar, furniture, utensils.

JOHN MACDONEL, Wits.:

Knew Claimts. Place, he had 15 acres clear, 4 Cows, &c., they were all left behind.

N. C.
January 26.

1058. Claim for Estate of ALEXR. GRANT, deceased, late of Tryon Co.

John MacDougal, Son in Law to Alex. Grant, decd., appears, saith: The late Alex. Grant was in Sr. John's Regiment, died in the year '77, left a Widow & 2 Infant Daughters. The Widow died in '80. Claimt. married Catharine, the Eldest Daughter, in '84, she was under age in '83.

Alex. Grant was a nat. of Scot. Came to Amer. in '74, settled in Johnson's Bush, joined Sr. John at first. Died at Montreal in the King's Hospital in 77, left 2 Daurs., Catharine & Isabella & a Widow. The Widow died in '80. Catharine mar-

ried Claimt. in '84. Isabella is unmarried & under age and lives with Claimt at New Johnstown. Agrees that Claimt. shd. receive her share.

Claimt. joined Burgoyne in '77 & served some time. Lived some time with Col. Campbell & served again in the 84th Regiment. Alex. Grant had 100 acres Tent. Land, had cleared 5 acres.

DUNCAN GRANT, Wits.:

(19).

Knew the late Alex. Grant, he joined Sr. John at first, died in Service. He had 100 acres Tenant Land, 5 acres Clear, utensils, furniture.

1059. Claim of JOHN McDOUGAL, from Broken Book, late of Tryon Co.   N. C. January 26.

Claimt. says: He was at the Cedars in the Fall '83.

Is a nat. of Scot. Came to America in '73, settled on White Creek. Had a farm near Saratoga. Was imprisoned 10 weeks in 1776. Joined the Brit. in '77, served with Burg., after he was taken came into Canada, lived with Col. Campbell. Afterwards served in 84th Regt. Now lives in New Johnstown.

Had 2 oxen on his farm which he sent to a friend to keep, they were taken by the Rebels. Crop in the ground. Left some Cloathes & a little furniture on his Place when he went away.

Produces affidt. from Alex, Munro taken before Willm. Faukner that Claimt. had a yoke of oxen, that Witness was present when they were sold by order of Congress, & to his loss of Crop in the ground.

1060. Claim of JAMES MACPHERSON, late of Tryon Co.   N. C. January 26. (20).

Claimt. says: He was at Cataraqui in '83.

Is a native of Scot. Came to America in '75, joined the King's Army at first at New York in '77. He was taken Prisoner in ye Jerseys, was bailed out, went to Johnson's Bush. Had some Land of his Father in Law, cleared 6 acres. In '80 joined Sr. John, servd till end of War. Produces his Discharge as Seargt. Produces 2 Ord. Discharges, one in the East Indies.

He had cleared 6 acres of Land in Johnson's Bush, this was in '77. When he went with Sr. John he left 2 Cows, 1 Horse, some Wheat sown, Watches & Cloathes left at New York. When he went to the Jerseys, he left these things, put into the stores, he never had them again.

ALEX. GRANT, Wits.:

Knew Claimt., he came to Johnson's Bush in '77, he had been a Prisoner. He cleared some land. He had a piece of Land from his Father in Law, had 2 Cows, 1 Horse, left on the Place when he went with Sr. John in '80.

1061. Claim of JOHN MACDONELL, from Fort Augustus, late of Tryon Co.   N. C. January 26.

ALEX. MACDONELL, his only Son, appears:

Says his Father died July, '86, he is his only son, his Mother is dead. His Father was in Sr. John's 1st Battn. Gave a Claim to his Commanding Officer.   (21).

His Father was a nat. of Scot., came to America in '73, settled in Johnson's Bush, joined Sr. John at first, served all the War. Claimt. joined the Brit. in '76, has served all the War in Queen's Rangers. Now lives in 2nd Township. Has one Sister married to Jos. Clarke.

His Father had 200 acres Tenant Land, 9 acres clear. Produces Certificate to the Loyalty of Claimt. & to the Death of his Father from Capt. Arch. Macdonell.

RANOLD MACDONELL, Wits.:

Knew the late John Macdonell. Knew his Place, 4 or 5 acres clear, 1 Cow, 1 Heifer.

Says the late John Macdonell made a Will in Favour of Claimt. & that Captn. Alexr. Macdonell has the Will.
Is told the whole will be paid to Claimt., if Mrs. Clarke objects she must inform us. Witness says she does not.

N. C.
January 26.

1062. Claim of JOHN MACDONELL, from Dalechreggen, formerly of Tryon Co.

Claimt. says: He went into the Colonies to bring his Family when the other Claims were sent, under the 2nd Act.
(22.) Sent a Claim to General Hope as soon as he came back.
Was in Sr. John's first Battn., he was at Carleton Island in '83.
Is a nat. of Scot., came to America in 1774, settled in Johnson's Bush, joined Sr. John at first, servd all the War.
Had 100 acres, 10 acres clear, mare, 1 Cow, Cloathes, furniture.

RONALD MACDONEL, Wits.:

Knew Claimt., he joined Sr. John at first & servd. He had a good Clearance, there was 10 acres clear, remembers mare & Colt.

N. C.
January 28.

1063. Claim of DUNCAN MACDONELL, late of Tryon Co.

Claimt. says: He was at Sorell in ye Fall '83.
Is a nat. of Scot., came to America in '73, settled in Johnson's Bush, joined the Brit. in '80, servd first as Volunteer in Sr. John's Regt., then joind the 84th & servd till end of War.
Now lives on River Raisini.
Had 100 acres Tenant Land, cleared 12 acres, 2 young Cattle, 2 Cows, 1 Horse, furniture.

JOHN MACDONELL, Wits.:

(23).

Knew Claimts. Place in Johnson's Bush, he joined Sr. John in his 2nd Expedition into that Country. Thinks he had 8 acres clear, 2 Cows, 1 Horse, 1 Hog, some young Cattle.

N. C.
January 28.

1064. Claim of JOHN MACDONELL, from Auchingleen, late of Tryon Co.

Claimt. says: He was at Sorell in the Fall '83.
A good man. Is a nat. of Scot., came to America in '73, settled in Johnson's Bush, joined the Brit. in '76, servd in '84, 7 years. Pro-

duces his Discharge in '82 on acct. of age & Infirmities. Lives in New Johnstown.
Had 100 acres, had cleared 2 acres; 2 Cows, 1 ox, furniture.

DUNCAN MACDONELL, Wits.:
Knew Claimts. Place, 2 acres clear, 2 Cows, 1 ox, furniture, left all behind.

1065. Claim of JOHN MACDONELL, from North Uist, late of Charlotte Co.   N. C. January 28.

Claimt. says:
He was at Montreal & delivered his Claim to his Captn. in the Fall '83. Produces Certificate from Captn. Richd. Duncan to that effect.
Is a nat. of Scot., came to America 2 years ago. Was settled at Fort Ann when Rebellion broke out. Joined the Brit. in '77, servd till end of the War. Now lives in New Johnstown.
Had 125 acres Tent. Land in Argyle Patent near Fort Ann. Had a Lease from George Way, Lease was for 100 yrs., had it 3 yrs. before the Rebellion, had cleared 15 acres, built house, barn & Stable. 3 Cows, 3 Heifers, 2 Horses, Hogs, grain, utensils, furniture.

(24).

1066. Claim of DONALD MCMULLIN, late of Tryon Co.   N. C. January 28.

Claimt. say: He was at St. John's in the Fall '83.
Is a nat. of Scot. Came to America in '73, settled in Johnson's Bush. Joined the Brit. in '77. Went to Fort Stanwix as a Bateau man, has been since in the Engineers Department, till '83. Produces his Discharge. Now lives at River Raisini.
Had 50 acres, had cleared 4 acres, 4 Cows, 2 horses, 1 Heifer, 7 Sheep, 6 Hogs, furniture, utensils.

JOHN HAGART, Wits.:
Knew Claimt., he joined Genl. St. Leger in '77. Knew his Place at Johnson's Bush, 4 acres clear, 4 Cows, 2 horses, &c.

1067. Claim of JOHN HAGART, late of Tryon Co.   N. C. January 28. (25).

Claimt. says: He was at St. John's in '83.
Is a nat. of Scot. Came to America in '75, settled in Johnson's Bush. Came within the Lines in '80. Has been in the Engineer Employment. Lives on River Raisini.
Had 9 acres clear, 3 Cows, furniture & Tools.

1068. DONALD CAMERON, late of Tryon Co.   N. C. January 28.

Claimt. says: He was on Carleton Island in '83.

Is a nat. of Scot., came to America in '73, joined Sr. John at first, servd all ye War.
Produces Discharge from 84 Regt.

Had 3 Cattle on some Lands of Angus Cameron, he was obliged to leave them when he joined the Brit.

ANGUS CAMERON, Wits.:
Claimt. had 3 head of Cattle. Claimt. is Witness' Son. The Cattle were on Witnesses Lands, they belonged to the Son, he bought them, left them, they were lost entirely. The Son never got a farthing for them.

N. C.
January 28.
(26).

1069. Claim of CATHARINE McGRUER, Widow of Donald McGruer, late of Tryon Co.

DUNCAN MACDONELL, Witness, says: Catharine McGruer is sick & cannot attend & her Children are sick. She resided at Mashishi in '83. The late Donald McGruer came from Scot. in '73, settled in Johnson's Bush, joined the Brit. Troops at first servd till his Death. died at Sorell. Left a Widow & 2 Daughters, one 12 yr. old, the other 6. They came to Canada in '82. They now live on River Raisiné.
Donald McGruer had a Tent. Farm, 3 acres clear, 3 Cows, furniture, Tools.

JOHN MACDONEL, Wits.:
Knew Claimt., he died in the service. Knew his Place, 4 acres clear, 3 Cows.

N. C.
January 28.

1070. Claim of DONALD FRASER, late of Tryon Co.

Claimt. says he was at Carleton Island in '83.
Is a nat. of Scot. Came to Amer. in '75, went to Johnson's Bush. He & his Son joined Sr. John at first, served all the War. Now lives on River Raisiné. Had 6 acres clear on Col. Butler's Sons Lands.

N. C.
January 28.

1071. Claim of ALEX. GRANT, from Strathspey, late of Tryon Co.

Claimt. says: He was at Mishimakinac in '83.

(27).

Is a nat. of Scot. Came to Am. in '74 Lived at Kats Kill. joined Sr. John at first, served all the War. Produces his Discharge from the 84th Regt. Lives at New Johnstown. He had Lease from Mr. Cummins to live upon his Land at Kats Kill, had lived there 1 year. Had 1 Cow. 1 Calf, 5 Sheep, Lambs, Cloathes, money he brought from Scotl., 65 Dollars, left behind & lost them all. Refers to Capt. Maclean for Character.
Capt. Maclean speaks in the most favourable Terms of him & gives him an Excellent Character.

1072. Claim of GEO. LOUCKS, late of Tryon Co. N. C. January 28.

Claimt. says: He gave his Claim to Capt. Duncan in the Fall '83. Produces Capt. Duncan's Certificate to that effect.
Is a nat. of Amer. Lived at Turloch, Tryon Co. when the Rebell. broke out. Joined the Brit. in '77, served till end of the War. Now lives at New Johnstown.
Had 300 acres about 15 miles from the Mohawk, given him by his Father 8 years before the War. Claimt. cleared 30 acres, built frame house, barn & Barracks. Vals. the clear Land at £4 per acre. Had 3 horses, 1 Colt, 4 Cows, 2 Heifers, 2 Calves, 10 Sheep, 6 Hogs, furniture, utensils, grain. Left all behind, they seized all his things & sold them. (28). A good man.

HENRY MACKLEY, Wits.:

Knew Claimt. He joined the Brit. in '77 & served all the War. Knew his Place, he had it from his Father, he had been upon it 8 or 9 years before the War, had cleared about 30 acres, built a farm house. Agrees in acct. of Stock. It was all sold at Vendue. Witness was Prisoner near the Place & heard of the Vendue.

1073. Claim of JOHN SHAVER, late of Tryon Co. N. C. January 28.

Claimt. says: He gave his Claim to Capt. Duncan in '83.
Is a nat. of Amer., lived at Turloch, Tryon Co., when Rebellion broke out, joined in '77, served all the War. Now lives in New Johnstown.
Had 200 acres at Turloch about — miles from the Mohawk, bought 3 years before the War of Henry Hanes for £200 York Curcy. He had 6 yrs. to pay. The time was not out when he came away. He had cleared 7 acres, built an house. Vals. his clear Land at £6 per acre, including his House, 2 horses, 2 Cows, 1 Heifer, 1 Sheep, Cloathes, furniture, utensils. Left all behind, were sold at Vendue by the Rebels. (29). A good man.

JACOB MASKLEY, Wits.:

Knew Claimt., he joined the Brit. Army in '77, served all the War. Knew his Place, he had 200 acres, bought it of Henry Hanes, about 7 ac.es clear. Agrees in acct. of his Stock. Has understood the Things were sold at Vendue.

1074. Claim of HENRY MASKLEY, late of Tryon Co. N. C. January 28.

Claimt. says he delivered his Claim to Captn. Anderson in '83. Produces Capt. Anderson's Certificate.

Is a nat. of Am., lived at Turloc, Tryon Co., when Rebellion broke out, joined in '77, served all the War. Produces his Discharge. Now lives at New Johnston.

Had 150 acres at Turloc, lease Land, hired of John Lawyer, taken many years ago by his Father. His Father gave it to Claimt. during his life Time, he died in the year '80, has one Bror. now living, 2 Sisters now here. Claimt. had an assignment of the Lease from his Father, it was a long Lease at £3.15 per Ann.

(80).

Had it 4 or 5 years before ye Rebellion, 40 acres clear, a frame house & Barn. Had 1 Horse, 5 Cows, Oxen, farming utensils.

A good man.

HENRY MASKLEY, Wits.:

Claimt. is a Cousin of Wits., he joined the Brit. in '77 & served all the War. Knew his Place at Turloc, his Father, Michl. Maskley, made it over to Claimt. some years before the War. He was then very sick, he did it by writing. Witness knows the man who drew the Writing. The old man was to have his Life in it. It was Lease Land, about 30 or 40 acres clear. The Claimt. was also to have the Stock, 8 Horses, 5 Cows, some young Cattle. There was one Elder Brother who had some Lands which his Father helped him to pay for, but the old man certainly made over this Estate to Claimant with the Stock.

N. C.
January 28.

1075. Claim of STEPHEN & DANL., BURRITT, late of Arlington, Vermont.

Stephen Burrett appears, says he is Son of Daniel Burrett. Daniel Burrett resided at Arlington from 15 July, '83; to March, '84, resides there now.

Stephen Burrett says he resided at St. John's in the Fall '83.

He is a nat. of America, lived at Arlington when the Rebellion broke out. Claimt. & his Father both joined the Brit.

(81).

in '77, served the Campaign under Burgoyne. After the defeat Claimt. was taken Prisoner, he was kept a Prisoner about 12 months, made his Escape, got into Canada.

Settled at St. Johns, was frequently employed on secret service. Served 3 years in Rogers Rangers. Now lives at St. John's. Produces Certificate from Geo. Smith to his having been employed on secret service & doing that duty well.

Claimt. had 2 Oxen, 2 young Cattle, one Cow, 1 Horse. They were on his Father's Lands in Arlington. They were taken with all his Father's Cattle after they joined Burgoyne, some plundered & some sold at Vendue. Claimt. had some grain of his own, about 70 Bushels of Wheat, taken at same time.

Produces Certificates from Govr. Chittenden that Claimt. joined the Brit. in '77 & was afterwards imprisoned a twelve month.

Seems a good man, bot. 2 of his inhabitancy

Produces affidt. from 2 persons in Arlington to the Property of Daniel & Stephen Burrett as stated in their Schedule.

Produces Certificate from Lieut. Ferguson that Claimt. served 3 yrs. & to his having discharged his Duty as a good Soldier & subject ı every occasion.

1076. Claim of WILLM. WALLACE, late of Tryon Co.   N. C. January 29.

Claimt. asys he was at Niagara in the Fall '83. (32). Is a nat. of Amer. Lived on the Mohawk when the Rebellion broke out. He set out to join Burgoyne soon after the first Battle at Saratoga. Had charge of an Express from Fort George. When going to Genl. Burg. he was taken Prisoner within a mile of the Camp, was robbed & treated with great severity, in Consequence of an Indian who was his Companion having fired on ye party who surprized them, the Indian was killed. Claimt. was terribly wounded & stript, carried Prisoner to Albany, kept Prisnr. till March, '78. Made his Escape, got to Canada, was afterwards in the Indian Department. Was Deputy Commissary of the Stores, continued in that employment during the War. Now lives at Montreal.

Produces a long act. of his Conduct when he joined Genl. Burgoyne & of his sufferings, very Circumstantial & apparently authentic.

He had £185 Cash about him, he had been collecting this sum for several years. Meant to have bought a farm, it was in Gold & Silver. He would not leave it in the Country. It was taken from him when he was taken Prisoner & given up to Gen. Gates. He had a small house on the Mohawk & some Land on which he had Permission to keep Cattle. 3 Cows left on this Place, furniture, Cloathes, large Quantity of Leather, 300 lbs. Sole Leather, worth 15 pence per Lib.

Refers to Sr. John Johnson for Loyalty & Character. Sir (33). John spoke very favourably of him, said he was industrious & in a way to save money. Sr. John such an opinion of his veracity that he said he should have given Credit to his Story.

1077. Claim of GEO. BARNHART, late of Ulster Co.   N. C. January 29.

Claimt. appears, says he was at Saut de Recollects in ye Fall '83.

Is a nat. of Amer., lived in Ulster Co., joined Sr. John's Regiment in the year '80. Left his home in 1778. Was in the Indian Co. & served with Capt. Brant. He had been imprisoned

for assisting Col. Butler before that time. He served in Sr. John's 2nd Battl. till end of the War, was Seargent.

Produces a Petition of his in '78 to ye Comrs. at Pughkepsie, praying to be released, on the back of which they return for ansr. an acct. of the Crimes with which he was charged.

He had a Lease of 180 acres on the Delaware, he took this Lease in 1770 of Wm. Cockburn, who acted for Van Plank, it was Leased for 2 Lives, Claimt. & his Sons, at £5 per Ann. 25 or 30 acres clear when he took it, he cleared a great Deal more, 70 acres more. He lived on this farm, built house & Barn.

No. 2—Had another Lease Farm of 170 acres for 2 Lives (34). near the former. Claimt. bought the Improvements in '73, gave a span of horses & £30 York Cur., 6 or 8 acres clear. He put a man upon it who cleared more. Claimt. was to have ½ the Profits.

No. 3—Had another Lease Farm 80 acres, bought the Improvements in '75. The War had begun, paid £30 for it, about 10 acres then clear. Had a large Stock on the Farm where he lived, 9 Horses, 28 horned Cattle, 44 Sheep, 50 or 60 Hogs, Flour & Grain of various kinds, Wool, Deer Skins, Leather, furniture, utensils. These things were seized & sold at Vendue. They were sold while Claimt. was a Prisoner in the Country.

JACOB KAIRN, Wits.:

Knew Claimt., he was a neighbour of Witness's on the Delaware. He was always Considered very Loyal. He left home in 1778, first served with Capt. Brant, came afterwards into Canada & served in Sir John's Regiment.

Knew the Place where he lived, remembers his buying the Improvements before the War, there was a good piece clear, he cleared near double the Quantity himself, a good 50 acres perfectly clear, the whole Farm was about 150 acres.

(35). Knew No. 2—He bought the Improvements 2 years before the War, thinks 20 acres clear. He had put a man upon this.

He had a very good stock, thinks 19 or 20 horned Cattle, thinks 9 Horses, a great Deal of Grain, Deer Skins, Leather, some was destroyed by the Rebels, but most was sold at Vendue.

Witness's Daughters was present at the Vendue & has sent him an acct. of it. Claimt. was in very good Circumstances. He was the richest man there about except Mr. Burch.

N. C.
January 30.

1078. Claim of DAVID BEVERLEY, late of Charlotte Co.

Claimt. says he was at Isle au Noix in '83.

Is a native of America, resided at Granville in Charlotte Co. when Rebellion broke out. Joined the Brit. in '77 at Skeensboro, served till end of War. Produces his Discharge. Now lives in 7th Township, New Johnstown.

Had a Lease of 300 acres in Grandville, in Charlotte Co., took the Lease of Mr. Campbell in '73. It was a Lease forever at one Sh. per acre. Went upon it in '73, had 10 or 15 acres clear, built house & Barn. Had 4 Cows, 1 yoke young oxen, 3 Horses, 7 Hogs, 5 Calves, utensils, furniture. They were taken by the Rebels the Day after he joined Burg.

(86). JOSEPH AVERY, Wits.:

Knew Claimt., he was always a Loyalist, joined Genl. Burg. at Skeensboro, served till end of the War. Knew his Place at Grandville, he took it some time before the War, not much short of 30 acres Clear. Part of it entirely Cleared. Witness lived with him in 1776, he had then 6 Cows, some Horses. Knew that his stock was taken by the Rebels. Witness was present at the time, he was then a boy. They took every thing they could lay hold of, he had 5 or 6 Cows at that time.

ALEX. FISHER, Wits.:

Knew Claimts. Farm at Grandville, there was a good Clearance. He had a pretty good Stock, he had Cows & horses.

1079. Claim of JOHN MCCAFFREY, late of Tryon Co.   N. C. February 1.

Claimt says: He was at Cote de Lac in '83 & gave his Claim to his Commanding Officer. Produces Certificate to that effect from Lieut. Allan McDonell.
Is a nat. of Ireland. Came to America 40 years ago, was settled near Sr. Wm. Johnston's Land. Joined the Brit. in '77, served all the War. Produces his Discharge. Now lives in 2nd Township.
Had 50 acres of Land, had not made a purchase but had settled himself there, cleared 3 acres, planted young orchard, built a small house. 2 Cows, 1 ox, 2 Calves, 1 Mare, 4 Hogs, Joiners Tools Compleat, Cloathes. Left everything behind. (37). A fair man.

1080. Claim of JOHN ROSS, late of Tryon Co.   N. C. February 4.

Claimt. says: He was at Carleton Island in '83.
Is a nat. of Scotl. Came in '73, lived at Johnson's Bush. Joined the Brit. in '80, served till end of War. Produces his Discharge. His Father joined Sr. John at first. Says he staid to take care of his Mother. He had 3 Cows & 1 Heifer. The Rebels took them after he went away. He had earned these Cattle by his Labour.

THOMAS MUNRO, Wit:

Knew that Claimt. had 2 Cows, 2 Heifers. He earned them by his Labr. Left them behind. They were taken soon after he went into Canada.

1081. Claim of PHILIP ROBLIN, late of Orange Co.   N. C. February 4.

Claimt. says he was at Sorell in the Fall '83.
Is a nat. of A. Resided in Orange Co. Joined the Brit. at New York in 1779 . He had always acted as a friend of Govert. in consequence of which he had been confined & tried. Was in the Barrack employment. Staid till evacuation, then came to this Country. Now lives at Bay of Quinty.
Had 15 acres of Land with 1-10 in a Grist Mill & Saw Mill in Smith's Cove, Orange Co. They came to his wife on the death of her Father, Garret Miller. Left by Will. Claimt. had been in possession 2 yrs. The Lands were plough land & meadow. Lands worth £5 York per acre. He had a share in the Profits of the Mills. (3*).
No. 2. Had 150 acres Lease Land. Lease was for 6 years from Phil. Livingston. Claimt. had taken it before the war. It was cleared chiefly when he took it. He pd. £6 per ann. Rent.

Bought the Improvemts.; gave £6 for them. He made some Improvements, fenced it, built some new buildings. He lived on this Place. Above 100 acres clear; 10 acres orchard. House &

2 Lots of Land at New York. Took the 2 Lots in 1779. Built a house.

Had 4 Horses, 1 yoke oxen, 6 Cows, 15 Sheep, 35 Bee Hives, Wheat, furniture, utensils. Says he left all these things on his Place at Smith's Cove.

Produces Certificate from Elihu Marven, Commissr. of Sequestration, that he seized the Property of Claimt. for use of the state, to Wit, Farm, Horses, Sheep.

(39.) Produces affidt. sworn before Peter Van Alstine at Bay of Quinty by Nicholas Wessels to Claimt.'s Property, nearly as stated above by Claimt. Do. from George Galloway, sworn before W. R. Crawford at Cataraqui.

February 5.   1082. Claim of WM. LEAHY, JUR., late of Charlotte Co.

Claimt. says: He is a nat. of A. Lived at Fort Edward. Joined the Brit. in '81. He was very young which was his reason for not joining before. Served in Jessup's Corps. Produces his Discharge. Now lives at Osswegatchie. Produces certificate to Loyalty from Mr. Sherwood & Barth. Carley.

A fair man. Had some Cattle on his Brother's Lands at Fort Edward; a pr. of 3 yr. old Steers, a mare, Cow & Calf. They were taken by the Rebels. Says he sent an affidt. of 2 Witnesses that he had

the Property. This affidt. was as he supposes sent with a New Claim.

N. C.
February 5.   1083. Claim of JACOB VAN CAMP, late of Albany Co.

Claimt. says: He was at Montreal in '83. Gave his Claim to the Comamnding Officer to be sent home.

Is a nat. of A. Lived at Saratoga when Rebellion broke out. He was Prisoner when Burgoyne came. He had been confined at Hertford. Kept close Prisr. for 5 months. This was in 1777 which prevented his joining Burg. Came into Canada in '80.
(40).   Served in Sr. John's Regt. Produces his Discharge. Lives at New Johnstown.

Had 100 acres Tent. Land. Took it 4 years before ye war, of Esq. Campbell; Lease forever. Had cleared 20 or 25 acres. Had 4 horses, 2 Cows, furniture, utensils, a Wagon. Taken from him in 1777 on acct. of his being a Tory. It was at this Time he was put in Prison.

JOHN BOICE, Wit:

Knew Clamt. He was always considered a Loyalist. Heard of his being imprisoned at Hertford in 1777. He came with Witness into Canada in '79 or '80. Served in Sr. John Johnson's

Regt. Knew his Farm. He had been in Possession before ye Rebellion. He had a large clearance. Heard of his stock being taken.

1084. Claim of PETER VAN CAMP, late of Albany Co., Decd. February 5.

JACOB VAN CAMP, his eldest son, appears: Says his Father died in '83, without a Will. Wits. is his eldest son.

His Father was a nat. of A. Lived at New Town, Albany Co. He had always declared himself in Favour of Govert. He was too old to serve. He had been ready to give all the assistance in his Power to Loyalists. He came into Canada in '80. He had 4 Sons & 4 Sons-in-Law, in the Army. Claimt. was in Sr. John's first Battn. He died at Montreal. Left Claimt., his eldest son, (41). Mary, married to John Boice; Phoebe, married to Saml. Street, of Osswegatchie; Simon, in the States; Thomas do.; Hetty, married to Wm. Leahy; John at Johnstown.

His Father had 100 acres Tenant Land at New Town, Albany Co. He had lived on it 18 or 20 years. Most of it was improved. It was a Lease forever at £5 Rent. He had Horses.

JOHN BOICE, Wits:

Knew Peter Van Camp. He was not very loyal at first, but soon joined the King's Party & became very Loyal. He was fined & Imprisoned. He came into Canada in 1780. He could not stay any longer.

He had a fine Farm. He had been upon it a Long time. It was about 100 acres. It was almost all clear. No more woodland left than was necessary. Witness helped clear a good deal of it himself. There were good builds., 2 orchards. He was driven from it by the Committees.

Knew of his losing 2 Horses. Heard of his losing farming utensils.

1085. JOHN BOICE appears. Says he sent a Claim with the February 5. others in March, '86. Says he recd. a Letter from Peter Hunter to know whr. he delivered his Claim to his Commanding officer, as Claimt. was in Sr. John's first Battalion. (42).

Claim was for Leased Land of Sr. John's 40 acres improved. Bought the Improvements. Gave £81, 4 Cows, 2 yoke of oxen, 1 yoke of Steers, 2 Heifers, 7 Sheep, furniture, utensils. Says his Claim was brought down from Captn. Andersons by Philip Shaver, who brought a good many at the same time, all that belonged to Sr. John's own Co. He assured Claimt. he had delivered it to Capt. Greenway.

Is told he must send down Mr. Hunter's Letter & must send us down Mr. Anderson's acct. of it & Mr. Shavers. Philip Shaver swears that he brought Boice's Claim with the others in March '86 & delivered Feby. 15. Produces Certificate from Mr. Anderson

70 AR.

that Claimt. perseveres in an acct. of his Lossess to him & was sworn to the truth of them by him in March, 1786.

N. C.
February 5,

1086. Claim of JOHN WIST, late of Albany Co., Lodged in England.

Claimt. says: He delivered his Claim to Capt. Leake in '84 & to Capt. Gomersal.

Is a nat. of A. Lived on Rancellor's Manor. Joined Genl. Burg. Served all the war.

(43).
A fair man.

Had 105 acres Tent. Land on Roncellor's Manor. Bought the Improvements for £30 in '75. Lived 2 years upon it. Cleared 15 acres more. 15 acres were clear when he bought it. 3 horses, 3 Cows, 2 Calves, 5 Sheep. All taken in 1777.

WILLIAM JAMSON, Wits:

Did not know Claimt.' Farm. Remembers his having a good stock before he went to Rancellor's Manor, but cannot speak to particulars. He had been a neighbour of Wits. before he went to Rancellor's Manor.

N. C.
February 6.

1087. Claim of JOHN LAWRENCE, late of Charlotte Co.

Claimt. says: He sent his Claim home by Major Leake. Gave it to him in the Beginning of Novr., '83.

Is a nat. of Ireland. Came to America 18 years ago. Was

settled in Camden Dist., Charlotte Co. Says it is not in Vermont. He joined the Brit. in '76. Served two years. Was then in the Commissary Department & had the care of his House & office at Montreal. Now lives at Osswegatchie.

No. 1. Had 188 acres in Campden. They were the property of his wife, Margaret Emberry. He married her in '75. She is now with him & Claimt. has children by her. She was the widow of Philip Emberry.

Philip Emberry left the Estate to his wife & her children by the Testator. He died in '73. There are two children; a Daughter married to Fisher, a shoemaker in Montreal. A son named Samuel who lives with Claimt. He is of age. He came within ye Brit. Lines in '75. His wife took possession immediately after her first Husband's death. It was a Tenant farm. Hired of Lawyer Duayne. A Lease for ever at 6 pence per acre. 45 acres clear, a good House & Stable. Claimt. lived there some time till he removed into Albany Co.

(44).

He let the Land when he went into Albany Co. The Lessee was to pay Landlord's Rent & all charges & £4.10 per ann.

Withdraws Claim for 2nd Article.

No. 3. Had 100 acres Lease Land Albany Co. Bought the Improvements for £50 York in '75. Went and lived there.

15 acres clear when he bought it. He cleared 2 acres more. It was a Lease for 46 years. Was to pay £50 for it, but he had not paid anything except one year increased Rent. The Tenant was

indebted to ye Landlord. He took this Debt upon himself on purchase of the Improvements, but has not paid the money. Had 3 Cows, 1 mare, 4 Colts, 2 yoke oxen. It appears 1 Cow taken for a fine. The other 2 disposed of for his family. The 2 young oxen taken by the Rebels. Some of the Colts saved. Withdraws his Claim for utensils & furniture. *Seems a good man.*

DUNCAN FISHER appears: (45).

Says he came to America in '75. He married Catharine Emberry. She is entitled to 1-3 of the Improvemts. under her Father's Will. *Is very well contented that the whole should be paid to claimt.*

JOHN DULMAGE, Wits:

Knew Claimt. He was always counted Loyal. He joined the Brit. in '76. Served 2 years. Was in Burgoyne's Campaign. Continued after that for some yrs. at Montreal.

Knew the Farm in Camden District. Remembers Philip Emberry in Possession. He left it to his Wife, now married to Claimt. & her children. She took Possession on her first Husband's death. This was Lease Land.

Knew No. 3. He bought the Improvemts. on that Farm in '75. He had 4 Oxen, young Cattle &c.

1088. Case of JOHN DULMAGE, late of Charlottte Co. February 6.

Claimant says: He is a native of Ireland. Came to America in 1756. Was settled in Charlotte Co. when Rebellion broke out. Joined the Brit. in '76. Served in Major Jessup's Corps. Served the whole war. Has ½ pay as Lieut. Lives at Osswegatchie. Produces Certificate to his services & Loyalty from Major Jessup.

Had a Lease of 200 acres in Campden. Took the Lease about 7 years before the war. It was a Lease forever at 3 pence per acre. He had cleared about 35 acres, built 2 dwelling houses & several Barracks & Buildings. His family were driven off by the Rebels in '78. (46).

Lost 3 Cows & some Hogs, utensils, furniture. Every single article was taken from his Family after he went away. Produces a Certificate from David Embery that Claimt.'s farm was taken Possession of by the Rebels in '78. *Seems a respectable and good man.*

PAUL HECK, Wits:

Knew Claimt.'s Farm in Camden District, 200 acres; 35 acres or more cleared. There were good buildings. It was an exceeding good farm. He was in good circumstances and had a good stock.

1089. Further Evidence in Case of JOHN WILSON—VI Vol. 19, P. 42. February 7.

JOHN DULMAGE, Wits:

Knew Wilson's Patent. Claimt. was one of the Patentees. Witness understood that Claimt.'s share was 1,000 acres. Claimt.

(47).

had a good house & Barn & had made considerable Improvements. Vals. Woodlands from 12 to 20 sh. York. Does not consider this as applying to large Tracts of Land. He had Horses and cows & pretty good stock. He was in good circumstances.

N. C.
February 8.

1090. Claim of JACOB STANBURNER, late of Tryon Co.

Claimt. says: He was at Sorell in the Fall '83. Is a nat. of Germany. Came to A. very young. Settled at the Schoharie at the Head of the Delaware. Had four Sons who joined the Brit. in '77. Claimt. was imprisoned on acct. of having sent his Sons into the Army. Kept close confined a twelve month thmen let out on parole. His Place was seized & all his effects plundered, so that he could not return home. Continued in Connecticut some time. Several years sculking about. In '82 made an attempt to get into Canada. Staid a year up the Country but could not meet

Q. if admissible with an opportunity, that he went there for that purpose & he afterward returned to New York, but did not arrive there till Aug., '83. Came away on Evacuation. Claimt. says he went up the north River with a full view of getting into Canada. He staid between Œsopus & Albany. This he thinks was in the year '82.

He says he cd. not get from Connect. while he was on his parole there, tho. he made several attempts & went to the sea side with a view of meeting with some Boat to take him to Long Island.

Had 500 acres in Harpersfield, Tryon Co. Bought in '72. Gave £50 for 300 acres & £30 for the other 200 acres. Cleared 25 acres. Had all the stock mentioned in his Schedule. All seized in '77. Now lives in New Johnstown.

(48).

ISAAC STEWART, Wits:

Knew Claimt. when he lived at the Head of the Delaware. He was always Loyal. He sent two of his sons with Wits. in '77 to join the Brit. There were 2 young Boys who came afterwards & served in Sr. John's Regt. Heard of the Imprisonment of Claimt. Heard that he made frequent attempts to get into Canada. He came to New York before the Evacuation.

Knew his Farm, but does not know the number of acres. There was a good clearance. He had a plentiful stock. All his things were plundered by the Rebels after his sons joined the Brit. Army. Says there were great Difficulties in getting into Canada.

N.C.
February 9.

1091. Claim of ISRAEL TOMPKINS, late of Saratoga.

Claimt. says: He was at Isle au Noix in the Fall '83.

Is a nat. of A. Lived at Stillwater. Joined Genl. Burgoyne. Served all the war.

(49).

Produces Major Jessup's Certificate to his services. Had a Cow & Calf on the Lands of John Aurie. Claimt. had the land on shares with him. Had Corn & Flax &c. sown. Claimt. came away before Harvest.

1092. Claim of HENRY BEAKER, late of Albany.   N. C. February 9.

Claimt. says: He was at Isle au Noix in '83.

Is a native of A. Lived on Schoharie Creek when Rebellion broke out. Joined Sr. John Johnson in '76. Served all the war. Produces his Discharge. Lives in the 5th Township.

Claimt.'s Father had 40 acres of land. Bought of Esq. Lawyer 7 or 8 years before the war. Says he paid £130 York for it. There were 50 acres. He paid some ready money, some at one time & some at another. £30 remained unpaid, for which 10 acres were given up, which has reduced the No. of acres to 40. His Father died in the King's service at Carleton Island. He joined the Brit. at first. Claimant is eldest son. All this Land was clear. Vals. it at £6 per acre. Heard that a Deserter of Burgoyne's Army was in Possession of it.

His Father had 8 Horses and all the effects mentioned in Schedule. Claimt. has 2 sisters & one Bror. in the Colonies. One Brother Conrad in New Johnstown.

ANDREW SOMMERS, Wits:

Knew Claimant's Father, Bostine Baker. He & his two sons joined the Brit. at first. Knew his Lands on Schoharie Creek. He bought it long before the war. Claimt. is the eldest son. It was a large Farm, about 50 acres. Nearly that number of acres clear. Vals. the best clear Land there at £10 York. The Land there was very valuable. His Father had a good stock. Name in Anstey's List.   (50).

1093. Claim of ALEXR. MCINTOSH, late of Tryon Co.   N. C. February 11.

Claimt. says: He sent his Claim by Capt. Wm. Fraser. Resided in the Fall '83 above Sorell.

Is a native of Scotl. Came to A. in '73. Was settled at Harpersfield, Tryon Co. Joined the Brit. in '78. Joined Major Jessup's Corps in 1780. Served till Regiment was disbanded.

Produces his Discharge. Lives at Osswegatchie.

Had 150 acres at Harpersfield; Tenant Land, on a Lease of 8 years without Rent & then for ever, paying 1 Six pe. pr. acre. He had 12 acres clear. Had house & barn. Had 9 Cows & 4 Calves, 1 mare, furniture, utensils. His Witness John McKay is so ill that he cannot attend. He produces a Paper from him setting forth that Claimt. joined the Brit. in 1778, and that he had the Property above stated.   Seems a fair man.

1094. Claim of CATHERINE CRYDERMAN, Widow of Valentine Cryderman, late of Tryon Co.   N. C. February 11. (51).

Claimt. says: She did not come into this Country till '85.

This is a Claim for the Estate of her late Husband. Says her Husband was a Loyalist, very true to King. He was too old to go as a soldier. He was taken up & put in prison in '76, by which he lost his Scenses. He lived some time afterwards and died the yr. '80. He sent 3 sons into the Army.

He left Michael, his eldest son who served with Sr. John Johnson, 4 other Sons & 3 girls; all in this Country. Three sons have been in the Army. The younger children are under age now. All live with their Mother in New Johnstown, except Michael who lives at Bay of Quinty.

Valentine Cryderman was a German. Came to America many years ago. Lived in Johnstown when the Rebellion broke out. He was always Loyal. In 1776 he was taken up & kept a close Prisoner 3 months & used terribly ill. He was required to take an Oath, which he refused. He became so ill in Consequence of his sufferings, that he never recovered. He lost his senses & was confined to his Bed a long time. Died in '80.

(52). Her Husb. had 125 acres Lease Land in Johnstown. Produces a Lease of 125 acres in Secondago from Wendell & others to Martin Walter forever at £6 per ann. Y. Cur., 1774, with assignment to Valentine Cryderman for £40, 1774. 8 acres were clear when he bought it. He cleared 22 acres more. Lost 2 Horses, furniture, cloaths, &c. She was obliged to sell her Cows & some other stock.

JAMES MORDEN, Wits:

Knew Valentine Cryderman. He was very Loyal. He suffered much from Imprisonment that Witness thinks it occasioned an Illness which proved fatal to him. Knew his Farm. Remembers him settling there. There was not much clear when he purchased.

Seems a good family.

JOSEPH CRYDERMAN, 2nd Son, appears:

Says the whole Family agree that his Mother shall receive the sum allowed.

N. C. February 11.

1095. Claim of JAS. MORDEN, late of Tryon Co., Decd.

JAMES MORDEN, eldest son, appears: Says he has 4 Bros. & 2 Sisters, all in this Country. Claimt. is eldest of them all. They were all under age in '83.

(53).

Joseph Morden was a native of England. Came young to Am. Was settled on the Mohawk. He joined Sr. John at first. He died in service in '77. Claimt. joined in '79. He served till end of the War. Had another Bror. that served. All live in Bay of Quinty. All agree that Claimt. shd. receive what is allowed.

His Father had a Tenant Farm. Near 70 acres Clear. It was a Farm hired of one Holland. His Father had been in Possession seven years. His Father lost 2 horses, a yoke of oxen, 4 Cows, His Father left them & they were taken by the Rebels. Some furniture.

JOSEPH CRYDERMAN, Wits:

Knew the late Joseph Morden. He came in with Sr. John at first. He died in the service. Knew his Farm. There were

70 acres clear. It was Tenant Land. He had had it many years before the war. He had a good stock on the Farm. Knows the eldest son, Joseph. He served from '79 till end of the war.

1096. Claim of JOHN ANNABLE, late of Tryon Co.   N. C. February 12.

Claimt. says: He was in Sr. John's first Battalion & gave his Claim to his Commanding officer, Captn. Anderson, in Octr., '83. Produces Copy of such Claim, dated in Octr., '83, as given in at that time.

Is a native of England. Came to America in '74. The war was near beginning, but it was before the affair at Lexington or Bunkers Hill. He settled on some Lands belonging to John Turnecliff, near the Mohawk. Came into Canada & joined Sr. John in '76. Has served all the War. Produces his Discharge as Seargent. Lives at New Johnstown.   (54).

No. 1. In 1774 he & James Massie went & settled on some Lease Lands taken of John Turnecliff, near the Mohawk. Had girdled 100 acres. Had about 12 acres Clear for crop. Built a house.

James Massie joined the Brit. in '76. He served in Sr. John's Regiment several years. Went to England. Claimt. says he was very ill when he heard of him last.

They bought 200 acres Woodlands about 50 off on the Antigo River. This was in '75. They had paid £25 York. Says he had a Deed from Mr. Wells. The Lands sold at £25 York per 100 acres. Claimt. had paid for clearing 6 acres. They had 19 Head of Cattle, 7 Horses, utensils, furniture.

Says he & Massie were taken Prisoners from their Farm in May, '76. Were carried to Albany; kept 3 weeks in Confinement. They made their Escape & got into Canada. Never returned to their Place again. All the above Stock was on their Farm. Says he had £50 when he came upon the Lands & settled first, Cattle & Money. Massie had £50 also.   (55).

JOHN BROOKE, Wits:

Knew Claimt. He was a neighbour to Wits. Knew his Farm, taken of Turnecliff. There was a good clearance. He had bought 200 acres on the Antigo River. Had paid for 100 acres. Massie was his partner. Cannot say when it was bought. It was in 1774 or 1775. They had 19 head of Cattle, large & small, 7 Horses. Remembers them being taken up & carried to Gaol. They never got to their Farm again & thinks all their Property was lost. Sr. John Johnson Certifies to the services of Claimt. & Massey.

N. C.
February 12.

(56).

1097. Claim of JOHN GLASFORD, late of Tryon Co.

JANE GLASFORD, Wife of Claimt., appears: Says her Husband is near 80 yrs. of age & very infirm & Could not Come. Her Husband was at Mashishe till he moved into the Upper Country. Her Husb. is a nat. of Scotl. Came many years ago when he was a Boy to America. He was settled on the Susquehana when the Rebellion broke out. Two sons joined Captn. Brandt & served with him in the Indian Country. Her Husband was to old to serve, but he sent his Sons to serve, and always declared himself in Favr. of Govert. The Rebels came in '79 & plundered them, & stript them of everything. She was almost starvd in her own house. They were all obliged to come away. Came to Niagara. Their House was burnt as soon as they left it. They now live at Osswegatchie.

He had 300 acres. Agree for them with Mr. Banyard & Mr. Wallis 7 or 8 years before the war. They were to pay £40 York for each 100 acres. They have given their Bond for the money and he gave his obligation to give them a Deed of the Land. They had not paid anything but the Bond is against them. Her Husb. had Cleared & fenced 40 acres, built a good house & Barn & Corn

house, planted an orchard. Had 1 Horse, 15 Sheep, 5 Hogs, all their furniture which was very good, Grain in the House & Barracks, 6 Cows, 5 Cattle. Some taken by Brant's Indians. Produces affidt. from Saml. Street that Claimt. had a valuable Farm on the Susquehana with a good stock. That he was plundered by a party of Rebels under Genl. Herkeman & to the services of his Son. Sworn before Justus Sherwood who certifies to Mr. Streets eredibility.

(57).

JAMES CROWDER, Wits:

Appear to be a good family.

Knew Claimt. Witness was a near neighbour of his on the Susquehana. He was always a good Loyalist. He had 2 Sons that served. His Place was plundered by Genl. Harkeman on acct. of his being a Loyalist. He was driven from his Place on acct. of his being a Loyalist. Came into Canada in '79. He had been settled some time on the Susquehana. He had about 40 acres clear. He had a considerable stock. He had Horses, Cows & Sheep. He was one of the ablest men in the Place.

N. C.
February 12.

1098. Claim of JOHN GLASHFORD, JUR., late of Tryon Co., Decd.

SARAH, his Widow, appears: Says her Husband died about a twelve month ago.

Says her Husb. was in Sr. John's first Battalion. Gave his Claim to his Commanding officer in '83. Produces Capt. Munroe's Certificate to that effect.

Her Husband was a native of America. Lived on the Susquehana when Rebellion broke out. Joined Capt. Brant's Indians. Came with them into Canada. There joined Sr. John's Regt. &

served till end of the war. Produces his discharge. He died a year ago, leaving 6 children, all living with Claimt. Now living at New Johnstown.

He had 100 acres of Land on the Susquehana. They were to have a Deed & paid for it, but they had not paid. He had Cleared 12 acres, built a house. He had 2 Cows, 2 oxen, Cloathes, furniture, utensils. (58) A good family.

LITTET GLASFORD, Wits:

Says his Bror., John Glasford, had a farm on the Susquehana. He had cleared 10 or 12 acres. He had some Cows & young Cattle. Witness was informed that he lost everything. He came almost naked into Niagara. He has left a Widow & 6 Children. The eldest son is about 20 yrs. of age.

1099. Claim of JAMES CROWDER, late of Tryon Co.   N. C. February 12.

Claimt. says he gave his Claim to his Commanding Officer in '83. Produces Certificate to that effect.

Is a nat. of Am. Lived on the Susquehana. From the first declared in favour of Brit. Governmt. Joined Butler's Rangers in '77; served 4 years, then served in Sr. John Johnson's Regt.

Produces Col. Butler's Certificate to his services & Loyalty. Produces his Discharge from Sr. J. Johnson's Regt. Now lives at New Johnstown. A very good man.

Had 100 acres on the Susquehana. Had bargained for them. Cleared 25 acres, built house. He had 3 Cows, 2 Heifers, 1 Bull, 9 Hogs, 4 Horses, utensils, furniture. Left all this stock on his Place when he went away. (59).

PAUL GLASFORD, Wits:

Says he knew Claimt. He was always considered as a Loyalist. Knew his Place on the Susquehana. He had 30 acres clear. He had a pretty good stock. Had horses & Cows.

1100. Claim of JOHN STARING, late of Tryon Co.   N. C. February 12.

Claimt. says he was in Sir John's 1st Battalion & gave his Claim in '83.

Is a nat. of America. Lived on the Mohawk River. He was

always friendly to Brit. Govert. Was an apprentice when Rebellion broke out. As soon as he was at Liberty he meant to have joined the Brit. Was taken Prisoner & kept confined but got away & joined Sr. John Johnson in Canada in 1780. Served till the war was over. Produces his Discharge. Now lives in New Johnstown.

His Grandfather, Henrick Markil, left him £50 York, to be paid in money or Land. He died in the year '81. Claimt. has never been paid this. Says his Grandfather was driven from the Lands before he died. He was a Loyalist.

(60).

He had 2 horses, 1 Cow. The Cow was left on his Uncle's Lands on the Mohawk. His Uncle is there now.

He left some Blacksmith's Tools at his shop in Johnstown before he came off to Canada; worth £12 York. vince.

JACOB MARKILL, Wits:

Speaks to Claimt.'s Loyalty. Says Henry Markill left Claimt. £50. It was to be paid in money.

Very little.

Henry Markill, Wits. Father, was a Loyalist & his Estate has been Confiscated. Claimt. had an horse which he lost. He had some Blacksmith's Tools. He set up a Blacksmith's shop at Johnstown before he came to Canada.

N. C.
February 13.

1101. Claim of DAYLE SELICK, late of Manchester, Vermont.

Claimt. says he was at the Isle au Noix in the Fall '83.

Is a nat. of America. Lived in Conect. Govt. when Rebellion broke out. Joined the Brit. in '77. Served all the war in different Regiments.

Produces his Discharge from Jessup's Regiment. Lives at Osswegatchie.

(61).

Had 100 acres of Land in Hoberton, given him by his Father in '77. It was new Land. Claimt. had done nothing. His Father went up from Connecticut to get Lands in Vermont after Troubles began. His Father bought a large Quantity. Gave Claimt. 100 acres. His Father is still in Hoberton.

Claimant had not been to live in Hoberton, but resided at Manchester, after he came up from Connecticut. There was some Rum of his father's which was taken away. Claimant says his Father gave it to him, 1 Heifer, 2 Sheep, which had been his Father's.

He & his Father had a place to work upon, where they had planted a crop.

N. C.
February 13.

1102. Claim of JOHN MORCELIS, late of Tryon Co.

Claimt. says. He was in Sr. John's 1st Batt. & gave his Claim to Capt. Duncan.

Is a nat. of A. Lived at Turlock when Rebellion broke out, 15 miles from Schoharie. Joined the Brit. in '77. Served all the war. Lives at New Johnstown.

Had 150 acres at Turlock, bought 4 or 5 years before the war. Gave £90 York for it. He had 8 years allowed for payment. Had not paid any part. Had cleared 19 acres, built House & Barn.

(62).

Had 50 acres in Anderstown given him by his Uncle many years ago. He never saw it, nor was there. It was wild land, Had been given him by his Uncle for his having worked with him 14 years.

A fair man.

Had 4 Horses, 3 Cows, 3 Calves, 3 Heifers, 6 Hogs, utensils, furniture. Left at Turlock, when he went away. The Rebels got it all.

CHRISTOPHER REDDICK, Wits:

Knew Claimt. He joined the Brit. in '77. Knew his Place of Turlock. He had 30 acres Clear. He had a very great stock, Horses, Cows &c.

1103. Claim of JOHN FRASER, from Boleskine late of Tryon Co.   N. C. February 13.

Claimt. says: He was at Yamasco Blockhouse in the Fall of '83.

Is a native of Scotl. Came to America many years ago. Lived on the Mohawk when the Rebellion broke out. Joined in '77. Served all the war. Now lives at Osswegatchie.

Produces Certificates from Capt. MacAlpine to Claimt.'s Loyalty, that in '77 he engaged above 30 men to come into Canada, but they were obliged to disperse & to Claimt.'s effects having been taken by the Rebels on that acct.   (63).

Certificate to his services & good Conduct from Major Jessup. Do. from Major Name.

He had 100 acres Tenant Land from Sr. Wm. Johnson. He had lived upon it 10 years before the war. He bought the Improvemts. for £90; 40 acres when he bought it. Claimt. cleared as much again. A House, Barn & Stable & orchard, & 2 Barracks, 4 Cows, 2 Heifers, 4 horses, 1 Colt, 6 Sheep, 6 Hogs, Grain, 12 tons Hay, furniture, utensils.   A good man. Very strong certificates.

After he went away these Things were taken and Vendued by the Rebels.

THOMAS ROSS, Wits:

Knew Claimt's Farm. He had been a long time upon it. It was a fine old Farm. He had above 50 Acres Clear land & Well fenced. He had a very good stock, 4 cows, 2 Heifers, 3 Mares, 1 Stallion. He was in very good circumstances.

1104. Claim of THOMAS ROSS, from Drumvaich, late of Tryon Co   N. C. Feby. 13.

Claimt says: He gave a Claim to Major Grey in '83.

Is in Nat. of Scotl. Came to Am. in 1773. Was settled in Johnsons Bush, joined Sr. John at first. Servd all the War. Produces his Discharge. Lives at New Johnstown.

Had 100 Acres Tenant Land, had Cleared 15 Acres, built house, Barn & Stables. Had 2 Cows, 1 Calf, a little furniture & Utensils.   (64).

JOHN FRASER Wits.

Knew Claimt. Knew his Farm. He had 12 or 13 acres Clear. A good man. He had 2 Cows & 1 Heifer.

N. C.
Feby. 13.

1105. Claim of WIDOW RYCKMAN, late of Tryon Co.

Tobias Ryckman, eldest son of John Ryckman, decd., appears. Says his Father was at Sorell in the Fall 83.

His Father was a Nat. of Am., lived at Tarpan, Orange Co., when the Rebellion broke out. He joined the Brit. at New York in 77. Servd as a guide to the Army during the War. He came to Canada in 80 or 81. He died in 84, leaving Susannah his Widow. Claimant Tobias Ryckman & 6 other Chidren. Witness servd. some time as a guide.

The Whole Family came into Canada with their Father. Now live near Cataraqui.

His Father had a House & some Land at Tappan, he was a Tanner & Shoemaker. He bought this Place many years ago. His first Purchase was of 4 acres, he bought some more afterwards, Wits. cannot say how much. There was a Stone house & framed Barn, & small framed house.

(65).

Produces a affidt. Sworn at Cataraqui to his having had this landed Estate, at Tappan, And ye stock as stated in the Schedule. Witness says they had Deeds of the Land, but they have been destroyed by fire since they came to this Country. Vals. it at above £200 York.

It has been sold by the Comrs. at a Vendue, one Herring bought it. His Father had 9 Wagon Loads of Leather just brought from Philadelphia. His Father had been imprisoned in Fisk Kill Gaol. The Rebels took the Leather at that time.

Produces an Affidt. that John Ryckman had been imprisond for his Loyalty & speaks of his having offerd a Reward of 100 Dollars to People to fetch off his Leather.

He had a No. of doz. Hides & Skins. The dry Hides Cost £100 York. He had three horses, the Rebels took them. He had a house at New York, which he built after he got there. He had two Witnesses who knew his Father's Property, they could not come, but were sworn before Peter Vanalstine near Cataraqui & he produces their affidts. as before stated.

Seems a fine man.

Says the Family Agree that he shall receive the whole.

N. C.
Feby. 14.

1106. Claim of JACOB WAGGEMS, late of Tryon Co.

(66).

Claimt. says: He was in Sr. John's First Batt. & gave his Claim to Capt. Darly.

Is a Nat. of Germany, came to A. 30 years ago, Was settled in Johnstown When Rebellion broke out, joined in 77, servd all the War. Produces his Discharge. Now lives at New Johnstown.

Had 100 acres Tenant Land, 20 acres Clear, 2 horses & 2 Colts, 2 Cows, 2 Heifers, 1 Calf, 4 Sheep, furniture.

JOHN FARLING Wits.

Knew Claimts. Farm. He had lived there some time before the War. Had a fine Clearance, thinks he had near 20 acres Clear.

He had 2 Horses, 2 Cows, &c.

1107. Claim of MARTIN ALGIER, late of Tryon Co.   N. C. Feby. 14.

Claimt. says: He gave his Claim to his Commanding officer in 83.

He is a Nat. of Germ., but came very young to America, lived near Johnstown when Rebellion broke out, joined in 79. He had been a Prisoner five months or would have joined sooner, he was in his March to join when he was taken Prisoner. Servd afterwards till end of War. Produces his Discharge. Resides at New Johnstown.

Had 100 Acres Tenant Land in Albany Patent, had cleared 10 Acres, built a house & Shop & Barn. Had 2 Cows, 2 horses, 2 Sheep, Weavers Loom, furniture. Left all behind.   (67). A good man.

JOHN FARLING Wits.

Knew Claimt. Heard he was imprisoned when Coming to join the Army. He afterwards joined & servd. Knew his Farm. He had 10 acres Clear before the War.

He had 2 horses & 2 Cows &c.

1108. Claim of MICHL. WARNER, late of Tryon Co.   N. C. Feby. 14.

Claimt. says: He gave his claim to his Commanding officer in 83.

Is a Nat. of Germany, has been 30 years in America. Was settled on the Mohawk when the Rebellion began, joined the Brit. in 77, Servd. all the War. Produces his discharge. Lives at New Johnstown. Had 100 acres Tenant Land in Albany Patent. Lived upon it 7 or 8 years before the War, had cleard. between 40 & 50 acres, built house & Barn, had a fine orchard. Had 6 Horses, 6 Cows, 3 Heifers, 2 Steers, 1 Bull, 8 Hogs, furniture, Utensils, left all behind when he joined the Brit.   (68).

MARTIN ALGIER Wits.

Knew Claimt. He had been long settled in the Albany Patent. He had 40 acres Clear. He had a very good stock, 5 or 6 Horses, 5 or 6 Cows & other Stock.   A good man.

1109. Claim of CHRISTIAN SCHICK, late of Tryon Co. Lodged in England.   N. C. Feby. 14.

Claimt. says: He sent his Claim by Capt Leake in 83.

Is a Nat. of Germany, came to Am. many years ago, was settled in Johnsons Bush when the Rebellion broke out. He sent his apprentices & journeymen to join Sr. John at first. He joind. in 1779, served 4 years in Sir John's Regiment, now lives at Johnstown.

No. 1. He had 200 acres Tenant Land, for which he paid £12 York per ann. He had this many years before the War. Had

Cleared about 40 acres. Bought these Improvements of Wm. Stevens. N. 6. He gave £44 for ye Whole farm in 72. Charges now £148 for 148 acres Wild. Very little property Clear when he bought it.

He had also some town Lots in Johnstown in a Lease from Sr. Wm. Johnstown at £8 per ann. There were 18 acres Clear Land in these Town Lots. He produces a Recpt. for the Rent in 1776 of the Town Lots & the other Lands.

(69).

He had 2 houses on No. 1. He built one himself in 1777, the other was there when he bought it. He did not live there, till he quitted his Town Lot. He Cleared all the Land in the Town Lots himself, built House & Blacksmith Shop & Stable. Cannot set any value on his Improvements on No. 1 or No. 2.

Values his Property too high.

He says he removed from the Town Lot to his farm after the Troubles began. He then built a house & Shop in 1777. He had 3 Cows, 1 Ox, 10 Horses, 5 Sheep, 5 Hogs, Utensils, Furniture, Blacksmith's Tools & Shop on his Farm. He had a large quantity of Iron bought during the War & paid for in Continental Dollars. It was one Sleigh Load. Says he left most of these things behind when he went away.

MICHAEL GOTTINGER Wits.

Knew Claimt. He was always Loyal. He was several times imprisond. because he would not take an Oath to the American.

Thinks they forced him to take one at last.

He had a farm out of the Town. 30 or 40 acres Clear. Had a House, Barn & Blacksmiths Shop.

Vals. Improvements at £5 per acre. Knew his Town Lot, 8 or 9 acres Clear. Remembers 6 Horses & 3 Cows. He had Blacksmiths Tools, 2 sets. Thinks the Rebels had them, many of his things were sold at Vendue.

JOHN CRISTY Wits.

(70).

Knew Claimts. Place near Johnstown & his Town Lots. There was a Considerable Clearance, most of his Town Lots was Clear. He was in Considerable Business as a Blacksmith.

N. C.
Feby. 15.

1110. Claim of JOHN PICKELL, late of Albany Co.

Claimt. says he was at St. Johns in the Fall 83. Was born in America. Lived in Kingsburg near Fort Edward. From the first declared to Favour of the Brit. He had been imprisond & given Bond. Claimt. & his 3 Sons & one Son in Law, joined the Brit. army in 1777, servd. all the war in different Regiments. Produces his Discharge from Rogers & Rangers. Now lives in Caldwells Manor.

He had 250 acres Tenant Land near Fort Edward, leased of Henry Franklin. Took the lease 4 years before the War. He had

40 acres Clear. Had built house & Barn. Saved most of his Horses & Cattle which he sold, but says, but says he lost 1 Cow

& Calf & 2 Steers which the Rebels got, 6 Hogs.   A good man.

DANIEL BEEDLE Wits.

Knew Claimt. He & his Sons joined the Brit. army in 1777. Knew his Farm. He had been upon it 5 years before the War. He had 21 acres Grass Land and 36 Arable. Knew his Stock. He was in a good way of living & had a good Stock.

1111. Claim of DAN'L. BEAGH, late of Albany Co.   N. C. Feby. 15.

Claimt. says: He was at Mashishi in 83. Is a Nat. of Germany. Came very young to Am. Lived at New Town, Albany Co., when the Rebellion broke out. Joind. the Brit. Army in 77. (71). Servd. all the War. Produces his Discharge. Now lives at Caldwells Manor.

Had 200 acres Tenant Land, hired of Anthony Van Schoick, took it in 73, it was for 3 Lives at 6 pence per acre. Had 20 acres Arable Land exactly. There was some Intervalle Land from which he cut 7 Ton of Hay Annually, about 5 acres of it. Built House & Barn. Had a Yoke of Oxen, 1 Cow, 1 Calf, 1 Horse, 7 Hogs, Left all these things behind in his place when he went away. The   A good man. Rebels had tem.

JOHN PICKET Wits.

Knew Claimt. He joined the Brit. Army in 1777. Knew his Place. He had been there long before ye War. He had a large Clearance & intervalle Land. Knew his Yoke of Oxen, Horse, &c.

1112. Claim of ALEX. MUNRO, late of New York.   N. C. Feby. 15.

Caimt. says: He was at Montreal in 83. Gave his Claim to Genl. Maclean who was going to England in the Fall 83.

Is a Nat. of Scott. Came to Amer. about 30 years ago. Lived at New York, when Rebellion broke out. Joined Major Jessup on the North River. Came with a party of 85 men. Joined in 76. Servd. all the War. Produces his Discharge, Produces Certificate from Major Jessup to Claimt's. Loyalty & that he joined him in the Autumn 76 & servd. the Whole War. Now lives at Montreal.

Had a House & Lot in Larie Street. It was a good Town Lot. It was the property of Nancy Macleod when Claimt. married (72). She is now living at Montreal. He has no Children. She bought it herself for £250 York about 1764, it used to Rent at £15 per ann. before she bought it. It was Considerably improved afterwards. This House was burnt in the first fire at New York. The Deeds were burnt at same time. Thinks he could have sold it for

A very good man. £300 at least. Lost all his Furniture, Cloaths, &c., at the same Time by the Fire. Produces Inventory of all his Furniture, says he remembers all the particulars then set down to above £200 York. Never got anything for the spot of Land afterwards.

WILLIAM CAMERON Wit.

Knew Claimt's. House at New York, it had been his Wife's.

Witness understood she had purchased it some time before he married her. It was a pretty good House in Larie Street. The Houses & Lots were very valuable then. Thinks it might have been sold for £500 York before the War.

The House was very well furnished. She had kept a public House & had exceedingly good furniture, no person in their station of life had better. The House & furniture were destroyed by the Fire.

N. C.
Feby. 15.

1113. Claim of JACOB VANALLIN, late of Tryon Co.

Claimt. says he was in Sr. John's 1st Batt., gave in his Claim in 83, to his Commanding officer, which is Confirmed by Certificate of Lieut. Munro.

(73).

Is a Nat. of Amer. Lived on the Mohawk River when Rebellion broke out. At first he kept himself quiet. Paid fines for not serving with them. Came into Canada in 80 and servd. till end of the War. Produces his Discharge as Corporal. Lives in 5 Township.

Had 12 acres in the Mohawk. It was given him by Vincent Scot. Cogintoitch for work done by Claimt. It was estimated at £20 York, says he had a Deed. This was just before the War. He had cleard. a little, it was a part of Scot's Lot. He had 160 acres & a good deal of it Clear.

Claimt. had 2 horses, 2 Cows, 3 Sheep, 3 Hogs. He kept them at the House of an Indian. Capt. Aaron left them there

when he joined Sr. John Johnson in 1780. That Country was plunderd by the Rebels & all parties.

PHILIP SHAVER Wits.

Knew Claimt. He lived at the Mohawk. He joined Sr. John in 80. He had some Land from a man that he was Partner with. There were 12 acres. There was a little Clearance. He had Horses & Cows at an Indian place where he lived.

N. C.
Feby. 15.

1114. Claim of JOHN COOK, SR., late of Tryon Co.

Claimt. says: He desired his Son-in-Law Jacob Ross to send his Claim home in 83. Gave him an acct. He was a Soldier in Sr. John's 1st Battalion & gave in the Claim to Capt. Anderson,

Who lodged it with the Agent. This acct. is in some measure Confirmed by Certificate from Capt. Anderson and that the acct. given in by the Claimt. in March 86 to be sent to ye Comrs. was the same as that given in to Capt. Anderson by Jacob Ross in 83.

Is a Nat. of Germany. Came to Am. 34 years ago. Lived at Johnstown when Rebellion broke out. Always declared for the King. Had 2 Sons in the Army. Came to Canada in 81. He was warnd. to quit on Pain of Death in 10 days. His place was Plunderd. Now lives in New Johnstown.

Had 250 acres Tenant Land. Had them many years ago in a Lease from Harry Holland. It was a Lease forever at £5 Rent. He had lived 18 years upon it. Had 50 acres Clear, a good House & Barn & fine Orchard. Had 4 working horses, 2 Colts, 2 Cows, 2 Oxen, 14 Sheep, 10 Hogs, Utensils. All these things were taken by the Rebels, many of the things were sold at Vendue, after he was warnd. off.

MICHAEL KORMAN Wits.

Knew Claimt. He & his Family were always Loyal. His eldest son joined Sr. John at first. Claimt. was driven from his Place during the War, on acct. of his Loyalty & came into Canada. Knew his Farm. He had been upon it a long Time. Thinks about 40 acres Clear. He had a very good Stock. Witness understood the Rebels had the whole.

1115. Claim of MARTIN WALDEC, late of Tryon Co. N. C. February 15.

Mary his Wife appears, says her husband is confined to his bed, he broke his leg terribly in several places & is now unable to move. He was in Sr. John's first Batt. & gave his Claim to Capt. Burns in 83.

He is a Nat. of Germany. Came many years ago to Am. Lived near Johnstown when Rebellion broke out. He joined Sr. John at first. Had servd. all the War. Now lives at 5th Township.

He had a Tenant Farm in the Albany Patent. He had been in Possession 9 or 10 years. Thinks more than 25 acres were Clear.

Built house, barn, Stable, &c.

He had 4 horses, 5 Cows, 3 Heifers, 5 Sheep, 8 Hogs, furniture, Utensils, Cloathes. Most of these things were on the Place when her Husband went away. Witness staid 3 years after the Husband went. The Rebels took most of these things in 1777 & sold them at Vendue. Witness was not able to dispose of any part. She came to Canada in 80.

MICHAEL KARMAN Wits.

Knew Claimt. He joined Sr. John at first & servd. all the War. He has met with a terrible accident lately which Witness

71 AR.

(76).

fears will prove fatal. Knew his Farm. The lots were in general 250 acres. Thinks he had 30 acres Clear. He had 4 horses, young & old, 3 or 4 Cows & Coming in Stock in 1776.

N. C.
February 15.

1116. Claim of LUKE BOWEN, late of Tryon Co.

Claimt. says: He was in Sr. John's 1st Batt., was at Isle Au Noix in the King's works as Carpenter in the Fall 83.

A fair man.

Is a Nat. of Am. Lived near Johnstown at a Place call Philadelphia Bush. Joined the Brit. Army in 77. Servd. all the War. Lives at the 5th Township.

Had 125 acres in the Albany Patent. Had been in Possession 5 years. Had 22 acres Clear. Had House, Stable & Barracks.

Had 5 Head Cattle, 2 Sheep, 10 Hogs, Utensils, Clothing. The Rebels took them after Depart of Burgoyne.

MICHAEL KARMAN Wits.

Knew Claimt. He joined the Brit. Army in 77. Knew his Farm. He had 12 acres Clear. He had Cattle & a little Stock.

N. C.
February 15.

1117. Claim of WILL AGNEW, late of Tryon Co., Evidence de bene esse.

PHILIP SHAVER Wits.

(77).

Knew Claimt. He lived about 13 miles from Johnstown. He joined the Brit. Army in 78. He was in the Commissary Department & Continues in that Line at Sorell. He had a lot of Land, a good Clearance upon it. He had been in Possession some time before the War. He used to give assistance to Loyalists. He supported Wits. 5 months when on a Scouting Party.

N. C.
February 16.

1118. Claim of JOHN AULT, late of Tryon Co.

Claimt. says: He was in Sr. John's first Batt. & gave his Claim to Capt. Burns.

Is a Nat. of Ger. Came to Amer. 36 years ago. Lived at Johnstown when Rebellion broke out. Sent 3 Sons to the Brit. Army in 1777. He joined in 80. Servd. till end of War. Lives in 5 Township. He had some Lands but sold them.

Lost 2 Horses, 7 Sheep, 3 Hogs, furniture, Cloathes, Provisions. The Rebels had some of these things. The Indians had the rest.

PHILIP SHAVER Wits.

Knew Claimt. He was always a Loyalist. He did not join till 80. Had 3 Sons in the Kings Army. He had Parted with his

Lands. He was Plunderd by Indians of some of his things & the Rebels took what the Indians left.

1119. Claim of JOSEPH KINGSBURY, late of Connecticut.   N. C. February 16.

Claimt. says: He was at Yamesca block house in 83. Is a Nat. of Am. Lived at Plainfield in Connecticut, when Rebellion broke out. Says he came into this Country with General Arnold, as a soldier with him & servd. several months. He deserted when the Rebels were going back from this Country. Continued in this Country till 80 then enlisted in Jessups Regt. Servd. till end of the War. Now lives at Yamosca.   (78).

Had a pr. of Oxen, 2 Cows, 1 Horse, 20 Sheep on his Father's Lands at Plainfield. His Father is dead, but he supposes these things may be now in his Mothers Possession. He left them there when he came as a soldier with the Rebels.

1120. Claim of PHILIP EMPEY, JR., late of Tryon Co.   N. C. February 16.

Claimt. says: He was in Sr. John's 1st Batt. & gave in his Claim with his Father in 83.

Is a Nat. of Am. Lived on the Mohawk. Joined the Brit. at Fort Stanwix in 77. Servd. all the War. Produces his Discharge. Lives at New Johnstown.

He had some Lands which his Father had given him & he had some stock of his own upon it.

2 Mares, 5 Head of Cattle, 6 Sheep, 4 Hogs, Utensils, furniture. Left all behind when he went away. There was a separate house on this Land. When Claimt. lived. The lands are inserted in his Father's Claim.   A good man.

STRIFFIL EMPEY Wits.

Says he is a Brother to Claimt. His Father had given Claimt. some lands & he had Stock of his own upon them. He had 2 Horses, Cattle & other Stock, they were his own. He left them behind on these Lands, when he joined the Brit. Troops.   (79).

1121. Claim of JOHN LAWRENCE, late of Tryon Co.   N. C. February 16.

Claimt. says: He was in Sr. John's 1st Batt. & gave in his Claim in 83, to Sr. John Johnson.

Is a Native of Ireland. Came to America in 1766. Was settled in Johnstown when Trouble broke out. Was imprisond. a long time in 76, near 10 months. Joined the Brit. in 78. Servd. all the War. Resides at New Johnstown.

Had a House & Lot at Johnstown. It was a Gift from Sr. Wm. Johnson. Claimt. built the House & improved the Lands.

A good man. There were 5 acres, all fenced & improved. There were near 2 acres of it laid out in a garden. Claims for his Improvements £60. Does not Claim the Soil Rights.

Had 2 Cows, 1 Heifer, 1 Horse, furniture, Utensils, Some Hay & Some Logs.

RICHARD MANDEVILLE Wits.

(80). Knew Claimt. He was always Loyal. He was a long time imprisond. He had a House & Lot in Johnstown. There were 2 acres of Garden Ground. He had a House which he supposes Claimt. built. He had a Cow & some other Stock.

PROCEEDINGS

OF

LOYALIST COMMISSIONERS

LONDON, 1784.

Vol I.

BEFORE COMMISSIONER WILMOT

Claimants.

	MSS. Folio.
Billup, Colonel Christopher	63
Conolly, Lt.-Col	36
Dean, Peter	21
Doty, Rev. John	55
Ellegocd, Lt.-Col. Jacob	48
Graham, Lieut. Governor John	1
Hamilton, James	11
Hamilton, Mrs. Mary	29
Hooper, Joseph	42

	MSS. Folio.
Lightenstone, John	33
Lovell, John	28
Morehead, William	31
Robertson, James	14
Rose, Peter	58
Saltmarsh, John	59
Stewart, Duncan	61
Walker, Justice	26

THE EVIDENCE.

1783.
19th December.   1122. Case of Lt. Govr. JOHN GRAHAM, Georgia.

Has been in America since 1753. He went out with a view to succeed to the Estate of a relation there, but did not succeed to it. He then went into trade, but left of Business & began Planting some years before the trouble. Previous to the Rebellion he was one of the Council & Receiver of the moneys arising from the sale of Ceded Lands.

(1).   In August, 1775, he had first an opportunity of showing his Loyalty by opposing sending Delegates to Congress from Georgia. This was the Commencement of the troubles in Georgia. They succeeded in opposing it at this time. Soon after the matter was Carried agt. the Loyalists.

In the latter end of 1775 he was appointed Lt. Governor in Jany. 1776, they were surrounded by an armed force & all the Council taken Prisoners. He did not receive his Commission until March, 1776, of Course could not act until then. There never was a Lt. Govr. before that time, but cannot say that appointment was thought necessary on acct. of the troubles, perhaps it might. After being taken Prisoners they were Paroled next day, before the appearance of the Scarborough Man of War on the Coast of Georgia, he thinking they were come with troops to protect the Province, but finding otherwise, when they sailed. He went on shore to bring his family to Savanah. He came to England in May 1776 & remained until April 1779. He returned to Georgia in June 1779 & remained until the Evacuation.

In 1782, He went into the Back settlements to quiet the settlers which he effected with 300 men.

Certificates to Loyalty as also an extract of a letter from Lord G. Germain in which he speaks highly of the Conduct of the Govr. & Lt. Govr. of Georgia & Services of Sir James Wright, of Genr. Leslie, Col. Monereel, Gen. Clark, &c. Some of them speak to his property, as very Considerable Property.

(2).   1224 acres called Mulberry Grove Plantation, Contained Swamp, Pasture & Upland. He has lost all his papers of every sort & refers to a book which contains a copy of an act assembly, 10th July, 1780. The object of which was to quiet all those people who had lost their titles. Govr. Graham's papers were lost in this way, they were buried in the ground in an Iron Chest from the year 1776 to 1779. When taken up they were all perished by damp. The act directs how such persons shall proceed.

The Plantation of Mulberry Grove was purchased some years before the troubles for £1500, including some other lands. There were then no Dams upon it. He banked it about 140 acres. He cleared a considerable part of, quantity of the Upland & built a very good house on it. Laid out a very considerable sum of money on it, besides about £1500 on a garden. The 140 acres rice ground, he looks upon worth £14 pr. acre. But wishing to be under their rate he says £8 pr. acre, which is £1320. 70 acres, River Swamp he asks at £5 pr. acre, £350. 200 acres of Pasture at 50s. is £500. 814 at 40sh. is £1628. Dwelling House & Barns & outhouses, £750. This valuation had been put on his Property in 1776. He values them much higher but abides by their valuation.

Mulberry Grove new Plantation with the Expenses of Clearing, Banking, &c., is valued by appraisers at £27,932, his own valuation is much higher.

The appraisment is made by Mr. Hull, Mr. Wright & Mr. Skinner in 1776. They say that the property would have sold for more before the troubles. Govr. Graham says, he thinks their estimate extremly moderate. The valuation put by the Appraisers on the 847 uncultivated acres in £1500. Govr. Graham says the two Plantations cost him about £2000 Stg. (3).

The Monteith Plantation containing in the whole about 6000 acres, he purchased at different times, of different people, he cannot say what he gave for them, for 557 he gave 10sh. pr. acre, 900 he bought for 15sh. pr. acre, some others he bought of Sir. James Wright & gave 20sh. pr. acre, the money is not paid. The original title to these lands is by Grant.

A Tract of 1453 acres on the Alatamaha River bought of Sir James Wright at 20sh. pr. acre, no part cultivated. He owes the money to Sir James Wright, he bought them on speculation.

1500 acres bought of the Atty. Gen. of Georgia at Public Sale for £500, they are uncultivated.

---

350 acres River Swamp likewise unsettled, he got these in Exchange.

44 in the purchase from Sir James Wright likewise unsettled.

1000 acres on the River St. Mary's, he bought a great while since & are likewise unsettled.

500 acres on Gt. Ogeechu unsettled. He bought this at public sale.

500 acres on St. Thomas, likewise unsettled. He cannot say what he gave for these two tracts. (4).

2019 bought of many different people, they were cultivated by Capt. Demery & many thousand laid out on them. He only values them at £1000. He was offered £1000 many years ago for them by Major Butler.

1000 on Great Ogeechu, they belong to Capt. Blake & he bought them at Public Sale, but for a mere trifle, they were uncultivated.

Three town lots in Fridaria at £5 each. These were granted to him and uncultivated.
2000 acres in 3 tracts, on Gt. Satella.
2000 acres on Alatamallia.
1000 acres in St. Pauls Parish.
3 Town Lots in Brunswick.
Two Dwelling Houses. Purchased a Town Lot in Savanah. 8 acres in the Island of Tibre.

No part of his lands were unpaid for, But that bought of Sir James Wright as mentioned. He has left no debts in America which affects his lands He does owe some money in America & has stated it.

Negroes—He had 262 Negroes in 1776, valued at £58.5.9, Georgia money each, he recovered 209 & has given credit for it in his Schedule so that 53 appear to have been lost, but admits the 32 died on his Plantation. Only 21 were carried off by the Rebells, he values these 21 at the above price or £54 Stg. He takes no notice of Births, but the mortallity was great as the Rebells emploied them on an unhealthy spot.

When he went away in 1776, he left considerable Crops, both of that and preceeding years. Part of 1775 was left in his Barns (5). & is included in the appraisments to which he refers, that part on his own Plantation is valued at £1729.18. Crops 1775, the Monteith Plantation valued at £282. Crop 1775 on Mulberry Grove £158.10.

Live Stock, &c., &c.

Some cattle was sold by his Attys. for which he has deducted £1500. Thinks they did not sell so much.

Crop 1776 was in the ground when he came away, he cannot say what it produced, but judges from former years that the Crop of his own & Monteath Plantation was worth £2750.

Crops of 1777 & 1778, was estimated £5500.

Crops 1779 at £2250.

All the River Swan Plantation at £750. Crop 1782, he values at £750. An additional charge for Rice &c., &c. £2000.

Has not charged the crops on these 130 acres for the years 1776, 1777 & 1778, but if it is allowed in any case, it will be allowed in his.

Furniture & other articles, he refers to the Schedule & says every thing contained in it is lost.

Debts he owed as an Individual £2197.12.6.

Partnership £15085.

December. 1783.
Being asked what his income would be from all his Plantations, he says they do not compete in that way in Georgia, but as well as he can guess the gross produce might be about £2700 stg. from the three Plantations. For the deductions he refers to a calculation he gave the Board in the Case of Sir James Wright.

(6). His opinion is £1000 higher than the valuation but is willing to abide by it.

Does not say he could have sold his property for what he values it at, but that he would not have taken that sum.

Being asked as to the Comparative value of Sir James Wright's Property with his, he says he thinks it was worth double. Sir James had double the number of Negroes & twice the quantity of land. In 1776 he made a settlement of his Estate on his wife & Children to save Confiscation.

His estate was mortgaged to Clarke & Milligen, but when the trouble broke out they restored the Mortgage Deed, being dissatisfied with the Security.

George Derbege, late of Georgia, Proves the authenticity of some papers & an Act of Assembly passed 10th July, 1780.

Has Known Lt. Gov. Graham since 1760, he was then in trade

& was afterwards appointed one of the Council by his recommendation, he appeared to be a man of Property & was an extensive Planter.

He took an early & decided part in favour of Great Britain & mentions several active services performed by Govr. Graham. He was appointed Lt. Govr. in 1775 & continued in that situation until the Evacuation. He behaved extremely well in Council, when Savanah was besieged & indeed upon all occasions, but being in a Civil situation he was not often exposed to personal hazard.

(7).

Sir James is very well acquainted with his Plantation. The Rice Lands in Mulberry Plantation is worth £12 pr. acre. He values the whole of it at £1700 more than Gov. Graham does. The River Swamp 847 acres, he values at £6 pr. acre. The other land from 45 to 50sh. pr. acre. He values the high land although it is not cleared.

Sir Jas. being asked at to the estimate he gave in of the expense of Banking &c., he Confirms it.

With respect to Lands at Altamata, he confirms Govr. Graham's acct. & says they were worth in 1775, 30sh. pr. acre.

Remember Govr. Graham's Negroes being taken away, does not Know the number, but he has heard he got all back but about 20.

JOHN JAMIESON, late of Georgia.

He Knew Govr. Graham's Plantation in Georgia. The Mulberry Grove Plantation was much cultivated in 1775. The House was not finished in 1777. He says he has been consulted as to the value of this Plantation. Says it is good land, but thinks it is not worth more than two thirds of Sir Jas. Wrights. He valued Sir Jas. Wright's at £15. He values this at £10 pr. acre. This relates to the 140 acres. The 70 acres at £5 pr. acre. The 200 at 45sh. & the 814 at 40sh. pr. acre.

He does not Know the new settlement of Mulberry very perfectly. Knows the Monteith Plantation. The Improved Swamp he thinks is worth ½ as much as Sir Jas. Wright's, he therefore puts it at £7.10. Provision land 40sh. The uncleared swamp at 50sh. 3359 Pine Land he values at 12s. 6d., thinks that the full value.

(8).

Mr. Jamieson includes all the buildings in the valuation. Knows the 1453 acres bought of Sir Jas. Wright, he values them at £3 pr. acre, if cultivated they were worth £10. He has seen lands in that County for which he would not have taken that sum.

He cannot speak particularly to the other lands. Govr. Graham's Negroes were very good.

ANDR. ROBERTSON was a Planter in Georgia.

In the spring of 1780, 70 or 80 Negroes were taken of the Plantation of Govr. Graham by one Johnson & 100 Rebells, some of them returned. He says Johnson was a Methodist Preacher. Knows nothing else Govr. Graham's case.

SIMON MUNRO—Speaks of the value of 1500 acres in Altamaha. He does not know that any of it was Cultivated, but has heard the former Proprietor say that part of it was Cultivated. He likewise Knew Govr. Graham lost all his Papers, he saw some of the remains. Says that Govr. Graham had the next largest property in the Province to Sir Jas. Wright.

Says Mr. Graham was in good business in 1762, perhaps worth £5000. It was a cheap Country to live in. Georgia money bore a discount of 8 pr. cent. to stg.

1783. 22nd December (9).

This Memorial the office of Superintendent of Indian Affairs & Lt. Govr. of the Province of Georgia. He has received notice respecting the loss of his Salary as Lt. Govr. & expects soon to loose the other. No salary was annexed at 1st to the office of Lt. Govr., but soon after he came to England his Majesty gave him a sallary of £300 pr. an.

A Letter from Gray Elliot, Esq., read by which it appears that the salary would be discontinued from midsummer last.

This office was given to him without solicitation & that in 1775. He certainly thought the British Gover't. in America would prevail.

A subsequent Commission read dated in 1780, when the Peace of the Province was restored & he was re-appointed.

His Commission as Superintendant of Indian Affairs, was left with his Deputy at St. Augustine, it was signed by Mr. Ellis & must have been signed in 1782.

A certificate produced by which appears that Lt. Govr. Graham held that office with a Sallary of £500 pr. an., £80 for a

(10).

house & £30 for Stationary. The perquisites were casual, but he believes they would have been £500 pr. an. He did not stay in the Country 3 months after his appointment, it was an old established office. He succeeded Mr. Cameron, who succeeded Mr. Stewart, looks upon this as lost. Has been informed that half pay has been granted to persons that held such offices, but he has made no application to the Treasury for it. His Commission extended to no other Province. He was appointed by the Crown at the recommendation of Sir Henry Clinton & Gen. Leslie, both these situations were during pleasure.

He mentions the loss of his Negroes Killed by the enemy.

Decision.

The Board are of the opinion that Lt. Govr. Graham is a zealous & active Loylist, carried Arms & renderd service to the British Govrt.

Mulberry Grove Plantation they value at	£2300
Mulberry Grove New Settlement at	2600
Monteith Plantation they value at	5750
Capt. De Reneys lands, 2019 acres at	1000
A Lott in Savanah, 8 acres on Tybu	150
Twenty-one Negroes	945
Crop, 1775	1548
Live Stock	2281
Crop, 1776, 800. Crop, 1782, 375	1175
Cattle &c., &c.	112.10

```
Carriage & Horses ..........................  120
Furniture ....................................  500
Plantation Tools ...........................  150
                                            £18631.10
State Debts, as a Private man.........£2197.12.6
Partnership Debts...    ......  ......  ...... 1585.10.1

Total debts due ...... ...... ...............£3783. 2.7
```

1123.   Case JAMES HAMILTON.   1783. 22nd December

He went from Ireland when 8 years old, is now about 30. Went first to Pensilvania. His mother was married and settled in Maryland at this time. At the Commencement of the troubles (11). he was married & settled on a Plantation, he bought about eleven years ago of his Father-in-law. The first opportunity he had was in the year 1778. He refused to sign the Association. He next refused the state oath, for this & some disrespectful Conversation, he was taken up, but Bailed. Afterwards with the Consent of his Bailsman he joined the British Army at Charles Town neck 29th March, 1780. He was afterwards employed by Major Andise to circulate Manifestors in the back Country, but not being able to get there he returned & remained until Charlestown was taken. He was afterwards at the Battles of Hanging Rock, Cambden & Gilford, upon the Baggage Guard. He was chose Capt. of Militia by a party of men Whose Capt. was wounded, he received no pay.

He came to Ireland from Charlestown with the consent of Gen. Leslie.

Certificats to Loyalty & Character from Lord Cornwallis, Lord Rawdon, Colonel Hamilton, Colonel Philips, &c., &c.

Has an allowance of £25 pr. an. from the Treasury Property.

Says he never had the titles to his land made out, but a Bond to have titles made out by his father in Law, John Bailey in 1771. He gave about £240 Stg. for it.

640 acres on the waters of Yadkin River & Rowan County, N. Carolina. Swears that he pd. for it in hard money. It was uncultivated when he bought it. He cleared twixt 30 & 40 acres & built a Log house on it. He cannot say the expense of Clearing (12). was, he values it at 25sh. pr. acre & could have sold it before the troubles for that sum. He left the Bond with his wife who was in the estate, but since learns that one Hall has taken the Property & that his wife is turned of. Has not heard from her since 1781. Does not Know if the estate is Confiscated.

He had Five Negroes in 1779, two of them went away to the Cherokee nation. He emploied a person to get them back, who was told by the officer who Commanded the fort that he could not get them as I had not taken the oaths to the States, and this Rebel Capt. sent them down to his own Plantation. One ran away soon after & the Sheriff of the County refused to deliver him up for the same reason. The other two he left at home with his wife when he came away, but supposes they were taken from her. He values them at £60 N.C. He left 10 Horses at home besides, some Certified by Ld. Cornwallis taken for the use of the Army. Explains that he rode one to the British & Left nine on the Plantation. Values them at £12 Currency each. He was a Horse dealer, these were working horses, a brood mare & 3 Colts.

He had 50 head of Cattle on his Plantation old & young, values them at 40sh. each. 60 Hogs, he values them at 7sh. 30 Sheep at 9 or 10sh., Currency each.

(13).

A Rifle Gun which the Rebels took because he would not take the State Oath, he values at £4.10.

Clothing £27.12. Says he lost that amount including 17 yards of Cloth.

BENJN. BOOTH BOOTE.

Has Known Mr. Hamilton since the year 1780. Knows nothing of his Property, but believes him a very Loyal subject.

ALEX. BURNSIDE.

Knows Mr. Hamilton, but nothing of his Property, has seen one Negroe with him & a waggon & Team.

CAPT. MCCULLOCH.

Knows nothing more of Mr. Hamilton's Property, than he has heard people from the same part of the Country say, that he was a good liver. Thinks he was as Loyal as a man can be & that it is Probable the Americans would seize all his property.

Decision.

The Board is of opinion that James Hamilton is an active & zealous Loyalist, that he has bore arms. Allow him for his 640 acres of Land £320.

Negroes	£168.10
Horses	44
Cattle	56
Hogs	12
Sheep	8
Furniture, Clothing & Linen	17
	£305.10

1783.
23rd December.

1124. Case JAMES ROBERTSON.

(14).

He went from this Country to Georgia in 1767. Where he has always resided. He servd. his Clerkship there, was admitted to the Bar in 1772 & followed the Profession until the Commencement of the troubles.

In 1774 he signed a Protest agst. the violent Proceedings of the opposite party. He signed many other resolutions which prevented that province from entering into the Confederacy. He retired into the Country in 1776, where Sir James Wright was obliged to go on Board Ship.

In 1775 he was chosen delegate from Province to Congress, but refused it. But went up the Country as overseer to Mr. Hume.

Produces a Warrant by which he was seized in June 1776, by order of the Rebel State. This was when Sir P. Parker & Sir Hy. Clinton lay at Charlestown Barr. He was then told he should remain in Confinement until he joined them. At last they brought to him an oath that he would be true & faithful to the American States & that he had not secreted any arms. He found after the Repulse of Charlestown, that he would still be confined if he did not take the oath. He then took it & thinks it justifiable.

He does not think this oath involves in it an abjuration of the King of Gr. Britian.

He was then set at liberty & returned to his former situation in the Country where he remained until Oct. 1777, taking no part with or agst. Great Britian. When he was called upon to take an oath to the American States & abjure his alleegance to Great Britian, this oath was only tenderd to suspected persons. Produces a summons to attend on that business & an order to depart the Province in consequence of non Compliance. He accordingly did depart & took his Passage for New Providence. Produces a Permit allowing him to depart, dated Savanah 10th Decemr., 1777. A power was at that time granted to persons banished to have an attys. to sell half their Property & to leave the remainder as a pledge. He was admitted to the Bar at Providence. Where he staid 3 months, then went to St. Augustine where he remained until the reduction of Georgia. Upon the establishment of Civil Govert. Having before held the office of Atty. Genl. he was applied to return & to act in several other departments. (15).

He returned & acted as Atty. Gen. & Advocate Gen., until the return of Sir Jas. Wright in 1779. Upon his return the Council was new modeld & he was left out, in order that he might be more serviceable in the House of Assembly. Soon after he was chose member for Savanah & remained so for above a year.

He then went into the Council & remained until the evacuation, He servd. as Lt. Col. of Militia until 1779 & afterwards as Col. Afterwards he went to N. York, he never received pay, but Rations while on actual service he staid in N. York 3 months & arrived in London, Nov. 1782. He applied to the Treasury & received an allowance of £50 pr. an., from Jany. 1782.

He is now appointed Chief Justice of the Vergin Island, with a sallary of £200 pr. an. Does not Know what the emoluments may be, the Profits of his Profession he considers to be about £200. He is a single man. He understands that his £50 pr. an. as an American Sufferer is to cease, but wishes to have a sum to carry him out. (16).

Property.

1936 acres of Land in one body but different tracts in Christ Church Parish about 14 miles from Savanah. These lands were purchased by him before the War & lost £570 str. They were uncultivated when he bought them & remained uncultivated when he left the Province.

All his lands were bought before the Rebellion, but one Bay Lott in Savanah. All these titles originated in Grants & in all these Grants had a clause of Forfeiture, but it was now insisted upon otherwise as a Professionable man he would have thought it a bad title. He thinks his lands well worth £1000 & could have sold them for that before the trouble.

150 acres on Great Ogeechu purchased from Lever Shethop, they cost him £75 & he values them at £100. There was a house on them & 15 acres cultivated on it, but he neglected it The original title was by Grant. He purchased it in 1774.

(17).
600 acres puchased in 1774 of Joseph Cannon, he paid £40 for them. There had been a Saw Mill & a little cultivation. He did not cultivate it himself, being asked how lands bought in 1774 for £40 could be worth £200 in 1775, he says that persons sold in necessity to take what they could get. He values them at £200 because adjoining lands were valued at that price, there was some little cultivation on these lands.

200 acres in St. Andrews Parish, he bought this at a sale in 1772, where he was the best bidder and gave £13 for it. He values this at £100, it was under similar circumstances. It had been settled, in some degree cultivated. He had laid out no money on it. He was offered £100 by a person who had lands adjoining.

A Bay Lott bought in 1781, in the Town of Savanah. It cost him £62.10sh., part of it was paid in Gold & half in Lawful money of the Country. Thinks it was worth £100 before the troubles.

A Lott in the Town of Brunswick, Granted to him by Sir James Wright, 4th Augst. 1772. The expense of the Grant was £5. He values it at £10.

Personal Property—Three Negroes, Two Children & a Woman.

She died of the Small Pox. One of the Children likewise died, the other he believes is in the Country. He left them at Charles Town. For he might have brought them away. He values them at £100. The woman & one child cost him that money. Furniture he values at £80 & thinks he is under the mark.

Public business done for the Province of Georgia, this was not pd., because no taxes were levied out of which he should be pd. He states two Debts which amount to £600.

The loss of the office of Atty. Gen. at £125 pr. an. He had no Mortgage on his estate & does not owe more than £15 in that
(18). Country.

His Estate was not settled. His Property was Confiscated. He has seen his name in a copy of the list.

There is an article at the end of the Memorial, in which Mr. Robertson states many other losses, &c., &c. But says he does not do it with a view to press it for Compensation, but merely to show that he has been carded in his statement of Losses. He says he has not the smallest hopes of recovering his Loss or any part of it in America.

Sir James Wright has Known the Claimt. for 12 or 13 years he was then clerk to the Atty. Genr. He was afterwards appointed to the Bar & before the troubles Sir Jas. made him a Lt. of

Militia. He was a practicing Atty. at the Commencement of the troubles & was appointed Acting Atty. Genr. in 1773. Mr. Hume the former Atty. Gen. being drove of by the troubles.

He was Lt. Col. during the seige & Sir James thinks him a truly Loyal & deserving subject. He acted from principal. Never heard of his taking an oath, if he did he thinks it must have been from necessity.

Sir James Wright knows nothing of his Property. He believes Mr. Robertson had no settled Plantations, but that he had a House which he purchased in the Town of Savanah.

Lieut.-Gov. Graham was well acquainted with Mr. Robertson & considers him as a zealous & firm friend to the cause of Great Britian. He was chosen a delegate to go to Congress in 1775, but refused. He understood that he took an oath of neutrality to the Rebel States.

Does not Know much of his Property only that he had some lands. He cannot say what he made of his business, but that he was well emploied & in Partnership with Mr. Hume. But does not Know what share of the Profits Mr. Robertson had, betwixt the years 1779 & 1782. He exerted himself as much as anybody & was very active at the seige. (19).

John Jamieson has known Mr. Robertson many years. Looks upon him as a very active & Loyal subject. Never heard of the circumstances of his taking an oath to the Rebel States. Believes he was banished for not doing it. Says that about the time they declared Independance they tenderd an oath of neutrality to many people. Being asked to the substance & purport of this oath, says the terms & purport of the oath are that the person should take no active part agst. the Americans & that they should not detain or secret any arms.

Property—does not particularly Know the 1936 acres, but he Knows adjoining lands. Has heard that a third was back swamp the whole was uncultivated. The Swamp was worth 20sh. pr. acre. The Pine lands from this situation was worth 10sh. pr. acre.

Mr. WILLIAM TELFAIR—Speaks to the acct. delivered in by Mr. Robertson to the Assembly in 1782 for the Public business done. Believes the sum was £100. It passed the House of Assembly, but cannot say if it was paid. Does not Know what Mr. R. gained by his Profession. (20).

Several other Witnesses were named to speak to Profession & appointments, but he says that demand is done away by his appointment in the Virgin Islands. He waves that part of his claim and offers no further evidence.

Decided.

The Board find that early in the Rebellion the Claimt. took (as he alledges this Constraint) an oath to the Rebel States of Georgia, but that he afterwards exerted himself in the British cause, servd. as Col. of Militia are therefore satisfied of his Loyalty.

Property—That he lost 150 acres in Christ Church Parish.
Value £75
600 acres in St. Philips Parish, Value......... 40
200 acres in St. Andrews Parish 50
A Town Lott in Brunswick............. 10

A Negroe... 45
Furniture, &c. 80

Total Loss.   £300

1125. Case PETER DEAN.

1784.
28th January.

(21).

He went to America in 1774, before he landed he heard of the troubles to the Northward from the Pilot. He landed at Charles Town in Jany. 1774. The troubles began in that Province in 1775 & Govert. was subverted in 1776. He then took an active part in favour of Govert. His first act of Loyalty was signing a Protest agst. the Proceedings of the Rebels. The Rebels spiked the guns that they might not be fired of the King's Birthday. He assisted in restoring them. He turned out under arms with 100 men to defend the Govr. & prevented some people from being tarred & feathered. When the Govr. retired, he went into the Country to avoid the resentment of the people, but was discovered making his escape in the night, when he was imprisoned for 14 days. Brought before a Rebel Committee who tendered an oath to him which he refused, in consequence he was ordered to depart the State in 60 days. In Oct. 1777, he was banished the state, but allowed to sell half of his Property & retained the other half as a security that he should not bear arms agst. them. In 1778 he was declared guilty of high treason agst. America & the other half of his Property was confiscated & sold. He then went to the

W. Indies to reside until the British Govt. was restored. He went to Savanah in 1779 & took an active part in the seige. He was in the hottest part of the engagement when De Stacey was repulsed.

At that time he acted as Lt. of Militia, but had neither Commission or Pay. He was afterwards elected a member of Assembly & served in the capacity doing every thing in his power to re-establish the British Govrt. he remained at Savanah unt'l the Evacuation in 1782.

He was by an Act of their Assembly banished and all his property confiscated—he is mentioned by name in the Act. He then went to C. Town to settle some business where he remained after the Peace.

(22).

He went to Georgia after the Peace with a view to settle there, but was refused admission & produces some papers to prove it.

Certificate to Character & Loyalty from Sir James Wright. He carried out little or no money in 1774. He went out as Clerk to a Mercht.

Property.
319 acres in Georgia for which he gave £73 in 1781. He says the King's Govt. was so well established that he had no fears.

Half of 500 acres purchased in 1781 for which £125 was given.
He married an American Woman by which he got a considerable sum of money which enabled him to buy these lands.

In 1781 he bought 4 Negroes for £160, the Americans took them & one carried of by them in 1772, which he values at £60.

About the time of the evacuation he lost 1000 Staves. Which he values at £— he says the common price was £10 pr. 1000. Says this charge ought to be £85. These were lost in the Country. He likewise lost 9000 in the Town, which he values at £90. He left them at the evacuation.

Part of the 1st tract of land was cultivated, but no part of the 2nd.

He charges the amount of Crop on Mr. Deans Plantation in New London, left at the evacuation. Does not charge the land as Mrs. Dean is in Possession. There were 50 acres Planted with Rice, the produce he values at £300. (23).

60 acres of Corn values the produce at £180.

600 Bushels of Pease at 2sh. £60.

10 acres of Potatoes at £50.

50 oars lost on his Plantation at 5sh. pr. oar, £12.12.6.

He bought 7 horses for his Plantation, for which he gave £82, five of them were working horses, one chaise & one saddle horse. They were all taken by the Americans.

He lost 3 Cows & 2 calves, he pd. £7 for them.

He lost 17 Hogs which he values at £17.

He lost 110 acres from a Plantation he rented at 5sh. is £23-7.6 the half of these & of them next articles belong to Mrs. Blight.

Lumber left on 3rd Plantation valued at £40.

---

8 acres of Corn & Pease at £36.

Six months rent pd. in advance for this Part £25. Rent was frequently pd. in advance in America.

320 Pine trees cut of his Lands & used in building Ft. Prevost. He has frequently applied to Gen. Clarke, but has never been pd. values them £40.

Hire of 3 Negroes emploied in said work for 65 days, which he values at £28.10. They had not rations from Governt.

Hire of 3 other Negroes in the same work for 65 days £19.10.

Amount of Rent of a House in Savanah, used as Barracks for the King's Troops for 3 years & upwards. Values this at £142.13sh. Produces a valuation of the above by several persons. Damages done the same house while used as Barracks estimated by the same persons at £163.11.2. (24).

Capt. Thos. Moor, late Barrack Master of Savanah, says, Mr. Dean's house was used as Barracks & he never was pd. for it, because he applied late. Mr. Dean got the house by his wife.

Says all Negroes had rations when emploied by Govrt. Says the rent of Mr. Dean's house was £40 pr. an. That it was much damaged during the seige. Says Mr. Dean is a very good man.

JOHN JAMIESON.

Has Known Mr. Dean for some years. He was a very Loyal subject. He knows the Lady he married. She was an only child

& her father was a man in good circumstances & had several negroes. He believes Mr. Dean was banished & his estate Confiscated.

JAMES HERRIOTT.

(25).

Knows Mr. Dean very well. He went over to America in 1774. He was a very Loyal subject. He had about £3000 by her. He Knows the 315 acres in St. Mathews Parish. Thinks it worth 10sh. pr. acre. Is not well acquainted with the 500 acres. He Knows he bought some Negroes & believes he lost them, but Mrs. Dean's Negroes are with her. His Wives Father was a Loyalist. Mr. D. lost some Staves at the evacuation.

JAMES HEWITT.

Knows Mrs. Deans estate in New London, believes 60 or 70 acres were Planted with rice & there was a great deal of Corn. Being asked what he thinks the value of the year's crop lost at the evacuation he says it would not exceed £200 St.

He Knows there were several oars there. Sold him some horses in 1781. Cannot tell the price they were left behind.

He had a few Cows & Hogs. He values hogs at 10sh. He Knows the Plantation which he rented of Pembroke, there was Corn & Lumber on it. All Mr. Deans Negroes were emploied on the works, the Labour of a Negroe is worth 2sh. pr. Diem.

JAMES ROBERTSON.

Knows Mr. Dean. He always bore the character of a Loyalist. Recollects his buying some land in St. Mathews Parish, believes he gave about £70 for it. Knows that persons were obliged to such Negroes to the Public Works. The Legislature did agree that they would pay a reasonable price for the labour of Negroes. Mr. Robertson says if the King's Govert. had remained in Georgia, Mr. Dean would have pd. for the Labour of his Negroes.

Decided.

The Board are of opinion that the Claimant is a Loyalist. That all his lands were purchased during the troubles. That he lost Negroes to the amount of £205.

(26).

Staves 50, do 45	£ 95
Crop on Mr. Dean's Plantation	200
Oars	7.10
Horses	36
Cattle	6
Hogs	16.10
Oars & Lumber on Pembroke's Plantation	14. 2.6
Corn	18
Trees Cut by Govert.	20
Hire of Negroes	47
Rent of House for Barracks	141.13
	£816.15.6

1784.
January 29th.

1126. Case JUSTICE WALKER.

Went from London in 1775 to Philadelphia. He only carried £15 out with him & hired himself aprentice to a Sugar Baker for 72a AR.

£36 pr. an. His wife followed him to America with £80. A few

weeks after he landed the Rebels beat up for Volunteers. They called upon him to sign the Association & he was in consequence turned out his place, as he refused. He joined the British at N. York. Served in the Militia & went from Philadelphia with British in 1778. He left behind him what was worth £100, it consisted of Furniture, Beef, Beer & Rum. He has applied to the Tressury & received £20 in full.

WILLIAM BURTON.

Resided at N. York & Knew Mr. Walker, he kept a small tavern there. He likewise kept a Shop in Philadelphia, but does not Know his Property. He bought Liquors from him. Burton thinks his Furniture, Liquors, &c., might be worth £50. Looks upon him as a very honest man & a Loyalist. He could make little at N. York as everything was dear. He believes he had 3 (27). Children & a wife, but does not Know if he brought anything to America. He supports himself by working in a Sugar house. He heard that Walker was tried by Rebel Colonel White & sentenced to be whipt & sentenced to be flogged for having some Hessians hid in his cellar. Does not know that he ever took an oath. Altho it is stated in the Memr. that he did. There are several certificates annexed by which it appears that he was esteemed a Loyalist & had taken the oath of alleegance to America. Mr. Gallaway signs such a certificate—Decision. The Board are of opinion that the Claimant is a Loyalist. That he lost Furniture, Liquors, &c., value £45. He has received £20 in full from the Treasury.

1127. Case JOHN LOVELL. 1784.
29th January.

Was Born in Boston & resided there when the troubles began. (28). Gen. Gage emploied him on some private services. This he did knowing with his principles were with the Govert. He frequently attended meetings at Boston & when measures hostile to Great Britian were proposed he always opposed them. Gen. Gage wanted to procure some papers which were in the Possession of the Rebell Committees. He procured them & delivered them to the Gen. This was attended with considerable expence which has never been repaid him. In this service he ran the Risk of being tarred & feathered.

He took up arms as an associator under Generals Gage & Hour & continued there until the evacuation. Had no witnesses to prove this, but the Genrs. can prove it. He is desired to send Certificates from them. As to property he cannot conceive that it is lost, so long as the King & Parlt. have offered to negotiate for it. And as he shall go to America & make his Claim. He looks upon his landed Interest to be worth £2000. There is about 3000 acres. He is only Tenant for life. It lays at Oxford Dudley, Belher Town, Cold Spring, &c. He got it by marriage. She is dead, but he has 3 children in America, who are in Possn. He left the improved part at £20 pr. an. All his title deeds were taken by Gen. Ward. He left goods &c., were taken out of his house when wife died, worth £150.

He was bankrup in 1769 & Compounded with his Creditors. Being asked whether he was worth a farthing, if his debts were paid, he says he is if he could receive what is due to him, they lay in Canada & he means to go there for the recovery of them, about £1800 Stg. They were all due before 1769. He admits that exclusive of these debts in Canada he owes more than his Property is worth.

He has received at different times from the Treasury £150 and by the Report of Messrs. Wilmot & Coke £30. He makes no application, but for the money & time spent these eight years.

Decision—All this claim rejected.

He seems to have Received more from Govert. than he ever lost.

(29).

1781. January 30th.

1128. Case MRS. HAMILTON.

Mary Hamilton—Her husband was a native of Scotland & died in 1780. He went to New York as a Surgeon about nine years ago. She was married to Mr. H. before he went. She never was in America. After he had been in America 5 years he returned & took out medicines to the value of £200. She Knows nothing of his Property in America. When he came to England in 1779 or 1780 he said he had lost every tning about £1000.

He died aboard the Centaur about 3 years ago. She says he never bought land, but his Property was in Furniture, Horses, &c., &c. America was in Rebellion When he went there. She says he was ill used on acct. of his Loyalty. Her husband left a Will with a power for his agent to receive any money might be due him. He owed his agent Mr. Raumont £100.

It turns out to be a letter of Atty. & that she had administered to the will. When he came home he applied to the Treasury, but received nothing.

Mr. Urqhart advised her to apply to this Board.

She has no support at present but £18 pr. an. as a Surgeon's widow.

Mr. John Bowman is a Navy Agent. He never knew Mr. Hamilton, until about 4 years ago. When he came home from America. Where he had been Surgeon to the Zebra, Capt. Collins. He Knows nothing of Mr. Hamilton or of his Property in America. Capt. Collins is at Plymouth. Mrs. Hamilton has a pension of £20 pr. an. He has settled all Mr. Hamiltons affairs in the ship where he died. He was in debt to Mr. Bowman, but his effects on board more than pd. him. Mrs. Hamilton administred & he acted under a power of Atty. from her. There was above £20 pd. her, being the ballance. He Knows nothing of the Profits of his business while in America, but says being Surgeon of a Man of War is of Considerable emolument.

(30).

GEORGE URQUHART.

Was acquainted with Dr. Hamilton when he came from America. He knows nothing of his losses, but by his relationship with him. In 1779 he had heard him say that he lost £1000. He has heard him say that he had a Negroe, Horses, Furniture, Cattle, Piggs, & a considerable quantity of Plate. There is a certificate from Capt. Collins of the Navy to Mr. Hamiltons Loyalty.

Mr. Urquhart thinks that Mr. Hamilton has adminestred. There was no Will. Mr. Hamilton went formally to America 25 years ago.

Mr. Urqhart is a Professional man & admits that his a very weak evidence. Capt. Collins is not in town, but can be heard on a future day. Mr. Urquhart will endeavour to find him & if his evidence will be of use to bring him before the Board.

Mrs. Hamiltons Husband appears to have been loyal. All the Claim rejected. (31).

1129. Case WILLIAM MOREHEAD.   1784.
                                          January 30th.

The Claimant is a native of Ireland. He went with his wife & two children to Philadelphia in 1773. He carried out above £100 with him. He sold a lease he held under Ld. Mount Castle In 1774 he purchased 180 acres about 100 miles from Philadelphia. He paid £10 for the land, there was about 18 acres cultivated when he bought it. He continued in Possession about four years, when he was driven away because he would not take up arms agst. the Comr. They seized him & every thing he had.

He fled to the British Lines. He would have taken arms for the British if his health had allowed, but he remained sick for six months & then came to Ireland in 1778. Does not Know if his Property is Confiscated or not as he never had inquired about it since he left. He cultivated 10 acres more which did not cost him much as he sold the Produce. Says he has valued the land low at £60. He had—acres in tillage when he left it. He values the crop at £30. Says the crop was on the ground. He values his Cows at £10 & his Cloaths at £20. He had a wife & 5 children at that time. Swears positively to his having given £100 for the land. Being asked why he valued it so low, says he thought it right to do so, but says if he was to have sold it he would have valued it above £100 considerably. He is a Protestant.

He never had a deed from the person he bought from, but had the promise of one.

He has no letter or Witness, but says as he hopes for salvation what he says is true. (32).

HENRY WAKEFIELD.

Has known Mr. Morehead nine years, lived within 7 miles of him in America upon a Plantation, but cannot say whether it was his or not. He had seen Cows upon the land. Has heard that he was oppressed & obliged to fly on acct. of his attachment to Govert.

He met Morehead in the street the other day or should not have been called upon as a Witness. In general he confirms Moreheads acct.

Decision.

The Board are of the opinion that William Morehead is a Loyalist. That he lost a Plantation which they valued £60. Crop & Stock they value at £40.

1784.
January 30th.

1130. Case JOHN LIGHTENSTONE.

He was born at Petersburgh of English Parents, went to America in 1775. He followed the sea & was mate of a vessel. Soon after he commanded a vessel out of N. York. At the Commencement of the troubles he was settled in Georgia & Commanded the Scout Boat. Produces his Commission from Sir Jas. Wright in 1768, in 1776 she was taken from him by the Rebels. They offered to continue him in Command of her if he would follow their measures, which he refused. He apprehended that it was an appointment for life & says he cleared £200 pr. an. by it. When Sir James Wright went away he went to the Island of Skidaway & was very cautious of showing himself. He afterwards went to Halifax & to N. York & continued with the army until 1782. Sir James Wright appointed him to Command a Troop of Horse. He received 15sh. 6d. pr. diem & Continued in this situation until the Evacuation of Savanah.

(33).

He was at the taking of Savanah by the British & was then D. Q. M. Genr. for which he received pay. He was at the taking of most of the Towns in America. Certificates from Sir Jas. Wright & Capt. Barkley to Loyalty. Sir Jas. talks of the Confiscation of his Property.

381 acres purchased contained in many Conveyances, the titles were produced, they were principally cultivated. He did not give quite 20sh. pr. acre for them, but they are much improved. He made the Buildings & Indigo Vaults himself. He was offered £500

for 320 acres, but refused it. He values these lands at 40sh. pr. acre.

150 acres in Wrightborough, no part of which is cultivated, it was his Property by Grant in 1774. He meant to have Cultivated it if the troubles had not happened.

The expense of taking out the grant was about £10. Values this at 20sh. pr. acre.

Crop of 40 acres left in 1782. Mr. Lightenstone values at £100. 480 Bushels corn valued at 2sh. 6d. pr. Bushel. 200 Bushels of Pease at 2sh. 6d. 3 acres of Potatoes £10. Corn in Store £5.

Horses, Cattle, Hogs at £100. 18 Head Cattle at £40. 8 Sheep 13sh. each. 30 Hogs 10sh. One Horse during the siege £11. Two horses at the Plantation £10. One Dragoon Horse £22. Swears they were all taken from him by the Rebels.

(34).

10 Negroes lost, 3 died natural death, 2 were drowned making their escape from the Rebels.

A Flatt & two Boats belonging to his Plantation he values at £20.

Furniture & Plantation Tools worth £60 at least, thinks he could swear to double that sum.

Clothes, Plate, money and arms taken from him at Rhode Island in 1776. He estimates at £43. He did not purchase these for double that sum. Values the loss of his employment £200 pr. an.

Receives from the Treasury £60 pr. an.

JOHN JAMIESON.

Knows the Claimant & believs him well attached to the British Cause. He has been on the Plantation. He only knows the number of acres from himself. He thinks it is moderately charged. Has sold such land for more than £3 pr. acre. He knows he had Negroes, but cannot say how many. Knows nothing of the Crop, but thinks it must be moderate.

GEORGE BURRY.

Knows the Claimant since 1771 & that he had a Plantation on the Island of Skidaway, but no particulars.

STEPHEN HAVEN.

Has known Mr. L. for some time. Knows a few of his Negroes were away & came to St. Augustine. He knows that one was Drowned by accident. Admits that he might have sold his Negro before he was drowned.

(35).

Mr. Lightenstone called in again. Being asked if he owes any money in America. He says he owes £257 for stores & other articles, but says there was no incumbrance or settlement on his estate. He is a Widower with one child which is now at St. Augustine & married. Being asked how much is due him in America he says £74, by which it appears the Ballance agst. him in America is £183.

ROBT. MCCULLOCH.

1874.
February 3rd.

Knows Mr. Lightenstone since April 1777. He knows he lost two Negroes during the siege. One was sent out with the Wood Cutters & taken, the other died of blows he received from some soldiers, he died in McCulloch's house. Knows that he was Plundered of some furniture at Burtons Landing by the French, does not know the value, but the house was well furnished. He says no man is more Loyal, has a better character or is more deserving than Mr. Lightenstone.

Decision.

That Mr. Lightenstone is a zealous & active Loyalist & that he lost 381 acres of Land, which the value at £350.

150 acres which they value at ....£	30
Crop, Corn, Pease, Potatoes, &c.	50
Cattle, Horses, Hogs & Sheep.	50
Negroes.	360
A Flatt & Boats...	10
Furniture, Plantation Tools, &c.	50
Plate, Arms & Clothes at Rhode Island	40

(36).

Has an allowance of £60 pr. an. from the Treasury.
He owes in America on a Ballance £183.

1784.
February 2nd.

1131. Case Lt. Col. Conolly.

Is an American Born & was settled in Virginia from the year 1770. He was in the Millitary Line, Some time last War & served agst. the Indians.

He had a Patrimonial estate originally in Pensilvania, which he sold and purchased in Virginia. At the commencement of the troubles he commanded the Militia in Augusta County.

His first act was to join Ld. Dunmore. Which he did when he was on board ship in July 1775.

He was then dispatched by Lord Dunsmore in Boston, where he got immediately, on his return from Boston he was appointed Lt. Colonel Commandant & the Command of an expedition given him 5th Nov., 1775. He was taken the 19th of the same month, he remained Prisonr. five years. He was not Particularly ill treated. His exchange was effected in Octr.. 1780. When he went to N. York. He was again taken Prisonr. in Sept., 1781, in the vicinity of York Town & remained Prisonr. until March, 1782. He was kept in Gaol from Jany. to March & then Paroled on Condition that he should go to England which he did accordingly.

(37).

He mentions a circumstance of Loyalty by which he did some service. Early in the Rebellion, he enduced four persons of consequence to take part with Govert. But Congress afterwards got them over to their cause. He was frequently offered a command by the Rebels. Congress offered him the command of the 2nd Virginia Regt.

He has received whole pay to the 24th Oct. last, but does not know if he is to receive half pay or not.

General Washington made him offers if he would come into their service. He was intimate with Gen. Washington before the War.

Colonel Conolly has made several applications to the Treasury for temporary support, but their being a doubt whether or not he would receive half pay, no report has been made in his favour.

300 acres on Charles Creek, Augusta County. He has no title to these lands but Pre-occupance, which was common in the County. They were in Virginia before the Division, but are now in Pensilvania.

There is a custom in Pensilvania that Preoccupance give a title, this title is indisputable, they occupied Lands in this manner. They put Poor People upon Lands & found them stock, at the end of seven years they were to return them with half the produce.

He might have taken out Warrants at any future time. He gave Lands in this way to Two men & stock to the amount of £60 each.

(38).

There was only one man on his 300 acres, the other two men he believes are now in Possession under the Rebel States.

He values the 300 acres at £500. He thinks they are worth more than 30sh. pr. acre. He had made some small improvements on the land before he put these men into Possession.

When he saw them last there was about 60 acres cultivated in each of the tracts. Being asked what expense he had been at, he says each tract cost him about £120 Pen. Cury.

The same circumstances apply to Raven Creek, where he had 400 acres which he likewise values at £500.

A House & Forty of Land adjoining the Town of Pittsburgh, with Furniture, &c.

Col. Conolly bought this in 1770 & pd. £60 Currency for it. The title to this was the same with that of the 300 & 400 acres. He values the whole of this at £500. Being desired to value the House & Land separates from the furniture, he says the House & Land was worth £300. The Furniture was worth £200.

4000 acres of Land in the County of Fencastle. They were granted to him in 1772, by Lord Dunmore, he has lost the papers. Says he sold 400 lotts at ½ a— Spanish Dollars each & one Dollar pr, an. Quit rent for each Lott. No cultivation had taken place on that part which remained by him, but each person who had a Lott was bound to cultivate 7 acres out of the Body of Land & at the end of 7 years to restore these 7 acres to him.   (39).

He values his Interest in these Lands at £4000. When in Gaol in 1778, he was offered 1000 Pistols for 2000 acres he had on a Warrant of Survey in 1772, but the Grant was never taken out, it was not Convenient for him to take out the Grant at that time. So he Postponed it. These lands lay adjoining the 4000 acres. There was no Improvements on these Lands. The expense of the Warrant & Survey was about £40 per curry. He values them at 5sh. pr. acre £500.

He claims Pay as Major Commandant of the Militia on actual service from 16th Decmr. 1773 to 16th June 1775, being 547 days at 15sh. pr. Diem. Amounting £307.13.9d.

Likewise for extraordinary Presents to the Indian Chiefs assembled at Pittsburgh £150.

Likewise expenses on the Public business of the Colony £100.

He claims £19 for the expence of 10 Pack Horses from the 10th May to 20th Novr., 192 days at 2sh. each.

These were all debts due to him by the Province, but they refused to pay him on acct. of the part he took in the troubles. He therefore claims it from Govert.

There is likewise included in his acct. £100 for Wheat, Flour, &c., which likewise should come agst. the Province & makes the whole £849.13sh.

He states no debts. Says there were no Mortgages on his Estate & says he is personally named in the act of Confiscation.   (40).

EARL OF DUNMORE.

Knew Col. Conolly in Virginia. He commanded the Militia of Augusta County, before the Rebellion & was concerned agst. the Indians. Lord Dunmore employed him in making a treaty with the Indians. He did this business well and was of great use. Looks upon Col. Conolly to be well attached to the British Govert.

He appointed him Lt. Col. Commandant in the year 1775. Ld Dunmore knew he was confined for several years. Confirms the acct. he gives of the Grant of 4000 acres. Ld. Dunmore being asked as to the demand he had upon the Province, says he believes part of it is just & that it ought to have been paid & thinks it never was. Says he certainly would have received it but for the Rebellion.

MAJOR STOCKTON.

Has Known Col. Conolly since 1776. He was in Gaol with him at York Town & at Philadelphia with him. Believes him to be a very Loyal subject. While he was in Gaol, with him two persons offered to buy some land from him. They appeared serious & offered to pay for it in gold & silver, the sum was he thinks 1000 Pistols.

1784.
February 5th.

(41).

JOSEPH GALLAWAY, Esq.

Being called upon by the Board to satisfy them as to the custom which Col. Conolly said existed in Pensilvania respecting the title of lands by preoccupancy.

Says the Proprietors hold their title by Patent from the Crown. They established a land office in order to dispose of their lands, to whom persons wishing to purchase must apply. Upon their applying to the office they received a Warrant to the Surveyor to survey & locate.

Lately they sent only a Copy of the application not a Warrant. Upon a return of the survey the title to the Purchase is reckoned so far Compleate, that he has a right to take out a Patent & Confirmation when ever the resedue of the purchase money is pd. He says the Warrant & survey was always pleaded in their Courts & was held legal title.

There have been instances of people cultivating a (few) acres

& that these persons have always had a right of preemption. He has known, he has known the Contrary. Mr. Galloway says the title of Mr. Conolly was better than that of the people eploied by him.

Decision.

The Board are of opinion that Colonel Conolly is a zealous & active Loyalist & renderd essential service to Govrt.

His Lands appear mostly to be held under a bad Title. They allow him £120 for his buildings & Stock in the 2 first tracts.

For the House & 40 acres they allow £48.

Furniture there £150.

(42).

4000 acres by Grant £475.

He has no allowance at present from the Treasury.

1784.
February 3rd.

1132. Case JOSEPH HOOPER, Marblehead.

As soon as the restraining act passed he Signed a Protest & induced others to sign it, contrary to the Resolutions of the Town of Marblehead, where he resided. He followed the business of a Rope maker & was a Mercht. His house was called Tory Hall from his known adherance to Govt. He was obliged to go armed for some time before he left America. The troops left Marblehead a short time before the battle of Lexington. He continually lived with the officers of the British Army.

After the battle of Lexington, Capt. Bishop in the Lively Ship of War blocked up the Port & he was chosen by the Town as a friend to Govert. to mediate for them.

After this he was constantly attacked & insulted and frequently put in danger of his life. Then attempts were made to burn his house in the night. He killed one man in the attempt.

On the 1st of May 1775 a Town meeting was held at Marblehead & all adherent to the British cause, were ordered to renounce their alligance, he was the only person in the Town who refused to make a temporary submission.

They immediately drew up a form of recantation, which a friend of his who was of the committee, brought to him & told him he must sign before the Friday following or his life would be the forfeit. He then thought it prudent to get off, which he did in a Ship of his fathers to Bilboa in Spain & lay 42 nights on some dried Fish. He came from Spain to England, since which time he has never been to America. (43).

Certificates from Gen. Gage & Judge Brown to Loyalty to Property from others, but they cannot be received.

SIR WM. PEPPERELL.

Believes Mr. Hooper to be a Loyalist & has understood that he has suffered considerably by his Loyalty. He supposed him to be a person of Property, when he was in America & still thinks he was.

His Father was a very steady Loyalist.

The Claimant called again to speak to Property says he built a House, he bought the land in 1772 of Benj. Matson Esq., says he thinks the Land cost him before he began to build, twixt £3 & 400 Stg. The building of the House cost him £2500 Stg. The out Buildings, fence, &c., cost him £500. It was just finished before the troubles. He values the whole at £3500 & is concious it must have cost him more.

Plate, Furniture, Wine, Liquors, Linnen, in his opinion were worth at least £500.

A large Rope walk he swears was his own property. He values this with tools & implements at £2500, it cost him that & he could had £2000 from a person to take him into Partnership. The Rope Walk he hears is not destroied. He thinks it would let for £70 or £80 pr. annum. His father is not in Possession. He says all his Property at Marblehead is confiscated as will appear by an affidavit of his Fathers which was produced & read. His Father was active last August. It appears by the same that the Property was the sons. He had a right in two other Rope Walks. He left all his Papers at Salem. He values this Interest at £300. (44).

A House & Land at Newbury Port, his title to this is in right of his Wife, it belonged to her. It belonged to her Father & Mother, it has been valued at £1875, there is a mortgage on it for £600.

He values his loss to him at £1000. Does not know that it is Confiscated his Wife is in Possession.

150 acres Lands at Marblehead, these he would only have at his Father's death. He has a Deed of Gift for them. He values them at £500.

For Hemp Cordage, English & West Indian goods. He swears he had those in his Rope Walk to the value of £400. Furniture, Plate, &c., &c., in his Father in Law's house £189.

He had two Negroes which are liberated by the Congress. Succeeded to two by his Father in Law, one lives with his Wife & one is dead.

(45). He had 5 Horses, two he drove in his Phaeton, one he rode. These cost him £20 each & 2 cart horses. He values them at £50.

He had two carriages which he values at £80.

Upon a ballance there was £400 due him in America.

He claims Loss of business in his Rope Walk for 9 years at £700 pr. an. Says he made that by his business. He realized about £400 pr. an., by his trade in the Fisheries, &c.

The Interest of his estate for 9 years at £300 pr. an. He formerly had £100 pr. an. from the Treasury from 1777. He is reduced by Mr. Wilmot & Coke to £80.

SAM'L. CARWEN, Esq.

Has Known Mr. Hooper since his infancy. Mr. Carwen lived at Salem only 4 miles from Marblehead, says the Hooper family were always esteemed Loyal. He does not himself know any acts of their Loyalty. He knows he carried on the Rope business & always considered him as the owner of the Rope Walk. He cannot put any value on his Rope Walk or on his House. He knows the woman he married. Believes her Father is a Loyalist he does not know what fortune she had, believes her father had failed some years before. Mr. C— came away before Mr. Hooper. He has heard nothing of Mr. Hoopers conduct by which he displeased the Rebels. Says Mr. Coombs could give the Board some information, but he is at present out of town.

(46).

Says he knows nothing more of Mr. Hoopers case & Mr. Monro is desired to inform Mr. Hooper that the Board will require further evidence to Coroborate Mr. Hoopers testimony.

February 24th. PETER FRY, Esq.

He lived at Salem. Hooper lived at Marblehead. He was a rope maker. He believes the Rope Walk was his own. It was made at a very considerable expense. He thinks it might have let for £100 pr. an. He thinks he could have bought & built the whole for £2000 Lawful. He always considered both Father & Son as very Loyal subjects. Knows his House, it was one of the best houses in Town. It would have cost him £2500 S. with the out buildings He was at great expense in clearing the ground for the foundation. If he had been to buy the house he would have thought £2000 a high price for it. At auction he thinks it would have sold for £1500, it was well furnished. He thinks that the furniture, plate, &c., might be worth £350. He has heard that Mr. Hooper had a concern in another Rope Walk. He has rode round the House at Newbury Port. Mr. Hooper got it by his Wife. He thinks it might be worth £7 or 800. He Knows Mr. H. had Negroes, but does not know the number. He had two or three Carriages. Being asked as to the price of Carriage Horses, he says £10 is a high price. He says that he might make £500 pr. an. of his Rope Walk, sometimes more. He does not know if Mr. Hoopers Property is confiscated & doubts if the proscription Laws prevents persons who are attainted from inheriting property. Says he never knew of Property coming by a man's wife being confiscated when she remained in this Country. This goes to the Estate at Newbury Port & the principle which he lays down as to Inheritence applies to the estate in reversion to him at his father death. (47).

Decision.

That Mr. Hooper is a Zealous & Steady Loyalist.

They value his House at...	£1450
Plate, Furniture, Liquors, Linnen, &c., &c.	300
His Rope Walk at	1450
Part concern in two others	150
Tar, Hemp, Cordage & Merchandise	200
Two Negroes	80
Carriages	40
Balance Debts	400
Allowance from the Treasury	80 pr. an.

1133. Case LT. COLONEL JACOB ELLEGOOD.   1784.
February 4th.

He is a native of Virginia. When Lord Dunmore first Issued his Proclamation sent letters to Col. Ellegood who Commanded the Militia of this County. In consequence he brought him in 600 men in Novr. 1775. They were all in arms & were part of those who had before attacked Lord Dunmore. They then took the oath to Govert.

Owing to the influence Colonel Ellegood had over them Lord Dunmore proposed to him to raise a Regiment for the defence of Norfolk. He accordingly raised the Regt. & Had a Commission from Ld. Dunmore to Command it. They were called the Queens Royal American Regiment. He Commanded this Regt. at the Battle of Great Bridge, where the British were defeated, after which it was found necessary to abandon Norfolk. (48).

He had an order to conduct some Women, &c., to the Eastern Shore when he was taken Prisonr, he was kept 4 weeks Prisonr at Northampton and afterwards at Williamsburgh & other places. Upon the whole he was detained Prisonr with them 5 years & 4 months, frequent applications were made for his exchange, but they never would exchange him. He came into the British lines on Parole in 1781 & remained on Parole for the whole War. Sir Henry Clinton wished to have carried him out with him, but could not get him exchanged. His services were stopt by his being made a Prisoner, but he did all he could until then.

Some letters & Papers produced in which Colonel Ellegoods Character is highly spoken of.

His Property he says is only confiscated for Life & his family are still in Possession of it.

Property—

(49). The Plantation on which he lived called Rosehall. 1000 acres on Lyn Haven River, Princess Ann County. He followed no Profession, but lived on his own Property. He was able to live very well on the produce of it, as many persons now in London can testify. He makes the whole together with the Buildings at £4000 Stg.

He had a very valuable Fishery adjoining to the Estate. Another Plantation he inherited from his father about 980 acres called the Chapel Plantation. There was not more than 40 acres cultivated. He gained considerable from this Estate by cutting Timber &c. 80 acres were cleared, about 40 only in cultivation. Both these Plantations are in the Possession of Mrs. Ellegood. Being asked as to the value of this Estate, he says he would not have taken £3430 for it which is between £3 & £4 pr. acre.

He cleared between £2 & 300 pr. an. by cutting timber, &c. He thinks he has lost more than £400 pr. an. from the two Estates & only claims for Loss of income for the last 8 years, as he admits that the Estate is not lost to his family. Says he should think himself recompenced by £300 pr. an. Mrs. Ellegood was not dispossessed of the Estate but about one year & half, she quitted it in 1775 & returned in 1777 or 1776. The Estate was stripped of everything, Stock, Furniture, &c. She afterwards recovered some things by order of the Governor & Council, which have not been charged by Colonel Ellegood.

(50). She recovered five or Six Beds, some Negroes, &c. Mrs. Ellegood has always been treated with great civility, but has been so highly taxed that he has been always obliged to remit her money from home.

The Property as he understands now stands thus By an act of the State of Virginia, passed about 1778. The Property of Loyalists who had joined the British, who had wives & children to go immediately to them. One third to the wife as if the Father was dead. He conceives that his family are in Possession of his Estate under this act and he is Prohibited from ever returning in that Country as a Subject.

He means to go & settle in Nova Scotia.

Personal Property—

He had 150 Sheep taken from him. 50 head of cattle. 8 Horses taken by the Rebels, some of them carriage, some riding horses. 8 or 10 of the Cattle were fat oxen. He could have sold them to the fleet for more. 3700 weight of Pork it was salted for the use of his family to be sent to Norfolk.

It was used by a Rebel family. He values it at £37. 80 live Hogs at 10sh. 300 barrels of Corn. He is sure as to the quantity. It was his whole crop. He values it at 2sh. pr. Bushel. 250 Bushels Wheat at 4sh. 1000 Bushels oats at 1sh. Some Oak Timbers valued at £80. Plantation Tools, Waggons, Carts, &c., £40. Spirits & Cyder £25. Household furniture lost £40. All these articles were taken away at the same time by the Commanding officers of the Rebel Troops after the Battle of Great Bridge in Decmr. 1775.

(51).

He lost four Negroes the best fled to the fleet to Lord Dunmore to avoid being sent to the mines when he died. The other run away in Consequence of Proclamation Issued by the Rebels. He values the 4 at £225, but would not have taken £400 for them. Being asked what is the average price of Negroes in Virginia about £80 each. Colonel Ellegood Presided in the Virginia Committee. There was no Mortgage on his Estate & he has made no demand for debts due him.

He received full pay from Novr. 14th 1775, the date of his Commission to 25th June 1778, at 17sh. pr. Diem & from June 25th 1778 to 24th Novr. 1782. He only received half pay & conteives that he is so injured to the amount of £926.18.6.

Colonel Conolly who is in the same situation has received full pay. Conceives himself entitled to full pay up to Sept. 1783. He never received anything from the Treasury until Jany. last, since which he has received £200 pr. an.

Debts—He has two Bonds, but does not wish to state them as he thinks it will be of no use to him. He had repeated offers from the Rebels in 1775. They offered him a Regt. & in 1782, when at New York, they offered him restitution. if he would relinquish the cause of Great Britain. but he constantly refused them.

THOS. MACKNIGHT.

Knew Colonel Ellegood very well. He was settled in Virginia when the troubles broke out. He inherited his Estate from his father. He was Colonel of Militia of this County. His father was County Lt. nearly similar to Lord Lt. of the County here.

(52).

The Plantation where he lived was very extensive. Speaks of Lord Dunmore writting to Col. Ellegood to take part with the British Govert. in consequence of which he came to the Head of 600 men of the Militia of that County Princess Ann. He was afterwards made Lt. Col. Commandant of a Regt. & went to the Battle of the Great Bridge. He raised great part of the Regt. He was a man in whom Lord Dunmore placed great confidences. The witness has known some spirited exertions of Colonel Ellegood.

His Plantation was a very valuable one. He thinks there were not more then 2 or 3 Houses in the County better than his. There were 4 or 500 acres cleared. The house was a good one & neatly furnished. He was very popular & considered as one of the first men in the Country. He knows he had another Plantation. Being asked to the value of the 1st says about £4000 & upwards. He would not have scrupled to have given that if he had wanted to have purchased it.

(53)

He had been more than once on the other Plantation. Thinks it would not have sold for so much as the other at a Public sale. He left Virginia in 1775 & has heard nothing of it since. But has heard of the Law which Col. Ellegood mentioned by which tne Property of Loyalists is given to the family being on the Spot. Believes it was a Public Law of the Province.

He cannot speak to the particulars of his Personal Estate, only that Colonel Ellegood lived well & had several Negroes & that his Plantation was well stocked.

JAMES PARKER, Esq.

Was born in this Country & resided in Norfolk as a Mercht. since the year 1747. He knew Col. Ellegood very well. Mr. Parker married his sister in the year 1760. He knows his Property very well. Failing of his children, the Swamp Plantation would have come to his Wife & another sister.

He knew the Plantation on which he lived. Believes it contained above 800 acres, but not more than 1000. About 400 acres were Cultivated. Col. Ellegood apllied to the Witness to survey the Estate, but it never was done. He thinks it would have amounted to nearly 1000 acres.

If Col. Ellegood had been obliged to sell it he could not have got above £4 pr. acre for it, tho' it was worth more. Remembers land selling for more than £4 pr. acre, but sales were common on credit. He thinks that the other Plantations was not worth near so much in the state that it was. Thinks it was worth 50sh. or £3 pr. acre. There was 8 or 900 acres of it little or none cultivated. He thinks there was but one Negroe Hutt & believes there was no part of this in cultivation for crops.

He does not recollect any part of it in tillage. Lumber from this Estate was a Considerable part of Col. Ellegoods income. He cannot speak particularly of the stock, he knows there was some, but believes there was little in Proportion to the extent. Has always known Col. Ellegood to be a Loyal subject & that he (Parker, advised Ld. Dunmore to write to him, knowing the weight he had in the Country & knowing him to be a firm friend to Govert.

(54).

JOHN SAUNDERS.

Lived on his own Plantation in Princess Ann & had no Profession. Colonel Elegood married his sister. Knows his Loyalty & Property. He was a very active Loyalist. He Commanded the Regt. in which Mr. Saunders was Capt., the Regt. was raised cheifly by Col. Ellegoods Interest, it was never completed as Col. Ellegood was taken Prisonr.

He knows both the Plantations, but most particularly that on which he lived. He cannot say what would be the annual income but it enabled C. E. to live very well.

The Plantation he lived at, He values at £4 or 5 pr. acre. Thinks the Swamp Plantation was worth 50sh. pr. acre. The Farm was well Stocked. Col. Ellegood had several very good horses. The Witness had sold him one for £25.

Decision.
The Board are of opinion that the Claimant is a very zealous & active Loyalist & performed material service to Govert., &c. &c.
Personal Property to the amount of £658.10.
Negroes 100
Has an allowance from the Treasury of £200 pr. an.

1784.
February 6th.
(55).

1134. Case the REVD. JOHN DOTY.
He was born at Albany, but educated at New York. He conconsidered himself bound by the oath of allegiance, which he had taken several times to his Majesty, to adhere to government which he did do at the commencement of the troubles.

He was Rector of St. Georges Church, Senectady, in the year 1775. He did both in & out of the Pulpit exort his Parishioners to good Govt. This soon drew upon him the resentment of the opposite faction, but they did not molest him until after the declaration of Independance. When his Church was shut up & soon after he was brought before the Committee & accused by the young men of Plotting agst. the State, this was in Summer 1776. He denied the charge of Plotting, but declared that he was & should be Loyal. They threatened to send him to Albany to Gaol, however he was discharged & allowed to remain unmolested for a few weeks, when he was again taken by two armed men, out of his bed, they hurried him & some others into a Waggon & carried them to Albany. When they came to Albany they proposed an oath to him he believes of neutrality. He refused to take it. He believes those with him took it. Notwithstanding that he refused to take the oath they released him & allowed him to return to Schenectady where remained until General Burgoynes defeat. When despairing of any further succor or happiness he procured permission from General Gates to retire into Canada.

(56).

Gen. Gates offered him a living of £200 pr. an. He was appointed by Sir. Guy Carleton Chaplain to Sir John Johnstons 1st Batt. Where he continued until 1782. When his wife & he came to England for his health & was permitted to appoint a Deputy Chaplain during his absence. He has now half pay, but that is mortgaged for a year to come to a gentleman at Montreal who advanced him some money to bring him home. He was appointed a Missionary in 1773 & has continued so ever since, the emolument of which is £40 pr. an., but he is going again to Canada with the addition of £10 pr. an. He has £40 pr. an. from the Treasury.

He Produces a Commission from Sir Guy Carleton & a letter from Dr. Morice, Secretary of the Society for Propogating the Gospel, speaking very highly of Mr. Doty & saying that the Society had him to go again to Canada.

Property—353 of Land produces Lease & Release by which it appears that it was purchased in August 1775 of John Hagan, for the consideration of £80 Lawful. Mr. Doty says he bought it in 1774, but the Deeds were not made out for some time as the Estate was sub-divided. No Part of this was cultivated, but it was cultivated all round it. This was the whole of the expense

(57).

about £45 S. It is part of 9000 acres granted to the Vendor in 1771. Part of this 9000 acres was cultivated, he values the Land at 13sh. 6d. pr. acre. It is confiscated £238.5. Stg.

Personal Property—He had a Chamber organ, which he put into the Church for security. He had a tolerable Library. He cannot exactly say the value of the Library or organ, thinks together they were worth £30. He says that his Land & Personal Property he thinks was worth £150. His living was worth £40 pr. an.

That he lost Property for which he pd. in the end of 1774 £45.
Personal Property £30
His living 40

He has an allowance as a Missionary ....: 50 per an.
Half pay as Chaplain to Sir John Johnsons Corps 60
From the Treasury 40

1784.
February 6th.

1135. Case PETER ROSE.

Is a Swede & went to America in 1776 to Boston. He was a Shoemaker. At the Commencement of the troubles he associated for the defence of Boston, as appears by the Certificate of Sir William Pepperell. Upon the Evacuation of Boston, he went with the troops to Halifax & came to England the latter end of 1777. He was obliged to leave behind him at Boston some little matters of furniture, which amount to as pr. Schedule £14.2.8.

(58).

He has Book Debts due him to the amount of £140.0.7. £40 of which is due him by the army.

He gained considerable by his trade. He brought over £250. Which he has since lost. He says in 1774 he was worth £200, but admits he was worth more when he came home. He says he ruined himself by keeping a Public house in Town. He gained more than £100 year before the troubles. He makes a charge of the Loss of three apprentices, one ran to the Rebels, one to the West Indies & he left one behind £50 each.

Certificates to Loyalty from respectable People. Says his principal Loss was his trade. He now makes 10 or 11sh. pr. week, as a journeyman. He has an allowance of £20 from the Treasury.

JOHN BARNARD.

Is a Furrier. He knew Mr. Rose in Boston when he kept a great many workmen. He had the best business in Town. He believes him to be a Loyalist. He worked for all the Army. He joined the Association. He knew him first in London. He went out 7 years before the Witness & carried out all he had to America. He does not know what it amounted to.

Decision.

The Board are of opinion that the Claimant is a Loyalist that he lost Furniture, &c., worth £14. He has an allowance of £20 pr. an. from the Treasury.

(59).

73A AR.

1136. Case JOHN SALTMARSH.   1784,
                                                           7th Feby.

Is an Englishman & went to America in 1768. He was settled at Norwich in 1775 & followed the trade of Breeches maker, Glover & Dyer. He was applied to for to teach the Americans the use of Arms, but refused although they offered to pay him for it. They offered to make him a Capt. with the Pay of 10sh. pr. diem. In Consequence they abused him & would not employ him. He quitted the place in June 1775 & went to New York where he was emploied by Gen. Tryon & Capt. Vanderput to get Intelligence. He was apprehended in Oct. 1776. He lay near three months in Prison in which time he was very ill used & many offers made to him. He did not get out of bondage until 1777, which year he took an oath which he says that he had no writings, so as to give

intelligence to the British Army. On this he was permitted to depart & joined the British fleet in 1777. He has been twice wounded He came to Ireland in March 1779.
in passing the Lines of the Enemy, which has affected his health.

He never received but £10 for his services. He has been in England since May, 1779.

He had no land. His stock in trade was worth in 1775, £500 Currency in Breeches, Gloves, Skins, &c. He left 250 dollars behind in his Trunk, besides he took away about 3 or 400 Dollars.

He says he sold 960 Dollars for £20.

Says at Norwich he gained £160 Stg. pr. an. by his business.   (60).
He says there is no person in England to prove these facts. Certificates from Govr. Tryon, Capt. Vandeput & Jones to Loyalty & receiving intelligence from him.

When he went to America he was gunner at Hythe. When he returned ten years pay was due him which Lord Townshand ordered to be paid up & he received for arrears of pay above £190 S.

About the year 1780 he had an allowance of £80 pr. an. given to him, which was reduced to £30 pr. an.

DUNCAN STEWART.

Has frequently seen Mr. Saltmarsh in America. Understood that he was a breeches maker. He has frequently seen him traveling from Norwich to New London.

JEREMIAH MILLER.

He has known Mr. Saltmarsh for 7 or 8 years. He then lived at New London & carried on the trade of Breeches Maker & carried on a Considerable business. Believes him a true Loyalist. He heard that he was taken up & confined in Norwich Gaol. Lived 7 or 8 miles from his father's house, being asked if he thinks he could make £200 by his trade he says it is a great deal. Says he was a rattling loquacious man. The time he knew him was 1775 & 1776.

Decision.
That the Claimant is a Loyalist.

(61).
Allow him.
Stock in trade £120
Cash 50

170

He is a Gunner at Hythe £18.15. pr. an.
He had from Govert. £80, now 30. pr. an.

1784,
7th Feby.

1137. Case DUNCAN STEWART, ESQ.

Claims for Loss of Office only.

In 1764 he obtained the office of Collector of Customs at New London & went to America in Consequence. His Commission produced it is dated 12th April, 1764. He was in England for a year & ½ about 1771 when the troubles broke out in 1774 & 1775. He was in the Execution of his office at N. London until 1777. He was always able to quell any disturbance which was there. He staid as long as he could in hopes that Govert. would be established. He was obliged to come away in July, 1777. The Americans never offered him an Oath but frequently an Employment in their Service.

Many respectable Certificates received to Mr. Stewart's Loyalty & good character.

The sallary of his office was £80 pr. an. the fees about £500 pr. an. The Sallary was continued until Oct., 1782. The fees gradually decreased for some time before he left America & finally ceased. He received £120 in addition to his sallary which was stopt. & Messrs. Wilmot & Coke allowed him £150 pr. an. He has seven children. He lost some.little Furniture but he does not state. No Money due him in America.

(62).

He has spent since 1777 £3000 more than he received & States for the Consideration of the Board this as a Loss occasioned by the troubles.

JEREMIAH MILLER.

He knew Mr. Stewart in New London, his Brother was Mr. Ss. Clerk. He looks at the acct of fees given in which is extracted from Mr. Stewart's Books. The Witness believes it a true & just acct. He has compared it with the original books & knows it to be an exact copy. He says the office was worth at least £500 pr. an.

Decision.

That Mr. Duncan Stewart is a Loyalist.

He lost the sallary of his office £80 pr. an., Fees & perquisites of do. £450 pr. an. He had formerly an allowance of £200 pr. an. It is now reduced to £100 pr. an.

1784,
9th Feby.

1138. Case COLONEL BILLUP.

Genr. Sterling being an Invalid is first examined. He has known him since 1776. When the Witness Commanded at Staten

Island Col. Billup Commanded the Loyal Militia. He served under him with spirit & activity in 1780 Lord Stirling attacked the Island & Col. B. lost part of his Property. A return of which he has amongst his Papers in Scotland. His Loss on this occasion was from to £6 to 900 Currency. When matters went ill Coll Billup used to say he would take £3,000 for his Property but he has heard that it was well worth £5,000 New York Currency.

(63).

COLONEL CHRISTOPHER BILLUP, the Claimant.

He was born on Staten Island. When the troubles broke out he was Representative in the Gen. Assembly of N. York & opposed all the measures of the Rebels. He prevented the Country he represented from joining them.

In 1775 the assembly refused to send delegates to Congress & he was very Instrumental in carrying that point. He tried by all means in his power to keep the people on the Island quiet until the British Troops arrived, which he affected when Gen. Howe landed in 1776.

He gave him every assistance in his power, as he was Colonel of the Militia before the Troubles & Continued so the whole War. He was in one Action & Produces an American Newspaper in which there is a paragraph much to the honor of Colonel Billup. He never received any pay.

GEN. ROBERTSON.

Knew Colonel Billup when he was a Member of the Assembly, when he did everything in his civil capacity to prevent it. When it did happen he put himself at the head of the British Troops on Staten Island & by his spirit & knowledge of the Country was very useful in driving them off. Some time after he fell into their hands when they imprisoned him & treated him cruelly. When he Governor he appointed him to act as Judge which he did with great uprightness.

(64).

He is a very good man has a large family & had good Property. He had a very good Estate on Staten Island. It suffered much by both Armies, but he cannot say the value.

Claimant called in.

He was Imprisoned 7 or 8 weeks during which time he was chained to the floor & kept on Bread & water during the War he has been prisoner about 8 months & has refused great offers from the Rebels.

Property.

He had 1,078 acres on Staten Island & produces a survey taken by himself & a friend in 1772.

There was a large House on it built by his Grandfather. The half of the Estate was Cultivated, the half Wood Land. Besides his own house there were four other houses in the hands of Tenants. In its then state he would not have taken £13,500 Currency for it & thinks it was worth that sum. Produces several title deeds. It appears to have been granted to the Govr. of the Province to his

(65).

Great Grand Father in 1687. The Estate was settled & a Recovery was suffered by his father 1744, by which means the Estate was cutt of & came to him in fee. The Recovery produced, by which it appears that this Property was left to him in fee.

He had the absolute disposal of the Estate if the troubles had not happened.

The first injury done to the Estate was by the Hessian Troops in 1776. A Schedule of the damage done is produced. It appears to have amounted in 1776 & 1777 to £1,441.16. Currency. Admits that several of the articles are charged at an advanced Price on acct. of the troubles, but he cannot say how much they are overcharged. After 1780 when he was attained he sold his lands to different people for £8,200 Currency & has received all but £200 by this means he lost £5,000 Currency.

He sold them for this sum after the Injury done to them in 1776 & 1777. This is the whole of his landed Property.

He states a loss of £1,500 expended during the War. Speaks in Currency. He produces a Schedule of his Personal Property taken from him by the Rebels amounting to £1,500 Currency, but says they are charged high being the prices during the troubles.

Certificates read from Govr. Tryon, Gen. Campbell, Colonel Simcoe, &c., &c.

GEN. SKINNER.

(66).

Knew Col. Billup. He always took a very active part. He always took an active part both in a Civil & Millitary Capacity. He shewed a great deal of spirit on many occasions. He was Colonel of Militia. He knew his Estate, believes it might contain 12 or 1,400 acres. There was a very good house upon it. Upon a supposition that it contained 1,078 acres & half of it cultivated he thinks it might be worth £1,000 currency or between 7 & 10. He would value the whole including buildings at £7 or 8 pr. acre, Colonel Billup says no part of his Estate was mortgaged. He owed no money in America, his Estate was confiscated in 1779.

PROCEEDINGS

OF THE

LOYALIST COMMISSIONERS.

EVIDENCE OF CASES EXAMINED WHILE I WAS ABSENT IN SCOTLAND REDUCING THE 80TH REGT. AND ATTENDING THE GENERAL ELECTION, 1784.

COPIED FROM MR. PARKER COKE'S BOOK, SEPTEMBER, 1784.

LONDON, 1784.

Vol. II.

BEFORE COMMISSIONER WILMOT.

Claimants.

	MSS. Folio.		MSS. Folio.
Atherton, Phineas	46	Martin, Lynn	65
Broadhead, Thomas	55	Richards, Owen	1
Chalmers, Lt.-Col. James	9	Rothery, Mrs. Mary.	60
Dare, Thomas	52	Wallace, Sir James	48
Galloway, Joseph	15	Warden, Hugh	4
McLelland, Robert	57	Watson, John	6

EVIDENCE.

1784.
9th Feby.

1139. Case OWEN RICHARDS.

He was born in Wales & went to America in 1774. He was a Custom house officer, Settled at Boston as a Tidesman. Produces the appointmt dated 8th April, 1768. His Sallary was £25 pr. an. & 1sh. 6d. when emploied. He was sent to Marblehead when the Port of Boston was shut. He was unable to do any duty after the Battle of Bunker Hill. He always did his duty like a Loyal subject & therefore he was treated more severely. He staid at Marblehead near a year & left Boston at the Evacuation.

(1).

He came to England in April, 1777 & applied to the Treasury who gave him £30 pr. an., which was Confirmed by Messrs. Wilmot & Coke & he still receives it. He has never received any sallary since he left America.

Certificates to the proper discharge of his duty from Mr. Hallowell, &c. & from Gover. Hutchinson & Chief Justice Oliver, they speak fully to Loyalty. Mr. Hallowell says in his Certificate that he had a house in Boston.

Property.

He had a house in North End Boston. He bought it of Clement Collins & produces the Conveyance dated 27th March, 1759. Consideration appears to be £158 Lawful Money. He pulled down & almost in new. The Repairs cost him £150 Stg. He values it at £250, he was offered £230 for it before the battle of Lexington by a Sergt. of 64th Regt. Believes he was a settler to the Army.

(2).

The Committee appointed to sell Estates took Possession of this House & made the people who were in it pay rent to them. He has heard this frequently & it is the only evidence of Confiscation. He values his Furniture & Plate at £30. He had three beds & 12 silver spoons. All this was left at the Evacuation. He left his wife in the house & she died soon after. He says he had another House in Middle Street, but his title is found nothing. He says he administered to it. He had lent money on it. Mr. Prince the owner died & left him executor. He left a child the effects of Mr. Prince are indebted to him in £70.

He has received £30 pr. an. from Treasury & £20 in advance.

He owes nothing in America & has nothing due him but what the Prince family owe him.

WILLIAM MURRAY, Sworn:

Has known Owen Richards since 1773. He lived at Boston at that time & was a Tide waiter. He lived at the north end & believes in his own house. When the troubles broke out he took part with the British & carried arms for the defence of the Town of Boston. The Witness was likewise a Tide waiter, that place was worth £45 pr. an.

They were both paid off at Halifax in 1776 & the Witness has never received any pay since. He conducted himself like a good subject & was so obnoxious to the Rebels that he believes he was Tarred & feathered before 1773. Speaks to the house he lived in. It was a good house. He had done some repairs to it. Being asked what repairs he had done to it & what he had laid out on it, he says has heard him say £60.

It was well furnished but cannot value it. Owen Richards being again called in, Says: he was tarred & feathered in 1770, on acct. of a seizure he had made. Says Murray was present when he paid the last bill for the repairs of his house. Swears postively that he laid out £140 Stg.

(3).

Decision.
That the Claimant was a Loyalist.
He was a Custom House Officer with a
Sallary of ....£25 pr. an.
He lost a House in Boston Value..................... 230
Furniture, &c. 20
He has due him in Boston 70
Has an allowance from the Treasury of £30 pr. an.

1140. Case HUGH WARDEN.

1784.
10th Feby.

He went to America in June, 1775, but had been in America from 1763 to 1770. He went to Virginia to recover his debts which were about £2,000 Stg. He recovered about £200. No man was more active in Conversation than he was. He was in several engagements as a Volunteer & received no pay. He was at Kemps landing & did duty at Norfolk & Great Bridge. He then went on Board a ship & remained 4 months. He went to Boston but as the Troops had left it he followed to Halifax & arrived there in April, 1776. He took goods with him on speculation. Rum, Sugar, Mollases, &c. He arrived in England in Nov. 1776 & went to N. York in 1777. He went out with a cargo of Merchandise. He had no landed Property. He Claims Property but what was lost by the fire at N. York. He believes all the People who owed him money in Virginia were responsible people. He lost Merchandise by the fire at N. York, amounting to £3,500 Stg. Says he thinks it was sett on fire by design & that the Committee who set to enquire into the cause of it thought so. He saved £2,000. He had better than £5,000 worth in his store.

(4).

JAMES PARKER, ESQ.

Knew Mr. Warden betwixt 1765 & 1770, he was then Clerk to

a Mercht. Mr. Warden always showed himself a Loyal subject. He was a Mercht. Clerk in 1770. He came out in 1775 to recover his debts. He thinks they could not be considerable.

He was at New York at the time of the fire. He knows he had a store but cannot estimate the value of it.

ROBERT GILMOUR, ESQ.

Knows Hugh Warden. He joined Ld. Dunmore as a Volunteer in the year 1775 at Norfolk. He carried Arms in Mr. Gilmour's Company. He remembers him at New York when he was burnt out. He had there many valuable articles in his store but he cannot say what amount. He then heard that he had lost £4 or 5,000, but should imagine that it could not be more than £2 or 3,000. Says he thinks the fire was accidental.

(5).

ROBERT STEEL.

He never was in America & therefore knows nothing of Mr. Warden's Loyalty or of his debts.

He can from circumstances collect that he lost £3 or 4,000 by the fire. He is a Mercht. & principally furnished Mr. Warden with goods. He shipped him off betwixt £9 & 10,000 in 1777 & 1778. He lost £2,100 by him unless he is reimbursed. He gave him a discharge which is to operate unless he gets something from this Board. He gave up everything for the Benefit of his Creditors after the fire which induced them to give him a discharge. He looks upon him to be a very honest man, or he would not have

trusted him. In Jany., 1778, he wrote the Witness to get him ensured agst. fire to the amount of £2,500 or 3,000 but he could not do it the Premium was so exorbitant.

Mr. Warden received formerly £80 pr. an. but is now reduced to 50.

Decision.

The Board are of opinion that the Claimant is an active & zealous Loyalist, that he bore Arms.

He states Debts due him to the amount of £737.0.0.

1784, 10th Feby.

1141. Case JOHN WATSON.

He went from Scotland in 1767 & settled as a Surgeon at New Castle on the Delaware.

(6).

In 1777 he took an active part with the British Govrt. He was then settled at New Castle, he remained quiet & unmolested until that time. Says he had Publicly expressed his sentiments in favour of the British Govrt. Upon which in 1777 he was insulted as a Tory. When Sir Wm. Howe Landed at the Head of Elke he was obliged to go out as Surgeon to a Provincial Regt. This he was obliged to do or go to Prison. He told a friend that he hated the Rebels & meant to make his escape to the British Army. He did & joined the Army under Sir Wm. Howe at the head of Elke 24th Augst., 1777. He remained with the British all the War.

He never received Pay from the Rebel Army nor from the British until he could not help it. He was made mate of the Hospital with an appointment of 5sh. pr. Diem.

He conducted Major Ferguson into the Enemy's Country on two Expeditions in conjunction with another Genl. He filled out a Galley & lost her by Capt. Laird, but he was paid for her by

Capt. Laird & Sir Hy. Clinton. In 1780 he was promoted to be apothecary to the Hospital & received 10sh. pr. Diem. This appointment was made at New York. He has received the 10sh. pr. Diem up to the 24th Decr. last. He does not know whether or not he is to receive any more pay or not. He has no Certificates but says he can procure them or Colonel Robinson who is a Witness can speak to his Loyalty.

Property.

He had no landed Property. His whole Property almost consisted of Drugs & Debts. He had a very large shop full of Drugs & which were all taken by the Rebels in the Winter of 1777. He values them at £290.17.6. Pen Cury or £173.10 Stg. He has charged them at the price they cost him. This includes all the Furniture of the shop. Instruments Stills, &c. (7).

All his Furniture his Wives & Children Cloathes & some Provisions, he values at £110 or £65.10 Stg. He had a new Chaise, two young horses & a Cow. The Horses cost him £55 Cury, the Chaise £40 & the Cow £5, in all Stg. £59.14.

He had a Negro & child which he lost by intrusting a person who sold them.

States debts to the Amount of £1015 Currency. They are all book debts, he had a very extensive Practice there & it was a sickly Country. Says he cleared £1,000 pr. an. by his business in 73, 74 & 1775.

Several affidavits sworn at Newport are Produced & read.

COL. THOS. ROBINSON.

He knew Mr. Watson a little before the War. Little more than that he lived at New Castle. He believes he has been a Loyal subject. He first knew him when he came to Gen. Howe's Army at the Head of Elke in 1777. He was a very active man & believes he was always ready to give every service in his power. He remembers his being made apothecary to the Hospital at New York & believes it was from his good behaviour. Does not know whether or not he was in good business before the War. He thinks a man in that Profession might make £100 pr. an. but does not think Mr. Watson did as he was not so emminent as some others. (8).

The Claimant being again Called.

He produces his Commission dated 6th Septr., 1780, signed by Sir Henry Clinton, by which he was appointed apothecary to all the Hospitals in America.

Decision.

That Claimant is a Zealous & active Loyalist, that he lost Drugs, Instruments, &c. to the value of £150.

Furniture, Cloathes, &c £50
Horses, Carriage, Cow, &c. 45
Profession .... 300 pr. an
Debts due to him 606

N.B.—This gentleman will probably receive half pay.

1784,
11th Feby.   1142. Case LT. COLL. JAMES CHALMERS.

(9).

He was born in Scotland & went to the W. Indies about 13 years of age. He went to America in 1759 or 1760 & took with him about £10,000. He soon after married Miss Jekyll by whom he got 3-4ths of the land enumerated in the Schedule. He settled 1st in Pensilvania & afterwards went to Maryland. He states some circumstances which prove that he was Possessed of his lands in fee.

At the Commencement he was offered a Regt. in the Rebel service. He did everything in his power to keep his neighbours to their allegance. He was frequently summoned to attend their Committees & armed his family to repell force by force. He then lived on his own Plantation within 4 miles of Chester. He was first molested in Summer 1776. He was insulted & much bruised by the Populace. This was in Consequence of his Loyalty. He never was imprisoned by the Rebels. He passed his time at home until 1777, when he joined the Royal Army at New York. He says he might have staid at home as he had done. But he conceived he might be of use to Sir Wm. Howe after he got to New York. He attended Sir Wm. Howe to the Chesapeak. He had before given intelligence on Paper to the British Army of the weakness of that Country. He went to Philadelphia when Sir Wm. Howe appointed him to raise a Regt. without his solicitation.

(10).

He did raise a Corps & was Lt. Col. Commandant with pay of Lt. Colonel he received 400 men. In the retreat through the Jerseys under Sir Henry Clinton he flanked the Army, & in Florida a detachment of his Regt. behaved with great spirit & suffered greatly, but he was not present. He was sent to Rhode Island but afterwards was embarked for Pensicola, but he was stopt at Jamaica. In consequence of which several of his Regt. died of the Small-Pox. He was at the taking of Charlestown & returned to New York with Sir Henry Clinton where he remained until the Provincial Regts. were disbanded. He arrived in England in October last. Has received full pay to 24th Octr., 1783. He expects half pay from that date.

All his deeds & papers are with Mrs. Chalmers in America, but he promises to send them at a future time. He is now going to Nova Scotia. He is banished & his Property Confiscated both in Maryland & Pensilvania, 1,098 acres the Plantation on which he lived 600 acres of which were cultivated. He had been at great expense in improving these Lands. He values them at £5 pr.

acre. He thinks himself justified in putting this value on these lands, because he sold worse lands for more money. This was 4 miles from Chester. He was entitled to 3-4th from his Wife & he purchased the other fourth about 16 years ago & gave £4 Currency for it. It was then destitute of wood. He says £4 Currency is about 50 sh. Strg. He says he shall prove that he was offered £600 Cury for it. The Mode of letting Land there was with Negroes & Stock.

300 acres in the forrest of Dean in the same County within six miles of the other. He says his lands have not been sold. He

had this by his Wife. She had the whole of this. They are very good Lands. 150 acres of them are cultivated. He says with all the circumstances attending them they were the best Lands in America. These he likewise values at £5 pr. acre £1,500. He was offered £2,000 Currency some years ago for them to be paid in half Joes.

A House Lott in the County Town of Chester, containing about two acres including garden, out houses, &c. These were his Wives Land. Her title was from her Grandmother. He values that £325, & says it is a very moderate valuation.

Personal Property.

15 Negroes he aprehends that 5 or 6 were seized in his absence to pay the taxes, which are heavy. The Negroes were on the home Plantation. They were sold Publickly. He values these Negroes at £35 each. Mrs. Chalmers has sent 4 or 5 into the Delaware State where they remain her Property. Says he has undervalued these Negroes because Mrs. Chalmers might derive some benefit from them. He says some of his friends purchased for Mrs. Chalmers the Negroes which were sold by the Sheriff at Public Vendue.

He Produces a letter from Mrs. Chalmers in which she says she fears the Estate will be sold next Spring & she assigns for reason that the moderate men have retired from Assembly and more violent men have taken their places.

22 Horses taken & Sold, 3 of them were worth £70, he values the whole at £200.

24 Head of Cattle seized & sold £50.

Plantation tools & Furniture lost £200.

Debts, Two Bonds one for £160 the other for £90, due by Minors.

Produces List of Debts which he owes to the Amount of £1462. He has not charged interest since 1776.

REVD. JOHN PATERSON.

Resided in Kent County. He knew Col. Chalmers. He was of his Parish for many years. Believes that he was uniformly Loyal from Principal. He knows both the Plantations which Col. Chalmers had. The 1098 was a very fine Plantation, about 600 acres Cleared. He got the Lands by his Wife, he purchased a share before he knew him.

Being asked to the value he thinks it worth from £8 to 9 pr. acre Currency. Thinks he might have sold it for that before the trouble. Two of his neighbours told him that Colonel Chalmers had refused an offer which they made him of £600 pr. an. & believes it to be true.

Knows the Plantation on the Forrest of Dean it was good land but not much improved, from 100 o 150 acres Cleared & improved. There was no buildings on it & it was not so good land as the other. He has known him offered £6 pr. acre for it in 1773, & thinks it worth that sum.

He Knows the House & Lott in Chester. He lived within sight of it. The House was tolerably good but a little out of repair. He thinks it was worth £500 Currency. Remembers him offered nearly that sum.

In 1774 Coll Chalmers returned to him in person who were titheable. He & his overseer were two of the number, the remaining 12 were Negroes. He has heard Mrs. Chalmrs say that several were sold by the Sheriff. He lived in great intimacy with Mr. Chalmers. His Negroes were not in General very valuable. The

---

Negroes were mostly brought from the W. Indies. He thinks they might be worth £45 Stg. Some of the Negroes were sent secretly into Delaware County, about 5 or 6, but they returned to the Plantation. Some of his best horses were taken by the Rebels for their Army. He cannot say what number. He says C. Chalmers had at least 20 horses before the Rebellion. He can't speak to the Cattle.

None of the furniture was taken away before he left the country, therefore cannot say what is lost. But the furniture was probably good.

RICHARD SMYTH.

(14).

He is a Native of Maryland & well acquainted with Col. Chalmers before the troubles. He stood forward among the first in favour of the British Govert.

He knows the Plantation, believes it to be from 1,200 to 2,000 acres. Thinks it worth from £4.10. to £6 pr. acre. The Property was Confiscated & is intended to be sold. He thinks there is a Description of Loyalists to whom indulgence will be shown. He does not think Coll. Chalmers is one of that description, as he was very active from the beginning.

Decision.

The Board are of opinion that Lt. Col. Chalmers is an active & Zealous Loyalist.

That he was possessed of 1,098 acres of Land which they value at £3,843.0.0
300 acres which they value at 1,083.0.0

A House & two acres in Chester 275.0.0
That he lost 22 Horses 120.0.0
24 Head of Cattle 36.0.0
Plantation Tools, Furniture, &c. 100.0.0
Col. Chalmers states debts due him 250.0.0
He owes in America £1,462.0.0
He has half pay as Lt. Colonel.

1784, 12th Feby.

1143. Case JOSEPH GALLOWAY, ESQ.

Is a native of America. In the year 1774 he was speaker of the Assembly of Pensilvania. He had been in that situation for 13 or 14 years having given up the Profession of the Law. The Congress met in Octr., 1774. Early in which year he had been selected to accept of a Delegation to Congress. So early as the Stamp Act Mr. Galloway saw a disposition to resist the Govern-

(15).

ment of Great Britain in the Americas. He wrote a Pamphlet against it which he produces to show his good disposition to the power of the Crown.

He joined in a Petition to Govert. to take this Province of Pensilvania into their own hands as they found the Proprietary Govrt. very weak, making a Compensation to the Proprietors, but after being considered here it was adjourned sine die & no answer was given. He was never of this assisted by Dr. Franklyn. He was always a friend to Monarchy. He agreed to go into a Congress appointed by the Lawful Assemblies at the solicitation of the Province of Pensilvania.

It was thought better to appoint Congress from the Genr Assemblies than to permit it to be done by Conventions which they saw would be the case. The Assembly agreed to send delegates to this Congress & he expected to have met Delegates of this Description.

The Governor of Pensilvania took no part in this. Most of the Governors objected but some suffered their assemblies to appoint. The Provinces of New Jersey, Pensilvania & some other Provinces did send Delegates, but the Majority of Delegates were sent by Conventions in the particular Provinces. He is of opinion that if the Assemblies had sent Delegates there would have been no Rebellion. The Province of Pensilvania appointed him & four others to go to Congress. He agreed on Condition that he might draw his own instructions. He has not a Copy of these instructions but are printed in a Pamphlet which makes part of his case. The Instructions were very short. They then asked to be represented in the British Parlt. He regulated his conduct entirely by his instructions to the best of his judgement. He signed the association for a non importation agreement in the first Congress. Notwithstanding that he endeavoured to prevent it when debated in Congress. He was supported by the Delegates from New York & some others. He was told by his friends out of Doors that it

(16)

would not be safe to refuse to sign it.

He proposed in Congress a Plan of Union betwixt Great Britain & her Colonies. A Copy of which is contained in the Pamphlet alluded to. Mr. Galloway afterwards laid this Plan before the House of Commons in 1779. This Plan was entered in the minutes of Congress & carried by one Vote. Congress afterwards set it aside & ordered it to be erased from the minutes. Upon this he protested in writing, but they refused to receive his Protest. A letter from Lt. Govr. Colden to Lord Dartmouth, dated 7th December, 1774, read in which he mentions this plan proposed. It is in a Pamphlet wrote by Mr. Galloway entitled a Candid Examination into the Claims of America. Upon all occasions he opposed every violent measure proposed by Congress. Frequently communicated his opinion to Dr. Franklyn & several other people out of Doors.

(17)

A leter from Dr. Franklyn produced, also one from Mr. Galloway to Dr. Franklyn, 9th Septr., 1774. He satt all the time of the first Congress and did not concur in the first Petition sent by Congress but there was no division upon it.

He wished it to be more full & disliked many things in it. But he believes he signed it, being signed by all the Delegates. This Petition contained many grievances which in his opinion did not exist. When he returned the Assembly he Communicated what was done & was again unanimously elected speaker, but he declined it thinking he could be of more use upon the floor. He was in hopes he could have made the Assembly reject the measures of Congress, & for that purpose he made several motions. He carried two of them & lost a third by a report then circulated from England that the King had been insulted & Lord North's house pulled down by the Mob. Early in 1775 he published his Pamphlet alluded to, which charges Congress with direct views to Independance. Upon his being supposed to be the Author he received a Box with a letter in it, a Policy of Insurance was opened that he was not alive in six days. In the Box were these words *hang yourself or we will do it for you.* This had no effect upon his conduct. A letter from Govr. Franklyn to Mr. Galloway, dated 12th March, 1775, produced & read. He always delivered his sentiments in Congress in favour of the supremacy of Parliat. and he wrote that part from his notes taken in Congress.

(18).

Several other letters from persons of distinction in America produced & read. An answer was made by Mr. Dickenson to Mr. Galloway's Pamphlet to which he made a reply which is subjoined to the original Pamphlet. Immediately after in April, 1775, he was obliged to leave Philadelphia & retire to his Country seat. He did not resign his seat in the Assembly, but continued until Octr., 1775, before he quitted the Assembly. Before this the Assembly chose him a 2nd time Delegate to Congress, he requested that they would erase his name & he absolutely refused to go. They then appointed another person in his room. He continued in his own house from April, 1775 to Decr., 1776.

He considered himself in great danger & was in a degree imprisoned in his own house. Two or three mobs came to his House with a view to Tarr & feather him but were diverted by his friends. The last mob was 13 Dutch men who getting Drunk quarreled whether they should Tar & Feather or hang him. The Innkeeper gave him notice of it. This Mob was hired by Mr. Adams.

(19).

Having advice of this Plot he quitted his house & did not sleep at home. He could not join the British before Sir Wm. Howe came near to Philadelphia in 1776. He joined the Army at Brunswick. He came in with 5 or 6 friends, all People of Property. He gave all the information he could to Gen. Vaughan. He continued with the Army while they remained in the Jerseys. Afterwards he remained in New York until he went with the Gen. to the Chesapeak in June, 1777. He was not in any Military Capacity when he went to Pensilvania. He was emploied in getting horses for the Army & in getting Charts of the roads. He sent out above 80 spies. He informed them of 1,500 horses, but his plan was imperfectly executed & they got only between 3 & 400 horses.

He accompanied Lord Cornwallis to Philadelphia & was afterwards of great use in erecting the Batteries agst. Mud Fort & finished the business in six days. During his whole residence at Philadelphia he was confidentially emploied in procuring intelligence of the movements of the enemy. All which he communicated to the general or his aid de camps. From his knowledge of the Country he made whilst at Philadelphia a Gen. Chart of all the roads. He was likewise emploied in numbering the Inhabitants & distinguishing the Loyal from the disaffected. He was likewise desired to fix the price of forage & wood by which he saved a great deal of money to the Public. He was about this time apptd. Superintendant of Police. He produces his Commission. It is dated in Decemr., 1777. He was likewise Superintendant of the Port & Prohibited Articles. This concludes all Civil Services. (20).

A Letter from Sir Wm. Howe to Mr. Galloway produced, dated 18th May, 1778, speaks of him in the highest possible terms.

A Commission dated 1st July, 1777, from Sir Wm. Howe giving him Rank of Colonel. When he got to Philadelphia he offered to raise a Regt. of Horse on which the Gen. sent him a Warrant to raise a Troop. He did it accordingly. He afterwards raised two companies of Refugees. These were Farmers' Sons, &c., & served without pay. They did very essential service & took many

Prisoners. He promoted an Association of the Loyalists which amounted to 13,000 men. Col. Rankin, who was one of them proposed to Sir Wm. Howe through Mr. Galloway to bring in the whole Congress. The association were then about 600 & Congress was sitting at York Town under a Guard of Invalids, perhaps 30 or 40. These Associates were to seize them in the night & carry them on board ship. He says he thinks the Plan was practicable because Washington's Army were at a great distance & there was no Militia in the Country they were to pass through. No answer was given to it. He did not mention this plan to him but to his aid de Camp. He had once before made such a proposal to him & received no answer. The offer was to bring in the Govr. & Magistrates of New Jersey Prisoners. He says he could have done it with great ease. Although it was more difficult than to bring in the Congress. He never received any pay for his Military services, for his Intelligence or Services. *Mr. Galloway desires that this may be taken out of the evidence, as it may contain a charge against the commander-in-chief.*

In consequence of these services the State of Pensilvania passed a Law in 1778 attaining his person & Confiscating his Estate. He came to England from New York in Decr., 1778 from which time he has received an allowance £500 pr. an. from the Treasury. Before he left America he opened a Chanel for intelligence which he laid before his Majesty's Ministers that he never asked, wished or received any reward. (21).

Mr. Galloway again Examined:

He refers to a Printed Copy of the Procedings of Congress held at Philadelphia 5th Septr. 1774, & a Printed Copy of a Book containing Mr. Galloway's instructions when appointed by *13th Feby.*

the Assembly to attend Congress, also a Letter from the Associated Loyalists to Walter Ellis, Esq. This he produces to show that he had been very instrumental in promoting this Association, likewise a book Containg many original & important Letters received by Mr. Galloway & Communicated from time to time by him to his Majestys Ministers. He has two or three more Volumes of these.

(22). Property:

The first Lot Contained in his Memorial is by Conveyance dated 9th June, 1870, from Israel Pemberton £2700 Pen. Curry., subject to a quit rent of 44 Dollars.

This Lot Contains two or three pieces of ground. The first title applies only to 39 feet, the remainder of the same land he bought at the same time of a Mr. Meredith for £600 Curcy. This includes the whole, of which he values at £8000.

Produces the deed from Israel Pemberton but has lost the other deed from Mr. Pemberton. He fancys it was lost in the hurry of putting some Papers into a Cart when Mr. Galloway left his Country house. He supplyes this defect by an Act of the State which recognises this to be the Property of Mr. Galloway

& stating him to have been seized of this Lott & Converting it into the residence of the Governor. When Mr. Galloway bought the 1st Lott from Mr. Pemberton there was an Excellent House upon it to which he added Stables, &c., it was a modern house & lately built. Mr. Gal. lived in this House himself, it had never been Lett. Mr. Pem's house was next & had been Lett for £500 pr. an.

There is amongst Mr. Galloway's Papers a valuation of this & the other Lott at £8000 by these persons of Credit. He produces a letter from his Agent refusing to assent to the valuation as too low. It was made by three Quakers on their Assertion for the purpose of laying it before the Board. He says he can bring Evidence of the Character of the Parties who valued it. He thinks it was Worth in that money in 1774. Admits that Property (23). sells higher in Philadelphia since the Event of the War. He thinks in the year 1774 he might have taken some thing less than £5000 for it. Which he thinks its value.

Estate Containing 29 & ½ acres. Rich Meadow. It appears by an article twixt Mr. Galloway & 7 others that he is Entitled to 29 acres & ½, the division was made by a deed of Partition upon record in Philadelphia. Produces a Lease by which it appears that he let these lands for £3 pr. acre, the Lease is dated in 1769, the agreement in 1752. Which recites that he purchased two fourteenth parts, the 1st was £3, the 2nd £100, he purchased another 7th part, the Consideration of which was £106. At the time Mr. Galloway bought this it was called Crippled land & was overflown with Water. It required a very great expense to reclaim it. When he bought one 7th for £3 the title was disputed, they prevailed & he then gave for another 7th £106. He laid

74a AR.

out £4 an acre in improving it. He could cut from 3 to 4 Tons of hay per acre. Each Ton was worth at least £3. There is a valuation of this Land by two persons of Character. They value it at £50 Currency pr. acre. This valuation is amongst Mr. Galloway's papers. Govr. Roberdeau who is a man of good Character had lands adjoining & will prove the value.

Boon Island Estate. The title is by deed dated in 1764, Whereby one person Conveys to Mr. Galloway & another Gent. this land at £25 pr. acre. Jas. Colthurst & Mr. Galloway after divided by deed of Partition Mr. G's share after purchas'ng part of Mr. Colthurst amounts to 29 acres, 3 Ro., 3y, this has likewise been valued by the persons who valued the former. Lot at £45 pr. acre. £40 pr. acre. (24).

Estate within nine miles of Philadelphia Containing 208 acres, 100 Perches, fine Meadow Land. Title is to 18 acres by purchase & the recital of the other 186 acres as being in Possession & they were afterwards divided by Writ of Partition, the Deed recites that.

In the year 1761, Mr. Galloway had before purchased the 186 acres but does not recite the Consideration money, that for the 18 acres seems to have been £300. This Estate was let for 40 sh. pr. acre. This likewise Crippled Land when he bought it. The 186 acres gave £5 pr. acre when he had improved the Estate by stopping the Water. He bought the remaining 18 acres at Vendue for £307.18. He would not have taken £35 pr. acre for it in 1774, it is valued at that.

Hog Island Estate is within nine miles of Philadelphia. Title Warrant dated 1766 to survey 3350 acres, it is to John Reed & likewise a Conveyance to same year of 333 acres to Mr. Galloway, the purchase was £120, he likewise gave £150 to three persons who had an Equable right. It let for £1.10 sh. pr. acre, he let it on an improving lease, they paid £100 the first year, £200 pr. an. afterwards. He thinks his Tenants laid out £2000 upon it. The same persons value this at £27 pr. acre. In 1774 the Lesee offered him £10,000 for it, but he then asked twixt 11 & 12,000. The present valuers have valued it at £8991. Upon casting up at £27 per acre it is £9157.10 sh. (25).

SchuyKill Estate. Within 4 miles of Philadelphia. Title Conveyance dated in 1756, Whereby Joseph Situty Conveys to Mr. Galloway 29 acres, the Consideration for 9 acres is £80 Currency. He gave him the 20 acres for having been of use to him in recovering the Land at Law. The improvements Cost Mr. Galloway about £400. This is valued by Owen Jones & the other valuers at £45 pr. acre. Mr. Galloway built a good house on this tract.

One 24th Part of Durham Iron Works purchased 1st Jany., 1763. Explained to be a gift from his Wife's Father in Law & therefore no Consideration is expressed. The whole tract has yielded £1200 pr. an. Mr. Galloway's part was valued in 1773 at £786.7.

Tract of Land bought of James Hamilton in 1774, 183 acres 7 perches. Consideration money Expressed in the Deed viz., £325.10.6. He bona fide paid the money.

(26).
One 10th part of undivided tract with Peter Gasgil, there was an original agreement twixt him & Mr. Gasgil in 1772. Whereby Mr. Gasgil Emploied Mr. Galloway to recover 10 pr. cent of the lands recovered which Mr. Galloway Construes into ten acres out of the 100. Mr. Gaskel conveyd this tenth part at Bath last year. The Possession was recovered in 1773 or 1774. The reason that Mr. Gaskel did not Execute the Conveyance sooner—Mr. Galloway is desired to come tomorrow & to bring the original agreement.

MR. GALLOWAY again Examined:

14th Feby.
Gives his reasons for claiming this Land from Mr. Gaskel. He apprehended by the treaty of Peace that Mr. Gaskel is made an alien from America & has no right to hold lands in Pensilvania. Should therefore Mr. Gaskel purpose to sell the lands & they should refuse to permit him upon the Idea that he is to be Considered as an Alien, then this would be a loss to Mr. Galloway & is a Loss in Consequence of the Rebellion. It would be the same thing if the State was to take his Property into their own hands. He gives an Answer to one objection made yesterday that it was too large a Compensation as a fee to Mr. Galloway for assisting him to recover his Property. He says that it is very Common & that Lord Shelborne gave to Mr. Hurst one third for locating 10,000 acres. Says he has given a third himself to persons for working lands—being asked if he ever had a quantity of land given to him for Professional services, he says several times. He once before had 20 acres given to him.

(27).
He says likewise that a Mr. Pennington refused the same offer before it was made to Mr. Galloway. He produces a letter dated the 1st May, 1772, from Mr. Gaskel to him, to show at that time he gave full powers to Mr. Galloway to act in this business & he then agreed & promised to give Mr. Galloway for his trouble *five per Cent upon all Monies received & upon the value of all lands received.* Mr. Gaskel's affairs were very voluminous & very Complicated. He accordingly appointed Agents to act under him in America & paid those Agents. He remitted money several

times to Mr. Gaskel & always deducted his own ten per Cent. Says he did not receive the ten per Cent as Council, but as Agent, being asked whether he Considers the words ten pr. Cent upon the Value of these lands to mean a tenth part of these lands, says that if Mr. Gaskel did not choose to sell the lands he looked upon himself as entitled to a tenth part of the Lands. But if he had sold the Lands then he should have expected a tenth part of the money. The whole of Mr. Gaskel's lands 204 feet in breadth & about a mile in length. It lay in the Town of Philadelphia, but this land was not built upon, being in dispute, although it was built round. It adjoined to the most valuable part of the Town. He says it was valued in 1775 at £75,000. A fourth part belonged to Mr. Hurst. Mr. Galloway claims a tenth of the residue which is £5625 Crcy. (28).

One tenth of 22,609 acres of land in the Province of Pensilvania in Company with Mr. Gaskel Exactly in the same Circumstances. Mr. Galloway's share is 2240 acres, these lay a Considerable distance from Philadelphia. Believes there was no Cultivation on them. Mr. Gaskel's title was by Warrant & survey from the Proprietors about 80 years from this time, he values these lands at 10 sh. pr. acre & would not have taken that sum for them. He thinks they could have sold for that sum. In 1773 that price was given for these rights. He produced a Deed to prove it.

One Moiety of 32 acres in Company wth Robt. Levan near the Delaware Containing 6871 acres. The Title is by Warrant & survey. These lands are taken up in the new mode of granting lands in Pensilvania, formerly there used to be a Warrant but now there is none. The return of the survey at this time gives a Complete title. Many of the Deeds are in the Custody of Mr. Levar, the Survey & location Cost him to his share about £300 Currency. He produces a receipt the surveyor to one part. They were taken up between 1765 & 1769. He produces a Certificate from a Notary Public dated 18th Octr., 1783, by which it appears that upon application to get papers out of the Public Offices, the present Governors of America have answered in the negative. He valued this when he took out the lands at 20 sh., he now values it at 15 sh. (29).

A Tract of 81 acres near the Susquehanah, Charged at the price which Mr. Galloway gave for it, which is £17.11.8d: He produces no papers to show title, but produces a Receipt by which it appears that he paid so much money.

A Tract of 280 acres on the Susquehana. He had two fifteenths & pd. for his share £36.0.5. He produces a Warrant & survey dated 28th Novr., 1768, but there is no receipt for the money paid.

A Tract of Land in Virginia, called Indiana. Computed at more than 300,000 acres. He is entitled to this under a deed from George Croghan, Esq., to one Moiety of 3 tenths of one 19th part, or 2300 acres, Valued at £5 pr. acre. He produces a Paper to show that he purchased this in 1768. His share Cost him £320. There were a great many people settled upon it. He laid out no money upon it, yet in 1774 he says it was worth £5 pr. acre, which makes £5750. He admits that he gave the market price in 1768 for it. He can give no reason for this increase of value but mentions an Instance of the Proprietors of Pensilvania buying from the Indians ten millions of acres for 10,000 Dollars & selling them out again for £620,000.

A Tract of 1157 acres on Lake Osewago, the title to this land is an agreement betwixt Mr. Galloway & Mr. Groghan. A Conveyance is produced from Mr .Groghan in which there appears no Consideration, it is dated 30th May, 1770. It was given by Mr. Groghan to Mr. Galloway as a Compensation for business (30).

done. He cannot put any value on it because he does not know the lands, but he asked Genr. De Lancey as to the value & he said that Lands in that situation were worth 10 sh. pr. acre.

This finishes the Land to which Mr. Galloway is entitled in fee.

His Life Estate is Mrs. Galloway's real property. Mrs. Galloway had it by the Will of her Father. He produces papers of survey & Partition, but there are no Deeds.

He is entitled to this Estate as Tenant by Curtesy.

It lay within 17 miles of Philadelphia, Containing 1753 acres regularly settled with Inhabitants & a Country Seat upon it —on which he lived—there were six well improved farms. His Wive's father died in 1770 & left his whole Estate to Mrs. Galloway & her Sister in fee as Tenants in Common. Produces a deed of Partition to show his Wive's share settled by a Jury. She had the half of 1753 acres. Mr. Galloway has not the Will with him but thinks he can produce it. She had another Estate on Durham & some lands on the Delaware, but as the Lands on the Delaware produced nothing he charges no Loss for rent. Mr. Galloway's further Examination postponed to Monday to Examine Mr. Lawrence who attends as a Witness.

(31).

JOHN LAWRENCE, ESQ.:

He was Second Judge of the Supreme Court at Philadelphia. Knew Mr. Galloway's house perfectly well. He remembers the building of it. It was a very Expensive house. He does not know what Mr. Galloway gave for it. Confirms the acct. of Mr. Morris giving £3500 for the adoining Lott to Mr. Penn, without a house on it. Mr. Morris' Lott was about the same size with Mr. Galloway's. He values Mr. Galloway's two Lotts with the House upon it at £6000 Currency in 1774, but thinks it would now sell for £8 or 9000.

He Knew Mr. Galloway's Estate at Schuy Kill, has land near it, only 18 acres, but has been offered £150 pr. an. for it, it is within 4 miles of Philadelphia.

Mr. Lawrence's land there is improved. Mr. Galloway's is not, he thinks it is worth £40 pr. acre & that it would have sold for that in 1774.

Being asked if he knows Owen Jones, Thos. Clifford & Henry Dunken who valued Mr. Galloway's Estate, says he does, that they were Quakers, men of unblemished Character & believes they understood the subject very well. They are men of very high character. He does not know whether they have valued at the present value or that of 1774, but in order to guess he desires to know what they value the house in Town at, being told £8000, he says they must have taken it at the present value & therefore supposes that they have valued the whole in the same manner. He knows the other two Valuers, William Jenkins & Abraham Lindsay & says he Knows them to be men of Character. There are two other persons who valued Mr. Galloway's life Estate,

(32).

Abel James & John De Normandy, says he Knows them to be men of very good character. Abel James is one of the 1st Merchts. in Phild., John De Normandy is a Phisician.

The Claimant again called in & Sworn:

Produces several papers to show his right to Mrs. Galloway's Estate for Life. Amongst others he produces the Will of Mr. Growden, Father in Law of to Mrs. Galloway, by which he leaves all his Estate Equally between Mrs. Galloway & her Sister. A Partition appears likewise to have been made betwixt the two Sisters. Mr. Galloway gives in a paper Contaning his title to the above Estate & likewise a valuation to it to which he refers & says it is very mod rate acct. of the value.

16th Feby.

The D.rham Tract he says Consists of 1038 acres, it is well Cultivated. There was a valuation of this Estate made in 1773 which Estimates the remaining Estate—two parts being sold of —at £5938.7.7. The annual value is likewise valued at £460 Currency. This value was put on it by very intelligent & respectable persons, one of which John De Montford valued Mr. Galloway's Estate. The Valuation produced in order to prove that it is low. He swears that he sold part of this Estate in 1774 for £231, which was valued in 1773 at £174.

(33).

Her Estate of Trivose Belmont King's Place & Richleau together 1723 acres. His Country House was on one of these, built by his Father in Law. Trevose being in his own occupation 444 acres. The other farms Lett for £183 & the rent was to have encreased.

The Valuers in 1773 have put no value on these, but he values it at £8615, which is £5 pr. acre. He values the yearly income from these lands, including which he held in his own possession at £425 pr. An.

The Delaware Estate Consists of 160 acres of Wood. There was a Farm house on it. A small part only Cleared, 10 or 15 acres. He charges no annual rent for this Estate, but he values it at £1500 Str.

Richland Estate, of which Mrs. Galloway's share was 508 acres. There was no part of this Cleared & it yielded him a profit, for which reason the Valuers had not put a value on it. He thinks it would have sold for £1219.4.

(34).

He claims a rent for these Lands from the time he was Compelled to take refuge within the British Lines. He gives as a reason that many persons have been in Possession of their Estates until 1781, or later, when he lost his in 1776—delivers a paper Containing the reasons likewise a paper Containing the particulars of his Claim amounting to £9073.17. Currency, which is £1600 pr. acre from the 1st Jany., 1776, to the 1st Jany., 1784. He then gives Credit for some rents he recovered in Philadelphia. He then lived in his own House.

He likewise Claims £6880 for the rents due on Mr. Galloway's Estate. The particulars are left Calculated the same time to the same time.

He claims Debts, Mortgages, &c., £7839.12. Crcy., refers to a Schedule which is left. In this he Includes Principal &

Interest. Several Debts are due him from Loyalists, but they are not included in this Demand. He Claims for Property lost or sold in Philadelphia.

When the King's Troops quitted the Province the same valuers valued this part of the Personal property they Estimate it at

£361.14. It sold for this in 1778. It Consisted of a Chariot, Household furniture, &c.

Property left at his Country seat & destroyed by a Mob which he values at £734.18. He brought a Considerable part of his furniture into Philadelphia, but was forced to leave a great deal, he has no Estimate for that—he wrote to his Agent to value it—but he writes that it was impossible & that Mr. Galloway must do it as well as he can from recollection. He has done it accordingly & produces a Schedule of the property Lost. He is sure that he lost all the Articles Contained in that Schedule & more & says he has put a very moderate value on them.

(35). He had no mortgage on his Estate or Incumbrance of any kind. His Life Estates were subject to an annuity of £100 pr. an., which he thinks he has given Credit for in his papers.

An Act of the State of Pensilvania Produced by which his name is attainted & his Property Confiscated.

The only Incumbrance on his Property was the ground rent pd. for his House & the Quit rent pd. for his lands to the Proprietors. He submits whether he should not charge Professional income which he declined in 1769 & was £2000 pr. an. He would have practised after the Loss of Estate.

Speaker of Assembly was worth £200 pr. an.

Feby. 17th. Abel Evans lived in Pensilvania for ten years prior to the troubles. He has been on the Borders of the Indiana Tract—is desired to wait until Gen. Vaughan is Examined.

GEN. VAUGHAN:

In Decemr., 1776, de was detached with Ld. Cornwallis in pursuit of Gen. Washington towards Brunswick. When they came to Brunswick the Rebels had left the place & were on their March to Philadelphia. After he had been there a short time he was told that two Gentlemen were come to surrender themselves. Mr. Galloway was one of them. He said he was well affected to Govrt. & wished to take that opportunity of surrendering himself. Mr. Galloway stayed with him all night & then went to Ld. Cornwallis. He Communicated at that time some intelligence, but not very much material information. He thought from his discourse that he was a well wisher to Govnt. He was a good deal with the general afterwards & he found him a sensible, Zealous, steady man.

(36).

He believes he was a very useful man afterwards in Philadelphia. He never had any reason to suspect his Loyalty during the whole time that he was under his Eye.

ABEL EVANS again called in:
Thinks he must have been on a part of the Indiana tract, so much of it as he saw was very valuable & a good deal of it settled.

His Father bought a Tract in this Country of 500 acres, for which he gave £350 Currency. He Knew some part of Mr. Galloway's Estate. He thinks the Indiana Tract not so valuable as what his Father bought, should ımagine it was worth £25 Curry. pr. 100 acres.

He knows the Trevose tract belonging to Mrs. Galloway. He does not Know the number of acres, it was in high Cultivation. There was a very good Stone House on it & a great many more buildings, thinks it all together worth £8 pr. acre. He thinks the Four Plantations which went under the name of the Trevose Farm were Extensive & Contained as many acres as are stated.

(37).

He Knew the Delaware Estate, 160 acres, it was chiefly Wood, a little of it was Cleared. He thinks that this Estate in 1774 was worth £15 pr. acre. The Woodland in that Situation is the most Valuable, it was close to the River & within 15 miles of Philadelphia. He has Known Woodland to sell for more than £15 pr. acre before the troubles. Being asked how much the Trevose Farm including the four Plantations would produce annually he says twixt 3 & 4 per Cent upon the Value.

GEN. ROBERDEAU:
He was particularly acquainted with the Sessuken Estate. He had land adjoining, but Mr. Galloway's was better than his, it was Equal in quantity, he believes about 29 acres.

It was Extremely valuable from its situation & he has Known Three Tons of hay produced from the first mowing. He thinks Mr. Galloway's of the produce moderate—being asked as to the value—he says he thinks it was worth £50 pr. acre. He has let his for £3 pr. acre & Interest being at 6 pr. Cent he thinks it Worth £50 pr. acre.

Mr. Galloway's land is better than his. He is not so well acquainted with Boon's Island, but believes it was similar. He has never been on the Trenchum Estate but has been on the adjoining lands, they were as good in quality but were further—9 miles—from Philadelphia. He does not Know the Hog Island Estate, but has sailed round it, but believes it to be the same sort of land. He Knew his House in Market Street, it was appropriated for the Governor.

(38).

It is an Elegant House, but cannot speak to the Value. He Knows all the Valuers, they are men of Character. He Knows the hand writing of two of them. They are men very Competent to put value ın Estates & are all men of Credit & reputation.

Gen. Gage (Lieut.), Govr. of Massachusetts Bay in 1774. He never saw Mr. Galloway but once in his life, when he wanted to Enforce a Meetinᵍ Act in Philadelphia. Mr. G. was of the opposite part, but told the Genr. that he would do all in his power to have the troops quartered. Knows nothing of Mr. Galloway since the troubles. Gen. Gage says he did not promote sending Delegates to Congress but did all he could to prevent it. Considering it a leading step to Rebellion.

LORD CORNWALLIS:

He recollects perfectly Mr. Galloway joining the Army. Cannot immediately recollect the particular intelligence he gave. He appeared particularly Zealous & attached to the British Govnt. He was always esteemed as well affected & does not believe that he was suspected by any person for want of sincerity on acct. of his Connection with Congress. When Lord Cornwallis took Possession of Philadelphia he went with him to assist, &c. He attended him at all times & gave Every assistance in his power and appeared to be a very Zealous Loyalist. He never had the smallest Suspicion of him.

Mr. Galloway gave very material intelligence & he thinks was of great use in taking Mud Island. He rendered, in his Lordship's opinion, very important service to the cause of Great Britain. Lord Cornwallis thinks Mr. Galloway took part with Great Britain from principal & believes him to be a true & Zealous Loyalist.

GOVERNOR FRANKLYN:

He came over in 1757 With his Father to request the King

to take the Govnt. of Pensilvania into his Hands. Mr. Galloway, as Speaker of the Assembly, had been very active in promoting that Measure.

Dr. Franklyn relied upon Mr. Galloway to preserve the same disposition in the Assembly. Remembers Mr. Galloway publishing a paper at this time Called Americans in support of the British Govert. which made him very obnoxious. He went by the Nick name of Americans by way of reproach & they used to abuse him as a Ministerial hireling. He has Known Mr. Galloway since he was a boy & has Every proof that since the Commencement of the troubles Mr. Galloway was a Loyalist. He has frequently Corresponded & Conversed with him on the subject. He always found him a Staunch friend of Govnt. & that he uniformly endeavoured to give more Weight to the Crown in America, thinking that it would be for the benefit of the people. Mr. Galloway told him before he went into Congress unless they would allow him to draw his own instructions. He believes they did so & understood the purport of these instructions was to form a union twixt the two Countries. He is sure Mr. Galloway would not have accepted the Delegation upon no terms but a union twixt the ―――――. He Knows that Mr. G. did promote a Plan of Union in Congress & sent it over to Dr. Franklyn, who sent it to Lord Dartmouth. That Plan was formed on a Constitution dependance on Great Britain. This plan was frustrated in Congress & Mr.

G. became unpopular from having proposed it. Gover. Franklyn says he approved of Mr. Galloway going into Congress, that he never opposed his Assembly sending Delegates—because he was Convinced a Congress would be held & he thought it an object that it should Consist of respectable men. Mr. Galloway being abused for his Conduct published a Pamphlet in his own defence which has been before stated, it was called a Candid Examination, &s. He thinks he ran great hazard in Publishing his sentiments at such a time. He was soon afterwards obliged to leave his Country House & fly to the British Arms. Dr. Franklyn & Mr. Galloway had an interview a short time before this when Dr. F. pressed him to go again into Congress. Mr. Galloway sayed that he had a great opinion of Dr. Franklyn, but that he did not think his person safe & that he did not approve of the Conduct of Congress. Dr. Franklyn would have given security for his personal safety, but Mr. Galloway would not agree. Dr. Franklyn accused his son of having poisoned Mr. Galloway's sentiments. Upon the Whole he believes Mr. Galloway's Conduct to have been uniformly Loyal & he has given the most Unequivocal proofs of it. He is not acquainted with any services he did after he joined the British Troops because he was then a Prisoner. He believes that he joined the King's troops from principal, for although Mr. Galloway might be personally afraid of danger, yet he Knows that any time he might have made his Peace with the Rebels.

(41).

He is not sufficiently acquainted with Mr. Galloway's Estate to speak to the value of it, but he Knows he had very Considerable Property. Gover. Franklyn says that his Loyalty & attachment to this Country are so undoubted that when Congress was sitting Mr. Galloway frequently Communicated secret intelligence to him which the Govr. sent at different times to the Ministers here. The Americans suspected this & it was frequently made matter of accusation agst. him. Declaration of Independence was made July, 1776.

(42).

Col. Montressor called by the Board.

He was aid de Camp to Sir Wm. Howe in 1776 & afterwards Chief Engineer. He remembers Mr. Galloway joining the Army & believes he did Communicate intelligence thro' him to the Commander in Chief, but cannot recollect what it was. Mr. Galloway accompanied the Army to Philadelphia & went in Col. Montressors Vessel, he frequently Communicated intelligence thro' the Witness to the Commander in Chief. It was always meant to be important & frequently was so, he was active in procuring it. Remembers his making a proposal to Drain the Waters of the Delaware & he suggested a person who was to Execute it. Mr. Galloway's assistance was very material at the seige of Mud Fort

& admits that although it would have been done without him, it would not have been done so soon. Upon the Whole he had a reason to think Mr. Galloway a Zealous Loyalist & always Endeavoured to promote the success of the British Arms & meant to render service to Government, but the Witness cannot say whether he did service or not, as the Commander in Chief must be the best judge of that.

JAMES MOODY:

(43).
His Father bought a Tract in this Country of 500 acres, for which Mr. Levans. He Knew it because he went there with an intention of taking some of it for himself, but he found it was taken by one Mr. Levans, it was perfectly uncultivated, but the soil was very good, particularly the Meadow, in the State it was then in it was worth 12 or 15 sh. pr. acre Curry. He cannot speak to any other part of Mr. Galloway's lands.

SIR WILLIAM HOWE:

Mr. Galloway joined the Army in 1776. He Communicated intelligence at different times, but it was not very material. He Considered him at that time as attached to the British Governmt. He Conducted himself as a Loyalist from the time he came in, & upon Several occasions was of material service. He was Emploied in a Confidential situation & he found him Zealous in the Cause of Govnt. He cannot say upon his Oath that he ever Communicated any material intelligence. He was Emploied for some time by Sir Wm. Howe in getting intelligence by Spies, but Sir Wm. soon altering his opinion of him he removed him from that situation. He remembers his Brother Consulting him as to the Navigation of the Delaware. He gave some information respecting it which Ld. Howe did not follow. He went with Lord Howe & him on the Expedition agst. Philadelphia at their request.

He remembers his making a proposition to bring the Governor & all the Magistrates of New Jersey to Philadelphia—Prisoners. He should have been very glad to have adopted it had it been practicable, but he thought it was not. He does not recollect his giving material intelligence the night before the Battle

(44).
of Brandy wine. Mr. G. had said that this intelligence was so material that the Battle was undertaken in Consequence of it. Sir Wm. says he does not recollect it, & is sure that he did not act upon it, for the Battle was determined long before that night to attack them the next Morning. He was appointed Superintendent of the Police which he Executed very well & Sir Wm. gave him his thanks in Writing. All his Emoluments at Philadelphia were about £600 pr. an. Strg. He never pd. him any bill or incidental Charges for secret services. Says he was not anxious for rewards.

He made proposals to Sir Wm. Howe in 1778 to raise a Troop of Horse from the County of Bucks which he consented to, thinking it would be some Emploiment to him, but upon Exam-

ining into the Troop it was found to Consist Chiefly of Deserters. He has no doubt about his Loyalty or his desire to promote the King's service as far as he can judge from his actions, but he does not believe that his heart was materially Concerned in it.

Decision JOSEPH GALLOWAY:

The Board find that Mr. Galloway was a Member of the first Congress, but they are of opinion that during that time he Endeavoured to promote the Constitutional dependence of the Colonies in Great Britain. That he has since Conducted himself as a Zealous Loyalist & rendered services to the British Govnt.

They find him possessed of a Lott & a House in Philadelphia, now the Residence of the Governor of Pensilvania, which the Board value at £3900 (45).

They find him Possessed of Specken Estate which they value at	£ 750
Boon's Island Estate which they value at	650
Tenecam Estate which they value at	3500
Hog Island Estate they value at	3600
Schuylkill Estate they value at	900
The Board found him likewise possessed of a 24th Share in the Durham Iron Works, which they value at	300

183 acres purchased in 1774 of James Hamilton, the Board find him possessed of this & value it at 195.11.

One 10th of an undivided tract with Mr. Gaskel disallowed.

Moiety of a Warrant & Survey with Robt. Levens, the Board values at	£300.00.0
81 acres near the Susquahana valued at	10.12.9
2-15ths of 280 acres on the Susquehana	21.12.3
23000 acres in the Tract Called Indiana	400.00.0
1157 acres on Lake Oswego rejected.	

(46).

Mr. Galloway is entitled to the life rent of his Wife's Estate as follows:

The Durham Tract, Value £3000, Annual Value	£200.0.0
The Estate of Trevose, Value £4000, Annual value	240.0.0
The Delaware Estate, total Value	1000.0.0
Richland Estate, total Value	750.0.0

Claims the passed rents of these lands—disallowed.

Furniture, &c., left when the King's troops quitted the Province	£217.0.0
Property left at his Country House	400.0.0

Loss of his Profession which he Confesses he had quitted—Rejected.

Mr. Galloway has an allowance from the Treasury of £500 pr. An.

1144. Case PHINEAS ATHERTON.

1784.
February 20.

He was in America when the troubles broke out. He lived in London. He went to Montreal in 1775 & joined Sir John Johnston. He had been in America great part of the last War & had served under Lord Amherst. Soon after he went to Montreal he got a Lieutenancy & served until the Army under Gen. Burgoyne surrendered at Saratoga. He had Leut's. pay & when Prisoner he went to look after his own Estate & lived at Cambridge. He lived in England from 1770 to 1775. Says he lost his Estate to a friend who pd. no rent, but it turns out to be his Mother's Estate, who is alive & living in the house. He says that was the Case in 1778.

(47). His title is by Deed from his Father, made as he thinks in 1758, his Father died in 1760. He built a House on it at the time his Father gave it to him. His Mother has lived upon it from 1760 to 1778 & never paid him a farthing of rent. He Swears that it is his property, but Cannot say whether it is Confiscated or sold.

The Property Consisted of 100 acres, 20 of which were Cultivated, he built a house on it, but cannot say what it Cost him. When at Lancaster the Rebels told him he should not live upon it because he had taken Arms agst. them. He has applied lately to Whitehall for support, but obtained nothing.

Colonel Kingston Knows him & Confirms him in saying that he was Prevost Martial in the Northern Army with an appointmt. of 5 sh. pr. Diem & he behaved very well.

COLONEL WILLARD:

He was Colonel of a Provincial Corps last War & lived in the Town of Lancaster. He Knew Phineas Atherton from a Boy, he lived six years with him, this Property was his Father's & he has heard that his father gave it to him by Deed before his death to pay his debts. He believes that his Father lived upon it by permission from his Son & that the Son built the House, it might Cost £20 Stg. He Knows the land, he has been frequently upon it, he thinks about 30 acres were Cultivated, he values the Land & house at £100 St. He mentions 5 acres more which he thinks were Worth £5 pr. acre. Phineas Atherton being asked to these 5 acres—he says they were his & given to him by his father.

(48). Decision:

The Board are of opinion that Phineas Atherton was Possessed of 105 acres of Land which they value at £110.0.0.

1784.
February 21.   1145. Case SIR JAMES WALLACE.

He was on Board several of his Majesty's Ships in different Stations in America from 1762 to the Conclusion of the last War & during the troubles until the Evacuation of Philadelphia. He married in Georgia in the year 1778 or 1779, by Whom he got the Plantation which he now claims. His Conduct & Loyalty are so well Known tnat no acct. of them is necessary.

The Plantation he got with his Wife was called the Ogerchu Plantation. He never was upon it since it belonged to him, it was well Cultivated & Consisted of 1900 acres. Sir James Wright managed it for him.

Sir James Wallace likewise Claims for 5000 acres in different Tracts obtained by Grants about the year 1763 from Govnt. for his services in America, these matters were managed for him by Governor Graham & the Govr. attends to speak to his Case, he does not Know the names of these lands but refers to Govr. Graham for particulars. He owed no money in Georgia.

SIR JAMES WRIGHT:

The Plantation which Sir James gave with his daughter was the Orange Grove. There was a settlement made upon the marriage in this manner to Sir James Wallace & his Wife for life, for their joint lives & to the survivor, then to the Issue of the marriage, if no Issue to the survivor in fee. There are yet no children. (49).

This settlement was made in 1779. The Plantation was more than 500 acres, 200 of which was River Swamp, the remainder was Provision & pasture land. It was valued by Mr. Hall & Mr. Jamieson at £1900. The 200 acres Swamp were worth £7 or 8 pr. acre. Sir James thinks the Provision Land was worth 40 Sh. pr. acre. At the time he gave this to Sir James Wallace the Province was in the King's peace & he was in Possession.

He Knows nothing of the unsettled Grant, although he had signed the Grant. He Knows he had such Lands in Consequence of the King's Proclamation Issued in 1763.

He Knows that Sir James Wallace lost 7 Negroes, one killed by the Rebels, the other six were taken away at different times

twixt 1779 & the Evacuation.

The Negroes were likewise in the settlement, they were Personal Property in Georgia.

He Knows nothing of the Crop stated to be lost on this Plantation at the Evacuation, it is stated to be a Crop of Rice on 60 acres, if so he thinks it would produce 2 Barrels or 2 Barrels & ½ pr. acre, this was managed by his son.

There is a Claim for insurance of 30 Negroes, he Knows that the Negroes were shipped and that the Insurance was paid, the sum was £163.0.0. (50).

This Plantation was Confiscated as the Property of Sir James Wright. The Estate considered the settlement as void & would not allow any transfer of Property, after the Battle of Lexington, the Estate is sold under Confiscation.

LIEUT. GOVNR. GRAHAM:

He Knows the Orange Grove Plantation & has understood that it was given as a marriage Portion by Sir James Wright with his daughter. He has understood that the Plantation was 500 acres, 200 of it Swamp. He Conceives the improved part to be worth £8 pr. acre, the other Wood & provision land he thinks worth 20 sh. pr. acre.

He understands that this Estate was valued at £18 or 1900. He Knows the Appraisers & thinks they were very proper people to value the Estate.

(51).

In 1775 he applied to the Governor & Councel of this Province for the quantity Sir James Wallace was entitled to as a Past Capt. by Proclamation.

He says he paid £83.2.4 for Sir James Wallace & has been repaid it by him. The Grants were never taken out as he supposes from the troubles, but believes they were signed as the application was made prior to the troubles—the quantity a Past Capt. was entitled to was 5000 acres & he thinks he took the whole number for Sir James. It was Contained in four Grants. He never saw the lands, neither does he Know where they were. No Expense but £83 has been incurred.

He Knows that Sir James Wallace had several Negroes with the Estate. He was a Witness to the Deed of settlement, but does not know the Contents. He knows that Sir James Wright sent Sir Jamses Negroes with his own to Jamaica, he has heard that they were insured, but does not know that fact.

Decision—

The Board find Sir Jas. Wallace had a right to Plantation called Orange Grove, 500 acres, which they value at £1250.

He had Grants for 5000 acres which he had not time to Cultivate, but allow him the Expense, £83.0.0.

They allow him for 7 Negroes, one killed. six taken, £315.0.0.

Crop lost at the Evacuation, £150.0.0.

Claim for insurance of Negroes rejected.

1784. February 23.

1146. Case THOMAS DARE.

(52).

He is a native of England & went out to America in 1768 or 1769. He was appointed by the Commissioners of the Customs at Boston Weigher & gauger & afterwards Tide Surveyor in the Port of New London. He Continued in that situation until obliged to quit America in 1776.

He never bore arms but refused a Commission from the Rebels. He continued as long as he could, but was obliged to go to Halifax in June 1776 & from thence to England where he arrived in May. He was mobbed & obliged to go out of Town for several nights. The duties of his office had been at a stand for some time. The Collector staid longer than he did. He was a man of more influence. He admits that he could have staid longer if he could have afforded it. He was in no danger of Personal safety. He has a Wife & one child.

He was possessed in right of his Wife of a House & Water Lott in the Town of New London & ten acres of Land. He has no Deeds, he says he left them in his Bureau in America. That Deed when explained appears to be a Copy of his Wife's Father's Will. Who left his this Property to his Wife & her Heirs. She is dead but has left a Son. He does not know whether his Property is Confiscated or not. He has enquired but cannot learn. He values the House & Water Lott in the Town at £400 St. The House was not a large one, but beautifully situated. He values the 10 acres at £100 Str. He married in 1770 or 1771. Part of the ten acres was Woodland part Grass. He turned a Horse upon it but never cultivated it. Thinks it would not have sold for 100 at that time. The Wood which he used in his family came from thence. This House was burnt in 1781. When Genl. Arnold was there. He lost the furniture in the House where he lived. He can safely swear that it was worth £50, but he took no notice of it at the time thinking that he shd. return.

The Sallary of his office was £40 pr. an. which was continued till Octr., 1782. The emolumnts were trifling. Thinks the office was worth £60 pr. an. He had an allowance from the Treasury until his Sallary was stopped when he applied to Messrs Wilmot & Coke who reported an allowance of £40 pr. an., from the time his salary ceased, which he still continues to receive. He has been Ensign & Lt. in the North Devon Militia for five years. He received the Pay of Lt. up to the time of Peace.

(53).

DUNCAN STEWART, ESQ.

He was Collector for the Port of New London. Knew Mr. Dare. He was a Tidesman previous to the troubles. Remembers his being Robed & ill treated & that he was obliged to secrete himself. He left New London before the Witness, being in want of Money. He did his duty very well. His Sallary was £40 pr an. He might have been removed by the Commission. Remembers one man being removed. He remembers Mr. Dare living in a House said to be his wives. Has heard that the Property was in dispute twixt Mr. Dare and the second Husband of his Mother & that it was either left to Arbitration or litigated & in the end it was determined in favour of Mr. Dare. This was the general idea of the Town. Believes likewise that he had a little land. The House was very well situated, he values the House, Lot & ten acres at what it is estimated at, thinks the House & Water Lott worth £400. His whole Conduct was that of a Loyal subject—attached to the British Government.

(54).

Decision.

The Board is of the opinion Mr. Dare acted like a Loyal Servant of the Crown.

That he lost a House, Lott, & ten acres of Land which they value at £350.

That he lost Furniture which they value at £35.

He was Tide Surveyor of the Port of New London with a Sallary of £40 pr. an. Fees £20

He has an allowance from the Treasury of £40 pr. an.

1147. Case THOS. BROADHEAD.

1784.
February 24.

He is an English man & went to America in 1766. He settled in S. Carolina in 1774 or 1775. He went first to Pensilvia. When the troubles began he lived in Ninety Six & was not

(55).

disturbed until 1781. He never took arms or an oath to the Rebels. It was tenderd to him but he put it off from time to time until at last they forgot it.

He is unable to bear Arms being a Cripple in one of his feet. At the Siege of Ninety Six Gen. Green wanted him to join the Rebel Army, but he refused & lay out during the night to conceal himself. He says that they offered to make him a Lieut. if he would join them. As soon as Ninety Six was evacuated he joined the British. He was emploied as a Labourer in the Armoury & received Rations & £4 a month.

He was discharged by the Army in April, 1782 & came away in the August following. He applied to the Treasury for support & receives £10 pr. an.

Produces a Certificate from Gen. Cannington which proves his having been emploied by the British Army & a pass from the Mayor of Falmouth to Show when he landed in England.

He had 200 acres of Land at Ninety Six which he bought of Wm. Robinson. He had a deed for it but he lost it in America. He gave £200 S. Car Cury for it & a month's work. He values the month's work at £15 S. Car. He cleared about nineteen acres in it. The remainder of the Land was wood. He built a House on it. It cost him nothing but his labour & that of a few friends. He purchased the land in 1775. He cannot say what it cost him in clearing. He left his Wife & family on the Estate. He has heard that she is dead but does not know it for certain. He values his House & Land at £100 S. Thinks it would have sold for that.

He had Four working Horses & they cost him near £400 S. Car. Cury. Swears they were worth £10 S. each. He had six Milch Cows & Six Calves. 10 Head of young Cattle. He values them at £25 each S. Car.

(56).

He had 100 Hogs, he values them at 10sh. each. Ten Sheep he values at 20sh. He gave that for them. He had 100 Bushels of Wheat in his Barn which he values at 4sh. 6d. pr. Bushel. He left a Crop growing which he values at £20. Furniture £10. He cannot say his Property is forfeited, it was not when he came away.

JAMES WALKER.

Knew Thos. Broadhead. He always took him for a Loyal Subject. Knew since 1776. He has heard that he purchased a tract but never was on the Land. Does not know the number of acres. Has seen him have two horses.

WILLIAM MARTYN.

Knew Broadhead in 1777. He lived in Ninety Six district. He bore the Character of a Loyal Subject. He knew the place where he lived. It was on Sleepy Rock. He heard Mr. Robertson say that he had bought it of him. He left the Country in 1779 & then Broadhead had not cultivated much of the Land. It was tolerably good. He lived within six miles of him. He had a Wife & believes she is in America. From the little knowledge he had of the Land he cannot put a value on it, but thinks he has heard him say that he valued it at 10sh. pr. acre. He has Lands in the neighbourhood which he values at 20sh. pr. acre. He does not recollect his Cattle & horses. Upon being asked he says he was not considered a man of substance.

Decision.

That the Claimant is a Loyalist. He was possessed of 200 acres of Land which the Board value at £50. Crop, Corn, Stock, & Furniture £95.

He has an allowance of £10 pr. an.

(57).

1148. Case ROBT. MCLELLAND.

1784.
February 24.

He is a native of Ireland & went to America in 1767 & settled in Craven County S. Carolina. He resided ther when the Rebellion broke out. He lived on his own Land. After Lord Cornwallis took Charles Town he joined Coll. Turnbull. Before this he had taken the oath to the Rebels. He was compelled to do it. He could not live in the Province without doing it. He has mustered with the Rebels but never took Arms agst the British. After he joined the British he continued with them until he lost his eye sight by the explosion of some gun powder. He was Lt. in the S. Car. Rangers under Major Doyle. He never received but £13 as pay.

There are many Certificates to Mr. McLelland's Loyalty & Services.

He acted as Commissary in driving in Cattle & received a dollar pr. Diem for it.

He had 350 acres on Little River, Craven County. It was granted to his father soon after he went there & he died 2 years after. He left no will & the Land descended to him. When his Father died 11 acres were cultivated, he added more than 10 acres. He then Lett it & went to Charlestown to follow his trade. He was to take no rent, but the person he allowed to live on it was to take care of it which he did not do. He allowed one of the houses to be burnt down. He values it at £500 S. Since the house was burnt down it has laid Waste. He says it was at least worth £300. He would not have taken that for it.

(58).

200 Acres on Watery Creek. The Deed to this is keeping the Bond of the Purchase is contained in the Grant. He gave near £100 for it ten years ago. 9 or ten acres were Cultivated.

He says he left this Deed in the office with Mr. Lee, but it cannot be found at present. The deed respecting 350 acres was left in America. He paid for the 100 acres in money & part in Horses. He values them at £200S. He never lived on them or derived any benefit from them.

100 acres situated on Nixons Creek. This was a Grant to his Sister Margaret McLelland. He bought it of her & thinks he gave £60 for it, about 11 or 12 years ago. There were 4 or 5 acres cultivated before his Sister run it, but it was abandoned. He got one Crop from it. The Deed is lost.

100 acres on Rocky Creek belonging to his Wife. It was granted to her when she was a single woman. It was cultivated & a House on it. He built the House. The Land is good. His

(59).

Wife is now in Bedlam, insane. He lived in the House for some time. He left this deed with Mr. Lee. He values this at £100. He had 4 Negroes. One he never paid for. One he gave about £40 for in horses & Cattle. The other two he had from his Brother. He values them at £50 each. He had six Working Horses. He values them at £70. He values his Furniture & Cattle at £100. He had more than 200 Hogs. He would not have taken £40 for them. He lost a great deal of Bacon, 8 Head of Cattle, 120 Bushels of Corn, Plantation Tools worth £10. Furniture he values at £15. He does not know if his land is Confiscated, but swears it is in the hands of a Rebel. He applied to the Treasury about a year & half ago & receives an allowance of £40 pr. ann.

Decision.

The Board are of opinion that Robt. McLelland is a Loyalist. They value 350 acres on Nixon Creek at £87.10. 200 acres on Watery Creek £50; 100 acres on Little River at £25; 100 acres on Rocky Creek £40; Negroes, £90; Stock, £75. He has an allowance of £40 pr. an.

1874.
February 25.

1149. Case MARY ROTHERY.

(60).

She is a native of Virginia & married Mr. Rothery at Norfolk in Virgina about 20 years ago. She was a Widow living at Norfolk at the commencement of the troubles. She came to Engd. in Augst., 1774, on acct. of the storm she saw coming on. The tea had been thrown into the sea before she came away, & the Town of Norfolk was in equal Divisions. Many families would not suffer Tea to drank in their houses. She has often blamed the Americans in Conversation. She was not driven away. She might then have remained with great personal safety. She has been absent the Whole War. She says she hears her Estate is not Confiscated on acct of the Minority of her Son. She Claims for it in her Memorial as she did not then know the fact. Now she only Claims for the injury done the Estate. Many of her houses are burnt at Norfolk. When she came awey she left Mr. John Elebeck & Co. in Management of her affairs, but she has never received any Profit from her Estate since the War.

By her Husband's Will the Houses in Norfolk were left to her for Life & afterwards to her Son who is now 19 years of age. Other persons speak to the value. She has seen the valuation & thinks it moderate. The rent of all the Houses & Warehouses amounts to £173.6. & the whole loss is computed at £3,067 Virg. Cury. The Houses were Lett low on acct. of the troubles. She was obliged to Lower the rents when she came away. She did not receive the rents up to the fire & she does not believe that her Agents have received them. She never applied to Ld. Dunmore for Payment. She has a Copy of the Will at Liverpool which she promises to send. As her lands are not confiscated no acct. is taken of them only the Houses destroied.

She states Book debts due her to the amount of... £1,000
Bond debts to the amount of.......................... 800

All the Books & Papers were in the hands of Mr. Elebeck & were taken by a French Squadron.

The lost Property burnt in Norfolk, £40 Currncy. She left seven Negroes with Mr. Elebeck when she came away. She says one went on Board the Shoemaker Privateer. He was the most valuable, an other is with a Relation, she does not know what is become of the others. She has heard that Lord Dunmore made all the Negroes free. She valued the 7 at £400 Curncy. (61).

When she came to England the Treasury gave her £180. Her case was afterwards heard by Mr. Wilmot & Coke last year who ordered her an allowance of £40 pr. an. from.that time which she continues to receive.

She owed no money in America.

WILLIAM FARIER.

He lived at Norfolk in Virginia. He knew Mrs. Rothery in 1774 & she appeared to be well affected to Govrt. being the reason why she came to England. Says he believes she had not much respect shown to her on acct. of the Loyalty of her father & he

believes that was the reason a Schedule of the Property Burnt is read to him & he says he believes it was the property of Mr. Rothery.

The Land is not Confiscated. He doubts whether they would allow her to have the Property again, but he is clear the son may have it. He came from Norfolk August last. The troubles were not very high at Norfolk in Augst., 1774.

He knows there were some negroes left but he cannot say what became of them. Mrs. Rothery's Husband was considered as a Man of Property & substance.

MR. BARTLET GOODRICH.

He lived at Baltimore & knew Mrs. Rothery. She came away before the troubles. He knew Mr. Orange her father. He lived at Liverpool. He was one of the Gent. appointed to investigate the Claims of Loyalists for Virginia. He is desired to look into the Schedule as she claimed this Property before that Committee. He says she did. He knew one of the Houses. When the Claim was given in it was thought very moderate, provided she came within the description to Claim. He says their Committee thought no person entitled to claim but those who had been active or driven away. This Gent. accts.for Mrs. Rothery saying she could not stay on acct. of the Division. He says there was a great Division in that neighbourhood about Inoculation & that her father took an active part in this business which made him very unpopular. He (62).

believes this made Mrs. Rothery's situation uncomfortable, but it had no connexion with the troubles. Nothing was done in Virginia until the Blockade of Boston. The Committee did not reject her Claim but it appeared very vague & doubtful.

MRS. ROTHERY, the Claimant.

Being asked as to the Division she before mentioned she says that it was caused partly by the disputes about Inoculation & partly by the dispute 'twixt the two Countries. She persists in this acct.

Mr. ROBERT GILMOUR.

(63). Knew Mrs. Rothery at Norfolk. She left it in the Summer of 1774. There was at that time no appearance of Rebellion, but there was a dispute about Inoculation, & several mobs assembled about it. There were no Political disputes at that time. There was no Disturbance at Norfolk until 1775. Mr. Orange had taken a strong part in this Inoculation business & had made himself very unpopular. He says he believes the Claim is just. The Committee received the Claim from Mr. Goodrich. Mr. Gilmour was one of the Committee. They thought her Claim very doubtful, because she came away before the troubles.

COLL. ELLEGOOD.

He knew Mrs. Rothery at Norfolk. Thinks she came to Engd. in 1774, but not before Congress met, which was in Septr. He knows the Houses which she had in Norfolk. Believes that she is

well affected to Gt. Britain, but does not think that the troubles were any reason for her quitting America. He says that the Committee in examining this Claim made several deductions from the value of the Houses. When the Claim was brought in they doubted whether it should be received, as in their opinion she did not come within the description of an American Refugee. Thy neglected many Claims on that ground. The whole of the Allowance for the Houses amounted £1,610 Stg. The land remains & is Confiscated but, she had no allowance from the Assembly of the Province because she was considered to be a Tory. If she had been looked upon as a Whig she would have been pd. for them.

(64). HENRY FLEMING.

He lived at Norfolk in 1774 & knew Mrs. Rothery there. She had a large dwelling House, several Ware houses, a Smiths Shop & a Warf all burnt in the year 1776. He supposes they were all worth £2,000 Stg. Thinks they would have sold for that before the burning of the Town. He knows she had several Negroes but does not know what is become of them.

He thinks the reason for her leaving Norfolk in 1774 was her foreseeing the troubles which have since divided the two Countries. He says the Committee met in June, 1774, & in August., 1774, the Town was under the direction of the Committees. He explains

that he means June & Augst., 1775, because it was after the Battle of Bunker's Hill. Says the Tea was throughn into the sea the beginning of 1774 & had thought that the Committee had sett immediately after, but upon the different dates being explained he says he meant 1775.

1150. Case LYNN MARTEN.   1784. February 25.

GENERAL PRESCOTT.

Knew the Claimant to be a very active & zealous Loyalist & a very useful man. He was in decent circumstances & had been Master of a Mercht. Ship. He carried Arms at Rhode Island & did his duty unexceptionally. He was made Capt. of the Port & had a Dollar a day for it. He had Property but cannot say how much. He never knew a better man in his life.

(65).

LYNN MARTEN, THE CLAIMANT.

Is an American & lived in New Port, Rhode Island, that was his home when not at Sea. But he was master of a Ship when the troubles broke out & was at sea. When he came home in Octr., 1775, the Island was under Rebel Govert. He wished to be quiet or take no part with them. They offered him the command of a Battery but he refused it. He remained quiet until the British Troops came to Rhode Island which was the 8th Decemr, 1776. He joined them Immed'ately. The Rebels offered an Oath to Mr. Morton, but he refused it. They sent some soldiers to carry him to Prison, but being known to the officer they did not do it. When he joined the British Sir Henry Clinton appointed him to the Command of a Schooner. He had 40sh. pr. month for it.

In 1778 he was appointed by Sir Robt. Pigot, Capt. of the Port of Rhode Island with a Sallary of 5sh. pr. diem. He continued in that situation until the Place was evacuated in 1779. He went to New York where he remained until June last when he went with his family to Quebec where they now are. Certificate from Sir R. Pigot which goes fully to his Loyalty & Conduct.

He had an appointment from Sir Hy. Clinton at New York for which he had 5sh. pr. Diem. As soon as the Rebel Govert. was established in Rhode Island they confiscated his Property real & Personal & sold it at Public Vendue.

(66).

Property.

A Lott of Land & Dwelling House in the Town of New Port. Produces the Deed for the Lands dated 26th Feby., 1772. It was a Conveyance from Aaron Lopez & Constce his Wife in Consideration of 191 Spanish Dollars or £42.19. He built the House himself which cost him 2,200 Dollars or £472. It was only finished in the summer 1773. He had a Pew in Trinity Church which cost him 30 Dollars. His furniture, &c. which was destroied he values at £20. He produces a Schedule of it.

He came to England last Decemr., & made no application at Whitehall, neither does he mean to do it long as he can get his Bread.

WM. BROOKS SIMPSON.

He lived near Mr. Marten in Rhode Lsland. He knew the Lott of ground & the house upon it. He thinks it well worth 2,000 Dollars £400. It was a very good house. He believes that it is Confiscated. He produces a Rebel Paper in 1781 when this Property is offered for sale. He had a Pew in Trinity Church worth 40 Dollars. He believes him to be a man of good character, Loyalty & in good circumstances before the troubles.

JOHN ANDREWS.

(67).

Me lived in New Port & knew Mr. Marten there. Recollects his House there if he had wanted a home he would have given 2,000 Dollars for it. He understands that it is Confiscated. He promises to send an Act of Confiscation to the Board.

It was passed in 1777 or 1778, he does not know what Personal Property Mr. Marten lost. He brought away great part at the Evacuation.

Decision.

That Mr. Lyon Marten is an active & zealous Loyalist & that he bore Arms.

He lost a Lott & Dwelling House in Newport which
the Board value at £400
A Pew in Trinity Church   5
Furniture lost & destroied   20

PROCEEDINGS

OF

LOYALIST COMMISSIONERS

LINCOLN'S INN FIELDS, 1784.

Vol. III.

BEFORE COMMISSIONER WILMOT.

Claimants.

	MSS. Folio.		MSS. Folio.
Alexander, Thomas	64	Kingsley, Zephaniah	8
Andrews, John	109	McQueen, William	113
Blenkinhorn, Henry	114	Miller, Thomas	37
Brookes, John	52	Pennington, William	7
Clarke, Rev. Mr.	108	Peronneau, Henry	17
Cooper, Robert	41	Phipoe, Thomas	103
Cooper, Rev. Robert	69	Rogers, Thomas	34
DeLancey, Brig.-Gen. Oliver	94	Ryan, Thomas	116
Edmonston, Rev. William	62	Stenhouse (Stonehouse), Alexander,	36 & 111
Forsyth, Mrs. Penelope	66		
Greatorex, Samuel	48	Skinner, Brigadier-General	77
Green, Francis	29	Thomson, George	59
Green, James	73	Thorp, Edward	1
Harrison, Gray	44	Wilson, Richard	26
Johnson, James	101	Wright, Jermyn	91

EVIDENCE.

1784.
February 26.

1151. Case EDWARD THORP.

He was born in America & lived in Stamford in Connecticut. He kept a store & traded by sea. He had two vessels one third of which belonged to him. He traded with these vessels in Jamaica. He always declared his opinion in favor of Great Britain & was imprisoned several times in 1775. He had the oath frequently tendered to him. He was first imprisoned on a charge of having given intelligence to Capt. Vaade of the Asia. He was kept in Prison for five days.

(1).
The same year he was obliged to give Bond for £1000, that he would not act agst. the Americans. Another who joined with him is likewise a Loyalist & they both came away in 1776. They agreed not to deal with him & he was obliged to come away, in consequence he removed to New York.

Property consisted at that time of these two Vessels besides Land.

4 Lotts, Dwelling House, Store house, Barn, &c. in the Town of Stamford & six acres of Land. He bought the Land & built upon it. He bought it 20 years ago. He has lost all his Deeds. He bought it of one Israel Smith. He says he gave £440 or 50 for it. He swears he gave at least £420. The House was then partly built. He cannot say what it cost him to finish the house. The Barn cost him £100 Cury. & the House at least as much more. The Store & 2 Shops cost him at least £150.

A House ½ a mile west of the above in the Town of Stamford with 14 acres of land, he bought of Joseph Hensly about 14 years ago. He gave £55 for the House & Garden & 7.10 an acre for the Land that is £105, in all £160. He has a Witness to prove this.

He thinks the first Lott with the Buildings worth £800. He was offered £750 for it 16 years ago. by a person from Long Island, but he cannot recollect his name. He then asked £900 for it. He thinks the 2nd Lot with 14 acres of Land worth at least £250.

(2).
He had a Tan Yard & Slaughter house, besides they were built on the Town land & owner, he had no title to the Land.

Two acres of meadow he bought of his uncle Nathan Terrius. He bought it 20 years ago & believes he gave £11 an acre for it. He bought other Property at the same time. He values them at £18.

600 acres at Lymington on the Missisippi, 100 acres of this was his right as a Srgt. last war. He bought the rights of 5 other Sergts. He bought 100 acres for 9 dollars about 16 years ago. He gave 6 dollars for another 100 acres & the same price for the remainder. He was never at any expense in cultivation & only Claims what it cost him. He had only a Warrant for these Lands.

3rd part of a Lot on the Missisippi, obtained by his partner, had been at no expense & makes no claim. He values the Tan Yard & Slaughter house at £60.

Personal Property.

Hides, Leather & Bark, he values at £45.

3rd Part of a Ship taken by the Rebels about 5 or 6 years ago. She was a trading vessel from Jamaica to Floriday. She was taken in Mississippi. He values his Loss in this Ship at £1000.

3rd Part of a Schooner in the same trade, taken at the same time. His Loss in her £600. Two Sloops Wholly his seized in 1775 in the Port of Stamford. One was a Packet to carrying goods & Passengers to New York. The other was a very old one. He values the two at £120. He says the Schedule produced was estimated by himself.   (3).

Dry Goods, Rum, Mollasses & Sugar lost in the store he values at £260 at least. Household furniture he values at £188. Plantation Tools £12. He lost two Horses which he values at £20 each. He lost likewise 2 Cows, 2 Calves & 6 Swine.

He had Bonds & Notes due him in America to the Amount of £600. Book Debts £1250. He admits that he owes £900 in America.

He receives £30 pr. an. from the Treasury. Says his Lands are Confiscated & sold.

JAMES HUBBARD.

Knew Mr. Thorp many years before the war. His Loyalty is undoubted & he was always well attached to the British Government from the first of the troubles. Says he went on board the Asia & took with him the names of many Loyalists. Mr. Thorp was a merchant many years before the troubles & dealt in dry goods & West Indian goods. He had considerable degree of business. He does not speak of his Property, but of his owning a house & Store & Several Buildings. He was bred a Shoemaker. He should value the house, buildings & Land in the first Lot at £450 or 500 S. or £600 Curcy. He knows the 2nd Lot he always occupied it and was generally thought the owner of it. Mr. Hubbards father owned part of this Lott & sold the House & 2 acres for £120. Thinks that with the 14 acres this might be worth £200. He understood that he had 2 acres of Meadow which he values at (4). £12 pr. acre. He had likewise a Tan Yard & Slaughter house, can't value them.

He knows nothing of his Lands on the Mississippi, neither can he speak acurately to his shipping concerns. He can't speak to the value of his stores, but thinks he could not have much, perhaps £200 or 300. He was a very obnoxious man, nobody was more active. He left his wife, but thinks she could not bring off any of the Property. He has been frequently in Thorps house. He thinks the furniture would have sold for £125.

Knew nothing of his horses &c., does not doubt but his Property is confiscated. He was at Stamford last year & was told by Colonel Davenport that all the Property of Loyalists was confiscated & most of it sold. He thinks it very reasonable to suppose that all his papers were lost as he did not go home before he joined the British Troops. He had then been on a Tour on his business

He has one child, either at Stamford or New York, but Mr. Hubbard thinks the child will not be permitted to inherit the fathers Property. He did not assist Mr. Thorp in making his estimate.

Mr. JARVIS.

Is an American, born at Stamford, since a Cornet in the Queens Rangers. He knows Mr. Thorp very well. He thinks him a steady Loyalist very active & very obnoxious in consequence of it. He knows part of his Property, the House he lived in.

There was a House, a Store, a shoemakers & Taylors Shop, a Barn, &c. & about six acres of Land. It was always looked upon to be Mr. Thorps Property. It was a good Situation & in appearance good Land. He thinks the Land worth £40 pr. acre & altogether that it was worth £600 or £650.

(5). He knows the other House in Stamford, but neither the House nor land was so good. There was more in this Lot than in the other supposing 14 acres. He thinks the house not worth £100, nor the Land not worth more than £20 pr. acre. If it was his he would value it at £250, but thinks it would not sell for so much. He knows he had a Tan Yard & Slaughter House, but cannot value them. Knows he had concern in Vessels, but cannot speak accurately.

He knows nothing of his store but he values his Furniture at £150 or £200. He has heard in America that his Property is confiscated & sold.

The REVD. MR. PETERS.

He lived at Hebron in Connecticut about 30 miles from Stamford. He has known Mr. Thorp above 20 years. He always looked upon him to be a very Loyal Subject. The Witness was drove away in 1774, but has had letters from New York by which he is convinced that Mr. Thorp was driven away & lost his Property on acct. of his Loyalty. He has been in Mr. Thorps house. He lived well & his house was well furnished. He was always looked upon as a man of substance & has often heard the neighbours say, that he was a man worth £3 or 4000 of the money of the Province. He thinks the house & Lot where he lived would have sold for £500.

Decision.

(6). The Board are of opinion that the claimant Edward Thorp is a zealous & active Loyalist. They find him possessed of 4 Lotts, House, &c. in the Town of Stamford value £375.

A House & 14 acres, ½ a mile from the above the Board value at £150.

Two acres of Meadow they value at £14.

Tan Yard, Slaughter house, Hides, Leather, Bark, &c., they value at £50.

A vessel used as a Packet to N. York, Laying in the Harbour of Stamford, they value at £50.

Dry Goods, Rum, Mollasses, &c. £150.

Furniture £70. Horses, Stock, &c. £20.

States Debts to the amount of £1850.

Says he owes £900.
Is allowed £40 pr. an. by the Treasury.

1152. Case WM. PENNINGTON.   1784. February 27.

Is a native of England. He went to America in 1764, as Comptroller of the Port of Brunswick in N. Carolina. He was appointed by the Lords of the Treasury, his sallary was £40 pr. an. He continued at Brunswick until Feby. 1776. He never was molested personally.

In Sept. 1776 the envoluments of his office ceased as all business was stopt at the Custom House in Feby. 1776. He to wait— of Govr. Martin & Gen. Clinton on board the Scopion and afterwards on board the Thitus until August, when he arrived at New York. He having first been at C. Town. He sailed soon after for Cork & arrived in Sept. When he went to Engd., where he remained ever since. He does not pretend to any acts of service. Says he never had an opportunity of doing service to his Country.   (7).

The fees of his office amounted to near £100, making his office amount to £150. He received the salary to Oct. 1782. He likewise received £60 pr. an. from the Treasury from 5th April 1777. He still continues to receive £60 pr. an.

He had a house in Brunswick which belonged to Gen. Tryon. He went into it in 1771. When the Gen. said he was welcome to that house as long as he remained in America. He did not then give it as a Property. He produces a certificate from Gen. Tryon that he had given him the house & that it cost him £100.

Furniture lost in the House he values at £50. Govr. Martin remembers Mr. Pennington reported as Comptroller of the Port of Brunswick. He is perfectly satisfied with his Loyalty.

Mr. Pennington produces his deputation from the commrs. of the Customs to prove his holding the office.

Decision.

That the Claimant was a Loyal servt. of the Crown. That he held the office of Comptroller of the Port of Brunswick sallary £40 pr. an. Envoluments £100 pr. an.

That the lost Furniture to the value of £50.

He is allowed £60 pr. an. from the Treasury.   (8).

1153. Case ZEPHANIAH KINGSLEY.   1784. February 27.

JAMES SIMPSON, Esq.

Knew Mr. Kingsley in the beginning of the troubles, when things went agst. this Country. He was uniformly Loyal. He believes he was so from principal. He subscribed to the raising a troop of Horse & made himself obnoxious by his zeal. He cannot speak to his property only that he lived in a good House which he believes was his own & adds that he was a very emminent Mercht. in Charlestown & in very extensive trade.

THOS. SKELTOWS, Esq.

Knew Mr. Kingsley very well before the troubles. He believes him to be a very Loyal subject. He was uniformly so &

has been a very great sufferer by his Loyalty. He considers him as a man in extensive business & of considerable Property, but he cannot tell how much. He knows he had several houses in Charlestown & some Lands. He believes his Lands have been Confiscated and knows that his name is in the Confiscation List.

Zepheniah Kingsley the Claimant being a quaker his affirmation is taken.

(9).
He is a native of England & went to America in 1770. He carried over a Cargo Goods with an intention to Establish himself there. When the troubles came on he did everything in his power to oppose the Rebellion. He suffered much persecution in consequence he was three times imprisoned. They often applied to him to bear arms, but he always refused. He admits that the principle of his Religion excludes him from bearing arms. In 1778 he signed a paper purporting to be a Test Oath & concious it bound him to take a part with them, but he never did. When Gen. Provost was coming to Charlestown they took away 300 Barrels of rice & some Hogsheads of Tobacco, but they paid for rice in depreciated Currency.

During the Seige he was made overseer of the Negroes which was the only service he ever did for the Americans. He is desired to explain his signing the test. He says they insisted upon his affirming to be true &c., but he always refused & would have left the Province sooner than do it. But it was done by a friend of his

in this way & then he gave him a Certificate that he had affirmed &c. He did not consider it as at all binding upon him after the reduction of the place. He subscribed £100 9s. towards raising a Corps of Horse. He does not know when, but it is confiscated & part of it sold & apprehends that he shall not be permitted to return. He receives from the Treasury £100 pr. an. from Jany. 1783. Certificate &c. from Govr. Bell to the Claimants Loyalty & to the Persons who have valued the Property.

(10).
Property—He has no Papers or Titles to Produce. He left them with his wife who gave them to Mr. Taylor, who now lives in a good Brick House, built by Mr. Kingsley in 1775. Mr. Taylor is a friend of his & he can have his papers whenever he chooses to send for them. He is desired to write for them.

£300 stg.
Lot 1st. in the Memorial. The house possessed by Mr. Taylor he gave above £4000 for it. The Cost in building above £3000. He values it at £2500. It is valued in 1782. He thinks the House would now sell for £3000.

Lot 2nd in the Memorial House, &c. in King & Broad street, he was likewise possessed of this in fee. He purchased it in 1777. He bought the 1st Lot just after Bunkers hill & then began to build. He produces the title Deeds to this Lott. He gave only £300 Stg. for it. He produces a Conveyance from himself to Gilbert Chalmers to this Lot in consideration of £1500 in 1781. Mr.

Chalmers Estate was Confiscated as well as Mr. Kingsleys, so that he could not pay for it. So the deeds have been returned, it is appraised at £1500. He let this Lot at 50gs. pr. an.

Lot 3. Two good Houses 60 feet in front. This Lot includes 554 acres of Land, but they are valued separately. The Two Houses at Beaufort are valued at £1200. The land at £450. He bought the two Lotts in 1778 & gave 2200 Dollars of Continental paper money for them. He cannot tell what the money was worth at that time. He let the two Houses for 60 gs. pr. an. He thinks he bought them cheap & admits that he bought them cheaper on acct. of the Rebellion.

(11).

He purchased the 554 acres in 1781. Thinks he gave about £200 S. for them, very little cultivation on them, this was matter of speculation in hopes that this Country would prevail.

A Tract of 1800 acres in St. Peters Parish, Granville County. He gave 54000 Continental Dollars for this in 1778, there were several Buildings in this & 7 or 800 acres were cleared. He had sold this to Mr. Briggs of Charlestown in 1780 for £4500, but he could not complete his purchase & the Deeds were returned. He bought this cheaper on acct. of the troubles. He made the purchase under a Rebel Govt. He bought it on Speculation, it is appraised at £4000. A Comr. Lot of Land in White Point 94 feet

in front &c. He had sold this for £1300 S. He purchased this the latter end of 1776 & gave for it £70,000 Currency in Continental fectly attached to the British Govert. He believes he has more money, that money was then depressed there for one. He bought the Low Water Lot at the same time & he values the two Lots at £2500 Strg. He setts that value on them because he sold them for that sum. The valuers did not set a value upon it.

He admits that all the Land he bought except the Front Lot was bought on speculation, upon the prospect of a change of Govert. The 1st Lot he bought to live in.

House & Lot in Furniture, St. James Parish Georgia. He bought in 1776, there was 40 acres. He bought it for a trifle. He gave goods to the amount of £100 for it. ♦He values it at £200 S. He bought in on Speculation.

(12).

A House, out buildings & 20 acres at Indian Land about 70 miles from Charlestown. He bought this for the purpose of carrying on his business in 1776. He gave £270 & values it at £250.

Personal Property—He supplied about £200 to certain persons in imprisonment this is either generosity or a Debt.

He lost different articles taken from him during the Rebellion. Rice, dry goods, Tobacco, &c. to the amount of £2080. He cannot give a particular acct. of this. It is extracted from the Books, at Charlestown, this he charges to the acct. of Mr. Rutledge the

---

American Governor & Assigns as a reason that he thought their Estates would have been confiscated not those of the Loyalists.

He claims £1911.10.6 paper money made under the Kings Government which thinking as good as the Bank he kept. He admits that he might have paid it away without Loss, but having

(13).

no doubt he chose to keep it. He gave it to Govr. Ball about a year ago, thinking that the Govr. would make some allowance for it.

Debts—He has Debts due him in America to the amount of £6500. He admits that he owes about £1200 currency in America & £10,000 Stg. here.

Negroes, he has several but makes no claim for them, as some are in Jamaica, Some in Charlestown. His agent is allowed to keep them on the Idea that they belong to his children. He made a Deed of gift of them to his Children before he Came away.

DOCTOR GARDEN.

Has known Mr. Kingsley 15 years & believes him to be perfectly attached to the British Govert. He believes he has never signed any paper acknowledging allegiance to the United States. He is sure the oath of abjuration was never tendered him. He looks upon him to be a very steady Loyalist & very kind to the Loyal Prisoners, that conduct made him very abnoxious. He knows that he subscribed to raise a Corps in 1781 or 1782.

(14).

He can only speak to that part of his Property in Broad Street where he lived—he built in 1778 or 1779, the old House was burnt down in 1778—the old House & Lott Cost £1600 S., he knows this because he lent the money to pay for it. He thinks the House & Lot in its present state would be sold for £2000. The fire was accidental. The 2nd House was more Commodious than the 1st, as it stood in 1774 it would have sold for £1500 or 1600, as it stood in the best part of the Town for trade. This House has been Confiscated & he believes sold for £4000 S., the value of which is about £2000. The payment is made in Treasury Indmts. which sell for 95 pr. cent Discount. He has known it let from £150 to £400 pr. an., it was valued at £150 pr. acre in 1770.

It now letts for £300 pr. an. Supposing the House to have been burnt down in 1778, he thinks the ground would have sold for £500. At the time the house was built the Rebel Govermt. prevailed in Charlestown. He knows the Valuers, they were all good men, two of them were good judges of Land. He knows the 2nd Lot in King & Broad Street, he heard of his having bought it, but cannot say what it Cost him. The House was a very bad one, the Lot was very valuable. He had often thought of buying this Lot & would have given £1200 or £1500 for it. He meant to have built on it. He thinks it would have let for £30 or 40 S. All lands sold cheaper from 1776 to 1778, but they rose on the Evacuation of Philadelphia on the Idea that Gt. Britain meant to Evacuate all America. He says this is Confiscated &

he believes has been sold. He says many good people took the Oath of Allegiance without Scruple, who afterwards spilt their blood for Gt. Britain, out he thinks Mr. Kingsley would have quitted the Province before he would have signed the abjuration.

ROBERT MCKENZIE:

He was Capt. in the Militia. He knew Mr. Kingsley & the lands he had on White Point in South Bay, thinks he bought it in 1778, it was in the Town of C. Town. He thinks the Lot, exclusive of the Water Lot, was worth 3 sh. pr. square foot, which brings it to £1800 S. He thinks it was worth that in 1774 or 1775, does not think lands in Charlestown were so valuable in 1778 as in 1774. His uncle had lands in that situation & was offered that money for them. He thinks it was worth £1200 in 1778. The value of the Water Lot was Ideal. He does not know what value he put on it, but thinks it worth £400 S. This Property is Confiscated, but never heard that this Lott has been sold. He cannot speak to any other part of his property. He knows Mr. Taylor, he was Mr. Kingsley's Partner, has been told that he had bought the house, but has no doubt that he has paid the fair value of it, believes there is no Colusion in it. He knew Mr. Kingsley's house after it was new built, thinks it was not worth more than £1500 S., in 1774 it would have sold for £2000 Sterg.

(15).

ROBERT BALLINGALL:

He was originally a Plasterer. He knew Mr. Kingsley very well. He knew most of his property in the black Swamp, the Witness advised Mr. Kingsley to buy it. He does not know the number of acres, but he believes there were 2000. He was present when he purchased them, he thinks in 1779, the man who sold the lands was then in Prison for Loyalty, but has now made his peace & remains in the Country. There was a good House on it & about 400 acres Cleared. Mr. Kingsley gave about £50,000 for it. He advised Mr. K. to give as much as £4000 for it. He thinks they were well worth it. He has heard that he sold these Lands to one Bugg who could not pay the money & he took the Lands again. He does not know the sum they sold for. The purchase was made during the Rebel Govnt. Believes the reason he purchased was that Paper Money depreciated so fast that he thought it wise to lay it out. He knows the Tract on Port Royal Island, but not so well as the other, he thinks it is more than 500 acres.

(16).

Mr. Ballingall has given a Certificate to the valuation of these Two Lots, in which he says that the valuation is a low one, that Certificate is annexed to the Memorial. He says he thinks every acre in Port Royal is Worth 20 Sh., & therefore the valuation is a low one, because it is valued at £400. He is not able to speak of any other part of his Property.

Decision—The Board is of the opinion that Mr. Zephaniah Kingsley is a Zealous Loyalist.

1154. Case of HENRY PERRONEAU.

1874, February 28.

Is a native of Charles Town, at the Commencement of the trouble he was Joint Public Treasurer. In 1770 he was appointed sole Treasurer & in 1771 another person was joined to him in the

(17).

appointment. He produces his appointment by Govr. & Council which read:—Benj. Dart is joined with him in that appointment, it is dated 1771. Produces a Paper dated March, 1776, by which he is prohibited from Issuing any more money from the Treasury about ten days before a Member of Congress called upon him & intimated that such an order would come & asked if he would obey any Orders from Congress, he answered that he would not on any account. He ackordingly paid no attention to it. He was dispossessed of the office the 26th March, 1776, & soon after paid the Ballance to the Rebel Governor Rutledge. He produces an order imposing the Oath of Allegiance & Abjuration & a Copy of the Oath, this ordinance was published on the 13th July, 1777. All his friends prior to this desired him to take part with them, but he Constantly refused & said that he would sooner forfeit his Life & Property. He was banished in Consequence & was put in Prison for refusing to Comply. He was often threatened but did not receive any personal insult until he was banished. His Connections were Considerable & they prevented the Mob from attacking him.

(18).

He was banished in April, 1777, when he went to Holland & came from there to England. As soon as he came here he applied to the Treasury who allowed him £200 pr. an. from 1st Jany., 1778. On the Reduction of Charlestown he was ordered out again & received one year in advance & passage money, he arrived there 3rd June, 1781, & Continued until the Place was Evacuated. He held a little office there for which he received 10 sh. pr. Diem, it Continued untill he received £107 & he never received any more money while he was there. When he returned his Case was again heard by Mr. Wilmot & Coke, who again reported him th same allowance from the 1st Jany., 1783.

Certificates—A very full & Handsome one from Gover. Ball to the Loyalty & Character of Peronneau.

Property—Lott of Land on the West side Meeting Street, C. Town. Part of this came to him by his Father, the other part he purchased. He has no deeds or papers.

He left all his papers with his Attornies in America. Produces a Receipt for all deeds, Papers, &c., from his Agents. He has two Witnesses to prove the hand Writing. He derived his right from his Father's Will, of which he can produce a Copy. He says he was seized in fee of both parts. There is a good Brick Dwelling house on it. He values it at £2500 S.

A Lott on the South Side Broad Street left by his father's Will to a younger Brother who is dead & to whom he is heir at Law. He values this Lot at £300, this value was put on it prior to the troubles.

One half of a Lot on the North Side of Queen's Street, this he became entitled to by the Death of another Brother, who was banished & died lately at Plymouth. Produces the Copys of his Will. He values the ½ at £600, the other half belongs to his Sister.

76a AR.

A Pew in the Parish Church of St. Michael's, values it at £100. (19).

Mr. Perenneau says he has great hopes that the Confisca- Confiscation is taken off and tion will be taken off his property, the Sale having been suspended he allowed to by the Legislature. He says he wishes it may be true & now return. only claims de Bone Esse.

He had three Slaves which were Confiscated but not sold, he values them at £200, these he thinks will share the fate of his lands, if he gets the lands that he will likewise get the Slaves.

He l_st Indigo which he values at £587.13.4. It was shiped at C. Town for Amsterdam, but not ensured & the ship was lost. He likewise lost some taken by the King's ships in 1777 under the Prohibitory Act valued at £268.13.10. He charges loss by depreciated at £2766.16.6, this by the British Calculation it comes to £523 less.

He owed no money in America.

Debts due him with Interest amount to £9881, Legacy & book debts, he thinks they will not Confiscate. He Considers so from

many Letters he has received. He states the Loss of office at £800 pr. an., it arose from 2½ pr. Cent. from all sums pd. in & out of the Treasury. This office was not restored to him on the Capture of Charlestown as Civil Govnt. was not restored there.

Mr. Peronneau says he never heard of any but two Oaths in America, there was no Oath of Neutralty.

ROBERT WILLIAMS, ESQ.: 1st March.

Has Known Mr. P——. for 40 years. He knows his lands, the Lott his house stood on came by his Father, thinks in 1774, & many years before it was worth from £2700 to £3000. (20).

He Knows another Lot on the South side of Broad Street, does not know how he became possessed of it, thinks this Lot was worth more than £300, there was a store upon it & a very bad House. This Gentleman was one of the Committee who valued these Houses, they put really the same value upon them. He knows the Lot North side Queen Street, he thinks the whole of the Lot worth £1300. He says he believes it belonged to his Brother, who was likewise a Loyalist. If he had wanted to buy land at that time he would have given that for it. He thinks the Pew was worth £100 S. He only speaks of the value of the Lands, it was the general reputation of the Country that the House in which he lived & the Pew were the Property of Mr. Peronneau & that the other Lots belonged to his Brother. His Loyalty is indisputable. He has heard that he disobeyed the

orders of the Rebel States. His name was in the Confiscation list.

He knows of but of two Oaths which are in the Possession of the Board.

JAMES SIMPSON, ESQR.:

Has Known Mr. Perenneau for many years, he has many reasons for knowing Mr. P—— is very Loyal from Principal, he more than believes it & will explain how to the Board if they wish it, the reasons which induced him to form that opinion. All his friends & Connections were violent of the other side & he refused to obey the orders of Congress.

(21). He cannot speak particularly to Property, but believes he was a man of great Property. He thinks the Lot on which Mr. Perenneau's house stood was worth £2500. Upon hearing the Dimensions he thinks Mr. Pen. must have sold of a part & that described should be worth £2200.

DOCTOR GARDEN:

Speaks to the Indigo being put on board an American Vessel the 1st a June, 1777, for Amsterdam, & was lost on the Coast of Holland. Half of the Indigo belonged to Dr. Garden. The 2nd was shipped in July, the same year & was taken under the Prohibitory Act. Most of the Property on board was Rebel Property.

Dr. Garden admits that if he had applied in time, the Loyal property would have been returned. But Mr. Powell, who was one of the owners, was too late of making application. He could not insure the Property at Charlestown as they would not insure the Property of Loyalists. The value of the 1st Cargo was £600 Str., of the 2nd £250. Dr. Garden speaks to a Loss Mr. Pen. sustained by receiving payment of some Bonds in depreciated paper money. Upon all the bonds he says it amounted to £23,835 Cury. He was Attny. to Mr. Perenneau, he believes his Loyalty & attachment to Great Britain was firm & indisputable. Dr. Garden says that the Seven Bonds pd. to him amounted to £2300, but he cannot say how much the Loss was. Mr. Perenneau says it was £19,000. Dr. Garden says it could not be more than £14,000.

JAS. ED. POWELL:

(22). He speaks to the value of the Treasurer office, he has heard it estimated by many people at £1200 to £1500 pr. an. Stg. He had the half of it. He Knows of the Indigo shipped for Frantz, he thinks it was worth £250 Stg. It was an American Vessel, she belonged to the Island of Nantucket. She was taken on the Banks of Newfoundland & Condemned. There was a great deal of Property on Board which belonged to Rebels. He did lodge an appeal but did not prosecute from his inability to lay down £60 to answer the charges of the appeal.

ROBT. WM. POWELL, ESQ.:

He Knows Mr. Perenneau, he & Dr. Garden were appointed by him his Attys. They shipped some Indigo for Mr. Perenneau

and has heard of its being taken. He speaks to both the Cargoes, were Consigned to Amsterdam, value £2620, but the whole did not belong to Mr. Pen. The 2nd Cargoe was sent to Frantz, valued at £737, one third of which was his. He & Dr. Garden sold Mr. Perenneau's furniture to buy this Indigo, they were induced to send it on the faith of its being restored, the Paper produced signed by Mr. Lowndes & Mr. Pennman. Mr. Powell proves the hand writing of Mr. Pennman. He believes his father did appeal, but could not proceed for want of money. He says the reputed income of the Treasurer's office was £2000 pr. An., Mr. Pen. had half of it. He knows the whole of Mr. Perenuas Landed property & values the Lott on which his house stood at £2500. He knows the small Lot on Broad Street & values it at £300 or 400, speaks of it before the troubles. He says the half Lot in Queen St. is worth £600 to £650 Strg.

He knows he left 3 Slaves in Charlestown, a Mother & two Daughters, he values them at £250 Strg.

JOHN HOPETON, ESQ.:

Knew Mr. Perenneau very well, he was joint Treasu., it was Considered as a better office than Governor, but he had only half of it. It was his opinion worth £2000 pr. An. He knows Mr. Perenneau's Dwelling house & Considers it worth £2000 Strg. Mr. Pern. lived in it ever since he knew him. He knew the Lot on Broad Street, it came to him from his Brother, he thinks the

Buildings were of no value, but the Land worth £300 Str. He knows the Lot North side Queen Street, he values the whole of the Lot at £1000 or £1200 Str. the Buildings were not in very good repair. He had a Pew in St. Michael's Church worth £100. He remembers a Negro Woman with two Mullatto Daughters, worth 300 gs.

JOHN LEWAGE, ESQ.:

He lived at C. Town & knew Mr. Perenneau very well, he was joint Treasurer which was worth about £450 pr. an. to him, the whole he thinks was worth £900 pr. an., exclusive of the money left in their hands, the other advantages £600 pr. an. He always looked upon Mr. Perenneau to be a very honest man & believes he was very Loyal because he refused to Conform to their Govnt. Being asked if he thinks the Interest of money in the Treasurer's hands a fair perquisite, he says always till lately it was thought fair.

ROBERT PERENNEAU, ESQ.:

Being desired to give an acct. of the Emoluments of his office he mentions first 2½ pr. Cent. on all monies received or paid, to the best of his recollection there was no Commission on the Taxes, he estimates this at £500 pr an. 5 sh. for making Entries & 20 sh. for Clearing all ships, the Interest of money in their hands

was £1000 at least. He believes the Commission money was £500 pr. an, the Clearance of Ships £400 pr. an., the Emoluments of the office independent of interest were £800 pr. an. At the time he refused to obey the orders of the Assembly many people came to him, if he would obey their orders he might retain their money in his hands, if not they would make him acct. for the

Interest. This was in 1771 & was occasioned by a dispute twixt the Govnr. & Assembly. It happened during the King's Govnt. but no reform was made.

Decision—
The Board are of opinion that Mr. Henry Peronneau is a Zealous & meritorious Loyalist. House & Lott on the West side of the Meeting house in Charlestown—

(25).

The Board values at ....£2000 Sterg.	
A Lott on the South side Broad Street, they value at	250
Half a Lott North side Queen Street they value at	500
A Pew in the Parish Church	100
3 Slaves at..	180

½ of the office Treasurer of the Province £400 pr. an. allowance, £200 pr. an. from the Treasury.

N.B.—Since the case has been decided Mr. Peronneau has informed the Board that his Property is restored to him.

1784.
2nd March.

1155. Case RICHD. WILSON.

He is a native of Ireland. He served all last War in the 22nd Regt. In 1775 & 1776 he was Lt. of Fort Johnstone in N. Carolina, in 1775 he received an order to dismantle the Fort, which was done accordingly. Produces his Commission signed by Govr. Marten.

In 1775 Gen. Gage gave him the Commission of Lt. of Royal Fencibles, he Continued so until July, 1782, Commission produced. After the last War he settled as a Planter & Continued as such until 1771. When the troubles breaking out he joined Gen. Tryon & in 1773 he was made Lt. of Ft. Johnstone. He produces a Warrant dated July, 1772, from Major Bruce ordering him to raise a Compy. of Loyal Americans & was afterwards made Capt. of it as appears by a Commission signed by Sir Guy Carleton in 1783.

(26).

He expects half pay but as yet has received none. The Regt. was reduced the 24th Octr., 1783.

Property—Previous to the troubles he was possessed of property in Lock Woods folly in the County of Brunswick. Produces a paper signed by Govr. Tryon by which it appears that he had 200 acres in that situation in the year 1770. He says that he had a Grant for it which Cost £4 or £5 Cury., he never lived on this Plantation. No part of it was Cultivated, he was at no Expense about it.

He had two Lotts in the Town of Brunswick he got by his Wife whom he marrried in 1767. He refused 100 gs. for the Land on Lock Woods folly, he thinks he could have sold it for £200 Cury.

His Wife is dead but he had 4 Children by her. The Lots were Cultivated & were valuable, she had them by deed from her Father—after her marriage. She died in 1776. It was given to her & her Heirs. His wife was not mentioned & all the Children are dead, it was left to his Wife's Brother failing her heirs.

He had a Plantation in Mecklenburg Coty., N. Carolina, 300 acres. He got this in 1771 from his Wife's father, he gave him no deed. He does not press this, he is not able to put any value on it. He holds no more Landed property in the Province. (27).

He built a House at Ft. Johnstone & was assured by Govr. Collet that he might sell it, or should be repaid the Expenses. He built it in 1773 & it Cost him 500 Cury., likewise £30 Cury. for Stables. He lost three Saddle Horses which he values at £35 the 3, a Cow & Calf £5 Cury., a large Canoe £7 Cry., a quantity of lumber, Garden fences, &c., he values at £55, he lost all these articles at the destruction of Ft. Johnstone, the Estimate is signed by Collet. He lost 24 new Saddles in the Fort, they were given him for a debt, he values them at £60.

Has no allowance from the Treasury, as he expects half pay he thout it wrong to apply.

GOVR. MARTEN, Sworn:

Knows very little of the Claimant, he was appointed by desire of Govr. Collet Lt. of the Fort. It was a mere Provincial appointment. There was no ground for this appointment on the Establishment. He believes him Loyal, he had no pay as Lt., he inhabited a new house within the Fort. He has heard Capt. Collet speak well of him.

JOHN STEPHENS:

He was Purser of the Cruizer Sloop in Cape Fear River. He was at Fort Johnstone when it was dismantled in 1775. Mr. Wilson was Dr. of the Fort, he bore a good Character & he believes he was Loyal. He knows the House he lived in, he was there (28). at the time he was building & altering it. Knows nothing of the Gover's. Assurances to repay the Expense on it that it was Considered as the King's House. It was called Mr. Wilson's House & might Cost him £200 S., it was decently furnished. He had saddle horses & a Cow, understood from himself & from other people that he had Property in Brunswick. As soon as they left the Fort the House was burnt & Every thing destroyed by the Rebels.

Decision—

The Board are of the opinion that Richd. Wilson is a Loyalist.

He built a House for the Convenience of the Fort
    which they value at £200.0.0
Furniture, Horses, &c 100.0.0

1784.
2nd March.

1156. Case FRANCES GREEN, ESQ.

The Memorial being read which is a very long one, he swears to the truth of the facts therein set forth. He proceeds to produce his vouchers to prove it.

A Letter from Gen. Gage to Govr. Turnbull of Connecticut, stating that in Consequence of his Loyalty he had been violently attacked & ill treated, to this an evasive answer was received.

(29).

A Boston Gazette dated July, 1774, by which it appears that the Americans Considered him as an Enemy & treated him very ill, the particulars of which are recited. A Certificate from Sir Wm. Howe speaking highly of Mr. Green's Character, Loyally & Property from report dated in 1782. A Commission from Sir Wm Howe in 1775 by which Mr. Green is appointed Capt. of an Associated Company of Loyalists & orders of the same date to take charge of a certain district & to order Arms, &c., &c.

Certificates from Gen. Gage, Govr. Wentworth, &c., to the Loyalty & services of Gen. Green. Certificate from Lt. Col. Hamilton who Commanded the 59th Regt. at Boston in 1774 & 1775 to Mr. Green's good behaviour with the Army last War.

From the Commander in Chief in Nova Scotia in 1776 that Mr. Green was appointed a Magistrate in 1776.

Proclamation by Gr. Tryon in 1778 by which Letters of Marque were granted to Loyal Subjects. Certificate from Govr. Franklyn to Zealous & Active Loyalty. Col. Balfour & Mr. Fisher to the same purpose.

He never received any pay or advantage during the Rebellion.

He fitted out a Vessel in 1778 which was of great use to the Army by giving material intelligence of the French fleet.

Mr. Green received £100 pr. an. from the Treasury from 1780 which was afterwards increased by Messrs. Wilmot & Coke to £150 on acct. of his Loyalty & Services.

His Property has been Confiscated & his name is in several Acts.

(30)

House, Lands, &c., in Pomfret, Connecticut. He bought this of Abel Clark. Produces a Conveyance from Abel Clark to Eliza, his Wife, for £300 Lawful money. He believes there were 10 or 12 acres, Bought of Josiah Warner in December, 1772. Consideration in the deed £52.2 sh. Lawful. It Contained 30 acres or there about, he laid out nothing on it & believes it was a Lott of Woodland.

Lands in Heborn. Taken under an Execution in 1772, the owner was indebted to him in the sum of £100, the Land. 26 acres, was set off to pay his debt & Conveyed to him by the Sheriff, the Debt & Costs was £103.12.10, this was uncultivated & is in the hands of Mr. Huntingdon, late President of Congress, who was his Atty. in that Country. A Letter read from Mr. Peters in which the whole matter is recited.

Lands in Great Barrington bought in 1773 of John Harvey, the Consideration in £50 Cury., it is Cultivated.

Lands in Parrys Town, New Hampshire, among several Proprietors share 300 acres or there about. Produces a Deed of Exchange with his Br. It seems to have been done for their mutual Convenience. It is not Cultivated, but he thinks it more valuable on that acct. He values this Lot at 40 sh. pr. acre, the Lands he gave in Exchange were worth £300, they Lay near Halifax, they were uncultivated, but part was salt meadow.

Lands in Stevens Town, New Hamps.

These were left to him by his uncle, he produces a Copy of the Will, 240 acres, these are likewise part of an original proprietors right & are under the same advantageous Circumstances. The Copy of the Will is not an authentic one, but he swears he was entitled to this under his uncle's Will & that he had been in Possession from the time he was 7 years old. He values the lands at 40 Sh. pr. acre. (31).

Lands near Pessody's River, 2032 acres with a Public road through it as per Grant under the Seal of the Province of New Hamps., signed by Govr. Wentworth in 1774, this was given as share as Lt. last War. The Condition was 1st to make a road thro' it, which has been done & Cost him £30. Had no limit to settle. Values this at 20 Sh. pr. acre.

He had Pew in the Church in Brattle Street, Boston, he paid £44 for it & layed out £20. March 3.

Mr. Green Produces letters from N. Hamps. in which it is said that the great part of his property is not sold & expressing a distant hope that it may be restored.

Personal Property—He had a Ship Building at Wells to the East ward of Portsmouth, the person who was building the Ship owed him £620 & he agreed to take the Ship for the debt. After he came away he understood that his Atty. took the ship in the state she was in for the debt, by which Compromise he lost £400. The person who was building the ship was not a Loyalist.

His Agent made the Compromise without his Consent, this is included in his list of debts.

Furniture lost at Boston to the amount of £100. (32).

Claims Debts to the amount of £5464.14.9, but his Agent has received some & he cannot say but he may have received more.

He owes £1000 Currency to different persons in America. Produces a Bond to show that he owes £2000 to Messrs. Lane & Fraser & about £1400 to the Widow of Mr. Hayley, for which he has given & is liable.

He claims £4099.8.5 for his share of the Ship Tryon, he had one third of that Ship. She was Worth £8000 & in her different Cruizes she did great service to Govnt., he swears he was half owner of her.

He has served as a Volunteer upon many occasions & has served this Country with his Pen as well as with his Person.

These two Circumstances are not mentioned in the Memorial

REVD. MR. PETERS:

He knew Mr. Green in 1774. He says he sold the land by Execution but never got the money, the reason assigned was that he had signed an address to Govr. Hutchinson. They seized Mr. Green & treated him very ill. He had a Conversation afterwards with the Rebel Governor who said they had treated him very properly, this violence prevented his receiving the £100, so that he lost from his attachment to this Country.

He found him a Loyalist & an out Law when he came to Boston the Septr. following. He knows nothing of his Lands, the note was for £100 & there was Interest due.

(33). When the Witness was at Boston, which was only for three weeks, Mr. Green was very active. He believes he was in the Association & in the Militia, has heard that the House in which Mr. Green was a Partner was in great business & good Credit.

Decision—

The Board is of opinion that the Claimant, Francis Green, Esq., is a Loyalist.

Lands near Pebody's River, New Hamps., allow Expense of making a road & of a Grant, £40.

An Allowance from the Treasry of £150 pr. an.

1784.
6th March.

1157. Case THOMAS ROGERS.

Is a native of Ireland. He went in 1772 to Maryland, in 1774 he went to South Carolina & was settled at the Commencement of the troubles in Craven County. He carried out £150 in Linin Cloth. He took arms in 1775. Majesty he associated under Colonel Fletcher with many other Loyalists soon after they fought the Rebels at Ninety Six. He was taken prisoner at Lindley Fort, in 1776. He was brought to tryal in the fall of this year & sentenced to death. Two or three men hanged, he was reprived. He (34). never took the oath, but went & lived with his Brother & remained quiet until Charlestown was taken, when he joined Major Ferguson. He remained in his Majesty's service until 1781, when he came home. He never was more than Sergt. in the army & never received any pay. He has £20 pr. an. from the Treasury.

His certificates are all at the Treasury. He has Witnesses to speak for his Loyalty.

300 acres North side of Tyger River, Ninety Six district. He has no papers or deeds. He was pludered of them all. He bought these Lands of Andrew Thomson in 1774 & gave 17Sh, Stg. pr. acre for it, part in cash part in cattle, £22 in money & 7 cattle. He had not time to cultivate any part of it.

150 acres on Jennings Creek, Ninety Six District. He bought these in 1776 from Enoch Loyd. He gave 20sh, pr. acre Vir. curcy.

---

for it, but had only paid 18gs. A Horse worth £120 currency. 3 Cows & Calves. 18 or 20 acres were cultivated. The Rebels have it in Possession, but cannot say it is sold or not. One Alexander lived upon this.

He had Two Horses, they were taken soon after Col. Fergusons defeat. He had three mares, 25 Cows & heifers, 4 fat Hogs, 4 sheep, 4 Lambs, a Rifle gun & Pouch, wearing apparell value £12 & a Loom.
States debts to the amount of £10 & only owed six dollars.

COLONEL GIBBS.

Has known Thos. Rogers since 1774. He then lived at Ninety Six district. He thinks he had been a very true Loyalist as far as his understanding goes. He first took up arms with Col. Gibbs & persevered with him the whole war. He was in many actions & was an excellent soldier. He has heard that he was taken Prisoner. He understood that he bought a Plantation from And. Thomson, it was within 4 miles of Mr. Gibbs mother, it was good Land, but uncultivated. He thinks in 1774 these lands would have sold for 15sh. pr. acre. He believes Mr. Rogers to be a very honest man. He knows 150 acres he possessed before the War. Thinks it worth 15sh. pr. acre. Does not know that it is confiscated, but is satisfied he can never retain it. He had some horses & Cattle but cannot say the number, he thinks in 1774 he might be worth £3 or 400 Stg.

(35).

SAML. GREATOREX.

He knew the Claimant in 1780. He had seen him before, but did not know him until 1780. He knows him to be well attached to the british Govert. He has. been in several actions with him when Rogers behaved very well. He knows nothing of his Property, but of one horse. He has often heard in America that he had two Plantations & some stock. He thinks the horse was worth £15.5. He did not know that he lost this horse, only that he had him.

The Claimant Thos. Rogers called in, he adheres to the 17sh being Sterling.

Decision.

The Board are of the opinion that the Claimant is a zealous & active Loyalist.

300 acres on the North side of Tyger, they value at £50.
150 acres on Jemms Creek, they value at £40.
Personal Property at £60.
States debts due him in America £40.
He has an allowance of £20 pr. an.

(36).

1158. Case ALEXR. STENHOUSE.

1784, 6th March

Dr. Stenhouse went from Scotland to America in 1736 & settled on his own acct. in 1759, in 1764 he came to the Town of Baltimore & remained there until 1776, when he practiced Physick. He always supported the King's cause. He could not take one active part being so much engaged in business. He was called upon by the Rebels to take arms & desired by his Customers to take their part, but constantly refused, by which conduct he was

deprived of the exercise of his Profession & treated with contempt by his former friends. In April 1776 he left Baltimore & went to Philadelphia with a view to go to New York, but not being able to get there, he came in a Vessel to Lisbon & Landed in Engd. in July, 1776. He never was Imprisoned. He lost some Property but makes no claim for it, but is advised by the board to make a claim for all his Losses, not being prepared with an acct. of these Losses he is indulged with a future hearing.

1784.
8th March.

1159. Case THOS. MILLER.

(37).

He is a native of New Jersey. In the summer 1775 when resident at New York as a mercht. he was called upon to sign the association & being apprehensive of experiencing similar ill treatmeant with others, he returned to Long Island & exerted himself in influencing the Country to his Majesty's service & succeeded in getting material intelligence & supplys of Provisions to the King's Troops & ships. In July 1776 the committee received accts. by some Deserters of the Claimts. zealous attachment to the British Govert. He was proscribed & advertised, he says upon his getting one of the advertisements he thought it prudent to conceal himself in Queens County until the arrival of Gen. Howe. In August Gen. Howe appointed him to conduct the Two Brigades under Major Gen. Grant, in Oct. following his health grew very bad & he came to Engd. He returned in Decmr. 1777 to Long Island, when he was appointed by Gen. Tryon to settle the disputes among

the Refugees who were put on Rebel Estates & the familys which were left behind. He came to Engd. in 1780 & was allowed £80 pr. an.

Certificates to Loyalty & Exertions in favour of Gt. Britain from Govr. Tryon & Major Gen. Grant.

(38).

Property—Quarter Part of a House in New Brunswick, Mr. Kemble, Mr. Evans & Mr. French had the other part. He says that all his Books & papers were destroied by the New England Soldiers who made a Barrack of his house. This Property was purchased of a Mr. Lyne about the year 1764 for £250 N.Y. Curcy. They added Buildings which cost £500 N.Y. Curcy. It was a lease about 60 years to run, when the claimt. quitted the Country. He values his share at £150 Curcy. It was rented at £47 pr. an. He estimated the value in the rent & Interest on the money at 7 pr. cent.

Six rights of Land in the Township of Milton, taken up under the Province of New Hamps. in 1763. Say they were originally granted by Gov. Wentworth to upwards of 70 persons. This is now part of Vermont. The rights which fell to the Claimt. were about 330 acres. Produces an Authentic Copy for the Receipt for the said Lands from Messrs. Franklyn & Underhill. Until 1776 no improvements were made. When about 40 acres of meadow were cleared by some German families who had settled there without leave in 1768. He gave a Lease to three of these Germans, of the whole 6 tracts for 12 or 15 years. He says the expenses of surveying, &c., amounted to £200 Curcy. They were to allow him no rent.

He values the 1980 acres at 20Sh. pr. acre. Says he has desired his Br. who now lives in New York to claim these rights of the State of Vermont.

One 8th part of 17280 acres in W. Florida now in the Possession of the Spaniards valued at £252 Stg.

1000 acres on the River Mobile now by the treaty in the Province of Georgia, valued at £1800 Stg.

200 acres at £5 pr. acre. 800 at 20Sh. pr. acre.

Claims £63 Curcy for Negroe hire, horse hire & boat hire in the service of Govt. in 1775 & 1776.

Book debts to the amount of £4570 Curcy. (39).

He owed £6 or 800 S. at New York.

JOHN BLACKBURN mercht. in London.

Was acquainted with the Claimt. some years ago in London. He knew him in 1768 & 1774, when he commanded a mercht. ship & was always consigned to his care. The claimt. went out to New York with Gen. Tryon in 1775, with the intention of fixing there. He kept a store there during the time he traded to London.

Knows nothing of his Landed Property.

WM. DAVIS.

Has known Mr. Millar upwards of 20 years, both as a mercht. & Master of a Ship. He kept a store in 1762 or 1763. He came to Engd. & went out with Gen. Tryon. He believes that he was always much attached to the cause of Gt. Britian. Knows nothing of his Landed Property only has heard that he had some in Florida.

THE REVD. SAML. SEABURY.

Speaks to the six rights Land. Does not know how the Claimant came possessed of them. He has known Mr. Millar 30 years, always considered him to be a staunch Loyalist.

LT. COL. WM. JOHNSON.

He knew the Claimt. in 1768 or 69. Says that he was posseessed of Lands in the River Mobile, but cannot speak to particulars. The value of Land Consisted in their goodness & situation.

ED. BUSH WEGG, Esq.

Knew the claimt. in 1764. He heard of his buying a 6th or 8th of a large tract in W. Florida. (40).

ROBERT FARMER.

Resided in 1779 & 80 on the Claimts. Plantation in W. Florida says there was 1000 acres, it is now by the Treaty in Georgia. There were 400 acres cleared, which he values at £5 S. pr. acre. 600 acres uncultivated, he values at 20sh. pr. acre.

THOS. MILLER.

Says he has heard of the $\frac{1}{4}$ part of the house being Confiscated.

SAM'L. KIMBLE.

Had a fourth share of the House it was bought in 1763 & cost £200 curcy.

Decision.

The Board are of the opinion that the Claimt. Thos. Millar is a Zealous & active Loyalist & rendered services to Govnt.

He was possessed of ¼ share of a House in New Brunswick which they value at £84.10sh.

He has an allowance of £80 pr. an. from Treasury.

1st November. 1786.

Six in Miltown Township, disallowed as it appears within the state of Vermont.

States Debts to the amount of £4570 curcy.

He owed £600 or £800 S. at New York.

1784. 8th March.

1160. Case ROBT. COOPER.

Is a native of America. He was born in Prince Fredk. Parish, George Town, South Carolina in 1775. He was at School in 1777.

(41).

He came into the Possession of a Property by the Death of his Father who died in 1774. In 1779 he went to the House of a Loyalist, Mr. Coulson in N. Carolina. He left his own Plantation to avoid doing duty with the Americans. Says he was under the necessity of serving with them for 2 months out of fear. They never desired him to take the oath, in June 1780, he joined a detachment under Major McArthur at the Cherans & Continued to serve as a Militiaman until the Evacuation of Charlestown. He served as Clerk in the Engineers Department for 10 months. He produces a Certificate of this from Col. Monereof.

Certificates also to his Loyalty from Ld. Cornwallis, Col. Gibbs, &c.

Property—

550 acres of Land on Blackennings Swamp, they were left to him by his father in 1774. He believes his father purchased the Plantation, but does not know what he gave for it. Says his Brother is in America & lives on a Plantation, left to him by his Father. Says his Brother was a Rebel. He values the 550 acres at 25sh. pr. acre. There were about 40 acres Cultivatd. He was offered 4 Negroes for it in 1779. The Negroes were worth £40 or 50 pr. Head.

He had 32 Head of Cattle on his Plantation, which he valued at £3 pr. head.

45 Head Hogs, he values at 45sh. each.

(42).

2 Negroes, one he hired to a man when he quitted his Plantation, the other came to him at Charlestown in 1781 & he hired him for 9d. pr. diem, to the Engineers Depart. He says he lost him, he believes he went to the Rebels.

COL. GIBBS.

Knew Mr. Cooper in 1781 at Charlestown. He was then in the Engineers Department & had negroes under his care. Says he has heard the Claimt. say that he had been with the Americans before the British took Charlestown.

Imagines that he had been in action agst. the British. He had a sister married to Mr. Coulson a Loyalist in N. Car. Colonel Gibbs thinks he advised to leave the Americans & to join the British.

He says the Claimts. Father died in 1782. He saw a copy of his will in the office at C. Town in 1782, by which the Claimt. was left 550 acres of Land Black. Swamp besides some Stock

for his Life, does not know the land but has heard in England that there were Indigo Valts on it.

He knows that the Claimt. had Negroes at Charlestown. Has known him have 8 exclusive of one seduced from him in Charlestown by a Rebel. Says he thinks the Claimt. has not valued his Lands so high as he ought. Lands in that situation were worth 40sh. pr. acre. Does not know that the Claimts. Property has been Confiscated, he believes not.

COL. FORTUNE.

Has known Mr. Cooper since 1781. At the Congress at the time he was a Volunteer with the British Troops. He understood at that time that he was a young man who had a Property at G. Town. He also knew him at Charlestown, when he served as an overseer in the Engineers Department. Since he came to Engd. he has heard of the Claimts. having served with the Rebels. He says the Claimt's Brother was a Rebel & pressed him to return, but he refused. Says that he believes that the Claimt. during the time that he was with the British Troops, was well attached to the cause of Great Britian. He has heard Col. Gibbs say that he had not half valued his Lands. Believes when he was with the Americans he served in his Brothers Company. (43).

ANDREW DEVAUX.

Knew the Claimt. in 1781 & had heard of his serving with the British before he came to Charlestown. He never heard the

Claimt. say that he served with the Rebels.

He heard that his Father left him a Tract of Land some Cattle & some Hogs.

He was on the Plantation in 1781, their were Indigo Valts on it. It was not then Confiscated.

Decision.

The Claimt. is a Loyalist.

He was possessed of 550 acres of Land value £450. 38 Head of Cattle £38. A Negroe £45.

1161. Case GRAY HARRISON, Esq.   1784, 9th March.

One of his Majestys Council & late Treasurer of the Province of Massachusetts Bay. (44).

Is a Native of Boston & has lived there most part of his Life. He was a Mercht. there many years ago. Has been Treasurer of the Province since 1753. As soon as the Tea was destroyed he endeavoured to prevail on the People to make Compensation for it. When Gen. Gage arrived he accepted of the office of one of the New Council, this was in 1774. He staid at Boston in the Executive of his business, until Gen. Howe quitted it. Went to Halifax & from thence to Engd. in 1776. In the latter end of 1774 he published a Pamphlet entitled "the Two Congress's Cut up."

Property—

Three Houses in Cornhill, Boston. He bought them of Charles Kelly in 1764, produces the Deed. Consideration £1016, besides

---

the sum of £600 due to him. He laid out about £150 on these houses. Produces his books by which it appears that he pd. in the year 1765 £1533.14 for these houses. Produces a Certificate of the sale of these houses in 1779 for £35.600 Currency, which he Estimates at £2000, he would not have taken that for them. They were worth £2000 before the troubles. He let them for £112. S. pr. an. He says he thinks them well worth £2000 Stg. before the troubles.

(45).

Three Houses in Boston which he was put into legal Possession of by Judgement of Court, which he recovered agst. John Hancock, Esq. Hancock has since been put into Possession by an act of the Province. Hancock owed him £956.16. He values the houses at £1875 Stg.

10th March.

Two Houses in Westerly street. Produces the Conveyance, dated 1st Jany. 1757. Whereby John Adam as administer for Jacob Parker conveys to Mr. Gray in consider of £333.6.8. Lawful a Messuage & Tenement in the West part of Boston in Fee. This Tenement was divided into two Lotts which he let for 40 Sh. pr. acre in 1763. He laid out £50 curcy & mon. He values the two Tenements at £600 curcy. They were worth that sum in 1774 These Houses are now in the Possession of his Son in Law. Who writes him that they may be sold & therefore desires to have a deed for them. Says that he Americans found his Will by which he had devised the houses to Eliz his Daughter & wife of Saml. Allen Otis for Life & his children. They have therefore permitted

---

Mr. Otis to remain in it, but he writes that he apprehends it will be sold. Mr. Otis has taken part with the Americans & does not doubt his keeping Possession of the Houses, he therefore does not claim them as a Loss.

(46).

A Tract of Land in Colchester. Produces the Deed from John Denny in Consider of £100 Lawful money, dated July, 1766, 23 acres, with buildings, he does not know if there was any cultivation or what buildings. He says the hurry of his public business did not allow him to attend to private concerns. He values them at £75 Stg. the money he gave.

500 acres good land in Hamps. He came possessed of them in 1770. A mortgage Bond, Princp. & Interest Assigned to him by Rich. Grindley. He received judgement on it & was put in Possession of the Land. Produces his book by which it appears he pd. that sum for it. He never received any benefit, nor does

he know that any part of the tract was cultivated. He was offered £400 Curcy. for it. In 1774 he would not have taken less than £400 Stg.

By an act of New Hamp. in 1782 the Estates of all those who had joined the British are confiscated.

A Right & Share of land in New Boston Conveyance, 2nd June 1767 from Wm. Story. Consider £40 Lawful. He believes it contained 300 acres, does not know if any part was cultivated, it is valued at £30 Stg. He makes a claim for 8 years rent of his

House at £232.10 Stg. pr. an. £1860.
Office of Treasurer & Receiver worth pr. an.

Treasurer	£200
Extraordinaries	150
House & Carts	50
Advantage on cash in hand	100
	£500

Furniture Lost. £75.
Horse £40. Chaise £35.
Seven 9 pounders, 4 three pounders, he values them at £207.
States Debts, Princip. & Interest £2336.8.3.
He owes nothing in America. No Incumbrance on his Estate. (47).
He receives £200 pr. an. from 1776. He had £200 given in advance on his arrival in July 1776.

COL. JOHN CHANDLER.

He first knew the Claimt. in 1752. Always esteemed him a Loyalist. He never heard any circumstance in his conduct to be of a different opinion. He was very zealous in endeavouring to prevail in the Public to pay for the Tea. Speaks of the Pamphlet Mr. Gray published. On every occasion he showed great attachment to Great Britain. The office ot Treasurer he thinks was worth annual allowance £200 Curcy. to £250. Extras £100 to £150. House & firing £66. Advantage by money £600 pr. an. He cannot speak with cirtainty of Mr. Grays Property.

COL. WILLARD.

He knows the Brick houses in Cornhill. They were reputed to be Mr. Grays, cannot value them. Knew the 500 acres in Peterborough. They were uncultivated & there were no buildings on the tract. The neighbourhood has well improved. He values them at 20 Sh. pr. acre one with another. It was good land close to the Town.

He sold lands for Mr. Flucker, Mr. Oliver & Mr. Brown, contiguous to Mr. Grays at 20 Sh. pr. acre. He sold them in Lots of 100 acres. He thinks he could have sold the 500 acres in one Lot for £500 Stg. Mr. Gray did not wish to sell this Tract. He (48) has sold land in this district at 40 Sh. pr. acre, the value raised by situation.

WM. PERRY, late a Mercht. in Boston.

He went in 1774 with Mr. Grass Son to view the 500 acres, the son took Possession of them for his father, it was a valuable

77 AR.

tract. He knew Mr. Gray had houses in Boston, but can't value them. He says some of the Lands was Cultivated, some reason.

1784.
11th March.

1162. Case SAMUEL GREATOREX.

He is a native of England, went to America in 1769, he settled in Rockingham County in 1770 & remained there until the Rebellion. He kept a Store.

In 1775 he was one of 400 Who Associated & Mr. John Davis was appointed to Command them. He Continued with them until

1780, during which time they were Emploied. but one of their number having informed on Col. Smith, of the Americans, that they had associated for the defence of the british Govert. Eleven of them were taken up, 4 were hanged in Oct., 1780. He had information that the Rebel Constable had orders to take him up, upon which he fled to 96 S. Car. He had been three times examined by Col. Smith before the Association was known of. He says he is sure he would have been hanged had he not made his escape. He joined Col. Tarleton, 1st Jany., 1781.

Was with the Kings Troops a fortnight after the Battle of Cowpers. Served with a great number of Loyalists. He joined Ld. Cornwallis the next day. He was at the Battle of Guildford & was frequently emploied by Ld. Cornwallis as a spy & to carry despatches. After Guildford he & a Mr. Lancaster carried Ld. Cornwallis Despatches to Ld. Rawden at Camden, they were afterwards sent by Ld. Rawden to Col. Balfour at Charlestown with dispatches, he remained at C. Town until the Evacuation.

Certificates from Ld. Rawden, Ld. Cornwallis & Col. Conger. to Loyalty.

He was Waggon master to the Barracks. Majr. Gens. department for 3 months & received a dollar pr. day. He & a Mr. Sharpless carried out to America £500 worth of goods. Mr. Sharpless died & left him the share of goods.

Property—

400 acres of Land on the Potomack, he gave deer skins for them in 1778, to the value of 10sh. pr. acre, if he had paid for the Land in money he could not have got it for less than 9sh. pr. acre. 50 acres were cleared, he cleared 5 acres himself.

There were two small houses on it, he built a store, which with the clearing the 5 acres cost him £10 Virg. Curcy. Values them at 10sh. pr. acre.

600 Deer Skins, swears they cost him 7sh. 6d. to 8sh. each.
200 Fur Skins, he values at 3sh. each.
A ton of Butter & a great many other articles an acct. given in amting to £1230.11.9 Stg. Exclusive of the 400 acres of Land.

He has £30 pr. an. from the Treasury from Mid Summer 1783. Does not know if his Property is Confiscated.

JOHN OLIVE.

Is an Englishman, he lived in Fredtown as a servt. to Mr. Smith in 1779 & 80. Greatorex bought deer Skins, Butter & Cheese to sell again.

77a AR

COLONEL FORTUNE.

Knew Claimt. in S. Carolina in summer 1781. He was an Assistant to Mr. Lancaster the Waggon Master. He knew that he had Rum, Sugar & money about him. He came to C. Town after the battle of Guilford. He had a Crop of Corn on Jas Island at the Evacuation. Thinks the Crop & Stock on Jas Island was worth £600, but he had a Partner Dill a great Rebel who held half the Concern.

In Midsummer last he applied to Col. Fortune to draw out his Memorial. He drew out the original from his own mouth, he then told him there were 600 Deer Skins, but nothing passed as to the value more than as those Skins vary in price, they were charged in the rough at £150. Don't recollect them to have heard that they were Patron Skins. He didn't recollect what the Claimt. said to him about the Loss of Money. He had the Original Schedule of the Claimts. Losses before him when he drew out the Memr. Don't recollect anything being said of Debts. (51).

He was applied to by the Claimt. in Oct. to draw out the second Memr. & Schedule the original one was left with him at that time.

Mr. Greatrex named the prices to the several articles as the Witness wrote them down. When they spoke of the Deer Skins the Claimt. said he had 600 Patton Deer about 10sh. each. Thinks he made some observation of the value being put down in the former Schedule at £150 & at £300 in the latter. Recollects that the whole of the charge in the first Schedule was £1400. Something passed about the Depreciation of money, but don't recollect if anything passed as to Debts, don't recollect if they were included at that time.

John Martin was at the Claimts. House in 1776, on Potomack March 22. River. He believed he had been some years there in Possession. He says the Claimt. kept several Pack horses.

Decision.
The Board are of the opinion that the Claimt. Samuel Greatorex is a Zealous & active Loyalist.
Allow him £500 for Deer Skins & Stores.
He has an allowance of £30 pr. an.

1163. Case JOHN BROOKS. 1784. March 15th.

Is a native of England. He went to Quebec in 1774 as a private Agent to Govr. Skim, who was then in England, but he had a large Landed Property in the Province of New York, at a Place called Skimborough. He arrived there in June or July 1774 & continued in the Execution of his business until May 1775. Says (52). that the Gover. Sen., Major Skim lived in the house with him. That he had frequently declared his disapprobation of the measure carrying on to a Mr. Danl. Tucker, who used to assist at the house & who he has reason to think was a spy.

On the 8th of May, he & the Major were taken Prisoners by a Party of Americans from New England, also the grs. Two Daughters & their aunt. The Ladies were Conducted to Salisbury, New England about 100 miles from Skimsborough, when they were left under the care of a Genl. & the Claimt. was carried to Hartford, New England. He remained there on Parole with the Major about a fortnight, When he went to Salisbury & had leave to return with the Ladies to S. borough under the care of Two American officers, A Capt. Biddle & Sheriden. Remained there until Sept., 1775, during which time he was under constant apprehension from the dislike the people had to him & was obliged to go to Philadelphia and apply to Mr. Jay to get some order from Congress to prevent his being any more molested, but notwithstanding this he still continued to be insulted & then from Skimborough he went in quest of intelligence to Albany then went to Philadelphia & formed a friendly connxion with a Dr. Kearsley a Zealous Loyalist. He was taken Prisonr. in Philadelphia, 8th Oct. 1775, in consequence of he & Dr. Kearsley being suspected of giving information. Committed to Lancaster Gaol & kept there 725 days. Dr. Kearsley was also taken up & kept much longer in Gaol. This gent. died at Carlisle the day after he was permitted to come out on acct. of his ill state of health. The Claimt. made his escape 3rd. Oct. 1777. Says that during his Confinement he was treated in a most rigorous manner, not suffered the use of Pen Ink or Paper or to have conversation with any person whatever. After making his escape he went to Philadelphia then in Possession of the British & presented himself to Sir Wm. Howe, who after hearing his story asked him if he would raise a Compy., when he said he could not for want of money, Sir Wm. Howe then ordered him to be paid 10gs. He staid at Philadelphia till the 10th Decr., when he ob-

(53).

tained Sir Wm. Howes pass to go to New York. He got to New York 22nd Decmr., when on his arrival he found himself in great distress, but fortunately he secured great assistance from a Mr. Chamin the Commissary who knew his family & connections. 3rd May 1778 he got a Wart. as Capt. from Col. Emerick at N. York to raise his 2nd Troop of Light Dragoons & went to Philadelphia to Recruit, he got 14 men, but the Evacuation happening at that time, he returned with the army to New York, after having put his men on board a Transport on his arrival at New York to the Agent, when he raised 5 more. Says he did not receive anything for raising those men. Remained in an inactive state till the 20th, Novr., 1778, when he came to Engd. He received as Capt. Pay £9.7sh. Stg., it was only two months Pay & that he did not receive more as the Troop was not completed. He arrived in London, Feby., 1779, and presented a Memr. to the Treasury stating his sufferings. He obtained a letter from Mr. Robinson to the Commander in Chief, New York. The Treasury ordered him £50 for Passage Money, Septr. on applying for a greater assistance he got a Hundred more in Aug., 1780 & then went to New York in June 1781. He delivered the letter to Sir Hy. Clinton. Says he was detained from Sept. 1779 to Aug. 1780 soliciting the additional sum of £100 the 1st £50 not being enough to pay his debts. The

(54).

Letter from the Treasury which he took out was to recommend him to a Command in the army or in the Provincial Troops.

He did not succeed in this, but was appointed to receive 5sh. pr. diem from 25 July 1781 on the Refuges List, which he received till Decmr. 1782. When he embarked for England & had six months paid in advance.

Property—

Says he Lost Cloths & other articles as stated in his Schedule to the amount of £114.7.5. They were taken from him by the Rebels at Skimsborough. Was appointed D. Inspector of the Woods by Gen Skim the end of 1774. Understood he was to have received £100 pr. an. Was only six months in the employ.

States Losses £553.15.6 for sundry sums has drew on Persons while in Confinement & for his support from Decmr. 1777 to Decmr 1783 it cost £200 Stg.

(55).

GOVR. FRANKLYN. 16th March.

He knew the Claimt. in 1778, brought the Witness a letter from Gen. Skene, recommending the Claimt. to him as a Loyalist & as a man who had suffered in the Kings cause for any assistance he might stand in need of. The Witness recommended him to Sir Hy. Clinton. He does not know whether Sir Hy. did anything for him. He soon came to England. Govr. Franklyn says that the Claimt. carried out with him a letter of recommendation from the Treasury to Sir Hy. & had 5Sh. a day as a Loyalist. Does not know how long he received the allowance.

JOSEPH GALLOWAY.

Was not acquainted with the Claimt. till after he got out of Gaol in 1778. Heard of his being concerned with Dr. Kearsley in writing letters respecting the state of the Country to persons in England. Believes him to be an exceeding zealous Loyalist. Says that in 1778 or 1779 the Claimt. applied to him for a recommendation to Ld. North & thinks he received £150 on assurance that he would not more be troublesome to Govert., but then Mr. Galloway observes he expected to be provided for in the Military Line, in consequence of the Letter to Sir Hy. Clinton & which he did not succeed in.

ANDR. ALLAN, Esq. late Attoy. Gen. of Pensilvania & member of the Committee of Safety.

(56).

Says he never knew the Claimt. till he was apprehended in 1775 by a sett of People called the Committee of inspection of Correspondence and fearing that he might from the enraged State of the mob, be very illtreated he the Witness got him brought before the Committee of Safety to be examined & then by the resentment of the multitude was lessened. Says that Mr. Brooks was apprehended on acct. of his being concerned with others in holding a Correspondence with the People in England. Says that he is satisfied that Mr. Brooks was committed for his Loyalty to his King, that he was confined at Lancaster & is satisfied that he must

have suffered a great deal of hard usage during his confinement.
Thinks he might have been Confined upwards of two years.

MILES SNOWDEN.

He has known Mr. Brooks since 1775. Knew him at Philadelphia for a month, he was an Agent to Govr. Gen. Skene. Says he was apprehended in consequence of some letters which were given to the Witness, addressed to Mrs. McCawley which enclosed others for Mr. Charles Jenkinson. Knows they were for him & their being put under cover to Mrs. McCawley was to prevent suspicion. Says the Claimt. was very long confined & has heard of his being very ill-treated & suffering very hard usage in Gaol.

(57).

GOVR. SKENE, late Gr. of Teconderago.

Says that in 1774 he agreed with Mr. Brooks of whom he had heard a very good character to take care of his Lands in America. Having got the appointmt. of Inspector of all Lands not Private Property within the Province of Quebec, as also of the Woods in 1764. Appointed Mr. Brooks his Deputy & meant to have allowed him £100 pr. an., as his Private Agent & Deputy Inspector. Thinks he would have well deserved £50 pr. an. as to Inspection. He speaks very highly of Mr. Brook's great zeal & attachment to the cause of Great Britain. He gave his promise to Mr. Brooks to appoint him Deputy-Inspector before he left England. The troubles prevented his giving Mr. Brooks a formall deputation Govr. Skene speaks very highly of Mr. B.'s Loyalty.

It was some time in 1774 that Mr. Brooks was settled in the

Witness's Estate; in July, 1775, when Govr. Skene was a Prisr. Mr. Brooks at the risk of his life went to him to give an acct. of the Govrs. Daughters & family which had been driven from his House & offered his assistance to him. Says that at his desire Mr. Brooks emploied himself in procuring Information which he knows he transmitted to Sir Wm. Howe & Gen. Gage. Knows of his being taken up at Phila. on acct. of his being concerned with Dr. Kennedy in transmitting intelligence from Philadelphia. Says
(58). that it was at his desire Mr. Brooks went to Phila. Can't speak particularly to Loss of Property, but was very well supplied with Cloths and used to dress genteely.

G. MCKAGE.

Knew the Claimt. in 1777 in Lancaster Gaol. Was in goal with him all the time which was 7 months. Says he heard the Goaler say something about the Claimt. being confined for taking part with the British. Never had an opportunity of speaking to him because he says Mr. Brooks was closely confined.

Decision.

The Board are of the opinion that the Claimt. John Brooks was an active & Zealous Loyalist & Suffered two years imprisonment thereby. Lost Clothes & other articles value £100.

Has received £150 from the Treasury & 5sh. pr. diem allowance as a Refugee at New York from 25th 1781 until June 1784, besides Capts. half pay to the amount of £9.7.

1164. Case GEORGE THOMPSON.

1784.
March 16th

He is a native of Scotland. He went to Charlestown in 1772. Was there in 1775 as a Mercht. Was desired to sign the Association but refused doing it so they left him quiet until 1777. Says that a man of his name having signed the Association, he in order to avoid the better getting clear of the Americans when they pressed him to sign the Association pointed out his namesakes name by which means he avoided signing it. Afterwards when pressed to take the oaths he positively refused & told them he would rather lose his life than do so. Went from C. Town to Cape Francois & from thence to Jamaica. Came to Engd. Octr., 1777.

(59).

Received £100 pr. an., till he went out in 1780 to Charles-Town to December 1782, when it was evacuated. Came to Engd. in Jany. 1(83, and is allowed £50 pr. an. by the Treasury.

Certificates from Ld. Wm. Campbell & Col. Balfour to Loyalty.

Property.
250 acres of Land in Craven County, purchased in June, 1775,

---

from Frances Comerelle for £130 Cur. But says the cost him £100 S. 15 acres Cleared. He never was upon them nor did he ever derive any benefit from them. Valeus them at £116 S.

1,000 acres bought of Wm. Miller. Produces Lease & release dated 29th Sep., 1774, whereby Wm. Miller in considr. of £700 Lawful sold Mr. Thompson this tract in Ninety Six & a Mr. Danl. Holmes lived on it. No advantage from it. There fifty acres Cleared but cannot value them, but says he has charged them in £300 Strg.

100 acres in Craven County. Produces Lease & release, dated 16th June, 1775, in consider of £100 Cury from Archd. Rich. Values this at £100 S. no Cultivation.

(60).

2,300 In S. Carl. 4 Grants in £1774 & 1775. No Cultivation. Values them at 6sh. pr. acre, £69 S. Says they cost him about £100 S.

No Incumbrance nor no Debts which would affect the Lands. He believes all his Lands have been Confiscated.

In March 1777 when he came away he had Debts due to him to the amount of £161.6. Says that he had a Store which was pulled down by the Rebels, which cost £42 S. & that his expenses in removing from C. Town to Cape Francois & then to Jamaica & Engd. amounted to £431.11. Says that he had Debts due him when obliged to quit C. Town at the Evacuation £309.10.11. These were debts due by the Rebels.

Says he had also Debts due him in 1777 £3,000 S., besides the £161.9, but his Books were destroied. He cannot speak to the particulars.

DR. GARDEN.

Has known Mr. Thomson since 1774. Says that he was universally esteemed at C. Town & by his Conduct was very obnoxious to the Rebels. That he was distinguished by the name of a very principal Loyalist. That he was a shop keeper & dealt in the Grocery way.

THOS. HARPER.

(61)

Says he was very well acquainted with Mr. Thomson, does not recollect the time he left C. Town. That he was settled as a storekeeper and appeared to be in good business. Knows nothing of his Landed Property nor of the destruction of the store. Always understood that he quitted Charles Town on acct. of his Loyalty.

Decision.

The Board are of the opinion that the Claimt. Mr. Thomson is a Loyalist.

250 acres in Craven County, they allow him £20.

250 acres in Craven County they allow him £20, which appears to have been the cost in 1775.

1,000 acres in Ninety Six. Value £100, the cost in 1774.

100 acres in Craven County, £15.

2,300 acres in S. Car. Grants allow expenses £25.

Store pulled down £20.

Has an allowance of £50 pr. an. from Treasury. it was reduced from £100.

1784.
17th March

1165. Case REV. WM. EDMONSTON.

Is a native of England. Rector of the Parish of St. Thomas, Maryland, prior to the troubles. . Says on the first breaking out of the troubles, when subscriptions were made for collecting Arms & Ammunition early in 1774, he exhorted his Parishoners to Continue their allegiance to the British Govnt. & circulated Pamphlets among them which had been written for the purpose of shewing them the evil intended by those who prevented violent measures. In December 1774 he was brought before the Committee & charged with having in his. exhortations to the People told them that by taking the Oaths to the insurgents they were guilty of Treason agst. the King. Says they required him to sign a recantation of all he had said which he refused, but the paper being altered by some of his acquaintances prevented any ill usage by signing it in 1775.

(62).

When the Association Paper was going about a friend asked him if he meant to sign it, & if he did not that his House would be pulled down thereupon he left the place & his wife & family & embarked in Novr., 1775 in Engd.

Property.

500 or 600 acres in Cecil County. He had by his Father's Will in 1753, Copy produced. 250 acres Cleared. Values them at £1600 Strg. Would not have taken this sum for them before the troubles.

550 acres in Baltimore County, which he values at £1,100. This Property by an acct. of Assembly in 1782, which he produces was given to his Daughter the other to his Wife who are now in Possession. The last 550 acres he bought in 1772, pd. £1500 Cur. The improvemts. cost him £600 or 700 Curncy. He cannot return to America. He has no other Property to state.

His Negroes & other matters having by virtue of the Act of Assembly given to his Wife & Daughter.

Produces the Appointment of Rector. Says his living was worth Communibus Annis £300 Strg., exclusive of surplice fees which were £75 pr. an. The latter were always increasing.

GEO. CHALMERS.

Was well aquainted with Mr. Edmonston. Confirms his being Rector & says he was very active in persuading his Parishoners to remain quiet particularly agst. Associating & delivered his sentiments on some occasion from the Pulpit. He believes he went so far as to have refused administering the Sacrament to many who had taken part agst. us. He persevered in his Loyalty until he was obliged to leave the Province.

His Living was worth £300 pr. an. including Surplus fees.

ROBT. ALEXANDER.

Knew the Claimant. Confirms what he said respecting his being brought before the Committees. Was very much respected & speaks highly of his Loyalty.

The Living was worth £270 Strg. Surplus Fees £50. The Witness was a member of the Committee who examined him in Decmr. 1774.

DR. STONEHOUSE.

Was well acquainted with the Claimt. Has heard him go as far in the Pulpit as he could do to inculcate a Principle of Alleegance amongst his Parishoners. Knows he had Lands. He cannot speak to the value. Thinks the Living was worth £4 to 500 Cuy.

Decision.

The Board are of opinion that he is a Zealous Loyalist. His Property does not appear to be lost.

Has lost his Living worth £300 Strg. pr. an.   (64).

1166.   Case THOS. ALEXANDER.   1784. 19th March.

Was Born in Scotland. He went to Boston in 1761, followed the hoisery business. Kept a store in 1774. When the troubles broke out he was a Lt. in the Associated Company at Boston in Feby., 1775. At the Evacuation he went with the Compy to Halifax & from thence to N. York in Septr. 1776. At New York he traded & tho not of any Corps he frequently bore arms & was wounded at Brandy Wine. He was then with the Queen's Rangers. He came to England in 1778 returned in 1780, in Feby., 1781 went to Virginia & was appointed Harbour Master of Portsmouth & Norfolk by Gen. Leslie, Continued in this situation until the Ports assd. were evacuated by Gen. O'Hara.

Then went to Yorktown where he was appointed to his former station for York & Gloucester by Ld. Cornwallis. Was taken Prisoner with his Lordship. Was allowed 10sh pr. day for this office & was pd. up to the time of the surender.

He is allowed £50 pr. an. from the Treasury from 5th April, 1783.

Property.

Was possessed of a Store on the Long Warf, Boston, which he purchased of Capt. Green in 1771 for £150 Str. Laid out £5 in repairs. Says he could have sold it before the troubles for £300 Stg.

He left Stores behind him at Boston viz.

(65). Furniture, Salmon, Stocking Loom, Twisting loom, Rum, Sugar, etc. £219.10.6.

He prevaricates a good deal respecting the prices of the different articles. He charges the selling prices. States due him at Boston £135 S.

ALER. SELKIRK.

Has known the Claimt. 12 years. He was a Zealous Loyalist. He thinks his store was worth £100 Stg.

JOS. ROBERTS.

Knew Mr. Alexr. at Boston in 1775. He kept a store, does not know that it was his own. Heard at New York that he left a great deal of Property at Boston.

Decision.

The Board are of opinion that the Claimt. Thos. Alexander is a Loyalist & bore Arms. Allow Furniture & Merchdz, £120, State Debts to the Amount of £135.

Has an allowance from the Treasury of £50 pr. an.

1784.
March 20th.

1167. Case MRS. PENELOPE D' ENDI.

She is the Widow of Wm. Forsyth, a native of Scoland. Went to Norfolk 2 or 3 years before the troubles. She married in 1775 & her Husband kept a shoemaker's shop in 1775. her Husband joined no Association and quitted his residence when Ld. Dunmore & the troops left it. He continued with the Army until Aug., 1776, but did not bear arms on acct. of his bad state (66). of health, he died on his passage to the West Indies. She has no Children. She is a native of Virginia. Came to England two months ago from N. York. Her Husband's Property was on board a Schooner belonging to him, it was put in board when Ld. Dunmore came away & burnt she says by British Sailors.

Property—Says the sundry articles mentioned in her schedule amounting £675 Cury. are valued very moderately & is certain that her Husband Lost them.

ROBT. GILMORE.

Knew the Claimts. Husband William Forsyth and of his joining Lord Dunmore at the Commencnt. of the troubles, he was a Shoemaker at the time. Norfolk was fortified Mr. Forsyth assisted with other Loyal subjects, believes he was always well attached to the British Govnt. Says all his Furniture & some Leather was on Board a Schooner of his own. She was lost on Groyns Island, 50 miles from Norfolk. Says she lay on the shore

to be Greased & was burnt by Sir Ant. Hammond least the Americans should get her. The Schooner was about 70 Tons & he thinks worth £100 Stg., he cannot speak to the other Losses.

REVD. JOHN AGNEW:

Resides near Norfolk. Knew Mr. Forsyth for several years, says he was most sincerely attached to the British Govnt. He bore arms when Ld. Dunmore was in Possession of it, he continued with the fleeet some time. Says that he was in a bad state of health owing to his remaining some days in an open vessel into which he had put his Property. Confirms what Mr. Gilmore says about the loss of the Schooner, that he was in good business & had good furniture. Knows that he had a negro man & woman & says they were worth £130 Cury. & much more. He had two Houses he thinks worth £40, a Riding Chair £20, Leather & a number Pairs boots Worth 50 sh. or 65 a Piece, the other articles are reasonable.

(67).

CAPT. STAIR AGNEW:

Knew Mr. Forsyth at the Commencmt. of the troubles, that he was settled there & sold shoes, he was well attached to Gt. Britain, bore arms & quitted Norfolk with Ld. Dunmore. He died he believes on his Passage to the W. Indies. Was in bad state of health he believes from the hardships he underwent at Norfolk Constantly mounting guard.

Mr. Forsyth bought a Schooner in which he put all his Property & which was burnt at Groins Island, he believes to prevent her falling into the hands of the Enemy, the schooner had Salt, Leather & Furniture on board. Knows that the negro man was lost & as he thinks at the Great Bridge, he was put into the works by Ld. Dunmore. Knew the Negro Woman. She & the man were well worth £130 V.C., also that he had two horses, a riding chair & harness, he thinks they might be worth £50. Although he carried on Shoe Manafactory he lived like a Gentleman.

(68)

Property:
Two negroes	£90.
Schooner	80.
2 horses & Chair	30.
Leather	45.
Books	22.10
Cow	2
Furniture, Clothes & Linen	100.

£369.10

Decision:
The Board are of opinion that the Claimt. is a Loyalist. Her deceased Husband a Zealous one & bore arms.

1784.
20th March.

1168. Case REVD. ROBT. COOPER.

(69).

Is a native of England, went to Charlestown in 1758, got a Living that yr. in Prince William Parish, at the Commencmt. of the troubles he was Rector of St. Michael's C. Town, says on his being required to observe a fact which he refused in Feby., 1775, the Committee of the State then considered whether he ought to be deprived of his living, the majority were in his favour. In June he was applied to sign the Association which was to renounce his allegiance to the King, he signed it with the reserve of his allegiance but about then after a Committee of three gentlemen waited on him & told him that if he did not sign it erasing the Condition annexed to his name, he should be considered as an Enemy and the Consequence might be very disagreeable, he then out the Condition and his name remained on the list as a subscriber. He Continued after this to execute the functions of his office without any molestation, taking care giving any cause of Complaint by the Language he held till the beginning of June, 1776, when he on Sir P. Parkers appearance he was called upon to attend the Muster which he at this time declined. An oath was tendered to the Inhabitants for the defence of the place but was not regularly tendered to the Claimt.

It was proposed to him by the Capt. of the Compy. in which he was inrolled, but he refused to take it. The Claimt. continued to pray for the King at Public Prayers and the day of the attack by Sir Pr. Parker, 28th June, 1776, having done so he was the Sundy following dismissed from the vestry, he remained in C. Town till April, 1777, without receiving any Injury, but being obliged to quit his Parsonage house, in April, 1777, he was called upon to take the Oath of Alleegance to the States, & abjuration of the King, he refused it & in consequence was obliged to quit the place in 60 days & went to Holland & from there to England where he arrived June, 1777.

(70).

He applied to the Treasury & received an allowance of £100 pr. an. until the reduction of C. Town, 1781, he returned to Charlestown & on his arrival he was appointed by the vestry to the Church of St. Phillips & Continued there until the evacuation when he came to England, he received £130 from the Treasury for his passage out to C. Town, he has a pension of £60 pr. an. from 6' Jany., 1783.

Property—500 acres of Land in Craven County, on Rocky Creek Waterer. Grant produced Nov., 1781. No Cultivation, he never saw them, he values them at 4 Sh. per acre, he was at £5 expense.

Produces Copy of the Will of Robert Perennau, Deceased, dated 2nd April, 1782, by which he devizes to his Brother Henry & his sister Ann Cooper his House & Lot north side of Queen Street, Charlestown, to hold as Tenants in Common in fee. He also devizes to his niece Ann Cooper, the Claimt's. daughter, & her Heirs, his Lot of Land South side of Queen Street, C. Town in fee. This Property has not been sold. Says that Robt. Perenneau was a Loyalist & this Property was confiscated as his Property. He values the undivided property held with Mr. Perennau's at £500 Stg. The Lot his Daughter's Property at £200 S.

He sustained a Loss of some Indigo Shipped on board the Live Oak & carried to Newfoundland, part of the Cargo formerly stated by Mr. Perennau, £200. Says he sustained a loss of £12,071.12.9 by Bonds pd. of in depreciated Cury. & upon Interest pd. to the amount of £1,577.13.10 Cur.

States debts due amounting to £27,758.9.2 Cury., besides two Bonds Amounting to £1,700 Sterg.

(71).

Says Mr. Jas. Perennau, from whom he Claims, was an officer in the American Service.

Values his living at more than £200 pr. an., the Salary was £117. Surplice fees £100 pr, an., his Parsonage house would let for £60 pr. an.

SIR ED. HEAD, BART.:

Has Known the Claimt. since 1764, he was Loyal from the Commencmt. of the troubles. Says he made himself obnoxious by Continuing to Pray for the King. Says that he read the services in that form the very day that Sullivan's Island was attacked.

He says he believes the Claimt. did sign an Association but appears little acquainted with the nature of it. He says an oath was tenderd to the Claimt. after Sir P. Parker's attack, abjuring the King & swearing allegiance to the States, that in Consequence of his refusal he was forced to leave the State. He believes sincerely that the Claimt. was strongly attached to Great Britain & that his conduct was guided by that attachment. Gives a similar acct. of the Living with the Claimt. & says he Lost his Church for Praying for the King.

HENRY PERENNAU:

March 22nd.

He has known the Claimt. 24 years, he always Conducted himself as a Loyal subject, believes he acted from principal, he was minister of St. Michael's Church & received a Sallary of £825 Cur., he was deprived of this from his Loyalty:

(72).

JOHN SAVAGE, ESQ.:

Has Known the Claimt. 20 years & always considered nim as a Loyal subject. He was Incumbent of St. Michael's Church, thinks sallary & perquisites, it was worth £200 Stg.

DR. GARDEN:

Has Known the Claimt. Long, he lost his living after Sir P. Parker's attack, believes him very Loyal, he was the Claimt's. Attry., & Shipped some Indigo for him on Board the live Oak, Worth £200 Stg.

He says Mr. Cooper lost Considerably by Paper Currency. Can't say how much. Believes the Living was worth £200 pr. an. He is asked if the Americans were obliged to accept payment in Paper Money, he says that all persons were equally bound to take it.

JAS. ED. POWELL:

Says he understood that the Claimt. had an interest in the Indigo shipped on the live Oak under his Care to the amount of £200, he entered an appeal in Newfoundland but could not follow it out for want of money.

ROBT. WM. POWELL:

(73).

Says the Claimt. returned to Charles Town in 1781, when he was elected to St. Philip's Church & continued Possessed of that Living until the Evacuation.

Decision—The Board are of opinion that the Claimt. is a Loyalist.

Mr. Cooper has informed the Board that his Property is returned to him with an Amersemt of 12½ pr. Cent.

1784.
24th March.

1169. Case JAS. GREEN.

Is an Englishman, & went to America in 1763, he settled soon after his arrival at Newburn, N. Carolina. He was 1st a Master of a Vessel, says he refused to join the insurgents in the resolves or to sign their Association, they made him take an oath in Novr., 1775, that would not give information or assistance to the British Govrt. whilst he staid in the Province. If he had not taken this oath he would have been sent to Prison.

Early in 1776 he went to Cape Fear, having obtained a clearance for that place from the King's Collector, but says that at that time an ordinance had been passed in the Province that no vessel should be permitted to sail unless they undertook to bring back Warlike stores. Says upon Sailing from Newburn he cleared out for Cape Clear & gave a Bond in the penalty of £295 that he would deliver his Cargo at Cape Fear, he did not and never meant lt. He intended to apply to the Govr. & to leave the Country. He left effects in the hands of a friend who was his security to the amount. Upon his arrival at Cape Fear he did deliver Gr. Martin's furniture & baggage & went with his own (74). vessel to Antigua & had papers from Govr. Morton. he first intended to go to London but altred his mind, by this means the Bond was forfeit. The Rebels seized the effects left in the hands of his friend. He left other effects behind to the amount of £408, he went to Antigua thinking himself safe with this Pass, but when he came into the Harbour he was seized by Capt. Keeler who took his ship & libelled him in the admiralty Court, but he could not appear because he was obliged to give security which he Could not do.

He made a Claim on the Treasury for this 4 years ago. Sir Gray Cooper said it was a very hard case & that he Shd. have an answer but he never has had any. The Vessel & Cargo was his sole property, they were worth about £1,400 Strg., no person speaks to the value but himself.

GOVR. MARTEN:

The Claimt., he believes, cleared out as he States & believes him well attached to the British Govrnt., he apprehended that his Letter was to secure him from the clearance, he is not sure if he Knew of the Prohibitory act at the time, but rather thinks not. He gave him this to protect him as he wanted a Clearance, he cannot form a judgement of the value of the vessel, he would (75). have been liable to have been seized not having a Clearance from Cape Clear & Govr. Marten gave him this to supply the want, had delivered his cargo at Cape Fear, the ships there would have

THOS. MCKNIGHT, ESQR.:

Knew a little of Mr. Green & believes him to have been a Loyalist. When he returned to Cape Fear from C. Town in July or August, 1776, he found Mr. Green at Cape Fear.

The Claimt. Called in, Assigns as a reason for getting the Pass that he had no Clearance & apprehended it was necessary, he did not know of the Prohibitory Act until he came into Antigua Harbour, the Schooner & Cargo was his own Property, she was 40 tons burthen, he values her at £510. The vessel & outfit cost him that, the Vessel cost £328, or £287, S., admits he

thought it a great price, he had on Board 1,200 Bushels Corn, he values the Indian Corn at 13sh. Antigua Cur., which is much the same as North Car. Cur., he gave about 3Sh. pr. Bush. for it & values it at that price, it would have sold for at Antigua, values it at 15Sh. pr. bushel, he thinks it cost him 4Sh. at New burn. Boards, Pork & Tar, valued at £28 the price they would have sold for at Antigua, but they cost him near that sum at Newburn.

States Debts £305 Cury, he has recovered none of them, he owed nothing.

Property—A Lot in Newburn. Consisted of $\frac{1}{2}$ an acre with- 76). out any building on it, he purchased it but left the deed in America, he gave £14 for it, he left all his papers with a friend, he bought it in 1774.

The lot lay in the Centre of the Town & was valuable, he paid the money for it. He had one Horse for which he gave £31.10sh.

5 Head of Cattle, 6 Sheep, but supposes that they both have encreased, he has been in England 4 years & has had no allowance till within a yr., he Receives £40 pr. an. from the Treasury from Jany., 1783.

Decision—The Board are of opinion that the Claimt., Jas. Green, is a Loyalist.

He lost a Schooner which they value at £200. Corn at £150. Pease £30. Pork £10.

His Lot disallowed for want of Evidence. Has an allowance of £40 pr. an. from the Treasury from Jany., 1783.

1784.
25th March.

1170. Case BRGR. GENR. SKINNER.

Is a native of New Jersey. When the troubles broke out he was Atty. Gen. & Speaker of the House of Assembly. He was appointed in 1754. In April, 1775, soon after Lexington, he was insulted in the Execution of his Office & the Septr. following at Morres Town he was called before the Town Committee & found guilty of being inimical to the Libertys of America, but on his declaring himself generally a friend to Liberty & his Country— friends in the Committee took advantage of these expressions & (77). obtained his discharge, from this time until Jany., 1776, he met with various obstructions in the execution of his office. In Augst, 1775, he had an offer made to him of the Command of the Provincial Troops by the Provincial Congress with the Rank he chose, which he refused. In Jany., 1776, upon the Discovery of some papers which the Claimt. had Copied for Gr. Franklyn Concerning the Proceedings of Congress, he was obliged to fly & went to New York. His Wife & family returned to Amby, but were in three months forced to quit by order of the Provincial Congress.

The fourth of Septr., 1776, he received a Commission from Sir Wm. Howe of Brigr. Gen. of all the Provincial Troops, he Continued as such until the arrival of Sir Guy Carleton, when he was ordered to Pemlos Hook & then to Long Island. He was in an Engagement on Staten Island 1st August, 1777, with Gen. Sullivan under the Command of Gen. Campbell, he had been previously in a Canonade at Tera town in Decem., 1776, & two at Brunswick early in 1777. Says in 1777 when he entered Jersey he found six Batteries were raising, he was instrumental in getting them Collected. The Batteries were to be 500 men each, in 1778 they were reduced to four & these were nearly Completed to 400 each.

Gen. Howe Commissioned the offirs. Principally by his advice. (78). Says the 1st year he was at the Expense of £100 S. in raising his own Compy., which Consisted of 56 Rank & File, it Cost him 30 or 40 gs. pr. an. to raise men over the Royal Bounty from 1777 to 1781. He Constantly furnished Lord Cornwallis & the Comr. in Chief with intellignce. Says Lord Cornwallis will speak thereon. He was always payed the Expense of procuring intelligence by the Comr. in Chief.

He Received Pay as Brigr. from 4th Sep. in 1776, to Oct., 1783, only as Col. from April, 1781.

He does not know if he is to receive pay. From last fall to has received at the rate of £200 pr. an. from the Treasury.

Property—

A Farm one mile from Perth Amboy Consisting of 598 acres of Land at £10 pr. acre, £5980 Cury., derived this Property from his Father who made no Will, it descended to him as the oldest

Son. The Laws of Engd. prevailed in the Province. Says that 200 acres were a Gift from Geo. Woolax to his Father, he purchased the remainder 30 years ago. He lost all his papers at Amboy, they were taken from Mrs. Skinner. Has heard that the deeds were cut up by the soldiers to make Pocket Books. It was a farm House, 250 acres in tillage, 160 Wood, the remainder Salt Meadow. About 20 acres had ben a Swamp, it Cost him £8 an acre to Clear, values the Estate at £10 Cury. pr. acre, says it would have sold for that in 1774. He has known Lands in that Neighbourhood sell for more. In tracts as large as his it sold in 1778 for £9700, when the depreciated money was 4 to 1. (79)

A House & Lot in Amboy settled by his Wife's father in 1751 on his marriage, this was settled on him & his Wife for their lives & the survivors in fee. It was a good Brick House three stories high. Built in 1732 or 33. He married in 1751. In 1775 he let this House for £50, there was another building on the Lott which he made his office, if he had Let the whole he should have asked £70 pr. an. The Whole Contained an acre & ½, it sold in 1778 for £3500, depreciation 4 to 1, thinks it would have sold in 1774 for £2000. Values it at £1800. Such a House could not have built for £1200.

Two Lotts in Amboy, 2 acres, values them at £100 Cury.,

he owned them as his father's heir at Law.

A Small Farm near Swan hill, Consisted of 100 acres, it was Sandy Land, on the S. side of the Bairiton, it was of no use but for Wood, he purchased it in 1763, he gave £90 Cury. for it, thinks it would have sold for more in 1774. Values it at £200 Cury.

1000 acres in Sussex County, purchased in 1765 from a Mr. Charles Stewart & a Mr. John Scott. They Cost 8 sh. pr. acre Cury., a part was Cultivated. This Tract is in W. Jersey, does not know how much is Cultivated, from 1764 to 1773 he derived no benefit from it. Thinks 50 acres might be Cultivated. Thinks in 1774 he might have sold the tract for 20 sh. pr. acre, he was offered that by a Quaker in 1773 or 174. He values it at 30 sh. (80). pr. acre, £1500 Cury. If Mr. Webster, the Quaker, had come up to 25 sh. in 1774 he would have taken his offer.

3-8 of one 24th of the Eastern division of the Province of New Jersey, he derived this from his Father. He cannot value it.

3-8 or one 24th of the Proprietory Estate in Perth Amboy,

78 AR.

the whole about £8000, it Consisted of a very large House, Genry. made use of by the Govr. Vals. his share at £125 Cury., derived this from his Father.

3-8 of a 24th Tract of Land called Rumages, it Lyes in Berghen County, this he had from his Father.

60 acres in Courtland Manor which was 1-5th of 3000 acres, this was Cultivated & left to him by his Mother.

1-5 of a 10th of undivided Estate in New York Province. His Mother had ten Brs. & Sisters, about 750 acres was his Proportion, derived this under the Will of his Mother, who was one of the 10 Children of Col. Stephen Courtland. Never derived any benefit from it. The Whole of this tract of Land had been in litigation with the Inhabitants of Bedford, who had been in Possession under a precluded Grant from Connecticut, part only had been recovered when the troubles Commenced, but as fast as actions were brought possession was recovered. This Tract was all settled, does not know how much was recovered or the value. Mrs. Skinner derived from her Father which he valued at £2000 Cury. He refers to the particulars to Mr. Andr. Elliot. His Estates were Confiscated in 1778, the incumbrances on them as pr. acct. of particulars, £2149.18 Cur.

Stock on the Farm Consisting of 8 Horses at £20; 45 head of Cattle, £6; £270.15 at £3, £45, £475 Cury.

Furniture, including Table Linen, Valued at £1000 Cry.; Library, £500 Cury.; Sallary of Atty. Gen., £60; Profession & fees, £1000 Cury.

Produces Copy of the order turning out Mrs. Skinner.

EARL CORNWALLIS :

Says his first personal Knowledge of the Claimt. was in Novr., 1776, at that time he joined his Ld. Ship in the Jerseys with the rank of Brig. Gen. Says he went through the hardships of the

service with Cheerfulness & was of the utmost assistance to him. That he was intrusted in matters of the most Confidential nature by his Ld. Ship & always found him a most Zealous man. In Decemr., 1776, when they of the Country, the Claimt. raised men & Ld. Cornwallis says that one day 100 men joined him, that he nearly raised 6 Batts. Does not think that he ever met a man who had so perfect a Knowledge of the Country as the Claimt. Ld. Cornwallis says he does not think it possible that any man could show more real Zeal & attachment towards Gt. Britain than the Claimt. That he had once a week a perfect acct. from him of the State of Washington's Army.

BRIGR. GN. SKINNER. In August, 1775, he was called upon by Mr. Dickenson, who was Mgr. in the American Service, he asked him to dine with him which he refused, fearing that some Conversation might be held at the table disagreeable to him, but he dined alone with him next day. Says before he did so, Mr. Carter, Secretary to the Provincial Congress & 2 other Gentlemen, Mr. Ellis & Mr. Stewart, Deputed by that body, acquainted him with their being authorized to offer him the rank of Major Genr. which should be Confirmed by the Gen. Congress, or if he preferred it, the Govnt. of the Province or any station within it upon his own terms. That he has seen the minute of Congress ordering the Deputation to wait upon him.

In June, 1776, he secured a Commission from Gr. Franklyn after he was taken Prisoner, appointing him Major Gen. of the Militia of the Province and Delegating to him all his Millitary power when he went to the Jerseys. After the arrival of Sir Wm. Howe he did endeavour to put the Commission in force with some effect, but the Evacuation of the Province made such a Commission afterwards useless.

GOVR. FRANKLYN:

Says that the Claimt. was Atty. Gen. & Speaker of the Assembly of the Province when the troubles broke out in 1775, in which situation he had been for several years previous to the Rebellion. He says the Conduct of the Claimt. on all occasions was such as to deserve his fullest Confidence, from time to time he received intelligence the most material from him. Confirms what Mr. Skinner said respecting his giving him a Commission to act as Mgr. Gen. Says he was an active, Zealous subject & that he did everything in his power to render service to the B. Govnt. (83).

DANL. COX, ESQ.:

Has known the Claimt. since 1755, remembers him being possessed of a very large farm in Perth Amboy, understood it came from his Father, has known Lands to sell for ———— pr. acre. Should Estimate the Claimts. Lands at £10 or 12 pr. acre. He is well acquainted with the Lands in the neighbourhood, he does not recollect lands sold so low as £5 Curcy.——Dollars at 7 sh. 6d. pr. acre. In the neighbourhood of Gen. Skinner's Farm he thinks land was not Worth less than £10 Curcy. pr. acre.

Says he knows his possessing the house at Amboy & believes he had it from his Father in Law, Mr. Kerney, it was part of Mrs. Skinner's Fortune, thinks it worth £1600 or 1800 Prov. Gr. Skinner is entitled in right of his Wife to a ninth of all Lands purchased by her Father, after he made his Will a Codicile was added to the Will. (84).

Says Genr. Skinner had a very good Library, he cannot say what number of volumes, but thinks they must have cost £200 or 300 Strg. Speaks of the Claimts. holding a share, thinks it was a 4th of 1-24 of .ne Eastern Division of New Jersey.

ISAAC OGDEN, ESQ.:

Was acquainted with the Claimt. in 1775 & many years before. Says that he heard in 1775 from some member in Provincial Congress that they wished him, the Witness, to serve therein, which he refused & that they then told him that Mr. Skinner would be offered the Post of Major Gen. & used that argt. to induce him to serve as a member of Congress. The Witness believes that Gen. Skinner's practice was worth £500 Stg. pr. an. Would have given the Claimt. £300 pr. an. for the Atty. Gns. Ship, this office led the Claimt. into great practice.

DAVID OGDEN, ESQ.:

Has known Gen. Skinner from his Infancy, he was Atty. Gen. & Speaker of the Assembly when the troubles broke out. Says the Claimt. was most sincerely attached to the British Govnt. Says the farm at Perth Amboy was always reported to be the Property of Claimt. Does not know if it was devised to him from his Father, or had it as his oldest son, thinks there were 500 or 600 acres. The Witness was not on the lands since he recovered them with Gr. Skinner's Father more than twenty years before the troubles, by what he can recollect there might be 200 acres of pretty good land, the remainder was a sandy soil, the whole might be worth from £8 to 12 N. York Crcy. pr. acre, at the Commencement of the troubles it would have sold for that, he would have given £11 for it & thought it Cheap.

(85).

Knows the House & Lott at Amboy very well, always understood the Claimt. had the title to it, believes he purchased it, but cannot speak positively. Thinks it might be worth £1500 or 1600 Curcy., believes he let the House for £60 pr. an., he kept his office in it, otherwise he would have got more. Has heard of the Claimt. having Lands in Sussex County, knows nothing of them. Always understood that the Claimt. had something more than ¼th of a ½ 4th of the Eastern division of New Jersey, believes he had it from his Father. Some time before the Rebellion a

24th Share of unappropriated Lands was deemed worth £1000 to 1200. Those rights in 7 years rose from £25 to £100 Curcy. pr. Hundred acres. Speaks of good rights, vide Mr. Cox's Explanation. Says from hearsay there were about 2,000,000 acres of unappropriated Lands belonging to the Proprietors, great part of which were mountaneous tracts. There were no Conditions of Cultivation on the Grants issued by the Proprietors of the Province of New Jersey, but they were at liberty to Locate the Lands where ever the Grantees chose. He knows the House stiled the Proprietory Estate in Perth Amboy, in which the Claimt. states he had a share, he cannot tell how to put a value upon it. Says there was a Contest twixt the Proprietors of the Province & a body of settlers who were fixed upon the tract called Banragio Situated in Bangor County, many suits were held in Consequence & at last a Compromise took place twixt the settlers & Proprietors & they agreed that the settlers should retain their Possessions & Convey the unlocated Lands to the Proprietors, this accordingly was done. Thinks the Whole Tract was 44,000 acres & that what remained to the Proprietors on the Compromise was about one half. Says that the Land which rested with the Proprietors was very inferior to that Possessed by the settlers, but thinks the value

(86).

of it 20 sh. pr. acre. Says he has been frequently at the Claimts. house, which was well furnished & he had a good Library. Books in genl. were dear in New Jersey. Cannot estimate the value of his Library.

ANDR. ELLIOT, ESQ.: 27th March.

Has known the Claimt. upwards of 30 years. Says that the Claimt. had a Farm near Amboy, does not know the number of acres, but thinks from 4 to 600 acres, a good deal of Wood & Salt meadow, cannot speak of the value. Says he had a mortgage of £120 Cur. on 12 acres of the Land which the Claimts. Father told him were well worth this sum, this mortgage was 15 years ago. Knows the house in Amboy which the Claimt. got by his Father in Law, Mr. Kearney, has heard what Mr. Kearney gave for his house, but has forgot. Mr. Kearney died in 1775 & devised Lands in Monmouth County which he held in Partnership with Mr. Barnet & also the Lands in Midsex. & other Lands in Partnership with Dr. Lewis Johnston, not far from the other Lands, a 4th part to his Daughter, Eliz. Skinner, for ever, & after devising the other 3 4ths he directs the 3rd lands to be sold as soon as can be.

(87).

After his Decease & directs the application of one 4th of the money in trust for his Daur., Susa. Kearney, by a Codicil to the Will 2nd Augt., 1775, he devised other Lands purchased after the making of his Will unto all his Children, Sons & Daughters, share & share alike forever. Mr. Kearney had been twice married. He purchased from Br. Capt. Michl. Kearney in 1774 a very fine farm in Monmouth, does not know the quantity, says it used to be valued at something more than £4000, the Witness has been often on it, there was a great deal of Cultivation on it. Speaks of the large farm in Mid Sex called Van Narchus Farm, it was held in Partnership with Mr. Ricketts, it was as noble a farm as any in America, does not know how many acres. Gen. Skinner has Four Sons & Four Daughters.

PHILIP COURTLAND, ESQR.:

Is Cousin of the Claimt. Speaks of 1-5 of the 10th of an undivided Estate in New York Province left to the Cliamt. by his Mother, part in West Chester, part in Dutchess County, does not know his share in Courtland Mannor, it Consisted of 11,000 acres. The undivided Land in N. York Province was about 25,000 acres, Gr. Skinner share about 500 acres, he does not know what part was Cultivated, thinks no part was sold by Claimt, great part was Cultivated. He values it at £3 pr. acre, the uncultivated at 20 sh. Crcy.

(88).

LT. MOODY:

Speaks to Lands in Sussex County. Some he says which were improved were very valuable. Not knowing what number of acres of the 1000 which Gen. Skinner claims were Cultivated, he cannot fix any value. The Cultivated Lands were worth £3 pr. acre Cury. From what he has heard from Gen. Skinner of the quantity of those Lands he supposes they could not be worth Less than from 20 to 30 sh. pr. acre.

PHILLIP SKINNER:

Is son to the Claimt. Speaks of the Copy of the order issued in July, 1776, to his Mother & family to remove from Amboy. Says that they packed up some papers, but which did not prove to be those which related to his Father's Property.

Claimt. called in:

He is desired to furnish better evidence of the value of his Property in New Jersey, Amboy & Ramagio.

30th April.

Produces an Estimate of his Wife's Property which appears to exceed greatly what he stated in his Schedule, £3941, instead of £2000.

CAPT. KEARNEY, R. NAVY:

(89).

Says he is uncle to Mrs. Skinner. Sold about 1000 acres in April, 1775, for £3000 N. Jersey Cury., they were worth £1000 more, 200 acres were Cultivated, a good House & Barn, it rented for £45 Cury. before it was put in the good state he had it in, thinks he should not have let it under £80 or 90 pr. an.

Mr. VANMAITRE:

Says he has heard & believes that Capt. Kearny sold to his Br. some Lands, does not know the quantity, but thinks about 800, he knows the land, has been often upon it, thinks the farm house, &c., worth £3400 Cury. Lands at Toppnumans he values at 36 sh. Cur. pr. acre, does not know the number of acres, but believes about 300, he values them at £540 Cury., he cannot speak to the value of the Lands of Barnegas.

SIR HY. CLINTON, K.B.:

Says that Gen. Skinner Conducted himself with great Zeal during the War, he has frequently received material information from him, and found great use from his Extensive Knowledge of the Country & Character of the Americans. Says upon the whole Gen. Skinner was particularly active &. Zealous in the cause of Great Britain.

Decision. Case Brg. Gen. SKINNER.

The Board is of opinion that the Claimt. is a most active & Zealous Loyalist. He bore Arms as Brigr. Gen. & *rendered Most Essential Service to the British Govnt.*

(90)

He was possessed of 598 acres near Perth Amboy
which the Board value at £3000.0.0
Two Lots in the Town of Amboy 40.0.0
100 acres near Swan Mill 80.0.0
For Life Estate by Mrs. Skinner 1500.0.0
Stock, £169; Furniture, £500; Library, £200. 869.0.0

Part of Courtland Mannor	600.0.0
3-8ths of a 24th Share of the Eastern division of N. Jersey	180.0.0
For Life 4 Shares of Lands at Bornagel	50.0.0
1000 acres in Sussex County	600.0.0
Office Atty. Gen. for N. Jersey	36.0.0
Profits of Office	500.0.0

Gen. Skinner has an allowance of £200 pr. an.

1171. Case JERMYN WRIGHT, Esq.   1784. 27th April.

Was born in England, went to America in 1758. He was a Planter & Mercht. He Swears that the Contents of his Memorial are true to the best of his Knowledge. Bore Arms 1st in Feby., 1776, he had a 100 men under his Command. Left Georgia in April, 1782. Has an allowance from Octr., 1782, of 200 pr. an. Certificate from Col. Graham, 16th Regt., & several other officers.

Property.

11000 acres & upwards in the Province of Georgia within ten miles of each other, there were about 600 acres Cleared in the Whole & 350 Planted with Corn, Indigo, &c., &c., but a small quantity under rice, about 80 acres. He had six different Plantations & some Land was Cultivated on each. He values the 11,000 acres at £8000 S., the Timber alone would have put that money into his pocket. There were houses on all the Plantations. He had a Mansion house on two of them & Common buildings for Negroes on all the rest. He laid out £1000 on the Buildings. He left all his deeds with Major Wright & Mr. Robertson, his Attys. Estimate of the value of these Lands produced by these two Gentlemen, sworn to at St. Augustine, £8000. Says that a sufficient number of acres were Cultivated to secure the lands from forfeiture. (91).

Says he considered Cultivation on one Plantation to answer the Condition of another Grant, he had 19 Grants, but his Cultivation was on six, Specified in the Schedule. Says the 13 Grants without Cultivation were equally valuable with the six Cultivated.

Lands in S. Carolina:

13,000 acres, he valued them at £20,000, but now values them at £10,000, they were principally grants, only one was a Proprietory Grant, the No. of Grants 15, the deeds are in the hands of his Attys. Supposes there were 500 acres Cultivated on the Whole. Many of those Tracts had buildings on them. He had only one Mansion House in this Province. He had taken his Negroes of before the Rebellion & had left the Province 7 years before the Rebellion. These Lands produced nothing, but he sometimes sold some, he once sold 1000 acres for £1000 Strg., 89 or 90 acres were Cultivated on this Plantation, thinks they were Worth £10,000, yet £5,000 would have tempted him. (92).

The same Custom prevailed in S. Carolina as in Georgia as to Cultivation. One half of the Plantations were settled, being asked to describe them in the Schedule he mentions Four Tracts which he is sure were settled, but believes now there was an encumbrance on this Estate, three mortgages, perhaps from £2000 to 3000, but more is owing to him, no encumbrance in Georgia.

He claims £9409 for damages in 1776, when driven away, including Debts, £2000. Besides he lost 54 Negroes over & above those mentioned in the Protest which he values at £40 each.

Negroes are in Genl. worth more; some double.

Loss of Dry goods as in the Schedule. Charges Expenses of Living.

State £4000 Debts in Car. & Georgia, but only Charges £2000, has no Witness, but papers & Certificates.

He believes his Property is Confiscated both in Georgia & Carolina.

2nd May. SIR JAMES WRIGHT:

Brother to the Claimt. Says his two older Brothers T—— & Charles, settled their Lands on the Longest Liver. He has been upon one of their Plantations, the land was worth in the degree of Cultivation they say 5 sh. pr. acre.

(93). He had 14,000 acres in S. Car. before the War, they would have sold for £7 or 8000. S.

1784.
8th November. ———. DEARLE:

Wm. Dagrell, late Clerk of the Schooner St. John. He was on the Coast of America in the years 1774, 1775 & 1776, the Schooner lay in the River St. Mary's in those years & he saw Mr. J. Wright's Property, he had great tracts of Grass & Corn Lands, he had 4 or 500 acres Cultivated with Corn & Yams. Has been in his House, it was but one story high & 9 or 10 rooms on a floor, it was well furnished. He had a great many Negroes at his place & seemed to be the richest man in the Country. He had a Stockade round his house. When he was there when Col. Macintosh attacked his Plantation when some of his Negroes were

Killed & some Wounded, he was taken Prisoner.

1784.
18th December. Decision—

An Active & Zealous Loyalist.

Six trackts in the Province of Georgia Containg 3900 acres, of which 600 acres are Cultivated, £2000 Sterg.

4 Tracts, 2660 acre in S. Carl., with 500 acres Cultivated at £3500, there was a Mortgage on this Property of £2000 Strg.

Personal Estate, £3705.

(94). He has an allowance of £200 pr. an.
States Debts due him £2000.

1784.
3rd May. 1172. Case Brigr. Gen. OLIVER DELANCY.

Swears to the Whole of his Memorial being true. Says that he was Emploid by Sir Wm. Howe to Command in Long Island

He had a Civil as well as a Millitary Command. In 1775 he lived at Greenwich, N. York Island, & in Consequence of avowing principals of Loyalty was frequently mobd.

He underwent great fatigues, hardships & dangers during the Rebellion & materially injured his health by his exertions in the British Cause.

Gen. Delancy has at present half Pay as Colonel, 12 sh. pr. Diem, & an allowance from the Treasury in the name of Mrs. Delancy of £200 pr. an. & One Hundred in the name of Miss De Lancey. He raised a Battal. which he Commanded himself.

Property—

He Esteems his Property in America Worth more than £100,000 Sterg. Has delivered in a Schedule to be Examined upon.

Lots in Pearl Street 18 feet long, 16 feet wide, it came to him from his Elder brother, who had it from his Father. He has no written evidence of this but refers to Mr. Watts. He has lost many papers, but still has many Deeds which he has preserved. Values this Property at £100 Cury.

N.B. The Whole Evidence refers to the Schedule.

Three Lots in Field Market, one Lett to Grey & Cunningham, 2nd to Hy. Ludlow, these he bought of Mr. Pachero. Values the 3 Lotts at £900, independent of the houses which were burnt in 1776. Says he is Confident it was done by design. (95)

Lot in New Street Cost £100, let for £16 pr. an., values it at £25. The Lots on the West side of the board way bought of John Richards, Conveyance produced, these he values at £3000, in the Whole with the Buildings. After the fire he Let a house in one of these Lots for £40 pr. an.

Lot let to Grey & Cunningham bought jointly with the next Lot, the Whole Cost £730, which he says is double the next Lot, this is given to his Son.

4 Lotts, Bush Lots, Title from the Corporation, he has laid out a good deal of money on them, these were burnt, he values them at £1000. £100 was Charged for a Water fence not burnt, but taken away by the King's Troops, thinks they would have sold for so much.

A Lot in New Street, he had by his Br. & Built a Brick house which Cost him £300, burnt by the Rebels.

4 Lotts North side Damnation Alley, he gave £700 for them & afterwards sold part for £1200, he had inproved it by that time. Values the remaining part at £800.

An Island—One Moiety he bought in 1754 for £250, the 4th May. other half Cost him £225, he values it at £1000. Mr. Dunbar, the Genrs. Clerk & on this occasion his assistant, says it is valued very low, having been offered £550 for the smallest part.

Many other tracts talked of in Evidence but in a manner little more satisfactory than the Schedule already sworn to.

Gen. Delancey gives a List of his Losses by Fire.

Proprietory Lands he Claims under Deed to him & Mr. Caylee 5th May. by Humphrey Bowles in Considn. of £6000 Strg.

Many thousand acres Cultivated & uncultivated Lands are Claimed in New Jersey, valued at 40 to 50 sh. pr. acre.

Gr. Skinner says the Proprietors in N. Jersey were restricted as to the quantity of Lands they should take up.

Bonds & Debts, £19,942.8.3¼ Curcy.

No part of his Estate is Mortgaged. He agreed to pay £1200 for Mr. Scott & Mr. Johnson, the only encumbrance on the Estate.

His Estate has been confiscated mostly. Mostly sold—he holds it lost to him.

His Estate produced £3 to 4,000 pr. an. to him. He had 531 Tenants—says if the troubles had not happened his Estate would now have been worth £10,000 pr. an.

He had Bonds in Connecticut for £21,000.

He had 23 Slaves when he was drove away.

Loss by fire at New York in Novr., 1777, £23,591—

The half of a 24th share of the Proprietry Land usually sells for £16.00.

His Estate was, in general, highly cultivated and settled—he did not do much to the cultivation.

(97).

Says he has sustained a Loss of 22 Slaves, one was burnt in his House. Three have died natural deaths. Since he came away one was killed by severe treatment by the Hessians, he values them at £40 each.

Says there was furniture burnt in his House belonging to Colonel Conger valued at £973-16-7.

House burnt at Kingston £400. Acct. for Forage given into the Treasurer £1,126.16. Stock £275. Brother's Picture.

This Estimate he delivered to the Treasury in 1778 by Sir Wm. Draper, but he never heard more of it—and makes the claim now. His House, &c., was burnt by the Rebels who came there on purpose—some of the houses, etc., were burnt at New York, which he is sure was done by Design.

The Expense of Patenting Lands in N. York Province was

£25 pr. Thousand acres.

JOHN SMYTH, ESQ., Perth Amboy.

Says Gen. DeLancey had the ½ of 2-24th & 7-8th—a 24th share, if nothing was done upon it, was worth a thousand Cury.

He should not imagine that Gen. DeLancey had 40,000 acres —he gave half of one 24th Share to his son just before the troubles—he thinks Gr. DeLancey's Lands were worth 25sh. pr. acre one with another.

GEN. ROBERTSON.

(98).

Has known Gen. DeLancey many years before the Rebellion, he thinks he was one of the first men in N. York Province in point of fortune and situation. He had great merit in stepping forward in raising Provincial Troops—his example had great effect.

His was one of the first fortunes in the Province. It is a difficult to estimate America Estates—he bought a great deal of Lands in New Jersey. He believes his House was burnt out of enmity. He was held a man of great integrity & honor. He kept a good Table & lived with great splendour. Thinks the fire was by accident.

JOHN MOODY.

Lived in Sussex County. Speaks of the old Farm—thinks upon an average it would have sold for £3 or 4 pr. acre. Never understood that he purchased a great deal of Land. He had many Tenants—always bore the character of a Loyalist & used his influence to support this Govrt.

GEN. STIRLING.

Has known Gen. DeLancey many years. He was a Colonel the War before last. He was always well attached to his Govnt. Gen. Sterling went to America this War in 1776 & found him then very active. He knows his House at Bloomingdale. He thinks it was worth £16 or 1800 with the furniture £2,000 or near that.

BR. GR. SKINNER.

Believes the Claimt was a very active Loyalist. He never served with him. He thinks it very possible that he may have hurt his Health by it. He thinks he took the part of Govnt. from principle.

The General had large property or rights in N. Jersey. He purchased from one Duckora more than two 24ths of the whole Province. These rights were granted by Charles the 2nd to the Duke of York & by him to the two First Proprietors, Lork Berkeley & Lord Cartant.

Gen. Skinner knows the 1060 at Wreck a bank which in a Division came to Deckene. Thinks it was worth £5 pr. acre. He m ans the Lott where Joseph Farmer was settled.

(99).

COL. GUY JOHNSON. May 7th.

Has known Gr. DeLancey since 1758. He behaved very well the former War in 1775. He saw him insulted by the mob for the expressions he had used in 1774. In 1776 he raised a Regt. & his conduct has been very Loyal.

SIR HENRY CLINTON. 12th May.

Speaks with great respect of the Genr. & in high terms of his Loyalty.

Decision in the Case of Brigr. Gr. DeLancey.

The Board are of the opinion that the Claimt is an active & zealous & meritorious Loyalist. He bore arms & rendered services to Great Britain.

No.	1. Lot in Pearl Street, N.Y., rented at £8 pr. an.	£ 84 Stg.
	3. Three Lots in Field Market with the Houses	563
	4. Lot in New Street with House	253
	5. Lots & Houses in Broad Street	1,660
	6. Lots in Damnation Alley	1,400
	7. Lot in Lombard St.	160
	8. DeLancey's Island	310
	9. 15 acres, 3 Lots Salt Meadow	85
(100).	10. Pew in Trinity Church	20
	11. Half of William Woodcock's House	22
	12. 242 acres & some Stock in Courtland Manor	675
	14. Lands in Albany County--Tryon County, etc.	1,125
	17. Appeal Patent Expence	169
	18. ¼th of 2,000 acres in Schnectedy	225
	20. Part of the Manor of Cosby Cost	675
	23. 6,288 acres in Minisent Patent Part of	549
	Appear to have been cultivated	310
	25. Part of Minisent Patent Cost	113
	26. 8,927 acres in Minisent Patent & Dur. Park	2,250
	27. Proprietry Lands in N. Jersey, bought of Bower	10,725
	28. do purchased from Reunora	408
	29. House at Bloomingdale	690
	30. Property Lost at Bloomingdale	2,848
	31. Negroes	820
		£24,940
	States Debts due to him	£11,219 Stg.

Mrs. DeLancey has an allowance of £200 pr. an. His Daughter, Miss DeLancey, an allowance of £100 pr. an.

Mr. DeLancey had half pay as a Colonel. Confiscation is proved, but no proof of Sale.

1784. 7th May.

1173. Case JAS. JOHNSTON, ESQ.

(101).

Is a native of Great Britain. Went to America in 1764. He went as a Clerk to a Prophmotory in S. Carolina. He was compelled to leave the Country in 1777. He was a civil officer when the War broke out. Clerk of the Crown. He had 60 days to quit the Province. Went to Bordeaux & and from thence to Engd. He returned to Carolina in 1781. He returned in consequence of orders given him.

At the end of 1871 he was appointed attny. gen. upon the Death of Sir Egerton Leigh. Does not produce his Commissions, but promises to do it. The value of the office of Clerk of the Crown £350 Stg. It was for Life. He bought it of Mr. Cumberland whose Life was in the Patent. He got about £750 pr. an. by his profession in the year before he left the Country.

Certificates from Ld. Wm. Campbell & Gen. Lister to his doing the duty of Atty. Gen. with honour, &c.

Likewise from Col. Balfour & a Letter from Ld. Germain. He

Lost £2,000 Stg. in his Passage accounted for in this way here.

He & a Son of Sir Jas. Wright sold all their Property & bought a vessel & cleared out for Bordeaux. They arrived safe & the person who sold the vessel & effects failed & they sustained great Losses.

States Debts to the amount of £2,500 & has likewise suffered by depreciation, but considers that as a debt & does not claim it. He only mentions this & the other debts in order to have the benefit at any future time.

He owed no money in America.

He receives £120 pr. an. from the Treasury.

Makes no charges but for Loss of Possession.

GOVR. BALL.

Has kown Mr.. Johnson 10 or 11 years. Ever since he knew him he was Clerk to the Clerk of the Pleas & Clerk of the Crown. When the times were critical he lived a good deal at Gr. Bull's House in the Country. Was a very zealous Loyalist from principal & was very obnoxious. He went out again with Gr. Bull & he appointed him Atty. Gen. in 1782, & Clerk of the Crown. Worth £3 or 400 Stg. pr. an. The Clerk of the Pleas was worth £900 pr. an. He had the office of Clerk of the Crown & Peace at the time of the Rebellion, by Commission given in 1770. Atty. Gen. Office was no profit. He was diligent & rising man & he was in good practice. He might in 1774 make £700 or 800 pr. an. Clerk of the Crown was a Patent office. (102).

THOS. KNOX GORDON, ESQ.

Has known Claimt since 1771. He was in good practice. He might make £700 or 800 pr. an. Fees were very high.

ED. SAVAGE, ESQ.

Knew Mr. Johnson. He was second Judge & went Circuits. He had a good deal of business. He would have made a fortune but for the troubles.

JAS. TRAILL, ESQ.

The Claimt was in great Practice in 1774. He was Clerk of the Crown. Perfectly Loyal & was banished. Clerk of the Crown was £400 pr. an. Mr. Johnson made by his practice at Least £700. (103).

1174. Case THOS. PHIPOE, ESQ., S. Carolina. 1784. 10th May.

Is a native of Ireland & went to C. Town in 1771 with Knox Gordon & Mr. Savage. He practiced the Law there at the time of the Rebellion. He dates the Commencement of the Rebellion from the Battle of Lexington. By the advice of Mr. Knox Gordon he Continued at Charlestown & was a member of the Rebel Assembly. He was Member for Prince Fredks. Parish, who were all Loyal.

He continued there under the Rebels userped Govrt. till April, 1781. When he joined Ld. Cornwallis. During the time he lived under the Rebel Govrt. he says he did everything to promote the Cause of Gt. Britain. He was always emploied by those who were tried for sedition. No other Lawyer dared to plead for them. He remained at Ch. Town until July, 1782, when he came to England.

When the British took the Town Gen. Paterson gave him his House & in Sept. 1780, Ld. Cornwallis made him a Capt. of Militia. He took an oath to the Rebels, but did not consider it as binding. Says he might have refused it with safety if he had quitted the Province. He was imprisoned in 1779 for pleading for a particular Person.

1,500 acres on Sampet. for which he refused £500. He gave £1,000 Currency for it in 1776. There were but 3 or 4 acres cultivated. All his Deeds are in Carolina. He bought them from Elisha Tamplet.

(104).
1,000 acres of ox Swamp.
500 acres in Wacoman.
428 acres in Edisto River.
260 acres in Walnut Creek.

He bought all these in 1777 of Lauchn. McIntosh with depreciated Paper Money. No Cultivation.

150 acres on Muddy Creek. He bought these of the Sheriff in 1775. No Cultivation. He paid £18.5 for them. They were 95 miles from Charlestown.

He left C. Town in April, 1780. During the Seige he sent his Furniture out of the Town with an intention to send them to George Town. They were taken by the British. He then thought the British would take the Town. He joined them 14th April, 1780. A Letter from Ld. Cornwallis respecting this furniture.

A good Law Library. A Chariot. A Negroe & Pew. He values the last at £100 Stg. His Library at £28 or 30. His Property is confiscated & himself banished. His name is in the list. He has some prospects of his debts being settled.

In August, 1780, he bought a House in C. Town for £1,500 Strg. & sold it in 1782 for £1,100.

Says he got betwixt £1,000 & 2,000 per an. by the Profession of the Law. He made at Least £900 in 1773-74 & 75.

(105).
In the Assembly he occasionally made Councilliatory propositions to promote a Union. He voted agst. the Banishment Act & spoke against it. He says that whilst a member of the Assembly he was an Enemy to all their Councils & measures.

Certificates from Colonel Phillips to Loyalty & to his being his Council & obtaining his pardon from the Govr.

KNOX GORDON, ESQ.

Mr. Phipoe went to Charlestown from London with him. Knew very little of him before. Believes he had spent a fortune before he went out. He was admitted to the Bar on his arrival. Got but little business at first, but before the King's Govrt. was overturned he had as much business as anybody. Supposes he made £900 or 1,000 pr. an. The King's Courts were open in 1775, but he continued to Act in the Rebel Courts. Mr. Phipoe mentioned to him that he had an offer to be chose of their Assembly & asked his opinion. Says that some time before he had suspicion of his Loyalty. He talked with him on the subject & found him Loyal. He signed the Association which he was sorry for. The King's Govert. had not left the Province in 1775. When Mr. P. mentioned his intention, he would not have advised him to become a member of the Assembly if he had thought it was necessary to take an oath to the States. Thinks he did not give him advice so late as 1777 to go into Assembly & he thinks in such a situation as the Country was in 1777 he should not have given him that advice. Mr. Phipoe he believes always was Considered by the Assembly as well inclined to the British. (106).

DR. GARDEN.

Has known the Claimt ever since he came to Charlestown. He practiced Law at the Commencement of the troubles, did not thus know much of him until 1776. Then thought he had fixed sentiments of Loyalty. When Sir Hy. Clinton & Sir Pr. Parker came agst. C. Town Mr. Phipoe went into the back Country. In 1777 he was elected by a part of the Country most disposed to the British Govrt. He was always agst. violent measures. Remembers Mr. P. quitting C. Town in 1780. He considered Mr. P. a friend to Gt. Britain, but the Americans did not consider him as hostile.

MR. BURKE.

Was left Agent to Mr. Phipoe at the Evacuation. Says Mr. P. was Loyal after the reduction of Charlestown. He sold the House for £1,100 which Cost him £1,500. Lachlan MacIntosh, a half-Pay Lt., sold Mr. Phipoe lands in 1778 for which he gave him £1,500 Cury. in depreciated Paper Money. He is asked whether he sold his Lands to a Loyalist or a Rebel. He says that no Loyalist could buy Lands at that time.

DR. FIFE.

Looks upon Mr. Phipoe as a Loyalist. He did every thing in his power at the Commencement of the troubles. He did not know that he had taken the oaths to the American States. Knew (107). he was a Member of the Assembly. He told him he went in to serve Gt. Britain. When he joined the British he believes it was from Principal.

EDWD. SAVAGE, ESQ.

Says that if Interest had been out of the way his wishes were for Gt. Britain. Says he was the most obnoxious man to the new State. He made about £8 or 900 pr. an. by his Profession.

REVD. JAS. STEWART.

In 1777 the Witness was prosecuted, Mr. Phipoe pleaded his cause without fee or reward. He refused money when he offered it.

MRS. FORTUNE, Wife to Colonel Fortune.
Knew him in C. Town. He was called the *Torrie Lawyer*.

He befriended her and Col. Fortune in 1777, when the Rebels took almost their all because they were Loyalists. She desired him to give his advice in writing, but he declined saying that if it was found out he would be hanged.

DR. SARSERY.

Has known Mr. Phipoe since the Surrender of C. Town. Since that time he has been very active & rendered every service in his power to the British Govrt.

22nd May.
Evidence Ld. Cornwallis Sen. Book No.—

1784.
12th May.
1175. Case REVD. MR. CLARKE.

(108).
Swears in Genr. that he believes every word of his memorial is true. He had the living of Dedham worth £50 pr. an. & 20£ pr. an. from the Society for propagating the Gospel. His Living was for Life. The Memorial Contains an acct. of very Loyal & Meritorious Conduct & sufferings in Consequence he has almost lost the use of his speech by his Confinement.

Says he lost £2,000 Stg. in Personal Estate, part of this a Bond.

About £120 or 130 Stg. exclusive of the Bond. His Father died in 1768. He was drove from America because he would not consent to Independance. He was tried & Condemned to Transportation & put in Prison for ten weeks. He receives £60 pr. an. from the Treasury.

£ pr. an. from the Society for Propagating the Gospel.

The REVD. MR. PETERS.

Has long known Mr. Clarke by Character & person from 1772. He had the Living of Dedham. He was always a staunch Loyalist. He was deaf in 1772, but very able to do his duty.
He had the Living of Dedham. He was always a Staunch Loyalist. The Living is moderately stated.

REVD. GEO. BASSET.

Rector of Trin. Church Rhode Island. Knows Mr. Clarke had the Living of Dedham. Remembers his being brought to Rhode Island to be Transported. His voice was extremely good & Strong when he first knew him, but in 1778 he had almost lost it. Always understood that he lost it in consequence of ill treatment.

(109).

Decision.

The Board are of opinion that the Claimt is a meritorious Loyalist.

He Lost Personal Estate value £120.
The Living of Dedham value £50 pr. an.
He has an allowance from the Treasury of £60 pr. an.

1176. Case JOHN ANDREWS.

1784.
13th May.

Is a native of New Jersey, in 1778 he carried an express from Sir Robt. Pigot to Lord Howe & Sir Hy Clinton. Produces a Certificate from Sir Hy. Clinton & Sir Robt. Pigot to that fact. In consequence he was tried & banished. He has done other services, but was always pd. He believes he is to have £40 pr. an. from the Treasury.

Property—Lot of Land at New Port purchased it from Capt. Howland 16 years ago. Consider 1,600 Drs. & laid out 600 Drs. more in expenses & buildings. A valuation produced on oath by James Nixon & James Clark at 2,500 Drs.

He had 8 large Hogs heads of sugar burnt at Bedford. 18 Hogs heads of Rum. Pd. 2,200 Drs. for both. Part was seized by the Rebels.

He left in his Store, 56 barrels Beef & Pork, pd. 60 sh. pr. barrel. He values them at 90sh. or £4-10.

(110).

64 Casks Flour, pd. 45sh. pr. barrel.
55 Head Cordage, Cost 40sh. pr. Head.
2,000 Weight Cheese, pd. 16d. for it York Cury.
2,000 Weight Cocoa, Cost him 60sh. pr. Cwt.
20 Kegs butter, Cost 8d. pr. pd.
7 Bags Hops, Cost £25.
A Blood Horse. 2 Blood Mares. A Colt taken by the Rebels. Gave £32 York for the horse. £22 for one mare, £20 for the other. Pd. £45 for the whole. Not more than £50S. Charges £100S. Wages pd. 8 men when Carrying the express. He received ten Gs. from Sir Hy. Clinton. Claimed his money at N. York, but received only One Dollar pr. day for two years & Rations. No Mortage or incumbrance.

JAS. NIXON, Late of Rhode Island.

Always considered John Andrews as well affected to Govrt. He carried Despatches for Govrt. He had a House & Lot worth 2,200 Dollars. Says he valued it at 2,500, but now thinks it worth 2,200. He would have given that. Says his Property is Confiscated. It appears so from an Official Paper.

BROOK SIMPSON.

Thinks his House in New Port worth £500 Stg. Thinks Mr. Clarke & Mr. Nixon have over valued it, but they are men of good Character & judges of Land.

Decision.

(111).

It appears that Mr. Andrews is Reported for £40 in full to carry him to America.

A Zealous and Active Loyalist.

House & Lot in New Port £420. Merchandise £1058. Horses, £40.

1177. Case ALEX. STANHOUSE.

1784.
13th May.

Is a native of Scotland, went to America in 1756, settled in 1759 as a Physician in Baltimore County & in 1764 in Baltimore

79 AR.

Town. Remained there until 1776. Avowed his principals from the Earliest moment.
Those who would not join the insurgents were Considered as Enemies. He was abused as a Torrie & Sent Coventry. In 1776 he went to Philadelphia to Embark for England. Came to Lisbon July, 1776, & from thence to Engd.

Property—A House & Lot in Baltimore.
The Proprietors granted to him for a Debt. £80 in 1773 or 4. The value when he quitted it was £1,000 Cury. The last year it was worth £2,000.

Debts—About £3000 Sterg. He made £707-10-6S. in 1775 by his practice, & in 1776 nothing it decreased with the troubles.

He gained by two other branches of business £274S. Total gives £956-11-4S.

Has an allowance of £80 pr. An.
Produces the acct. of his gains by his Business.

(112).

GEO. CHALMERS, ESQ.

Knew Dr. Stanhouse in Baltimore. Believes that he was uniformly Loyal. Believes he Lost his practice by the part he took. He cannot speak to his Property, but Knows Dr. Stanhouse had very handsome business. Thinks his gains might be £600 pr. An. S.

JAMES CHRISTIE, ESQ.

Believes he was obliged to quit Baltimore & good Business as a Physician on acct. of the part he took with Gt. Britain. He had the 2nd practice in Baltimore. Thinks he might some years make £500 per an.

1178. Case WM. MCQUEEN.

1774.
15th May.

Went from Scotland to America in 1773. When the troubles broke out he was on his own Plantation in N. Carolina. First joined the King's Standard Jany., 1776.

Swears in Genr. to the truth of his Memorial. Bore arms in a Troop of Horse 1780, without pay. Ld. Cornwallis gave him a Capt. Commission. He was in 2 or 3 Engagements & served in the Ranks after 1780.

He was sent with dispatches by Major Craig to Lt. Cornwallis Was taken, tried & Condemned, but made his escape to C. Town & Stayed until the Evacuation.

Has an allowance of £30 pr. An.

(113)

Was Inspector of Refugees at C. Town for one month with a Sallary of 5sh. pr. day.

Certificates—Ld. Cornwallis, Major Craig, Col. McDonald & C. Colton to Character, Loyalty, e c

He carried out £500S. with him.

250 acres of Land at Hedge Creek, Anson County, he gave £100 Cury. in 1774. 50 acres Cleared. He Cleared 20 acres. He values it at £150 Cury.

63 Head of Cattle, 20 Milch Cows, 2 riding Horses, 13 Work Horses, 86 Hogs, 8 Sheep. Furniture £60. Carpenter's Tools

£15. 400 Bushels Corn 3sh. 30 bushels Wheat & all the other articles in the Schedule. The Whole real & Personal Property is valued at £795-10. Believes his Property is Confiscated. He owed no money.

KENNETH STEWART.

The Claimnt took part with the King's Govrt. at Cross Creek in 1776.

Knew his Farm, it was large & Considerable Clearances & some buildings. Cannot value it. He had a large stock, about 60 Hd. Cattle, Several Horses. Thinks his furniture worth £40 or 50 Cury.

DR: SHAW.

The Claimt was always Loyal. He was Prisoner with him in 1781.

Has been on his farm. It was in good Condition 50 or 60 acres Cleared. The House was tolerably furnished.

ANGUS MARTIN.

Lived neighbour to Claimt in America. Bore arms & was uniformly for Govnt. Heard he went with dispatches. Knew he owned his Farm, 150 acres. A Considerable Clearance. Says it was worth £150S. His House was decently furnished.

(114).

MURDOCH MCDONALD.

Lived near the Claimt in 1776. He had a good Farm. Considerable Clearance. Good Stock, & his House well furnished.

1179. Case HY. BLENKENHORN.

A German, went to America in 1762. Was at C. Town when the Troubles broke out. Took charge of the Rebels Waggons when they went agst. Savannah.

1784.
15th May.

Joined the British when Charlestown was taken & served in Capt. Phipoe's Compy. The oathes were tendred him, but he was sick & they excused him.

He gave £70,000 Paper Money for a House in C. Town in 1777 or 1778.

He had two Negroes. One of them was away. Came home in the fleet & had 260 Weight of Indigo & a cask of rice. The ship was taken. He values the rice at £5, the Indigo at £79-4.

States Debts Amounting to £526-11-6.

THOS. PHIPOE.

After the reduction of Charlestown the Claimt was in his Compy. He was trusted with arms & behaved well. He bought 2 Horses in 1777 or 1778. Does not know the value.

(115).

JAS. DARBY.

Says the Claimt kept the Brown Bear in C. Town, a Carriers Inn. He was Capt. of the Ship which brought him home. She was taken. He had rice & Indigo & some furniture on board. All Lost.

JAS. MOORE.

Knew he Kept a store for drg goods after C. Town was taken. Believes him an honest man.

SOPHIA GUTHORP.

Claimt married her Daughter. He Kept a Store & Tavern at Charles Town. He lost two negroes there.

Col. Fortune. Knew the Claimt at Charles Town, he was a friend to the Loyalists. More Loyalists resorted to his House than to any in Town.

1784.
May 15th:

1180. Case THOS. RYAN.

Is an Irishman. He went to America 14 years before the troubles. Lived at New York as a Car Man when the troubles broke out.

He refused to sign the Association. Was obliged to absent himself until the British Troops took the Place.

Came to Engd. last Michlmass for his health. He never bore arms.

(116).

Certificates to Loyalty from Govr. Tyron & Mountford Brown. States his Losses at £178.

A Cart & Two Horses. Hay Clothes. Furniture. Cash. Loss of Business, &c. Suport of his family for two years. Has received £20 in full from the Treasury.

JOSEPH ALICOCKE.

The Claimt was an honest Car Man at N. York. Very industrious & always Loyal. Knows nothing of his Property.

Decision.

The Claimt is a Loyalist.

He Lost Personal Property to the Amount of £80. Has received £20 in full from the Treasury.

PROCEEDINGS

OF

LOYALIST COMMISSIONERS

MONTREAL, 1788.

VOL. I.

MISCELLANEOUS EVIDENCE.

Claimants.

	MSS. Folio.		MSS. Folio.
Allen, Joseph	35	Liddel, Andrew	30
Bogart, Gilbert	5 & 27	Lyman, Henry	20
Bradshaw, James	28	McGlaughlan, William	3
Brooke, Richard	1	Mackie, Alexander	40
Brown, Governor William	41 & 42	Maybee, Mrs. Eleanor (Mrs. Hoffman)	17
Buck, George	11	Middagh, John	6
Buis, Stephen	15	Middagh, Martin	7
Christy, John	16	Middagh, Stephen	7
Cross, John	34	Miller, Jacob	14
Crowe, Richard Robert	50	Nicholson, Alexander	4
Curtis, John	32	Ogden, Nicholas	45
Day, Bernabas	23	Schermerhorn, William	31
Derry, James	50	Shaw, James	33
Derry, John	49	Sills, Conrad	20
Dixon, Robert	3	Smith, John	25
Evans, Mrs. Margaret (Mrs. Fitzsimmons)	44	Spencer, Jeremiah	12
Grass, Michael	9	Walker, Daniel	39
Jackson, Henry	29	Waggoner, John	34
Jackson, James	24	Wartman, Abraham	18
Keller, Frederick	22	Wentworth, Governor	41
Keller, William	21	Worth, Benjamin	43

THE EVIDENCE.

N. C.
February 18.
1181. Claim of RICHARD BROOKE, late of Tryon Co.

Claimt. says. He delivered his Claim to Mr. Powell in the Fall 83. Mr. Powell was too late to lodge it in England. Produces the Acct. which was sworn to before Judge Fraser Nov. 1st, 83, and Claimt. says the Acct. was delivered at that time or near it.

(1).
Is a Nat. of England. Came to America about the beginning of the War, but there had been no battle at that time. He went to several Places, and at last fixt on Tryon Co. This was in the Fall of 1774. He Continued there till the Rebellion broke out, from the first he declared in favour of Brit. Govnt., in 1776, he was taken up & imprisoned & kept 7 months in prison in Johnstown, in 1777 he was imprisoned again, he was imprisoned a 3rd time in Albany Gaol in 1778 from whence he got discharged on bail & Came to Canada, has Continued there ever since. Now lives in Montreal.

His name in Anstey's list.
Had 400 acres in Tryon Co., purchased in 1774 of Richd. Wells, of Philadelphia at £50 Pens. Cur. per 100 acres. Paid the whole in Gold & Silver in 12 months, says he had Cleared & improved & fenced 70 or 80 acres, built a good house, 3 Stories high, a large Barn & good out buildings. Vals. Clear land at £4 York as very low.

Lost near 30 Head horned Cattle, 4 horses, valuable Tools, utensils, furniture, Plate, 10 Tons Hay, a great quantity of Cheese. Part taken when he was imprisoned the first & 2nd time, the

Seems a good man.
rest when he was sent to Albany. They were all sold at Vendue. Says he sold an Estate in England for £1,000 before he came to America & brought most of it with him.

WILLIAM FAUKNER, Wits.:

Knew Claimt. He settled in Tryon Co. in 1773 or 1774. He always was Considered as very Loyal, and acted as such, he was several times imprisoned on acct. of his Loyalty, the last time Witness thinks was in Albany Gaol, from Albany he went to Canada & his Whole Property was Confiscated.

(2).
He had a Tract purchased of Mr. Wells in the Fall 1774. Witness remembers him living upon it in 1774. He made large Improvements—there were 40 acres clear in the end of 1775. There was an extraordinary good Barn and good house. He had a large stock at this time—12 milk Cows and other Cows. He came over in very good circumstances—with a great quantity of Tools etc. The house appeared well supplied with all sorts of necessaries. Has understood that all his Property real and personal has been sold.

Claimt. produces a letter from a Friend of his dated Albany March 3, 1787, informing him that a Frenchman had bought his Farm.

1182. Claim of WM. McGLAUGHLAN, late of Tryon Co. N. C.
February 18.

Claimt. says he was in Sr. John's first Battn. was at Coteau de Lac & delivered his Claim to his Commanding officer.

Is a nat. of Ireland—came to Am. in 73—was settled in Cherry Valley—joined the Brit. at first—served all the war—now lives in New Johnstown.

Produces Discharge. Produces Recommendation from Capt. Anderson & Certificate to his Character. Says Sr. John Johnson told him he would give him a like Recommendation. (3).

Had 100 acres. He had bargained for it in 1774—he had not paid for it, but had paid for the Improvmnts—pd. £30 York. Says there was not so many acres as 20 acres clear. He cleared 5 acres more, there were above 25 acres clear. There were buildings upon it. A good man.

Had 3 milch Cows—2 Heifers—5 Horses—Utensils—furniture—Left all behind him. They were all lost.

TIMOTHY OBRIEN Wits.

Knew Claimt's. Place at Cherry Valley—he was in a prosperous way. There were good clearances. He had a good stock.

1183. Claim of ROBERT DIXON, late of Albany Co., decd. N. C.
February 18.

WILLIAM FAUKNER Wits.

Says Robert Dixon was a soldier in Jessops—thinks he was at

the River Le Chenay the Fall before the Regiment was discharged He died last May 12 month. His wife died last year. He has left 2 sons, 2 Daughters all very young and helpless—they live with their uncle John Cameron at New Johnstown—speaks very well of him as a man proper to have the rect., of what may be allowed for the children.

John Cameron appears—Says he is Brother in Law to Robert Dixon—he died last May 12 months—his wife is since dead. He has left 4 Infant Children who live with Witness.

The late Robert Dixon was a nat. of Scotl—came to America some years before the war. He was settled at Saratoga. He joined the Brit. Army in 1776, and served all the war. He had settled on some Lands at Saratoga as Witness was informed, but he does not know the Place. Witness seems a good man, but at Present there is no Evidence. (4).

1184. Claim of ALEXR. NICHOLSON, late of Remington Vermont—Lodged in England. N. C.
February 18.

Claimt. says he was at Isle au Noix in the Fall 83, then gave in a Claim to be sent to Major Jessop—delivered another to Capt.

Gomersall in 84.

Is a nat. of Scotl— came to Amer. in 74—settled in Pounal— joined in 77—served all the War, except the time he was Prisoner. Now lives a Bay of Quinty.

Had 200 acres that lay near William's Town, it lay on the Lines between Massts. & York Govt. Claimant bought it of Thomas Euston in 1776 after the war began—it was wild land—it was to cost 1 dollar per acre, but he was to pay it part in work—part in money. He had began some little Improvements.

He had 2 horses, 2 Cows, 1 Heifer, 2 Hogs, Joiners Tools, at Pounal. They were taken and sold after the Battle of Bennington, when Claimt. was taken Prisoner.

JOHN DEFOE, Wits.

(5).

Knew Claimt. There were some Lands which were call'd his. Knew that he had 2 Horses, 2 Cows, at Pounal & Joiners Tools He was taken Prisoner at Bennington Battle and the Rebels took his stock. The rebels sold him as a slave and he was obliged to work out his Freedom.

N. C.
February 18.

1185. Claim of GILBERT BOGART, late of Orange Co., de bene esse, vi infra.

TOBIAS RYCKMAN, Wits.

Says Claimant was in the Engineers Department during the War. He was at Sorell in the Fall 83. He lived at Tappan Orange Co.—he had 2 houses, and a large Barn, and 30 acres of Land in Tappan. Witness has seen his purchase Deeds. He had Horses, Horn Cattle—very good furniture. He joined the Brit. very early and his Property was seized and sold by the Rebels.

N. C.
February 19.

1186. Claim of JOHN MIDDAGH, late of Ulster Co.

Claimt. says. He was in Sr. Johns 2nd Battalion—was at a considerable distance from Montreal in the Fall 83.

Is a nat. of A.—lived in Ulsetr Co. when Troubles broke out. He from the first declared for Brit. Govnt.—Suffered a great Deal from the Rebels on that acct. Was driven from his house in 1777, and was obliged to sculk in the woods for almost a whole winter—

(6).

had a brother who was executed for raising men for the King's service, in 1779 Caimt. came to Niagara, joined Sr. Johns Regt., served till end of the war. Produces his Discharge—now lives at New Johnstown.

A good man.

Had taken up some lands on the Head of the Deleware—was to have had a Lease from Judge Livingston. He had been in Possession some years before the War—had cleared 10 acres—Had built a House, and had a share in a Horse Mill worth £2. He saved his Cattle—Lost Utensils, furniture, Cloaths, 2 Canoes.

Produces Certificate from Capt. Munro to his Loyalty, which also mentions the execution of his Brother.

STEPHEN MIDDAGH, Wits.

Says Claimt. and Wits. and 2 other Brothers were very active for Government from the first. One Brother was executed. Claimt. joined the Brit. Army at Niagara, he and his Family.

He had taken up lands at the Head of the Deleware 2 years or more before the War—cleared 10 acres, Lost Utensils, furniture.

1187. Claim of STEPHEN MIDDAGH, late of Ulster Co.   N. C. February 19.

Claimt. says—he was in Sr. Johns 1st Battn.—gave his claim to Capt. Munro in the Fall 83. Produces Capt. Munro's Certificate to that purpose and to his Loyalty.
Is a nat. of A.—lived upon the Delware when the Rebellion broke out. He first joined Butlers Corps in 1776,—was discharged on acct. of illness in 1779. As soon as he got well he joined Sr. Johns Corps. served till end of the War—produces his Discharge. Now lives at 5th Township.   (7).

Had taken up some Land at the Head of the Delaware—had cleared 5 acres—had built a house, a share in a Grist Mill. Lost 1 Horse, 1 Cow, Utensils, furniture, Cloaths, Stack of Corn.   A good man.

JOHN MIDDAGH, Wits.
Gives the same acct. as his Brother. He had 5 acres Clear. Lost Horse & Cow, furniture, Tools, all taken by the Rebels.

1188. Claim of MARTIN MIDDAGH on behalf of Henry, Charles, Rachel and Mary Bush, children of the late Henry Bush, late of Ulster Co., decd.   N. C. February 19.

Martin Middagh says—Henry Bush died in the year 1779 or 1780. He and his wife both died at Mashishe, nearly at the same time.
He is a native of America. He lived at Marbletown when the Rebellion broke out. He came from thence to the Delaware. He always declared in favr. of Brit. Govt. He joined the Indians under Brant—thinks this was in the year 1777. He was always ready to join the scouting parties and joined in many occasions. Came into Canada in 1779, brought his family, died at Mashishe in 1780. He married Witness's Sister and has left t children all Infants. Witness is the Guardian of them all—3 live with him, one Rachel lives with Capt. Rich'd. Duncan.   (8).

The late Henry Bush had a farm at Marbletown left him by his Father's Will. His Father died some years before the war He had been in Possession from the time of his Fathers death till he came to the Delaware.
There were 5) acres—it was new ground, not cleared —he had begun building, but did not do much. He lift Machishe on the commencement of the Rebellion, being persecuted by the Rebels and came to the Delaware. He then took some Lands and cleared 5 or 6 acres.

He lost 2 Horses. He left a Weavers Loom and Tackling, utensils and furniture. He left all these things on the Delaware when he went to Capt. Brant—a Loom was worth £6.

JOHN MIDDAGH, Wits.

Says Henry Bush was from the first a steady Loyalist. He joined with Capt. Brant and was in several scouting Parties. He was very near losing his Life by a party of Rebels who fired at him.

(9).

He came into Canada with the other Loyalists who were driven from their homes.
He had 50 acres of Land at Marbletown under his Father's Will. His father had a considerable Estate besides a lot of it cleared in Marbletown—this was left to other children. Some little was done on these 50 acres—the house was began. From thence he came to the Delaware—Cleared 4 or 5 acres. He lost his moveables—1 weavers Loom and Tackling Compleat, furniture.

N. C.
February 20.

1189. Claim of MICHAEL GRASS, late of Tryon Co.

Claimt. says. He was at Sorell & Cataraqui in the Fall 83. He sent a Claim home by Mr. Kyler & Capt. Gomersal.

Is a native of Germany—came to America in 1753. Was living in Tryon Co. when the Rebellion broke out. From the first took part with the Brit. Govert.—in 1777 he went to New York where he continued to reside & on all occasions turned out as a Volunteer. Had an appointment as 1st Lieut. in one of the Companies of City Militia in 1780. Produces his appointment from Major James Patterson—came away from New York before the Evacuation, being appointed Captn. of Militia for a Company of Loyalists who were going from New York to Canada. Produces the Commision from Sr. Guy Carleton in July in 1783.

In consequence of his appointment he came to Canada—has been employed in settling the Loyalists at Cataraqui for which he hsa rec'd nothing—above 900 Persons came under his Direction. Now resides at Cataraqui.

(10).

Withdraws his claim from his Farm inserted in his first Schedule—as he has saved it, and for several articles of personal property which he has recovered—produces a new acct.

Had a house at New York—he built it after he went to New York in 1780. It was on Ground belonging to one Bateman. Says this was a vacant lot & he built upon it in Consequence of Permission given by the Mayor agreeable to a Proclamation of Sr. Henry Clinton—the building Cost him 165 guns. Lost furniture to a considerable amount. This was in the House at the Farm in Tryon Co.—While Claimt. was at New York. The Rebels seized all his furniture & Stock & sold it at public Vendue—he had very good furniture—a stock of Sadlery goods worth at least £150. They took his farming utensils at the same time—Lost 4 horses—5 Cows 8 Sheep.

A very good man.

Produces at the Foot of his acct. the affidavits of 2 persons to the Truth of the acct. now given in. Sworn at Cataraqui.

PETER CARLOW, Wits.

Knew Claimt. when he lived on the Mohawk—he was always very Loyal. He went off to New York, to join the Brit. Troops because he was called upon to join the Rebels.

He was in good circumstances—he was a farmer & sadler. He had a very good stock. He used to have a quantity of Tools & Sadlery goods. He had horses & Cows—had a wagon & Carts.

(11).

1190. Claim of GEO. BUCK, late of Tryon Co. Lodged in N. C. February 20. England by Capt. Gomersal.

MICHL. GRASS, Wits.

Says Claimant has met with an accident lately which has made him quite a cripple & he is unable to travel to Montreal.

He is a native of Germany—Came to America quite a child— lived in Tryon Co. He was then a cripple & could not serve, but he was very Loyal. Went to Canada in 81. on acct. of his Loyalty. He was driven from his Farm by the Rebels. He now resides at Cataraqui.

Witness speaks very favourably of him.

He had no Land of his own but was on hired Land. He lost a Horse & a Colt & Cow & some grain. Witness remembers that he had the Horse, Colt & Cow & thinks that he lost them by being driven from his Place. He came into Canada helpless & stript of all his Property.

1191. Claim of JERMIAH SPENCER, late of Clarendon. N. C. February. Lodged in England, Vermont.

Claim says—He was in Caldwells Manor in the Fall 83. He sent his claim home by Capt. Gomersal.

Is a nat. of Am. —lived in Clarendon when Rebellion broke out—joined the Brit. Army at Castleton & Fort Edward—attended the army 5 weeks with Cart & Oxen after Burgoyns Capitulation. He returned home—he was taken prisoner 3 or 4 months—he got back to his Family—after that he sculked about. He was frequently employed by scouting Parties. He came into Canada in March, 82.—staid till June, then fetched his Family in July.

In the fall he joined Rogers Rangers. He and 3 sons joined at the same time—served till Regt. was disbanded—says he was about 13 months in the Corps. Produces his Discharge in Decr. 83, stating that he had served for a year.

(12).

Says his Sons were so young that they could not enter into year service without him. He staid to be of service in Scouting Parties.

Had 100 acres in Otter Creek purchased in 1768 of Randol Rice for 16 dollars—it was half a right—afterwards got Grants from New York & New Hampshire—at expense 60 dollars—he cleared 40 acres—built a Log house.

Produces Certificate from M. Lyon, Clerk of County of Confiscation that Claimts. real and personal Estate was Confiscated in 78.

Lost mare & colt—4 Cows—3 calves—2 Steers—3 yearlings— some Flax &c., Taken by the Rebels.

(13).

SIMSON ——— Wits.

Knew Claimt—Considered him always as a Loyalist. He went into Burgoynes Camp with Wits. served in the army with his Team during the Campaign —returned home, but was prosecuted

& imprisoned & driven from his Place. Thinks he came into Canada before the war was over.

He had 100 acres in Clarendon—Witness says he had 300 acres, when he knew the Place, but he sold 200—Witness understands he kept his home Lot—thinks there were 30 or 40 acres clear. He had a good stock of Cattle.

LIEUT. HASELTINE SPENCER, Wits.

Knew Claimt.—Considered him always as a Loyalist—he joined Genl. Burgoyne with his team & Continued with Burgoyne during that Campaign. He came into Canada before the war was over. He and 3 sons were in Rogers Rangers. His sons were very young. He had about 100 acres of Land at Clarendon—about 40 acres clear—remembers him in Possession some years before the war—he had been settled in that Country a long time. He had a horse or two & 4 or 5 horned cattle when Witness was at his Place last, which was in 1777.

(14).

N. C.
February 21.

1192. Claim of JACOB MILLER, late of Tryon Co.

sent a claim to England by Capt. Gomersal.

Is a nat. of Germ.—came to Amer. many years ago. Lived at Turloch when Rebellion broke out. He joined the Brit. Army in 1777—served all the war now lives at Bay of Quinty.

He had 150 acres of Land at Turloch. He purchased them of Nicholas Stamberg of Schoharie in 1769—he was to pay £90 York. He gave a Bond for payment had no pard. He had cleared 20 acres—built house & Barn—He lost 3 horses, 10 head of Cattle, 4 Sheep, 12 Hogs, furniture, Utensils. Left all these things on his

Farm. Left a Crop in the Ground.

FREDERIC FOX, Wits.

Knew Claimt—he was always Loyal—he joined the Brit. at Fort Stanwix.

He had 150 acres at Turloch—he had been in Possession 6 or 7 years before ye war. He cleared 21 or 22 acres. He had built Claimt. says—He was at the River De Cheyne in the Fall 83. House and Barn. Knew his Stock—he had 3 horses, about 10 head of Cattle &c.

N. C.
February 21.

(15).

1193. Claim of STEPHEN BUIS, late of Albany Co.

Claimt. says he was at Isle au Noix in the Fall 83. Is a nat. of A.—lived at Newtown, Albany Co.,— joined the Brit. in 80— says he was to young to join before. He lived with his Father & a year after his death he joined the Brit.—served till end of War. Produces his Discharge . Now lives at Cataraqui.

His Father had a house for 80 years of 120 acres. Claimt. took Possession on his Father's death in 1779. His Father had been in Possession 20 years. The Rent was £6 York per ann. When Claimt. came to Canada, his mother was turned off the Place and came to Canada. She saved the Cattle.

There were 70 acres clear—there was a good Log house, Barn A good man.
& good orchard.

Produces affidt. of John Conklin taken by W. R. Crawford at Cataraqui to Claimts being possessed of a Farm as above stated.

Do of PETER THOMAS.

JOHN BUIS, Witness.

Knew the Farm which belonged to Claimts Father, & which came to him on his Father's Death—there was a good deal clear. His Father had been in possession many years—there was a good house & Barn—he supposes there were 50 or 60 acres clear.

1194. Claim of JOHN CHRISTY, late of Tryon Co. N. C. February.

Claimt says— He was at Carleton Island in 83. Is a nat. of Am.—lived at Johnstown when the Rebellion broke out—he joined the Brit. in 1780. He had one son who had joined before—he had 2 other sons in the service. Claimt. served 3 years produces his Discharge—lives at New Johnstown. (16).

He had taken some Land of Sr. Wm. Johnston, in Kingsbury Patent on Lease, 100 acres. Took Possession in 1775—cleared 15 acre—built house & Barn.

No. 2. Had also agreed to purchase some Lands of Sr. Wm. Johnson in Mayfield. The agreement was made in 73 or 74—had not got a Deed, or paid for them, but had cleared about 15 acres. When he left his Place, he left 2 horses, & 20 horned cattle—his family saved 10 young Cattle, farming utensils. These things were taken by the Rebels & sold at Vendue—soon after Claimt. went away.

Produces an affid't of Allen Cameron taken before Capt. Anderson to Claimts. Loyalty, & property as above stated.

CHRISTIAN SCHICH, Wits.

Knew Claimt in Tryon Co.,—he came up from New York to settle on Sr. Wm. Johnson's Lands, some time before Sr. Wm.'s Death. He had 2 Farms then as Witness understood. He used to attend the market as a Farmer with grain &c., & used to have his Farming utensils repaired by Wits., but Witness never saw his Farms. He seemed to be in a very good way. Has seen some Horses & Cattle that belonged to Claimt. (17).

He came into Canada in 80—left some of his Family behind, but they saved only part of his property. Witness speaks of his Character as being a very honest man.

Further Evidences in Case of ELEANOR MAYBEE, v. Vol. 21, February 21. f. 112.

Joseph Hoffman, her present Husband appears—says he was informed by several persons that the late Peter Maybee had 150 acres of Land, of which he had the soil Right, in Dutchess Co.— has heard a great deal was cleared. Heard he let it when he went to Albany Co., to one Miller. There was a great deal of Rent due which Peter Maybee never rec'd.—has understood that Miller was driven away from his Farm. Thinks Peter Maybee had left Dutchess Co. 9 or 10 years before the war began.

N. C.
February 25.
(18).

1195. Claim of ABRAHAM WARTMAN, late of Pensilv., dec'd.

John Wartman 2nd Son of Abraham Wartman appears—says his Father died last fear. His eldest Brother Peter is at Cataraqui —his lamed from an accident & could not come, but Witness is authorized to act for him & produces a Letter of attorney to enable him to do so.

The late Abraham Wartman was at Coteau de Lac, in the Fall 83, & sent a claim home to England by Capt. Leake.

The late Abraham Wartman was a native of Germany—came young to America—lived in the Susquehana when Rebellion broke out. He joined the Brit. in 1777—he served 3 years in the Army. He was then discharged on acct. of age & came to Canada & was employed in the King's Works as artificer—he afterwards settled in Cataraqui—died last year, leaving Catharine his widow & 3 Brothers all at Cataraqui.

His mother came to Canada with her Husband—his eldest Bror. came in at the same time, & was employed in the King's Works. Witness & the youngest Bror. came in at the same time, they were both too young to serve. The eldest Brother of all was killed in service in 1788.

His Father had a Farm in the Susquehana—he had taken up some Land at the office at Philadelphia it was on the disputed Lands. He took Possession seven or eight years before the war— he built house, Barn & outhouses—thinks there were 24 acres clear.

(19).

He had mare & colt & Horse, yoke of oxen do of yearling, 2 Heifers, Sheep, Hogs, furniture & utensils. These Things were taken after his Father & eldest Brother joined the Brit.—Witness & his Mother were at Home & were obliged to quit & the Rebel took all the Things above mentioned.

N.B. The whole is to be paid to John Wartman.

CONRAD SILL, Wits.

Knew the late Abraham Wartman—he was very Loyal.—He & his eldest son joined Col. Butlers Corps in 1777—he served two years—then he & his Family came into Canada. His eldest son was killed in service. His Property was all lost, after he came away. He had some Proprietors Land in the Susquehana it was disputed land—thinks he had cleared 30 acres—a fine young orchard—he had a house, Barn &c. Gives same acct. of stock.

A good family.

N. C.
February 25.

1196. Claim of CONRAD SILLS, late of Pensv. Lodged in England.

Claimt. says—He was at Mashishi in the Fall 83—gave a Claim to Capt. Leake in Jany. 84.

Is a nat. of Germany—came very young to America—Lived on the Susquehana, joined the Brit. in 1777—was at Fort Stanwix

—served 3 years— then came into Canada—he sent three of his sons as soon as they were old enough into Sr. John Johnson's Regt. Now lives at Bay of Quinty.

He had 300 acres on the Susquehana—he built an house— he had cleared 20 acres—it was disputed Land—he had 6 Horses, 4 cows, 2 calves, 1 Bullock, Sheep, Hogs, furniture, utensils, grain &c.

A good man.

(20)

JOHN WARTMAN, Wits.

Knew Claimt.—He joined the Brit. Army in 1777—Knew his Lands.

LAWRENCE SILLS, Wits.

Says there was a good clearance on his Father's Lands— remembers the stock & agrees with his Father in the acct.

1197. Claim of HENRY LYMAM, late of Pensilvania. Lodged in England.

N. C. February 25.

Conrad Sills Witness appears—says that Claimt. is so ill, with the Ruematism that he could not come.

Says Claimt. was at Coteau de Lac in the Fall 83.—sent a claim by Capt. Leake. He is a native of Germany—came very young to America—settled on the Susquahana. He joined the Brit. in 17777—he served three years—then came to Canada. He was an old man—they gave him an Employment at Coteau dr Lac. He now lives at Bay of Quinty.

He had some Land on the Susquahana and a good stock.

JOHN WUSTERS, Wits.

(21).

Knew Claimt.—he was always Loyal—joined the Brit. in 77. Knew his Lands on the Susquahana—he had better than 12 acres clear—he had built a house & Barn—he had oxen & Cows & Sheep.

Witness is told to inform him that he sh'd send a Certificate that he is not able to come from his apothecary.

1198. Claim of WILLIAM KELLER, late of Albany Co. Lodged in England.

N. C. February 25.

Claimt. says—He was at Isle au Noix in 83—gave his claim to Major Mathews that Winter.

Is a nat. of America—lived in Houssac when Rebellion broke out—joined the Brit. in 80—served in Rogers Rangers till end of War. Produces his Discharge. Now lives at Bay of Quinty.

He had 100 acres of Land in Houssack. It was the Pataroon's Land. His Father had a Lease for 15 years—gave it Claimt., who got a new Lease in his own name. He was a long time in Possession, before the war. He had near 50 acres clear—he had built house & Barn &c.

Lost 2 horses & a colt, 2 Cows, 1 Heifer—these were lost before he left the Country—he left when he came away—2 other horses, 2 Cows, his Furniture & utensils were taken away in 1777.

Seems a good man, but not to be allowed much.

(22). Produce an affidavit from his Brother Frederic Keller taken before Jephtha Hanley to Claimts. having the Property above stated.

N. C.
February 25.

1199. Claim of FREDERIC KELLER, late of Albany Co. Lodged in England.

William Keller says—his Brother was at Isle au Noix in the Fall 83.

He is a nat. of Amer. He joined the Brit. in 80—served till end of the war. Produces his Discharge—now lives at Bay of Quinty. He had lived with Witness at Housac—had no Lands—he had a horse & Cow, 2 Sheep. He left the horse & Cow behind where he joined the Brit. Army.

N. C.
February 25.

1200. Claim of BERNABOS RAY, late of Goshen, New York. Lodged in England.

Claimt says he was at Cataraqui in 83. Sent a Claim by Capt. Gomersal.

Is a nat. of A., lived in Essex Co. when the Rebellion broke out. He was in a bad state of health at first & would not take any part. He was summoned before a Rebel Committee in 79. Had a Judgement agast. him & was obliged to find security of £1,000 Feb. following, viz., in 1780, he got into New York & Continued there till the Evacuation. Then came to Canada. Now lives at Cataraqui.

(23). He had 40 acres near Goshen. Purchased after the War began. He gave £200 York for it. He paid the whole. Part by money, part by Paper, & part by giving a Bond. Vals. it at £200 York.

He had Improvements on another Farm adjoining. He bought the Improvements at the same time with his other Farm, he gave £30. He came to an agreemnt with Roger Clark to let this Place to him before he went to New York. He took Possession but has now parted with it. Lost the Stock mentioned in his Schedule, at different times. Greatest part was lost as he was carrying it into New York. The 2 horses & Wagon loaded with Beef were taken near the New Bridge, by the Rebels in the Winter of 1779. He intended to have sold the Beef at New York. He had been used to

Carry Provisions into New York for some time.

Carpenters Tools, Hogs, &c., they were taken from the Place at Hackinsac where Claimt had got leave to reside. His Wife was there. The Rebels took them & sold them at Vendue after Claimt went into New York. All the Things except the two first Articles were lost in this way.

Produces an affidt from John Burdet sworn before Major Van Alstine that Claimt had the above Property.

N. C.
February 25.

1201. Claim of JAMES JACKSON, late of Skeensborough.

(24). Claimt says He was at Isle au Noix in 83. Is a Nat. of England. Came to America in 1770. Lived at Skeensborough when

Rebellion broke out, joined the Brit at Skeensboro where Burgoyne was. He did not serve at that time, but assisted the Army there. He came into Canada in 81. Served in Jessups Corps till end of the War. Produces his Discharge. Now lives at Cataraqui.

He had 208 acres at Skeensborough Lease Land. He had the Lease in 70. He had cleared between 30 & 40 acres, built house, barn & stable, &c.

Lost 5 Cows, 1 Heifer, 1 Bull, 3 Horses, furniture, utensils. They were taken in 1777. The Cattle were sold at Vendue. This was on acct. of his having Assisted the Brit. Army. Says he should have left the Country sooner, but Illness prevented.

Produces an affidt from Wm. Prindle sworn before Major Van Alstine, to Claimts Property in a great measure as above stated, & that he was possesst of 2 Mulattoes.

Claimt says his wife had 2 Mulattoe girls about 8 yrs. old. One was sold when Major Skeens things were sold. They had been given to his wife by Miss Skeen. The other was stole.

JOHN SMITH, Wits.

Knew Claimt at Skeensboro. He was a very good Loyalist. He afforded great assistance to the Brit. Army at Skeensboro. His effects were seized on Acct. of his having assisted the Brit. Knew his Farm, he had been a long time in Possession. He had about 30 Acres Clear. His Wife had two Mulatto Girls. Witness always supposed they belonged to him. Knew his stock. He had a good stock, heard of 5 Cows, 2 Heifers, being driven off by the Rebels.

(25).

1202. Claim of JOHN SMITH, late of Skeensboro.   N. C.
February 25.

Claimt Says. He was at St. Johns in the Fall of 83. Is a Nat. of Eng., has been 37 years in Am., lived at Skeensboro when Rebellion broke out. He came into Canada in the year 80, & joind Rogers Rangers. Says he was old, or he should have joind at first. His principals were known and he was driven off from his place. He had frequently harboured Persons who were sent out on secret service. Served 2 yrs. in the Rangers. Now lives at Bay of Quinty.

Produces Certificate to his Character & to his having served in the war before the last in the 44th Regt. & to his Loyalty & service during the late Rebellion, signed by a great many of his neighbors, by way of recommending him to Charity, he having lost his House & Property by fire last May, 12 months.

(26).

He had 111 acres Tenant Land in Skeensboro. He had the Lease 1768. It was a Lease forever at 1s. pr. Acre. He had cleared 24 acres, a good house, a large Barn & Stable.

Lost 1 Horse, 2 Cows, 16 Hogs, Grain, Hay, &c. This was at Kingsbury. He had got some lands there from a friend, after he quitted Skeensboro. He left all these Things there when he went into Canada.

80 AR.

JAMES JACKSON, Wits.

Knew John Smith. He was always a good Loyalist. He had a Farm at Skeensboro, 24 acres Clear. He had been a good while in Possession. After he was driven from Skeensboro. He had some lands & a little stock at Skeensboro, 2 Cows, 1 Horse, Hogs, &c., all left behind when he came away.

N. C.
February 25.

1203. Claim of GILBERT BOGART, late of Orange Co.

Claimt says. He was at Sorell in 83. Is a Nat. of Amer., lived at Goshen when Rebellion broke out. Never joined the Rebels. Came into New York in 1777. Continued at New York. Served in the Engineers Department. Produces Certificate from Alex. Mercer, dated Jan., 80, that Claimt then did Duty in that Department.

(27).

He sometimes went out as a guide, particularly when Major Blowwett, a Rebel Major, was taken. Continued at New York till Evacuation. Now lives at Bay of Quinty.

He had 30 acres at Goshen. He bought it 6 or 7 years before the War. He gave £300 York for it. He has paid all. Had a Deed. His Deed is now at Home. Built 2 Stone houses & one

His name is in Anstey's list.
A very good man.

framed House & good Barn, the whole was well improved. There were fine orchards, fine meadows. Vals. it at £350. Says he could have got more.

Had 12 Cattle, 4 horses, 9 Hogs, furniture, Clothes, utensils. Taken after he went to New York.

Produces an affidt from Susannah Baker before Major Van Alstine to Claimts Property above stated. Produces 2 affidts to his Loyalty & services as a Guide, & to his having been driven from home & Coming within the Lines at New York & serving in Engineers Department. See Page 11th.

N. C.
February 25.

1204. Claims of JAMES BRADSHAW, late of Kingbury, Charlotte Co.

David Bradshaw, eldest son of Claimt, appears. Says his Father is very old & infirm & Could not attend.

His Father was at Sorell in the Fall,83. He is a Nat. of Ireland. Came to America many years ago. Was Settled at Kingsbury when Rebellion broke out. He had always declared in Favour of Brit. Govrt. He had been a Capt. of Brit. Militia in 1777. He was put in Gaol on acct. of his Loyalty in 1779.

(28).

Came into Canada. He was too old to serve. He continued with the Loyalist till he went up to Bay of Quinty. He lives there now.

He had 500 acres in Kingsbury. Produces a Conveyance from Benjaman Wildman to Claimt of 1-46 of 23,000 acres in Albany Co. in Considr. £60-1762.

He had 56 acres in good Improvements & well fenced. He had a House & Barn. Vals. Clear land at £3 pr. Acre. The wood land at 16 shills. York, exclusive of buildings. His Father had

80a AR.

also a share in a Saw Mill. Lost his furniture & farming utensils. Says the House & Barn were burnt when Major Carleton retreated from that Country.

Produces affidt. from Ensign Thos. Sherwood to Claimts having been imprisoned in Œsopus Gaol & to his having been indited.

Produces 2 Affidts. to Claimts property agreeing with the above acct.

Moses Williams, Wits.

Knew Claimt, he was always Loyal, suffered a great deal on that acct. Knew his Place, it was a large Farm, thinks 50 acres Clear, it was a noble House & good buildings. The House & buildings were burnt on Major Carleton's return. One Esq. Moss, a Rebel, has got Possession of it, he was a Committee man.

1205. Claim of Henry Jackson, late of Albany Co.   N. C. February 25. (29).

Claimt. says he was at the River DeChine in the Fall, 83.

Is a Nat. of Am., lived at Trenhausik, near Albany when Rebellion broke out, joined the Brit in 81, Served till the end of the War. Produces his Discharge. Now lives at Osswegatchie.

He lived at the Farm of one Cline. He lived on Shares with him. Had some Stock of his own. He was driven off on acct. of having harboured Scouts. Left 2 horses, 4 Cows, 2 Heifers, 2 Steers, 21 Sheep, Utensils, furniture, Corn Loom. A Party of Rebels came to take Claimt. He made his Escape, but they took his things.

Thomas Lake, Wits.

Knows Claimt, he was always a Loyalist, he used to assist persons kept on Secret service. He had a farm at Town—on shares with one Cline and had stock of his own, 4 Cows, 4 Young Cattle, 2 horses, a good many sheep. Witness had been at his Place and Knew of his having this Stock.

Has heard from Several Persons that Claimt was obliged to quit his Farm & leave his stock behind him.

1206. Claim of Andrew Liddel, late of Schenectady.   N. C. April 15. (30).

Claimt says. He was at Quebec in the Sumr., 83, left it in June, came to Montreal. Went to Chambly & was there during that Fall.

Is a Nat. of Ireland. Came young to America. Lived in Sheneckadie when Rebellion broke out. Always against the Rebels. Joined Genl. Burgoyne, served that Campaign, was taken Prisoner—Coming to Canada after Burgoyne's defeat. Kept in Albany Gaol 7 months. Made his escape, got into the Province. Now lives at Caldwells Manor.

Had furniture in a house at Scheneckady—a hired house—hired of Esq. Duncan, taken in 1774 for 7 years. Claimt. was to have the Improvemts. He had built a Blacksmiths Shop, this was an Improvement for which he should have been paid at end of his Lease. Worth £40.

His furniture & Blacksmiths Tools were all taken when he joined Burgoyne. Was robbd of Cash when Coming into this Country When he was taken Prisoner. The party that robbed him was commanded by one Lieutenant Fairchild.

Says his Blacksmiths Tools could not be replaced for £100 York. Says the same as to his furniture.

HUMPHREY HARGRAVE, Wits.

(31). Knew Claimt Scheneckady, always Loyal, he joind Genl. Burgoyne. He was a Blacksmith, had a Shop & Tools. He Kept 2 apprentices. He had his house well furnished. His things were taken by the Rebels. Some plundered, some sold at Vendue.

April 16. Further Evidence in Case of WILLM. SCHENNERHORN, v. Vol. 21, p. 117.

HENRY DELLENBACK, Wits.

Knew the late Wm. Schermerhorn. He lived at Hilberg on Rancellors Manor. Knew the Farm on which he lived, there was a good House, fine Clearance. Understood he had other Lands. About 40 or 50 acres Clear about his House. Heard that he lost all his Stock by the Rebels. There was a new framed house & a good Barn. Farms run there at 100 or 200 acres.

N.º. 1207. Evidence in the Claim of JOHN CURTIS, late of Manchester, Vermont.

Claimt Sworn Says, that he was at St. Johns in the Fall 1783.

Is a native of America, lived at Manchester when the Troubles broke out. Always declared in Favour of the British, but was obliged to turn out once with the American Militia & served with them three months at Mount Independence. Joined Genl. Burgoyne in 1777. Came to Canada just before the Convention. Served in Col. Peters Corps & afterwards in Sir John Johnsons Regt. till the end of the War. Produces his Discharge. Now (32). lives on Caldwells Manour.

Produces Deed dat. 20th March, 1775, Whereby Moses Soper in Consideration of £31 Currt. lawful money in hand paid, Conveys to Claimt 65 acres in Manchester. Says when he made the purchase it was all wild land. Afterwards Cleared 5 acres. Lost when he joined the British, Cloaths & Watch, Farming utensils, Corn in the ground.

Produces Govr. Chittendens Certificate dated 1st March, 1788, that the Estate of Claimts had been Confiscated for his adherence o the Enemies of the State.

N. C. 1208. Claim of JAMES SHAW, late of New York.
May 10.

Claimt. says He came from New York in the Sumr., 83, never landed at Quebec, went to Sorell—was there that winter.

Is a Nat. of Ireland, has been in America 30 yrs., was at New York when Rebellion broke out. Had a House at New York. Was a Vendue Master. Always took part with the Brit. Was in the

New York Militia. Produces Govr. Tryons Certificate that Claimt took ye oath of allegiance Jany., 77. Certificate mentions Claimt. as being of the New York Militia. Produces Certificate to his Loyalty from Stephen Delancey, Albert White, Pat. Smith, & that they heard of his having lost his Property. Has Lands at Gaspie, but resides at Sorell now.

Claims for furniture. He sold his own House. There were 2 houses of his Wifes, but they are in Possession of his Wifes Relatives. Lost furniture left behind at New York, worth £100 Ster. Cloathing of himself & Wife. Says he had about £60 York in hard money, which he lost. He cannot exactly say where, but it was lost in the hurry in moving his Things from New York, had it just before he left New York. Had recd. part for some Rum which he sold.

(33).

A good man in distress,

1209. Claim of JOHN CROSS, late of Shaftsbury, Vermont.

N. C. May 14.

Claimt says he was at St. Johns in 1783. Is a nat. of America, lived at Shaftsbury when Rebellion broke out, in 77 came within the Brit. Lines at St. Johns. Produces a Pass from Brigadier Fraser, June, 77. Next year enlisted into Rogers Corps, servd 4 years. Now lives near Isle au Noix.

(24).

Had some Land at Cawash in Gilhall Township where he lived before he went to Shaftsbury. Gave 30 Dollars for 100 acres. Cleared about 5 acres. When he went to Shaftsbury, left his furniture at Cawash, which he was forced to leave behind. A Horse lost at Bennington by his Wife. He does not know who had it.

BENJAMIN SAWYER WITS.

Very little.

Knew Claimt. when he lived at Cawash. He had 100 acres, purchased about 73—some of Wits.—had about 4 or 5 acres Clear. Vals. Cleared Land at 10 dollars per acre. He left it about 75.

1210. Claim of JOHN WAGGONER, late of Saratoga.

N. C. May 16.

Claimt says He was at St. Johns in the Fall, 83, gave a Claim to a Mr. Tailor who promised to send it by Sr. John Johnson who was going to England.

He returned to the Colonies & staid all the Winter. Did not send any Claim because he thought Tailor would send it. Tailor is a Merchant.

Produces the acct. drawn up by Tailor, indorsed, to be presented to ye Comrs. Says this was drawn up in the Fall 83, & he left it with Tailor to send.

Is a native of Am., lived at Saratoga, joined Genl. Burgoyne, came into Canada in the Spring 1777, served in Jessops Corps, was taken prisoner after the first Battle of Stillwater. Was kept in Prison 2 Months & 2 Days. Staid in the Colonies after that. Came here in the Fall 83. He then went for his Family. They came in the summer following. Now lives at Masisco Bay.

(35).

Had 112 acres of Land at Saratoga. Had bought them of John Gelan & gave them up to him when he came into Canada. Bought 9 years before the War. Had Cleared nearly half. Had planted an orchard. Had 5 horses, 2 Bullocks, 12 Cows, Sheep, Hogs, Utensils, furniture. Left it all at Saratoga When he went to Canada. The Rebels got it, except a little that the Brit. had

N. C.
May 26.
1211. Claim of JOSEPH ALLAN, late of Monmouth Co., New Jersey, Lodged in England.

Claimt. says—He was at New Brunswick in the Fall 83. Gave a Claim to Mr. Hardy to be sent to England, which was accordingly sent, but not delivered by Mr. Hardy's Agent, Chevalier Rooms.

Is a nat. of Amer., lived at Monmouth Co. when Rebellion broke out. When the Brit. Army were at New Brunswick in 1776 he carried in Recruits to General Skinner & Col. Morris, but he continued at his own Place till 1780, tho' he was frequently taken up & imprisond.

In 1780 he was imprisond, broke Gaol & got to New York.
(36). Joined Major Ward. Served in the Associated Loyalists. Claimt raised a Company & had the Command of them at Bergen from 81 till the Evacuation of New York. Came at the Evacuation to Nova Scotia, afterwards to Canada. Now settled at Bay of Quinty.

No. 1. Had a Track of Land Called Lawrence Neck in Monmouth Co., produces Deed from Abraham Schenk to Claimt. of a Moiety of Lawrence Neck in Considr. of 140,000 feet of Inch Pine Boards dated 1770.

Produces Deed from Peter Benson to Claimt of a Part of Lawrence Neck containing 490 acres by Estimation in Considr. £420 York dated 1770. This was the other Moiety. Claimt says he made great Improvements, built a House & a large Barn. Not much Clear when he bought it. There were 100 acres Clear when he left it.

There was a house & barn where he lived. Another house on the Farm which he let to one Holmes who was to Clear 10 acres annually for Claimt. Vals. the Land at £2.15 pr. acre Jersey. House, &c., as in Schedule.

Produces apraisment by 3 Appraisers at the Price above mentioned.

No. 2. Had 15 acres of Land with a Saw Mill. Produces the Deed from Abraham Shenk mentioned in No. 1 wherein mention
(37). is made of 2 Tracts besides Lawrence Neck. Says this was 15 acres & a saw mill. Vals. it at £75. So valued by the apraisers.

Produces Certificate from the Court of Monmouth Co. of Sale as a Moiety to pay a Mortgage of £86 to the Loan office, & that the Surplus was paid to the Agent of forfeited Estates. Produces certificate of sale of the other Moiety.

Produces an affidavit from one James Allan who had been a Juror on a Survey taken of the Estate & that it contained about 1300 acres.

Had a Sloop of 30 Tons. Produces a Bill of Sale of it in 1771 for £160 York. He had bought a new set of sails. This was taken by a Rebel officer from Claimt in 1776, who took the Riggings & Sails. They Stript off the Rigging, drove the sloop into a Creek where she rotted.

Produces an affidt. from Wm. Gifford Confirming this acct. & that the persons who took ye sloop said they would put it out of Claimts Power to go away in her. Claimt says he meant to have gone in her to New York. Vals. her at £200 Jersey. Had 10 head of Cattle, 3 Horses, furniture, Cloathes, utensils .

When Claimt was a prisoner in 1780, these things were all taken from the house by a Scouting Party of Rebels. Produces an affidt. from Margt. Reynolds who had been a Servt. in his House of his Loss as above stated. Do. from 2 other Persons.

Says the Debts due by him were not paid out of his Estate, but he expects to be called upon for them. The Debts due to him on Bills, notes & Book Accts. amounted to 419. 14. 6. (38).

Produces a Certificate from John Stillwell Agent of forfeited Estates, that he had recd. the Said Bills, Notes, &c., for the use of the State.

ELIJAH GROOMES Wits.

Knew Claimt, he was always loyal. He sent recruits to the Brit. Army in 76. He went to New York in 1780 & served in the Associated Loyalists. He was Called a Captain. Knew his Lands at Lawrence Neck, remembers him in Possession. He built a house & Barn & another out house & made Improvements in Clearing Land.

After the Purchase there was a great Quantity of Clear Land. Some were meadow, Some upland. Vals. Clear Land at £4 or 5 per acre Jersey Cury., inclosed lands 40sh. per acre. A very large stock of Creatures. The Rebels took his Stock. Witness Knows that a good many were sold at public Vendue.

1212. Claim of DANIEL WALKER, late of Charlotte Co., Vermont. N. C. May 28.

Claimt says He was at the River Du Chine in the Fall 83. Is a nat. of Amer., lived at Otter Creek, Vermont, when Rebellion broke out. Joined Genl. Burgoyne. After his defeat came to Canada. Served under Major Jessop till end of the War. Produces his Discharge. Lives at Cataraqui. (39).

Had 300 acres in Durham, bought 5 or 6 years before the war of Thos. Green for 675 Spanish Dollars. He had also a Warrant from Col. —— 5 acres Clear when he bought it. 80 acres Clear when he left it. He had built one House & Barn. Vals. it at 25sh. per acre wild land, improved £3 pr. acre. The New York Title was reckoned ye best at Durham. Produces Certificate from Govr. Chittenden that all the Estate of Claimt had been Confiscated. Says the Estate has been sold by Comrs.

Capt. Mack bought it.

Had 3 Horses, 23 Cattle, 23 Sheep, 8 Hogs, utensils, furniture, Cloathes. Left all these Things on his Farm when he went to join the Brit army. They were all taken by the Rebels. His Wife was there & was turned off the Farm.

Produces affidt. from Robt Perry & David Shorey to Claimts having been possessed of the above Property & that his estate was worth £738-7-6 Halifax.

(40).

Produces Certificate from Jos. McDonald, Surgeon, & Saml. Adams to Claimts Illness from Fatigue & trouble which his Loyalty had exposed him to.

May 30.

Further Evidence on the Claim of ALEXANDER MACHIE.

Major Hughes remembers Claimts Father, he had a Considerable Estate on the Susquahana above Harris's Ferry. Witness has been at the House, it was a good House. It was in a very fine part of the Country. There seemed a great deal Clear. A very large Tract on the River. It was in 1756 & 1757, when Witness saw this Estate. Claimts Father was reckoned a man of the most. Considerable Property there abouts.

February 14.

Further Evidence in case of Govr. WM. BROWN.

JOHN FISHER, Esq.

Is acquainted with Govr. Wm. Brown. He was one of the Mandamus Council. Did not know his Property in Connecticut. Knew his House at Salem, a large good House near the Town house, one of the best Houses in Town. Thinks £1000 Str. a very moderate Valuation.

Catherine Sargents was a Small house.

Knows not the Wharf & Warehouse. Knew he had a farm at Stage Point very valuable.

(41).

GOVR. WENTWORTH.

JOHN FISHER, Esq.

Knew his Place at Wolfsboro. The building of the House Cost him a great Deal. There were great Improvements, a garden fenced with Stone, and Park. House alone must have cost £4000. It was a beautiful situation. The largest House Witness has seen in America. A great Deal of Timber Mills. The Govr. is ———
——— is valuable, it is on Connecticut River, more valuable than any in Vermont. Lime is well settled. Lime is worth more than a dollar an acre, about £80 a right, too low a Calculation. The other Township not so good as Lime.

MR. PACKER.

Knew him well, never heard of his ——— he executed office of high Sheriff till the time of his Death. Govr. Went. was in possession of it.

It was imagined that the Heir at Law was encouraged by Mr. Langdon, a man of great Weight with that Party, in Consequence of which the Heir brought his suit and recovered.

114 acres in Rockshire an old settled Town.

Dito in Barrington.

GOVERNOR BROWN. (Claim of.)

JOSEPH CHIME, Wits. (42).

Knew the Governors Estate in Connecticut. It was a large Tract of Land, a good many Tenants upon it. The Tract was between 9 & 10,000 acres, 14 miles from New London 10 from Norwich, 8 from Connecticut. Good Lands for Ship Timber.

SAML. FETCH, Wits. February 17.

Knew a great deal of Govr. Browns Estate in Connect., it was a large Estate, about 10,000 acres, frequently past by the Estate. The situation made the Land valuable. Lands sold by the acre.

Vals. the Tract, if there are Improvements such as has heard at £3 pr. acre.

1788.
1213. Case of BENJAMINN WORTH, late of New Jersey. August 30.

Claimant Sworn.

He is a native of America, lived in Somerset Co., New Jersey, joined the Brit. at Amboy in 1777, servd. under Genl. Campbell on Staten Island, was among the Persons called Express Riders, servd. two years, then servd. with a Team, with the British army. Came to this Province a little before the Evacuation.

Had 150 acres in Somerset County. Came to him on his Fathers death, two years before the War. His Father had been a long time in Possession. Chiefly Clear. Land sells at from £6 to 4 (43). pr. acre that Currency.

Lost 3 Horses, 5 Cows, farming utensils, sold for the benefit of the State.

Produces Aaron Durhams Certificate. Says the only reason for his not attending as when we were here, was because he had not got his Vouchers from the States, now has them. Mr. Bell Certifies to his good Character and says he always understood Claimt. had been Loyal. Major Milledge Certifies to his Loyalty.

MRS. MARGARET MARTIN, Wits.

Knew Mr. Worth in Somerset County. He had a good farm, had it on his Fathers death, remembers him in Possession. There was an Extraordinary good House. They had very good stock. Remembers his having Horses.

1788.
1214. Case of MARGARET FITZSIMMONS, formerly Evans, late October 6. of North Carolina.

Claimt. Sworn.

Says her first Husband, Thomas Evans was an Englishman, settled very young in America, settled near Salisbury in North Carolina. He sent a Claim by Morses Vessel in the year 1783, When the rest of the Claims were sent. That vessel was lost.

(44). Her Husband joined the British at first, servd all the time, raised a Company, served as Capt. Went from Carolina to Florida. He left four Children all Infants, the eldest Samuel about 19. All live with their mother at Rawdon.

Her Hsband had 100 acres, bought the Improvements when they first came. There was a good House. Eight acres Clear, took up other Lands and Cleared 40 acres.

Had five Negroes taken by a Company of Americans. He had joined the Brit. Army. He had Eleven Horses, Twenty Cattle, Furniture, Stock. All lost and taken by the Americans.

SAMUEL MACHYDEW, Wits.

Knew Thamas Evans, he joined the British early, servd. six

years. He raised a Company—served as Captain. He was wounded at the time of Colonel Moores defeat.

He heard that the claim was sent by Morses Ship and that the Ship was lost. He had two Farms—he had 50 acres clear. He had five or six negroes—the Rebels got them—they took part, the res. ran away. He had very good Stock and did not save it—a great many Horses and Cattle.

Quebec, 1788. March 19.

1215. Evidence on the Case of NICHOLAS OGDEN, late of New Jersey.

(45). Says he is a Native of America—resided at New York when the Rebellion broke out. From the first he declared against the measures of the Rebels. Had been threatened to be Tarred and Feathered, in the Summer 1775. He made himself particularly obnoxious by rescuing Dr. Cooper who was attacked by a mob— he became so obnoxious that he was obliged to fly. He went into Jersey in 1776, came again to New York.

There were warrants against him for conspiring against the Life of General Washington.

Claimt. was tried by a Committee of Congress for that offence but discharge for want of Evidence.

He remained with the British in New York till the Evacuation, except a short time he was imprisoned.

Served in the Militia as assistant Brigade Major now lives at Shelburne.

Claimant married Hannah Cuyler daughter of Henry Cuyler of New York. He died some years before the war leaving six children. By Will he left his Estate to be divided amongst his six children, and in case of either of their deaths without Issue or under age the Share of such Person to go to the survivors equally. Henry and Barnt Cuyler and John Smith were Executors.

Henry the Eldest Son died leaving children—Mary, Alida and Barnt died without children. Hannah wife of Claimant and

Hester wife of Captain Fenck are the two Survivors. Captain Fenck now lives at New Brunswick. (46).

Henry Cuyler had considerable Estates in Sussex and Somerset, New Jersey. He was in partnership in taking up Lands with Oliver DeLancey at different Periods.

Produces a paper signed by James Parker and Abraham Ogden, which states that the Lands located by DeLancey and Cuyler were 15,666 acres of which 2,470 had been sold and mortgages had been given back for securing the money. Henry Cuylers share in the residue was 6,598 acres, a a great deal of which was Leased out, these Leases were before 1776. Henry Culylers Executors had taken possession of his Estates, but Claimant had never settled with them.

James Parker and Abraham Ogden are now Trustees of the Estate, and in Possession except of the Lands Leased or sold. The Lease Lands were improved by the Tenants. The Residue continued unimproved. Claimant in right of his Wife is entitled to ⅓ of Culyers Estate.

There has been no particular Confiscation of Claimants share but Claimants name is in the general Act of Attainder.

The Lessees continued in possession, but the Leases, as well as the mortgages which were in Possession of Colonel Barton, agent for Henry Cuyler were destroyed by the Rebels.

Abraham Ogden and James Parker were appointed Trustees by Act of Assembly. Claimant thinks there were several Incumbranches in the Estate. These Lands were in Sussex County. (47).

Henry Cuyler had also some Lands in Rocky Brook as one of the Proprietors in Dockwrays Patent. He had four Lots as his share, in the whole 856 acres fully improved. They are not Confiscated, and Claimant supposes they may be recovered.

Produces Certificate from James Parker and Abraham Ogden that Henry Cuylers Estate was worth £14,114 in 1776 and is now worth £8,310. N.B. This looks as if the whole Loss conceived to be from the sinking in value of the Estate.

Produces Certificate from Colonel Barton, who is prevented from having broke his leg from coming—that no located Lands for Henry Cuyler in Sussex County—that he sold many for which he took Mortgages, and leased 20 Farms, which mortgages and Leases were destroyed by the Rebels. Values the Lands sold at 35/ p. acre—Says the Farms were 150 acres each—the Leases for 21 years without Rent for 5 years, and then at a shilling.

When Claimant removed from Newark in Jersey to New York in 1776. Claimant had joined Lord Cornwallis at that time.

Left part of his Furniture at a house which he had lived at Newark. This was worth £70 or 80 Currcy.

ISAAC OGDEN Wits:

Says Henry Cuyler left his Estate in New Jersey to his 6 children. He and Oliver Delancey had proprietors Rights and had located Considerable Tracts in Sussex County—a good part had (48).

been Leased out as Witness was informed. Thinks Henry Cuyler deceased was clear from Debts, he died some years before the Rebellion.

Henry Cuyler his son was in Debt, but thinks there were other estates bound with that Debt and not the Lands in New Jersey. Witness does not know for what particular purpose the Trustees have been appointed — nor how far Claimants share has been Confiscated, or whether it would be spar'd as being the Estate of the wife.

Claimant was in a House at Newark which he left in a Hurry and imagines he must have left part of his Furniture.

Major Beckwith Certifies that Claimant was a good man, always considered him as well affected. Witness knew him in 1778 at New York. He had then a Command in the Militia, he was employed confidentially and gave Intelligence that was of Service.

Halifax, 24th Nov., 1788.

(49).

1216. Evidence on the Claim of JOHN DERRY, late of West Chester County New York.

Claimant Sworn Says—he was at Cumberland in the Fall of 1783—sent a Claim to Col. Delancey but it got too late. Was ill and could not come to St. Johns.

Is a native of Ireland—came to America Forty years ago—lived near Venplanks Point. He served in Delanceys Crops.

Had no Lands of his own—lived on a Farm—Lost three Cows—6 Sheep—on his Farm. Had a mare taken by a Rebel Colonel. Was plunderd of £16 by a Rebel. Household furniture.

JAMES DERRY, Wits.:

Says he lived with his Father. He joined the British and served some years. Swears to the Property mentioned in the Schedule.

Halifax, 24th Nov., 1788.

1217. Evidence on the Claim of JAMES DERRY, late of New York.

Claimant Sworn—Says he sent a claim home to Colonel Delancey—Lived near Venplanks Point.

Is a native of America—joined Col. Delancey Corps. Served all the War—now lives at Cumberland.

He lived with his Father—had Creatures of his own—one mare—one yoke of oxen—eight head of horned Cattle—Six Sheep.

John Derry the Father says he had this Property.

November 24.

(50).

1218. Evidence on the Claim of RICHARD ROBT. CROWE, late of New Jersey.

Claimant Sworn—Says he lived some time at Parsburgh—he came from there to New Brunswick to attend the Commissions. The Commissioners had left the Place—three or four days before. Claimant saw Mr. Hunter—told him his case—he desired Claimant to send his Deposition and Evidence to the Commissioner afterwards. Claimant was an hour with Mr. Hunter and conferred with him on his Losses.

Claimant had no opportunity to send to the Commissioner in Canada. Says he lives at a very retired place where there is little

little Communication with the rest of the Province.

Is a native of Ireland—came to America with General Braddock in the year 1775. Was a Lieutenant in the 48th Regt. was afterwards at the taking of Quebec, Louisburg and Havannah.

Was settled in Monmouth County near Amboy when Rebellion broke out—he refused entering into the American Troops. They offered him the rank of General. He was put in Gaol first at Brunswick—he got away to Philadelphia—he was imprisoned there, and sent back to New Jersey—and was tried and was acquitted. He then went home where he was very ill. As soon as he could he joined General Vaughan at Amboy afterwards served to end of the Rebellion. Came here in 1783—he had a Company in the Black Poiners. Has now half Pay. Resides at Parrsburgh. Refers to Captain McKenzie.

(51).

No. 1. He had 142/76 acres in Amboy purchased by Claimant in 1763. Produces a Survey with two Lots marked with Claimant's name—Containing the Quantity of acres above mentioned. Says he paid £736 for these two Lots and a third Lot of 117 acres which he has since sold. Says he gave a great price, it was then Chiefly Woodland, he cleared a good deal on the price he sold the rest. Was Wood Land. Says Wood land was very valuable then. He used to send wood to New York and Amboy. Values it at £400. Jersey.

No. 2. Had 561 acres in South Amboy. Produces Deed from Nicholas Evanson and James Milvan of 561 acres in South Amboy to Eyre Evans Crowe in Consideration of £1,109 Currnt. Proclamation money dated 1766.

Claimant says he bought the place for his Brother. His Brother was in England. Says in his claim sent home he mentions this Estate and claimed it in his Brother's name. Claimant expected his Brother would come out to America and bought this Estate for him. Says he bought the Estate very cheap. He paid the money which his Brother reimbursed, he had made great Improve ments upon it.

Produces copy of Inquisition against him and order to sell Claimants Real Estate. The Estate was sold in Consequence of his Conviction. Values the Estate at £300 more than he gave for it. His Brother lives at Tydenham—he writes to him at Mr. Bombacks No. 16 Shelburne Lane, London.

(52).

No. 3. 327 acres in Pensilvania Cumberland Co. Produces Deed from John Young to Claimant of 337 acres on the Delaware in Consideration of £120 dated 1767. There was a house and some Improvmts. on it when he bought it. He made no additional Improvmnts. Had a Soldiers Right in New York Government. Produces Deed from Ed. Low to Claimt. of his Right on Lake Champlain for £5 dated 1766, nothing was done upon it. Had an order for survey for 2,000 acres in New York Gover. as an officer last war.

Claimant lived at No. 2. He had a large stock there. Three yoke of Oxen—Six Horses—twelve Sheep—Farming Utensils—Furniture—Stone Ware worth £100. He has given a more particular account in his Claim sent home. He left these behind when he was sent to prison. The Rebels took them off.

He had a Kiln and large Shop. The Kiln cost £50 building. He carried on the Stone Ware Business at his own expense. His Brother had nothing to do with this.

Produces affidavit from Samuel Warne to Claimants Loyalty and Property. Ditto from Issaac Bonnell and Certificate to the Credibility of Samuel Warne.

(53).

EYRE EVANS CROWE. Sworn.

Says he lodged a Claim for his Brother and another for himself He has not appeared to be examined on his own Claim.

Richard Robert Crowe was examined at Halifax and there gave an account of his Loss of 561 acres in South Amboy, which appears to have been purchased in the name of Eyre Evans Crowe. Witness says he is willing this should go under his Brothers Claim.

His reason for not coming to be examined was not having evidence to prove his title. He had remitted money to his Brother to make a Purchase intending to have gone there himself.

It appears by an Entry in the Commissioners Book that he attended at the Board in January 1787 and said he waited for Papers from America.

(54).

PROCEEDINGS

OF

LOYALIST COMMISSIONERS

CARLTON ISLAND, NIAGARA, LONDON, 1188-9.

Vol. II.

MISCELLANEOUS EVIDENCE.

Claimants.

	MSS. Folio		MSS. Folio
Austin, William	25	Gummersoll, Thomas, & William Demasine	29
Bertram, Alexander	29	McKenzie, Colin	1
Brant, Mary, Children of	7	McMeeking, Thomas	2
Culter, Ebenezer	13	Oliver, Ichebod	31
Cumming, Alexander	22	Pell, Jos.	32
Demasine, William, and Thomas Gummersoll	29	Peterson, Jenet	23
Ellerbeck, Emanuel	1	Schermerhorn, William	5
Eves, Oswald	17 & 21	Sherwood, Thomas	12
Garetvile, Andrew	8	Shewman, William	11
Gibson, James	21 & 23	Van Every, McGregor	10
Girty, George	10	Wallace, Alexander	26
Girty, Simon	5	Watkins Hy.	33

THE EVIDENCE.

Carlton Island, 8th May, 1788.

1219. Further Evidence on the Claim of COLIN MCKENZIE, late of Crown Point, New York.

Gave claim to Mr. Cuyler in 1783.

Sarah McKenzie wife to Claimant Sworn—late Sarah Powers— Says her late Bro. Wm. Powers died in Canada in 1784. He joined Gen. Burgoyne before the Convention in May 1777 at St. Johns.

He left no Children & his Wife was dead. They have no Parents alive nor Brothers nor Sisters. They were born in America.

(1).

No. 1 1050 acres in Santen township Vermont. His Father had bought it. There were 2 houses—a Saw mill half his & 50 acres cleared. It is sold under Confiscation. It is valued at 10sh. York per acre.

Waves personal estate as she cannot say the quantity.

No. 2. 360 acres in Bredport Vermont, from his Father. No improvements on this. It has been sold under Confiscation. The late Wm. Powers was in Possession of the lands. To be paid Colin McKenzie.

Carleton Island, 5th May, 1788.

1220. A Claim Lodged in England.

Evidence on the Claim of EMANUEL ELLERBECK, late of Pugh-Keepsie, New York.

Claimant Sworn. Says he sent a Claim home in 83. He is a native of England & came to America in 1774 & in 1775 lived at Pikeepsee. He joined the B. Army soon after New York was taken in the Spring 1777. He was in Gaol the Winter and got freed by inlisting, but deserted to the British. Afterwards he joined the New York Volunteers, & carried to Canada. Says he is known to Major Beckwith & to Col. Beverly Robinson. They emploied him on secret service. He now lives at Cataraqui.

Chest Tools brought from England, sixteen Guineas, a Horse and a mare, a Negroe, a House bought in the War in New York, & a vessel in the King's service £200 Curry. Total amount Claim £500 York.

Niagara, 12th May, 1788.
(2).

1221. A new Claim Lodged in England.

Evidence on the Claim of THOMAS MCMEEKING, late of the W. Branch Delaware River, Tryon Co., N. York Province.

Claimt. Sworn. Says that in 1783, until July 1784, he was at Niagara. In July 1784 he went to Quebec & gave his Claim to Major Mathews.

He is a native of Scotland, and came to America in July 1774. When the War broke out he lived in Tryon Co. In March 1781 he joined the British Army at Niagara. Says that he was desired by Joseph Brantt to remain in the Country for the purpose of getting intelligence & of supplying the British scouts with provisions.

He had a large family which he could not remove. His Mother lived with him and broke her leg so as to be an object.

He was obliged to take Arms once with the Rebel Militia for one night, before that he had been under Arms with Capt. T. McDonell of Sr. J. Johnsons regt., & was in Consequence imprisoned by the rebels.

In 1781 he was taken by the Seneca Indians and brought into Niagara. He inlisted on his coming into the British Lines in the Johnsons Forresters and served in them for a year. He afterwards lived on a farm.

He is now settled at Niagara. (3).

He had a Tenant farm from Goldsburg Runyard & had made all his Improvements during the War. His claim is for Provisions &c., furnished Indians and Scouts.

No. 1. Capt. Arm and Capt. David, 2 Indians with a Party, June 5. 1779. took from his Plantation stock &c., as by Schedule amounting to £166.9, New York Currcy, it was his own Stock. He was then in Albany Gaol for furnishing Provisions to a British Party. Produces Certificate from John Burch dated Niagara 4th June, 1782, to the truth of the above charge & that Claimant was always Loyal & was in Gaol for giving Provisions to a British party when his stock was taken.

Certificate from Sr. Wm. Johnson Jnr that he was present when a Party of Mohawk Indians plunderd the Plantation of Thos. McMeeking that he Thos. McG. was in the Albany Gaol.

Niagara, 2nd Aug., 1783.

5th April, 1780. He furnished to Capt. Brant and his party, Provisions to the amount of £9. 12-10 New York Currcy., was never paid for it.

Niagara 14th June, 1782. Certificate from Joseph Brant, that Claimt. was always Loyal, that he frequently gave him Intelligence furnished his partys with Provisions.

Oct. 18th, 1780. The Seneca Indians took from him stock, &c., to the amount of £142. 19, at this time he was brought Prisoner to Canada. Part of his Stock belonged to Thos. Carson but he has pd. him £24 York for it, & 3 Cattle belonging to Hugh Alexander, not paid for, has paid Pr. McMeeking of Butlers rangers £10 of the cash, being his. Says that nothing but his being a friend to Gt. Britain kept him settled where he was, which exposed him to these Losses. (4).

Certificate dated Niagara 18th Oct., 1782 from Lt. Joseph Ferris. that Claimant often furnished parties under his Command with Provisions thinks he had seen the Delaware Indians take 8 Sheep from him.

Niagara 11th June, 1782. Certificate from Lt. David Brass that Claimant was a Loyalist from the beginning of the Rebellion & frequently furnished him & his party with Provisions.

Further Evidence on the Claim of WM. SCHERMERHORN. Niagara, 13th May, 1788.

John Boice Sworn.

Says that before the War he lived near the Property of Claimt. at the Beaver dam 18 miles from Albany. He fled from his Property on acct. of his Loyalty.

81 AR.

(5).

He had a farm at the Beaver dam, leased from Ten Broocke of Albany, 30 acres were cleared with a good house and Barn. Understands that it has been sold.

The rebel Committee took a span of excellent Horses from him. His wife remained until near the end of the war & lived on the farm. He cannot say whether they took his stock or not. He was confined a long time in Gaol & suffered much.

Niagara, 12th May, 1788.
N. C.
Further evidence.

Evidence on the Claim of SIMON GIRTY, late of Westmoreland County, Pensilvania.

Claimant Sworn. Says that in 1783 he was in the Enemies Country at Fort Pitt.

He is a Native of Pensilvania. In 1775 he lived at Fort Pitt, he was the Interpreter in the Indian department. He was asked repeatedly to join the rebels & had offers made him which he rejected.

They put him into prison on suspicion of being friendly to Gt. Britain & was tried, but was acquitted. He attempted to come in soon after but failed. He afterwards came in with Capt. McKee & Mr. Elliot, to Detroit. He has ever since been in the emploiment of Gt. Britain as an Indian Interpreter, & has been often emploied in secret service.

Before he joined the B. Army he was voted a Lt. in Col. Crawford's regt. in the rebel service, & served in it for 6 months. He found it necessary to accept of that commission or to go to Gaol He resigned this Commission before he came to Canada. He now resides at Detroit. An Interpreter of the Indian department.

(6).

Produces his titles much defaced, but says they have been examined by Mr. Pemberton.

No. 1. 300 acres of Land at Hanahs Town—says that he bought it about 1774 for a small sum of money—Moyer from whom he had bought it had been driven off by the Indians. He gave only £6 York for it—25 acres were cleared with a House, Stable and Barn— Says he was offered £1,000 by Col. Croghan but did not like the security—Swears that it would have sold for £1,500 N. York Cury. Says that one Hannah took Possession of this & for what he knows is still in Possession—it might cost him £50 or £60 more in Trouble & Lawyers fees.

No. 2. 273 acres in Pottsburg— he had Improved them for 5 years i.e. he put a Farmer there some years before the War—20 or 25 acres Cleared & a House—he valued this at £273 Currcy.

No. 3. 3 Tracts of Land in Kentucky—300 acres each—Says that two people by the name of Simon Bullee and John Steward took Possession of these Lands under agreement from him—Says that these are soldiers in the Virgena Militia—he gave them cloathing & got other men to serve for them in the Militia— it will cost him a trifle. He values it at £600 N. Y. Curry., very few acres were clared.

81a AR.

He claims 4 Horses which he says he left at his house on No. 2. (7).
It was on No. 2 that he resided when the War began—only being a
single man—he was almost always emploied among the Indians.

GEO. GIRTY BR. & Claimant.

Remembers some land his Br., had at Hannah's Town, he
bought it from one Myers—before the Rebellion—has been on the
Lands—his Br. had a Tenant on it—there was a house & 30 acres
cleared —the Americans have it now & a Town built on it.

No. 2 His Br. lived there—it was good land and his Br. had a
good clearance on it—about 30 acres cleared—has heard that his
Br. had Lands in Kentucky.

1222. Further Evidence in the Claim of the CHILDREN of Niagara,
MARY BRANT. May 12. 1788.

Wit——— BRANDT SWORN.

Says that some years before the War he sold a lot of 1,200 acres
good land near Anthonys Nose to Sr. Wm. Johnson. He sold it for
£1,200 York Curry & thinks it was well worth that. Sr. Wm.
pd. the price for it—understood that Sr. Wm. made over his Estate
to some of the children of Mary Brant. He thinks that 80 acres
were cleared & under improvmt—there was a House & Barn on it.
Wits. was in that Country since the War & understood that it was
sold under Confiscation.

William Showman says that the children of Mary Brant had Carlton Island
very considerable tracts of land on the Mohawk river—he cannot 22 May, 1788.
distinguish what was the children's and which hers. (Thinks (8).
that). Knew lots No. 8 and 12 in Stone Arabia—he thinks it was
worth 40sh. York per acre—knew a farm in Stone Arabia purchased from one Snells was good land & Considerable Clearance.

1223. Evidence on the Claim of ANDREW GARETVILE, late of N. C.
Albany Co. Niagara, 12 May, 1788.

Claimant Sworn—Says he was a Soldier in Jessup's Corps in
1783, & was quartered at the River de Chinne.

He is a native of America —In 1775 he lived at Albany. He
joined Major Jessup's Corps in 1780. He never had been within
the B. lines before that time.

He had served 5 months in the Rebel Continental troops. He

came to the British Army because he was ill used—he remained
so long on account of his Mother who was an old Woman—he fled
with some friends of Gt. Britain—he is now a Soldier in the 53
Regt. of fort.

He proposes remaining in Canada if the 53rd Regt. should be
drafted.

No. 1. A Town Lot in the ——— of Ransellor 40 feet front
by 80 feet deep with a large House thereon. He had it by his (9).
father's Will who died in 1778, his mother had the life rent & died
in Sept. 1779. There was a House, Barn & Garden. He left it in
charge of his Cousin Henry Bradt. Says that his father was offered

£700 Curry. for this in 1775. He values it at £500 York—has heard that it was sold at Vendue—when it was known he was in Canada.

No. 2. Ten acres of Land a mile from Albany—he had from his Gd. Father Andr. Bradt, he cannot say who has them. There was an orchard on this & a meadow—he values it at £50 Y. C.

Furniture £20—2 Horses and 2 Cows —all left when he went away.

May 17. JOHN BRAT, Wits., Sworn.

Knew claimant in Albany—he is his relation—his father left him a House in Albany—a Barn and a piece of ground—it was a frame house.

Wits. Joseph Winter—Says he knew the house Claimed by Andr., Garretville—it was left him by his father & mother, it was a good lot with an orchard & a good house close to Albany.

Niagara, 14th May, 1788.

Evidence on the Claim of GEORGE GIRTY, late of Fort Pitt, Pensilvania.

Claimt. sworn. Says he was at Detroit in 1783.

He is a native of Pensilvania. At the commencement of the War he was a Hunter & on the Banks of the Mississippi. Says that he never joined the rebels.

In May, 1778, he was taken by Coll. Willing, a rebel officer, near the entrance of the Ohio. They took his canoe & five hands and put him in Irons. They carried him to New Orleans, where they kept him 12 months, when he broke Gaol, & escaped through the Indian Country to Detroit. He then was taken into the Indian department as an Interpreter with the pay of 2 Dollars per diem, in which situation he still continues.

(40).

He resides with the Delaware Indians. Produces the affidavit of James Sherlock, an Indian trader, 14th Nov., 1787, that he was present when G. Girty was Robb'd of a Boat with a considerable quantity of Peltries some guns & Steel Traps.

Claims Skins taken from him because he was a friend of Gt. Britain, viz., 2,000 Beaver Skins 900 Otters, 6 rifles, 35 Beaver Traps, 7 Horses & 2 Saddles. All these were taken from him.

Niagara, 15th May, 1788.

1224. Evidence on the Claim of McGREGOR VAN EVERY, late of Scohary, N. Yorke.

DAVID VAN EVERY, oldest son to Claimt, Sworn:

Says his Father died at Niagara in Sept., 1786. He left a

wife, Mary Van Every, & 7 Children.

His Father joined the British Army in 1781. Five of his son were in the King's service from the first of the War. His father attempted to join the Army early but was seized & imprisoned. He was always friendly to Gt. Britain.

His mother tells him they lost 2 Horses, & 2 Cows & some young Cattle, farming utensils & Furniture. All these were taken from them on acct. of their Loyalty.

Mary Van Every, Wid. of Claimt., says her husband lost 2 Horses, 4 Cows, furniture, & farming utensils. Her Husband was six months in Gaol.

Capt. John McDonnel, of Butler's Rangers, says that McGregor Van Every & five of his sons served in the same Corps with him. They were all Loyal people. (11).

Mary Van Every lived always as Claimt.'s Wife & mother to the children.

1225. Evidence on the Claim of WILLIAM SHOWMAN, late of Tryon Co., N. York. Carleton Island 22 May, 1788.

Claimt. Sworn. Says he was a Soldier in Sir John Johnson's 2nd Battn., & gave a Claim to Sir John.

He is a native of Germany, but has been in America 42 years. He lived 4 miles from Johnstown in 1776. He did not come to Canada until 1781, but says that all the War he was Emploied in getting Recruits for the British, or in assisting Scouts. He was tried giving aid to the British & Condemned. Seems a good man.

He served in Sir John's part of the War, & now lives in the Bay of Quinty.

No. 1. 50 acres Cleared on a Lease forever, from Sir Wm. Johnson. He had been settled 18 years. With a House & Barn. A rebel lives on it.

He had 4 Horses, a Cow, a Stocking Loom. But he kept a Public House.

No. 2 125 acres of Land, near his other farm on the Albany Patent. He bought in 1774. He pd. £175 Curry of the price which was to have been £50. He cannot say who has it. (12).

Further Evidence on the Claim of THOS. SHERWOOD, late of Fort Edward, Kingsbury, N. York Province. Owegatchee, 23 May, 1788.

Wits., ALEXR. CAMPBELL, Sworn:

Says that Claimt. possessed a Leasehold farm before the War. The Lands belonged to Mr. Smith of New York. Believes that his bargain was that he might have purchased ——— time for 2 Dollars pr. acre.

Witness knows that he had a large Clearance on this farm. His Bro. in the ——— of N. York told him there was 100 acres cleared.

In 1786 Wits. carried a power of Attorney to Claimt.'s Bro. to act for him. They told him that the Lands were Confiscated & that the Lands were all sold. Mr. Sherwood cannot return into the State of N. York on his own affairs on acct. of the active part he took in the course of the War.

1226. Evidence on the Claim of EBENEZER CULTER, late of Groten, Massachusetts Bay, now of Annapolis Royal, Nova Scotia. London, 21st November, 1778.

Claimt. Sworn Says, that he was not prepared for Examination when the Commrs. were in Nova Scotia. Memorial read.

(13).

Says he is a native of America. In 1775 he resided at Groten in Massachusetts Bay where he carried on Trade. He continued to import British goods after the non-importation agreemt. In consequence the mob destroied his property & ill used him & exposed him publickly. He got into Boston the 13th June, 1775, before which time he had been confined & tried for being friendly to Gt. Britain.

He carried arms in one of the Associated Company in Boston & went to Halifax with the King's Troops. During the whole of the War he remained within the B. Lines or in England. In 1775 he joined C. Wellard on an Expedition to procure stock for the Garrison of Boston with pay of half a crown per day. Says that he acted in many hazardous situations as a Volunteer, and was Clerk in the Qr. Mr. Gens. Department for some months.

He had an allowance from Govert. of £80 per ann. until 1782, when it was reduced to £40, & continues to receive that allowance.

One half of the profits of a Store at Groten in Co-partnery with his Brother Jonas Culter. His yearly profits were £150 per ann. Nine years, £1,350.

His Br. Jonas was left in Possession in Sepr., 1774. He died in 1781 & left a Wife.

Claim for the Estate of ZACCHEUS CULTER, his Brother.

Zaccheus Culter joined the B. Army in 1775, & remained within the B. Lines & in England until he was took going from London to S. Carolina in 1780.

He left no Will. He had no family. There were 2 Bros. besides Zaccheus & Claimt. 1st Elisha Culter, the eldest, lives in New England, always friendly to the Americans, 2nd Jonas Culter dead without issue. Has left a wife in New England 3rd Claimt.

(14).

Produces Letters of Administration dated London 25th Septr. 1782. Says that in Consequence of this Letter of Ad. he has divided his personal property amongst his creditors in England.

No. 1. One acre & a half of Land in Amherst, with a Dwelling house, Barn & Tan House. Says that he believes the original Deeds are lost, but produces authenticated Copys from the Records of Hillsboro County signed by Moses Nichols, Recorder of Deeds, 25th Decr., 1783.

Copy of Conveyance from Thos. Brown to Zaccheus Culter, dated 4th Feby., 1772, in Considn. of £100 Lawful of a certain piece of Land near the place of Worship in Amherst with the Buildings thereon.

After the purchase his Br. made considerable repairs. He now values this at 180 Ster., because he finds it so valued in his Br.'s memorandum Book. It has been sold under Confiscation.

No. 2. 60 acres of Land in Amherst. Same proof of title produced Copy of Deed from Saml. McKim in Considr. of £200 Lawful, 6th July, 1773. This he values at £225, the value stated in his Bros.' memorandum Book. Knows of no Improvement after purchase. Sold under Confiscation.

No. 3. 14 acres in Amherst. Produces same title, viz., Copy Deed from Saml. Flagg of Salem in Consider. of £80.7.10 lawful 1st Sep., 1774. Nows of no improvmts. after purchase. It was all cultivated land. It is sold under Confiscation. (15).

No. 4. 2 Lots of Land in Amherst containing 124 acres of Land, produces the title as before, dated 2nd March, 1775, from Saml. McKim in Consider. £240 Lawful. Can say nothing of the improvmts. on this, but it is sold under Confiscation.

No. 5. 150 acres in New Boston. Produces like title as above from Robt. White in Considr. of £200 lawful. Claimt. cannot speak to improvemts. It is sold under Confiscation.

No. 6. Piece of Land with a Shoemaker's shop in Amherst, produces like title from Danl. McGerth in Considr. £4.13 lawful, 23rd Decr., 1774.

Knows nothing of Improvmts., is sold under Confiscation.

Claimt.'s name & that of his Bro. is in the Act of to Confiscate Estates of Certain persons.

Produces valuation of certain Lands, etc.

No. 7. 46 acres of Land in Northborough; produces Deed dated 10th Feby., 1774, from Michl. Martyn Zaccheus Culter in Considr. of £100 Lawful, the Share of Sd. Martyn in the Estate of Northborough.

Produces an order from the Justices of the Supreme Court of Massachusetts to sell the lands of Mich. Martyn, & Certificate that was sold.

Produces appraisment of the Property of Michl. Martyn, £236 lawful.

No. 8. 2 Pews in Amherst Meeting House. Produces an acct. of Sales when the select men of Amherst are credited £45 lawful. (16).

No. 9. Stock in Tan yard at Amherst. A charge appears in the Mem. Book of the deceased Bro. of £200 Lawful for stock in his Tan Yard. Likewise Memorandum of his Stock on the Farm of 60 acres as in the Schedule, as also the furniture is mentioned. Value £178.11.7 This memorandum book was made out at Halifax in 1776. It contains an acct. of all his Property, real & personal, & contains an acct. of Debts, £1,495.11.4, Interest, £807.10.6 of this has been pd. into the Treasury. Produces an acct. of Sales of personal Estate.

Wits. SAML. ROGERS, sworn:

Says he has known Claimt. before & during the late War. He

was always esteemed a zealous Loyalist. He likewise knew his late Brother, Zaccheus Culter, who was likewise Loyal. Believes he was lost at Sea in 1781.

He recollects the Memorandum Book of the late Zaccheus Culter. It was made out by the Wits. & the late Mr. Culter in 1776 at Halifax. Thinks it was made out to keep in his recollection the Property he had left behind & the value in his own opinion of the property. Before the War Zaccheus Culter was considered a thriving man, & in tolerable circumstances.

(17).
22 November.

Wits. has always considered Claimt. Ebenezer Culter a man of good Character.

Claimt. produces a Certificate from Nahum Baldwin, Trustee of the Estate of Zaccheus Culter, dated Hillsborough, April 4, 1787, that he had in Possession notes & Book debts of the said Zaccheus Culter to the amt. of £381.8.11 Ster. to which acct. has added 7 years interest.

Claimt. also produces a note from Wm. Clarke to Zaccheus Culter for £150.7.10 lawful with Interest, dated 7 March, 1775.

November 21st.

1227. Evidence on the Claim of OSWALD EVES, late of the City of Philadelphia.

Daniel Cox, Esq., produces a Power of Attorney from Oswald Eves, dated 5th Nov., 1783, appointing Mr. Cox & John Potts, Esq., his Attorney, to act for him in all matters respecting his losses & to receive Compensation, &c., &c.

Mr. Eve went home to New York to the Bahama Islands at the Evacuation at the Head of a number of Loyalists. Mr. Cox believes that his attention to his New settlement & a belief that his case might be heard by Attory. has prevented his attendance either in London or on the Commission in America.

Wits. DANL. COX, Sworn:

(18).

Says that he was personally acquainted with Claimt. before & during the War. He has good reason to believe that he was always well attached to Gt. Britain. He never took any part agst. Gt. Brit.

He joined the B. Army when they marched into Philadelphia & remained with them the whole War. Mr. Cox knows that he built a Galley for the King's service. It was generally understood that Mr. Eve gave the information in consequence of which the Vigellant was brought agst. Mud Fort. He was an active, zealous Loyalist.

Mr. C. understood that Claimt possessed a Property as described; from its vicinity to Philadelphia it must be valuable.

No. 2. Mr. C. knows that Claimt. possessed a House as described. They must have been valuable.

Mr. C. has good reason to believe that Mr. Eve had had personal Property to the amount of £352.10 Ster.

Produces Estimation of Abel James & Robert Morris affirmed to before Wm. Bush, 17th Octr., 1783. It is exactly the sums claimed.

Mr. Cox says he made out the Claim from the valuation. Abel James is known to Mr. Cox. He is a man of Character & conversant in the value of property.

Wits. ANDR. ALLEN, ESQ., Sworn:

Knew Oswald Eve after the Army came to Philadelphia. Says that he considered him a person of some property. He came off with the B. Army. He had some Property on the Northern bounds of Philadelphia.

MR. THOS. YORKE, sworn: (19).

Knew that Mr. Eve was in Possession of No. 1. It was reputed Claimt.'s property. He cannot speak positively as to value, but on a supposition that there were 200 acres of Land & the Buildings he saw on it in 1776. He thinks that it is overvalued at £3,000 Str.

Remembers No. 2. Believes it was his property. The House was good. Mr. Yorke has reason to know that Claimt. is settled on Cat Island, Bahama Islands. He is a strictly honest man.

In 1777 Claimt. was not to appearance in the same flourishing state he had been in. November 22.

CAPT. CHARLES R. NAVY, Sworn:

Recollects Claimt. at Philadelphia. He was useful in the construction of the —— Galley. This Galley proved useful the whole War. She was built on Eve's place, which was ingenious. Speaks to Claimt.' Loyalty & readiness to be useful to forward the

King's service.

JOSEPH GALLOWAY, Sworn:

Says he knew Oswald Eve at Philadelphia. He was a Loyal man. February 23.

No. 1. Recollects that Claimt. had a Powder Mill near Frank Port. He never was on the spot. He carried on the business of making gun powder. No. 2. Mr. G. does not recollect. Says that Mr. Eve was insolvent about the year 1767. He went to the W. Indies & returned, before the War. It was understood that he had brought Property with him from thence.

Further Evidence on the Claim of OSWALD EVE. February 28th, 1789.

Wits. WM. AUSTIN, Sworn:

He has been in No. 1 It was six miles from Philadelphia. (20). Cannot speak to the Quantity. Thinks Land in that situation might be worth from £15 to £20 Pen. Cury. per acre. Does not conceive the Mills could be of any great value; perhaps £200 Cury. Does not know that the House in Front St. or the Store was on his Property.

No. 2. Was very small. The House might be worth £150, & the Land £60 per acre, £240, £390.

Mr. Eve was in bad circumstances in 1768, but he made a good voyage to the Bay of Honduras which might clear him of Debt. He cannot speak to his circumstances in 1777. Abel James, Robert Morris; the 1st is a land Jobber, the 2nd is a very honest man.

Mr. Eve had given up the business of Ship Chandler before the War. The House in Front St. belonged to one Pigeon.

London,
27 November,
1788.

1228. Evidence on the Claim of JAMES GIBSON & his Partners, late Merchts. in Suffolk, Virginia.

Archd. Hamilton, Esq., appears & produces a Power of Atty. from Saml. Donaldson, the only surviving Partner of the House of Jas. Gibson, Donaldson & Hamilton, dated Petersburgh, Virginia, 12th July, 1788.

In the original Claim the only demand is for property destroyed by the BritishArmy. That of course is delayed until the Demand shall be transmitted from the Treasury or the Commrs. shall be authorized to proceed in the examination of such Claims.

(21).

There is now produced a Claim for certain Lotts of Land amounting in value to £1,113 Virginia Cury, but as this Claim has not been entered upon by the Commrs. prior to the 1st Aug., 1788. It cannot now be heard. Carrd to P. 75.

February 27th.
1789.

Further Evidence on the Claim of OSWALD EVE.

ENOCH STOREY, sworn:

Says Claimt. had a Ship Chandler's Store & a House in Front St., Philadelphia, & believes they were his own. The house might be worth £400 Pens. Cury. The Store was of brick on the Warf & might be worth the same sum. He has understood & believes that Mr. Eve had a Powder Mill & some property in the Country but Mr. Storey cannot speak to the value. Mr. Eve was in a good

way as a Ship Chandler, but Wits. should not consider him as a person possessed of much Property.

28 November,
1788.

1229. Evidence on the Claim of ALEXR. CUMMING, late of South Carolina.

John Simpson produces Power of Attorney from Alexr. Cumming, 4th Novr., 1783, to James Graham & John Simpson; it is a general Power.

JOHN SIMPSON, Sworn:

Says Mr. Cumming was in England in 1784. He came home to be examined on his Claim, but as his private business required his return to Jamaica & the Comrs. could not enter into his Claim he returned to Jamaica. Says he did not think it necessary to apply for leave to go abroad.

(22).

Mr. Simpson has known Claimt. since 1771, & he has always Conducted himself as a Loyal man. He was a School Master at Beaufort, S. Carolina. He now resides in Jamaica.

The Loss of a Negroe, a Carpenter; lost at C. Town. Loss of Professin as a School Master from £300 to £500 per ann. Ster. States Debts due him £1,627.7.1.

Negroe, hire of Caesar, £780 S. Car. Cury.
"   "   of Jake, £900.

Wits. ROBERT WELLS, sworn:
Says Alexr. Cumming had some Negroes. He kept a School at Beaufort. Understood that he had 20 Schollars at £14.6 Ster. each per an. At first he restricted himself to that number. Afterwards understood that he increased his number to 30 Schollars or thereabout. This sum was for teaching only.

Wits. CHARLES SCHEM, sworn:
Knew Claimt. during the troubles. He was always a Loyal man. Wits. was banished Carolina at same time as Claimt. on acct. of his Loyalty. They went together to Jamaica. He left 2 valuable Negroes, Jake & Cæsar. In peaceable times Jake might be worth £100. He was sent to Claimt. at the Evacuation but his hire was a dollar per diem, Cash. Believes that the Negroe Cæsar died or was killed before the Brit. took C. Town. Says that in the year 1782 Mr. Cumming gave Wits. a Power of Atty, to settle with Mr. Russel, Claimt's Agent, but although Mr. Russel had received all his Debts in paper Currency yet he would never settle with Wits. Mr. Russel had it not to settle. Mr. Russel likewise received the hire of Negroe Jack, but never paid Mr. Cumming.

(23).

Mr. Cumming had 25 Boys, Schollars, in 1775. He received £100 S. Car. Cury, equal to £14.16 Ster, for each, & 4 girls at £50 Cury, £7.3 Stir., for Teaching.

1230. Further Evidence on the Claim of JENET PETERSON, Wid. of John Peterson, late of Philadelphia.

London, December 11th, 1788.

Claimant sworn:

Says that she did not understand when her Claim was made that there would be any Compensation for personal property, and when on Examination in N. Scotia she could not produce the necessary proof. She now Claims.

No. 1. The Stock in Trade of her late Husband, consisting of New Furniture. She says that there was a considerable quantity of ready made Furniture in her late Husband's store at the Evacuation of Philadelphia, to the value of more than £100 Ster. Says that neither her Husband or herself never recovered one farthing's worth of this property & she was informed by a person with whom She left the Key of the store that the goods were taken by the mob.

No. 2. Swears there was to the value claimed & that they shared the same fate as No. 1.

(24).

No. 3. She swears to the quantity & Loss.
No. 4. A great quantity of Tools & Lumber, &c. Seems that they left the amount claimed including Benches & other fixtures.

Wits. ADAM COCKBURN, Sworn:
Says he knew the Deceased, John Peterson, at Philadelphia, before the Evacuation. He had been in his work shop & stores & had emploied him in some alterations in his shop. He carried on trade as an undertaken & cabinet-maker & joiner.

London, 15th December, 1788.

Further Evidence on the Case of WM. AUSTIN, late of Philadelphia.

Claimant, WM. AUSTIN, sworn:

No. 3. Says he had one thousand Gallons of Spermmacette Oil at Cooper's Ferry. He had purchased this about a month before the British took Possession of Philadelphia—who is now in America as a Cabinet maker at Philadelphia. He pd. a Dollar pr. Gallon & paid the amount.

(25). One Coll. Haight, an officer in the Rebel service, took it from thence, 3 weeks after the British took Philadelphia—the British had no Post then. Believes that he knew it was Claimt.'s Property; his Servt. had given information of its being hid. Claims £225 Ster. the cost.

Wits. HENRY LUM, Sworn:

Says that he was in N. Jersey when the British took possession of Philadelphia. He resided at Mount Holly. Says that he heard Wm. Paxton, an Inhabitant of Mount Holly say that he had purchased some oil from Coll. Haight which he had taken at Cooper's Ferry soon after the British took Possn. of Philadelphia. He has since heard in that part of America that Wm. Austin had lost some oil at Cooper's Ferry.

London, 18 December, 1788.

1231. Further Evidence on the Claim of ALEXR. WALLACE, Esq., of Thos. White, Esq., of New York.

Claimt. MATTHEW WHITE Sworn:

Says he is the second son of the late Thos. White of New York. He is 23 years of age. He came to England in 1778, & has been in England ever since. He resides in London; in business.

It appears by Evidence of Thos. White, eldest son of Thos. White, deceased, that he waved his Claim to No. 35, 28 acres of Land at King's bridge, as he could produce no proof of Title.

(26). Wits. now wishes to produce proof to this Title. Says that he has been told by Mr. Alexr. Wallace that his Father did possess this property, but knows nothing of the Title. It is Located to Dr. McKnight, however. No. 34 appears to be in the possession of Charles McKnight. Believes No. 35 was wood land.

From No. 1 to 30. The Estates called the Vineyard. Says that although Mrs. White has regained possession for £3,500 Currency, in 1784, yet he considers the Loss & the family to be what the Estate is nearly worth, as it is now his Mother's property. She is still unmarried. Mrs. White has mortgaged the Estate for the purchase money.

Produces Certificate from Gerard Bancker, Treasurer of the State of New York, that by the returns of the Comrs. for Sales, Mr. White's Estates have sold for 3,500 Cury., dated N. York, 16th Octr., 1788.

Produces Valuation of House, &c., in Elizabeth Town & Certificate of Sums pd. into the Treasury of New Jersey as debts which were due Thos. White, Esq.

The House is valued by Ed. Thomas & Geo. Price at £1,500 N. J. Cury, 28th May, 1788.

Mathew White has an allowance of £25 per an. Danl. White had £25 given him, which a Commissn. was procured for him.

Wits. DAVID OGDEN, Sworn:

No. 34. Says he recollects a House & Lot of Land in Elizabeth Town, N. Jersey. Mr. White purchased the Lott & House in 1766. He paid the Sheriff £400, Mathias Williamson £700 or 800 N. J. Cury., being the amount of a mortgage on the Property before Mr. White purchased from the Sheriff.

(27).

Both the Sheriff & Williamson sold the property. Mr. W. after the purchase from the Sheriff commenced a suit agst. Williamson. Thinks it old under value, as the title was disputed twixt Mr. White & the purchase from Williamson. Thinks this Property is worth £1,800 including House & Barn.

Wits. GEO. FRANKLIN, Sworn:

Remembers a House in Elizabeth Town, the property of the late Thos. White. It was a Tavern. Thinks from the appearance of the House it shd. be worth from £1,500 to £2,000 Cury.

Wits. COMS. HATFIELD, Sworn:

No. 34—Knew Mr. White's House in Eliz. Town, believes Mr. White pd. £1200 for this House & Lands. Thinks the House & Land should have Let for £100 pr. an.

He Values it at £1800 N. J. Curcy. Thinks it would have let for £100 pr. an. One Sam Smith has possession of the House as a Tavern.

Wits. CHEVALIER JONETH, Sworn:

He did Know a House of Mr. White's in Eliz. Town. Conceives the House Cost £1600 or £2000 Cury. building. He thinks the House would have sold for £1400 with the Land. It was let for a Tavern, but thinks it was too good for a Tavern.

Wits. WM. WADELL, Sworn:

Knew the Property called the Vineyard in N. York, it was valuable. The Property was in Possession of Mr. White or his Tenant all the War. Since the War he understood that has been sold to Mrs. White. Thinks this Property was worth £11.000 Cury.

(28)

Wits. JAS. JANNEY, Sworn:

Says he knew Mr. White's Property called the Vine Yard in N. York. When it was purchased it was Considered a good purchase. Understood Mrs. White had been favoured in the purchase of it under Confiscation. He heard that Mr. White had Property in Kings bridge Woods, it was Wood land, should think Woodland in that situation was worth £20 pr. acre.

Has heard that the Wood was destroyed by the British Army.

Mr. White had Considerable sums due him on Bonds. Cannot speak to the Amount.

Wits. JOSEPH CHEW, Sworn:

Says the late Thos. White was a determined, Loyal man. Says that he was at great expence & trouble in Clothing the New Corps. Wits. often distributed Charity to poor Loyalists for Mr. White.

London, 14th January, 1789.

(29)

1232. Further Evidence on the Claim of WM. DEMASINE & THOS GUMMERSALL.

Thos. Gumersal produces different Extracts from Proceedings in Court agst. Wm. Durmasin & Thos. Gumersall in New Jersey. Has no further Evidence to offer as to the property.

London, 13th February 1789.

1233. Further Evidence on the Claim of ALEXR. BERTRAM, late of Philadelphia.

Claimt. Sworn:

Says he could not produce Evidence in N. Scotia & prays to be heard further & produce Witness's.

8 first Patents—He purchased them 1772, he paid £10 Pen. Cur. pr. Hundred acres to the person who had the Location, & £5 Ster. pr. Hundred acres to the Proprietor. This was all his expence, besides a Penny pr. acre Quit rent pr. acre.

No. 9—Says that his Pottery let for £30 pr. an., the Houses for 60-90 Pen. Cury.

Says he was offered £100 pr. an. for the ground these buildings are on.

No. 10—Was purchased by his Wife in 1777 for £700 Pen. Cury. by his advice, the purchase was paid, it has been sold.

No. 11—Was Mortgaged to Claimant in 1773, she got a deed in 1776, he paid £800 Pen. Cury. for it. This sold under Confiscation.

No. 12—He likewise purchased & paid the price.

No. 13—He purchased in 1776, it is sold.

(30)

No. 14—Says he purchased when there was no War in the Province. Says he paid for it in Lawful money.

No. 15—The property is sold since his last Examination, £450 Cury.

No. 16—These 92 acres are sold. Says he pd. for his share £376 Cury.

No. 17—The title was not Completed—as the Patent was not made out he paid £10 pr. hundred acres for it, purchased from the person who had located.

No. 18—In like situation.

No. 20—He gave £10 Cury. for this & claim £100 for it.

Wits. JOSEPH GALLOWAY, Sworn:

Says that £10 Cury. pr. Hundred acres was a Common price for lands located. The Warrant & Survey was Considered a Complete Title.

If the Lands Cost 3sh. & 6d. Cury. in 1773 they might have doubled in value by 1776.

No. 9—Mr. G. does not recollect the Property, but if situated as described he thinks it was valued low at £800 P. Cur., the situation was very good, it was worth 12 years purchase.

No. 10—Property in Second St. was valuable, if 47 feet by 200, with a Brick House, it is low valued at £700. Sales of property in 1775-6 & 7 were not frequent & property did not sell for its value. Mr. Bertram was Considered a thriving man & of good Credit in Philadelphia. He kept a Shop, he might be worth some money. (31)

No. 15—Is valued moderately, as the land was good there.

No. 16—Lands in Northampton were worth £4 pr. acre. The Wasted Lands are too highly valued.

Wits. CAPT. DANL. COUSINS, Sworn:

No. 11—Remembers his purchasing this property, it had been mortgaged to him, he thinks it was worth £1000 Cury. It was sold under Confiscation.

No. 13—He recollects it was worth £50 pr. acre, it was Claimts. It rented for £60 pr. an.

1134. Proofs of the Claim of ICHEBOD OLIVER, late of N. Jersey. _{N. C. London, 16th February 1789.}

The Comrs. saw the Claimt. near Annapolis in Octr., 1786, & on an affidavit of his age he appears to have been under age in 1784.

Mayor Thos. Beverley Certifies that he served in a provincial Corps some years of the War. He now resides in Wilmot, N. Scotia.

Claims ¼ of his Father's Homestead & ½ of a Tract near Rawyag. 1-3 of a Tract of Salt Meadow under the Last Will of David Oliver, his father, dated in 1766, which is produced.

Produces appraisment of 71 acres & ¼ & 8 acres Salt Meadow at £752 N. J. Cury. Joseph Burd & David Brant. Likewise appraismt of ten acres—¾ late the property of Ichabod Oliver in N. Jersey, £107.10, by the same persons. (32)

Aaron Dunham Certifies to the Sale of Ichabod's real Estate for £402.19.6. Cury. _{11th April, 1786.}

Further Evidence on the Claim of JOS. PELL, late of W. Chester, N. York Province. _{London, 16th February, 1789.}

Wits. JAMES DELANCEY, Sworn:

Says that in or about 1778, Jos. Pell purchased from his Attys., Thos. Jones & G. Staunton, 32 Lotts in the suburbs of N. York, he paid £3225 N. York Cur., he paid the price in Cash. Mr. Delancey understood that he sold 10 Lotts of these. It was part of the Agreement that Mr. Pell was to sell to the Tenants on these ten Lotts at the price he paid Mr. Delancey. Mr. Delancey valued the Lotts at £100 Cury. each prior to the War.

The ground of 2 Lotts was occupied by a Street so that in fact he lost 20 Lotts. They were sold as Mr. Delancey's Property, & are included in Mr. Anstey's acct. of Mr. Delancey's Property sold under Confiscation. A small Consideration was paid to Mr. Delancey for the houses.

But he understands that Mr. Pell laid out some money on the Property. Wits. declares that no part of these 32 Lotts is Claimed by him.

London,
6th February,
1788.

1235. Further Evidence on the Claim of HY. WATKINS, late of N. Yorke.

Wits. JAS. DELANCEY, ESQ.

(33)

Says that in 1781 his Atty., Jas Kingston, at N. York, sold to Claimt. a House & Lott in Little Queen Street, New York, for the sum of £350 N. York Cury., which was paid to Wits. Atty. in Cash. This Property has been Confiscated & sold as Mr. Delancey's Property.

Claimt. brought an action agst. Wits. to recover the price paid but Plaintiff was Cast with Costs.

London,
4th March.

1228. Further Evidence on the Claim of MR. JAS. GIBSON of Virginia.

MR. JAS. PARKER Examined.

Says he knew Mr. Jas. Gibson, late of Suffolk, he lived in England all the War. His Partners, Messrs. Hamilton & Donaldson, were in Virginia. They were both Loyal men.

The Copartnery had Property in Suffolk. The Houses were burnt by Genl. Garth in 1779.

(34).

Mr. Gibson had lived in Suffolk many years & believes the Property belonged to Mr. Gibson & partners.

No. 1—The Lot where Mr. Gibson lived was —— acres & might be worth £150 Ster., the Buildings worth £1000 Ster. He had some Warehouses, the property of the Co., at the near side. He cannot speak of the value of the Warehouses, nor to the quantity of Land.

Mr. Gibson's Property was destroyed on acct. of Naval Stores which were in the Town of Suffolk, & it was necessary they should be burnt. The Army went to Suffolk to destroy the Magazines for the supply of the American Army.

Lt. Coll. John Hamilton says that he knows Mr. Gibson & his partners were possessed of Considerable property at Suffolk in Virginia, Consisting of houses, Warehouses, Gardens, Lotts & Stock in trade.

He cannot speak to what has been destroyed & what Confiscated. He thinks that the demand made by Messrs. Gibson, Donaldson & Hamilton is very much within the Value.

MR. HAMILTON, Atty. for the Partners.

Produces an Abstract of the Title Deeds of Lotts in Suffolk on which the Houses destroyed stood.—The Proofs of Sale he has good reason to believe that this property was in Possession of the Copartnery at the Commencmt of the War and that they did not dispose of them.

7th March—Certifies to Certain Signatures of persons in public office in Virginia.

(35).

Likewise Inquisition found agst. Jas. Gibson & Co. wherein Certain Lotts of Land in Suffolk are mentioned. Enter Valuation of the Lotts in Suffolk & Certificates of Confiscation & Sale.

PROCEEDINGS

OF

LOYALIST COMMISSIONERS.

Vol. III.

MISCELLANEOUS EVIDENCE.

Claimants.

	MS.S. Folio.
Bayard, Robert	33
Bunton, Capt. J.	4
Gibbs, Mrs.	13
Jamieson, Neil	27 & 29
Knox, William	1
McLean, David	31
Orde, Capt.	6
Pepperell, Sir William	26
Savage, Arthur	11
White, Mr.	10
Wright, Govr. Sir James	14 & 23
American Claims, Epitome of	34
Memoranda—1785	34
House of Commons Proceedings, June 26th, 1786	35
Anstey Commission	41
Minutes of Claims, 25th Nov.	44
Correspondence	54
Statement of Reports, &c.	73
List of Blank Certificates, &c.	75
Total Loss, &c.	76

82 AR.

THE EVIDENCE.

1236. Case of MR. WM. KNOX, late Secretary of the Province of New York & Planter in Georgia.

Loyalty.

Mr. Knox has been a Servt. of Government since 1771 as deputy Secretary of State in the America department.

Landed Property—

Landed Property.	1st Grant in 1769, 600 acres produced	600
	Conveyance 1760, from N. Switzer to W. Knox	250
	do do from M. Miller to do.........	50
	do 1761 S. & E. Moore for 50 acres...	50
	do 1761 Dorlay for 50 acres	50
	do 1761 N. & M. West, 50 acres	50
(1)	Bought of Mr. Smith by Lt. Govr. Graham...	1,000
	Grant 1760 to Wm. Knox for 50 acres...	50
		2,100

It appears that Mr. Knox may have forfeited these grants by non performance of Conditions.

Settled Plantation.

Two settlements Rice Ground 240 acres, a Valuation produced of the property of Mr. Knox, 1776, £15,825 G. Currency, Equal to Sterling, £15,825.

Negros were carried off by overseer.

Value Land alone... £7230		deduct Value of	
Negroes 122 6560		102 Negroes 50 each	
Stock Rice, &c...... 2115		sold... 4756	
15905			

Crop upon the ground in 1782 by letter from Mr. Hall, Agt. for Mr. Knox, it appears by acct...2000
That Crop of 1781 produced £1400.

Mr. Knox paid G. Clark for the office of Secretary £3000, the amount of fees rented at £1000 pr. an. Mr. Knox received for 2 years & since the King's troops were at New York about £600.

Mr. Knox enjoys a pension of £600, his Wife a pension of £600, during pleasure, apparently for Losses in America, but being in Possession of the pension had the bad effect to him of his receiving no Consideration for losing his income as under Secretary of State. Mr. Knox is of opinion that had he been without Pension he would have received £750 pr. an. upon the Loss of office.

LT. GOVERNOR GRAHAM.

(2) Two Plantations of Mr. Knox's upon the River Savanah Contained above 200 acres of rice ground & a Considerable quantity of Corn, Meadow, & Wood, the Wood was valuable. Has heard Mr. Hall manager that he might return £2000 in the year 1782, but the Estate never yielded near that. The Plantation might

82a AR.

produce 2 Barrels of Rice pr. acre, worth from 40 to 50 sh. pr. Barrel, which sum fully the yearly value of the Plantation. Thinks the Plantation of Knox br. Worth £4000, at least £3000. He might have given ready money payments as usual in that Country, by instalments. Good rice ground worth £10 per acre. There were no mortgages or Incumbrance upon Knox br.

Mr. Graham made a purchase of 1000 acres from Mr. Smith adjoining the Knox br. for £500. He looks upon that part to be equal to the former possession. Mr. K's grant was in the State of Nature & of no yearly value, but might have been sold perhaps for 7sh. 6d. per acre, perfectly unsettled.

Property all registered in the Province of Georgia.

Knows M:. Knox Overseer took off some of the Negroes to the Rebels.

Produces an estimate of Knox br. Plantation which he makes Worth £7056—yet Continues of Opinion that would not advise his friend to give more than £4000—nor would he have given more than £3000.

When Lt. Gr. Graham wrote Mr. K— that he would advise him to take £4000 Ster. & that in answer Mr. K. wrote that his overseer, Mr. Hall, had behaved so well to him lately that he would not sell for less than the valuation.

(3)

GOVERNOR WRIGHT: Sep. 24th.

Visited Knoxborough Plantation at the desire of Mr. Knox three or four times a year. He had two Plantations from which he had a little profit for some years—until 1764 when they improved Considerably. The Plantation more adapted to Lumber produce than rice—that for one or two years he made 200 barrels of rice upon each plantation which would sell from 45 to 50 sh. pr. Barrel, that he would not have made use of Mr. Knox's Plantation but for Lumber, it was most valuable.

Mr. Knox had about 115 Negroes upon his Plantation, very good ones—Worth £50 on an average. Know his Over Seer, Griffin, carried off some Negroes to the Americans.

Supposes Crop 1782 could not be Worth more than £500, he thinks with the number of Mr. Knox's Negroes he could Cultivate his rice ground & carry on the lumber trade, as he holds a Negro equal to the work of four acres of rice.

Thinks Mr. Knox's rice ground was worth from £6 to 7 pr. acre—his high Land 20 sh. pr. acre. The Plantation of Knox br. he thinks is Worth £6000 Ster.

1237. Case of CAPT. J. BUNTON, of the Navy. 19th Sept., 1783.

Evidence of Claimt.

Declared traitor to the United States by act of Assembly of Rhode Island. Driven from his Property 1775, his property Confiscated. Has served most of the War on Board of his Majesty's Ship.

(4)

177 acres by the Will of his Father—Valued at £2250 by three men of Character—one of which pd. that sum for an Equal share of the same farm.

Land & House belonging to Mrs. Bunton in the Town of Newport.

Lett to Richards Eighteen Silver dollars ...	4.1.0
do to Littlefield twenty Silver Drs...	6.4.6
do to Hanah Allan Seventeen do	3.6.6

in all 62 Dollars which he holds to be half his Wife's property. a house, part of the improved property, was burnt by the Hessians, value £40.0.0.

1600 acres in the Province of Mayne—papers all lost—uncultivated—£720—has been offered for it 3200 Dollars.

4600 Dollars agst. the Estate in Mortgage upon the 177 acres —is money laid out upon that, subject when the Estate is sold. Ct. B. believes it would be sold with that incumbrance.

Personal property Consists in small articles which he has put an under value upon —amount £1800.

Received by Mrs. Bunton for the use of his house & farm by the Naval Hospital.

(5) Evidence of MR. WALLER.

As Purveyor of Naval Hospital he took Capt. Buntons farm in 78, 60 or 70 tons of Hay & 150 Bushels Indian Corn.

MR. G. ROHNER.

He knows the Valuer of the Property to be of good Character & that one of them gave 10,000 Dollars for an Equal share

MR. ALUMFORD.

Knows the Valuers & believes it was valued & properly—His house & Stock.

Knows Capt. B. succeeded to a Considerable property, in right of his Wife—but only in genl. terms.

MR. LEWIS MUMFORD.

His father being Executor to Mr. B. Will has seen it, where he leaves Capt. B. ¼ of 5000 acres in Prov. of Mayne.

22 Oct. The Schedule of personal property was formed at different times when the property was taken in 1775—before he quitted his house—he fixed the value since that time at the market price.

Charges his Indian Corn at 3 sh. pr. Bushel.
Oats at 1sh. 3d. pr. Bushel.
250 Bush. ——————— 4sh.
Potatoes 1sh. 3d. pr. Bushel.
Flax Seed, 50 bushels, ready for Market at 4sh. 6d.
Apples, 350, 1sh. 3d. pr. Bushel.
50 Loads of Hay at 50sh.
70 bushels Turnips, 1sh. 3d. pr. bush.

Amount of Stock, &c., a Barn, £400, thinks it Cost him £150, Dary house & Crib, Cost £140, gave £45 for his Negroe, debts due him, £137.

1238. Case of CAPT. ORDE.

(6) Sepr. 26th, 1783.

Married Miss Stevens in 1781. She was an Orphan & had been so a great while, of Course had taken no part in the disturbances. The Barnwells were her nearest male relatives. Upon the death of Messrs. Middleton & Reeve, Messrs. Barnwell Carson & Gibbons assumed the management of Mrs. Ordes affairs. By the advice of Mr. D——, Mr. Boone, Gd. to Mrs. Orde, apptd. Mr. Joiner & Mr. Barwell Agents—upon this appointmt arriving in America in 1775. Mr. Barnwell refused to act upon it or to allow Mr. Joiner to act upon the Idea that Mr. B—., Mr. C—. & Mr. G—. were trustees upon Mr. Stevens Will. Upon that part of the Country falling into the hands of the British Miss Stevens appointed Mr. Tatnall, a steady friend of Governmt., to act as agent in 1781—his marriage took place when he apptd. Mr. Tatnall & Mr. Gibbs his Agents. Believes Miss Stevens went to America in 1781 to take Possession of her property as a british subject.

Understands that his property in S. Carolina is not sold, upon the Idea that it is his only for life, but Mrs. Orde in settlemnt. understands his property in Georgia is sold for £1235

LT. GOVRENOR BULL.

(7)

All Miss Stevens Connections he can speak to are strong favourers of the American Cause. No remittance being made might proceed from breach of trust rather than from any particular motive. As far as Gr. Bull's Knowledge goes believes that Copy of the Will would be allowed as Evidence in a Court in S. Carolina. Knows the Signature of the Secretary, Mr. Wins Stanley.

Knows the Plantation upon St. Helena & Crepot, not Extensive, but kept in good order & well Cultivated.

Lot of ground in Beaufort is about half an acre.

Average of Negroes for some years prior to '77 was in his opinion £70.

Thinks two gs. an average price of Cattle, Sheep half a guina, Horses, £5.

MR. GIBBS.

Was apptd. Atty. jointly with Mr. Tatnall in 1781 by Capt. Orde.

The Plantation of St. Helena & Cassas were in good order, she thinks they were Worth £1200.

There were 100 or 99 Negroes upon the Plantations, mostly very good ones. Was present at the marriage of Capt. & Mrs. Orde in 1781.

79 or 80 Negroes were saved for Capt. Orde, all those in Cassaw were saved, all those on St. Helena were carried off by the Rebels, most of them escaped back.

Knows there were Copys taken of her Brother's Will, believes the Copy produced to be true.

(8) Mr. Geo. Elliot.

Knows Mr. Stevens family for 30 years & Property. Knows the Plantation upon Cassaw in the year 73—had been an Indigo Plantation, is now for Stock & Corn. The Island was from 12 to 1300 acres. Values it at 40 or 45 sh. pr. acre. At St. Helena at 700 acres—some of the best Indigo Land in the Province, such land sold from 45 to 55 sh. pr. acre, medium 50 sh.

Rented the Lott at Beaufort at ten pounds pr. an. Would have bought it but could not make a title—it was held by Mortgage—if the title had been good would have given £350.

Mr. James Carson.

The House he was partner in at Charles town remitted in 1773—seven Casks Indigo—Value upon the spot £400. That he bought the Crop of Indigo 1774 from Dr. Carson & Mr. Gibbs for £959.10.8. He believes the Estate of Stevens made 16 Casks of Indigo in 1773 & has heard that the Estate was Worth that year £2000.

That Messrs. Clark & Miligen upon Mr. Carson's representation, advised Miss Stevens about £4000 Sterling, part of which Capt. Orde has repaid.

Mr. Charles Shaw.

(9) Resettled at Beaufort in S. Carolina. Knew the Estates of Stephens in that neighbourhood, the Estate at Cassaw was Considered as one of the most valuable Estates in that Country—from its being an Island—his Uncle & Partner, Messrs. Shaw & Stewart, have often purchased the whole produce from 1766 to 1773. It amounted to from £1000 to £1500 Sterling—his Uncles house often paid that sum for produce, he thinks the Stock sold might pay the Expense of Cultivation, &c. Speaks much from Idea of guess.

The Negroes were very good & might sell at Credit for £60 or 70—which might be reduced very much by getting sold for ready money. Thinks the two Plantations might have been sold at £3 pr. acre, if two years Credit could be given.

Lott at Beaufort—Knew the Lot, it might be worth £150. No buildings upon it.

Mr. Gibbs—on Mr. Orde's Case.   15th Oct., 1783.

Mrs. Gibbs gave Govr. Orde an acct. in Writing upon her return from visiting the Plantation which she received from the people upon the Plantation. She thinks there were more—believes the Loss of Negroes after she took possession of the Plantation was about twenty.

Mrs. Gibbs sent Capt. Orde £500 arising from Sale of Indigo, Cattle & Sheep.

She Swears the Stock of Horses left on Cassaw & St. Helena was Worth above £700. The Cattle was drove of by order of the Commissioners—under the Confiscation & sold for £5 a Head in the year 1782.

1239. Notes MR. WHITE'S Case. 7th Octr., 1783.

Joined Sir Wm. Howe's Army at Trenton in Decr., 1776. Was sent out from Brunswick on the 14th Jany., 1777—as appears from his pass produced—for the purpose of raising men & ——— (10) the Enemy. The second day he was taken up on Suspicion by Gr. Washington—also after some days Confinement he was dismissed on his Parole to remain in the Jerseys ten days—after that time to remove to N. York with his Wife & family.

Bought 600 acres of Land in March, 1776, from Cornls. Low. Left his titles with Mr. Skelton at N. York. Mr. Skelton sent them to his father in Law, Mr. Lowrie, in Jersey, pd. for it £4000 New Jersey Cury., paid down £2500 & gave a Bond to Mr. Low for £1500, which he still owes & expects to have a demand made upon him for it.

This Property was mortgaged for the £1500 to Mr. Low.

Mr. THOS. SKELTON. Oct. 8, 1783.

Mr. White came to the Jerseys in 1775 & Married soon after— was in business—bought a Plantation—in 1776 of Mr. Cornl. Low —was present at the agrement the price was £4,000, N. York or N. Jersey Cury.—received a deed from Mr. White when he went to Jamaica.

After two or three months Mr. Thos. Lowrie sent for it, as Atty. for Mr. White—he sent it by some person to Mr. Lowrie whom he did not recollect —has heard he got £2,000 or 3,000 Sterling by his Wife—has heard Mr. White say he owed a considerable part of the purchase money.

Mr. ARTHUR WADMAN, late Capt. 26th Regt. (11)

Believes he was a Loyal Subject.

Knows he purchased a Plantation from Mr. Low—left his family in the Jerseys in May 1775, to join his Regt. at **Ticonderago** & was taken Prisoner with his servt. on Lake George five days afterwards. Mr. White made the purchase before this time.

1240. Case ARTHUR SAVAGE. 10th Oct., 1783.

An officer of the Customs at Falmouth & Boston—Produces Certificate of Govr. Hutchinson & Wentworth setting forth his good behaviour as an officer of the Customs & his suffering from it.

300 acres of Land at North Yarmouth—was left him by his father—by Will—has not that Will—it was a share of a Tract of 3,400 acres granted many years ago to Mr. Pratt—600 acres was

bt. by the Claimts. father—does not know what he pd.—it yielded him no yearly profit.

(12)

40 acres near Brunswick he got possession of for a debt of £40 Sterling—upon Mr. Ss. quitting the Country in 1771 he desired his Atty. to let the person from whom he had, have it—at a rent—has heard nothing more of it.

One 3rd of 2 Lots at Peterburgh in right of his wife valued at £10 Sterling pr. his two letters produced, which treat of that property—but no rights produced—unless for ten years.

His furniture & Plate lost at Boston & at Falmouth was worth he thinks £300 including what he sold at Halifax & in England— left furniture &c. at Boston which cost him £200.

Comptroller at Falmouth—was apptd. in 1765 remained in possession until 1771 & enjoyed Sallary & perquisites until 1775— when Falmouth was burnt—has only received the Sallary from that time to 1782 £50 per an., the fees were he thinks about £150 Ster., has received £80 per an. from 1st May 1776 to 1782, & at this time £60 per an., allowance.

Mr. HERON.

40 acres of Land in Brunswick—has a Conveyance to some Land to Mr. Savage—he has it as a security for £28—it appears to be a sale.

Mr. Waldo—Collector of Customs at Falmouth.

Mr. Savage always behaved with great Loyalty & fidelity in the execution of his office—is unaquainted with Mr. Savages Ld. property—thinks uncultivated land near N. Yarmouth may be worth 4sh 6 per acre—never heard Mr. S— was in possession of Lands in N. Yarmouth—thinks his office of Comptroller might be worth £183 Ster.

Mr. HOLLAND of New Hampshire.

Cannot undertake the value of of Mr. S.'s land—good Wild Lands in N. Yarmouth T. Ship might be worth ten or fifteen shillings per acre.

Case Considered.

(13)

The 40 acres at Brunswick were in his possession in Consequence of an execution, but had received no advantage from it, & had disposed of his right to it as a security for a debt.

Some land near Peterburgh in right of his wife—no sufficient evidence—that he lost furniture to the value of £100. The office of Depty Surveyor & Searcher of the Port of Boston was at the disposal of his Principal Mr. Chamire was merely a temporary appointment.

21st Oct., 1783.

1241. Case of MRS. GIBBS.

She took no active part in the Rebellion—nor never did anything to promote the cause. The Grove was burnt by accident while possessed by the British Commissiary—it was the only house she had to live in.

Was allowed £50 per an. for the hire of her Plantation in the hands of the British. For the last six months she received £160 —at the rate of—she received it for six months.

Has never had any acct. of her personal property, of her husband. It is not Confiscated—she left atty's in South Carolina.

Mr. JAS. CARSON, S. Carolina.

As one of Mrs. Gibbs Atty's. he had occasion to know her husband died without a Will. Mrs. Gibbs was always in Conversation a friend of the British Govt., £50 pr. an was paid Mrs. Gibbs as rent for the Grove by the Commissary Gen. Mr. G. applied for Compensation for the house burnt by accident but was refused it—upon the whole thinks Mrs. Gibbs Husband was a favourer of the Rebellion's cause in Gen. (14)

1242. Case of Govr. SIR JAMES WRIGHT. 20th Oct., 1783.

Appt'd. Lt. Govr. 1760, & Govr. 1761—remained so until 1782—resided from Oct. 1760 to July 1771—Came home with leave of absence—went out to his former situation for the Convenience of Gov't. & at the disin of the Ministers in De Cene 1772—remained until forced off in March, 1776—got to England in June 1776—remained until April 1777, when he was again ordered out by Ld.

Sackville & resided until July 1782—Produced a Letter from Ld. Mansfield very Complimentary of his behaviour at Savanah, & an extract from Ld. G. Germain's Letter after the defence of Savanah—very Strong.

There Savanah Plantations are 780 acres formed of five acre Lotts or Garden Lotts, purchased by him & valued in May 1776 tivated state—they were cultivated by him & valued in May 1776 by John Jamieson & James Rossman—Mr. Jamieson is now—— £8,400. (15)

The reason of the appointmt. was because he knew the Rebells could seize them & wished to know their value so that he might get satisfaction from America—really thinks they would have sold for £8,400.

Cowoother Plantation appraised at £2,100—purchased Jany. 1767 from Jonathan Cochran 500 acres for £5,000 S. Carolina Cury. When he purchased this Plantation it had a good deal of cleared ground some wood—when he purchased it produced no yearly income—lay 14 miles S. from Savanah—it was appraised by the same Gentlemen—thinks it worth the appmt.

Mount La——Purchased July 1767, from Elis. Butler, Esq. for £1,000 Lawful money Georgia, Contains 500 acres of which 200 acres are improved rice Land & 300 acres high Land—was unimproved when he purchased it—left it in high Cultivation—thinks it worth £2,000 Sterling.

River Plantation 210 acres of rice ground & 300 high land—received part of it as exchange from Mr. Butler—a grant of 100 & one of 232—he did not comply with the Conditions upon themselves but upon the adjacent grounds much more—these Lands are Timber Lands, valued at £2,100—purchased in Apl. 1768, from Joseph Butler, for £1,000 Lawful money. Contains 200 acres rice land & 300 acres high land, worth £2,150. (16)

Tract of Land —— purchased of Mr. Free —— containing 528 acres —— on river Swamp. —— never cultivated. This purchase Sir James thinks it was worth £1,700—received no yearly value, was offered £1,700 by his Son & £1,600 by Mr. Hall—no incumbrance or Mortgage on any part of his property excepting two debts—Beton one a note £1,855—Bond Benj. Smith £2,042—3,927.

5,200 acres of Land 12 different tracts, purchased by me—produces titles to 4,600 acres the Considr. of the whole £1,520—no yearly income from these Lands the Conditions of the grants had not been fulfilled—500 acres purchased at the same time in the year 1781, with three houses for £280.

Sir James values 1,600 acres in Wrights p. at 10sh. per acre.

Values 2,000 acres in S. Carolina at 30sh. per acre.
Values 1,000 acres in Sateller at 10sh. per acre—4,600 acres value £4,300—the 500 which would make the quantity 5,100 acres he cannot speak————————Grants from Crown prior————————steps taken towards Cultivation ————————————Complyed with—————————— uncultivated land Grants stand him in 3sh. per acre————as far as Sir Jas. Wright has seen or judge by the reports of the surveyors of what he has not seen they were worth 10sh. per acre—a purchase for £280 purchased in 1781.

(17)

500 acres with the houses for £280 in all—Sir James swears to the possession of two 45 acre Lotts near Savanah & Dwelling houses—in the town—the houses were let—one pd. £45 yearly rent—another £15—the other the best, was possessed by a Widow —he exacted no rent—thinks they would have sold for £700—cannot speak to the value of the two 45 acre lotts.

Six Lotts in the Town of Brunswick were granted in the year 1772—Conditions not complied with—Cost Sir. Jas. the fees of office.

Sir James Says 29 were taken & killed by the rebels when they destroyed his Barns--the remaining 14 were lost during a period when one Jackson had a party near Savanah for the purpose of taking negroes if Loyalists.

In the year 1777, there appears to have been 523 negroes delivered over to the America Comrs. upon the reduction in 1778, & afterwards 323—the 200 he swears are totally lost to him & his family—totall loss—200 value at £52. 15 per head makes the loss £10,000.

43 Negroes killed or carried off by the rebels at £52-15—thinks 3 to 100 should be allowed for deaths per an. He thought it prudent & advisable to send his Negroes to Jamaica as to the best market the insurance of £10,000 being the value of 2,000 negroes—£997-8.

In 1777, the Attys. left by Sir James Consequence of Confiscation. Clean rice 2,456 at per Bbl. 50 sh.
rough rice ——— 1851 at ——— 31sh. 6d:
"Sir Jas.," Barrels were always 550 weight the Common Barrels were only 500.

While Sir Jas. was at Cockspur on Bt. Ship, he wrote to his manager, to send a Boat Ld. of rice to Tybu which he did & shiped 106 Barrels & ordered them to gold Tybu but upon the way down the Rebells seized the rice—in March 1776 the difficency he accts. for being taken away by the rebells. Sir James Burrell, held 9 Bushels & one Peck—1020 Bushels Indian Corn at 3sh. pr. Bushell £153—oxen & other Cattle, working oxen on Savanah Plantation 35—well worth £4 each—other Cattle 31 at £1-10. each. Sheep 18, £1, Horses 16 at £7.

(18)

Ogeechu—26 Horses £7, 20 Sheep £1, 54 Hogs at 15sh. 90 Cattle at £1.10—54 working Cattle £4. Total Stock £889—Tools £875. His Plantations were well provided with Tools—he believes they were worth £875—including a Store of New Tools.

Sir Jas. lost Carriages & Horses in 1776 to the amt. of £311—produces an Inventory of furniture lost when he left Savanah in 1776—he says that furniture cost him in London some years before £771. There Town furniture was appraised by his attys. at £491—he lost in 1782, he swears cost him more than £400 but has no Inventory or appraisement.

Bonds & mortgages which Sir James Considers as very good debts £1,879.

Sir James—having made £7,670 in 1776 he supposes the Rebel Comrs. may have made 6,000 per an. which for years 77 & 78 amts. £12,000.

Left upon the ground in 1782—300 acres would have produced 1,000 barrels at £2-10..2,500.
would have sold at £7. per bbl. Paper.
money received in payment............................... 201.13
Crop peas, potatoes &c., he rates at..................... 650.
Acct. No. 8 to be Considered. 4,943.
Crop &c. destroyed by the French & American Troops during the seige of Savanah .... 3,300.

(19)

Explanation by Sir JAS. WRIGHT.

Nov. 6.

Says that the number of Working oxen, was necessary upon his Plantation—as his machines for pounding the rice were worked by them—the Common price of Working oxen was £4—he is satisfied he had that number from Letters & memorandums of his overseers at his return in 1779—Indian Corn Sir James supposes from the quantity of ground under Indian Corn & from the Custom of the Country that the 1020 Bushels were clean Corn.

It is the practice in Georgia to pack the rice in Barrels as it is manufactured—Sir Jas. therefore says that his Clean rice was Certainly in Barrell the rough rice was some part in Stock some part thrashed—his rough rice was worth to him near one third his Clean rice—from his Convenience to Manufacture it.

Mr. JOHN JAMIESON, late of Georgia.

23 Oct., 1873

In 1776 he was emploied by Sir Jas Wright to appraise his negroes —Sir Jas. did this upon his being forced to fly from Georgia—he naturally wished to ascertain the value of his pro--perty, by judges & honest men—the paper marked A he believes is the original valuation—he thinks they were well worth what he put them at.

(20)

Amount of Mr. Jamieson's Valuation—
At Savanah... £1,270
Farm..   2,400
Cedar hill.. 17,900
Laurel Grove   2,855
E different Plantations 19,063
F House Negroes   785
He did not appraise the town Negroes.   27,163

Mr. Jamieson appraised the Plantation of Sir Jas. Wright at the desire of Mr. Tuthall, Mr. Hume & Mr. Hall, Attys. for Sir Jas.

but that he did not examine the grounds at that time but that he did it from recollection & guess, but he meant to put the real value & thought them well worth the value.

Recollects the three Savanah Plantations—believes they contained twixt 335 acres of ground & perhaps 400 high ground—the Lands were in high Cultivation—Mr. Jamieson would have given £10 an acre for the rice ground on the Savanah.

Mr. Jamieson & Mr. Mossman formed their opinion of the value from the accts. of Crop 1776. 1100 Barrels made on the three Savanah Plantations he had this information from Sir John Wright.

(21) Mr. Jamieson finds himself at a Loss to put a particular value upon the high Land as he has suffered much since that period— 312 acres at 40 sh. The mode Mr. Jamieson followed for valuing the Ogeechee Plantations was—taking the rice Lands at £8 per acre & the high Land at 30 sh. per acre—1,800 rice Swamp — & 2,000 high Land—Thinks he included the Barns & Buildings in his valuation. Mr. Jamieson formed his former valuation of the produce of the year 1776. Mr. Jamieson thinks in the gross produce of £2,750 the clear profit may be £1,500.

Never was upon any of Sir Jas. purchases of uncultivated Lands formed his Ideas from hearing—that a Tract upon the Carolina Side of 2,000 & believes it was very good—he valued at 30sh per acre—don't recollect any such sold—the remaining part

of uncultivated Lands he valued at 10sh per acre—17 years ago Mr. Jamieson purchased 500 acres of unclt. Land & paid 10sh per acre.

Lt. Gover. Graham.

Knows Sir James Wrights settled Plantations at Savanah & Ogeechee—the Savanah Plt. was very highly improved, they contained about 800 acres of which 330 acres might be rice grownd— that one year—under Govrs. management as Atty. joined with others—it made 1,100 barrels of rice—makes his rice lands as valuable as any in theProvince—he thinks that although they are very (22) highly valued, yet he thinks that from situation & Character they might be sold for £8,000—thinks the rice land was worth £15. per acre—he thinks the high Land separate from the rice Ld. they were worth £3 pr acre, but as they are situated joined to the rice Land he values them at £5. 133 acres Bs. swamp was worth £6 or £6. 10 pr. acre—does not suppose there was so much.

Cowoother Plantation & Mount Laurel Contained about 200 acres rice swamp in each & there might be 2,400 acres highlands to the eight Plantations.

Gr. Graham.

He values the rice Land on the Ogeechee Plantations worth from £8 to £10 an acre—has reason to think the 8 Plantations made 200 barrels of rice—the high Land was mostly Pine Barren, but from its situation & Convenience might be worth £20 pr. acre.

Rice sold by the Cwt.—upon an average at 8sh pr Cwt. the Ogeechee Plantation produced nothing of value but rice.

Purchase from Mr. Freer.—he never was upon it but believes it was 520 acres—some part of it cleared—Sir James never cultivated it—has heard Sir Jas. say that he gave £600 for it. Knows Sir Jas. purchased Lands at Gts.—good lands there worth 10sh. per acre. Knows he had great Tracts of Grants—understood that in 1776 Sir Jas. Wright had 100 Negroes or upwards—he lost many—as they were all sold by the rebells, but many returned. His Negroes were on a parr with the other peoples. He knows he had several carriages &c. in town. (23)

There was a fine crop of rice in 1782, he planted the usual quantity. He knows the Barns upon the Ogeechee, plantation now all burnt but one—he thinks the houses upon a plantation might cost £400.

Case of SIR JAMES WRIGHT Considered. 24 Oct., 83.

The Board are perfectly satisfied of the Claimts. Loyalty.

Sir James Wright's property both real & personal appears to have been Confiscated by an Act of the Assembly of Georgia in 1782. And it appears that part of that property was sold in Compliance with the said act.

It appears that Sir James was entitled to & in Possession of three Plantations near the Town of Savanah. Plantations Containing 780 acres or thereabouts. It seems to have been in the most complete state of cultivation & of the most valuable quality.

The Board allow Sir Jas. for this Property £5000.

Four Plantations on the River Ogeechee were in the Possession of Sir James Wright, it does not appear that they were by any means so valuable as those near Savanah. There appears to have been granted Lands to the Amount of 332 acres in these Plantations, but as Sir Jas. seems to have turned them to the most advantageous use they are held as Cultivated as the Conditions of the Grant require. (24)

Sir James purchased a tract of 500 acres of ground in 1768 from Mr. Freer, in 1769, 270 acres of which was river Swamp for £600 & Sir James not having been at any expence upon it they allow him only the original purchase money & 500 acres on Ogeechee. Dwelling Houses & two 45 acres Lotts bought in the year 1781, are disallowed on the ground that were purchased since the commencement of the troubles.

4,600 acres of uncultivated Lands purchased before the year 1775. The Amount of the Consideration by the Deeds appears to have been £1,520, & as Sir Jas. seems to have taken no steps towards Cultivation they allow the Original Value, only.

Sir James was in possession of 19,354 acres of uncultivated Lands by Grant & had Complyed with no one Condition. The Board do therefore put no value upon them. Grants from the Crown. 6 Lotts in the grounds marked out for the Township of Brunswick seems to have cost Sir James £48, & as the term for compliance with the conditions was not expired before the Rebellion broke out, they allow him the original Cost.

Sir James Wright lost 200 Negroes in 1776 & in following disturbances in the Province of Georgia at £45 a head, £9,000.

It appears that Sir James Wright lost 2,562 barrels of Clean rice in 1776 & 1777 which at 40sh. pr. Barrel is £5,124, and 1851 Barrels of rough rice at 10sh., is £925.10. Sir James Lost 1,020 bushels Indian Corn at 2sh. pr. bushel, £102.

Sir James lost Stock to the Amount of £546.10. The Estimate, the Tools, Maschines, Carts, &c., &c., lost upon his different plantations at £500.

The Board are of the opinion he should be allowed half the original Cost of his furniture £585.15.6.

There appear to have been debts upon Bond &c. due to Sir James Wright to the Amount of £1,879. Principal £1,538.5.10. The Board allow Sir James £1,200 for the Crop upon the ground at the Evacuation. Savanah Plantation, Coach Horses, &c., £150.

Sir James Wright's Conduct in the Council of War held at Savanah upon that place being summoned to surrender by Comte D'Eslaing & his zeal & activity during the seige contributed materially towards the preservation of that place.

Sir James Wright was Governor of Georgia with a sallary of £1,000 pr. an. & £300 perquisites.

1243. SIR WM. PEPPERELL. (Note *the first part of Statemt gone.*) This Gentleman stepped forth the 1st Person of great property in N. England, by accepting the situation of Mandamus Councellor & taking a decided part in support of the British Govert.

On ½ sold viz. what he had in fee, the other ½ lost a Life Interest in reversion.

Entail. Sir Wm. has lost the life Interest in reversion. Has lost his Interest in this House which they value at £2,000. Reversion in Fee by Andr. Pepperell Will. A House & Garden £690.

Has lost his 8 acres	£ 30
An Orchard 25 acres	100
Crocketts, 40 acres	100
Tenneys, 20 acres	50
A House & 20 acres, Wm. Page	80
400 acres Wood	1450
200 acres, Amos Williams	600
20 acres upon the road	80
300 acres in Kittny.	1125
Tavern & 10 acres	400
	£6,705

Property Entailed to which Sir Wm. has a Life rent right in reversion & is in the Possession of Lady Pepperell.

A Mill & 300 acres let at £122 Str.	£1,500
300 acres ¼ of a Mile S. East of the above	230
1,200 acres above Sanco falls	1,975
700 acres deep brooke Lott	540
700 acres Long Reach	540
600 acres Guinea Lott	463
350 acres Bernes Lott	200

490 the old Orchard	445
Foxwell's right 870 acres	600
Blue Point Farm 3 or 400 acres	600
4-8 of Cookes Right	1,568
700 acres	540

9,201
6,705

15,906

538. Examination NEIL JAMIESON, late of Norfolk.　　23rd February 1790.

No. 1. The Co. of Glasford Gordon Monteith & Co. Possessed Certain ware houses at Portsmouth in Virginia in which he was intrusted ¼ of ½, viz., £140. The total value to the Co. was £610. This Property was destroyed by the Americans in 1776, soon after Norfolk was destroyed.

Mr. Jamieson explains that his reason for now bring forward his Claim is because he was informed in a Letter from Mr. Betts 11th Feby, 1790, that this article was not cognizable by the Comrs. when he was formerly examined.

He rests the Claim on his former examination, &c., says this damage was done to him on acct. of his Loyalty.

No. 2. ¼ of a Moiety of Houses at Gt. Bridge, £12.10. Destroyd before the Burning of Norfolk. At the Attack of Gt. Bridge he cannot say whether these Buildings were burnt by the British or Americans, rather thinks that they were destroyed by the British.

No. 3. ¼ Share of Tobacco burnt at Richmond. Says the quantity burnt was 53 Hogsheads. It was at Manchester. There were some thousand Hogsheads burnt at the same time.

This he proves by the affidavits of Messrs. Lyle & Banks—Factors at Manchester. He Claims payment for this Loss as Property destroyed by the British Army. It had been deposited in payment of Debts.

Mr. Jamieson at the time this Property was destroyed was banished from Virginia & his property Confiscated.

He does not know when the Tobacco was lodged. The Claim is grownded on the affidavit of James Lyle, the Warehouse Keeper. He considers 20sh. pr. Ct. as a fair average price. The Tobacco from James river was during the War chiefly sent to France. Claims principal & Interest £373.16.10.

Refers to Examination on the Claim of Henderson McCaul & Monteith & Co. for proof of his share in the Company 1-12 of Warehouses burnt by the Rebels at Richmond in June, 1780. His share, principal & Interest, £189.

Refers to Examination on the Claim of Henderson McCaul & Co. for proof of his proportion of Stock in trade in this Copartnery.

Mr. Jamieson explains that by an Old Law of the Province of Virginia it is enacted that all Tobacco shall be lodged in a Public

Ware house & be inspected before it is shipped and that no Tobacco can be shipped before it has been in one of these Warehouses α inspected.

1890
2nd March.

Further Examination on NEIL JAMIESON.

Mr. Jamieson examined and Says.

No. 4. That his Claim for Warehouse at Richmond is as Partner in the House of Henderson McCaul & Co. He is concerned ¼ in this House. Mr. Jas. Lylle was likewise Partner 1-11h Share in this House.

The Compy had several Houses in Richmond, and as examinant has been informed they were burnt by the British Troops. And he has good reason that the Houses called James Lyles in the affidavits of Dowery, Wood & Smith Bleakly were the Property of the Copartnery.

James Buchanan who Certifies to his Loss is a Gentleman of good Character. Well known to many persons from Virginia.

Mr. Neil Jamieson. Enquired into Mr. Jamieson's Losses and the Amount included in the Amended List.

The two first articles of Claim have been reconsidered by the Comrs. who formerly in Consequence of Report of his Loyal ——

(30)

The next article in this demand is for one Fourth Share of the value of Fifty Hogsheads of Tobacco, the Property of the Claimant deposited in a public Warehouse at Manchester in Virginia, where that Commodity was necessarily stored, in order to be inspected previous to Exportation, and which Lord Cornwallis in the year 1781 found it expedient to destroy, as one means of Weakening the Resources of the People of that Colony, then in a state of actual Rebellion.

The Act of Parliament of the 16 Geo. 3rd Cap. 5th having prohibited all Trade and Intercourse with the Colonies during the Continuance of the Rebellion within the said Colonies.

And two subsequent Acts having declared all Ships & Vessels whatsoever, together with their Cargoes, which shd. be found trading in any Port or Place of the said Colonies, or going to trade, or coming from trading, forfeited to his Majesty, as if the same were the Ships or effects of open Enemies, &c.

The Commissioners from their Construction of the spirit and Tendency of the said Acts, Consider the acquirement of the Tobac-

---

co in Demand as obtained by the Claimant contrary thereto, since the Intention of exporting the same must be admitted, which could only be done in Defiance to the sd. Acts.

Even the Plea of having received this Tobacco in Payment of Debts would not in the opinion of the Commissioners be sufficient to protect Property thus circumstanced so far as to make this Government answerable for its Destruction, especially when mixed beyond the Possibility of distinguishing between it and the Property meant to be destroyed.

(31)

With respect to the Claim for Damages done to a Warehouse & Buildings at or near to Richmond, belonging to a Partnership in Britain, wherein the Claimants owned an Eleventh Part, the said Damages having been sustained in Pursuance of an order from Lord Cornwallis, whereby the public service was to be promoted the Commissioners consider this as a Property for which the Claimant as a Loyalist should be indemnified, and finding the value of the Damages sustained to have been £1,100, they recommend Payment to Mr. N. Jamieson of the Eleventh Part thereof. viz., £100.

1244. DAVID MCLEAN. *Part of this claim gone.*

—her husband is dead & left no Will. She has not administered.

DUNCAN MCRAE.

Knew Dvd. McLean was at Moors Bridge & thinks that he was not an officer. He cannot speak to value. Says that McLean was put in Gaol & obliged to pay for railing burnt by the Loyalists. Says the demand was for £12 Cur. The Charge is laid at £40 Cur.

He bought the Negro while Cross Creek was in the Possession of the Americans. He pd. for him in Beef & Pork in 1779.

COMM. DOWD.

Says he was cast £14 for damage done by the Royalists to railling. (32)

Decision.
Her Husband was a Loyalist & bore Arms.

300 acres in Anson County	£30
Tools	5
Cattle	17
Hogs	3
Negroe one	20
2 Horses	10
2 Horses	10
Saw switch	20
Clothes	10
Furniture	

1245. Schedule of Robert Bayard Esq., Losses as per Vouchers herewith Delivered to John Foster, Esq., Secretary to the Board of Commissioners, viz.,

Mrs. Bayard's annuity of £700 pr. an. N.Y. Cury. Sterlig. from Septr., 1776, to 1783	4,900. 0.0.	2,756. 5.0.
His Proportion of Lands in Company with my Brother William Bayard in the Saratoga Patent as pr. proof Deliverd in by him	1,512. 0.0.	850.10.0
His proportion of a Certain Tract of Land in Company with his Brother, William Bayard, and his Brother in Law, Col. Wm. Sheriff in the Patent of Wasweighnunck pr. proofs delivered	600. 0.0.	337.10.0

(33)

by Wm. Bayard. 2,000 acres of Land purchased of Captain Gamble in the Patent of Whiteborough as per Deed proof Col Kemble	200. 0.0.	112.10.0.
Loss on effects sent into the County for Security	300. 0.0	168.15.0.
His office of Judge of the Admiralty for the Province of New York, Mrs. Burnard's Annuity of £700 per an. payable Quarterly proof as per Will of Jas. McEvers Esq, Deceased. Mrs. Bayard, aged 42 years	8,085. 0.0.	4,547.16.3.
Rent of Mrs. Bayard's House & Grounds of Blooming Dale on the Island of New York at £350 per an., during her life, proof General Delancey	4,042.10.0.	2,273.18.1½
	19,639.10.0.	11,047. 4.4½

AMERICAN CLAIMS.

Claims recd. 2,173, £7,209.759 exclusive of 153 containing no specified Claim.

12 April '86   Liquidated.   563,   £3,090,373,   Liquidated at £876,421 Professions not included in this List.

Not yet heard 1610, £4,119,384, exclusive of Debts, £2,349,870.

109 Professional men reported before 25 March, 1786, who claim £48,000, which was liquidated at £33,000.

(34)   Memoranda, 1785.

A Packet to be at Portsmouth by the 20th August, Canteens, Linen, Stores.

From Mr. Forster.

Box of Stationery, Box for my own Books &c., &c. Copy of Decisions. Copy Report & regulations. List of Claims numbered, distinguished those reported upon, which proven & which not. The Claim vouchers, &c., of those persons who are in Nova Scotia, numbered as delivered with observations. Laws of Confiscation, restoration & Sale—if these are not duplicates of the acts. they should be copied, i.e., that part which respects Confiscation & Sale, into one book, private information which affects Claimts. in Nova Scotia. Whether examined or not. Two good Clerks, at £— pr. an. to be emploied in the office in Lincoln in fields for some time before they go. Their appts. not known,

or if that should be necessary let it be put on the head of extra expence. Acting Secretary to be sent to London by Sunday for the night. The 30th to practise in the office.

House of Commons, Monday,

June 26, 1786.

On Motion for the House to go into a Committee upon the Appropriation Bill.

Mr. Dempter observed, that in the Claim respecting the £178,500 granted for the Relief of the American Loyalists, it did not appear that the cases of some persons whose circumsances loudly called for Relief, had not come under Consideration; that in particular should be glad to be informed if those, who possessed Estates in America & had resided in Great Britain during the War, were to participate in the present Grant or were to be excluded, as was the case last year. He also wished to be informed if it was intended to make an allowance of Interest on the Claims as they were liquidated, which appeared to him a most material object to those unhappy sufferers, as it would establish a credit, on which they might procure money, to be advanced to them and by that means they would be enabled to engage in trade or other means of lively hood, and become useful subjects of the empire. Whereas to issue 30 and 40 pr. cent on the sums liquidated would in most cases have no other effect, than to relieve their immediate necessities, or perhaps only discharge debts contracted by necessity,

(35).

---

whilst they were waiting the investigation of their Claims, but would not enable them to emerge from the distresses to which they were reduced. Mr. Dempster desired further to be informed if any Relief or Compensation was to be given at present in the cases of Office & Professional Losses.

The Chancellor of the Exchequer immediately answered that with respect to the first question, it was not intended that any part of the sum appropriated by the Bill under Consideration should be applied to those who before the war and during the course of it had resided in Great Britain, that he thought they neither could pretend to the merit nor from their situations, were they in such circumstances of distress as those who had taken an active part in our cause in America, or were expelled from their habitations in that Country, that he did not mean to say they were ultimately to be excluded, nor would he take upon him to prejudge, what the House in the future circumstances of the Country, might think proper to do in their behalf, by granting compensation, either in part or for the whole of their Losses, but at present he was of opinion, there could be no injustice in postponing their cases. That with respect to the allowance of Interest upon Claims as they were liquidated, he could not agree to it, as it would pledge the House for the full paymnt of them at some future period, which was a principal it had not hitherto recognized; but that if the sums issued as temporary allowances could be appropriated in a manner more proportionate to the Losses, it might be done by a Treasury order to the Commissioners to revise them, which he should have no objection to, provided it did not increase the expence to the nation, but that it would be a matter of some difficulty, as there were persons who had a Claim to support, from their merits & sufferings for their adherance to this Govr'mnt,

(36).

although they had lost but little property. That with respect to professional Losses they did not appear to him to be equivalent to losses of property, and might more properly be recompensed by annuities, than by a Grant of Money, and therefore it was not intended to Comprehend them amongst those whose losses of property had been Liquidated.

(37). Mr. Dempster thereupon called upon the Minister to recollect, that in the last Session, he had declared, that he intended to grant some relief to those persons, from the reduction of the pensions, issued to such as were to receive a partial Compensation. this he understood had not been done, and therefore professional men had not hitherto received any manner of Relief. To this the Minister made no reply.

Mr. Coke then rose and observed that when he entered upon the execution of his duty as a Commissioner to investigate the cases of those unfortunate sufferers he was far from having a predilection in their favour, but that in the course of his Enquiries, he had discovered such merit and sufferings, and such fidelity and attachmnt to this Governmt, that he now entertained the warmest Sentiments in their favour, that he always considered

the House as pledged to grant the full amount of the Losses, as they were liquidated, and under that Idea, he had been intent to pass them down & reject them unless they were proved in the most satisfactory manner. That he was surprized after the House had been called upon to grant £700,000 for the purpose erecting useless Fortifications, there could be any hesitation to comply with a demand so evidently founded in the principles of Justice and humanity. He begged the House to consider, that they were undoubtedly pledged for the paymnt of 40 and 30 pr. Cent. or about the third of the sums which should be liquidated, this would
(38). amount to about Seven Hundred thousand pounds, supposing the same proportionate deductions were made in the Claims which remain to be examined, as in those which have been already liquidated. But he must go further. Parliament were certainly pledged for more, for those Gentlemen to whom 30 & 40 p. Cent had been paid, had at least part of their temporary allowances continued to them which he conceived could not be withdrawn, until something further was done in their behalf, and that it would at any rate be impossible to get Clear of their demands for less than a Million of Money, and would the house for the sake of saving another Million, suffer such a Stigma to be handed down in the Annals of this Country, as must blast its reputation to the latest Posterity. That an allowance of Interest at the rate of 3 pr. Cent might be granted without any additional burthen, and indeed

would be a saving to the Country, for as the Parliament during the last, and the present Session had granted £300,000 toward the relief, the two Million he proposed to grant was reduced to £1,700,000, the Annual Interest of which amounted only to £51,000, and £55,000 was the sum at present appropriated to them, and every payment would occasion reduction in the Interest. That an annual Lottery for Eleven years would Compensate the whole, and although there might be grounds of objection to Lotteries, he saw no great harm in indulging the People in a manner of gaming to which they had so strong a propensity, but at any rate, he thought (39). it was incumbant on the Justice of the House, to grant the whole of the sums liquidated by the Commissioners.

Mr. Wilmot began with observing that when he entered upon his duty as a Commissioner, the Conduct and the situation of the Loyalists had raised in his mind a predilection in their favour, which continually increased as he proceeded in the business. That for near four years past, his daily and almost his hourly labour had been employed in that service, and during the course of it, he had received such proofs of fidelity & attachment and sufferings and distress, as in his opinion justly entitled them to every mark of favour and attention, which the Government could confer. That he was glad to hear, that those who were not in America during the War, although they were postponed, were not finally excluded.

With respect to those who were present, when ever a question came before the House upon which he was to decide as a Member of Parliamt, he should cheerfully accede to every proposition in their favour. That it was his earnest wish the house could replace them in situations equal to what they had lost in America. But that was not possible, double the sum liquidated by the Commissions would not indemnify them, and besides most of them had, to lament the loss of a Husband, Father, Son or Brother, who fell in defence of the cause of this Country. He said he could not ap- (40). prove of the Proposition to allow Interest because it would be injurious to those whose merits and services entitled them to assistance and support from the Government, although they had lost but an inconsiderable property in America, nor could he acknowledge, that the Claims had been passed down, in order to induce Parliament to grant the whole of what was liquidated at least he had never been influenced by that motive. That he had considered his duty as a Commissioner was like an impartial Juryman, diligently to enquire into the cases which were brought before him and to make his report without regard to Consequences or whether the whole or what part of the Claim was to be granted. That with regard to professional Losses, he differed from the Right Honourable Gentlen. Mr. Pitt, in thinking they ought to be post-

poned, especially if they were to be recompensed by Annuities, as Annuities would cease upon the Death of the persons to whom they were granted, whereas in the case of property, the Right would descend to their posterity, and he concluded with repeating that when their case came properly under the consideration of the House, as a member of Parliament, they should meet with his firm support.

Whereas JOHN ANSTEY, ESQ., of the Kingdom of Great Bri- (41). tain has been Specially appointed under the Authority of an Act of the British Parliament entitled an Act for appointing Commissions, further to enquire into the losses and sacrifices of all such persons who have suffered in their rights, properties, and professions, during the late unhappy dissentions in America, in Consequence of their loyalty to his Majesty and attachment to the British Government to repair to the United States of America for certain purposes in the said Act mentioned.

And Whereas the same has been duly notified and Explained to his Excellency George Clinton, Governor of this State, by his Excellency, John Adams, Minister Plenipotentiary, resident at the Court of London, notice is hereby given that the said John Anstey has accordingly entered upon the Execution of the trusts and powers in him vested.

And Whereas several of the description of those called in England, Loyalists, have resorted from distant parts of the Country to put in their Claims at the Office in Broad Street in this City, and applications have been made from time to time to the said John Anstey to receive and admit the same, Whereas no such authority is in him vested for that purpose.

(42). Notice is therefore hereby further given, That the said office is open for the sole purpose of liquidating the amount in value of the losses sustained in this state, by hearing, inquiring and examining into such facts and circumstances and collecting such information as may be material for the better ascertaining the several claims which have been presented under the authority of the above mentioned, or any former Act, to the end and intent that ample justice may be done in the premises that the bounty of the British Government may be upheld in all cases, and confined to its proper objects, and Compensation adequately and impartially administered to the several Claimants in just proportion according to their pretensions as the proofs thereof shall be found to require.

And Whereas the unliquidated loss of the said Claimants, and the number of Claims are considerable in this State, Whereby it becomes necessary to regulate the order of preference in the Examination. It is proposed that the arrangement of the same shall be made according to the local situation of the subject matter of loss, in respect to the particular district within which such loss has been or hereafter may be fully ascertained in consequence of sale by the Commissioners of Forfeiture, and that the enquiry shall commence with the Southern district of this State, and therein in the first instance with the cases of Brigadier General Oliver Delancey, Mr. Isaac Low, Mr. Hugh Wallace, Mr. Alexan-

(43). der Wallace, Colonel Beverly Robinson, Colonel George Morris, Robert Bayard, Esq.. and Colonel James Delancey in the order following, that is to say, Monday, the 15th day of May instant, is alloted for the enquiry into the case of Brigadier General Oliver Delancey, of Mr. Isaac Low, on Tuesday the Sixteenth day of May instant, of Mr. Hugh Wallace, on Wednesday the Seventeenth day of May instant of Mr. Alexander Wallace, on Thursday the eighteenth day of May instant, of Colonel Beverly Robinson, on Friday the Nineteenth day of May instant, of Colonel Roger Morris, on Saturday the twentieth day of May instant, of Robert Bayard, Esq., on Monday the twenty second day of May instant, of Colonel James Delancey, on Tuesday the twenty third day of May instant. On which days such further directions and

appointments will be severally and respectively made, as the occasions and circumstances of each case may require, and all persons in any way interested in the enquiry as above directed, either as Friends, relatives or agents, to prove the titles of the Claimants, or as Creditors having demands on the Estates Confiscated, either by way of Mortgage, Bond debts, or otherwise, are hereby requested to attend, at the same office in Broad Street, in the order of time above mentioned, with their respective proper vouchers to the end that the same may be examined into, and the actual loss of each Claimant ascertained accordingly. (44).

N.B. The names of other Claimants as they occur in the order of Examination will be published in this paper, and the days appointed for the enquiry, fixed from time to time as occasion may offer whereof proper notice will be given.

Office of Claims, Broad Street, New York, 11th May, 1786.

Minutes, 25th Novr.

Rejected—Reas. assd. that he resided at N. Brunswick & could find no opportunity to send his Claim Home. N.B. He states in the first part of his affdt. that he resided at St. Johns.   No. 1392.

Received in part being for Losses under the Prohibitory Act —2nd as to the residue of the Claim.   1405.

Rejected—Reas. Assd. that he did not know that his property was Confiscated till the Month of Feby., 1784, & Knew of no opportunity of sending Home his Claim to England after He Knew of the Confiscation. Resided all the while at New York. ,   1414.

Rejected—Reas. Assd. that he did not Know Whether he Could not support his right to his Property as it was not Confiscated in his Name & thought he might recover for most of the property agst. Jas. Delancey. Resd. at New York.   1416. (45).

Rejected—Reason Assigned Ignorance of the Act. Resided at New York and Halifax.   1418.

Rejected—Reason Assigned that they were obliged to attend to the removal of their Families, which prevented their attention to forward their Claims in time. Resided at Penobscot & St. Andrews, N.B.   { 1422. 3. 4.

Rejected—Reason Assd. that he did not fully understand the mode of application. Resided at Penobscot & St. Andrews.   1425.

Rejected—Reas. Assd. that he was not sufftly. acquainted with the Design of the Act. Resided at Penobscot & St. Andrews.   1426.

Rejected—Reason Assd. that she had no Connexions in England to whom she could forward her Claim and did not Know how to proceed. Resided at Penobscot.   1427.

Rejected—Reas. Assd. that he had not seen the Act or heard the Purport. Resided at Penobscot & St. Andrews.   1428.

Rejected—Reas. Assd. that he had not seen the Act or Knew the Purport. Resided at Penobscot & St. Andrews.   (46). 1429.

Rejected—Reas. Assd. same as in preceding No. Loss of Propy. the same.   1431.

Rejected—Reas. Assd. that she resided at Penobscot—Endeavouring to dispose of her Husband's Property—N.B. The Clts. Husband, John McPhaill, is stated to be in England.   1432.

Received in part—As the Loss of the Sloop Welcome under the Prohib. Act. 2nd as to Residence of the Claimt. as he states   1433.

no Reason but his not being sufftly. acqtd. with the Design of the Act.

List of Persons to be Wrote to, to state Where they resided.

(47).

No. 188 Jacob Loder.
191 Eupheme Harned.
192 Jeremiah Mabee.
208 Nathan Frink.
209 Jon'n. Mowyr.
225 Nathan Roberts.
228. John Dove.
230 Andrew Patcher.
232 James Sayer, Where resided & What Age.
234 Jasper Stymest.
238 Charles Vincent.
240 John Lyon.
243 Andrew Pickens.
246 John Billea.
251 Rachel Kent.
252 Alexander Clark.
254 Richard Squire.
272 William Gray.
231 Thomas Flewelling—left Long Island.
248 Anthony Egbert.
253 Richd. Lippincott, Beaver Harbour.
354 John Taylor.

The Commrs. of American Claims desire that you would inform them in Writing the time when you left New York & what was the particular place of your residence in this Province after your arrival from New York until the 25 March, 1784.

(48).

366 Benjamine Allward.
367 Abraham Waters.
369 William Babcock.
370 Willm. Underhill.
372 Isaac Hatfield—King's Co.
373 Charles Heall.
378 John Lawson.
379 John Hill.
380 Samuel Piers.
384 John Wilson.
383 Thomas Merritt.
388 Timothy Daniels, likewise to send an Acct. of his Losses.
390 Dennis Coombs & to send a Schedule of his Losses.
394 John Yeomans.
395 Thomas Peters, with an acct. of his Losses.
401 Mariane Bedwell.
405 Philip Foree.
407 Archelaus Carpenter.
414 George Wheeler, to send in Writing the Persons Name to whom he entrusted his Claim to be sent to England. Resides at Mangerville.

416 Peter Fick, Mangerville.
420 Peter or Wm. Welling, King's Co.
421 Dow Vanstine, Fredrickton, likewise to send an affidavit as required by Persons lodging New Claims.
424 Timothy Wetmore, St. John.
426 John Flewellin, King's Co.
428 Samuel Tilly—to know by whom he sent his Claim to England. Resides St. John.
433 Henry Underwood.
437 Adam Ireland.   29th November.
438 Peter Hance.
439 Joseph Flewelling.
441 David Harkey.
442 Andrew Harrison.   49).
443 Shewbell Snifton, with an Acct. of his Losses.
444 Thomas Hacock, late of the King's Amr. Regt.
447 Daniel Southick.
448 Abraham Elston, & if he lost anything.
450 Samuel Reynolds, Queen's County.
455 Joshua Lamerce, King's Co.
458 Jabez Husted.
460 Frances Fluallen.
463 Anthy. Terrils, Queen's Co.
469 Joseph Russell, with an Estimate of his Losses.
471 Thomas Barker, St. John.
725 Jeremiah Worden, St. John.
727 Henry Vandeburgh.
728 Peter Vandeburgh.
1556 John Day, King's Co.
1580 James Beyea or Boyce, King's Co.
1598 Benjn. Bradford—to Know if his Vessell was Condemned under the Prohibitory Act, or if he took any steps to recover from Captain Thornburgh.
1727 John Maston.   30th November.
1732 Elihu Crowfoot as heir to John Crowfoot & in behalf of the Heirs of Peter Jackson & of the Widow of Ebenezer Haly to Know his own age & when John Crowfoot Died, the Age of the Heirs of Peter Jackson & when he Died & the Age of the Heirs of Ebenezer Daly & when he Died.   (50).
1733 Do.
1738 Aron Olmstead, St. John.
1739 Ebezer Slocum.
1744 John O'Blereny, King's Co.
1745 John Ogden, Queen's Co.

         New B. Claims, 21st Nov., 1786.

Rejected—reason Assigned that he could not make out an Estimate without his Br., resided at Annapolis—as far as relates to John Vroom, Defend as to Peter.   No. 153.

Received—reason Assigned that Elias Hardy required 2 Guineas to carry his Claim home which he had not to give, therefore sent his Claim to Capt. Vandeburgh.   184.

93.	Received—Sent his Claim by Elias Hardy.
194.	Received—Sent his Claim by do.
202.	Rejected—Reas. Assd. that he resided in the State of N. Jersey.
199.	Rejected—Reas. Assd. that he lived at the Entrance of the River St. John.
210.	Rejected—Reas Assd. Ignorance, that he did not think that the Act extended to Losses of the nature of his or to services.
213.	Rejected—Reas. Assd. that he resided at the City of St. John.
214. (51).	Rejected—Reas. Assd. that the Claimt. resided at Stratford, Connect., New York & City of St. John.
215.	Received—Sent his Claim by Hardy.
216.	Rejected—Reas. Assd. that he resided at the City & Co. of St. John.
217.	Rejected—Reas. Assd. that he resided at St. John.
222.	Rejected—Reas. Assd. that he did not think the Comrs. were empowered to Enquire into Loss of Personal Property.
226.	Rejected—Reas. Assd. that he did not Know that his property was lost, but was in hopes of recovering it.
233.	Received—Sent his Claim by Hardy.
239.	Rejected—Reas. Assd. that he resided at St. John.
241.	Rejected—Reas. Assd. that he lived at New York & St. John.
246.	Received—Sent his Claim by Hardy.
250.	Rejected—Reas. Assd. that he resided at N. York & St. John.
256.	Rejected—Reas. Assd. Sickness & other Infirmities which prevented his leaving New York where he resided till 1st May.
273.	Received—Sent his Claim by Hardy.
274.	Rejected—Reas. Assd. that he was not in Circumstances to prosecute his Claim in England.
275.	Rejected—Reas. Assd. that he was not in Circumstances to prosecute his Claim in England.
329.	Received—Reas. Assd. being Arrested & Imprisoned at New York.
332.	Received—Sent his Claim by Hardy.
333. November 27.	Rejected—Reas. Assd. Poverty & Inability to go to England. Resided in New York & City of St. John.
360. (52).	Rejected—Reas. Assd. Why rejected the Claim being for secret Services & Demands upon the Commissary Department. Resided at New York & St. John.
364.	Rejected—Reas. Assd. that he resided at New York & N. B's., N.B. This Claim is from a German Soldier, being for a house built upon property of his own.
368.	Rejected—Reas. Assd. that he resided at New York & N. B's., N.B. The Claim is for Services & loss of a Schooner Employed in a lucrative business.
371.	Rejected—Reas. Assd. that he could not procure Witnesses in England of his Losses. Resided in New York & St. John.
456.	Rejected—Reas. Assd. that the Claimt. resided at Conway, Six miles from St. John.
457.	Rejected—The Whole of the Claim is for a House bought during the War.

Rejected Reas. Assd. that he resided at New York & N.B. 459.
N.B., the Claim is for 18 months Imprisonment.
Received—as it appears to be the Claim of a minor. 461.

Received to be summarised. Resides at St. John. Resided 462.
in the Island of Bermuda.
Rejected—Reas. Assd. that he could not procure proof of his 472.
Losses. Resided at St. Georges, N. B'k.
Rejcted—The Claim is for a House built at Penobscot dur- 474.
ing the troubles for which he recd. payment in part. Resided at
St. Andrews.
Rejected—Sent h's Claim by Captn. Vandeburgh, but the 521.
Claim being for Crop in the Ground & articles plundered it would
be all Dis'd.
Rejected—Reas. Assd. that he resided at Shelburn. 527.
Rejected—Reas. Assd. that he could not procure the neces- (53).
sary proof to Support his Claim in time. Resided in New York 720.
& N. B'k.
Rejected—Reas. Assd. that he resided at New York—N.B. 721.
The Claim is for £1000 for Articles too tedious to mention.
Rejected—Reas. Assd. that he resided at the Mouth of the 722.
River St. John.
Rejected—Reas. Assd. that he resided at New York & Long 723.
Island.
Rejected—The Claim is for Services in Col. Delancey's Re- 724.
fugees. Resided in New Brunswick.
Rejected—Reas. Assd. he never heard of the Act. Resided at 729.
St. John & Connecticut.
Rejected—Reas. Assd. that he resided at Staten Island & St. 730.
John, N.B., the Claim is for Stock plundered.
Rejected—Reas. Assd. that he did not hear of the Act. Re- 731.
sided at St. John & Connecticut.

Rejected—The Claim is from the same person as the former 732.
as Heir at Law to his Brother.

Feby. 6th, 1787.

Information on Canada from Capt. Gummersall. Says he
left Canada in 1784. He carried home the Claims from all Loyalists at Cataraqui & other parts of Canada to the Amount of £180,-
000 N. York Cury. He thinks that in gen. those people who resided above the old settlemt. in 1783 & 1784 were incapable of
availing themselves of the former Act. He confirms this opinion (74).
to the officers & soldiers in or near the Forts in Upper Canada.
Says that Montreal is Convenient for the attendance of the
Claimts.
Extract of a Letter from Lord Sidney, one of his Majesty's
Principal Secretaries of State to his Excellency, Genl. Haldimand.
"You will furnish me with a List of those unfortunate Persons who have taken refuge in your Province, distinguishing the
Places from whence they fled, and as nearly as you can recollect,
the value of real Property which each Person has lost. In mak-
ing this Investigation, however, it is necessary that you should not

permit the service of his Majesty's paternal feelings for the sufferings of those who have adhered to 'their Loyalty, to prevent every exertion in their own power to reap the Benefit of the 5th Article of the Provisional Treaty with America."
Rec'd. in Canada, 1784.

Halifax, 26th Jany., 1786.
(From Col. Dundas.)

Dear Sir,—

(55).
The Brisk Sloop of War being ordered to sail for England gives me an opportunity I much wishd of Communicating on the subject of our Business here, & I must join Mr. Pemberton's request to my own that you would give us your opinion and the opinion of your Colleagues on a material point which I shall Endeavour to state as fully as I can.

It is what New Claims are to be received under the late Act of Parliament. Being strongly impressed with the Idea that Door was opened only for some few hard Cases, upon our arrival here we fixed Bounds where we believed the Accounts of the passing of the Act of Parliament might have reached. The Whole Province of Nova Scotia we Considered to be in that predicament & that they had time to have lodged Claims formerly. On this Idea we sett aside very many when the appearance of some very honest & respectable men who swore that they did not hear of the Act & could not Claim in time, began to stagger my Colleague, these were settlers in the interior parts of the Province who had been Closely Employed all the Winter 1783-4 in————. From New Brunswick we have affidavits that the Earliest they could possibly present their Claims was in April, as no person went from that Country to England before a Capt. Vanburgh, who Carried over some Hundreds, all of which were too late—the back parts of Canada is likewise in this predicament, at Quebec & Montreal they were informed in due time, farther up I really believe they suffered from Ignorance.

(56).
We find that Genl. Parr never received one Letter informing him of the Act & from the miscarriage of that Letter no steps were taken in this Province for informing the distant settlers. I had wrote to Forster very fully on this subject by a Brigg bound to Antigua, but she is this day drove back by bad weather & I shall send my letter by the Brisk. We shall Continue to Minute our opinions on the different New Claims & to Collect all Information we can upon that subject, our final Determinations shall be delayed until we hear from you—indeed we have given the Claimants to understand that until the receiving of Claims is expired we shall not make public what Claims we receive. Some few have sent Claims from the United States & some old Claimants who are become subjects of the States are Come here for the purpose of having their Claims heard. We are agreed here that no Compensation should be given them, this opinion I think we shall give in our first report. We shall, however, report on the different Cases, but by way of Observation distinguish those who reside

within the or mean to go there—as they have a Choice which

Govert. to prefer. We think the Bounty of Great Britain should be Confined to her own good subjects. We now have Claimants from every part of the province as the Communication by Land & Sea is now open. We shall find full Business for another Winter at this place. If New Claims should be received in the extent that the words of the Act of Parliamt will admit of & although I remain of Opinion that the Door should be kept shut except for a very few particular cases, yet I think we shall be doing what would be unjust—observe I think it necessary & therefore can be guilty of unjustice—those who would suffer are people who in three years will be as well off as they were formerly, in the meantime they are miserable & really think Govert. could not lay out £500,000 better than in giving it to the Industrious Inhabitants of this Infant Country. Should the old Claimants come to us as we have reason to expect we shall report 150 or 200 Cases by the month of May. We find the Climate here very severe & very Changeable. Mr. P. has had a little cold for some days, but otherways we go on vastly well, he makes no difficulties. We had Govr. Parr with us yesterday, who admires my Colleague very much, he says he Certainly was intended for a soldier & would have made a good one. We want nothing but our Wives

(57).

& the Comptation of many fine girls may make my Colleague Choose a help Mate, they set their Caps at him, but he seems partial to the females of Old England. In writing to you upon the subject of our business I have made it ever the rule, to be as full as possible, which must be my excuse for repetitions & inaccuracy. A very strong expression often Conveys an Idea better than one perhaps more proper, the ground of our sistem here is good intention & close attention, this with caution against fraud is all we can pretend to—Wishing much to go hand in hand with our friends at Home, we hope for your opinions freely, which as we highly value we shall pay the greatest attention to. I find in my Colleague ability & infinite attention, honest & honorable perhaps he gives some who appear before us more Credit for Candour than they deserve, or perhaps those who know better would. Could we agree with you in drawing a proper Line for receiving New Claims we shall have no other difficulty, let me observe one thing more on that subject, the line to which I am still partial, viz.—that of receiving very few—will be attended with the Consequence which Administration wished to avoid when they extended the period for receiving Claims, as all those who present Claims will be offended should they not obtain a hearing. Of course this indulgence will prove the source of much unpopularity to the odl Country, which in the first instance will be wreaked upon

(58).

us. The prospect of more business from New Claims than I expected makes me more dispair of seeing Home this year. We then shall in all probability again Winter here & visit Canada next Summer, from whence we may get Home in Octr., 1787, which will probably be before you are ready to wind up matters. From the few lines you wrote me while at Falmouth on what passed twixt you & Rose, I expect good News on that head by the

(59). spring Ships, which will arrive here about the middle of April—perhaps you may have an opportunity of writing sooner by asking for a packet to be sent out early in March, this would be no expence of Govermt. & would be most acceptable to those provinces who Complain much that they are neglected when a Packet is sent monthly to New York. It is likewise probable that a ship of War will sail early in the spring—perhaps the Brisk, as she belongs to this station. Forster will learn by applying at the Admiralty or of Lord Howe's Secretary. We may thus hear from you early. Would you write two lines to Ly. Eleanor at Carron hall, Falkirk, if this should happen, accept of best Complts. to all our Friends & believe me, &c., &c.

Copy to MR. WILMOT.   31st Jany.

We have made Mr. Hunter write to Mr. Forster upon every Circumstance which has occurred, as we Consider such Communications most desirable as the means of the Proceedings of each Board being known to the other.

(60). Had not the period for presenting Claims been extended we should have found our business short & easy—now we shall be obliged by some strong general Resolutions almost to shut the Door. Two Causes are in generally alledged for non deliverance of Claims, viz., ignorance of the Act, which cannot be true, as notice of it was published in the different news papers at Halifax, Shelburne & St. Johns, the other is the improbability of sending their Claims home—in some situations this last excuse must have some weight—as the time allowed was a most inconvenient one. No Ship sailing from these Ports during the months of Jany. or Feby.—there are some few hard Cases, but in genr. the Claims are from People who would never have Claimed had we not have come out, & who think they may gain & cannot lose. With such speculative Claims we shall make free. We are at this moment almost Idle—the Claims near this place are exausted & the Season of the year will not allow a move. The expedition with which we have got through the Claims near Halifax makes us look forward to the probability of our getting home next year.

(61). We shall therefore divide our time in the most Convenient manner possible twixt Annapolis, St. Johns, New Brunswick & Shelburne, at which last place we shall be by the month of August, & if our business bears the same aspect in the spring which it does now we shall request that a ship be ordered to that place which is an excellent Porte, to be ready to sail for England by the 1st Octr. The Claimants in Canada shall be informed of the time when we shall be at St. Johns, N.B., which is no great distance for them to come and the Communication is by Water, those at the Bahama Islands may come to Shelburne, the difficulty of going to these two Countries & the time it would require makes it absurd for us to think of going to them—and unless we could go to the Dwellings of each Individual it would still be attended with some inconvenience.

These are at present our Ideas—by May we shall be able to report the Cases heard & the number of New Claims received & rejected, the latter will be most numerous.

Halifax, 15 May, 1786.

DEAR SIR,—

The Mercury Frigate being ordered for England on a very few hours notice gives me an opportunity of acknowledging the Recpt. of your Letter of the 30th November, 1785, and duplicates of yours of the 8th & 9th March, 1786. These letters arrived here the 12th instant in the St. Lawrence, with many other necessary Papers, all of which are mentioned in Mr. Hunter's Letter to Mr. Forster, dated yesterday.

I could have scarcely supposed it possible for men to have agreed more in opinion than we seem to have done in carrying on the Business of the two Boards.

In the Business of New Claims we differ in words, in the spirit and Practice I think we nearly agree.

In our rule as to Agents we Consider ourselves at Liberty to admit those who satisfy us their utmost Endeavours were used to forward their Claims in time, but in near 1800 Claims which have been presented at this office, we have had opportunities of seeing and discovering every species of trick.

Upon the granting of Lands in 1783 the new settlers were required to give in to a Justice of the Peace an account of their former Situations on Oath to guide the equal distribution of Land, this in some hundreds of Cases has been construed into lodging a Claim for Compensation, and the respectable Justices are in some Instances returned to become very good American subjects.. (62).

The distinction of becoming an American subject or residing in the States of America certainly may be made—was the word subject transformed into Inhabitant it would be more comprehensible and better express the opinion of my Colleague and me. Arriving here by dozens from New York, Boston & Philadelphia, where they have resided since the Peace, and in many Cases are in possession of their Property, we cannot prove their being subjects to the extent to which that word perhaps will go when used to deprive a man of his Property.

But Considering, Great Britain treats the Loyalists with unexampled Liberality in Compensating their Losses. Considering that most Enviable Situations are prepared for them in this Province, in Canada and other parts of the British Dominions, that more than two years of provisions have been given to those who have left the States at the Peace, is it unfair to Conclude that those Inhabitants who have remained are subjects, and that they enjoy more than they have lost, and that they only come to us to take the chance of making as much of Great Britain as they can. I should wish the word Subject, which I think allows of many quibbles, should be changed to Inhabitant, in which we shall all agree. (63).

You mention the appointment of Mr. Anstey—and although we have not yet received his Instructions, as we understand he is arrived at New York, we shall make every use of him we find necessary.

I am glad to find you have received the Pension List, it required a Revision. I am happy to find that fresh Cases for temporary support are rare indeed. I should not be sorry should the Books be closed. The Teller when he finds he is pressed here would readily agree to be paid for crossing the Atlantic to have a hearing where he is not known.

We understand that the Packet intended for this place at the beginning of March was detained and had not sailed the 26th, so I have it in my power to answer what may be contained in your Letters by that opportunity, as yet no Conveyance is established equal to Rashley's Ships.

In answer to yours of the 8th & 9th March, Governor Parr did not receive our official Letter, but our Advertisement was published in November, 1783, and every person who came from New York at the Evacuation might have known of the Act, as it was published from authority in the News papers at New York, and persons who knew of it joined every Settlement in this province.

(64). The sum you mention, £30,000, will be sufficient to pay 30 or 40 p. Cent upon our first Report.

You say you do not understand under including—my Idea of including subjects of the United States into our Report. What I have before said will in some degree explain that matter. When we are satisfied that they are avowedly Subjects, i.e., when they declare themselves so, we disallow the Claim, but as this never happens, we consider, our observation of Inhabitants of the States coupled to what we shall say on that subject in our Report tantamount to disallowing the Claim, leaving it in the power of Government to send some Treasurer into the States of America should they think it political, and here I must say that I think the person who has returned to the States, lately after having sold his lands bestowed on him by Governmnt and after having benefitted by their Bounty for two years, is less an object for the further

Bounty of Government than the person who has remained.

There are many in this predicament and some have returned to this Province upon our arrival with a Lie in their mouths which we can see through.

Most Certainly no Cases shall be included in the List Classed for Compensation but such as are satisfactorily proved—and although we include them in our Report we know one step more is yet necessary, viz., the List of Cases satisfactorily proved, before Compensation is made.

(65). I have received no Copy of a Letter & Estimates which you mention in yours of the 8th March, unless the List for Compensation which I received at Falmouth, I therefore suppose it is in a Letter not yet come to my hand—or upon Considering your letter, I imagine you allude to yours of the 26th Aug., 1785.

I wish he would pay us—but I am satisfied to continue my Labours while I can without any material Inconvenience. I am glad to find the Compensation in Consequence of our Enquiries has generally given Satisfaction. It is pleasant that should be the case, yet I do not expect it, neither will it affect any part of our Conduct—the Persons you name are *Growlers*.

I agree with you that Life Estates should be Considered, and we shall be glad that Mr. Forester would transmit any particular mode you may have followed, for establishing the value of such Interset, if you have any Rule more than giving a certain proportion of the value of the whole due for Life Interest.

I should beg that the Board at home would turn their attention to the subject of Debts paid into the Treasury of the different States during the War, for which Treasury Receipts can be and are purchased. After much thought on it, I must declare I think they are most just demands and easily ascertained until 1783. When the Treaty of Peace gives the Creditor a Right to sue for his Debt before that, I must think Debts might be Confiscated and paid into the Treasury, as well as Landed Property might be Confiscated & sold.

This goes by a Trusty Servant I send home to attend Lady Elenora to this Country, he will soon return if she should be sailed, and at all events he will not be three weeks in Britain, and will take the greatest care of anything entrusted to his care. (66).

Halifax, 1st June, 1786.

DEAR SIR—

The Brig Ark being to sail for the River Thames to-morrow or next day, although the Packet is under orders to sail the 10th, I cannot help sitting down to write you a few lines was it only to acknowledge the receipt of your Letters of the 26th August, 30th Nover. 85, 30th Jany., 1st & 18th Feby., 7th, 8th & 9th March, 1786. No Letters by the New York Packets are come to hand, neither have we heard from Mr. Anstey—the Letter forwarded by B. Watson has likewise miscarried.

The Packet will carry from hence our first Report containing 156 Cases with Lists for Compensation amounting to £72,541 Property—£2,470 Profes. Income—all Estates for life we have valued & made part of the property Lost. We have thought it proper to add a 7th Class in which is included all Inhabitants of the States of America which we Consider to have from various reasons preferred the one Country to the other, but who are all well disposed to Benefits from the Generosity of Great Britain—the amount of this 7th Class is £4,666.6.8 Property—£120 Income, temporary residents are not in this 7th Class. We have added (67). to the Schedule the No. of New Claims presented under the Act passed in 1785—it is tremendous. We are unable to determine which of the New Claims in Canada & New Brunswick we shall receive or Reject, from a want of Information concerning the situation of many places in these Provinces & an accurate account when the Act was well known—but I am sorry to say that in my opinion the numbers to be received will be very great. As we find ourselves from Inclination & from Justice to the Loyalists, bound by the very liberal sentiment of Rules of your Board—it would indeed be unjust not to give the Industrious settler in the Provinces an Equal advantage with the Drone at Home—who is but a very despicable member of Society. I am confident that the admission of one sett of Claimants, to wit, those who have suffered by the neglect of their Agents, will admit of 500 New Claims

at least— but if Great Britain wishes to encourage these Provinces, I do not see where she could bestow her money better for that end—only if the Business of our Mission is not executed so speedily as may be expected, I trust you will defend us & give us at least 12 months more for these 500 Cases, which will bring our return to July, 1788—should we be so long. Although we both enjoy our Healths & are as happy as banished men can be, you will believe that we shall slave hard to see an end to our Labours. You would be shocked to see the Impudence of Demands made from the States—under the Head of Losses under the Prohibitory Act—at Least £200,000 has been claimed by persons who were trading from the States under American Papers & who never thought of doing Great Britain any service—on the Contrary, owners of Privateers against us. Rascally Yankee thinks such Claims a good speculation, he may gain & cannot Lose. I trust you will not hold us guilty of a harsh or severe action in a General Rejection of all such Claims, & rejoicing that such Property has been put into the Pockets of British Sailors. The Indulgence granted to Mr. McKnight by inserting that Clause will cost Great Britain very dear—many have lodged Claims under this Clause, giving as a reason for their not formerly Claiming that they never expected such Losses would be Compensated, and as Governmnt have by inserting a particular Clause in the Act of 1785 ordering or directing such Claims to be enquired into,

the Loyalist has good reason to agree with Parliament that the former Act did not include these Losses & of course we must receive their claims.

So soon as the Packet Sails Mr. P. & I propose going for three weeks to Shelburn, as we have been given to understand that a visit from us will give general satisfaction, at that New Settlement, on our return in July we shall proceed to hear New Claims in this Province & expect to be able to leave this early in Septr., hearing the Claims of the Old, Lame & Lazy on our way by Annapolis to New Brunswick—where we hope to be by the first Octr—& to have our Hands full all Winter. Could we make the Claimants shake off their Indolence & attend us we should get on fast, but it is the nature of the Beast. I beg my best Complts. to all round the Green Table.

I have read all this Letter to my Colleague who agrees most compleatly, indeed in receiving Claims for Losses under the Prohibitory Act—he is rather of opinion that no limited time is fixed for receiving such Claims & that the Words in the Act may be construed into power to receive them while the Commission exists., but we have shut the Door. Upon a representation of Brig. Genl. Hope that the New Settlers in Canada would still be deprived of reaping any advantage from the extension of the time of receiving Claims, we recommended that he should appoint some man of Character to receive & minute all Claims which should

arrive at Quebec before the 1st May, 86, but too late to be forwarded in time to this place, & we assured him that we should represent the situation of these people Govert. Gen. Hope requests that the time may be extended for these people to the 1st August. We shall write a particular Letter on this subject to Mr. Pitt, in which all Gen. Hope's Letters shall be stated & Copys shall be sent to Forester. As far as we can at present form an opinion we go along with Gen. Hope—as far as relates to settlers in the remote parts of Canada.

I mention these matters that should Parlt. not have entered into the Business of our Commission before you receive this, you may be possessed of all matter which may be material. (70).

In answer to your Query whether it was our practice to Disallow Claims for uncultivated Lands when there appears some Cultivation on part of the same Patent not the property of the Claimant. In N. York where the Patent was always made out to many, at the rate of so many acres to each—Cultivation was required of each Patentee. In N. England & other Provinces when Lands were granted in Townships, Sales of Lands & Cultivation in consequence, making Rods, Building Churches & Mills was commonly held Compliance with Conditions. I believe I need hardly tell you that my own opinion has ever been inimical for allowing anything for Grants uncultivated, as I can see no justice in Goverts. paying for what they had lately given. But I trust that I have been able uniformly to regulate my Conduct

by the Opinion of the majority of the Board.

P.S.—I still find that one part of your letter remains unanswered, viz.—If a Claimant is a subject of America, why, not simply disallow his Claim—The Sett of men I meant have resided within the British lines some part of the War & are now Inhabitants of the States—they have to serve the end of the moment—conformed to which ever party was uppermost. We cannot prove them subjects of America more than of Gt. Britain, (71.) as they have sworn to both sides. We have on our Lists for Compensation formed these gentry or Light troops into a 7th Class & given Govert. our opinion on our Report—so that they may be Compensated or not as Parlt. thinks fit—occasional residents are not in the 7th Class.

Yours, &c., T. D.

36 Berners Street,
Oxford Road, 2nd Dec., 1790.

Sir,—

The Business of the American Commission being now nearly brought to a Conclusion, I think it my Duty to request you that in Conformity to your Directions, the Evidence Books have been

been gone through and every Case of magnitude examined, and the Whole of Mr. P. and your Books minutely looked into to see that each Case in entered and the additional examinations Copied.

The New Claims are put up by themselves properly indorsed, as are likewise the Claims that have been heard, in fact every Paper relative to the Business has been looked into and put in its right place. Boxes are preparing and the whole will be ready to pack up in a very few days. The Minute Book has also been compleated and I have signed each Days Business.

(72).

The rest of the letter is mostly taken up with personal matter. There are several Books which Mr. Forster does not think proper should be sent to the Treasury, viz.—A Duplicate of the lists of Old & New Claims, Compensation Lists, &c., which if I do not receive your Commands to the Contrary shall be sent with your other Books.

JAMES BETTS.

A statement of the Reports made to the Lords Commissioners of the Treasury by the Commissioners appointed for inquiring into the losses and services of the American Loyalists. Numbers of persons who have lodged their claims in terms of the Act of Parliament 2,063

	Property	Debts	Income
	s.d.	s.d.	s.d.
The amount of such claims	£7,046,278.15.1	£2,354,135.12.4	£88,631.1.4

Account of the number of claims already examined with the total amount of the sum claimed and the neat sum liquidated.

PROPERTY

No. of Claims.	Claims Property.	Debts.	Losses found, debts not included.	Income claims, alledged income.	Benefices and Offices for life.	Offices during pleasure and proficiency.	Losses total.	Estates for life.
1st Report 149	£ 534,705.02.02	£136,225.18.01	£201,750.04.07	£18,518.17.00	£1281	£9,745	£11,026	£31,610
2nd Report 149	693,257.06 05	212,398.13.00	150,935.10.00	10,725.13.00	617	6,428	7,645	550
3rd Report........ 87	682,718.07.05	163,591.15.10	191,989.00.00	6,505.00.00	135	3,807	3,942	8,090
385	£1,910,681.06.07	£512,216.06.11	£544,674.14.07	£35,749.10.00	£2,033	£19,980	£22,613	£40,262

The above 385 claimants are classed as follows :   (73).

Persons who have borne arms.. 79
Persons who have rendered services 47
Not particularly classed.. 259
                                                                          ———
                                                                          385

Losses by capture of vessels under the Prohibitory Act :

In the first report .... £ 858.12.10
In the second report..1,258.00.00
                                                                  ————————
                                                                  £2,116.12.10

A List of Certificates sent to Colonel Dundas for his signature. Signed 12th Septr., 1790.

1024.	Mathew Benson	£ 39. 0.0.
1144.	Cameron, John	36. 0.0.
1175.	Derington, John	30. 0.0.
1225.	Fitz, Peter	12. 0.0.
1240.	Fletcher, Six	40. 0.0.
1261.	Frymire, Philip	30. 0.0.
1275.	Gilbert, Samuel	717. 0.0.
1319.	Garretville, Andrew	144. 0.0.
1359.	Hamilton, John	30.12.0.
1364.	Harriss, Jane	80. 0.0.
1382.	Hofftalin, James	105. 0.0.
1389.	Hurlburt, Moses	25. 0.0.
1437.	Kern Revd. J. M.,	39.12.0.
1471.	Lissatt, Patrick	30. 0.0. (74).
1568.	McPherson, Mary	28. 0.0.
1569.	McPherson, Donald	14. 0.0.
1676.	Noncosser, Adam	27. 0.0.
1700.	Palmer, Lewis	120. 0.0.
1716.	Perkins, Isaac	13. 4.0.
1816.	Stinson, John	90. 0.0.
1858.	Symons, James	45. 0.0.
1897.	Smith, Jacob	68. 0.0.
1899.	Swartflager, Fredk	45. 0.0.
1950.	Tomkins, Israel	12. 0.0.
1959.	Vanderburgh, Peter	21. 0.0.
1977.	Van Alsteni, Lambert	34. 0.0.
1984.	Van Camp, Peter	132. 0.0.
1995.	Willard, Abijah, for ch	360. 0.0.
2029.	Willard, Abijah, ch.	420. 0.0.
2065.	Waggoner, John	60. 0.0.
2090.	Camp, Abiather	767.12.0. (74).
2107.	Mulloney, John	704. 0.0.
2114.	Sterns, Joshua	85. 0.0.

List of Blank Certificates sent to Col. Dundas to be signed by him, and to be filled up hereafter as applied for.

No. 1.	Leonard Askew	£ 81.11.3.
2.	Samuel Adams	31.12.6.
3.	Saml. & Jas. Anderson	35. 0.0.
8.	Thomas Blakeney	28. 0.0.
9.	Fredk. Boush	70. 0.0.
16.	John Bates	150. 0.0.
18.	George Bisset	(75).
20.	T. J. & W. Cochrans	1,000. 0.0.
22.	William Chisholm	400. 0.0.
32.	Isaac Du Bois	100. 0.0.
33.	James Darby	400. 0.0.
46.	Col. James Grierson	818. 4.0.
47.	James Gammell	221. 9.0.
49.	Lt. Joanus Graham	500. 0.0.

	53.	Goulds & Monk	150. 0.0.
	63.	Jenkins, Saml. Hunt	147.10.0.
	76.	Neil McArthur	848.14.0.
	77.	William Maclin	17.14.0.
	81.	John Murray	765. 0.0.
	82.	Alexr. Morison	32. 0.0.
	85.	Thos. McMicking	100. 0.0.
	87.	Charles Ogihie	164. 0.0.
	88.	William Ogihie	219. 8.0.
	91.	Samuel Penney	7.17.6.
	92.	Joseph Peddle	103.11.10
	93.	Richard Perm	2,538. 0.0.
	96.	Phyn & Uree	650. 0.0.
	110.	David Thompson	270. 0.0.
(75.)	112.	William Taylor for S. Woodward	31.10.0.
	114.	Aaron Vardy	56. 5.0.
	121.	Stephen Watts	300. 0.0.

Total Loss found by Commrs. at home £2,696,338. 0.5.
  do by N. Scotia Commrs. 336,753. 2.6.
  do by Navy & Army Commrs. 66,124.14.11.

             £3,099,215.17.10.

  Amount of Pensions for Loss of   Per Ann.
Income on the 15th March, 1790   25,785

(76). Annual Allowance for Loss of
Income on the 1st April, 1790   28,673

               54,458

  Total sum Claimed on the above
Loss found by the Commrs. at home 7,958,644.12.11.
do. by the Commrs. who have been abroad 1,064,039.11. 7.
do. Army & Navy Commrs.   305,725. 6. 4.

   Total Sums Claimed   £9,328,409.10.10.

N.B. Debts not included.

PROCEEDINGS

OF

LOYALIST COMMISSIONERS.

COMMISSIONERS' REPORTS,

1784-90.

	MSS. Page.
Wilmot, Parker, Kingston, Dundas and Marsh, Second Report, Dec. 23rd, 1784	1
Wilmot, etc., Third Report, May 19th, 1785	5
Wilmot, etc., Fourth Report, July 12th, 1785	5
Wilmot, etc., Fifth Report, April 7th, 1786	5
Wilmot, etc., Sixth Report, July 25th, 1786	14
Wilmot, etc., Seventh, Eighth, Ninth and Tenth Reports	15
Wilmot, etc., Eleventh Report, April 5th, 1788	15
Wilmot, etc., Twelfth Report, May 15th, 1789	19
Dundas and Pemberton (First) Report, June 10th, 1786, and Correspondence	34
Dundas and Pemberton, Second Report, Sept. 30th, 1786	54
Dundas and Pemberton, Third Report, March 26th, 1787	57
Dundas and Pemberton, Fourth Report, Jan. 24th, 1788	62
Dundas and Pemberton, Fifth Report, June 5th, 1788	66
Dundas and Pemberton, Sixth Report, May, 1789	69
Dundas, Pemberton and MacKenzie, Report, March 25th, 1790, statements (3), reports (3), and final statement, April 23rd, 1790	78

COMMISSIONERS' REPORTS.

To the Right Honourable the Lords Commissioners of His Majestys Treasury.

The Second Report of John Wilmot Esquire, Daniel Powkes, Esquire, Colonel Rt. Kingston, Colonel Thomas Dundas and John Marsch, Esquire, Commissioners appointed by an Act of Parliament passed in the Twenty third year of the Reign of His present Majesty entitled an Act for appointing Commissioners to enquire into the Losses and services of all such Persons who have suffered in their Rights, Properties and Professions during the late unhappy Dissensions in America in Consequence of their Loyalty to His Majesty and Attachment to the British Governmnt.

(1).

In addition to the several Descriptions of Losses which we examined in our first Report as—in our opinion, not falling within the Compass of the Inquiry directed by the Act, the Claims which have since undergone our Consideration, have occasioned us to form our Judgements upon and subjoin the following, viz.,

1. Losses and sustained by the removal of effects by passages from place to place, and by the Maintenance of the Claimants and their families during and since the troubles. Losses and expences of this nature being considered as the ordinary and unavoidable consequence of War and it having been the practice of Governmt. throughout the Troubles to provide passages for Loyalists and to grant temporary support to such as prayed for and stood in need of it, but when they have been attended with peculiar hardships or have proceeded expressly from the loyalty of the party they have been allowed.

2. Claims for indented servants not being peculiar to the Loyalists and being a species of traffick which we conceive not to be a fit object for our Consideration.

(2).

3. Demands on the Provincial Assemblies whilst under the British Government.

4. Losses by the Annihilation of the value of paper money issued by the Provincial Assemblies whilst under the British Government. The two last Descriptions of losses being occasioned by the subversion of the respective Governments and not peculiar to Loyalists.

5. Sundry Claims have been offered to us for lands lying within the territory called Vermont, but it appearing to us that the inhabitants of that district have throughout the troubles considered and maintained themselves as a body distinct from and independ of the United States and have not recognised or allowed any Laws of confiscation to operate or be carried into effect there, and as we do find that any persons have been persecuted or deprived of their property by the authority of the inhabitants on account of their loyalty or attachment to the British Government, we have not considered Claims for losses within this Territory as objects of our Inquiry. (Obs. subsequent information has made it necessary to depart from this Rule.)

We have the satisfaction to find that some of the Claims prefered to us have been withdrawn in consequence of the Claimants having obtained the restitution of their property. We learn that the Legislature of the State of South Carolina has passed an Act for restoring the confiscated property and permitting the return of certain persons, a copy of which Act has been laid before us, whereby it appears that an Americiament of £12 pr. Cent. on the value and other Charges are laid on the Estates of Sundry of the persons therein named and the Estates of others are directed to be restored free of such Amerciament but subject to the other Charges; it is also provided that in Cases where the Estates have been sold under the Authority of the Confiscation Laws and the Purchasers refused to give up their Contracts, the Indents or specie received for the use of the state for the Purchase Monies are to be delivered to the original Proprietors in lieu of their Estates. Some Claims have been withdrawn in consequence of the Claimants having obtained the benifit of this act, but other Claimants named in the same act, have for the present declined to withdraw their Claims, alledging that by reason of the depreciated value of the Indmts. in cases where the Estates have been sold and the purchasors refuse to deliver them up, the benefit to be derived under the Act will be uncertain and very inconsiderable in Proportion to the value of their Property Lost.

(3).

We have at the first of the Schedule annexed a List of such Persons as have withdrawn their claims, distinguishing such as have taken the benefit of the above mentioned act.

Exclusive of the Cases contained in the Schedule we have enquired into many others which we find ourselves obliged to keep open for want of further Evidence and Information which we have a prospect of obtaining.

At the foot of the schedule we have alco noticed the claims which we have already separately to your Lordships as Fraudulent, and made with intent to obtain more than just Compensation withn the meaning and pursuant to the Directions of the Act of Parliament. We are extremely concerned to have fo.ind ourselves under the necessity of representing one of the Claimants to have been guilty in our opinion of Wilful and Corrupt Perjury in his Examination before us which we conceived it our Duty to do with a view to deter others from similar attempts to impose upon the Bounty and Generosity of Government.

(4).

Office of American Claims, December 23, 1784.

To the Right Honourable the Lords Commissioners of His Majesty's Treasury.

The third Report of,&c.

In the Schedule hereunto annexed we have stated for the Information of your Lordships the result of our Inquiry into the Losses and services of Sundry Persons whose Claims have been under our Examination since the date of our last Report, and have subjoined a List of such further Claims as have been withdrawn. Office or American Claims,
May the 19th, 1785.

(5).

Fourth Report of Similar Import, dated 12 July, 85.

To the Right Honourable the Lords Commissioners of His Majesty's Treasury.

The fifth Report of John Wilmot, Esquire, Coloned Robert Kingston, John Marsh, Esquire, & Robt. Machenzie. Esquire Commissioners appointed by Act of Parliament passed in the 25th year of the Reign of His present Majesty entituled "An Act for appointing Commissioners further to enquire into the Losses and services of all such Persons who have suffered in their Rights, Properties and Professions during the late unhappy Dissensions in America in consequence of their Loyalty to

His Majesty and attachment to the British Government.

(6). In obedience to the directions of the Act of Parliament whereby we are appointed we severally took the Oaths of Qualification therein prescribed and having immediately entered upon the execution of the Powers thereby vested in us, we caused public Notice to be given by advertisements in the London Gazette and in the English, Irish and Scotch News Papers of the further Time allowed by the act for the receiving of Claims from such Persons as were absent from Great Britain & Ireland, and were incapable of presenting Claims within the Time for that purpose limited by the former Act.

Under this authority we have since admitted one hundred and ten new Claims, sundry others we have thought ourselves obliged to reject, the Claimant not appearing to have been situated precisely under the circumstances required by the Act to entitle their Claims to Admission.

The time for receiving New Claims not expiring till the first day of May next is not in our Power at present to form a Correct Judgement of their number or Amount and we defer any specification of those already admitted till the whole shall be received, our principal motive for making a Report at this Time being to lay before your Lordships the progress of our Examination into Claims presented under the first act, in order that if Parliament

should think fit to extend its further Bounty to the sufferers during the present Session your Lordships may be in possession of the necessary statements for that purpose.

(7) It was stated to your Lordships on the first Report that the sum of £7,046,278.15.1 was the Total Amount of such of the Claims as contained specific Estimates of Loss, but that there were several others in which no such Estimates were given; since that time in some of the latter that deficiency has been supplied, one of which on account of its peculiar magnitude and Importance we think proper to mention. We mean that of Mr. Harford, which amounts to near Half a Million Sterling. It is needless to observe that these must considerablely increase the amount of the Claims as stated in the first Report.

Colonel Dundas and Mr. Pemberton after having taken the oathes of Qualification at this Board departed for Nova Scotia and arrived in the month of November at Halifax, where they have since been employed in the execution of the Act, We have not yet received from them a formal Report of their proceedings to be laid before your Lordships, but their last letters gave us to understand that they would probably be enabled to transmit a report in the month of May next, and we think it proper to mention that they represent in very Strong terms their opinion that if those Claimants who shall be included in their Report can be admitted to a participation of any Bounty Parliament may grant during the

present Session, it would be a most seasonable Relief to the Progress and Improvement of their infant settlements, would eventually prove beneficeal to the whole Province.

The Act having empowered us to appoint a proper Person or Persons to repair to any part of the United States of America to Enquire such Facts and circumstances as we should think material for the better ascertaining the several claims which had been or should be presented to us we did accordingly on the 28th day of November last appoint John Anstey, Esqr., Barrister at Law to repair to the United States of America for that purpose, which appointment we had the Honour to Communicate to your Lordships in our letter of the 29th day of November last, and your Lordships having been pleased to signify to us your approbation thereof and of the Salary and allowance we submitted as proper to be made to Mr. Anstey for such service, he took his departure in the February Packet for New York, furnished with such Instructions as were judged necessary for his guidance in the execution of his Employ. (8)

We have every reason to believe that the Wisdom of Parliament in authorizing the Employment of a Person or Persons for the purposes above mentioned will be fully examplefied in its effects that the Inquiry will be relieved by it in a considerable degree from the Disadvantage under which it laboured from the want of such Channel of Communication as expressed in the first

Report, and that the measure adopted will prove materially conducive to the two great ends we keep in view, of aiding the helpless and detecting the fraudulent Claimant.

In the Schedule subjoined we have stated the result of the Inquiry into such Cases as have been examined since the Commencement of the present Act.

In the first Report it was observed that in order to render Estates for Life, the Subjects of a just Compensation, it seemed necessary to fix an estimate upon them by way of *Annual Income*, but as instances of Estates in America let at Rack rents were extremely rare and the ascertaining by any reasonable average the general produce of Lands in the occupation of the Proprietors was found impracticable, the Commissioners proceeded no further in cases of Estates for Life than to state the value of the Fee Simple of the Property, including the Annual Income in the very few Instances where it was ascertianed, and the Interest of the Claimant therein, judging it proper to leave to the future Discussion and Direction of the Legislature in what manner the value of such Interests should be calculated and stated for Compensation, and in the Schedule to that Report, and in those annexed to the (9) subsequent Reports, Losses of Life Estates were classed under the Head of *Losses of Income* as distinguished from those Losses which were enumerated under the Head of *"Losses of Property"* the latter Designation being confined to such articles wherein the Claimant enjoyed the absolute and entire ownership in perpetuity.

The Distribution of the sum of £150,000 granted by Parliament in the last Session was held to be applicable to the latter species of Losses only, wherefore it followed that no Proportion thereof fell to the share of those who had sustained the Loss of Life Estate.

(10) This exclusion which we apprehended to have been an accidental and unforseen consequence of the Mode in which Life Interests had been stated in the Report, and of the circumstance of their present value not having been reduced (into sums certain) has drawn the Subject of Life Estates again into our Contemplation, and we are of opinion that the class of sufferers are more particularly entitled to an early participation in the Bounty of Government for the Property being Temporary and consequently susceptible of daily Diminution, Delay necessarily tends to the gradual Reduction and, in case of Death, to annihilation of their claim.

To avoid this Inequality and to enable such Claimant to partake in any future Grant of Parliament we have thought it just and expedient to estimate the present value of such Life Estates in gross sums, as well in the cases included in the Reports under the former Act, as in those we have since Investigated.

These Estimates have been formed in the following manner. We have first found the value of the Fee Simple of the Property whereupon we have computed Interest at Four Pounds and a quarter per cent., being the rate of Interest which the Public Funds on an average now yield—the amount of which Interest we have considered in the Light of the Claimant's annual Income from (11) the Estate, and we have calculated the present value of such Income for the Life or Lives during which the Estate lost was held, allowing Interest in such Calculation at Four Pounds and a quarter per Cent., and taking the age or ages as they stood at the time of the Loss.

We have distinctly stated in the Schedule the particulars of Loss sustained in Consequence of an Act passed in the 16th year of the Reign of His present Majesty entitled "An Act to prohibit all Trade and Intercourse with the Colonies of New Hampshire, &c." by Persons who were Inhabitants of the said Colonies and who have satisfactorily proved their Loyalty considering such Losses as a separate Branch of the Inquiry.

The Claims for Debts due from subjects of the United States as well from the magnitude of their amount as the peculiar Hardship and Injustice under which the Claimants labour respecting them form a subject which appears strongly to press for the attention and Interposition of Government. The Treaty of Peace having provided that "Creditors on either side should meet with no

lawful Impediment to the recovery of the full value of their debts in Sterling Money," Losses of this nature have not been considered as within the Inquiry directed by the Act, because we cannot consider any Right on Property as lost to the Party when the Government of the Country has expressly provided and stipulated for a remedy by a Public Treaty. We think it however incumbent upon us to represent that the Claimants uniformly state to us the insuperable Difficulties they find themselves under as Individuals in seeking the Recovery of their Debts, according to the Provision of that Treaty, whilst themselves are the objects of Prosecution in the Courts of Justice here for Debts due to the subjects of the United States. Under such circumstances the situation of this Class of Sufferers appears to be singularly distressing; disabled on the one hand by the Laws or Practice of the Several States from recovering Debts due to them, yet compellable on the other to pay all Demands against them, and tho' the stipulation in the Treaty in their favour has proved of no avail to procure them the Redress it holds out in the one Country, yet they find themselves excluded by it from all claim to Recompense in the other. (12)

On the same principal that we disallow claims for Debts, we have not considered any Interest in Confiscated Lands whether by Debts, Marriage Settlement or otherwise as lost to the Parties, in cases where such Parties are not named in or are not the immediate objects of the Confiscation Laws, tho' we apprehend it may be difficult for them without the aid of Government to have those Rights ascertained and secured.

We have thought it our Duty to represent this to your Lordships as we apprehend it to be one of the objects of our Inquiry to furnish Government with such Information as may promote His Majesty's Endeavours to procure from the United States of America Restitution of or Recompence for the Estates and Effects of the Sufferers under the Provisional Articles as stated in the Preamble of the Act which first instituted this Inquiry. (13)

The Review directed by your Lordships of the Pensions granted to such of the Claimants who received Sums of Money upon Account out of the Grant of Parliament made last Session and the Report of our opinion as to the Reduction proper to be made therein, our Examinations from time to time into Claims for Temporary Support and a variety of other matter out of the Ordinary Course which has occured since the Commencement of the Present Act, have formed an Accumulation of Business in addition to that of the Inquiry under the Act which has necessarily engrossed a Considerable share of our Attention. We nevertheless flatter ourselves that the progress made under the Circumstances has been

such as to leave it scarcely necessary for us to say that neither exertion or Perseverance has ben wanting on our Part to advance it.

Office of American Claims,
    Lincolns Inn Fields,
        April 7th, 1786.

To the Right Honourable the Lords Commissioners of His Majesty's Treasury.

The Sixth Report of, &c.

(14) We beg leave to lay before your Lordships in the Schedule hereunto annexed a view of the further progress of our Inquiry since the date of our last Report.

The Act of Parliament above mentioned having authorized us to receive the Claims of Persons who should upon Oath prove to our Satisfaction that they were absent from the Kingdom of Great Britain and Ireland and by unavoidable accident or particular circumstances to be judged of by us were utterly incapable of preferring their Claims during the time allowed by the former Act, provided that no such Claims should be received after the first day of May, 1786—we Report to your Lordships that in Consequence thereof 652 New Claims have been presented to us of which 652 New Claims have been presented to us of which we have received 134, and rejected 13. but finding that the Remainder, except some few which we have reserved for further Enquiry, were pre-

sented on the behalf of Persons resident in Nova Scotia or Canada. We have thought it expedient to transmit them to the Commissioners acting in Nova Scotia, and to refer the admissibility of such Claims to their Determination. The Amount of the Losses of Property specified in the New Claims received by us is £215,080. 14.11., and the Amount of the Losses of Incomes therein stated is £1,605 per Annum, and they contain Claims for Debts to the Amount of £44,620.18.1. We defer giving the particulars of (15) the Claims thus received until we shall be enabled to perfect the List of New Claims by the Reception or Rejection of those we have judged it necessary to reserve for further Investigation.

Office of American Claims,
 Lincolns Inn Fields,
  25th July, 1786.
      JOHN WILMOT.
      ROBERT KINGSTON.
      JOHN MARSH.
      ROBERT MACKENZIE.

The Sixth Report, together with the 7th, 8th, 9th, & 10th, are similar to the Third Report, simply a preface to the Schedule's attached.

To the Right Honourable the Lords Commissioners of His Majesty's Treasury.

The Eleventh Report of JOHN WILMOT, ESQUIRE, &c.

In the Schedule here to Annexed we have stated for the Information of your Lordships the result of our Inquiry into the Losses and Services of Sundry Persons whose Claims have been under our Examinations since the date of our Last Report, and have subjoined a List of such further Claims as have been withdrawn.

Having mentioned in our first Report of the 10th of August, 1784, that we had not at that time dispensed with the personal attendance and Examination of the Claimants, we think it proper to acquaint your Lordships that, as this Enquiry is drawing near to a Conclusion, we have thought we might with more propriety, and indeed have been under a necessity of relaxing from that Rule, in cases where we have satisfactory Proof of the total Inability of the Party to attend in Person either thro' sickness, age, or Poverty, taking all due Care to prevent Imposition and false Representation on the one hand, and on the other to enable Persons so circumstanced to avail themselves, as far as it might be safe, benevolent Intention of Parliamnt.   (16)

We have taken the opportunity since our last Report to compleat the Enquiry into some cases which had remained undecided for want of further Proof and which Consequently encreases both the number of Claims and the gross amount of the sum liquidated beyond what the Current business would have occasioned.

It appears from the Statement subjoined that the total amount of the sum liquidated up to the 5th of April, 1788, is £1,887,548 and have likewise subjoined a Statement of all the Classes into which we have divided them with the number contained in and the sums alloted to each, by which Governmt will see the different circumstances of the Claimants, and be better able to determine what Relief or Compensation each Class shall respectively receive. We have thought proper to make a separate class, the 9th, of those Loyalists who are subjects or settled Inhabitants of the United States and beg leave to observe that some of them are cases of great merit and peculiar Hardship. There is likewise another Description of Persons concerning whom we have been under Considerable Difficulties as stated in our 5th Report of the   (17)
17th April, 1786, namely of Loyal British Subjects who appear to have Relief under the Treaty of Peace, but represent the utter impossibility of procuring it. We have stated these Losses therefore in a separate Class, 11th, in order to facilitate the endeavours of Government to procure from the United States of America a Retilation of Recompence for the Estate and effects of the sufferers under the Treaty of Peace, or if not, that Governmt and the Legislature may be enabled to make them Compensation at home if it should be thought Proper.

Mr. Anstey has nearly Completed his Progress in the United States and we have the Satisfaction of Confirming what we promised ourselves on his appointment that it will relieve the Enquiry from many difficulties under which it laboured and that it will tend much to aid the honest and to detect the fraudulent Claimant. By this means we shall be enabled to supply the Defects of Evidence in many cases and to do justice to those who there was reason to think had sustained considerable Losses, but who otherwise would not have been able to have substantiated their Claims. We are now proceeding in the Revision of the Claims from those   (18)
States which has already visited, and we expect he will bring with him the Result of his Enquires in the other States in the Course of the summer.

It is impossible to say with exactness what may be the addition to the sum already liquidated from the few cases remaining unexamined from the Revision above mentioned and from the Enquiry now carried on in Canada, but from the Estimate we are able to form, assisted by the opinion of the Commissioners in Canada as to the Claims under their Consideration, this addition may amount to between 2 and £300,000 more, which estimate we thought it might be material to furnish Governmnt with a general view, tho the above Circumstances will prevent us from bringing the whole Business to a Conclusion till the Return of the Commissioners and of Mr. Anstey from the Continent of America and which we expect in the ensuing Autumn.
April 5th, 1788.

To the Right Honourable the Lords Commissioners of His Majesty's Treasury.

The Twelth Report of John Wilmot, Esquire, &c.

As this probably will be the last Report we shall have the Honor of submitting to the Consideration of Governmnt, we are desirous of making a few observations on some parts of the Business Committed to us before we proceed to state what have been the immediate objects of our attention under the last Act for continuing our Commission.

(19) We beg leave to observe in the first Place, that we have with the utmost care and attention taken a general review of the whole of our proceedings from the Commencemnt of the Enquiry, taking into our reconsideration as well, the general Principles and Rules which have guided us in the Conduct of it, and which we have from time to time Communicated to your Lordships, as the application of them to each particular case. We have thus had an opportunity of relaxing from and making exceptions to such Rules and Principles as we found by a rigid application bore too hard upon Individuals and we herewith transmit a Copy of these Rules and Resolutions as adjusted on such Revision and rendered Conformable to the practice we have since adopted.

We have thus endeavoured to supply any defects, to correct any mistakes and to reconsider any points in which perhaps too great humanity towards the Individuals on the one hand or an over anxiety to reduce exaggerated Claims on the other, may have led us into error, being sensible that an investigation of so arduous and intricate a nature, the utmost circumspection was necessary to enable us to render impartial Justice to the Individuals and to the Public. On this head we must remark the material assistance we have derived from the Enquiries of John Anstey, Esqr., who returned from the United States in September last, after having collected much Information respecting the general subject of (20) our Commission, and the respective Losses of the Claimants and without which it would have been impossible for us to have done Justice to many Individuals, for though there was in most cases Evidence sufficient to warrant a payment upon account, yet in few was it so Complete in every article, as without further Information to have warranted the Paymt in full that has since taken place.

We thought it our duty to state in our second report of the 24th December, 1784, that the State of South Carolina had by an Act of the 24th March, 1784, restored the Confiscated Property of Certain Loyalists, subject to the Restrictions therein mentioned that in Consequence thereof many had withdrawn the Claims they had before presented to us. We find however that in many instances the Parties have not been able to reap that advantage they expected, and which the Act above mentioned held out to them. In some Instances the Property restored has been so wasted and injured as to be of little value, in others the Amercements and Charges have been so nearly equal to the value of the Fee Simple of the Estate, and in many where the Indmts being the species of money received by the States have been restored to the former Proprietors an inevitable and Considerable Loss has been sustained by the Deprication. In all these cases therefore we have made a minute enquiry into the real Benefit that has been secured from such Restitution, whether of the Property itself or of the Indmts in lieu of it, and having endeavoured to ascertain as nearly as the Circumstances would admit, the value of what was Lost and the value of what has been restored, we have Considered the Difference as the real loss of the Party. (21)

We have found likewise that the Information we have received concerning Property in the State of Vermont, viz., that it was not Confiscated in Consequence of Loyalty as stated in our second Report was not well founded and of course have considered the Loss of Property in that State where the Title value and confiscation have been proved as an object of Enquiry and Compensation.

We have taken notice on former occasions of the reasons which induced us to decline enquiring into debts due to the Loyalists, but as this is a matter that has been repeatedly stated by the Loyalists themselves to Government and indeed has been more than once the subject of Debate and of Motions in Parliament, it does not become us to give any opinion upon it.

We beg however to observe that we have thought it our Duty to be very scrupulous in enquiring into and deducting from the liquidated Losses any Debts that were owing from the Loyalists in cases where by the Provision of those Laws which Confiscated the Property or by the Treaty of Peace with the United States, such Debts ought to be answered out of the Confiscated Estates of the Loyalists, for it appears to us that it would be not only Contrary to the Clearest Principles of Justice but to the very language of the Confiscation Laws that they should be held to Convert to the use of the State the Property of the Loyalists otherwise than subject to the Payment of their Debts. The aggregate of those Debts thus deducted form a heavy sum Total, the burthen Whereof had this operation been neglected would in effect have been transferred to this Country; whereas on every princi- (22)

85 AR.

ple of Justice it ought to remain on the respective States possessing the Property of the Claimants, originally chargable with those Debts; it seems however just that the Loyalist should be protected against such Debts or be enabled to discharge them otherwise he may eventually pay them twice over and the Bounty of this Country may in some cases merely enable him to pay those Debts again which have been already deducted out of his Compensation.

Whether the Laws as they now stand are sufficient for this purpose, or whether any further provision is necessary or expedient, or whether, if the Courts of Justice are not open in the United States, some explanation or Negotiation with them should be resorted to is not for us to determine. We have not thought ourselves at Liberty without further Instruction, to depart from a broad principle of Reason and Justice, especially when such a Departure would have had the effect of throwing an immence Burthen upon this Country, which neither in Justice or Honor she ought to bear.

(23)

These observations apply to those cases, in which there is no doubt of there having been a sufficiency to discharge all Debts due from the Owners of the Estates Confiscated. There are other cases of a more complicated nature, in which it has been matter of general difficulty to ascertain whether there was or was not a sufficiency for that purpose. In such cases we have made Deductions with a sparing hand, and after hearing everything the Party had to urge on the subject, have given an equitable Consideration to the peculiar Circumstances of each Case. We have been very cautious in taking the exaggerated accounts of those Debts as presented to or allowed by the Commissioners of Confiscation in the United States. We have seldom gone further than to deduct such as the Claimant on his examination on Oath before us has admitted to be justly due unless other corroborating or circumstantial Evidence sufficiently established them. For tho' in the first Instance it might appear that such Deduction might be made with Propriety as the different States have admitted them against themselves, yet the various circumstances of pretended Trespasses and Damages of fabricated Accounts and arbitrary Balances, blending Principal and Interest together, the uncertainty and fluctuation of the value of their nominal Money, the facility with which claims of this kind were made by Creditors and admitted by Commissioners, which Characters not infrequently united in the same Persons, at different times, not to mention the facility of committing direct Frauds under Governmnt. Energy; all these circumstances have made us extremely careful in making Deductions of this nature and have induced us to give the turn always in favour of the Claimant.

(24)

We now proceed to lay before your Lordships a general Statement of the Claims and liquidated Losses up to the present time, divided into Classes, and shall in another statement give our account of the Sums which have been already granted, and the amount of what remains for Consideration.

8ʹa AR

The Commissioners appointed to repair to Nova Scotia and Canada, having completed the Business committed to them and returned to this Country last Autumn have made a Separate Report of their Proceedings to which we beg leave to refer. But in order to give a more comprehensive view of the whole we purpose to unite the Proceedings of both Boards in our general Statement in the appendix to this Report.

(25)

First General Statement of the Claims made by and Losses Liquidated of American Loyalists.

Losses of Property Claims under the Acts of 1783 & 1785.

	No. of Claims.	Amount of Claims.	Losses allowed.
		£ s. d.	£ s. d.
1. Loyalists who have rendered service to Great Britain...................	176	1,904,632 4 0	640,690 19 0
2. Loyalists who bore arms in the service of Great Britain....................	252	1,040,506 6 0	263,135 6 0
3. Loyalists zealous and uniform.......	414	1,744,429 18 0	531,616 4 0
4. Loyal British subjects resident in Great Britain.....................	31	342,139 4 0	140,927 0 0
5. Loyalists who took oaths to the American States but afterwards joined the British	22	137,718 3 0	36,530 0 0
6. Loyalists who bore arms for the American States but afterwards joined the British.................	13	103,362 19 0	26,738 1 0
7. Loyalists sustaining losses under the Prohibitory Act.................21 N.B.—Of the number there are included in other classes, 15.	6	31,427 1 0	14,412 13 0
8. Loyal British proprietors...........	2	537,854 0 0	290,000 0 0
9. Loyalists now subjects or settled inhabitants of the United States, some of whom are persons of great merit and have met with peculiar hardships	21	51,578 0 0	20,077 0 0
10. Claims disallowed and withdrawn : 1. Disallowed for want of proof of Loyalty .... 5 2. Do. for want of satisfactory proof of loss................... 189 3. Do. being fraudulent......... 9 4. Do. being for debts only......16 5. Withdrawn..................24	243	20,589 10 0 653,819 3 0 104,618 15 0 .... 145,582 12 0	....
11. Loyal British subjects who appear to have relief provided for them by the Treaty of Peace, but state the utter impossiblity of preserving it........	2	....	13,270 0 0
12. Claims presented but not prosecuted	448	959,387 19 0	....
Claims under the Act of 1788.			
13. Claim of John Penn, Jnr. and John Penn, Sen., Esq. (v. Special Report)	1	944,817 8 6	500,000 0 0
14. Do. of Lord Fairfax, do.	1	98,000 0 0	60,000 0 0
15. Do. of the creditors on the Ceded			

(26).

Losses of Property Claims under the Acts of 1783 & 1785.—Continued.

	No. of Claims.	Amount of Claims.	Losses allowed.
		£ s. d.	£ s. d.
Lands in Georgia	11	45,885 17 5	45,885 17 5
6. Do. of the other persons specially named in the Act of 1788	14	77,246 0 0	29,977 0 0
	1,657	£8,943,594 19 11	£2,613,260 0 5

(27).   LOSSES OF INCOME.

Claims for losses of income which have been allowed	252	92,388 0 0	75,234 0 0
Do. for a person now a subject or settled inhabitant of the United States	1	600 0 0	500 0 0
Do. where the parties have died since their claims were examined	15	4,683 0 0	3,838 0 0
Do. which have been disallowed	30	9,865 0 0	
Do. for loss of income allowed, referred by the Act of 1788	1	894 0 0	800 0 0
	299	£108,430 0 0	£80,372 0 0

(28). The Act of Parliament having directed us to enquire into the Loyalty and services as well as into the Losses of the Parties, we have thought it our Duty to distinguish them into different Heads or Classes with a reference to that subject, not presuming to judge whether Parliamnt might make any or what Distinction in the ——— Distribution of its Bounty, but being desirous of stating all the Circumstances applicable to different Descriptions of Persons without going into invidious Distinctions of the Comparative merit or political Tenets of Individuals in the early stage of the Dissentions, which we apprehended the Act of Parliament neither warranted or intended. It is to be observed, however, that whatever is the Comparative merit either of the Classes themselves or of the Individuals that compose them, they have all, and each of them, sustained the Losses st. against their respective names in Consequence of Loyalty to His Majesty and attachment to the British Government.

It may perhaps appear singular that, so many of the Claims presented, viz., 448, have not been prosecuted, but it may be owing in the first Place to the Circumstance of many of these Claimants having recovered possession of their Estates, and in the next Place to the uncertainty at the Commencemt of the Enquiry as to the nature of our Commission and the species of Loss which was the object of it, and perhaps to the circumstances of others that they were not able to establish the Claims they had

presented.

Besides those Claims which were referred to us by the last Act of Parliament there are two of the above Classes, viz.—the 9th and 11th, to the objects of which Parliament hath not yet allotted any Compensation. With regard to the 9th Class, viz., of those who are subjects or are settled Inhabitants of the United States, we cannot presume to anticipate the opinion of Government, but we cannot help observing that there are many Persons included in that Class of great merit and under Circumstances of peculiar Hardship. With respect to the 11th Class, viz., of those who appear to have relief by the Treaty of Peace, but it is to be observed that it consists of the value of Reversionary Interests expectant on the determination of the Lives now in, being the value of the Life Interests being included in some of the other Classes. It is proper to observe likewise that the Fee of the Property in these Instances has been seized, Confiscated, and sold by the respective States within whose Territory the Property lies, and notwithstanding the Provisions of the Treaty of Peace we are afraid there is little probability of the Recovery of such Reversionary Interests by the Persons entitled in Remainder. (29).

We submit therefore to the Consideration of Government and of Parliament whether it will be more eligible to make those Persons who have lost their Life Interests a Compensation only for the Loss of those Interests, or to make a Compensation for the Fee Simple of the Property, to be paid to Trustees, subject to the

same uses to which the Estates were settled; by which means for a Comparatively small additional Consideration those entitled in Remainder will have no future Claim on the Justice or Liberality of the nation, if they should recover their Property, on the death of the Tenants for Life, and this Country will become Creditors of the different States for the value of the Reversionary Property, whenever an arrangement shall take place between the two Countries of their respective Interests and Pretensions.

It remains to be observed that the Claims for Losses sustained for furnishing Provisions, &c., for the Service of His Majesty's Army and Navy in America during the last War, are not included in the foregoing Statemnts. The Members of the Board specially appointed by the 9th Clause of the last Act to enquire into such Claims are now in the Progress of their examinations, which being Completed, will make the subject matter for a Separate Report. (30)

Second General Statement of the Sums which have been already granted & of what remains for Consideration.

Sums already granted—Amt. of Grants of 1785, 1786 & 1787 for Compensation for Loss of Property ... 454,260.19.0

Do. Grant of 1788 for Ditto 1,462.977. 4.0

1,917.238. 3.0

Amount of Pensions to which the 252 Persons mentioned in the former Statement would have been entitled under the Address of the House of Commons of the 9th of June, 1788, if none of them had been otherwise provided for 35.339. 0.0

(31).	Amount of the Net Pension after making Deduction in various Instances on account of the Provisions enjoyed by both Parties	27.528 0.0

Amount of What remains for Consideration.

Claims heard under former Acts but which have not participated in the Act of 1788.—No. of Claims 60 .... 108.995.11.0

Losses Liquidated
Do. of Earl of Coventry & Lord Viscount Weymouth, Trustees under the Will of Earl Grenville, deced. 60,000. 0. 0

V. Special Report—
Do. of Subjects or settled Inhabitants of the United States, many of which are Cases of great merit or peculiar Hardship 34,868. 6. 0
Do. of Persons who appear to have Relief provided for them by the Treaty of Peace but state the utter impossibility of procuring it 13,270. 0. 0
   N.B.—The above Statement includes the Claims examined by the Commissioners in Nova Scotia and Canada.

Claims under the Act of 1788.

	Claim of John Penn, Jur., & John Penn, Senr., Esqrs., v. Special Report	500,000. 0. 0
	Do. of Lord Fairfax, do	60,000. 0. 0
	Do. of the Creditors on the Ceded Lands in Georgia	45,885.17. 5
(32).	Do. of other Persons specially named in the Act of 1788	29,977. 0. 0

£852,996.14. 5

Claim for the Loss of Income pr. Ann .... £800. 0 .0

We have only further to observe that Conformable to your Lordship's Directions signified in a Letter from George Rose, Esq., of the 6th of August, 1788. We have made Deductions from the Annual Allowances for Temporary support enjoyed by the Parties in proportion to the sums received by them respectively out of the grants of Parliamnt, taking all the circumstances of those Cases into Consideration. We have also received the Annual allowances of those who either had made no Claim for Loss of Property, office or Profession, or whose Claims have been disallowed. But however Connected this is with the general Sub-

ject of Relief and Compensation to the Loyalists, yet as it is not one of the objects referred to us by the Act of Parliament Constituting our Commission, we shall reserve what we have further to say on this Head for a Separate Report.

We have thus, we trust, brought the whole of the important Business committed to us nearly to a Conclusion, little now remains to be transacted than what Parliament may think necessary for the final Payment of those Claimants who have not yet partaken of the National Bounty.

Great as the length of time is which hath been consumed in the prosecution of this Enquiry, it may without difficulty be accounted for by a survey of the multiplicity and complicated nature of the objects to which the Acts of Parliament extended our Scrutiny; and when to those are added the Investigation— delegated to us by your Lordships—of the numerous Claims for present Relief and Temporary Support—which alone formed a heavy Branch of Business demanding daily attention—the several Reviews and Modifications of the Pension Lists and the various other extraneous matters which have incidentally devolved upon us, we trust we shall on a due Consideration of this Extensive of Inactivity and unnecessary Delay. We have felt with anxious Solicitude the urgency as well as the Importance and delicate Scene of Employment, at least stand exculpated by the Publick nature of the Trust reposed in us, and to this Impression our Exertions towards the speedy, faithful and honorable Execution of it, have been proportioned. We cannot flatter ourselves that no errors have been committed, but we have this Consolation that the most assiduous Endeavours have not been wanting on our part to do Justice to the Individuals and the Publick. Supported by this Reflection in our retirement from this most arduous and invidious Employment, we shall feel no inconsiderable Satisfaction in having been instrumental towards the Completion of a Work which must ever reflect Honor on the Character of the British Nation.

(33).

(34).

JOHN WILMOT.
ROBT. KINGSTON.
JOHN MARSH.

Office of American Claims,
    Lincoln's Inn Fields,
        15th May, 1789.

To the Right Honorable the Lords Commissioners of His Majesty's Treasury:

A Report of Colonel Thomas Dundas and Jeremy Pemberton, Esquire, two of the Commissioners appointed by Act of Parliament passed in the Twenty fifth year of the Reign of His present Majesty entitled "An Act for Appointing Commissioners further to enquire into the Losses and services of all such Persons who have sufferd in their Rights, Properties and Professions during the late unhappy Dissentions in America, in Consequence of their Loyalty to His Majesty and attachment of the British Governmt"—and who were directed by the said Act to repair to Nova Scotia or any other of His Majesty's Colonies in America.

(35).

We did ourselves the Honor of informing your Lordships by a Letter dated 36th November, 1785, that we had enterd upon the Business of our Commission, since which time we have been employed in examining different Claims, all of which have been lodged under the Act of Parliamnt passed in 1783.

We have seen no reason to vary from the Rules which the Commissioners at home have stated to your Lordships in their first Report respecting those Losses which should, or those Losses which should not be Considered as fit objects for Compensation, and in our proceedings we have adhered to the same method and have observed the same Rules of Evidence which have been before adopted and which have been also stated to your Lordships by the Commisioners in their former Reports.

(36). The only or most important addition which in the Course of our Enquiries we have thought it necessary to make to the method formerly pursued, has been an attentive and strict examination into the present place of Residence of those Claimants whose Cases we have examined, the reason for our so doing has been, that since our arrival here no inconsiderable number of Claimants have come from the United States of America for the sole Purpose of being examined by us, in order that from our Report to procure Compensation for the Loss they have sustained. Persons, some of Whom from their former Loyal Conduct had the fairest pretensions to Favour, from Great Britain, and who in fact have suffered for the cause which they for a time supported, but who have since made their peace, and either never left, or afterwards returned to the United States, and are now living there in the undisturbed Enjoyment of many, if not all, the Rights and privileges of American subjects.

We have placed such Persons under a New or Seventh Class by the Description of Inhabitants of the United States, meaning thereby, fixed settled Inhabitants, distinguishable from those who have been unwillingly detained or those whom we consider as

only temporary or occasional Residents.

We are of opinion that Persons thus described are not entitled to the Benefits of the Act, and we beg to submit to your Lordships our principal Reason for entertaining that opinion.

(37). It appears from the manner in which Compensation has been offerd to the American Loyalists to have been the Intention of Great Britain that the Persons who have sufferd in her Cause should be placed in a Situation Equally advantageous with that which they enjoyed before the late Troubles.—With this view, immediately after the Peace it was made publick throughout the Continent of America, that Commissioners were appointed to Enquire into the Loss and Service of Loyalists, at the same time it was equally notorious that Grants of Lands would be given them on the Easiest Terms in the remaininig Colonies—and Provisions of various kinds supplied till they could subsist on the produce of those Lands.

These were the liberal Terms offerd by Great Britain in the choice of the Persons to whom offered to accept or refuse and these various advantages would, it might be fairly expected prove to those who accepted them, a sufficient Recompense for what they had lost or what they would expect to enjoy as Inhabitants of the

United States—But these Terms could not, as we think, be meant unless for those who had lost the advantages of their former situation.

Those Persons therefore who have remained in America enjoying in great measure the benefit of their former situation appear to us to have made their Election, and to have refused the Terms which were offerd as not worth their acceptance, and we cannot but Conclude that they set an higher value on what they have retained than what Great Britain offered.

We presume therefore that we should have been well warranted in totally disallowing all such Claims, but as it may be urged in favour of these Claimants that they adhered to Great Britain while their adherence would be serviceable, and that they were in the words of the Act sufferers for their Loyalty, for these Reasons we have not disallowed such Claims, but have reported them to your Lordships; tho' we must at the same time beg leave to repeat, that as far as our opinion goes, such Persons cannot be Considered as proper objects for the Bounty of Parliamnt. (38).

We beg leave to observe to your Lordships that there are other Claimants whom we distinguish in our Schedule as residing in the United States, by which we mean Persons who have been unwillingly detained there, Persons who have gone with a

view of procuring Evidence of their Losses, or for the purpose of recovering Debts or the like, and who mean, as we are Convinced, to return and to remain under the British Governmnt.—We look upon these as Cases of mere temporary occasional Residence, and there is no reason in our opinion for denying or delaying Compensation to Persons whom we so describe.

The Schedule which accompanies this Report contains the Cases of 151 old—Claimants, the whole number who have yet proved their Losses.

We hoped that it would have been practicable during the last Winter for different Claimants to have attended us, not only from the remote parts of the Province and from the neighbouring Province of New Brunswick, but that some might have also come from Canada and the Bahama Islands, and we expressed these hopes in the different notices which we have been assiduous in dispensing, but from the extent of the different Provinces, from the nature of the Climate which renders Communication between different Places often very difficult, and for part of the year absolutely impracticable, from the Poverty of some of the Claimants ,far unequal to the Expence of a long and teidous journey, from the Infirmity of others and often an unwillingness on the of the industrious Settler to quit his new settlement which might be materially Injured by his absence; from these and the like Causes many persons have been prevented from attending us, and consequently our progress has been less Con- (39).

siderable than we wished.

In order to pursue and finish the Business with all the Expedition in our Power, and fully to answer the purpose of our

Commission, we shall in the course of this Summer visit several of the principal Places in this Province, and it is our Intention to pass the ensuing Winter in the Province of New Brunswick, and to repair to Canada in the Spring following.

(40).
We do ourselves the Honor of transmitting herewith Lists of those Claimants whose Losses have been satisfactorily proved, classed for Compensation in the same manner as those which were laid before Parliamt in the year 1785—with the addition only of the Seventh Class before mentioned.

The sum at which these Losses ascertained by us amounts to £66,864.13.4, Exclusive of the sum of £4,666.6.8—at which we estimate the Losses of Persons Inhabitants of the United States.

We beg leave to express our Earnest Wishes that to those Persons who shall be thought under our Report entitled to Compensation, such Compensation may be speedily afforded. We have reason to believe the situation of many of them so distressful as to require almost immediate Relief, and we cannot but think too that as reasonable Assistance now afforded to the New Settlers would not only Excite their Industry, but would be doubly useful to them in forwarding their Improvements, and would therefore in the same proportion contribute to the general advantage of these Provinces.

The Act of Parliamnt passed in the year 1785 has on two points opened a very wide and extensive Field for Enquiry. In the first place by the Clause authorizing us to enquire into the Losses sustained under the Prohibitory Act, and in the next Place by the Clause allowing further time for those Persons to deliver in their Claims who prove to our satisfaction their Inability to have availed themselves of the former Act.

(41).
Under the first Head respecting the Prohibitory Act, we have received Claims for such Losses without requiring any Reason for their not having been formerly delivered; because the Legislature having found it necessary to give us a power of Enquiring into Losses of this nature by a particular Clause in the last Act, it must be inferred that it was not before within our Jurisdiction and Consequently there was no neglect in those Persons who omitted to make application from which they had no right to expect success.

In our Examinations under this Head, it has been our Constant practice to require a Copy of the Condemnation before a Judge of the Admirality Court properly authenticated, and to guide us in ascertaining the value of the Cargo we have required the production of the original Invoices when they could be possibly obtained.

We beg to inform your Lordships of some very singular Claims that this Clause has occasioned, for in Consequence of it being known in the United States—and as soon almost as the Knowledge of it could have arrived there—Claims to a great amount have been transmitted to us, ships taken by British

Cruizers; and we find those Claims came from Persons who were during the War and still are Inhabitants of the United States, of whom some were active in the Rebellion, and concerned in fitting out Privateers against His Majesty's Subjects; and we find that many of the Vessels and Cargoes for the Losses of which Compensation is Claimed were Cleared from American Custom Houses, and were Sworn to as the Property of American subjects. (42).

We have without Hesitation rejected all these Claims, Considering the Experimnt as nothing more than an attempt to impose on the generosity of Great Britain.

On the Second Head respecting the admission of New Claims, the difficulties which have risen have not been few or inconsiderable. We are authorized to receive such Claims from those Persons only who prove to our satisfaction their utter Inability to have Claimed under the former Act, but in deciding whom we should, or whom we should not Consider as standing in this predicament, a great variety of Circumstances have demanded our attention, and we have found it unavoidably necessary to receive

a much greater number than was foreseen or expected. We shall endeavour to explain to your Lordships the Decisions we have hitherto made on this subject and the Reasons on which the most material of these Decisions are grounded.

When the delivery of a Claim has been prevented by ship wreck or distress at Sea, we have clearly considered these as unavoidable accidents and admitted the Excuse.

In respect to those particular Circumstances which may in like manner amount to an Excuse, we beg leave to represent to your Lordships that from the local information we have acquired (43). of these Provinces, we are fully satisfied that the period allowed for lodging Claims under the former Act of Parliamt. was ill calculated to answer the purpose intended, and there were, as we believe, many Loyalists settled in places so remote from the principal Towns for parts of the year absolutely inaccessible, that the Knowledge of the Act could not possibly have reached them in Time—and in some places hardly before its Expiration.

It is on this account that we have thought the Excuse alledged of Ignorance of the former Act of Parliamt in many Instances ought to be allowed.

So far as relates on this Head to the New Claims from Per-

sons residing in this Province, we have found that the former Act of Parliamt was known here in October, 1783—and was published in the Halifax News Papers on the second of November following. We have therefore thought it right to Consider all Persons resident in Halifax, Shelburne, Anapolis or other principal Towns of this Province, or in places having an open Constant Communication with such Towns, as having had notice of the Act in time to have availed themselves of it, and we do not allow to persons so situated any benefit from their alledged Ignorance. But we find also that there are New Settlements in places so remote, so cut off from all intercourse with the principal Towns (44).

that it was not possible for the Act of Parliamnt to come to the Knowledge of Persons there situated time enough to have given them an opportunity of transmitting their Claims to England — an opportunity which in this Province rarely occurs, and in some places not at all for many months of the Winter. We have therefore thought Persons so circumstanced entitled to Indulgence, and have admitted the Excuse from Ignorance of the Act.

We find in many Instances the neglect or inattention of an Agent assigned for a Reason for a Claim not having been formerly delivered, as to which our Rule has been when the Claimant has used all the diligence in his Power and there is not the least degree of blame or neglect imputable to him to suffer such excuse to prevail, and we have been induced to adopt this Rule from

Considering that, added to the various difficulties and distresses in which Loyalists were at that time envolved, many of them had no friends who could assist in forwarding their Claims, the office of Agent was frequently declined and very few could be found to undertake it, so that the methou adopted by Persons thus Circumstanced, tho' not attended with Success, was the most prudent that could have been expected and the choice they made of an Agent perhaps the only one in their Power.

When a Right to Property has descended to an Infant, and the Infant continued under age during the time prescribed by the Act, we have allowed this as a sufficient Excuse.

In a few Instances the Reason given has been—Confinement in Prison within the United States, on Charges grounded on the Parties Loyalty, such an Excuse we have readily admitted.

These in general have been the Cases to which we have thought the Indulgence of the Legislature might be extended, and have admitted Claims when these excuses have been assigned, subject however to further Enquiry on the Personal Examination
(45). of the Claimant as to the facts which Constitute the Excuse.

The Cases to which we have held that the benefits of the Act could not be extended have been of the following Description : —

We have not to persons resident in this Province allowed the excuse of Ignorance of the Act of Parliamnt—unless with those

particular Exceptions before stated.

We have not allowed the plea of Inability from Poverty or Sickness, or of Ignorance in what manner to proceed.

We have not admitted Claims when we have been Convinced that the Claimant lost the advantage of the former Act by his own neglect or inattention.

We have not allowed a Wrong Interpretation of the Act as furnishing a sufficient excuse, such as that it extended to the Loss
(46). of Real Estates only, not Personal, which Reason has been assigned in many Instances.

We have not allowed the excuse—very frequently offerd founded on a misconception or misinformation respecting the former Act, such as that it required a personal attendance in England on the delivery of a Claim.

Our Decision on the Reception or Rejection of New Claims has been hitherto confined to those arising in this Province, Cape Breton, the Island of St. John, or those sent from the United States, the number of which is as follows, 642 presented, out of which number 199 have been rejected.

The number of New Claims which have been presented from New Brunswick amounts to 402, the number of those from Canada. 716. It will require more local knowledge of the different settlemts in these two last Provinces and fuller Information on many particulars than we at present possess before we can finally decide on the Admission or Rejection of these Claims.

We have used our utmost endeavour to make the Act of Parliament Public thro' the different Provinces with a view that the Parties interested might avail themselves of the Indulgence of the Legislature within the time prescribed, but we are sorry to say that end has not been Completely accomplished, for we have been informed by several Letters which we have received in the Course of the Winter from Brigadier General Hope, Lieutent Governor of Canada,—Extracts which we have annexed to this Report— (47). that it was absolutely impossible to Communicate the Knowledge of the Act to the Remote parts of Canada so as to enable Persons residing there to transmit their Claims to us by the first of May.

These representations have induced us to recommend to General Hope that a proper Person should be appointed at Quebec to whom those Claims from the remote Parts of Canada which it was impossible to transmit to us in time might be delivered. We directed, however, that none should be received after the first of May, and that they should be forwarded to us with all possible Expedition after their delivery at Quebec.

In Consequence of our Recommendation, General Hope has appointed such Person and for such Purposes as we desired. But as our present Power may not extend to the Examination of Claims so delivered from their not being delivered to us personally or at our office on or before the first of May, we earnestly recommend that a Clause be proposed in the next Act giving us authority for that purpose.

Your Lordships will also see that by a further extract from General Hope's Letters that he is of Opinion that unless the period is extended to the first of August, 1786, as to those Persons resident at Niagara and upwards the purpose of the Act would still be defeated.

Altho we are far from taking upon ourselves to decide whether this Indulgence should be granted or not, yet we think it our duty to say that if it is denied some meritorious Loyalists (48). may still be depri ed of the advantages intended for them by Governmnt.

We likewise beg leave to annex to this Report an Extract of a Letter we have received from Lieutent Governor Patterson, of the Island of St. John, in the Gulf of St. Lawrence, and to add our opinion that some Loyalists in that Island may likewise suffer should they not be favoured in the same manner as those settled in the back parts of Canada.

We have at th' foot of this Schedule annexed a List of Such Persons as have Withdrawn their Claims, and the name of one Person whose Claim we have Considered as fraudulent and made with intent to o....in more than a just Compensation.

We have likewise added in the Schedule a State of the New Claims which have been presented to us under the last Act of Parliament.

Your Lordships will see that the Business in which we are engaged in very considerably encreased by the admission of New Claims, but we venture to assure your Lordships that we shall endeavour by a Constant and Laborious attention on our part, and by every exertion in our power to expedite and accomplish the purposes intended by our Commissioner.

(49). We think it a duty incumbent upon us in Justice to the sereral Governors and officers in Command in these Provinces to assure your Lordships that we have received from them every mark of attention and every kind of Assistance which our Business required.

THOMAS DUNDAS.
J. PEMBERTON.

Officer of American Claims,
  Halifax, Nova Scotia,
    10th June, 1786.

Extract of Letters from Brigadier General Hope, Lieutenant Governor of Quebec, to the Commissioners of American Claims at Halifax, Nova Scotia.

Quebec, 29th January, 1786.

"It is utterly impracticable at this Season to convey to Niagara notice of your arrival or intended method of proceeding so as to have any reply in time to be transmitted to you by the period specified.

The principal Settlements are from Johnstown to Cataraqui. Johnstown is about 100 miles from Montreal, Cataraqui about 500.

Quebec, 18th April, 1786.

(50). You will next permit me to observe altho' I am perfectly sensible of the Justice of your Intentions and that in the Latitude given for the receival here of Claims until the 1st of May you have accommodated your proceding for the benefit of Loyalists settled in the remote parts of the Province as far as the nature of your Appointmnt and the terms of the Act of Parliamnt will admit, yet from the situation and Circumstances of the Communication of this Country and more particularly so at (this) Season it will still be totally out of the power of those persons whose Relief you have principally consulted in authorizing the receival of Claims at this place till the 1st of May to profit these by within that time.

Being so thoroughly satisfied that your Intentions in this respect could not be answered in the way you propose, In the notice therefore which I thought proper to publish, together with yours on the Subject, Copy whereof I beg leave to enclose, I have taken upon myself to extend the period of receiving Claims from Persons in those situations to the first of August and I shall hope through your Sanction and support that means will be found to obtain the Examination and admission of Claims so received.

To answer the purposes in the receival of Claims here I have authorized Mr. Craigie my private Secretary and Commissary General to follow your Directions for whose punctual and ready Execution of such Instructions as you may find necessary to give on the subject I shall hold myself responsible.

Along with this Letter I transmit to your office a Packet containing sundry Claims received here after the departure of the former express, but before there was any signification of your last notice. They are, I believe, chiefly from Persons in some retired Quarters with which the Communication was at that time difficult and uncertain, or from Persons in Quebec and Montreal who had arrived from such places after the time of sending off the Express. (51).

At the Council Chamber in the Castle of St. Lewis on Friday the 27th January, 1786,

Present: Frances Levesque, Edward Harrison, Adam Mabam, George Pownall, Jos. G. C. De Lery, Henry Caldwell, Frances Baby, Esquires.

The Council resuming the Consideration of the several Papers received by his Honor the Lieutenant Governor from the Commissioners at Halifax laid before them the 21st instant and seeing from the Situation and circumstances of the Loyalists who have

taken Refuge in this Province the impossibility of their repairing to Halifax to support the Claims they will have to make for their Losses, think it their Duty to request his Honor earnestly to recommend in his next Dispatches to the Commissioners their coming to this Province as soon as the Communication of the River St. Lawrence will admit to the end that the beneficent Intentions of Parliament respecting those worthy subjects should not be defeated, but have their full effect.

I Certify the above to be a true Copy of a Minute of Council held this day as entered on Record in my office. Witness my Hand (52). the 27th day of January, 1786.

Signed   J. WILLIAMS, C.E., Quebec.

Extracts of Letters from Lieutenant Governor Patterson, Charloton Island of St. John Gulf of St. Lawrence to the Commissioners of American Claims at Halifax, Nova Scotia.

Charloton, 25th January, 1786.

On the 22nd of last month I was honored with your Dispatch of the 17th November.

The lateness of its arrival rendered an earlier reply useless as there has since then been no possibility of sending to the Continent and tho' I purpose shortly to make an attempt to that effect,

yet it is far from being certain I shall be able to accomplish my design. As to New Claimants from this Quarter under the present Act they are totally excluded. It was a remarkably late arrival from the Continent that brought your Dispatches. The Communication shut up immediately after. Such a Consequence as this which I purpose to attempt cannot be depended on, tho' I have hitherto succeeded in the like, nor is it by any means certain that an express can reach Halifax before the 1st May, who leaves this after the Communication opens so far from being the case that I am certain it would not take place once in ten years.

(53). The other settlements in the Gulf are if possible in a worse situation as I do suppose they are as yet Ignorant of the benevolent Intention of your Commission.

I shall therefore hope, as it must be the design of the Legislature to render equal justice to all, that you will have the goodness to represent this matter in its proper Light, and the necessity there is of a further prolongation of the Time for preferring New Claims, and in case you shall concur in this opinion it is needless to point out to Gentlemen of your Comprehension that the granting exactly of another year would not give the desired Relief as it is most reasonable to suppose the Countries I have mentioned would in that case be in 1787 exactly in their present Situation.

Charloton, 20th May, 1786.

The Season also has renderd it impossible for any New Claims to be given in to your office by the time limited. These were prevailing—Inducements for my wishing to be honored with your presence and for a prolongation of the time.

To the Right Honorable the Lords Commissioners of his Majesty's Treasury:—

THE SECOND REPORT OF., &C.

(54). We did ourselves the Honor of informing your Lordships by our Report dated the 10th of June last, of the Progress we had then made in the Business of our Commission, of the Rules we had adopted, and the manner in which we meant our future proceedings should be regulated. We at the same time transmitted to your Lordships a Schedule Containing the Cases of 151 Claimants, the Whole Number who at that time had proved their Losses before us. We have since that period been Employed in Examining several Claims lodged under the Act of Parliamt passed in 1783, as also a Considerable number of New ones arising Chiefly in this Province, which for the reasons before stated to your Lordships we have thought it right to admit.

Accompanying this Report we have the Honor of transmitting to your Lordships a Schedule Containing the Cases of 40 old Claimants and 64 New ones, the Whole Number that we have had it in our power to examine since the date of our former Dispatches. We have in our Schedule particularly distinguished the Claims formerly lodged from those admitted under the Act of Parliamt. pased in 1785—and in respect to these later Claims it gives us pleasure to remark that out of 64, the Number already examined, 39 were Claims by Persons who have borne Arms or rendered services to Great Britain, and we beg leave further to add that as far as has fallen within our observation we have every reason for thinking that many of the Persons of this Description are now becoming very good and industrious settlers. It will we presume give no small Degree of Satisfaction to Parliamt to find that their Generosity in these Instances extends to Persons whose former Zeal and Activity might well entitle them to Extraordinary Favour, and who show themselves by their present Conduct likely to make the best use of the Bounty they may receive.

(55).

We stated to your Lordships in our former Report the various difficulties which prevented the personal attendance of sundry Claimants not only from the other Provinces, but even from the distant parts of this. In order to obviate some of those difficulties we have in the course of this Summer visited Shelburne and we propose travelling thro' the Country by Land on our way to New Brunswick that we may by these means have an opportunity of hearing several Meritorious Persons who might otherwise be prevented by Age or Infirmity from attending us.

We have Examined the Cases of some few Claimants from Canada, New Brunswick and the Bahama Islands, but in general our Enquiries hitherto have been Confined to Persons residing in Nova Scotia, and except the Cases of some few Claimants who may attend us in our Journey thro' the Country and others whose Situation near the Bay of Fundy makes it more Convenient for them to visit us in the City of St. John, We have in great measure finished the Business of this Province, and are preparing with all Expedition to proceed to New Brunswick.

(56).

As the Loyalists settled in New Brunswick are very numerous, forming as we understand the principal Part of the Inhabitants of that Province—We have every reason to expect the number of Persons whose Claims we shall there have to examine will be very Considerable, and we think our Enquiries there cannot be Concluded in less than seven or eight months, so soon as that Business is ended and with all the expedition in our Power we shall proceed to Canada.

We herewith transmit to your Lordships additional Lists of Persons whose Losses have been proved to our Satisfaction classed for Compensation in the same manner as those Lists which accompanied our first Report.

It gave us great pleasure to find that Parliamt had granted during the last Session a sum for partial Compensation to the American Loyalists in Consequence of the Commissions' Report, and we beg leave to repeat to your Lordships our firm Persuasion

86 AR.

that the timely Assistance will not only be of the greatest Service to the Claimants themselves but is likely in its Consequences most essentially to promote the Prosperity of these Colonies.

THOMAS DUNDAS.
J. PEMBERTON.

Office of American Claims,
Halifax, Nova Scotia,
September 30th, 1786.

(57). *To the Right Honorable the Lords Commissioners of his Majesty Treasury:—*

THE THIRD REPORT OF, &C.

We did ourselves the Honor of informing your Lordships by our Second Report bearing date the 30th September, 1786, of our Intention to leave Halifax and to proceed to the further Execution of our Commission to the Province of New Brunswick. We have now to add that according to the Plan we had proposed we travelled thro' Neva Scotia by Land and by that means gave an opportunity to several Persons to have their Claims examined which benefit they otherwise must have lost.

Immediately after our arrival in this Province in October last we proceeded in our Enquiry with the utmost expedition in our Power, and arranged our Business in such a manner as on full Consideration best adapted to the general Convenience of the Persons Concerned

We have since that Time Continued our Examinations of their Claims which were lodged under the Act passed in 1783 and have heard and decided 110 cases of that Description which with our opinion as to the Terms allowable to each Claimant are inserted in the Schedule accompanying the Report.

We have also proceeded in our examination of New Claims arising Chiefly in this Province and lodged under the Act passed (58). in 1785, and in this Branch of our Enquiry we have again met with those Difficulties which we formerly stated to your Lordships in determining what Persons should be admitted to this Benefit and who should be Excluded.

In general we have pursued those Rules which we stated to your Lordships in our first Report, dated 10th June, 1786, but as our Ground of Decision under which a Considerable number of Claims have been admitted arises from the Situation of this Country and depends on local Circumstances we shall beg leave to explain to your Lordships more fully the Reasons on which that Decision has been adopted.

A very Considerable number of Claimants who came to this Province in the Summer 1783, came from New York before the Act of Parliamnt in favour of the Loyalists could be known there.

On their arrival many of them did not Continue in this City when the principal Settlement was then forming, but went up the

River St. John and settled in the interior or remote parts of the Country, dispersed in different places as they had an opportunity of procuring Lands. In this Situation they Continued during the ensuing Winter, some more quitting their Homes, others only occasionally and for a Short Time. During this period the Communication between the different parts of this Province was very uncertain and difficult and particularly about the Time when the last opportunity offered of sending to England from this Province (59). All intercourse with the interior Parts of the Country was then absolutely impracticable. We have therefore thought it not unreasonable to extend the Benefit of the Act to Persons so situated on a persuasion that in many Instances they had no possible means of obtaining Knowledge of the Act, and that in a still greater number of Cases where the Act was in some degree Known, they had not an opportunity of availing themselves of it, and transmitting their Claims in time, and therefore when either of the above Grounds of Excuse has been fully proved to us on oath, we have thought such Claims ought to be admitted.

But we have not extended this Kind of Indulgence to Persons who, during the Winter, or any part of the Winter resided in this Town, or within the Neighbourhood as within those Limits

---

we are satisfied the Act was in general Known, and that there were opportunities for the Loyalists to have sent their Claims to England, which opportunities if lost, were lost thro' their own Neglect.

Though the number of Persons whose Claims have been admitted under this Rule of Decision is Considerable, yet the sum allowed to each of them is in general trifling—and we have the satisfaction to think it will be received by Persons the greater part of whom have risked their lives in support of the Cause to which they adhered, and from whose Continued and prosperous Industry the greatest advantages are likely to be derived to this Province.

Of the New Claims which have been admitted we have examined since our last Report 239. Which with the sums allowed in each are included in the Schedule hereunto annexed, distinct from the Claimants under the former Act. (60).

We have likewise transmitted to your Lordships Lists of those Persons who have proved their Losses to our Satisfaction Classed for Compensation in the same manner as we have before done in our former Reports.

We beg to express our Earnest Wishes to your Lordships that some Compensation may be allowed on our Report as soon as possible as we are satisfied such Relief would at this Time be of great general advantage and the situation of many Individuals we believe to be so distressed as to require immediate assistance.

Some few Claims arising in this Province as well as in Nova Scotia may still remain unheard, but in these Instances we incline to think the Parties have left the Country or have abandoned their Claims as being too trifling to pursue, or from a Consciousness that they Could not be supported; of this we can, we think Confidentially assure your Lordships, that no Claimants resident in this or the neighbouring Provinces can reasonably or with Truth Complain that they have not had an opportunity of attending us and having their Cases examined since our arrival in America.

(61). We beg leave to inform your Lordships that we have found the Loyalists of this Province impressed with the deepest sense of Gratitude to His Majesty and the British Parliamnt for the attention shown to their Situation in appointing a Commission to be executed abroad, and we perceive the most sanguine expectation universally prevailing, that this Instance of National Liberality to Individuals will be attended with general Advantage to their improving Settlements, and we are, as we presume, the better Warranted in stating this Information to your Lordships as we have found these Sentiments publickly and explicitly declared by the Lieutenant Governor, His Counsil and the House of Assembly.

Having now in a great measure finished the Business of this Province we are preparing with all expedition to proceed to Quebec.

THOMAS DUNDAS.
J. PEMBERTON.

Office of American Claims,
   City of St. John, New Brunswick,
      26th March, 1787.

To the Right Honorable the Lords Commissioners of his Majesty's Treasury:

THE FOURTH REPORT OF, &C.

We did ourselves the Honor of informing your Lordships by our Report dated 26th March, 1787, how far we had at that time proceeded in the Execution of our Commission within the Province of New Brunswick, the number of Claims which we afterwards heard amounted to 18.

(62). Having thus as far as was in our Power Concluded our Business in New Brunswick we proceeded in His Majesty's Ship Thisbe for the Province of Canada as early in the Spring as the Navigation was practicable and arrived at Quebec on the 11th of May last when we immediately entered on the Business of our Commission.

On the first Commencement of our Enquires it became necessary to determine on the advisability of the several Claims presented under the Act passed in 1785, amounting in number to 716 which had been sent to us from this Province during our residence at Halifax and in doing this we adopted in general the same principels and proceeded on the same Rules as were formerly stated to your Lordships in our Report dated 10th June, 1786. But as the Admission or Rejection of a Considerable number of Claims depended much on local Circumstances——on which account as we formerly informed your Lordships we had found it necessary to delay our Determination respecting such Claims until on our arrival in this Country we had fully informed ourselves of the situation of the different Places at which the several Claimants resided, and the opportunities they had of sending their Claims to England in 1783.—We shall now endeavour to explain to your Lordships the principal Reasons which have weighed with us as on this very material Head of Decision.

We find on Enquiry that the Act of Parliamnt passed in the year 1783 in favour of the Loyalists was first printed in the Quebec Gazette on the 23rd of October in that year. We Consider this as the period when authentic Notice was first given of the Act in this Province. The time which the Loyalists had to entitle themselves to the benefit of the Act by transmitting their Claims home was very short. There was no direct and immediate Conveyance to England after the 16th November when the last ship sailed from Quebec; the only mode of Conveyance after that time was thro' the States by the way of New York, but as that mode of Conveyance was not so well regulated from all the different Ports of this Province as it is at present and was besides particularly uncertain and precarious at that time of the year, viz., from the 16th of November to the end of January following, within which period the Claims ought to have been forwarded so as to (63).

have any chance of arriving in time, these Considerations have induced us not to lay any great stress on this Circumstance of the possibility of a Conveyance thro' the States in determining what Claims we should or should not admit, and this we have been the readier to do as we are satisfied that almost the only Persons who could availed themselves of this opportunity and who consequently would in our Judgment have suffered from their neglect of it were those resident at or near Quebec or Montreal, and it would have been totally useless to have taken the Point into Consideration in their Cases as we rejected their Claims on another Reason, viz., that the Parties neglected a better and more immediate opportunity of transmitting them directly to England by the Ships that sailed from this Country in the Fall of the year 1783. (64).

It has then upon the whole appeared to us that the only persons who could gain Knowledge of the Act in time and had it in their power to avail themselves of the short opportunity that offerd of transmitting their Claims to England were those then resident at or near Quebec or Montreal, and when Persons so situated neglected to avail themselves of that Advantage we have Considered their subsequent Caims as inadmissable; But to those Persons settled beyond those Boundaries we have thought ourselves Authorized to extend the Privilege of the Act passed in 1785, indeed as to the far greater part of them, those who resided in the settlements remote from Quebec or in the upper parts of the Country or who were on Duty at the different Posts, there cannot be a doubt entertained but that they were from their situation utterly incapable of availing themselves of the former Act.

The schedule accompanying this report contains the cases of 77 old and 300 New Claimants distinctly and separately reported with the sum allowed to each.

(65). We have likewise transmitted to your Lordships Lists of those Persons who have proved their Losses to our Satisfaction, Classed for Compensation in the same manner as we have before done in our former Report.

We take the Liberty as we did in the Case of those Loyalists who reside in the two other Provinces of expressing our most earnest wish that the Persons entitled to an Allowance under our present Report may receive a speedy Compensation, as we are satisfied that a very deserving set of men most of whom are at present in necessitous and distressful Circumstances—Will derive the most reasonable Relief from such Assistance.

THOMAS DUNDAS.
J. PEMBERTON.

Office of American Claims,
Montreal, 24th Jany., 1788.

To the Right Honble the Lords Commissioners of His Majesty's Treasury:—

THE FIFTH REPORT OF, &C.

We had the honor to inform your Lordships dated 24th January last of the progress we had then made in the Execution of our Commission within this Province, since which time we have heard and examined the Cases of many other Claimants— Inhabitants of this Country which with some formerly heard amount in number to 356, the names of which Claimants with the sum allowed to each are included in the Schedule accompanying this Report; but as some particular Circumstances attend many of the Cases included in this Report, we think it necessary to state to your Lordships at large the opinion which we have formed on some of them, and the observations too, that occur to us with the request we have to make to your Lordships on that Head.

(66).

The Persons thus particularly Circumstanced are of three Descriptions. In the first place those who held Property in the State of Vermont, as to whom an opinion long prevailed which was adopted by the Board at home and reported to your Lordships that there had been no Instance of Confiscation of Real or Personal Property within the State of Vermont on account of the owners Loyalty. This opinion we are inclined to think from the evidence that has appeared in many Cases before us is

not invariably true. We have received many Certificates of the Confiscation and Sale of Lands within that State on account of the Parties Loyalty and when such Confiscation has not taken place, we believe it has been because the Partys Title to the Lands in Question was deny'd by the State as has been generally the Case of Lands Claimed Solely under Grants from the New York

Government, and when no Title was conceived to exist Confiscation was held unnecessary.

In such Cases however of Loss of Real Estate which have come before us accompanied with Certificates of Confiscation we have thought it Right to make the Party Compensation for his Losses, tho' from various Circumstances attending the Real Property of that Country, the value at which we have estimated it has not been Considerable. (67).

In regard to Personal Property possessed in that State we are satisfied by Evidence in many Cases that it has been Confiscated or Lost merely on account of the Possessors Loyalty, and we have therefore considered this a Loss Entitled to Compensation.

As to the other Classes of Persons whose particular Situation requires as we think to be stated they are those who sent New Claims to us after our arrival in Halifax but which did not arrive at our office till after the 1st May, 1786. When the time expired for receiving them. In our first Report we stated to your Lordships the apprehensions we had from the Accounts transmitted to us that it would be impossible for the Claimants resident in the different Parts of Canada to transmit their Claims to Halifax within the time limited by the Act, and we had therefore appointed an Agent at Quebec to receive such Claims with directions not to receive any after the first of May, 1786.

Claims were lodged in time with our Agent specially appointed by us. We hope your Lordships will have no difficulty in Considering this the same as if they had been received personally by us or at our Office. (68).

In the same Report we also stated to your Lordships a request from Lieutenant Governor Hope of extending the time still farther, namely to the first of August, in favour of those Persons resident in the still more distant and remote parts of the Province whose Claims could not arrive even at Quebec before that time. Convinced of the Reasonableness of this Request and the Truth of the Facts in which it was grounded we have examined several Claims of this Kind which were lodged on a public Notice from the Lieutenant Governor at the Secretary's office at Quebec after the 1st of May, and we hope the Reasons which prevailed with us to examine these Cases will have sufficient Weight with your Lordships to Approve and Confirm what we have done.

There still remain some few Cases upon which for want of necessary Proofs and other unavoidable Circumstances we have not been able to come to a final Determination, but we hope soon to report to your Lordships upon these few remaining Cases.

We herewith transmit to your Lordships Lists of those Persons who have proved their Losses to our Satisfaction, Classed for Compensation in the same manner as we have before done in our former Reports. (69).

THOMAS DUNDAS.
J. PEMBERTON.

Office of American Claims,
Montreal, 5th June, 1788.

To the Right Honble the Lords Commissioners of His Majesty's Treasury :—

The Sixth Report of, &c.

We have had the Honor of informing your Lordships by our former Reports of the progress we from time to time made in the Execution of our Commission abroad and in our last Report dated 5th June, 1788, we gave your Lordships an Account of a Certain number of Claims heard by us during our Residence in Canada which brought our Business in America to a Conclusion. This being the Case, and the object of our Commission being thus attained, we left the Province of Quebec and returned to England.

It may not be improper at this Close of the Business in America, to observe, that from various Notices which we caused to be given both publicly and to Individuals, from the length of time during which we Continued, and the manner in which we fixed our Residence in each Province, we are satisfied that every Claimant resident within His Majesty's Dominions who had a right to be heard—either from his Claim having been lodged under the Act of 1783, or from its having been admitted by us under the Act of 1783—had an opportunity of being heard and that this opportunity if lost was lost by his own Neglect.

(70).

We also informed your Lordships in our last Report that there were several cases in part heard which remained undetermined. These Cases we have reconsidered since our return to England. In some we have been furnished with additional satisfactory Information, in others tho' the Information is slight we have been able to collect sufficient Materials on which to form our Decision. Some few only have been disallowed from a total failure of Evidence to support them—but they have been all finally settled & determined.

We have also since our Return been Employed in taking a Careful Review of the whole of our Proceedings. In doing this we have made several alterations which Consist Chiefly in Additions to the sums before allowed, and these we have made in Cases where a former Insufficiency or total Defect of Evidence has been supplied and more particulary by relaxing from a Rule formerly adopted respecting Purchases made under particular Circumstances during the Troubles, which as well as the Propriety of relaxing from it having been fully stated by the Board at Home with whose Opinion we Concur, need not as we presume be repeated.

(71).

We beg leave further to state to your Lordships that the names of those Persons with the sum due to each whose Claims we have determined since our last Report, likewise the sums due to Complete Payment in full to Persons who had received Compensation in part and the additional sums which we have seen Reason to allow on Revision are all Contained in the Books or Lists for Compensation transmitted to your Lordships. The only Persons whose Claims we have examined and whose Losses we have liquidated, whose Names are not included in any such Lists are those whom we distinguished under the Title of Settled Inhabitants of the United States—being doubtful what might be the Determination of Governemt respecting Persons of this Description we have proceeded no further than to examine their respective Claims and to make an Estimate of their Losses.

The number of Persons thus examined by us in America amounts to 25—Whose Names with the sums allowed to each will be added to a List of Persons of the like Description who have been heard by the Board at home, and in this manner they will be all jointly submitted to future Consideration.

We have likewise added the names of those Persons to whom we have allowed for Professional Losses to the List of Persons of the same Description heard by the Board at home which has been transmitted to your Lordships.

The Business of our Commission being now brought almost to a Conclusion we have drawn up a Statemnt of the Whole which we shall annex to this Report in order to give your Lordships at once a full and distinct view of all our proceedings in America, in the Execution of these Powers with which we have been intrusted. (72).

But as it will appear from the Annexed Statement that the number of Claims lodged in our office under the Act of 1785 does greatly exceed the number that has been brought to a hearing, it may be proper to account for this Circumstance and to explain the Causes from which it has proceeded.

In the first Place in this number of unheard Claims are included those which at first were only deferred for want of Information on which to form our Judgement respecting their admissibility and which have Contained in the same state, the necessary Evidence required by us not having been afterwards supplied.

To these may be added a Certain Number of Claims which have been admitted by us on which the Parties never appeared for an Exam nation altho' if resident within His Majesty's Dominions they all as we believe received our Summons for their Attendance.

But the far greater part of the Claims thus unheard Consists of those which we have held inadmissable under the Act of 1785—the Parties not only not having proved their utter Incapacity to have lodged their Claims under the Act of 1783, but it having on the Contrary clearly appeared that they were so situated as to have it in their Power to have transmitted their Claims to England within the limited Time. (73).

To these may be added a Number of Claims to which appeared on perusal to have been delivered for Losses sustained in Nova Scotia, New Brunswick and Canada. For as we did not Consider our Enquiry to Extend to Losses sustained beyond the Limits of the United States we of course did not proceed to the Examination of those Claims.

From all those various Causes it has happened that the number of Claims unheard has become altogether so Considerable.

We shall now beg leave to refer your Lordships to the Statement itself, having as we presume sufficiently accounted for that part of it respecting unheard Claimants which appeared to us to require a more full and particular Explanation.

(74). Office of American Claims,
Lincoln Inn Fields, May, 1789.

THOMAS DUNDAS.
J. PEMBERTON.

FIRST GENERAL STATEMENT OF CLAIMS MADE AND LOSSES LIQUIDATED OF AMERICAN LOYALISTS.

LOSS OF PROPERTY.

Claims under the Act of 1783 and 1785.

	No. of Claims.	Amount of Claims.	Losses Allowed.
1. Loyalists who have rendered services to Great Britain	74		£ 99,765 7 6
2. Loyalists who bore arms in the service of Great Britain	857		125,146 0 0
3. Loyalists zealous and uniform	293		88,676 14 0
4. Loyalist British Subjects resident in Great Britain	1		700 0 0
5. Loyalists who took oaths to the American States, but afterwards joined the British	12		1,635 0 0
6. Loyalists who bore arms for the American States but afterwards joined the British	7		4,484 15 0
7. Loyalists sustaining losses under the Prohibitory Act	3		1,554 0 0
	1,247	£919,322 9 5	£321,961 16 6
8. Loyal British Proprietors			
9. Loyalists now subjects or settled inhabitants of the United States, some of whom are persons of great merit and have met with peculiar hardships	25	55,988 3 7	14,791 6 0
10. Claims disallowed and Withdrawn { 1 disallowed for want of proof of Loyalty	3	1,704 4 2	
2 do for want of satisfactory proof of losses	109	78,478 17 3 1,513 0 0	
3 being fraudulent	1		
4 for debts only	3		
5 withdrawn	13	7,032 17 2	
11. Loyal British subjects who appear to have relief provided for them by the Treaty of Peace, but state the utter impossibility of procuring it. N. B.—The amount of the claim in these cases is included in other classes			
	1,401	1,064,039 11 7	336,753 2 6
12. Claims presented under the act of 1783, carried out by or transmitted to the Commissions in America and not prosecuted	99	£71,134 0 3	

STATE OF THE ENQUIRY OF THE COMMISSIONS OF AMERICAN CLAIMS WHO WERE
DIRECTED BY ACT OF PARLIAMENT TO REPAIR TO NORTH AMERICA.

—	Claims lodged.	Amount.	Claims unheard	Number examined.	Property claimed.	Losses found.
Claims under the Act of 1783				432	675,004 15 8	212,146 2 6
Claims under the Act of 1785	1,799	707,346 1 0	830	969	389,034 15 11	124,607 0 0
Total	1,799	707,346 1 0	830	1,401	1,064,039 11 7	336,753 2 6

(77).

To the Right Honble the Lords Commissioners of His Majesty's Treasury:—

The Report of the Commissioners appointed to Enquire into the Losses sustained by many of His Majesty's Loyal Subjects who have presented Memorials and Claims to the Commissioners of the Treasury for the said Losses—previous to the third day of June, 1788—Either by furnishing Provisions or other necessary Articles for the Service of His Majesty's Navy and Army in America during the late War, or by having their Property used, seized or destroyed for carrying on the Public Service there, and for which they have hitherto received no Compensation.

(78).

In pursuance of the Powers with which we were invested by an Act of Parliamnt passed in the 28th year of the Reign of His present Majesty to Enquire into Losses particularly described in the above Preamble, and in obedience to the directions of the said Act, requiring us to give an account of our Proceedings in Writing to the Lords Commissioners of His Majesty's Treasury, and to His Majesty's Principal Secretaries of State for the time being, we have the Honor to Report.

That upon the Memorials and Claims which had been presented to your Lordships previous to the 3rd day of June, 1788, being transmitted to us, We immediately proceeded to the Examination of them taking such measures as were most Conducive to Dispatch.

The number of Claims before us became very Considerably Encreased by the adition of those of a like nature that had been, previously presented to the Commissioners in Britain and in America under former Acts, which Claims being Considered as Demands against Governmnt and not as Losses in Consequence of Loyalty remained unexamined.

As it was not in our Power to get through the Enquiry during the Continuance of the Act by which we were first appointed and particularly as many of the Claims that had been entred into were necessarily left open for further Evidence we judged

(79).

it more Expedient to Keep such Report as we might then have made, than to offer one incomplete to your Lordships.

The duration of our Powers being extended by the last Act we have been enabled to enquire into and determine upon all Cases brought forward to this date.

Some four names however still remain upon the List first transmitted, but after the publick and direct Notices which have given there is reason to Conclude that the Parties of their Re-

presentatives have been either wilfully negligent, unable to prove, or disinclined to appear in support of their Demands.

(80). There also remain many articles of Claim for supplies furnished to the Navy and Army in America extracted from the accounts of Losses formerly presented to the Commissioners which were not Enquired into for the Reasons before mentioned. These are individually of small amount, the proofs already adduced are not sufficient to act upon and no further Evidence has been offerd; besides which the charges for the most part are such as could not in all probability have been substantiated to effect.

Throughout the whole of our Enquiry we have endeavoured to discriminate between Demands for articles applicable to the Wants of the Navy and Army and such as may have been used or seized for Carrying on the publick Service, from those not applicable to such wants, and from those by which the Public service could not be benefitted. In like manner we have distinguished between Property destroyed by order and for the Convenience or safety of the King's Troops from destruction indiscriminate and unwarranted, which can only be attributed to the unavoidable Incidents of War.

We must also observe that in the Investigation of Facts at

a time so distant and of Transactions during the active operations of Troops when Receipts for supplies furnished, or taken, may not have been given with the Precision they ought, and sometimes not all. We have studiously formed our Judgemt upon the merits, and a due Consideration of all the Circumstances of each Case without exercising the strictest Rigor upon the Evidence produced, or relaxing unguardedly from the Caution due to the Interest of the Publick.

(81). In Justice to the Claimants to whom Compensation is recommended, it is incumbent upon us to observe, that the greatest Disproportion between the sum Claimed, and the sum admitted, is mostly to be atributed to the Discriminations we have made of Losses applicable and unapplicable to the wants of the Navy and Army, and of those by which the Public Service could or could not have been promoted. Other Causes of this Disproportion arises from the misapprehension of many with respect to the Nature of Losses to which the Act of Parliament extended and from several Claims having been presented by Agents in the name of Persons who have given no proof of Loyalty at any period, or who, by remaining Citizens of the United States of America, from the acknowledgment of their Independence to the present

Time, have not been Considered as His Majesty's Loyal Subjects from whom or in whose Behalf alone the words of the Act imply that the Memorials and Claims lodged at the Treasury had been presented.

The Statement hereunto annexed Comprize the result of our whole Enquiry and will also show the number of Claims remaining unexamined for the Reasons specified, viz:—

Amount of Sums Claimed and Admitted. No. 1.
Claims transmitted from the Treasury to which the Parties have not appeared. No. 2.
The number of Claims presented to the Commissioners and not Enquired into either by reason of the Parties not appearing, or, if the Evidence formerly produced not being sufficient to act upon. No. 3. (82).

How far we have succeeded in our Endeavours to fulfil the gracious Instructions of Parliamnt will best appear by a Reference to our Proceedings Contained in Books that will be Completed and transmitted to the Treasury as soon as possible.

         Thomas Dundas.
         J. Pemberton.
         R. MacKenzie.

American Office,
25th March, 1790.

No. 1.

Amount of Sums Claimed and Admitted.

No. of Claims examined.	Total sum claimed.	Total sum admitted.
216	£305,725 6 4	£66,124 14 11

No. 2.

Claims transmitted from the Treasury to which the Parties have not appeared.

Names.	Observations.	
Phyle & Armstrong..................	Messrs. Champion and Dickerson, who appear by the Memorial to have lodged the claim, have denied any knowledge of or connection with the claimants.	(83).
John Van Boskirk and other proprietors of Bergen Neck..................	Mr. Van Schaack, who lodged the claim, has been repeatedly summoned to attend.	
Lawrence Powell.....................	John Rolph, the Attorney, has been summoned at various times, but never attended.	

No. 3.

Number of Claims presented to the Commissioners and not Enquired into either by Reason of the Parties not appearing or of the Evidence formerly produced not being sufficient to act upon—78.

THOMAS DUNDAS.
J. PEMBERTON.
ROBERT MACKENZIE.

American Office,
25th March, 1790.

American Office,
30th March, 1790.

SIR,—

(84). We request you will annex the Enclosed Papers No. 1, 2 and 3 to our Report transmitted to their Lordships on the 27th inst. in place of those then sent. They are in Substance precisely the same, but Convey at the Head of each a fuller Description of the matter reported.

We are, Sir, Yours &c.,
THOMAS DUNDAS.
J. PEMBERTON.
ROBERT MACKENZIE.

GEORGE ROSE, Esq., &c., &c., &c.

No. 1.

STATEMENT

Of the number of Claims Examined, of the Total Sum Claimed, and of the Total Sum Admitted by the Commissioners appointed to Enquire into the Losses sustained by His Majesty's Loyal Subjects Either by furnishing Provisions or other necessary Articles for the Service of His Majesty's Navy or Army in America during the late War, or by having their Property used, seized or destroyed, for Carrying on the Public Service there, &c.

No. of Claims examined.	Total sum claimed.	Total sum admitted.
216	£305,725 6 4	£66,124 14 11

(85).

TOTAL SUM ADMITTED.

Sixty Six Thousand, One hundred and Twenty four Pounds, Fourteen Shillings and Eleven Pence.

THOMAS DUNDAS.
J. PEMBERTON.
RT. MACKENZIE.

American Office,
30th March, 1790.

No. 2.

REPORT

Of Claims transmitted from the Treasury for Supplies furnished to the Navy or Army in America, or for Property used, seized or destroyed for carrying on the Publick Service there, to which the Parties have not appeared.

Names.	Observations.	
Phyle & Armstrong....................	⎧ Messrs. Champion and Dickerson, who appear by the Memorial to have lodged the Claim, have denied any knowledge of or connection with the claimants.	
John Van Boskirk and other proprietors of Bergen Neck..................	⎧ Mr. Van Schaack, who lodged the claim, has been repeatedly summoned to attend.	(86).
Lawrence Powell.....................	⎧ John Rolph, the Attorney, has been summoned at various times, but never attended.	

THOMAS DUNDAS.
J. PEMBERTON.
ROBERT MACKENZIE.

American Office,
30th March, 1790.

No. 3.

REPORT

Of the number of Claims for supplies furnished to the Navy or Army in America or for Property used, seized or destroyed for Carrying on the Publick Service there, which have not been Enquired into, either by Reason of the Parties not appearing or of the Evidence formerly produced not being sufficient to act upon. 78

THOMAS DUNDAS.
J. PEMBERTON.
ROBERT MACKENZIE.

American Office,
30th March, 1790.

STATEMENT (87).

Presented to the House of Commons 23rd April and a Copy sent to the Treasury same day, of the Claims Examined by the Commissioners appointed to Enquire into the Losses sustained by His Majesty's Loyal Subjects, Either by furnishing Provisions or other Necessary Articles for the Service of His Majesty's Navy or Army in America during the late War, or by having their Property used, seized or destroyed for Carrying on the Publick Service, &c.

Pursuant to an Order of the Honorable House of Commons dated 22nd April, 1790.

No. of Claims examined.	Total sum claimed.	Total sum admitted.
216	£305,725 6 4	£66,124 14 11

Signed, THOMAS DUNDAS.
J. PEMBERTON.
ROBERT MACKENZIE.

American Office,
23rd April, 1790.

NOTE.

Cadleton Island, p. 23, evidently ought to be Carleton Island.
69 District, p. 168, l. 14, should be, 96 District.
Oswargatche, pp. 388, 389, 390, read Oswaigatache.
Van Matu, p. 610, read Van Mater.
Another Graham, p. 678, 1, 3, read Arthur Graham.
Christian Sarg, p. 687, read Christian Sing.
David Olden, p. 725, read David Ogden.
Gen. Wheeler, p. 907, read George Wheeler.
J. Gust Hope (4) p. 957, Evidently Brig. Genl. Hope is referred to.
Schennerhorn, p. 1268, read, Schermerhorn.
Alumford, p. 1300, read Mumford.

GENERAL INDEX.

Aaron, Capt., 1120.
Abacca, Island, 191.
Abacco, 163, 296.
Abbots, Joseph, 234.
Abbott, John, 576, 1022.
" Capt., 948.
Abbott's Creek, 280.
Abels, Major, 799.
Acadian Settlers, 22.
Acherly, Isaac, of New York, 766.
Achington, 1018.
Ackerly, Obadiah, of New York, 795.
Ackerman, Abraham, 429, 561.
Adams, 752, 753, 754.
" Evi, 598.
" John, of Pits, 263, 602, 1216, 1318.
" Mr., 660, 947, 1168.
" Nathaniel, of New York, 806, 808.
" Capt. Samuel, 437.
" Dr. Samuel, 338, 460, 484.
" Samuel, 381, 462, 1272, 1333.
Adventure, Schooner, 274.
Aesopus, (Oesopus), 486, 654, 816, 864-5-6-72.
" Gaol, 769, 927, 1267.
Agnew, John, 1227.
" Capt. Stair, 1227.
" William, of N.Y. Prov., 452.
Airdie, John, 622.
Akerman, Peter, 55-6.
Alatamalia, 1127.
Alatamaha River, 1127.
Albany, 29, 105-6, 152, 213, 262, 315, 333, 345, 347-8-9, 361, 365, 366, 380, 387, 401, 425, 456, 457, 551, 552, 562, 563, 618, 654, 682, 860, 865, 927, 928, 929, 937, 938, 940, 944, 952, 992, 993, 994, 995, 1000, 1026, 1034, 1064, 1109, 1153, 1267, 1284, 1281-2.
Albany Bush, 460, 467.
Albany County, 144, 344, 345, 346, 347, 359, 368, 372, 376, 391, 392, 400, 404, 407, 408, 409, 415-7-8, 422, 423, 433, 441, 443, 445, 455, 457, 468, 470, 474, 857, 858, 903, 936, 941, 942, 943, 950, 953, 960, 967, 968, 1001-2-3-4-5-6, 1016, 1020-4-8-9, 1030-1-4-5-6-7-8, 1041-2-7, 1050-1-2-3-5-9, 1070-5-7-8, 1081, 1118, 1260-3-4, 1266, 1283.
Albany Fort, 425, 562.
Albany Gaol, 345, 414, 436, 454, 462, 469, 470, 486, 1267.
Albany Patent, 1117, 1121, 1285.
Aldborough, Patent of, 123.
Aldbrunt, Henry, 403.
Alexander, Adam, 162.
" Hugh, 994, 1281.
" John, 170.
" Robt., of S. Carolina, 169, 172, 647, 901, 1225.
Algier, Martin, 406, 1117.

Alicoke, Joseph, 1252.
Allan, Andr., 1221.
" Hannah, 957, 1300.
" James, 1270.
" Joseph, of New Jersey, 1270.
Allegainy Mountains, 55.
Allen, Lt. A., 260.
" Andr., 1288.
" Amos, 576.
' David, 753.
" Dr., 704.
" Elizabeth Bland, 926-7.
" Col. Ira, 577.
" Col. Isaac, of New Jersey, 109, 248, 269-70-1, 297-8, 833.
" I., 680.
" John, 249, 592.
" Jonathan, 576.
" Joseph, 32, 262.
" Judge, 895.
" Lt.-Col., 184, 470, 702, 793, 871.
" Mr., 927.
" Mrs., 250.
Allford, Benj., 141.
Alling, Stephen, 81.
Allington, 1024.
Allison, And., 45.
" Samuel, 832.
Allward, Asher, of Jersey, 854.
" Benjamin, of New Jersey, 810, 855, 1320.
" Samuel, 810.
Alward, Joseph, 802.
Amboy, 93, 126-7, 179, 180, 198-9, 320, 547-8, 581, 619, 711-2, 725, 760, 802, 863, 914, 1277.
Amboy, South, 1277.
Amelia Township, 175, 180, 244.
Amey, Jonas, 1023, 1041-2.
Amherst, 1286-7.
" General, 738.
" Lord, 309, 1182.
" Sir ———, 309.
Amity, John, 126.
Amot, James, 733.
Amsterdam, 346, 1203.
Anderson, Alexander, of N.Y. Prov., 387.
" Capt., 406, 410, 440, 459, 1043, 1120-1, 1261.
" David, 849.
" Elizabeth, 849.
" George, of S. Carolina, 849.
" Jane, 849.
" Capt. James, 599.
" James, 175, 849-1333.
" John, 387, 849.
" Jonathan, 745.
" Capt. Joseph, of Vermont, 424.
" Mrs. Mary, 387.
" Mr., 1105.
" Samuel, of Vermont, 391, 424, 486, 1333.
" Susan, 849.

[1379]

Anderson, William, 849.
Anderstown, 1114.
Andree, Major, 166, 896-7, 1131.
Andrew, Janet, 1000.
Andrew, (Sloop), 910.
Andrews, John, of Rhode Island 187, 195, 716, 1192, 1249.
" Nichol, 55.
Angevine, John, of New York, 784, 790.
Angus, Capt., 484.
Annable, John, 1111.
Annapolis, 11, 22, 68, 109, 112, 147, 215-6, 312-3-4-6-7, 533-4, 540-2-4, 599, 652, 710-1, 723, 747, 748, 755-8, 853, 872, 1295, 1321, 1326, 1330, 1355.
Annapolis River, 22.
Annapolis Royal, 1285.
Anson County, 44, 102, 550, 695, 704, 1250, 1313.
Anstey, John, 217, 292, 366, 377, 398, 418, 451, 476, 768, 771-4, 809, 903, 908, 1295, 1317-8, 1327-9, 1339, 1343-4.
Anteli, Edward, 925.
Anthony, Elizabeth, 51.
" Joseph, 51.
Anthony's Nose, 472, 1283.
Antigo River, 1111.
Antigonish, 130-1, 829.
Antigua, 154, 305-6, 630, 929, 1230-1, 1324.
Antill, Ed., 93.
Appleton, W., 643.
Apthorp, 629.
Apthorp, Charles Ward, of New York, 622.
Arbuthnot, Admiral, 39, 608, 616.
Archer, Jekel, 501.
Argo, (ship), 305, 862.
Argyle, 160, 376, 718.
" County, 554-5.
" Patent, 1097.
" Township, 466, 949.
Ariadne, (ship), 905.
Ark, (brig), 1329.
Arlington, 86, 398, 434-5-7-8, 1100.
Arm, Capt., 1281.
Armory, John, 916.
Armstrong, Capt., 338.
" David, 538.
" John, 223.
" Major, 260, 681, 1049.
" Phyle &, 1373-5.
" Col. Thos., 338.
Arnold, Gen. Benedict, of North Kingston, 29, 31, 80, 231, 303, 347-9, 365, 425, 436, 447, 566, 601, 722, 865, 896, 1123, **1185**.
Arnold, Stephen, 204, 818.
Arnot, Isaac, 117.
Arundel, 660-1.
Aseltine, Peter, 1007.
Ash, Lawrence, 587.
" Mercy, 587.
" Mr., 914.
Ashford, New, 444-5-9.
Ashley, 643.
" Capt., 391.
" Nathaniel, 705.
Asia, (Man-of-War), 42, 82, 138, 199, 313, 378, 423, 635, 829, 830, 864, 872.

Askew, Capt., 909.
" Leonard, 1333.
Aswegatchy, 933.
Atherton, Phineas, 1181-2.
Atkins, Henry, of Massachusetts Bay, 190.
Atkinson, Samuel, 328.
" Theo., 48.
Atwater, Mr., 87.
Auchingleen, 1096.
Auger, Frederick, 973-4, 1001.
Augusta, 28, 163-4, 527, 695, 700, 704, 705, 717-8, 792-3-7, 1144.
Augusta, Fort, 704-5, 793-4.
Augustine, 182, 193, 694, 706, 714-8, 734, 800.
Ault, John, 1122.
Aunt, Jacob, 558.
Aurie, John, 1108.
Austin & Co., 221.
" Joel, 993-5.
" Joseph, 201.
" Penderson, 509.
" Samuel, 566.
" Thos., 669.
" Wm., of Philadelphia, 125, 565, 614-5-6, 1289, 1292.
Auston's Ferry, 566-7.
Avery, Gordon, 981.
" Joseph, 1102.
" Samuel, 92, 623.
" Solomon, 776.
Aylesford, 738.
Ayscough, Capt. James, 909, 910-1.

Baache, (Bache, Beecher or Beach), Abraham, 117-8, 120, 626.
" Nathan, 249.
" Theophilet, of N.Y., 117-8, 249.
Baagan, Gooldsbury, 338.
Babbet, Daniel, of New York, 808.
Babcock, David, of Orange County, 147, 655.
" Phineas, 486.
" William, 1320.
Baberty, Madame, 1047.
Baby, Frances, 1359.
Bachoit, John, senr., 538.
Back Creek, 46.
Back Street, Boston, 622.
Back Water Creek, 43.
Backus, Ebenezer, 721.
Badcock, Benjamin, 751.
Baden, Peter, 166.
Badgely, Stephen, 883.
Bagnell, Samuel, 417.
Bagsby, Henry, 327.
Bahama Islands, 163, 174, 190, 296, 339, 684, 704-5, 727-8, 798, 1288-9, 1326, 1353, 1361.
Bailey, John, 1131.
" Rev. Mr., 746-7.
Bain, Dr. James, 25.
Bakeman, Jacob, 456.
Baker, Bostine, 1109.
" Charles, 509.
" John, 790, 1019.
" Remember, 437.
" Robt., 862.
" Susannah, 1266.

INDEX.

Baker, Capt. Walter, 331.
Baldridge, John, 363.
Baldron, 357.
Baldwin, Isaac, 202, 290.
" John, 531.
" Mr., 365, 586.
" Nahum, 1288.
" Simeon, 202.
Balentine, Fairly & Co.,
Balfour, Capt., 629.
" Col. N., 165-9, 182, 242, 652, 678.
  700, 704, 718-9, 728, 1208, 1218,
  1223, 1245.
" Nisbet, 61, 700.
Ball, Col., 61.
" Elias, jr., 165.
" Govr., 1200, 1202, 1245.
" Jacob, 960.
" Mr., 131.
Ballantine, Col. Wm., 159, 182.
Ballingall, Robert, 1201.
Balston, 1054-5.
Ballstown, 330, 468, 933, 937, 1033, 1052, 1072.
Baltimore, 154, 1189, 1211, 1225, 1249.
Bancker, Gerard, 1292.
Bandt, Capt., 420.
Banes, Capt., 853.
Bangan, Mr., 395.
Bangell, Adam, of N.Y. Prov., 372.
" John, 372.
Banker, Floras, 419.
" Gerard, 723.
Banks, Lyle &, 1311.
Bannel, Solomon, of Massachusetts, 755.
Bannister, John, 102.
" John, senr., 105.
" Thos., of Newport, 102.
Banragio, Banger Co., 1236.
Banvard, Mr., 1112.
" Wm., 971.
Barbadoes, 304-5.
Barbadoes Neck, 626, 691-2.
Barbadoes Precinct, 747.
Barber, (or Barker) Abraham, of N.Y. Prov., 383.
Barclay, Andrew, 661.
" Rev. Dr., 546.
" Major Thos., of New York, 495-8, 545.
" Mrs. Susan, 545-6.
Bardolph, Abraham, 815.
Bardwell, Ebenezer, 113.
Barham, Alex., of Philadelphia, 122.
" Mrs., 122-4-5.
Baristle, Andrew, 435.
" Danl., 435.
Barker, Henry, 404.
" John, 103.
" Oliver, 1091.
" Thos., of N.Y., 234, 882, 1321.
" Thos., senr., 883.
Barkley, Capt., 1142.
Barlow, Edmund, 285.
" Thos., 539.
Barn, John, 555-6.
Barnard, John, 1154.
Barnard, Samuel, jr., 114.
Barnegas, 1238.

Barnes, Capt., 351.
" Fl., 108.
" Jas., 266.
" Joshua, 854.
Barnet, 916.
" Conrad, 931.
" John, of N. Johnstown, 478, 931.
" Mary, 931.
" Mrs., 931.
" Mr., 179, 1237.
" Saml., 920.
" William, 931.
Barnett, Ephram, 253.
Barnhart, George, 397, 1101.
" John, of N.Y. Prov., 476.
Barnsley, Rev. Mr., 636.
Barnwell, Mr., 1301.
Barr, Dr., 102.
" Oliver, 238.
" Saml., 90.
Barret, Mr., 511.
" Saml., 570-2.
Barrington, 509, 617, 732, 1273.
Barrit, E., 251.
Barron, Ellis, of N. Jersey, 140.
" Govr., 654.
" James, 532-3.
Barron Plain, 282.
Barrs, the, 219.
Bartlet, Ann, 196.
" Capt., 611.
" Edward, of Philadelphia, 195.
" John, 195-6.
" Mrs. Sarah, 196.
" Thomas, 196.
" Zachariah, 314.
Bartley, John, 179.
Barton, John, 253.
" Col., 104, 227, 597, 1275.
" Joseph, 148.
" 223, 235.
" Lt.-Col. Joseph, of N. Jersey, 599, 600.
" Kiln, 388.
" Mrs., 603.
" Patent of, 123.
" Thomas, 723.
Barry, Capt. John, 567.
Barrymore, Major, 229, 289.
Bary, Mr., 59.
Bashley, Major, 751.
Bashwick, 898.
Baskerkis, Col., 299.
Bass, Abraham, 425.
Bassert, Christ., 266.
Basset, Geo., 1248.
" Mr., 607.
Bateman, Col., 882.
Bateman's Precinct, 768, 882.
Bates, Abraham, 828.
" John, 1333.
Bathmore, 148.
Bawdin Township, 60.
Bawl, Defeat of, 54.
Bawnbrook, 271.
Baxter, Stephen, 897.
Bayard, Col. John, 429, 665, 1016.
" Mr., 949.

Bayard, Mrs., 1313-4.
" Nicholas, 514.
" Robert, 1313-8.
" Saml., jr., 108.
" Samuel Vetch, of N.Y., 579.
" William, 514, 1313-4.
Bayfun, Thomas, 759.
Bay Shore, 609.
Bazby, William, 890.
Beach (or Baache), 117-8, 626.
Beacon St., Boston, 622.
Beady Fork Roan River, 46.
Beagh, Danl., 1119.
Beaker, 1109.
Beaman, Ebenezer, 878, 880.
" Elizabeth, 878-9.
" Joseph, 878.
" Sarah, 878-9.
" Mrs. Elizabeth, 879, 880.
" Abigail, 878.
" Stephen, 779.
" Thos., 878-9, 880.
" Thos., jr., 878.
Beardsely, Revd. John, 252.
Beardmore, Mr., 789.
Beardslee, Zephaniah, of Connecticut, 838.
Bear Lane, Boston, 38.
Bearman, Major, 768, 776, 778, 790-5.
Bears, William, of N. Jersey, 899.
Beasts Patent, 962.
Beattie, Mr., 249.
Beaufort, 1199, 1290-1, 1301-2.
Beaver Dam, 715-6, 965, 1281-2.
Beaver Harbour, 102, 119, 120, 135, 294, 297, 307, 317-8, 564, 787, 908, 1320
Bebee, Charlotte, 331.
" Edw., 331.
" Easse, 331.
" Emerson, 331.
" Job, 331.
" Jos. of Pensilvania, 331.
" Sarah, 331.
" Secord, 331.
Beckwick, Geo., 877.
Beckwith, Major, 1276, 1280.
Bedel, John, of N.Y., 834.
Bedford, 216, 791, 878, 1046, 1234.
" County, 229, 295, 536, 933.
Bedlam, 1188.
Bedwell, Mariane, 1320.
Beecher, Capt., 287.
" Theophelackt, 286.
Beechman, John H., 948.
Beedle, Daniel, 1119.
Beehler, Jacob, of Georgia, 109.
Beekman Street, N.Y., 147.
Beers, Isaac, 785.
" Saml., 251.
Behahan, Richard, 49.
Bekman, Thomas, 618.
Behler Town, 1139.
Bell, Andrew, of N. Jersey, 619.
" Duncan, 203, 1023.
" George, 178, 681.
" Isaac, cf Connecticut, 199, 224, 826, 829.
" James, 199.
" John, 619.
" Mr., 548, 1273.

Bell, Mrs. Susannah, 200.
" Wm., 1023.
" Wm., jr., 1025.
Bellia, John, of N.Y., 889.
Belling, Aron, 219.
Belleisle Bay, 244, 259, 819, 841, 849, 873.
Bellop, Col., 835, 908.
Bellows, Benj., 89, 90.
Belvedere township, 857.
Bender, George, 1074.
" Philip, 984.
Benedict, Comfort, of Connecticut, 716.
" Lt. Eli, " 282.
" Elijah, " 483.
" John, " 439.
" Jas., 205.
" Joseph, 435.
" Josiah, 282-3.
" Thadius, 1049.
Benezer, Saml., 724.
Benjamin, George, 252.
" Mr., 502.
Benjwood, 263.
Bennet, David, 539, 540.
" & Golding, 1048.
" Isaac, of N. Jersey, 547.
" William, 648.
Bennington, 365, 426, 474, 479, 577, 654, 857, 940, 951, 952, 1011, 1063, 1071, 1269.
" Battle of, 142.
Benson, Brig. Major, 165.
" Christopher, of N.Y., 177.
" Fr., 106.
" James, 345.
" Mathew, 1333.
" Mr., 850.
" Peter, 1270.
Benzel, Adolphus, 447-8.
" Ann Alice, 447.
Bergen County, 246, 299, 308, 429, 430, 449, 450, 541, 542-3, 554, 555, 560, 627, 895, 898, 1019, 1035.
Bergen Neck, 1373-5.
Bergen Point, 774.
Berkeley, Lord, 1243.
Berkley, 590-3.
Berkman, Mr., 457.
Berks, 449.
Berkshire, 445, 754.
Berman, Capt., 89.
Bermudas, 111, 131, 194, 613, 634-5, 639, 853, 1323.
Bernard, Govr., 752.
" Sir Francis, 734-5, 922.
" John, 922-3.
" Rachel, 41.
Berners Street, 1331.
Bernes Lott, 1310.
Berrington County, 787.
Berry, John, 767.
" Mr., 784.
Berton, Peter, of N.Y., 862, 866, 872.
Bertram, Alex., of Philadelphia, 672, 686.
Besboro, 857.
Best, Mrs. Catherine, 386.
" Catherine, jr., 386-7.
" Conrad, of Hoseck, 386.
" Hannah, 386-7.

Best, Hermanus, of N.Y. Prov., 386-7, 942, 1080.
" Jacob,386.
" Jacob, jr., 386.
Bethary, Patent of, 122.
Bethun, Angus, 1066-8.
Betsy, (sloop), 274, 83.
Betts, Azor, of N.Y., 216, 830, 864, 866-7, 872.
" Betts, Benj., of N.Y. Prov., 338.
" Capt., 243, 584.
" James, 21, 1332.
" John, 258.
" Mr., 230, 827, 1311.
" Pr., 209.
Beverley, David, 1102.
" Major Thos., 1295.
Beyea (or Boyce), James, 1321.
Bickle, Nicholas, of New Jersey, 837-8.
Biddle, Clem, 601.
Bigby, Ebenezer, 847.
Biggs, Mr., 851.
Bilboa, Spain, 1147.
Billea, John, 1320.
Billings Farm, 739.
" & Fosster, 248.
Billings port, 929.
Billop, Col. Christopher, 74, 1156-7-8.
Birch, Genl., 544, 585.
Bird, Col., 261, 321.
Birdsill, Danl., 321.
Bisham, John, 124.
Bishop, Saml., 83-4.
" Jonathan, 290.
" Silvanus, of Connecticut, 290.
" Capt., 1147.
Bison Creek, 581.
Bisset, George, 1333.
Black, David, of Boston, 659, 664.
Black River, 159, 245.
Black, Wm., 661.
Blackburn, John, 1213.
Blackeney, David, 841-2.
Blackennings Swamp, 1214.
Blackster, Ann, 81.
" James, 81.
Blackwater, 521.
Bladen County, 235.
Bladsley, Benj., 319.
Blakely, Chambers, of S. Carolina, 676-7.
Blakeney, Thomas, 1333.
Blaker, Mr., 468.
" Mrs., 1041.
Blanch, Mr., 556.
Blanchard, Abner, 1022.
Blaney, Joseph, 641, 721.
Blandon County, 550.
Blasons, Lawrence, 983.
Blaworth, Thomas, of N.Y. Prov., 554.
Blazing Star, 93.
Bleakly, Smith, 1312.
Bleakney, David, of S. Carolina, 259.
Blenheim, 404.
Blenkenhorn, Hy., 1251.
Blewer, Jacob, of Mecklenburgh, 527.
" " of N. Carolina, 710.
" John, 524-6-7.
" Peter, of N. Carolina, 524-6.
Blight, Mrs., 1137.

Bliss, Joshua, 866.
Block House, Yamaska, 1035, 1053.
Bloomary, 255.
Bloomfield, Timothy, 810.
Blooming Dale, 622-3-9, 1243, 1314.
Blowers, Atty.-Genl., 33.
" Ch., 528.
" Mr., 105.
" Mrs., 490.
" Sampson Salter, of Massachusetts Bay, 98, 490, 734.
Blown, Mr., 365.
Blowwett, Major, 1266.
Blue Point, 1311.
Blundell, Chr., 856.
Board, James, 748.
Boddington, William, 46.
Bodet, Point, 359.
Bodwin, Govr., 114, 274.
Bogart, Gilbert, of Orange County, 899, 1256, 1266.
Boggs, Dr. James, of N. Jersey, 35-6, 119, 609, 619-20-9, 690.
" Mary, 36.
Boice, John, 1083, 1104-5, 1281.
Bollerhouse, G., 68.
Bombacks, Mr., 1277.
Bond, George, 703.
" John, of S. Carolina, 701.
Bonds, George, of S. Carolina, 181.
Boneau, Mr., 800.
Bones Creek, 97.
Bongun, Capt., 993.
Bonnell, George, of Georgia, 706.
" Isaac, 761, 1278.
Boon Island, 1171.
Booth, Benjn., 1132.
Bootman's Farm, 606-8.
Bordeaux, 632, 1244-5.
Borden, Joseph, 789.
Bordman, William, 58-9.
Borgaert, John, 446.
Borgert, Albert, 561.
Bosquet, Isaac, 202.
Boston, 32-3-7, 113, 145, 247, 272-3-6, 313-6, 343, 490-1-2-3, 495, 505-6-7, 511, 537, 568-9, 570, 584-5-6-8-9, 599, 600-5, 610, 622-3-4, 635-7-8-9, 655-6-9, 660-1-3-4, 682-6-7, 734-5-8-9, 752-3, 791-4, 831-2-5, 851-2-3, 918-9, 921-2-3, 1144, 1154, 1160, 1208, 1209, 1210, 1216, 1225, 1286, 1303-4, 1327.
Boston, Blockade of, 763.
" Evacuation of, 597.
" Gaol, 611, 659.
" Neck, 303.
" New, 1287.
Bostwick, Isaac, 202.
Bosworth, Thos., of N. York, 504.
Botsford, Amos, of Connecticut, 310, 785, 873.
Botsford, Sarah, of N.B., 310.
Bouch, Fredk., 469.
Bouck, Adam, of N.Y. Prov., 443.
Bouge, Adam, 441.
Boulby, (Boulbey or Boulsby), Edward, of Morris County, 148.
" George, 149.
" John, 149.

Boulby, Richard, 149-50.
Boush, Fredk., 1333.
Bowditch, Ebenezer, 720.
" Jos., 720.
Bowdoin, Govr. James, of Massachusetts, 145.
Bowen, Danl., of N. Jersey, 708.
" Luke, 1122.
Bower, Adam, 662.
" Bartholomew, 657.
" Gasper, of N.Y. Prov., 420.
" Mr., 297.
Bowerman, James, 930.
Bowers, Charles, of S. Carolina, 527.
Bowery Lane, N.Y., 116.
Bowker, John, 389.
Bowles, Humphrey, 1241.
Bowley, Thos., 148.
Bowman's Creek, 1032.
Bowman, John, 1140.
" Peter, 76.
Bownell, Isaac, 725.
Bownet, David, 689.
Boyce, George, jr., 157.
" (or Beyea), James, 1321.
" Peter, 145.
Boyd, Henry, 29.
" Mr., 807.
Boyde, Col., 694.
" Sarah, 613.
Boyer, Peter, 721.
Boyle, Thomas, 844.
Boyne, (ship), 172.
Braddock, Genl., 1277.
Bradford, Benjn., 1321.
" West, 494, 564, 612.
Bradk, Arent, 966.
Bradt, Andr., 1284.
" Aunt, 984.
" Henry, 1283.
" John, 1284.
Bradle, Mr., 310.
Bradley, Abraham. J.P., 290.
" James, 785.
Bradport, 328.
Bradshaw, David, 1266.
" James, of Charlotte Co., 1266.
Bradsley, Revd. John, 836.
Brady, John, 844.
Brae, Nathn., 306.
Bragan, Isaac, 212-3.
Braket, Mr., 687.
Brainton, 655.
Braintree, 686-7.
Brant, David, 1295.
" Elizabeth, 472.
" Capt. Joseph, 397, 459, 471, 1101-2, 1280-1.
" Kingsland, 472.
" Magdaline, 472.
" Margt., 472.
" Mary, 472, 1283.
" Mrs. Mary, 983.
" Peter, 472.
Branford, 82.
Branian, Thos., 879.
Brandley, George, of Halifax, 108.
Brandon, Lord, 43.
Brandt, Capt., 477.

Brandy Wine Battle, 296, 564, 611.
Branning, Samuel, 718.
Brass, Lt. David, 1281.
Brat, John, 995.
Bratt, Danl., 941..
Brathwait, Wm., 148.
Brattle Street, 1209.
Bready, Luke, of N.Y. Prov., 405.
Breeches, 124.
Bremer, Alex., 625.
" Peter, of Tryon Co., 466.
" Herman, 570.
Bremner, George, of N.Y. Prov., 400.
Brewster, Joseph, 99.
" Mr., 595.
" Saml., 749-50-1.
Brian, Capt., 526.
" Creek, 109.
" Mrs. Rachel, 939.
Brians, Col., 280.
Briar Creek, 707, 914.
" " Battle of, 695.
Bridgefield, 300-1.
Bridetown, 305, 810.
Bridgewater, 656, 619-20.
Brien, Saml., 925.
Briggs, Gray, 77.
" Mr., 1199.
" Wm., of N. York, 146.
Brindley, George, 735, 506.
Brinley, Dr., 463.
Brisband, James, 769.
" John, of N. York, 769.
Brisbane, Mr., 583.
" Robert, of N.Y. Prov., 456-7, 488.
Briscoe, Isaac, of Arlington, 435-6-7-9, 1018.
Brisk (sloop of war), 1324.
Brison, John, of S. Carolina, 699, 701.
Bristol, 222, 295, 589.
Britain, New, 709-10.
British Tar (Brigantine), 906.
Britton, Capt., 69, 70.
Broadhead, Thomas, 1185.
Broad River, 33-4, 718-9, 792, 800-1.
" fork of, 61.
" Street, N. York, 1200-2-3-5-6, 1244, 1318-9.
Brock, Elias, 719.
Brodesne, Wm., 602.
Brook, Richd., 416.
Brooke, Abraham, 106.
" H., 636.
" John, 1111.
" Richard, 1254.
Brookhaven, 99, 100, 750.
Brookhaven, South, 594.
Brooklyn, 710.
" Battle of, 118, 567.
" Ferry, 585.
Brooks, John, 1219, 1222.
" Mr., 1221-2.
" Saml., 617.
Broome, John, 87.
Brosie, Christ., 446.
Brown, Alexr., 885.
" Mrs. Ann, 244.
" Benj., 640-2-4.

Brown, Beriah, 304.
" Catharine, 244.
" Colonel, 205, 351, 581, 694-5-7, 705, 728, 792-3-4, 835-6.
" Danl. Isaac, of N. Jersey, 541.
" David, of Boston, 656, 861.
" Ebenezer, 1049.
" Elizabeth, 924-5.
" Genl., 829.
" George, 244, 887.
" Capt. H., 83.
" Revd. Isaac, of Newark, 688.
" James, of Antigonish, 131.
" James, of S. Carolina, 244.
" Jean, 244.
" John, 722, 997, 1077.
" John, of Georgia, 60.
" John, of N. York, 769.
" John, of Virginia, 512.
" Jonas, of Georgia, 792, 797.
" Jos., 251, 386.
" Josiah, 852.
" Judge, 1147.
" Major, 574, 747-8.
" Malcolm, 191.
" Mary, 238, 1004.
" Mr., 909, 1217.
" Montfort, 1252, 636.
" Peter, 688.
" Dr. Peter, of N. Jersey, 689.
" Col. Saml., 639, 640-2, 720.
" Thomas, of Boston, 39, 164, 726, 1286.
" Lt. Col. Thos., of Georgia, 182, 190-1-2-3, 339, 696, 705-6, 715-27, 792, 797.
" Titus, 792, 813.
" Wm., of Virginia, 66, 512, 633, 635.
" Wm., of Salem, 638.
" Govr. Wm., 127, 130, 209-10-11, 251, 644, 720, 809-10, 829, 1272-3.
" Zachariah, 416.
Browne, Joseph, 258.
Brownson, Capt. Gideon, 577.
" Saml., 1013, 1026.
" Saml., jr., 1031.
" Timothy, 576.
Brownton, Col., 232.
Browster, Joseph, 477-8.
" Margt., 477.
" Martha, 477.
" Mrs. Mary, of Pensilvania, 477.
" Simon, 477.
Bruce, D., of N. Jersey, 427.
" Brigden, 185.
" Major, 764, 1206.
Brucken, Gerard, 100.
Brudenel, Revd. Mr., 584.
Bruen, Major, 588.
Bruff, Margt., 140.
" James Earl, 139, 140.
" Oliver Charles, of N. York, 139.
" Peter Schuyler, 140.
Bruin, David, 530.
Brun (Frigate), 211-12.
Brunson, Saml., 1013.
Brunswick, (U.S.), 111, 296, 741, 837, 1127, 1176, 1207, 1277, 1303-4.

Brunswick, Port of, 1197.
" Town, 1306.
" Township, 1309.
Brum, Major, 92.
Brumford, Joe, 615.
Bruse, Coms., 203.
Brush, Crean, 611, 725.
" Meadow, 231.
Bryant, Needham, 242.
Bryson, John, 176.
" Wm., of S. Carolina, 176.
Buchanan, James, 1312.
Buck, Bun, 1043.
" George, 1259.
" John, of Ulster Co., 992-9.
" Philip, 964, 974.
" Sarah, 1042.
Bucks, County of, 94, 124, 260, 294-6-7, 710, 724, 741-2, 827, 840, 895.
Buffington, Jacob, of Pensilvania, 564-5, 902.
Buis, John, 1261.
" Stephen, 1260.
Bull, Aaron, 836.
" Govr., 677.
" Lt. Govr., 1301.
" Gr., 1245.
" Jacob, of N. York, 871.
Buller, John, 618, 789.
Bullia, James, 890.
Bullee, Simon, 1282.
Bullein, Dr. Nathaniel, of S. Carolina, 180.
Bulleen, Dr. N., 339.
Bullis, John, 534.
Bulyea, Abrm., of N.Y. Prov., 299.
" Henry, of N.Y. Prov., 890
" James, 264-5.
" Joseph, of N.Y. Prov., 891, 264.
" Robert, 265, 891.
Bunekerhoff, Dr., 857.
Bunker Hill, Battle of, 52-5, 113, 610, 656, 660, 934, 1033, 1084, 1111, 1160, 1190, 1198.
Bunton, Capt. J., R.N., 1299.
" Mrs., 1300.
Burash, 891.
Burch, John, 996, 1281.
" Justice, 983, 990.
" Philip, 1001.
Burchs, Mr., 1000, 1102.
Burd, Joseph, 1295.
Burdet, Capt., 229.
" John, 1264.
Burdets Ferry, 262.
Burgoyne, General, 39, 86-8, 328-9, 330-5-6-7-9, 345-6-7, 350-1, 360-2-3-5-6-9, 371-8, 381-6, 388-9, 391-8-9, 400, 414-7-8, 421-3-4-6-8, 432-3-4-7-9, 445-9, 451-2-5-7, 462-6-7-8-9, 474-7-9, 483-4-7, 551, 575-8-9, 658, 662, 762, 816, 865, 870, 896, 900-3, 917, 923-4-7-8, 931-3-9, 940-1-2-3-4, 949, 950-2-3-9, 960, 1002-3-6, 1051, 1065, 1073, 1084, 1090-1, 1101-6-8, 1153, 1182, 1260-5-7-8-9, 1271, 1280.

Burke, Govr. Thomas, 241-2.
" Mr., 1247.
Burler, Col., 961.
Burling, Samuel, of N. York. 137.
Burlington, 71, 298-9, 415, 577, 649, 685.
" County, 787-8.
" Gaol, 307.
" Patent, 331.
Burn, Silvanus, 721.
Burnaby, Sir Wm., 656.
Burnard, Mrs., 1314
Burnes, James, 779.
Burnet, Stephen, 579.
" Township, 47.
" Mr., 533.
Burnham, Ed., 82.
" John, 214.
Burns, Capt., 329, 353-4, 409.
" John, 577.
" Rouse, 505.
Burnside, Alex., 1132.
Burt, Judge Benj., 91-2, 300-1.
" Christr., 205-6.
" Darius, 300.
" David, of Connecticut, 206-7, 301, 892-3.
" Ebenezer, 113.
" Goold, 300.
" Hulday, 300.
" Joseph, 300.
" Mrs. Rebecca, of Connecticut, 300.
" Rebecca, jr., 300.
" Sarah, 300.
" Seaborn, 205, 300.
" Susannah, 301.
Burtis, Mrs. Mary, 807.
Burton, 260, 283, 295, 300-9, 813, 827, 865-7.
" Colonel, 103.
" County, 298.
" John, 251.
" Joseph, 520.
" Township, 816
" Wm., 1139.
Burrell, Sir James, 1306.
Burrett, Stephen, 88.
Burritt, Danl., 1100.
" Stephen, 1100
Burroughs, Mr., 119.
Burry, George, 1143.
Burwick upon Tweed, 474.
Bush, Henry, 1257.
" Mary, 1257.
" Wm., 1288.
Busherville, 924.
Bushton Hill, 457.
Buskertrus, Buskinton or Buskirk, Colonel, 245, 299, 308, 561, 814.
Bust, Nathan, of Cambridge, 60.
Butler, Capt., 1101.
" Colonel, (Butler's Rangers), 331-2, 351-2-3, 392, 458-9, 478, 480, 537, 959, 962-3-5-7, 974, 983, 993-4-6-8, 1000-1, 1262, 1281-5.
" Edmund, of N.Y. Prov., 551, 563.
" Elis, 1305.
" Genl., 96.
" Hannah, 761.
" John, 45-9.
Butler, Joseph, 1305.

Butler, Major; 1127.
Butterfield, Thos., 577.
Butters, Purchase, 856.
Byrne, Capt. Wm., 351-3-4, 410, 473.
Cabin Point, 732.
Cable, And., 140.
" Anthony, 909.
" Danl., 909.
" Jabez, 911.
" James, 909, 911.
" Jane, 909.
" John, jr., 909.
" John, of Connecticut, 909.
" Marianna, 909.
" Mrs. Ann, 909.
" Isaac, 239.
Cabot, Mr., of Salem, 509.
Cadiz, 156.
Cadleton Island, 23.
Cafford, John, of Albany Co., 415.
Cain, John, 216.
" Wm., 888.
Cairn, East, 612.
Calcraft, Col., 1052.
Calder, Govr., 360.
Calder, Janet, 1059.
" Wm., 1059.
Calderhead, Mr., 133.
Caldwell, Capt., 1040.
" Henry, 1359.
" John, 1065.
" Robert, of N.Y. Prov., 329, 336, 1063.
" Wm., of Pensil, 840.
Caldwell's Manor, 456, 462, 467-8, 941, 1119, 1259, 1267, 1268.
Calehan, James, 910.
Calif. Dr. John, 312-16.
Callaghan, James, of Merimichee, 841.
Callahan, Charles, of Massachusetts, 745.
" Mrs. Rebecca, 745.
Calvert, Campbell & Co., 722.
Cambridge, 58, 59, 623, 658, 852, 943, 1182.
" District, 407, 950.
Camden, 155, 185-6, 401-2, 524, 526-7, 646-7, 652, 677, 841, 934-5, 1106, 1131, 1218.
" Battle of, 549.
" District, 34, 159, 718.
Cameron, Alexander, 1092-4.
" Allen, 1261.
" Angus, 1093-8.
" Mrs. Ann, 397.
" Capt., 712.
" Christian, 1081.
" Donald, 1097.
" Duncan, of New York, 940.
" John, of N.Y. Prov., 86, 357-8, 394-7, 1057-9, 1255, 1333.
" Mr., 1130
" Miss, 175.
" William, of N.Y. Prov., 374.
" " of N. Jersey, 400-9, 1120.
Camp, Abiather, of Newhaven, 80, 284-5, 1333.
Campbell, Alexander, 926-7, 1285.
" Alex., of N.Y. Prov., 359, 361, 401, 481-2.
" Major Allen, 926-7.

INDEX. 1387

Campbell, Archd. & Co., 133.
" Arch., 401.
" Capt. Archd., 313.
" Lt.-Col. Archd., 695, 727, 914.
" Dr. Archd., of Virginia, 131, 646.
" Genl. Archd., 326.
" Brig.-Major, 119.
" Catherine, 926.
" Lt. Colin, 306.
" Col., 60, 163, 170-1, 248, 463, 527, 700, 833, 1071, 1094-5.
" Daniel, 30, 396, 453.
" Dugald, of Albany Co., 144.
" Duncan, of N.Y. Prov., 414, 482.
" Mrs. Elizabeth, 926.
" Genl., 28, 109, 585, 715, 1232, 1273.
" Govr., 326, 663.
" Gr., 183.
" Hogg &, 54.
" Isabell, 926.
" James, 926-7, 1084.
" Major James, 711.
" John, 926.
" Brig.-Genl. John, 59, 306.
" Col. John, 926.
" Lt. John, 306.
" Moses, of N. York, 926.
" Mr., 1102-4.
" Capt. Peter. of N. Jersey, 250, 832.
" Col. Saml., of Wilmington, 54, 160.
" Sarah, 250.
" Thomas, 250, 833.
" William, 57, 125, 1244.
" Lord Wm., 799, 1223.
Campbell's Bush, 462.
Campeau, Thomas, 701.
Campo Bello, 900-1-8.
Campton township, 915.
Camtuch, 728.
Canfield, Saml., 202.
Canless, Thos., 252.
Canno, Joseph, 1134.
Canoe Brook, 64.
Canso, Gut of, 582.
" (Ship), 172-3, 272, 831.
Cape Breton, 11, 85, 106, 188, 734, 1357.
Cape Fear, 1230-1.
" Fort at, 54.
" River, 44, 50, 736, 1207.
" Fern, 652.
" Francois, 1223.
Capon, Hopestill, 569.
Carden, Major, 829.
Carey, Col. James, of S. Carolina, 646, 652, 678.
Carl, Thomas, 831.
Carles, Griffin, 195.
" Thomas, 246.
Carleton, 238, 244, 267, 904.
" Colonel, 329.

Carleton, Genl., 346, 400, 425, 447, 450-6.
" Govr., 349.
Carleton, Sir Guy, 35, 58, 68, 80, 95, 180, 155, 166, 248, 490, 518, 574, 620, 654, 655, 763, 785, 789, 799, 803, 843, 865, 889, 901, 917-8-9, 1153, 1206, 1232, 1258.
" Island, 386, 394, 409, 423, 431, 436, 442-3, 450, 470, 953, 1027, 1030, 1065, 1096-7-8, 1103, 1267.
" Major, 388, 432, 947, 1029, 1267.
Carley, Bartholamew, 1090, 1104.
Carlisle, 832.
" Bay, 332-3-5-6-7.
Carlow, Peter, 1258.
Carman, Michael, of N.Y. Prov., 410-2.
" Michael, senr., 411.
" Michael, of N. York, 956.
" Saml., 596.
Carns, Jacob, 477.
Carpenter, Archilaus, 880, 884-8, 1320.
" Cons., 881.
" Jacob, 880.
" Jas., 195.
Carron Hall, 24, 1326.
Carscallen, Edward, 1023-28.
Carson, Jas., of S. Carolina, 1302, 1305.
" Mr., 1301.
" Thos., 1281.
" Wm., 658.
Cartant, Lord, 1243.
Carter, James, of S. Carolina, 694.
" Mr., 1234.
Carter's Hook, 863.
Cartwright, Mr., 86, 357-8.
" Richard, 1001.
Cartwright's Patent, 1059.
Carwen, Saml., 1148.
Carvie, Ross, 885.
Cary, Jas., 187.
Casamur, Silvanus, 440.
Casamure, Soveraines, 441.
Casco Bay, 172-3, 272, 304, 904, 919.
Caskeat Patent, 883.
Cass, Josiah, of N.Y. Prov., 328.
Cassas, 1301-3.
Casselman, Warner, of N.Y. Prov., 454.
" William, 454.
Castle, Abel, 438.
" David, 913.
" William, 56.
Castles, Wm., of Albany, 654-8.
Castleton, 1259.
Caswell, Lemmuel, 399, 1090.
Cataraqui, 13, 254, 368, 402, 414, 420-3, 431-4-6-7, 447, 451-2-3, 466, 470, 474, 480, 950, 1001-5-6-7, 1021-6-8, 1032-5-8-9, 1047, 1072-3, 1080, 1095, 1104, 1116, 1258, 1260-1-2-4-5, 1271, 1280, 1323, 1358.
Catawba River, 44.
Catch, Robert, 774.
Catchum, Jonathan, 812.
" Samuel, 812.
Catharine (Brigantine), 156-7.
Cathcart, Lidia, 670.
Cat Island, 1289.

Catline, Mr., 219.
Caven, Jacob, of N.Y. Prov., 397.
Cawash, 1269.
Cayley, Mr., 1241
Cayton, Capt., 929.
Cedar Hill, 1307.
" Mountain, 205.
Chace, Geo., 302.
" James, of Massachusetts Bay, 302.
Chadobachto, 152.
Chadwick, E. M., K. C., 25.
Chaleur, Bay of, 152, 330-1-6-7-8, 344-5-9, 350-1, 923, 1063.
Chalmers, Lt.-Col. James, 174, 1164-5-6.
" George, 1225, 1250.
" Gilbert, 1198.
" Mrs., 1164-5-6.
Chamber St., N.Y., 429.
Chamberlain, Theophelus, 717.
Chamberlin, Lewis, 136.
Chambers, Col., 535-6.
Chambers Town, 535-6-7.
Chamblee, Port, 940.
Chambly, 345, 1063, 1267.
Chamin (or Chamire), Mr., 1220, 1304.
Champion Dickerson, 1373-5.
Champlain, Lake, 29, 89, 91, 152, 329, 349, 359, 364, 378, 385-8, 394, 399, 405, 409, 417, 436, 475-7-8, 450, 467, 470, 482-3, 918, 926, 936, 940, 941, 1277.
Champnay, Ebenezer, 464.
Chandler, Dr., 53.
" Eliz., 310.
" Jas., 565.
" John, of Connecticut, 310-11, 785.
" Col. John, 1217.
" Jos., of Connecticut, 310.
" Jos., of Newhaven, 286.
" Mary, of N.S., 310
" Mr., 287.
" Col. Thomas, 91.
" Thomas, of N.B., 310, 857.
" Wm., 310, 587.
Chapel Plantation, 1150.
Chapman, Thos., 258.
Charles, Capt. in R.N., 1289.
" Creek, 1144.
" Point, 492.
Charlestown, 51-2-4, 61-3, 96, 143-4, 155-6-8-9, 160-2-8, 170-4-5-6, 180-1-2-5-7, 193, 241-2-4-8, 259, 266, 280, 513, 524-5-6-7, 535, 548, 558, 618-9, 657-8, 662, 674-5-6-7-8-9, 680-7-8, 692-3-4-5, 700, 702-3-6, 707-8-9, 711, 714, 719, 728-9, 730-2-3-4, 792-3, 800, 833, 841, 849, 862, 885, 900, 914, 1131-4, 1164, 1187, 1197-8-9, 1200-1-2-3-4-5-6-10, 1136, 1214-5-8, 1223-4-8, 1230, 1245-6-7-8, 1251-2, 1290-1.
" Barr, 1133.
" Seige of, 164.
Charlotborough, 263.

Charlotte, 857-8.
Charlotte Co., 45, 328-9, 347-8, 350, 362-9, 377, 383-8, 398, 400-1-5-6-8, 421, 433-6 447-8, 466, 469, 470, 475, 534, 865, 934, 1004, 1012, 1020, 1023-5-7, 1030-4-6, 1044, 1063, 1078, 1080-4-9, 1090-1, 1104-6-7 1266, 1271.
Charlotte Precinct, 882, 883.
Charlotte River, 86, 958.
Charlottenburgh, 486.
Charlton, 642-5, 1359, 1360.
Charlton, Richard, 126.
Charming Polly, (Brig), 159.
Chart. Gen., 1169.
Chartres, Geo., 1034.
Chase, Reuben, of N. York, 817.
Chatham, 83, 198, 241, 711.
" Township, 82.
Chattenden, Govr., 435.
Chatterton, S., of Chaleur, 331.
Chaucer, Alexr., 425-6.
Chauncey, Charles, 786.
Chauncys, Jos., 311.
Cheat River, 55.
Cheery, Sarah, 990.
Cherokee Country, 727.
" Nation, 800-1, 191-3, 1131.
Cherry Valley, 392, 454-5, 475-6, 996-7, 1002, 1065, 1255.
Chesacook Patent, 749.
Chesapeake, 218, 565, 1168.
Chesapeakes, 154.
Cheshire Co., 616, 820, 821.
Chester, 504, 1164-5.
" Adam, 958.
" County, 123-4-5, 494, 511, 564-5, 611, 901, 902, 904, 1072.
" East, 146, 300, 499, 502, 553-4, 722-3-4, 743-4-5, 761.
" West, 261-4-6, 281-8-9, 497-8, 500, 538, 567, 571, 593, 680-1, 698, 723, 755-6-8-9, 779, 780-3, 789, 791, 811-13, 819, 820-2, 874, 1276, 1295.
Chestnut St., Philadelphia, 833.
Chestnut's Land, 202.
Chew, Joseph, 1294.
Chilson, B., 425.
Chiltenham, 124.
Chime, Joseph, 1273.
Chimney Point, 447.
Chisholm, Alex., of N.Y. Prov., 345, 378.
" Hugh, of Tryon Co., 379.
" John, of S. Carolina, 326, 977-9, 994, 1092.
Chitabucto, 499.
Chisencook, 715.
Chisholm, Wm., 1333.
Chittenden, Govr. Thomas, 438, 460, 484, 576-7, 954, 1015, 1100, 1271.
Christ Church, Middleton, 131.
" Parish, 296, 341, 1133.
Christie, Abijah, 1021.
" Brit. Commissary, 93.
" George, of N.Y. Prov., 479.
" James, 137-8, 1250.
" Commissary, 626.
Christy, John, 1261.

Church, Capt., 47.
" Street, Norfolk, 132.
Churton, William, 44-6-8-9, 50.
Chyler, Henry, 602-3-5.
City Island, 515.
Claments Township, 544.
Clap, Elisha, 311.
Clap, Danl., 879.
Clapp, Thos., 777.
Clarence, Duke of, 23.
Clarendon, 460, 1259, 1260.
Clark, Abel, 1208.
" Abraham, 117.
" Adam, 453.
" Alexander, 1320.
" Charles, 163.
" Francis, 1064-5.
" Genl., 1126.
" G., 1298.
" Isaac, 940.
" Jas., of Rhode Island, 52.
" John, 163.
" Major, 847.
" & Milligen, 1128.
" Mr., 1302.
" Robert, 159.
" Roger, 1264.
" Simon, 1073.
" Lt. Gov., 647.
" Nehemiah, of Connecticut, 835.
" Sherman, 104.
Clarke, Gen., 1137.
" George, 358.
" James, of N.Y. Prov., 105, 369.
" Dr. Joseph, of Connecticut, 251-8, 1095.
" Rev. Mr., 1248-9.
" Mrs., 1096.
" Nehemiah, 252.
" Thos., 329.
" Wm., 304, 1288.
" Brig.-Genl., 695.
" Dr., 924.
" Francis Rush, 752.
" Hugh, of N. York, 662.
" Lacon, 643.
" Robert, of N.Y. Prov., 474.
" Saml., 785.
" Simon. of N.Y. Prov., 471-3.
Clarkson, David, 902.
Claus, Colonel, 346, 418, 423-4, 471, 480, 959.
" John, 971.
Claverock, 423, 452, 942.
Clavinook, 1034.
Claw, Johannes W., 364.
" John W., of N.Y. Prov., 363.
" Peter, 363.
Clay, Chas., 77.
Clayborne, James, 460.
Clayborne James 1084.
Clear, Point, 383.
Clemant, Wm., 323.
Clement, Eliza, 977.
" Joseph, 965-6, 977.
" Lewis, 977.
Clements, 534.
" Capt., 883, 903.

Clements, Precinct, 747.
Clementson & Denton, 741.
Clenck, Mr., 904.
Clendenning, James, 975.
Cleveland, Genl., 885.
Clifford, Thos., 1174.
Cline, Eliz., 1028.
" John, 1028.
" Michael. of N.Y. Prov., 408.
" Mr., 1267.
Clinton, 56.
" Gebr., 185.
" Genl., 544, 767, 1197.
" George, 1318.
" Lord, 901.
" Sir Henry, 51-2-3, 61, 95, 130, 163. 185, 191, 208, 221, 253, 272, 307, 314, 347, 548, 555, 652, 728, 787, 788, 803, 843, 873, 901, 904, 1130-3, 1150, 1163-4, 1191, 1220-1, 1238, 1243-7-9, 1258.
Clobeck District, 1006-7.
Close, Abraham, 1049.
" Benj., 830.
Closson, Caleb, 1089, 1091.
Clough, Jos., 721.
Clow, Henry, of N.Y. Prov., 414.
Cloyne, Adam, 481.
Co Valdt, Abrm., 247.
Coater, Cor., 1012.
Cobb, Saml., 905.
Cobblegate Mountain, 776-9, 780-2.
Cobers Kiss, 962.
Cobham, Dr., 653.
Cobus Conk, 997.
" Kill, 971.
" Kite, 395.
Cochrane, Capt. John, of N. Hampshire, 620, 831, 849.
" Hon. Mr., 33.
" James, 637.
" John. 249, 637, 678.
" Jonathan, 1305.
" Mr., 448.
" Mrs. Sarah, 831.
" T. J. & W., 1333
Cockburn, Adam, 1291.
" Wm., 1101.
Cockermouth, 510-17.
Cockspur, 1306.
Codwin, Richd., 273.
Codwis, George, 207.
Coe, Benj., 313.
" Capt., 233.
" John, 84.
" Judge, 883.
" Thomas, 255-6, 315.
Coffee Town Creek. 259.
Coffin, John, of Boston, 243, 921.
" Dr. Nathan, 276.
" Wm., 1050.
Coke, 20.
" Daniel Parker, 14, 508, 1140, 1148. 1156, 1160, 1185-9, 1202-8, 1316.
Colchester, 639, 640, 721.
Colden, Alexr., 31, 940-1, 1071.
Colden, Alice, 858.
" Cadwallader, 259, 821, 855-7-9.

Colden, Cadwallader, Senr., 856-7-9.
" Catharine, 858.
" David, 857, 855-6-8, 860, 878.
" Eliz. Ann, 858.
" Lt.-Govr., 855, 1167.
" Colden, Mary, 858.
" Mrs., 878.
" Richd., 580.
Cole, Simon, of N.Y. Prov., 465.
Coleman, Robert, 184.
Colepit Hill, 716.
Colier, Sir George, 632.
Collenger, Christr., 432.
" Sarah, 431.
Collet, Govr., 1207.
Collin, George, 492.
Collins, Mrs. Ann, 82.
" Capt., 933, 1140-1.
" Clement, 1160.
" James, of N. Jersey, 93, 142, 572-4.
" Gov. John, 303.
" John, 1050.
Colquhoun, Sir James, 663.
Colter, John, 363.
Colthurst, Mr., 1171.
Colton, C., 1250.
" Col. James, 236.
Colvertt, Capt., 1000.
Colwell, Capt., 833.
Comb (or Combe), William, 44.
Comerelle, Frances, 1223.
Commander, Thos., of S. Carolina, 164.
Commerce (Sloop), 482, 862-6.
Compton, John, of N. Jersey, 904.
Conajohary, 475.
Conally, Lieut., 1069.
Concklin, Abraham, of Saratoga, 467.
Concord Gaol, 464, 754.
Condet, Thomas, 985.
Congaree, 33-4, 525.
Conger, Col., 63, 184-5, 398, 525, 699, 700, 702, 793, 1218.
Conkie, Israel, 96, 114.
Conklin, Jos., 1018.
" John, 1261.
Conkright, Abraham, 1033.
" Hercules, 1026.
Conly, Thos., 250, 833.
Connascreek, 628.
Connecticut River, 89, 350, 588, 617, 641, 739, 1272.
Connell, Hugh, of N.Y. Prov., 454.
Connolly, Lt.-Col., 478.
" Ense., 454.
" John, 375.
Connor, Constant, of Boston, 40.
" John, 230.
" Michael, 330.
Connos Creek, 633.
Conogharie, 1010.
Conojohay, 453-4.
Conolly, Lt.-Col., 1144.
" Col., 1145-6, 1151.
" John, 1082.
Conqueror (ship), 229.
Conrad, John, 123.
Cons Schohary, 420-1.

Conterman, Jacob, of N.Y. Prov., 402.
Conway, 220, 247, 1322.
Cook, Chas., 311.
" John, 1120.
" Joseph, 717.
" Mr., 34, 474.
" Philip, 1052.
" Wm., 249.
" Zedicia, of Connecticut, 825.
Cooke, Chas., 138.
" John, 45.
" Jos., 282.
" Samuel, 82.
Cookes Right, 1311.
Cooks Boro, 1048.
" Michl., 1048.
Cooksbury, 433.
Cooley, Mr., 113.
Coomb, Abraham, 286.
Coombs, Dennis, 1320.
" John, 352.
" Mr., 1148.
Coon, John, 962.
Coons, John, of N.Y. Prov., 353..
Cooper, Ann, 1229.
" Dr., 53, 1274.
" Farm, 739.
" Sir Guy (or Gray), 762, 1231.
" John, 428.
" Lancelot, 295.
" Mr., 1214-5.
" Rev. Robt., 1214, 1228-30.
Cooper's Ferry, 567, 1292.
Coovert, Abraham, 235.
Coppendoch, 706.
Corbet, Mr., 44.
Corbyn, Mrs., 925.
Corell, Capt., 951.
Corinth, 328, 916.
Cormick, Stephen, 250.
Cornelius, John, 1039.
Cornell, Albert, of N. Jersey, 430.
" Saml., 856.
Cornhill, 1216-7.
Cornwall, 376.
" James, 82.
" George, 108.
" Lewis, 878.
" Robt., 663-4.
" Township, 393-4, 426.
Cornwallis, 22, 172-3, 188, 308.
" Earl, 803, 1234.
" Fort, 696-7, 704-6.
" Lord, 22, 43, 77-8, 96, 126, 135, 155, 164, 186-7, 191-2, 241-5, 254-5-6, 280, 308, 526, 537, 554, 561-2-5-6, 574, 617-8-9, 626, 632, 646-7, 648, 657, 677, 689, 691-2, 710-11, 718-9, 722, 732, 802, 810, 814, 842, 869, 885, 894, 908, 1131, 1169, 1176-8, 1187, 1214-8, 1226, 1232, 1246-8, 1250, 1275, 1312-13.
Cornwell, Geo., of N.Y. Prov., 538.
Cornwell, Saml., of N. York, 795-6.
Cornyn, Thos., 994.

Corry, Catharine, 434.
" George, 434.
" Gilbert, 874-6.
" Griffyn, of N. York, 874-6.
" James, of N.Y. Prov.
" John, 434, 874.
" Lewis, 874.
" Mrs. Margt., 434.
" Morris, 874.
" Oliver, 91.
" Sarah, 434.
" Mrs. Sarah, 874-6.
" Silvaneus, 876.
" Thos., 874-6.
Costigan, Francis, 92.
Coteau du Lac, 356, 364-9, 370, 404-5, 411-5, 459, 1030, 1054, 1062-4-7, 1093, 1255, 1262-3.
Cotter, James, 1021.
Cottle, Jas., 331.
Cottinger, Michael, 1118.
Cotton, Col., 168, 277.
" Seth 114.
Coty Dam Creek, 841.
Coulson, Mr., 1214-5.
Coulter, Andr., of N.Y. Prov., 336.
Council, John Temple, 594.
Counter, Jacob, 844.
Country Harbour, 677.
County Harbour, 33.
Courtland, John, 228.
" Nathl., 1072.
" Philip, 100, 1237.
" Col. Stephen, 1234.
Courtland's Manor, 216, 228-9, 230, 264, 285, 299, 301-2, 321, 514-6, 698-9, 766-8, 783-4, 795, 874-6, 888-9, 891-2-3-7-8, 1234-7-8, 1244.
Court St., Portsmouth, 66.
Courtwright's Patent, 662.
Courtwright Township, 85-6.
Courwins, Saml., 867.
Cousins, Capt. Danl., 1295.
" James, 213.
Couvert, Abrm., 322.
Covell, Capt. Simeon, 485, 954 1051
Coventry, Earl of, 1350.
" Harbour, 674.
Coverley, Anthony, 920.
Covert, Abraham, of N. York, 766, 771, 784, 796.
" Isaac, 783.
Cowell, Ebenezer, 976.
Cowgill, Capt. John, of N. Jersey, 227.
Cow Pens, 718.
Cowoother Plantation, 1305-8.
Cowper, Mr., 886.
" W., 642.
Cowperthwaite, Hugh, of Jersey, 824
Cox, Danl., 68, 518, 932, 1235, 1288.
" Farm, 739.
" James, 136.
" John, of N. Jersey, 615, 929.
" Saml., 959.
" Thos. Ashton, 929.
Cozens, Capt., 929.
Cozin, Walter, 177.
Crafte, Thos., 569.

Craig, Col., 54.
" Isaac, 932.
" James, of Massachusetts, 588.
" Major James Henry, 96, 241-2-4, 549, 1250.
Craigie, John, 344.
" Mr., 485, 1359.
Cranch, Richd., 470-2.
Crane, Jeremiah, 531.
" Nicholas, of S. Carolina, 156-8, 675.
" Stephen, 140.
Crank, William, 719.
Cranke, Abraham, 261.
Crannell, Bartholomew, of N. York, 234, 842-6.
Cransut, Barth., 636.
Crantwell, Philip, 158.
Craven Co., 326, 647, 1187, 1210, 1223-4-9.
Crawford, Archibald, 813.
" Capt. Edward, of Georgia, 28-9, 714.
" Colonel, (rebel) 97.
" James, of N. York, 138, 791, 813.
" John, of N. York, 139, 791, 813.
" " senr., 791.
" Mrs. Margaret, 138.
" Martha, 139.
" Robt., 813, 1104.
" Thos., 139.
" W. R., 1261.
" Wm., 690.
Crayderman, Catherine, 1109.
" Joseph, 1110-1.
" Valentine, 1109-10.
Creek Nation, 800.
Cregg, John, 95.
Crepot, 1301.
Cresler, Adam, 978.
" Baltiza, 962.
" H., 961-2.
Crine, Peter, 33-4.
Crisdale, John, 433.
Crislor, Philip, 1056.
Cristy, John, 1118.
Crockar, Col. George, 295.
Crocker, Josiah, 664.
Crocketts, 1310.
Croft, Mr., 348.
Croghan, Col. George, 858, 1173, 1282.
Croghan's, Col., Patent, 857.
Cromilin, Charles, 267.
Crosby (or Crosbie), Col., 51, 798.
" Benjamin, 815.
Crosley, Moses, 708.
Cross Creek, 97, 235, 338, 1251, 1313.
Cross, Henry, of N. Y. Prov., 437, 448.
" John, of Vermont, 1269.
" Michael, 1005.
Crossfield, Stephen, 47.
Crossle, Philip, 352.
Crossny, Hendrick, 856.
Crosswick, 71.
Crouch, Geo., 869.
Crous., Peter, of N. Y. Prov., 409.
Crouther, Isaac, 1033.
Crow, Elizabeth, 204.

Crow, Isaac D., 249.
" Samuel, 204.
Crowder, James, 1112-3.
" Wm., of N. Y. Prov., 470.
" " jr., 471.
Crowe, Eyre Evans, 1277-8.
" Richd. Robt., of N. Jersey. 1276.
Crowell, Capt. Joseph, of N. Jersey, 227, 596, 603.
" Thos., 119.
Crowfoot, Elohu, 1321.
" John, 1321.
Crown Point, 50, 332-7, 345-9, 369. 400-1-5, 434, 447, 450, 926-7, 934-5, 949, 1023-7, 1280.
Crowson, Abraham, of Saratoga, 487.
Cruden, Mr., 794.
Cruikshank, Alexander, of N. York, 927.
" Ann, 927.
" Mrs. Catherina, 927-9.
" Elizabeth, 927.
" Sarah, 927.
Crysdale, John, of N. Y. Prov., 433.
Crysler, Adam, 961.
" John, of N. Y. Prov., 481.
Cuffe (or Cuffy), Town Creek, 158-9, 170-1.
Cuffy Town Waters, 841-2.
" Waters of, 62.
Cullachy, 1068.
Cullen, Wm., 926.
Culler, Samuel, 582.
Culter, Ebenezer, of Massachusetts Bay, 1285.
" Elisha, 1286.
" Jonas, 1286.
" Zaccheus, 1286.
Cumberland, 150, 213, 295, 568, 763-5-6-7, 770-4-7-9, 781-3-4-9, 790-5, 842, 857-8, 1276.
" Bay, 11.
" County, 150, 272-4-5, 535-7, 611, 708, 932-3, 1277.
" St., Norfolk, 123.
Cumming, Alex., of S. Carolina, 1290.
" Thomas, 276, 1000.
" Wm., 44.
Cunliff, Joseph, 256.
Cunningham, Archd., 139, 655-8.
" Capt., 585.
" Brig.-Genl., 157-8, 168-9, 170-1, 183-4-5, 191, 276, 676, 680, 692-3-4, 701-9, 727, 792, 841.
" & Grey, 1241.
" Mr., 696.
" Patrick, 800.
" Rachel, of N. S., 283.
" Robt., 680, 718.
Curless, Wm., 307.
Curry, Joseph, of Courtland's Manor, 285.
Curry's Bush, 482.
Curtis, Elnathan, 867.
" James, 214.
" John, of Vermont, 318. 1268.
" Thomas, 343.
" Walter, 343.
" Wm., 208-9.
Curtmens, Peter, 806.
Custard, Joseph, 297.

Custer, Adam, 997.
Cutter, Amey Rohame, 508.
Cuyler, Abraham, 106, 347, 575.
" Alida, 1274.
" Barnt, 1274.
" Col., 344, 443, 453, 654-5.
" De Lancey &, 136.
" Hannah, 274.
" Henry, 137, 1091, 1274-6.
" Henry, jr., 1274.
" Hester, 1275.
" Mary, 1274.
" Mr., 214, 374, 386.
Cuzler, Richd., 288.
Cypher, Mr., 289.

Dafoe, Abraham, 417, 1011-12.
" Conrad, 417.
" Daniel, 417.
" John, of N. Y. Prov., 417, 425.
" John, senr., 417.
" Mrs. Mary, 417.
" Michael, 417.
Dagrell, Wm., 1240.
Dalchreggen, 1096.
Dale, Robt., of N. York, 625.
Dales, Francis, 46.
Daly, Mrs., Ebenezer, 1321.
Damascus Patent, 122.
" Suburbs of, 124.
Damnation Alley, 1241, 1244.
Damsell, (sloop), 198.
Dan, Selick, 816.
Danburgh, 226.
Danbury, 231, 282-3-4, 300, 716-7, 821, 838, 850-1, 909, 915.
Daniels, Timothy, 769, 1320.
Danks, Shadrack, 577.
Dann, Saml., 464.
Darby, Capt., 1073.
" Jas., 1251, 1333.
Dare, Thomas, 1184-5.
Darlinch, 395.
Darling, Joseph, 252.
Dartmouth, 50, 700, 716.
" County, 517.
" Lord, 630, 1167.
Davenport, Col., 1195.
" John, 571.
" Saml., of N. Y. Prov., 571.
David, Capt., 1281.
Davidson, John, 80.
Davies, Benj., 833.
" Randal, 753.
Davis, Andr., 45.
" Benj., of Boston, 637.
" Danl., 640.
" Eli., 47.
" Geo., 124-5.
" John, 1218.
" Mr., 768.
" Wm., 804, 1213.
Dawes, Thos., 569.
Dawkins, Capt. George, of S. Carolina, 33, 156-8, 674-5-7.
" George, senr., 34.
" & MacKay, 242.
Dawson, Capt., 589.
" Mr., 499.

Day, John, 1321.
" Peter, 262.
Dayrich, Philip, 938.
Deabury, David, of N. York, 547.
Deal, Adam, 1080.
Dean, Hugh, of Maryland, 173, 697.
" Joseph, 214.
" Peter, 1136.
" Saml., 590.
Deans, Mr., 1138.
" Mrs., 1137-8.
Dearle, Mr., 1240.
Debby, (sloop), 873.
De Blois, George, of Newbury Port, 40.
" " of Salem, 491.
" " jr., of Port Massachusetts, 492-3.
" Gilbert, 492.
" Lewis, of Boston, 273, 492-3.
" Stephen, 492.
Debois, P., 329.
De Cene, 1305.
De Chazeau, Adam, of Boston, 38.
De Chine, 1044.
De Cow, Ann, 298.
" Isaac, 298.
" 298.
Dedham, 570-1, 1248.
D'Endi, Mrs. Penelope, 1226.
Deep Brook Lott, 1310.
Deep Creek, 102.
Deer, Jno., 127.
Deerfield, 112-3-5, 219, 220.
Deers Island, 306.
D'Estaing, 109.
D'Eslaing, Comte, 1310.
Defiance, (sloop), 906.
De Foe, Abrm., 1011-12.
Defoe, John, 1256.
De Forest, Ephraim, 226.
De Gorma, Jacob, 775.
De Herster, Gen., 167.
Delancey, Col., 229, 262-5, 289, 300-1, 755, 764-5-6-7-8-9, 770-1-4-5-6-7-8, 779, 780-1-2-3-4, 789, 790-1-5, 807-11, 822-5, 870-1, 881-8-9, 897, 1008, 1276, 1323.
" Danl., 652.
" Elizabeth, 858,
" Genl., 98, 211, 263-7, 301, 502, 1174, 1241-2-3, 1314.
" James, 453, 500-1, 545, 668-9, 744, 870, 1295-6.
" Col. James, 101, 141, 166, 571-2, 723-4, 758-9, 1318-9.
" John, 140, 1046.
" Mr., 429.
" Mrs., 546.
" Brig.-Genl. Oliver, 137, 347, 600-2-3-5, 698, 1240-1, 1275, 1318.
" Peter, 546.
" Stephen, 346, 424, 450, 744, 1269.
" & Cuyler, 136.
Delaney, And., 140.
" Andr. Blanchard, 140.
Delap, William, 537.

Delaware Co., 21, 35, 521, 992, 1040, 1101-2-8, 1162-5, 1175-7, 1180, 1256-7.
" Indians, 1281-4.
" River, 249, 356-8, 403, 427, 458-9, 477, 492, 519, 613-5, 824, 902, 929, 1067-8, 1277, 1280.
" West Branch, 337.
De Lery, Jos. G. C., 1359.
Dellenback, Henry, 1268.
Delwinny, Oliver, 329.
Demarest, Joannes, 544.
Demasine (or Demaine), Wm., 254, 315, 1294.
Demerery, 723, 761.
Demery, Capt., 1127.
Demill, Dr. Peter, of Connecticut, 199.
Demming, Eli, 577.
" John, 39.
De Montford, John, 1175.
Dempster, Mr., 1315-6.
Dennis, Robert, 520.
Denny, John, 1216.
De Normandy, John, 1175.
Dent, Adam, 387.
Denton, Clementson &, 741.
" Gilbert, 821.
Depue, John, 998.
De Peyster, Lt.-Col., 477, 957, 986.
Derbage, George, 193, 1128.
Derby, 349, 350.
" Elias Heskel, 721.
" James, 721.
Derington, John, 1333.
Derry, 389.
" James, of N. York, 1276.
" John, " " 1276.
Desbarres, Govr., 85, 188, 915.
Desbrosses, James, 116.
Des Brousses, Elias, 333-5.
Despard, Major, 732.
De Stacey, 1136.
Detlor, Peter, 1024.
" Valentine, 1024-7-8.
Detroit, 453, 477-8, 959, 985-7, 994-5-6, 1082, 1282-4.
Detters, Lewis, 906.
Devagne, Mr., 401.
Devaux, Andrew, 1215.
DeVaznes, Mr., 408.
De Veber, J. P., 889.
Devoe, Frederick, 540.
Devonshire (man-of-war), 504.
De Vow, Danl., 285.
Dewar, Wm., 347, 377.
DeWitt, Garton, of N. Y. Prov., 458.
Diamond, Jacob, 1031-7.
Dibble, Danl., 283, 717.
" Ezra, 283, 717.
" Jonathan, 215.
Dickens, Andrew, 837.
" James, 765.
Dickenson, Deacon, 220.
" Elias, 90.
" Gilbert, 815-6-7-9.
" Hannah, 218.
" Henry, 217.
" James, 115, 815.

88 AR.

Dickenson, Joel, 113
" Jonathan, 99.
" Mr., 84, 335, 1168, 1234.
" Nathaniel, 112, 218.
" Samuel, of N. York, 114, 218, 220, 815, 817.
Dickerson, Champion &, 1373-5.
Dickman, James, 600.
Dickson, Jos., of Connecticut, 847.
" Nathanl., 852.
" Robert, 745.
Dies, Ezra L'homme, 595.
Digby, 43, 68, 95, 216, 540-7, 565, 587, 600, 615-6, 754-5-7, 765, 879, 880.
" Admiral, 127, 585.
Dilworth, James, 305.
Dimker, Henry, 614.
Dingman, Garnet, 1038-9.
" Groddus, 1041.
" Richard, of N. Y. Prov., 471.
Dingwell, John, 1088.
" John, 1088.
Dinquy, Solomon, 876.
Diver Pond, 183.
Dixon, John, of N. Y. Prov., 108, 455.
" Robert, 1255.
Dixon's Mill, 241.
Dobson, Isaac, 980-9.
Dockwrays Patent, 1275.
Dr. France, Land called, 124.
Dodds, Jonathan, 530.
Dodge, Thos., 862.
" Wm., 464.
Dogherty, John, 405.
Dolana, Thos., 453.
Dole, Jas., 315.
Dolier, Pierre, of N. Jersey, 429, 430.
Dolphin, (schooner), 52, 862-3.
Dommet, Rev. Joseph, 221.
Dominica, 195, 746, 863.
Donaldson, Saml., 1290-6.
" William, of Virginia, 194, 731.
Dongan, Magdalin, 115.
" Thos., 115.
Dorchester, 506, 510-17, 617, 692-3, 849.
" Benjn., 287-8.
" Lord, 13, 23, 345, 405, 1063.
Dorington, John, of N. York, 886.
Dorlay, Mr., 1298.
Dorlock, New, 481.
Dorset, 576-7.
" Manc., 1050.
Doty, Rev. John, 361, 1153.
Doughty, Robt., 857.
Douglas, Benj., 785.
" Lt.-Col. John, 28, 60, 164, 715.
" Mr., 310.
" Saml., 464.
" Wm., 81.
Douke, Peter, 820.
Dove, John, 1320.
Dover, 213.
Dowd, Comm., 1313.
Dowery, Mr., 1312.
Down, Abraham, 1021.
Downey, John, 145.
" Roger, 474.
Downing, John, 721.

88a AR.

Downs, Thos., 145.
Doyle, Col., 732.
" Major, 170, 1187.
Drake, Jeremiah, 321.
" Mrs., 504.
" Wm., 76, 820.
Draper, Sir Wm., 1242.
Draten, Col., 970.
Dressler, Andr., 402.
Dringworth, Henry, 648.
Drowning Creek, 235.
Drummond, Capt., 1031.
" Lord, 603.
" Major, 627.
Drumvaich, 1115.
Dry Creek, 582.
Duane, Jas., of N. York, 100, 160, 515-6.
" Joannes, 496.
" Mr., 1024.
Duanes Bush, 1067.
Duayne, Lawer., 1106.
Du Bois, Isaac, 1333.
" Petro, 495.
Du Chene, 1050.
Ducke, Jacob, 932.
Ducker, David, 572.
Dudley, family of, 638.
Duff & Walsh, 157.
Dulmage, John, 402, 1107.
Dumayne (Demaine or Demasine), Wm., of N. Jersey, 254, 315, 1294.
Dun, Capt., 872.
Dunbar, Issa, 751.
" Major, 379.
" Mr., 1241.
Dunbarton Township, 271.
Duncan, G., 281.
" John, 360, 475-6, 481.
" Mr., 40, 1267.
" Capt. Richd., of N. Y. Prov., 352, 359, 378, 383, 395-6, 402, 427, 474, 481, 847, 1099, 1257.
Duncanson, Capt., 663.
Dundas, 20-1.
" Major A., 1091.
" Col., 77, 180, 495, 585, 634-8, 919, 1324, 1333.
" H. C., 127.
" Col. Thomas, 14, 1336, 1351-8, 1362-4-6-7, 1370-3-4-5-6.
Dunham, Aaron, of N. Jersey, 79, 80, 112-6-7-9, 136, 142, 150, 180, 228, 251, 270-8, 320, 351, 558, 560-2, 598, 618, 620-9, 688, 692, 708, 712, 725, 825, 837-8, 895, 926, 930, 1273, 1295.
" Lieut. Asher, 538.
" Wm., 126.
Dunken, Henry, 1174.
Dunlap, Capt., 336.
" Creek, 933.
" John, 123-5.
Dunmore, 857-8.
" Lord, 55, 65-7, 131-2-3, 447, 535, 630-2-3-4-5, 657-8, 666-8, 720, 731-2-3, 986, 1082, 1144-5-6-9, 1150-1-2, 1162, 1188-9, 1226-7.

INDEX. 1395

Dunn, James, 732.
Dunning's Neck, 732.
Dupuy, John, 984.
Du Quesne, Fort, 222.
Dunsmore, David, of S. Carolina, 171.
Durboge, George, 915-6.
Durham, 1271.
" Township, 369, 421-2.
Durfee, Joseph, of Norfolk, 50.
Durnford, Andrew, 558.
Duscta, 395.
Dusenbur(y), John, 1037.
Dusenburg, Wm., 877.
Dutchess (Duchess) Co., 146, 229, 233-4-5, 240-6-7, 291-2, 312-3, 368, 453, 474, 533 635, 756-7, 766-7, 771-6-8, 784, 790-5, 806-8-9, 815-7, 823, 830, 842-3, 870-1, 881-2-4-7, 896, 1005, 1061, 1237, 1261-2.
Dutchess of Gordon (man-of-war), 42, 177, 359, 504, 541, 553, 622, 829, 830, 864, 914.
Dutchman's Point, 467.
Dyer, Col., 500.
Dyke Land, 22.

Eamer, Philip, of Tryon Co., 406.
Eagle Brook Plain, 220.
" (ship), 901, 929.
Eagles, John, of N. York, 853.
Earle, Capt. Edwd., of N. Jersey, 814.
" Hannah, 815.
" Justus, of N. Jersey, 814.
East Cairn Township, 612.
" Chester, 146, 165-6, 300, 499, 502, 553-4, 722-3-4, 743-4-5, 761.
" Haddam, 207.
" Hoosack, 917.
" River, 40.
" Township, 110.
Eastbury, 82.
Eatens Neck, 294, 850-1.
Ebenezer, 109.
Eccles, James, of N. York, 776.
Edgecomb Co., 648, 730.
Edinburgh, 730.
Edisto River, 1246.
Ediston, 185.
Edmonston, Rev. Wm., 1224-5.
Edward, Fort, 30-1, 336, 345-7-8-9, 360-4-5, 376-7-8, 390-2-8, 423, 442, 468, 486-7, 924, 937, 943-4, 1285.
Edwards, Isaac, 44.
" Pierpont, 310, 786.
Egbert, Anthony, 1320.
Egg Harbour, 833.
Eikengen, Lawrence, 908.
Elebeck, John, 1188-9.
Eleker, John, 467.
Eliot, A., 628.
Eliston, Mr., 605.
Elizabeth (Brigantine), 585-6-7, 632-6.
" River, 76.
" Township, 711-2, 743.
Elizabethtown, 115-7, 139, 151, 254-5-6-7, 388, 554, 603, 678-9, 711, 842, 1293.
" Point, 198.
Elk, 295, 1163.
Elphinstone (Privateer), 513.

Elston, Abraham, 1321.
Ellan, Mr., 341.
Ellegood, Jacob, 132, 631.
" Lt.-Col. Jacob, 1149, 1150-1-2, 1190.
" Mrs., 1150.
EHerbeck, (Ellibeck), Emanuel, of N. Y. Prov., 1009, 1280.
Ellice, Alex., of N. Y. Prov., 361.
' James, 361.
" Robt., 361.
Elliott, Andrew, 126, 608, 1234-7.
" Geo., 1302.
" Gray, 342, 1130.
" Capt. Mathew, 985-7-8.
" Mr., 1282.
Ellis, Danl., 72-3.
" James, 992.
" Mr., 1130, 1234.
" Walter, 1170.
Elliston & Piratt, 195.
Emberry, Catharine, 1107.
" David, 1107.
" Margaret, 1106.
" Philip, 1106-7.
Embree, Joseph, of N. York, 782.
" Saml., of N. York, 775-7, 782-3.
Embury, John, 1027-8.
Emerald Frigate, 66.
Emerchies, Col., 766.
Emerick, Col., 567, 770-7-8, 795, 835-6, 870, 897, 1220.
Emerson, Samuel, 511, 616.
Empy, John, of N. Y. Prov., 440.
" Philip, 1123.
" Striffil, 1123.
England, Wm., of N. Y. Prov., 487.
English, David, 886.
" Neighbourhood, 178, 262.
Enoch, County of, 49.
" Loyd, 1210.
Enoe River, 43-4-5-6.
Enor Rae River, 170.
Enson, George, 519.
Ensterick, Wm., 547.
Enceru River, 192.
Erie, Fort, 985.
Ernestown, 434-5, 442, 466.
Erskine, Sir Wm., 73, 119, 267, 567, 628, 670-2, 684-5, 741, 758, 787.
Erving, John, 37.
Eselstine, Peter, 368, 1002.
Esen, Michael, 688.
Esopus, 458.
Essex, County of, 65, 134, 530, 558, 627, 639, 711, 714, 1264.
Estel, Richd., 602.
Esther Town, 420.
Ettler, Peter, senr., of Massachusetts, 686.
" " jr., 687.
Ettleman, David, 280.
Etons Neck, 294, 850-1.
Euchee River, 797.
Eucra River, 728.
Eustace, Capt., 901.
Euston, Thomas, 1256.
Evans, Abel, 1176.
" David, 196, 223.

Evans, John, 129, 130.
" Mrs. Hannah, 129.
" Mrs. Margaret, 1273.
" Samuel, 1274.
" Thomas, 1274.
Evanson, Nicholas, 1277.
Evens, Mr., 1212.
Everett, John, 1007.
Everitt, Capt., of Cataraqui, 431, 916.
" Mrs. Mercy, 431.
Eves, Oswald, of Philadelphia, 1288.
Ewing, John, of Portsmouth, 39, 66.
Exeter, 247.
" Gaol, 816.

Fairbanks, Rufus, of N. Hampshire, 517.
Fairchild, Benj., 376-7.
" Lt., 1268.
" Saml., 376-7.
Fairfax, Lord, 192, 1350.
Fairfield, 224-5-6-7, 283-5, 350, 654, 799, 847-8, 867, 909, 910.
" County, 850, 1049.
" Gaol, 207.
" North, 850-1.
" Township, 224, 238-9.
" Wm., 1019, 1021.
Fairweather, Handorf, 812.
" Thos., of Connecticut, 231, 812.
Falcon (ship), 235.
Falkirk, 1326.
Falkner, Ralph, of N. Y. Prov., 416.
" Wm., of N. Y. Prov., 415.
Falliett, George, 858.
Falwell, Wm., 72.
Falmouth, 173, 272-3-4-5-6-7, 304-5-6-7, 632, 904-5-6-7, 1303-4, 1325-8.
" (Brig), 305-6-7.
" County, 172.
" Harbour of, 274, 304.
Faltnell, Josiah, 342.
Fame, (schooner), 316, 789, 790.
Fannen, Col. John, of S. Carolina, 717, 720.
Fanning, Col. David, of N. Carolina, 53-4, 119, 239, 241-4, 259, 261, 284, 363-8, 594, 629, 652-3, 736, 768, 770, 859, 869, 889, 890, 1007.
" Col. Edmund, Lt.-Govr. of N. S., 41, 241.
" Wm., 44.
Fannings, 139.
" Borough, 767-9, 770.
Fannock, John, 193.
Farend, Stephen, 891.
Farier, Wm., 1189.
Farington, Col., 859.
Farling, John, 1116-7.
Farlinger, John, of N. Y. Prov., 406.
Farman, Gabriel, 232.
" **Morris**, 127.
Farmer, A. W., 497.
" Joseph, 1243.
" Robt., 633, 1213.
" Saml., of Virginia, 634.
Farnham, Capt., 316.

Farr Place, 739.
Farren, Ebenezer, 149.
" Phineas, 149.
Farrington, Philip, 443.
" Stephen, 443.
Fasset, John, 576-7, 1015.
Faukner, Wm., 1095, 1254-5.
Favourite (schooner), 305-7, 905.
Faymire, Nicholas, of N. Y. Prov., 440.
Fear, Cape, 235.
Feb, Joseph, 130.
Felton, Fras., 726.
Fencastle County 1145.
Fencher, Richd., 43.
Fenck, Capt., 1275.
Fennel, John, 1083.
Fenny, Peter, of N. Y. Prov., 364, 1063.
Fenwick, Col. Edwd., 862.
Ferguson, Alexr., 1087.
" Col., 728, 688, 833-4, 1211.
" Israel, 452, 1075.
" Farrington, 1075.
" Lt., 432, 1100.
" Major, 701, 1162, 1210.
" Mary, 162.
" Peter, 1092.
" Richd., 1075.
" Wm., of N. Y. Prov., 391-2.
Ferman, Saml., 126.
Fern, Cape, 652.
Ferris, Col., 662.
" Lt. Joseph, 235, 286, 322, 887 910-11, 1281.
" Mr., 266.
Ferry Point, 81.
Fessenden, John, 741, 879.
Fetch, Jno., 82-3.
" Saml., 1273.
Fezelow, Phoenix, 930.
Fick, Peter, 1321.
Field, Daniel, 980, 990.
" George, 979, 980, 990.
" Market, 1244.
" Nehemiah, 521.
" Rebecca, 979, 981.
Fields, Nathan, 980-1.
Fife, Dr., 1247.
Fifth Township, 354, 410, 449, 471-3.
Finckle, Goerge, 368, 1002-6.
Finlay, Hugh, 487.
" James, 582.
" Mr., 348.
Finlason, Mrs. Eliz., 926.
Firman, John, 151.
" Genl., 72-4.
First Township, 355-6-7-8, 371-5-8-9, 397, 434.
Fish Creek, 106-7.
" John, 464-5.
" Kill, 320, 453, 749, 767-8, 834-5, 882.
" Kilns, 698.
Fisher, Alex., of N. Y. Prov., 362, 1103.
" Col., 374.
" Donald, 362-3.
" Duncan, 1107.
" Finlay, of N. Y. Prov., 362.
" John, 1272.
" Mr., 565, 1208.

Fishing Creek, 64, 124.
Fitch, Jonathan, 785.
Fitchburg, 642-3.
Fitchet, Richd., 442.
Fitstown, 443.
Fitz, Peter, 1333.
Fitzgerald, John, of N. Y. Prov., 452.
Fitzpatrick, Peter, 1076.
Fitzrandolph, Asher, 94.
" David, of N. Jersey, 93.
" Ed., 93.
" Joseph, 93.
" Nathanl., 93.
" Richd., 203.
" Robt., 135, 142.
FitzSimmons, Margaret, of N. Carolina, 1273.
Flaake, Harmnus, of N. Y. Prov., 346.
Flag, John, 509.
Flagg, S., 641-5, 1287.
Flagler, Simon, of N. York. 887.
Flat Bush, Long Island, 118.
Flats, German, 332, 345, 420-1, 969, 1028.
Flecher, Edward, of Long Crane, 143.
Fleerboome, John, 555.
Fleet St., Boston, 622.
Fleiger, John Henry, 49.
Fleming, Catharine, 381.
" Henry, 1190.
Fletchall, Thos., 718.
Fletcher, Capt., 332.
" Col., 703, 1210.
" Isaac, 295.
" Sex, 1043, 1333.
Flewelling, Abel, of N. York, 821-2.
" Francis, of N. York, 822, 888, 1321.
" John, 873, 1321.
" Joseph, 822, 878, 1321.
" Thos., of N. York, 877, 1320.
Flint, Dr., 663.
" Jos., 721.
Florida, Gulf of, 52.
Floyd, Richd., 100.
Flucker, Mr., 1217.
Follcott, Mr., 479.
Folliott, Bartlet, 300.
Foltin, Capt., 301.
Foord, Ebenezer, 204.
" John, of N. Jersey, 203, 314.
" Oswald, 203-4.
" Saml., 203.
Forbes, Alexr., 885.
" Elijah, 785.
" Thomas, 190.
Force, Philip, 1320.
" Thomas, 899.
Ford, Col., 140, 256.
" Ebezener, 802, 810.
" John, 803, 810.
" Mr., 192.
" Thos., 140.
Forde, Isaac D., 360.
Fordham, Manor of, 854.
Forge, the, 391.
Forked River, 926.
Forman, Saml., 690.
Formerly, McClement.

Forster, Mr., 84, 266, 1314, 1324, 1326-7-9, 1330-1.
Foresyth, James, of Tryon Co., 404.
" Thos., 361.
" Wm., 1226-7.
Fort Hill, 622.
Fortune, Col., 61, 1215, 1219. 1248.
" Mrs., 1248.
Fosster, Billings &, 248.
Foster, Col., 940, 941.
" Ebenezer, of N. Jersey, 142, 894-8-9, 900.
" Ed., jr., of Boston. 39, 40.
" Ed., of Boston, 37.
" John, 76, 1313.
" Laurence, 898.
" Mr., 931.
" Moses, 455.
" Stephen, 898.
Fourth St., Philadelphia, 250.
" Township, 368, 395-6, 419, 441, 454, 481.
Fowler, Abigal, 761.
" Adam, 583.
" Amos, of N. York, 792.
" Caleb, 281, 880.
" David, 553.
" Edmund, 723.
" John, of Massachusetts, 288, 293, 724.
" Jonathan, of N. York, 756.
" Josiah, of N. Y. Prov., 288.
" Rachel, 723, 761.
" Mrs. Sarah, 722, 761.
" Solomon, of N. York, 722, 761.
" Wm., 880.
Fox Chase, 901.
" Frederic, 1260.
" Grace, 547.
" Hill, 149.
" Thomas, 517.
" Mr., 348.
Foxcraft, Mr., 528.
Foxwell, Mr., 1311.
Foyke, Daniel, of N. Y. Prov., 402.
" Francis, 402.
Frairy, Nathan, 220.
Fralick, Adam, of S. Carolina, 168, 171, 693.
" Hannah, 419.
" Jacob, 419.
" Mrs. Nancy, 170.
Frank Port, 1289.
Franklin, 429.
Franklyn, Dr., 1167-8, 1179.
" Geo., 1293.
" Govr., 130, 178, 269, 542-7-8, 600, 841, 901, 929, 1178-9, 1208, 1221, 1232-5.
" Henry, 1118.
" Joseph, of N. Y. Prov., 448, 450.
" & Underhill, 1212.
" Walter, 880.
Franks, Catherine, 478.
" Fredk., 478.
" Margt., 478.
" Mary, 478.

Franks, William, of N. Y. Prov., 478, 480.
" Wm., jr., 478.
Frantz, 1204.
Frany, Nathan, 114.
Fraser, A., of S. Carolina, 165.
" Capt. Alex., 436.
" Brig.-Genl., 468, 1269.
" Capt., 332, 927.
" Donald, 1098.
" Eliphalet, 134.
" Genl., 360, 479, 926-7, 939.
" Isabel, 1071.
" James, of N. Jersey, 133.
" John, of N. Y. Prov., 355, 1115.
" Judge, 365, 401, 1072, 1254.
" Kenneth, 1031.
" & Lane, 1209.
" Lt., 336.
" Major, 718.
" Simon, 1071.
" Capt. Thos., 343-4, 486, 956, 1052-4-5.
" Capt. Wm., 409, 414, 486, 1109.
" Wm., senr., 1052-3-5, 1071.
Frederick, Barnet, of N. Y. Prov., 473.
" County, 192.
" Lodowick, of N. Y. Prov., 473.
Fredericksburg, 421, 443, 767, 771, 809, 815-7, 823.
Frederickton, 245, 260, 277, 283-4, 298-9, 309, 814, 882, 903-8, 1218, 1321.
Free, Mary, 765.
" Mr., 1305-8.
" Wm., of N. York, 888-9.
Freebody, Mr., 103-5.
Freehold, 70, 152, 297, 302.
" Upper, 73, 136-7, 320, 787.
Freeman, Constantine, 921.
" David, 46.
" Henry, 141.
" Isaac, 142, 919.
" John, of N. Y. Prov., 465, 484.
" John, senr., 484.
" Mr., 920.
" Saml., J. P., 273-4.
" Thos., 485.
Freetown, 589, 592.
Frelick, Benj., 967-8.
Frelinghugson, Frederic, 619.
French, Charity, of Albany, 213.
" Col., 130.
" Lt. G., 441.
" Jeremiah, 575.
" Joseph, 584.
" Lt.-Col., 1049.
" Major, 349.
" Mr., 1212.
" Village, 288.
Freth, Peter, of 96 Dist., 63.
Fridaria, 1127.
Friel, Deborah, 959.
" John, 959.
Friendship (sloop), 52.
Frink, Nathan, 1320.
Fritz, Abraham, 525.
" Elizabeth, 526.

Fritz, John, 526.
" Margaret, 526.
" Mary, 526.
" Peter, of S. Carolina, 525-8.
Frog's Neck, 211, 300, 758-9, 789, 815, 877-8.
Frock Morton, Lt. John, of N. Jersey, 151.
Front Street, Phila., 1289.
Frost, Edward, of Tryon County, 353.
" Capt. James, of Rhode Island, 327, 918.
" John, 903.
" Joshua, 593.
" Millar, 918.
" Mrs., 327.
Fry, Capt., 997.
" Col. O., 57, 419, 420.
" Peter, 492-4, 607, 1148.
Frymiern, Nicholas, 444.
Frymire, Philip, of N. Y. Prov., 469, 1333.
Full, Thomas, of Boston, 656.
Fuller, Jonathan, 91.
Fundy, Abraham, 937.
" Bay of, 268, 308, 310-6-7, 658, 1361.
" Gulf of, 22.
" Major, 1074.
Furman, Govr., 151.
" John, 877.
" Saml., 151.
Fury, Sloop, 902.
Fuset, John, 484.
Fyker, Henry, of N. Y. Prov., 431.

Gadbeer, Wm., 899, 900.
Gadnar, Mr., 165.
Gaft, George, 155.
Gage, Genl. Thomas, 32-9, 113, 380, 491-3, 505-7, 586-9, 590-9, 624, 639, 726, 738, 752, 762, 803, 817, 878, 890, 922, 986, 1139, 1147, 1177-8, 1206-8-16.
" Town, 240-6, 273, 291-2, 303-7, 806-8, 815, 830, 861, 874, 881-6, 892, 903.
Gale, Leviny, 174.
Galley, Anthony, 123.
Gallinger, Michl., of N. Y. Prov., 407.
Galloway, George, 1104.
" Isaac, 614.
" Jas., 840.
" Joseph, 109, 1146, 1166-7, 1181, 1221, 1289, 1295.
" Mr., 565, 1139, 1170-1-2-3-4-5-6-7-8-9, 1180.
" Mrs., 1174-5-7.
Galmchi, Mrs., 88.
Galpin, 101.
Galusin, 640.
Gamage, James, of Boston, 655.
Gambier, Admiral, 685.
Gambin, 904.
Gamble, Capt., 1314.
Gamblin, Admr., 608.
Gammell, James, 1333.
Garden, Dr., 1200, 1204, 1224, 1230, **1247**.
Gardener, Jacob, 1016.

Gardener, Capt., 789.
" Henry, 725-6.
" Silvester, 38.
" Thomas, 861.
" W., 639, 640-5.
Gardiner, 305.
Garetville, Andrew, of Albany Co., 1283, 1333.
Garlow, Peter, of N. Y. Prov., 419, 421.
" Philip, 360.
Garner, Jacob, 800-1.
" John, 148.
" Richd., 601.
Garnet, Lt., 415.
Garret, Joshua, of S. Carolina, 155, 183-7.
Garretville, Andrew, 1283, 1333.
Garrignes, Saml., 222.
Garrow, Jacob, 774.
Gasgil, Peter, 1172.
Gaskel, Mr., 1181.
Gaspe, 195, 1269.
Gaston, Squire, 89.
Gate Farm, 739.
Gates, Genl., 648, 1153.
Gauger, Weigher &, 190.
Gavin, Wm., 342.
Gay, Ebenezer, 568.
" Capt. John, 577.
" Joshua, 569.
" Martin, of Boston, 568, 572.
Gayton, Capt. Geo., R.N., 66.
Geddes, Charles, 599.
" John, 203, 802.
Gedney (or Gidney), Elizabeth, of Rochelle, 108.
" John, of Rochelle, 108.
" Joseph, of N. Y. Prov., 553, 853-4.
" Capt. Joshua, of N. Y. Prov., 233-4, 734, 816, 882-3.
General Gage, the, (sloop), 745-6-7.
Genevay, Capt., 950.
George, Fort, 311, 336, 380-4, 391.
" Lake, 336, 380-1-3, 425, 738, 959.
" Town, 165, 1214, 1246.
George's Island, 657-8.
Georgias Hill, 722.
Germain, Lord, Geo., 762, 915, 1126, 1245, 1305.
German, John, 1003-4.
" Flatts, 332, 345, 420-1, 969, 1028.
" Town, 670, 901.
" " Battle of, 741.
Gerty, (or Girty), George, of Fort Pitt, 988, 1283, 1284.
" Simon, of Pensilvania, 988, 1282.
Gibbons, Joseph, 342.
" Mr., 1301.
" Willm., 685.
Giberson, Gilbert, of N. Jersey, 135.
Gibertson, Mr., 760.
Gibbs, Col., 1211-4-5.
" Mr., 1301.
" Mrs., 1304.
Gibson, Dr., 836.
" James, of Virginia, 646, 1290-6.
" John, of N. Y. Prov., 462.
Gifford, Wm., 1271.
Gilbert, Anthony, 890.

Gilbert, Bradford, 302.
" John, 287.
" Mr., 899.
" Nathaniel, 590.
" Samuel, 1333.
" Thos., of Massachusetts, 96, 589, 592.
Gilchrist, Mr., 30.
" Peter, of N. Y. Prov., 466, 1034.
Gilfillan, T., 691.
Gilhall Township, 1269.
Gill, John, of Pensilvania, 294.
" Mathew, 930.
Gilleland, Wm., 436.
Gillet, A., 640.
Gillespie, Mr., 97.
Gills, James, 673.
Gillsland, William, 400.
Gilman, John Taylor, 616.
" Samuel, 617.
Gilmore, George, of N. York, 682.
" Hugh, 933.
" Robt., 1162, 1190, 1227.
Glasford, James, 1079-80.
" Jane, 1112.
" John, of Glasgow, 631, 1112-3.
" Littet, 1113.
" Mr., 1311.
" Paul, 1113.
Glasgow, 630-1-6, 730.
Glastonbury, (Glasstenberry), 82-3, 909.
Gleeson (Gleason), John, of N. York, 778-9.
Glen, John, 360, 475, 1077.
Glen Morrison, 390, 1068, 1093.
Glossenbury, 909, 910.
Gloster Co., 72.
Gloucester Co., 615, 857-8, 929, 930.
Gochen (Goshen), 749, 843, 1264-6.
Goddard, Mr., 287.
Godfrey, James, 568.
" Mathew, 721.
Goforth, John, 95.
Goicon, 239, 240.
Golden, Joseph, 228.
Golding & Bennet, 1048.
" John, 229.
" Nathanl., of N. York, 768.
Goldthwaits, Col., 312.
Goodall, Nathan, 645.
Goodrich, Bartlet, 1189, 1190.
Goodwin, Mr., 646.
Goodyear, Thos., 288.
Gorden, Charles, 950.
" James, of Georgia, 631, 792-7.
" Knox, 1245-6.
" Major, 620.
" Mr., 1311.
" Robert, 1064.
" Thomas, 178.
" Thos. Knox, 1245.
Gore, the, 510.
Goreham, Wm., J. P., 274.
Gosling, Ann, 179.
" David, 178-9.
" Elizabeth, 179.
" Howe Carleton, 179.
" James, 179.

Gosling, Mary, 179.
" Sarah, 179.
" Wm., 179.
Gosport, 76.
Gouch, Thomas, 627.
Goulds & Monk, 1334.
Gover, Lt., 156.
Governors Island, 508, 617.
Gracie, George, 661.
Gradin, Philip, 76.
Grafton Co., 511, 616-7.
Graham, Arthur, 677-8.
" Dr., 807.
" Col., 1239.
" Ennis, 399.
" Mrs. Hannah, 677.
" James, 1290.
" Lt. Joanus, 1333.
" Lt.-Govr., John, 342, 1126-7-8-9, 1130-5, 1183, 1298-9, 1308.
" Lt.-Col., 126.
" Thomas, 1086-7.
Grand Bay, 247, 280, 869.
" Duke of Russia (ship), 656.
" Isle, 91.
" Lake, 814.
" River, 998.
Grant, Alexr., of Tryon Co., 370, 397, 1087-9, 1092-3-4-5-8.
" Major Alex., 312.
" Angus, of N. Y. Prov., 373.
" Archibald, 1058.
" Donald, jr., of N. Y. Prov., 372.
" " senr., of Tryon Co., 372-3.
" Duncan, 390, 1093-4.
" Elizabeth, 313.
" Finlay, 372, 1067-8.
" Genl., 544.
" George, 403.
" Helen, 313.
" John, 1080-9.
" Jonathan, 879.
" Lucy, 313.
" Major-Genl., 1212.
" Peter, 358, 1061.
" Robt., 312.
" Mrs. Sarah, 312.
" Thos., 334-5, 398.
" William, 1072.
" Zebulon, 648.
Granville, 177, 303, 723, 741, 919, 921, 1102-3.
" Co., 527, 748.
" Lord (Earl), 46, 648, 1350.
Grass, Capt., 449, 1032.
" Michael, 420-1, 1073, 1258-9.
" Mr., 1217.
Graves, Adam, 55.
" Admiral Samuel, 37, 108, 154, 172, 656.
" Capt., 195.
" George, 55.
Gray, Capt., 657.
" Isaac, of Pensilvania, 129.
" Major James, 346, 394, 402, 426-7, 475, 481, 931, 1074, 1115.
" Mr., 1217-8.
" Capt. Robt., 131.
" Wm., 1320.

Great Barrington, 1208.
" Bridge, 131, 210, 632, 668, 1311.
" Cove, 530.
" Meadows, 64, 530, 559.
" Neck, 81, 530-2, 559, 560.
" Pasture, 243, 282.
" Swamp, 243, 560.
" Valley, 612.
Greatorex, Samuel, 1211, 1218-9.
Green, Capt., 674.
" Col., 759.
" Elizabeth, 302, 897.
" Ephraim, 228.
" Francis, 1208, 1210.
" Genl., 266, 646, 702, 714, 901, 1186.
" Harbour, 147.
" Henry, of S. Carolina, 709.
" Jas., 1230-2.
" John, of N. Y. Prov., 45, 442.
" Lancaster, 843-4.
" Mr., 69, 665, 1208-9, 1210, 1231.
" Robt., 236.
" Thos., of St. Johns, 102, 1271.
Greenfield, 219.
Greenland, 512.
Greenock, 306.
Greenoughs, Thos., 38.
Greenwich, 141, 807, 848, 861-4.
" (sloop), 909.
Greenwood, Gertrude, 671.
" Saml., of Boston, 37, 108, 638.
Greevy, Guyon, 500.
Gregory, Mr., 884.
Greig, Major, 357.
Grenville family, 45.
Grey & Cunningham, 1241.
" John, 602.
" Wm., of N. York, 819, 887.
Greyhound (ship), 504.
Grierson, Fort, 697.
" Col. James, 696-7, 1333.
Griffis, Evan, 499.
Griffith, Evan, 930.
Griffyn, Benj., 877.
" Isaiah, 956.
" James, 552.
" Joseph, of N. York, 956.
Grime, Hugh, 116.
Grimerose, 263.
Grimes, Major, 1049.
Grindley, Rich., 1216.
Griswold, Seth., 291.
Grooms, Elijah, 1009, 1271.
Groon, Burzilla, 787.
Groton Township, 463.
" 463-4-5, 623, 1286.
Groughton, 938.
Grover, Bruzilla, 71-2-3-4, 787.
Groyns Island, 1227.
Gruse, Joseph, 827.
Guesbertson, Guesbert, 137.
" William, 137.
Guess Benj., 535.
Guildford, 160, 293, 1131, 1218-9.
" Battle of, 155, 241, 549.
Guinea Lott, 1310.
Gummersal (Gomersal), 453, 1106.

INDEX. 1401

Gummersal, Capt. Thos., of N. Jersey, 254, 315, 383, 418, 421-2-3-4-8, 430-6, 442, 450, 479, 480, 923, 1037, 1255-8-9, 1260-4, 1294, 1323.
Gunel, Thos., 856.
Gurney, Mr., 885.
Gut of Canso, 582.
Guthorp, Sophia, 1252.
Guthridge, John, 67.
Guy, Major, 1032.
Gwaldomay, Jas., 442.
Gwattse, Abraham, 441.

Hacket, Allen, 143.
Hackinsack, 149, 245-6, 262, 541-2-3-4, 600, 692, 747-8-9, 814, 1019, 1264.
Hacock, Thomas, 1321.
Haddam, East, 207.
" Israel, 198.
Hadley, 643.
Hagan, John, 1153.
Hagart, John, 1097.
Hagarty, Patrick, 599, 603-4.
Hagginis, John, 1055.
Haight, Caniff, 25.
" Col., 1292.
" James, 864.
" John, 200, 223.
" Joseph, 654.
Haldimand, Genl. Sir Fredk., 86, 347, 359, 365, 397, 575, 682, 915-8, 957, 1023, 1051, 1063, 1323.
" Govr., 577, 948, 957, 1053.
Hale, Josiah, of Glastonbury.
Halebe, Capt., 889.
Half Moon Dist., 432, 468.
Haliburton, Dr., of Rhode Island, 52, 154, 653.
Haliday, Samuel, 782.
Halifax, 11, 21, 37-9, 56-8, 97, 109, 119, 144, 156-7, 211, 219, 229, 242-4, 277, 313, 316-7-8, 339, 397, 423-4, 466, 485, 490-1-2, 579, 581, 599, 624, 635-8, 655-6-7-8-9, 661-2-3-4, 670-4-8, 680-1, 690-1-2-3, 714, 730-1-8, 745, 746, 752-5-8, 760-4, 803, 814-9, 823, 851, 862, 904-7, 918, 920-2, 935, 985, 1012, 1084, 1154, 1161, 1209, 1216, 1278, 1286, 1304, 1319, 1324-6-7-9, 1338. 1355-8-9, 1360-2-4-7.
Hall, Mrs. Ann, 925, 931.
" Caleb, 321.
" Elizabeth, 923.
" Mr., 653, 1183, 1298-9, 1306-8.
" Stephen, 124.
" Wm., 520.
Hallam, Lt., 157.
Halleback, 1073.
Haller, Thomas, 1069.
Hallet, Danl., 212.
" Joseph, 212.
" Capt. Saml., of Long Island, 211, 233.
" Wm., 212.
" Wm., jr., 212.
Hallet's Cove, 212.
Halley, Mr., 828.
" Seargt., 799.

Hallock, Mrs. Hannah, 515.
" John, 515.
" Mr., 698.
" Saml., 292.
Hallowell, Mr., 1160.
Halstead, Wm., 679.
Halton, 857.
Hamblin, Silas, 1077.
Hamilton, Archd., 1290.
" Attorney, 1296.
" Colin, of N. York, 423.
" Dr., 1141.
" Govr., 987.
" James, 1131-2, 1172.
" Capt. John, 182.
" John, of S. Carolina, 841.
" Lt.-Col. John, of S. Carolina, 241-2, 265, 277, 423, 680, 695, 700, 756-8, 770, 841-2-9, 1131, 1208, 1296, 1333.
" Mr., 1140, 1296.
" Mrs., 1140.
" & Woods, 719.
Hamlin, Isaac, 903.
Hammel, Danl., of Windsor, 534, 545, 682.
Hammond, Sir Andrew, 51, 658, 720, 785, 1227.
" Mr., 527, 540.
Hampshire, 660.
Hampstead, 267.
Hampton, Jonathan, 601.
" New, 882.
Hance, Peter, 1321.
Hancock, John, 659, 918, 1216.
" Mr., 40.
Hand, Tadock, 437.
Hanford, Mr., 239.
" Mrs. Sarah, 238.
Hanger, George, 811.
Hanging Rock, 829, 1131.
Hankhurst, Jonathan, 807.
Hankinson, Kennet, 690.
Hannah, James, 414.
" Mr., 1282.
" (Schooner), 657.
Hannahs Town, 988, 1282-3.
Hannon, George, 295.
Hanover, 67, 149, 244, 1074.
" County, 68.
" Square, Newhaven, 82.
" Township, 153, 188-9, 787.
Hansen, Nichs., 966.
Hansen's Patent, 965.
Hard Labour Creek, 63, 158.
Hardenburg, Col. Joannas, 992.
Hardenburghs Patent, 268.
Harding, George, of Philadelphia, 517.
" Martha, 741-2.
" Thos., 741-2.
" Thos., of N. York, 872.
Hardinge, Jasper, 518.
" Richd., 518.
" Robt., 518.
Hardwick, 96, 738-9, 740, 687.
Hardy, Elias, 177, 211, 217, 225, 233, 254, 285, 697, 755, 808, 814-5-9, 821-3-6, 835, 880-1-7, 890, 900, 1270, 1321-2.
Hare, John, 970.

Hare, Margt., of N. York, 970.
" Wm., 970.
Harford, Mr., 1338.
Hargrave, Humphrey, 454, 1268.
Hargreaves, Wm., of Virginia, 656-8.
Harkey, David, of N. Carolina, 869, 1321.
Harkinson, Kenneth, 609.
" Wm., 151.
Harlow, Mr., 687.
Harn, Andr., of N. Carolina, 280.
Harned, Eupheme, 1320.
Harper, Col., 979.
" Mr., of Hilsboro, 49.
" Robt., 336.
" Thos., 1224.
Harpersfield, 357-8, 1108-9.
Harrington, James, 545.
Harris, James, 639-640.
" Jane, 1062, 1333.
" Mr., 182.
" Capt. Peter, of N. York, 635.
" Richd., 725-6.
" Robt., jr., 181.
" Mrs. Sarah, 635.
" Thos., 1010, 1012.
" Tyne, 43.
Harris's Ferry, 1272.
Harrison, Andrew, 1321.
" Edward, 1359.
" Gray, 1215.
" Victor, 984.
Harrison's Patent, 472.
' Precinct, 744-5.
" Purchase, 780.
Harrod, Benj., 40.
Hart, Henry, 731.
" Mr., 45.
" Simon, 524.
Hartehey, Col., 835.
Hartford, 128, 207, 756.
Hartman, David, 1030.
Hartshorn, Lawrence, 36, 95, 119, 127, 619, 627.
" Richd., 628.
Hartwood, 131.
Harvey, John, 1208.
Hastings, Sylvanus, 90.
Hatch, Jethro, 868.
Hatfield, Col., 110-1-4.
" Coms., 1293.
" Isaac, 1320.
" Isaac, jr., of N. Y. Prov., 755.
" James, of N. Jersey, 678.
" Job, 554.
" John Smith, 256, 554.
" Mr., 768. 778, 790-5.
" Peter, 84.
" Saml., 554.
" Wm., 520.
" Mrs. Wm., 520.
Hathaway, Benony, 255.
" Israel, 592.
Hathorn, Col. John, 264.
Havannah, 1277.
Haven, Stephen, 1143.
Haver, Christian, 942-3.
Haverford, 123.
Haverhill, 617.
Haverstraw, 390.

Haviland, Genl., 738.
Hawfields, 45-6, 50, 736.
Hawke, (Sloop), 492-3.
Hawley, Abel, 437.
" Abijah, 88, 578.
" Agar, 438.
" Capt., 437.
" Gideon, 438-9.
" Ichabod, 435-9, 1018.
" Jeptha, of Arlington, 329, 434-8, 442-3, 476, 1264.
" Josiah, 434-5-9, 440.
" Peter, 437.
" Ruth, 436-9.
" Thomas, 207.
Haws, George, 1062.
" Widow, 871.
Hay, Lt. Manson, 291.
" Rodney, 336.
" Mrs. Sarah, 573-5.
" Sidney, 436.
Haycock, Danl., 240.
Hayes, Joseph, 274.
" Smal., 558.
Hayley, Mr., 1209.
Hayman, Gabriel, 561.
Hays, Mr., 401.
Hayward, Danl., 189.
Haywood, Robt., of Halifax, 70.
Hazard, Nath., 311.
" Robt., of Boston Neck, 303.
" Capt. Thos., 303.
Hazen, Mr., 316.
Hazens, 239.
Heacock, Thos., of N. Y. Prov., 239.
Head, Sir Ed., 1229.
Heall, Charles, 1320.
Heanor, Henry, of Ulster Co., 971.
Heaslip, James, of Albany Co., 965.
Heath, Genl., 744.
Hebron, Conn., 1196.
Heck, Paul, of N. Y. Prov., 401, 1107.
Heddon, Margt., 894.
Hedge Creek, 1250.
Helback, 995.
Helena, (Brig), 118.
Heliker, Abraham, 468.
" Ann, 468.
" Blackners, 468.
" Japed, 467-8.
" Jeremy, 468.
" John, of Saratoga, 467.
" Olive, 468.
" Oness, 468.
Hellellog, Garret, 596.
Hellgate, 211, 501, 808.
Helzenger, Michl., 962.
Henchman, John, 125, 616.
Henderson, Arthur, S. Carolina, 143-4.
" Caleb, 438.
" David, 144.
" James, of Pensilvania, 143-4, 498.
" Maccaul & Co., 632.
Hendrichson, Garnet, 690.
Hendrick, Conrad, 886.
" James, 886.
" John, 886.

Hendrick, Sarah, 886.
Hendricks, Mrs. Sarah, 886.
Hendrie, Govr., 732.
Hennesy, David, 244.
" James, 244.
Henricks, Barker, 117.
Henny, Josiah, of Penobscot, 59.
Henry, Mr., 154, 556.
" Gov. Patrick, 67.
" Philip, 280.
Henshaw, S., 572.
Herbert, John Malcolm, 732.
" Mr., 34.
Herd, Genl., 232.
Herkeman, Genl., 1112.
Heron, Mr., 501, 1304.
" Peter, 555.
Herring, Abraham, 556.
Herrington, Mr., 511.
Herriott, James, 1138.
Hertford, 529, 562-3, 835-6, 1104.
" Goal, 865.
Hevisdue, 820.
Hewat, Capt. Andrew, of Georgia, 340, 583.
Hewitt, James, 1138.
Hewlet, Col., 861.
Hichcox, Lt., 83.
Hickey, Jeremy, 108.
" Mrs. Lavina, 108.
Hickford, Dr., 101.
Hickock, Benj., 283.
Hickory Lane, 671.
Hicks, Danl., 480.
" Edward, of Susquehana, 480.
" Geo., 857.
" Gilbert, of Pensilvania, 94, 581.
" Isaac, 95.
" James, 724.
" John, 711.
" Joseph, 95, 480, 534.
" Lewis, 1036.
" Mills &, 144.
" Mrs., 104.
Higley, Mr., 602.
Hilberg, 1024, 1268.
Hilhouse, James, 623.
Hill, Capt., 768.
" James, 730-1.
" John, of N. York, 584-7, 1320.
" Joshua, of Sussex Co., 519, 521, 697.
" Mrs., 522, 730-1.
" Richd., 585.
" Solomon, 622.
" Thomas, 918, 921.
" Wm., of Boston, 495, 784.
Hillsborough, 43-4-5-6-8-9, 50, 241-4, 269, 271, 511, 616, 736, 857-8, 1286-7.
" Lord, 507, 639.
Hilton, Benj., of N. Y. Prov., 562.
" John, 562-3.
" Township, 895.
" Wm., 563.
Hilltown, 827.
Hindman, Samuel, 1063.
Hine. Noble, 202.

Hirolyhy, Lt.-Col. Timothy, of Connecticut, 130.
Hitchcock, Aaron, 202.
" Joseph, 812.
" Saml., 202.
Hoaksley & Platt, 945.
" Robert, 944.
Hoaxley, Mr., 366.
Hobb, Augustine, 719.
Hoberton, 1114.
Hockley, Wm., 518.
Hoffman, Joseph, 1261.
Hoffnail, Jobert, 1004.
" Michael, of Kingsbury, 487, 944-5-7.
Hofftalin, James, 1070, 1333.
Hog Island, 539, 733.
Hogal, Eliz., 1009.
Hogel, Capt. Francis, 363.
Hogg & Campbell, 54.
" Robt., 54.
" Saml., 832.
Hogle, Busteyon, 1009.
" James, 1009.
Holland, 1003, 1202.
" Harry, 1121.
" Henry, 916.
" John, 696, 916.
" Major, 271, 780-3, 795.
" Mr., of N. Hampshire, 1304.
" Lt. Richd., 260, 271.
" Major Samuel, 327.
" Samuel, of N. York, 810, 914.
Hollandville, 327, 915.
Holloways, Mr., 520.
Holmes, Benj. Mulberry, of Boston, 41, 154, 571.
" Capt., 190.
" Ebenezer, 1047.
" James, 1046.
" John, 926, 1061.
Holt, Benj., of Vermont, 86, 578.
Holton, John, 573.
Holly, Mount, 1292.
" Ruben, 388.
Homan, John, 595.
Homvall, Israel, 854.
Honduras, Bay of, 1289.
Hood, Capt., 727.
" Langden, 660.
Hooper, Joseph, 1146-7-8-9.
" Robt., 606.
" Thos., 761.
Hoosack, 386, 417, 941, 1263.
" East, 917.
Hoosick River, 1038.
Hope, Lt.-Govr. & Brig.-Genl., 23, 337, 959, 960, 1330, 1357-8.
" J. Gust., 957.
" Town, 330.
Hopeton, John, 1205.
Hopkins, Mark, 293.
Hopper, Mr., 634.
Hornebec, Mr., 928.
Horner, John, of Beaver Harbour, 119.
" John, of N. Jersey, 787.
Hornet, Widow, 198.
Horse Neck, 141, 626-7, 723, 761-2, 770, 909, 910-1.

Horton, 22, 166, 180, 503, 537, 698.
" Samuel, 770.
" Solomon, of N. York, 770.
Hoskins, Abiel, 592.
" John, 592.
" Mr., 601.
Hosmer, Joseph, 464.
Hough, Barnabas, 1019, 1022.
" John, 1028.
Houghton, Mrs. Ann, 920.
" John, 90, 919.
" Richard, 919.
" Roland, 919, 921.
Houlopan, Cape, 320.
Hour, Gen., 1139.
House, Geo., 983.
Houston, Debr., 341.
" Mr., 341.
Hover, Casper, 1003.
" Henry, 1073.
" Martin, 1023.
Hoverland, Andrew, 983.
Howard, Alex., 787.
" County, 280.
" John, 214.
" Capt. John, 883-7.
" Justice, 45-8.
" Lt., 1031.
" Martin, 52.
" Mr., 700.
" Peter, 196.
Howe, Admiral, 821.
" Capt., 632.
" Lord, 42, 211, 350, 670, 901, 920 1249, 1326.
" Silvanus, 879.
" Genl. Sir Wm., 32, 42-3, 53, 66-7, 71, 94, 108, 113-8, 130-7-9, 141, 154, 205, 211-18 238, 253, 267, 273, 282, 307, 429, 450, 495-7-8, 499, 503-4, 535, 541, 555, 564, 565-8, 570, 594-7, 600, 605, 628, 633-8, 652-5-9, 666, 670-8, 689, 700, 739, 741-4-7, 756-8, 762, 832, 853, 864, 871-8, 900-1, 925, 1048-9, 1162-3-8-9, 1179, 1180, 1208, 1212, 1220, 1232-5, 1240, 1303.
Howell, John, 1021.
" Silas, 149.
Hoyt, Capt., 211, 238.
" Eben, 830.
" Goold, 209, 210, 722.
" Isaac, 717.
" Israel, of Connecticut, 243, 823.
" Jacob, 192-3.
" James, of Connecticut, 209, 722, 798, 866.
" Jonathan, 510.
" Joseph, 510.
" Josiah, 319.
" Stephen, of Conecticut, 206, 209.
Hubbard, Isaac, 223-4.
" James, 1195-6.
" Margrt., 224.
" Mathew, of Connecticut, 223.
" Wm., 224, 825.
Hubbit, Nathan, 582.
Hubble, Major, 865.

Hude, James, 618.
Hudson, Ann, 186.
" Elizabeth, 186.
" James, 186.
" Higgenbotham, 186.
" Joel, of Cambden Dist., 34.
" Joel, of S. Carolina, 185.
" John, 186.
" Ludwick, 185-6-7.
" Martha, 186.
" Mary, 186.
" Samuel, 186.
Hudson's Ferry, 718.
" River, 11, 30-1, 398-9, 857, 941, 1041.
Huff, Paul of N. Y. Prov., 453.
" Squire, 369.
Huffman, David, 423.
" Joseph, of Albany Co., 422.
Huggerford, Dr. Peter, 84, 285, 836.
" Elizabeth, 84.
" Major Thomas, 759, 761.
Hughes, Major, of Montreal, 117, 943, 1002.
" Samuel, 65.
Hughston, James, of N. York, 583-5.
Hull, Mr., 1127.
Humberton, County, 837.
Hume, Jas., 715.
" Mr., 1133-5, 1308.
Humphreys, Ashton, 222-3, 250, 566.
" Henry, 883.
" Publisher, of Philadelphia, 53.
Hungerford, Mr., 819.
Hunt, Abraham, 249.
" Col. Berry, 743-5.
" Catharine, 38.
" Israel, 567.
" James, 167, 723-4.
" Jesse, 744.
" John, 919.
" Joshua, of N. Y. Prov., 567.
" Moses, 889.
" Nathan, 250.
" Saml., 38.
" Shepherd &. 804.
Hunter, David, 1055.
" Fort, 459.
" John, of N. York, 133, 646, 781.
" Mr., 102, 1276-7, 1326-7.
Huntersfield, 961.
Huntingdon, 252, 477, 789, 910.
" County, 127, 618, 837.
" Mr., 1208.
" Saml., 639.
Hurd, Aaron, 795.
" John, 508.
" Mr., 795.
Hurlburt, Moses, of N. Y. Prov., 438, 469, 1333.
Hurry, Willm., 861.
Hurst, Mr., 178, 1172.
Husted, Jabez, 1321.
Hustin, Mrs., 873.
Huston, Mary, 822.
Hutchinson, Anna, 188.
" Capt., 270.
" Col., 241, 700, 714-5-8.

Hutchinson, Francis, 188.
" Hon. Forster, (Govr.,) of Boston, 40, 97, 490-1-3, 590, 624, 638, 726, 735, 1160, 1210, 1303.
" Isaac Stev., 710.
" Israel, 721.
" James, 710.
" John, 153, 188-9.
" Margaret, 188.
" Mrs. Margaret, of N. Jersey, 98, 152, 188.
Hutchinson's, 761.
Hyatt, Abraham, of N. York, 936.
" Col. John, 771.
" Nathanl., of N. York, 783.
Hynd, Wm., 721.
Hyster, Genl., 915.
Hyte, Col., 567.
Hythe, 1155-6.

Impey, Adam, 1070.
" Philip, 1069.
Independence, Mount, 1268.
Indian Creek, 153.
" Island, 316.
" Lands, 386.
" Nation, 191-3.
" Purchase, 193.
Indies, West, 21, 76, 133, 305-6, 320, 343, 513, 566, 634-5, 684, 746-7, 793, 900-5, 929, 1164, 1289.
Industry, (sloop) 720.
Inever River, 701-3.
Ingersoll, Tom, 785.
Ingles, Dr., 53.
Inglish, Alex., 660.
Ingraham, Abijah, 903.
" Benj., of N. York, 902.
" Stephen, 81.
Innes, Col., 62, 653, 677, 728.
James, 744.
" Mr., 124.
" Peter, 744.
Invermorrison, 1092.
Ipswich, New, 616.
Iredell, Abraham, 200, 221-3.
Ireland, Adam, 781, 1321.
Irvine, Edward, 253.
Irving, Lt., 391.
Irwin, Mat, 566.
Isle aux Noix, 355, 398, 483, 935-6, 1002, 1026, 1037, 1050-8, 1063, 1102-8-9, 1114, 1255, 1260-3-4, 1269.
" Jesus, 346, 458.
Ivers, Thos., 273.
Ives, Capt. David, of N. York, 864-5.
" Titus, 865.

Jacks, Jas., 110.
Jackson, Danl., 824.
" David, 1020.
" Henry, of Albany Co., 434, 1267.
" James, 433, 1020-9, 1264-6.
" John, of Pensilvania, 564.
" Mr., 1306.
" Peter, 1321.

Jamaica, 52, 267, 326, 496, 647, 800, 918, 1290-1, 1303-6.
" Town, 583-4.
James, Abel, 614, 670-1, 1175, 1288-9.
" Col., 800.
" Creek, 171-2, 1211.
" Francis, 138.
" Island, 54, 171, 244, 1219.
" River, 137-8, 170, 720, 1311.
Jamieson, John, of Georgia, 342, 1129, 1137, 1143, 1305-7-8.
" Mr. 1183.
" Mrs., 631.
" Neil, of Virginia, 133, 514, 630-4-5-6, 646, 668, 721,
" Neil, of Norfolk, 1311-2.
" Stephen, 722.
Jamson, Wm., 1106.
Janney, Jas., 1293.
Jarvais (or Jervais), Chas., 250, 833.
" Morison, 200, 210.
" Mr., 828, 1196.
" Lt. Stephen, 283.
Jay, Mr., 545.
Jebare, Joseph, of N. York, 943.
Jeddon, 185.
Jefferson, John, 334.
Jeffrey, Jas., 721.
Jeffries, John, 335.
Jekyll, Miss, 1164.
Jellet, Joseph, 1091.
Jenkins, Richd., of N. York, 146.
" Saml. Hunt, 1334.
" Thos., 95.
" Wm., 1174.
Jenkinson, Charles, 1222.
Jennings Creek, 1210.
" Mr., 550.
Jenny, (schooner) 274.
Jenny, Simpson, 422.
Jerico, 753.
" Patent, 122.
Jessup, Col. Ebenezer, (Jessup's Corps), 30, 47, 106, 376, 769, 860, 923-4.
" Joseph, of N. Y. Prov., 376.
" Major Edward, (Jessup's Corps), 13, 106, 329, 330-5-7-8, 245-6-7, 365, 376-7, 383-6-8, 398-9, 423, 433, 451-5-6-7, 467-8, 483-4-5-7, 924-8, 942-4-5-7-9, 956, 1003, 1013-4, 1021, 1031-6, 1050-5, 1061, 1073-7, 1089, 1107, 1115-9, 1255, 1265-9, 1271, 1283.
Jessup's Patent, 152, 376.
Jessupsburg, 1075.
Jesus, Isle, 346, 458.
Jewel, Robt., 684.
Jewett, Dummer, 721.
Johnes, Dr. Butler, 89.
John St., N. Y., 147.
Johns, Danl., 577.
Johnson, Alexr., 277.
" Col., 471, 662, 957, 1052.
" Col. Guy, 351, 1243-5.
" Hannah, 568.
" James, 1011, 1027.
" John, 126-7, 186.

Johnson, (Johnston), Sir John, 85, 254-7, 328, 332-5, 346, 351-2-3-4-5-6-7-8-9, 360, 361-2-4-8-9, 370-1-2-3-4-5-8-9, 381-2-4-5-6, 390-3-5-6-7, 400-1-2-3-4-6-7-8, 410-1-4-5-8-9, 421-3-4-5-7, 432-4-9, 440-3-4-9, 454-8-9, 463-6-7-9, 470-1-2-5-7-8-9, 481-2-4-6, 575, 662, 934, 940-8, 956-9, 960-5, 999, 1001-2-5, 1025, 1034, 1048, 1051-2-4-7, 1062-4-5-7-9, 1070-3-4-6-8, 1080-1-3-7, 1101-9, 1110, 1153, 1181, 1255, 1263-8-9, 1281-5.
" Jonas, 731.
" Mr., 1242.
" Phebe, 277.
" Philemon, 287, 985.
" (Johnston), Sir Wm., 47, 354-5-6, 369, 410-11-12, 472-3. 856, 956-8-9, 965, 970, 1005-6, 1021, 1052-3-4-7-8, 1063-4-6, 1079, 1103, 1115, 1213, 1261, 1281-3-5.
Johnson's Bush, 1089, 1093-7-8, 1115.
Johnston, Adam, 456.
" And., 127-8.
" County, 648.
" Dr., 258.
" Gersham, 95.
" James, 97, 433, 1244.
" John, 179, 818.
" Dr. Lewis, 1237.
" Robert, 79.
" Sarah, 110.
" Wm., 42-3.
Johnstone, Fort, 1206-7.
" Hall, 47.
Johnstown, 355-6, 364, 370-5, 383-4-5, 390-3-4-5-7, 403-6-8, 410-11, 444, 459, 471, 480, 926, 934, 953-9, 1021, 1052-3-4-5-6-8, 1062-4-7-8-9, 1083, 1117, 1122, 1261, 1285, 1358.
" New, 351-2-3-4, 368-9, 370-1-8, 383-5, 397-2-3-5-6-7, 403-4-5, 406-7-8-9, 410-11-14, 421-3, 432-9, 440-1-4-9,454-431-3, 432-9, 440-1-4-9, 454-6-8, 463-7-9, 471-2-7-8-9, 481-2.
Jolly, (Sloop), 905.
Jones, Alpheus, 753.
" Asina, 753.
" Charles, 703.
" Col., 190.
" Danl., of N. Y. Prov., 398, 751.
" Edward, of Pensilvania, 827, 895.
" Edward, senr., 827.
" Elias, 751.
" Elisha, 751-2, 796.
" Elisha, jr., 754, 794, 911.
" Col. Elisha, of Massachusetts, 762, 794-6, 820, 911, 917.
" Eliphalet, 278, 389.
" Ephraim, 751, 911-12, 917.
" Isaac, 753, 787.
" Israel, 751.

Jones, James, of S. Carolina, 707, 729, 982.
" John, of N. Y. Prov., 336, 380-4, 391-2, 521, 944-5-7, 950, 1078.
" Jonas, of Massachusetts, 751, 762, 911.
" Capt. Jonathan, of N. York, 31, 105-7, 153, 578, 827.
" Josiah, of Massachusetts, 751-2-4, 762-3, 820, 911, 917.
" Mr., 130, 604.
" Mrs., 107.
" Mrs. Mahittable, 753, 794, 912.
" Nathan, 751-3.
" Owen, 1171-4.
" Robert, 753.
" Sereno, 753.
" Simeon, of Massachusetts, 751, 762, 820, 917.
" Simon, 911.
" Stephen, of Massachusetts, 751-2, 762, 821, 911.
" Thos., 1295.
" Unice, 753.
" Upham, 753.
Joneth, Chevalier, 1293.
Jordan, Charles, 28.
" Mary, 281.
Judas Island, 243.
Judith, Point, 52.
Judson, Chapman, 874.
Juniper Creek, 97.
Justice, George, 690.
Justuson, Isaac, of N. Jersey, 615, 930.

Kairn, Jacob, 1102.
Kat Kill Mountains, 313.
Kayadosseras (or Kaidosseras, Kaimdussen, Kaiody rascras), 456. 860.
" (Kayodoscens or Kydoseros) Patent, 944, 948, 1053.
Kearney, Capt. Mich., 1237-8.
" Mr., 620.
" Phil., 858.
" R., 151.
" Susa., 1237.
Kearsley, Dr., 1220-1.
Keating, Mr., 793.
Keelar, Silas, 205.
Keeler, Capt., 1231.
" Thos., 207-8.
" Timothy, 206.
Keeport, 328.
Keesway, Mr., 167.
Keeler, Christian, 1038.
" Frederic, 1264.
" John, 1038.
" Wm., 418, 1263-4.
Kelly Burgh, 465.
" Charles, 1216.
" H., 174.
" Hugh, of Maryland, 55.
" James, of N. Y. Prov., 388.
" John, 115, 857-8.
" Mrs., 637.
" Will, 601.

Kelsay, Wm., 708.
Kelsey, James, 1082.
Kemble, Col., 1314.
" Mr., 1212.
Kemp Hausen, (Kniphausen), Genl., 71-3, 309.
Kennebecasis, 227, 230, 262-3, 271, 288, 800-2, 812, 837, 870, 886, 891.
" River, 198, 203, 222.
Kennebeck, 921.
" Purchase, 273.
" River, 323.
Kennedy, Alex., 1086-7.
" Capt., Arch., 626, 1070.
" Dennis, 534.
Kennet Square, 611.
Kent Co., 162, 1165.
" David, 802-3.
" Rachel, 802, 1320.
" Stephen, of N. Jersey, 204, 801, 811.
" Township, 867-8.
" Wm., 203, 802.
" Zernia, 802.
Kentner, Geo., 478, 480, 1001.
Kentucke, 477, 1282-3.
Kenty, Bay of (Kquenty, Quinte), 346, 363-8, 383, 417-8-9, 420-1-3-4.
Kenyon, Lloyd, 16.
Kenzie, Mrs., 298.
Kepp (or Kess), Isaac, 747-8.
" Thomas, 756.
Kerch, David, 775.
" Job, 775.
" Rob., of N. York, 774.
" Wm., 774.
Kerin, Mr., 691-2.
Kern, Rev. John Michl., 262, 1333.
Kerney, Mr., 1235-7.
Kerr, Ebenezer, 104-5.
Kershaw, Joseph, 186.
" Joshua, 568-9.
Kess (or Kepp), Isaac, 747-8.
Ketchum, Abijah, 474.
" Daniel, 474.
" James, of Connecticut, 224.
" John, of Connecticut, 252-7, 263.
" Jonathan, of Connecticut, 230, 812.
" Joseph, 258.
" Saml., 231, 258, 812.
Kettle Creek, 170, 727.
Kettler, Andries, 445.
Key, Mrs., 311.
Keys, John, 856.
Kidd, Alex., of Philadelphia, 684.
" Mr., 260.
Kimble, Saml., 573, 1214.
Kimmerly, Andr., 442.
Kinderhook, 363-4, 428, 445-6-7, 451, 470, 1043.
" (Kenterhook), District, 1016.
" Patent of, 446, 451-2.
Kine, George, of Pensilvania, 109.
King, Capt., 515-6.
" Elenas, 516.
" Mrs. Elenas, 516.

King Fisher (H. M. Sloop), 302, 862.
" George, 510.
" Henry, 611.
" James, of N. York, 774.
" Julius, 43.
" Mrs. Kesia, 774-5.
" Col. Richd., of 96 Dist., 143, 162, 680, 702, 714, 792, 849.
" Street, Marblehead, 606.
" Thos., 43.
King's Bridge, 116, 233, 289, 698, 755-6-7, 770, 791-6, 818, 864, 897, 1292-3.
" County, 224, 241, 280, 807, 1320-1.
" District, 903.
" Road, 334.
Kingsborough, (or Kingsbury), 104, 251, 277, 298-9, 348, 400, 432, 487, 857, 949, 1010, 1012-13, 1025-9, 1031, 1065, 1089, 1090, 1118, 1261-5-6, 1285.
Kingsbury, Joseph, 1123.
" Patent, 398.
Kingsland, 472.
Kingsley, George, 507.
" Mr., 193, 1197-8-9, 1200-1.
" Zephaniah, 1197-8, 1201.
Kingston, 20, 224-5-6, 242-3, 293, 812, 823-4-6, 848, 982, 1242.
" Jas., 1296.
" North, 303-4.
" Col. Robert, 14, 1182, 1336-8, 1342, 1351.
Kingwood, 409.
Kipp, Benj., 764-5.
" Capt., 771, 897.
" James, 764-5.
" Jesse, 765.
" Saml., of N. York, 763-6.
" Thos., 764-5.
" Wm., 764-5.
Kirshaw, Mr., 187.
Kirwin, Col., 499.
Klyne, John, 927-8-9.
Knapp, Capt., 764-7.
" Joseph, of N. Y. Prov., 468.
" Titus, of N. Y. Prov., 777.
" Tobias, 776.
Knight, Elijah, 91.
Knox, Mr., 678.
" Mr., of Shelburn, 731, 841.
" Wm., of N. Y. Prov., 1298.
Knoxborough, 1299.
Korman, Michael, 1121-2.
Kortwright Township, 85-6.
Kquenty, (Kenty or Quinte), Bay of, 420-1-3-4.
Kunberel, Mr., 187.
Kyler, Abraham, 562.
" Col., 654-5.
" Cornelius, 769.
" Mr., 1258.
Kyln, Mr., 933.

L'Assomption, 424.
Laber, Charles, 81.
La Chine, 345, 371, 386, 390, 424-5, 1003, 1027, 1033-4, 1057-8, 1062-4, 1073, 1093.
Lackens, Jno., 223.
La Colle, Riviere, 349.

Lacy, Mr., 900-1.
Lagransie, Amie, 446.
Laird, Capt., 1162-3.
Lake, Jacobus, 1109.
" Mr., 178.
" Major, 347.
" Thomas, 1267.
Lamb, Mrs. Hannah, 677.
" Isaac, 389.
" Jesse, 1082.
" Joseph, 159, 678.
Lambton, Wm., 558.
Lamerce, Jashua, 1321.
La Mott, Capt., 936.
Lancaster, 283-4, 415-6, 434, 777, 1222.
" Co., 109, 129, 160, 879, 987.
" Mr., 1218-9.
Landon, Asa, 1084.
Lane & Fraser, 1209.
" George, 568.
" John, of N. Y. Prov., 330.
" Peter, 568.
Lanesboro, 796.
Langan, Lieut. P., 418.
Langdon, Mr., 1273.
Langwood, Fort, 58.
Lansen, Francis, 551.
Lansing, Abraham, 402.
" Jacob, 941.
" Lt. Philip, 160, 348, 390, 929, 931-6, 1075.
Lanson, Capt. Jacob, 380.
La Prairie, 346, 931.
Larie St., New York, 178, 1119, 1120.
Larraway, Isaac, 1030.
Lasley, Hannah, 832.
Latta, Wm., of Massachusetts, 660-3.
Laurel Grove, 1307-8.
" Swamp, 608.
Laurence, Col., of Halifax, 690.
" Joseph, 787.
" Martha, 567.
" Mr., 643.
Law, James, 764.
Lawrence, Adam, 856.
" Lt.-Col. Elisha, of N. Jersey, 35, 73, 135-6-7, 151-2, 504, 652.
" John, 101, 132-6, 200, 717, 1049, 1106, 1123, 1174.
" Jos., 609.
" Martha, 85.
" Mary, 247.
" Mr., 334.
" Neck, 1270-1.
" Samuel, 463.
" Major Thomas, 136.
" Wm., of N. York, 830.
Lawson, John P., of N. Y. Prov., 240, 1320.
" Isaac, 304.
Lawyer, John, 352, 361.
Leahy, Wm., 1104-5.
Leake, Ann, 853.
" Capt., 406, 440, 937, 953, 1034-7, 1080, 1106, 1117, 1262.
" John, 321, 951.
" Major, 349, 398, 401-2-4-7, 415, 418, 424-8, 434, 447, 457, 479, 934, 940-1-2, 970, 1027.

Leake, P., 419.
Leaky, Wm., senr., of N. York, 389.
Leary (Larie) St., N. York, 178, 1119, 1120.
Leave & Co., 866.
Lebanon, 223.
Lecker, Geo., 705.
Lee, Fort, 262.
" Genl., 68, 256.
" Mr., 1188.
" Robert, 306.
Lefferts, (Lefarts, Lefergtts, Leffert), Aldoma, 917.
" Dirk, 212, 1053.
" Mr., 106, 923.
" Nicholas, 585.
Lefroy, Genl. Sir Henry, 24.
Leggat (Leggett), Capt. John, 235, 242, 674, 705.
" George, 494-5.
" James, 779.
" Mrs. Mary, 494.
Legge, Robt. G., 213.
Leigh, Sir Egerton, 1244.
Legmour, Thos., 130.
Le Marr, Thos., 163.
Lemon, Alexr., 295.
Lennekin, Zebedee, 323.
Lent, Abraham, 555.
" James, 556.
Leonard, Capt., 198.
" George, 105, 221, 699, 866, 873, 989.
" John, of Monmouth Co., 31, 70, 297, 318, 610, 788.
" Magdalen, 71.
" Mr., 831.
" Mrs., 298.
" Paulus, 664.
" Saml., 818, 917, 925.
Le Roome, John Chevalier, 177, 211, 304, 785, 1270.
Lerpsbergh, Mr., 395.
Lescom, Mr., 661.
Leslie, Gen., 54, 242, 526, 618-9, 1126, 1130, 1226, 1244.
" Govr., 43.
Lessumes, Isaac, 731.
Lester, Gen., 308.
Levan, Robt., 1173.
Levans, Mr., 1180.
Levesque, Francis, 1359.
Lewage, John, 1205.
Lewellens, Abel, 67.
Lewis, Barnet, 844.
" Capt., 215.
" Curtis, 564, 611-2-3.
" David, of N. Jersey, 342.
" Francis, 862.
" Mrs. Hannah, 611.
" Mrs. Jane, 343.
" John, 612.
" Lewis, 612.
" Reuben, 611.
" Robt., 451.
" Saml., 203.
" Thos., 902.
Lewiston, Mr., 845.

Lexington, Battle of, 42, 218, 272, 4
  492-3, 599, 624, 687, 752, 762, 798, 922,
  1111, 1147, 1160, 1232.
Liddel, Andrew, of Schenectady, 1267.
Lidias, John Henry, 421.
Lifford, Derrick, 30.
Light House Post, 633.
Lightenstine, John, 1142-3.
Lightman, Henry, 662.
Limburner & Co., 705.
Lime (Lyme) Township, 510, 517, 617,
  639, 640-2, 721, 1272.
Linch, James, of Tryon Co., 459, 486.
Lincoln, 272.
Lincoln's Inn Fields, 20, 327, 664, 1341-
  2, 1351, 1370.
Lincolnshire, 643.
Lindley, Fort, 1210.
Lindsay, (Lindsey), Abigail, 1061.
  " Abraham, 1174.
  " Derby, 1061.
  " John, 1061.
  " Samuel, of Pensilvania, 535-8.
Linsycombe, Gideon, 46.
Lippincott, Capt., 317.
  " Richd., of N. Jersey, 307,
  1320.
Lion (Ship), 190.
Lisbon, 93, 565, 803.
Liscolm, Nehemiah, 660-4.
Lisle, James, 722.
Lissatt (Lisitt), Patrick, of Pensilvania,
  160, 1333.
Lister, Murray, 844.
Litchfield, 124, 290-1, 439, 440, 816, 865-
  7, 1015.
  " Gaol, 207, 882.
Little George (Vessel), 799.
  " Jas, 196.
  " Falls, 475.
  " Queen St., N. York, 1296.
  " River, 241, 1187-8.
Littlefield, Mr., 1300.
Littraer, Geo., 340.
Lively, Reuben, of S. Carolina, 175, 692.
  " (Sloop), 548, 831.
Liverpool, 1188.
Livingston, Flora, 1067.
  " Gilbert, 235.
  " Govr., 67, 79, 98, 112, 151,
  561, 894.
  " Henry, jr., 757.
  " John, 1067-8.
  " Judge, 1088, 1256.
  " Mr., 971.
  " Neil, 1067.
  " Philip, 356, 483, 749, 1103.
  " P. Henry, 234.
  " Robt. Gibb, 870-1.
  " V. B., 1067.
Livingston's Manor, 907.
Lloyd, Benj., 595.
  " John, 278.
  " Mich., of N. York, 790.
  " Mr., 902.
  " Col. Richd., 593.
  " Wm., 157, 595.
Lloyd's Neck, 210-2, 223-4, 231, 243, 251-
  2, 263, 302, 667-8, 716-7, 825, 847-8,
  850, 861-5-6, 873-7, 893.

Locke, Mr., 219.
Lockwood, Col., 847.
  " Gresham (or Gersham), 861-4.
  " James, 903.
Lockwood's, 1206.
Loder, Danl., 828.
  " Jacob, of Connecticut, 828, 1320.
Logan, James, 414.
Loggan, Stoffel, 35.
Loghouse, 467.
Lombard St., N. York, 1244.
London, New, 721, 1273.
  " (Schooner), 513.
  " Wall, 148.
Londonderry, 506, 832.
  " Township, 63, 849.
Long Cane Settlement, 143, 174-5.
  " Christopher, 156-7-8-9.
  " Geo., of 96, 143.
  " Hill Division, 113-4.
  " Island, 52, 78, 84, 98-9, 100-2, 139,
  201-7-9, 214-6, 223-4, 232-5, 243-
  6, 258-9, 261-7-8-9, 270, 282, 290-
  3, 300-2-3-9, 314, 349, 445, 453,
  497, 540-7, 562-7, 583, 593-4, 612,
  655, 708, 710, 716, 722-3, 745-9,
  750-5-6-8, 760-1-8, 789, 790, 806-8-
  9, 811-12-13-17, 822-5-6, 828-9, 830-
  5, 843, 850-5-6, 860-2-4-7, 871-4-
  6-8, 880-2-4-5-6, 892, 909, 1007,
  1212, 1232, 1240, 1320-3.
  " Island, St. John's River, 228, 264-
  6, 281.
  " Island, Battle of, 764-5.
  " James, 139.
  " John, of Pesamaqudy, 315-6.
  " Reach, 813, 821, 842, 885, 1310.
  " Sault, 403, 411, 470.
Longfield, Mr., 760.
Longneck, 300.
Longworth, Isaac, 128, 627.
Lonsberry, Thos., 246.
Lord, Henry, 217.
Lorraway, Isaac. 1015-6.
Losberg, Genl., 764-777.
Lott, Abraham, 917.
Loucks, Abrm., of N. Y. Prov., 428.
  " Geo., 1099.
  " Jacob, of N. Y. Prov., 428.
Louisburg, 1277.
  " Seige of, 914.
Louring, Eben, 832.
Lovel, Ebenezer, 89.
Lovelace, (Loveless), Archd., 152.
  " Ebenezer, 152.
  " Elizabeth, 152.
  " James, of Albany, 107, 152.
  " Mrs. Lonas, 152.
  " Lucy, 152.
  " Thos., 107, 152.
  " Wm., 152, 817.
Lovell, John, 1139.
  " Timothy, of Vermont, 88, 579.
Low, Cornl., 1303.
  " Ed., 1277.
  " Isaac, 944-5, 1318.
  " John, 1004.
Lowndes & Pennman, 1205.
Lowrie, Thos., 1303.
Lucas, Amor, 1031-2.

89 AR.

Luce, Will, 554.
Lucretia, (Brig), 626.
Lucy, (Schooner), 656.
Ludington, Col. Henry, 776.
Ludlow, Chf. Justice, 267-9, 270, 584.
  855-6-7, 860, 878.
" Genl. D., 594.
" Col. Sir Gabriel G., of N. York.
  232, 267-8, 598, 838, 860, 972.
" Hon. G. Duncan, 99, 267.
" Henry, 1241.
" Mrs., 267-8.
Lufbry, Nathaniel,
Lukin, Jesse, 1001.
Lukins, John, 201.
Lum, Henry, 1292.
Lumon, Major, 103.
Lutkins, Hendric, of N. Jersey, 747.
Lyde, Edward, of Boston, 144.
" Nath. B., 145.
" & Rogers, 144.
Lydons, John, 1041.
Lyle & Banks, 1311.
" James, 1311-2.
" Lt.-Col., Mathew, 28.
Lyman, 509. 617.
" Danl., of Newhaven, 82, 786.
" Henry. 1263.
" Lt., 131.
Lymburner & Co., 705.
" John, 311.
" Mathew, of Penobscot, 311.
Lymington, 1194.
Lyn Haven, River, 1150.
Lynch, James, of Tryon Co., 459, 486.
" Thos., 84.
Lynches Creek, 165.
" Lake, 165.
Lynn, 40.
Lyon, James, 225.
" John, 227, 1320.
" Joseph Oliver, of Fairfield, 225-6.
" Henry, 226.
" M., 1259.
" Peter, 226.
Lyons, Mr., 245.
Lytle, Mr., 48.

McAdam, Ann, 167.
McAllister, Samuel, of S. Carolina, 182. 702.
" Terrence, of N. York, 85.
McAlpine, Capt., 368, 392, 414, 457, 462.
  487, 937, 959, 960, 1059, 1115.
" Danl., 948.
McAntyre, Dr., 40.
McArthur, Brig.-Genl. Arch., 60, 155.
  163, 174, 191, 339, 582.
  696, 705, 715, 718, 728.
" Donald, 1074.
" Duncan, of N. Y. Prov., 368.
" Major, 96, 1214.
" Neil, 1334.
McArthy, Mrs. Jane, 409.
" John, of N. Y. Prov., 409.
" John, jr., 409.
McAuley, Robt., of N. Y. Prov., 436, 449.
McBean, Angus, of Vermont, 346-9.

McCaffrey, John. 1103.
McCaskell. Alexr., 102.
McCaul, Henderson, 1311-2.
McCawley, Mrs., 1222.
McConnil. Wm., J. P., 295.
McCrea, Capt., 1049.
" John, 348.
McCrummell. Donald. 549, 550.
McCulloch, Capt., 1132.
" Robt., 1143.
" Thos., 133.
McDonald, Capt. Alex., of Pensilvania, 253, 370.
" Allan, 86.
" Lt. Allen, 356, 404.
" Capt. Archd., 369.
" Brig.-Genl., 235-6.
" Capt., 85.
" Col., 1250.
" Genl., 102, 280.
" Capt. John, 353, 382, 404.
" Jos., 1272.
" Keneth, 1066.
" Lewis, 217.
" Murdoch, 1251.
" Ronald, 375.
" Thos., of N. Y. Prov., 281.
" Wm., 175, 183.
McDonell. Alex., of N. Y. Prov., 378-9, 392-4.
" Alex., 1086.
" Allan, 1103.
" Capt. Allen, 379.
" Angus, of N. Y. Prov., 394.
" Angus, 1058.
" Capt. Angus, 419, 440.
" Capt. Archd., 449.
" Capt., 394, 444, 482.
" Donald, 371, 392-3, 1058, 1060, 1088-9.
" Duncan, of N. Y. Prov., 390-3-5.
" Hugh, 393, 1086.
" Corpr. John, 392.
" Capt. John, of Tryon Co., 357-9, 1285.
" Kenneth, of N. Y. Prov., 374.
" Ronald, of Tryon Co., 371-4.
McDougall. Dun., 374.
" John, 1095.
McEvers. Jas., 1314.
McEwen. Patrick, of S. Carolina, 841.
McGee, John, 443.
" Sergt. John, 355.
McGeer, Cornelia, 336.
" Martha, 336.
" Mrs. Mary, 335.
" Wm., of N. Y. Prov., 335-6.
McGerth, Danl., 1287.
McGill. Dd., 344.
McGilles. Donald, 1060.
McGlaughlan, Wm., 1255.
McGowan, Patrick, 259.
McGrath, 1039.
McGregor, Donald, 364.
" Donel, 1062.
" Hugh, of N. Y. Prov., 378.
" John, 369.
" Peter, of N. Y. Prov., 368-9.

INDEX. 1411

McGrown, John, 355.
McGruer, Catharine, 1098.
" John, 1054.
McGuire, Ed., 192.
" John, 112.
McGwin, Daniel, 1007.
McIlmoyle, James, of N. York, 933.
McIntosh, Alexr., 1109.
" John, of N. Y. Prov., 373.
" Launchn., 1246.
McIntyre, Dr., 128.
" Duncan, 379, 1076.
" John, of N. Y. Prov., 460, 485.
" John, senr., 486.
" Robt., 486.
McKage, G., 1222.
McKay, Angus, of Tryon Co., 381.
" Capt., 449, 457.
" Hugh, 1060-1.
" John, of Tryon Co., 357-9, 396, 1109.
" Mr., 150.
" Wm., 1060.
McKee, Alexr., 987.
" Allen, 986.
" Capt., 1282.
" John, of Connecticut, 207.
" Wm., 207.
McKee's Purchase, 856.
McKenly, Susanah, 479.
McKenny, James, 377.
McKenzie, Capt., 1277.
" Colin, of N. Y. Prov., 450, 1280.
" Duncan, of Tryon Co., 357-8.
" John, 358-9.
" Capt. John, 357.
" Lt. John, 486.
" Lawr., of N. Y. Prov., 330.
" Robt., 1201.
" Mrs. Sarah, 1280.
McKeoughs, Tim, of Antiginish, 131.
McKim, Saml., 1286-7.
McKisson, Lawyer, 431.
McKnight, Dr. Charles, 1292.
" Mr., 1330.
" Thos., 1231.
McKoy, Capt., 940-1.
McLaren, Ewen, 1077.
McLauren, Major, 191.
McLean, Brig.-Genl. Allen, 254, 475-6.
" David, 1313.
" Donald, of Tryon Co., 356.
" Genl., 58, 316, 323.
" Gr., 371.
" John, 53, 282.
" Mr., 453.
" Murdoch, of N. Y. Prov., 355-6.
" Neil, 374.
McLellan, John, 48.
McLelland, Margaret, 1187.
" Robt., 1187.
McLennan, John, of N. Y. Prov., 379.
McLeod, Genl., 244,704.
" Mr., 236.
" Capt. Norman, 363, 371, 574.
" Wm., of Tryon Co., 370.
McMartin, John, of N. Y. Prov., 385.
" Lt., 385.

McMartin, Malcolm, of N.Y. Prov., 385.
McMaster, Danl., 57.
" James, of Boston, 56.
" John, 56.
" Patrick, 56.
McMeeking, Pr., 1281.
" Thomas, of N. Y. Prov., 1280, 1334.
McMullin, Donald, 1097.
" Wm., 223.
McNab, Lt. Allen, 465.
McNaughton, Alex., of N. Hampshire, 540.
" John, 1076.
McNeal, Major Charles, 146.
" Hugh, of Pensilvania, 295.
" James, 295.
McNeil, Capt., of Cross Creek, 338.
" Major, 241.
McNerin, John, of N. Y. Prov., 404-5.
McNight, Charles 117.
McPhaill, John, 1319.
McPherson, Alex., of N. Y. Prov., 382.
" Alister, 382.
" Donald, 1333.
" Mary, 1333.
" Murdoch, 1088.
McQueen, Wm., 1250.
McQuin's Patent, 602.
McRae, Duncan, 1313.
McTaggart, James, 1035.

MacArthur, Chs., 1043.
" Deborah, 1043.
" John, 1074.
MacCloud, Brig.-Genl., 695.
MacDonald, Capt., 1046, 1093.
" Duncan, 1081.
MacDonell, Alex., 1066.
" Allan, 1066.
" Capt. Angus, 1087.
" Duncan, 1093-6-7-8.
" John, 1064, 1093-4.
" Keneth, 1063.
" Randel, 964.
" Roderic, 1066.
" Ronald, 1067.
MacDougal, John, 1034.
" Peter, 1033-6.
" Wm., 664.
MacDowen, And., 858.
MacEwen, James, 732.
MacGillis, Donald, of Tryon Co., 1087.
" Hugh, 1087.
MacGreer, James, 749.
" John, 749.
MacGroah, Wm., 1079.
MacIntosh, James, of N. York, 939.
MacKay, Dawkins &, 242.
" G., 326.
" Hugh, 904.
MacKaye, Ensn. Malcolm, 338.
MacKee, Alex., 1082.
MacKenny, John, 1033.
MacKenzie, Capt., 619, 1092.
" R., 1373-4-5-6.
MacKnight, Thos., 1151.
MacKinney, John, 1036.
MacLeod, Isabel, 1078.

MacLeod, Wm., 1078.
MacNaughton, Donald, 1077.
MacNeal, Capt. Danl., 736.
MacNeill, Elizabeth, 918.
MacQui, Danl., 952.

Macarter, Wm., 536.
Macarthur, Duncan, 1064.
Macauly, Robt., 436, 449.
Macbain, Andrew. 1070.
" Isbel, 1070.
Macbride, Wm., 586-7.
Maccaul & Co.. Henderson, 632.
Macdonald, Capt., 662.
Macdonald, John, of N. York, 816-9.
" Soirle, of N. Carolina, 549, 550.
Macdonell, Alex., 1095-6.
" Capt. Arch., 1083, 1096.
" Capt., 1065.
" Capt. J., 1088.
" John, 1068, 1095-6-7-8.
" Roderick, 1068.
" Ranald, 1096.
" Ronald, 1057.
" Rory, 1067.
Macdowal, John, & Co., 632.
Macewen, Capt., 660-1.
" James, 664.
Macgarth, Col., 527-8.
Macgee, Henry, of Pensilvania, 537.
Macgevah, Wm., 1079.
Macgregor, John, 1064.
Macguire, John, of Pensilvania, 495.
Machydew, Samuel. 1274.
Macintosh, Col., 1240.
Mackay, Don'd. 1078.
" Capt. John, 260.
" John, 1059, 1061.
Mackenzie, Capt., 752, 1058, 1074-8.
" Robt., 561, 744, 1338, 1342.
" Wm., of Tryon Co., 148.
Mackim, James, 1028.
Mackinnon, Capt., 694.
Mackinstin, Samuel, 827.
Mackrahin, Capt., 1063.
Maclaghey, Pat., 858.
Maclauren. Major. 674-5.
Maclean, Capt., 1089.
" Donald, 1060.
" Genl., 1119.
" John, 767.
Maclellan, Wm., 729, 996.
Maclellan's Creek, 549.
Maclelland, Robt., 1188.
Macleod, Genl., 244, 704.
" Malcolm, 1078.
" Nancy, 1119.
" Capt. Norman, 363, 371, 574.
Macley, Henry, 1099.
Maclin, Wm., 1334.
Maccloud, Lt. Donald, 551.
Macloud, Alex., 548.
" John, of N. Carolina, 548.
Macmiken, Thos., 994.
Macnamara, John 747.
Macnaughton, Alex., of Georgia, 914.
Macneil, Archibald, of Massachusetts. 918.

Macneil, Mary, 918.
" Nancy, 918.
" Sarah, 918, 920.
" Wm. Henry, 918.
Macnut, Eva, 1040.
" James, 1040.
Macpherson, John, 1031, 1054.
" Peter, 1033.
Macquin, John, 565, 613.
Macquire, Jas., 499.
Macylmoil, James, 937.
Maagash, 711.
Maban, Adam, 1359.
Maceon, Mr., 860.
Machiche, 328, 330-1, 337-8, 344, 392-3-5, 434-7, 443, 455-8, 466, 478, 487, 1001, 1014-17, 1027, 1031-4-6, 1040-1-2, 1059, 1079, 1112, 1119, 1257, 1262.
Machie, Alex., 1272.
Mack, Capt., 1272.
Mackrel, Michl., 698.
Madam Kiswick, 309.
Madeira, 118.
Madiville, Henry, 474.
Magadary River, 901.
Magan, Wm., 680.
Maganogwuck, 314.
Magee, Robt., 949.
Mahogany, 831.
Mahony, Township, 124.
Maidstone, (Ship), 789.
Mail, Peter, 158.
" Philip, 158.
Majery, Rachel, 605.
Major, Sarah, 647.
Major's Island, 285.
Majorfield, 806-9, 810-11, 824-5-7-8, 838-9, 850, 867, 870-3. 880.
Majorville, 282, 307, 817-9, 854, 872, 889, 899, 904, 908.
Mal Bay, 332, 397, 476.
Mallory, Caleb, 868, 873.
" Enoch, of N. Y. Prov., 470.
Mallowney, John, of Philadelphia, 156-7.
Man, Isaac, of N. Y. Prov., 333-4.
" Isaac, jr., 334-5, 924.
" Williams, 976.
Manadrix, 350.
Manchester, 214, 575-6-7-8-9, 632, 1114, 1268, 1311-2.
Mandeville, Richd., 1124.
Mangerfield, 222, 251.
Mangerville (Maugerville), 71, 232, 247, 253, 257-9, 272-7, 283-8-9, 299, 302, 1320-1.
Manhood, Col., 111, 712, 824, 908.
Manley, John, 147.
Mann, Benj., 464.
" Thos., of Gaspe, 31.
Mannel, Henseck, 430.
Manning, Wm., 802.
Mansfield, Isaac, 600-6.
" Nathan, 82.
Maple Island Creek, 531.
Mapletown, 940-1, 1071.
Marble Mountain, 298.
Marblehead, 605-6-7, 721-5-6, 1146-7-8, 1160.
Marbeltown, 993, 1257-8.

March, Wm., 91.
Marchington, Mrs., 612.
" Philip, of Pensilvania, 494, 567, 612-4.
Marguard, A. D. C., 764.
Mariann, (Schooner), 906.
Mark, Conrad, 526-8.
Markes, Hen., 1022.
Market St., Philadelphia, 1177.
Markil, Henrick, 1113.
Markill, Henry, 1114.
" Jacob, 1114.
Markle, Jacob, 472.
" John, 481.
" Wm., 472.
Markley, Jacob, of N. Y. Prov., 395, 1099.
" Henry, of Tryon Co., 395, 1099, 1100.
" Michl., 396, 1100.
Marks, Conrad, of S. Carolina, 63, 662.
" Lawrence, of S. Carolina, 157, 184.
" Nehemiah, 786.
Marlboro St., Boston, 919.
Marlborough St., Newport, 587.
Marlbro, New, 586.
Marlandale, Henry, of Pensilvania, 162.
Marlland, Major, 841.
Marsch, John, 1336, 1342.
Marschs, Nichs., 960-1.
Marsh, 20.
" Abraham, of Albany Co., 953.
" Col., 652-3.
" Danl., 134.
" Elias, 179.
" James, 1018.
" John, 14, 1251.
" Jonathan, 711, 743.
" Joseph, 204, 1020.
" Mr., 687.
" Saml., 530.
" Wm., of N. Y. Prov., 575, 1050.
Marshal, George, 841.
" Wm., 577.
" Henry, 327.
" John, of Georgia, 60.
Marshfield, 505-6-7.
Marsten, Benj., of Massachusetts, 605.
Marston, John, 721.
" Mrs., 606-8.
Martha (Ship), 492-3.
Marten, Lynn, 1191-2.
Martin, Alex., 102.
" Angus, 1251.
" Capt., 919.
" Justice Edmund, 598.
" Govr., 42, 154, 235, 695-6, 1197, 1206-7, 1231.
" Isaac, 597.
" John, 179, 1219.
" Lyman, 327.
" Mrs. Margaret, 1273.
" Peter, 1002.
" Robt., 818.
Martindale, Henry, 680.
Martyn, Mich., 1287.
" Sd., 1287.
" Wm., 1186.

Marven, Elihu, 1104.
Marvill, Col., 751.
Mary (Brig), 195
Maryon, Genl., 763.
Marysburgh, 443.
Masco, River, 89.
Mase, Mr., 929.
Masisco Bay (Messisque Bay), 386, 407-9, 457, 1080, 1269.
Mason, 465, 616.
" Danl., 104.
Mason's Patent, 508, 617.
Massachusetts Bay, 32, 40, 112, 131, 272, 302-4, 322, 337, 389, 444-8, 463-5, 490, 586, 639. 725, 1285.
" Port, 493.
Massey, Genl., 39.
Massie, James, 1111.
Mastic, 594.
Mastick River, 595.
Mastin, Danl., 526.
" John, 870.
Maston, John, 1321.
Mattack, Joseph, 124.
Matchepenix, 128.
Mather, D., 628.
Mathews, Col., 840.
" David, Mayor of N. York, 63, 106, 139, 160-6, 343, 500, 554-6, 559, 574, 1006.
" Dr., 159, 174.
" Genl., 732.
" Major, 365, 986, 990, 1280.
" R., 575-7, 682.
" Wm., .329.
Matson, Benj., 1147.~
Mattack, Joseph, 124.
Mawhood, Col., 111.
Maxwell, Genl., 679.
" Major, 524.
" Wm., 729, 730.
May, John, 186.
Maybee (Mabee), Eleanor, 1022, 1261.
" Jeremiah, 1320.
" Lewis, of Tryon Co., 983.
" Peter, of N. York, 765, 1023, 1261-2.
" Solomon, 817.
Mayfield(s), 1021, 1261.
Mayhew, Peter, 327, 916.
Mayor, Jacob, 988.
Mayor Ville, 223.
Mea. John, 270.
Mead, Capt., 485.
Meadows, Genl., 871.
Meagher, Martin, of N. Carolina, 153.
Meaker, John, 238.
" Stephen, 238.
Mecklenburgh, 162, 441, 524-6, 710-11, 1207.
Medford, 623.
Medley, Col., 715.
Meek, Wm., of S. Carolina, 183, 717.
Meighler, Danl., 170-1.
Melesquan, 743.
Melford, Mrs. Mary, 575.
Mellows, David Henry, of N. York, 159.
Melyanum, (A. D. C.), 777.

Mening, Mr., 645.
Mercer, Alex., 1266.
" Capt., 821.
" Genl., 218.
" Joseph, of N. Carolina, 255.
Merceran, Andrew, of N. Jersey, 277.
" Phebe, 277-8.
Mercury, (Frigate), 1327.
Meredith, John, of Pensilvania, 709.
" Mr., 1170.
Meriamachee (Merimichee), 817-8, 841.
Merrick, Elnathan, 438.
" Robt., 288.
Merriman, Genl. S., 799.
Merritt, James, of N. York, 781-3.
" Jeremiah, 779.
" Nathan, of N. Y. Prov., 261.
" Rogers, Taylor &, 221.
" Thomas, 770, 1321.
Metz, Henry, of N. Y. Prov., 423-4.
Meyers, John W., 1050.
Mices, Capt., 936.
Michean, Benjamin, of N. York, 834.
Michelher, Daniel, 661.
Mickam, 779.
Middagh, John, 585, 1256, 1257.
" Martin, 1257.
" S ophen, 1256-7.
Middlesex, 198, 319, 464.
" County, 126, 277, 642, 751-2-3, 760, 802, 818, 894, 908, 938.
" Ferry, 339, 340-1-2.
" Island, 340.
Middleton, 82, 103, 119, 120, 130, 508-9, 520-1, 609-10, 616, 617, 627-8-9, 633, 690, 900.
" Dr., 433.
" Mr., 1301.
Midelle St., Boston, 38.
Midlock, Charles, 44.
Migler, Daniel, of S. Carolina, 62.
Milby, William, 520.
Miles, Abigal, 319.
" Justin, 202.
" Mr., 318.
" Samuel, 201, 320.
Milford, Barnabas, 81.
" New, 439, 867, 908.
Milhouse, John, 647.
" Mr., 678.
Miligen, Mr., 1302.
Mill Meadow, 105.
" River, 220.
" St., Newport, 104.
Millar, Abijah, 216.
" James, 216.
" Mr., 887.
" Moses, 811.
" Thos., 968-9.
Milledge, Major, 137, 153, 529, 531, 1273.
" Major Thos., 153.
Miller, Adjutant, 1032.
" Fore. 329, 345, 409, 439, 444, 449, 944.
" Garret, of Charlotte Co., 934, 1103.
" Jacob, 1260.

Miller James, of Portsmouth, 65-7.
" Jeremiah, 1155-6.
" John, 420, 687, 877.
" Manwell, 168.
" Mr., 1213.
" Moses, of N. York, 807-8.
" Peter, of N. Y. Prov., 407, 935.
" Thos., 1212-3-4.
" William, 698, 1223.
Millet, Joseph, 242.
Millidge, Major Thomas, 65-7, 199, 315.
Milligen, Clark &, 1128.
Millikin, Benj., 324.
Millross, Andrew, 1068.
Mills & Hicks, 144.
" Hope, 584.
" John, 700.
" Justice, 717-8.
" Mr., 707.
" Thomas, of N. York, 673.
Millston River, 269.
Milton, Township of, 1212-4.
Milvan, James, 1277.
Minchin, Major, 474-5.
Minet, Mr., 511.
Ming, Thos., 862.
Miniford's Island, 167, 515.
Minisink, 602-3.
Minot, Mr., 923.
Minten, Benj., 514.
Misseroe, George, 508.
Mishimakinac, 1098.
Mississippi River, 1284.
Mitchell, Hugh, 360.
" Peter, 57.
" Wm., 112.
Mock, John, of N. York, 937.
Mobile River, 1213.
Mohawk Indians, 376-7, 1281.
" River, 332, 351, 362, 372, 402, 419, 420, 432, 453-4, 472-3-5, 856, 963, 983, 990, 998-9, 1035, 1053, 1062-4-5-9, 1070-4-7, 1099, 1101, 1110-5-8, 1120-3, 1258, 1283.
Moirle, Jonathan, 139, 140.
Moncreif, Col., 834, 1214.
Moncreel, Col., 1126.
Monk, Goulds &, 1334.
Monmouth, 307, 609.
" Battle of, 71, 690.
" County, 35, 71, 119, 135, 151, 208, 317, 320, 342, 504, 609, 628, 649, 690, 760, 787-8, 917, 925, 1009, 1237, 1270-7.
Monongahela, 55.
Monro, C., 786.
" Charles, 326.
" Hugh, of N. Y. Prov., 384, 944.
Montague, Capt., 513, 862.
Monteith, Mr., 1311.
" Plantation, 1130.
" Walter, 631.
Montgomery, Alex., 861, 903.
" Alex., jr., of N. York, 861-4.
" Archibald, 861-4.

Montgomery, Capt., 391, 714.
" Col., 312.
" David, 861.
" Fort, 53, 247, 281, 308, 313, 821, 830, 915, 1048.
" John, 861.
" Hugh, 861.
" Mary, 861.
" Mr., 297.
" New, 869.
" Sarah, 861.
" Susannah, 861.
Montreal, 11, ᴌᴏ, 355-6-7-8, 362-3-8-9, 372-8, 382-4-7, 392, 401-3-7, 411, 418-9, 436, 442-3, 444-7-9, 453-9, 466, 471-3-4-8-9, 480-1-2, 662, 682, 738, 917-8, 924, 931-3-5-8, 943, 1027, 1032-3, 1057-8, 1062-3, 1055, 1064-5-8-9, 1073-6-9, 1083, 1097, 1104-6-7, 1119, 1181-2, 1259, 1267, 1323-4, 1359, 1365-6-7.
Montreson, John, 71.
Montressor, Major, 53.
Montru Cornu, 165.
Moody, Capt., 760.
" James, 271, 1180.
" Lt. James, 128, 1237.
" John, 1243.
Moor, Maurice, 924-5.
" Saml., 743.
" Wm., 840.
Moore, Col., 1274.
" Jas., 1253.
" John, 800.
" Joseph, 135.
" S. & E., 1298.
Moore's Creek, 550.
" " Battle, 54.
" " Bridge, 96-7, 102, 244-5, 280, 704, 1313.
Moors, Capt. Joseph, 465.
Morany (Ship), 405.
Morcelis, John, 1114.
Morden, James, 1110.
" Joseph, 1111.
Mordoff, George, 1005, 1021.
More, Saml., 142.
Morehead, Thos., 660.
" Wm., 1141.
Morehouse, Danl., of N. York, 301, 893.
" Saml., 893.
Moreton, Mr., 685-6.
Morice, Dr., 1153.
Moris, Rich'd, 69.
Morison, Malcolm, 314.
" Alex., 1334.
Morr, Miss, 923.
Morrell, John, of N. Y. Prov., 259.
Morris, Chief Justice, 601.
" Col., 235, 628, 771, 782, 815-6-7, 830, 1270.
" County, 67-8, 128, 140-9, 150, 227, 298, 307-8, 887.
" House, 756.
" Col. George, 1318.
" Lt.-Col. John, of N. Jersey, 342, 608, 666, 917, 925.
" Col. Lewis, 776, 854.
" Mr., 541, 1174.

Morris, Richd., 116.
" Robt., 601, 1288-9.
" Col. Roger, 246-7, 1318.
" Roger, 767.
" Wm., 715.
Morrisiana, 285, 290, 571, 764-8-9, 771-4-6-7-8-9, 780-2-3, 790-5, 807, 822-3, 854, 864, 881.
Morrison, John, 832.
Morristown, 126, 254-5-6-7, 315, 561.
Morse, Capt., 295.
" Col., 58.
" Mr., 1274.
Morson, Arthur, 632.
Mortman, Dennis, 698.
Morton, Govr., 1231 .
" Mr., 684, 1191.
Mortule, Jacob, 472.
Mosher, Lewis, of N. Y. Prov., 485.
Moss, Mr., 684, 727, 1267.
Mossman, Mr., 1308.
Mott, Mr., 610.
Mouleton, 865.
Moulton, Joanna, 145.
" Jonathan, 145.
Mound Neck, 586-7-8.
Mount Castle, Lord, 1141.
" Desert, 40.
" Holly, 1292.
Mount, James, 609.
" Mich., 787-9.
Mountain Creek, 695.
Mourese, John, 682.
Mowat, Capt., 172-3, 273-5-6, 305, 316, 905-6.
" J. C., 304.
Mowyr, Jon'n., 1320.
Moxen, Mary, 484.
Moyer, Mr., 1282.
Moyes, John, 124, 672.
Mud Fort, 1169, 1179, 1288.
" Island, 1178.
" Lick, Waters of, 169.
Muddy Creek, 1246.
Mudler Creek, 169.
Mulberry Grove Plantation, 1126-8-9.
" Street, Philadelphia, 566.
Mulle, Mrs. Phebe, 108.
" Saml., of Long Island, 108.
Mulliner, Thos., 789.
Mulloney, John, 1333.
Mulloy, Hugh, 30.
Mumford, Lewis, 1300.
Munday, Jos., of N. Jersey, 314.
" Nicholas, 314.
" Reuben, 314.
Munn, Alex., of N. Carolina, 53.
Munro, Alex., 1095, 1119.
" Donald, of N. Y. Prov., 344.
" Hugh, of N. Y. Prov., 382, 951, 1078-9.
" Capt. John, 344-5, 475-6, 1256-7.
" Lieut., 1120.
" Mr., 952, 1148.
" Nathan, of N. Jersey, 92.
" Simon, 1129.
" Thomas, 1103.
Munson, Jared, 576.

Munson, Mr., 578.
" Thaddeus, 576.
" Walter, 288.
Mur, Joseph, 179.
Murcheson (Murchison), Duncan, 356, 1057-8.
" John, 1057.
" John, jr., 1058.
Murdof, Geo., 1006.
Murison, James, 596.
Murphy, Capt., 190, 662.
" John, of S. Carolina, 694.
Murray, Alex., of Virginia, 76.
" Betty, 77.
" Col., 880.
" Dun., J.P., 284.
" Joel, 868.
" John, 753, 1334.
" Major, 1047.
" Wm., 1160.
Murray's Ferry, 164.
Murrayfield, 879.
Murrels, Will., 678.
Murrison, Ann Woolsey, 98.
" Benj., 98.
" George, of N. York, 98.
" James Delancey, 98.
" Mary, 98.
" Mrs., 101.
" Silvester, 98.
Muscongus, 920.
Musgrave, Col., 758.
" Joseph, 564.
Musk Wash, 793.
Musquash Island, 240, 265, 822, 850.
Myer, David, of Massachusetts, 907.
" Johanns, 246.
" Thos., of Massachusetts, 905-6-7.
Myers, And., of S. Carolina, 185, 676-7, 857.
" John, of Virginia, 332.
" Mr., 1283.

Nacissus (Frigate), 209.
Nairn, Major John, 933.
Naked Creek, 102.
Nane, Moses, 339.
Nansemond Co., 720.
Nantucket, 316.
Nash, Abner, 45-9, 50.
" Huch Meadow, 78.
Nassau, 296, 339, 351.
Naughton, Andr., of N. Y. Prov., 337.
" Mrs. Loes, 924.
Nautulus, (H. M. Ship), 131, 316.
Neal, Danl., of Massachusetts, 107.
Nealey, Major Christopher C., of S. Carolina, 169, 193, 707-8, 727.
Nealy, Capt., 317.
Neave & Co., 863-6.
Nelles, Henry W., 999.
Nelson, Jered, 327.
Nelson's Ferry, 326.
Neptune, (Schooner), 343-4.
Neschat Haw, 1070.
Nettleton, Danl., 469.
New Ashford, 444-9, 455.
" Boston, 1287.

New Bridge, 561-2.
" Britain Township, 709, 710.
" Brunswick, N. Jersey, 92, 248, 572-3-4, 585, 626, 1212-4.
" Cambridge, 950.
" Carlisle, 328-9, 330.
" Dorlock, 481.
" Fort, 220.
" Hampton, 882.
" Hanover Co., 244-5.
" Haven, 80, 98, 286-8, 310, 349, 716, 785-6, 825, 867, 892.
" Ipswich, 616.
" Johnstown, 351-2-3-4-6, 368-9, 370-8, 383-5, 391-2-3-5-6-7, 403-4-5-6-7-8-9, 410-11-14, 421-3, 432-9, 440-1-4-9, 454-6-8, 463-7-9, 471-3-7-8-9, 481-2, 1069, 1079, 1087, 1093-4-7-8-9 1102-4-8, 1110-15, 1121-2, 1255-6, 1261.
" London, 52, 80, 159, 639, 640-1-6, 721, 1184-5, 1273.
" Marlbro, 586.
" Milford, 201-3, 439, 867-8, 908.
" Montgomery, 869.
" Orleans, 1284.
" Paisley, 414.
" Perth, 329, 462.
" Providence, 174, 696, 727-8, 1133.
" Rochelle, 108-9, 166, 499, **538-9, 767.**
" **Settlements, the, 23, 468.**
" Stanford, 1089.
" Street, N.Y., 1241-4.
" Tarlock, 1056.
" York Island, 211, 1241.
Newark, 52-4, 78, 128, 528-9, 530-1-2, 558-9, 597, 688-9, 842, 891, 1275-6.
Newborough (New Burgh, Newboro), 430-1, 493-4, 821-2, 873, 889.
Newburn, 42-5, 1230.
Newbury, 112, 259.
" Dock, 873.
" Port, 190, 1148-9.
" Township, 112.
Newcastle, 877, 1162-3.
Newcomb, Adonijah, 234.
Newell, James, 203.
Newfield, 251.
Newfoundland, 21, 68, 1204, **1229.**
Newport, 51-2, 102-3, 194, 304, 327, **484,** 587-9, 593, 679, 692, 907, 918-9, **1191,** 1249, 1300.
Newton, 227, 232, 269, 319, 623, 432, 598, 601, 716, 862, 1105, 1260.
" Creek, 864.
Niagara, 22-3, 152, 332, 387, 392-7, 415-6, 470-7, 957-9, 960-1-2-3-4-8, 971-5, 981-2-3-9, 992-5-7-8, 1001, 1067, 1070-9, 1101, 1112, 1256, 1280-1-4, 1357-8.
Niasa River, 242.
Nicholas, John, 1028.
Nichols, Moses, 616, 1286.
" Theophelos, 251.
Nicholson, Alex., 417, 427, 1255.
" Wm., of Philadelphia, 124.
Nickels, James, of S. Carolina, 169.
Nickelson, Jno., 612.
Nicoll, Henry, 596.

Niger (Frigate), 211-2.
Ninety-six District, 61-2-3, 143, 156-7-8, 162-8, 171-4-5-6, 183-4-5, 259, 276, 525-6-7, 675-6-7-8, 692-4, 701-2-3-4-9, 727-8, 734, 793, 800, 833, 841-2-9, 662, 674-9, 680, 699, 707, 714.
Nixon, Jas., 1249.
Nixon's Creek, 1187-8.
Noble, Silvanus. 203.
" Town, 682.
Noel, Mr., 927.
Nonsuch, 753.
Norfield Par., 847.
Norfolk, 50, 131-2-3. 512-3-4, 630-1-2-3-4-5, 646, 656-7-8. 666, 720-1-2, 732, 1149, 1150-2, 1162 1188-9, 1190, 1226-7, 1311.
Norman's Kits, 963.
Normand's Kill, 465.
Norrid, Mr., 323.
North Castle, 228-9, 262, 281, 764-8-9. 777-9, 813, 822; 877-8, 880, 1072-3.
" Fairfield, 850-1.
" Haven, 287, 785.
" Kingston, 303-4.
" Lord, 144, 497. 668.
" River, 119, 246, 261-3-5, 321, 608, 626, 699, 821, 872.
" (Sloop). 745.
" Ward. 669.
" Yarmouth, 919, 920-1, 1303.
Northampton, 1295.
" County, 201, 260, 270.
" Township, 124.
Northborough, 1287.
Northumberland, 201, 981, 1082.
Norton, And., 152.
" John, 92.
Norwalk, 207-8-9, 217, 224-5, 230-1, 242-3, 257, 318-19, 756, 798, 812-13, 824, 867.
" Harbour, 722.
Norwich, 639, 641-6, 998, 1155, 1273.
Notick, 753.
Nottingham Township, 53.
Noyes, Elizabeth. 568.
" Joseph, 274-6,
Nunkasor (Noncosser), Adam, of S. Carolina, 687, 1333.
Nutting, John, of Massachusetts Bay, 58-9.
O Blereny, John, 1321.
O'Brien, Mrs. Fanny, 108.
" John, of N. York, 771.
" Thos., of Shelburne, 108.
" Timothy, 1255.
O'Hara Gen., 1226.
O'Neal, John, 169.
" Dr., 240.
Oak Point, 852.
Oakham Co., 588.
Oaknabaki, Lake, 262.
Oathardt, Henry, 446, 4b2.
Obenholt, John, 972.
" Widow, 972.
Oceanachy Mountain, 43.
Odell, Abijah, 722.
" Abraham, 286.

Odell, Rev. Jas., of N. Jersey, 297-8, 884.
" John, 744.
Oesopus, 864-5-6.
" Gaol, 872, 927, 1267.
Offilay, Danl., 294.
Ogden, Aaron, 65.
" Abraham, 69, 1275.
" Albert, 829. 830.
" Andrew, 829, 830.
" Benj., of N. York, 829, 1047.
" David, 69. 79, 128, 188, 627, 725, 926, 1236, 1293.
" David, jr., of N. Jersey, 70, 528, 532-3, 666.
" Dr., 129.
" Isaac, 64, 917, 1235, 1275.
" Isaiah, 530.
" Jacob, 529.
" John, of N. York, 679, 886, 1321.
" Jonathan, 433.
" Josiah, 129.
" Judge, 601.
" Nicholas. of N. Jersey, 150, 1274.
" Rachel, 829.
" Robt., 189, 601-2.
" Robt., jr., 529, 531.
" Saml., 128.
Ogeechee (O'Geetchie), 706-7, 1308-9.
" " River, 715-6, 1309.
Ogeechu, Great, 1127, 1134.
Ogelvie, John, 706.
" Peter, 706.
Ogilvie, Charles, 1334.
" Wm., 1334.
Ohio River, 150, 477, 1284.
Okes, Joshua, 750.
Olcott, Timothy, 90.
Old Orchard, 1311.
Oldfield, Mr., 742.
" Lt. Thos., 741.
Olive, John, 1218.
Oliver, David, 1295.
" Chief Justice, 590, 1160.
" Fredk., of N. Y. Prov., 418.
" Ichebod, of N. Jersey, 1295.
" Mr., 1217.
Olmstead, Aron, 1321.
Olmsted, Danl., 205-6.
Onida Indians, 360, 417.
Onsley, Newdigate, 696.
Ontario, Lake, 23, 254.
Oram, James, of Pensilvania, 885.
Orange Co., 42-3-5, 84, 147, 239, 240, 276, 390, 430, 452, 554, 665-6, 749, 750, 843, 883-6-9, 1103, 1256, 1266.
" Grove Plantation, 1183.
" Mr. 1189, 1190.
" Street, Boston, 851-2.
Orangeburg, 702, 714.
Orangeburgh Dist., 168.
Orchard, Joseph, 188.
Orde, Capt., 1301.
" Mrs., 1301.
Orel, Thos., 330.
Orleans, New, 1284.
Ormsby, Mathew, 538.

Oro. 865.
Oromokto, 848, 908.
Orr. Thos.. of N. York. 924.
Orser, Arthur. 1108-9.
" Jos., 1108.
Osborne, 76.
" Capt., 905.
" Dr. Cor., 845-6.
" Joseph, 874.
" Hoziah. 226.
" Isaac. 226.
" Samuel. 569.
" Thos., 215.
Osser, Isaac, 1073.
" Solomon. 1073.
Oswiagatche (Oswegatchy. Osswegatchie), 388-9, 390-8, 401, 447. 468-9. 933. 944, 1011. 1053, 1068, 1081-4. 1104-5-7-9. 1112-14-15. 267.
Oswego. 11, 85, 351, 379, 401-3. 414. 420-8, 441-3. 454, 479, 998. 1005-6. 1020, 1038-9. 1067, 1087-9.
" (Osewago). Lake, 1173, 1181.
Otego Patent, 415-17.
Otis, Saml. Allen, 1216.
Otter Creek, 349, 369, 422, 1090. 1259. 1271.
Ottera, Felix, 195.
Overing, Harriet, 195.
" Lt. Henry, 194.
" Henry John, 194.
" Mrs. Mary, 195.
" Polly, 195.
" Robt., 195.
Oxford, Dudley, 1139.
" Road, 1331.

Pachero, Mr.. 1241.
Packer, Mr., 1272.
" Thos., 511-12, 593, 616-17, 636-7.
Paddock, Adin, 39.
" Mr., 831.
Pagan, Mr., 315-6.
" Robt.. of Massachusetts. 304-5. 304-5-6-7.
" Thos.. 275-6, 306, 317.
" William. 306, 866.
Page (Paige, Wm., 741, 1310.
Paine, Mr., 447.
" (Parne), Robt. Trent. 274. 592.
" Saml., of Massachusetts Bay. 32, 507.
" Timothy. 739.
" Wm., M.D., of Massachusetts. 803, 904.
Paisley, New, 414.
Palmer, Benj., 166-7, 515.
" Beriah, 937.
" David, of N.Y. Prov., 432.
" Edmund Fowler. 516.
" Edmund, senr., 516-7.
" Lieut. Gideon, of N. York. 760, 789.
" Lewis, of N. Y. Prov., 514-6. 1333.
" Martin, 43.
" Rachel. 761.
" Wm., 821.

Palmerston, 456.
Panton, George, of Trenton, 53.
" James, 947.
" Rev. Mr., 498.
Pape, Col., 902.
Papu Chink. 995.
Paris, Col. Richd., 164-5-6, 170, 694, 702.
Parisburgh. 341.
Parke, Nathan, of N.Y. Prov., 459.
Parker, Capt., of Phenix, 137-8.
" Col., 634, 715.
" Isaac, 114, 465.
" Jacob. 1216.
" James. 126-7, 979, 1152, 1161, 1275, 1296.
" Jno., 508.
" Mr., 1152.
" Nathaniel, 113.
" Nathaniel, jr., 220.
" Sir Peter. 803, 1133, 1228-9, 1230, 1247.
" Sarah, 671.
" Thos., 176.
" Wm., 318.
Parker's Ferry, 718.
" " affair of, 182.
Parks. Cyreneus. 1010.
" Hook, 299.
" James. 979, 1011.
" Nathan. 458-9.
Parkson. Mathew, 809.
Parletin. Mathew, 239.
Parmeter. Josiah, 589.
Parmintown. 923-4.
Parr, Governor. 11, 33, 51, 68, 667, 1328.
" Genl., 1324-5.
Parr's Borough. 505, 1276-7.
Parroch. James, 670.
" John, of Philadelphia. 125, 567, 614-6, 669, 685.
" Mary. 670.
" Sarah, 671.
Parrott. James. 950, 1009.
Parry's Town, 1209.
Parsal. John, 1019.
Parsons, Capt.. 44.
" Genl., 101.
" Island 808.
Partelow, Amos, of N. York, 809.
Partridge Field. 752.
Pasacoting. 602.
Pasamaquady. 96, 108, 112, 315.
" Bay, 900.
Pasolet River. 160.
Pass, Jos., 301.
Passaic River. 531.
Pataroon Land. 419, 965-7-8, 1263.
Patchen. Andrew. 847.
Patcher. Andrew. 1320.
Patet, Dunham, of N.Y. Prov., 456.
Patroon Patent. 417.
Patterina. Patent. 123.
Patterson (Paterson), Col., 809.
" Genl., 547, 585, 689, 1246
" Major James, 1258.
" Rev. John. 1165.
" Lt.-Govr., 1357-9.
" Mary. 343.

Patterson, Wm., of N.Y. Prov., 332, 985.
Pattersquash, 594-6.
Patteson, Jas., 625.
Paulet, 1019.
Pauling, Major, 1047.
Paxton, James, 581.
" Joseph, of Pensilvania, 96, 580, 724.
" Township, 1082.
" Wm., 724, 1292.
Peabody, Saml., J.P., 272.
Peabody's River, 1210.
Peacocks, David, of N.Y. Prov., 482.
Peaks Kill, 261, 285, 321-2.
Pearce, Wm., 925.
Pearl St., N.Y., 1241, 1244.
Pearson, Christopher, of N.Y. Prov., 331.
" (Pierson), Col., 277, 527, 707.
" Mary, 331.
" Col. Richd., 700-2.
" Robt., 249.
" Col. Thos., of S. Carolina, 175, 184, 703, 728.
" Township, 273.
Pearstown, 274-5.
Peavis, G., 193.
" Col. Richard, 181, 702, 704, 709, 728-9, 190.
" Richd., jr., 162.
Peck, Caleb, 1062.
" Capt., 911.
" George, 910-11.
" Wm., 910-11.
Pecking's Ford, 183.
Peddle, Joseph, 1334.
Peddleford, Seth, 660.
Peder, 695, 714.
" River, 705.
Pedgeon, Isaac. 648.
Peers, Henry, 777.
Peggy, (Schooner), 52, 154.
Pelham. 499.
" Manor, 167, 496, 500-2.
" Street, Newport, 104.
Pelican, (Ship), 565.
Pell, Caleb, 553.
" Henry, 501.
" John, 47.
" Joshua, of N. Y. Prov., 496-8, 503, 553, 745, 1295.
Pell's Neck, 538, 540.
Pemart, Francis. of N.Y. Prov., 320.
Pemberton, Benjamin, 922.
" Israel, 1170.
" Jeremy, (Commissioner), 20-2. 411. 467, 472, 550-2, 579, 580, 712, 1282, 1324, 1338, 1351-8, 1362-4-6-7, 1370-3-4-5-6.
Pembroke. 506.
Pembroke's Plantation, 1138.
Pemlos Hook, 1232.
Pempany. Major, 165.
Pencel, John, 1040-1.
Pendergarst. Thos.. 655.
Pendleton. John. 67, 722.
Penfield. Jon., 83.
Penkney, Israel, 166.
Penman & Lowndes, 1205.
Penn, Govr., 201, 933.

Penn, John, 122, 1350.
" John, jr., 1350.
" Mr., 1174.
" Thos., 122.
Penne, Joseph, 179.
Pennington, Mr., 1172.
" Wm., 1197.
Penney, Samuel, 1334.
Penobscot, 41, 58-9, 107, 304-6-7, 311-12, 315-7, 322-3-4, 721. 747, 763, 905-6-7, 920-1, 1319, 1323.
" Bay, 316.
" River, 40.
Pensacola, 191, 800.
Pepar, Alex., 43.
Pepperell, Andr., 1310.
" Lady, 1310.
" Sir Wm., 679, 1147, 1310.
Pequanack Township, 189.
Perbeck, Col., of Halifax, 109.
Percy, Lord, 303, 762, 878, 880.
Percival Ward, 341.
Perreneau, (Perroneau), Henry, 1201-3-4-5-6.
" Robert, 1229.
Perine, John, of N. Jersey. 760.
" Perine, Wm., of N. Jersey, 320.
Perkin, Christ., 124.
Perkins. Isaac, of N. Jersey, 202, 1333.
Perm, Richd., 1334.
Perry, John, 555-6.
" Paul, 592.
" Robt., 422, 1014, 1030, 1272.
" Saml., of N. York, 457, 923.
" Wm., 1217.
Perseus. (Man-of-war), 67.
Port. Saml., 71-3.
Perth Amboy, 203, 1233 5-6-8, 1242.
" New, 462.
" Valley, 537-8.
Pessody's River, 1209.
Peterborough, 1217.
Peterburgh, 1304.
Peters, Col.. 328, 336, 405-7, 934, 1268.
" James, J.P., 260-3.
" Rev. Richd., 112, 311, 1196, 1208, 1210, 1248.
" Thos.. of N. York, 806, 1320.
" Peters. Wm., 722, 806.
Petersburgh, 1142, 1290.
Petersham, 878-9.
Peterson, Abraham, of N. Jersey, 449.
" Christian, 1035-6.
" Mrs. Jenet, 1291.
" John, of Philadelphia, 322, 1291.
" Nicholas, jr., 1035.
Petit, Nathaniel, 982.
Petrie, Hanioist, 969.
Petticoat Jack (Peticodiac) River, 213-4 259, 842.
Philadelphia, 53, 66, 110, 122-3-9, 156-7, 195-6, 201, 211-12, 222-3, 250-3, 260, 270-1, 294-7-9, 317, 331, 430, 447, 493-4-8-9, 517-8. 521. 535-7, 550, 564-5-6-7, 581, 613-4-5-6, 655-7, 666-7-9, 670-1-2, 684-5-6, 692, 708, 752, 760-7, 777, 787, 790, 806, 824-5-7, 832-3-4-7, 840, 885, 892-5, 900-1, 929, 932-3, 1146, 1222, 1277, 1288-9, 1291-2-4, 1327.

Philips Borough, 889, 890.
" Capt., 323.
" Col., 61, 281, 571-2, 781, 890-7, 1131.
" Ed., 854.
" Elisha, 1025, 1032.
" Fred., 84, 1046.
" Col. Fred., 698.
" Gen., 566, 657, 722
" Mr., 130, 266.
" Mills, 100.
" Philip, 879, 884-5.
" Richd., 964.
" Wm., 956.
Philips' Manor, 266, 289, 571-2, 770-1-8, 780-1, 808, 881, 1008.
" Patent, 767, 784, 790.
Philipsburgh, 266, 567, 571-7, 811, 889, 890-6-7.
Philipstown, 388-9, 1081.
Phipoe, Thos., 1245-7-8, 1251.
Phipps, Col., 58.
Phoenix, (Man-of-war), 137-8, 218, 246, 265, 571.
Phyle & Armstrong, 1373-5.
Phyn, James, of N.Y. Prov., 361.
" & Uree, 1334.
Phyns, Mr., 482.
Pickard, Wm., 963, 973.
Pickell, John, 1118.
Pickens, Andrew, of N. Jersey, 837, 1320.
Pickering, Lawyer, 57.
Picket, Danl., 202-3.
" David, of Connecticut, 826.
" John, 1119.
Pickle, John, of N.Y. Prov., 424.
Picknell, John, 424.
Pierce, Capt., 429.
Pierpont, Robt., 611.
Piers, Samuel, 1320.
Pierse, Right, 868.
Pierson, (Pearson), Col., 277, 527, 707.
Pigeon, Mr., 1289.
Pigot, Genl. Sir Robt., 43, 50-1, 103-5, 194, 709, 1191, 1249.
Pimlico, Sound, 701, 720.
Pinchers, Mr., 493.
Pine, Alpheus, 896.
" Stephen, of N. York, 896.
" Street, Philadelphia, 932.
Pinset, Eve, 1039.
Piper, Capt., 103.
Piratt, Elliston &. 195.
Piscatua (Piscutawn, Piscataway), 125-6, 818, 908.
Pitcher, Moses, 611.
Pitsfield, 752-3-4, 794-6.
Pitsford, 577.
Pitt, Fort, 150, 985-6-7-8-9, 1082, 1282-4.
" Mr., 1317.
Pitt's Town, 213-4, 941-2, 951.
Pittsburgh, 214, 988, 1082-3, 1145.
Pixford, Charles, 249.
Plain, the, 202.
Plainfield, 1123.
Plass, Peter, of N.Y. Prov., 457.
Platet, Dunham, 457.
Platt, John, 946-8.
" Mr., 944.

Platt, Nathanl., 757.
Pleader, Hink, 420.
Plumb's Point, 64.
Plunket, Dr., 980.
Plymouth, 491, 605, 687, 716, 922, 1202.
" Purchase, 921.
Poggy, (Sloop), 608.
Point de Bas, 351.
" Bodet, 359.
" Clear, 383.
" au Fear, 1002.
" Judith, 52.
" au Lac, 1067.
Pole, Jeremiah, 306.
Pollock, Wm., 58.
Polly, (Sloop), 569.
Pomeroy, Joseph, 328.
Pomfret, 1208.
Pompton, 149.
Pondfield, 167.
Pondridge, 791.
Pool, Saml., 59.
Popple(s)dorff Willelmus, 147.
Port Roseway, 11, 135.
" Royal Island, 1201.
Porter, Col. Asa, 327-8
Portsmouth, 56, 65, 194, 509, 511-12, 593, 617, 632-3-4-6-7, 657-8, 705, 731-2-3, 1209, 1226, 1311, 1314.
Post, John, 299.
Potomack, 1218-9.
Pott, Mr., 304.
Potter, Asher, 916.
" Mrs. Elizabeth, of N. Jersey, 178.
" Ellis, 198.
" Henry, 179.
" John, 832.
" Joseph, 168.
Potts (Pots), Jeremiah, of Massachusetts, 904-6.
" John, 1288.
" Saml., 277.
" Thos., 228.
Potts' Neck, 498.
Pottsburg, 1282.
Poughkeepsie, (Pughkepsie), 240, 262-3, 635-6, 654, 816, 830, 843-4-5-6, 860, 882, 1101, 1280.
Powell, Brig.-Genl., 386, 391, 400.
" Caleb, of N.Y. Prov., 291-3.
" Felix, 577.
" James Ed., 1204, 1230.
" Lawrence, 1373.
" Lawyer, 935.
" Martin, 576.
" Mr., 362-3, 416, 1204, 1254.
" Robert Wm., 1204, 1230.
" Samuel, 292.
" Solomon, of N.Y. Prov., 292.
" Wm. Dunmore, 931-2.
Powers, Jonas, 328.
" Sarah, 1280.
" Wm., 1280.
Powkes, Daniel, 1336.
Powlet Township, 1021-2.
Pownall, 214, 417, 424-7, 1012, 1043.
" George, 1359.
Pownallborough, 323, 745-6-7.
Pratt, Mr., 1303.

Preble, Wm., 274.
Prentice, Danl., 1080.
Prepack Tract, 128.
Prescott, Charles, 752.
" Genl., 271-2, 831, 1191.
" Jas., 464-5.
" John, 934.
Preston, 155, 182, 700.
" Capt., 490-1-5.
" Mr., 583.
" (Ship), 656.
Prevost, Augustine, 332.
" Col., 109.
" 1137.
" Genl., 180-2, 339, 694-9, 704-6, 718, 1198.
Price, Capt., 223.
" Ezekiel, 464.
" Francis, 601.
" Geo., 1293.
" Joseph, 608.
" Michl., of N. Jersey, 608.
" Robt., 601.
" Wm., 261.
Primeus, (Sloop), 910.
Prince Edward Esland, 11.
" Fredk. Parish, 1214, 1245.
" George's Creek, 924.
" Dr. John, of Salem, 493-4.
" Dr. Jonathan, 645.
" Mr., 1160.
" Street, Boston, 37.
" Town, 111, 320, 739, 740, 753.
" William, 821.
" " Parish, 1228.
Princess Ann Co., 1150-1.
" St., Boston, 38.
Prindle, Joel, 1030.
" Joseph, 1029.
" Timothy, 1029, 1030.
" Wm., 1029, 1265.
Prior, Edward, 177.
Pritchard, Azariah, of Connecticut, 349.
Proctor, Saml., 709, 734.
Prossor, P., 391.
Protectworth, 510, 517, 637.
Prous, Joseph, 410.
" Peter, of N.Y. Prov., 410.
Providence, 585, 684, 728.
" New, 696, 727-8.
" (Schooner), 77.
" Township, 901-2.
Provincial Patent, 433.
Pugsley, Gilbert, of N.Y. Prov., 266.
" John, of N. York, 777.
Pulsopher, David, 90.
Purdy (Purdie), Capt., 774, 864.
" Charlotte, 431.
" David, 430.
" Gabriel, of N. York, 780.
" Gilbert, of N.Y. Prov., 230, 430, 781, 884.
" Gilbert, jr., 431, 781.
" Henry, 554, 780.
" Jacob, 781.
" Mary, 431.
" Mecadia, 431.
" Mercy, 431.
" Nathanl., 782.

Purdy, Rhoda, 431.
" Samuel, 431, 781.
" Saml., jr., 781.
" Winnifred, 781.
Pushtain, Kiln, 1026.
Putnam, Genl., 650.
" Herbert, 25.
" James, of Worcester, 32, 587-9, 790.
" Judge, 586, 803-4.
Puttney, 865.
Pye, Elizabeth, 341.
Pyncheon, Wm., of Boston, 114.

Quaker Hill, 349.
Quasencooke, 408.
Quebec, 13, 30, 332-7, 344-5-7, 363, 405, 425-6, 485-7, 662, 682, 705, 900, 918, 920-3-4, 936, 944, 965, 1020, 1031-4, 1051, 1191, 1219, 1222, 1267-8, 1277, 1280, 1324, 1331, 1357-8-9, 1364-5-7.
" Seige of, 346.
Queen Ann's County, 140.
" Street, N. York, 108, 668, 1202-3-5-6, 1229.
Queen's County, 198, 232-3, 267, 289, 540, 808, 814, 823, 840, 855, 860, 877, 884-6, 1212, 1321.
Queensborough, 60, 282, 399, 582.
Quig, Hugh, 887.
Quin, John, of N.Y. Prov., 375.
" Michael, 375.
Quinby, Moses, 768.
Quinmans Patent, 389.
Quinte (Quinty, Kenty, Kquenty), Bay of, 346, 363-8, 383, 417-8-9, 420-1-3-4-8-9, 430-2-3, 450-1-3-5, 465, 478, 480, 1050, 1072-3-5, 1103, 1110, 1255, 1260-3-4-5-6, 1270.
Rachel, Charles, 1257.
Racoon Creek, 615.
Radley, Alderman, 140.
Rahway, 133-4-5.
Rain-bow, (Man-of-war), 56, 904-5.
Rall, Defeat of, 71.
Rambo, Benj., 123.
Rambler, (Ship), 567.
Ramshack (Ramsbag), 767-8, 770, 783, 790.
Ramsey, James, 996-7.
" Mr., 321-2.
Rancellor (Ransellar), Col., 368.
" Mr., 942, 1283.
" Stephen, 457, 960.
Rancellor's Land, 465, 995.
" Manor, 368, 388-9, 960, 1007, 1016-7, 1024, 1034-7, 1073, 1106, 1268.
" Patent, 963.
Randal, Geo., 727.
" Simeon, 818.
" Thos., 625-6.
Randolph, Col., 650.
" Harrison, 67.
" Robt., 94.
Ranger (Sloop), 863.
Rankin, Col., 1169.
" James, 112.

Rankin, John, of York Co., 112.
" Wm., 112, 499.
Rapalgie, Abraham, 898-9.
Rareton River, 802.
Rashleigh & Co., 686.
Rashley's Ships, 1328.
Raumont, Mr., 1140.
Raven Creek, 1145.
Rawdon, 162, 175-6, 181-4, 692-3-4-9, 701-2-3-9, 1274.
" Lord, 61-2, 155, 524, 646-7-8, 677-8-9, 1131, 1218.
" Township, 168-9, 170.
Rawlinson, Francis, 61.
Raworth, Saml., 715.
Rawyag, 1295.
Ray, Bernabos, 1264.
" Danl., of N. Carolina, 96.
" Geo., 601.
Raymond, Isaac, 319.
" Silas, of Connecticut, 242, 824.
Reaburn's Creek, 241-2.
Read, Capt. Wm., 28, 914.
" Wm., 46, 167.
" Wm., of N.Y. Prov., 499, 502.
" Wm., of Georgia, 581.
Reading, 226-7, 835.
Readsborough, 858.
" Patent, 857.
Rebecca, (Brig.), 630.
Red Bank, 208-9, 608-9.
Reddick, Christopher, 1115.
Redford, 159.
Redheasel, Genl., 917, 1084.
Redout, Maria, of Connecticut, 850.
Reece, Anthony, of Connecticut, 900.
Reed, Duncan, 387.
" Lawr., of N. York, 333.
" Mrs. Mary, 387.
" Richd., 606.
Reedy Branch, 849.
" River, 191-3.
Rees, Danl., 980.
Reeve, Mr., 1301.
Rehobath, Farm, 298.
Remingtown, 802, 1255.
Renfrew Co., 664.
Renown, (Ship), 741.
Resolution, (Schooner, 316.
Return, (Sloop), 320.
Reynolds, Ebenezer, 809.
" Margt., 1271.
" Samuel, 1321.
Rhode Island, 21, 42, 50-1, 92, 102, 272, 302-3-4, 318, 327, 345, 463, 490-1, 587, 656, 663, 803, 831, 918-9, 938, 1299.
Rhodes, Mr., 598.
" Saml., 518.
" Town, 708.
Rice, Evan, 445.
" Ezekiel, 145.
" Randol, 1259.
Richards, Charles, of Jersey, 842.
" James, 520.
" Jesse, 615, 930.
" Mr., 1300.
" Nathaniel, of Newark, 78.
" Owen, 1160.
" Paul, 286.

Richards, Thomas, 78, 530.
Richardson, Asa, of Charlotte Co., 1012, 1014.
" Joshua, 581.
Richie, Ann, 71-2.
" John, 664.
Richmond, 332, 671-2, 834-5, 1311-2.
" Col., 665.
" (Frigate), 51, 173.
" Isaac, 138.
" James, 137.
Richmoor, Col., 1050.
Ricketts, Mr., 1237.
Ridehazte, Genl., 917, 1084.
Ridgefield, 204-5-6, 300, 892-3.
Rierson, John Francis, 543-5, 748.
Ritchie, Andrew, of Boston, 599.
Ritenhouse, Wm., of S. Carolina, 676.
Rivers, 925.
Riviere du Chene, 388, 468, 484, 949, 1006, 1016-8, 1024, 1034, 1260-7, 1271, 1283.
" la Colle, 349, 483.
" au Raisin, 364, 372-3-4, 382-3-4, 393-4-5-7, 409, 415, 1062, 1077, 1081-6-8, 1092-3-6-7.
Rivington, James, 669.
Robbler, John, 534.
" Thos., of N.Y. Prov., 533.
Roberdeau, Genl., 1177.
Robins, James, 1017, 1037.
" John, 649, 652.
" Mr., 1002, 1031.
" Richard, of Monmouth Co., 649, 652.
Robert, (Brigg), 625.
Roberts, Charles, 898.
" Israel, 222.
" John, 222-3.
" Jos., 1226.
" Nathan, of Pensilvania, 222, 1320.
Robertson, Alex., of Pensilvania, 150.
" Andr., 1129.
" Daniel, of Albany Co., 362, 392.
" Gorr., 490.
" Lt.-Genl. James, 118, 144, 303, 318, 453, 584, 594, 1132-8, 1157, 1242.
" Mr., 1135, 1239.
" Neil, J.P., 734.
Robie, Thos., of Massachusetts Bay, 725.
Robinson, Capt., of Thisbe Frigate, 70, 670.
" Col. Beverley, 105, 216, 261, 312-3, 674-5, 749, 809, 823, 841, 871, 889, 890, 900, 1163, 1280, 1318.
" Esther, of N.B., 283.
" Genl. James, 555, 574, 637-8.
" Lt.-Col. James, 718.
" Sir John Beverley, 24.
" Joseph, of S. Carolina, 242, 478, 799.
" Lt.-Col., 191.
" Luke, 550.
" Mr., 1220.
" Robert, 595, 1069.

INDEX. 1423

Robinson, Thos., 174, 273, 1186.
Roblin, Owen, of Orange Co., 1006.
" Philip, of Orange Co., 1103-6.
Rochelle, 108, 503, 540.
" New, 499, 538-9, 767.
Rockingham, 88, 511, 617, 1218.
" Upper, 89.
Rockshire, 1273.
Rocky Bridge, 722.
" Brook, 1275.
" Comfort, 715.
" Creek, 1187, 1229.
" River, 143-4.
Rodney, Geo. Bridges, 871.
Roebuck, (Man-of-war), 520, 720.
Rogers, Col., 764.
" David, 245. .
" Fitch, 210, 225.
" James, of S. Carolina, 244, 828.
" Col. James, 91, 896.
" Major James, 13, 89, 330-1, 417, 432-7, 449, 470, 756-9, 941, 1010, 1011, 1029, 1031, 1043, 1265-9.
" John, 952.
" Lyde &, 144.
" Mr., 122, 241.
" Nehemiah, of Branford, 82, 210.
" Robert, 103, 832.
" Lt.-Col. Robert, 228, 417, 853, 896.
" Saml., 1287.
" Sarah, 98.
" Thos., 1210-11.
" Wm., 832, 1017-8, 1020.
Rohner, G., 1300.
Roland, Israel, 477.
Rolph, John, 1373-5.
Rolton, West, 243.
Rombogh, Jacob, of N.Y. Prov., 414.
Romulus, (ship-of-war), 66.
Room, Jacob, 542.
Roome (Roem), John Chevalier Le, 177, 211-17, 304, 785, 1270.
Ropelgre, Garret, 140.
Rose, Gersham, 390.
" George, 580, 1350, 1374.
" (Man-of-war), 589.
" Matthias, 1020-6.
" Peter, 1154.
" Roger, 328.
" Samuel, 479.
" (Ship), 53.
" Wm., of N.Y. Prov., 356-8.
Roseband, Menard, 419.
Rosehall, 1150.
Rosevelt, Mr., 555-6.
Roseway, 21, 315.
Ross, Alex., of Falmouth, 274, 1081.
" Ann, 1081.
" Daniel, 1054.
" Donald, 978, 1054-5, 1081.
" Mrs. Eliz., of Massachusetts, 274-5.
" Finley, 1060, 1081.
" George, 554.
" Jacob, 1120.
" John, of Tryon Co., 1103.
" Major, 375.
" Mary, 919.

Ross, Mr., 988.
" Thos., of N.Y. Prov., 382-4, 1115.
" Col. T., 275.
Ross's Wharf, 863.
Rossboone, Bat., 1050.
Rossiter, Mrs. Eliz., 494.
" Thos., 494.
Rossman, James, 1305.
Rothery, Mary, 1188-9.
" Mr., 1188.
" Mrs., 1190.
Roudge, Jas., 915.
Rowand Co., 280, 1131.
Rowarth, Major Saml., 582.
Rowe, John, 80-1.
Rowland, 141.
" Revd. John Hamilton, of Virginia, 666.
Rowney Creek, 124.
" Hugh, 328.
Roxbury, 585, 622.
Roys, Evan, of Massachusetts Bay, 444, 455.
Rug, John, 204.
Ruggles, John, 740.
" Richard, 740.
" Brig.-Genl. Timothy, of Massachusetts, 32, 96, 586, 588-9, 624, 738, 752-4, 762-3, 790.
Ruiter, Capt. Henry, of N. York, 941.
" Herr, 943.
Rullege, Govr., 727.
Rumages, 1234.
Rumbrother, 308.
Rumney Township, 915-6.
Runaway River, 64.
Rundle, Jabez, of N. York, 784.
Runyard, Goldsburg, 1281.
Rupert, Christr., 244.
Russel, (Russell), Elijah, 654.
" Joseph, 1321.
" Mr., 1291.
" Nathan, 52.
" Wm., of Tryon Co., 463.
Rutherford, Wm., 76.
Rutherforth, Walker, 602.
Rutland, 1014-5.
Rutledge, Govr., 191, 1202.
" Mr., 1199.
Ruttan, Peter, of N. Jersey, 429, 430.
Ruyter, John, 941.
Ryan, Dennis, 331.
" Thos., 1252.
Ryckman, John, 1116.
" Tobias, 1116, 1256.
" Widow, 1116.
Ryder, Ens., 429.
" Robt., 515.
Rydner, Conrad, 246.
Ryerson, Cornelius, 857.
" Francis, 543-5, 748.
St. Andrews, 304-6, 311, 315-6-7, 322-3, 901-5-7, 1134, 1319, 1323.
St. Ann's, 239, 253, 270, 282, 290, 326-82, 841, 892-3, 898, 902.
St. Augustine, 28, 33, 60-2-3, 96, 155, 165, 183-6, 241, 339, 582-3, 695, 700-3-7, 714-5, 727-8, 914, 1130, 1143.

St. Augustine, Bar of, 190.
St. Brides, 666.
St. Christophers, 513.
St. Eustatice, 326.
St. Eustatius, 195.
St. Francis, Lake, 13, 415.
St. Gall, 339.
St. George, Manor of, 594-5.
" Parish, 28-9, 581-2.
St. George's, 316, 322-3, 1323.
St. Germains, Lord, 43.
St. Helena, 1301-2-3.
St. James Parish, 1199.
St. John, Col., 258.
St. John, Island of, 130-4, 151, 649, 1357, 9.
St. John's, Antiqua, 929.
St. Johns, 11, 22, 42, 102, 113-5, 201-5-7-9, 211-15-18, 222-9, 232-5, 282, 319, 321-2, 336, 400, 434, 455, 463, 595-8, 607, 628, 682, 698, 787, 843, 850-8, 861-9, 901, 937, 941-2, 1276, 1280, 1319, 1321-2-3-6, 1361-4.
" Lake Champlain, 89, 329, 349, 350-9, 364-5, 378, 385-8, 394, 409, 417, 432, 448, 456, 462, 482-3-4-5, 936-9, 1020-4-5-6-9, 1030-1-2, 1043, 1050, 1070-5, 1084-9, 1091, 1100, 1268-9.
" East Florida, 583, 714-17.
St. Johns River, 71-4, 190, 217, 228, 233, 242-8, 258, 261-2-4-5, 275-7, 280-1, 293-5, 309, 314, 660-1, 862, 800, 1322, 1363.
St. Kitts, 684.
St. Laurent, 384.
St. Lawrence, Gulph of, 130, 151, 1357-9.
" River, 344, 1327, 1359.
" Suburbs, 932.
St. Leger, Col., 352, 1053.
" Genl., 1097.
St. Lewis, Castle of, 1359.
St. Lucia, 914.
St. Mark's Parish, 326.
St. Martins, 440.
St. Mary, Parish, 648.
St. Mary's, 706.
" Bay, 105, 593, 759.
" River, 83, 340, 1127, 1240.
St. Mathew's Parish, 296, 1138.
St. Michaels, (St. Michells), 428, 1015-16, 1093, 1203, 1228.
St. Ours, 363.
St. Peter's Parish, 340, 1199.
St. Phillip, Parish, 296.
St. Stephen, Parish, 648.
St. Therese, 457.
St. Thomas, 1127.
" Parish, 1224.
St. Vincents, Port, 477.
Sacandago, 472.
Sacchorader, Christian, 871.
Sackville, Lord, 1305.
Sagar, John, 418.
Sagre, Jonathan, 79.
" M., 128.

Salem, 154, 491-2-3, 509, 599, 638-9, 641-2-4-5, 720-1, 738, 824-5, 922, 1048, 1147-8, 1272, 1287.
" Gaol, 230.
Saladu (Saludu) River, 176, 728, 792.
Salisbury, 45, 1084, 1220, 1274.
" Mr., 586.
Sally, (Sloop), 909, 911.
Salt Ketches, 182-8.
Saltmarsh, John, 1155.
Sanco Falls, 1310.
Sand Born, 616.
Sanders, Wm., 432.
Sanderson, John, of S. Carolina, 679, 693-9, 719.
" Joseph, 113.
Sanford, Benj., of Newhaven, 82.
Sandford, Ephraim, 1048-9.
" Mr., 741.
Sands, Mr., 334.
Sandy Hook, 35, 628, 633, 692, 862-3, 917.
" River, 719.
Sandys, Mr., 908.
Santee, 164-5, 326.
" River, 763.
Santen Township, 1280.
Sarasy, Saml., 720.
Saratoga, 152, 329, 337-8, 390, 409, 414, 447, 451-6-7, 467, 474-5-8-9, 484-5-7, 769, 917, 923-4-8, 933-7, 940-3-4-8, 950-2, 1002, 1017, 1020-6-7, 1031-6-7, 1041-2, 1059, 1077, 1104, 1108, 1255, 1269, 1270.
" District, 1003.
" Patent, 333-5, 1313.
Sarg. see Sing.
Sargents, Catherine, 1272.
Sarsery, Dr., 1248.
Sassafras St., Philadelphia, 670-1.
Satella, Great, 1127.
Sateller, 1306.
Sault de Recollet, 401, 1101.
Saunder, John, 701, 1152.
" Samuel, 671.
" Wm., 721.
Savage, Arthur, 1303.
" Capt., 150.
" Edward, 1245-7.
" John, 1230.
" Mr., 1245, 1304.
Savan(n)ah, 28, 60, 109, 158, 163-9, 248, 254, 296, 338-9, 240-1-2, 513, 558, 582-3, 676, 695, 706, 715, 741, 793, 833, 914, 1127, 1133-4-6-7, 1142, 1305-6-7-8.
" Plantation, 1306-8-9.
" River, 340, 793, 1298.
" Seige of, 527, 582, 674.
Sawyer, Benj., 1269.
" Commodore, 173.
Saxton, Nathan, 576.
Say, G., J.P., 235.
Sayer, James, 1320.
" Jonathan, 559.
" Mr., 257.
Sayre, Cadwallader, of Pensilvania, 283.
" Francis Bowes, " 283.
" Harriet, " 283.

Sayre, James, 283.
" John, 260.
" Rev. John, of Connecticut, 283.
" Mary, of Pensilvania, 283.
Scamuel, Abar., 851.
Scataco, 474.
Schader, Wm., 278.
Schem, Charles, 1291.
Schenectady, 330, 359. 360-1, 414, 441, 453, 474-5-6, 562, 936-7, 959. 960, 992, 1153, 1244, 1267.
" Patent of, 361.
Schenk (Schank, Shank), Abraham. 585, 1270.
" Capt., 918, 944.
Schermerhorn, (Schormorhorn), Ryn., 408.
" Wm., 1024-5, 1073, 1268, 1281.
Schich, Christian, 1117, 1261.
Schohary (Schoharie), 359, 360. 400 1-4, 420. 441-3-4, 475. 961-2. 997, 1108, 1114, 1260, 1284.
" Creek, 1109.
" River, 361. 961, 997.
Schooley's Mountain, 298.
Schoolgrave, Christian. 408.
Schulctham, (Sloop), 138.
Schumaker, Samuel. 669.
SchuyKill Estate. 1171.
Schuyler, Col., 390.
" (Skyler), Jacob. 963.
" (Skyler), Genl. Phil.. 347, 377, 424, 456. 485-6, 931-2-6, 963, 970, 1059.
Scofield, Amos. 791.
" David, 264, 848.
" Jonathan. of N. Jersey, 257, 263. 848.
Scott, Capt.. 332.
" David, of N.Y. Prov., 329.
" Dorcas, 484.
" Ebenezer. 208.
" James. 933.
" John, 1233.
" Major. 269.
" Mr., 1242.
" T . 483.
" Walter. of N. York. 935.
Scribner, Elias, 208.
Seabury, Saml., 1213.
Seager, John, 995.
Sealey, Benj., of Connecticut, 873.
" Capt.. 417.
" Mr., 351.
Seaman. Stephen. of N. York, 778.
Sebray, David. 546.
Second St., Philadelphia. 671.
" Township. 378. 405.
Secord, James. 594, 989.
" John. 989.
" Peter, 874.
" Solomon. 89.
" Wm., of N. York. 889.
Sedds, Andrew, 524.
Seers, Joseph 780.
Segar. John. 963.
Segondaga, 371.

90 AR.

Selick, Dayle, of Vermont, 1114.
Selkirk, Alex., 664, 1226.
Selkrig, Andrew, 661.
Semms, Wm., 44.
Semple, John, 46.
" Mr., 222.
Seneca Indians, 1281.
Senegal (Frigate), 798-9.
Sergeant, Jonathan, 559.
Serles, John, 47.
Seron, Christopher, of N.Y. Prov., 441.
Servaniss, James, 299.
Servos, Danl., 957, 962, 978.
Sessuken Estate, 1177.
Seth's Ground, 282.
Seton, Mr., 287.
Seventh Township, 917.
Sévine River, 168.
Sewell, John, 318.
Sexton, Janet, 250.
Shaftsbury, 953, 1269.
Shannon (Schooner), 492.
Sharp (Sharpe), Guysbert, of Kinderhook, 447, 451.
" Lieut., 1035.
" Jos., 601-3.
" Samuel, 126, 601-3, 818.
Sharpless, Mr., 1218.
Shaver, John, 1099.
" Philip, of N.Y. Prov., 351-3-5, 1120-2.
" Mr., 1105.
Shaw, Charles, 1302.
" Dr., 1251.
" Francis. 40.
" James, of N. York, 1268.
" John, of N. York, 884.
" Mrs., 40-1.
" Samuel, 903.
" Timothy, 879, 884-5.
" Wm., 195, 714.
Sheaffe, Mrs., 343.
" S., of Boston, 343.
" Thos., of N.Y. Prov., 337.
Sheddie, Conrad, 158.
" Mrs. Mary, 158.
Sheels, Wm., 309.
Shell, John, of Tryon Co., 352, 1056.
Shelbourne, 21, 43, 52-6. 61-2, 107-8, 110, 122-9, 134-5, 144-6-7-9, 154-9, 160-6, 194, 340-2-3, 497, 514-8-9, 520-1-2-5-6-7, 549, 550-1-8, 567, 571-4, 608-9, 610-11, 628, 655-6-8, 660, 666-7-8, 678, 691, 731-2, 815, 900. 1274, 1323-6, 1330, 1355, 1361.
" Lane, London, 1277.
Sheppard, Moses, 35.
Shepherd, Elias, 708.
" & Hunt, 804.
Sherard, Capt., 348.
" Seth, 1029.
Sherborne, Lord. 1172.
Sheriff, Col. Wm., 624, 1313.
" Major Wm., 309, 921.
Sherlock, James, 1284.
Sherman, James, 82.
" Sarah, 82.

Sherman, Simeon, of Saratoga, 337.
" Ward &, 799.
Sherman's Valley, 253.
Sherwood, Adrel, 376-7
" Capt., 407, 483.
" Dial, 1090.
" Isaac, 205.
" Capt. Justus, 469, 470, 699, 820, 957, 1084, 1112.
" Mr., 1104.
" Seth, 847, 1089.
" Ensign Thomas, of N.Y. Prov., 1032, 1089, 1090-1, 1267, 1285.
Shethop, Lever, 1134.
Shewman, Wm., of N.Y. Prov., 442.
Ship Harbour, 156-8-9, 674-7-8.
Shipman, Elias, of Newhaven, 83.
Shipper St., Philadelphia, 124.
Shobert, Geo., of S. Carolina, 677.
Shoemaker, (Schumaker), Mr., 929.
" " Samuel. 110. 669, 673, 932.
Shoolbred, David, 918-9.
Shoram, 328.
Shoreham Township, 865-6.
Shorey, David, 422, 1030, 1272.
Shortwell, Benj., 895.
" Joseph, 895.
Shotwell, Joseph, 142.
Shoum, John, of Broad River, 34.
Showers, Michl., 973-4-5.
Showman, Wm., of N.Y. Prov., 1283-5.
Shrewsbury, 35-6, 94, 208, 317-8, 608. 925.
Shuberburgh, Isaac. 269.
Shumway, John, 577.
Shunk, Peter, 994.
Sickel, Thos., 941.
Siddons, Anthony. 124.
Sidney, Lord, 1323.
Silliman, Genl., 799.
Sills (Sill), Conrad, of Pensilvania, 1262-3.
" Lawrence, 1263.
Silvester. Amos. 920.
Simcoe, Col., 741, 877, 897.
" Major, 824.
Simmons, Moses. 779.
Simms, Judge, 601.
Simpson, Alexr., of N.Y. Prov., 453-4, 1010.
" Drummond, 215.
" Henry, 871.
" James, 181, 190, 1203, 1197 1290.
" Mr., 716.
" Robert, 215.
" Sarah, 215.
" William Brooke, 187, 1191 1249.
Sinclair, Capt. John, 295.
Sing (Sarg) Christian, of S. Carolina, 674-5-6. 687.
" Peter, 674.
Sisco, Thos., 1048.
Sisseboo, 751-4-5, 763, 795.
Siteman, Henry, of S. Carolina, 184.
Situty, Joseph, 1171.

Skelton, (Skeltows), Thos., 1198, 1303.
Skench, Ruloff, 628-9.
Skeene, (Skeens, Skene), Andr. Philip, 330.
" Govr., 654, 1219, 1221-2.
" Major, 330, 1265.
" Philip, 329, 931-6, 1084.
Skeensborough, 30, 86, 329, 330, 345-6, 351, 362, 380, 398, 462-6, 470, 483-7, 578, 900, 924, 933, 950, 1013, 1020-9, 1071-5, 1091, 1102, 1219, 1220-1, 1264-5-6.
Skimming, John, 943, 950.
Skinner, Brig.-Genl. Courtland, of N. Jersey, 68, 126-7, 141, 151, 188, 199, 203, 248, 253-4, 270, 429, 541-8, 633, 711, 712, 802, 811, 832-3-4, 894, 917, 982, 1009, 1158, 1232-4-5-6-7-8-9, 1242-3, 1270.
" Eliz., 1237.
" Mr., 619, 858, 1127.
" Mrs., 1233-4-5-8.
" Philip, 1238.
" Stephen, 277, 711.
Skran, Barnabas. 965.
Sleepy Rock. 1186.
Sly, Geo., 895.
Sloane, Robt., of S. Carolina, 714, 734.
Slocum, Abraham, 303.
" Charles, 303-5.
" Ebenezer, of Rhode Island, 303.
" " of N. Brunswick, 303-4.
" " 1321.
" Ellis, of W. Greenwich, 303.
" George, 303.
" Hanah, 303.
" Margt., 303.
" Mauss, 303.
" Sarah. 303.
" Mrs. Sarah, 303-4-5.
Small, Col., 54-8, 590, 762.
" John, 919.
" Major, 89.
Smith, Abraham, of N. York, 775.
" Adam, 1000.
" Alex., of Philadelphia. 932.
" Arthur, of N. York, 748.
" B., 301, 456.
" Bayard, 124.
" Benj., 206, 230, 281, 1306.
" Col., 762, 1218.
" Danl., of Connecticut, 867.
" Danl., of Tryon Co., 1006.
" Dr., 1032.
" Eli Hugh, 421.
" Elias, 481.
" Elijah, 775.
" Brig.-Genl. F., 194.
" Frederick, 964, 972.
" Genl., 878.
" Gideon, 293.
" Jacob, of N.Y. Prov., 300, 418, 1333.
" James, 69, 70, 750.
" Mrs. Janet, 214-15.
" John, 69, 178, 287, 290, 405, 474, 518, 616, 751, 925, 1274.

Smith, John, of N. Jersey, 269.
" John, of Skeensboro, 1265.
" Joseph, 398, 425, 947, 1050, 1089.
" Jos. Hitt, 164-6.
" Joshua, 553-4, 697.
" Joshua H., 743.
" Keeting, 680.
" Lawyer, 147.
" Lieut., 873.
" Mr., 213, 575, 889, 1218, 1298-9.
" Mr., of N. York, 1285.
" Michl., 178.
" Nathan, 200, 576.
" Pat., 1269.
" Philip, 419.
" Richd., 415.
" Samuel, 272, 425, 582, 734.
" Samuel, of N. Jersey, 711, 743.
" Town, 445, 654-5.
" Wm., 398, 550, 595.
" Wm. C. I., 214-5.
" Chief Justice Wm., 188, 213, 321, 361, 941-2.
Smith's Cove, 1103.
Smithfield, 328.
Smitts, Daniel, 1005.
Smyth, Geo., 350, 381.
" Dr. George, of N.Y. Prov., 364, 483.
" John, 1242.
" Patrick, 365, 380, 390-1, 486-7.
" Patrick, of Fort Edward, 377.
" Patrick, of N.Y. Prov., 347.
" Richard, 1166.
" Towen, 390.
Sneider, Col., 982.
" Marks, 1037.
Snell, Ann, 171.
" Barnet, 170-1.
" Catharine, 170.
" Christopher, 170.
" Danl., 170.
" David, 170.
" George, of S. Carolina, 170.
" Mr., 1283.
" Nicholas, 472.
Snider, Elias, of Pensilvania, 270.
" Elve, 1027.
" Peter, of Pensilvania, 270.
" Simon, 1037, 1041.
Snifton, Shewbell, 1321.
Snow, (Vessel), 685.
Snowden, Miles, 1222.
Snyder, Henry, 857.
" John, 1059.
Snyder's Bush, 440.
" Patent, 857.
Solomon, Mr., 613.
Somerset Co., 111, 174, 269, 1273-5.
Somersetshire, 323.
Sommers, Andrew, 1109.
Soper, Moses, 1268.
Sopus Co., 427.
Sorel, 128, 329, 333-6, 347-8, 363, 373-4-5, 381-4-5, 422, 431-3, 441-9, 453-5-7, 462-5, 486, 682, 923, 934, 1012, 1032-5, 1051, 1061, 1072-7-8, 1086, 1098, 1103-8-9, 1256-8, 1266-8-9.
" Wm., of Shelburne, 815.

South Amboy, 1277.
" Bay, 30-1.
" Beach, 100, 595-6.
" End Square, 754.
" Haven, 750.
" Mountain, 536.
" River, 128, 484-5.
Southampton, 188.
Southfield, 720.
Southick, Daniel, 1321.
Southwark, 123-4-5, 518.
Spalding, Leonard, 91.
Spanish River, 745.
Sparkes, John, 123.
Sparks, Rolland, 939.
Sparling, Peter, 934-5.
Sparham, Dr. Thos., of N.Y. Prov., 447-8, 450-1.
Spencer, Abel, 421.
" August, 421.
" Barnabas, 421.
" Benj., of N.Y. Prov., 421, 460.
" Dorit, 421.
" Lieut. Hazelton, 421, 460, 1259.
" Jeremiah, 422, 1259.
" John, 421.
" Sarah, 421.
" Town, 682, 860.
Spicer, Ezekiel, 1044.
Spoon island, 897.
Spooner, Ephraim, 687.
Spotis Wood, 128.
Spring St., Newport, 104.
Springfield, 520, 559, 644.
Sproat, David, 123.
" I., 566.
" J., 933.
Sproule, Capt., 201.
Spry, Capt., 58.
Squeers, Mr., 819.
Squire, Richd., 796, 1320.
Staats, Capt. Garret, 563.
Stacey, Thos., 195.
Stage Point, 642-5, 1272.
Stamberg, Nicholas, 1260.
Stamford, 199, 200, 215, 223, 294, 319, 826-7-8, 1194-5-6.
Stanburner, Jacob, 1108.
Stanhouse, Alex., 1249.
" Dr., 1250.
Stanley, Wins., 1301.
Stanton, (Staunton), Geo., 870, 1295.
" Richd., of N. Jersey, 626.
Stanwix, Fort, 352, 395, 419, 440, 481, 969, 970-1-4, 1001, 1054, 1065, 1074-6, 1081-6-8, 1097, 1262.
Staples, Francis, of N.Y. Prov., 309.
" R., 640.
Staring, John, 1113.
Stark, Aaron, 640.
" Fort, 347.
" Genl., 271-2.
" (Starke), Gr., 360.
" John, 1019.
" Major, 847.
" R., 67.
Stark's Rangers, 578.
Starr, Major, 282.

Staten Island, 67, 93-4, 118-19, 203, 211, 232, 242, 254, 270-1, 313-14, 320, 495, 554, 600, 625, 630, 649, 666-8, 678-9, 689, 690, 712, 747, 760-1, 801, 830-4-5, 855, 894-5-8, 908, 925, 1157, 1273.
Stawe, Mathew, 717.
Stead, 303.
Stebbens, Meadow, 220.
Stebbins, Josiah, of Connecticut, 204-6.
Stedman, Charles, 869.
Steel, Robt., 1162.
Stenhouse, Alexr., 1211, 1249.
Stephens, John, 1207.
" Richd., 960.
Sterns, (Stern), Conrad, 524.
" Jonathan, 92, 611.
" Joshua, 1333.
" Nathan, of N.Y. Prov., 345.
Stet, Mary, 332.
Steven's Creek, 700-1-7, 720.
" Town, 1209.
Stevens, John, 602, 774, 972.
" Miss, 1301.
" Mr., 97, 1302.
" Simon, (or Simeon), 47.
Stevenson, Dr., 174.
" John, 609.
" Shove, of N. Jersey, 609.
Steward, Mr., 1025.
Stewart, Alexr., 195.
" Anthony, 174, 901.
" Charles, 1233.
" Col., 191, 728.
" David, 384.
" Duncan, 1155-6, 1185.
" Isaac, 1108.
" Rev. James, 1247.
" John, 148.
" Kenneth, 1251.
" Mr., 583, 733, 1130, 1234, 1302.
" Wm., of N. York, 943-9.
Stiff, James, 270.
Stile, Isaac, 558, 560.
" John, senr., 558-9.
" Mary, 558.
" Wm., of N. Jersey, 558.
Still Water, 333-5-7, 483-4, 931-3-5-6, 1108.
" " Battle of, 1269.
Stillwell, James, of N. Jersey, 690.
" John, 307, 318, 628-9, 630, 690, 1271.
Stinson, James, of Massachusetts, 322.
" John, of N. Hampshire, 271, 1333. t
" Saml., 272.
Stirling, (Sterling), Genl., 678, 811, 1243.
" Lord, 320, 601, 618-9, 887-8.
" Wm., Earl of, 70.
Stirlingshire, 24.
Stockbridge, 293.
Stockton, Arnice, 111.
" David, 111.
" Elizabeth, 111.
" Helen, 111.
" James, 111.
" Joseph, 111.
" Major, 1146.
" Mrs. Mary, 111.
" Nancy, 111.

Stockton, Rachel, 111.
" Richard, 111.
" Sarah, 111.
" Mrs. Sarah, 111.
Stokes, Chief Justice, 254.
Stone Arabia, 360, 396, 441, 454, 472-3, 1283.
" Bobby Patent, 354.
" Charles, 293.
" Cole, 337.
" Wm., 802.
Stoneburne, Jacob, 403, 1108.
Stonecody Township, 941.
Stonehouse, Dr., 1225, 1250.
Stoney Creek, 361.
" Hill, 282.
" Point, 808, 817.
Storey, (Storeys, Story), Enoch, 1290.
" Mr., 286.
" Wm., 1217.
Storms, Gilbert, 1036, 1041-2.
Stout, David, 154.
" John, 681.
" Peter, 857.
Stoutenbouyt, Peter, 857.
Stoutenburgh, Isaac, 116, 167, 233, 595-6, 669, 723.
Stover, Martin, 1042.
Stow, Edward, of Massachusetts, 851.
Stowell, Isaac, 90.
Strange, James, 592.
" Lott, 302.
Stratford, 251-2-3-7-8, 318, 594, 616-7, 838, 873, 1322.
" Co., 508-511.
" Township, 251.
Strathspey, 1098.
Stratton, Township of, 46.
Street, (Streets), Jacob, of Tryon Co., 411.
" Nehemiah, of Norwalk, 824.
" Saml., 1105, 1112.
String, Laurence, 615.
Stringer, Rev. Wm., 122.
Stronberg, Jacob, 401.
Strong, Selah, 100.
Stromson, Benj., 744.
Strum, Henry, of S. Carolina, 661.
" Henry, jr., 661.
Stuart, David, 1078.
" James, of N.Y. Prov., 403.
Stuby, Martin, 466.
Studholme, Major, 222.
Sturges, Lewis B., 1049.
Style, John, 558.
Styles, Moses Halsy, 189.
Stymest, Jasper, 1320.
Submacady, 714.
Suburbs of Damascus, 124.
Sudbury, 753.
" Street, Boston, 98.
Suffolk, 33, 98, 593-4, 684-5, 1290-6.
Sullivan, Fort, 51.
" Genl., 490, 681, 895, 908, 1232.
Sullivan's Island, 1229.
Summer St., Boston, 145.
Summers, Andrew, of N.Y. Prov., 404.
" Philip, of Jersey, 870.
Sumerset, Co., 619, 620.

Sumpter, Genl., 648.
Sunbury, 866.
" Co., 235.
" Townships, 272.
Sunderland, 437-8.
Susquehana, 331, 471-8, 480, 868, 963-4-9, 992-7, 1030.
" River, 387, 392, 404-5, 415, 440, 471, 486, 858, 968, 972-4, 981-5-7-9, 990-8, 1001-3, 1034-8-9, 1040-1, 1079. 1080-2, 1112-3.
Sussex, 69, 227-8, 257, 519, 521-2, 598, 600-1-3, 1070, 1233-6-7, 1243, 1275.
" Court House, 601.
Sutherland, Capt., 841.
" Hector, 392.
" James, 273-6.
" Mrs. Jean, of N.Y. Prov., 392.
" Mr., 927.
" Mrs. Nancy, 926.
" Lieut. Walter, 394, 1075.
Sutton, John, 263.
" Joseph, 281.
Swamp Plantation, 1152.
Swan, Lawyer, 701.
" Ponds, 192.
" River, 1128, 1230.
" Saml., 652.
" (Sloop of war), 35, 909.
" Thos., of Massachusetts, 938.
Swanee, Waters of, 185.
Swartfager, (Swartflager), Fredk., of N. Y. Prov.. 478, 1333.
Swartout, Jacobus, 234-5.
Swarts, (Swartz), Henry, 1032.
" Simon, 1032.
Swarts' Patent, 962.
Sweden, Saml., 744.
" Stephen, of N. York, 743.
Sweet, Joseph, 606-7.
" Sarah, 607-8.
Swift, (Privateer), 798.
" (Schooner), 656.
Swinter, Thos., 326.
Switzer, N., 1298.
Sydney, 85.
Symons, James, of Massachusetts, 323, 1333.
Synott, Capt., 45.

Tabilet, Cath.. 300.
Tabout, Cornelus, 152.
Tague, Jacob, of N.Y. Prov., 332.
Tailor, George, 628.
" Gustain, 202.
" John, 628.
" Joseph, 491, 570.
" Mr., 1269.
" Wm., 548, 570, 580, 609, 628-9.
Talbot, Capt., 350.
" Co., 139, 140.
Talmage, Mr., 595.
Tamplet, Elisha, 1246.
Tamworth, 832.
Tanbrooks, Genl., 337.
Tanney, Jas., 311.

Tappan, 1256.
Tarbell, Saml., of Massachusetts Bay, 463.
" Thos., 464.
Tarborough, 729, 730.
Tarleton, Col., 718, 741, 811, 877, 1218.
Tarpan, 1116.
Tartar, (Frigate), 182, 281, 889.
Taswell, Judge, 49.
Tatnall, Mr., 1301.
Taulus Hook, 299.
Taunton, 590, 660-1-3-4.
Taylor, Alex., 482-3-4.
" Elizabeth, 867.
" George, 119, 120.
" James, 46, 132.
" Mrs. Jane, 409.
" Jared, of Massachusetts, 455.
" John, 860.
" Joseph, of N. Jersey, 617, 788-9, 904.
" Major, 717.
" Mary, 920.
" Mr., 684, 1198.
" Mr., of Halifax, 195.
" Mrs., 921-2-3-5.
" Nathaniel, of Massachusetts, 734, 921-2-4.
" Robt., 132.
" & Rogers Merrit, 221.
" Saml., 224.
" Thos., 283.
" Timothy, 742.
" Wm.. 65. 118-9, 120, 133, 151-2, 180, 343, 542, 600, 618, 625, 655, 691, 735, 894, 1334.
" Wm., of Halifax, 108, 318.
" Wilson, of Montreal, 918.
Tebew Point, 553.
Teed, Isaac, 784.
Teinmouth, 87.
Telfair, Gov. Edward, 163.
" Wm., 1135.
Teller, Abraham, 321.
Tempane, Major, 429.
Ten Breech, John, 574.
Ten Brooke, Mr., 1282.
Ten Mile Creek, 982.
Tenacomb Island, 684.
Tench, James, 691.
Tenderhook, 428.
Tennant, Wm., 277.
Tenneys, 1310.
Terhues, John, 542.
Teriacomb, 686.
Terpton, John, 328.
Terre Bonne, (Tarbonne), 372, 1057.
Terrill, (Tirrell), Anthony, of N. York, 809, 823, 1321.
' Wm., of N. Jersey. 125, 823.
Terrytown, (Tera Town), 139, 1232.
Thacher, Capt. Elisha, 154.
Thames River, 641, 1329.
Thering, Nathanl., 746.
Third Township, 353, 397, 402-3, 419, 452, 482.
Thisbe (H. M. Frigate), 70, 1364.
Thomas, Arthur, of Philadelphia, 613.
" Capt., 297.
" Col., 192-3-4, 288-9.

Thomas, David, 463.
" Ed., 1293.
" Evan, of Pensilvania, 296, 895.
" Josh, of Pensilvania, 260.
" Michl., 973.
" Mr., 139, 238.
" Mrs., 506.
" Nathaniel Ray, of Massachusetts, 505, 511.
" Peter, 1261.
" Thomas, 744.
Thompson, Archibald, 979.
" Benj., 852.
" Col., 763.
" David, 1334.
" Dorothy, 969.
" Ebinezer, 616.
" Elizabeth, 852.
" George, 1223-4.
" Israel, 386.
" Thos., 852.
" Wm., 212.
Thornburgh, Capt., 1321.
Thorndike, Luckin, 721.
Thorne, (Thorn), Joseph, of N. Jersey, 898, 908.
" Robt., of N. York, 881.
Thornton, 509, 617, 637.
" David, 692.
" John, of S. Carolina, 170, 276.
" Thos., of S. Carolina, 692.
" Thos., jr., 692.
Thorp, Edward, 1194-5-6.
" Elisha, 239.
" Job, 899.
" Mr., 1196.
Thorwin, Israel, 87-8.
Three Rivers, 391, 487.
Thresher, Saml., 590.
Thurming Township, 48.
Ticonderago (Teconderago), 335, 346-9, 380-4, 405, 426, 436, 457, 865-6, 923-4-6, 939, 959, 1222, 1303.
Tilden, Jonathan, 145.
Tilley, (Tilly), Saml., of Courtland's Manor, 229, 265, 823, 1321.
Tillinghost, John, 103.
" Mary, 51.
" Philip, 51.
Tilton, Clayton, of N. Jersey, 208.
" John, 628, 633.
Tinsley, Capt., 717-8.
Tire, Patent of, 123.
Tisdale, John, 590.
Titus, Isaac, of West Chester, 216.
Tobago, 905.
Tobey, Saml., 663.
Tobias, Christian, 757.
" Joseph, of N. York, 756-7-8.
Todd, John, of Georgia, 28, 582.
" Michl., 81.
Tolley, John, 519.
Tollman, Thos., 87.
Tolten, James. of N. York, 766.
Tomhanock, 434.
Tomlinson, Joseph, 251.
Tomkins, (Tompkins), Israel, of Saratoga, 1108, 1333.

Tongre, Gen., 339.
Tongue, Joshua, 892.
Tooker, Jacob, of Elizabeth Town, 554, 679.
" Jos., 554.
Tool Bridge, 236.
Topper, Dr., 845.
Toppnumans, 1238.
Topsham Township, 916.
Totten, Gilbert, 764.
" Joseph, 47.
Tottle, Stephen, 552.
Town Creek, 164.
Towner, Ithiel, of N.Y. Prov., 388.
Towns. Joseph, 160.
Townshend, (Townsand), Ben., 789.
" Ebenezer, 81, 825.
" Gregory, 32, 619, 735.
" Lord, 1155.
" Mr., 103, 668.
Trail, Col., 180.
Traill, Jas., 1245.
" P., 885.
Trant. Mr., 77.
Trapahagen, Henry, 76.
Travers. Moses, 874.
Traverse. Patk., 338.
Trawbridge. 255.
Tredwell, Abel, 850.
" Epheraim, 850.
" Fredk. Saml., 850.
" Mary, 850.
" Mathew, 850.
" Nathanl., 850-1.
" Rebecca, 850.
" Rueben, 850.
" Ruth Caml., 850.
Trenchard, Henry, of N. York, 780.
Trenhausik, 1267.
Trenton, 53, 71-3, 94, 203, 248-9, 269, 617-8, 649, 787-8, 832, 873, 917, 925, 1303.
" Falls, 925.
" Manor, 35.
Trepes Hill, 967.
Treple, John, of N.Y. Prov., 400.
Trevose Tract, 1177.
Trimble, Jas., 223.
Trip, Mr., 631.
Troop. Col. Dier, 501.
Troopsbury, 126.
Troy, 68.
Tryon County, 148, 331-2, 346, 351-2-3-4-5-6-7-8, 360-1-8-9, 371-2-3-4-5-6-7-8-9, 381-2-4-5-7, 390-2-3-4-5-6-7, 402-3-4-5-6-7-8-9, 410, 414-5-6-9, 420-3-4, 431, 440-1-2, 454-9, 462-3-6-9, 471-3, 480-1-2-5-6, 662, 744, 856-7-8, 934, 957, 979, 983, 996, 1028, 1032-3-9, 1040, 1051-2-4-5-6-7-8, 1060-1-2-3-4-6-7-8-9, 1070-3-5-6-7-8-9, 1080-7-8, 1092-3-5-6-7-8-9, 1103-8-9, 1110, 1113-4-7, 1120-1-2, 1244, 1254-5-8-9, 1260-1, 1280-5.
Tryon, Genl., 80, 210, 226, 230-1-2, 243, 282-3-4-5, 300, 310, 348, 654, 681, 771, 785, 828, 853, 882, 914-5, 1155, 1197, 1212-13.

Tryon, Govr., 42-3, 159, 177, 209, 359, 493, 500-4, 540-1-5, 553, 571-9, 580-2-4, 593-4, 611, 622-5, 668-9, 705, 718. 728, 743, 755-6, 764, 811-2, 829, 830, 859, 910, 1049, 1206-8, 1252, 1269.
" Wm., 877.
Tubbs, S., 640.
Tucker, Danl., 1219.
" Isaac, 214.
" Joseph, 306.
" Joseph & Co., 304.
" Moses, 712.
" Nathanl., 572.
" Dr. Robt., of N. Carolina, 652.
Tunbridge Township, 47-8.
Turbill, Jon'n, 90.
Turloch, 1099, 1115. 1260.
Turnbull, Col., 718, 1187.
" Govr., 1208.
Turnecliff, 1111.
Turner, Col., 169.
" Edward, 980-1.
" John, 684-5.
" Joseph, 196.
" Mr., 642.
" Mr., of Montreal, 384.
" Moran, 981.
" Morris, 981.
" Saml., 286.
Turner's Patent, 391.
Turtle Bay, 309.
Tuskal River, 561.
Tusket, 718.
" River, 78.
Tuthall, Mr., 1308.
Tuttle, Elisha, 1043.
" Mr., 287.
" Stephen, of Albany, 29, 31, 70, 107.
Tweed, John, of N. York, 783.
Twills, Godfrey, 222.
Twiss. Capt., 940-4, 959.
Two Creek, 841.
Tyger River, 1210.
Tying, Col., 274.
" Ed., 273.
" Mrs., 273-4-5.
" Wm., of Massachusetts Bay, 272-6, 903.
Tyler, Gerard. 445-9.
" Wm., of N.Y. Prov., 329, 345, 350.
Tything, Hack, 341.
" More, 341.
" Stopen, 341.
Tybu (Tyber?), 1306.

Ulster Co., 259, 260-8, 397, 403, 430, 458-9. 476. 495. 545, 774-5, 821-2, 856-8, 872, 896, 952, 982, 1007, 1088, 1101, 1256, 1257.
Underhill, Abraham, 577.
" Augustine, 576.
" & Franklyn, 1212.
" Mr., 302.
" Nathaniel, of N. York, 811.
" Wm., of N. York, 896, 1320.
Underwood, Henry, 869, 1321.
Union & Eastbury Town, 80.

Union River, 323-4, 577.
Union, St. Boston, 568, 570-2.
" Township, 840.
Updegrave. John, 603.
Upham, Col., 716-7, 847.
" Major, 202, 263, 865, 873.
Uphraim, Col., 861.
Upper County, 442.
" Freehold, 73, 136-7, 320, 787.
" Rockingham, 89.
Upshaw, Arthur, 733.
Uree, Phyn &, 1334.
Urim, Capt. Wallis, 929.
Urquhart, George, 1141.
" John, 344.
" Mr., 383.
" Wm., of N.Y. Prov., 382-3.

Van Allen, Wm., 561.
Van Allin, Jacob, of Tryon Co., 1120.
Van Alstine, Abraham, 446.
" Alex., 446.
" Cornelius, 961.
" Isaac, 445, 1015-6, 1030-4.
" James, 1033-4.
" John, 445-6.
" Lambert, of Connecticut, 440, 1333.
" Lambert. jr., 440.
" Lydia, 1033.
" Major, 13, 1035, 1264-5-6.
" Martin, 445.
" Peter. 418, 452, 654, 1104, 1116.
Van Amburg, Abraham, 872.
Van Buren, James, of N. Jersey, 543.
Van Buskirk, (Boskirk). Col., 562.
" John, 308, 1373-5.
" James, 665.
" Lawrence, of N. Jersey, 307-8.
" Lawrence. of N. York, 665.
" Mrs., 665.
Van Camp, Jacob, 1104-5.
" Peter, 1105, 1333.
Van Cleek, Col., 845-6.
" Leonard, 844-5.
" Peter, 843-4.
" Mrs Sarah, 843-4.
Van Courtland, Philip, 269, 595-6, 669, 723.
Van Denbogist, John, 844.
Van Dusen, Conrad, of N.Y. Prov., 368, 1003-7.
" John, 360.
" (Vandeusent), Wm., 863.
Van Emburg, Adoniah, 692.
" James, of N. Jersey, 691.
Van Every, David, 1000, 1284.
" McGregor, of N.Y. Prov., 1284.
" Mary, 1284-5.
Van Horn, Gabriel, 246.
Van Maple, Henry, 310.
" Mary, of N. York, 309.
Van March, Charles, 340.
Van Mater, Chrinesyonce, of N. Jersey, 610, 627-9, 633.

Van Norden, Gabriel, of N. Jersey, 542, 561.
Van Onslow, Abraham, 292.
Van Plank, Hy., 477.
" Mr., 1101.
Van Plank's Patent, 397.
Van Rensselar, James, 401, 446, 452
" Jer., 360.
Van Rypun, Garret, 627.
Van Schaack, Mr., 1373.
" Peter, 445.
Van Schoick, Anthony, 1119.
Van Slaak. Innis 446.
Van Slick, Mr., 1022.
Van Tassel, Isaac, of N. York, 289, 881.
" Wm., 289.
Van Vleet, Genet, 364.
Van Vleit, Cornelius, 883.
Van Wart, Jacob, of Courtland Manor, 301, 898.
Van Waters, Cranyance, 610.
Van Winkle, Mr., 627.
Vans Kerk, Col., 754.
Vander Voort, Mr., 333-4
Vaade, Capt., 1194.
Valentine, Adjt., 355-8, 368.
" David, 215.
" Mr., 443, 478, 754.
" Saml., 568.
" Township, 919, 921.
Valentine's Hill, 264.
Vandecar, Ralph, of Albany Co., 452.
Vanderbeck, Abraham, of N. Jersey, 245.
Vanderburgh, Henry, of N.Y. Prov., 247, 846, 1321.
" Peter, of N. York, 830, 1321.
" Capt. Richard, 225-8, 232-3, 240-7-8, 257-9. 260-4-5, 272, 280-2-8-9, 291-2-6-9, 301-2-8-9, 806-8-9, 811, 813-6-7-9, 822-5-6-7-8, 830-8, 847-8, 851-5, 860-2-4-5-9, 870-1-2-4-6-7, 881-2-6-8-9, 890-3-6-7-8, 904-9, 1321-3-4, 1333.
Vandeput, (Vanderput, Vanderport), Capt., 118-9, 504, 1155.
Vanderlip, Wm., 997.
Vandine, Dowe, of Long Island, 232, 1321.
" Wm., 232.
Vandyke, Col., 824.
" Major, 708.
Vanmaitre, Mr., 1238.
Vanrypee, Mr., 841.
Vanskort, Mr., 795.
Vanstine, Dow, 1321.
Vant, Adaim, 1025.
Vanvockes, Jacob, 561.
" Nan, 561.
Vardy, Aaron, 1334.
Varren, 956.
Vaughan, Col., 560.
" Major-Genl., 203, 530, 541, 562-3, 712, 802, 816, 1176, 1277.
" Wm., 57.
Veal, Abraham, 548.
" Jacob, 759.
" Thos., 66.

Venplank's Point, 1276.
Venters, Moses, 82.
Vernon, Elias, 902.
" Gideon, of Pensilvania, 900-4.
" Moses, 902.
Verns, Mr., 93.
Verplank, Philip, 230.
" Sarah, 453.
Vescher, Mat., 360.
Vesper, (Sloop), 195.
Vesscher, Mat., of Albany, 563.
Vincent, Charles, of N. York, 767, 870, 1320.
" Egbert, 545.
Vine St., Philadelphia, 521.
" Yard, N. York, 116-7, 1292-3.
Virgin Island, 1133.
Voluntown, 682.
Vought, Christian, 76.
" John, 76.
Vroom, John, 1321.
Vrooman, Isaac, 856.
" Swarts, 962.
Vrooman's Patent, 961.
Vulture, (Sloop), 316.

Wacoman, 1246.
Waddell, Alderman, 204.
" Henry, 151.
" Robt., 115.
" Wm., 699, 1293.
Wadman, Capt. Arthur, 13(3
Wadsworth, Judge James, 83.
Wager, Allen, 602-5.
Waggems, Jacob, 1116.
Waggoner, John, of Saratoga, 1269, 1333.
Wagstaffe, Thomas, 878.
Wailey, Mr., 899.
Wait, John, 89.
Waite, Geo., 934.
" Mrs. Jane, 934.
" John, of N. York, 934.
" Jonathan, 89.
Wakefield, Henry, 1141.
Waldec, Martin, 1121.
Walden, Thos., 511.
Waldo, Mr., 1304.
Waldroff, Mrs. Margaret, 480.
" Martin, 481.
Waldroft, Martin, of N.Y. Prov., 480.
Waldron, Isaac, 897.
Walis, Eleazer, 207.
Walker, Adam, of Massachusetts Bay, 586.
" Danl., 90, 422, 1015.
" Danl., of Vermont, 1271.
" Gideon, 1015.
" Jacob, 975.
" James, 1186.
" John, 122.
" Justice, 1138-9.
" Silas, 895.
" Thos., 277.
Walkeys, Henry, of N. York, 668.
Wall, Geo., 710, 742.
" Mrs., 611.
" Mrs. Margaret, 724.
" Patrick, of Boston, 610, 724.
" Street, N. York, 117.

Wallace, Alex., of N. York, 1292, 1318.
" Anthony, 354.
" Capt., 50.
" Hugh, 632, 1318.
" Sir James, 1182-3-4.
" James & Co., 729, 730.
" John, 729, 730.
" John & Co., 720.
" Michael, 632, 729, 730.
" Wm., of S. Carolina, 174, 734, 1101.
Wallbough, 269.
Waller, Mr., 1300.
Walley, Thos., 39, 570.
Wallingford, 80-6, 287.
Wallis, Hugh, 603.
" Mr., 1112.
Walliser, Anthony, of N.Y. Prov., 354, 403.
Wallkill, 262-3.
Walmsley, Thos., 294.
Walnut Creek, 1246.
Walrand, Jacob, 420.
Walsh, Duff &, 157.
Walters, (Walter), Mrs. Elizabeth, 147.
" John, 918.
" John, jr., 147.
" John Francis, 147.
" Mr., 92.
" Philip, of N.Y. Prov., 396.
" Rev. Dr., 139, 145-6-7-8-9, 194, 553, 573-4, 610, 655-6-8-9, 678-9, 691, 731.
" Will, 518.
Waltham Stowe, 190.
Walton, Jno., 297.
" Mr., 553, 926.
" Wm., 208.
Wannamaker, Eliz., of N. Jersey, 299.
" Richard, 299.
Wantage Township, 596.
Wanton, (Sloop), 137-8.
Ward, Charles, of Apthorp, 629, 1013.
" Ebenezer, 531, 560.
" Edmund, 165, 697.
" Edmund, of Connecticut, 83.
" Edmund, of East Chester, 502-3.
" John, 1012.
" Major, 665, 872, 1035, 1270.
" Mr., 453.
" Nathl., 559.
" Saml., 560, 854.
" & Sherman, 799.
" Stephen, 166, 745.
" Thos., 147.
" Uzal (Uziel), 65, 79, 529, 531-2, 560.
Ward's House, 743-4.
Wardell, John, 208-9.
Warden, Hugh, 1161-2.
" John, 608-9.
Ware River, 739.
Waring, Nathan, 319.
Warne, Samuel, 1278.
Warner, Christian, of Albany Co., 967.
" Josiah, 1208.
" Levi, 1018, 1020.
" Michl., 1117.
" Sir Peter, 473.
Warnock, Hy., 478.

91 AR.

Warren, Admiral, 698.
" Sir P., 390.
Warrens Bush, 470, 1038.
Wartman, Abraham, of Pensilvania, 1262.
" John, 1262-3.
" Peter, 1041.
Warwick, 602-3.
" River, 603.
Washamadock, 264-5-6, 281, 299, 301.
Washburn, Ebenezer, of Charlotte Co., 422, 1014.
" Israel, 663.
" John, 215, 602-3.
Washington, 363, 402, 752.
" Fort, 756, 867, 886.
" Genl. George, 137, 160, 177, 287, 544, 572, 609, 628, 851, 1144, 1176, 1274, 1303.
Washydoemack River, 880.
Wasweighnunck, 1313.
Water St., Portsmouth, 66.
Waterbury, 233.
" Mrs. Sarah, 827.
" Silvanus, of Connecticut, 827.
Waterea, 156.
Wateree River or Creek, 647, 678, 1187.
Waterous, John, 301.
Waters, Abraham, 1320.
" Col., 696.
" of Cuffe, 62.
" George, 742.
" Mr., 61.
" Saml., 653.
Watertown, 905.
Watkins, Henry, of N. York, 1296.
Watrivers, Reuben, 881.
Watson, Alderman, 188.
" Alex., 548.
" Brooke, 51, 504, 798, 13:9.
" John, 1162.
" Marston, 605-6.
" Mr., 1163.
Wattemeer, Capt., 468.
Watts, John, 264, 469, 916.
" Mr., 1070, 1241.
" Stephen, 1334.
Watwing Plains, 255.
Way, George, 1097.
Wayne, Genl., 824, 865, 873.
Wearing, Fredk., 458.
Weatherford, Martin, of Georgia, 163, 705-7.
Weaver, George, of 96 Dist., 156, 674-5-7.
Webb, Charles, 200.
" David, 200.
Weber, Christian, of N. York, 942.
Webster, Col., 679, 908.
" Mr., 327, 1233.
Weedman, Lt., 223.
Weeks, James, 291.
" Revd. Mr., 608, 726.
Wegar, Aberhard, 443.
" Everhart, of N. Y. Prov., 443.
" Thos., 443.
Wegg, Ed. Bush., 1213.
Weigher & Gauger, 190.
Weir, David, 343.
" Mr., of Falmouth, 304.

Weiser, Fredk., of N. Jersey, 573-4.
Welcome, (Sloop), 316, 1319.
Wellard, C., 1286.
Wellbanks, Abraham, 522.
Welling, Peter, 1321.
" Wm., 1321.
Wells, 865.
" Col., 759.
" Harrison, 615.
" Mr., 1111, 1254.
" Robt., 1291.
Welsh, Joseph, of Massachusetts, 658.
" Saml., 1012.
Welstead, Sarah, 98.
Welsv, Wm., 794-8.
Went. Adam, 1025.
Wentle, Harmans, 406.
Wenton, Col., 50.
Wentworth, Benning, 915.
" Govr. John, of N. Hampshire, 32, 48, 102-5, 115, 491, 506-7, 517, 540, 590-3, 616, 629, 636, 752, 762, 821, 831-2, 915, 938-9, 1208-9, 1212, 1272, 1303.
" Mark Hawking, 509.
Werjar, Ephraim, 1048.
Werjars, Jacob, 1047.
Wertham Township, 258.
Wesner, Mr., 603.
Wessels. Nicholas, 1104.
West Bradford, 494, 564, 612.
" Chester, 84, 216, 261-4-6, 281-8-9, 497-8, 500, 538-9, 567, 571, 680-1, 698, 723, 755-6-8-9, 761-2-4-5, 775-7-9, 780-3-9, 791, 811, 813-9, 820-2, 874, 880-6, 896, 1237, 1276, 1295.
" Indies, 21, 76, 133, 305-6, 320, 343, 513, 566, 634-5, 684, 746-7, 793, 900-5, 929, 1164, 1289.
" M., 1298.
" N., 1298.
" Rolton, 243.
" Town, (Weston), 753, 917.
Westbrook Gaol, 975.
Westerfelt, Abr., 246.
Westerwelt, Stephen, 561-2.
Westfield, 141.
Westminster, 611.
Westmoreland, 150, 201, 259, 477-8, 537, 786-9, 963-4, 1282.
Westonbrook, Patent, 100.
Wethersfield, 1018.
Wetmore, George, of Antigonish, 829.
" Mrs., Rachel, 829.
" Timothy, 829, 1321.
Weymouth, Lord Viscount, 1350.
Whailen, David, 1065.
Wharton, Elisha, 609.
Whatley, Mr., 570.
Whealley, Moses, 801.
Wheaton, John, 959.
Wheeler, Abraham, 239.
" George, 1320.
" Joseph, 804.
" Josiah, 238.
" Josiah, jr., 238.

Wheeler, Obadiah, 239.
" Sarah, 238.
" Tolman, 238.
Wheeler's Point, 65, 78.
Wheler, Catharine, 908.
" Edward, 908.
" Elizabeth, 908.
" Geo., of N. York, 907.
" John, of N. Jersey, 890.
" Mrs., 891.
" Nicholas, 907.
" Mrs. Polly, 907.
" Reinhard, 908.
White, Albert, 1269.
" Alex., of Tryon Co., 1051.
" Amelia, 115.
" Mrs. Ann, 115.
" Capt., 1037.
" Charlotte, 115.
" Col., 1139.
" Creek, 329, 344-5, 924, 1033-6, 1063, 1095.
" Danl., 115, 507, 1293.
" Hartshorn, 151-2.
" Henry, 138, 333, 335, 632.
" Hill, 99.
" Hugh, 332.
" John, 243.
" Joseph, 328, 389.
" Mathew, 115, 1292.
" Michael, 295.
" Mr., 91, 209, 1303.
" Mrs., 1292-3.
" Plains, 53, 84, 108, 205, 290, 500-3, 553, 698, 775-7, 781-3, 806-7-8, 818, 853-4.
" Battle of, 281, 681, 771, 780, 811, 854, 870.
" Point, 1199, 1201.
" Saml., 856.
" Stephen, 520.
" Thos., of N. York, 115, 1292.
" Thos., jr., 115, 1292.
Whilpley, Oliver, of Connecticut, 848.
Whippener River, 68.
Whitcock, Dd., 226.
Whiteborough Patent, 1314.
Whitehall, 1182.
Whitehead, Reason, 45-6.
Whitfield, 832.
Whiting, Nathan, of N. York, 697.
" Saml., J. P., 252.
" Wm. Joseph, 99.
Whitlock, Capt. John, 292-3-4.
Whitman, Robt., of N. Y. Prov., 483.
Whitney, Nathan, jr., 699.
" Saml., of Connecticut, 318-9.
" Stephen, 319.
Whittingham Towns, 857.
Wickam, Wm., 448.
Wiggins, John, 240, 260, 822.
Wilcox, Capt., 654-5, 944.
Wildman, Benj., 1266.
Wiley, Jacob, 890.
" Mr., 50, 859.
Wilington, 112.
Wilkins, Isaac, of Newark, 502, 514, 529, 668, 680.

INDEX.   1435

Wilkins, Mr., 498.
" Mrs., 498.
Willard, Col. Abijah, 204, 213-4, 313, 642-3, 849, 878, 1182, 1217, 1333.
" Benj., 91.
" Elias, 932.
" Oliver, 623.
Willet, (Willett), Capt., 878.
" Isaac, 166.
" John, 690, 856-7.
" Mrs. Martha, 741-2.
" Saml., 742.
" Thos., 690.
" Walter, of Pensilvania, 741.
William Henry, Fort, 380.
William & Mary, Fort, 831.
William's Bridge, 723.
" Town, 1256.
Williams, Abner, 705.
" Amos, of Newark, 63, 1310.
" Benj., 663.
" Capt., 778.
" Col., 218, 947.
" Daniel, 108.
" David, 439, 1018.
" Dr., 947.
" Edward, of S. Carolina, 182.
" Elijah, 220, 821.
" Elisha, 754.
" Frederick, of N. York, 363, 758, 762.
" Henry, 164.
" Major Henry, of N. Carolina, 695-7, 704.
" Isaac, of N. York, 680, 724.
" J., 1359.
" Jacob, 705.
" James, 64, 317-8, 590, 649, 664, 700-1.
" Jane, 705.
" John, 281, 343, 1017.
" John Chester, 114.
" John Robert, 840.
" Joseph, of N. Jersey, 317.
" Capt. Judah, 213.
" Mathew, 64.
" Mr., 550, 720.
" Mrs., 219, 220.
" Moses, 432-3, 1267.
" Nathan, of N. Jersey, 64.
" Obediah, 317.
" Robert, 890, 1203.
" Ruben, of N. York Prov., 289.
" Samuel, of N. Carolina, 704.
" Sarah, 705.
" Seth, 590.
" William, 705.
" Wilson, 705.
Williamsburgh, 55, 131, 423-4-7, 475, 684, 1149.
" Gaol, 731-3.
Williamson, Genl., 158, 191.
" James, 941.
" Mathias, 1293.
" Mr., 425.
Willing, Col., 1284.
Willisbro, 400.

Willocks, Geo., 71-2.
Wilmington, 54, 112, 241-2-4-5, 253, 549, 613-8-9, 652-3, 832.
Wilmot, 20, 179, 308, 537, 708, 749, 1295.
" John, (Commissioner), 14, 508, 1140-8, 1156, 1160, 1185-9, 1202-6, 1317, 1326, 1336-8, 1342-4, 1351.
Wills Township, 470.
Willsbrough, 436-7.
Wilson, Charles, 818.
" Cornelius, 277.
" David, 536.
" Ezekiel, 206.
" Judge I., 746.
" John, 181, 1107, 1320.
" John, senr., 818.
" John, of N. York, 783.
" John, of N. Jersey, 817.
" Jos., 559.
" Mr., 345, 1207.
" Phebe, 277.
" Richd., 1206.
" Robt., 277.
" Zebedee, 891.
Wilson's Creek, 181.
" Patent, 1028, 1107.
Wilton, Patent of, 123.
Wiltse, Benoni, 389.
Winat, John, 339.
Winchelsea, Lord, 803.
Windham Township, 69.
Windron, Hendrick, 990.
Winds, Genl., 894.
Windsor, 255, 337, 551, 679, 682-9, 690-1.
Wing, Mr., 399, 400.
Wing's Lane, Boston, 622.
Winlow, James, 592.
Winney, Peter, 983.
Winning, Mathias, 198.
Winock, Anna, 919, 920.
" Joshua, 919, 920.
Winslow, Col., 853, 871, 897.
" Ed., 246, 268, 1049.
" Isaac, of Boston, 623.
" Isaac, senr., 624.
Winslow's 739.
Winter, Joseph, 1284.
" Road, 894.
" St., Boston, 569, 570-1.
Wintermute, John, 974.
Wise, Joshua, 658.
Wiss, John, 1034.
Wist, John, 1106.
Wiswall, Revd. John, of Falmouth Co., 172, 188.
Withrow, Jacob, 168.
" John, of S. Carolina, 693.
Witman, Mrs., 866.
Witmore, Timothy, 878.
Witney, Judge John, 82.
Wittser, Benoni, 389, 1081.
" James, 924.
Wolcott, Oliver, 207, 290.
Wolf, Genl., 914.
Wolfesboro, 508-9, 511, 593, 616-7, 637, 1272.
Wood Creek, 1013.

Wood, Capt. F., 284.
" Jonas, of N. Y. Prov., 458.
" Mr., 1312.
Woodbridge, 93, 141, 198, 203-4, 314, 801-2-3, 810, 818, 855, 894-5-8-9, 900.
Woodbury, 123-5, 198, 483, 617.
Woodcock, John, of Albany Co., 428, 1038-9, 1040.
Woodhut, Mr.; 610.
Woodlax, Geo., 1233.
Woodmansey, Mr., 926.
Woodruff, Jonathan, 711.
" Samuel, 140.
Woods, Hamilton, 719.
Woodstock, 623, 993, 1000.
" John, 1040.
Woodward, Anthony, 71-2-3-4, 297, 787-8.
" S., 1334.
Woolwich, 615-6, 929, 930.
Wooster, Col. Joseph, 838.
Worcester, 32-3, 148, 520, 586-7-8, 642, 721, 738, 740, 803-4, 878-9.
Worden, Jeremiah, 1321.
Worth, Benj., of N. Jersey, 1273.
Wrag, (Wragg), John), 946.
" Richd., of N. Y. Prov., 946-9.
Wraight, John, 971.
Wright, Capt., 524, 942
" Chas., 894.
" Danl., 443.
" David, 894.
" Gideon, 526.
" Hanah, 198.
" Major James, 109.
" Govr. Sir James, of S. Carolina, 60-1-2, 163, 339, 340, 525, 582-3, 695-9, 714-5, 792-8, 1126-7-8-9, 1130-2-3-4-5-6, 1240-2, 1182-3-4, 1245, 1299, 1305-7-8.
" Jermyn, 1239.
" Jesse, of Massachusetts Bay, 449.
" John, 109.
" Jonathan, 868.
" Joseph, 480.
" Major, 1239.
" Mr., 500, 906, 1127.
" Saml., 425.
" Uriah, 225.
" Wm., of N. Jersey, 198.
Wright's Patent, 1306.
Wrightborough, 1142.

Wrightman, Col., 303.
Wrightsman, Peter, 43.
Wusters, John, 1263.
Wyboosenk, 968.
Wylly, Capt. Alex. Campbell, of Georgia, 296.
" William, 296.
Wyoming, 140.

Yadkin River, 1131.
" Road, 97.
Yale, Govr., 310.
Yamaska, (Yamasco), 414, 1014-5, 1033, 1043, 1077, 1123.
" Block House, 1035, 1053, 1115.
Yammaceraw, 339, 340-1-2.
Yardley, Thos., 95.
Yarmouth, 318, 553, 644.
" North, 919, 920-1, 1303.
Yates, Richd., 335.
Yeack, Saml., 1014.
Yeomans, John, 816, 876, 1320.
Yerxa, John, of N. York, 888-9, 892.
York Co., 112, 833-6.
" Duke of, 23, 1243.
" Town, 77, 112, 280, 295, 566, 658, 885, 1226.
" William, 361.
Yorke, Col., 106.
" Island, 130.
" Thos., 1289.
Young, Adam, 998.
" Andrew, 540.
" Atty-Genl. Col., 28.
" Israel, of N. Y. Prov., 540.
" John, 160, 530, 999, 1277.
" Mr., 60.
" Peter, 1005, 1011-2.
" Saml., 160.
" Thos., 184.
" Thos., of S. Carolina, 700-3, 719, 720-9.
" **Capt. Thos., 707.**
" Col. Thos., 717-8.
" Col. Wm., 170, 184.
Yurex, Isaac, 1072.
Zabariski, Peter, 544.
Zubly, David, 342.
" David. jr.. of Georgia, 338.
" Dr. John Joacim, 339, 340-1-2.